THE ANNUAL OBITUARY 1987

THE ANNUAL OBITUARY 1987

Editor
PATRICIA BURGESS

St J

St James Press

Chicago and London

For further information, write:
ST. JAMES PRESS
233 East Ontario Street
Chicago 60611, U.S.A.

or

3 Percy Street
London W1P 9FA, England

British Library Cataloguing in Publication Data

The Annual Obituary 1987.
1. Biography—Periodicals
920′.02′05 CT100

ISBN 1-55862-021-4

First published in the U.S.A. and U.K. 1990

Typeset by Irish Typesetting & Publishing Co. Ltd.
Galway, Ireland

CONTENTS

EDITOR'S NOTE

Where would a Hollywood filmstar rub shoulders with a Russian general, a flugelhorn player sit alongside a fighter pilot, and a war criminal be a short hop from an archbishop? Where else but the *Annual Obituary*. As ever, the mixture is an eclectic one, covering people from all walks of life who have made their mark in a huge variety of ways.

Each entry consists of a descriptive essay followed by a detailed, who's who-style biographical note, which, where appropriate, includes lists of exhibitions and major works, plus extended bibliographies and filmographies. The result is fascinating reading for the casual browser combined with authoritative information for the serious researcher.

Special thanks are extended to Paul Stevens for research, Mary Jean Evers, Tony Henderson, Kelly Boyd and David Carter for who's who biographies, Miren Lopategui for proof-reading, and the diligent team of contributors who wrote the 331 essays.

Patricia Burgess
London

Alphabetical Index of Entrants

Index of Entrants by Profession

The index is divided into the following categories:

Actors, Actresses and Entertainers

Anthropologists and Archaeologists

Architects and Planners

Art Historians, Collectors, Critics and Dealers

Artists and Craftsmen

Astronomers and Astrophysicists

Aviators, Aviation Experts, Aerodynamicists and Astronauts

Biographers and Memoirists

Biologists, Botanists, Naturalists and Zoologists

Business Executives and Industrialists

Chemists and Biochemists

Children's Writers

Clergy and Religious Scholars and Theorists

Composers, Arrangers, Songwriters and Librettists

Criminals

Dancers, Choreographers and Dance Critics

Designers

Diplomats

Directors

Earth Scientists (including Geographers, Geologists, Meteorologists, Seismologists, Oceanographers and Demographers)

Economists, Financial Specialists and Bankers

Educators, Educationists and Educational and Foundation/Association Administrators

Engineers and Technologists

Essayists

Explorers

Farmers, Horticulturists and Agriculturists

Heads of State, Presidents, Premiers and Governors General

Historians, Classicists, Genealogists and Folklorists

Illustrators, Cartoonists and Animators

Intelligence Officers and Agents

Journalists and Editors (including Travel Writers)

Judges, Lawyers and Criminologists

Labour Leaders

Librarians, Museum Curators, Archivists and Antiquarians

Literary Scholars and Critics

Mathematicians

Medical Practitioners and Researchers

Military Officers and Strategists

Musical Performers and Conductors

Novelists and Short Story Writers (including Humorists)

Performing Arts Critics and Scholars

Philanthropists

Philosophers

Photographers

Physicists

Playwrights and Scriptwriters

Poets

Politicians

Producers and Administrators (Film, Stage, Radio, TV and Music)

Psychiatrists and Psychologists

Public and Government Officials

Publishers, Newspaper Proprietors and Literary Agents

Radio and Television Personalities

Royalty and Socialites

Social, Political and Human Rights Activists

Social Workers

Sports and Games Figures

Theatrical/Music Impresarios, Managers and Agents

Translators

Contributors

Simon Adams
Jamie Ambrose
Ian Armour
Antonia Boström
David Brady
Edmund Bradley
Mary Cadogan
Joanna Chambers
Scott Coombs
Margaret Cornell
Tim Cornell
Christopher Downing
Jane Ehrlich
Mike Gautrey
Teresa Gautrey
James C. Hart
Rodney Hoare
Doug Jesseph
Maria Lauret
Elizabeth Lee
Jehanne Lequesne
Lucinda Lubbock
Roger Mills
Trevor Mostyn
Linden Nicoll
Paula Nuttall
Ian Poitier
Zandra Rathbone
John Simley
Caroline B.D. Smith
Philip de Souza
Paul Stevens
Paul Tweddle
Jane Walker
Peter Ward
Ian Weightman
Sara Wheeler
Sue Wilson

THE ANNUAL OBITUARY 1987

JANUARY

YVES ALLÉGRET

French Film Director
Born **Basle, Switzerland, 13 October 1907**
Died **Paris, France, 31 January 1987**

To call Yves Allégret a major figure of the *cinéma qualité* French film period (1940s–1950s) would be relegating him to a status that is not all it appears to be. However, although only a handful of his films stand out, they are considered to be celluloid high points of the days of *la Libération*. Less majestically, Allégret is partly responsible for launching the career of his then-wife, Simone Signoret.

Introduced to the film industry by his older brother Marc, also a director, Allégret quickly learned the trade by assisting such masters as Cavalcanti and Renoir. He directed his first feature during the German Occupation, after a series of aborted projects and unimpressive short documentaries. This effort, *The Girls of France*, was shown at the 1939 New York World's Fair. Light comedies and other projects, some of which were censored and unfinished, followed, dogging Allégret's career through to the Liberation.

It was not until 1948, with *Dedée d'Anvers*, starring Signoret, that his reputation was firmly established, particularly as a proponent of *film noir* social criticism. His attempt possibly to repeat the Marcel Carne/Jaques Prévert pre-war poetic fatalism successes was misguided, partly because the climate had changed, and partly because his style was more cerebral and analytical. *Dedée* and his next film, *Une si jolie petite plage* (1949), established a downbeat atmosphere of bitter disillusionment and cynicism about the human race. Allégret's "psychological realism" could be said to counter the other attributes of his films: excellent performances and a technically polished structure. His third film in the trilogy, *Manèges* (1950), an exposé of bourgeois nastiness, was to be the last of his more respected works.

Many critics consider the rest of his career populated by soulless commercial literary adaptations, or "off-the-peg variety of romantic nihilism" to quote Gilbert Adair. However, *Les Orgueilleux* (The Proud and the Beautiful), from a Jean-Paul Sartre story, won the Bronze Lion award at the 1953 Venice Festival. "The milieu is still the depths: heat, squalor, disease and desperation," says film critic Pauline Kael. "Allégret uses the story atmospherically in an effort to approximate the ironies, inconsequences, accidents and stupidities of life, and the atmosphere *almost* redeems the movie."

In the 1960s came castigation of Allégret's films by New Wave directors, most notably François Truffaut, who derided the charmless pessimism of the whole *cinéma qualité* period that flattened a decade and a half of French film. Allégret never regained the tenuous foothold he had in the industry; as the grim style of *film noir* faded, his switch to slick, American-style films and Zola adaptations made little impact. Instead, he remains a B-figure of the uncertain climate of realism, a producer of superb performances in funereal scripts by such great actors as Gerard Philippe, Jean Marais, Allida Valli—and Signoret—and his trilogy, which still packs a powerful punch, even by a cynic's commercial standards.

Born Yves Allégret. **Pseudonym** Yves Champlain. **Marriage** Simone Signoret, actress, 1944, (divorced, 1949). **Children** Cathérine. **Career** In film industry, 1929 onwards, first as assistant, then assistant director, costume designer, and later as director; assistant to brother, Marc Allégret, 1929; installed sound for film producer Pierre Braunberger, Billancourt Studios, 1930; also assistant to Jean Renoir, Augusto Genina; art director on short advertising films; with Communist Associated Theatre Troupe, the Groupe Octobre, 1930s; first feature film, 1941; also directed for television. **Awards and honours** French César for career achievement, awarded posthumously, Paris, March 1987. **Films** (short) *Ténériffe*, 1932; (co-costume designer) *Ciboulette*, 1933; (short) *Prix et profits*, 1934; (short) *Le Gagnant*, 1935; (co-director) *Vous n'avez rien à déclarer?* 1936; (technical adviser) *Forfaiture*, 1937; (co-director) *L'Émigrante*, 1939; *La Roue tourné*, 1941; *Tobie est un ange*, 1941; (as Yves Champlain) *Les Deaux Timides* (*Jeunes timides*), 1942; (begun by Jean Choux) *La Boîte au rêves*, 1943; *Les Démons de l'aube*, 1945; *Dédée d'Anvers, (Dédée)*, 1947; *Une si jolie petite plage*, (Riptide), 1948; *Manèges* (The Cheat), 1949; *Les Miracles n'ont lieu qu'une fois*, 1950; *Nez de cuir*, 1951; "La Luxure (Lust)", episode of *Les Sept péchés capitaux* (*The Seven Deadly Sins*), 1951; *La Jeune folle* (*Desperate Decision*), 1952; *Mam'zelle Nitouche*, 1953; *Les Orgueilleux* (*The Proud and the Beautiful*), 1953; *Oasis*, 1954; *La Meilleure part*, 1955; *Quand la femme s'en mêle*, 1957; *Méfiez-vous fillettes* (*Young Girls Beware*), 1957; *La fille de Hambourg* (*Port of Desire*), 1958; *L'Ambitieuse*, 1959; *Oasis*, 1960; *La Chien de pique*, 1961; *Germinal*, 1962; *Terreur sur la savane*, (*Konga-Yo*), 1962; *Johnny Banco*, 1966; *L'Invasion*, 1970; *Mords pas—on t'aime*, 1976. **Television** (includes) "Georges Maigret" series. **Publications** "Why I Choose the Unusual", *Films and Filming*, London, October 1955. **Cause of death** Undisclosed, at age 79.

WILFRID BLUNT

British Author and Museum Curator

Born **Surrey, England, 19 July 1901**

Died **Surrey, England, 8 January 1987**

Eldest brother of art historian and Soviet spy Anthony Blunt, and son of an Anglican clergyman, Wilfrid Blunt was a prolific writer whose mature interests ranged far beyond the experimental art he dabbled in in his youth in the studio of Othon Friesz in Paris.

Educated at Marlborough, Oxford and the Royal College of Art, Blunt went on to become art teacher at Haileybury School and then at Eton College. Here his conservative spirit and promotion of italic handwiting endeared him to the then headmaster, Robert Birley. From 1959 until 1985 Blunt enjoyed what must have been a most civilized job as curator of the Watts Gallery at Compton in Surrey. The museum left him even more time to pursue his interests in botany, art history and travel than had schoolmastering.

As well as reorganizing the Watts Gallery, Blunt wrote and travelled widely for the rest of his life. His books on botany include *The Art of Botanical Illustration*, *The Illustrated Herbal*, a book on Kew Gardens, and a biography of Linnaeus entitled, *The Compleat Naturalist*. Of this the *Time* critic wrote that it "admirably illustrates how Linnaeus's single-mindedness and plodding devotion to stamens and pistils laid the foundation of modern beauty".

Blunt's travel books include *A Persian Spring*, about a journey of his own to Persia in the 1950s. This was followed by *Isfahan* and *The Splendours of Islam*. Of his *Golden Road to Samarkand* J.S. Phillipson of *Best Sellers* wrote: "This is a beautiful book, engagingly written. With a witty and lucid prose Mr Blunt holds us charmed. We travel in time from the Asia of Alexander the Great in the fourth century BC to a glimpse of Samarkand today, many of its historical places restored and in the opinion of the author, who appears to know very well where he speaks, well worth seeing. Every person discussed is fascinating." Blunt also wrote biographies of Ludwig II of Bavaria, the Algerian Abdel Kader, Lady Muriel Paget, Sir Sydney Cockerell and John Christie of Glyndebourne. Last but not least was his biography of Watts himself whom, following Lord Leighton, he called "England's Michelangelo".

Blunt the writer clearly possessed not only an enormously wide range of interests and knowledge, but was also gifted in his ability to convey to readers his own sense of the magic and romance of life and of the places and people about which he wrote.

The author of Blunt's obituary in the London *Times* described him as "a great bear of a man, genial but mischievous" who, for all his gardening lore, had no time or patience for gardening in the everyday sense. Happiest of all beside an ornamental garden urn, he was not one to bend or dig.

Shortly before his death Blunt wrote: "In my eighties I have had much pleasure in writing the first two volumes of my autobiography. The third and final volume will probably never be written; I haven't the energy to embark on it in my eighty-sixth year and, since I feel the need to write very frankly or not at all, too many people are still alive to make even posthumous publication possible for many years to come." Critics of the first volumes, *Married to a Single Life* and *Slow on the Feather* comment on Blunt's unusual frankness about his own homosexuality. Of his brother Anthony, Wilfrid Blunt continued to write with undiminished affection. "I could never adequately repay," he wrote in a letter to the *Times* in 1979, "the kindness he has shown me."

Born Wilfrid Jasper Walter Blunt. **Parents** Arthur Stanley Vaughan, clergyman, and Hilda (Master) Blunt. **Education** Marlborough College, 1915–20; Worcester College, Oxford, 1920–21; Royal College of Art, London, ARCA, 1923; also studied in Paris under Othon Friesz. **Career** Art master, Haileybury School, Hertfordshire, 1923–38; left Haileybury briefly to begin training as an opera singer; drawing master, Eton College, Berkshire, 1938–59; curator, Watts Gallery, Compton, Guildford, Surrey, 1959–85. **Memberships** Fellow, Linnean Society. **Awards and honours** Veitch Gold Medal, Royal Horticultural Society, for *The Art of Botanical Illustration*. **Publications** *The Haileybury Buildings*, 1936; *Desert Hawk*, 1947; *The Art of Botanical Illustration*, 1950; *Tulipomania*, 1950; *Black Sunrise: The Life and Times of Mulai Ismail, Emperor of Morocco*, 1951; *Sweet Roman Hand: Five Hundred Years of Italic Cursive Script*, 1952; *Japanese Colour Prints*, 1952; *Georg Dionysius Ehret*, 1953; *Pietro's Pilgrimage*, 1953; *Sebastiano*, 1956; (with Sacheverell Sitwell and Patrick Synge) *Great Flower Books, 1700–1900, 1956; A Persian Spring*, 1957; (with James Russell) *Old Garden Roses*, 1957; *Lady Muriel*, 1962; *Of Flowers and a Village*, 1963; *Cockerell*, 1964; *Omar: A Fantasy for Animal Lovers*,

1966; *Isfahan: Pearl of Persia*, 1966; *John Christie of Glyndebourne*, 1968; *The Dream King: Ludwig II of Bavaria*, 1970; *The Compleat Naturalist: A Life of Linnaeus*, 1971; *The Golden Road to Samarkand*, 1973; *On Wings of Song*, 1974; *"England's Michelangelo"*, 1975; *The Ark in the Park*, 1976; *The Splendours of Islam*, 1976; *In for a Penny*, 1978; (co-author) *The Illustrated Herbal*, 1979; *Married to a Single Life: An Autobiography, 1901–38*, 1938; *Slow on the Feather: An Autobiography, 1938–59*, 1986; also contributed articles to journals. **Cause of death** Undisclosed, at age 85.

RAY BOLGER

American Actor

***Born* Boston, Massachusetts, 10 January 1904**

***Died* Los Angeles, California, 15 January 1987**

To any member of the international film-going public, the mere mention of Ray Bolger's name conjures up the elastic-bodied, genial Scarecrow in the 1939 film version—is there really any other?—of *The Wizard of Oz*. The film's renowned lyricist, E.Y. Harburg, said about the casting: "No one else was ever considered." As *Oz* is shown annually on television around the world, not to mention at cinema retrospectives, Bolger's legion of admirers has grown, as has the awareness that his talents not only as a dancer but as an actor/comedian were not fully appreciated.

Raymond Wallace Bolger, born in Boston, had been proverbially stagestruck from childhood, although his career seemed destined for a more ordinary path; he worked for a bank after high school classes, then for a life insurance company upon graduation. However, his continual visits to the theatre fed his enthusiasm for dancing. He received unorthodox evening training after work with the night watchman at Boston's Horticultural Hall, who had once been a professional "hoofer". Bolger was later to recall regretfully that he was not a promising quick-study: "My ears could hear the rhythms and I could do them. But subconsciously I just didn't want to do what the others did. I felt it in a different way...it was my build and nervous temperament."

Bolger's "build", 5 feet 10½ inches and very lean, exaggerated his loose-legged and easy style. That distinctive "temperament" led to his first public performance: an amateur show put on by some of the insurance company's employees. After that, his free-wheeling dance routines were not limited to that platform; he was fired for hoofing up and down the halls. A career change was obviously called for, so while Bolger took a succession of jobs, from selling vacuum cleaners to peanuts, he auditioned for repertory roles and gave his first paid performance at 19: as second comic with the Bob Ott Company. As they utilized a dozen routines, Bolger learned a wide variety of roles and styles. "I was hired as a comedian," Bolger said years later, "becoming a dancer in self-defence. I was doing a comedy monologue and didn't know how else to get off, so I danced off!" Bolger's modesty and affability were characteristic throughout his career, and he was well-liked by his co-performers. He continued to maintain that his first love was comedy acting and that dancing was merely a means to obtain the parts.

Bolger played small towns, and no bouquets were forthcoming. However, in 1924, as one of "A Pair of Nifties", a vaudeville act typical of the times, he eventually won a brief spell at the Rialto Theater in New York City along with partner Ralph Sanford. The following year he went solo, dancing between films shown at a Paramount chain movie house. When he got a tiny part in

The Merry Whirl, his New York "début", he was discovered by agent Gus Edwards; two years on the celebrated Orpheum circuit followed.

Bolger's individualistic dancing style continued to develop; it was astonishingly agile and flexible. His next role, in *George White's Scandals of '31* at the Apollo, truly launched his career, but it was a bigger part in the popular *Life Begins at 8.40*—for which Harburg wrote the lyrics—that attracted the notice of Manhattan critics, known to be a jaded lot. He was proclaimed "an engaging comedian whose dancing never failed to steam up the audiences". In *On Your Toes* (1936) he was "a jazz Nijinsky" and "Astaire in mufti", for Bolger's athletic fashion had developed a romantic grace. His mastery of various techniques was spotlighted in the play *Slaughter on 10th Avenue Ballet*, choreographed by George Balanchine. Bolger considered it the most difficult dance of his career, but notices were enthusiastic. *Tenth Avenue* set him on the road to Hollywood.

These performances were followed by roles in musical films, such as *The Great Ziegfeld* (1936) and *Rosalie* (1937), but his talents as a character actor were not showcased to his satisfaction, although *The Wizard of Oz* (1939) cemented his name in the minds of the public. Although many other films followed, including *The Harvey Girls* (1946), *Where's Charley?* (1952) and *Babes in Toyland* (1961), his love for the stage often brought him back to Broadway. "I like the movies," he said, "but there aren't so many good spots in them for a fellow like me. I have to keep working. Besides, a dancer's legs can't go on forever."

Where's Charley? at the St James Theater in 1948 made Bolger's name as respected on Broadway as it was in Hollywood, perhaps more so, as the stage brought out his performing gifts more effectively than his film roles which were, generally speaking, secondary to more popular, "love interest" actors. The soft-shoe song, "Once in Love with Amy", became a kind of theme song for him. This success was of great personal satisfaction to Bolger; in addition, the play had been produced by his wife, Gwen Rickard, with whom he had a long and happy marriage. The play brought several awards, one of which was a Tony.

During World War II Bolger organized USO tours. Afterwards, he remained busy for the next several decades in stage, screen and the then upstart medium, television, with his *Ray Bolger Show* in 1953. He was elected to the Theater Hall of Fame in 1980. Bolger's last performance was in 1985 as a narrator in *That's Dancing*, a film collection of dance classics that included, ironically, a Scarecrow dance cut from the final version of *Oz*—one that was his favourite number in the film. He was to survive the other members of the *Oz* troupe: Judy Garland, Bert Lahr, Jack Haley—even their nemesis, the Wicked Witch of the West, played by Margaret Hamilton.

Born Raymond Wallace Bolger. **Parents** James Edward and Anne (Wallace) Bolger. **Marriage** Gwendolyn Rickard, vaudeville actress, 1929. **Education** Dorchester High School, Massachusetts; Senia Roussakoff School of the Dance, *circa* 1922. **Career** Worked for First National Bank while still at school; joined New England Mutual Life Insurance Company, Kelly Peanut Company, then became vacuum cleaner salesman, after graduating; appeared as dancer in amateur shows; became professional dancer, musical comedy star and actor on stage, films and television, 1922 onwards; stage début, with Bob Ott Musical Comedy Repertory Company, Boston, 1922; New York début, *The Merry Whirl*, 1926; film début, *The Great Ziegfeld*, 1936; television début, *The Comedy Hour*, 1952. **Awards and honours** Newspaper Guild Page One Award, 1943; Best Musical Comedy Performance for *Three to Make Ready*, Drama Critics' Poll, 1946; Tony Award for *Where's Charley?* 1949; Donaldson Award for *Where's Charley?* 1949; Decency in Entertainment, Notre Dame Club, Chicago, 1967; Medallion of Valor, Israel, 1970; nominated to Theatrical Hall of Fame, 1980. **Stage** (all in New York, unless stated) With Bob Ott Musical Comedy Repertory Company, Boston, 1922; vaudeville tour, 1924–26; *The Passing Show of 1926* (tour), 1926; *A Night in Paris*, 1926; *Ritz-Carlton Nights*, 1926; *Heads Up*, 1929;

George White's Scandals, 1931–33; *Life Begins at 8:40,* 1934–35; *On Your Toes*, 1936; *Keep Off the Grass*, 1940; *By Jupiter*, 1942; organizer, United Service Organization's Camp Shows, American military, naval bases, worldwide, 1943–45; *Three to Make Ready*, 1946; *Where's Charley?* 1948–51; *All American*, 1962; *The Ray Bolger Show*, (tour), 1965; concert appearance, 1967; cabaret, 1968; *Come Summer*, 1969; concert appearance, 1980; *That's Dancing*, 1985. **Films** *The Great Ziegfeld*, 1936; *Rosalie*, 1937; *The Girl of the Golden West*, 1938; *Sweethearts*, 1938; *The Wizard of Oz*, 1939; *Sunny*, 1941; *The Harvey Girls*, 1946; *Look for the Silver Lining*, 1949; *Where's Charley?*, 1952; *April in Paris*, 1953; *Babes in Toyland*, 1961; *The Daydreamer*, 1966; *The Runner Stumbles*, 1979. **Television** *The Colgate Comedy Hour* (guest appearances), 1950–51; *The Ray Bolger Show* (originally called *Where's Raymond?*), 1953–55; *The Bell Telephone Hour* (guest appearance), 1960; *The Judy Garland Show* (guest appearance), 1963; *Washington Square*, 1976; *The Entertainer*, 1976; *The Runner Stumbles*, 1979; *Captains and Kings* (mini series); *The Partridge Family*; *The Love Boat*. **Recordings** *The Wizard of Oz*; "Once in Love with Amy"; *All American*. **Cause of death** Cancer, at age 83.

GERALD BRENAN

British Writer

***Born* Malta, 7 April 1894**

***Died* Malaga, Spain, 19 January 1987**

Gerald Brenan, a British author of penetrating studies of the history and culture of Spain, including *The Spanish Labyrinth*, *The Literature of the Spanish People* and *South from Granada*, made his books memorable with a blend of curiosity and liveliness, extensive research and firsthand experience gleaned from his many years living in southern Spain. After various abortive attempts at novels and biography, some under the pseudonym of George Beaton, he started writing his finest work in the early 1940s, while back in England for a time. Brenan first went to Spain in 1920 and lived there for much of his life, dying there at the age of 92.

The life of Edward FitzGerald Brenan did not follow a conventional pattern. Born in Malta, where his father was stationed with an Irish regiment, his ancestors were mainly well-to-do, with incomes from ship-building and cotton-spinning, his mother Helen being the daughter of a Belfast linen manufacturer. He had one brother, Blair. Fond of his gentle mother, he found his father domineering and irritable; later he had to struggle against both parents' disapproval of his lifestyle and chosen career as a writer. Until the age of eight, Brenan's family went wherever his father was posted, including South Africa, Ceylon, India and Ireland, where the young Brenan stayed at his grandmother's country estate. All these places had their influence on the boy and the foundations were laid for a yearning to get away to distant and exotic places.

His early education was supplied by his mother who gave him lessons in reading, history and geography. At preparatory school in England from 1903 he enjoyed reading boys' adventure books and, becoming absorbed by geography, he would draw imaginary islands. At Radley College he developed his interest in geography and remote, deserted places, drawing maps of deserts and cities of the East. He also became drawn to poetry, an interest he would keep all his life.

Up to this point, apart from the many moves from country to country—not unusual for a military family—Brenan's early years were not untypical of an English middle-class childhood. However, at Radley he was already feeling out of sympathy and stifled by the narrowness and hypocrisy of English public school life with its élitism, strict code and over-emphasis on games and religion. In his own words: "I was given the usual Spartan education meted out to English middle-class boys, which consists in their being taught nothing and made as miserable as possible."

At the end of his last term in 1912 he broke the mould. Wishing to avoid being sent to the military academy at Sandhurst, and under the influence of such books as W.H. Davies' *Autobiography of a Supertramp* and Henry Thoreau's *Walden*, he and his friend John Hope-Johnstone, former tutor to the children of British painter Augustus John, went off to France in rebellious spirit and with little money, intending to walk to the Far East. This was both a great adventure and a formative experience, acquainting Brenan for the first time with poverty and awakening his compassion for the poor, which he later wrote about with great awareness and sympathy. Staying in doss houses and eating in tavernas, the pair pushed an old cart until they acquired a mule named Mr Bird. They walked through Italy, then into Austria, where they were suspected of espionage and arrested. Once released, Brenan proceeded alone to Yugoslavia, then to Venice, returning to England in 1914 when he ran out of money.

He was sent to Gemany to continue his education but war broke out and he joined the 5th Gloucesters, fighting with them from 1915 to 1918. A young man of barely 21 when he joined up, he was at first enthusiastic, but his experience of the slaughter and appalling conditions took its toll of his once buoyant morale. Although modest about his war years, he served with distinction and attained the rank of captain, fighting in the battles of the Marne and the Somme, and was awarded the Military Cross and the Croix de Guerre. He was wounded at Ypres, but returned to take part in the final Allied offensive. He wrote of this part of his life, up to the age of 25, in his first volume of autobiography entitled *A Life of One's Own*, containing portraits of family and friends and showing his movement towards nonconformity. A reviewer for *Time* magazine in 1963 commented: "Self-love in writers is common enough, but there is no exhibitionism in the steadfast egotism of Gerald Brenan. This has the paradoxical effect of giving his superb autobiography the quality of authenticity that belongs only to the highest kind of fiction—it is his work, take it or leave it."

His second volume, *Personal Record*, covering the years 1920 to 1972, begins in the year he went to live in Spain, choosing to live simply in the remote village of Yegen in Granada, known as the Alpujarra, and beginning his long and sympathetic relationship with Spain and its people. Like the first volume, the book is full of frank portraits of family and friends, but now included lovers and his relationship to them. His aim was to educate himself, not yet having formed his wish to be a writer, and to this end he spent his time in long reading and solitude, broken only by walks in the surrounding countryside. Although money was short, he made occasional visits and longer stays in England. There he spent time with the Bloomsbury Group, named after the area of London in which they lived. This talented group included writers and artists such as Virginia Woolf, her sister Vanessa Bell, Roger Fry, Duncan Grant and Lytton Strachey. Brenan found them rather cliquish and inward-looking but became more involved through his intense love affair with the painter Dora Carrington, who was always known by her surname only. She lived with Lytton Strachey and married Brenan's war-time friend Ralph Partridge. In England, Carrington, Strachey and Partridge lived together in a cottage and were inseparable, despite Partridge's growing involvement with another woman and Strachey's homosexuality. In 1932, soon after Strachey's death from cancer, Carrington shot and killed herself. Before this time, however, relations between Brenan and Carrington had become distant. Brenan described their "once rapturous, then tormenting, and always unstable relation" in *Personal Record*. This book, written in the 1960s, also focuses on his struggles to be a writer, and it sold very well, earning him ten times more in royalties than had his previous books together. From the time of his relationship with Carrington, Brenan was rarely without the stimulation of a sexual relationship.

In 1931 Brenan married an American poet, Gamel Woolsey, whom he had met in Dorset on the south coast of England. The couple, who evolved a calm and companionable relationship, settled in Spain in a beautiful house at Churriana, outside Malaga. They lived there modestly until the outbreak of the Spanish Civil War, when, on the recommendation of Bertrand Russell, Brenan served for a time as special correspondent for the *Manchester Guardian*, writing government propaganda and cycling into Malaga each day for news. He felt that the Civil War was "...a purely Spanish affair, to be seen in terms of Peninsular rather than European history, and distorted by the existence of two great power dynamos, Nazi Germany and Communist Russia, which operated from outside." In his own politics, he was always a liberal, saying, "I am an individualist and value liberty above everything else."

Curiosity about the reasons for the Civil War were part of Brenan's inspiration for his distinguished book *The Spanish Labyrinth* (1943), a lucid social and political study of Spain from 1874 until the outbreak of the Civil War, containing also an epilogue on the war. A wide-ranging book, it is factually accurate, well researched and, as in his other books on Spain, he attempts to probe and define the Spanish character. From 1939 to 1954 Brenan and his wife lived in Aldbourne, Wiltshire, and it was here that Brenan completed the book. During these war years he also served in the Home Guard, and then as an air raid warden in London, but declined active service in the invasion of Normandy.

He began to read much medieval French and Spanish poetry at this time and in 1949 published *The Literature of the Spanish People*, which covered the different periods of Spanish literature in great detail and traced its influences. His aim was to draw "the attention of English and American readers to Spanish literature", and his success in doing so was confirmed by the critics, one of whom, writing for the *Saturday Review*, commented, "the author of this fine study...is rapidly moving into the position of the first English-speaking Hispanicist of this period".

In 1945 and 1949 Brenan made visits to Spain, and he and his wife returned permanently in 1953. His travel book, *The Face of Spain* (1951), put together from a diary where he had noted his "everyday experiences and impressions", describes his return to his home in Andalusia after a long absence and his visits to Madrid, Granada and Toledo, again attempting to explore and express the real character of Spain and the Spanish. Following his return to Spain, he wrote *South from Granada*, recalling his earlier years in Yegen. The book is about Spanish peasant society but successfully integrates visits from some of his Bloomsbury friends, including the Woolfs, Lytton Strachey and Roger Fry. This book was well received but Brenan was less successful with his fiction, about which he had never felt confident, although a novel, *Jack Robinson* (1933), written under a pseudonym, had received good reviews. A later novel, *A Holiday by the Sea* (1961), set in England and with a middle-aged central character, Tom Fisher, a man who has published nothing, drew the following comments from a *Times Literary Supplement* reviewer: "...one reads it with sympathy and at times even with exhilaration, yet one finally lays it down with the depressed feeling of a crossword-solver whom the last clue still eludes". *The Lighthouse Always Says Yes* (1962) also had a dissatisfied central male character who was criticized for being too negative.

Brenan's wife Gamel died of cancer in 1968. The following year he sold their Churriana home and built a house 13 miles away overlooking the village of Alhaurin el Grande, where he lived with poet Lynda Nicholson Price, 50 years his junior, and later with her husband. There he and Price wrote a biography of the holy man and poet *St John of the Cross* (1973), an expansion of his own earlier essays and inspired by his interest in Spain and religious experience. He had earlier started a biography of St Teresa of Avila.

A small book, *Thoughts in a Dry Season* (1978), assembled from notes Brenan had made over the years, confirms his tendency to aphorism and shows the broadness and singularity of his mind as he ranges over love, death, religion and art. In a review of this book, V.S. Pritchett described how Brenan's personal presence pervaded his prose: "The tall man whose glasses flash as if he were sending out signals, as he slippers about the room talking fast and softly...pops up between the lines of the printed page....He will punctuate his talk with the most elegant of smoker's coughs and the most enticing of suggestions or gossipy innuendos."

In 1984, at the age of 90, Gerald Brenan returned to England and went into a nursing home in Pinner, Middlesex, because British friends felt he wished to be in his native country, but Spanish admirers protested and he went back to Spain only a month later, apparently at his own wish. The Andalusian government and the town council of Alhaurin el Grande showed their appreciation of him by helping to pay for a nurse and housekeeper to look after him, as he had been living with only modest means despite the sale of his books.

Brenan's only child was a daughter, Miranda, the offspring of a pre-marital relationship with a Spanish woman. Brenan adopted the child and she later married and lived in Paris. In 1982 he was made a Commander of the British Empire, and in 1986 a group of Spanish and foreign historians set up a Gerald Brenan Foundation to perpetuate the study of his works. He is remembered for his love of life and for his generosity of spirit, open to those many visitors who came to consult him. His books, revealing the complex history and make-up of Spain, are admired by historians and literary critics alike. Cyril Connolly in a review of *South of Granada* analysed the appeal of Spain for Gerald Brenan thus: "The beauty of [the book] is that the young man who fled to these remote uplands was healed by them: he found the ancient rhythm, the beliefs, the folklore, the pagan survivals, the Virgilian poetry, the life-cycle that he had craved and he emerged with a philosophy as well as an education."

Born Edward FitzGerald Brenan. **Pseudonym** George Beaton. **Parents** Hugh Gerald, Irish Army officer, and Helen Brenan. **Marriage** Elisabeth Gamel Woolsey, poet, 1930 (died, 1968). **Children** One daughter, Miranda, from pre-marital liaison. **Education** Winton House Preparatory School, 1903–08; Radley College, Hertfordshire, 1908–12. **Emigration** Lived for long periods in Spain from 1918; settled there permanently, 1953. **Military service** Captain, 5th Gloucesters, Western Front, 1915–18; lieutenant, Home Guard, World War II. **Career** Author, traveller, historian, specializing in books on Spain; first publications, satires, "The Bestiary", *Nation*, *circa* 1924. **Related activities** Special correspondent, *Manchester Guardian*, 1936–39; broadcaster, children's playwright, BBC, 1950s. **Awards and honours** Croix de Guerre, World War I; Military Cross, World War I; Commander of the Order of the British Empire, 1982. **Publications** (as George Beaton) *Jack Robinson*, 1933; (as George Beaton) *Dr Partridge's Almanack for 1935*, 1934; *The Spanish Labyrinth* (history), 1943; *The Face of Spain* (travel), 1950; *The Literature of the Spanish People*, 1951; *South from Granada*, 1957; *A Holiday by the Sea* (novel), 1961; *A Life of One's Own* (autobiography), 1962, revised edition, 1975; *The Lighthouse Always Says Yes* (novel), 1966; (co-author with Lynda Price Nicholson) *St John of the Cross* (biography), 1973; *Personal Record, 1920–1972*, 1974; *Thoughts in a Dry Season*, 1978. **Cause of death** Undisclosed, at age 92. **Further reading** *Twentieth Century Authors* (first supplement), 1955; Cyril Connolly, *The Evening Colonnade*, 1973.

CARLO CASSOLA

Italian Novelist and Essayist
***Born* Rome, Italy, 17 March 1917**
***Died* Monte Carlo, 29 January 1987**

Carlo Cassola, award-winning Italian novelist, was born into a middle-class intellectual family in Rome but was drawn all his life to provincial Tuscany—spending holidays there from childhood, settling there once his studies were complete, fighting there with the partisan resistance to the Fascists in World War II—and it was in the small Tuscan towns and suburbs that he set much of his writing. He said: "In these places I later had the most important experiences of my life, including that of partisan struggle."

Cassola's mother was herself from Tuscany and his father from the north of Italy. He had an early interest in literature and in the 1930s was impressed with the work of Irish writer, James Joyce, and the French author, Marcel Proust. In 1935 he enrolled at the University of Rome School of Law and lived in the city until 1940. He married Giuseppina Rabage with whom he had one daughter. Cassola started teaching history and philosophy in high schools in 1942, continuing to do so until the early 1960s, when he began to establish his literary reputation, giving up teaching for full-time writing and journalism.

He began writing before the war and his first two volumes of short stories, *La Visita* and *Alla Periferia* were published in 1942. A short essay, "Il film dell'impossibile", expressed his early literary aims and its title suggests how difficult they were to achieve. He said he was trying "to create a purely existential narrative, one, that is, which gave a sense of existence." Through expressing the universal flow of time, he wanted to achieve a timeless beauty and, to this end, stripped his writing of conventional story-telling techniques, such as plot, characterization, development, analysis, commentary, descriptive and ornamental detail, and ideology, seeing all these as distractions from his aim. He recorded the lives of the simple people of Tuscany, living unremarkable but hard lives in ordinary towns and suburbs, often through their own colloquial speech. This technique, understated and non-selective, where nothing actually "happens", owed much to James Joyce's *Dubliners*. Cassola's early work is seen as a forerunner of the French *nouveau roman* (new novel), with its non-story technique. This distilling of his material made some of his stories very short indeed and gradually brought him to a complete standstill. He had five years when he wrote nothing at all, but during the war, he fought with the communist partisans against the Fascists in the Tuscan countryside, an experience which inspired some of his most successful work.

Cassola's post-war novels began to win acclaim. The emergence of a clear story-line seemed to indicate a change, although he kept his unpretentious style, low on analysis and commentary. The semi-autobiographical *Fausto e Anna* (Fausto and Anna, 1952) tells of urban, middle-class Fausto, a character not unlike himself, who decides to give up his comfortable life and girlfriend, Anna, to go and fight with the partisans against the Fascists. The first part of the novel is about the young couple's growing relationship, while the second part concerns his experiences with the partisans, his disillusionment with the brutality and destructiveness of war, and his unsuccessful attempt to reclaim Anna, who has married another man. The book was criticized by the Italian Left because of its ambiguous attitude to the achievements of the partisans, but it gave a voice to those who were anti-Fascist but who, nevertheless, felt some doubt and confusion about the role of the partisans. After the fall of Fascism, Cassola joined the Partito d'Azione, a coalition of anti-Fascist and non-communist forces.

Cassola also found himself in disagreement with the literature of "engagement" which was gaining ground at that time, preferring his own personal integrity to the commitment of espousing a cause or movement wholeheartedly. He said: "The war and the resistance had not altered me; rather, after so many changing events, did I feel more strongly than ever the need to take refuge in my own little private world...I believed...that a writer must express only his own nature and only his own personal story." He was, however, influenced by neo-realism, a powerful current at this time in Italy, of which the leading exponents were Elio Vittorini (1908–66) and Cesare Pavese (1908–50), whose books also deal with Fascism, war and resistance mainly through the lives of ordinary people, using an unpretentious conversational style and whose work shows the influence of American writers such as Steinbeck and Hemingway.

Another personal book, considered by many to be his best and held high in his own affections, was *Il Taglio del Bosco* (The Cutting of the Woods, 1950), an autobiographical novella in as far as it explored his own feelings of loss following the death of his wife, although these were expressed through the character of a simple woodcutter.

With *La Ragazza di Bube* (Bebo's Girl, 1960), Cassola won the prestigious Strega Prize and popular success both at home and abroad. This book tells of a girl, Mara, and Bube, a 19-year-old ex-partisan who has become involved in the killing of a policeman. Only Mara stands by him and loyally waits for him to complete his 14-year sentence. After the publication of this novel, Cassola's books were guaranteed best sellers and often translated into English and other languages. During the course of his career he won several other Italian literary awards.

Much of Cassola's appeal and skill lies in his sympathetic portrayal of ordinary people pursuing their lives in the only way they know how, with little economic means and with limited powers of self-analysis and self-expression, but nevertheless true to themselves. This is why the simple Tuscan people, living at the periphery of events—hence the frequent setting in suburbs—seem to embody his vision of life so well. The kind of non-intellectual stoicism and wisdom that his characters display, especially the women, has annoyed some critics who see his central women as predictably resigned and rarely open to any kind of development in their lives.

His earlier post-war books, including *Fausto e Anna* and *La Ragazza de Bube*, were given atmosphere and excitement through their partisan background, but Casola's work in the 1960s seemed to return to his earlier no-story style, sometimes described as flat and colourless, and drawing complaints from critics of monotony and repetition as he reworked his earlier themes. One such critic described his style by saying that "the rhythm of the narration seems to coincide with the rhythm of life itself", but goes on to say "the reader is made increasingly uneasy by a sense of aridity in the lives of Cassola's protagonists—a sense of lost opportunities and in the last analysis of an inability to live life in any full or meaningfully human sense of the term."

Cassola's book *Un Cuore Arido* (An Arid Heart, 1961) illustrates her point. Anna, whose daily life is minutely recorded, chooses a lonely but self-sufficient life by staying in her native village rather than following her fiancé to America. One commentator described this book as "woven out of the minutiae of everyday life...an almost unbroken dialogue punctuated by long silences...the sinuous rhythm of the tranquil prose, the limpid clarity of Tuscan colloquial speech...intensify Cassola's muted, poetic picture of those quiet, remote Italian towns in which life, for all its secret turbulence, seems as if arrested in time and space."

Two short stories, "Storia di Ada" (Ada's Story) and "La Maestra" (The Schoolteacher), published together in 1967, also have central female characters who come to terms with the severe limitations in their lives. Ada, a farm girl, loses a hand in an accident and marries an illiterate soldier who goes into hospital with an illness that may be incurable. The small-town schoolteacher, Fiorella, finds meaning through an illicit relationship with a doctor. A later novel,

Paura e Tristezze (Fear and Sadness, 1970), also has at its centre a woman living a bleak life but nevertheless able to enjoy simple moments. *Monte Mario* (Portrait of Helena, 1973) moves away from Tuscany and portrays a contemporary urban relationship, set in Rome.

From 1975 Cassola became concerned about conservation. He published three essays on nationalism and nuclear terror, the best of which was "La Lezione della Storia" (The Lesson of History, 1978), and he took part in some disarmament campaigns. His novels began to reflect his preoccupation with these themes, perhaps most effectively in *Il Paradiso degli Animali* (Animals' Paradise, 1979).

Despite being involved in and influenced by various literary and political trends, Carlo Cassola was respected for maintaining his artistic independence. He was a prolific writer and very popular, but will probably be best remembered for his more structured stories, most of which were written between 1950 and 1960, and for giving a voice to the quiet stoicism of simple people.

Born Carlo Cassola. **Marriage** Giuseppina Rabage. **Children** One daughter. **Education** University of Rome School of Law, 1935. **Military service** With partisans, Tuscany, World War II. **Career** Teacher and author of novels, short stories, essays, 1942 onwards; teacher, secondary schools, 1942–61; professor of history and philosophy until 1971; first publication, *Alla Periferia*, Florence, 1942. **Related activities** Contributor to periodicals, including *Il Mondo*, *Contemporaneo*, *Corriere della Sera*, particularly post-World War II. **Awards and honours** Prato Prize, 1955; Salento Prize, 1958; Marzotto Prize, 1959; Strega Prize, for *La Ragazza di Bube*, 1960; Naples Prize, 1970; Bancarella Prize, 1976; Bagutta Prize, 1978. **Publications** *Alla Periferia* (short stories), 1942; *La Visita* (short stories), 1942, second edition, 1962; *Fausto e Anna* (novel), 1952, second edition, 1964, translated by Isabel Quigly as *Fausto and Anna*, 1960; *I Vecchi Compagni* (novel), 1953; *Il Taglio del Bosco* (short stories), 1955, second edition, 1970; (co-author with Luciano Bianciardi) *I Minatori della Maremma* (essays), 1956; *Viaggio in Cina* (essays), 1956; *La Casa di Via Valadier* (novel), 1956; *Un Matrimonio del Dopoguerra* (novel), 1957; *Il Soldato*, 1958; *La Ragazza di Bube* (novel), 1960, translated by Marguerite Waldman as *Bebo's Girl*, 1962; *Un Cuore Arido* (novel), 1961, translated by William Weaver as *An Arid Heart*, 1964; *Il Cacciatore (novel)*, 1964; *Tempi Memorabili* (novel), 1966; *Storia di Ada*, 1967; *Ferrovia Locale* (novel), 1968; *Una Relazione*, 1969; *Paura e Tristezza*, 1970; (co-author with Mario Luzi), *Poesia e Romanzo*, 1973; *Il Romanzo* (essays), 1973; *Monte Mario*, 1973; translated by Sebastian Roberts as *Portrait of Helena*, 1975; *Foglio di Diario* (essays), 1974; *Gisella*, 1974, second edition, 1978; *Troppo Tardi*, 1975; *Il Gigante Cieco* (essays), 1976; *Ultima frontiera* (essays), 1976; *La Disavventura*, 1977; *L'Antagonista*, 1977; *L'Uomo e il cane*, 1977; *La Lezione della Storia* (essays), 1978; *Un Uomo Solo*, 1978; *Il Superstite*, 1978; *Contro le Armi*, 1980; *Vita da Artista*, 1980; *Romanza Totale* (essays), 1981; *La Zampa d'Oca* (essays), 1982; *Colloquio con le Ombre* (essays), 1982; *Gli Anni Passano* (essays), 1982; *Mio Padre* (essays), 1983. **Cause of death** Undisclosed, at age 69. **Further reading** L. Russo, *Inarratori*, 1958; S. Pullini, *Il Romanzo Italiano del Dopoguerra*, 1960; G. Mariani, *La Giovane Narrativa Italiana Tra Documento e Poesia*, 1962; G. Ferrenti, *Letteratura e Ideologia*, 1964; A.R. Alberto, *Scritori e Popolo*, 1966; R. Macchioni-Jodi, *Cassola*, 1967; M. Grillandi, *Letteratura Italiana: I Contemporanei*, 1969.

WILLIAM DEVLIN

British Actor

***Born* Aberdeen, Scotland, 5 December 1911**

***Died* Somerset, England, 25 January 1987**

William Devlin was a scholarly Shakespearian actor who astonished his friends and the world twice in the course of his professional career. The first was when, aged only 23, he sprang to fame overnight as the youngest great King Lear ever to appear on the London stage. The second was when, some 25 years later, he suddenly announced that he was "giving it all up", retiring to live in the little village of Monksilver in Somerset. Here he apparently spent a very happy last 20 years of his life fishing, playing golf and busying himself with the affairs of the Monksilver Parish Council.

Hugh Hunt, Devlin's friend and colleague of many years, felt that Devlin's "easy-going, unambitious and comfort-loving nature", together with his scholarly interests, might better have suited him to the life of an Oxford don, but that "his darkly handsome face and superb voice" doomed him to an actor's career. Devlin was famous for having his morning newspaper warmed for him by the fire before he settled down to the day's crossword puzzle. He read Greek, Latin and Old English for pleasure; his favourite author was Chaucer.

Devlin however, distinguished himself on the stage from an early age. The son of an Irish architect settled in Aberdeen, he was educated at Stonyhurst public school where his performance as Stanhope in *Journey's End* earned him a mention in *Punch* magazine. At Oxford in the early 1930s he starred in most of the Oxford Union Dramatic Society's productions, playing, for example, Tybalt in John Gielgud's production of *Romeo and Juliet* alongside such professional actresses as Edith Evans and Peggy Ashcroft. After only a year at the Embassy Theatre School of Acting, Devlin took the London theatre world by storm in his "majestically composed" performance in Hugh Hunt's production of *King Lear* at the Westminster Theatre.

Devlin's Lear—his straggling beard streaked with grey to add age to his face—was one of the great classic performances of all time. The critic James Agate wrote that Devlin's own age became immaterial. "His understanding of the text and his sense of beauty are everywhere apparent." Agate later phoned the Westminster Theatre to ask whether it was his review in the *Sunday Times* that was responsible for the "House Full" notices posted outside the theatre every night.

Age almost immediately became Devlin's great forte. The following year his Peer Gynt won high praise from W.A. Darlington, theatre critic of the *Daily Telegraph*, who wrote about Devlin's "intellect, magnificent voice and extraordinary range of facial expressions". A couple of years later his elderly Gladstone in the biographical play put on at the Gate Theatre in London was another outstanding success, even though Devlin himself complained that the more he made himself up to look like Gladstone, the more like Disraeli he actually appeared. Devlin went on to play any number of Shakespearian roles at the Old Vic Theatre, including Cassius, Banquo, Leontes, Richard III and, again, Lear.

During the war Devlin joined the Cavalry and learnt to ride a horse, but in fact spent most of his time on active service in Italy and North Africa riding a motorcycle as a military policeman. When he returned to the theatre he worked with Hugh Hunt to set up the Bristol Old Vic theatre company, where he starred in the parts of Lear, Macbeth, Othello, Brutus and Shylock. In these years he also played Lear and Macbeth in Boston, Agamemnon at Stratford-upon-Avon and Emilius in Peter Brook's European tour of *Titus Andronicus*. Despite some film and broadcasting work, for which his voice was particularly suited, Devlin somehow never achieved the spectacular fame which his early talent appeared to predict.

Perhaps success came to William Devlin too young. Perhaps he really was so unambitious and unworldly as to prefer, once he could afford it, the gentlemanly life of a small village squire. There is a hint that in the innate conservatism of his views, Devlin may also have found himself at odds with some of his colleagues. In the late 1950s, for example, he attacked a left-wing attempt by members of the actors' union, Equity, to become involved in a dispute between the Musicians' Union and the BBC. Whatever the significance of this, one thing is certain: having played most of the "older" roles in his youth, Devlin would have been hard put to catch up on the "youthful" parts in his old age. Perhaps, too, there was something in his early understanding of the tragedy of Lear that freed him to make the most of his own later years in the life most suited to his nature.

Born William George Devlin. **Parents** William John, an architect, and Frances Evelyn (Crombie) Devlin. **Marriages** 1) Mary Casson, actress, 1936 (divorced); 2) Meriel Moore, 1948 (died, 1981). **Children** One daughter. **Education** Stonyhurst College; Merton College, Oxford, BA, 1933; Embassy Theatre School of Acting, 1933–34. **Military service** Trooper, Horsed Cavalry, 1939; commissioned, Royal Wiltshire Yeomanry, 1941; served with 8th Army in Africa and Italy; demobilized as major, 1945. **Career** Actor for leading British theatre companies, 1931 onwards; also broadcaster and television actor; acting début, Oxford University Dramatic Society, 1931; London début, 1934; television début, *The Tiger*, 1936; New York début, *You Never Can Tell*, 1948. **Related activities** Secretary, Oxford University Dramatic Society, 1931–33; member, Equity Council, 1957–65. **Other activities** Member, Monksilver Parish Council, 1967, chairman, 1971, 1973–74. **Stage** With John Gielgud's Company, 1934–35; Old Vic Company, 1935–36; played leading roles at Old Vic, London, 1935–39, 1945–53; *The Lost Leader*, Dublin, 1937; *Zola*, 1937–38; *The Tiger*, 1937–38; *Mr Gladstone*, 1937–38; *Ascent of F6*, 1938; *Mourning Becomes Electra*, 1938; leading man with Old Vic Company, Bristol, 1945–48; *You Never Can Tell*, New York, 1948; *King Lear*, Boston, 1948; *Macbeth*, Boston, 1948; *Adventure Story*, 1949; season at Memorial Theatre, Stratford-upon-Avon, 1954–55; *Titus Andronicus*, European tour, 1957. **Cause of death** Undisclosed, at age 75.

LOVAT DICKSON

British Biographer and Publisher

***Born* Victoria, Australia, 30 June 1902**

***Died* Toronto, Canada, 2 January 1987**

For many years senior director of the London publishing firm Macmillan and Company, Lovat Dickson always said that he "gravitated naturally into publishing" and "never thought of doing anything else". Such a gravitation seems not wholly inevitable, given Dickson's background. Born the son of a mining engineer, his childhood was spent in Australia, Rhodesia and Canada—his schooldays in England—and his youth was spent working as a farm labourer, a shipyard driller's assistant and a clerk dealing with the pensions of Canadian war widows. Bad health finally prevented Dickson from following his father as a mining engineer and launched him instead on a new path as founding editor of the *Blue Diamond Weekly*, a newspaper for the mining workers of the Blue Diamond Mine at Brule in the Canadian Rockies, of which his father was then manager.

From Brule, Dickson went on to Alberta University where he graduated in English with flying colours and was appointed as a lecturer under Professor Broadus. To Broadus's dismay, however, Dickson left Alberta two years later in 1928 to work as editor of the *English Review* under the ownership of the Canadian mining millionaire, Frederick Hammond.

In his autobiography, *The Ante-Room*, Dickson later described his "moment of clarity" on sailing into Dover as he saw clearly the mistake he was making. Although, he says, he already knew that people were more important than words, happiness than success, he was by then already too addicted to the "subtle drug" of words to change direction. This addiction came, he said, both from the books "too exciting for a young mind to bear" that his father read to him in childhood, and even more from the solace he found in the written word in the long, lonely months following his mother's death in 1917.

Books were to remain the focal centre of Dickson's long and successful career as editor of the *English Review* and the *Fortnightly Review*, and later as a publisher. As director of his own company from 1930 until 1938, he published a number of best sellers, including Eiluned Lewis's *Dew on the Grass*, Von Rintelen's *Dark Invader* and, in the teeth of strong Nazi opposition, a translation of Ewald Banse's *Germany Prepares for War*.

It was a book that later turned out to be something of a hoax that really made Dickson's fame and fortune, however. When he published *Pilgrims of the Wild*, a passionate account of the struggle for existence of the wild life in the Canadian backwoods, he believed, as did everyone else, that the author "Grey Owl" was indeed a native of the Ojibway tribe. Sales from this book quickly topped the 35,000 mark. "Grey Owl", brought to England by Dickson, proved a charismatic and popular speaker. In his traditional Red Indian garb—buckskin trousers, moccasins, feathers and flowing black hair—he enchanted his female audiences in particular. The high point of his visit came with a visit to Buckingham Palace where he apparently held the little princesses enthralled with his tales of the wild, clapped George VI fraternally on the shoulder and departed a universal hero.

Only when "Grey Owl" died unexpectedly a short time later and was revealed in the undertaker's parlour as the cockney-born Englishman Archie Belaney was the whole story blown. Belaney's aunts, then living in Hastings, explained that their nephew had been adopted by the Ojibway Indians and given the name of "Grey Owl". Dickson, who wrote two books on the affair, defended his protégé whom, he said, had spent the greater part of his life with the Indians, spoke their language and had married one of their women.

Fortunately, publisher and author survived the scandal unimpaired. Dickson became a director of Macmillan's in 1941 and handled for them Richard Hillary's *The Last Enemy*. His own study of H.G. Wells earned him the praise of C.P. Snow. His autobiographical work, *The Ante-Room*, was described by the Canadian novelist Robertson Davies as "a book of uncommon literary distinction in which a man reveals himself in spare, elegant prose which carries us far below what can be achieved by undisciplined confession". Of the second volume, Dickson's obituary in the London *Times* said that it was "lively with sketches of authors and publishers and...brings out Dickson's never failing sense of fun".

Born Horatio Henry Lovat Dickson. **Parents** Gordon Fraser, a mining engineer, and Josephine Mary (Cunningham) Dickson. **Marriage** Marguerite Isabella Brodie, 1934. **Children** One son, Jonathan Alexander Brodie. **Education** Alfred Beit School, Salisbury, Zimbabwe, 1909; Berkhamsted School, Hertfordshire, England, 1913–17; Haileybury School of Mines, Ontario, 1919–20; Alberta University, Edmonton, Canada, BA, 1927, MA, 1929. **Military service** Royal Air Force cadet-officer, 1917. **Career** Series of temporary jobs, including miner, driller's help and farmhand, until starting at Alberta University; administrative clerk, Board of Pension Commissioners, Montreal, *circa* 1918; sales department, Paramount Pictures Corporation of Canada, 1920; founder and editor of weekly newspaper, *Blue Diamond Weekly*, Brule, Canadian Rockies, 1921; lecturer in English, Alberta University, Edmonton, 1927–29; also, assistant to Professor Broadus, University of California, Los Angeles, summer 1928; associate editor, *Fortnightly Review*, London, England, 1929–32; editor, *Review of Reviews*, London, 1930–32; managing editor, Lovat Dickson Ltd, London, 1932–38; editor, *Lovat Dickson's Magazine*, 1934–37; assistant general editor, Macmillan & Co Ltd, London, 1938–41, director, 1941–64; director, Reprint Society, 1939–64; director, Pan Books Ltd, 1946–64, retired 1964; also author, 1938 onwards. **Awards and honours** Lieutenant-Governor's Gold Medal, 1927; joint winner, Shakespeare Prize, 1927; honorary LLD, Alberta, 1968; honorary DLitt: Western Ontario, 1976, York University, Toronto, 1981. **Publications** (in London unless stated) *The Green Leaf*, 1938; *Half-Breed, the Story of Grey Owl*, 1938; *Out of the West Land*, 1944; *Richard Hillary*, 1950; *The Ante-Room* (autobiography), 1960; *The House of Words* (autobiography), 1962; *H.G. Wells: His Turbulent Life and Times*, 1969; *Wilderness Man*, 1974; *Radclyffe Hall at the Well of Loneliness*, 1975; *The Museum-Makers*, 1985. **Cause of death** Undisclosed, at age 84.

HUGO FREGONESE

Argentinian Film Director

Born **Mendoza, Argentina, 8 April 1908**

Died **Buenos Aires, Argentina, 11 January 1987**

Hugo Fregonese was one of those B-film directors, born abroad and swallowed up by the, at times anonymous, Hollywood film industry without having had a chance to carve out a particular style. After years spent earning a medical-school education at Buenos Aires University (1920–28), Fregonese became a journalist, then editor of a sports magazine for a year. From 1932 to 1935 he was involved in the cattle industry; he then decided to continue his education at New York's Columbia University. By 1937 he was hired by Columbia Films as a technical adviser for Latin-American-theme pictures; at last he had found his vocation. Fregonese learned what he could about the basics of film-making, then returned home a few years later to direct his own films, such as *Pampas barbara* (Savage Pampas, 1943) and *Where the Words Die* (1946). It is interesting to conjecture what might have happened to his style of directing had he stayed in Argentina.

He returned to Hollywood in 1944 and quickly gained a reputation of turning mundane material into stylishly presentable B-pictures, mostly westerns and thrillers. In fact, he became a kind of foreign exponent (as did many other directors from other countries) of American B-picture values: quick violence and shadowy atmospheres feeding a rightfully paranoid attitude of the main characters. At Universal he directed *One-Way Street*, an emotionally turgid work with James Mason, and *Saddle Tramp*, both in 1950. This began a series of westerns which culminated in his best, *Apache Drums*, produced by Val Lewton. This film, about a community threatened by unseen killers, began a partnership between Lewton and Fregonese which, unfortunately, did not come to fruition as Lewton died not long after.

Fregonese did not remain under contract to a particular studio; he moved back to Columbia where, in 1952, he directed *My Six Convicts* for Stanley Kramer, and *Blowing Wild* (1953), a rather bleak-in-mood piece with Barbara Stanwyck and Gary Cooper. Although he was selected to do other films for the studio, he seems not to have produced anything remarkable enough to pull him out of the B-picture level, and his reputation for creating a kind of tortured acting from his stars underlined the specific genres he shot. Nevertheless, given the small budgets and banal storylines, Fregonese could turn out films with a strong visual style.

In 1953 he relocated once more, this time to 20th Century-Fox, where he made a remake of the Jack-the-Ripper story, *Man in the Attic*, with Jack Palance. Fregonese's tendency towards nightmarish imagery suited the material well; it is considered to be one of his better films, showing off Palance's attributes to good effect. Other films which stand out during this period are two made in 1954: *Black Tuesday*, a gangster film about a killer on the run, with Edward G. Robinson, and *The Raid*, a Civil War thriller about Confederate soldiers escaping prison and wreaking vengeance upon a small town in Vermont. The latter starred Anne Bancroft and Van Heflin, and remains one of Fregonese's more convincing films.

Fregonese set his sights upon other countries where he could develop more freedom in his choice of material; however, it appears not to have improved his career. In the UK he directed *Seven Thunders* (also known as *The Beast of Marseilles*, 1957) and in 1961, *Harry Black and the Tiger*, an adventure story shot in India with Stewart Granger. He also worked in Italy and Germany, then returned briefly to Hollywood where his work suffered a decline, despite his remake of *Savage Pampas* (1966) with Robert Taylor, and a series of his favourite genre, the western. By 1970 he was back in Argentina, where he directed several unremarkable films before he ended his career.

Born Hugo Fregonese. **Marriage** Faith Domergue, actress (divorced, 1954). **Children** Two. **Education** Studied medicine, Buenos Aires University, 1920–28; Columbia University, New York, 1935. **Career** Journalist, editor, sports magazine, 1929–30; in cattle industry, 1932–35; technical adviser, Columbia Pictures, Hollywood, 1937; returned to Argentina, becoming full-time film director, particularly of westerns, 1939 onwards; later worked in Hollywood and Europe before returning to Argentina. **Films** (as director, unless stated) *Bariloche*, 1939; *El delta*, 1939; (assistant director) *Frente a la vida*, 1939; (assistant director) *Hermanos*, 1939; (assistant director) *Corazon de turco*, 1940; (assistant director) *Novios par las muchachas*, 1941; (assistant director) *El cura gaucho*, 1941; (assistant director) *Melodias de America*, 1942; (assistant director) *El viejo hucha*, 1942; (assistant director) *La guerra gaucha*, 1942; (co-director with Lucas Demare) *Pampa bárbara*, 1943; (assistant director) *Delirio*, 1944; (assistant director) *Su mejor alumno*, 1944; *Donde mueren las palabras*, 1946; *Apenas un delincuente*, 1947; *De hombre a hombre*, 1949; *Saddle Tramp*, 1950; *One Way Street*, 1950; *Apache Drums*, 1951; *Mark of the Renegade*, 1951; *My Six Convicts*, 1952; *Untamed Frontier*, 1952; *Blowing Wild*, 1953; *Decameron Nights*, 1953; *Man in the Attic*, 1953; *Blowing Wild*, 1953; *The Raid*, 1954; *Black Tuesday*, 1954; *I girovaghi*, 1956; *Seven Thunders/The Beast of Marseilles*, 1957; *La spada imbattibile*, 1957; *Live in Fear*, 1958; *Harry Black/Harry Black and the Tiger*, 1958; *Marco Polo/L'avventura di un italiano in Cina*, 1961; *Apache's Last Battle/Old Shatterhand*, 1964; *Die Todestrahlen der Dr Mabuse*, 1964; *Savage Pampas/Pampa salvaje*, 1966; *La malavida*, 1972; *Más alla del sol*, 1975. **Other work** *Una moneta spezzata*, 1963; *Joe, cercati un posto per morire!/Find a Place to Die*, 1968; (guest) *Veni conmigo*, 1972. **Cause of death** Heart attack, at age 78.

SIR VICTOR GODDARD

British Air Marshal

***Born* England, 6 February 1897**

***Died* Kent, England, 21 January 1987**

Air Marshal Sir Victor Goddard, KCB, CBE, was a distinguished officer who saw active service throughout both world wars in a career that spanned almost 40 years. A trained engineer, Goddard both experienced and oversaw a large number of technological changes and advances from the beginnings of military aviation to the airborne nuclear age. In his retirement he wrote a number of books and became deeply interested in supernatural and extra-terrestrial matters.

Robert Victor Goddard was born near the end of the last century, the son of a distinguished medical practitioner. He began his education at St George's School in Harpenden, before moving on to the Royal Naval Colleges, Osborne and Dartmouth. Consistent with such an education, Goddard entered the navy as a midshipman and saw service with the Battle Fleet from the early months of World War I. In 1915, however, his passionate interest in technology and innovation led him to join the newly formed Royal Naval Air Service, thereby swapping his allegiance from the sea to the air. The following year he transferred to the Royal Flying Corps (the precursor of the Royal Air Force), serving in France, where he undertook hazardous night reconnaissance missions in a blimp. Such experiences, which themselves were part of a pioneering and learning process, gave Goddard valuable firsthand insight into the problems of night reconnaissance, standing him in good stead for his activities in France 25 years later.

Goddard elected to remain in the RAF at the end of the war, but in 1921 he decided to continue his education, going up to Jesus College, Cambridge, where he studied for a degree in engineering. He then moved on to Imperial College, London, to widen his technical skills still further before returning to Cambridge as an instructor to the university's prestigious air squadron. In 1929 he passed out of the Staff College before taking command of a bomber squadron in Iraq, participating in operations against the rebel Kurdish tribesmen. For these actions he was awarded the Order of Al Rafidain by King Faisal. Upon his return to England in 1931 he was appointed chief instructor of the officer training engineer's course, a part which made use of his technical background and operational experience. After a spell at the Royal Naval Staff College, he was appointed deputy director of intelligence at the Air Ministry in 1935, a post he held until the outbreak of war in September 1939.

Goddard was again sent to France as an administrative officer in the RAF contingent of the British Expeditionary Force, a position he held until he was appointed senior air staff officer in early 1940. Goddard found himself beset by political and military restrictions which hampered the effectiveness of RAF action; its role was generally limited to leaflet drops and reconnaissance, with little offensive action being permitted. As a senior administrative officer, Goddard found himself at the centre of a bureaucratic minefield of regulations and red tape, though he did much to ensure the effectiveness of the RAF response to the German blitzkrieg by overseeing the dispersal of the squadrons to a large number of separate air fields. The French, Dutch and Belgian Air Forces failed to do this and paid a high penalty. Nevertheless, in spite of this prudent action, the RAF squadrons in France were quickly overcome, and when it was clear that they did not exist as a coherent fighting force, Goddard returned to Britain. He later recounted these experiences in his book *Skies to Dunkirk*, published in 1982.

While in France Goddard had been deeply involved in trying to coordinate the RAF and Army responses to the German attacks and as a result of this experience—in the most trying and confused conditions—was appointed director of military cooperation at the Air Ministry. It was in this post that Goddard made one of his most significant contributions, using his administrative skill and firsthand knowledge of the problems to lay the foundations for what quickly became considered an essential part of operational planning and action—close ground support and air cover. It was at this time that Goddard became well known to the British public as a regular broadcaster on the BBC reporting the air war. On 22 May 1941 Goddard made a famous statement on the invasion of Crete by German paratroops, which was very quickly proved wrong: "Never fear, airborne forces by themselves will not capture that island. Please do not suppose that some new and unexpected danger has just emerged. We are prepared for airborne forces. They are extremely vulnerable to good defences." There can be little doubt that Goddard thought he was following the official line but the public, already exasperated by other erroneous reports and communiqués, protested as the full tragic story of the battle for Crete emerged. Indeed, Churchill in the House of Commons felt compelled to disassociate himself from such war commentaries. In his next broadcast, made from his sick-bed, Goddard recanted his views and apologized for any misleading statements he had made.

In September 1941 he was appointed chief of air staff to the Royal New Zealand Air Force, arriving in New Zealand shortly before the Japanese attack on Pearl Harbour. The outbreak of war put Goddard—the only senior British commander in the region—in the front line once again and he, working closely with the US Admiral Halsay, did much to stem the Japanese advance in the Guadalcanal and Solomon Islands campaigns, skilfully eking out his precious resources and putting them to best effect. For his actions in this campaign he was awarded the US Naval Distinguished Service Medal, a rare award for a foreign officer. In 1943 he was transferred to RAF HQ Delhi, before being placed in charge of all administration in the entire South-East Asia Command, a necessary but inglorious position which he held until 1946.

The dawn of the post-war age posed new problems in the field of cooperation between the Allies, and Goddard, with his experience of administration and technical knowledge, was posted to Washington as RAF representative where he did much to improve cooperation and closer association between the air forces. In 1948 he returned to the UK to become a member of the Air Council for Technical Services, a newly created body which aimed to coordinate and foster development in the rapidly expanding technological branch of the air force. The post was allowed to lapse in 1951 when Goddard retired from the RAF. This was not, however, the end of Goddard's association with aviation, for he was immediately appointed principal of the College of Aeronautics, a position he enjoyed until 1954. Moreover, he was also the long-serving president of the Airship Association, being one of the first men to operate such aircraft in a military context.

After his retirement he turned to writing, publishing the controversial *The Enigma of Menace* in 1959, in which he advocated the swift proliferation of nuclear weapons as a means of providing an effective universal deterrent. In 1975 he published *Flight Towards Reality*, which touched upon his lifelong interest and belief in the supernatural. He particularly recalled an incident in 1946 at a party in Shanghai when he heard a naval officer telling of a dream he had had in which Goddard, two other men and a woman were killed in an air accident when the aircraft in which they were travelling iced over and crashed on a rocky beach near mountains. That night Goddard flew a Dakota—Earl Mountbatten's personal aeroplane "Sister Ann"—to Tokyo with two men and a woman as passengers. The aircraft did ice over and crash landed on a rocky beach at the foot of a mountain range; however, owing to Goddard's forewarning and precautions, which included strapping his passengers into the luggage rack, no one was injured. This remarkable story became the outline plot for a 1955 film, *The Night My Number Was Up*, although Goddard himself was offended when it portrayed the air marshal panicking as the aircraft was about to crash. Stiffly, Goddard noted he had remained calm throughout.

In his retirement Goddard devoted much of his time to the Wrekin Trust and had been instrumental, together with Sir George Trevelyan, in its foundation in 1971. He also spent many years investigating, studying and lecturing on flying saucers and other unidentified flying objects. He was convinced that he had himself undergone "time-slip experiences"—momentary transferences to future time—and came to "a deep conviction of the reality of the world of spirit".

Air Marshal Sir Victor Goddard was a man who was heavily involved in and, indeed, initiated many of the technological and tactical advances made by the air force in a period of rapid and fundamental change. A man of great technical, administrative and operational experience, he made a significant personal contribution to the RAF's thought and development, while his great love of the air and all types of aircraft stayed with him throughout his life.

Born Robert Victor Goddard. **Father** Charles Ernest Goddard, a doctor. **Marriage** Mildred Catherine Jane Inglis, 1924 (died, 1979). **Children** One daughter and two sons. **Education** St George's School, Harpenden; the Royal Naval Colleges, Osborne and Dartmouth; studied engineering, Jesus College, Cambridge University, 1921; Imperial College of Science, London University; Royal Naval Staff College, 1929, 1935. **Career** Midshipman, Royal Navy, 1914; joined Royal Naval Air Service, 1915, also with Royal Flying Corps (now the RAF), World War I; instructor, air squadron, Cambridge University, 1925; commander, bomber squadron, Iraq, 1929–31; chief instructor, officers' engineering course, 1931; deputy director of intelligence, Air Ministry, 1935–39; air officer in charge of administration, General Headquarters, British Expeditionary Force, France, 1939; senior air staff officer, 1940; director of military cooperation, Air Ministry, 1940–41; chief of air staff, New Zealand, and commander, Royal New Zealand Air Force, South Pacific, 1941–43; air officer in charge of administration, Delhi, 1943, then air command, South-East Asia, 1943–46; representative, Royal Air Force, Washington, USA, 1946–48; member, Air Council for Technical Services, 1948–51, retired, 1951; principal, College of Aeronautics, 1951–54. **Other activities** Occasional broadcaster, 1934 onwards; worked for Wrekin Trust from 1971. **Offices and memberships** Governor, St George's School, Harpenden, 1948–64, chairman, 1948–57; governor, Bryanston School, Dorset, 1957–78; president, Airship Association, 1975–84, vice-president, 1984 onwards. **Awards and honours** Order of Al Rafidain, *c.*1931; Commander of the Order of the British Empire, 1940; Companion of the Order of the Bath, 1943; Knight Commander of the Order of the Bath, 1947; US Naval Distinguished Service Medal. **Publications** *The Enigma of Menace*, 1959; *Flight Towards Reality*, 1975; *Skies to Dunkirk*, 1982. **Cause of death** Undisclosed, at age 89.

RENATO GUTTUSO

Italian Painter

***Born* Bagheria, Italy, 2 January 1912**

***Died* Rome, Italy, 17 January 1987**

The foremost Italian representative of Social Realism, Renato Guttuso has also sometimes been considered an exponent of Socialist Realism on account of his communist sympathies. However, although his political commitment was manifest in his art, this was never merely a vehicle for propaganda; neither his passionate concern for the human condition nor his insistence on artistic quality were compromised by the demands of political statement.

Guttuso was born in Bagheria, near Palermo in Sicily. He began painting as a young boy and was self-taught. In 1931, after studying law, he left the impoverished south of Italy and embarked on his artistic career, initially working as a picture restorer in Perugia and at the Galleria Borghese in Rome. He settled in Rome in 1932, and apart from brief periods in northern Italy, the Italian capital remained his home. His Sicilian origins nevertheless retained a lasting influence on both his art and his character, the Sicilian landscape determining the forms and vivid colours of his paintings, the Sicilian qualities of passion and obduracy present in his own vigorous and uncompromising nature.

Guttuso's political sympathies found expression in the formation of the Corrente Group in 1938, which he set up with Ernesto Traccani, Renato Birolli, Enzio Morlotti and other artists opposed to the bland academic style promoted by the Fascist authorities. Guttuso's early work consisted principally of still-lifes; in Italy at this time, as he later observed, "to paint bottles...was in itself a protest".

His art developed, strongly influenced by such twentieth-century movements as Expressionism and Cubism, and by earlier masters, notably Goya. Guttuso was apt to see in contemporary events the parallels of great masterpieces; thus his "Flight from Etna", with its vigorous design of figures and horses, reflects Picasso's "Guernica". This work earned Guttuso third prize in the Premio Bergamo of 1939, despite its controversial character. Even more overtly critical of the Fascist regime was the neo-cubist "Crucifixion" of 1941, one of the central works in modern Italian painting. Of it Guttuso noted: "I want to paint the death of Christ as a scene of our time, as a symbol for everyone who, for their ideas, has to suffer agonies, prison and death." In other works dating from World War II Guttuso attacked the brutalities of the German Army of occupation in Italy, while serving with the communist partisans from 1943 to 1945.

After the war, in 1947, he founded a second artistic group, the Fronte Nuovo delle Arti, and returned to a more realistic style, somewhat out of keeping with current trends towards abstraction. His works tended to be didactic in content and featured exploited peasants and workers, as in the monumental "Battle of Ponte Ammiraglio", a history painting showing a scene from Garibaldi's Sicilian campaign, exhibited at the Venice Biennale of 1952.

In the 1970s Guttuso reaffirmed his interest in the history of art with allegorical works merging the past with the present, art with real life. "Der Unterhaltung mit den Malern", for instance, depicts a number of great painters, including Velázquez, Rembrandt and Picasso, together with three female figures from the latter's paintings.

In later life Guttuso played an active role in politics. He belonged to the pro-Soviet World Peace Council and in 1972 was awarded the Lenin Peace Prize. In 1973 he became a town councillor of Palermo and in 1976 a communist senator of the Italian Republic. In the course of his career his art was awarded a number of prizes, and was the subject of several retrospective exhibitions.

Born Renato Guttuso. **Marriage** Mimise (died, 1986). **Education** Studied law, Palermo Law School, Sicily, and the School of Rome, 1933; self-taught in art. **Military service** Italian Army, 1935; with Communist partisans, 1943–45. **Career** Painter, 1931 onwards; first exhibition, Rome, 1931; picture restorer, Galleria Perugia and Galleria Borghese, Rome, 1932; first London exhibition, Hanover Gallery, 1950; first New York exhibition, ACA Gallery, New York, 1958; first Moscow exhibition, Pushkin Museum, 1961. **Related activities** Founder, with Ernesto Traccani, Renato Birolli, Enzio Morlotti and others, Corrente Group, 1938–42; founder, with Birolli, Morlotti, Ericle Fazzini and others, Fronte Nuovo delle Arti, Rome, 1947; professor of painting, Academia delle Belle Arti, Rome, 1961; titular professor of design, Liceo Artistico

Rome; guest professor, Kunstschule, Hamburg, West Germany, 1968. **Other activities** Town councillor of Palermo, 1975; Senator of the Italian Republic, 1976–83. **Memberships** Communist Party, from 1942; Moscow World Peace Council; Lenin Peace Prize committee. **Awards and honours** Second Prize, for "The Crucifixion", Bergamo Competition, 1942; Prize for Young Artists, 24th Biennale, Venice; Second International Prize for "La Spiaggia", 28th Biennale; Marzotto Painting Prize, Rome, 1960; honorary doctorate, University of Parma, 1971; Lenin Peace Prize, Moscow, 1972. **Individual exhibitions** Galleria del Milione, Milan, 1934; Galleria la Cometa, Rome, 1938; Galleria Zodiaco, Rome, 1943; Galleria Margherita, Rome, 1946; Studio Palma, Rome, 1947; Hanover Gallery, London, 1950; Leicester Galleries, London, 1955; Galleria d'Arte Selecta, Rome, 1957; Galleria Odyssia, Rome, 1957; ACA Gallery, New York, 1958; Heller Gallery, New York, 1958; Vetrina di Chiurazzi, Rome, 1958; Galleria del Milione, Milan, 1959; Galleria il Fiore, Florence, 1959; Vetrina di Chiurazzi, Rome, 1961; Galleria Minima, Milan, 1961; Pushkin Museum, Moscow, 1961; Hermitage Museum, Leningrad, 1961; Galerie Welz, Salzburg, 1961; Stedelijk Museum, Amsterdam, 1962; Galleria la Nuova Pesa, Rome, 1962; Bagheria, Sicily, 1962; Palazzo della Pilotta, Parma, 1963; Galleria del Milione, Milan, 1963; Palais des Beaux-Arts, Charleroi, Belgium, 1963; Galleria del Milione, Milan, 1966; Nationalgalerie, West Berlin, 1967; Kunsthalle, Recklinghausen, West Germany, 1967; Kunsthalle, Darmstadt, 1967; Musée National d'Art Moderne, Paris, 1967; Palazzo dei Normanni, Palermo, 1967; Deutsche Akademie der Kunst, Berlin, 1967; Galleria Toninelli, Rome, 1968; Galleria la Medusa, Rome, 1968; Galleria del Milione, Milan, 1968; Galleria l'Annunciata, Milan, 1968; Galleria Gissi, Turin, 1968, Galleria il Gabbiano, Rome, 1969; Galeria Michael Hertz, Bremen, West Germany, 1970; Musée d'Art Moderne de la Ville, Paris, 1971; Galerie Wolfgang Ketterer, Munich, 1971; Galleria la Medusa, Rome, 1972; Neue Gesellschaft für Bildende Kunst, Berlin, 1972; Galleria Schwarz, Milan, 1972; Galerie Michael Hertz, Bremen, West Germany, 1973; Galleria di Palazzo d'Accursio, Bologna, 1974; Studio Mures, Molin di Falcade, Italy, 1974; Il Collezionista d'Arte Contemporanea, Rome, 1975; Kunstverein, Frankfurt, 1975; Palazzo del Podolo, Todi, Italy, 1976; Kunsthalle, Cologne, 1977; Moderna Museet, Stockholm, 1978; Museo della Basilica di San Francesco, Assisi, 1978; Narodni Galerie, Prague, 1979; Muzej Savremene Umetnosti, Belgrade (toured Eastern Europe), 1979; Marlborough Fine Art, London, 1979; Palazzo del Turismo, San Marino, 1979; Galleria del Milione, Milan, 1980; Gastaldelli Arte Contemporanea, Milan, 1980; Marlborough Fine Art, London, 1980; Galleria d'Arte Moderne, Bologna, 1981; Galleria Rondanini, Rome, 1981; *Opere dal 1931–81*, Centro di Cultura, Palazzo Grassi, Venice, 1982; Gastaldelli Arte Contemporanea, Milan, 1984; Villa Croce, Geneva, 1985; Palazzo Reale, Milan, 1985; Cittadella dei Musei, Cagliari, Italy, 1986. **Selected group exhibitions** *Quadriennale*, Rome, 1931; *Cinque Artisti Siciliani*, Galleria Mediterranea, Palermo, 1937; (with Orfeo Tamburi) Galleria Barbaroux, Milan, 1941; *Biennale*, Venice, 1950; (with Giacomo Manzu) Galleria la Nuova Pesa, Rome, 1961; *Italianische Meister des 20 Jahrhunderts*, Vienna, 1962; *Dunn International*, Tate Gallery, London, 1963; *Salon de Mai*, Paris, 1966; *Kunst und Politik*, Badischer Kunstverein, Karlsruhe, West Germany, 1970; *Kunst um 1970*, Neue Galerie, Aachen, West Germany, 1972. **Collections** Galleria Nazionale d'Arte Moderna, Rome; Galleria d'Arte Moderna, Palermo; Tate Gallery, London; Kunstakademie, Berlin; Hermitage Museum, Leningrad; National Museum, Prague; National Museum, Warsaw; Museum of Modern Art, New York; Museu do Arte Moderna, Sao Paulo; Gallery of New South Wales, Sydney. **Publications** *Contadini di Sicilia*, Rome, 1951; *Mestiere di pittore: scritti sull arte e la societa*, Bari, Italy, 1972. **Cause of death** Undisclosed, at age 75. **Further reading** Morosini, *Disegni di Guttuso*, Rome, 1941; Gino Severini, *Prefazione a Renato Guttuso*, Rome, 1942; Douglas Cooper, *Renato Guttuso* (exhibition catalogue), London, 1950; Pablo Neruda, *Poema a Renato Guttuso pittore realista*, Rome, 1951; Giuseppe Marchiori, *Renato Guttuso*, Milan, 1951; John Berger, *La Spiaggia di Renato*

Guttuso, Dresden, 1957; Morosini, *Renato Guttuso*, Rome, 1960; Elio Vittorini, *Storia di Renato Guttuso*, Milan, 1960; *Renato Guttuso* (exhibition catalogue), Moscow, 1961; Alberto Moravia, *Renato Guttuso*, Palermo, 1961; Pier Paolo Pasolini, *Disegni di Guttuso*, Rome, 1962; Mario de Michele, *Guttuso, l'occupazione delle Terre*, Milan, 1970; Enrico Crispolti, *La Crocifissione di Renato Guttuso*, Rome, 1970; Franco Grasso and others, *Catalogo della mostra antologica del l'opera di Renato Guttuso*, Palermo, 1971; Werner Haftmann, *Renato Guttuso*, Rome, 1971; Leonardo Sciascia, *Renato Guttuso: Disegni 1940–72*, Naples, 1972; Antonio del Guercio, *Renato Guttuso: I disegni dell'amore*, Milan, 1974; Maurizio Calvesi and others, *Guttuso: Opere dal 1931–81* (exhibition catalogue), Venice, 1982; introduction by Alberto T. Galimberti, *Renato Guttuso* (exhibition catalogue), Milan, 1984; *Renato Guttuso: Il bosco d'amore*, Rome, 1985; Vittorio Rubin and Cesare Brandi, *Renato Guttuso* (exhibition catalogue with essays), Cagliari, 1986.

IGOR ILYINSKY

Soviet Actor and Director

Born **Russia, 1902**

Died **Moscow, USSR, *circa* 24 January 1987**

For most Russians of today, both young and old, the familiar name of Igor Ilyinsky commands admiration and respect. Broadly admired as an actor for the talent he showed in the art of stage and screen acting, he was also deeply respected for the contribution he made throughout his long career to Soviet theatre and film. Indeed, for some his name is synonymous with its very history and development.

In a professional career that spanned some 60 years from the early days of the Revolution, Ilyinsky's two greatest performances in the eyes of most critics were as the pompous bureaucrat Byvalov in the film *Volga-Volga*, directed by Grigory Alexandrov in the 1930s, and as the highly principled peasant in Tolstoy's play *Power of Darkness* at the Maly Theatre some years later. These two roles epitomize Ilyinsky's renowned versatility and encompass the broad scope of his acting skills. In the power-crazed petty official Byvalov, Ilyinsky found a vehicle to display his remarkable talent for satire. He built upon his broad experience of political comedy and farce to help turn what was already a work of genuine satire into a classic of the Soviet screen. In Tolstoy's play, on the other hand, Ilyinsky showed himself to be not only a master craftsman of the stage, but also an expert exponent of serious drama, with an acute understanding of human psychology, and a natural ability to convey that understanding to an audience. With its insight into the everyday hardships and moral rigours of peasant life under the tsars, *Power of Darkness* could not be further from *Volga-Volga* in content and style. Ilyinsky, an all-rounder of the acting profession, was at home in both.

His early career was spent in the attempt to "find himself" in the arts, but if it was an attempt to claim a single character-type as his own, it failed. Stylistic diversity became the overriding hallmark of his acting career. In the early 1920s, however, he took parts in a wide range of stage-works—Gluck pastorales, Mozart operas, Molière comedies, Schiller tragedies, French farces, even Viennese operettas—and spent relatively short periods in a wide variety of Russian theatres. It was no doubt as a result of so diverse an "apprenticeship" as this that he adopted the view that "when working on a new part, you have to plunge in naked, like a new-borne babe, forgetting all about any other roles you have ever played. Then the role itself, and your experience of life—of life, not of the theatre—will be able to suggest much that is new and unexpected."

Ilyinsky's early acting models were Charlie Chaplin and Buster Keaton, but unlike those geniuses of the silent film, he confined himself neither to the film medium nor to comedy and slapstick. His portrayal of the rogues and bumpkins of Gogolian farce went hand in hand with that of the more serious types of Tolstoyan drama. Comparisons were made as much with Chaliapin and Ulanova as with Chaplin and Keaton. Popular, too, were his recitals and dramatic readings.

But it was probably his friendships with the revolutionary poet and dramatist Mayakovsky, and the innovative actor and director Meyerhold, that exerted the greatest influence on Ilyinsky's artistic development. Meyerhold it was who introduced him to the "political agitational theatre" of the early days of the Revolution, to the uncompromising satire and burning passion of early Soviet drama. In 1921 Ilyinsky found himself playing the part of the Menshevik Soglashitel in Mayakovsky's comedy *Mysteria Bufa* under the directorship of Meyerhold, a performance for which he won high praise from the drama critic Lunarcharsky and from Mayakovsky himself. It was in the light of such performances that Meyerhold once wrote to his friend, "Who but you stands first?" Remaining faithful to his artistic guide, Ilyinsky stayed at the Meyerhold Theatre until 1935, only occasionally departing to play at such other notable venues as the Kommissarzhevskaya Theatre and, of course, the Moscow Arts Theatre.

In 1938, however, he moved to the Maly Theatre, where he remained until his retirement in 1985. In later years he turned his hand to directing, revealing a further talent not always shared by even the greatest actors. Some of his productions, Thackeray's *Vanity Fair* (1958) for instance, Ostrovsky's *The Forest* (1974), and Chekhov's *The Cherry Orchard* (1982), remain in the Maly repertoire to this day. His commitment to his craft was acknowledged in 1967 on the occasion of the fiftieth anniversary of the Revolution, when he was awarded the Order of Lenin. While many artists of Ilyinsky's generation believed such honours to be worthless—merely rewards for political and intellectual subservience to the State—in Ilyinsky's case it denoted a genuine recognition of his artistic integrity and worth. His self-confessed goal, thoroughly Chekhovian in its implications, was "to help goodness and truth with laughter and tears on the stage. To do nothing against one's conscience in art." It was the key to a highly successful career.

Born Igor Vladimirovich Ilyinsky. **Career** Actor, comedian, singer and satirist on stage and in films, 1918 onwards; stage début, *Lysistrata*, 1918; with director Meyerhold, 1918–35; film début, *Aelita*, 1924; actor, director, Maly Theatre, 1938–85. **Awards and honours** Order of Lenin, 1967. **Stage** *Lysistrata*, 1918; *Mysteria Bufa (Mystery-Bouffe)*, 1918; *The Great-Hearted Cuckold*; *The Storm*; *The Shrew*; *The Bedbug*; *The Inspector-General*; *The Powers of Darkness*; (director) *Vanity Fair*, 1958; *John Reed*, 1967; (director) *The Forest*, 1974; (director) *The Cherry Orchard*, 1982. **Films** *Aelita*, 1924; *The Tailor from Torzhok*, 1925; *The Trial of the Three Millions*; *St Jorgen's Day*; *Volga-Volga*; *Carnival Night*; (director) *An Old Acquaintance*. **Publications** (autobiography) *Sam o Sebe* (About Myself), 1960. **Cause of death** Undisclosed, at age 85.

VINCENT IMPELLITTERI

American Mayor

***Born* Isnello, Italy, 4 February 1900**

***Died* Bridgeport, Connecticut, 29 January 1987**

In September 1950 New York Mayor William O'Dwyer, his administration racked by political scandal, resigned from the city's highest office. His chair was filled by a modest, unassuming, yet industrious man named Vincent Impellitteri, an Italian shoemaker's son who, though he had served for four years as City Council president, often substituting as mayor in O'Dwyer's absence, was virtually unknown to most New Yorkers. But while Impellitteri, dubbed "Impy" by city newspapers, first entered office as a temporary replacement, he went on to win a special election in November, gaining a 225,000-vote victory as an independent candidate in a three-way race. It marked the first and only time in New York City history that a candidate had been elected to the office of mayor without the backing of a major political party. Though the Impellitteri administration was beset with financial crises and brushed by political scandal, the mayor's valiant and enduring struggle against the city's mighty Tammany Hall political machine captured the respect and admiration of millions of New Yorkers.

Born in the village of Isnello, Sicily, at the turn of the century, Impellitteri was brought to New York's Lower East Side when he was one year old. Soon afterwards the family moved north to Ansonia, Connecticut, where his father set up a cobbler's shop. At Ansonia High School the young Impellitteri excelled in extra-curricular activities. In addition to managing the baseball and basketball teams, he served as left tackle on the football squad and played fife in the school fife and drum corps. During the summers he worked as a moulder's assistant at a local mill. When he graduated in 1917 he joined the US Navy, serving overseas as a ship's radioman at the beginning of World War I.

Following his discharge in 1919, Impellitteri enrolled in the school of law at Fordham University, working nights at a Broadway hotel to pay his way. He also became a member of the Fordham Democratic Club, and from that point on, considered himself an "organization Democrat". In 1922 he became a naturalized US citizen, and two years later received his law degree. He was admitted to the Bar in 1925, and in 1926 married legal secretary Elizabeth McLaughlin. In addition to supporting her husband in all his personal endeavours, she acted as an invaluable assistant in his campaign headquarters in 1950.

Impellitteri's first legal posting, with the Manhattan firm of Griggs, Baldwin & Baldwin, and his moonlight job as counsel to Local 282 of the Teamsters' and Chauffeurs' Union, brought him into contact with a host of important Democratic figures and ultimately helped to advance his political career. He left the firm in 1929 to serve as an assistant district attorney. After nine years he returned to private law practice, and for the next three years concentrated on criminal defence. In 1941 he was appointed law secretary to State Supreme Court Justice Peter Schmuck—a position he attained through college political contacts—and then to Justice Joseph Gavagan. He remained with the latter until 1945.

When Impellitteri was chosen as a candidate for City Council president—the number two job at City Hall—in 1945, few New York politicians took him seriously. Many contended that Democratic leaders had simply thumbed through the city's official "Green Book" directory until they came upon the name Vincent Impellitteri. But as a judicial clerk, Impellitteri had gained a reputation for honesty, ability and party loyalty, and while he was not favoured for the council post by the Manhattan Democratic machine known as Tammany Hall, Mayor William O'Dwyer insisted upon his selection. In the end, the Italian-born, Roman Catholic candidate proved a successful balance for the O'Dwyer ticket, and Impellitteri was swept into office along with the mayor in the 1945 election.

Impellitteri worked quietly under O'Dwyer for the next four years, replacing the mayor during his frequent holidays and also serving as president of the Board of Estimate. In 1949, in return for his loyalty and hard work, he was renamed to the ticket, and polled 1.3 million votes compared with only 1.2 million for O'Dwyer. But while the latter's ability to govern became increasingly impaired by his involvement in an organized crime scandal, and city leaders met often to consider alternative candidates, Impellitteri's name was never mentioned. The press offered the opinion that Impellitteri's straightforward "Mr. Clean" image and his snubbing of gambler and racketeer Frank Costello, known as the "tsar" behind the scenes at Tammany Hall, had something to do with it.

In September 1950 events at City Hall took a sudden turn. Amid a growing political scandal and grand jury investigation, O'Dwyer stepped down as mayor, accepting President Truman's appointment as ambassador to Mexico. Impellitteri was left to serve as acting mayor until a special election could be held.

When the time came, Impellitteri found that his on-going squabble with Tammany Hall had cost him the Democratic nomination. As a further inducement not to run, he was offered a handsomely paid judgeship on the State Supreme Court. But he refused to bow to Tammany pressure, and quickly established his own party—named the "Experience" party to emphasize that he had already functioned as New York's mayor under O'Dwyer, an advantage none of his opponents could claim—and gathered more than 67,000 nominating petitions in support of his candidacy. While political observers offered little hope of an Impellitteri victory, New Yorkers saw the shy, deliberate candidate as a welcome change from the flamboyant—and frequently corrupt—politicians they were accustomed to, and a massive volunteer organization sprang up to support him. He also received the strong endorsement of Robert Moses, head of city planning and construction in the O'Dwyer administration, and that of a number of other important Tammany leaders.

Vincent Impellitteri was sworn in as New York's 101st mayor on 14 November 1950. He began with high ambitions, but quickly found he had inherited a host of municipal problems, and his lofty plans to expand public transportation and city housing were hampered by entrenched budgets and post-war inflation. In addition to calling for the coordination of Federal, State and City efforts in civilian defence, and the establishment of an independent transit organization, he activated a Parking Authority to help alleviate New York's serious traffic congestion, and introduced plans to create long-term financial stability for the city government. And in a determined drive to root out corruption—a move described by the New York Herald Tribune as a "masterful stroke"—he appointed former United States Attorney Thomas F. Murphy as police commissioner. The *New York Times* characterized the new mayor as a man who "doesn't jump into decisions" but "seems to make up his mind very deliberately". Impellitteri, the editor wrote, "gives the impression of dogged earnestness and good intentions".

Soon after his election, Impellitteri made peace with city Democratic leaders, though he continued to deny patronage to Tammany's ringleader Carmine de Sapio. This steadfast refusal eventually led to his political downfall. He was also criticized for his timidity or "lack of forcefulness" in legislative manoeuvres, and while he himself was never implicated, several members of his staff were touched by the political scandal that had plagued O'Dwyer's administration.

When Impellitteri sought re-election in the 1953 Democratic primary, public concern over rent hikes, tax and transit fare increases, and school overcrowding conspired against him, and he was easily defeated by Tammany's candidate, Manhattan Borough President Robert F. Wagner.

Wagner appointed him to a criminal court judgeship, which he retained until 1965. Thereafter he returned to private law practice, taking little active part in politics.

An affable, optimistic man who admitted he was "keenly disappointed" but never bitter after his failed bid for re-election as New York's mayor, Impellitteri sank back into virtual obscurity following his retirement from politics. When he walked through the streets of New York, passers-by occasionally smiled at him and called him "Impy" or "Judge", but most did not recognize him at all. He spent his leisure time playing golf, swimming and attending the opera and theatre with his wife. He also served on the boards of numerous professional and civic organizations, and for his efforts in defeating Italian communism in the 1940s, was made an honorary citizen of the Boys' Republic of Italy.

Born Vincent Richard Impellitteri. **Parents** Salvatore, a shoemaker, and Maria Antonia (Cannici) Impellitteri. **Marriage** Elizabeth Agnes McLaughlin, a legal secretary, 1926 (died, 1967). **Education** Ansonia High School; Fordham Law School, graduated, 1924. **Emigration** Left Sicily for USA as child; naturalized, 1922. **Military service** Radioman, US Navy, 1917–19. **Career** Admitted to New York Bar, 1925; practised law, Griggs, Baldwin & Baldwin, 1925–29; assistant district attorney, New York, 1929-38; returned to private practice, 1938–41; law secretary to State Supreme Court Justice Peter Schmuck, 1941–43; law secretary to State Supreme Court Justice Joseph Gavagan, 1943–45; New York City Council president (Democrat), 1945–50; acting mayor of New York City, 1950; corruption scandal and split in Democratic Party machine led to his successfully running for mayor as independent, 1950, mayor of New York City, 1950–53; criminal court judge, 1953–65; thereafter returned to private practice. **Related activities** Co-leader of "Letters to Italy" campaign aimed at undermining Italian Communist Party support, 1948; made occasional radio broadcasts to same purpose; one of President Nixon's New York City campaign co-chairs, 1972. **Offices and memberships** American Legion (past commander); Veterans of Foreign Wars; Catholic War Veterans; New York Bar Association; New York County Bar Association; American Bar Association; Rapallo Lawyers' Association; New York City Lawyers' Association; Gamma Eta Gamma; Knights of St Columbus. **Awards and honours** Citations for interfaith work from: Catholic War Veterans, 1946; Interfaith Movement, 1948; Jewish War Veterans, 1949; honorary citizen, Boys' Republic of Italy, 1950. **Cause of death** Heart failure, at age 86.

MARGARET LAURENCE

Canadian Novelist

Born **Neepawa, Manitoba, 18 July 1926**

Died **Lakefield, Ontario, 6 January 1987**

It has been the fate of Canadian authors throughout history that, as soon as they made an international reputation for themselves, they were automatically assumed to be American or French writers—Canada somehow never figured on the map of world literature. Recently this situation has changed due to the contribution of Canadian women writers like Margaret Atwood, Alice Munro, Joan Barfoot, Marian Engel, Anne Hébert and Mavis Gallant. Less familiar, but in many ways equally if not more important, is the name of Margaret Laurence whose work anticipated the major feminist themes of contemporary novelists in a series of books of which some were too advanced for the readership of her day. Her last novel, *The Diviners*, for example, was censored in Canada by a number of school boards. Laurence later said: "I was desperately hurt. I thought I'd get back at them in a novel. But after two years of mulling it over, I realized you don't write fiction to get back at somebody. It was a lousy idea." All the same, she never wrote another novel. The experience of being blacklisted silenced her for good.

Margaret Laurence was born Jean Margaret Wemys in the prairie town of Neepawa, Manitoba, in 1926. Her parents were of Scottish highlands ancestry, but both of them died when Laurence was still a girl. From an early age she found comfort in writing, first for the school magazine and then, after graduating from United College in Winnipeg with a degree in English, for the *Winnipeg Citizen*, where she got a job as a reporter. But Margaret Wemys, as she was then, had a taste for adventure which even journalism could not satisfy. Failing to find excitement in the job, she did what many women did instead in those days: she got married. Jack Laurence was a civil engineer whose work frequently took him abroad and this attracted his young wife. They married in 1947 and went to England first, then to Somaliland and Ghana: the promise of a better life was being fulfilled.

In Africa Margaret Laurence began to write. Her first book, *A Tree for Poverty*, was really a practice run but an important one. It was published in Somaliland in 1954 and contained Somali folktales and poetry, translated by Laurence. From this first venture she gained the courage to do her own writing, resulting in a travel book entitled *The Prophet's Camel Bell* (1963). In 1968 another "African" book of hers appeared—*Long Drums and Cannons: Nigerian Novelists and Dramatists 1952–66*—which introduced much hitherto neglected or ignored oral and written literature to the English-speaking world. Here too, Laurence was also ahead of her time in that she made African writing accessible to the West long before it became fashionable to do so. She did it because she was there and because she was sensitive to cultures other than her own, but she also did it at a time when such cultural traffic was particularly important because of the struggles for independence which were being fought all over the African continent. Laurence also set her first novel, *This Side Jordan* (1960), in Africa, dealing with precisely such a struggle for independence in Ghana, complicated by internal strife between country and city people and between tribal traditionalism and modern ways. Two collections of short stories, *The Tomorrow Tamer* (1963) and *A Bird in the House* (1970), also had African themes in them, thus completing the African part of Laurence's *oeuvre*.

In 1957 Margaret Laurence, her husband and their two children returned to Vancouver and Canadian life. The constant travel and moving about had taken their toll on the marriage, with husband and wife reacting very differently to their foreign environments; he saw the situation merely as a matter of work, whereas she relished the experience of exploring a new way of life and was reluctant to give it up. In 1962 the marriage broke down and they separated. Margaret Laurence went to England with the children and began work on the Manawaka novels which are regarded as her greatest achievement. The first of these, *The Stone Angel*, was published in Canada, London and New York in 1964. It is the story of a 90-year-old prairie woman talking about her life, trying to understand her own past and that of the country which is changing so rapidly. This was the pattern Laurence used time and again: people's efforts to come to terms with themselves, to weigh up experience and opportunities lost, paths taken and paths unexplored. Of course, in this way she could also say things about Canada as a country which itself was still vastly wide and open to all kinds of possibilities.

In Manawaka, many critics saw Laurence's hometown of Neepawa. Sheldon Frank wrote in the *New Republic*: "Controlled by the hard-working and God-fearing Scottish businessmen and their wives with their acute sense of status and propriety, Manawaka is a hard place for most of its inhabitants. Everybody knows everybody else's business, and for those without a secure niche in the social hierarchy it is a town good only for leaving." And this is exactly what happened in the second novel, *A Jest of God* (1966), also set in Manawaka, which told the story of an unmarried schoolteacher, Rachel Cameron, and her awakening to sexuality and the wider world. At the beginning of the novel the 34-year-old Rachel is still living with her mother and dying a slow death in the stifling conventionalism of the town. At the end she has escaped into a new and freer life, even though the love affair which initially lured her out of her shell has proved unreliable as a source of happiness. *A Jest of God* was made into a film, *Rachel, Rachel*, and it was followed by a third Manawaka volume entitled *The Fire-Dwellers*, published in 1969.

Laurence's last novel, *The Diviners* (1974) is also about Manawaka, reintroducing characters which had already appeared in the other novels but focusing on Morag Gunn, a Canadian novelist in middle age, who, in a series of flashbacks called "Memorybank Movies", reminisces about her life, weaving past and present together. The American novelist and poet Marge Piercy wrote in a review that, like Margaret Atwood and Alice Munro, Laurence "set out a powerful gritty sense of place, of daily life based on economic realities and conflicts, of different ethnic peoples contending in a setting these writers know from the weeds in the yard—by name—to the mortgages and the buried history. All three create a strong breed of women characters who must earn a living, who have a keen sense of self or battle hard to find it." Another critic called *The Diviners* "an unusually honest account of a woman's inner life", even if the storyline had a "tendency to melodrama". This may sound innocuous enough, but the novel also deals with abortion and has explicit passages about Morag's sexual escapades. For this reason it was deemed unsuitable to be read by schoolchildren and was therefore removed from a number of libraries.

Having moved back to Canada after publication of *The Fire-Dwellers*, there was no way Laurence could now watch developments from a safe distance. The alarm that the novel had caused in the more rural parts of Canada in a way proved the point of her Manawaka novels—that provincial life was stifling and dangerous—but it nevertheless affected her personally to such an extent that she could not write another. Having made her home in the hamlet of Lakefield, Ontario, Laurence turned to children's fiction instead. She published four books for children during the 1970s, plus a volume of adult essays, *Heart of a Stranger* (1976). However, she could not get back to her "real" work, the Manawaka epic which had been cut short with *The Diviners*.

Margaret Laurence stopped writing about Canada and its imaginative landscape in the mid-1970s, just when Atwood and others were gathering steam. In many ways this block was her greatest tragedy, even though towards the end of her life she did witness a resurgence of interest in her work. Both the *Journal of Canadian Studies* and the *Journal of Canadian Fiction* devoted a whole issue to her in 1978 and 1980, and book-length critical studies began to appear in the early 1980s. Margaret Laurence died too young, at the age of 60. But despite the ugly censorship episode, she was, in the end, vindicated in her belief that "human society wherever it is, anywhere in the whole world, needs fiction and poetry in the same way that human cultures forever have needed their storytellers and their poets and their singers of songs...There really is room for an unlimited number of different points of view."

Born Jean Margaret Wemys. **Marriage** John F. Laurence, a civil engineer, 1947 (divorced, 1969). **Children** One son, one daughter. **Education** United College, University of Manitoba, Winnipeg, Canada, BA in English, 1947. **Career** Journalist, *Winnipeg Citizen*, 1947; after marriage lived in Somaliland and Ghana, 1950–57, in England, 1962–69; became compiler and translator of folktales and poetry; turned to travel writing; first publication, *A Tree for Poverty: Somali Poetry and Prose*, 1954; author of novels, short stories and children's books, 1960 onwards. **Related activities** Writer-in-residence: University of Toronto, 1969–70, University of Western Ontario, London, 1973, Trent University, Peterborough, Ontario, 1974; chancellor, Trent University, 1981–83. **Awards and honours** Beta Sigma Phi Award, 1961; University of

Western Ontario President's Medal, 1961, 1962, 1964; honorary fellow, United College, University of Winnipeg, 1967; Canada Council Senior Fellowship, 1967, 1971; DLitt: McMaster University, Hamilton, Ontario, 1970, University of Toronto, 1972, Carleton University, Ottawa, 1974, Brandon University, Manitoba, 1975, Mount Allison University, Sackville, New Brunswick, 1975, University of Western Ontario, 1975, Simon Fraser University, Burnaby, British Columbia, 1977; Companion, Order of Canada, 1971; LLD: Dalhousie University, Halifax, Nova Scotia, 1972, Trent University, 1972, Queen's University, Kingston, Ontario, 1975; Molson Prize, 1975; B'nai B'rith Award, 1976; fellow, Royal Society of Canada, 1977; Periodical Distributors' Award, 1977; City of Toronto Award, 1978; Canadian Booksellers' Association Writer of the Year Award, 1981; Banff Centre Award, 1983. **Novels** (all published in Toronto, London and New York) *This Side Jordan*, 1960; *The Stone Angel*, 1964; *A Jest of God*, 1966, published as *Rachel, Rachel*, New York, 1968, as *Now I Lay Me Down*, London, 1968; *The Fire-Dwellers*, 1969; *The Diviners*, 1974. **Short stories** *The Tomorrow-Tamer*, Toronto, London, 1963, New York, 1964; *A Bird in the House*, Toronto, London and New York, 1970. **Other** (editor and translator) *A Tree for Poverty: Somali Poetry and Prose*, Nairobi, 1954; *The Prophet's Camel Bell* (travel), Toronto and London, 1963, published as *New Wind in a Dry Land*, New York, 1964; *Long Drums and Cannons: Nigerian Novelists and Dramatists 1952–66*, London and New York, 1968; *Jason's Quest* (juvenile), Toronto, London and New York, 1970; *Heart of a Stranger* (essays), Toronto, 1976, Philadelphia, 1977; *Six Darn Cows* (juvenile), Toronto, 1979; *The Olden-Days Coat* (juvenile), Toronto, 1979; *The Christmas Birthday Story* (juvenile), New York, 1980. **Cause of death** Undisclosed, at age 60. **Further reading** Clara Thomas, *Margaret Laurence*, Toronto, 1969; Clara Thomas, *The Manawaka World of Margaret Laurence*, Toronto, 1975; Joan Hindsmith, *Three Voices: The Lives of Margaret Laurence, Gabrielle Roy and Frederick Philip Grove*, Toronto, 1975; W.H. New (editor), *Margaret Laurence: The Writer and Her Critics*, Toronto, 1977; Patricia Morley, *Margaret Laurence*, Boston, 1981; George Woodcock (editor), *A Place to Stand on: Essays By and About Margaret Laurence*, Edmonton, Alberta, 1983.

HARRY LEADER

British Bandleader

Born **London, England, 28 January 1906**

Died **Brighton, England, 19 January 1987**

All the best bandleaders had a signature tune, a piece of music that instantly distinguished them from their competitors and which as often as not opened and closed their shows on the radio. In Harry Leader's case, the command, "Music, maestro, please," was the catchphrase that introduced him and his band to generations of dancers, and many an avid listener to his broadcasts on the Light Programme, as it then was, and later on television. For over 20 years the "maestro" was one of the most popular of British bandleaders.

It was a position he had to fight hard for, for it was not until 1940, when Leader was in his late twenties, that his band obtained its first residency, at the Hammersmith Palais de Danse. There, night after night during the war, Leader and his band entertained a city at war, constantly changing its repertoire in tune with popular demand. Later residencies, notably at the Astoria

Danse Salon in the Charing Cross Road, from 1944 to 1959, and then out of London for four more years at Brighton's Regent Ballroom, were equally popular.

Leader was born in a grocery shop in London's East End, the son of a professor of music from the St Petersburg Conservatory who had settled in Britain. His father taught him the violin, and in his early working life Leader doubled up as a grocery boy and a cinema accompanist to silent movies. In the 1920s, under the influence of jazz, he switched to alto saxophone and was soon playing gigs in the many jazz clubs that sprung up in London's West End. Tours of Europe with various dance bands followed before he established his own dance orchestra in the mid-1930s. The band played and recorded prolifically, and with some success, selling more than 400,000 copies of "Little Man You've Had a Busy Day", a considerable number in pre-war Britain.

Much of Leader's success can be put down to his numerous compositions. With his wife, Rona, he wrote more than 350 songs, and his shows—he had a television show of his own in 1948—were notable for their variety of material. He was also a considerable talent spotter, rescuing Terry Parsons from the platform of the 27 bus *en route* from Highgate to Teddington and turning him into the crooner Mat Monro.

A chairman of both the Music Conductors' Association and the Performing Rights Society, Leader was in danger of turning into an institution in his later life, for as the popularity of the dance bands waned, his career waned with them. But for the many Londoners who relieved the tensions and dramas of war on the dance floor at Hammersmith, he was a maestro who will be remembered fondly for his music, please.

Born Harold Leader. **Father** Former professor of music, St Petersburg Conservatory, Russia, who later ran grocery shop, East End of London. **Marriage** Rona. **Education** Grammar school, London; studied violin and trumpet with father. **Career** Musician, prolific recording artist on all major labels, songwriter and bandleader; played alto saxophone at clubs in London's West End; also played flute, clarinet and novelty instruments; set up own dance orchestra, 1940; resident at Hammersmith Palais, London, 1940–44, at Astoria Danse Salon, Charing Cross Road, London for 15 years, at Regent Ballroom, Brighton for four years; featured frequently on BBC radio; own television show, 1948; toured England and Europe. **Offices and memberships** Chairman: Music Conductors' Association, Performing Rights Society; member: Mechanical Copyright Protection Society, BBC Club, Songwriters' Guild of Great Britain, Variety Club of Great Britain. **Awards and honours** Honorary adviser to the American Biographical Institute's National Board of Advisers. **Compositions** Joint-composer, with wife Rona, of over 350 songs, including "Tonight's the Night", "Dragon Fly", "South Paw Special", "Dance Dance Dance Back to Those Old Kentucky Days" and "Lead the Way". **Cause of death** Undisclosed, at age 73.

V. G. LEVICH

Soviet Physical Chemist

Born **Kharkov, Russia, 30 March 1917**

Died **19 January 1987**

As a scientist, Professor Levich was best known for his work in establishing physico-chemical hydrodynamics as a recognized scientific discipline. But in his time he also attained world renown for his fight to be allowed to emigrate from Russia. He was one of the early, celebrated "refuseniks", scientists who were refused permission to leave the country.

Venyamin Grigorievich Levich was born at Kharkov, more than 400 miles south of Moscow, and it was at Kharkov University that he gained his degree in 1937. From there he went to the Lenin State Pedagogical Institute in Moscow where he obtained his doctorate in 1943. His thesis was on electrolytic cells, and most of his further studies focused on concentration polarization and the possibilities of using rotating disc electrodes. However, at the same time he joined the research into atomic energy, but when he realized it might later compromise him if he had access to classified information, he withdrew from all such work.

The year 1950 saw the publication of his first book, *Static Physics*, but it was in 1952 that his masterpiece came out. *Physico-Chemical Hydrodynamics* incorporated several separate branches of science in its study, and established the subject as a new discipline. For this four-volume work Levich did extensive research into gas-phase-collision reactions, the photo-emission of electrons in solutions and the quantum mechanics of electron transfer between ions.

At this stage he was working as a member of the staff at the USSR Academy of Sciences Institute of Physical Chemistry, but in 1958 he moved to the academy's Institute of Electrochemistry. His professorship came in 1963, when he was the first professor of chemical mechanics at Moscow State University. He would undoubtedly have climbed higher, but in 1972, with the agreement of his wife and sons, he asked permission to emigrate to Israel.

The reaction was sudden and extraordinary. He was told he had no chance of emigration as he knew classified information. He was no longer considered fit to instruct the young, his chair was abolished and he became a simple scientific worker. His former colleagues ostracized him, his work was no longer published, and when American scientific texts arrived in the USSR his name was carefully removed in every reference.

News of Levich's persecution reached the West, and fellow scientists kept up a behind-the-scenes protest until an unwritten agreement was reached: provided the protests stopped, both his sons and their wives would be allowed to emigrate at once, and Levich and his wife would follow after a year. (At that time one of his sons had been illegally transferred to an Arctic military camp.)

All went well at first: the sons and their families left, but when the time came for Levich and his wife to go, permission was suddenly refused. Yet Levich had not been one of the vocal scientists attempting to change the system in Russia; his only crime was wishing to emigrate. The reasons given were that he had learnt classified information in the 1940s and that he owed his education and prowess to the USSR.

In response to this refusal, British scientists arranged a conference in Oxford in 1977 for over 100 scientists from 13 countries. It had three purposes: to review progress in physical chemistry and electrodynamics, to honour Levich as a pioneer in this field, and to demonstrate solidarity with him. Levich was not allowed to attend the conference, in spite of last-minute pressure from American scientists. However, he did write to those present. In his letter he suggested that the "evil forces" in his country were "awaiting the final solution of my problem in a natural way, taking into account my age [60]" and the health of his wife Tanya who had suffered a heart attack not long before.

Up till then the protests by Western scientists had been comparatively restrained, but now it was decided to be more vocal. "Dear Friends," Levich had written, "do not be discouraged. It is the support of many of you that has resulted more than once in the salvation of human lives and freedom." Quiet pressure had not succeeded, so following the Oxford conference, particularly as there had been an enthusiastic response from oppressed scientists, it was felt a more activist approach should be tried. Some American scientists threatened to boycott Soviet–American scientific conventions. Then, in 1978, a second conference, similar to the one in Oxford the year before, was held in Washington, D.C.

The change in tactics paid off. Three weeks later the Leviches were in Vienna. They eventually settled in Tel Aviv, where a chair had been kept for this most distinguished Jewish immigrant. He enjoyed several other honours, and the following year accepted the Albert Einstein Chair of chemical physics at New York City College on condition it allowed him the chance of returning to Tel Aviv frequently. He still held that chair when he died.

Levich was completely at home in the West, but his wife's health remained a problem. She had to have major surgery soon after they first arrived in the USA and never completely recovered. After her death in 1984, Levich travelled frequently, but more for solace than pleasure, and his work provided distraction from grief.

Born Venyamin Grigorievich Levich. **Marriage** Tanya (died, 1984). **Children** Two sons. **Education** Kharkov University, 1937; Lenin State Pedagogical Institute, PhD, 1943. **Emigration** Left USSR for Israel, 1978. **Career** Theoretical physicist, specializing in physical chemistry and hydrodynamics; staff member, Institute of Physical Chemistry, USSR Academy of Sciences, 1940–58; staff member, Institute of Electrochemistry, USSR Academy of Sciences, 1958–63; professor of chemical mechanics, Moscow State University, 1963–72; status reduced to scientific worker, 1972–78; professor, Tel Aviv University, 1978; Albert Einstein professor of chemical physics, New York City College, 1979–87. **Offices and memberships** Corresponding member, USSR Academy of Sciences, 1958–87. **Publications** (include) *Static Physics*, 1950; *Physico-Chemical Hydrodynamics*, 1952, translated into English, 1959; four-volume treatise on theoretical physics. **Cause of death** Undisclosed, at age 69.

MARY LINDELL

British Wartime Resistance Fighter

Born **Sutton, Surrey, 11 September 1895**

Died **On a visit to Germany, 8 January 1987**

The real life story of Mary Lindell, Comtesse de Milleville, reads like any thriller of Frederick Forsyth or Eric Ambler—almost too full of adventure to be true.

Born into a conventional upper middle-class home in that most conventional of milieux—Sutton in Surrey—Mary Lindell served in the Red Cross in World War I, and while recovering from a gas attack in a Russian hospital in Brittany, met her future husband, the Comte de

Milleville. By World War II she was well established in French society, but she immediately rejoined the Red Cross, proudly wearing the Croix de Guerre and the Tsarist medals won in the First War. Her natural air of command and her social position took her at once to the top. With the occupation of France, she—almost automatically—obtained a personal introduction to the German commander of her region and a permit for herself and a companion to travel freely across the country. With this she became one of the major lines of escape to the free zone for British airmen shot down over France and, on one occasion, for an injured German pilot whom she delivered to his barracks. Ultimately, of course, her activities were spotted and she was imprisoned for a time by the Germans.

In July 1942 she escaped via Spain to London but not to a safe haven. Within three months she insisted on being parachuted back into France to the Limoges region where she arrived in time to contact her old organization and arrange, among others, the escape of two of the famous Cockleshell Heroes, the Royal Marine commandoes who carried out the limpet mine attacks on German shipping at Bordeaux. For almost two years she was one of the foremost Resistance organizers and her own escapes and near escapes became a legend. The most notable was her attempted escape in 1944 from a moving train, in which she broke her neck. This finally landed her in Ravensbrück concentration camp, despite the efforts of the German surgeon who treated her injury. But not even Ravensbrück could daunt her indomitable courage and she worked tirelessly in the camp's infirmary until the end of the war.

Thereafter she lived in Paris, still working for the Royal Air Force Escaping Society. She was awarded a second Croix de Guerre and the American Medal of Freedom for her war service, and in 1969 the somewhat grudging award of the Order of the British Empire from her native country. Mary Lindell invariably travelled in Red Cross uniform and always proudly displayed her medals. *La petite Anglaise*—as she was known locally—was a true European, unstinting in her service to her native and her adopted countries, and earning the undying gratitude of many of her compatriots.

Born Mary Lindell. **Marriage** The Comte de Milleville. **Children** Two sons (one deceased) and one daughter (deceased). **Military service** Red Cross nurse in World War I and World War II; also, worked for the French Resistance, transferring British airmen from German-occupied France to the free zone, 1939–44; worked as nurse while imprisoned at Ravensbrück concentration camp, 1944–45. **Related activities** Worked for many years as Paris representative for the Royal Air Force Escaping Society. **Awards and honours** Croix de Guerre and Tsarist Order of St Anne, for services to Russian wounded, World War I; Croix de Guerre and American Medal of Freedom, World War II; Order of the British Empire, 1969. **Cause of death** Undisclosed, at age 91.

NORMAN McLAREN

Canadian Film-maker and Animator
***Born* Stirling, Scotland, 11 April 1914**
***Died* Montreal, Canada, 26 January 1987**

For far too many years the art of animation has been considered to be the more frivolous sibling of film-making. Animation and art were two terms rarely connected by those outside the field. Norman McLaren helped to change such a conception, and furthered the possibilities of the medium to an enormous degree. He perfected techniques (some pioneered by the New Zealand animator Len Lye) of drawing, scratching and painting directly on to the celluloid strip, as well as other animation innovations. McLaren also experimented with three-dimensional film and the "sonic" equivalent of direct film. The result was a body of work, most not over ten minutes long, which were celebrations of joy, wit and great beauty.

Although McLaren was considered to be a Canadian film-maker—indeed, the first of real stature who emerged from the country—he was actually born and educated in Scotland. While studying interior design at the Glasgow School of Art, he began to make short films there in 1934. When he made the switch from documentary to animation a few years later, he created an anti-war film with an animated sequence which won first prize at the Scottish Amateur Film Festival. (McLaren's strongly-held pacifism remained a theme in his work throughout his life.) That year, 1936, John Grierson, who had seen his *Colour Cocktail*, invited McLaren after graduation to join the General Post Office (GPO) Unit in Canada. (Len Lye was also there at the time.)

Grierson, considered to be the father of the British documentary movement, was not only a renowned teacher, but a firm believer in giving artists the freedom and opportunity to develop their own styles; McLaren could probably have found no finer mentor. For the next two years he worked on live-action documentaries, and was introduced to techniques he would then develop. In 1938 he made his first professional animated film, *Love on the Wing*—also the first example of his drawing-directly-on-film method.

His reputation spread; when he was 24 he made several publicity shorts for the National Broadcasting Company (NBC) television network in New York, several for the Museum of Non-Objective Art and some independently, staying until 1941. However, living there seemed to confirm his interests in settling down in Canada; he returned shortly after and eventually gained citizenship there. He was rehired by Grierson at Canada's National Film Board to establish an animation department there. He was to make short films to "help the war effort". Grierson wanted, wisely, to inject a little lyricism into the staid images promulgated by the country's wartime propaganda film studio. His instinct was, as usual, sound; McLaren's films pleased audiences enormously, and he also inspired those he worked among. He was a teacher of great talent, with his patience and, above all, enthusiasm, which remained his trademark. At the NFB studios the emphasis was on film movement and technique exploration, not storyline, not predigested colours and methods, nor slick, static images which dominated mainstream, popular cartoons at the time (and do now, with the advent of Hanna Barbera, to a frightening degree). The animation studio was established by 1944, as were enduring principles of film-making made possible by the NFB's respect for freedom and opportunity. Owing to the financial set-up of the board, public support was essential (and forthcoming) for the board to encourage people like McLaren, an important factor which helped make the NFB *the* fountain of the world's best animation for decades.

McLaren's 1941 films, *Mail Early* and *V for Victory*, were lively, pulsating expressions of advertising art at its best—without a camera—and are among his classics. In 1949 he made, along with collaborator Evelyn Lambert, *Begone Dull Care*, a jazz film with Oscar Peterson on piano, which was a superb illustration of film working *with* music and via free-form choreography instead of against. It also abolished conventional framing in order to give the images the fluidity of music. Later that year he was sent by UNESCO to China in order to instruct artists in the preparation of simple audio-visual images which were used to encourage tree planting, improve standards of community sanitation and teach the villagers about health care.

In 1952 McLaren's *Neighbours*, an allegory about the futility of violence, won the Best Documentary Short Subject Academy Award. In it he developed a process of animating film of live actors called "pixillation", using a stop-motion technique to give a kind of robot-effect. The process is still used today.

Other films continued to attract attention, reinforcing McLaren's stature in the film-making world. After seeing the four-minute *Blinkety Blank*, a semi-abstract little ballet, François Truffaut described it as "...an absolutely unique work having no resemblance to anything achieved in 60 years of cinema history...(combining) all of Giraudoux's fantasy with Hitchcock's brilliance and Cocteau's imagination."

With *Mosaic*, McLaren engraved figures on film. As in all his work, there was no speech; form, movement and music spoke for themselves. According to film writer Jonathan Rosenbaum, McLaren had "a solid grasp of syncopation and imagination that flirts with abstraction without ever entirely succumbing to it, and a tendency to limit his visual patterns to bone essentials—and then does his witty best to make the most of them."

In 43 years at the NFB, the quiet, rather shy and always kind film-maker made more than 50 films, each different from the last because he was continually stretching the boundaries of his art, and expressing its accessibility to those who studied it and those who viewed his results. He wrote articles on the techniques of animation, from sound to "Synthesis of Artificial Movements in Motion Picture Projection", in film magazines in Canada, the US and France. He was presented with over 200 awards.

In 1978 McLaren's desire to create even greater access to the basic understanding of animation led to five instructive, beautiful films, *Animated Motions*, which are still considered by many in his field to be a "bible" of concepts. "I'm terrified of letting an audience get bored," he once said. Audiences never were—and never would be.

Born Norman McLaren. **Education** Schools in Stirling, Scotland; Glasgow School of Art, 1936. **Emigration** Left England for United States, 1939; left United States for Canada, 1941, became Canadian citizen, 1952. **Career** Film-maker, 1934 onwards; first film, *Hand Painted Abstraction*, 1934; worked for John Grierson, General Post Office Film Unit, 1936; made live-action documentaries, 1936–38; first professional animated film, *Love on the Wing*, 1938; worked as freelancer, also for Museum of Non-Objective Art, also made publicity shorts, New York, 1939–41; set up animation department, National Film Board of Canada, 1941; head, animation department, National Film Board of Canada, 1941 onwards. **Awards and honours** First prize, for anti-war film with animated sequence, Glasgow School of Art, 1934; Best Documentary Short Subject Academy Award for *Neighbours*, 1952. **Films** *Hand Painted Abstractions*, 1934–35; *Seven Till Five*, 1934–35; *Camera Makes Woopee*, 1934–35; *Colour Cocktail*, 1934–35; *Hell Unlimited*, 1936–37; *Defence of Madrid*, 1936–37; *Book Bargain*, 1937–39; *News for the Navy*, 1937–39; *Many a Pickle*, 1937–39; *Love on the Wing*, 1937–39; *The Obedient Flame*, 1939; *Dots* (film without camera), 1939–41; *Scherzo*, 1939–41; *Loops* (film without camera), 1939–41; *Rumba*, 1939–41; *Stars and Stripes* (film without camera), 1939–41; *Boogie Doodle* (film without camera), 1939–41; *Mail Early*, 1941; *V for Victory*, 1941; *Five for Four*, 1942; *Hen Hop* (film without camera), 1942; *Dollar Dance*, 1943; *C'est l'aviron*, 1944; *Keep Your Mouth Shut*, 1944; *La Haut sur ces montagnes*, 1945; *A Little Phantasy*, 1946; *Hoppity Pop* (film without camera), 1946; *Fiddle-de-dee* (film without camera), 1947; *Poulette grise*, 1947; *A Phantasy*, 1948–52; *Begone Dull Care* (film without camera), 1949; *Around Is Around*, 1950–51; *Now Is the Time*, 1950–51; *Neighbours/Les Voisins* (pixillation), 1952; *Two Bagatelles* (pixillation), 1952; *Blinkety Blank* (film without camera), 1954–55; *Rhythmetic*, 1956; *A Chairy Tale/Il était une chaise* (pixillation), 1957; *Le Merle*, 1958; *Serenal* (film without camera), 1959; *Short and Suite* (film without camera), 1959; *Mail Early for Christmas*, 1959; credit sequence for *The Wonderful World of Jack Paar* (television), 1959; *Lignes verticales/Vertical Lines* (film without camera), 1960; *Opening Speech/Discours de bienvenue de McLaren* (pixillation), 1960; *New York Lightboard*, 1961; *Lignes horizontales/Horizontal Lines*, 1962; credit sequence, intertitles for *Caprice de Noel/ Christmas Crackers* (pixillation), 1963; *Canon* (pixillation), 1964; *Mosaic/Mosaique* (film without camera), 1965; *Pas de deux* (live action), 1967; *Spheres*, 1969; *Synchromy*, 1971; *Ballet adagio*, 1972; (co-director with Alexeieff and Parker) *L'Écran d'épingles*, 1973; *Le Mouvement image par image*, 1976–78; *Narcissus* (live action), 1981–83. **Publications** *The Drawings of Norman McLaren*, Montreal, 1975; contributor to periodicals, including *Cahiers du cinema*, *Quarterly of Film, Radio and Television*, *Film*, *Sequences*, *Film Library Quarterly*, *Film Culture*, *Écran*, *Films and Filming*, *Wide Angle*. **Cause of death** Undisclosed, at age 72. **Further reading** Hardy Forsyth, *Dots and Loops: The Story of a Scottish Film Cartoonist*, Edinburgh, 1951; *Norman McLaren*, Montreal, 1965; Maynard Collins, *Norman McLaren*, Canada, 1975; Robert Russett and Cecile Starr, *Experimental Animation*, New York, 1976.

JOHN BARTLOW MARTIN

American Journalist, Author and Criminologist
***Born* Hamilton, Ohio, 4 August 1915**
***Died* Highland Park, Illinois, 3 January 1987**

"The best living reporter." "The ablest crime reporter in America." For a man who turned out a million words a year at his peak, the writings of John Bartlow Martin were criticized surprisingly seldom. Described as a "devoutly liberal Democrat, unabashed and unregenerate", the gravest accusation the reporter and political speechwriter seems to have sustained throughout his nearly 50 years of writing was that "his sympathies echoed through many of his works". Considering the fact that his works concentrated on the people outside society—criminals, prisoners, the homeless—Martin could be forgiven by many for being overly sympathetic. Yet even if his own views sometimes showed beneath the typescript, Martin remained first and foremost a reporter of facts. From Illinois coalfields to presidential campaign planes, the Ohio native always retained his diffidence and reserve.

Born in Hamilton, Ohio, in 1915, Martin endured a childhood which was, in his own words, an unpleasant one: "Most of my childhood memories are dark." His parents argued a good deal and the death of a brother added to the familial strain. Perhaps to escape his unhappy family environment, Martin graduated early from his Indiana high school and entered DePauw University, but this collegiate beginning was shortlived; before the end of his first year, Martin had been expelled for drinking in his room. For a while, he became a copy boy for the

Indianapolis bureau of the Associated Press wire service, where he earned $9 a week. Soon, however, he was allowed to re-enter the university, where he graduated with a degree in political science in 1937.

Having written for the *Indianapolis Times* during his university years, Martin had no trouble obtaining a job there as a reporter after his graduation. But reportage and rewrites on orders were not to his liking; by 1938, using the profits from his first freelance magazine article, Martin moved to Chicago with "one suitcase, a portable typewriter, and the desire to write". His freelance career began slowly—at first. There were, he recalled, "two or three articles to *Esquire*, then a great number of factual crime pieces for such magazines as *True Detective*". As any journalist knows, breaking into a magazine like *Esquire* is no mean feat; however, Martin considered that his first real quality piece did not occur until 1943, when he sold "The Making of a Nazi Saboteur" to *Harper's*.

The best known of his early articles and the one which brought his name to the attention of the national magazines was a story called "Who Killed the Centralia Miners?" published in *Harper's* and *Reader's Digest* in 1948. The article analysed the facts surrounding the Centralia, Illinois, mining disaster which killed around 100 people. Prior to its publication, however, Martin had already written the first of his dozen or more books: *Call It North Country: The Story of Upper Michigan* was published by Alfred A. Knopf in 1944, and was described by the *New York Herald Tribune* as "one of the best regional books to come out of the woods in a long time. A careful, well-written, understanding job." It seemed that, before his fame as an investigative reporter had been established, John Martin had already gained a reputation for sympathy.

A second regional book, *Indiana: An Interpretation*, followed in 1947 to equally high praise, but it was *Butcher's Dozen* (1950)—six accounts of actual crimes—that set the writer back on the path of criminal journalism. This book was the forerunner of one of Martin's most famous works, *My Life in Crime*, published two years later. Benefiting from his matured technique, the result was an in-depth analysis of the criminal personality. "I don't know whether there has ever been published a book quite like *My Life in Crime*," wrote Joseph Henry Jackson in the *San Francisco Chronicle*. "Here is the whole story of a professional American criminal, a man in his middle forties, who has spent his entire life in crime, told unreservedly and frankly." Martin had once stated that the common factor in his writing was interest in the individual. *My Life in Crime* and his next book, *Why Did They Kill*?, an analysis of three juveniles sentenced to life imprisonment for murder, proved that his interest in the individual had never flagged. This ability to concentrate effectively and explore one topic was combined with another Martin characteristic: fearlessness. In the 1950s his *Break Down the Walls* dealt unashamedly with the workings of the prison system and the failures of it to deal with the serious sexual problems of inmates. It was Martin's intention, one reporter said, not only to analyse the prison system, but also "to awake and arouse the public from its habitual apathy" about the conditions "inside". It was the writer's conviction that once the causes of criminality were understood, then the need for maximum security institutions would be unnecessary.

Such convictions, coupled with his consistent work in the Democratic Party, led to Martin's appointment by John F. Kennedy as ambassador to the Dominican Republic from 1962 to 1964. When that post came to an end, the writer remained politically active, drafting speeches for Lyndon Johnson, Hubert Humphrey and Robert Kennedy, just as he had done for Adlai Stevenson during his presidential campaign of the 1950s. It seemed only natural that these political experiences would be turned into print: thus, the 1970s saw the publication of Martin's *Life of Adlai Stevenson* and *The US Policy in the Caribbean*. *The Televising of Heller* followed in 1980, a novel which examined the behind-the-scenes problems of a political campaign. Charles Peck of the *Washington Post* stated that the book "skilfully suggests the endless dispute over how much time and resources ought to be devoted to creating and projecting a candidate's image when he already has a good record of service".

Martin was a modest man whose reserve masked a great deal of intensity; his writing provoked controversy as well as admiration. In the words of J.K. Galbraith, "No one then, and I think none since, could make a point more succinctly, support it more sharply with evidence and then, of all things, stop."

Born John Bartlow Martin. **Parents** John Williamson, building contractor, and Laura (Bartlow) Martin. **Marriage** Frances Rose Smethurst, 1940. **Children** Cynthia Ann, Daniel Bartlow, John Frederick. **Education** DePauw University, BA, 1937. **Military service** US Army, 1944–46. **Career** Copy boy, Associated Press, 1934; reporter, *Indianapolis Times*, 1937–38; freelance writer, 1938–62; consultant on Caribbean affairs to the Department of State, 1961; special envoy of US president to Dominican Republic, 1961, 1965; US ambassador to Dominican Republic, 1962–64; freelance writer, 1964–87. **Related activities** Senior fellow, Center for Advanced Studies, Wesleyan University, 1964–65; visiting fellow in public affairs, Princeton University, 1966–67; visiting professor, Graduate School and University Center of the City University of New York, 1968; professor of journalism, Medill School of Journalism, Northwestern University, 1970–80, professor emeritus, 1980–87. **Other activities** Campaign staff member and speech writer for Adlai Stevenson, 1952–56, John F. Kennedy, 1960, Lyndon B. Johnson, 1964, Robert F. Kennedy, 1968, Hubert H. Humphrey, 1968. **Memberships** Delta Chi; Sigma Delta Chi; Authors' Guild. **Awards and honours** *Sigma Delta Chi* Magazine Award, 1950, 1957; *Benjamin Franklin* Magazine Award, 1954, 1956, 1957, 1958; Indiana Authors' Day Award, Indiana University Writers' Conference, 1967, for *Overtaken by Events*; Ohioana Book Award, 1967, for *Overtaken by Events*; honorary LLD, Indiana University, 1971; honorary LHD, Knox College, Galesburg, Illinois, 1975. **Publications** *Call It North Country: The Story of Upper Michigan*, 1944; *Indiana: An Interpretation*, 1947, reprinted 1972; *Butcher's Dozen*, 1950; *Adlai Stevenson*, 1952; *My Life in Crime*, 1952; *Why Did They Kill? 1953; Break Down the Walls*, 1954; *The Deep South Says Never*, 1957; *Jimmy Hoffa's Hot*, 1959; *The Pane of Glass*, 1959; *Overtaken by Events*, 1966; *The Life of Adlai Stevenson*, 1976–77; *US Policy in the Caribbean*, 1978; *The Televising of Heller*, 1980; contributor to *Harper's*, *Reader's Digest, Saturday Evening Post*, *Redbook*, *Cosmopolitan*, *McCall's*, *Esquire*, *True Detective*, *Life*, *Look*, *Collier's*, *The Atlantic* and other magazines. **Cause of death** Throat cancer and emphysema, at age 71.

DAVID MAYSLES

American Documentary Film-maker

***Born* Brookline, Massachusetts, 10 January 1932**

***Died* New York City, New York, 3 January 1987**

"My God, this was a real film...not any of that intellectual shit" was John Lennon's quoted reaction to *Gimme Shelter* when he saw it at Cannes. The controversial result of the prolific partnership of David and Albert Maysles, it is ironic that the film, and their work in general, should have stimulated such a furious debate which centres around that lofty philosophical chestnut, the Nature of Truth, with discussion of Reality and Artistic Responsibility thrown in for good measure.

The product of a conventional, middle-class Massachusetts upbringing, David Maysles read psychology at Boston University before serving in the US Army in West Germany. On his return, a brief flirtation with Hollywood and conventional film-making in the shape of *The Prince and the Showgirl* and *Bus Stop* was enough to convince him that the business of working with scripts, actors, lights and the other trappings of orthodox cinematography was not for him.

He turned to documentaries and, with *Youth in Poland*, began the collaboration with his brother Albert that was to last nearly 30 years and produce some two dozen films. Their use of a near-silent, exceptionally light, hand-held camera, which could be operated almost imperceptibly, formed their basic equipment, allowing for a considerable degree of spontaneity and a lack of self-consciousness on the part of their subjects. David used a highly sensitive directional mike to record the sound while Albert operated the camera.

Their use of lengthy continuous action put them at the vanguard of the 1960s development of *cinéma vérité*, a label they firmly rejected. "Direct cinema" was the acceptable alternative, avoiding the theoretical baggage of "truth" and suggesting the immediacy which their techniques certainly provided.

Starting with a theme, the Maysles would allow their subject to lead them intuitively to insights they had not predetermined, shaping and structuring the final product by editing the huge quantity of footage gathered. *Salesman*, a study of four door-to-door Bible salesmen in small-town, middle America, and *Grey Gardens*, an observation of two eccentric, elderly ladies of a branch of the Bouvier family, both fed the unending argument between documentary makers and critics about whether objectivity is at all possible in the medium. Typically, both films aroused strong reactions, ranging from trenchant accusations of exploitation, dishonesty and tastelessness to fulsome praise of their makers' artistry, compassion and devotion.

Gimme Shelter, perhaps David Maysles' most controversial film, followed the course of a Rolling Stones concert, culminating in extreme violence and the murder by Hell's Angels of a black youth in the huge crowd at Livermore, California. The footage was used by the court trying the case to establish the facts—testament, argued the makers, to its validity and objectivity. Their *oeuvre* is catholic in its range, including subjects as varied as Marlon Brando, Truman Capote, the Beatles and Vladimir Horowitz. If it is part of the function of cinema to challenge and provoke, the Maysles association has produced artefacts of undeniable power and, whether or not their films constitute The Truth, they undoubtedly articulate a particularly stimulating minute observation of reality.

Born David Paul Maysles. **Marriage** Judith. **Children** One son, John Philip, and one daughter, Celia. **Education** Brookline High School; Boston University, BA in psychology. **Military service** United States Army, Military Intelligence School, Oberammergau, West Germany, World War II. **Career** Began in feature films; assistant to producer on *Bus Stop* and *The Prince and the Showgirl*, 1956; moved over to documentary films; first film with brother, Albert Maysles, *Youth in Poland*, 1957; reporter on television series, *Adventures on the New Frontier*, late 1950s – early 1960s; founder, with brother Albert, Maysles Production Company, 1962; worked on full-length documentaries, plus industrial and corporate promotional films, 1970–82. **Awards and honours** Joint recipient with brother, Guggenheim fellowship in experimental film, 1965; Best Short Story Documentary, Academy Award nomination for *Christo's Valley Curtain*, 1973. **Films** (with brother) *Youth in Poland*, 1957; *Showman*, 1962; *What's Happening*, 1964; *The Beatles in the USA*, 1964; *Meet Marlon Brando*, 1965; *With Love from Truman*, 1966; *Salesman*, 1969; *Gimme Shelter*, 1970; *Christo's Valley Curtain*, 1972; *Grey*

Gardens, 1975; *Running Fence*, 1977. **Publications** Contributor to periodicals, including *Movie*, *Film Quarterly*, *Sight and Sound*, *Filmmakers' Newsletter*, *Documentary Explorations*, *Millimeter*, *Quarterly Review of Film Studies*. **Cause of death** Stroke, at age 54. **Further reading** M. Issari, *Cinéma Vérité*, Michigan, 1971.

EWART MILNE

Irish Poet

***Born* Dublin, Ireland, 25 May 1903**

***Died* Bedford, England, 14 January 1987**

Conflict seems to have been the keynote of Ewart Milne's long and unsettled life. Always in conflict with the Ireland of his birth, he was also in conflict with the socialism he adopted as his creed in the 1930s and, finally, as shown most movingly in his long prose poem "Time Stopped" published in 1967, he was in conflict with his own feelings.

To be born an Irish Protestant at the beginning of the twentieth century was, in a sense, to be born into a state of conflict. This Milne initially rejected. Feeling himself a misfit in his youth and wishing to have no part in the sectarian strife that was tearing his country apart, he left Ireland on leaving school in 1920 and went off to sea. "I think my early circumstances, when Ireland was still part of the British Empire, but like my family was torn apart by Home Rule and all the rest of it, were very important indeed...," Milne later wrote. "I think the traumatic period of the Irish Civil War had a far greater effect on me than I believed at the time." He also said that he "sort of looked in on Trinity College, Dublin" but that the mounting sense of strife in Ireland encouraged him to say "a plague on both your houses" and to leave.

Milne was to spend most of the next 15 years travelling around the world. In a later allegorical poem he talked of being "shanghaied aboard" for "the round trip" on the "steamship Earth". "Where we were bound for had been left blank."

Rejecting Ireland, Milne finally found his cause in socialism and in Spain. Following his friend Charles Donnelly to Madrid, he worked as an ambulance driver for Medical Aid in the Spanish Civil War. Here, however, he became increasingly disillusioned with the Republican cause, quarrelled with his fellow poet, W.H. Auden, over the question of means and ends and finally left Spain after the collapse of Medical Aid and the fall of Barcelona. Some of Milne's most moving poems were written in memory of scenes he witnessed during that war.

The 1939–45 war saw Ewart Milne back in England managing an estate in Suffolk and helping to run a school for refugee diplomats' children with Thelma Swinburn who was to become his second wife. It was after her death in 1964 that Milne wrote "Time Stopped".

I sat by her bedside and watched her die
And the hopeless and defeated one   that was I
The helpless one the condemned one   that was I
Left over   left to live on   mercilessly
Left with the fallen bricks of my house of poetry.

The London *Times* obituary described Milne's poem as a "harrowing elegy to his second wife written in agonized recognition of her infidelity to him, revealed only after her death". These words brought an angry refutation from Douglas Cleverdon (q.v.) who claimed that Milne's own lechery was notorious and thus his bitterness and disillusion somewhat hypocritical. Milne, he alleged, not only made a pass at his [Cleverdon's] wife within minutes of meeting her for the first time, but also grumbled about the selfish and nubile young women who rejected his amorous advances when he was in his sixties. Whatever the truth of this, it seems somehow in character that conflict should have surfaced around Milne's obituary notices, just as it did throughout his life.

With Ireland also Milne was never really to make his peace. When he returned full of hope in 1962 and published his optimistic and romantically nationalistic *Garland of the Green* it was not well received. But although he finally chose England, his poems were always, according to one critic, infested with "that rhetoric verging on blarney which is germane to being Irish". Milne himself confessed surprise to find that almost all the poems in his final volume, *The Folded Leaf* (1983), were "made up of pieces about my boyhood in the early years of this century spent in Dublin and Ireland".

Born Charles Ewart Milne. **Parents** Charles Frederick, a chartered accountant, and Edith Jane (Williams) Milne. **Marriages** 1) Kathleen Ida Bradner, 1927 (divorced, 1945); 2) Thelma Dobson, 1948 (died, 1964). **Children** Charles Beresford by first marriage; Justin David and Kevin Charles by second marriage. **Education** Pembroke Street National School, Sandymount, 1909–10; Nun's Cross School, Rathnew, County Wicklow, 1910–15; Christ Church Cathedral Grammar School, Dublin, 1915–19. **Career** Seaman, Elder Dempster Line, 1920–35; student-teacher, 1925; began writing seriously, 1930 onwards; early efforts appeared in anthology, *Goodbye Twilight*; contributor and book reviewer, *Irish Times*, Dublin, 1936 onwards; co-founder, with Leslie Daikan, *Irish Front* (later *Irish Democrat)*, 1936; staff writer, *Ireland Today*, 1937–40; first publication, *Forty North, Fifty West*, 1938; farm manager, Suffolk, England, 1942–61; book reviewer, *Irish Press*, Dublin, 1968–70. **Other activities** Ambulance driver, Spanish Civil War, 1936. **Verse** *Forty North, Fifty West*, Dublin, 1938; *Letter from Ireland*, Dublin, 1940; *Listen Mangan: Poems*, Dublin, 1941; *Jubilo: Poems*, London, 1944; *Boding Day: Poems*, London, 1947; *Diamond Cut Diamond: Selected Poems*, London, 1950; *Elegy for a Lost Submarine*, Burnham-on-Crouch, Essex, 1951; *Galion: A Poem*, Dublin, 1953; *Life Arboreal*, Tunbridge Wells, Kent, 1953; *Once More to Tourney: A Book of Ballads and Light Verse, Serious, Gay and Grisly*, London, 1958; *A Garland of the Green*, London, 1962; *Time Stopped: A Poem Sequence with Prose Intermissions*, London, 1967; *Drift of Pinions*, Portree, Isle of Skye, 1976; *Cantata Under Orion*, Portree, Isle of Skye, 1976; *Deus Est Qui Regit Omnia*, Mornington, County Meath, 1980; *Spring Offering*, Portree, Isle of Skye, 1981; *The Folded Leaf*, Portree, Isle of Skye, 1983. **Other** *Drums Without End* (stories), Portree, Isle of Skye, 1985. **Cause of death** Undisclosed, at age 83. **Further reading** Hugh Ford, *A Poet's War: British Poets in the Spanish Civil War*, Pennsylvania, 1965; Frank Kersnowski, *The Outsiders: Poets of Contemporary Ireland*, Texas, 1975; J.C.R. Green (editor), *Ewart Milne: For His 80th Birthday*, Portree, Isle of Skye, 1983.

GALO PLAZA LASSO

Ecuadorian Farmer, President and Statesman
***Born* New York City, New York, 17 February 1906**
***Died* Quito, Ecuador, 28 January 1987**

Something of a dilettante in the best sense, Galo Plaza Lasso successfully combined a domestic career as a skilled agriculturist with a high-profile political role as statesman on both the national and international stage. Tellingly, he achieved this in the context of the stormy history of Ecuador where, amid the string of coups and counter-coups, dictatorships and military juntas which have become almost the hallmark of any Latin-American republic, he preserved a genuine commitment to liberalism and a firm belief in the Western democratic model.

Politics was in the family. His father, General Leonidas Plaza Guttierez, was president twice himself, and was noted for his progressive and anti-clerical outlook, although in his attitude to his family he was paternalistic, authoritarian and very conservative. It was during the General's tour of ministerial duty in the United States that Galo Plaza was born in New York City, and the North American connection was maintained and strengthened when, after elementary and secondary education in and around Quito, the Ecuadorian capital, the young Galo was forced to flee to the United States with the rest of his family when one of the country's sporadic and ultimately inconclusive revolutions broke out.

His academic career, studying agriculture and economics, at the University of California was undistinguished, although he apparently excelled in playing football with "bone crushing enthusiasm". The General intervened in a bid to preserve his eldest son for future glories and put a stop to his energetic participation in the "dangerous Yankee game" by sending him to Maryland University as a transfer student, thus rendering him ineligible for varsity sports. (Galo Plaza later turned to the gentler art of amateur bullfighting as an alternative.)

After Maryland, where, as he freely admitted, he was more interested in playing the horses than grappling with the rigours of modern dairy-farming methods, Plaza studied diplomacy at Georgetown University School of Foreign Studies in Washington. He combined this with a position as civil attaché in the Ecuadorian legation until the patrician General, in fine Victorian tradition, decided to cut off his son's allowance to foster self-reliance—almost immediately following the crash of 1929 and the ensuing Depression which engulfed the country.

It was not until after the death of his father in 1933 that Plaza returned to Ecuador to take over the management of the family's properties which, though extensive, were at that time virtually bankrupt. His implementation of the techniques absorbed at college, together with the practical retail experience gained selling apples on New York street corners during his "self-reliance" period, put the business into the black within a few years.

He applied the same flair to politics and the end of the decade saw him as defence minister under President Mosquera Narvaez. Renewed turbulence on the domestic front forced a return to the United States in 1942 and, although he returned soon afterwards, he remained out of public life until his appointment two years later, under the newly installed President Velasco Ibarra, as ambassador to the United States. The President's subsequent seizure of dictatorial powers prompted his resignation and the following year's presidential elections saw Plaza installed as chief executive after a closely fought, four-cornered contest.

During his term, Plaza's progressive approach, combined with considerable business acumen, reaped large dividends for Ecuador. Political stability and a heavy programme of investment in domestic production led to a doubling of exports with no serious inflationary side effects. The country became the world's leading exporter of bananas, which provided the mainstay of Ecuador's economy until oil exports began nearly 30 years later. Plaza crowned this notable political achievement by withdrawing gracefully at the end of his four-year period of office, prohibited by the constitution from immediate self-succession—the first freely elected president to do so in the country's history.

Although he stood again (unsuccessfully) for the presidency in 1960, Plaza subsequently turned his political attentions outwards and confined his domestic activities largely to farming. Recognizing his considerable administrative and negotiating skills, the United Nations appointed him chairperson of a variety of working committees and observation groups, most notably as UN mediator in Cyprus between Ankara and Athens. He ultimately resigned the latter post when the two sides refused to accept his compromise solution of an independent state for Cyprus, but not before receiving widespread commendation for his diplomatic efforts from the international community.

His term as secretary-general of the Organization of American States (OAS) gave him the opportunity to promote solidarity among Latin-American nations in a bid for hemispheric cooperation. His perceived Western bias laid him open to the charge from other member states of being the puppet of the United States, an accusation he vigorously rejected. On the contrary, he maintained, only by standing together could the Latin-American nations negotiate successfully with their more powerful neighbour to the north.

Galo Plaza's powerful personality, combined with a shrewdness of mind that enabled him to navigate the often treacherous and choppy waters of statesmanship, earned him the enduring respect not only of progressive forces in his own country but of the international community at large. He represents a period of calm, strength and sanity in the turbulent history of Ecuador.

Born Galo Plaza Lasso. **Parents** General Leonidas Plaza Gutierrez, former president of Ecuador, and Avelina (Lasso) Plaza. **Marriage** Rosario Pallares Zaldumbide, 1933. **Children** One son, Galo, and five daughters, Elsa, Luz, Rosario, Marcela and Margarita. **Education** Colegio Nacional Mejía, Quito, graduated 1925; University of California; University of Maryland, left 1929; Georgetown University School of Foreign Service, 1929. **Emigration** Left Ecuador for US, 1925; returned to Ecuador, 1933. **Career** Worked in real estate; junior assistant purser, Grace Line; farm manager, 1933 onwards; elected to Quito municipal council, 1937; mayor of Quito, 1938–39; minister of national defence, 1939–40; ambassador to the US, 1944–46; member, Ecuador Senate, 1947; president of Ecuador, 1948–52; secretary-general, Organization of American States, 1968–75. **Related activities** Co-founder, Independent Citizens Party, 1947; chairman, UN observer group, Lebanon, 1958; chairman, working group, UN Economic Commission for Latin-America, 1958–59; chairman, UN commission to study problems of evacuating Belgian treaty bases in Congo, 1960; vice-chairman, Oxford Conference, 1961; UN mediator, Cyprus, 1964–65; held talks with president of Haiti on behalf of Carnegie Endowment for Peace, 1966; lectured widely at American universities. **Awards and honours** Foundation of Americas award, 1955; Elise and Walther Haas award, University of California, 1967; distinguished alumnus award, University of Maryland, 1968; portrait hung in Chicago's Agricultural Hall of Fame, 1968; Key Man of Americas award, 1969; decorations from governments of US, Mexico, Colombia, Chile, China, Costa Rica, Cuba, Bolivia, Guatemala, Venezuela, Paraguay and Peru; honorary degrees from University of Maryland, Columbia University, Washington University, Harvard University, University of New Mexico, Williams College, Hamilton College and the New School for Social Research. **Publications** *Problems of Democracy in Latin-America* 1955; (with Stacy May) *The United Fruit Company in Latin-America*, 1958; *Latin-America Today and Tomorrow*, 1971. **Cause of death** Heart attack, at age 80.

DOUGLAS SIRK

American Film Director

***Born* Hamburg, Germany, 26 April 1900**

***Died* Lugano, Switzerland, 14 January 1987**

When it became necessary—and sometimes fashionable—for scholars and critics to reassess underrated or ignored film directors in the late 1960s and 1970s, Douglas Sirk's name leapt to the top of the list. The master of melodrama, previously dismissed as trivial and novelettish, is regarded as having one of the finest narrative styles, laced with sharp insight into American societal values, of any modern *auteur*. Melodrama gained credibility under Sirk's hand. Where his films were once consigned to the late-night TV slot, they are now, along with their maker, objects of cult status, as well as of film festivals and retrospectives.

Certainly his background influenced his attitudes and mastery of film form. Born in Germany of Danish parents, Claus (changed later to Hans) Detlef Sierck studied law at the University of Munich, philosophy at Jena, and painting and art history with Erwin Panofsky at Hamburg. This last talent was directed into a great flair for set design, lighting and composition (his hallmarks), sharpened even more by his successful career in the theatre. From 1923 to 1929 he was the artistic director of the Schauspielhaus in Bremen and, at the age of 29, became the manager of the respected Altes Theatre in Leipzig. He spent three years there producing over 100 classic plays, often audaciously translated. Sirk's name was a popular and highly regarded one.

His creative and leftist sympathies becoming increasingly frowned upon by the Nazi regime, Sirk joined the somewhat safer UFA Studio. The films he made during that three-year period are unremarkable, competent costume pieces of which the audiences could not get enough. His second feature, *Das Mädchen vom Moorhof* (1935) was a blowsy remake of the silent Swedish jewel, *Tosen fran Stormytorpet*, directed by the great Viktor Sjöstrom. In his *Schlussakkord*, a mawkish love story made the following year, film scholars may note that Sirk broke away from his usual literary values, embracing purely filmic ones, hence it is something of a landmark. While it is incorrect to describe Sirk's style in this period as "expressionist", as many people do, it is evident that his theme of unmasking hypocrisy and his love of mirror shots began here. His *Zu Neuen Ufern* (1937) established Zarah Leander as a major star. Ironically, while Sirk fled, with so many artists, from Germany, Leander stayed on to become the heroine of many a film made under the aegis of Joseph Goebbels.

Sirk arrived in Hollywood (via Holland and Paris) in 1937, and was signed on as a freelance director/scriptwriter at Columbia Studio from 1939 to 1948. His time there was troubled; only his independent films gave him the freedom to rise above the "B" scripts he was given, as he was allowed to edit, restructure and shoot the material to his satisfaction. The low-budget *Summer Storm* (1944) and *Scandal in Paris* (1946) are two examples. A disheartened Sirk returned to Germany for a year. Finding the film climate was no better, he returned to direct at Universal in 1950. He became the "in-house" director, who was also responsible for showcasing the studio's stars, such as Robert Stack, Dorothy Malone, Lana Turner, John Gavin, Jane Wyman and Rock Hudson, many of whom had been abused by flimsy scripts.

Even under his restrictions, which were numerous, the films made during this time still carry Sirk's stamp. Of all the German émigrés to Hollywood, he seemed to be the most stimulated by the American social climate and its changing priorities, reflected in his cycle of glossy melodramas. Many of his films were shot by cameraman Russell Metty; this partnership was as crucial to the "look" of his films as those of, for example, Woody Allen/Gordon Willis, Viktor Sjöstrom/Julius Jaenzon and Ingmar Bergman/Gunnar Fischer and Sven Nykvist.

His first major film, *Magnificent Obsession* (1954), with Rock Hudson and Jane Wyman, had several of his major themes. A playboy becomes a doctor to cure a woman whose blindness he had caused. Sirk was to feature over half a dozen doctors in his films, with illness representing social breakdown. Self-delusion, dead-end relationships, ambiguity in his heroes and sexual difficulties (such as repression, frustration and fear of impotence)—everything was here, everything reflected in his now famous mirror shots.

"There is a wonderful expression: seeing through a glass darkly," Sirk once explained. "Everything, even life, is inevitably removed from you. You can't reach or touch the real. You just see reflections. If you try to grasp happiness itself, your fingers only meet glass. It's hopeless." This sense of despair permeates nearly all Sirk's films, a sharpness redeeming the formula glossiness of the scripts. He was able to get the best out of his actors, and made the melodrama an ideal genre to reflect what he saw as the disintegration of American values, especially in ways the producers couldn't perceive. One of the strongest ironies of Sirk's career was the fact that he left one repressive climate only to labour under a quieter one of the Hollywood machine.

It is interesting to compare the films Sirk made under producer Ross Hunter, who enforced happy endings and his own particular style (*All That Heaven Allows*, 1955, and *Imitation of Life*, 1959), with the two works which were produced under a more sympathetic executive who let Sirk have his way: *Written on the Wind* (1956) and *Tarnished Angels* (1957), from a Faulkner short story. The last two, particularly, have substance and sharpness which redeem the most idiotic of plotlines.

Although Sirk made films in other genres, such as westerns and war pictures, he was to return to the melodrama. His last film, *Imitation of Life*, was the studio's greatest success. However, after its release, Sirk, ill in both body and spirit, left for Germany, where he remained active in the theatre and taught at a film school in Munich. He later moved to Switzerland, which remained his home until his death.

Born Claus Detlef Sierck. **Education** Studied law, philosophy and art history at the universities of Munich, Jena and Hamburg, until 1922. **Emigration** Left Germany for Austria and France, 1937; emigrated to US, 1939. **Career** Writer, *Neue Hamburger Zeitung*, 1920; assistant dramaturg, Deutsches Schauspiele, Hamburg, 1920; appointed dramaturg, 1921; became theatre director, 1922; directing début, *Bahnmeister Tod*, Bossdorf; artistic director, Bremen Schauspielhaus, 1923–29; director, Altes Theater, Leipzig, 1929–36; film directing début, Ufa Studio, Berlin, 1934; head, Leipzig drama school, 1936; scriptwriter, Austria, France, Holland, 1937–39; moved to United States, 1939; under contract to Warner Brothers, 1939; writing contract with Columbia, 1942; worked independently with group of German émigrés; film director for Universal, 1950 onwards; retired from film-making, 1959; returned to Europe and worked for Residenz-Theater, Munich, Thalia Theater, Hamburg, 1960–69. **Other activities** Translator of Shakespeare's sonnets, 1922. **Films** (directed as Detlef Sierck) *'t Was een April* (*April, April*), 1935; *Das Mädchen vom Moorhof*, 1935; *Stützen der Gesellschaft*, 1935; *Schlussakkord* (*Final Curtain*), 1936; *Das Hofkonzert*, 1936; *La Chanson du souvenir* (*Song of Remembrance*), 1936; *Du neuen Ufern* (*To New Shores*, *Paramatta*, *Bagne de femmes*), 1937; *La Habanera*, 1937; *Liebling der Matrosen*, 1937; *Dreiklang* (story only); *Accordfinal* (Bay), 1939; *Sehnsucht nach Afrika* (actor only), 1939; *Boefje*, 1939; (directed as Douglas Sirk) *Hitler's Madam*, 1943; *Summer Storm*, 1944; *A Scandal in Paris*, 1946; *Lured*, 1947; *Sleep My Love*, 1948; *Slightly French*, 1949; *Shockproof*, 1949; *Mystery Submarine*, 1950; *The First Legion* (also co-producer), 1951; *Thunder on the Hill*, 1951; *The Lady Pays Off*, 1951; *Weekend with Father*, 1951; *No Room* *for the Groom*, 1952; *Has Anybody Seen My Gal?* 1952; *Meet Me at the Fair*, 1952; *Take Me to Town*, 1952; *All I Desire*, 1953; *Taza, Son of Cochise*, 1953; *Magnificent Obsession*, 1954; *Sign of the Pagan*, 1953; *Captain Lightfoot*, 1954; *All That Heaven Allows*, 1955; *There's Always Tomorrow*, 1955; *Never Say Goodbye*, 1956; *Written on the Wind*, 1956; *Battle Hymn*, 1957; *Interlude*, 1957; *The Tarnished Angels*, 1957; *A Time to Love and a Time to Die*, 1958; *Imitation of Life*, 1959. **Cause of death** Undisclosed, at age 86. **Further reading** Jon Halliday, *Sirk on Sirk*, New York and London, 1972; *Edinburgh Film Festival 1972: Douglas Sirk*, Edinburgh, 1972.

SIR GEORGE THALBEN-BALL

British Organist

***Born* Sydney, Australia, 18 June 1896**

***Died* London, England, 18 January 1987**

"When I was 60—around the time of Suez I think it was—I hadn't even got my second wind. Trouble is, I only feel about 50 now, and my musical recall is as good as ever."

Other people retire at 60. When Sir George Thalben-Ball retired from his position of organist at London's Temple Church in 1981 at the age of 85, the knighthood he received to mark 62 years of service did nothing to diminish his reluctance to leave his post. He continued to get up early every Wednesday morning to travel to Birmingham where as city organist he had been giving free lunchtime recitals since 1949, totalling over 1000. The doyen of organists, he was probably the biggest single influence on Anglican church music in the twentieth century. Among those who petitioned for his knighthood were Edward Heath, former prime minister, and Robert Runcie, Archbishop of Canterbury. The Queen Mother and Prince Charles both sent letters of support.

Thalben-Ball was born in Sydney, Australia, where his parents were on an extended working holiday. During the return journey to Cornwall three years later, Thalben-Ball managed to have himself kidnapped in Ceylon. Later, in the safety of Muswell Hill, Sir George won the Grove Scholarship to the Royal College of Music, where he studied composition with Sir Frederick Bridge and Sir Charles Stanford, and the organ with Sir Walter Parratt. He won the Hopkinson, Challen and Tagore gold medals as well as the Lafontaine Prize from the Royal College of Organists.

By the age of 16 he was already organist at the Whitefield's Tabernacle. He subsequently played at Holy Trinity, Castlenau and Paddington Parish Church before succeeding Sir Walford Davies at the Temple Church which became the focus of his professional career. He became a professor at the Royal College of Music, curator-organist at the Royal Albert Hall, and was city organist in Birmingham from 1949 to 1982. He was awarded the CBE in 1967.

In 1927 he recorded with boy soprano Ernest Lough one of the oldest records ever to receive a golden disc: "Oh, for the Wings of a Dove". As an organist he had a superlative technique and few people realized that he was also a fine pianist capable of playing Rachmaninov. He began playing at a time when organists were expected to play orchestral arrangements which are unfashionable today but demanded great skill, especially in the art of registration. He was not a showman but knew how to convey a sense of occasion.

Thalben-Ball performed at promenade concerts, on radio and television, and gave recitals all round the world. He was also an adjudicator, examiner, and conductor. "When he conducts an unaccompanied anthem," wrote his biographer, "he uses the smallest inflexion of hands and face and virtually tunes the choir with his eyebrows." He was a great champion of contemporary music and wrote organ compositions and several psalters. For a number of years he was a music adviser to the BBC, responsible for the daily service, and he composed the corporation's VE Day anthem. One of his more hair-raising assignments for the BBC was a live recital for the overseas network one morning at 3.30 a.m. He overslept, woke up half an hour before the broadcast, but made it to the studio on time, giving the recital in his pyjamas.

Thalben-Ball asked to be buried in the Cornish village of St Mawgan where he spent his early life and where his mother is buried. He was a legend in his lifetime, and his prodigiously full career will remain an inspiration to all aspiring professional musicians.

Born George Thomas Thalben-Ball. **Parents** George Charles and Mary Hannah (Spear) Thalben-Ball. **Marriage** Evelyn Chapman (died, 1961). **Children** One son and one daughter. **Education** Private schools in Australia; Grove Scholar, Royal College of Music, London, England; studied piano under Fritz Hartvigson and Fanny Davies, harmony and composition under Sir Frederick Bridge, Sir Charles Stanford and Dr Charles Wood, musical history under Sir Hubert Parry, organ under Sir Walter Parratt and F.A. Sewell. **Emigration** Left Australia for England as a child. **Career** Organist: Whitefield's Tabernacle, London, Holy Trinity Church, Castelnau, London, Paddington Parish Church, London, 1911–19; acting organist, Honourable Society of Temple, London, 1919, organist, 1923–81, organist emeritus, 1982; civic and university organist, Birmingham, 1949–82; curator-organist, Royal Albert Hall, London; made many recordings at venues such as Birmingham Town Hall, Temple Church and All Souls, Langham Place. **Related activities** Professor and examiner, Royal College of Music; examiner to the Associated Board of the Royal Academy of Music and the Royal College of Music; member of the Council and examiner, Royal College of Organists; examiner on behalf of the Cape University, 1925; adviser and consultant on religious music, BBC, 1941–70; joint editor, *BBC Hymn Book*, 1951; jury member, Concours International d'Orgue, Grand Prix de Chartres, 1973; contributor, *Australian Hymn Book*, 1977, *Hymns and Psalms*, 1983. **Offices and memberships** President: London Society of Organists, 1936, Incorporated Association of Organists, 1944–46, Royal College of Organists, 1948; member, board of governors, Royal National College of the Blind. **Awards and honours** Chappell and Hopkinson Gold Medallist; Lafontaine Prize, Royal College of Organists; Doctor of Music Cantauriensis, 1935; associate, Royal College of Music, fellow, Royal College of Music, 1951; fellow, Royal College of Organists; fellow, Royal Society of Choral Music, 1956, diploma, 1963; Bard Ylewyth Mur; Freeman of the City of London; honorary bencher, Inner Temple, 1959; EMI Gold Disc, 1963; Commander of the Order of the British Empire, 1967; fellow, Royal Society of Arts, 1971; honorary DMus and Gold Medal, Birmingham, 1972; fellow, Royal Canadian College of Organists; honorary fellow, Royal Academy of Music, 1973; knighted, 1982. **Major tours** Guest organist, Les Amis de l'Orgue, Paris, 1937; toured Australia as guest organist in connection with jubilee of the formation of the Commonwealth, 1951; toured South Africa, 1954; guest of honour, American Guild of Organists' Convention, New York, 1956; toured New Zealand, 1971; guest, Philadelphia, 1973; toured US and Canada, 1975. **Compositions** (include) *Sursum Corda*, for chorus; orchestra and trumpet fanfares (commissioned by the BBC); *Tune in E*, *Elegy*, *Variations on a Theme of Paganini*; *Toccata Beorma Poema*. **Cause of death** Undisclosed, at age 90.

ARCHBISHOP VALERIAN TRIFA

Rumanian Clergyman

***Born* Campeni, Rumania, 28 June 1914**

***Died* Cascais, Portugal, 28 January 1987**

Valerian Trifa was ordained a priest of the Rumanian Orthodox Church shortly after his arrival in exile in the United States in 1950. In 1952 he became a bishop and then, in 1970, archbishop of the Rumanian Orthodox Episcopate based in Grass Lake, Michigan. For years he was a highly respected churchman and leader of his community. He was a member of the Holy Synod of the Orthodox Church, of the central committee of the World Council of Churches, and was on the governing board of the National Council of Churches. In 1955 it was Archbishop Trifa who gave the opening prayer before the United States Senate.

The archbishop's downfall began in 1975 when the US Justice Department opened a case against him alleging that he had obtained entry to the country on false pretences. When applying for American citizenship, Trifa claimed that he was a displaced person, and had been in a concentration camp in Germany. What the Justice Department had now discovered was that Trifa had spent the year 1939–40 on postgraduate studies at the University of Berlin and had been treated as a privileged person while in Germany.

The real case against Valerian Trifa rested on his pre-war membership of the Fascist Iron Cross movement in Rumania. This he did not deny, claiming in 1973: "For those circumstances in that time I think that I didn't have any alternative but to do what I thought to be right for the interests of the Rumanian people." Although a speech by Trifa in Bucharest on 20 January 1941 was alleged to have sparked off four days of violence in which over 300 people were killed, and although he also admitted editing an anti-Jewish newspaper and making pro-Nazi speeches, there was no attempt made to build a war crimes case against him.

The Justice Department's case against Valerian Trifa dragged on for almost a decade. In 1980 the archbishop voluntarily surrendered his citizenship, hoping that this would close the case. Then, in 1982, during a hearing before an immigration judge in Detroit, he announced that he would agree to be deported to save his Church from the continuing financial burden of his case. It was another two years before he could find a country that would accept him. Only in 1984 did he finally find refuge in Portugal.

To the end Valerian Trifa remained publicly unrepentant. He said that he felt himself to be a victim of the Jewish preoccupation with the Holocaust—a preoccupation that he warned might backfire against them. "I am a man," he said in 1984, "who happened to get put in a moment of history when some people wanted to make a point."

Born Valerian Dionisie Trifa. **Parents** Dionisie and Macinica (Motora) Trifa. **Emigration** Left Rumania for the United States, 1950; naturalized, 1957; surrendered American citizenship, 1980; deported from the United States, 1984; allowed to settle in Portugal, 1986. **Education** University of Jassy, Rumania, Licentiate in Theology, 1935; University of Bucharest, Rumania, 1936–38; University of Berlin, Germany, 1939–40. **Career** Ordained a priest, Rumanian Orthodox Episcopate of America, 1950; elevated to bishop, 1952; bishop, Rumanian Orthodox Episcopate of America, Jackson, Michigan, 1952–70, archbishop, 1970–87. **Related activities** Member, governing body, National Council of Churches, 1960 onwards; member, central committee, World Council of Churches, 1968–75. **Other activities** Member, Iron Guard, Rumania, 1940s. **Cause of death** Heart attack, at age 72.

EARL WILSON

American Journalist

***Born* Rockford, Ohio, 3 May 1907**

***Died* Yonkers, New York, 16 January 1987**

Broadway and Hollywood never had a more popular or inexhaustible chronicler of celebrity derring-do than Earl Wilson. The doyen of gossip columnists from 1942 to 1983, he wrote some 11,424 issues of his "It Happened Last Night" column. His collection of anecdotes and titbits was avidly followed by those within the entertainment industry—theatre, film, radio, television—those who wanted to be, and those who were content to simply read about who said or did what to whom, when and where. At the height of his popularity, in the 1960s, Wilson's column was syndicated in as many as 175 newspapers across the United States.

His informal pieces, not so much gossipy as conversant in tone, were put together in 18-hour days. Wilson would phone his news sources and retrieve reports from assistants in the day, and prowl through bars, cabarets, clubs, theatre openings, first nights and other hot-spots with his wife until 2 or 3 a.m. His name was synonymous with the show-biz pulse. Unlike other columnists, such as Hedda Hopper (in Hollywood), Wilson was liked and respected; when rivals lost their audiences over the years, his continued to thrive.

The Ohio-born writer's career began innocuously enough as a $15-a-week sports writer for the *Piqua Daily Call*—a result of writing stories for free during his high-school years. After a journalism degree from Ohio State University, Wilson worked for papers in Columbus and Akron, and for the International News Service. In 1923 he graduated to the *Washington Post*, then moved in 1935 to the *New York Post*, where he remained for the next seven years. Wilson was best known for his show-biz column; few people realized that he was also responsible for breaking many "serious" front-page stories. For example, he was first to break the news that an anti-polio vaccine was in the works in 1935. He had a reputation for being a tenacious reporter, a trait which proved worthwhile in ferreting out secrets from otherwise publicity-shy stars, and their "friends" and co-workers.

In addition to his syndicated work, Wilson was also a radio commentator, hosting entertaining and chatty talk shows. He wrote many books, mainly based on his newspaper columns. They provide valuable insights to the New York and Los Angeles theatre scenes, as well as being well-written pieces in their own right.

Born Earl Wilson. **Parents** Arthur Earl, farmer, and Cloe (Huffman) Wilson. **Marriage** Rosemary Lyons, 1936 (died, 1986). **Children** Earl Lyons Jr. **Education** Heidelberg College; Ohio State University, BS, 1931. **Career** Columnist, radio commentator and editor; wrote for various newspapers, including *Piqua Daily Call*, *Columbus Dispatch*, *International News Service*, *Akron Beach Journal*, *Washington Post*, 1923–35; writer, New York, 1935; drama, amusement, nightclub editor and columnist ("It Happened Last Night"), *New York Post*, and syndicated in up to 175 newspapers, 1942–83. **Related activities** Radio commentator for various stations, including WOR-Mutual, 1945; host of part of *Tonight Show*, NBC-TV, 1957. **Offices and memberships** Sigma Delta Chi; Alpha Tau Omega. **Publications** *Jungle Performers*, 1941; *I Am Gazing Into My Eight-Ball*, 1945; *Pike's Peak or Bust*, 1946; *Let 'Em Eat Cheesecake*, 1949; *Look Who's Abroad Now*, 1953: *NBC Book of Stars*, 1957; *Earl Wilson's New York*, 1964; *The Show Business Nobody Knows*, 1971; *Show Business Laid Bare*, 1974; *Sinatra*, 1976; also contributions to magazines and journals, including *Saturday Evening Post*, *Esquire*, *Liberty*. **Cause of death** Stroke, at age 79.

PHILIP YOUNG

American Civil Servant

***Born* Lexington, Massachusetts, 9 May 1910**

***Died* Arlington, Virginia, 15 January 1987**

Philip Young, a trusted associate of President Eisenhower, and his personnel manager throughout the first five years of his presidency, was a man whose career never really fulfilled its early potential. It was only during the Eisenhower period that he came into any real prominence, and for the last 20 or so years of his life he remained in the comparative obscurity of private consultancy.

Young came from a privileged background. His father was the long-standing chairman of the General Electric Company and the initiator of the Radio Corporation of America; he was also the eponymous author of the Young Plan for German reparations after World War I. Philip Young followed the typical educational pattern of his time, graduating from Harvard School of Business Administration in 1933, then continuing there for a year as a researcher in the history of business. For the next four years he worked as a business economist in the Securities and Exchange Commission in Washington, then moved over to the Treasury to work as a special assistant in the sales of US military hardware abroad. This inevitably led him, with the outbreak of World War II, into the Office of Lend-Lease Administration and wartime service in the Navy Supply Corps.

In 1948 Young was appointed dean of Columbia University Business School in the same year that General Eisenhower became the University's president. Eisenhower was impressed with the young dean's reforms at the school, turning it into a graduate rather than a first-degree department and opening its advanced classes for the first time to women. It was a natural progression that when Eisenhower became president he appointed Young as his personnel manager with a seat in his Cabinet. But these were the dangerous days of the McCarthy anti-Communist witch-hunts and Young was given the task, among others, of administering Eisenhower's Executive Order 10450 designed to search out officials with suspected subversive tendencies. The partisan aspects of the activity flared up into a major political scandal when the Democrats discovered that the security boys were keeping files even on members of Congress. Young himself inevitably came under attack for being involved in what the Democrats called "numbers games", and he was forced to resign his chairmanship of the Civil Service Commission in early 1957.

There can be little doubt that Young was made the scapegoat of what was a notorious period of US administration. In fact, the president implicitly admitted this by immediately compensating him with the political appointment of US ambassador to the Netherlands, a post he occupied throughout the remainder of Eisenhower's presidency. For five years thereafter he was executive director of the US Council of the International Chamber of Commerce until he returned to private business consultancy in 1965. Over the years Young was active as director or trustee of a number of institutions, including his old school and university, and the Netherlands–America Foundation. Most notable among these was his chairmanship of the charity, Project Hope.

Born Philip Young. **Parents** Owen D., chairman of General Electric Company, and Josephine Sheldon (Edmonds) Young. **Marriages** 1) Faith Adams, 1931 (died, 1963); 2) Esther Sarah Whitmey (Lady Fairey), 1964 (died, 1978); 3) Diana Morgan, 1982. **Children** Two daughters, Faith and Shirley, from first marriage. **Education** Choate School, 1927; St Lawrence University, Canton, New York, AB, 1931, LLD, 1948; Harvard School of Business Administration, MBA,

1933. **Military service** Lieutenant-commander, United States Naval Reserve, 1944–46. **Career** Research assistant in business history, Harvard Graduate School of Business, 1933; business economist and analyst, Securities and Exchange Commission, Washington, 1934–38; special assistant to under-secretary of the Treasury, 1938–40, assistant to secretary, also chairman, president's liaison committee of military procurement, 1940–41; assistant executive officer, division defining aid reports, Office of Emergency Management, 1941; deputy administrator, Office of Lend-Lease Administration, 1941–43; assistant to administrator, trade relations adviser, Foreign Economic Administration, 1943–44; executive director, American Assembly, 1950–53; chairman, United States Civil Service Commission, presidential adviser on personnel management, also member, White House staff, 1953–57; US ambassador to the Netherlands, 1957–60. **Related activities** President, United States Council of International Chamber of Commerce Incorporated, 1961–65, trustee, 1965 onwards; member, United States of America BIAC to the Organization for Economic Coooperation and Development, 1962–68; member, advisory board on International and Comparative Law Center, South-West Legal Foundation, 1963–67. **Other activities** Vice-president, Astraco Incorporated, 1947–48; treasurer, Van Lear Woodward & Co. Incorporated, 1947–48; dean, Columbia Graduate School of Business, 1948–53; Class C director, Federal Reserve Bank, New York, 1950–53; trustee, Equitable Life Assurance Society of the United States, 1951–53. **Offices and memberships** Trustee emeritus, St Lawrence University, 1943 onwards; Business History Foundation, 1949–53; Edison Institute, 1950–53; trustee, Choate School, 1950–54; director, Project Hope, 1962 onwards; president, Netherlands–America Foundation, 1963–68, chairman of the board, 1968 onwards; council of American Museums in Britain, 1974; trustee, New York State Historical Association. **Awards and honours** Grand Cross Order Orange Nassau, Netherlands; gold medal, Holland Society of New York; Alumni Seal award, Choate School, 1958. **Cause of death** Heart attack, at age 76.

FEBRUARY

ALESSANDRO BLASETTI

Italian Film Director
***Born* Rome, Italy, 3 July 1900**
***Died* Rome, Italy, 2 February 1987**

The real extent of both Alessandro Blasetti's contribution to and his popularity in the world of cinema (the latter in his own country) has not been appreciated, as the Italian industry's taboo on anything produced during the Fascist period has buried his work. Too few people outside Italy have seen his films, although they were hits of the 1930s and 1940s. In all, Blasetti made nearly 50 films and was considered a leading figure in Italian cinema. As he was never a disciple of the neo-realist movement, however, other film-makers of that period (such as Visconti and DeSica) have overshadowed his reputation. Although Blasetti made historical and light comedy works, he was considered something of a master in shifting styles and genres.

University studies led to a doctorate in law, but Blasetti switched to journalism in 1924, becoming film critic of *L'Impero* newspaper. In 1926 he founded the magazine *Il Mondo dello Schermo* (Screen World), *Cinematografo* (Cinematography, 1928) and *Lo Spettacolo d'Italia* (The Sights of Italy) the same year, periodicals which called for new directions in Italian cinema. In 1928, along with film-makers Goffredo Alessandrini and Umberto Barbaro, he helped found a cooperative. His first work in this cooperative was *Sole* (Sun), which demonstrated the influence of both Soviet and German film styles, which were then dominant all over Europe.

Sole demonstrated an effective use of the moving camera as formal strategy, as well as a mastery of montage techniques and close-ups to create meaning in disparate material. The subject, a drama of conflict over the draining of marshes (a particular project of Mussolini's) was reminiscent of Soviet films dealing with progress and change. It was propagandistic, but surprisingly fresh. Between 1932 and 1934, Blasetti directed the first Italian film school at the music academy of San Cecile, which was to become Centro Sperimentale. In 1934 he directed the second of his best films, *1860*, an historical account of Garibaldi's conquest of Sicily through the eyes of two peasants. Specifically Italian, nationalistic themes were arguably those Blasetti handled the most skilfully. The non-conformist recounting and realistic portrayal of both the people and the landscape made *1860* one of the best films of the era. Some consider it to be a forerunner of the neo-realist school, although Blasetti himself had, ironically, no interest in the movement.

Other films well regarded by both critics and the viewing public followed: *Vecchia Guardia* (Old Guard, 1934) was a sentimental story exalting the early Fascists, which put him at odds with Mussolini's regime. It had similar sharp, social insights as in other films of his, such as *Terra Madre* (Mother Earth, 1931) and *Un Avventura di Salvatore Rosa* (Salvatore Rosa's Adventure, 1939). After *Aldebaran*, that same year, Blasetti turned from contemporary themes to costume dramas. *La Corona di Ferro* (The Iron Crown) was an epic, called "a Byzantine Western" by critic Elliot Stein, while his *Quattro Passi fra le Nuvole* (Four Steps in the Clouds, 1942), anticipated once more the post-war new realism. The film, scripted by Cesare Zavattini, was a bittersweet comedy about the grey existence of a salesman sparked by an agreement with a young mother to pose as her husband. It confirmed one of Blasetti's most important contributions to the cinema: creating distinctively Italian themes, Italian films. It is considered his finest film.

Blasetti's output since the early 1950s, which included some big hits in Italy, was never considered particularly creative. However, the short-story, episodic structure of his *Altri Tempi* (In Olden Days/Infidelity), made in 1952, became the standard method of Italian production for the next two decades. He gained more international fame when he played himself in Visconti's *Bellissima* (1951), a brilliant satire of the film industry starring Anna Magnani.

Throughout his 35-year career he made a number of documentaries, and an autobiographical film, *Io, io, io...e gli altri* (Me, Me, Me...and the Others, 1965), which will be mandatory viewing when his life and work are eventually given the evaluation they deserve.

Born Alessandro Blasetti. **Children** One daughter. **Education** Doctor of Law, Rome. **Career** Lawyer, until 1924; journalist and film critic, *L'Impero*, 1924–26; founded monthly, *Il Mondo dello Schermo* (Screen World), 1926, (later became *Cinematografo* (Cinematography), 1928); formed film-making cooperative, Augustus, with Goffredo Alessandrini and Umberto Barbaro, 1928; also founded *Lo Spettacolo d'Italia* (The Sights of Italy), 1928; became full-time feature and documentary film director and scriptwriter, 1928 onwards; producing, directing début, 1929; director, first Italian film school, music academy San Cecile, Rome, 1932–34. **Films** (as director, co-scriptwriter, co-editor) *Sole* (Sun), 1929; *Nerone*, 1930; *Resurrectio* (Resurrection), 1931; *Terra Madre* (Mother Earth), 1931; *Palio*, 1932; *La Tavola dei Poveri* (Paupers' Table), 1932; *Il caso Haller*, 1933; *1860* (*Gesuzza la Sposa Garibaldina*), 1934; *L'Impiegata di Papa* (Daddy's Cleric), 1934; *Vecchia Guardia* (Old Guard), 1934; (director, co-scriptwriter only) *Aldebaran*, 1935; *La Contessa di Parma* (The Countess of Parma), 1937; *Ettore Fieramosca*, 1938; *Caccia alla Volpe* (Foxhunt), 1938; *Retroscena* (Flashback), 1939; *Un'Avventura di Salvatore Rosa*, 1940; *Napoli e le Terre d'Oltremare* (unfinished), 1940; (as director and co-scriptwriter) *La Corona di Ferro* (The Iron Crown), 1941; *La Cena delle Beffe* (Fools' Supper), 1941; *Quattro Passi fra le Nuvole* (Four Steps in the Clouds), 1942; *Nessuno Torna Indietro* (No one Turns Back), 1943; *Un Giorno nella Vita* (A Day in the Life), 1946; *La Gemma Orientale di Papi*, 1946; *Il Duomo di Milano* (Milan Cathedral), 1946; *Castel Sant'Angelo* (St Angelo's Castle), 1946; *Fabiola*, 1948; *Prima Communione* (Father's Dilemma), 1950; *Ippodromi all'Alba* (Alba Racecourse), 1950; *Altri tempi* (In Olden Days/Infidelity), 1952; *La Fiammata* (The Flame), 1952; *Tempi Nostri* (Anatomy of Love), 1952; *Peccato Che Sia una Canaglia* (Too Bad She's Bad), 1954; *La Fortuna di Essere Donna* (Lucky to Be a Woman), 1955; *Amore e chiacchiere* (Love and Chat), 1957; (director only) *Europa di Notte* (European Nights) 1959; *Io amo, tu ami* (I Love—You Love), 1961; "La lepre e la tartaruga", episode of *Le Quattro Verità*, 1963; (director only) *Liolà, 1964; Io, io, io...e gli Altri* (Me, Me, Me...and the Others), 1966; *La Ragazza del Bersagliere* (The Bersagliere's Girl), 1967; *Simon Bolivar*, 1969; *Venezia, una Mostra per il Cinema* (Venice, on Exhibition for the Cinema), 1982. **Publications** *Come Nasce un Film* (How a Film Is Made), Rome, 1932; *Scritti sul Cinema* (Writings on the Cinema), 1982; *Il Cinema Che ho Vissuto*, 1982. **Cause of death** Undisclosed, at age 86.

MICHAEL BURKE

American Sports Executive

***Born* Enfield, Connecticut, 8 June 1918**

***Died* Aughrim, Ireland, 5 February 1987**

The conflict of behind-enemy-lines action, resistance fighting and espionage evolved into the battles of the sportsfield, and the executives' offices above them, for Michael Burke, who became one of New York's leading personalities in the late 1960s and early 1970s as president of the New York Yankees baseball club.

Burke, the son of a first generation American-Irish father and a mother who emigrated to the United States from County Kerry, Ireland, was sports minded from his early years. A halfback under scholarship for the University of Pennsylvania football team in the years immediately preceding World War II, he was contracted to play professionally, for the Philadelphia Eagles, but left for military service shortly after signing with them.

What followed was a tour of duty with the US Office of Strategic Services (OSS) that was so colourful it formed the basis of a post-war Hollywood movie, *Cloak and Dagger*, starring Gary Cooper. Burke had been instructed to penetrate enemy lines in Italy, and later, France, where in the latter missions he parachuted into occupied territory to team up with Resistance fighters and conduct espionage activities in preparation for the D-Day invasion in Normandy. For his exploits the young lieutenant was awarded the Navy Cross, the Silver Star and France's Médaille de la Résistance.

After the war, Burke served in the CIA, became briefly involved in radio announcing, and went to Hollywood for the production of the movie based on his wartime experiences. But in 1951 he returned to Europe with his second wife, Timothy, for the first of several extended assignments there. His first civilian work in Europe was as an adviser to John J. McCloy, the US high commissioner in Germany. When he returned again to the United States in 1954, it was as general manager of the Ringling Brothers and Barnum & Bailey Circus, at the invitation of Henry Ringling North, who had served with him in the OSS.

At Ringling Brothers Burke got his first taste of conflict within the ranks of executives who run public entertainment, and was often given the task of handling the unpleasant business that his boss, North, was loath to take on himself. In 1955, during an engagement in St Paul, Minnesota, his reputation with the circus crews was so low that, when instructed by North to dismiss several rebellious key personnel, a substantial number of department heads walked out and the "Greatest Show on Earth" was forced to close after the opening wild animal act had been performed. The show barely made it through the remainder of the year, and during the following year encountered labour problems that eventually altered its traditional staff structure. In the summer of 1956 Burke left when notified that he was to receive a 50 per cent cut in salary.

He joined the Columbia Broadcasting System that year, and soon took on the assignment of developing new areas of business as a company vice-president. While there, he suggested that CBS back the hit *My Fair Lady*, and took on European assignments for the network in Zurich and London. After he had returned to New York with CBS, he suggested in 1964 that the network purchase the Yankees, for $13.2 million. He became chairman and president of New York Yankees Inc. in 1966.

It will probably be as head of the Yankees organization that Burke will be best remembered, but his years there were not always productive. A new team in town, the New York Mets, which managed to assemble one of the most loyal followings of fans known in the sport, no doubt redirected a quantity of baseball fans from Yankee Stadium. Adding to the competition, during Burke's reign, the Mets managed to put together what has been described as the most amazing World Series-winning season ever, in 1969.

Meantime, the Yankees lost $11 million, and in the early 1970s proposals were made to move the team to a new stadium in New Jersey. Burke, who later described his stint with the Yankees as an "immensely happy time", managed one of his triumphs in 1972 by using the threat of the move to persuade the city to undertake a refurbishment of the ageing Yankee Stadium in return for the team continuing to play there. The project ultimately cost New York City $100 million.

With the CBS sale of the team the following year, Burke left the Yankees as president. He continued his relationship with the team until his death, however, as a partner in a ten-person syndicate that purchased the franchise. He soon decided to defer the day-to-day running to the colourful George Steinbrenner, and move to Ireland where, in 1960, he had acquired a 500-acre farm, and where he could satisfy "a strong rush of Irish blood in my veins". Before he could depart he was offered the post of running Madison Square Garden, where he served as president of the New York Knicks basketball team, chairman of the New York Rangers ice hockey club, and organized boxing and ice skating events. He remained there for eight years, until December 1981.

Burke professed to being a total New Yorker—"I feel I really come out of the crucible of New York, so that every marrow of my bones is made of New York," he once told an interviewer. Yet his Irish heritage was equally strong for him, and his final years were spent at Northbook Farm in what he described as contentment. "I always knew," he had said shortly after his retirement, "that at some point in my life I'd like to come here and have a house and live. Several months ago my internal signal went off, and I said, now's the time to do it."

Born Michael Burke. **Parents** Patrick and Mary (Fleming) Burke. **Marriages** 1) Faith Long, 1939 (divorced, 1945); 2) Timothy Campbell, 1946 (divorced). **Children** Patricia from first marriage; Michele, Doreen and Peter from second marriage. **Education** University of Pennsylvania, BS, 1939. **Emigration** Left USA for Ireland, early 1980s. **Military service** Lieutenant, US Navy, 1942–45; attached to United States Office of Strategic Services serving behind enemy lines in Italy and France. **Career** Professional footballer, Philadelphia Eagles, 1941–42; special adviser to US high commissioner for Germany, 1951–54; general manager, Ringling Brothers and Barnum & Bailey Circus, 1954–56; programme executive, CBS, New York City, 1956–58; president: CBS Europe, based in Switzerland, 1958–62; CBS Ltd, London, 1958–62; vice-president, CBS, New York City, 1962–73. **Other activities** Adviser to film based on own wartime experiences, *Cloak and Dagger*, Hollywood, late 1940s; New York Yankees: chair and president, 1966–73; partner and consultant, from 1973; president, Madison Square Garden, 1973–81; senior vice-president and director, Madison Square Garden Corporation. **Awards and honours** Navy Cross (USA); Silver Star (USA); Médaille de la Résistance (France). **Cause of death** Cancer, at age 70.

JAMES COCO

American Actor

***Born* New York City, New York, 21 March 1929**

***Died* New York City, New York, 25 February 1987**

"He was an acting comedian, and he was as funny as any actor I've ever met," playwright Neil Simon said of James Coco. "As a character, he was always in trouble in everything he ever did. He exposed himself in all the most vulnerable ways, and he was always able to play the foibles of anybody."

For those who knew his background, such a statement didn't come as a surprise; after 20 years of playing a fat man in numerous stage "flops", vulnerability and insecurity were no strangers to James Coco. What is unusual, however, is that in the fanatically health-conscious, streamlined world of American acting, the balding, roly-poly character actor was able to reach the realms of success. First, there was *Next* (1969), a play written for Coco by friend and playwright Terrence McNally; then Neil Simon's *Last of the Red Hot Lovers* launched him into fame, followed by other notable roles and an Academy Award nomination. In all his new-found glory, however, James Coco never forgot his years of struggling and frustration, an experience which was undoubtedly revealed in his exceptionally realistic portrayal of character roles. His realism also endeared him to thousands of theatre and movie audiences.

If there was ever truth to a stereotype, Coco's life was proof positive. Coco was born in the Little Italy section of Manhattan in 1929, and his Italian upbringing produced an overweight child who quickly grew into an overweight teenager, complete with all the associated problems. After becoming hooked on movies at the age of eight, Coco spent his adolescence hanging around the stage doors of various New York theatres, dreaming of stardom while seeking autographs from the stars already on stage—an escape from the rather tight reins held on him by his father Feliche, a shoemaker who made young James help out in his shop from the time the boy was ten years old. Unlike most stagestruck teenagers, Coco followed his desires in spite of his unlikely physique. Immediately after graduating from high school at the age of 17, he joined Claire Tree Major's Children's Theater, earning $40 a week for work as a stage manager and actor. For three years he toured the country with the company, playing such parts as Old King Cole and Hans Brinker, until eventually he returned to New York to join the endless numbers of young actors and actresses trying to eke out a living in off-Broadway stock companies.

As he put it in an interview with *Time* magazine, Coco's next years in New York were lean ones spent "living in $8-a-week rooms on West 57th Street and appearing in one flop after another." There were, as well, all the in-between jobs of the unemployed actor: stints as short-order cook, as a hotel switchboard operator, even as a Santa Claus impersonator at Gimbel's department store. Finally, at the age of 28, Coco landed a part in a Broadway play (Tabu in *Hotel Paradiso*), but even that was a minor role. There followed six Broadway shows, 25 off-Broadway ones, and even two Obie awards for the off-Broadway productions *The Moon in the Yellow River* and *Fragments*. But, as one interviewer put it, Coco was "entirely forgotten by audiences and casting directors when his shows were over". Still, he landed a film role in 1964, with the Warner Brothers' production of *Ensign Pulver*, yet by the end of the 1960s, Coco "had become used to appearing in plays where rehearsal periods were often longer than their runs". Resigning himself to a frequently unemployed career as a character actor, Coco turned to television commercials to earn a decent living, and became known to millions of American housewives as "Willie the Plumber", advertising Drano, a drain cleaner.

It was at this low point in his life that Coco audibly complained about his lot—with very favourable results. The story of his success, as he told a *New York Times* reporter, went like this: "We were sitting around the apartment one night and I think I'd just done another Drano commercial and I was feeling depressed and I said, 'Why doesn't anybody ever write a play for a fat character actor?' A few days later Terrence [McNally] phoned me and said, 'I'm writing a play for you'."

The play was *Next*, and Coco's role was that of Marion Cheever, a "flabby, pathetic little assistant movie-house manager who has to subject himself to a series of hilarious indignities at an army induction centre". "My God!" Coco thought. "What a beautiful role!" The role came to life twice: first in Elaine May's off-Broadway production, then (after a re-working of the script) at the Greenwich Mews Theater in February 1969. Marion Cheever brought Coco the success he had so long been awaiting. "This is gorgeous acting," read the *Times*. "Rich, stylish, impeccable. Mr Coco, with easy gesture and inflection, brings an entire man to life."

The year 1969 certainly changed the life of James Coco. While playing to rave reviews in *Next*, he found himself barraged with offers, principally small parts in films: the most notable was the Fishmonger in Otto Preminger's *Tell Me That You Love Me*, followed by the Doctor in *Such Good Friends*. The best result of *Next*, however, was the fact that it brought Coco to the attention of playwright Neil Simon, who saw the play at a time when he had just finished the first act of *Last of the Red Hot Lovers*. After seeing James Coco as Marion Cheever, Simon finished his own play with Coco in mind. Enter for Coco an 18-month run on Broadway in the leading role of Barney Cashman.

"He bounces around on-stage as a middle-aged New Yorker containing a wastrel screaming to be let out," *Time* magazine said of Coco's Cashman. "Mostly he resembles an overweight wrestling coach or the boy next door who ate too much of too many Sunday dinners." As an overweight married owner of a seafood restaurant, the character of Barney Cashman tries unsuccessfully to join the sexual revolution. Coco, to whom both professional and personal frustration had been a way of life, had no trouble in producing what the *New York Post* called a "magnificent characterization". The performance won him a Tony award, as well as parts in other Neil Simon works—films this time, including *Murder by Death* and *The Cheap Detective*.

In the meantime, Coco's career had taken another upturn. Due to his much-lauded "overnight" success, he appeared as a guest or guest-host on over 60 television talk shows. United Artists signed him to play Sancho Panza in *Man of La Mancha*, a film which starred Sophia Loren and Peter O'Toole. He also starred in several television shows, including his own short-lived series, *Calucci's Department*. There were, as always, numerous stage roles; one, at least, got Coco away from his comic stereotype. In *The Transformation of Beeno Blimpie*, the actor showed that if fat could be funny, it could also be frightening; Benno was a man who was slowly but surely eating himself to death.

It was another Neil Simon movie, however, that earned Coco an Academy Award nomination, and typified the essence of his talent in the bargain. *Only When I Laugh* starred Marsha Mason as an alcoholic actress and sometime mother who is surrounded by a circle of equally problematical actor friends. One of these is a fat homosexual: sensitive, sympathetic, and usually out of work. Desperately seeking a real acting job instead of the ridiculous TV commercials he is forced to take in order to survive, the character eventually succeeds in landing a proper role—only to have it end before it has even begun. Sound familiar? Whether or not James Coco was gay remains to be seen; he lived as a bachelor all his life. What is clear, however, is the reason for his success in *Only When I Laugh*: he had lived the part for over two decades of his own career. Is it coincidence, then, that the character's name happened to be "Jimmy"?

Coco's last projects consisted of a role in the film *The Muppets Take Manhattan*, an episode of the TV series *St Elsewhere*, which earned him an Emmy award for best supporting actor, and the publication of his popular book *The James Coco Diet*—an ironic work considering the fact that he continued to be described as podgy and cherubic throughout his lifetime.

Born James Emil Coco. **Parents** Feliche, a shoemaker and Ida (Detestes) Coco. **Education** Evander Childs High School, the Bronx; studied drama with Uta Hagen, Berghof Studio, New York. **Career** Stage manager, actor, Clare Tree Major's Children's Theater, 1946–49; employed in a variety of jobs, short-order cook, hotel switchboard operator, messenger, until eventually becoming full-time actor on stage, films and television; stage début, *Old King Cole*, Clare Tree Major's Theater; New York début, *Hotel Paradiso*, Henry Miller's Theater, 1957; film début *Ensign Pulver*, 1963. **Awards and honours** Obie Award for *The Moon in the Yellow River*, 1961; Obie Award for *Fragments*, 1967; Obie Award for *Benno Blimpie*, 1977; Academy Award nomination, People's Choice Award, Entertainer of the Year Award, Film Exhibitors' Award, all for *Only When I Laugh*, 1982; Outstanding Supporting Actor, Emmy Award for "Cora and Arnie", *St Elsewhere*, 1983–84. **Stage** *Old King Cole*, on tour, 1946–49; *Hotel Paradiso*, 1957; *Auntie Mame*, 1957; *Darwin's Theories*, 1960; *The Moon in the Yellow River*, 1961; *Everyone Loves Opal*, 1961; *A Passage to India*, 1962; *A Shot in the Dark*, national tour, 1962–63; *Arturo Ui*, 1963; *The Sponge Room*, 1964; *Squat Betty*, 1964; *5 a.m.—A World's Fair*, 1965; *Lovey*, 1965; *Man of La Mancha*, 1966; *The Devils*, 1965; *Astrakhan Coat*, 1967; *The Basement*, 1967; *Fragments*, 1967; *Here's Where I Belong*, 1968; *A Matter of Position*, 1968; *Next*, 1968; *Witness*, 1968; *Adaptation-Next*, 1969; *Last of the Red Hot Lovers*, 1969; *The Transfiguration of Benno Blimpie*, 1977; *You Can't Take It With You*, 1983. **Films** *Ensign Pulver*, 1963; *Generation*, 1969; *End of the Road*, 1970; *Tell Me That You Love Me, Junie Moon*, 1970; *The Strawberry Statement*, 1970; *A New Leaf*, 1971; *Such Good Friends*, 1971; *Man of La Mancha*, 1972; *The Wild Party*, 1975; *Murder by Death*, 1976; *Charleston*, 1978; *Bye Bye Monkey*, 1978; *The Cheap Detective*, 1978; *Scavenger Hunt*, 1979; *Moses*, 1980; *Only When I Laugh*, 1981; *The Muppets Take Manhattan*, 1984. **Television** *Johnny Carson Show*, *Raquel Welch Special*, guest appearances; *Marcus Welby, MD*, 1972; *The Flip Wilson Show*, 1972; *The Trouble With People*, 1972; *VD Blues*, 1972; *Calucci's Department*, 1973; *The Dumplings*, 1976; *The French Atlantic Affair*, 1979; *The Diary of Anne Frank*, 1980; *St Elsewhere*, 1983. **Publications** *The James Coco Diet Book*, 1984. **Cause of death** Heart attack, at age 57.

SIR WILLIAM COLDSTREAM

British Artist

***Born* Belford, Northumberland, 28 February 1908**

***Died* London, England, 18 February 1987**

Sir William Coldstream was a traditional, sensitive painter much respected by the public and by many of his fellow artists. Friends describe him as "a painter's painter". They talk about his "luscious nudes" and the quality of his drawing—often with measuring marks still showing. They say that he was a painter whom they were "proud to own as one of ours".

Coldstream studied at the Slade art school under Henry Tonks. In the 1930s he experimented briefly with "objective abstractionism" working from nature towards abstraction. "I did not alter or invent shapes, but selected very consciously from the objects I was painting, used a rather formalized colour and tone scheme, and usually left out the features if I was painting a head," was how he described his work at this time.

In reaction against the advent of Fascism, Coldstream turned in the mid-1930s towards a more lyrical naturalism. With Victor Pasmore and Claude Rogers he was responsible for the founding of the Euston Road School of Painting and Drawing. To the principles of this school—romantic delight in nature and the "exaltation of the commonplace"—Bill Coldstream alone was to remain consistently faithful.

His main concern was always to keep open the lines of communication between the artist and the layman—lines which he felt were threatened by the élitism and obscurity of much of the modern art movement. It was this which drove him to seek out the everyday subjects of his paintings—his still lifes, nudes, townscapes, scenes from the industrial north and from working class life—and to reject the developments in the use of form and colour taking place elsewhere in Europe.

From 1949 until 1976 Coldstream was Slade professor of fine art at University College, London. There he exercised an enormous influence on the development of art education. He was responsible for introducing postgraduate art courses and for starting the first university courses in film in Britain. Later, as chairman of the university national advisory committee on art education from 1958 to 1971, he produced what became known as the first and second "Coldstream Reports" which, in effect, transformed the whole teaching of art in Britain. Among other things, they introduced the excellent "foundation year" for prospective art students, thus making a degree in art into a four-year course.

After his retirement from the Slade and from his many other public duties as trustee of the National and Tate galleries, chairman of the art panel of the Arts Council, director of the Royal Opera House and chairman of the British Film Institute, Sir William returned with renewed vigour to his own painting. It was said that he often had as many as five canvases on the go at any one time.

It is, perhaps, as a spokesman for art and artists that Sir William Coldstream will finally be remembered. His image as a quiet, grey-suited and pre-eminently able administrator fits oddly with the conventional view of the artist. Therein, perhaps, lay his strength—that he was able to work with the non-artistic world and to negotiate effectively with those whose primary concerns are money and efficiency.

Born William Menzies Coldstream. **Parents** George Probyn and Lilian Mercer (Tod) Coldstream. **Marriage** Nancy Culliford Sharp, 1931 (divorced, 1942); Monica Mary Hoyer, artists' model, 1961. **Children** Two daughters from first marriage; one son and two daughters from second marriage. **Education** Slade School of Fine Art, University of London, 1926–29. **Military service** Royal Artillery, 1940; camouflage officer, Royal Engineers; war artist, 1943–45. **Career** Lecturer, Bow and Bromley Evening Institute, London, 1929; made documentary films for GPO film unit, 1934–37; founded (with Claude Rogers and Victor Pasmore) the Euston Road School of Drawing and Painting, 1937–39; teacher, Camberwell School of Art and Crafts, 1946–49; Slade professor of fine art, 1949–75. **Related activities** Chairman, art panel of Arts Council of Great Britain, 1953–62; chairman, National Advisory Council on Art Education, 1958–71; vice-chairman, Arts Council of Great Britain, 1962–70. **Offices and memberships** Member: East London Group, 1929, London Artists' Association, 1931, London Group, 1933; trustee: National Gallery, 1948–55, 1956–63, Tate Gallery, 1949–55, 1956–63; director, Royal Opera House, Covent Garden, 1957–62; chairman, British Film Institute, 1964–71. **Awards and honours** Commander of the Order of the British Empire, 1952; knighted, 1956; honorary DLitt: Nottingham, 1961, Birmingham, 1962; honorary DEd, Council for National Academic Awards, 1975; honorary DLitt, London, 1984; fellow, University College, London; senior fellow, Royal College of Art. **Group exhibitions** New English Art Club, London, 1929; *British Art Since Whistler*, National Gallery, London, 1939; *United Nations International Exhibition*, Paris, 1946; *Euston Road School*, Arts Council Gallery, London, 1948; *Critics' Choice*, Arthur Tooth and Son, London, 1958; *Painting and Sculpture of a Decade 1954–64*, Tate Gallery, London, 1964; *British Painting 1952–1977*, Royal Academy of Arts, London, 1977; *Eight Figurative Painters*, Yale Center for British Art, New Haven, Connecticut, 1981. **Individual exhibitions** (with H.E. du Plessis) London Artists' Association, Cooling Galleries, London, 1933; South London Art Gallery, Camberwell, London, and subsequent tour of UK, 1962; Anthony d'Offay Gallery, London, 1976; Fine Art Society, Edinburgh, 1976. **Collections** Tate Gallery, London; Imperial War Museum, London; University College, London; Ashmolean Museum Oxford; Somerville College, Oxford; Christ Church, Oxford; National Museum of Wales, Cardiff; National Gallery of Canada, Ottawa. **Cause of death** Undisclosed, at age 78. **Further reading** John Rothenstein, *Sir William Coldstream*, London, 1980.

JOHN COUNSELL

British Director, Actor and Theatre Manager
***Born* Beckenham, Kent, 24 April 1905**
***Died* Windsor, Berkshire, 23 February 1987**

The name of the Theatre Royal, Windsor, is, in the twentieth century, inextricably linked with that of John Counsell who devoted the bulk of his life to developing the theatre into a modern success story.

Counsell made his first appearance on the stage at The Playhouse, Oxford, when a youthful enthusiasm for the theatre first found practical expression in his activities with the Oxford University Dramatic Society. After completing his degree in history at Oxford, he worked in a department store where he gained practical business experience. It was not long, however, before he returned to the Oxford Playhouse Company, this time as an assistant stage manager, and began his life in the theatre in earnest. An initial tour to Canada as stage director for Maurice Colbourne's Shavian company led to a stint playing leading juvenile parts with the Northampton and Folkestone repertory companies. His first London engagement was at the New Theatre in 1930 as stage manager for Baliol Halloway's production of *Richard III*, and he remained in London for three years.

In 1933, Counsell returned to the Oxford Playhouse to act as stage director, scenic artist and director with the Oxford Repertory Company. However, in the autumn he left to take over as manager of the Theatre Royal, Windsor. His initial efforts there were a complete disaster, due largely to an over-ambitious policy which resulted in amateurish productions. He left Windsor to return to the West End and, until 1938, dabbled in films and broadcasting, while at the same time wooing enough financial backing to return to Windsor in 1938 to launch the Windsor Repertory Company.

The theatre's new policy of supplying middle-of-the-road productions of a consistently high standard was an instant winner. Success was assured when, six weeks after opening, the theatre received the first of many visits from its royal neighbours when King George VI and Queen Elizabeth attended a performance of Clifford Bax's *The Rose Without a Thorn*. Over the years the Royal Family visited regularly, finding that the theatre's proximity to Windsor Castle made it a convenient way of entertaining guests.

During World War II, Counsell took a commission in the Royal Artillery and served, from 1942 to 1945, in North Africa, France and Germany. He had two moments of glory: first, as draughtsman of Eisenhower's personal despatches for the Tunisian and Italian campaigns, and then, while a member of the planning staff of SHAEF (Supreme Headquarters of the Allied European Forces), he prepared all the papers relative to the surrender of Germany which General Jodl signed at Reims.

After demobilization in 1945, Counsell returned to Windsor, and with his wife, the actress Mary Kerridge, continued to build up the company. They launched a weekly repertory system that lasted until 1958, when they changed it to a fortnightly one. They celebrated their one thousandth production with Shaw's *You Never Can Tell* in which Counsell, his wife and their twin daughters all performed.

By this time the company had firmly established a reputation for producing fairly conservative programmes that consisted mainly of West End successes and revivals of popular classics. The annual pantomime also brought the theatre a well-earned reputation for traditional Christmas entertainment. Counsell launched such successful productions as *Bonadventure* (1949), *For Better, For Worse* (1952)—which established the reputation of the actress Geraldine McEwan—and also in that year, *Anastasia*, which spread Counsell's reputation as a director. His television production of the play won the *Daily Mail* newspaper's award for the best television play of the year.

Counsell was ideally suited to running and producing the kind of theatre that was wanted by the solidly middle-class audiences of Windsor. He was a practical and unassuming man; the nearest he got to scandal was in 1969 when he banned the pantomime *Robinson Crusoe*. He insisted that this was not on racial grounds, although he did admit that Man Friday "was susceptible to some people's feelings in that he appears subservient and, in a way humiliated".

Counsell was a capable businessman who turned the theatre into a profitable concern. Although the repertory company is no longer in existence—the shows are now cast from London—Counsell's influence on and contribution to the life of Windsor will forever remain in the spirit of its theatre.

Born John William Counsell. **Parents** Claude Christopher, preparatory school headmaster, and Evelyn (Flemming) Counsell. **Marriage** Mary Kerridge, actress, 1939. **Children** Two daughters. **Education** Sedbergh School; Exeter College, Oxford, 1923–26. **Military service** Royal Artillery, 1940, demobilized with rank of lieutenant-colonel, 1945. **Career** Worked in Whiteley's department store, London; briefly engaged as a tutor before making stage début, 1928; acted as stage manager, touring with Maurice Colbourne's Shavian Company; played juvenile lead with Northampton and Folkestone repertory companies, 1929–30; assistant stage manager, scenic artist and director, Oxford Repertory Company, 1930–33; director and joint manager, Windsor Repertory Company, 1933–34; engaged in broadcasting and films, 1935–36; toured in South Africa, 1936–37; re-formed Windsor Repertory Company and became manager, director and actor, Windsor Theatre Royal, 1938–40, 1945–87. **Offices and memberships** Member, Oxford University Dramatic Society, 1923–26. **Awards and honours** *Daily Mail* Television Play of the Year award for production of *Anastasia*. **Stage roles** *Mr Pim Passes By*, 1928; *Lover's Leap*, 1935–36; *Sweet Aloes*, 1936; *The Frog*, 1936–37; *You Never Can Tell*, 1962; *The Importance of Being Earnest*, 1966, 1975; *Mrs Warren's Profession*, 1968; *Hay Fever*, 1968. **Windsor productions** *Dear Brutus*, 1938; *The Rose Without a Thorn*, 1938; *Bonadventure*, 1949; *Who Goes There!*, 1951; *Anastasia*, 1952; *For Better, For Worse*, 1952; *Dry Rot*, 1954; *Grab Me a Gondola*, 1956; *Simple Spymen*, 1958; *You Never Can Tell*, 1962; *Chase Me*,

Comrade!, 1964; *Ring of Jackals*, 1965; *The Importance of Being Earnest*, 1975. **Other productions** *Birthmark*, Embassy and Playhouse theatres, 1947; *Little Holiday*, Kilburn Empire, 1948; *Captain Brassbound's Conversion*, Lyric, Hammersmith, 1948; *The Man With the Umbrella*, Duchess, 1950; *Who Goes There!*, Vaudeville, 1951; *His House in Order*, New Theatre, 1951; *Waggonload o' Monkeys*, Savoy, 1951; *For Better, For Worse*, Comedy, 1952; *Anastasia*, St James's, 1952; *Starlight*, Golders Green Hippodrome, 1956; *Grab Me a Gondola*, Lyric, 1956; *Three-Way Switch*, Aldwych, 1958; *How Say You?*, Aldwych, 1959; *Ring of Jackals*, Queen's, 1965; *Horizontal Hold*, Comedy, 1967; *Aren't We All*, Savoy, 1967. **Publications** (autobiography) *Counsell's Opinion*, 1963; *Play Directing*, 1973. **Cause of death** Undisclosed, at age 81.

LORD CROWTHER-HUNT

British Academic and Politician
Born **Bradford, Yorkshire, 13 March 1920**
Died **Oxford, England, 16 February 1987**

Norman Crowther Hunt, later Baron of Eccleshill in Yorkshire, was a university lecturer in politics who advocated major constitutional reform in the government of the United Kingdom. He combined a long academic career with a life of college administration, advisory work for the government and terms of office as a minister of state.

His scholarly promise was apparent while he was at Belle Vue Grammar School in Bradford, then at Sidney Sussex College, Cambridge, where he held a scholarship in history from 1939 to 1940. Wartime service with the Royal Artillery, in which he reached the rank of captain, interrupted his studies, but he returned to Cambridge and graduated with first class honours in 1949. He remained at Sidney Sussex as a research scholar until 1951, when he gained a fellowship and lectureship in politics at Exeter College, Oxford. In the same year he was awarded a fellowship by the Commonwealth Fund to study for a year at Princeton University.

Back in Oxford, he devoted a tremendous amount of energy to the day-to-day life of Exeter College. He was an enthusiastic and provocative teacher, never trying to conceal his own political views, which were socialist but not radically left-wing. His students did not find themselves dictated to or prevented from putting forward their own points of view. Discussion and debate were very much part of his style, whether formally in the tutorial, or informally in the relaxed atmosphere of the senior common room. He was a dedicated college member who worked hard to promote the life of the community in both social and academic terms. From 1954 to 1970 he held the office of domestic bursar, a post which demanded hard work and delicate diplomatic and administrative skills, trying to satisfy the often conflicting needs of staff, students and fellows.

Hunt planned many publications on political and constitutional matters, but various demands meant that they were curtailed. His first major book was a study of eighteenth-century political and social movements: *Two Early Political Associations: The Quakers and Dissenting Deputies in the Age of Sir Robert Walpole* (1961). Later publications were concerned with contemporary politics, the British Government and the civil service.

His writing and teaching benefited from his experience as an adviser and a minister for Labour governments. He had supported the Labour party from his youth, becoming a trusted adviser to

Harold Wilson, prime minister in the 1960s, first as a constitutional adviser in the cabinet office, and then in more wide-ranging roles. Wilson had great respect for Hunt's abilities and his understanding of the workings of politics and government, and appointed him to the Committee on the Civil Service, chaired by Lord Fulton from 1966 to 1968. Hunt is credited with authorship of a substantial part of the Fulton Report, although it is not clear how far he agreed with its general conclusions. The final report was criticized for its conservatism: "Whether or not new wine is being poured into the civil service these days...it is certain that the old bottles are there to receive it." This was the view of the report from within the civil service. Some good progress was made on improving recruitment, but generally there was entrenched resistance to radical change. It was not the only occasion when Hunt came across the conservative tendencies which make change very difficult in British politics.

Yet change was what he advocated. In the late 1960s economic failure by the government and significant political gains by the nationalist parties in Scotland and Wales resulted in the appointment of a Royal Commission on the Constitution. It was chaired by Hunt and later Lord Killbrandon, sitting from 1969 to 1973. After inquiring into various forms of "devolution" of power to Welsh and Scottish assemblies, the commission proposed limited devolution, giving them power over local government, planning and social services, but retaining central control. Hunt was the joint author of a dissenting memorandum. He advocated federal government for all the regions of England, Scotland and Wales. He was very disappointed when opposition forced the government to call a referendum in 1979, which failed to gain a big enough vote in favour of the assemblies in either Scotland or Wales. He remained as an adviser to Harold Wilson in the 1970s and was made a lord in 1973, when he legally changed his name to Crowther-Hunt. The following year he was invited to join the government as minister of state at the Department of Education and Science. He did not enjoy his work here since it was not as wide-ranging as his earlier appointments, and it was difficult to make much of an impact. His tenure at the DES was short-lived, and he became a minister at the Privy Council office, which dealt with broader issues, like the handling of the devolution question.

After his spell in government, Crowther-Hunt returned to Oxford to continue teaching and working for his college. He was appointed rector of Exeter College in 1982. In this position of responsibility for its general wellbeing, he launched a major appeal to bring in funds and introduced a scheme to bring promising young civil servants to the college for a sabbatical term. This scheme was beneficial to a succession of promising young administrators from the Department of Health and Social Security.

In 1980 Crowther-Hunt published jointly with Peter Kellner a book on the civil service, *The Civil Servants*, in which he defended the Fulton Report and its criticisms of the "amateur" approach to government which he believed to be a major fault in the service. It showed how deeply committed he was to the principles of good government which he had tried to live up to during his own long career. He did not always achieve his aims, but he was highly respected for his efforts.

Born Norman Crowther Hunt; legally changed surname to Crowther-Hunt, 1973. **Parents** Ernest Angus and Florence Hunt. **Marriage** Joyce Stackhouse, 1944. **Children** Three daughters. **Education** Wellington Road Council School; Belle Vue Grammar School, Bradford; Sidney Sussex College, Cambridge: exhibition in history, 1939–40; open scholarship, 1945–47; resident fellow, 1945–51; BA, 1947; MA, 1949; PhD, 1951. **Military service** Royal Artillery, rising to rank of captain, 1940–45; GSO3, War Office, 1944–45. **Academic career** Commonwealth Fund fellow, Princeton University, 1951–52; Exeter College, Oxford: fellow and lecturer in politics, 1952–83; domestic bursar, 1954–70; rector, from 1982. **Political career** Member (and leader of management consultancy group), Fulton Committee on the Civil Service, 1966–68;

member (and principal author of dissenting report), Royal Commission on the Constitution, 1969–73; constitutional adviser to the government, 1974; minister of state, Department of Education and Science, 1974–76; minister of state, Privy Council Office, 1976. **Offices and memberships** Delegate, Oxford University Extra-Mural Delegacy, 1956–70; visiting professor, Michigan State University, 1961; council member, Headington School, Oxford, 1966–74; advisory council member, Civil Service College, 1970–74; member, advisory council, BBC. **Awards and honours** Created life peer (becoming Baron Crowther-Hunt), 1973; honorary DLitt, Bradford, 1974; honorary LLD, Williams College, Massachusetts, 1985. **Publications** (as Norman C. Hunt) *Two Early Political Associations: The Quakers and the Dissenting Deputies in the Age of Sir Robert Walpole*, 1961; *Sir Robert Walpole, Samuel Holden and the Dissenting Deputies*, 1963; (editor) *Whitehall and Beyond*, 1964; (editor with Graham Taylor) *Personality and Power*, 1970; (as Lord Crowther-Hunt) (with Peter Kellner) *The Civil Servants: An Inquiry into Britain's Ruling Class*, 1980. **Cause of death** Undisclosed, at age 66.

SIR HUGH GREENE

British Broadcasting Executive

***Born* Berkhamsted, Hertfordshire, 15 November 1910**

***Died* Bury St Edmund's, Suffolk, 19 February 1987**

Sir Hugh Greene chose his own epitaph. He was, he declared: "The man who turned down the central heating and opened the windows at the BBC." As a controversial director-general of the BBC during the "swinging sixties", he attempted to free the corporation from the stuffiness of the Reithian regime and allow previously forbidden subjects on to the air—the satirical *That Was the Week That Was*, for example—without compromising the fundamental principles of a free and democratic society about which he felt the BBC should not be neutral. His admirers saw this as his achievement. His detractors, such as Mary Whitehouse, blamed him for a disgraceful period of permissiveness.

Hugh Carleton Greene, younger brother of the novelist Graham, started his career as a journalist and ended it as president of Bodley Head Publishers, and chairman of Greene, King and Sons, a Norfolk brewery. As a young journalist in the early 1930s he was sent to Berlin by the *Daily Telegraph*. There he experienced the full impact of Hitler's regime in Germany and his forthright dispatches led to his expulsion by the Nazis. During the war he continued to serve as a foreign correspondent in Europe and also worked for the intelligence service. In 1940 he joined the BBC as head of the German service and after the war he became controller of broadcasting in the British zone of Germany. He was the author of the constitutional blueprint for broadcasting in Germany which was emerging from the ruins of war, and his name is still revered in German broadcasting circles. At the time of his death he was engaged in a German television project.

In the mid-1950s Greene began to climb the ladder in the BBC's overseas service, and in 1955 became director of administration with a place on the board of management—a small group of directors who, with the director-general, form what Greene used to call the "cabinet" of the BBC. In 1958 he became director of news and current affairs for the British side of the Corporation. Then, when Sir Ian Jacobs' retirement was imminent, the governors chose Greene as the next director-general, and he took up the appointment in January 1960. He was the first to have come up directly through the ranks of the BBC.

Gerald Mansell, former deputy director-general, said: "It was difficult to appreciate the impact of Hugh Greene's appointment as director-general unless one experienced it at first hand. It was electrifying. A new age was being born, there was a clearer vision of what broadcasting was all about. Inhibitions were shed and taboos swept aside. Windows and doors were opened and cobwebs swept away. You felt glad to be alive and involved in what felt like a renaissance.

Greene's period in office was a time of great expansion and innovation during which he steered the now enormous organization into the age of mass communication. In the late 1950s the BBC's television audience had dropped to 27 per cent, and there was a rising clamour of discontent from those who claimed they never watched a service they were being taxed to support. In the two years following Greene's appointment almost every top TV position was refilled and Greene personally head-hunted the right kind of talent. Sydney Newman was made drama supervisor, and with Kenneth Adam and Huw Wheldon, Greene engineered the greatest explosion of TV activity ever known.

Under Greene's aegis the notorious live satire show *That Was the Week That Was* was launched. Gritty and realistic comedies like *Steptoe and Son* took over from cosy domestic series, and in *Monitor* directors such as Ken Russell were given a free range with arts films. *Top of the Pops* was started; *The Forsyte Saga* and *Civilization* commissioned. *The Wednesday Play* struck out with writers of such calibre and controversial outlook as David Mercer, Dennis Potter and Troy Kennedy Martin, and such televisual landmarks as *Cathy Come Home* and *Up the Junction* were created. Greene also played a crucial role in founding the Open University.

One scandalized veteran member of the board of management said of him: "But the fellow actually goes drinking beer in pubs with producers and engineers!" His dress was informal. He used first names in conversations everywhere. Up and down the corridors of the BBC he was simply "Hugh". This reflected his desire to rid the BBC of its previous pomposity. "When I left," he said, "I gave a special party for the caterers."

A second divorce, fatigue and perhaps the most mischievous move any politician has ever made against the BBC—Harold Wilson's appointment of the chairman of the Independent Television Authority, Lord Hill, as chairman of the BBC—combined to bring Greene's reign to a close in 1969. Lord Hill offered him a place on the board of governors as the price of his going. It would never have been enough. Greene lasted two years and then left to mastermind an influential public campaign against the Greek colonels. He accepted the chairmanship of his brother's publishers, the Bodley Head, in 1969.

As his biographer, Michael Tracey, has put it, Hugh Greene had key gifts as director-general, an ability "to let the creative create, the imaginative imagine, the witty amuse, the shocking shock, the failure fail". "Television today lacks a sense of adventure," Hugh Greene said himself, not long before he died. "We *enjoyed* ourselves."

Born Hugh Carleton Greene. **Father** Charles Henry Greene, a headmaster. **Marriages** 1) Helga Guinness, 1934 (divorced); 2) Elaine Shaplen, 1951 (divorced); 3) Tatjana Sais, actress, 1970 (died, 1981); 4) Sarah Grahame, 1984. **Children** Two sons from first marriage; two sons from second marriage. **Education** Berkhamsted School, Hertfordshire; Merton College, Oxford, MA. **Military service** Pilot officer, Royal Air Force Intelligence, 1940. **Career** Joined *Daily Telegraph* Berlin staff, 1934; chief correspondent, 1938; expelled from Germany, 1939; *Daily Telegraph* Warsaw correspondent, 1939; war correspondent, Poland, Rumania, Bulgaria, Turkey, Holland, Belgium and France, 1939–40; appointed head of BBC German Service, 1940; controller of broadcasting, British Zone of Germany, co-founder and first director-general, *Nordwest Deutscher Rundfunk* radio service, 1946–48; head of BBC East European Service,

1949–50; head of emergency information services, Federation of Malaya, 1950–51; BBC Overseas Services: assistant controller, 1952–55; controller, 1955–56; BBC director of administration, 1956–58; director, BBC news and current affairs, 1958–59; director-general of BBC, 1960–69; governor, BBC, 1969–71. **Related activities** Chair, Federal Commission of Enquiry into Organization of Broadcasting in Federation of Rhodesia and Nyasaland, 1955; reported for Israeli Government on Israel Broadcasting Authority, 1973; reported for Greek Government on constitution of Greek broadcasting, 1975. **Other activities** Chairman, the Bodley Head publishing company, 1969–81, honorary president, 1981–87; chairman, Greene, King & Sons Ltd, Westgate Brewery, 1971–78. **Offices and memberships** Vice-president, European Broadcasting Union, 1963–69; member, *Observer* Editorial Trust, 1969–76; chair, European-Atlantic Action Committee on Greece, 1971–74. **Awards and honours** Officer, Order of the British Empire, 1950; knight commander, Order of St Michael and St George, 1964; companion, British Institute of Management, 1966; honorary DCL, University of East Anglia, 1969; honorary DUniv, Open University, 1973, York University, 1973; Grand Cross, Order of Merit (Germany), 1977; fellow, British Academy of Film and Television Arts, 1984. **Publications** (with Graham Greene) *The Spy's Bedside Book*, 1957; *The Third Floor Front* (speeches), 1969; (editor) *The Rivals of Sherlock Holmes*, 1970; (editor) *More Rivals of Sherlock Holmes: Cosmopolitan Crimes*, 1971; *The Future of Broadcasting in Britain*, 1972; (editor) *The Crooked Counties*, 1973; (editor) *The American Rivals of Sherlock Holmes*, 1976; (editor) *The Pirate of the Round Pond and Other Strange Adventure Stories*, 1977; (editor) *The Complete Rivals of Sherlock Holmes*, 1983; (with Graham Greene) *Victorian Villainies*, 1984. **Cause of death** Undisclosed, at age 76. **Further reading** Michael Tracey, *A Variety of Lives: A Biography of Sir Hugh Greene*, London, 1983.

JOAN GREENWOOD

British Actress

Born **London, England, 4 March 1921**

Died **London, England, 27 February 1987**

Joan Greenwood, the elegant and charming English comedienne, started and ended her acting career on the stage, but she reached a larger audience through her success in films, most of which were made between 1948 and 1955, although it is generally felt that both the British and American cinema undervalued and underused her talents. She was tiny, just over 5 feet tall, blonde and strikingly attractive, but her most memorable characteristic was her husky voice, likened to "the sound of someone gargling with champagne", and with which she delivered her lines in a style at once captivating, provocative and beautifully measured.

Some of Joan Greenwood's most well-known films were made for the Ealing Studios in England, most notably her own favourite, the stylish *Kind Hearts and Coronets* (1949), a black comedy directed by Robert Hamer, which remains entertaining and undated to this day. The film follows an Italian with noble connections, Louis Mazzini, as he plots the demise of members of the family who stand between him and the title of Duke of Chalfont. Joan Greenwood plays Sybilla, one of the two women in Mazzini's life, between whom he has no wish to choose. He has known the headstrong Sybilla, now married to an unexciting man, since childhood. Greenwood's portrayal of Sybilla has been described as "feline, purring, yet deadly". Alec Guinness, that expert of disguise, plays eight of Mazzini's victims, while Mazzini himself is brilliantly played by Dennis Price.

Joan Greenwood appeared in several other Ealing films, including *Whisky Galore* (1949), renamed *Tight Little Island* for showing in America as the word "whisky" in the title was outlawed. The story comes from a novel by Scottish writer Compton Mackenzie, who based it on the true occurrence of a ship carrying 50,000 cases of whisky, apparently destined for the United States, being shipwrecked off a small Scottish island. The film carries the true story into hilarious fantasy and follows the frantic activities of the islanders to lay their hands on the "water of life" of which they have felt so cruelly deprived in wartime, and the equally frantic efforts of the authorities to prevent looting. Joan Greenwood plays a Scots girl, Peggy Maccroon, remembered by film-goers for her refusal to admit a customs official in the middle of the night with the simple and beautifully delivered line: "Post Office is closed".

These and other successful Ealing films, such as *The Man in the White Suit* (1951) and her performance as the playful, widowed Lady Warren in *Father Brown* (1954), both films also starring Alec Guinness, helped to establish an international reputation for Greenwood. In 1955 she made her Hollywood screen début as the formidable villainess, Lady Clarissa, in Fritz Lang's *Moonfleet*. She did not feel much at ease in Hollywood and described its lifestyle critically: "I couldn't put up with the endless make-up sessions...all the palaver of keeping out of the sun, dyeing one's hair and worrying about the size of one's bosom." She found Ealing more down to earth: "We used to wash our hair in buckets and we survived on toasted sandwiches, chocolate and soup." Peter Ustinov described the essence of Ealing Studios as reflecting a "jaunty disrespectful attitude" deep in the British character. "Everything at Ealing was defiantly small at the expense of the big, the conventional, the pompous."

Joan Greenwood's style was strongly personal, relishing the outrageous, often ironic, full of innuendo, always faintly astonished, and she delivered her lines, as one critic remarked, as if "she dimly suspected some hidden menace in them". Philip Kemp describes her appeal thus: "Being at once sexy and witty was Greenwood's forte. Petite and graceful, she moved with a delicate feline sensuality; her breathily husky voice, accentuating unexpected vowels, hovered always on the verge of self-parody. She countered questionable situations with an exquisitely enquiring stare."

Her acting was mannered yet eccentric and she excelled at playing titled ladies. Her film performance as Gwendolen Fairfax in Anthony Asquith's adaptation of Oscar Wilde's *The Importance of Being Earnest* (1952), illustrates how she handled such roles with skill and enjoyment, at once wickedly playful and entirely elegant. A *New York Times* reviewer described her Gwendolen as "a lady to her fingertips". It has been suggested that her talents were not of her time, recalling an earlier vanished age. However, she was able to bring them to more modern parts, such as the industrialist's daughter in *The Man in the White Suit*, her Scots girl in *Whisky Galore* and her suburban girl in *A Knave of Hearts* (1954), displaying powers of intuition, feeling and sureness of observation, as well as showing that she was not limited to playing supercilious ladies in comedies of manners.

Joan Greenwood, daughter of artist Sydney Earnshaw Greenwood, was born in London's Chelsea and educated at St Catherine's School, Bramley, in Surrey. From childhood, encouraged by her parents, she took dancing lessons, and continued as an adult to practise ballet as a hobby, which must have contributed much to her grace of movement. While still at school, she developed a talent for mimicry and went on to study at the Royal Academy of Dramatic Arts (RADA). At the age of 17 she made the first of her many appearances on the London stage as Louisa in Molière's *Le Malade Imaginaire* (The Hypochondriac). Her early roles were often lighthearted and she had success as Wendy in J.M. Barrie's *Peter Pan*, touring with the production and going on to play the title role as one of the smallest Peter Pans ever, ten years later. During the wartime Blitz, she appeared in a revue, *Rise Above It*, and the following year she was at the Strand Theatre in *Little Ladyship*. Soon after she played Little Mary in *The Women* at the Lyric, where the late actor Leslie Howard spotted her and was so impressed that he made her his leading lady in a film *The Gentle Sex* (1942). She began to play more mature roles, taking over from Deborah Kerr as Ellie Dunn in Shaw's *Heartbreak House*, with which she later toured. In 1944 she played Ophelia in *Hamlet* during a season with the Donald Wolfit Company and was cast as Celia in *Volpone*. In 1945 she increased her range by taking such diverse roles as Lady Teazle, Cleopatra and Nora, the last in Ibsen's *A Doll's House*. She was praised for her sensitivity as Nora and found the part a special challenge, especially as she toured with it in Helsinki, Finland and Copenhagen.

In 1954, returning to the stage after her spell in films, she made her first appearance in the New York theatre as Lucasta in T.S. Eliot's *The Confidential Clerk*. She described Lucasta as a character "who is all unsettled. She's a girl who rushes about with a nice mask on and who finally settles for just being safe." Her performance was described as "provocative, poignant and bewitching", and one reviewer described her as "a strawberry blond bombshell". Of her American surroundings she said: "New York is amazing...people leap at you, but it's sweet. I like bearhugs."

Back in England, in 1955, she played a witch in John van Druten's *Bell, Book and Candle*, and she took the title part in *Lysistrata* at London's Royal Court Theatre in 1957. In 1959 she packed St Martin's Theatre with her performance as Hattie in *The Grass Is Greener*. The following year, in the title part in *Hedda Gabler* at the Oxford Playhouse, she met again and played alongside actor André Morell. That summer, at the age of 39, she married him secretly in Jamaica, to the surprise of those who knew them. They had one son and their marriage lasted until Morell's death in 1978.

Later London stage performances included a comedy, *Oblomov*, with British comedian Spike Milligan, the role of a tight-lipped governess in *The Chalk Garden* (1971), and in 1982 she took over from Celia Johnson in *The Understanding* following Dame Celia's death. Later films included the part of Lady Bellaston in *Tom Jones* (1963) and *The Hound of the Baskervilles* (1978). She moved into television, appearing in a comedy series, *Girls on Top*, as a highly eccentric romantic novelist, and as a society lady in a BBC "Miss Marple" adventure, based on the Agatha Christie stories. She said of herself, "Now I'm an old hag, I get to play much more interesting characters."

Throughout her career, Joan Greenwood drew admiring responses from audiences and critics alike, described at various times as "an instinctive actress", "volatile", "a pretty elf", "a charmer" and "an out-of-this world comedienne". However, some of the films she appeared in were badly received, including *The White Unicorn* (1947), *The Smugglers* (1947), *Saraband* with Stewart Granger (1948), and a French film *Le Passe-muraille* (1950). Although excellently cast as Lady Caroline Lamb in *The Bad Lord Byron* (1949), reviews of the film contained the same adjective as its title.

Joan Greenwood saw herself as a rebel—she once ran off with a circus for a week during the filming of *Saraband* to perform with an acrobatic troupe—and she claimed that she found her security in acting because, paradoxically, she could lose herself "in being other people". It is regrettable that neither British films nor Hollywood seemed able to offer her the material worthy of her particular talents. Later in life, her film roles were mainly cameos, reminding audiences of what might have been.

Born Joan Greenwood. **Parents** Sydney Earnshaw, an artist and Ida (Waller) Greenwood. **Marriage** André Morell, 1960 (died, 1978). **Children** One son. **Education** St Catherine's School, Bramley, Surrey; Royal Academy of Dramatic Art, London, from age of 14, 1935–38.

Career Stage actress mainly in the West End, also at Oxford Playhouse and Chichester Festival, 1962; also appeared in films, on television and radio; stage début, *Le Malade Imaginaire*, Apollo Theatre, London, 1938; film début, *John Smith Wakes Up*, 1940; New York début, *The Confidential Clerk*, Morosco, 1954; Hollywood début, *Moonfleet*, 1955. **Stage** *Le Malade Imaginaire*, 1938; *Little Ladyship*, 1939; *The Women*, 1939; *Peter Pan*, 1941, on tour, 1942; *Rise Above It*, 1942; *Striplings*, 1943; *Damaged Goods*, 1943; *Heartbreak House*, 1943; *Hamlet*, 1944; *Volpone*, 1945; *A Doll's House*, 1945; *Frenzy*, 1948; *Young Wives' Tale*, 1949; *A Doll's House*, on tour, Helsinki, Finland, Copenhagen; *The Confidential Clerk*, 1954; *Bell, Book and Candle*, 1955; *Cards of Identity*, 1956; *Lysistrata*, 1957–58; *The Grass Is Greener*, 1959; *Hedda Gabler*, 1960; *The Irregular Verb to Love*, 1961; *Oblomov* (*Son of Oblomov*), 1964; *Fallen Angels*, 1967; *The Au Pair Man*, 1969; *The Chalk Garden*, 1971; *Eden End*, 1972; *In Praise of Love*, 1973; *The Understanding*, 1982. **Films** *John Smith Wakes Up*, 1940; *My Wife's Family*, 1941; *He Found a Star*, 1941; *The Gentle Sex*, 1943; *They Knew Mr Knight*, 1945; *Latin Quarter*, 1945; *A Girl in a Million*, 1946; *The Man Within*, 1947; *The October Man*, 1947; *Saraband for Dead Lovers*, 1948; *The Bad Lord Byron*, 1949; *Whisky Galore!* (*Tight Little Island*), 1949; *Kind Hearts and Coronets*, 1949; *Garou-Garou, le passe-muraille* (*Le Passe-muraille, Mr Peek-a-boo*), 1950; *Flesh and Blood*, 1951; *Young Wives' Tale*, 1951; *The Man in the White Suit*, 1951; *The Importance of Being Earnest*, 1951; *Knave of Hearts* (*Monsieur Ripois; Lovers, Happy Lovers; Lover Boy*), 1954; *Father Brown*, 1954; *Moonfleet*, 1955; *Stage Struck*, 1958; *Horse on Holiday* (voice only), English-language version of *Hest pa sommerferie*; *Mysterious Island*, 1962; *The Amorous Prawn* (*The Playgirl and the War Minister, The Amorous Mr Prawn*), 1962; *Tom Jones*, 1963; *The Moon-Spinners*, 1964; *Girl Stroke Boy*, 1971; "London 1912", episode of *The Uncanny*, 1977; *The Hound of the Baskervilles*, 1977; *The Water Babies*, 1978. **Television** (includes) *Country*, 1981; *Ellis Island*, 1984; *Caring*, 1985; *Girls on Top*; *Miss Marple*. **Cause of death** Heart attack, at age 65. **Further reading** Ivan Butler, *Cinema in Britain: An Illustrated Survey*, London, 1973; George Perry, *Forever Ealing*, London, 1981.

MAJOR-GENERAL PYOTR GRIGORENKO

Soviet Soldier and Human Rights Activist

***Born* Borisovka, Ukraine, 16 October 1907**

***Died* New York City, New York, 21 February 1987**

The death of Major-General Pyotr Grigorenko in February 1987 seemed to many both untimely and ironic; a man who had suffered for his beliefs in the sanctity of human expression, who had espoused the causes of the oppressed, did not live to see the day when perestroika and glasnost became synonymous with democratization. Grigorenko, this "madman" as the Soviet authorities once deemed him, had himself criticized the party advocating democratization. Such criticism led to his dismissal from the chair of military cybernetics and to banishment in the Far East. Had he lived to see the increasing democratization of his motherland, he would not have been out of place in the new Supreme Soviet or Congress of Peoples' Deputies. His legacy is, however, apparent for all to see, in that human rights are now firmly on the Soviet agenda.

Some would say that Grigorenko was a man of vision, a man born before his time, a man who placed truth and goodness above personal ambition and success; a rare breed, as he had been a long-serving member of the élite armed forces and had witnessed the suffering of many of his colleagues during the Stalinist purges.

The son of a peasant, he was admitted into the party in 1927, and after studying at the Workers' Faculty and the Technical Institute in Kharkov, he joined an engineer unit of the Red Army in 1931. He was destined for a distinguished career, when after three years he was admitted to the Academy of the General Staff. In 1939 he graduated with honours as a candidate of science and was sent to the Far East to fight in the Soviet–Japanese War.

Throughout Grigorenko's military training Stalin was purging his officer corps, but Grigorenko remained unscathed in body if not in soul, convincing himself that those who lost their lives were traitors. Later in life, however, he realized that Stalin had created, as he once said, "a system of complete lies and terror". Despite a reprimand for criticism of the purges of the High Command, he survived and was sent at his own request to command an infantry division in the Baltic. A distinguished war record followed. Among the many honours bestowed on him was the Order of Lenin. He paid a high price, however, as he was both wounded and shell-shocked.

With his war-time experience and a distinguished service record, it was natural that after the war he should be offered a post lecturing at the Frunze Military Academy in Moscow. His academic career was just as successful as his war record and he wrote over 60 papers. At the 20th Party Congress after the death of Stalin he was promoted to general and awarded the chair of military cybernetics. His works proliferated under Khrushchev's thaw, which gave him the opportunity to reappraise the role of the Soviet military. Indeed, a paper which reached the West in 1969 offered an analysis of the losses inflicted on the Soviet Army by the German invasion in 1941. Grigorenko maintained that the responsibility for such devastating losses lay entirely with Stalin and his staff. His purges had caused the near demise of the officer corps and had laid the country open to Nazi invasion.

Obviously encouraged by increasing freedom of expression, Grigorenko started reappraising Soviet life as a whole, and what some argue as his moral and spiritual regeneration took place. This course inevitably led him into conflict with the authorities and in 1961, at the Moscow Party Conference, he delivered a fierce attack on the party—"the most terrifying moment of my life", he later admitted in exile in the USA. He beheld a vision of a better, fairer life in which there was party democratization, fewer privileges for party officials and, above all, an end to the persecution of those communists who were bold enough to seek reform of the system. The speech sealed his fate and having survived the purges and the war, he was ignominiously relieved of his posts and transferred to the Far East. Numerous protests to the party followed, whereupon he was dismissed from active service as a "trouble-maker".

As if driven by a vision of a greater good which could transcend the evils of the past and present, in 1964 he set about establishing an unofficial organization, calling for a return to Leninism. He was arrested—a supreme irony in view of the identical appeals of the people in today's regenerated Soviet Union. He was committed without trial to a psychiatric hospital where, on predicting the downfall of Khrushchev by the end of 1964, the doctors proclaimed him "paranoid". Released in 1965 after the fall of Khrushchev, he continued his activities with renewed vigour, leading protests against the persecution of dissidents with no concern for his own life.

In 1968 Grigorenko condemned the invasion of Czechoslovakia and called for an end to one-party elections, but perhaps it was the fight for the rights of the Crimean Tartars to their homeland which will remain his major legacy. His campaign for their return to the Crimea after the enforced deportation under Stalin found him, in 1969, attending a trial of leading Crimean Tartars in Tashkent. Such selflessness and concern for the plight of the wronged was sufficient for the authorities to declare him insane and he was imprisoned once more in a mental institution. Despite campaigning on behalf of academician Sakharov and prominent Crimean Tartars,

Grigorenko did not receive a remission until 1974 when, after his third heart attack, the authorities saw fit to release him—a man bowed but not broken.

In several samizdat publications which were disseminated in his homeland and in the West, Grigorenko described in detail the degrading torture he regularly endured. "They pack me into a straitjacket while hitting me and strangling me," he once wrote. "They hit me, they strangle me again...I resist, hoping my heart will give up. I come to want death." His name in the West, now well known, provided some security against subsequent arrest for engaging in seditious activities, and in 1977 after his son had emigrated to the USA, Grigorenko and his wife, Zinaida, left to join him. Exiled and stripped of his citizenship, Grigorenko later said from his home in New York, "I wouldn't want history repeated, but I wouldn't have wanted my life any different."

His remaining days were spent just as tirelessly as previously, working on his memoirs, *In the Underground One Meets Only Rats* (1982), giving lectures and monitoring human rights in his motherland. Till his dying days he loved Russia, professing, "I have the right to live and die in my home country". The campaigns of a man who opened the eyes of the West to the plight of the Soviet dissident live on. He can, perhaps, now rest in peace—a vindicated man.

Born Pyotr Grigorevich Grigorenko. **Marriages** 1) Mariya, 1927 (divorced, 1942); 2) Zinaida Egorovna, 1948. **Children** Three children from first marriage; one son, Andrei, from second marriage. **Education** Workers' Faculty (Rabfak), 1929; Technological Institute, Kharkov, 1931; Military Technical Academy (engineering unit), 1931–34; Moscow Academy of the General Staff, 1935–39. **Emigration** Left USSR for USA, 1977. **Career** Served in Far East, taking part in Soviet–Japanese War; officially reprimanded for criticizing Stalin's purge of Soviet Army High Command, 1941; transferred at own request to German front, 1943; promoted to divisional commander, twice wounded and suffered shell-shock; lecturer, Frunze Military Academy, post-war, publishing many works on military history and cybernetics; promoted to general, 1956; professor, chair of military cybernetics, 1961; relieved of posts and transferred to Far East after attacking personality cult around Khrushchev, advocating reform of the Communist Party and democratization of Soviet life, 1961; dismissed from active service; founded Fighting League for the Re-establishment of Leninism, 1964; arrested and declared insane by KGB psychiatrists, 1964; confined in Moscow and Leningrad mental asylums, 1964–65; released to employment as labourer, 1965; expelled from Communist Party; continued campaigns for reform and denounced Soviet invasion of Czechoslovakia, 1968; arrested, declared insane and imprisoned, 1969–74; returned to civil rights activities on release; left USSR for USA, 1977; deprived of Soviet citizenship, 1977; continued fighting for reform of Soviet Union and Communist Party from exile. **Memberships** Communist Party of the Soviet Union, from 1927. **Awards and honours** Five orders, including Order of Lenin, and six medals. **Publications** *Mysli sumasshedshego* (*Thoughts of a Mental Patient*), Amsterdam, 1973; (memoirs) *In The Underground One Meets Only Rats*, 1982; plus numerous articles and other works on science and warfare. **Cause of death** Undisclosed, at age 79.

HENRY-RUSSELL HITCHCOCK

American Architectural Historian

***Born* Boston, Massachusetts, 3 June 1903**

***Died* New York City, New York, 19 February 1987**

Any reader checking through the catalogue at the British Architectural Library, Portland Place, London, will find a great number of entries under the name Hitchcock, Henry-Russell. Catalogue cards refer the reader to books dealing with subjects as diverse as Modern Movement architecture in England and Rococo churches in Germany. The reader will find not simply a number of different titles, but many editions of the same title, indicative of the longevity of their contents. The dedicated researcher will pursue a vast quantity of periodical articles and reviews, written by Hitchcock over the more than 50-year span of his remarkable career.

The father of architectural history in the US, Hitchcock was also the doyen of Victorian studies in Britain and promoted the study of under-researched areas of European architecture. More of his books deal with buildings in western Europe and Britain than with architecture in the US, though the scale may tip the other way with periodical articles.

Hitchcock has left a substantial legacy to posterity in the form of his writings. His 1958 classic, *Architecture: 19th and 20th Centuries*, looks likely to remain unsurpassed among synthetic works dealing with the period. In writing it he was fully aware of his own part in the story, beginning three decades earlier, with his youthful magazine articles on the new pioneers. He gives the following *apologia* in the preamble to the twentieth century section:

> Historians, whether of politics or the arts, should ideally stand at some distance from their subjects thanks to remoteness in time; in lieu of that, remoteness in space sometimes serves the same purpose. However, this historian has now reached the point at which he entered the scene; he must write as statesmen who write history are often forced to do, of events concerning which he had first-hand knowledge—and hence, alas, first-hand prejudices.

HRH, as Hitchcock inevitably came to be known, was born a "Boston Brahmin". Educated at the Middlesex School and Harvard University, he took his BA in 1924 and MA in 1927, which was just two years before his first full-length book, *Modern Architecture*, appeared. This work has become a classic study of the early Modern Movement—by an author who was at once a scholar and, evidently, a partisan.

However, Hitchcock was never completely dazzled by the *modernity*, and the "historical inevitability" of his subject matter as others often were. Thus, his writing is enthusiastic, yet dispassionate, untainted by a doctrinaire approach. An approach for which he has been damned with faint praise by David Watkin in his book, *The Rise of Architectural History*. The introductory section of *Modern Architecture* is a history of architecture from about 1750 to the present day, while at the end of the main text is a kind of epitome-history of architecture, from the very beginnings. It is an extraordinarily confident book by a young academic.

Parts of this book had previously been published in the *Hound and Horn*, a Harvard-based periodical which promoted modernism in all the arts. This magazine featured the early writing of such luminaries as T.S. Eliot, Sean O'Faolain, James Agee and Alfred H. Barr. Hitchcock was a member of the *jeunesse dorée* at the university, along with such men as Philip Johnson and Virgil Thompson. He was able to afford to travel in order to further his research, first arriving in Europe about 1920.

Hitchcock was an absolute stickler for verisimilitude, writing solely about those buildings he had himself visited. The epic trip he made around Europe with the architect Philip Johnson in 1931 resulted in an exhibition and a book that gave an English title to the new architecture: *The International Style*. Hitchcock is usually given the credit for inventing this evocative phrase; he certainly popularized it, but he undoubtedly had in mind the title of the first *Bauhausbücher*, published in 1925. Written by Walter Gropius, then head of the Bauhaus, it was called *Internationale Architektur*.

Hitchcock and Johnson's book, *The International Style: Architecture Since 1922*, was not the catalogue proper to the exhibition; it was a well-illustrated round-up of works in the new style from Europe, the US and Japan. Hitchcock later referred to it as "monolithic", meaning it was too one-sided in presenting solely the most modern architects. The effect of the book was to present the American public with a wholly other view of the development of contemporary architecture. As the architect Peter Eisenman, former member of the "New York Five", puts it, the difference between the names "Modern Movement" and "International Style" marked "a transformation from a pluralistic vision of the good society, into an individual conception of the good life".

HRH returned to his theme of promoting what he called "the new tradition" in 1937, with his exhibition *Modern Architecture in England*. This exhibition and accompanying book of the same name reflected a change in emphasis. In the catalogue Hitchcock wrote: "Today, it is not altogether an exaggeration to say that England leads the world in modern architectural activity." One architect that he singled out for special praise, Berthold Lubetkin, recollected a trip they made together to Europe in 1937:

> It was an amazing journey. He was absolutely a polymath—knew everything. It was very often that we would go somewhere, up a side street, and he'd say "Ah ha! If you turn left you will find such and such a village. Now there's nothing special about it. They've got a little church there, but the columns are imported from Constantinople." So we would go and see. And with the same authority he was talking about the monetary system of the Aztecs. An amazing chap from that point of view.

Sir John Summerson recalled his first encounter with Hitchcock, in the 1930s: "I first sighted Henry-Russell Hitchcock in the Café Royal, somewhere about 1935. I was aware of a big man with a trim beard and a voice which, to put it mildly, 'carried'." HRH was holding forth to Ernestine Carter about the possible sources of the red plush and scrolly giltwork decorative scheme in the restaurant. Summerson later met the two Americans socially and acquaintance deepened into a lasting friendship. The loud, booming voice and powerful physical presence are often commented on by those who knew HRH. Summerson later summed him up thus: "Formidable and madly egocentric but kind and often generous, a bon viveur, a bit of a dandy (he is known to have sported a cape at Harvard in the mid-1960s), always ready for a laugh, he was conspicuous in any company."

Hitchcock made many visits to Britain to undertake research for his next *magnum opus*, which was not to appear until well after the war. *Early Victorian Architecture in Britain*, published in 1954, was a pioneering work in more ways than one; for HRH it was the first of his books to demonstrate his abilities with purely historical material and it was, of course, one of the first scholarly works on a subject which was then regarded as rather a joke. One of the most highly praised features of this book was the thorough inventory of Victorian buildings provided, appearing just as they were being demolished wholesale. Gavin Stamp, chairman of the Thirties Society, illuminates Hitchcock's working method for compiling the inventories, saying that he rode about on the top deck of London buses making his notes.

In his active espousal of the cause of Victorian architecture, Hitchcock was certainly a pioneer spirit. Almost no other period of architectural history was so neglected before he and a few other like-minded scholars took up the cause. Hitchcock, with the Englishmen Nikolaus Pevsner, John Betjeman and John Summerson formed a vanguard in the study of the buildings erected during Queen Victoria's reign. Indeed, in 1958 HRH was a founder member of the Victorian Society in Britain and was president (1969–74) of the American Victorian Society. He was also a founder member and sometime president of the Society of Architectural Historians. To the British version of the SAH, he donated the Alice Davis Hitchcock Medal, to serve as a memorial to his mother. Summerson could not praise him too highly: "HRH is beyond doubt the greatest living architectural historian. What is more, he has written more about nineteenth-century British architecture than the rest of us put together."

That mythical reader who looked through the card index at the British Architectural Library might well pause on leaving the building to survey the marble wall of the foyer on which are inscribed the names of those who received a Gold Medal from the Royal Institute of British Architects. In vain would the name Henry-Russell Hitchcock be sought, as he was never, alas, offered this signal honour. This was due, no doubt, to petty jealousies in the British architectural establishment, stirred up by his larger than life personality.

Born Henry-Russell Hitchcock. **Parents** Henry Russell and Alice Whitworth (Davis) Hitchcock. **Education** Middlesex School, Concord, Massachusetts; Harvard University, AB, 1924, MA, 1927. **Career** Architectural historian and critic; assistant professor of art, Vassar College, 1927–28; assistant associate professor, Wesleyan University, 1929–48; lecturer in architecture, Massachusetts Institute of Technology, 1946–48; professor of art, Smith College, 1948–68; professor of art, University of Massachusetts, 1968; adjunct professor, Institute of Fine Arts, New York University, 1969–87. **Related activities** Director, Smith College Museum of Art, 1949–55; lecturer, Institute of Fine Arts, New York University, 1951–57; lecturer in architecture: Yale University, 1951–52, 1959–60, 1970, Cambridge University, 1962, 1964. **Offices and memberships** Fellow: American Academy of Arts and Sciences, Pilgrim Society; honorary corresponding member, Royal Institute of British Architects; Franklin fellow, Royal Society of Arts; president, Society of Architectural Historians, 1952–54; founder-member, Victorian Society; president, Victorian Society of America, 1969–74. **Awards and honours** Honorary DFA, New York University, 1969; honorary DLitt, Glasgow, 1973; honorary DHL: Pennsylvania, 1976, Wesleyan, 1979; award of merit, American Institute of Architects, 1978; Benjamin Franklin Award, Royal Society of Arts, 1979. **Publications** *Frank Lloyd Wright* (in French), 1928; *Modern Architecture: Romanticism and Reintegration*, 1929, second edition, 1970; *J.J.P. Oud*, 1931; (with Philip Johnson) *The International Style*, 1932, second edition, 1966; *The Architecture of H.H. Richardson*, 1936, third edition, 1966; (with others) *Modern Architecture in England*, 1937; *Rhode Island Architecture*, 1939, second edition, 1968; *In the Nature of Materials: The Buildings of Frank Lloyd Wright*, 1942, second edition, 1973; *American Architectural Books*, 1946; *Painting Toward Architecture*, 1948; *Early Victorian Architecture in Britain*, 1954, second edition, 1972; *Latin-American Architecture Since 1945*, 1955; *Architecture: Nineteenth and Twentieth Centuries*, 1958, fourth edition, 1977; *German Rococo: The Brothers Zimmermann*, 1968; *German Rococo in Southern Germany*, 1968; (with William Seale) *Temples of Democracy*, 1977; *Netherlandish Scrolled Gables of the Sixteenth and Early Seventeenth Centuries*, 1978; *German Renaissance Architecture*, 1981. **Cause of death** Cancer, at age 83.

SPIKE HUGHES

British Jazz Musician, Critic, Composer, and Broadcaster

Born **London, England, 19 October 1908**

Died **London, England, 2 February 1987**

The term "all-rounder" could have been devised with just Spike Hughes in mind, for rarely have so many talents come together in one man. But another description that is often applied to people like Hughes does not do him justice at all, for while he was indeed a jack of all trades, he was also a master of most of them.

The trades he pursued were varied. His father was the music critic Herbert Hughes, and from him he acquired a lifelong love of music that was encouraged on their frequent musical tours together around Europe (Hughes's formal education was minimal, although its lack was scarcely noticeable). Hughes began composing short works while still in his early teens, and at the age of 15 he studied composition for two years in Vienna with Egon Wellesz. In 1926, when he was barely 18, his cello sonata received its London première, and in the same year he wrote the incidental music for a production of Congreve's *Love for Love* in Cambridge. He followed this up the next year with the music for a production of Yeats's *The Player Queen*.

While in Vienna, he had filed reports on music for the London *Times* and in the 1930s resumed the career of a critic, writing for the *Daily Herald* for three years. Hughes subsequently made a name for himself as a regular radio broadcaster on both serious and light music and, in 1938, turned his attention to the new medium of television, composing *Cinderella*, the first opera to be written specially for TV. Hughes did not believe that opera was an élitist art, and throughout his life he did much to popularize opera with a series of books that introduced it to a wider audience. In these, as in all his writing, he combined scholarly erudition with a stimulating enthusiasm and readability.

Yet his musical tastes were not all highbrow, for he had always had a love for jazz. While in his teens, he had taught himself the double bass—he first played a German instrument made of tin—and soon found work with a number of dance bands in London. Auditioning for Decca Records with his band, the Decca-Dents, in 1928, he produced a number of tracks that personify the British chamber jazz of the period. In the next few years he was much in demand, writing and orchestrating for impresarios C.B. Cochran and Noël Coward and composing an entire jazz symphony, *A Harlem Symphony*, in 1931. The following year, he wrote the music for a jazz ballet, *High Yellow*, that was performed with Alicia Markova at London's Savoy Theatre. The score daringly combined jazz and classically trained players to considerable commercial success.

In 1933 he visited New York, where he composed and recorded 14 tracks with Benny Carter's All American Orchestra. His compositions were all masterpieces, his use of the tenor sax players Coleman Hawkins and Chu Berry strongly individual. Yet when he returned from America late in 1933, he largely abandoned professional playing. "I left jazz behind at the moment I was enjoying it most: the moment when all love affairs should end." Instead, he championed jazz in the columns of the *Melody Maker* until 1944, a role he picked up again in *The Times* from 1957 to 1967. As a trained musician, he possibly found the youthful excesses of jazz too much to cope with, and he was unduly aware of his own limitations as a bass player.

During the war, Hughes worked for the BBC German Service (he was fluent in the language), and was a popular reader on the radio series *Children's Hour*. The onset of middle age did little to dampen Hughes's enthusiasms, and in the 1950s and 1960s he turned to playwriting, producing a series of radio plays that were enlightened by his own compositions. In 1950, his first musical,

Frankie and Johnny, was broadcast, while three years later he arranged and conducted the folk music that accompanied a BBC TV series. Two volumes of autobiography written in the late 1940s attempted to sum up his many interests.

Yet Hughes will probably best be remembered as the propagandist for the art of coarse living, an art he described and promoted in a series of books that attacked a range of sacred cows. At first, the jokes were sharp and he hit his targets full-on. But as the series developed, his humour became more forced and the rapier was replaced by the bludgeon. Yet many readers were attracted by his witty attacks on bridge, cricket, gardening, travel and entertaining, and Hughes had no pretensions other than to entertain. In retrospect, that too was the principle that informed the rest of his highly productive life.

Born Patrick Cairns Hughes. **Pseudonym** Mike (for writings in *Melody Maker*). **Father** Herbert Hughes, music critic. **Marriage** Charmian. **Education** Studied composition in Vienna with Egon Wellesz, 1923–25. **Career** Music correspondent for London periodicals and newspapers, Vienna, 1924–24; played double bass with the Night Watchmen, 1929–30; performed and arranged for the impresario C.B. Cochran, 1931; toured with Jack Hylton, 1931–32; formed own dance band, the All American Orchestra (formerly the Negro Orchestra) 1930–33; music and radio critic, *Daily Herald*, 1933–36; worked for the BBC's German Service during World War II; jazz critic, *The Times*, 1957–67. **Related activities** Wrote, under the pseudonym Mike, for *Melody Maker*, 1931–44; BBC broadcaster, *Children's Hour* and other programmes; several plays with original incidental music broadcast by the BBC; contributed material for, and appeared in, several films. **Publications** (all London) *Opening Bars* (autobiography), 1946; (with B. McFadyean) *Nights at the Opera*, 1948; *Second Movement* (autobiography), 1948; *Great Opera Houses*, 1956; *Out of Season*, 1956; *Famous Mozart Operas*, 1957; *Famous Puccini Operas*, 1959; *The Toscanini Legacy*, 1959, revised 1969; *Glyndebourne: A History of the Festival Opera*, 1965, revised 1981; *Famous Verdi Operas*, 1968; (with C. Hughes) *Cold Dishes for all Seasons*, 1971; *The Art of Coarse Cricket*; *The Art of Coarse Travel*; *The Art of Coarse Gardening*; *The Art of Coarse Bridge*; *The Art of Coarse Language*, 1974. **Compositions** (with date of first performance/broadcast) Sonata for solo cello, 1926; incidental music for *Love for Love* by Congreve, 1926, and *The Player Queen* by Yeats, 1927; *High Yellow*, jazz ballet, 1932; incidental music for *The Swan* by Ferenc Molnar, 1937; *Cinderella*, opera for TV, 1938; *St Patrick's Day*, opera, 1947; *Frankie and Johnny*, musical, 1950; conducted and arranged folk music heard in BBC series *As I Roved Out*, 1953–54; many other compositions, including music for orchestra, jazz band and piano. **Recordings** (all Decca) *A Harlem Symphony*, F2711, 1931; *Six Bells Stampede*, F2844, 1932; *Nocturne*, F3563; *Pastorale*, F3606, 1933; *Arabesque*, F3639, 1933; *Donegal Cradle Song*, F3717, 1933; recorded with English groups, including *The Decca-Dents* and *Three Blind Mice*; other recordings between the above dates. **Cause of death** Undisclosed, at age 78.

NORA KAYE

American Ballerina

***Born* New York City, New York, 17 January 1920**

***Died* Santa Monica, California, 28 February 1987**

Nora Kaye, who for almost 20 years led one or other of the two leading American ballet companies, is acknowledged as having been one of the greatest American dramatic ballet dancers.

Born Nora Koreff of Russian parents, her first name was inspired by the heroine in Ibsen's play *A Doll's House*. Early on in her career she changed her surname to Kaye because she considered that an American dancer should have an American name—an interesting contrast to the previous generation of dancers in the West who tended to take Russian-sounding names when embarking on a ballet career.

Kaye's mother had ambitions for her daughter to become a dancer, so from the age of four she sent her to dancing classes. Her father, who had been an actor in the renowned Moscow Arts Theatre, also had a significant influence on her future career by encouraging her to take lessons in the Russian Stanislavsky tradition of acting. The outcome of this was that Kaye became an exceptionally dramatic interpreter of classical dance.

At the age of eight Kaye entered the Metropolitan Opera Ballet School and studied there for seven years. During this time she occasionally had the thrill of appearing on-stage in the operas and she was seen variously as a cupid in *Tannhauser*, a gnome in *The Sunken Bell* and a Nibelung in *Das Rheingold*.

In 1935, at the age of 15, Kaye graduated into the *corps de ballet* of the Metropolitan Opera. Later that year she joined George Balanchine's American Ballet when it became the resident ballet company at the Metropolitan. During this time Kaye continued her training, taking regular classes with the celebrated Russian choreographer Michel Fokine, which also enabled her to learn many of the famous roles he had created.

However, Kaye soon came to feel that the theatre had more relevance to real life than did the world of classical dance. She was quoted in *Time* magazine as saying that ballet was "something dragged up from 300 years ago that didn't make any sense and wasn't going any place". She switched to Broadway and began appearing in musical comedies, including *Virginia* (1937), *Great Lady* (1938) and *Stars in Your Eyes* (1939). She also appeared with the Radio City Music Hall *corps de ballet* during this period and danced at the International Casino.

When the American Ballet Theatre Company was being set up in 1939, Kaye changed direction again and joined as a member of the *corps de ballet* because, as she has said, "most of my friends were joining". It was a fortunate decision, as she soon came under the influence of the choreographer Antony Tudor (q.v.) who was to have a lasting effect on her career. Working with Tudor made Kaye reassess her ideas about the potential of ballet as a significant modern art form and she began to see its dramatic possibilities.

It was at this point that Kaye's serious career as a dancer began. In the company's first New York season in 1940 she appeared in the chorus of Tudor's *Dark Elegies*, and she also had a part in his ballet *Lilac Garden*. Other small roles followed and soon Tudor, who had spotted Kaye's potential from the beginning, gave her the important character role of the Russian Ballerina in *Gala Performance*. Kaye had great success with this part and the *New York Times* praised her "fine technique" and "most ingratiating comedy sense".

Kaye continued to take increasingly important solo roles and in 1942 she got her first big breakthrough. Tudor created his celebrated ballet *Pillar of Fire* with Kaye in the leading role of Hagar. This was a complex work on the theme of frustrated love and Tudor painstakingly rehearsed with Kaye for months until he was satisfied that her smallest movement or gesture clearly projected his heroine's inner conflict. The passion of Kaye's performance caused a sensation on the opening night with the *New York Times* describing her interpretation as being among "the greatest examples of tragic acting of its generation".

From then on Kaye became a prima ballerina, dancing principal roles with the company. She appeared in the classics, notably *Swan Lake*, *Giselle* and as Princess Aurora in *The Sleeping Beauty*, while continuing to interpret new roles created for her by Tudor and Jerome Robbins. Agnes de Mille created the role of Lizzie Borden for Kaye in her ballet *Fall River Legend*. Although illness prevented her from dancing at the première, when she appeared in this work later in the season she scored a huge success.

In 1946 the American Ballet Theatre visited London for the first time. On the opening night Kaye danced Odile in the Black Swan *pas-de-deux* and she received an ovation, with the critic of *The Times* reporting that she "excelled anything seen there for years". Ballet was a relatively new art form in Britain and the visit by the American company had a big impact on British dancers. Kaye formed an enduring friendship with the leading British ballerina Margot Fonteyn during the trip.

In 1951 Tudor and Robbins left Ballet Theatre to join the New York City Ballet and Kaye soon followed them. Her début with that company was in *Symphony in C* and Kaye sailed through the enormous technical difficulties of the piece triumphantly. The following season Robbins choreographed his controversial ballet *The Cage* for Kaye. This was based on the story of female insects who consider their male counterparts as hereditary prey. Kaye's performance was praised in the *Herald Tribune* as being "frighteningly inhuman, provocative and glittering". Her next role was created by Tudor in his ballet *La Gloire* (1952). Although it was generally felt, as the *Newsweek* critic put it, the ballet "failed to give Miss Kaye's great dramatic talents sufficient outlet", she scored a personal triumph in the work.

Kaye continued to dance the great classic parts but she will undoubtedly be best remembered for the roles which were created specially for her. She retired from the stage in 1961 but continued to act as adviser to the American Ballet Theatre, thereby greatly influencing their policies.

Married to the choreographer and director Herbert Ross, Kaye and her husband presented seasons at the Spoleto Festival of Dance in 1959 and 1960. The couple also collaborated on several musicals, and on the ballet films *Nijinsky* and *The Turning Point*.

Born Nora Koreff. **Father** Gregory Koreff, actor. **Marriages** 1) Michael Van Buren, 1943; 2) Isaac Stern, violinist, 1948 (divorced); 3) Herbert Ross, choreographer and director, 1959. **Education** Studied at Metropolitan Opera Ballet School under Margaret Curtis for seven years from the age of eight; also studied under Michel Fokine, Vilzak-Shollar and Margaret Craske. **Career** Occasional parts at the Metropolitan Opera from the age of eight; member of *corps de ballet* from 15; danced at Radio City Music Hall; actress in musical comedies, 1937–39; American Ballet Theatre, 1939–51, 1954–60; New York City Ballet, 1951–54; co-founder, prima ballerina, Ballet of the Two Worlds, 1959–60; retired as dancer, 1961; associate artistic director, American Ballet Theatre, 1977–87; production assistant to Herbert Ross on various films and stage musicals, including *Nijinsky*, *The Turning Point* and *The Sunshine Boys*. **Stage roles** *Virginia*, 1937; *Great Lady*, 1938; *Stars in Your Eyes*, 1939. **Ballet roles** *Dark Elegies*, 1940; *Lilac Garden*, 1940; *Les Sylphides*, 1940; *Swan Lake*, 1940; *Gala Performance*, 1941; *Peter and the Wolf*, 1941; *Pas de Quatre*, 1941; *Giselle*, 1941; *Princess Aurora*, 1941; *Pillar of Fire*, 1942;

Bluebeard, 1942; *Apollo*, 1943; *Capriccio Espagnol*, 1943; *Dim Lustre*, 1943; *Mademoiselle Angot*, 1943; *Romeo and Juliet*, 1943; *Aleko*, 1943; *Waltz Academy*, 1944; *Harvest Time*, 1945; *On Stage!*, 1945; *Gift of the Magi*, 1945; *Graziana*, 1945; *Firebird*, 1945; *Black Swan Pas de Deux*, 1945; *Facsimile*, 1946; *Les Patineurs*, 1946; *Fall River Legend*, 1948; *Petrouchka*, 1948; *Theme and Variations*, 1949; *Nimbus*, 1950; *Jeux*, 1950; *Symphony in C*, 1951; *Pas de Trois*, 1951; *Bourrée Fantastique*, 1951; *The Guests*, 1951; *The Cage*, 1951; *Mother Goose Suite*, 1951; *The Age of Anxiety*, 1951; *La Gloire*, 1952; *Two's Company*, 1952; *Haunted Hotspot*, 1952; *Roundabout*, 1952; *Paquita*. **Awards and honours** *Dance* magazine Award of Distinction, for *The Turning Point*, 1980. **Cause of death** Cancer, at age 67.

ESMOND KNIGHT

British Actor

***Born* East Sheen, Surrey, 4 May 1906**

***Died* Egypt, 23 February 1987**

Had the story of Esmond Knight's career been simply an account of a huge volume of theatre work playing everything from leads with the Royal Shakespeare Company to hoofing it in West End musicals; had it merely taken note of the large body of films in which he appeared with such luminaries as Laurence Olivier, Moira Shearer, Richard Burton and Kenneth More; had it even given us just his superlative one-man show *Agincourt—The Archer's Tale*, it would have warranted a place in theatre history. Add to this the fact that for 46 years he was almost totally blind, and his life becomes an example of remarkable determination and courage.

Knight lost his sight in action during World War II while serving as a gunnery officer with the Royal Navy. During an engagement with the German battleship *Bismarck*, he received a faceful of molten metal which knocked out his left eye completely and pierced the right with splinters of shrapnel. Disfigured and handicapped by blindness, he underwent rehabilitation at St Dunstan's Training School in Shropshire and within two years was back on the West End stage as the English soldier Courage in Eric Linklater's *Crisis in Heaven*.

Educated at Westminster School where his ambition to act was first awakened, he made his professional and West End débuts in the same year, appearing in Ibsen's *Wild Duck* at Pax Robertson's salon, and later in *The Merchant of Venice* at the Old Vic at the age of 20. He quickly established himself as a young actor with strength, virility and impressive stage presence, moving easily between the intimacy of small auditoria, such as the Arts and the Gate, to the vastness of Drury Lane, the largest theatre in Britain.

After the war and his injury, Knight returned to the theatre almost as if nothing had happened. This was made slightly easier by the partial recovery of his vision in 1943, although at best his sight was "like looking through clouds" and was to deteriorate inexorably over the rest of his life.

Fellow actors speak of Knight's insistence that they should pay no attention to his blindness and his dogged determination to ensure it would not affect his playing. He would spend hours memorizing every corner of the stage and relative distances on the set to enable him to move about freely and act as though he had no handicap at all. He even managed to turn himself into a competent painter and had several exhibitions to his credit.

The theatre is a notoriously unsentimental and fickle employer and it is testament to Knight's considerable talent that he went on to take full part in a demanding season at Stratford-upon-Avon where he played Leontes in *A Winter's Tale*, Christopher Sly in *The Taming of the Shrew*, the Ghost in *Hamlet* and the foul-mouthed Thersites in *Troilus and Cressida*.

The next three decades saw him in plays by Terence Rattigan, G.B. Shaw, Ibsen and T.S. Eliot, as well as Shakespeare. His particular speciality was a readiness to play the minor, integral parts in the classical canon which, though small, nevertheless require great skill and considerable experience, and which leading actors so often regard as beneath them.

Esmond Knight worked solidly throughout his 60-year career, appearing both on stage and television as late as 1985. He was working on a film adaptation of Olivia Manning's *Balkan Trilogy* in Egypt and died there, in harness, having earned the enduring admiration and respect of managements and colleagues alike.

Born Esmond Pennington Knight. **Parents** Francis Charles and Bertha Clara (Davis) Knight. **Marriages** 1) Frances Clare, 1929 (divorced); 2) Nora Swinburne, an actress, 1946. **Children** One daughter, by first marriage. **Education** Willington Preparatory School, Putney, London; Westminster School, London. **Military service** Gunnery Officer, Royal Navy, blinded in action, 1941. **Career** Actor; stage début, *Wild Duck*, Pax Robertson's salon, 1925; played juveniles, Old Vic, 1925–27; with Birmingham Repertory Company, 1927–28; film début, 1931; with Travelling Repertory Theatre Company, 1946; with Shakespeare Memorial Theatre Company, Stratford-upon-Avon, 1948; with own company, Bermuda, 1951; New York début, *The Emperor's Clothes*, Ethel Barrymore, 1953; with Royal Skakespeare Company, Aldwych, 1961; with Old Vic Company, 1962; at the Mermaid, 1965; at Edinburgh Festival, 1966. **Stage** *Wild Duck*, 1925; *Doctor Syn*, on tour, 1926; *Twelfth Night*, 1927; *The Return*, 1927; *Yellow Sands*, on tour, 1927–28; *Contraband*, 1928; *Thunder on the Left*, 1928; *To What Red Hell*, 1928; *Fashion*, 1929; *Maya*, 1929; *Improper People*, 1929; *Art and Mrs Bottle*, 1929; *The Man I Killed*, 1930; *Hamlet*, 1930; *Charlot's Masquerade*, 1930; *Mr Eno, His Birth, Death and Life*, 1930; *Salome*, 1931; *Waltzes from Vienna*, 1931; *Volpone*, 1932; *Love for Love*, 1932; *Waltzes from Vienna*, on tour, 1932; *Wild Violets*, 1932; *Three Sisters*, 1934; *Streamline*, 1934; *The Insect Play*, 1936; *Night Must Fall*, 1936; *The King and Mistress Shore*, 1936; *Wise Tomorrow*, 1937; *African Dawn*, 1937; *Van Gogh*, 1937; *The Melody That Got Lost*, 1938; *The Insect Play*, 1938; *Crest of the Wave*, 1938; *Twelfth Night*, 1938; *Through the Night*, 1940; *The Peaceful Inn*, 1940; *A Midsummer Night's Dream*, 1940; *Crisis in Heaven*, 1944; *Three Waltzes*, 1945; *Romeo and Juliet*, 1946; *Saint Joan*, 1946; *Man and Superman*, 1946; *In Time to Come*, 1946; *Electra*, 1946; *The Relapse*, 1947, 1948; *The Winter's Tale*, 1948; *Hamlet*, 1948; *Caroline*, 1949; *Who Is Sylvia?*, 1950; *Caesar and Cleopatra*, 1951; *Antony and Cleopatra, 1951; Heloise*, 1951; *Montserrat*, 1952; *The Emperor's Clothes*, 1953; *Age of Consent*, 1953; *Bell, Book and Candle*, 1955; *The Caine Mutiny Court Martial*, 1956; *Head of the Family* 1957; *The Country Wife*, 1957; *The Russian*, 1958; *A Piece of Silver*, on tour, 1960; *The Lady From the Sea*, 1961; *Becket*, 1961; *The Taming of the Shrew*, 1961; *Two Stars for Comfort*, 1962; *Peer Gynt*, 1962; *The Merchant of Venice*, 1962; *The Alchemist*, 1962; *Measure for Measure*, 1963; *The Wakefield Mystery Plays*, 1965; *Oedipus the King*, 1965; *Oedipus at Colonus*, 1965; *Left-handed Liberty*, 1965; *Four Thousand Brass Halfpennies*, 1965; *Dandy Dick*, 1965; *A Winter's Tale*, 1966; *Getting Married*, 1967; *The Black Swan Winter*, 1969; *Martin Luther King*, 1969; *Spithead*, 1969; *Mister*, 1969; *The Servants and the Snow*, 1970; *Mister*, 1971; *The Family Reunion*, 1973; *Agincourt—The Archer's Tale*, one-man show, 1973; *The Cocktail Party*, 1975; *Love's Old Sweet Song*, 1976; *Three Sisters*, 1976; *Agincourt—The Archer's Tale*, 1976; *Henry V*, 1976; *Crime and Punishment*, 1978; *The Family Reunion*, 1979; *Hamlet*, 1982; *Moby Dick*, 1983; *The Devils*, 1984. **Films** (include) *Romany Love*; *77 Park Lane*; *Waltzes from Vienna*, 1933; *Black Roses*; *What Men Live By*; *The*

Bermondsey Kid; *The Blue Squadron*; *Girls Will Be Boys*; *Dandy Dick*, 1935; *Someday*; *Pagliacci*, 1936; *Crime Unlimited*; *Contraband*, 1940; *This England*, 1941; *The Silver Fleet*, 1943; *Halfway House*, 1944; *Henry V*, 1944; *A Canterbury Tale*, 1944; *Black Narcissus*, 1946; *Hamlet*, 1948; *Red Shoes*, 1948; *Gone to Earth*, 1948; *The River*, 1950; *The Ringer*, 1952; *Helen of Troy*, 1954; *The Dark Avenger*, 1955; *Richard III*, 1955; *On Secret Service*; *The Prince and the Showgirl*, 1957; *Battle of the VI*, 1958; *Sink the Bismarck*, 1960; *The Spy Who Came in From the Cold*, 1966; *Anne of the Thousand Days*, 1969; *Where's Jack*, 1968; *The Boy Who Turned Yellow*; *The Yellow Dog*, 1973; *Robin and Marian*, 1975; *The Element of Crime*, 1985; also assisted in making several natural history films. **Television** (includes) *Dickens and Ibsen*; *Dr Finlay's Casebook*; *Elizabeth I*; *The Pallisers*; *Fall of Eagles*; *History of the English-speaking Peoples*; *Shades of Greene*; *Ballet Shoes*; *Quiller*; *I Claudius*; *1900*; *Voices from the Past*; *Kilvert's Diaries*; *Supernatural*; *Romeo and Juliet*; *Rebecca*; *Nelson*; *The Borgias*; *Troilus and Cressida*; *My Cousin Rachel*; *Drake's Venture*; *King Lear*; *The Grassless Grave*; *The Invisible Man*; *Blott on the Landscape*. **Publications** *Seeking the Bubble* (autobiography), 1943. **Cause of death** Undisclosed, at age 80.

KAROLOS KOUN

Greek Theatre Director

Born **Bursa, Turkey, 13 September 1908**

Died **Athens, Greece, 14 February 1987**

Karolos Koun injected the nascent modern Greek theatrical tradition with a powerful tonic which sustained it during a dark and troubled period of the country's history. As a teacher, performer and, above all, a stage director and producer, his influence was almost without parallel.

Born in Bursa, in Anatolia or Asia Minor (Turkey), Koun was educated at Robert College, Istanbul, and studied in Paris before moving to Greece in 1929 to teach English literature at Athens College. Here he staged student productions of works by Aristophanes, Euripides and Shakespeare.

Although there had been something of a theatrical revival in Greece during the 1920s, both performances and interpretation were still highly unsophisticated until the National Theatre was founded, at the instigation of George Papandreou, the Education Minister, in 1932. This generated a good deal of public enthusiasm and interest, as well as stimulating the independent theatre.

Koun founded one of the most successful of these independent groups, the Laiki Skini, or Popular Stage, while he was still teaching, in 1934. He is particularly remembered during this period for the marvellous production of *Erophili*, by the late sixteenth-century Cretan dramatist Chortatsis, which he staged with his first repertory company.

In 1941 Koun founded the Theatro Technis, or Art Theatre, which played a crucial role in the cultural life of occupied Athens and became one of the most important Greek dramatic centres after the war, although he closed it for a period during the civil war (1947–49).

His career from this point on was illustrious, controversial and iconoclastic. Productions at the Art Theatre, which was the first Greek theatre in the round, included the whole range of Ancient Greek classics and many foreign works, such as the Greek premières of Brecht and Pirandello plays, Ibsen's *The Wild Duck*, Lorca's *Blood Wedding*, Tennessee Williams's *A Streetcar Named Desire*, and many others.

Koun transformed the Greek classics from period pieces to dramas of critical relevance to the contemporary audience, and for this he was frequently in trouble with the authorities, particularly given the sensitive and paranoid political climate which prevailed for much of his career. In 1957, for example, his production of Aristophanes' satirical comedy *The Birds* at the ancient Herodus Atticus theatre in Athens had the priests as contemporary Orthodox clergy; it was booed off the stage.

He directed several other Greek companies, including the National Theatre from 1950 to 1953, where his productions included Pirandello's *Henry IV* and Chekhov's *The Three Sisters*. His style was full of verve, and he often used spectacular features, such as a chorus of whirling dervishes in his 1964 production of *The Persians* by Aeschylus.

Koun often directed and produced abroad. In 1962 he brought his Art Theatre company to the Théâtre des Nations in Paris where their production of *The Birds* was tremendously well received and Koun became an international theatrical celebrity. He brought them again to Europe in 1964, this time to the Aldwych Theatre in London, and directed *The Birds* as part of the World Theatre Season, returning the following year to do Aeschylus's *The Persians*, which he then took to the Paris Festival. Both plays then went to Moscow, Leningrad and Warsaw.

Further successes in England included *Romeo and Juliet*, which he directed for the Royal Shakespeare Company in Stratford-upon-Avon in 1967, and Sophocles's *Oedipus Rex* and Aristophanes' *Lysistrata* at the 1969 World Theatre Season. More European performances followed.

Despite being lauded in Europe, the colonels' regime in Greece did not favour the outspoken, individual style of artists such as Koun, and until their departure in 1974 the Art Theatre struggled desperately to survive, both in terms of finance (it was rescued by grants from the Ford Foundation) and in terms of public support (theatre-goers were frequently too intimidated to attend).

Happily, over 14,000 people went to see Koun's production of *The Birds* at the amphitheatre in Epidaurus to mark the demise of the hated regime.

Koun, who like many of his countrymen chain-smoked, founded a drama school attached to the Art Theatre, which over the years produced many of Greece's leading actors and actresses, including Melina Mercouri, who was culture minister in Andreas Papandreou's ill-fated socialist government. They called him "Teacher", and generations of Greek theatre-goers could have done the same.

Born Karolos Koun. **Education** Robert College, Istanbul; and Paris. **Career** Teacher of English Literature, Athens College, 1929–mid-1930s; staged student productions of Shakespeare, Euripides and Aristophanes while at Athens College; founder and director, Laiki Skini (Popular Stage), 1934; freelance theatre director, Athens, 1939–41; founder, producer and director, Theatro Technis (The Art Theatre), from 1941. **Related activities** Directorial work for many companies in Greece and worldwide, including the Greek National Theatre, 1950–53, and the Royal Shakespeare Company. **Stage** (all with Theatro Technis at various locations, unless stated, with dates of first production) included *Alcestis*, 1935; *The Wild Duck*, 1942; *The Glass Menagerie*, 1947; *The Blood Wedding*, 1948; *A Streetcar Named Desire*, 1949; *Henry IV*, Greek National Theatre, 1950; *Death of a Salesman*, 1950; *Three Sisters*, Greek National Theatre, 1951; *The Cherry Orchard*, 1955; *Twelfth Night*, 1956; *The Caucasian Chalk Circle*, 1957; *Plonto*, 1957; *The Birds*, 1959; *Arturo Ui*, 1962; *Rhinoceros*, 1963; *Exit the King*, 1963; *The Persians*, 1965; *Romeo and Juliet*, Royal Shakespeare Company, 1967; *The Frogs*, 1967; *Oedipus Rex*, 1969; *Lysistrata*, 1969. **Cause of death** Undisclosed, at age 78.

EDWARD LANSDALE

American Military Adviser

***Born* Detroit, Michigan, February 1908**

***Died* McLean, Virginia, 23 February 1987**

Edward Lansdale rose to the rank of major-general in the USAAF but was better known for his counter-insurgency activities in the Philippines and Vietnam. As a senior military adviser, Lansdale made a significant contribution to the defeat of the communist Hukbalahap rebellion in the Philippines, although he met with far less success when he employed similar techniques in Vietnam. Nevertheless, he remained an influential figure in the 1950s and 1960s, and was thought to be the man behind a number of fictional CIA operatives in novels of the period.

Born in Detroit, Lansdale graduated from the University of California at Los Angeles and embarked upon a career in business, becoming an advertising executive. During World War II he enlisted in the US Army, becoming a captain in 1943. It was during this war that he received his initial experiences of undercover operations, serving in the Office of Strategic Services (OSS). Having risen to the rank of major by 1947, Lansdale resigned his commission and immediately joined the USAAF with the rank of captain. Quickly promoted to colonel and drawing on his experience in the OSS, he was sent as a military adviser to the newly independent Philippines to work alongside the defence secretary, and future president of the Philippines, Ramon Magasaysay. On Lansdale's advice, Magasaysay set about undermining the Huk rebellion with a combined programme of social reform and military action, convinced that the best way of preventing a communist revolution was a democratic revolution to undercut communist support. Lansdale once said, "The Communists strive to split the people away from the government and gain control over a decisive number of the population. The sure defence against this strategy is to have the citizenry and the government so closely bound together that they are unsplittable." Indeed, his theory was proved correct and both the social and military aspects of his policies met with considerable success.

With this victory behind him, Lansdale was posted to Vietnam in 1954 as head of a US military mission and subsequently as chief of the Saigon station for domestic affairs of the Central Intelligence Agency. During the 1954 Geneva negotiations, Lansdale, as head of a team of agents, unsuccessfully attempted to thwart the Viet Minh take over in North Vietnam by a series of sabotage raids. Lansdale's report on one such raid made shortly before the withdrawal from Hanoi in October 1954 following the French defeat at Dien Bien Phu, later included among the Pentagon Papers, gave a flavour of the type of operation carried out; the team "had spent the last days of Hanoi in contaminating the oil supply of the bus company for a gradual wreckage of engines in the buses" and "in taking actions for delayed sabotage of the railroad". The team had a bad moment when contaminating the oil. They had to work quickly at night in an enclosed storage room. Fumes from the contaminant came close to knocking them out. Dizzy and weak-kneed, they masked their faces with handkerchiefs and completed the job. In South Vietnam Lansdale was a staunch supporter of President Ngo Dinh Diem and was instrumental in securing US backing for his government. One of Diem's closest advisers, Lansdale lived in the presidential palace until his recall to the Pentagon in mid-1956.

In January 1961 Lansdale, then assistant to the secretary of defence for special operations, returned to Vietnam on an inspection mission to investigate the current situation in the troubled country. Although critical of some aspects of Diem's government, Lansdale proposed substantial US support to stabilize Diem's regime and enable him to introduce a package of social reforms to win public support. In April Lansdale was appointed operations officer to a special committee set up by President Kennedy and headed by the defence secretary Roswell Gilpatrick, to investigate ways and means of preventing a communist victory in Vietnam. The final report of the committee did call for increased US support for Diem's regime but not as much as Lansdale had advocated. Despite Diem's repeated request for him to be posted to Vietnam, Lansdale remained in the US and retired from the Air Force with the rank of major-general in 1963, the same year in which Diem was overthrown and killed in a coup.

Lansdale, however, did return to Vietnam in 1965 with Henry Lodge who was to begin his second term as US ambassador. Lansdale's role as a special representative involved him in liaison work between the US and Vietnamese governments, and he again called for a programme of "rural reconstruction" to undercut support for the communists. Early in 1966 Lansdale's arguments prevailed when South Vietnam's president, Air Vice Marshal Nguyen Cao Ky, declared that his government would undertake a rural programme to reassert government control, improve conditions for the peasants and extirpate the Vietcong. Lansdale returned to the US in 1968 at a time when events made it clear that there was little use for his policy of combined social reform and counter-insurgency measures. Nevertheless, he maintained the validity of his approach, publishing *In the Midst of Wars: An American's Mission to Southeast Asia* in 1977, where he argued that the US could still play an influential approach in the Third World by exporting "the American way" and "winning the hearts and the minds of the people" by a blend of economic aid and military support.

Lansdale's activities were not restricted solely to Vietnam, for he also served as director of the CIA's undercover operations in Indochina, and in an interview with the *New York Times* in 1975 revealed that in November 1961 he had been instructed by Attorney General Robert F. Kennedy, acting on behalf of the president, to prepare plans to overthrow the Cuban leader, Fidel Castro. The plan, based on the use of Cuban exiles to ferment internal discord, was never put into practice.

According to Stanley Karnow in his highly acclaimed book *Vietnam: A History* (1983), Lansdale was the figure behind the character of Colonel Edwin Hillendale in Eugene Burdick and William J. Lederer's novel *The Ugly American*, and also behind Alden Pyle, "the naïve US official who believed that Vietnamese peasants instilled with the precepts of town-hall democracy would resist communism", in Graham Greene's *The Quiet American*.

Although Lansdale's policies ultimately failed in Vietnam, he was a highly influential figure in the politics of the region for over a decade. In his book *The Best and the Brightest*, David Halberstam described him as "the Cold War version of the Good Guy, the American who did understand the local ambience and the local nationalism", a fair description of a man who worked hard at an unfashionable and thankless task.

Born Edward G. Lansdale. **Parents** Henry and Sarah Frances (Philips) Lansdale. **Marriages** 1) Helen Batcheller, 1933 (died, 1972); 2) Patrocinio Yapcinco, 1973. **Children** Edward Russell and Peter Carroll by first marriage. **Education** University of California, Los Angeles. **Career** Advertising executive; joined US Army as captain, 1943; served in Office of Strategic Services, World War II; left army as major, 1947; joined US Air Force as captain, 1947; special adviser to Philippines government on counter-insurgent warfare, late 1940s–early 1950s; in Vietnam undertaking various counter-insurgent activities, including sabotage, for US Central Intelligence Agency (CIA), 1954–56; assigned to Pentagon, assisting in formation of the Special Forces, late 1950s; assistant to secretary of defence for special operations, early 1960s; returned to Vietnam to advise on combating communist guerrillas, 1961; retired from US Air Force as major-general, 1963; special assistant to US ambassador to Vietnam and US representative to South Vietnamese government committee on counter-insurgency and "pacification" of the

Vietnamese countryside, 1965–68; director of CIA undercover operations in Indochina. **Awards and honours** Distinguished Service Medal (twice); Legion of Honour; Philippines Medal of Military Merit. **Publications** *In the Midst of Wars: An American's Mission to Southeast Asia* (memoirs), 1972, plus various articles. **Cause of death** Heart disease, at age 79.

LIBERACE

American Musician and Entertainer

Born **West Allis, Wisconsin, 16 May 1919**

Died **Palm Springs, California, 4 February 1987**

Once upon a time in West Allis, Milwaukee, Wisconsin, there lived an Italian-born gourmet grocer who played the French horn. He was Salvatore Liberace, who married Frances Zuchowski, an acquaintance of Ignace Paderewski, the pianist who ran Poland. You would be right to sense exotic developments,

A son, then a daughter were born. In 1919 twins arrived; one died at birth, the other weighed 13 pounds. He, Wladziu, was set to the piano at four years of age, though his father's saturnine plan was for him eventually to become a physician or a mortician "like his uncles". At the age of seven, Wladziu won a scholarship to the Wisconsin College of Music, where he studied tuition-free for the next 17 years. In childhood he was tiny, sickly and mocked by his peers for preferring music to more conventionally violent boyish pursuits; then, when he was eleven, came a departure. The parents had separated and Wladziu brought in some money by playing the piano for silent movies. His already impressive repertoire enabled him to take requests and this, he realized, made him popular. He tried a little classical admixture, but the kids got bored. "When I told my teacher about it, she said, 'Don't give it to them in big doses—just a little at a time.' That's when I started my *Reader's Digest* versions of concertos and learned about trying to keep the audience's attention—by trying to make friends."

At 17, Walter Liberace, as he now was, appeared as soloist with the Chicago Symphony Orchestra. Engagements with dance bands and at local nightclubs continued to help the exchequer. At school he was growing more confident and popular, running cookery classes and a five-piece band, and beginning to suggest a sartorial extraversion which would become, to put it mildly, characteristic. He graduated in 1937.

The young man could now rely on a modest income from both popular and classical music. He called himself Walter Busterkeys to take care of the downmarket work, but truth would out. His personality, musical or otherwise, would not accept the split and, in 1939, when asked for an encore at a classical recital, he gave them "Three Little Fishes". That, he recalled, "really shook 'em up". It was a liberation. Now he was just "Liberace". He went to New York and played the big hotels where the audiences "were rotten, they were drunk and they were rich". He used the camp failsafe of pre-emptive criticism—"I heckled myself."

Spinal injury kept Liberace out of World War II. He spent the period playing the Milwaukee area with his brother George as his violinist, bandleader and business manager. His act developed, his reputation increased, and after the war it was back to New York's Plaza Hotel. Two vital props now appeared: an oversized Blüthner grand piano and an imitation Louis XIV candelabrum. (He got the idea from *A Song to Remember*, which starred Cornel Wilde as Chopin.)

Now earning a "decent salary" as a café–society entertainer, Liberace moved via Chicago to California. In 1951 he played a local Los Angeles television station. In the following year *The Liberace Show* went nationwide, and by 1953 he was TV's first matineé idol, carried by more stations than *I Love Lucy*, the ultimate accolade. He was suddenly the biggest solo attraction in American concert halls, breaking box-office records at the Hollywood Bowl and Madison Square Gardens, and selling vast numbers of record albums. He never forgot his first teacher's advice; whipping through the classics, "cutting out the boring bits", he could, on a good night, clock 37 seconds for "The Minute Waltz", before seeing to "The Beerbarrel Polka". Everything came with double octaves and lush trills. Somebody penned the suspicion that "He just plays 'Lady of Spain' over and over again in different keys". His costumes became increasingly outlandish and exotic, and as the money rolled in, his mother would be introduced in matching attire. For a while he cast off the glitter, but his bookings dropped dramatically, so back it came.

"...the summit of sex, the pinnacle of Masculine, Feminine and Neuter. Everything that He, She and It can ever want." Thus wrote the famous British journalist Cassandra (William Connor) in 1959. Liberace successfully sued him for libel and donated the £8000 to Cancer Relief. That same year he starred as a deaf pianist in the film *Sincerely Yours*, and in 1963 he was a memorably unctuous casket salesman in *The Loved One*.

Liberace resolved to work less and earn more. The Las Vegas act became his staple for half the year and he devoted spare time to the exercise of taste on his home there, his Hollywood mansion and other places he had collected. He bought, renovated, furnished and sold many homes, and patented a disappearing toilet. The visible kind he found "unglamorous". He once tried to sell off some of his superabundance of expensive gewgaws, through the Liberace Interiors and Objets d'Art boutique, but couldn't bear to part with any of it. The shop closed after five years in the red. More successfully, he opened his Hollywood mansion to the public at $6 per head, and this was followed by a Liberace Museum in Las Vegas. Here you could view his mother's knitting basket, a crucifix blessed by Pope Pius XII and a piano constructed of toothpicks. The profits went to the Liberace Foundation, which provided bursaries for aspiring musicians.

In the 1980s Liberace began touring again, and box-office records crumbled before him. Feathers, rhinestones and a $300,000 fur cape adorned the maestro. "Look me over," he bade his disciples. "I didn't dress this way not to be noticed." Indeed, he didn't. His sister once told an interviewer, "This glitter gulch...it's because we were so poor. You wouldn't believe all the stuff he bought mother and me...he wanted us all to live together, he wanted to make a world of the past...he doesn't care much for the real world." As fans flocked to kiss his bejewelled fingers, Liberace once joked, "I feel like the Pope". He encouraged this notion in himself by sleeping in a reproduction of the Sistine Chapel.

In later years he suffered from a kidney complaint and seldom appeared in public. In 1982 he settled out of court a case brought against him by his chauffeur. The young man claimed that Liberace had reneged on a promise of money in exchange for sexual favours. Other sexual scandals occurred, but none dented his popularity.

"Liberace," as somebody wrote acutely, "is to 'serious' music what popular newspapers are to news." It may be added, however, that he was less harmful than they. He looked back to Liszt and Chopin, and was himself spiritual grandpa to Elvis Presley, Mick Jagger, Elton John, Prince and the rest. A hard worker with a sound technique, he had fun making fun of himself. "It's a matter of time. If you stick around long enough, you end up making converts out of non-believers. I guess I've just worn out my critics."

Born Wladziu Valentino Liberace. **Parents** Salvatore, a grocer and French horn player, and Frances (Zuchowski) Liberace. **Education** Pershing Elementary School, Milwaukee, 1929; won scholarship to Winsconsin College of Music, studied under Florence Bettray-Kelly. **Career**

Pianist, entertainer on the concert platform, in variety, film and television, also, composer; played with local dance bands, accompanied silent movies under name Walter Busterkeys in late teens; professional début, piano soloist with Chicago Symphony Orchestra under Frederick Stock, 1936; entertainer in Milwaukee, also at clubs such as the Blue Angel, Chicago, and Le Ruban Bleu, New York City, 1940–45; film début, *East of Java*, 1949; television début, KLAC, Los Angeles, 1951, became biggest solo attraction in USA, appearing at the Hollywood Bowl from 1952, Carnegie Hall, 1953, Madison Square Garden, 1954, London Palladium, 1956, and Las Vegas; recorded for Columbia Records and Coral Records. **Other activities** Founder, Liberace Foundation for benefit of talented young performers; founder, Liberace Museum, in the Liberace Shopping Plaza, Las Vegas, Nevada, 1979; owner, Liberace's Tivoli Gardens Restaurant. **Awards and honours** Two Emmy awards; named Entertainer of the Year, 1973; six gold records. **Offices and memberships** American Society of Composers, Authors and Publishers; National Academy of Recording Arts and Sciences. **Films** *East of Java*, 1949; *South Seas Sinner*, 1950; *Sincerely Yours*, 1959; *When the Boys Meet the Girls*, 1965; *The Loved One*, 1965. **Television** (includes) *The Liberace Show*, 1952, in syndication, 1953–55, 1958–59, 1969; episodic appearances in *Batman*, *Hotel* and *Another World*; guest appearances, *The Ed Sullivan Show* and others. **Publications** (with Carol Traux) *Liberace Cooks! Recipes from His Seven Dining Rooms*, 1970; *Liberace*, 1973; ed. Tony Palmer, *The Things I Love*, 1976; *The Wonderful Private World of Liberace*, 1986. **Cause of death** Aids, at age 67. **Further reading** Bob Thomas, *Liberace: The True Story*, New English Library, 1989.

ALFRED LION

American Record Producer

***Born* Berlin, Germany, 21 April 1908**

***Died* San Diego, California, 2 February 1987**

The typical record label owner does not exist, but by any definition, Alfred Lion was the most untypical of them all. To describe him as a record label owner is rather like describing New York merely as a collection of buildings, for Lion was quite simply the most important patron and producer American jazz has ever had.

His importance lies in his enthusiasm. Lion was born in Berlin and there, in 1925, at the age of 16, he saw a poster advertising a concert for Sam Wooding's orchestra. Out of curiosity, he went along, and immediately and passionately fell for the jazz music he heard. He searched the record shops of Berlin for the few jazz records available in the city, and slowly came to acquire some knowledge of this Black American music. In 1928 he moved to New York, and for two years barely survived in a series of low-paid, manual jobs. Forced to return to Germany in 1930, although accompanied by over 300 records, he took a job with an import-export firm. For the next eight years he attempted to return to America—to be near to jazz and far away from Fascism—and, after a two-year stay in Chile, he returned to settle permanently in the US in 1938.

On 23 December Lion attended the "Spirituals to Swing" concert at the Carnegie Hall. Impressed by the boogie-woogie pianists Meade Lux Lewis and Albert Ammons, he decided to record them. A session was arranged for 6 January 1939, and Blue Note Records was born.

The subsequent success of Blue Note Records is due both to its personnel and its attitude to its musicians. Within months of starting the label, Lion was joined by Frank Wolff, a boyhood friend and refugee from Germany who found work in New York as a photographer. It was Wolff who took many of the startling black and white photos that adorn Blue Note record covers. Together, these two men defined Blue Note, what it recorded and how they presented it. Looking back in 1969, Wolff recalled that, "Somehow we set a style, but I would have difficulty to define same. I remember though that people used to say, 'Alfred and Frank only record what they like'. That was true. If I may add three words, we tried to record jazz *with a feeling*." That feeling extended to paying rehearsal fees to the musicians, an almost unheard of occurrence, and making conditions right for the musicians to produce their best work. If a set was not right, it was not released, no matter how much it had cost. On one master disc, Lion once wrote: "This session would be okay for release, but it is just not up to Blue Note's standard."

That standard was largely set by Blue Note's recording engineer, Rudy Van Gelder, who joined the company in 1953. Working first from his home in Hackensack, New Jersey, and then from Englewood Cliffs, Van Gelder achieved the highest results, although always happy to say that "the Rudy Van Gelder sound is really the Alfred Lion sound", for Lion always knew exactly what he wanted from a musician and oversaw every stage of the recording and production process. Another important member of the Blue Note team was typographer Reid Miles, who for eleven years in the 1950s and 1960s was responsible for a stream of innovative and award-winning sleeves. With photographs by Wolff, designs by Miles, artwork by such as Andy Warhol, and notes by revered critics like Leonard Feather, Ira Gitler and Nat Hentoff, Blue Note record covers set the standard that all other labels failed to match.

None of this success would have been possible had Lion and Wolff had cloth ears. And those they most definitely did not have. Their first few recordings in 1939 and 1940 were of traditional and swing musicians, including a notable session with Sidney Bechet, who, with his soprano saxophone reading of Gershwin's *Summertime*, provided the label with its first commercial success. Lion was drafted in 1941 and the label went into abeyance for two years, although distribution continued through the good offices of Commodore Records. It resumed in November 1943 with recordings of small groups of swing soloists who were emerging from the economic death of the big bands.

But Wolff and Lion were aware of new developments in jazz, and in September 1946 they halted recordings as they came to terms with the emergent bebop music. Guided by saxophonist Ike Quebec, who would remain as friend, adviser and later artistic director until his death in 1963, Lion and Wolff started to record the new wave of bop musicians in late 1947. Bud Powell, Fats Navarro, Tadd Dameron and others all found a home on the record label, while Thelonius Monk, Art Blakey and more all recorded their first sets as leader for Blue Note. Monk in particular is important, for Lion and Wolff appreciated his music and stuck with him despite his apparent lack of commercial promise. If they believed in a musician, lack of sales did not cause either to lose faith.

Throughout the 1950s, Blue Note attracted an enviable group of musicians to its roster. Miles Davis, Sonny Rollins, Kenny Dorham, John Coltrane and Milt Jackson were all established names whose careers were given a considerable boost by being recorded for Blue Note. Most importantly, a session in late 1954 with pianist Horace Silver gave birth to the Jazz Messengers and a new sound in jazz, one which combined the language without the clichés of bop with the feelings of gospel and blues music. This style of jazz—defined as hard bop—was to become a major part of Blue Note's programme and quickly became identified as "Blue Note jazz". Yet they also found room for the soul jazz of people like organist Jimmy Smith, and managed to promote both styles as being faithful to the Blue Note sound.

The 1960s saw new developments, for Lion and Wolff were alive enough to the emerging avant-garde scene to record sessions from such uncompromising musicians as Eric Dolphy, Andrew Hill, Cecil Taylor and Ornette Coleman. But such risks were more than compensated for in 1964, when the label achieved commercial success with two records—Lee Morgan's *The Sidewinder* and Horace Silver's *Song For My Father*—that spent considerable time on the pop charts and were to usher in the popular fusion music of the late 1960s. Characteristically, the profits from both records were soon invested in new records by unknown artists. Blue Note also promoted the music of such Miles Davis alumni as Herbie Hancock and Wayne Shorter, who were exploring modal-based music as a way towards greater harmonic freedom. In time, this music became known as the "Blue Note school" and was the second style closely identified with the label.

The decades of constant work at the forefront of the record industry took their toll on both Lion and Wolff, and in 1966 they decided to sell the label to Liberty Records. Lion retired from full-time work due to ill-health the following year, and Wolff remained with the label the few years before his death in 1971. It was the end of an era, and although Blue Note continued for a few years, it was practically dormant by the mid-1970s.

Lion, however, was to participate in one final chapter of the label, for after various spasmodic reissue programmes, the label was revived in 1985 under the adoring eye of Bruce Lundvall, a jazz enthusiast and president of Manhattan Records, a division of EMI. A wealth of new recordings was planned alongside a comprehensive reissue programme, and the rebirth of the label was celebrated at a five-hour concert on 22 February 1985 at the New York Town Hall. Lion was guest of honour, witness to the revival of a label that had done so much to document modern jazz in all its variety after 1945. Alone of record labels, Blue Note can claim to have defined two styles of music as its own and to have introduced style into jazz itself. A new generation of jazz enthusiasts in the late 1980s is growing up identifying the Blue Note sound of the 1950s and 1960s as the best of modern jazz. That achievement would not have been possible without the midwifery of Alfred Lion.

Born Alfred Lion. **Emigration** Left Germany for the United States, 1938. **Career** Founded Blue Note recording company, January 1939; co-director, with photographer Francis Wolff, Blue Note recording company, October 1939–65; recorded established artists, as well as encouraging new young musicians, such as Thelonius Monk, Tadd Dameron and Art Blakey; sold label to Liberty Records, 1966; retired due to ill-health, 1967. **Awards and honours** Guest of honour, EMI's relaunch of Blue Note label, New York, 1985. **Cause of death** Undisclosed, at age 78.

ALISTAIR MacLEAN

Scottish Novelist

***Born* Glasgow, Scotland, 28 April 1922**

***Died* Munich, Germany, 2 February 1987**

Alistair MacLean was a simple man with simple tastes whose wartime experiences produced the backcloth against which he wove the intricate plots of his rattling good stories. He never had any pretensions about what he was doing. He pronounced himself a "storyteller" as opposed to a novelist, and told people firmly, "The day I start to satisfy readers of *The Times*, I'm finished."

He was born into a family strongly headed by a Calvinist clergyman who insisted that only Gaelic be spoken in the home. As most of MacLean's early years were spent in a remote village in

Inverness where his father was the minister, there were few opportunities for outside influences. Only when he was eight and beginning his education was English permitted. Being forced to read specified authors, such as Sir Walter Scott, John Buchan and Anthony Trollope, his written English developed well but the legacy of speaking Gaelic remained with him throughout life. His accent remained so strong that many found him difficult to understand.

After attending the Inverness Royal Academy and later, following the family's return to Glasgow, the Hillhead High School, MacLean joined the Royal Navy for five years of "extended and involuntary (war) service" which took him virtually around the world from the Arctic to the Far East and a good many places in between. After the war he returned to Scotland and gained his MA in English at Glasgow University, subsequently becoming a "chronically" impoverished teacher. It was this poverty that led him to writing at the age of 32.

In 1954 he entered a short story competition run by the *Glasgow Herald*. His submission was a sad and evocative tale about a fishing family in the West Highlands of Scotland. From 900 entries it was selected for the first prize of £100—not a fortune but a very useful supplement to a teacher's income in the days when a pair of top quality men's shoes cost only £5 or so.

The tear-jerking effect of this prize-winning tale was noticed by a young editor at the William Collins publishing house. He watched his wife reading it and the tears rolling down her cheeks. After reading it himself he sought out MacLean and spent several months trying to persuade him to write a novel. His efforts were rewarded with the production of *HMS Ulysses* which was published the following September and, within three months of publication, it had sold a staggering quarter of a million copies. As MacLean put it, "I had a go and the go went!" A frankly autobiographical account of his war service on convoys, it did not please the British Admiralty, nor the critics. The latter found it unskilled and slipshod. MacLean gave up reading the critics and collected the money. It always remained his favourite book.

Caution, however, made him hold on to his job. Fearing it had all been a flash in the pan, he waited until his second book, *The Guns of Navarone*, which was based on a period spent in the Aegean Sea came out two years later. It was equally successful and the die was cast. MacLean resigned his job and left Scotland for Geneva in Switzerland where he found the climate more acceptable and the tax system more congenial. His third book, *South by Java Head*, was submitted in 1958 and nearly rejected. Collins sent their editor to visit and tactfully suggest that he put it to one side for the time being. While the editor was *en route*, however, the film rights were snapped up! The tactful discussion was dropped and no more was said. Publication went ahead and the film was made in 1959, the same year as that of *The Guns of Navarone*.

MacLean turned out books at the steady rate of one per year until 1963 when he was in dispute with Collins. Disillusioned, he returned to Britain around the time *Ice Station Zebra* came out. He settled on Bodmin Moor in Cornwall, about as far as one can get from Scotland while remaining in the UK. He bought and ran a small chain of hotels but eventually gave it up as "a most undemanding pastime". During this period he wrote some secret service thrillers under the name of Ian Stuart. Stuart was, in fact, his middle name. They sold, but were nothing like as successful as his adventure stories, possibly because he had not personally experienced as much of their backgrounds as he had of the earlier books. Within three years he was back in Geneva working as MacLean once more.

He continued writing prolifically, turning out an annual stream of typical MacLean books, continuing with his formula of very visual, action-packed adventures in which the hero is plunged into danger from the word go and moves from one crisis to the next until the denouement. However, although some books contain an element of mystery, more often these are not stories of the whodunnit genre but more a matter of *how* the hero will overcome evil and good triumph. There is rapid movement, violence and a fair amount of alcohol, but no sex because that "holds up the action". The majority of critics agreed with Richard Schickel who wrote, "MacLean's ideas of characterization have always been primitive, his humour a trifle strained, his tendency to over-complicate somewhat distracting. But he has an uncanny compensatory gift for keeping plots boiling and the suspense building."

MacLean would undoubtedly agree. This was precisely what he aimed to do. His advice to others was: "Keep the action moving so fast that the reader never has time to stop and think, 'This is impossible'." And it was precisely these qualities that made his adventures so suitable for films. Sea, ice and land—the very elements themselves—emerge as the crucial factors in MacLean's repertoire. In fact, after he had been persuaded to write his own film script of *Where Eagles Dare* his books emerged even more like straight screenplays.

Marvellous as they are to watch, MacLean's stories were not always easy or comfortable for the actors involved in their filming. David Niven's memories of *The Guns of Navarone*, in which he starred with Gregory Peck, were pretty harsh. In his autobiography, *The Moon's a Balloon*, he recalled that it had involved nine months of physically very arduous work "culminating with five weeks in England in November simulating a storm at sea by working nine hours a day in a huge tank of filthy water". With three days' work on the $7 million epic remaining, Niven fell seriously ill with septicaemia—and this was in the days before very effective antibiotics were generally available. Eventually, against medical advice, he finished the vital sequences of actually blowing up the guns, and had a relapse for seven weeks.

MacLean's total sales, including translations into many European languages, have topped 200 million. Together with the vast sums he received for film rights, this made him one of the richest writers of all time. But his colossal wealth seems to have been more of an embarrassment than a joy, probably because of his frugal background in Scotland, and he never truly found the cause for which he was seeking. He never returned to his native country except, as he put it, "to carry a coffin" and he died, as he had lived so much of his life, away from his roots.

His books and the movies live on, and MacLean will long be turned to when people are looking for a first rate yarn.

Born Alistair Stuart MacLean. **Pseudonym** Ian Stuart. **Marriages** Two; second wife, Marcelle Georgeus, 1972 (deceased). **Children** Three sons, by first marriage. **Education** Inverness Royal Academy, Inverness, Scotland; Hillhead High School, Glasgow; Glasgow University, MA, 1953. **Emigration** Left UK for Geneva, Switzerland, 1958. **Military service** Torpedo man, Royal Navy, 1941–46. **Career** English teacher, Gallowflat Secondary School, near Glasgow, 1954; organizer, tourist boats to Arran Islands, briefly, 1954; became full-time writer, 1955. **Other activities** Hotelier, 1963–66; film producer, briefly, 1970s. **Awards and honours** Winner, short story competition, *Glasgow Herald*, 1954. **Publications** (all published in London and New York) *HMS Ulysses*, London, 1955, New York, 1956; *The Guns of Navarone*, 1957; *South by Java Head*, 1958; *The Last Frontier*, London, 1959, published as *The Secret Ways*, New York, 1959; *Night Without End*, 1960; *Fear Is the Key*, 1961; *The Golden Rendezvous*, 1962; *Ice Station Zebra*, 1963; *When Eight Bells Toll*, 1966; *Where Eagles Dare*, 1967; *Force 10 from Navarone*, 1968; *Puppet on a Chain*, 1969; *Caravan to Vaccares*, 1970; *Bear Island*, 1971; *The Way to Dusty Death*, 1973; *Breakheart Pass*, 1974; *Circus*, 1975; *The Golden Gate*, 1976; *Seawitch*, 1977; *Goodbye California*, London, 1977, New York, 1978; *Athabasca*, 1980; *River of Death*, 1980; *Partisans*, 1982; *Floodgate*, 1983; *San Andreas*, 1984; *The Lonely Sea* (short stories), 1985. **Novels as Ian Stuart** *The Snow on the Ben*, London, 1961; *The Dark Crusader*, London, 1961, published as *The Black Shrike*, New York, 1961; *The Satan Bug*, London, New York, 1962; *Death from Disclosure*, 1976; *Flood Tide*, London, 1977; *Sand Trap*, London, 1977; *Fatal Switch*, London, 1978; *A Weekend to Kill*, London, 1978. **Screenplays** *Where Eagles Dare*, 1968; (with Don Sharp and Paul Wheeler) *Puppet on a Chain*, 1970; *Caravan to Vaccares*, 1974; *Breakheart Pass*, 1975; *Hostage Power* (for television), 1980. **Other** *All About Lawrence* *of Arabia* (juvenile), London, 1962, published as *Lawrence of Arabia*, New York, 1962; *Captain Cook*, London and New York, 1972; *A Layman Looks at Cancer*. **Cause of death** Heart attack, at age 64.

EDNA MANLEY

Jamaican Sculptor

Born **Bournemouth, England, 29 February 1900**

Died **Kingston, Jamaica, 6 February 1987**

"Regardless"—what a strange name for a house. Edna Manley, Jamaica's national sculptor, chose it for the home that she made for herself and her family in Kingston after emigrating from England, her homeland. There must have been a reason for "regardless". Regardless of what? One answer might be that throughout her life Edna Manley determined her own fate, despite other people's more conventional ideas of what was good for her. She was, as we would say today, "very much her own woman", as is evident in her professional achievements as a sculptor and her personal life at the centre of Jamaican politics.

Edna Manley was born Edna Swithenbank in Bournemouth on the south coast of England, then—in 1900—still a Victorian watering hole where polite society could be observed dressing up in those endearingly prudish swimming costumes one now sees only on old postcards. But maybe Edna did not get to enjoy beach life much, for her father was a missionary in the Methodist Church who gave her a strictly religious upbringing. The Reverend Swithenbank, however, died when Edna was still a girl and she and her mother settled in Penzance at the southernmost tip of Cornwall, where Edna went to West Cornwall College. It was here, in 1914, that she met a first cousin, Norman Manley—a handsome young man who managed to impress her with more than his looks: he was interested in politics and seemed to know much more of the world than she did—after all, she was only 14. The two got on well, but Edna was more than a little worried when Norman went to war with the Royal Field Artillery, fearing for his safety. She was much relieved when he returned unscathed, winning a Military Medal for his courage. They agreed to keep in touch and Norman went off to Oxford to study.

In the meantime, Edna, young as she was, had also been doing her bit in the war effort, breaking in Canadian horses at the Army Remount Department at Wembley in London. She was an excellent horsewoman and this job gave her an opportunity to see more of the world than just the southern tip of England. It was no wonder, then, that as soon as the war was over, Edna announced that she was leaving home officially and moving to London to study art. This did not meet with approval from her mother, but it was clear that opposition would be futile. Edna began the life of a New Woman, living independently without the support of either family or husband. She took a job in the City and attended art classes in the evening at Regent Street Polytechnic and at St Martin's School of Art.

Beginning with clay models of animals, Edna Swithenbank soon discovered that she had more facility with wood, so woodcarving became her *métier*. These were exciting times in British sculpture, for a whole new generation of artists was about to emerge: Edna studied, for instance, with both Henry Moore and Barbara Hepworth. She found St Martin's an especially stimulating environment to work in, but three years of this arduous existence were enough; London was a big and lonely place, and studying while also doing a full-time job was hard work. When Norman Manley got his degree from Oxford, the old flame between the two cousins was rekindled. After a brief courtship they married in 1921; a year later the couple sailed for Jamaica to begin a new life there.

Edna Manley has come to be known as "Jamaica's national sculptor" not only because she helped foster Jamaican art, but also because the island was so inspirational to her work that it fuelled her artistic development. Here she found her materials and themes, and, ultimately, also an identification with the Jamaican people, which led her to proclaim that she was herself of Black ancestry (her mother was Jamaican). This statement, like the way she had left home as an adolescent, again brought her into conflict with relatives in Britain, but she now felt the bond with the West Indies to be so much stronger than that of her English origins that she carried on—regardless.

The first exhibition of Edna Manley's work in Kingston was a great success. She was attracted to what were then called Negro or native types, but what we would now describe as ethnic forms and traditions, which she carved in Jamaican hardwood. One such sculpture entitled "Eve" was a big hit at a London exhibition in 1930, where it attracted attention because of the vigour and simplicity of its form. Ironically the critics took Edna Manley to be part of the new modernist (European) vogue for sculptural minimalism, whereas she herself knew just how far removed her artistic roots were from the élitism of that movement. She was, nevertheless, elected to be a member of the London Group with whom she had other exhibitions in Britain.

During the 1930s Edna Manley pursued her passion for Jamaica and Jamaican subjects with works such as "Negro Aroused" (1935), which was bought for the Institute of Fine Arts in Kingston, "The Prophet", "Diggers" and "Pocomania", all woodcarvings, and "Woman with Basket", purchased by the Dublin Municipal Gallery of Modern Art, a carving in stone. In 1943 she made "Horse of the Morning" and "Moon", two of her best-known pieces. She began to edit *Focus*, a journal of Jamaican art and poetry especially geared towards the promotion of young artists and writers, and she founded the Jamaica School of Art in 1950. Like her sculpture, this was an enduring achievement and, in effect, a monument of thanks for the island's artistic gifts to her.

By the end of the 1930s the other part of Edna Manley's life, as the wife of a prominent politician, had come into sharper focus as economic depression led to political crisis on the island. Norman Manley, founder of the People's National Party, was a mediator in the conflict and became an increasingly central figure in Jamaican politics. When, in 1959, he became chief minister of Jamaica, Edna's life also was taken over by matters of state. For about a decade she did hardly any sculpture at all, turning instead to drawing and teaching. Still, her career as a sculptor was not at an end. At the age of 72 she was the proud witness to the election of one of her sons, Michael, as prime minister of Jamaica. His brother Douglas, a social scientist, served in the cabinet with him and Edna passionately supported them both. She also started work again, doing her last woodcarving, "Journey", in 1974 but then taking up clay and fibreglass modelling as a new departure. At the same time her work became more overtly political than ever before. "The Message", one such political piece, as its title indicates, is now permanently on exhibition in the Commonwealth Institute, London.

During the course of her long and fertile artistic lifetime, Edna Manley had exhibitions in Germany, Guyana, the United States, Puerto Rico, Canada, Cuba and Haiti, as well as in Jamaica and England, and in 1977 she received an honorary doctorate from the University of the West Indies. She was tall, elegant and slender in appearance and—apart from her love of horses—had shed all the affectations of being "an Englishwoman abroad" in the process of becoming a true Jamaican. Despite her three years of art classes in London, as a sculptor she must be regarded as largely self-taught since she only really developed as an artist after leaving

England. How then did she manage to achieve international renown as well as the rare integration of political, professional and personal life? Undoubtedly her answer would be just the one word—"regardless".

Born Edna Swithenbank. **Father** The Reverend H.G. Swithenbank. **Marriage** Norman Manley, a lawyer and politician, founder of the People's National Party, 1921 (died, 1969). **Children** Two sons, Michael and Douglas. **Education** West Cornwall College, England; Regent Street Polytechnic, London; St Martin's School of Art, London. **Emigration** Left England for Jamaica, 1922. **Career** Broke in Canadian horses, Army Remount Department, Wembley, London, World War I; worked in the City of London while studying art; first sculptures, clay models of animals; became full-time sculptor, particularly of works carved in wood; first exhibition, Kingston, Jamaica; first London exhibition, Coupil Gallery, 1930; member, London Group, 1930. **Related activities** Founder, editor, *Forum* magazine, 1943; founder, Jamaica School of Art, 1950. **Other activities** Politician's wife, on husband entering politics, 1938 onwards. **Awards and honours** Gold Musgrave Medal for contribution to the arts in Jamaica, 1943; honorary DLitt, University of the West Indies, 1977. **Exhibitions** London Group, Germany and Guyana; Jamaica, 1980; London, 1980; one-woman show: French Gallery, Coupil Gallery, 1930, Atlanta, USA, Canada, Puerto Rico, Cuba, Haiti, Jamaica. **Work in permanent collections** "Eve and Dance", Sheffield; "The Message", Commonwealth Institute, London. **Public statues** "Mary", Holy Cross Church; "Crucifix", All Saints Church; "Angel", Kingston Parish Church; "Paul Bogle", Court House, Morent Bay and George VI Park, Kingston. **Official purchases** "Negro Aroused", Institute of Fine Arts, Kingston, 1935; "Woman with Basket", Dublin Municipal Gallery of Modern Art; University College of the West Indies. **Other works** "The Prophet", 1935; "Diggers", 1935; "Pocomania", 1935; "Horse of the Morning", 1943; "Moon", 1943; "Journey", 1974. **Cause of death** Heart failure, at age 86.

E.D. NIXON

American Civil Rights Activist

***Born* Montgomery, Alabama, 12 July 1899**

***Died* Montgomery, Alabama, 25 February 1987**

The American Deep South was a backward country as far as race relations were concerned in the 1950s. For returning Black veterans from World War II, as well as the Korean War, it was a shock to find that after discharging their patriotic duty they were still treated no better than Blacks ever had been in the South: as second-class citizens, or worse. Their wives and girlfriends found it easier to get work than these men did, but it was often cheap, degrading work. And all lived under the threat of violence if racial discrimination was questioned or if the *de facto* segregation which existed between Black and White was defied.

E.D. Nixon—"Dr E.D." as he affectionately came to be known much later—grew up in this environment. He had met Rosa Parks when he was working with the National Association for the Advancement of Colored People (NAACP) in his native Montgomery in the early 1950s. When Mrs Parks, a seamstress at a local department store, decided one day after work to ride home in the front of the bus instead of moving to the back where Black people were supposed to sit, she sparked off a *cause célèbre* of the Southern Civil Rights Movement. The Montgomery bus boycott, led by the then relatively unknown Reverend Martin Luther King, was the first major protest to follow the 1954 Supreme Court ruling which declared segregated schools illegal. Mrs Parks, Dr King and others in the NAACP thought it was time this ruling extended to transport and all other areas of life in which segregation was still the practice. But while the names of the seamstress and preacher have firmly lodged themselves in the popular memory, it is much less widely known that Edgar Nixon had chosen both Parks and King for the roles they were to play in the making of civil rights history.

Nixon, like so many Black activists of his generation, began his career in public life as a Pullman porter on the train from Montgomery to Chicago. In the 1920s he joined the Brotherhood of Sleeping Car Porters, the first and most powerful union of Black workers which was headed by the famous A. Philip Randolph. Nixon was primarily active in the brotherhood, until in 1944 he was elected president of the Voters' League of Montgomery. At that time it was unusual and often dangerous for Black people to exercise their right to vote in many of the Southern states. Alabama was no exception, and Nixon organized a march to the courthouse in 1944 to demand the right for Blacks to vote without intimidation and without the blatantly discriminatory "qualifying tests" which required Blacks to demonstrate an understanding of the constitution not demanded of White voters.

The success of this protest has gone unrecorded, but ten years later Nixon was the first Black man to run for office in Montgomery County since the reconstruction, losing by a narrow margin to a fellow Democrat. It was then that he became active in the Montgomery Improvement Association, a local Black group of which Rosa Parks was also a member. When she told him one day that she had been thrown off a bus for travelling in the "White section", Nixon decided it was time to take action. "I told her if she was ever arrested in such an incident, call me. When they did arrest her, it was on one of the old Jim Crow segregationist laws," he said, "and I knew then that something could be done." He asked Dr King to lead an overall bus boycott in Montgomery. "Martin King was young and smart, and he had a wonderful speaking voice. I knew it would take somebody young and intelligent with leadership ability," Nixon later commented. Because of Nixon's confidence and good judgement of character, Martin Luther King was effectively launched as *the* leader of the Southern Civil Rights Movement in 1955.

Meanwhile, E.D. himself continued working as a railroad porter, although he also remained active in the NAACP throughout the turbulent times of lunch counter sit-ins, freedom rides, protest marches, voter registration drives and the later race-riots in Northern cities. Only after he retired from Pullman's did Nixon begin to make full use of his administrative skills and organizational experience, when he became director of a local housing project. For this, and all his other work in rendering services to the Black community, he was awarded an honorary doctorate from Alabama University and presented with the NAACP Walter White Award in 1985. Four years earlier he had achieved the distinction of having his house at 647 Clinton Street, Montgomery, where he had lived all his life, put on the Alabama Register of Historic Buildings.

E.D. Nixon, a veritable son of Montgomery, Alabama, devoted his life to the mammoth task of making the American South a better place for Black people to live. His less public, but no less effective contribution to racial equality will long be remembered with admiration and warmth.

Born Edgar Daniel Nixon. **Marriage** Arlet Campbell. **Children** One son, Edgar. **Career** Railroad porter and civil rights activist, 1920s onwards. **Related activities** Joint-organizer, the Brotherhood of Sleeping Car Porters, 1920s; president, Voters' League of Montgomery, 1944; worked with National Association for the Advancement of Colored People, president, 1948–49; stood for county executive committee of Democratic Party, Montgomery County, 1954; organizer, Montgomery Bus Boycott, 1955; active in Montgomery Improvement Association,

1955–56; creator, director, Montgomery Housing Authority on retirement; pension security, 1977; vice-president, OIC; vice-president, Alabama Civil Rights Commission; vice-president, Committee on Ageing. **Awards and honours** Home placed on Alabama Register of Landmarks and Heritage by state historical commission, 1981; Walter White Award, National Association for the Advancement of Colored People, New York, 1985; Award for Outstanding Service, State of Alabama; Award for Outstanding Service of Youngstown; honorary doctorate, Alabama State University; also received 75 certificates and 21 plaques. **Cause of death** Heart failure, at age 87.

NOEL ODELL

British Geologist and Mountaineer

***Born* Brighton, Sussex, 25 December 1890**

***Died* Cambridge, England, 21 February 1987**

Though born a flatlander, the mountains were never far from Professor N.E. Odell—rarely physically and certainly never in heart.

Even at the age of 93, in 1984, he was observed at the Britannia Hut in Switzerland, which he had reached by cable car and a half-mile glacier crossing. While his own formal education in geology took place in the level campuses of Brighton College, the Imperial College of Science and Technology and Clare College, Cambridge, his practical application of that knowledge included experiences in mountain ranges on several continents—the most notable of which was his participation in the expedition to conquer Everest in 1924.

During that expedition, Odell served as a principal in the assault parties, and led searches for the bodies of Mallory and Irvine, who had been lost on their summit attempt. In two lone attempts he climbed to 27,500 feet without oxygen; a third took him to 25,000, unassisted. Upon his return from the expedition (by then a public hero for his tremendous efforts), he was granted a private audience with King George V at Buckingham Palace.

Odell returned to Everest in 1938 for another attempt on the world's highest summit, but inclement weather prevented the expedition from succeeding. In part, that was due to the philosophy of its leaders, H.W. Tilman and Eric Shipman, who argued that small, lightly equipped parties stood a better chance in Himalayan exploration.

Odell had been asked to participate in the 1938 attempt by Tilman, whom he accompanied on a 1936 effort that reached the previously unscaled 25,645-foot summit of Nanda Devi in the Uttar province of India. The altitude record the duo set by climbing that mountain stood for 14 years as the highest peak reached by man.

Though his fame came from adventures in the world's alpine regions, Odell was also a man of the lecture hall and laboratory. He held various lecturing assignments around the world, in such disparate places as New Zealand, Pakistan, Scandinavia and Canada.

Commercial exploration also formed part of his career, with geological surveys in Labrador, Greenland, Alaska and the Yukon, and assignments for the Anglo Persian Oil Company in his early years. He served twice in the British Army: during World War I (1915–19) with the Royal Engineers, when he was wounded three times, and during World War II (1940–42) as a major with the Bengal Sappers and Miners of the British and Indian armies.

Known for his modesty, despite the hero worship that hundreds of aspiring young climbers must have directed towards him, Odell was highly regarded in climbing associations around the world, holding membership to clubs in Canada, New Zealand, South Africa, the United States, Switzerland, Norway and Japan. The Royal Scottish Geographical Society's Livingstone Gold Medal was one of several distinctions he had received for his mountaineering.

Vigorous and active until the end, he has been described as the "lean, clear-eyed, keen-minded elder statesman among climbers" whose "earnest enthusiasm...carried him to record heights on the Earth's surface".

Born Noel Ewart Odell. **Parents** Reverend R.W. and M.M. (Ewart) Odell. **Marriage** Gwladys Jones, 1917 (died, 1977). **Children** One son. **Education** Brighton College, Sussex; Imperial College of Science and Technology, London; Clare College, Cambridge University, PhD. **Military service** Royal Engineers, 1915–19; major, Bengal Sappers and Miners, British and Indian armies, 1942–47. **Career** Geologist and mountaineer; geologist, Anglo Persian Oil Company, Limited, 1922–25; consulting geologist and mining engineer, Canada, 1927–30; university lecturer in geology, and tutor, Harvard University, 1928–30; research student and university lecturer, Cambridge University, 1931–40, fellow commoner and supervisor of studies, Clare College; lecturer, McGill University, 1948–49; professor, University of Otago, New Zealand, head of department, 1950–56; professor, Peshawar University, Pakistan, 1960–62. **Related activities** Staff lecturer, Council for Adult Education in Forces, 1942–47; British Council lecturer: Scandinavian universities, 1946, 1959, Swiss universities, 1947; visiting professor, University of British Columbia, 1948–49. **Other activities** Expeditions: geologist, Oxford University to Spitsbergen, 1921; geologist, leader, Merton College, Arctic, 1923; geologist, Mount Everest, 1924 (to 27,500 feet without oxygen, search for Mallory and Irvine); Norway, 1929; British Columbia, 1930; Nanda Devi, 1936 (to 26,640 feet); Mount Everest, 1938 (to 25,000 feet); geological exploration: northern Labrador, 1931, northeast Greenland, 1933, Lloyd George Mountains, Rockies, 1947, Saint Elias Mountains, Yukon, Alaska, 1949, 1977. **Offices and memberships** Associate, Royal School of Mines; member, Institution of Mining and Metallurgy; fellow: Geological Society, Royal Society of Edinburgh, Geographical Society, Alpine Club, Arctic Institute of North America; president, Arctic Club. **Awards and honours** Leverhulme Fellowship, 1934, 1938; Livingston Gold Medal, Royal Scottish Geographical Society, 1944; honorary fellow, Clare College, Cambridge University, 1983. **Publications** (contributor) Norton, *The Fight for Everest*, 1925; (contributor) H.W. Tilman, *Everest*, 1938; also made contributions to many journals. **Cause of death** Undisclosed, at age 96.

ANNY ONDRA

Czech Actress

Born **Tarnov, Poland (then Czechoslovakia), 15 May 1903**

Died **Hamburg, West Germany, 28 February 1987**

Anny Ondra was best known to English-speaking audiences through her appearances in *Blackmail*, Alfred Hitchcock's first sound film, and in his lesser known silent film *The Manxman*, both in 1929. She was, however, very popular all over Europe, especially for her light comedy roles in Czech and German films during the 1920s and 1930s. Her career was greatly advanced by her first husband and partner in Ondra-Lamač Films, Karel Lamač, a Czech actor and director.

Having made appearances in two British silent films in 1928, Ondra then worked with Hitchcock, playing Kate, an innkeeper's daughter, in *The Manxman*, a film about conflicts between love and duty, taken from the popular novel by Hall Caine and set in the Isle of Man, off the west coast of England. Hitchcock himself later told French director François Truffaut: "the only point of interest about that movie is that it was my last silent one...it was a very banal picture."

Although the film has been given little attention by critics, it is rich in imagery, psychologically convincing and admired by such eminent directors as Eric Rohmer and Claude Chabrol. Anny Ondra as Kate is loved by two men, fisherman Pete, played by Carl Brisson, and lawyer Phillip, played by Malcolm Keen. Despite loving Phillip, Kate finds herself pledged to Pete, mainly because he confides his feelings first. Pete at one point is presumed dead, releasing Kate and Phillip to become lovers, but Pete unexpectedly reappears and he and Kate marry. Kate subsequently gives birth to a daughter, who is, in fact, Phillip's child. Under great strain, Kate leaves Pete and tries to commit suicide, whereupon she is brought before Phillip, now a judge. The film ends with Kate and Phillip leaving together in spite of public disapproval and the collapse of Phillip's career as a judge. Of Anny Ondra's performance, Maurice Yacowar, in his book *Hitchcock's British Films*, commented:

> Miss Ondra may at first seem too shallow to be called the prototype of the cool blonde Hitchcock heroine that was to follow—the volcanic glaciers of Ingrid Bergman, Eva Marie Saint and Grace Kelly—but she earns the title in the scene where Phillip first sees her after the news of Pete's supposed death has arrived. She stands deep in the centre background of the shot, a mass of shadowy inn patrons around her. Upon Phillip's arrival she wheels around with a surprising, glowing and intense, "Phillip—we're free".

In his next film, *Blackmail*, another film about love and duty, Hitchcock cast Ondra as Alice White, girlfriend of detective Frank Webber. The pair have a row, after which Alice meets a charming artist who tries to seduce her. Terrified of rape, she stabs and kills him and Frank is put on the case. A blackmailer, who knows of Alice's involvement in the murder, becomes prime suspect himself and when he meets his death in a police hunt, the case seems closed. Alice wants to confess but Frank persuades her to keep quiet, putting his personal relationship with her before his duty as a policeman. This was Britain's first sound film and acclaimed as a masterpiece, full of Hitchcock's sense of irony and attention to detail. Initially, only the last reel was to have been in sound but Hitchcock claimed that he filmed all of it with the possibility of "a talkie" in mind. The use of sound posed problems for Anny Ondra who spoke limited English with a strong accent. She mouthed the lines and actress Joan Barry, just off camera, supplied the voice. Interestingly, as Maurice Yacowar states, "The film is not just *in* sound, it is *about* sound." Misunderstandings of what people say abound and real feelings are not spoken. In a memorable scene too, a breakfast-time conversation centres around the repeated word "knife", leaving the haunted Anny Ondra as Alice almost unable to lift the breadknife.

After her two Hitchcock films, Ondra returned to Germany. With the advent of sound, she returned to acting in Czech and German films in the two languages she spoke fluently and by this time she was receiving many offers of work.

Anny Sofia Ondráková was born to Czech parents in Tarnov, then in Czechoslovakia and now part of Poland, where her father was an army officer in the Austro-Hungarian Army. She gained early experience by acting in amateur shows and as a child actress in films by Czech producer/director Gustav Machaty. She studied drama in Prague, making her début as a dancer at the age of 16, as an actress in Wedekind's *Pandora's Box*, and as an adult film actress in *Dáma s malou nožkou* (Woman with Small Feet), directed by J.S. Kolar, all in 1919.

Her first film with Karel Lamač, *Gilly y Praze* was in 1920 and they married the same year. He helped establish her as a star and in 1930 they formed their joint film company in Berlin, which made more than 20, often "escapist" films, some of them bi-lingual co-productions with Czech or French film-makers, such as *Die vertauschte Braut* (The Substitute Bride, 1934) directed by René Lefèvre.

Although Anny Ondra often appeared in conventional roles of girls abandoned or unhappy in love, she was, as Lamač realized, at her best in comedy, as can be seen in films such as *Chytte ho* (1924). She was one of the first female comics of Czech films and had an influence on the development of comedy films both at home and internationally. As one critic observed, in her comedies she often played "a courageous girl, a little coquettish, a little naïve, who nevertheless manages to resolve intricate situations with humour. Her funniness is based on simplicity rather than on absurd situations."

Ondra and Lamač divorced amid great publicity in 1933 and that same year she married German heavyweight boxing champion, Max Schmeling, a union that lasted until her death at the age of 83. Schmeling appeared in two of her films, including *Knockout* (1935). Her professional association with Lamač continued, however, until 1939, when he was forced to flee Nazi Germany. They had made over 70 films together. After his departure she made only a few more, two of which were made in the early 1940s, but she did not appear in Nazi propaganda pictures. She made *Schön muss man sein* (You Have to Be Beautiful) in 1951, playing opposite Willi Fritsch, and her last film appearance was in 1957.

During the war, she and her husband lost the money they had made and thereafter lived modestly in a suburb of Hamburg, where Schmeling worked as a representative for the Coca-Cola Company.

Anny Ondra has been described both as "Buster Keaton in skirts" and as "a Czech porcelain doll" by film historians. She was a versatile performer, appearing also in comic operas and in dancing and musical films, and audiences all over Europe loved her for her charm and comic talent.

Born Anny Sofia Ondráková. **Marriages** 1) Karel Lamač, film director and actor (divorced, 1933); 2) Max Schmeling, boxer, 1933. **Career** Film actress, 1919–57; initially on the stage in Czechoslovakia and Germany; film début, 1919; films mostly directed by husband, Karl Lamač, with writer Vaclav Wasserman and cameraman Otto Heller in Czechoslovakia and Germany, apart from brief period in UK when she appeared in films directed by Alfred Hitchcock, 1929; co-founder, with Lamač, Ondra-Lamač production company. **Films** *Dáma s malou nožkou* (Woman with Small Feet), 1919; *Nikyho velebne dobrodružtvi*, 1919; *Zpěv zlata* (Song of Gold), 1920; *Dráteniček*, 1920; *Gilly y Praze*, 1920; *Setřelé pismo*, 1920; *Tam na horách*, 1920; *Outrávene světlo*, 1921; *Přchozi z temnot*, 1921; *Zigeunerliebe*, 1922; *Drvoštěp*, 1922; *Muž bez srdce*, 1923; *Tu ten kamen* (Tutankamen), 1923; *Unos bankéré Fuxe*, 1923; *Bilý Raj*, 1924; *Hřichy v manzelstvi*, 1924; *Chytte ho*, 1924; *Ich liebe dich*, 1925; *Do panskeho stavu*, 1925; *Hrabenka z Podskali*, 1925; *Karel Havlíčiek Borovský*, 1925; *Lucenrna*, 1925; *Sest Mušketýru*, 1925; *Vdavsky Nanynky Kulichovy*, 1925; *Aničko vrat se!*, 1926; *Trude, die Sechzehnjährige*, 1926; *Pantáta Bezoušek*, 1926; *Die Pratermizzi*, 1926; *Velbound uchem jehly*, 1926; *Kvet Sumavy*, 1927; *Milenky starého kriminálnika*, 1927; *Sladká Josefinka*, 1927; *Der erste Kuss*, 1928; *God's Clay*, 1928; *Der Eviny Evas Töchter*, 1928; *Saxaphon Susi*, 1928; *Blackmail*, 1929; *Glorious Youth* (*Eileen of the Trees*), 1929; *The Manxman*, 1929; *Das Mädel aus USA*, 1930; *Die grosse Sehnsucht*, 1930; *Eine Freundin so goldig wie du*, 1930; *Die von Rummelplatz*, 1930; *Die Fledermaus*, 1931; *Mamsell Nitouche*, 1931; *Er und seine Schwester*, 1931; *Baby*, 1932; *Kiki*, 1932;

Eine Nacht in Pardise, 1932; *Kanton Ideal*, 1932; *Die Grausame Freundin*, 1932; *Die Tochter des Regiments*, 1933; *Fraulein Hoffmanns Erzahlungen*, 1933; *Das verliebte Hotel*, 1933; *Klein Dorrit*, 1934; *Polenblut* (*Polska Krev*), 1934; *Die vertauschte Braut*, 1934; *Knockout*, 1935; *Der junge Graf*, 1935; *Grossreinemachen*, 1935; *Ein Mádel vom Ballett*, 1936; *Donogoo Tonka*, 1936; *Flitterwochen*, 1936; *Der Unwiderstehliche* (*The Irresistible Man*), 1937; *Vor Liebe wird gewarnt*, 1937; *Narren im Schnee*, 1938; *Der Gasmann*, 1941; *Himmel, wir erben ein Schloss*, 1943; *Schön muss man sein*, 1951; *Zürcher Verlobung*, 1957. **Cause of death** Stroke, at age 84. **Further reading** Maurice Yacowar, *Hitchcock's British Films*, Archon Books, 1977; ed. Ann Lloyd, *Movies of the Silent Years*, Orbis, 1984.

JANET QUIGLEY

British Radio Producer

Born **Belfast, Northern Ireland, 10 May 1902**

Died **7 February 1987**

Janet Quigley, an able, imaginative and strong-minded woman, was a pioneer in the field of radio broadcasting for women. She obtained a degree in English at Oxford University and after some years in publishing she joined the BBC in 1930.

During World War II she made her reputation producing programmes, mainly for women, on radio. *Women at War*, for example, first produced in 1941, discussed topics which were of concern to women in an honest and realistic way, rather than the euphemistic terms which had been used hitherto. The success of this programme, intended for women in the services, led to another for women at home—*The Kitchen Front*.

Quigley proved herself to be very aware of and sensitive to the new role being played by women during the war. At the time there were over 200,000 women in the forces and factories, about the same number in the Women's Land Army, and some 48 per cent of the workers in the civil service were women. Yet most of the war propaganda and war-effort slogans were masculine in tone and assumed that most women were still housewives and mainly concerned with domestic problems. Quigley's programmes did much to restore the balance. She was awarded an MBE for this work in 1944, but left the BBC in 1945 on her marriage to Kevin Fitzgerald, the Irish writer.

Returning to radio in 1950, she was appointed editor of *Woman's Hour*, a programme which had only had a woman editor for the three previous years. The work that had already begun in broadening the programme's scope was greatly accelerated by Janet Quigley. At this time the BBC was rather a prim institution and very much male dominated. A discussion of the menopause, for example, met with masculine howls of outrage. In spite of that, Quigley was determined that no topic should be considered outside the reach of her programme. "It is our duty to bring hush-hush topics into the open; no subject which concerns our listeners need be taboo," she memoed her department. Cruelty to children, marriage and divorce, spinsterhood and homosexuality were all discussed on her programmes, which horrified some men listeners and even some of her male colleagues. Undaunted, she continued to widen the scope of the programme, introducing discussions and reports on international affairs.

At that time the BBC was facing criticism that the Light Programme, as Radio 1 was then called, was consistently "too highbrow". There was also concern that the light entertainment broadcast by the new Radio Luxembourg—"our enemy across the Channel"—was winning away listeners. Kenneth Adam, the controller of the Light Programme, was consistently trying to make programmes more popular and searching for a "new look". By the end of 1950 he was trying to persuade Janet Quigley to reduce the length of *Woman's Hour* from 60 to 45 minutes. She held her ground, pointing out that all the evidence from listeners suggested that "far from wanting less...they wanted more". She won the battle. However, she did change the style of the programme, introducing more short features and varying the format considerably. As a result, she was praised in the press and thus preserved the programme in the way she wanted it. The *Star* called it "excellent", while the *People* wrote that the changes she had made "have all meant brighter down-to-business programmes for housewives". The recipe of making the listeners "laugh, cry and think was a very successful one", and one that continues to this day. Indeed, it is widely rumoured that *Woman's Hour* boasts as many male listeners as female.

Janet Quigley was in the vanguard of women in British broadcasting, and was the first woman to have her own team of editors. In 1956 she was appointed chief assistant of talks on BBC Radio, a position she retained until her retirement in 1962.

Born Jane Muriel Alexander Quigley. **Marriage** Kevin Fitzgerald, a writer, 1945. **Education** Studied English, Oxford University. **Career** Worked in publishing; BBC Radio producer of such programmes as *Women at War* and *The Kitchen Front*, 1930–45; editor, *Woman's Hour*, 1950–56; chief assistant of talks, 1956–62. **Awards and honours** Member, Order of the British Empire, 1944. **Cause of death** Undisclosed, at age 84.

FYFE ROBERTSON

British Journalist and Television Personality

Born **Edinburgh, Scotland, 19 August 1902**

Died **Sussex, England, 4 February 1987**

Fyfe Robertson was one of those unique men who could never be forgotten by those privileged to see and to hear him at work. Robbie, as he came to be known, was the son of a Scottish miner who had pulled himself out of the working class by becoming a minister in the Church of Scotland so Robertson and his five siblings were reared in the manse. As he said, "It was a case of high thinking but low living." This background had a profound effect on his career. He was unfailingly courteous and fair, yet utterly determined to root out injustice and elicit truth. Fear of slipping back into the insecurity his father had escaped never left him and it seemed almost inevitable that, having studied medicine for two years, he should move to journalism.

He came up the hard way, beginning with newspapers in Scotland and then moving to Fleet Street in London, the traditional home of the British national press. He worked on the *Sunday Express* and *Daily Express*, both very popular newspapers although not, at that time, tabloids. He was 39 when he joined Hulton's famous *Picture Post* in 1943.

Picture Post was a weekly magazine specializing in first-rate reporting accompanied by excellence in photo-journalism. It began shortly before World War II and gave the public a vital sense of the events of the next decade far more strongly than the, sometimes, rather bland newsreels to be seen in the cinema. Robbie was a strong member of the *Picture Post* team, which included such respected and renowned colleagues as Trevor Philpott, James Cameron, Kenneth Allsop and Macdonald Hastings.

Robertson spent 13 years with the magazine, during which he saw himself as the "serious cove, trying to turn scientific gobbledegook into King's English". Philpott described him as "an investigator, his curiosity natural and tireless. His skill with words was extraordinary and at times lyrical." One of Robertson's memorable contributions was an attack on the composition of bread in the UK. He commenced with a (then) shocking parody of the Lord's Prayer. Spread across two pages it read, "Give us this day our daily nitrogen tricholoride, chalk, bensyl chloride, potassium bromate...whilst removing 20–30 per cent of the valuable parts of wheat so that it can be fed to pigs...and ...sold back to us...prescribed to meet dietary deficencies."

Another was a national scandal: an exposé of Britain's groundnut scheme in Tanganyika. This was an ambitious development programme backed by the socialist government which failed dismally and was abandoned. Philpott described this story as a "finely-detailed revelation of blunder, waste, concealment, exploitation, bureaucratic cowardice and ministerial duplicity". Although believing in the value of the scheme, Robertson's sense of honesty led him to make the shambles public knowledge, despite paying a high price personally in loss of faith in the honesty of the government and its servants who, added Philpott, "had been careless with the truth and the people's money".

Robbie could, however, be pragmatic. Two years later Hulton refused to publish an article on atrocities in South Korea which had been filed by James Cameron. As representative for the *Picture Post* branch of the National Union of Journalists, he was forced to consider resignation. The union ruled that this was a matter of individual conscience. Three resigned, including Cameron, but the remainder, including Robbie, put family responsibilities first. They stayed.

Picture Post did not survive well once periodical publishing began booming in the 1950s. Its stark black and white images were no longer wanted by the public, and although it essayed colour it was now in competition with television. Once the commercial channel was under transmission, its days were numbered. It folded in 1956, leaving a remarkable team redundant. Robbie was then 52, of an age, he said, "when most men would be thinking about clipping hedges [but] I've never been much of a hedge clipper". At BBC Television a group of innovative producers were considering a new programme to fill the time slot between 6 and 7 p.m., previously known as the *Toddlers' Truce*. Independent Television was giving clear signals that it would not keep an empty channel after the first full year, so the BBC staff were looking for ways to compete.

The BBC riposted with *Tonight*, a 45-minute topical magazine programme hosted by Cliff Michelmore and Derek Hart. For its time it was truly adventurous, designed to be the voice of people rather than authority, asking questions ordinary people would ask themselves if they could. Over the years it shaped public opinion which, in turn, reshaped the programme and its content. For Robertson and his colleagues this was a vital new career opportunity even though, at the time, he saw it as a retirement job.

Michelmore, in his autobiography, *Two-Way Story*, written jointly with his wife, Jean Metcalfe, says, "When Robbie joined us he was a worrier. He worried only because he was such a perfectionist. His journalist training and practice...had taught him that no detail was unimportant when getting the background to a story." He wrote "concisely, accurately and with concern for his subject and for people".

Tonight and a companion late-night programme, *24 Hours*, ran for eight years, during which time Robertson filed over 750 documentary film reports. Those who saw *Tonight* will never forget the pleasure brought by the announcement of "Robbie". Across the black and white screen would walk the tall, lean, elegantly dressed Scot, complete with seamed features and deerstalker hat, and the slow, measured Edinburgh voice would begin the report. He said that he felt his appeal for the middle-aged and elderly lay in his clear slow speech with the "highly individual probing cadence" as he once had heard his accent described. But his appeal was ageless and universal.

Although perfectionist the most notable thing about his work for *Tonight* was the transformation from "serious cove" to "the old character who got sent to do funny stories about things he knew absolutely nothing about"!

When *Tonight* ended Robbie was 61 but still not ready for hedge-clipping. He made a number of serious documentaries on topics such as *The Trade in Animals*, *Why Zoos?* and *What Happened to Pity?* This last was an examination of the after-effects of the Aberfan Disaster in which a school full of pupils was engulfed by the slide of a mining waste tip in South Wales. Later still he produced a series of his own called simply *Robbie* in which he looked back over his life. His final television appearance came only a few weeks before his death—a tribute to his old colleague, Michelmore.

Robertson stands as one of the greats in journalism. Although his real fame came from his light-hearted work, Robbie himself would not regret it. He always counted himself fortunate to have had the opportunity of working in television and greatly enjoyed it. And perhaps the most important thing to remember is that television was very fortunate to gain journalists of his calibre at that time. He set standards that are still being followed.

Born James Fyfe Robertson. **Father** Church of Scotland minister. **Marriages** 1) Betty, 1928 (died, 1973); 2) Vera Ford, 1978. **Children** Two daughters, Elizabeth and Grace, from first marriage. **Career** Reporter and feature writer on various newspapers, including *Glasgow Herald*, *Sunday Express*, *Daily Express* and, most particularly, *Picture Post*, 1943–57; on closure of *Picture Post*, moved into television as reporter/presenter of BBC TV's *Tonight* programme, 1957; subsequently became national figure, making over 750 documentary reports for *Tonight* and *24 Hours*; later made own series, including *Robbie*, 1978, and *Robbie in Ripe Old Age*; last TV appearances were on *40 Minutes*, 1985, and a special edition of *This Is Your Life*, 1986. **Offices and memberships** Father of Chapel, National Union of Journalists, *Picture Post*. **Cause of death** Undisclosed, at age 84.

CARL ROGERS

American Psychologist

***Born* Oak Park, Illinois, 8 January 1902**

***Died* La Jolla, California, 4 February 1987**

Client: "I feel so angry with my mother, sometimes I think I want to kill her." Therapist: "I think I hear you say that you have a lot of anger towards your mother, a quite murderous anger. Is that right?" Client: "That's right."

The above exchange can be read as a caricature of Carl Rogers' life's work: client-centred therapy. Other than in conventional psychiatry or psychoanalytic practice, the therapist does not guide or "direct" patients so much as reflect back their thoughts and emotions in order to make them available for conscious introspection. This "invention" of Rogers' has been of enormous influence in post-war psychotherapy and counselling. Not only was Rogers, in a sense, responsible for the proliferation of group-therapies and the widespread use of counselling techniques in industrial and educational settings, but he can also be seen as the instigator of the self-help/personal growth industry that brought us psycho-babble and socio-speak. This proved to be a growth industry indeed, especially when, after the turmoil of the 1960s self-reflection, or the "culture of narcissism" as Christopher Lasch called it, it became a national vogue flourishing particularly well in Rogers' home soil of California. But if this conjures up pictures of decadent beachlife combined with the self-indulgence of perpetual therapy by way of ego-massage, then we have the wrong impression. Rogers' aims, in part developed from his own experience, were quite different.

He was born the fourth of six children and raised in an affectionate but very strict religious atmosphere, where hard work counted for everything. Like the stereotype of a budding intellectual, he was a solitary child who spent most of his time reading, developing an outside interest only in night-flying and silkworm moths, which he bred in captivity. When Rogers was 12 years old, his father bought a farm and experimented with scientific agriculture, an interest which young Carl adopted also. Upon entering the University of Wisconsin he was intending to study agriculture, but after an intense religious experience he decided to switch to theology and become a Protestant minister. Then a trip to China in 1922 with the World Student Christian Federation put paid to this ambition also. "I was forced to stretch my thinking, to realize that sincere and honest people could believe in very divergent religious doctrines. In major ways I, for the first time, emancipated myself from the religious thinking of my parents and realized that I could not go along with them." Carl Rogers decided to study psychology instead: "improvement of life for individuals would probably always interest me, but I could not work in a field where I would be required to believe in some specified religious doctrine", he recalled in *This Is Me*, an autobiographical essay of 1961.

In 1923 Rogers thus embarked on what was to become a long and distinguished career. He began in child guidance, where he increasingly came to profile himself as a clinical psychologist. His PhD thesis, *Measuring Personality Adjustment in Children*, was published in 1931. In the previous year he had been offered the directorship of the child study department of the Society for the Prevention of Cruelty to Children in Rochester, where he stayed for a decade. It is interesting to note that because psychology was then equated with experimental psychology and laboratory rats, Rogers' lectures at Rochester were initially listed under the headings of sociology and education, while he himself was more inclined to describe his approach as "guidance", meaning some form of social work. Through his work with underprivileged and delinquent children, Rogers discovered that an authoritarian, disciplinarian attitude does not bring about personal change.

From "guidance" to psychotherapy was but a short step, and in 1940 Rogers was appointed professor in clinical psychology at the University of Ohio. Here he did his most innovative work, ironically now almost doing away with any notion of "guidance" altogether and putting "client-centredness" in its place. He set out the principles of his theory in a controversial paper, "Newer Concepts in Psychotherapy", later published in his seminal book *Counselling and Psychotherapy* (1942). The latter, together with *Client-Centred Therapy: Its Practice, Implications and Theory* (1951), were the foundation of a whole new therapeutic movement, whose main characteristics were that it "emancipated" the patient (now "client"), took an optimistic view of human potential and based the process of change not on teaching or directiveness but on self-motivation in a positive, affirming environment. Crucial in this approach was the changed relation between the parties: doctor and patient became therapist and client who faced each other person-to-person on the assumption that clients know what is best for them and the therapist need only act as a facilitator in a natural process—"personal growth" or "self-actualization" in Rogerian terms. The therapist, Rogers stipulated, needs to work with empathy, genuineness and caring, and must not impose *any* demand of his/her own. Clients, on their part, he believed, had an innate capacity to achieve a full human existence and it was only *other* people's inappropriate demands that stunted their development; with emphatic listening, growth could be re-stimulated in its natural direction.

Reasonable, even commonplace as these ideas may seem now, they were hotly debated in the 1950s. A post-Freudian colleague of Rogers' was scathing when he said dismissively: "Rogers' method is unsystematic, undisciplined and humanistic. Rogers doesn't analyse and doesn't diagnose. We have no common ground."

Meanwhile, Carl Rogers had lived through the war years and served as a psychological consultant to the US Air Force, which resulted in another book, *Counselling with Returned Servicemen* (1946), setting out techniques for helping ex-soldiers re-adapt to civilian life. In 1945 he became professor of psychology at the University of Chicago, staying until 1957, when he moved on to Wisconsin and from there in 1963 to La Jolla, California, to remain there for the rest of his life. La Jolla offered him a resident fellowship at the Center for Studies of the Person, which he held from 1968 until the time of his death. Several more books were written there, among them *Carl Rogers on Encounter Groups*, which became yet another classic of post-war humanist psychology.

Encounter groups were also an innovation of Rogers'. They consist of six to ten members plus a counsellor, and participants are encouraged to express their immediate feelings about themselves and each other in order to "check against reality" the psychological blockages that people set up in their perception of the outside world as a defence of the personality. Breaking down these blockages will, according to Rogers, make growth possible and bring about permanent change, without the need to delve deep into the person's past, as in psychoanalysis.

Criticism of Rogers' work has centred on two aspects: first of all, its client-centredness, which can lead to extremes of therapeutic passivity and banality (see the opening paragraph of this essay) to the point of stagnation, and secondly the limited applicaton of Rogerian psychotherapy which is really only appropriate to the treatment of neurotics and of personal behaviours which are within the range of the normal. Psychotics and people who suffer from a mental illness have very little to gain by client-centred therapy, since they are too sick to direct their own healing process. It would be fair to say then that Rogers' client-centred therapy and encounter groups truly belong to the realm of psychology, not psychiatry, where there is by definition less cause for optimism in the possibility of change which is so characteristic of Rogers' conception of the human personality.

This leads us to wonder what Carl Rogers himself was like as a person. It is tempting to speculate that many of his theories in fact derived from his personal development, travelling an enormous distance from a strict religious upbringing centred on the Protestant work ethic to the sensual pleasures of life on California's west coast. For, despite his illustrious academic career, Carl Rogers did find time to establish a personal life with a wife and two children. In 1928 he had married an artist, Helen Martha Elliott, with whom he liked to spend long vacations in isolated spots in Mexico and the Caribbean. There they would both get on with their painting, while Rogers also enjoyed swimming, snorkelling and photography. The holidays proved he had learned his own lessons well. "In these spots," he wrote, "where no more than two to four hours a day goes for professional work, I have made most of whatever advances I have made in the last few years." Able to see academic work as a creative process that will develop naturally when given the space and time it takes to gestate—even on holiday—this was personal growth indeed.

Born Carl Ransom Rogers. **Parents** Walter Alexander and Julia (Cushing) Rogers. **Marriage** Helen Martha Elliott, artist, 1924 (died, 1979). **Children** David Elliott and Natalie. **Education** University of Wisconsin, BA, 1924; Union Theological Seminary, New York, 1924–26; Columbia

University, MA, 1928, PhD, 1931. **Career** Fellow in psychology, Institute for Child Guidance, New York, 1927–28; psychologist, Society for the Prevention of Cruelty to Children, Rochester, New York, 1928–30, director, child study department, 1930–38; director, Rochester Guidance Center, 1939; professor of psychology, Ohio State University, 1940–45; professor of psychology and executive secretary, Counseling Center, University of Chicago, 1945–57; professor, departments of psychology and psychiatry, University of Wisconsin, 1957–63; resident fellow, Western Behavioral Sciences Institute, La Jolla, California, 1964–68; resident fellow, Center for Studies of the Person, La Jolla, 1968–87. **Related activities** Visiting professor: Columbia University, 1935, University of California at Los Angeles, 1947, Harvard University, 1948, Occidental College, 1950, University of California, Berkeley, and Brandeis University; lecturer, University of Rochester, 1935–40; psychological consultant, Army Air Forces, 1944; director of counselling services, United Service Organizations, 1944–45; member of executive committee, Wisconsin Psychiatric Institute, University of Wisconsin, 1960–63; fellow, Center for Advanced Study in the Behavioral Sciences, 1962–63. **Offices and memberships** Founder member and fellow, American Association for Applied Psychology, chairman of clinical section, 1942–44, president, 1944–45; fellow, American Orthopsychiatric Association, vice-president, 1941–42; fellow, American Psychological Association, president, 1946–47, president of division of clinical and abnormal psychology, 1949–50; founder member, American Academy of Psychotherapists, president, 1956–58; founder member, Association of Humanistic Psychology; fellow, American Academy of Arts and Sciences; Phi Beta Kappa; Phi Kappa Alpha. **Awards and honours** Nicholas Murray Butler Silver Medal, Columbia University, 1955; cited for outstanding research, American Personnel and Guidance Association, 1955, 1961; special contribution award, American Psychological Association, for research in the field of psychotherapy, 1956; honorary DHL, Lawrence University, 1956, University of Santa Clara, 1971; Knapp Professorship, University of Wisconsin, 1957; selected as humanist of the year, American Humanist Association, 1964; distinguished contribution award, American Pastoral Counselors' Association, 1967; honorary PhD, Gonzaga University, 1968, University of Hamburg, 1975; professional award, American Board of Professional Psychology, 1968; distinguished professional contribution award, American Psychological Association, 1972; distinguished professional psychologist award, American Psychological Association Division of Psychotherapy, 1972; honorary DSc, University of Cincinnati, 1974, University of Leiden, 1975, Northwestern University, 1978. **Publications** *Measuring Personality Adjustment in Children Nine to Thirteen Years of Age*, 1931; *The Clinical Treatment of the Problem Child*, 1939; *Counseling and Psychotherapy*, 1942; (with John L. Wallen) *Counseling with Returned Servicemen*, 1946; *Client-Centered Therapy: Its Current Practice, Implications and Theory*, 1951; (editor, with Rosalind F. Dymond) *Psychotherapy and Personality Change*, 1954; *On Becoming a Person*, 1961; (editor and co-author) *The Therapeutic Relationship and Its Impact: A Study of Psychotherapy with Schizophrenics*, 1967; *Person to Person: The Problem of Being Human*, 1967; *The Interpersonal Relationship in the Facilitation of Learning*, 1968; (editor with William R. Coulson) C.E. Merrill, *Man and the Science of Man*, 1969; (editor with William R. Coulson) C.E. Merrill, *Freedom to Learn: A View of What Education Might Become*, 1969; revised as *Freedom to Learn for the 80s*, 1983; *Carl Rogers on Encounter Groups*, 1970; (with Willard B. Fish) *Humanistic Psychology: Interviews with Maslow, Murphy and Rogers*, 1971; *Becoming Partners: Marriage and Its Alternatives*, 1972; *Carl Rogers on Personal Power*, 1977; *A Way of Being*, 1980; contributed many articles to psychological, psychiatric and educational journals. **Cause of death** Heart attack, at age 85. **Further reading** Richard I. Evans, *Carl Rogers: The Man and His Ideas*, New York, 1975; Robert D. Nye, *Three Views of Man: Perspectives From Sigmund Freud, B.F. Skinner and Carl Rogers*, California, 1975, second edition as *Three Psychologies: Perspectives From Freud, Skinner and Rogers*, 1981; Howard Kirschenbaum, *On Becoming Carl Rogers*, New York, 1979;

Harry Albert Van Belle, *Basic Intent and Therapeutic Approach of Carl R. Rogers: A Study of His View of Man in Relation to His View of Therapy, Personality and Interpersonal Relations*, Toronto, 1980.

WILLIAM ROSE

American Screenwriter

***Born* Jefferson City, Missouri, 1918**

***Died* Jersey, Channel Islands, 10 February 1987**

Cinema critic Gavin Lambert said of *Genevieve* in 1954 that it was "one of the best things to have happened to British films over the last five years". Some of its fans might have been surprised to learn, with its quintessentially British flavour of wit, high style and discreet, light-hearted sexual intrigue, together with its profoundly British stars Kenneth More, Dinah Sheridan and Joyce Grenfell, that the film was written by a man born in the heart of middle-America, William Rose. It gained him an Academy Award Nomination for best screenplay and marked the beginning of an extremely fertile 14-year period in which Rose, now well into his thirties, wrote his most mature and successful scripts.

The son of a judge, William Rose was born in the last year of World War I in Jefferson City, Missouri. He lived there until moving east to attend Columbia University in New York. He developed a keen interest in European affairs and his Eurocentric sympathies led him to volunteer for the Finnish Army in their fight against Soviet invasion. At the outbreak of World War II he went immediately to Canada, joined up, and was sent to Scotland with the Black Watch to, as he saw it, "rescue the civilization which produced Shakespeare". He was involved in some of the toughest episodes of the war in Europe, including the Dieppe raid, and left the army with the rank of acting lieutenant-colonel.

Rose's decision to stay in Britain led him to join Ealing Studios, then at the height of its prodigious output of quality British films. After his first big hit with *Genevieve*, he went on to script another notable success in the shape of *The Ladykillers* with Alec Guinness, Peter Sellers, Herbert Lom and a youthful Frankie Howerd. Another Oscar nomination followed, but it was not until several years later that he won the coveted statuette for Hollywood's *Guess Who's Coming to Dinner?*, a much praised, rather frivolous treatment of American racism—but then as Doctor Johnson said of women preachers, like a dog walking on its hind legs, it's not so much that it's done well but that it's done at all.

The Cold War comedy *The Russians Are Coming, the Russians Are Coming* (1966) broke new ground for its time. In spite of the publicity department's self-consciously whacky approach ("Why the crazy title? If we told you, you'd only laugh!"), it proved very popular in the US. The huge commercial success of *It's a Mad, Mad, Mad, Mad World* successfully negotiated the cultural barrier of the Atlantic and has since gained the dubious commendation of appearing with monotonous regularity on the British television Christmas schedules. By negotiating a percentage of the gross, Rose made himself a millionaire.

By now a confirmed Anglophile, he retired to the tax haven of Jersey so as to follow the cricket scores, tell stories from his impressive fund of anecdotes, and enjoy being British—but without the tax burden.

Born William Arthur Rose. **Father** A judge. **Marriages** Two, both of which ended in divorce. **Children** One son and one daughter. **Education** Columbia University, New York. **Emigration** Left US for Canada, 1940; after World War II lived in Scotland; finally settled in Jersey, Channel Islands, 1960s. **Military service** Finnish Army, Russo-Finnish War, 1939–40; lieutenant-colonel, Canadian Black Watch, 1940–45. **Career** Screenwriter: Pinewood Studios, England, 1947–54; Ealing Studios, 1954–60s; began writing for Hollywood, 1960s; last film credit, *The Secret of Santa Vittoria*, 1969. **Awards and honours** Oscar nominations for *Genevieve*, 1953, *The Ladykillers*, 1955, and *The Russians Are Coming, the Russians Are Coming*, 1966; Oscar Award for *Guess Who's Coming to Dinner*, 1967; Laurel Award of the Writers' Guild of America, 1973. **Films** (US titles in parentheses) *Once a Jolly Swagman* (*Maniacs on Wheels*), 1948; *My Daughter Joy (Operation X)*, 1950; *I'll Get You For This* (*Lucky Nick Cain*), 1950; *The Gift Horse* (*Glory at Sea*), 1952; *Genevieve*, 1953; *Song of Paris* (*Bachelor in Paris*), 1954; *The Maggie (High and Dry)*, 1954; *The Ladykillers*, 1955; *Touch and Go* (*The Light Touch*), 1955; *The Man in the Sky* (*Decision Against Time*), 1956; *Davy*, 1957; *The Smallest Show on Earth*, 1957; *It's a Mad, Mad, Mad, Mad, World*, 1963; *The Russians Are Coming, the Russians Are Coming*, 1966; *Guess Who's Coming to Dinner*, 1967; *The Flim Flam Man*, 1967; *The Secret of Santa Vittoria*, 1969. **Cause of death** Undisclosed, at age 67.

DAVID SUSSKIND

American Producer and Television Personality

***Born* New York City, New York, 19 December 1920**

***Died* New York City, New York, 22 February 1987**

"A short, broad-shouldered man who likes to say 'I'm an iconoclast. A rebel.'" "A restless personality, who stubbed out cigarettes with the energy of a matador." "Combative." "Controversial." "Blunt." "Endearingly narcissistic."

Whatever one's opinion of him, David Susskind was a character who never elicited a lukewarm response. These adjectives—and many more besides—indicate the level of strong feeling which surrounded the crew-cut sporting TV producer and talk show host. Yet despite his ability to make people take sides, Susskind himself remained something of an enigma; never easy or content, he was, in his own words, constantly "damn frustrated". He enjoyed tremendous success from "the box"—a 28-year-run of his talk show and 47 Emmy awards are clear evidence of that. But when asked about television as a medium, Susskind replied that it was "lousy". "Ninety-five per cent of the stuff shown on it is trash," he said, a strange comment from the man who was the first person to provide in-depth interviews with Nikita Khrushchev and Richard Nixon, and who was responsible for such TV productions as *Death of a Salesman*, *Eleanor and Franklin*, and *The Moon and Sixpence*, starring Laurence Olivier.

Susskind is reported to have said that he wanted to become the "Cecil B. DeMille of television," yet Susskind's talents were never confined to the small screen; from the acclaimed *Raisin in the Sun* with Sidney Poitier to *Alice Doesn't Live Here Anymore* and *Fort Apache, the Bronx*, his film credits were outstanding in themselves. He also produced well-known stage plays, such as *Rashomon* and *A Very Special Baby* on Broadway. From the first, his life was full and extremely provocative—a far cry from what he envisioned as a young man, for once upon a time David Susskind said that "the only thing I wanted of life was a job at Harvard as a teacher".

Born in New York and reared in Massachusetts, young Susskind had from the beginning set his sights upon Harvard. His father, however, sent him instead to the University of Wisconsin for the first two years of college, in the belief that the experience would broaden his son's outlook on life. Whether it did or not remains to be seen. What the agrarian college did provide was a wife; by the time his two years at Wisconsin were completed, he and Phyllis Briskin were married. The couple moved to Cambridge, Massachusetts, and Susskind finally enrolled in his beloved Harvard, graduating in 1942 with a degree in government and history. His teaching days never materialized, however. World War II intervened, and the young graduate entered the US Navy, eventually serving as communications officer aboard an attack transport ship in the Pacific.

Despite the fact that he was present at Iwo Jima, Okinawa and other invasion points, Susskind decided that his naval experiences were too boring and made a teaching career seem even more passive by comparison. "I settled on show business as the most dynamic and interesting field I could get into," he told a *New York Post* reporter in 1959, "and went looking for a job in my navy uniform." His search for excitement resulted in a job as a press agent, first for Warner Brothers and then for Universal Pictures Corporation; next came a stint as a talent scout for Century Artists and the Musical Corporation of America (MCA). Eventually Susskind worked his way into MCA's television programme department, where he managed such personalities as Jerry Lewis and Dinah Shore. Finally, in 1952, he threw in his lot with a new company, Talent Associates Ltd., and thus began his career as a television producer, smack in the middle of what is now known as the "Golden Age" of television.

These were the days of corporation-funded drama, and David Susskind's first productions were on such series as *The Philco Television Playhouse*, *The Kaiser Aluminum Hour* and *The Armstrong Circle Theater*, where he became executive producer. Throughout the 1950s Talent Associates continued to thrive, adding *The Kraft Television Theater* and *The Du Pont Show of the Month* to its repertoire; the latter series included Susskind's production of the *Bridge of San Luis Rey*. By 1959 the company had been contracted for $9 million worth of live productions—more than the country's three major networks (CBA, ABC and NBC) put together. This feat led a *Time* magazine critic to state: "Susskind's frenetic pursuit of both the television dollar and television quality has left many a competitor gasping in his wake." Other critics, almost certainly including the envious, accused the argumentative little man of offering nothing better to TV viewers than the mediocrity he so vocally deplored. Yet among Talent Associates' new projects for 1958 had been a talk show hosted by Susskind himself. Entitled *Open End* for its first nine years (afterwards it became *The David Susskind Show*), it was this programme which more than any other of his projects transformed David Susskind into a household name.

As its original title indicated, the show had no set structure. Susskind and his guests simply talked to each other until they had nothing left to say. The approach was new and often controversial, leading many critics to dub it "Open Mouth". Beginning at 10 p.m. in the evening, according to one *New York Times* reporter, the show "often ran for four hours or until the talkers' eyes began to contract, they sank lower in their chairs and became nonsensical". Susskind himself saw it in a slightly different light: "The whole idea is that the public can hear the best and liveliest minds on any particular subject giving their honest opinions and prejudices." Whether honesty was the best policy is still a question up for debate: Susskind's blunt, off-the-wall questions often resulted in what he termed "awkward moments", "like Bette Davis flying off the handle and attacking me". Once, he called actor Tony Curtis "a passionate amoeba", whereupon Curtis threatened to punch him "right on his big nose". Other guests were not so violent. Nikita Khrushchev, whose interview in 1960 resulted in Susskind being targeted as a communist sympathizer, told the commentator before thousands of viewers, "I like your eyes. They're honest."

Perhaps it was Susskind's honesty, after all, combined with his skills learned as a talent scout, which allowed him to assemble and work successfully with some of the most impressive casts for his many films: Sidney Poitier, Michael Redgrave, Anthony Quinn and Trevor Howard, to name but a few. Typically of Susskind, however, he deplored "having to use" top names in any type of show. "I want to have my own marquee value," he said in 1959, "like Sam Goldwyn and Cecil B. DeMille. Then I wouldn't always have to bother about getting stars for every show. If people accepted it as a Susskind production, that would be ideal." Considering the fact that *Open End* only closed in 1986, and that his name became synonymous with "some of American TV's best work", one has the impression that Susskind had easily achieved this goal by the time of his death. And, as another reporter has noted, "one can't help but wonder what effect David Susskind might have had on the hallowed halls of Harvard if he remained true to his original ambition—to become a college professor."

Born David Howard Susskind. **Parents** Benjamin, an insurance agent, and Frances (Lear) Susskind. **Marriages** 1) Phyllis Briskin, 1939; 2) Joyce Davidson, 1966. **Children** Two daughters, Pamela and Diana, and one son, Andrew, from first marriage; one daughter, Samantha, from second marriage. **Education** Local public schools; Brookline High School, 1938; University of Wisconsin, 1938–40; Harvard University, BS in history and government, 1942. **Military service** Ensign, later communications officer, US Navy, 1942–46. **Career** Junior economist, War Labor Board, Washington, DC, briefly, 1942; press agent for Warner Brothers, then Universal Pictures, 1947; talent agent, Century Artists, 1949–52; founder, with Alfred Levy, of packaged television programmes, Talent Associates Ltd, New York City, 1952 onwards, except for leave of absence with Musical Corporation of America, 1952–53; television producer, 1953 onwards; first production for *Philco Television Playhouse*, of which he became executive producer, 1955; founder, with Levy, of film company, Jonathan Productions, 1955; producer of Broadway shows from 1956; of films from 1957; chat show host from 1958. **Awards and honours** Robert Sherwood Award, 1957; Peabody TV award for production of *The Moon and Sixpence*, 1959; Sylvania TV awards; Newspaper Guild awards; Christopher awards; elected to Hallmark Hall of Fame, for *The Price*, 1971; twelve Emmy awards for *Eleanor and Franklin*, 1976; TV Critics' Circle award for best drama of the year for *Eleanor and Franklin: The White House Years*, 1976. **Stage productions** *A Very Special Baby*, 1956; *Handful of Fire*, 1958; *Rashomon*, 1959; *Kelly*, 1965; *All in Good Time*, 1965; *Brief Lives*, 1967. **Films** *Edge of the City*, 1957; *Raisin in the Sun*, 1961; *Requiem for a Heavyweight*, 1961; *All the Way Home*, 1963; *The Pursuit of Happiness*, 1969; *Lovers and Other Strangers*, 1969; *Straw Dogs*, 1970; *Alice Doesn't Live Here Anymore*, 1974; *All Things Bright and Beautiful*, 1975; *Buffalo Bill and the Indians*, 1976; *Loving Couples*, 1980; *Fort Apache, the Bronx*, 1981. **Television** Host, TV discussion programme *Open End*, 1958–67; *The David Susskind Show*, 1967–86. **Television productions** *Philco-Goodyear Playhouse*, 1948–52; *Play of the Week*, 1959; *Festival of the Performing Arts*, 1962–63; *Esso Repertory Theater*, 1964–65; *Dupont Shows*, 1957–64; *Kraft Theater*, 1957–58; *Armstrong Circle Theater*, 1960–61; *Family Classics*, 1960–61; *Hedda Gabler*, 1961; *The Price*, 1971; *Look Homeward Angel*, 1972; *All the Way Home*, 1972; *If You Give a Dance, You Gotta Pay the Band*, 1972; *Harvey*, 1972; *The Shenyang Acrobatic Troupe Special*, 1973; *The Glass Menagerie*, 1973; *The Magic Show*, 1975; *Caesar and Cleopatra*, 1976; *Eleanor and Franklin*, 1976; *Truman at Potsdam*, 1976; *Harry S. Truman: Plain Speaking*, 1976; *Richard Rogers: The Sound of His Music*, 1976; *Alice*, 1976; *Eleanor and Franklin: The White House Years*, 1977; *Johnny We Hardly Knew Ye*, 1977; *On Our Own*, 1977; *The TV Circle Critics'*

Awards Show, 1977; *The War Between the Tates*, 1977; *Goldenrod*, 1977; *World of Darkness*, 1977; *Breaking Up*, 1977; *Tell Me My Name*, 1977; *Casey Stengle*, 1980; *Dear Liar*, 1980–81; *Ian McKellen: Acting Shakespeare*, 1981; *JFK: A One-Man Show*, 1984. **Publications** *Happy Shows for Happy People with Happy Problems.* **Cause of death** Heart attack, at age 66.

WYNFORD VAUGHAN-THOMAS

British Broadcaster and Television Personality

Born **Swansea, Wales, 15 August 1908**

Died **Fishguard, Wales, 4 February 1987**

The Welsh are natural poets and have produced a prodigious number of wordsmiths. This abundant talent springs from an innate delight in language for its own sake combined with a mellifluous eloquence to which any Welsh speaker's ear is attuned almost from the cradle. Wynford Vaughan-Thomas was as Welsh as they come and his name and voice became known throughout Britain and the English-speaking world. His combination of warm humanitarianism, Celtic passion and articulate wit made him one of nature's broadcasters and turned informed commentary into an art.

He overlapped with Dylan Thomas at Swansea Grammar School, and they became close friends until the poet's untimely death in 1953. After graduating from Exeter College, Oxford, he returned to his native city as a lecturer. A relatively silent spell as keeper of manuscripts and records at the National Library of Wales followed in what must have been a frustrating year, before he went on to become area officer of the South Wales Council of Social Services.

On a whim, he responded in 1936 to an advertisement for a post in the regional office of the BBC in Cardiff. It changed his life. His considerable linguistic ability found a natural outlet in radio and flourished under challenging assignments such as giving the Welsh commentary on the coronation of George VI.

It was World War II and a move to London's Outside Broadcast Unit that brought him quickly to prominence and popularity with his reports on some of the most thrilling and frightening episodes of the war. His work illustrated his particular talent for immediacy which, when combined with considerable physical courage, created some of the most memorable broadcasts of radio history. He was a pioneer, too, becoming the first to give a running commentary from a Lancaster bomber on an RAF raid on Berlin—like "jewels being thrown on black velvet, a beautiful, horrible sight".

Vaughan-Thomas was frequently involved in manoeuvres that took him into the front lines, sometimes under fire. His experiences during the Anzio beach landings led to a book, called simply *Anzio*, and he was again at the front for the Normandy landings. Reminiscing later, he said with typical self-deprecation, "I moved up with the French Army in the Alsace campaign and liberated the vineyards of Burgundy. We had three marvellous days in a cellar and I emerged with the Croix de Guerre."

Not all his experiences could be passed off so lightly. He was among the first to witness the horror of the concentration camp at Belsen; it marked him for life, according to a close friend and colleague, John Morgan, after which he could never again be solemn or take himself seriously. He derived considerable satisfaction from one of his last war broadcasts when, seated in the traitor William Joyce's chair from which, as Lord Haw-Haw, he had transmitted anti-British propaganda, Vaughan-Thomas used the familiar formula to announce, "This is Germany calling–calling for the last time..." as the city fell to the Allies.

His work during the war years ensured his membership of the BBC élite, and for the next three decades he was one of those who covered royal tours, coronations, and the growing number of independence celebrations as former colonies broke away from the Empire.

A skilful politician, Vaughan-Thomas was a natural choice for membership of the team bidding for the franchise of the new Welsh commercial television channel in the 1960s. His organizational abilities made him a great asset to Lord Harlech's consortium, which included several members of the burgeoning "Tafia"—Aled Vaughan, Richard Burton, Geraint Evans, Stanley Baker and John Morgan, among others. They won the contract and Vaughan-Thomas became the first director of programmes for Harlech Television (HTV), a position he held until 1971 when he was promoted to executive director of the company.

Vaughan-Thomas's commitment to Wales and Welsh culture never faltered and his patriotism was rewarded by the Gorsedd of Bards at the 1970 eisteddfod when he was made an honorary Druid. He became chairman of the Contemporary Arts Society for Wales and co-wrote *The Shell Guide to Wales* with Alun Llewellyn. It was also the subject of the major HTV series, *The Dragon Has Two Tongues*, an innovative piece of television work where he was placed in deliberate opposition to fellow presenter Professor Gwyn Alf Williams.

Vaughan-Thomas provoked lasting loyalty and strong affection among his friends and was universally popular. A noted raconteur, he was excellent company and could be relied upon to enhance any gathering with his eloquence and charm. His suggestion to John Morgan for his own epitaph was "time will not wither nor custom stale that infinite variety act which is myself", which, though it characteristically debunks his impressive wealth of gifted intelligence, aptly pinpoints one central fact of Vaughan-Thomas's life—he was never, ever dull.

Born Lewis John Wynford Vaughan-Thomas. **Parents** David, a musician, and Morfydd Vaughan-Thomas. **Marriage** Charlotte Rowlands, 1946. **Children** One son, David. **Education** Swansea Grammar School; Exeter College, Oxford, graduated 1931. **Career** Keeper of manuscripts and records, National Library of Wales, 1933; area officer, South Wales Council of Social Services, 1934–37; outside broadcasts assistant, BBC Cardiff regional office, 1937–39; reporter, BBC Outside Broadcasting Department, London, 1939–42; BBC war correspondent, 1942–45; freelance author, journalist and broadcaster, giving radio and television commentaries on most subsequent major outside broadcasts undertaken by BBC, 1945–67; programme director and board member, Harlech Television, 1968–71; continued to give commentaries and appear on television and radio into the 1980s. **Offices and memberships** President, Publicity Association of Wales, 1974; governor, British Film Institute, 1977–80; fellow, Royal Society of Arts, 1980–87; member, Welsh Arts Council; director, Welsh National Opera; chairman, Council for the Preservation of Rural Wales; member, Gorsedd of Bards; president, Contemporary Arts Society; patron, Great Little Trains of Wales. **Awards and honours** Croix de Guerre, 1945; member, Order of the British Empire, 1974; honorary MA, Open University, 1982. **Publications** *Royal Tour, 1953–54*, 1954; *Anzio*, 1961; *Madly in All Directions*, 1967; (with Alun Llewellyn) *The Shell Guide to Wales*, 1969; *The Splendour Falls*, 1973; *Gower*, 1975; *The Countryside Companion*, 1979; *Trust to Talk* (autobiography), 1980; *Wynford Vaughan-Thomas's Wales*, 1981; *The Princes of Wales*, 1982; *Wales: A History*, 1985; *How I Liberated Burgundy*, 1985. **Cause of death** Undisclosed, at age 78.

ANDY WARHOL

American Artist and Film-maker

***Born* McKeesport, Pennsylvania, 6 August 1928**

***Died* New York City, New York, 22 February 1987**

"In the future, everybody will be famous for 15 minutes." It is questionable whether time will show this, one of Andy Warhol's best-known dictums, to have been a true prediction, and in the final analysis, as Warhol himself might have observed, it does not really matter. More pertinent is the question of how long Warhol's own fame, considerable in his lifetime, will stand the test of posterity. At the height of his career, in the 1960s and 1970s, he was considered a key figure in contemporary American culture, a pioneer of Pop Art and a leader of fashion, his image enhanced by the aura of mystery which he carefully cultivated.

Warhol was deliberately evasive regarding his origins and early life, and this has produced much conflicting evidence; several dates and places of birth, for instance, have been given. It appears, however, that his real name was Andrew Warhola and that he was born in Pennsylvania of working-class, Czech-immigrant parents. He studied at the Carnegie Institute of Technology, graduating in 1949. He soon became highly successful as a commercial artist in New York, working primarily as an illustrator for advertisements. He was particularly well known for his camp and whimsical drawings of cats and shoes, and in 1957 won the Art Directors' Club Medal for a giant shoe advertisement.

By the beginning of the 1960s he had changed direction and had taken up painting, holding his first major one-man show in 1962. He began by making stencilled pictures of money, having been advised by an art dealer to paint whatever was most important to him. However, it was the famous, meticulously painted pictures of Campbell's soup cans which established his reputation among the artistic avant-garde, as well as bringing him great commercial success. He followed this with pictures of other mass-produced, familiar consumer goods, notably Coca Cola bottles and Brillo cartons, with depictions of such icons of contemporary popular culture as Marilyn Monroe, Elizabeth Taylor and Elvis Presley, and other subjects ranging from the horrific (electric chairs) to the inoffensively banal (day-glo flowers). In these works the image was repeated over and over again, with only infinitesimal variations.

Warhol was fascinated with monotony and uniformity, with repetition and mechanical processes. "I want to be a machine," he said. "I think it would be terrific if everybody was alike." To facilitate the mechanical repetitiveness of his art, and to permit himself to multiply images *ad infinitum*, he soon abandoned painting proper for silk-screening, the cheapest and technically the simplest of all printing processes. His silk-screen pictures no longer looked like "art", but like mechanical reproductions; moreover, the process enabled Warhol to fulfil his wish for "somebody else to do all my paintings for me". His artistic input could now be minimal, limited to selecting the image—torn from a newspaper or magazine—and sending it to the commercial silk screen-maker with his size and colour specifications. Like so much else about Warhol, however, there is a paradox here, in that there were actually extremely subtle variations in even the most repetitive prints—such as the rows of Campbell's soup cans—produced by the amount of ink and pressure applied in their manufacture.

These pictures were presented in a manner readily accessible to his public, using the techniques and subjects of advertising, in which Warhol's early career had given him considerable experience, and with which the twentieth-century consumer is at least superficially familiar. His mass-media approach was seen as questioning the traditional, élitist view of great art in general, and specifically as a revolt against the considerably more serious Abstract Expressionist style then current.

In 1963 Warhol made his first films and soon became a leader of the burgeoning New York underground film scene. In the light of his obsession with the automatic and mass-produced, his progression from repetitive painting to silk screening and finally to cinema seemed logical. The most talked-about of these early films was *Sleep*, a six-hour movie of a sleeping man shot from one viewpoint, without movement of the camera or cutting. Similarly, *Empire* was an eight-hour stationary view of the Empire State Building, a film so unwatchable that Warhol himself refused to sit through it.

Between 1963 and 1967 he made some 55 films, all using this same passive technique of simply letting the camera run, unblinkingly recording whatever was in front of it. The casts of these movies were "superstars of the underground" with names like Ultra Violet and Holly Woodlawn. They were taken from the entourage of egocentric artists, junkies, rock singers, transvestites, hustlers, fugitives and hangers-on with which Warhol surrounded himself in his East 47th Street studio, known as The Factory. The movies were characterized by lack of cinematic technique, and had no plots or scripts as such.

The most commercially successful of the films was *Chelsea Girls* (1966), a seven-hour movie shown on two screens simultaneously, featuring the Warhol "superstars" in various pseudo-documentary, voyeuristic hotel-room scenes allegedly shot in New York's Chelsea Hotel. It was the first underground film to be shown in a commercial theatre, and was dubbed "The Sound of Music" of the underground because of its box-office success. Warhol's last completed film was *Lonesome Cowboys*, for once made on location, in Arizona, and featuring the "superstars" posing in western garb among western movie sets. In 1967 he was shot and seriously wounded by Valerie Solanis, a Factory hanger-on, and subsequent Warhol films such as *Trash* and *Heat* were, in fact, made by his associate Paul Morrissey.

Despite the notoriety of his work and the personalities with which he consorted, Warhol was—paradoxically—a quiet and retiring figure, a devout Roman Catholic who lived with his mother in a Lexington Avenue apartment, and who did not wholly approve of the drug-orientated, drop-out lifestyles of the "superstars". He was, though, a sexual fetishist, liking, for instance, to lie alone in bed listening on the telephone to other people's accounts of their sexual encounters, rather than participating in sex himself: a manifestation of his self-confessed abhorrence of physical contact.

A slight, soft-spoken man, he wore a white wig to emphasize the blandness he cultivated. Opinions varied as to whether this persona was merely a pose, or whether, in John Rublowsky's words, it was "an armour that turns aside every probe before it can reach too deep—a shield that guards a raw edge of sensitivity". As another critic remarked, however, Warhol's very "banality endowed him with an air of mystery, since few people could bring themselves to believe that any artist could possibly be so banal". Perhaps the truth is most closely approached in Warhol's own comment: "If you want to know all about [me], just look at the surface: of my paintings and films and me. There I am."

It remains to be seen if Warhol will go down in history as an innovative artist who introduced valid and important new principles to mid-twentieth century art, or if he will simply be regarded as a minor figure, a poseur or even a charlatan, whose chief claim to fame was that his work mirrored the shallow and dehumanized culture of his times.

Born Andrew Warhola. **Parents** Andrew and Julia Warhola. **Education** Carnegie Institute of Technology (now Carnegie-Mellon University), Pittsburgh, BFA, 1949. **Career** Illustrator, *Glamour Magazine*, New York, 1949–50; commercial artist, New York, 1950–57; first individual exhibition, Hugo Gallery, New York, 1952; full-time artist, 1957 onwards; first silk-screen paintings, 1960–61; also, film producer, mostly with Paul Morrissey, at Warhol's "Factory", from 1963. **Related activities** Editor, *Inter/View* magazine, New York; publisher, co-founder, *Andy Warhol's Interview*. **Awards and honours** Art Directors' Club of New York Medal for shoe advertisements, 1957; Independent Film Award from *Film Culture* for *Eat*, *Haircut*, *Sleep*, *Kiss*, *Empire*, New York, 1964; Los Angeles Film Festival Award, 1964. **Individual exhibitions** Hugo Gallery, New York, 1952; Bodley Gallery, New York, 1956, 1957, 1958, 1959; Ferus Gallery, Los Angeles, 1962; Stable Gallery, New York, 1962; Ferus Gallery, New York, 1963; Leo Castelli Gallery, 1964; Stable Gallery, New York, 1964; Galerie Sonnabend, Paris, 1964; Leo Castelli Gallery, New York, 1965; Contemporary Arts Center, Cincinnati, Ohio, 1966; Galerie Sonnabend, Paris, 1965; Galerie Rubbers, Buenos Aires, 1965; Galerie M.E. Thelen, Essen, 1965; Gian Enzo Sperone Arte Moderna, Milan, 1965; Institute of Contemporary Art, Philadelphia, 1965; Galerie Buren, Stockholm, 1965; Jerrold Morris International Gallery, Toronto, 1965; Gian Enzo Sperone Arte Moderna, Turin, 1965; Galerie M.E. Thelen, Essen, 1966; Gian Enzo Sperone Arte Moderna, Milan, 1966; Institute of Contemporary Art, Boston, 1966; Contemporary Arts Center, Cincinnati, Ohio, 1966; Galerie Hans Neuendorf, Hamburg, 1966; Ferus Gallery, Los Angeles, 1966; Leo Castelli Gallery, New York, 1966; Galerie Rudolf Zwirner, Cologne, 1967; Galerie Sonnabend, Paris, 1967; Galerie Rudolf Zwirner, Cologne, 1968; Stedelijk Museum, Amsterdam, 1968; Galerie der Spiegel, Cologne, 1968; Rowan Gallery, London, 1968; Galerie Heiner Friedrich, Munich, 1968; Kunstnernes, Oslo, 1968; Moderna Museet, Stockholm, 1968; Neue Nationalgalerie der Staatlichen Museen Preussischer Kulturbesitz, West Berlin, 1969; Irvin Blum Gallery, Los Angeles, 1969; Leo Castelli Gallery, New York, 1969; Galerie Folker Skulima, West Berlin, 1970; Museum of Contemporary Art, Chicago, 1970; Stedelijk van Abbemuseum, Eindhoven, Netherlands, 1970; Musée d'Art Moderne de la Ville, Paris, 1970; Pasadena Museum of Art, California (toured United States and Europe), 1970; Galerie Bruno Bischofberger, Zurich, 1971; Gotham Book Mart Gallery, New York, 1971; Institute of Contemporary Arts, London, 1971; Musée d'Art Moderne, Paris, 1971; Castelli Downtown Gallery, New York, 1972; Multiples Gallery, New York, 1972; Margo Leavin Gallery, Los Angeles, 1973; Mayor Gallery, London, 1974; Musée Galliera, Paris, 1974; Baltimore Museum of Art, 1975; Wurttembergischer Kunstverein, Stuttgart (travelled to Kunsthall, Dusseldorf), 1976; *Andy Warhol: Photos*, Lisson Gallery, London, 1980; *Portrait Screenprints 1965–1980*, Gloucestershire College of Arts and Technology, Cheltenham, England, 1981; Galerie Schellmann und Kluser, Munich, 1982; Stadtische Galerie im Lenbachhaus, Munich, 1982; Fraenkel Gallery, San Francisco, 1983; Scottsdale Center for the Arts, Arizona, 1984; Edition Schellmann und Kluser, Munich, 1984; Flow Ace Gallery, Los Angeles, 1984; Judith Goldberg Gallery, New York, 1984; Galerie Kammer, Hamburg, 1984; Galerie Schellmann und Kluser, Munich, 1984; Galerie Daniel Templon, Paris, 1986; Edition Schellmann, Munich, 1986; Anthony D'Offay Gallery, London, 1986; Galerie Bernd Kluser, Munich, 1987. **Selected group exhibitions** *The Painter and the Photograph: From Delacroix to Warhol*, University of New Mexico, Albuquerque, 1964; *Il Pop Artists: The New Image*, Galerie M.E. Thelen, Essen, 1966; *Photo/Graphics*, International Museum of Photography, George Eastman House, Rochester, New York, 1971; *Photographic Process as Medium*, Rutgers University, New Brunswick, New Jersey, 1975; *Paris–New York*, Centre Georges Pompidou, Paris, 1977; *Mirrors and Windows: American Photography Since 1960*, Museum of Modern Art, New York, 1978 (toured the United States, 1978–80); *La Photo Polaroid*, Musée d'Art Moderne, Paris, 1980; *Instantanes*, Centre Georges Pompidou, Paris, 1980; *Lichtbildnisse: Das Porträt in der Fotografie*, Rheinisches Landesmuseum, Bonn, 1982; *Painter as Photographer*, John Hansard Gallery, Southampton, Hampshire, 1982 (travelled to Wolverhampton Art Gallery, Wolverhampton, Museum of Modern Art, Oxford, Royal Albert Memorial Museum, Exeter, Camden Arts Centre,

London, 1982–83). **Collections** Museum of Modern Art, New York; Whitney Museum, New York; Corcoran Gallery of Art, Washington, DC; Walker Art Center, Minneapolis; County Museum of Art, Los Angeles; Norton Simon Museum of Art, Pasadena, California; Art Gallery of Ontario, Toronto; Tate Gallery, London; Moderna Museet, Stockholm; Museum of Contemporary Art, Chicago. **Films** (Warhol as producer and director, Paul Morrissey as sometime assistant) *Tarzan and Jane Regained...Sort Of*, 1963; *Sleep*, 1963; *Kiss*, 1963; *Andy Warhol Films Jack Smith Filming Normal Love*, 1963; *Dance Movie* (*Roller Skate*), 1963; *Salome and Delilah*, 1963; *Haircut*, 1963; *Blowjob*, 1963; *Empire*, 1964; *Batman Dracula*, 1964; *The End of Dawn*, 1964; *Naomi and Rufus Kiss*, 1964; *Henry Geldzahler*, 1964; *The Lester Persky Story* (*Soap Opera*), 1964; *Couch*, 1964; *Shoulder*, 1964; *Mario Banana*, 1964; *Harlot*, 1964; *Taylor Mead's Ass*, 1964; *13 Most Beautiful Women*, 1965; *13 Most Beautiful Boys*, 1965; *50 Fantastics*, 1965; *50 Personalities*, 1965; *Ivy and John*, 1965; *Screen Test I*, 1965; *Screen Test II*, 1965; *The Life of Juanita Castro*, 1965; *Drunk*, 1965; *Suicide*, 1965; *Horse*, 1965; *Vinyl*, 1965; *Bitch*, 1965; *Poor Little Rich Girl*, 1965; *Face*, 1965; *Restaurant*, 1965; *Afternoon*, 1965; *Prison*, 1965; *Space*, 1965; *Outer and Inner Space*, 1965; *Camp*, 1965; *Paul Swan*, 1965; *Hedy* (*Hedy the Shoplifter or The 14-Year-Old Girl*), 1965; *The Closet*, 1965; *Lupe*, 1965; *More Milk, Evette*, 1965; *Kitchen*, 1966; *My Hustler*, 1966; *Bufferin* (*Gerard Malanga Reads Poetry*), 1966; *Eating Too Fast*, 1966; *The Velvet Underground*, 1966; *Chelsea Girls*, 1966; **** (*Four Stars*), 1967; (parts of ****: *International Velvet*, *Alan and Dickin*, *Imitation of Christ*, *Courtroom*, *Gerard Has His Hair Removed with Nair*, *Katrina Dead*, *Sausalito*, *Alan and Apple*, *Group One*, *Sunset Beach on Long Island*, *High Ashbury*, *Tiger Morse*, all 1967); *I, a Man*, 1967; *Bike Boy*, 1967; *Nude Restaurant*, 1967; *The Loves of Ondine*, 1967; *Lonesome Cowboys*, 1968; *Blue Movie* (*Fuck*), 1968; (Warhol as producer, Morrissey as director) *Flesh*, 1968; *Trash*, 1970; (co-director with Morrissey) *Women in Revolt*, 1972; *Heat*, 1972; (co-director, co-screenplay with Morrissey) *L'Amour*, 1973; *Andy Warhol's Frankenstein*, 1974; *Andy Warhol's Dracula*, 1974; *Andy Warhol's Bad*, 1977; (Morrissey as director) *The Hound of the Baskervilles*, 1977. **Publications** *Andy Warhol's Index Book*, New York, 1967; (with Gerard Malanga) *Screen Test: A Diary*, 1967; *A: A Novel*, New York, 1968; *Andy Warhol: Transcript of David Bailey's ATV Documentary*, London, 1972; *A to B and Back Again*, London and New York, 1975; *Ladies and Gentlemen*, Milan, 1975; *Andy Warhol's Exposures*, 1979; *Andy Warhol: Photographs*, New York, Zurich, 1980; (with Pat Hackett) *Popism: The Warhol '60s*, New York, 1980, London, 1981; *Andy Warhol: Schweizer Portraits* (text by George J. Dolezal), Thun, Switzerland, 1982; *Andy Warhol's Children's Book*, Zurich, 1983; *America*, New York, 1985; *The Diaries* (edited by Pat Hackett), New York, 1989. **Cause of death** Undisclosed, at age 59. **Further reading** Van Deren Coke, *The Painter and the Photograph: From Delacroix to Warhol*, Albuquerque, New Mexico, 1964, 1972; John Coplans, *Andy Warhol*, Pasadena, California, 1970; Rainer Crone, *Andy Warhol*, London, 1970; John Wilcock, *The Autobiography and Sex Life of Andy Warhol*, New York, 1971; Peter Gidal, *Andy Warhol: Films and Paintings*, New York, 1971; Van Deren Coke, *Photo/Graphics* (exhibition catalogue), Rochester, New York, 1971; Rosanne T. Livingston, *Photographic Process as Medium* (exhibition catalogue), New Brunswick, New Jersey, 1975; Daniela Palazzoli and others, *L'Arte nella societa: fotografia, cinema, videotape*, Milan, 1976; John Szarkowski, *Mirrors and Windows: American Photography Since 1960*, New York, 1978; Ralph Gibson (editor), *Art*, New York, 1979; Paolo Barozzi, *Voglio essere una macchina: la fotografia di Andy Warhol*, Milan, 1979; Michel Nuridsany, *Instantanes* (exhibition catalogue), Paris, 1980; Klaus Honnef (editor), *Lichtbildnisse: Das Porträt in der Fotografie*, Cologne, 1982; Marina Vaizey, *The Artist as Photographer*, London, 1982; Victor Bokris, *Warhol*, New York and London, 1988; Ultra Violet, *Famous for 15 Minutes: My Years with Andy Warhol*, New York and London, 1989; Fred Lawrence Guiles, *Loner at the Ball: The Life of Andy Warhol*, New York and London, 1989.

GLENWAY WESCOTT

American Novelist

***Born* Kewaskum, Wisconsin, 11 April 1901**

***Died* Rosemont, New Jersey, 22 February 1987**

Glenway Wescott's last work of original fiction, *Apartment in Athens*, was published in 1945, after which he virtually ceased writing altogether. Before this cessation his output was regular, albeit occasional. Two novels form the basis of Wescott's involvement in American fiction. The first is *The Grandmothers* (1927) and the second is the more highly praised *The Pilgrim Hawk* (1940). The opinions on these, and of Wescott as a writer, range from the laudatory to the dismissive. "Like Joyce's *The Dead*, Ford's *The Good Soldier*, and Porter's *Noon Wine*," wrote critic James Korges, *The Pilgrim Hawk* "comes as close to perfection as literary art is liable to allow." Others, notably Ira Johnson in his book *The Paradox of Voice*, felt that Wescott could not adequately fuse themes or develop character. He was admired by all for his technical skill and subtle narrative precision, and for his "lyric, disciplined, imagistic prose of sensibility". Still the assessment of him remains divided over his success as an artist and about his importance in American literature. Perhaps the best way to describe him is as a talented writer of great promise, but only moderate achievement.

Wescott was cast firmly in the mould of many other Midwesterners of the 1920s and 1930s, such as John Dos Passos, T.S. Eliot, Ezra Pound, Ernest Hemingway, and F. Scott Fitzgerald. More than the others, Wescott was more overtly concerned with his own past, his personal history providing the setting and theme of his writing. He came from what he described as a "poor farm" in northern Wisconsin, near the Canadian border. He attended the University of Chicago, becoming president of the poetry society and "pretending to be a genius...in order to get on in the world". He did not complete his course, but instead left the US for Europe. He returned in 1939 and settled in New Jersey by the end of 1942.

Wescott's ex-patriatism, its appeal and dilemmas, and his motivation for choosing it are consistently articulated in his fiction. Whether the conflict is between family duty and personal freedom, as in *The Apple of the Eye* (1924), the search for a proper relationship to the past, as in *The Grandmothers*, or the tensions between love as dependence and as liberty, as in *The Pilgrim Hawk*, Wescott continually explores the paradox of self and other.

The Apple of the Eye is a short story cycle revolving around the Wisconsin marshland and how it stunts the growth of the principal characters. In one story the only avenue of escape for a girl is suicide in the marsh, in another a boy fails to extricate himself from the lure of the past as represented by the marsh. *The Grandmothers* presents a history of Alwyn Tower, an American émigré and author who recalls his ancestors, guided by a collection of their photographs. Tower returns in *The Pilgrim Hawk*, where a whole world of relationships is revealed during one day in France. In *Apartment in Athens* the context is not love, but ideology, since it had an avowed propagandist intent. The prevailing climate surrounding this wartime story of a German officer and his Greek "host" made this novel difficult to balance. In all cases, especially those with Alwyn Tower, there is a close personal relationship between the writer and narrator. "Unquestionably," Johnson says, "the narrator...is no longer separated from other elements in the novel, but is the very principle on which its form relies."

When Wescott first began publishing in the late 1920s, he was received with enthusiasm and optimism as a young and gifted writer. What he had done to that point, once again, was in keeping with the approved "schooling" for writers. His early poetry was imagistic, his critical reviews appeared in the *New Republic*, *Poetry* and the *Dial*. His themes and experiments with form in his novels and short stories, his early blossoming and his ex-patriatism all put him squarely in the literary mainstream. One of the reasons he was not able to continue his work, or fully mature as a writer was his close identification with the narrative voice. Ironically, the development of the participating narrator, identical to the author's creative mind, inseparable from subject and form, was Wescott's greatest achievement. The two outstanding qualities of his prose and narrative strategy are the lyrical, symbol-making, mood-creating quality, and the rhetorical, aphoristic and epigrammatic organization. When in control of these, Wescott could produce tightly compacted passages which are remarkably lucid:

> Unrequited passion; romance put asunder by circumstances or mistakes; sexuality pretending to be love—all that is a matter of little consequence, a mere voluntary temporary uneasiness, compared with the long course of true love, especially marriage. In marriage insult arises again and again; and pain has to be not only endured, but consented to; and the amount of forgiveness that it necessitates is incredible and exhausting. When love has given satisfaction, then you discover how large a part of the rest of life is only payment for it.... To see the cost of love before one has felt what it is worth is a pity; one may never have the courage to begin.

Passages like this have the resonance of personal confession. And, indeed, so closely are the narrative voice and Wescott's imagination intertwined, that the only successful form of narration is one in which all action is received through the narrator. In *The Apple of the Eye* the point of view throughout the book is omniscient, the language, dialogue and characterization derived from that of the uncharacterized narrator. In *The Grandmothers* Alwyn Tower is the guiding voice, with no one outside to question his presumptions. *The Pilgrim Hawk* shares this trait, though by now Wescott is good enough at controlling the story to permit dramatic irony. It is still through Tower that we encounter and understand the characters, incidents and symbolism of the novel. The relation of this particular kind of structure to character, in Johnson's words, is that "the concentration, the focus, is upon only one character *essentially*"; that is, the reader is so dependent upon the narrative voice that all other characters and techniques are refracted and obscured by its presence.

This is a major problem for Wescott, treated at length by Johnson in his critical study. The main result is what he calls "inflexibility" in the style, which prohibits and obstructs character development outside the parameters of the author's "intellectual demands". Sometimes "there is a remarkable lack of ear not only for vocabulary, but for the syntax of idiomatic speech". The underlying problem is one of aesthetics:

> [Wescott's view is that] *truths* are necessarily general. *Images* are concrete—an entire story may be an image—and images have to be...converted into truths before they can be mentally digested and then made use of; and it is the use of these truths that justified the creation of the images.

Art, therefore, is not truth, but a derivation of it; and the ruminations of the author are the apparatus of that process. Four things follow from this. The first has already been mentioned: the participating narrator. Beyond that, no character beside the narrator can speak for him, her, or itself. In all four of Wescott's novels there is a central character or image—marsh, hawk, Tower —which serves this function. The only way to bridge the gap between truth and image is via a particular medium, but inevitably that medium will block any complete identification of the two.

Unfortunately, this defeated Wescott as often as not. It forced him to be excessively rhetorical and general in his rendering of character and theme. Korges, on the other hand, who described

The Pilgrim Hawk as "art which conceals art", found Wescott too likely to take centre stage and play the pontificator. Symbolism often seems forced on the story rather than present in it. Morton Dauwen Zabel complained that Wescott's proselytizing "over and above the volition of his drama soon involves him in a...serious enervation of tone, force and unity of his story, and in un exaggerated precocity which is the major weakness of [*The Pilgrim Hawk*]".

Where Wescott tried to sever the connection between author and narrator he produced his least successful pieces. The attempted objectivity in *The Babe's Bed* and *Apartment in Athens* simply exacerbated the problems they sought to correct. Sadly, then, Glenway Wescott—as fine a writer as he was—misses the mark of a major writer. He could not solve these artistic problems and, in fact, was immobilized by them. Johnson's summation is that Wescott was caught "between the pull of two opposing concepts of the novel form: one in which he has done his only significant fiction and which he rejects in spite of it having some deep personal appeal for him, and another which he admires and believes superior but in which he can do only the most inferior work. The latter method is a denial of his talents and perfected techniques, as well as a denial of the self."

Born Glenway Wescott. **Education** University of Chicago, 1917–19. **Career** While in teens worked for mass-production tailoring firm and cared for blind millionaire art collector; full-time writer of novels, short stories and poems, 1921 onwards; first publication, 1920; lived in France and Germany, 1925–33. **Awards and honours** DLitt, Rutgers University, New Brunswick, New Jersey, 1963. **Offices and memberships** President, Poetry Society, University of Chicago, 1917–19; president, National Institute of Arts and Letters, 1959–62. **Novels** *The Apple of the Eye*, New York, 1924, London, 1926; *The Grandmothers: A Family Portrait*, New York, 1927, published as *A Family Portrait*, London, 1927; *The Pilgrim Hawk: A Love Story*, New York, 1940, London, 1946; *Apartment in Athens*, New York, 1945, published as *Household in Athens*, London, 1945. **Short stories** *...Like a Lover*, Macon, France, 1926; *Goodbye Wisconsin*, New York, 1928, London, 1929; *The Babe's Bed*, Paris, New York and London, 1930. **Verse** *The Bitterns: A Book of Twelve Poems*, Evanston, Illinois, 1920; *Native of Rock: XX Poems 1921–1922*, New York, 1925. **Other** *Elizabeth Madox Roberts: A Personal Note*, New York, 1930; *Fear and Trembling* (essays), New York, 1932; *A Calendar of Saints for Unbelievers*, Paris, New York and London, 1932; (editor) *The Maugham Reader*, New York, 1950; (editor) *The Short Novels of Colette*, New York, 1951; *Twelve Fables of Aesop, Newly Narrated*, New York, 1954; *Images of Truth: Remembrances and Criticism*, New York, 1962, London, 1963. **Cause of death** Undisclosed, at age 85. **Further reading** Sy Myron Kahn, "Glenway Wescott: A Bibliography", *Bulletin of Bibliography 22*, Boston, 1956; William H. Rueckert, *Glenway Wescott*, New York, 1965; Ira Johnson, *Glenway Wescott: The Paradox of Voice*, Port Washington, New York, 1971.

MARCH

WALTER ABEL

American Actor

***Born* St Paul, Minnesota, 6 June 1898**

***Died* Essex, Connecticut, 26 March 1987**

In a stage and screen career spanning more than 60 years, Walter Abel distinguished himself as a solid and versatile performer, as adept in his work in Eugene O'Neill's early melodramas as in Edward Dmytryk's thrillers and Danny Kaye's comedies. Over the years, the craggy-faced, husky-voiced character actor played opposite a galaxy of top professionals, including Spencer Tracy, James Cagney, Gregory Peck, Kirk Douglas, Katharine Hepburn, Helen Hayes, Bing Crosby and Ray Milland.

Abel's vocation was clear from the beginning. By the time he had graduated from the American Academy of Dramatic Arts in 1917, he had already chalked up a list of commendable performances. He went on to make his professional stage début at the Manhattan Opera House in December 1919, as Second Lieutenant Vincent Moretti in *Forbidden*. This role launched him into New York's theatrical mainstream, where he was quickly accepted as part of the Greenwich Village theatre crowd. Soon he was spotted by Eugene O'Neill and given major parts in the first stage versions of two of his one-act plays.

In November 1924 Abel juggled two roles in O'Neill's "SS Glencairn" quartet—that of Olson, the Swedish sailor, in *Bound East for Cardiff*, at the Provincetown Playhouse, and the New England farmer in *Desire Under the Elms*, at the Greenwich Village Theater. In their biography of O'Neill, Arthur and Barbara Gelb praised Abel for "both his acting talent and his sprinting ability" in his handling of the roles. "He would speak his last line in *Bound East for Cardiff* from the stage of the Provincetown—'Nothin' but yust dirty weather all dis voyage. I yust can't sleep when wheestle blow.'—then sprint over to the Greenwich Village Theater, make a few slight changes in his costume...and utter three lines, including the curtain speech: 'It's a jim-dandy farm, no denyin'. Wished I owned it'." Brooks Atkinson of the *New York Times* described Abel's portrayal of Olson as "deeply sincere", and the actor went on to play the part several more times during the course of his career.

Abel found regular work on Broadway throughout the 1920s and early 1930s, playing major and supporting roles in scores of important shows. Among them were *Back to Methuselah*, *As You Like It*, *Love for Love*, *The Enemy*, *Hangman's House* and *The Seagull*. He first appeared on the London stage in *Coquette* in 1929. Returning to New York, he performed in a variety of

Broadway comedies and melodramas, including *A Divine Drudge*, *Wife Insurance* and *Invitation to a Murder*. In 1932 he toured with O'Neill's new trilogy, *Mourning Becomes Electra*. Then, while acting in the George S. Kaufman–Moss Hart play *Merrily We Roll Along*, he was offered a contract at RKO Pictures, and turned his energies to Hollywood.

Though he appeared in more than 60 films, Abel is best remembered for one of his earliest roles—that of D'Artagnan in Rowland V. Lee's 1935 version of *The Three Musketeers*. From then on his film offers multiplied. Notable pictures included George Nicholl Jr's thriller *The Witness Chair*, Fritz Lang's *Fury*, George Marshall's *Star Spangled Rhythm*, Mark Sandrich's *Holiday Inn* and the Bette Davis–Claude Rains classic *Mr Skeffington*.

In 1940, one of his most productive years, Abel appeared in five different films, including Mitchell Leisen's hit, *Arise My Love*, starring Claudette Colbert and Ray Milland. His portrayal of the newspaper editor is considered one of his best screen performances.

Following World War II, and throughout the 1950s, Abel acted in a wide variety of films, including Danny Kaye's *The Kid from Brooklyn*, Henry Hathaway's thriller *13 Rue Madeleine*, Leisen's *Dream Girl* and Nunnally Johnson's *Night People*. He also tried his hand at several westerns. At the same time the theatre continued to offer him challenging roles. During this period he played important parts in *The Mermaids Singing*, *The Wisteria Trees* and in a new adaptation of *The Cherry Orchard*. In the 1950s he also served as vice-president of the Screen Actors' Guild, at a time when Ronald Reagan was its president.

While Abel's stage career continued into the mid-1970s, embracing repertory and summer-stock performances, his later film appearances were few. Memorable pictures included *Mirage* (1965), starring Gregory Peck, *Zora* (1971), and his very last one, *Grace Quigley*, released in 1985. He made his final New York stage appearance in 1979 in a revival of Pinero's *Trelawny of the Wells* at Lincoln Center.

From 1944 until his death, Abel appeared regularly on TV and radio, and was last seen on camera discussing his early work with Eugene O'Neill. In his dramatic performances, he was most often cast as a "heavy"—either a hard-biting prosecutor or a contentious district attorney. Out of the spotlight and off the stage, however, the veteran actor's favourite recreations were quiet, contemplative ones—domestic landscaping and gardening.

Born Walter Abel. **Parents** Richard Michael and Christine (Becker) Abel. **Marriage** Marietta Bitter, a harpist (died, 1979). **Children** John and Michael. **Education** American Academy of Dramatic Arts. **Career** Actor on stage and screen, also director; stage début, while still a student, 1918; film début, 1918; professional stage début, *Forbidden*, Manhattan Opera House, New York, 1919; with the Theater Guild, 1922; London début, *Coquette*, 1929; television début, 1944; directing début, *The Imaginary Invalid*, 1964; made regular appearances in summer stock seasons. **Offices and memberships** Vice-president, Screen Actors' Guild, 1950s; president, American National Theater and Academy, 1960s. **Stage** *Harvest*, 1918; *Nocturne*, 1918; *A Woman's Way*, 1918; *Forbidden*, 1919; *Back to Methuselah*, 1922; *A Square Peg*, 1923; *As You Like It*, 1923; *The Spook Sonata*, 1924; *The Fashion*, 1924–25; *SS Glencairn*, 1924–25; *The Crime in the Whistler Room*, 1924–25; *Beyond*, 1924–25; *Michael Auclair*, 1924–25; *Desire Under the Elms*, 1924–25; *Love for Love*, 1924–25; *The Enemy*, 1925; *Hangman's House*, 1926; *The House of Women*, 1927; *Skidding*, 1928; *The Seagull*, 1929; *Coquette*, 1929; *First Mortgage*, 1929; *At the Bottom*, 1930; *I Love an Actress*, 1931; *Mourning Becomes Electra*, 1932; *When Ladies Meet*, 1932; *A Divine Drudge*, 1933; *The Drums Begin*, 1933; *Wife Insurance*, 1934; *Invitation to a Murder*, 1934; *Merrily We Roll Along*, 1934; *The Wingless Victory*, 1936; *What Every Woman Knows*, 1938; *The Birds Stopped Singing*, 1939; *West of Broadway*, 1939; *No Code to Guide Her*, 1939; *The Mermaids Singing*, 1945; *Parlor Story*, 1947; *The Biggest Thief in Town*, 1949; *Hamlet*, 1949; *The Wisteria Tree*, 1950; *The Long Watch*, 1952; *Noah*, 1953; *King David*, 1953; *Under*

Milk Wood, 1954; *The Pleasure of His Company*, 1958; *A Christmas Carol*, 1959; *Night Life*, 1962; *Twelfth Night*, 1963; (director) *The Imaginary Invalid*, 1964; *Affairs of State*, 1965; *Maggie*, 1966; *The Ninety-Day Mistress*, 1967; *A Conflict of Interest*, 1972; *Saturday Sunday Monday*, 1974; *Trelawny of the Wells*, 1975. **Films** *Out of a Clear Sky*, 1918; *The North Wind's Malice*, 1920; *Liliom*, 1930; *The Three Musketeers*, 1935; *The Lady Consents*, 1936; *Two in the Dark*, 1936; *The Witness Chair*, 1936; *Second Wife*, 1936; *Fury*, 1936; *We Went to College*, 1936; *Portia on Trial*, 1937; *Wise Girl*, 1937; *Green Light*, 1937; *Arise My Love*, 1940; *Michael Shayne, Private Detective*, 1940; *Miracle on Main Street*, 1940; *Dance Girl Dance*, 1940; *Who Killed Aunt Maggie?*, 1940; *Hold Back the Dawn*, 1941; *Skylark*, 1941; *Glamour Boy*, 1941; *Wake Island*, 1942; *Holiday Inn*, 1942; *Beyond the Blue Horizon*, 1942; *Star Spangled Rhythm*, 1942; *So Proudly We Hail*, 1943; *Fired Wife*, 1943; *Mr Skeffington*, 1944; *An American Romance*, 1944; *Follow the Boys*, 1944; *The Affairs of Susan*, 1945; *Kiss and Tell*, 1945; *Duffy's Tavern*, 1945; *The Kid from Brooklyn*, 1946; *13 Rue Madeleine*, 1946; *Dream Girl*, 1948; *The Fabulous Joe*, 1948; *That Lady in Ermine*, 1948; *So This Is Love*, 1953; *Island in the Sky*, 1953; *Night People*, 1954; *The Indian Fighter*, 1955; *The Steel Jungle*, 1956; *Bernardine*, 1957; *Handle With Care*, 1958; *Raintree County*, 1958; *The Confession*, 1964; *Mirage*, 1965; *Zora (Night of the Dark Full Moon)*, 1971; *Silent Night, Bloody Night*, 1971; *Grace Quigley*, 1985. **Television** (includes) *Man Without a Country*, 1973. **Cause of death** Undisclosed, at age 88.

BIL BAIRD

American Puppeteer

Born **Grand Island, Nebraska, 15 August 1904**

Died **New York City, New York, 18 March 1987**

In latter years, he grew to resemble an elf: bright, twinkling eyes set in a face of somewhat angular proportions; a grin which was at once both joyful and mischievous; a shock of silver hair. One visitor to his workshop said he alternately looked like a medieval wizard and one of Santa's helpers. For most of his professional life, however, he remained behind the scenes, letting his "little wooden ones" speak for him. For Bil Baird was a master puppeteer whose 3000 creations ranged from Charlemane the Lion to the marionettes of the "Dancing Goatherd" sequence in *The Sound of Music*. (Jim Henson, creator of the world-famous Muppets, once said that Baird taught him most of what he knew.)

Baird's fascination with marionettes began when, at the age of seven, he was given a puppet made for him by his father. By the time the young Baird reached high school, he had constructed a stage in his attic and, using an old automobile dashboard as a switchboard, he began to present puppet performances, such as *Treasure Island*. While attending Iowa State University, Baird continued to be involved in theatre work of all kinds: painting sets for the university productions and performing with a dance band—and putting on puppet shows during the intermissions. Baird graduated from the university in 1926 and spent the next year at the Chicago Academy of Fine Arts, specializing in set design.

It was here that Baird pared down the letters of his name—from "Bill" to "Bil"—primarily in order to belong to the Crowned Radish Club which insisted that its members possess first names of three letters. As Baird remarked later, "I never heard anyone pronounce the other 'l' anyway," so Bil he remained.

By designing sets for a Chicago opera company, Baird earned enough money for a bohemian year abroad in France, where he supported himself by playing the accordion in cafés and restaurants. Upon his return, he took a job with Tony Sarg, an established puppeteer, and from that time forward Baird's life became one long puppet show.

Despite its obvious appeal, a puppet master's lot was not always an easy one. While working for Sarg, Baird once had to take a production of *Ali Baba and the Forty Thieves* across the nation for 40 weeks of one-night stands—an experience which elicited the mournful remark: "I never knew there were so many trains in America leaving at five o'clock in the morning." Other facets of his work proved more enjoyable; while still in Sarg's employment, Baird worked on several of the gigantic balloons which have become the hallmark of the Macy's Thanksgiving Day parades.

After five years with Sarg, Bil Baird began to create and produce his own marionettes, which he took to the Chicago World's Fair in 1934 and afterwards used in commercial productions for such clients as the Atlantic Refining Company and Shell Oil. Bigger breaks were on their way, however, such as in 1936, when Orson Welles, who was producing Marlowe's *Dr Faustus*, commissioned Baird to create puppets representing the Seven Deadly Sins. A young actress named Cora Burlar was assigned to speak the parts of Envy, Gluttony and Sloth; soon she noticed that "the puppets on the *College Humor* magazine covers Bil was doing were beginning to look like me: slanty eyes, long legs, and all." The leggy actress became Baird's second wife and, until her death in 1967, Cora Baird served as a full partner in all subsequent puppet productions.

The first step in the Bairds' partnership consisted of transforming an old carriage house near New York's Hudson River into Fire Horse Manor, a puppet warehouse and workshop, followed by the conversion of an adjacent building into more storage space for the ever-growing number of stage sets, props and, of course, puppets—many of which had to be located via a card index. During these early years, all the work—carving, painting and dressing the puppets, building the scenery, writing scripts, and even composing and playing the musical scores—was done solely by Bil and Cora Baird, who both seemed to thrive amid the chaos of arms, legs and torsos waiting to be combined into new characters. According to Baird himself, the couple used Darwin's *The Expression of the Emotions in Man and Animals* as a textbook, and the approach worked well indeed: the Bairds had no lack of work on the vaudeville/nightclub circuit.

In 1943 their fame rose a stage higher when they began playing in the more famous clubs such as the Le Ruben Bleu, and especially when their puppets appeared on stage in the Ziegfeld Follies. Television was the next inevitable step for the Bairds and, after appearing as guests on numerous talk shows all over the country (including, of course, Ed Sullivan's productions), the puppeteers produced their own series of children's shows for CBS TV, including the well-known *Life with Snarky Parker*, *The Whistling Wizard* and the short-lived *Bil Baird Show*. The NBC and ABC networks poached the Bairds after that to create several television specials, the most famous of which was *Art Carney Meets Peter and the Wolf* in 1958; the show won Baird an Emmy Award.

The 1960s found the Bairds taking their art form abroad with a production entitled *Davy Jones' Locker*; they toured India, Nepal, Afghanistan and several Soviet cities. By this time the Bairds had their own team of sculptors and technicians, and had created the Bil Baird Theater in Greenwich Village, New York (now run by the non-profit American Puppets Arts Council).

After Cora's death in 1967, Baird spent much of the 1970s producing and performing commercial work, except for the production of several shows at his own theatre. In 1982, however, he bounced back into the public eye with a stunning performance of Igor Stravinsky's *L'Histoire du soldat*, a production which charmed critics and public alike. Whatever his projects,

Baird refused to acknowledge the idea that his puppets were simply comic "little people". "They are the way we accent what is important in people," he said.

Cora Baird had once declared that there was much more to Baird's fascination with puppets than simple make-believe. "Bil fell into this work because it combined all the things he liked—sculpture, dance, music, painting and the theatre." From the beginning, both Bil and Cora Baird took their work in deadly earnest and never allowed a puppet to be used until its character had been fully and firmly developed. Such dedication has certainly survived in Baird's best-loved characters: Charlemane the Lion, Groovy the Rabbit Disc Jockey and Hedda Louella McBrood are all remembered as stars of television's golden age of the 1950s.

Born William Britton Baird. **Parents** William Hull, a chemical engineer and playwright, and Louise (Hetzel) Baird. **Marriages** 1) Evelyn Schwartz, 1932 (divorced, 1934); 2) Cora Burlar, an actress and puppeteer, 1937 (died, 1967); 3) Patricia Courtleigh, 1969 (divorced); 4) Susanna Lloyd, 1974. **Children** One son and one daughter, Peter Britton and Laura Jenne, by second marriage; one daughter, Madeleine, by fourth marriage. **Education** High School, Mason City, Iowa; State University of Iowa, BA, 1926; Chicago Academy of Fine Arts, 1926–27. **Military service** US Army Reserve, 1925. **Career** Puppeteer, Tony Sarg Marionettes, 1928–33; writer, builder, 1933; creator and producer, Bil Baird's Marionettes, 1934–40; with wife Cora, founded puppet warehouse and workshop, Fire Horse Manor, 1937; puppet show presenter in vaudeville, on Broadway, 1943–59; founder, with wife, Bil Baird Theater, where trained many other puppeteers, 1966 onwards. **Related activities** Producer of more than 400 commercials, also of Apollo and Gemini spaceflight simulations, and several films. **Awards and honours** Emmy Award nomination from National Academy of Television Arts and Sciences for *Art Carney Meets Peter and the Wolf*, 1958; Outer Circle Award, with wife Cora Baird, for founding a permanent puppet theatre, 1967; Jennie Heiden Award from American Theater Association for excellence in professional children's theatre, 1974. **Offices and memberships** International Alliance of Theatrical Stage Employees; director, International Puppet Federation; American Federation of Musicians; American Federation of Television and Radio Artists; American Guild of Musical Artists; American Guild of Variety Artists; National Academy of Television Arts and Sciences, governor, 1957–61; Screen Actors' Guild; Sigma Chi Fraternity, Alpha Eta Chapter; Omicron Delta Kappa. **Stage work as puppeteer** *Ali Baba and the Forty Thieves*, on tour, US cities, 1927–28; (choreographer) *Rip Van Winkle* and *Alice in Wonderland*, US tour, 1931–32; *The A&P Show*, 1933; *Bil Baird's Marionettes*, 1934; *Horse Eats Hat*, 1936; *Dr Faustus*, 1936; *Ziegfeld's Follies*, 1941, 1943; *Nellie Bly*, 1946; *Flahooley*, 1951; *Ali Baba and the Forty Thieves*, 1955; *Pageant of Puppet Variety*, 1957; *Carnival of Animals*; *Surprise Box*; toured US, India, Nepal, Afghanistan and Soviet Union with *Davy Jones' Locker*, 1959–63; *Man in the Moon*, 1961; *Baker Street*, 1963–65; New York World's Fair, 1964–65; *Chrysler Show Go Round*, 1964; *Davy Jones' Locker*, 1966; *The Magic Onion*, 1966; *People Is the Thing That the World Is Fullest Of*, 1967; *Winnie the Pooh*, 1967; *The Wizard of Oz*, 1968; *The Whistling Wizard and the Sultan of Tuffet*, 1969; *L'Histoire du soldat*, 1969; toured India and Turkey for US AID, 1970; *Holiday on Strings*, 1970; *Peter and the Wolf*, 1971; *The Magic Onion*, 1972; *Band Wagon*, 1973; *Pinocchio*, 1973; *Alice in Wonderland*, 1975; *Once Upon a Dragon*, 1977. **Film work** *The Sound of Music*. **Television** *Life with Snarky Parker*, 1949–50; *The Whistling Wizard*, 1952–53; *The Bil Baird Show*, 1953; *The Morning Show*, 1954–55; *Babes in Toyland*, 1954–55; *Heidi*, 1955; *Art Carney Meets Peter and the Wolf*, 1958; *The Sorcerer's Apprentice*, 1959; *Winnie the Pooh*, 1960; *O'Halloran's Luck*, 1961; *Baird's Eye View*, 1961; *Puppet Revue*, 1979; also made many guest appearances: *Galen Drake Show*, 1957, *Discovery '65*, 1965, *The Ed Sullivan Show*, *The Jack Paar Show*, *The Mike Douglas Show*. **Publications** *The Art of the Puppet* (young adult), 1965;

Schnitzel, the Yodeling Goat (juvenile), 1965; *Puppets and Population*, 1971. **Cause of death** Bone marrow cancer, at age 82. **Further reading** Alan Stern and Rupert Pray, *Bil Baird's Whistling Wizard*, 1952; Carlyle Wood, *TV Personalities Biographical Sketch Book*, 1954.

DUC LOUIS DE BROGLIE

French Physicist

Born **Dieppe, France, 15 August 1892**

Died **Paris, France, 19 March 1987**

For an aristocrat born with the title of Prince to push forward the boundaries of science and to gain a Nobel Prize is highly unusual, and in the case of Louis de Broglie it is even more remarkable as he showed no interest in being a scientist for the first part of his life.

Louis-Victor Pierre Raymond de Broglie was the younger son of the fifth Duc de Broglie. His forebears had come from Piedmont in Italy, and the French branch of the family to which he belonged had produced prominent military, scientific and political figures. His grandfather was French prime minister in the 1870s, and a great-grandfather fought under George Washington as chief lieutenant of the Marquis de Lafayette.

The young Louis was a solitary child, with a prodigious memory, and he could recite whole scenes from classical French dramas. He created a fantasy world for himself and discoursed for hours with the people he created in his loneliness. Literature and history remained the chief interests of his youth, and after study at the Lyceé Janson-de-Sailly in Paris, he gained his bachelor's degree in history from the Sorbonne.

All this changed when he accompanied his elder brother, Maurice, to an international conference in physics held in Brussels in 1911. These were the exciting days when the quantum theory of Max Planck was being developed.

Spectra had been the key to the change. Light and heat are only emitted and absorbed in discrete "packets" of energy, called "quanta" by Planck. The energies were proportional to the frequencies of the light. The energy can only come in multiples of quanta, therefore, 2, 8 or 20, say, but never 15.6 quanta. It was a revolutionary concept and very successful in explaining the simple spectra.

This idea that light behaved as finite units in some ways was a return to the particle theory of light. For some phenomena, such as interference and diffraction, light behaves as if it travels in waves, but for others, such as photo-electricity and the fact that light travels through a vacuum without any medium, were more simply explained by considering it as particles.

De Broglie was inspired to study physics, and by 1914 he had gained his degree in science at the Sorbonne. Further studies were interrupted by World War I; from 1914 to 1919 he served with the Army Radio-telegraphy Unit. Then it was back to the Sorbonne to work for his doctorate, and in 1924 he submitted his thesis *Recherches sur la théorie des quanta* to the Faculty of Sciences.

This remarkable paper was the basis of the development of wave mechanics. In it he proved mathematically, working from the quantum theory and relativity, that not only did light waves sometimes behave like particles, but that all matter has associated waves. This meant that an electron, for instance, which gives a visible blip on a television screen and had been regarded up to then as a finite particle of matter, has waves as well. If there are two vertical slits close together and an electron is fired at them, when it goes through one its associated waves are aware of the other and this affects where it lands on the screen beyond. Or if an electron is fired at a sheet of nickel and bounces back, it is clear from the direction it takes that it is aware of the distances between the atoms and does not just bump off the atom that its matter happens to hit. The concept was extraordinary and revolutionary.

De Broglie's paper was almost ignored, but its importance was realized by Einstein, and in 1927 experiments in both the US and Britain showed the effect clearly. His brilliance was acknowledged, and in 1929 he was awarded the Nobel Prize for Physics. In fact, his innovation cleared the errors from the existing quantum theory and became the basis for the whole structure of the study of wave mechanics.

Much of de Broglie's further career was devoted to teaching. He remained at the University of Paris, and by 1926 was professor of theoretical physics at the Henri Poincaré Institute, a post he held until 1962. It was at the institute that he founded the Centre of Studies in Applied Mathematics to bring physicists and mathematicians closer.

In 1945, with his brother Maurice who was an experimental physicist well known for his X-ray research, he was appointed an adviser to the French Atomic Energy Commission. He actively promoted the peaceful use of atomic power, and helped influence public opinion in France in that direction.

De Broglie published prolifically, some of his 20 books being translated into English, including *The Revolution in Physics*, *An Introduction to the Study of Wave Mechanics* and *Matter and Light*. Although none of his later works matched the eminence of his first paper, many of them were outstanding. In his eighties he was still at work, refining his theories.

Primarily a deep thinker and man of silent reflection, he tended to avoid company and was rarely seen at international symposia. He never married. However, he was a keen correspondent and this meant he exerted a great influence on physicists in France and overseas. His writing was distinguished, and he had the honour of being elected to the French Academy, the top institution in language and literature, in 1944, thus continuing a tradition established by his grandfather, father and brother.

On the death of his brother in 1960, Louis de Broglie inherited the title, and became the seventh duke, but to most of his scientific friends and admirers he continued to be referred to as Prince de Broglie, the title he had borne when in the very forefront of scientific progress.

Born Louis-Victor Pierre Raymond de Broglie. **Parents** Victor and Pauline (d'Armaillé) de Broglie. **Education** Lycée Janson-de-Sailly; University of Paris, degree in history, 1910, degree in science, 1913, PhD, 1924. **Military service** Army Radio-telegraphy Unit, 1914–19. **Career** Lecturer, Faculty of Sciences, University of Paris; professor of theoretical physics, Henri Poincaré Institute, 1928–62. **Related activities** Founder, Centre of Studies in Applied Mathematics, Henri Poincaré Institute, 1943; adviser, French Atomic Energy Commission, 1945 onwards. **Offices and memberships** Member, Academy of Sciences, 1933, permanent secretary, 1942; member, Académie Française, 1944. **Awards and honours** Nobel Prize for Physics, for work in wave mechanics, 1929; Henri Poincaré Medal, Academy of Sciences, 1929; Max Planck Medal, German Physical Society, 1938; Kalinga Prize, UNESCO. **Publications** Over 20 books, including *Selected Papers on Wave Mechanics*, London, 1928; *An Introduction to the Study of Wave Mechanics*, London, 1930; *Matter and Light*, New York, 1939; *Non-linear Wave Mechanics: A Causal Interpretation*, New York, 1960; *The Current Interpretation of Wave Mechanics, a Critical Study*, 1964; *The Revolution in Physics*. **Cause of death** Undisclosed, at age 94.

RONALD W. CLARK

British Biographer and Journalist

***Born* Wimbledon, England, 2 November 1916**

***Died* London, England, 9 March 1987**

Ronald Clark was a prolific author with many publications on both sides of the Atlantic. He is probably best remembered for his works on mountains and mountaineers and his biographies of famous scientists.

Born into a banker's family in Wimbledon, south London, he attended the local King's College School, eventually leaving to make a career in journalism. In 1943, at the height of World War II, he joined British United Press as a war correspondent, serving with the First Canadian and Second British Armies in north-west Europe. After victory he worked as a foreign correspondent and reported on the war crimes trials at Nuremberg.

Finishing as foreign correspondent in 1948, he was determined to continue to make his living by writing books rather than articles. All he needed was a subject to inspire him. Being a keen climber, of the scrambling variety, and a collector of "mountain Victoriana", he used these interests as his "launch pad". In 1948 he published *Splendid Hills: The Life and Photographs of Vittorio Sella, 1859–1943*, and followed this in 1950 with *The Early Alpine Guides*. A series of books on mountains and mountaineers followed, some directed at children. They were readable and accurate, if not particularly original, but in some cases his photographs made up for deficiencies in the text. One of his more amusing subjects was described in *An Eccentric in the Alps*, published in 1959. This featured W.A.B. Coolidge, a crotchety Victorian cleric who wrote on Alpine history, whose importance seemed to lie mainly in his having an aunt who was among the first women climbers, and a beagle bitch of similar repute among her species.

Clark found that good, readable, straightforward biography suited him, and he turned to a scientist next, Sir Henry Tizard, who advised the British government during World War II. Clark's book *Tizard*, published in 1965, portrayed the man well and it also gave a clear picture of the times in which he worked. This was followed by biographies of the Huxleys, J.B.S. Haldane, Einstein, Bertrand Russell and others. They were eminently readable and accurate, and in several cases he managed to obtain new and important material to use in his verbal portrayals. He even wrote a book on William Freedman, the American cryptologist who cracked the Japanese naval and diplomatic code called "purple", and on Thomas Edison. His biography *Freud: The Man and the Cause*, published in 1980, is a formidable and valuable work in which he makes use of much important new matter.

The fact that others might have written on the same subject never worried Clark. He set out determined to find something new about his subject and to make the book readable—aims he generally achieved.

He was married three times, but had no children from any of the marriages. Towards the end of his life he suffered ill-health, but he worked on, and two biographies, one on Benjamin Franklin and the other on Lenin, were published posthumously.

Born Ronald William Clark. **Parents** William Ernest, a banker, and Ethel Clark. **Marriages** Three; one to Pearla Odden, an author. **Education** King's College School, Wimbledon, England. **Career** Magazine journalist for a short time; war and foreign correspondent for United Press, attached to the First Canadian and Second British Armies, north-west Europe, also at Nuremberg trials, 1943–48; writer, mainly of biographies and books on mountaineering, 1948 onwards; also, contributor to periodicals and newspapers, including *The Times*, *Guardian*,

Cornhill, *Blackwoods*. **Publications** *Splendid Hills: The Life and Photographs of Vittorio Sella, 1859–1943*, 1948; *The Early Alpine Guides*, London, 1949, New York, 1950; *The Victorian Mountaineers*, 1953, 1954; *Lion Boy: The Story of Cedric Crossfield*, 1954; *Come Climbing with Me*, 1955; *The Picture History of Mountaineering*, London, 1956; *Great Moments in Mountaineering* (juvenile), 1956; *Six Great Mountaineers: Edward Whymper, A.F. Mummery, J. Norman Collie, George Leigh Mallory, Geoffrey Winthrop Young, Sir John Hunt*, 1956; *True Book About Mountaineering*, 1957; (with E.C. Pyatt) *Mountaineering in Britain: A History from the Earliest Times to the Present Day*, 1957; *We Go to Switzerland* (juvenile), 1958; *The Royal Albert Hall*, London, 1958; *Instructions to Young Ramblers*, 1958; *Sir John Cockroft, O.M.*, 1959; *Great Moments in Rescue Work*, USA, 1959, published in England as *Great Moments of Rescue*, 1959; *We Go to Scotland* (juvenile), 1959; *An Encounter in the Alps*, 1959; *Eccentric in the Alps: The Story of W.A.B. Coolidge, the Great Victorian Mountaineer*, 1959; *Sir Mortimer Wheeler*, 1960; *Montgomery of Alamein*, 1960; *We Go to Southern France*, 1960; *Sir Julian Huxley, F.R.S.*, England, 1960, USA, 1961; *How to Use Your Camera*, 1961; *Great Moments in Battle* (juvenile), 1961; *The Birth of the Bomb*, USA, 1961, published in England as *The Birth of the Bomb: The Untold Story of Britain's Part in the Weapon That Changed the World*, 1961; *Sir Winston Churchill*, 1962; *The Rise of the Boffins*, 1962; *We Go to the West Country*, 1962; *Great Moments in Espionage*, 1963, 1964; *We Go to England*, 1963; *Explorers of the World*, 1964; *We Go to Northern Italy*, 1964; *Battle for Britain: Sixteen Weeks That Changed the Course of History*, 1965, 1966; *Tizard*, 1965; *The Day the Rope Broke: The Story of the First Ascent of the Matterhorn*, USA, 1965, published in England as *The Day the Rope Broke: The Story of a Great Victorian Tragedy*, 1965; (with wife Pearla Clark) *We Go to Southern England*, 1964; *The Air: The Story of the Montgolfiers, the Lilienthals, the Wright Brothers, Cobham and Whittle* (juvenile), 1966, 1967; *Queen Victoria's Bomb: The Disclosures of Professor Franklin Huxtable* (novel), 1967, 1968; *The Huxleys*, 1968; *J.B.S.: The Life and Work of J.B.S. Haldane*, London, 1968, USA, 1969; *The Bomb That Failed* (novel), 1969; *The Last Year of the Old World: A Fiction of History* (novel), 1970; *Einstein: The Life and Times*, 1971; *A Biography of the Nuffield Foundation*, London, 1972; *Sir Edward Appleton*, London, 1972; *The Alps*, 1973; *Einstein: The Life and Times*, 1973; *The Scientific Breakthrough: The Impact of Modern Invention*, 1974; *The Life of Bertrand Russell*, London, 1975, USA, 1976; *Men, Myths and Mountains*, 1976; *The Man Who Broke Purple*, 1977; *Freud: The Man and the Cause*, 1980; biographies of Benjamin Franklin and Lenin published posthumously, 1987. **Cause of death** Undisclosed, at age 70.

EDDIE DURHAM

American Jazz Musician and Arranger

Born **San Marcos, Texas, 19 August 1906**

Died **New York City, New York, 6 March 1987**

Despite his importance in the history of jazz, Eddie Durham is in many ways a neglected figure. Without his innovation on the guitar, there would have been no amplified guitar in jazz, and possibly no electric guitar either. His many arrangements are excellent, their existence a crucial link in the history of jazz. If for nothing else, Durham should be remembered as the man who scored possibly the most famous Swing Era arrangement of all time, Glenn Miller's "In the Mood".

Durham was a professional musician by the age of ten, playing first guitar and then trombone with the family group of the Durham Brothers, featuring two brothers and two cousins. He was married at the age of 16, and moved for more pay to a circus band in which he learned how to score trombone and trumpet sections. Gigs with various local bands eventually found him in Walter Page's Blue Devils with pianist Count Basie. The two moved quickly via the Elmer Payne band into Bennie Moten's Kansas City Orchestra in the summer of 1929. There Durham made an immediate impact, writing and arranging almost all the band's repertoire and transforming an essentially local band into one of national importance. His arrangements were sophisticated and articulate, with strong section writing and relaxed yet cohesive rhythms that were later to characterize most bands of the Swing Era. These rhythms were basically rhythmically repetitive riffs drawn from blues music as developed by the many Kansas City bands. It was largely due to Durham that this Kansas City style became the standard everyone else had to emulate. Some critics have called him the unsung hero of the Swing Era, for while the bandleaders got the credit, it was their best arranger, Eddie Durham, who did the work.

In 1933, at the height of the Depression, Durham made a brave choice and left Moten to work for Cab Calloway in New York. The engagement lasted only a week, and then Durham was on his own as a freelancer. He survived—well enough to be hired in 1935 as a trombonist by the Jimmie Lunceford Orchestra, for whom he produced several notable arrangements.

While in this band, Durham perfected the guitar experiments he had begun with the Moten band. He would insert a circular piece of aluminium the size of a 78 rpm record under his guitar strings in order to amplify the sound, and bring the microphone right up to the strings. The resulting sound was penetrating, and while those tracks with Moten featuring his adapted guitar are striking, those with Lunceford sound as if the instrument was electronically amplified. The importance of this development is easily overlooked, and in print it reads like a gimmick. But what Durham had done was to invent the amplified guitar. At this stage the amplification was not electric, but that was just a short step away—a step made by two of the people Durham demonstrated the device to. Floyd Smith and, more importantly, Charlie Christian went on to establish the place of the electric guitar in jazz.

But it was as an arranger rather than a soloist that Durham was most in demand, and in 1937 he left Lunceford to rejoin Basie whose band was in need of new and tighter arrangements to meet the critical gaze any new band received in New York. He stayed a year and his arrangements were a great success, one of them—"Swingin' the Blues"—credited as responsible for wiping out Chick Webb's band in an early 1938 big-band contest. For the rest of the 1930s and into the early 1940s—the heyday of big bands—Durham was much in demand as an arranger, and he readily found work with Glenn Miller, Artie Shaw and Lunceford again. But as the jazz climate changed, Durham's fortunes declined. His small group of Kansas City jazzers was shortlived, as was his 1940 big band, and he soon found himself director of the all-women International Sweethearts of Rhythm Band from 1941 to 1943, which, as he wryly remarked, at least kept him out of the army. He continued to freelance as an arranger during the 1950s, leading his own groups from 1957, and after a fallow period resumed regular playing when he joined Buddy Tate's band in 1969. In the 1980s he toured and recorded with the Harlem Blues and Jazz Band.

These later activities all seem somewhat of an anticlimax, and Durham rarely lived up to the promise he showed in the 1930s. Yet for his role in jazz instrumentation and arrangement he deserves to be fondly remembered.

Born Edward Durham. **Children** Marsha, Lesa, Edward Jr and Edward T. **Career** Toured in minstrel shows with the Durham Brothers Band, playing first banjo then guitar and trombone; toured with various bands, including Walter Page's Blue Devils; worked and arranged for Bennie Moten's Kansas City Orchestra, 1929–33; arranged for Willie Bryant, 1934; joined Jimmie

Lunceford's band, 1935; played with Count Basie's band, 1937–38; member of Kansas City Five and Kansas City Six; arranged for Glenn Miller, Artie Shaw, Jan Savitt and others, 1939–40; formed own big band, 1940; music director, International Sweethearts of Rhythm, 1941–43; later directed own all-female orchestra and other small groups; freelance arranger during 1950s and 1960s; joined Buddy Tate, 1969; appeared with Countsmen and toured Europe in 1980s with Harlem Blues and Jazz Band. **Compositions and arrangements** (for Jimmie Lunceford) "Pigeon Walk", "Lunceford Special", "Blues in the Groove"; (for Count Basie) "Out the Window", "Topsy", "Time Out"; (for Glenn Miller) "Slip Horn Jive", "Glen Island Special", "Wham". **Recordings** (as leader) *Eddie Durham*, RCA LPL1-5029, 1973–74; *Blue Bone*, JSP 1030, 1981; (as sideman) Kansas City Five, "Good Mornin' Blues", Com.511, 1938; Kansas City Six, "Way Down Yonder in New Orleans", Com.512, 1938; "Countless Blues", Com.509, 1938; E. Barefield, *Eddie Barefield*, RCA LPL1-5035, 1973. **Recorded arrangements** (with Durham as sideman unless stated) B. Moten, "Moten Swing", Vic.23384, 1932; J. Lunceford, "Avalon", Decca 668, 1935; J. Lunceford, "Hittin' the Bottle", Decca 765, 1935; J. Lunceford, "Harlem Shout", Decca 980, 1936; C. Basie, "Time Out", Decca 1538, 1937; C. Basie, "Topsy", Decca 1770, 1937; C. Basie, "Swingin' the Blues", Decca 1880, 1938; (arranger only) C. Basie, "Jumpin' at the Woodside", Decca 2212, 1938; J. Lunceford, "Lunceford Special", Voc./OK 5326, 1939. **Cause of death** Result of a fall, at age 80. **Further reading** S. Dance, *The World of Count Basie*, New York and London, 1980; M.L. Hester, *Going to Kansas City*, Sherman, Texas, 1980; S. Placksin, *American Women in Jazz, 1900 to the Present*, New York, 1982.

LLOYD GOODRICH

American Museum Director, Author and Art Critic
Born **Nutley, New Jersey, 10 July 1897**
Died **New York City, New York, 27 March 1987**

The subjects of an endless stream of books, catalogues and articles which flowed from the pen of Lloyd Goodrich from 1930 until his death in 1987 will leave the reader in no doubt of the focus of his interest: almost without exception he wrote on American art of the nineteenth and twentieth centuries. Given his extremely long association with the Whitney Museum of American Art, where he was employed from 1930 until his retirement in 1968, this may come as no surprise.

Born in Nutley, New Jersey, from an early age Goodrich was familiar with American painting: his family owned a Winslow Homer and his father's circle of friends included the painter Fred Dana Marsh, whose son Reginald, also a painter, became a close friend. Encouraged by his family to pursue a career as a painter, Goodrich studied for four years at the Art Students' League from 1913, spending 1916 at the National Academy of Design.

Increasingly doubtful of his talent as an artist, after World War I he entered the steel industry, but by 1923 he had abandoned this line and began editing religious works for Macmillan Publishers. At around this time he began to review books for *The Arts*, a publication subsidized by Mrs Gertrude Vanderbilt Whitney, and a friendship and partnership developed with the benefactress which resulted in her inviting him to join the newly founded Whitney Museum of American Art as a research curator in 1930. During his long career there he held the position of associate curator, associate director, director, trustee, and finally, from 1968, advisory director, preferring by then to devote more time to his writing. This suggests that he felt he had neglected his academic pursuits: quite the reverse may be noted. Although confining himself to American art, Goodrich was a prolific writer, publishing several weighty monographs on prominent American artists such as Thomas Eakins, Winslow Homer, Edward Hopper and Georgia O'Keeffe, as well as surveys of American painting, and a continuous flow of catalogues and articles, while also serving on the editorial boards of the *Magazine of Art*, *American Quarterly*, *Art Bulletin* and *Art in America*.

Goodrich's association with the Whitney Museum resulted not only in the expansion of the collections, notably with the gift of 2000 works by Edward Hopper from his widow in 1968, but also in a number of important retrospective and historical exhibitions focusing on the artistic heritage of North America.

Despite its earlier acquisitions of pre-1900 American art, the museum sold these holdings in 1949, and from that date concentrated on collecting twentieth-century American art, becoming the main American collection of contemporary painters like Rothko and de Kooning. Goodrich played a significant role in the support of contemporary art and artists, and was personally involved in commissioning artists for public spaces while associated with the New York regional office of the Public Works of Art Project in 1933.

Much later in his career he drew attention to the plight of the living artist, proposing that they should receive increased financial assistance through a system of fees and public patronage, stating "the important thing is that we should recognize the value of the creative artist to our society, and strive to reward him more adequately for what he contributes to our national life". Likewise, he was keen to protect the buying public by urging support of the bill to protect art purchasers against forgeries.

Actively involved in scores of national artistic associations and foundations, commissions, exhibition and advisory committees, Goodrich also found time to mount a series of important shows. Perhaps the one with which he is most closely associated, and which inaugurated the controversial new museum building designed by Marcel Breuer and Hamilton Smith in 1966, was *Art in the United States: 1670–1966*, prompting one reviewer to write that he had gathered "the finest collection of American painting and sculpture yet installed under one roof...borrowed from all parts of the country. Some rare loans...give proof of the affectionate trust that the Whitney and its director have generated in America."

The honours bestowed upon him include fellowship of the American Academy of Arts and Sciences and of the Art Students' League, a rare appointment for a non-practising artist.

Born Lloyd Goodrich. **Parents** Henry Wickes, lawyer, and Madeleine (Lloyd) Goodrich. **Marriage** Edith Havens, teacher of costume illustration, 1924. **Children** David Lloyd, Madeleine Lloyd. **Education** Art Students' League; National Academy of Design, New York. **Career** Shipyard worker; Vulcan Steel Products Corporation and Consolidated Steel Corporation; James R. Marsh's ornamental ironworks firm; editor, religious books department, Macmillan Publishing Company, New York, 1923–25; associate editor, *Arts* magazine 1925–27, 1928–29, European editor, 1927–28, contributing editor, 1929–31; research curator and writer, Whitney Museum of American Art, New York, 1930–47, associate curator, 1947–48, associate director, 1948–58, director, 1958–68, advisory director, 1968–71, consultant, 1971–87. **Related activities** Assistant art critic, *New York Times*, 1929; New York Office of Public Works Art Project, 1933–34; adviser on purchase of American art, Metropolitan Museum of Art, 1937; trustee, American Federation of Arts, 1942 onwards, vice-president, 1957–62, honorary vice-president, 1962 onwards; member, editorial board of *Magazine of Art*, 1942–53, chairman, 1942–50; member, editorial board of *Art Bulletin*, 1943 onwards, editorial board of *Art in America*, 1946 onwards; chairman, Committee on Government and Art, 1948 onwards; director, College

Art Association of America, 1948–52; member, editorial board of *American Quarterly*, 1952–53, National Council on Arts and Government, 1954 onwards, vice-chairman, 1962 onwards; vice-president, Sara Roby Foundation, 1956 onwards; founding member, Friends of the Whitney Museum, 1956; member, White House advisory committee for art, 1960–63; co-chairman, Joint Artists–Museums Committee; associate, seminar on American Civilization, Columbia; adviser, Committee of Artists' Societies selection committee; trustee: Halpert Foundation, American Friends of Tate Gallery; member: Whitney Museum board of trustees, National Collection of Fine Arts Commission, Committee on Religion and Art in America, advisory board of Carnegie Study of American Art, advisory panel on the visual arts of New York State Council on the Arts, Edward MacDowell Association board of directors, Smithsonian Art Commission, Michigan Cultural Commission, editorial board of *Art Bulletin*, editorial board of *American Art Journal*, international scientific council of *Enciclopedia dell'Arte*, regional board of Archives of American Art, Cornell University's College of Architecture council, advisory commission to the Stone Mountain Memorial Association, Atlanta. **Memberships** International Art Critics' Association, Association of Art Museum Directors, Drawing Society. **Awards and honours** *Art in America* award, 1959; DFA, Cornell College, Iowa, 1963; National Art Materials Trade Association award, 1964; DFA, Colby College, 1964; award of merit, Philadelphia Museum College of Art, 1964; fellow, American Academy of Arts and Sciences, Art Students' League, 1966 onwards; honorary member, American Institute of Interior Designers; Creative Arts award, Brandeis University, 1970. **Publications** *Kenneth Hays Miller*, 1930; *H.E. Schnakenberg*, 1931; *Thomas Eakins: His Life and Work*, 1933; *Winslow Homer*, 1944; *American Watercolor and Winslow Homer*, 1945; (editor) *Research in American Art*, 1945; *Albert P. Ryder Centenary Exhibition*, 1947; *Yasuo Kuniyoshi: Retrospective Exhibition*, 1948; *Max Weber: Retrospective Exhibition*, 1949; *Edward Hopper: Retrospective Exhibition*, 1950; *John Sloan*, 1952; (with Atsuo Imaizumi) *Kuniyoshi: Catalogue of Kuniyoshi's Posthumous Exhibition*, 1954; (contributor) *New Art in America*, 1957; (editor) *The Museum and the Artist*, 1958; (with John I.H. Baur) *Four American Expressionists: Doris Caesar, Chaim Gross, Karl Knaths, Abraham Rattner*, 1959; *Albert P. Ryder*, 1959; *Young America, 1960*, 1960; *Thirty American Painters Under Thirty-six*, 1960; (with John I.H. Baur) *American Art of Our Century*, 1961, published in England as *American Art of the Twentieth Century*, 1962; (with Edward Bryant) *Forty Artists Under Forty from the Collection of the Whitney Museum of American Art*, 1962; *The Drawings of Edwin Dickinson*, 1963; (author of preface) Andrew Wyeth, *The Four Seasons: Paintings and Drawings*, 1963; *Pioneers of Modern Art in America: The Decade of the Armory Show, 1910–1920*, 1963; *Edward Hopper: Exhibition and Catalogue*, 1964; (author of foreword) ed. John I.H. Baur, *Between the Fairs: Twenty Five Years of American Art, 1939–1964*, 1964; *Edwin Dickinson*, 1965; *Art of the United States, 1670–1966*, 1966; *Three Centuries of American Art*, 1966; *Raphael Soyer*, 1967; *Sao Paulo Nine: United States of America*, 1967; *The Graphic Art of Winslow Homer*, 1968; (with Patricia FitzGerald Mandel) *John Heliker*, 1968; *Winslow Homer's America*, 1969; *Fifty Years of Painting by Max Weber*, 1969; *Five Paintings from Thomas Nast's Grand Caricature*, 1970; *Georgia O'Keeffe*, 1970; *Edward Hopper*, 1971; (editor) *Realism and Surrealism in American Art: From the Sara Roby Foundation Collection*, 1971; *Americans: Individualists at Work*, 1972; *Reginald Marsh*, 1972; *The White House Gardens*, 1973; *Harold Sterner*, 1974. **Cause of death** Cancer, at age 89.

FREDDIE GREEN

American Jazz Musician

***Born* Charleston, South Carolina, 31 March 1911**

***Died* Las Vegas, Nevada, 1 March 1987**

It is always said of rhythm guitarist Freddie Green that he never took a solo and never played amplified guitar. The first is almost right, the second completely right, but what they both highlight is that Green was one of those rare musicians who found satisfaction with one role in one band and stayed loyal to both all his life.

Green was born in Charleston, South Carolina, in 1911 and began to teach himself banjo and guitar at the age of 12—he remained entirely self-taught. After a few local jobs, he moved to New York in 1930 and eked out an existence, working by day as an upholsterer and by night as a freelance musician. In various clubs he played for dancers and there picked up the ability to judge tempo and create a supple rhythm. His break came in late 1936 when impresario John Hammond (q.v.) heard him play at the Black Cat in Greenwich Village and recommended to Count Basie, who was putting together his first national tour out of Kansas City, that he employ Green. Basie already had a guitarist, Claude Williams, so reluctantly auditioned Green, but then hired him on the spot. For the first few weeks of the tour, Green was forced to sit in the wings until Williams left the band.

The date was 1937, and apart from a short interlude in 1950, Green stayed with Basie until the latter's death in 1984. It was a remarkable display of loyalty on both sides and it allowed Green to develop to perfection the role of the acoustic guitar in the rhythm section, investing it with such personality as to make it almost a solo instrument. Green rarely gave interviews, which he considered an intrusion in his private life, but he did once remark that "a performance has what I call a rhythm wave, and the rhythm guitar can help to keep that wave smooth and accurate". A descriptive statement masking a complex and skilled performance, for, as critic Chris Sheridan has noted, "there were three aspects of what might at first sight seem a simple matter. He freed the beat from metronomic clomping by creating a constantly shifting variation on the chord structure, he afforded his playing quite subtle variations in dynamics by slight changes in striking position, and he meshed his playing very carefully with his drummers."

In the Basie band Green teamed up with bassist Walter Page and drummer Jo Jones in what was known as the all-American rhythm section. Arranger Nat Pierce, a one-time writer for the Basie band, remarked that "they had a kind of throb going, no one instrument louder than the other, so it was a real section", while Harry Edison, a trumpeter with Basie from 1938 to 1950, remembered that "Freddie, Walter and Jo would follow Basie until he hit the right tempo, and when he started they kept it". In later years, when less reliable timekeepers played with the band, Green could always be relied upon to provide the rock-steady rhythm. In every way he was the heartbeat of the Basie band, his light, propulsive and understated accompaniment as precise as a metronome.

To say he never took a solo is not completely right, but the exceptions tend to prove the rule that he was, above all, a rhythm guitarist. His style remained constant, with the single-string playing in his accompaniment to folk-singer Brother John Sellers a rare exception. And although he did record several albums under his own name, and was much in demand as a session player with many famous musicians, the core of his work was with Basie. What is true is that throughout his life, he never touched an amplified guitar, much less an electric one, despite the sometime presence in the band of Eddie Durham (q.v.), who pioneered the acceptance of the first in jazz and thereby cleared the way for the introduction of the second.

Green knew little life outside the band, joining its softball team and striking up lifelong friendships with many of his colleagues. So it was a considerable shock to him when, in 1950, Basie disbanded the big band and set up a small group without him. One night he climbed back on to the bandstand, uninvited, and began to play. He was back in the band, and the sight of "Old Freddie Green sitting there like a sheepdog looking round to see that nothing is going wrong" was a familiar sight for the next 30 years.

Born Frederick William Greene. **Education** High school, New York. **Career** Self-taught musician from the age of 12; began performing as a banjo player; played guitar with Kenny "Kloock" Clarke, 1936; rhythm guitarist with Count Basie's band, 1937–87. **Related activities** Session musician; played with, among others, Benny Goodman, Benny Carter, Teddy Wilson, Lionel Hampton, Joe Sullivan, I. Jacquet, Lester Young, Billie Holiday, Brother John Sellers, Buck Clayton, Joe Turner, Jimmy Rushing, Jo Jones, Al Cohn and Joe Newman. **Awards and honours** Won *Down Beat* Critics' Poll, 1958. **Compositions** Contributions to Count Basie's repertoire include "Down for Double", "Right On" and "Corner Pocket". **Recordings** (as leader) *Mr Rhythm*, RCA LPM1210, 1955; (with Count Basie) "Good Morning Blues", Decca 1446, 1937; "Topsy", Decca 1770, 1937; "Down for Double", OK 6584, 1941; *Dance Session*, Clef 626, 647, 1952–54, including "Right On", 1953; "Two for the Blues", Clef 89131, 1954; *April in Paris*, Verve 8012, 1955–56, including "Corner Pocket", 1955; *Kansas City Shout*, Pablo 2310859, 1980; (with others) Kansas City Six, "Them There Eyes", Com. 511, 1938; P.W. Russell, "Dinah", HRS 1000, 1938; L. Young, "Blue Lester", Savoy 581, 1944; B.J. Sellers, *Brother John Sellers Sings Blues and Folk Songs*, Van. 8005, 1954, including "Boll Weevil"; J. Newman, *All I Wanna Do Is Swing*, RCA LPM1118, 1955. **Cause of death** Undisclosed, at age 75. **Further reading** R. Horricks, *Count Basie and his Orchestra: Its Music and Its Musicians*, London and New York, 1957; M.J. Summerfield, *The Jazz Guitar: Its Evolution and Its Players*, Gateshead, England, 1978.

WOODY HAYES

American Football Coach

***Born* Clifton, Ohio, 14 February 1913**

***Died* Upper Arlington, Ohio, 11 March 1987**

For nearly 28 years, when the name of the Ohio State University came to mind to even the most casual college football fan, the name of Wayne Woodrow Hayes was sure to follow. Legends are rarely made in one's own time (in spite of what the cliché dictates), but Woody Hayes unquestionably was—not only for his success, but also for his uniquely "charismatic" approach to the game. Truly, Hayes's legend is as strong as ever today, and it is still difficult to imagine anyone else being the head coach of the Ohio State Buckeye football team.

Woody Hayes had the reputation of being a gruff, fiery, temperamental, win-at-all-cost type of individual. Indeed, this could be considered a rather good characterization of him. He had, however, a much softer side. He had a certain charm that the parents of prospective recruits to the OSU football team often found hard to resist. He was also characterized by the rather prudish attitudes and values that were common to those in his generation who shared similar backgrounds. He shied away from all vices and, not surprisingly, had little tolerance for those who did not.

Hayes grew up in Newcomerstown, Ohio, the youngest of three children of a school superintendent. Even as a child he had the reputation of being the "toughest kid on the block" and a natural leader. He inherited a love of reading from his father, and was a superior student and athlete. He attended Denison University in Granville, Ohio, where he played football, baseball and basketball. Even at this stage in his life he had the reputation of being a poor loser.

His original aspiration was to be a lawyer, but the Depression (as it did for many) changed the course of his life. He became a high school teacher–coach instead, first in Mingo Junction, Ohio, then in New Philadelphia, Ohio. During his stint in the latter place he earned a master's degree in educational administration from Ohio State, in 1939.

He joined the US Navy in 1941 and served first as chief of exercise programmes for new recruits in Norfolk, Virginia, and then as commander of a patrol chaser and destroyer escort in the Pacific. He was discharged in 1946 with the rank of lieutenant-commander, but he never really left the military behind, as its influence dominated his thoughts and strategies as a football coach.

Upon his return to Ohio, he became head football coach at his alma mater, Denison University, beginning a head coaching career that would last for the next 33 seasons. Hayes stayed at Denison for three seasons, then moved on for two more to Miami University in Oxford, Ohio.

In 1951 Hayes was appointed head coach at Ohio State. His predecessor had resigned because the pressures of producing a winning football programme at OSU had driven him to the brink of a nervous breakdown. Hayes struggled during his first year and drew the wrath of fans and players alike. His teams gradually improved, however, and in 1954 he won the first of his two national championships. From here, Hayes began to build his dynasty: by 1962 his teams had won four Big Ten Conference titles, a conference record 17 straight Big Ten games, and two Rose Bowl games. In 1968 his team went undefeated and Ohio State was again named the national champion.

The year 1969 saw the beginning of the legendary clashes between Hayes's OSU teams and Bo Schembechler's University of Michigan Wolverine teams. Schembechler, one of Hayes's former protégés from Miami of Ohio, upset his mentor in the 1969 game after Hayes's team was again undefeated and in search of a second straight national championship.

One of Hayes's most notorious moments as a coach came during the Michigan game in 1971. Toward the end of the game, the Buckeyes (behind 10–7), were on a touchdown drive that would have given them the lead. Michigan, however, intercepted a pass that assured them of victory. Hayes was furious. He argued bitterly with the officials, maintaining that Michigan had been guilty of pass interference. Hayes was subsequently penalized for unsportsmanlike conduct, and then went on a rampage in front of a national televison audience. He hurled a yard marker on to the field and ripped a downs marker flag to shreds. Perhaps this was one of his more famous outbursts, but it was certainly not his first and was by no means his last.

In 1973, minutes before his Buckeyes were to meet the University of Southern California in the Rose Bowl, a newspaper photographer was crouching near a huddle of OSU players gathered around Hayes during pre-game warm-ups. After the huddle broke, Hayes ran over to the unwitting photographer, shoved the camera into his face and cursed him. The photographer required medical attention and later filed assault charges.

In 1977, in another important game with his arch-rival Schembechler, Hayes punched an ABC cameraman in the stomach during another frustrating loss to the Wolverines which cost Ohio State a trip to the Rose Bowl. Once again, Hayes's antics were nationally televised for all to see.

His conduct notwithstanding, Hayes continued to field successful teams on the gridiron during the 1970s. His teams went to five Rose Bowls (winning only one, however) and continued to be a national power. Still, Hayes's temper was bound to get the best of him.

On 29 December 1978, during the closing moments of a painful 17–15 loss to Clemson in the Gator Bowl, Hayes let his emotions do his thinking one time too many. As a Clemson player was chased out of bounds and on to the Ohio State sideline after intercepting a Buckeye pass, Hayes stepped up and struck the player as he tried to make his way back to his own sideline. Once again, the game was nationally televised and there was no doubting the evidence against Hayes. The next day he was fired and the end of an era came to Ohio State football. Even Hayes, who was rarely repentant, could see the logic in his fate: "I got what was coming to me," he admitted the day after his dismissal.

Despite his lapses into barbarism, Hayes was a thinking man's coach. He was an avid reader, especially of military histories, and the influences of this were more than evident in his style of coaching. He was a strong admirer of General George S. Patton and one might almost think their roles were interchangeable the way Hayes talked. In his defence of running the football (instead of passing it, the way most teams outside the Midwest did), Hayes said: "The most deceptive course in football is straight at the goalposts. When the Germans went through the Argonne, it wasn't an 18 sweep, it was a 10 trap." In his role as commander at Ohio State, battlefield tactics and discipline were an important part of the Buckeye game plan.

True to form, Hayes was also a staunch conservative when it came to politics. He was an unabashed admirer of the beleaguered former president Richard Nixon, calling him "undoubtedly the finest third string end who ever ran for president of our country". In 1974 he told an audience of graduate students his stand on the Watergate cover-up: "I would have done the same thing myself and I consider myself an honourable man."

In his later years Hayes remained close to Ohio State University and was still considered a hero by his fellow Ohioans. He spent his time in speaking engagements and was named professor emeritus by the OSU board of trustees. He kept his small office on campus until the end, and had a street named after him outside the Ohio State stadium.

Hayes, for all his flamboyance on the football sideline, was a modest man: "I am not very smart," he once said, "but I recognize that I am not very smart. So I outwork every SOB that comes down the pike." Perhaps he uttered his own epitaph when, the day after his dismissal, he said: "Nobody despises to lose more than I do. That's got me into trouble over the years, but it also made a man of mediocre ability into a pretty good coach." It is probably safe to say that even Michigan Wolverine fans wish Hayes never punched that Clemson player. He was certainly one of the most colourful personalities ever involved in college football, and the game sorely misses him. Regardless of this truth, in the minds of both fans and opponents of Ohio State football, Hayes will probably go on coaching forever.

Born Wayne Woodrow Hayes. **Parents** Wayne Benton, a school superintendent, and Effie Jane (Hupp) Hayes. **Marriage** Anne Gross, 1942. **Children** Steven. **Education** Denison University, Ohio, BA; Ohio State University, MA, 1939. **Military service** US Navy, becoming lieutenant-commander, World War II. **Career** Teacher–coach, Mingo Junction and New Philadelphia high schools, Ohio; football coach: Denison University, Ohio, 1946–48, Miami University, Oxford, Ohio, 1948–50; head coach, Ohio State University, 1951–78. **Awards and honours** Honorary PhD, Ohio State University, 1986. **Publications** *Football at Ohio State*, 1957; *Hot Line to Victory*, 1969; *You Win with People*, 1974. **Cause of death** Heart attack, at age 74. **Further reading** Jerry Brondfield, *Woody Hayes and the 100-Yard War*; Robert Vare, *Buckeye*.

ALLAN JAFFE

American Jazz Musician and Impresario

***Born* Pottsville, Pennsylvania, 24 April 1935**

***Died* New Orleans, Louisiana, 9 March 1987**

There is a splendid story, almost a fairytale, about how Allan Jaffe came to acquire his job as owner and manager of the Preservation Hall in New Orleans. Just married, Jaffe and his new wife Sandra were on their honeymoon and touring the United States in order to choose a place to live. They had reached New Orleans, where one night they heard a jazz band. This decided them both that here was where they wanted to stay. Jaffe was a graduate of the Wharton School of Finance and he had a flourishing business, but he gave it all up and, in 1961, devoted the rest of his life to the music he heard that night.

Like all fairytales, this one does have a happy ending. When Jaffe arrived in New Orleans, its indigenous jazz was going through one of its unfashionable periods. Musicians were hard pressed to find gigs to play or venues to play in, and the traditional music of the city was in danger of dying out. Jaffe rescued it from potential oblivion, and thus ensured that the music, and its practitioners, lived to play another day. He took over the ailing Preservation Hall and restored it as a venue where local musicians could play their own music. Under his guidance, the hall soon became both a tourist mecca and a living museum of New Orleans jazz, attracting music students, jazz fans, historians and the many casual tourists, all interested in the sounds played nightly within.

Jaffe was not the only person involved in the renaissance of New Orleans music, but as a colleague, Christopher Botsford, pointed out, "with his persistence and the close relationship he developed with his musicians and the love that he had for the music", he was always at the forefront of every attempt to promote New Orleans jazz. "In many ways, he's been the sparkplug of traditional New Orleans music for 25 years," remarked William Russell, curator of jazz archives at Tulane University. Jaffe organized tours of Preservation Hall musicians to such countries as Japan and Britain, attracting worldwide support for his venue and, more importantly, for the musicians whose livelihoods he was preserving. Jaffe worked as tour operator and manager, but he was also an unobtrusive sideman, playing a silver tuba somewhere in the background. As Botsford noted after his death, the work "was a real labour of love for him, but he did it because he had fun". Part of that fun was the fact that the hall was a financial success, but Jaffe put as much in as he took out, and many musicians had cause to give thanks for this generous support over the years. It was largely due to his dedication that New Orleans was reinstated in its rightful place as one of the major centres of jazz in the world.

Jaffe died at the tragically early age of 51. His funeral was in the classic New Orleans style, with a procession through the French Quarter led by many of the elderly musicians whose careers he had supported over the years. It was a fitting tribute to a man who once paid them the ultimate compliment when he said that "the old musicians appeared to me as folk heroes. It was like a chance to be part of the *Iliad* and the *Odyssey*."

Born Alan Jaffe. **Parents** Harry and Fanny Jaffe. **Marriage** Sandra. **Children** Benjamin and Russell. **Education** Wharton School of Finance. **Career** Jazz impresario; owner and manager, Preservation Hall, New Orleans; organized tours, Preservation Hall musicians, USA, Japan, Europe, from 1963. **Related activities** Jazz tuba player; toured with various musicians, Lincoln

Center, New York, Symphony Hall, Boston, Royal Festival Hall, London, Israel, South America, Japan; played with Olympia Brass Band, New Orleans. **Cause of death** Cancer, at age 51.

EUGEN JOCHUM

German Conductor

***Born* Babenhausen, Germany, 1 November 1902**

***Died* Munich, West Germany, 26 March 1987**

"I know very precisely what I want but I hope I am not a school master. I don't want to be a dictator, I only want to make an orchestra free—in some ways it is more difficult than to be a dictator. I am not a man who thinks that if an orchestra has the greatest discipline it's the best."

Eugen Jochum, one of the last representatives of the traditional German school of conducting and the founder of the Bavarian Radio Symphony Orchestra, was widely respected for his many recordings and the warmth and idiosyncrasy of his conducting of repertoire from Bach to Stravinsky. He was best known as a Bruckner specialist, recording a cycle of the symphonies and serving as president of the West German Bruckner Society.

Jochum was born the son of a talented organist and choirmaster and was destined from an early age for a career in music. It was a time in Germany when a new breed of conductors was emerging, with artistic high priests like Furtwängler concerned to maintain the exalted traditions of nineteenth-century German art.

He began to study the piano when, as he put it, "his feet were too short to reach the pedals". His formal training was at the Augsburg Conservatoire. He then served as a repetiteur in Munich's National Theatre, where he made his conducting début in 1926 with Bruckner's seventh symphony. "The performance of that symphony made my whole career," he said, in 1978. "You must know, I began playing the organ when I was four years old. And I played Bach and Reger and much church music. I liked very much Baroque churches. It was all very similar in feeling to Bruckner. So the style of Bruckner was not very difficult for me."

In the 1930s he was much encouraged by Furtwängler. In 1934, just as the Nazis came to power, he was appointed conductor of the State Opera in Hamburg, a Hanseatic city with a tradition of independence. There, as a devout Catholic and anti-Nazi, he was glad to be able to keep Jewish musicians in the orchestra and to stage works by banned composers like Stravinsky and Bartók.

"We in Germany are very lucky because we have so many opera houses," he said in an interview in 1978. "I think the young conductor must first go into the opera house because here he learns, you could say, how to drive a car. You can do an opera 20 times. I did my first *Rosenkavalier* in Kiel with hardly any rehearsal, I did my first *Meistersingers* without any rehearsal. If you conduct many operas you must have a good technique."

In the meantime Jochum had not neglected the symphonic repertoire. He founded the Hamburg Philharmonic Orchestra in 1934 and remained its director until 1949. His principal post-war engagement, though, was the Bavarian Radio Symphony Orchestra. He returned to Munich to found it in 1949 and elevated it to one of Europe's most innovative and stylish ensembles. Richard Strauss conducted it during its first year. During this period Jochum also had a close relationship with the Amsterdam Concertgebouw which he had first conducted during the Nazi occupation of the Netherlands. He left the Bavarian orchestra to assume joint conductorship with Bernard Haitink in 1961.

In later life he concentrated on guest appearances, notably making many recordings with the London Philharmonic Orchestra and the London Symphony Orchestra; he was appointed laureate conductor of the LSO in 1978. "I had twice to build up orchestras in my life—in Hamburg and Munich," he explained, "In Munich it was difficult because there were not many young musicians after the war. So I have decided that I want to be free in my last years. No more organizing."

Magisterially tall, like Furtwängler, on the podium Jochum seemed the most benign of conductors, often beaming radiantly. Yet in rehearsal he could be an exacting, meticulous tyrant, determined to have his own way. From his earliest recordings the bones of his interpretative style seemed set in the German Kapellmeister tradition into which he was born. He was closely associated with the Furtwängler approach—flexible, intuitive and imaginative. And like Furtwängler he could inspire individual performances of great spontaneity and insight.

Claudio Arrau has claimed that only Jochum really understood the tragic implications of parts of the first movement of Beethoven's *Fourth Piano Concerto*. "I shall never forget the performance with Jochum and the Concertgebouw," he told an American journalist. But it is for his performances of Bruckner he is best remembered. He took an essentially romantic view of Bruckner's music, and his readings frequently bowled over audiences and orchestras alike. But he said in a 1983 interview, "Today everyone thinks of me as a specialist in Bruckner symphonies. But I began with the music of Bach, Mozart and Beethoven and it is to their music I still feel closest."

Born Eugen Jochum. **Marriage** Maria Montz, 1927 (died, 1985). **Children** Two daughters, Veronica and Romana. **Education** Studied piano and organ at Augsburg Conservatory, 1914–22; studied composition at Akademie der Tonkunst, Munich, 1922–24. **Career** Conducting début, Munich, 1926; opera coach and assistant conductor, then first conductor: Kiel Opera House, 1926–29, Manheim National Theatre, 1929–30; generalmusikdirektor: Duisburg, 1930–32; Radio Berlin, 1932–34; conductor, Hamburg State Opera and founder, Philharmonic Orchestra, Hamburg, 1934–49; Bayerischer Rundfunk, forming Bavarian Radio Symphony Orchestra, 1949–61; chief conductor, Concertgebouw Orchestra, Amsterdam, 1961–63, making US début with them, 1961; subsequently avoided full-time appointments while continuing as regular guest conductor across Europe, North America and Japan; permanent guest conductor with Concertgebouw Orchestra, Amsterdam, West Berlin State Opera and Philharmonic Orchestra, and the Chicago Opera; conductor and artistic director, Bamburg Symphony Orchestra, 1969–73; laureate conductor, London Symphony Orchestra, 1977–79; appeared and/or toured with, among others, Berlin Philharmonic Orchestra, Concertgebouw, Bayerischer Rundfunk, Detroit Symphony Orchestra, Los Angeles Symphony Orchestra, New York Philharmonic, Bamberg Symphony Orchestra and Y Chamber Symphony Orchestra. **Offices and memberships** President, International Bruckner Society, from 1950. **Awards and honours** City of Hamburg Brahms Medal; International Bruckner Society Bruckner Medal. **Publications** Various articles, principally on Bruckner, in music journals and programme books. **Recordings** (include) Bach's Passions and *Christmas Oratorio*; Haydn's twelve London symphonies; all Beethoven and Brahms; all Bruckner symphonies, for Deutsche Grammophon and Philips. **Cause of death** Undisclosed, at age 84.

MARIA JOLAS

American Translator, Journalist and Publisher
***Born* Louisville, Kentucky, January 1893**
***Died* Paris, France, 4 March 1987**

Maria Jolas knew all the greats of the Lost Generation before World War II and founded the literary journal in which much of their work was first published. With James Joyce and his family she had a special relationship in which she was often called upon to act as a kind of guardian angel; after Joyce's death she rescued his papers from oblivion. During the 1960s she was a major figure in Parisian protests against the war in Vietnam, and in the 1970s she established a sound reputation for herself as translator of Nathalie Sarraute's hellishly difficult experimental literature.

Why did a woman of this stature never produce any writing of her own? With an ironic and slightly wry smile, Jolas explained in an interview: "I was reared when there was a good deal of sniffing and snorting about women writers. All one asked of a daughter was to look pretty and smell sweet. When I got a scholarship to the University of Chicago my family laughed their heads off and it never occurred to any of us that I should take advantage of it."

If this sounds antiquated, remember that it did happen a long time ago, in another era. Maria Jolas was born Maria McDonald in 1893 in Louisville, Kentucky, not the most enlightened of places by anyone's standards, and certainly not before the turn of the century. Because she was a girl, Maria was given a "genteel" education in music and the arts. Real intellectual work was not acceptable to the family, but the further study of music was approved of, so the young Miss McDonald was sent off to Berlin in 1913 to train as a classical singer. Unfortunately the outbreak of war interrupted her stay there, and she had to go home after only a year. For a while she worked as a secretary for Charles Scribner & Sons, but when the Armistice was signed and her music teacher moved to Paris, she got permission from her parents to resume her lessons with him. It was a fateful decision because Maria was to live in or near Paris for the next 65 years of her long and interesting life.

Maria McDonald met Eugene Jolas in 1925, when she was in her early thirties and well on her way to a professional singing career. Jolas, a half-French American reared in France, was the brother of a pianist friend and impressed her with his enthusiasm for experimental literature—something she also had an interest in. As their relationship grew more intimate, Maria became increasingly involved with Jolas's literary concerns. He wrote in English, French and German and published both critical essays and poetry, the latter with the help of his friend, the American author Sherwood Anderson. Jolas had recently met James Joyce through Sylvia Beach, Joyce's publisher, and although Joyce was 12 years older than Jolas, a close friendship developed, of which Maria also became a part. Six months after meeting him, Maria McDonald married Eugene Jolas, and the period of *transition* began. This was the title of the magazine founded by the Jolases for publication of new, experimental literature. Joyce's work in progress on what was to become *Finnegans Wake*, for example, was published in *transition*. But although Maria Jolas did an enormous amount of work for the magazine, she was not even listed on the masthead. "I said to my husband when we were married: 'I promise you I'll never write'," she recalled, "and then I found myself forced to write, first letters, then translations, as well as correcting proofs. But as a rule, in our circle the men did the creative work and the women kept house."

One of the many exceptions to this rule, as well as herself, was Gertrude Stein, another American writer who made friends with the Jolases. Stein did not always approve of their literary tastes, as was evident when she scolded Eugene for giving too much attention to Joyce: "Jolas," she said, "why do you continue to lay such emphasis in *transition* on the work of that fifth-rate politician?"

Despite her marital promise, Maria Jolas did contribute one article to the magazine on something she felt very strongly about: the new fashion for Black music. In her article she argued that Negro spirituals were being exploited by White singers because the singers knew nothing about Black people or Black culture in general. For Mme Jolas the question was less one of ownership (who is entitled to sing what material) than of cultural and political integrity. Her judgement in this matter was sound and has since been echoed many times by historians and performers of Black music.

The magazine created not only a lot of work, but also occasioned much business traffic, which made Eugene Jolas restless. He and his wife decided to move out of Paris to a small, pretty village in eastern France to get some peace. This village has since become historic for another reason: by pure chance the Jolases rented the very house which General de Gaulle was later to buy, in Colombey-les-Deux-Eglises (also the place where he is buried). Living in the country proved not all that practical. After a few years the Jolas family—by now including two daughters—moved back to Paris. As before, Eugene and Maria were vitally important to Joyce in his final years, Maria especially. She liaised between Joyce and his schizophrenic daughter Lucia, who was living in an institution in England. In these years Maria Jolas travelled frequently between Ireland, England and France to look after Joyce's affairs. After his death she also looked out for his family. She was the person who thought to rescue his papers from an attic in Montparnasse where the impoverished Joyces had been living. She had them wheeled across Paris in a pushcart, walking behind herself to make sure nothing got lost. Had it not been for her efforts, the librarians of the University of Buffalo would most likely be out of a job—Joyce's papers were deposited there.

But however interesting the Joyce connection, Maria Jolas had claims to fame of her own. One was the famous École Bilingue (the Bilingual School) in Neuilly which she ran for a number of years, feeling dissatisfied with the rigours of the established French school system for her own children's education. When the Germans invaded she evacuated a number of children to a château in the south of France. She and Eugene, however, went back to the United States for the duration of hostilities, to work for the Office of War Information.

Upon their return to France after the war the Jolases resettled in Paris, but they also bought a small house in the country on the right bank of the Seine about an hour's travel away. Here Mme Jolas enjoyed tending her flowerbeds, working on manuscripts and translations and watching village life. Here also in 1952 Eugene was buried. And here, but at the other end of the main street, lived the writer Nathalie Sarraute, whose work became so important to Maria Jolas in her later years.

Maria Jolas's engagement with experimental literature was of long standing, but her relationship with Sarraute seems particularly intense—and not only because they lived in the same village. Jolas translated about a dozen of Sarraute's immensely difficult novels, whose style is ostensibly without rhyme or reason and scattered with broken sentences, abrupt shifts and unconventional grammatical constructions. Yet she said about translating that it was "a lazy person's job. Someone else has done the thinking, and you accompany him like a pianist accompanying the singer, self-effacing if essential." Despite this humble view of the translator, Jolas's own approach was painstaking if nothing else. She believed that "it's a crime not to follow the text. To do anything but reproduce her [Sarraute's] sentence structure would be immoral—you know what I mean." Well, yes, we do in the case of Sarraute, otherwise known as "the most difficult writer in any language since Joyce"—surely that particular comparison was no coincidence.

In the post-war period Maria Jolas saw her literary acquaintance of Joyce, Stein, Samuel

Beckett, Franz Kafka, Dylan Thomas and William Carlos Williams gradually thinned out and replaced by a new and younger set, which included, apart from Sarraute, Marguerite Duras and Michel Butor, as well as Mary McCarthy. During the 1960s she was an active member of the Paris American Committee to Stop War (in Vietnam), and she translated *The French Student Uprising*, a sympathetic historical account of events in Paris in 1968.

Still immensely energetic in her old age, Maria Jolas must have been a sight to see on the streets of St Germain. A friend described her as a "tall, striking woman with a shock of white hair who walks with determination along the narrow streets of her *quartier*". She raised two daughters: Betsy who became a professor of music and composer, based in Paris; and Tina, an anthropologist living in the Vaucluse. Maria Jolas died at the age of 94, and was buried next to her husband in the cemetery at Chérence, the country retreat they had both cherished so much.

Born Maria McDonald. **Marriage** Eugene Jolas, a critic and poet, 1926 (died, 1952). **Children** Two daughters, Betsy and Tina. **Education** High school, Louisville, Kentucky; studied music in Berlin, 1913, and Paris, 1918. **Emigration** Left United States for Paris, 1918; lived in France except during World War II, but remained an American citizen. **Career** Secretary, briefly, for Charles Scribner & Sons, *circa* 1914; co-founder, with husband, quarterly literary review *transition*, 1926 onwards; editor, *A James Joyce Yearbook*; also, translator of many books, including the entire works of Nathalie Sarraute. **Related activities** Looked after James Joyce and his family; rescued James Joyce manuscripts after his death. **Other activities** Founder and manager, École Bilingue, Neuilly, France, until the outbreak of World War II; worked in Office of War Information in the United States during World War II; leader, Paris American Committee to Stop War, 1960s. **Cause of death** Undisclosed, at age 94.

DANNY KAYE

American Entertainer

Born **Brooklyn, New York, 18 January 1913**

Died **Los Angeles, California, 3 March 1987**

When Danny Kaye played the London Palladium in 1951, he was the hottest ticket in town and at the summit of his popularity. He had Broadway stardom behind him and some way yet to go in a considerable film career, but a strong body of critical opinion has it that the camera could never capture his on-stage excellence: "He gave a new meaning to the expression 'one man show'."

It had been a comprehensive apprenticeship. David Daniel Kominski was born in Brooklyn, New York, the son of Jewish immigrants from Russia. He showed no signs of wanting to be an entertainer until, some three years into high school, he and another boy ran away to Florida. David sang, the other played the guitar, and the impromptu tour made $7 net. The history of his early employment is disastrous: an insurance company sacked him for an error that presented some lucky person with $36,000 excess award, and Sally Rand the fan dancer dispensed with his services after he "dropped her visual obstacles at an unpropitious moment". He became a "toomler"—an all-round entertainer—in the Borscht Circuit summer camps and hotels in the

Catskill Mountains. For four years he tried without success to interest a Broadway producer in his abilities.

In 1933 he assumed the name of Danny Kaye and under that name was engaged by A.B. Marcus, who produced an annual review, touring "where no one else did". Consequently, he sailed for the Orient in 1934 and in response to the usual exigencies of such tours (the audiences and stagehands refused to understand English) he sharpened his singing, dancing and pantomimic techniques, performing without props and extemporizing stage-business. Back on the Borscht Circuit he met pianist-composer Sylvia Fine, whose witty, distinctive material was ideally suited to his delivery. Some of her songs appeared in *The Straw Hat Revue*, in which Kaye scored a modest hit on Broadway in 1939, and the following year they married. Sylvia Fine was to be responsible in large measure for her husband's later success, acting as his writer, personal director, coach, critic and sometime accompanist.

At the end of 1940 Kaye was stopping the show nightly in *Lady in the Dark* on Broadway. He sang a tongue-twister, rattling off 57 Russian composers in 38 seconds, the names slung together with maximum contortion by Ira Gershwin. In 1941 Kaye took the lead in *Let's Face It*, a musical comedy which included more verbal acrobatics prepared by his wife, including one song which "... is done in triple-talk. At least it seems to go a step beyond mere double-talk, in that it doesn't even pretend to be using words." This was now his recognized speciality.

When the United States entered World War II, a back injury kept Kaye out of the army, so he entertained the troops at camps and hospitals in the South Pacific. Sam Goldwyn had been offering him a film career for some time. Now he decided to accept, and the producer spared no expense. *Up in Arms* appeared in 1944, and in the years after the war Kaye was all the rage. *Wonder Man*, *The Secret Life of Walter Mitty*, *The Inspector General*, and *Hans Christian Andersen* (which spawned the hit songs "The Ugly Duckling" and "Wonderful Copenhagen") are thought to be the pick of the seven he had made by 1952. They are lavish in setting and provide showcases for his clowning, dancing and nonsense patter. Generally speaking, he took on multiple roles or characters with several personalities, all of which were well within his range. A questionable success, however, was the appearance of a sentimental, romantic strain. This applies notably to *White Christmas* (1953), which Fred Astaire turned down. Critics tend to suck their teeth about Kaye's films: really, they think, he should not have been wasting his talent— "Kaye is a zany, a man of grimaces, an explosion of nervous energy. But the screen has never been a very congenial instrument for personal extravagance...but he can do everything that is demanded remarkably well, especially for a man who is at heart out of his head."

It was an experiment he could afford to make though. When Kaye visited Britain in the late 1940s, his seasons at the London Palladium were a sensation, a tonic, they said, for the exhausted nation. He danced, sang and bantered with mercurial grace, and was lionized as pop stars would later be. In 1953 Kaye and his wife formed their own production company called Dena productions. Of the three films it made, *The Court Jester* is usually judged the best, and some think it Kaye's best ever. None of his films after that was much of a success. In 1963 though, he transplanted his one-man show to television and it ran for more than four years.

During the 1950s Kaye was appointed "ambassador-at-large" for the United Nations International Children's Emergency Fund (UNICEF), in which capacity he travelled the world campaigning and giving fund-raising performances. One of these trips is recorded in the documentary film *Assignment Children*. In 1967 he was to appear in Britain's prestigious Chichester Festival, where he was to have taken the lead in Goldoni's comedy *The Servant of Two Masters*. It would have been his first appearance in a classic play, the role was eminently suitable, and the show was sold out weeks ahead. There was surprise and resentment when Kaye broke his contract at very short notice, embarking instead on a visit to Israel during the Six-Day War. He had never emphasized his Jewishness hitherto, but during that period of crisis, he became an outspoken champion of Israel and earned himself a film ban in the Arab countries. After three years' absence, he returned to the Broadway stage in 1970 to play Noah in the Richard Rodgers musical *Two by Two*. In 1975 he appeared on television in *Peter Pan*, and in 1981 he played a holocaust surviver in *Skokie*, also on television. These were breaks in what amounted to retirement, during which he continued to work for UNICEF and other charities.

There is, of course, no shortage of evidence for Kaye's material achievements; as well as everything else, he flew his own plane on UNICEF missions, and was much honoured as an entertainer and a humanitarian. He leaves, however, especially on film, an impression that does not add up—a curiously unfocused asexual energy and an unquiet, emulative spirit. One critic called him a "wild, uneasy show-off", which is rather unfair—as if any entertainer wasn't some kind of show-off. Kaye said of himself that he would have liked to have become a surgeon, but was an entertainer because he was meant to be.

Born David Daniel Kominski. **Parents** Jacob, a tailor, and Clara (Nemerovsky) Kominski. **Marriage** Sylvia Fine, a lyricist and composer, 1940. **Children** One daughter, Dena. **Education** Thomas Jefferson High School, Brooklyn, New York. **Career** Worked as entertainer at private parties, on WBBC radio station, Brooklyn, on Borscht Circuit summer hotels and Catskill Mountains camps until 1933; toured with dancing act of Dave Harvey and Kathleen Young, 1933–39; film début, 1937; London début, cabaret at Dorchester Hotel, 1938; Broadway début, *The Straw Hat Revue*, 1939; became internationally known variety artist, 1940s onwards, recorded hit songs, many written by his wife; feature film début, *Up in Arms*, 1944; popular radio show inaugurated, 1945; début at London Palladium, 1948. **Related activities** Co-founder, with Sylvia Fine, Dena Productions, 1953; formed Belmont Television Company, 1963. **Other activities** Worked for United Nations Children's Fund, 1960 onwards; permanent ambassador-at-large for UNICEF; founder and managing limited partner, Seattle Mariners baseball team, 1976. **Awards and honours** Special Academy Award, 1954; Emmy Award, 1963; George Foster Peabody Award, 1963; first award for International Distinguished Service; Best Children's Special Award, 1975; Scopus Laureate, 1977; Jean Hersholt Humanitarian Award, 1982; Danish knighthood, 1982; Kennedy Center honors, 1984; Emmy nomination for *The Cosby Show*, 1986. **Stage** (includes) *The Three Terpsichoreans*, 1933; *La Vie Paree*, 1934; *The Straw Hat Revue*, 1939; *Lady in the Dark*, 1940; *Let's Face It*, 1941; performed for war bond rallies in camps and hospitals overseas, World War II; *Two by Two*, 1970. **Films** *Dime a Dance*, 1937; *Getting an Eyeful*, 1938; *Cupid Takes a Holiday*, 1938; *Money on Your Life*, 1938; *Night Shift*, 1942; *Up in Arms*, 1944; *The Birth of a Star* (*A Star Is Born*/*The Danny Kaye Story*), 1944; *Wonder Man*, 1945; *The Kid from Brooklyn*, 1946; *The Secret Life of Walter Mitty*, 1947; *A Song Is Born*, 1947; *Bob Hope Reports to the Nation*, 1947; *It's a Great Feeling*, 1949; *The Inspector General*, 1949; *Bernard Shaw's Village*, 1951; *On the Riviera*, 1951; *Hans Christian Andersen*, 1952; *Knock on Wood*, 1953; *Hula from Hollywood*, 1954; *White Christmas*, 1954; *Assignment Children* (short for UNICEF), 1954; *The Court Jester*, 1955; *Merry Andrew*, 1958; *Me and the Colonel*, 1958; *The Five Pennies*, 1959; *On the Double*, 1961; *The Man from the Diners' Club*, 1963; *The Madwoman of Chaillot*, 1969; *Pied Piper* (short for UNICEF), 1972. **Television** (includes) *The Danny Kaye Show*, 1963–67; *Look In*, 1975 onwards; *Pinnocchio*, 1976; *Skokie*, 1981; *The Cosby Show*, 1986. **Cause of death** Hepatitis, at age 74.

HENRY R. LABOUISSE

American Civil Servant and Lawyer

***Born* New Orleans, Louisiana, 11 February 1904**

***Died* Manhattan, New York, 25 March 1987**

Henry Richardson Labouisse had a long and distinguished career at the US State Department and as a United Nations official. A very able administrator and diplomat, he was much praised for his work on behalf of Palestinian refugees while head of the United Nations Relief and Works Agency for Palestine Refugees (UNRWA) in the 1950s, and for his years as head of UNICEF, the United Nations Children's Fund—work which took him all over the world. Following the news of his death, tribute was paid by UNICEF's executive director, James P. Grant: "Harry Labouisse contributed so much towards making the world a better place for all of us, especially for our children."

Trained as a lawyer, he was admitted to the New York State Bar in 1930, and practised law until he joined the State Department in 1941. He was a modest man, never a seeker of publicity for himself, doing much quiet reconciliatory and constructive work behind the scenes, and earning himself such nicknames as "The Good Samaritan" and "Quiet Oracle".

In 1961 President Kennedy appointed him as director of the International Cooperation Administration (ICA), the United States foreign aid organization. He had previously been considered for the post by Republican President Eisenhower two years before but his appointment was vetoed because of his Democrat affiliation. As head of ICA, Labouisse implemented a plan to raise the calibre of recruits to the agency in order to be able to reduce the numbers working within it. Later in 1961 Kennedy reorganized foreign aid agencies, forming one single Agency for International Development (AID) to consolidate the functions of the ICA and the Development Loan Fund, transferring military aid to the defence budget and aiming at involving other members of the Western Alliance in sharing the costs of foreign aid. Fowler Hamilton was appointed its administrator.

Labouisse had already been working at the State Department in a variety of roles since 1941, when he became assistant chief of the Division of Defence Materials, and its chief just over a year later. In 1943 he became deputy director of the Office of Foreign Economic Coordination and the following year was appointed head of the Eastern Hemisphere Division. In 1944 he went to the Office of European Affairs as special assistant to the director. He became chief of the Foreign Economic Administration mission to France in November 1944, also serving as minister of economic affairs at the American embassy in Paris. In the following year he became special assistant to William L. Clayton, under-secretary of state, and was once again special assistant to the director at the Office of European Affairs in 1946.

After World War II, from 1948 to 1949, Labouisse played a key role in setting up the Marshall Plan, the European Recovery Program. He was head of the mission sent to Paris by the State Department to help set up the Economic Cooperation Administration (ECA), the agency dealing with economic aid to Europe under the Marshall Plan; as the State Department's coordinator of foreign aid and assistance from June 1948, he was largely responsible for implementing the Marshall Plan aid. In May 1948 Labouisse headed the United States delegation at the meeting of the Economic Commission for Europe in Geneva, and a year later he became director of the Office of British Commonwealth and Northern European Affairs. Two years later he was appointed head of ECA's Special Mission to France.

Labouisse did very valuable work as director of UNRWA between 1954 and 1958. When he took over, the organization had some 887,000 Palestine refugees in its care, a third of whom were then in refugee camps in Egypt, Jordan, Syria and Lebanon. Labouisse's task was made more difficult by the hostility and suspicion of Palestine refugees and Arab countries towards UNRWA itself and towards the United Nations, especially those nations who had sponsored the partition of Palestine. There were also angry exchanges at UN meetings between Arab and Israeli speakers. Characteristically, Labouisse kept his speeches short and always tried to stay out of conflict. He once commented, "Too many speeches are made in this world."

In his first report to the United Nations in 1954 he said that a settlement of the refugee problem was being hindered both by Israel's refusal to take back refugees and compensate them for their losses and by refugees' refusal to take part in rehabilitation projects in case their right to return to Israel was jeopardized. Despite the ever-present difficulties, Labouisse was able to gain the confidence and even affection of many Palestinians, improving their living conditions and facilities for health, education and training, and setting up a grants scheme for refugees wishing to set up in farming or business. Although Labouisse drew tributes for his work from UN secretary-general Dag Hammarskjold and others, he was hampered all along by a shortage of funds from the UN and was reported as saying: "What we need is less compliments and more money."

In May 1959 he became a consultant to the International Bank of Reconstruction and Development, affiliated with the UN. In this role he headed a survey mission to Venezuela to assist in formulating a programme of economic development. He was recalled by Dag Hammarskjold to assist in setting up the UN force sent to the Congo in the 1960 crisis. In December that year, he was appointed special representative for Africa of the International Bank and early in 1961, he headed a mission in Uganda to study economic problems.

Following his six months at the ICA, Labouisse went to Athens in 1962 as US ambassador to Greece, where he remained until 1965, playing an important role in August 1964 in applying American pressure on Greek leaders to take a cautious approach in a crisis over Cyprus. He resigned his post when U Thant, now United Nations secretary-general, and the board of UNICEF asked him to become that organization's executive director. On receiving the Nobel Peace Prize that same year on behalf of UNICEF, Labouisse said that the prize had "reinforced our profound belief that each time UNICEF contributes, however modestly, to giving today's children a chance to grow into useful and happier citizens, it contributes to removing some of the seeds of world tension and future conflicts."

In August 1968, when both sides in the Nigerian civil war blocked urgent relief supplies, Labouisse again spoke out: "With strong and affirmative cooperative action on the part of all concerned, a great many lives can be saved. Without it, untold thousands of innocent people will die." Under his direction, aid was finally able to reach its destination on both sides of the conflict.

Some eleven years later he oversaw UNICEF's relief work in famine-struck Cambodia, where he reported 700,000 children and sick people "in extreme need", with malaria and dysentery wiping out many of those already weakened by hunger.

Labouisse was known as a quiet man, a good listener with a modest manner and was described in the *New Yorker* as "an easy-going, slow-speaking cigar smoker, medium-sized, florid and roman-nosed, who parts his iron-gray hair in the middle, in the Ivy League style of the twenties". His daughter, who made him a grandfather several times over, said that he was "not of the mint-julep-and-magnolia school" but rather a "Northernized Southern gentleman". His quiet, but effective contributions to the welfare of others mark him out as a notable humanitarian of his times.

Born Henry Richardson Labouisse. **Parents** Henry Richardson and Frances Devereux (Huger) Labouisse. **Marriages** 1) Elizabeth Scriven Clark, 1935 (died, 1945); 2) Eve Denise Curie, author and journalist, 1954. **Children** One daughter, Anne, by first marriage. **Education** Princeton University, BA, 1926; Harvard University, LLB, 1929. **Career** Attorney, 1929–41;

joined US State Department, 1941; assistant chief, Division of Defense Materials, 1941, chief, 1943; deputy director, Office of Foreign Economic Coordination, 1943; chief, Eastern Hemisphere Division, 1944; special assistant to director, Office of European Affairs, 1944, 1946; chief, Foreign Economic Administration mission to France and minister for economic affairs at American embassy, 1944; special assistant to under-secretary of state, 1945; head of mission sent to France to set up Economic Cooperation Administration, 1948; coordinator of foreign aid and assistance, 1948–49; director, Office of British Commonwealth and Northern European Affairs, 1949; head of Economic Cooperation Administration mission to France, 1951–54; director, United Nations Relief and Works Agency for Palestine Refugees in the Near East, 1954–58; consultant, International Bank of Reconstruction and Development, 1959–61; head of mission to Venezuela, 1959; special representative for Africa, 1960; director, International Cooperation Administration, 1961–62; ambassador to Greece, 1962–65; executive director, United Nations Children's Fund (UNICEF), 1965–79. **Offices and memberships** Member, New York State Bar. **Awards and honours** LLD: University of Bridgeport, 1961, Princeton University, 1965, Lafayette College, 1966, Tulane University, 1967; LHD: Brandeis University, 1983, Hartwick College, 1983; several decorations and awards, including Woodrow Wilson Award, Princeton University, 1978. **Cause of death** Cancer, at age 83.

RICHARD LEVINSON

American Television Writer

Born **Philadelphia, Pennsylvania, 7 August 1934**

Died **Los Angeles, California, 12 March 1987**

Few American television viewers are unfamiliar with the bumbling, bedraggled, yet clever and curiously charismatic figure of Police Detective Columbo. During the height of the mystery programme's popularity, some 37 million Americans tuned in each week, and *Time* magazine called it "at once the most classic and original" of television's cops-and-robbers series. In 1972 *Columbo*, one of the crowning achievements of the prolific Link and Levinson writing partnership, won the Hollywood Foreign Press Association's coveted Golden Globe Award. But while mysteries were one of the team's most successful vehicles, Levinson's first love was the television movie, a form which allowed him to explore, in a sensitive and realistic manner, a variety of controversial social and political issues. During the course of their 38-year collaboration, Link and Levinson won critical acclaim for a host of provocative films and serials.

Richard Levinson's talent for radio and TV writing revealed itself at an early age. He was 12 years old, a junior high school student in suburban Philadelphia, when he first met William Link. The two struck up a friendship and soon formed an amateur script-writing team. Both continued their education at the University of Pennsylvania, where they collaborated on film criticism for the college newspaper and co-wrote short stories for *Playboy* magazine.

Link and Levinson's first big break came in 1959, when their army drama *Chain of Command* was performed by the Desilu Playhouse. From there they went on to write episodes for programmes such as *Alfred Hitchcock Presents*, *Dr Kildare* and *The Fugitive*. In 1968 they created their first television series, *Mannix*. But it was their early teleplay *The Storyteller*, with its dogged policeman hero, which provided them with the idea for the winning Columbo character.

Made-for-TV movies were catching on, and the two were soon asked to write another mystery script, *Prescription: Murder*, introducing the appealing Detective Columbo. Two years later, in 1971, NBC decided to turn the popular *Murder* pilot into a series.

When *Columbo* first took hold, the American media rallied to analyse its success. According to *Time*, it owed much to the hero's dogged, deductive method of investigation—a riveting formula which let the audience in on the action by allowing them to know the culprit's identity, yet kept them watching until the hero uncovered the crucial clue and solved the mystery. "The title character's method of operation dates back at least to Sherlock Holmes," *Time*'s critics wrote. "There is no gunplay, no chase sequence...the only puzzle is how and when Columbo's seemingly bumbling pursuit will lead to *the* clue—the one mis-step in an otherwise perfect crime." William Link remembered that in creating Columbo, he and Levinson were exalting the ordinary, the unglamorous man, the "character who's very bright but doesn't seem to be...who's not got much of an education and no social graces, but takes advantage of his shortcomings". He added that Columbo himself was modelled after Pyotr Petrovich, the cunning yet obsequious detective in Dostoevsky's *Crime and Punishment*.

Throughout the 1970s Levinson and Link continued to collaborate on new and innovative projects, both serials and television movies. Among the series they created were *The Bold Ones*, *The Psychiatrist*, *Tenafly* and *McCloud*. They also tried their hand at writing stage plays. But TV movies offered the greatest challenge of all. One of their earliest and most memorable teleplays, *My Sweet Charlie* (1970), the story of an inter-racial relationship, won an Emmy Award. It was followed by *That Certain Summer* (1972), one of the first TV films to address the issue of male homosexual love. Merle Miller called it "a marvellous film—beautifully written, superbly acted, and directed and produced with tender care". The following year it won a Silver Nymph Award from the Monte Carlo Film Festival. Another award-winning teleplay, *The Execution of Private Slovik*, based on a controversial military trial, explored the workings of a man's conscience. A later film, *The Gun*, meticulously researched and sympathetically filmed, traced the history of a single handgun, from buyer to buyer until its final impoundment. The story that evolved was an impassioned plea for stricter gun-control laws.

"Each time out we tried to do something that hadn't been done before, something that would touch an emotional or social chord," Link explained. By addressing sensitive social questions in a small-screen format, he and Levinson could reach large numbers of often passive viewers, and encourage them to ponder the issues for themselves. Levinson himself was even more modest about his creative aims. "Bill and I have no pretensions to be artists," he once said. "We are not Günter Grass or Vladimir Nabokov. What we try to do is the highest quality popular entertainment we can do, with an occasional thought sticking through."

In later years Levinson and Link returned to the detective genre that had brought them their early success. In 1976 they developed and produced the *Ellery Queen* mystery series, and finally, the hit programme *Murder, She Wrote*. When asked why he thought the Sherlock Holmes-style murder mystery had come back into vogue, Levinson replied, "I just think the form has a lot of juice to it. People keep rediscovering it." He also added a practical note: "Car chases are becoming too expensive to film. On shows like *Murder, She Wrote*, most of the scenes are just two or three people in a room talking." During their lengthy mystery-writing career—one of the longest creative partnerships in Hollywood history—Levinson and Link won four Edgar Awards from the Mystery Writers of America for their chilling contributions to TV serials.

Born Richard L. Levinson. **Parents** William, a businessman, and Georgia (Harbert) Levinson. **Marriage** Rosanna Huffman, actress, 1969. **Children** One daughter, Christine. **Education** University of Pennsylvania, BS. **Career** Prolific writer, especially for television, in partnership with William Link, 1959–87. **Offices and memberships** Member and chairperson of playwrights' committee, Actors' Studio West; member of steering committee, Caucus for Writers, Producers and Directors. **Awards and honours** Emmy Award for *My Sweet Charlie*, 1970; Golden Globe Award for *Columbo* (series), 1972; Golden Globe Award for *That Certain Summer*, 1973; Writers' Guild of America Award for *That Certain Summer*, 1973; Silver Nymph Award, Monte Carlo Film Festival, for *That Certain Summer*, 1973; George Foster Peabody Award, University of Georgia, for *The Execution of Private Slovik*, 1974; four Edgar Awards from the Mystery Writers of America for contributions to the writing of mystery stories in television series. **Publications** (all with William Link) *Prescription: Murder* (three-act play), 1963; *Fineman* (novel), 1972; also contributed over 30 short stories to periodicals. **Stage play** (with William Link) *Merlin*. **Television series** (all with William Link) *Mannix*, 1967–75; *The Bold Ones*, 1969–73; *The Psychiatrist*, 1971; *Tenafly*, 1971; *Columbo*, 1971–; *Ellery Queen*, 1975–76; (also with Peter S. Fischer) *Murder, She Wrote*; also contributed scripts for episodes of *General Motors Presents, Westinghouse Desilu Playhouse*, *Dr Kildare*, *The Fugitive*, *The Rogues*, *The Alfred Hitchcock Hour*. **Teleplays** (all with William Link, include) *Chain of Command*, 1959; *My Sweet Charlie*, 1970; *That Certain Summer*, 1973; *The Gun*; *The Execution of Private Slovik*, 1974; *The Storyteller*. **Cause of death** Heart attack, at age 52.

ALFRED de LIAGRE

American Producer and Director

***Born* Passaic, New Jersey, 6 October 1904**

***Died* Manhattan, New York, 5 March 1987**

Hailed by Katharine Hepburn as "the last of the great gentleman producers", Alfred de Liagre enjoyed a career spanning over half a century, producing and directing for the American stage. Although later in life he spent nearly a decade working with the American National Theater and Academy, it is for his work in the commercial world, principally on Broadway, that de Liagre is best remembered.

De Liagre's early life offered no real indication of where his passion and talents lay. Having grown up in a solidly middle-class suburb of New Jersey, he studied at Yale University, graduating in 1926 along with fellow classmates John Ringling North, John Hay Whitney and Rudy Vallee. He spent the next few years "dabbling", trying his hand at journalism and aviation, before turning to the theatre. His show business début was in an acting job, playing a small part in the Marx Brothers' comedy *Cocoanuts*. It was during these early acting days that he first met Katharine Hepburn when they shared a dressing-room on alternate nights.

In 1933 de Liagre entered the Broadway theatre as producer and director of *The Three-Cornered Moon* with Ruth Gordon and Brian Donlevy. Having picked up a fair amount of experience in management and stagecraft in summer stock (repertory theatre), he acted as producer and director for a string of light comedies up until 1941.

His big break came in 1943 when he produced *The Voice of the Turtle*, the most successful comedy of its time. It was written by John van Druten of *I Am a Camera* (later to become *Cabaret*) fame. The show starred Margaret Sullavan and Elliot Nugent and became the piece with which de Liagre would be most enduringly identified for the rest of his life.

Two further producing ventures gave way to a return to direction with *The Mad Woman of Chaillot* (1948). The piece is notoriously difficult to stage, but de Liagre's brilliant production earned him a place in the French Legion of Honour. Further successes and acclaim came in this new role with *The Golden Apple*, which was named best musical by the New York Drama Critics' Circle in 1954, and *J.B.*, an adaptation of the biblical Book of Job, which won the Pulitzer Prize for Drama in 1959.

In 1960 de Liagre suffered what he later described as his favourite failure. It was a production called *The Tumbler*, staged by Laurence Olivier and starring Charlton Heston, Martha Scott and Rosemary Harris. The show ran for only four days, but mercifully the losses incurred did not break the bank.

Subsequent years were spent producing comedy, drama and musical comedy, but in the 1970s, frustrated by the increasingly daunting financial pressures of Broadway, he moved into subsidized national theatre. After a decade, he returned to the commercial world with Ira Levin's *Deathtrap* and the revival of Rodgers and Hart's 1939 musical *On Your Toes*, which marked the Broadway début of the ballerina Natalia Makarova.

De Liagre did not care much for modern theatre fashions which, since the 1960s, had galloped through a succession of styles. "Play craftsmanship has gone out of fashion," he once told an interviewer. "Playwrights today don't care very much about telling a story that has a beginning, a middle and an end. It's become a mood thing, and so many of them have gone into the same kind of abstract expressionism that you find in painting and sculpture."

Early on in his life, during the 1920s, de Liagre assumed the role of the high-living gentleman, throwing lavish parties in locales as exotic as Cannes and Venice. He also had a passion for vintage cars and enjoyed touring regularly. It would no doubt please him that it is this image of the perfect gentleman that remains in everyone's memory. On hearing of his death, Bernard Sachs, president of the Shubert Organization, said: "He was a traditional, old-fashioned gentleman. Once he gave his word, you never had to look for him a second time."

Born Alfred Gustav Étienne de Liagre. **Parents** Alfred, textile manufacturer, and Frida (Unger) de Liagre. **Marriage** Mary Howard, actress. **Children** Christina and Nicholas. **Education** Graduated from Yale University, 1926. **Career** Tried his hand at journalism and aviation before working at the Woodstock Theater, 1930; assistant stage manager, 1931; subsequently produced and directed in New York; worked with the American National Theater and Academy, 1970 onwards. **Offices and memberships** Director, Actors' Fund of America; member: American National Theater and Academy, League of New York Theaters, National Repertory Theater, Shakespeare Festival and Academy, John F. Kennedy Cultural Center, Committee of Theatrical Producers, Yale Drama School; president, American Theater Wing; co-founder, Plumstead Players. **Awards and honours** Chevalier of the French Legion of Honour for *The Mad Woman of Chaillot*, 1948; Pulitzer Prize for Drama for *J.B.*, 1959. **Stage** (producer and director) *Three-Cornered Moon*, 1933; *By Your Leave*, 1934; *Pure in Heart*, 1934; *Petticoat Fever*, 1935; *Fresh Fields*, 1936; *Yes, My Darling Daughter*, 1937; *I Am My Youth*, 1938; *No Code to Guide Her*, 1939; *Mr and Mrs North*, 1941; (producer) *The Walrus and the Carpenter*, 1941; *Ask My Friend Sandy*, 1943; *The Voice of the Turtle*, 1943; *The Mermaids Singing*, 1945; *The Druid Circle*, 1947; (producer and director) *The Madwoman of Chaillot*, 1948; (producer) *Second Threshold*, 1950; *The Deep Blue Sea*, 1952; (producer and director) *Escapade*, 1953; (producer) *The Golden Apple*, 1954; *The Caine Mutiny Court Martial*, 1955; *Janus*, 1955; *Nature's Way*, 1957; *The Girls in 509*, 1958; *J.B.*, 1958; (with Roger L. Stevens) *The Tumbler*, 1960; *Kwamina*, 1961; *Photo Finish*, 1963; *The Irregular Verb to Love*, 1964; (producer and director) *Janus* (revival), 1965; *Deathtrap*, 1978. **Cause of death** Lung cancer, at age 82.

BOBBY LOCKE

South African Golfer

***Born* Germiston, South Africa, 20 November 1917**

***Died* Johannesburg, South Africa, 9 March 1987**

It was Bobby Locke who helped to formulate that all-important principle of professional golf: "You drive for show, but putt for dough."

One of the greatest putters of all time, Locke built his game around his outstanding judgement of distance. He could afford to play safe at the longer holes, and was—for a good many years—the best chipper in the sport. Seldom appearing to be too concerned as to where the flag was, he simply got the ball on to the green and holed the putt.

His masterful short game earned him success worldwide: he had captured every title worth holding in his native South Africa by the time he was 20, and from there enjoyed success on both the American and European circuits.

Born in Germiston, near Johannesburg, Locke turned professional in 1938, at the age of 21. He won his third South African Open Championship that year, and as well as claiming the Irish Open, he finished third in the British Open. But in common with so many other sportsmen of his generation, Locke's blossoming career was interrupted with the onset of World War II. He did not so much as hold a golf club for almost three years. Instead, he spent 1800 hours as a bomber pilot in the Middle East, flying more than 100 missions in Liberator bombers.

Locke returned to professional golf in 1946. And even though the former svelte star was now a portly 200 pounds, he continued to dominate the South African scene. He also began to make his presence felt in both Europe and the United States.

After finishing a moderate fourteenth in the 1947 US Masters, Locke won the Carolinas PGA, the Houston Invitational, the *Philadelphia Inquirer* Open, the Canadian Open and the Tam o' Shanter tournament, before securing third spot in the US Open. It was a short season; but Locke finished second on the money list, and, not surprisingly, returned for more of the same in the years that followed. Among his most notable performances was his victory in the 1948 Chicago Victory National Championship, where he destroyed the field by a full 16 strokes.

Locke's intrusion on the American scene was, nevertheless, all too brief. His relationship with the US Professional Golfers' Association was soured in 1948 when he was banned from the circuit for missing two tournaments: a decision later described by one fellow professional as "the most disgraceful action by any golf organization in the past 30 years".

Locke, however, simply concentrated his efforts on the European circuit, where he was always warmly received and genuinely appreciated. The leading amateur in the British Open in both 1936 and 1937, he claimed his first British Open title at Sandwich in 1949; and for the following decade, he and Peter Thomson dominated that particular championship. Locke won again, at Troon, in 1950, setting a new championship record of 279 with rounds of 69, 72, 70 and 68; and he recorded his third victory in 1952, at Royal Lytham.

Thomson took three consecutive titles, from 1954 to 1956. But Locke—conspicuous now for his girth, and his preference for outmoded plus-fours—confounded the experts by snapping up his fourth British Open title in 1957. He nevertheless had to survive one moment of controversy when, after the final round, it was noticed that Locke had moved his ball two puttheads' distance from his line to allow space for a fellow competitor to complete his round, but had then forgotten to replace his own ball before putting out. The officials later met to discuss the matter, but—showing more flexibility than their American counterparts—decided he had derived no benefit, and allowed the result to stand. Locke was later made an honorary member of the Royal and Ancient—an honour extended to only a few professionals. Reluctant to linger on the scene, Locke's departure from the professional ranks was also hastened by a car accident, in 1960, which kept him in hospital for several months.

In all, Locke recorded more than 80 major tournament wins in a professional career that spanned over 20 years. A master of self control and politeness, he set the standards which others of his generation followed. Locke's courteous habit of touching his white-peaked cap in acknowledgement of the crowd's applause and appreciation, for example, was one of his major trademarks. But his poise and charm also concealed intense ambition.

Locke was one of the most unlikely-looking of golf's greats; and even his putting stance was a little unusual, with his left foot placed well in advance of his right. It nevertheless served him well when it mattered. And Locke's own assessment of his putting skills—that he was not a good short putter—was seldom put to the test.

Born Arthur D'Arcy Locke. **Father** Charles James Locke. **Marriages** 1) 1943; 2) Mary Fenton, 1958. **Children** One daughter, by first marriage. **Education** Benoni High School, South Africa. **Military service** Pilot, South African Air Force, Middle East and Italy, 1939–45. **Career** Amateur golfer, 1936–38; turned professional, 1938; professional at Observatory Golf Club, Johannesburg; first win, Transvaal Junior championship, at age of 14. **Offices and memberships** Professional Golfers' Association, London. **Awards and honours** Honorary member, Royal and Ancient Golf Club of St Andrews, Scotland. **Major championships** Amateur South African Championship, 1935, 1937; South African Open, 1935, 1937–40, 1946, 1950–51; leading amateur, British Open, 1936–37; Irish, Dutch, New Zealand Open, 1938; South African Professional Champion, 1938–40, 1946, 1950–51; Canadian Open, 1947; winner, four tournaments, USA, 1947; third, United States Open, 1948; British Open, 1949, 1950, 1952, 1957, runner-up, 1946, 1954; French Open, 1952–53; Mexican Open, 1952; Egyptian Open, 1954; German Open, 1954; Swiss Open, 1954; Australian Open, 1955; also, winner of many tournaments in the United States. **Publications** *Bobby Locke on Golf*, 1953. **Cause of death** Meningitis, at age 69.

GERALD MOORE

British Pianist

Born **Watford, Hertfordshire, 30 July 1899**

Died **Penn, Buckinghamshire, 13 March 1987**

Great songs by composers such as Schumann, Wolf and Debussy were written for equal partnership between voice and piano. Armed with the knowledge that the music itself was on his side, Gerald Moore completely changed the public's perception of accompanists. At a time when they were often treated as no more than page-turners, he elevated them to the level of creative partner. Accompanists are not failed soloists, he insisted. His defiant motto was, "I would rather be guilty of being too loud than the reverse."

Moore showed early promise as a musician. As a child he had perfect pitch and an ability to reproduce anything he heard by ear, although he hated actually practising the piano. "It seems to me that as soon as I could toddle I was seized and flung literally at the piano," Moore said. "I had my first lessons when I was six or seven." He later confessed, "I did not absorb music into my being until I was in my twenties."

Moore's parents moved to Canada in 1913 and there he studied with Michael Hambourg while earning money as a church and cinema organist. It was then that he started accompanying other performers. He accompanied Hambourg's son, Boris, on a tour of western Canada that took in such unlikely stop-overs as Moose Jaw. Paid $40 for as many concerts and dressed in an Eton jacket, Moore was billed as "The Remarkable English Boy Pianist".

He returned to London in 1919 and continued studies with Hambourg's son Mark, though it was always Solomon whom Moore regarded as his mentor and model. Solomon was to become one of Moore's lifelong friends.

In his "galley years" Moore made no attempt to specialize and played regularly with countless instrumentalists, including the Harrison sisters, Albert Sammons, Feurman and Suggia. Gradually he came to favour *Lieder* and song. It was while working with the perfectionist Yorkshire tenor John Coates that Moore became convinced of the importance of equality in partnership. It was a baptism of fire. Coates once snarled at Moore: "Have you never been in love, man? What's the matter with you? Put some feeling into it. The notes are not enough. You have to bring out the feeling behind the notes!"

Walter Legge's newly established London Lieder Club brought Moore on to the platform with such artists as Patzak, Husch, Kipnis, Trianti, Gerhardt, Schumann and Lehmann. This period set him on the road to legendary partnerships, such as those with Kathleen Ferrier, Elisabeth Schwarzkopf and Victoria de los Angeles, and Dietrich Fischer-Dieskau, who said that Moore had "taken me farther into the hearts of Schubert, Schumann, Wolf and Brahms than I have ever been before". He was Chaliapin's first accompanist in England.

With recognition came an increasing commitment to lecturing, television appearances, master classes and teaching. His début on disc in 1921 led to a lifetime of recordings. Among his writings are three volumes of an autobiography: *Am I Too Loud?* (1962), *Farewell Recital* (1978), and *FurtherMoore* (1983); he also wrote *The Unashamed Accompanist* (1943), *The Schubert Song Cycles* (1975), and "*Poets Lore*" *and Other Schumann Songs* (1981). His many awards include the Cobbett Gold Medal for services to chamber music (1951), the CBE (1954) and honorary doctorates from the Universities of Sussex and Cambridge. In 1964 he was made an honorary Royal Academician.

Gerald Moore gave his farewell recital in the Festival Hall on 20 February 1967 with Fischer-Dieskau, Schwarzkopf and de los Angeles. As his younger colleague the accompanist Geoffrey Parsons put it: "With music and words he has made the world far more aware of his and our role. In gratitude and homage to him no accompanist can ever be too loud."

Born Gerald Moore. **Parents** David Frank, mattress manufacturer, and Chestina Jane (Jones) Moore. **Marriage** Enid Kathleen Richard. **Education** Watford Grammar School, England; University of Toronto. **Emigration** Left England for Canada, 1913; returned to England, 1919. **Career** Concert pianist, choirmaster and organist; sought-after accompanist to many eminent musicians and singers, including Pablo Casals, Yehudi Menuhin, Feodor Chaliapin, Elisabeth Schumann, John McCormack, Elena Gerhardt and Kathleen Ferrier, 1921–67. **Related activities** Performed for Entertainments National Services Association (ENSA) and Council for the Encouragement of Music and the Arts (CEMA) during World War II; gave lectures, talks and lecture-recitals throughout the post-war years; gave frequent ensemble classes throughout the world; served on the Music Advisory Panel of the BBC, 1964–66, and on many scholarship and prize juries. **Offices and memberships** President, Incorporated Society of Musicians, 1962; member, Music Advisory Council of the Arts Council of Great Britain, 1964–

67; patron, Songmakers' Almanac. **Awards and honours** Cobbett Gold Medal for services to chamber music, 1951; Commander of the British Empire, 1954; honorary member, Royal Academy of Music, 1962; honorary DLitt, Sussex, 1968; Grand Prix du Disque, Amsterdam, 1968, 1970, Paris 1970; Granados Medal, Barcelona, 1971; Hugo Wolf Medal, Vienna, 1973; honorary MusD, Cambridge, 1973; fellow, Royal College of Music, 1980. **Publications** (all London unless otherwise stated) *The Unashamed Accompanist*, 1943, US, 1944, revised, 1957; *Careers in Music*, 1950; *Singer and Accompanist: The Performance of 50 Songs*, 1953, US, 1954; *Am I Too Loud?*, 1962; *The Schubert Song Cycles*, 1975; *Farewell Recital: Further Memoirs*, 1978; *FurtherMoore: Interludes in an Accompanist's Life*, 1983; *"Poet's Lore" and Other Schumann Cycles and Songs*, 1984; *Collected Memoirs*, 1986. **Recordings** *Am I Too Loud?*, Angel Records, 1955, Seraphim, 1966; many other recordings with various solo artists. **Cause of death** Undisclosed, at age 87.

ARCH OBOLER

American Radio Dramatist

***Born* Chicago, Illinois, 6 December 1909**

***Died* Westlake, California, 19 March 1987**

"These stories are not for the timid soul, so we tell you calmly and very sincerely, if you frighten easily, turn off your radio now. Lights out, everybody."

These chilling words, delivered by a strange and sombre voice, marked the beginning of one of early radio's most popular weekly series. With its graphic tales of horror, mystery and suspense, the *Lights Out* programme enthralled and delighted millions of late-night listeners in the 1930s, radio's golden age. At the same time, it earned a prominent and enduring place in radio history for a bright, ambitious, young playwright named Arch Oboler. Though he left *Lights Out* in 1938, moving on to write science fiction and fantasy for stage and screen, it is for his early radio thrillers that he is best remembered.

As a child growing up in Chicago, Oboler's scientific interests were far tamer than his later work might suggest. He dreamed of becoming a naturalist and filled his bedroom with turtles, frogs, salamanders, snakes and scorpions. At the age of ten his fascination with science and his skill in story-telling came together for the very first time, and he wrote and sold a story inspired by his beloved menagerie. In high school his scientific curiosity intensified. But when he graduated, he turned his sights to the drier—if more practical—field of electrical engineering, and enrolled at the University of Chicago.

Oboler's creative talents would not be silenced, however. He continued to write, and in 1934, while still a student, he submitted an original fantasy called *Futuristic* to the National Broadcasting Company. They were so overwhelmed by its quality that they bought it immediately and used it that same year as a launch programme for the opening of their Radio City headquarters in New York. For Oboler, there was no turning back. His career path had been chosen for him.

For the next few years he remained in Chicago writing original radio dramas. These included a series of playlets for the *Grand Hotel* programme, and a string of individual sketches for well-known screen stars such as Don Ameche, Henry Fonda, Joan Crawford and Edward G. Robinson. Next he accepted the post as *Lights Out*'s writer, and remained there for two full years—until he had exhausted his ready repertoire of horrific tales. During this time, he married a University of Chicago classmate. Appropriately enough, they spent their honeymoon touring New England's haunted houses.

Towards the end of his "horror" phase, Oboler had begun writing and producing a weekly drama series for NBC in Chicago. In the spring of 1938 he headed east to New York with the recorded script of his play *The Ugliest Man in the World* under his arm. Upon hearing it, NBC's production manager was so impressed that he offered Oboler his very own series, *Arch Oboler's Plays*, to include dramas of realism, fantasy, comedy, satire and tragedy—whatever Oboler envisioned. One of the high points of this venture came in 1939, with a special full-hour broadcast of a play called *The Lonely Heart*, featuring a well-known Russian actress and using the music of the NBC symphony orchestra. In addition, Oboler's play *Alter Ego*, starring Bette Davis, was cited as the best original air drama of 1938.

In 1940 Oboler began producing his first commercially sponsored series, Oxydol's *Everyman's Theatre*. That same year he published his first book, a collection of scripts titled *Fourteen Radio Plays*. Though Oboler had a host of admirers among the general public *and* in the radio hierarchy, both this book and its successor, *The Oboler Omnibus*, published in 1945, received only mixed reviews. A.N. Williams of the *Saturday Review of Literature* wrote that Oboler's published plays were proof that "radio [had] come of age". But James Fuller of the *New York Times* had serious reservations. "On the air there is no denying the impact of his passionate seriousness...but with the cooling-off process between performance and publication, the clichés emerge, as from a campaign speech revisited." Despite the criticisms, Oboler is generally credited with having been the first to develop an innovative theatrical technique—the use of monologue and stream-of-consciousness in radio drama. And in 1945 one of his programmes won the prestigious Peabody radio award.

At the same time that he was producing radio plays in New York, Oboler was exploring new creative spheres in Hollywood. While working at MGM, he wrote and directed a series of films, including *Escape* (1940), *Bewitched* (1945), *The Arnelo Affair* (1946) and *Five* (1950). In 1952 he wrote, directed and produced Hollywood's first three-dimensional movie, *Bwana Devil*, a story of railway building in Africa. Though *New York Times* reviewer Bosley Crowther found the story itself hackneyed and dated, the filming technique used was a revolutionary one. The innovations continued, and in 1958, at the height of his Broadway phase, Oboler helped bring the twenty-first century to the stage with *Night of the Auk*, a science-fiction drama set aboard a spaceship.

In the 1960s Oboler served as head of his own company, Oboler Productions, and continued to write for radio, films and the theatre. *The Bubble*, released in 1966, was Hollywood's first space-vision picture, and his 1969 book, *House on Fire*, recalled the terror of his early radio work. The ideas for some of his stories, Oboler said, arose from his dreams, while others came from listening to the music of great composers. He found additional inspiration by prowling the streets of Lower Manhattan.

In 1986 Oboler sold the rights to many of his original *Lights Out* episodes to a Minneapolis-based media concern specializing in the distribution of old radio programmes. When a *New York Times* interviewer asked him why he had refused to sell his stories to television in the 1950s, he replied with typical candour: "Basically, I think TV talks too much and shows too much," he said, adding that he felt his thrillers were still effective because, "I wrote about human beings, not special effects. What we fear most is the monster within—the girl who lets you down, the husband who is unfaithful. The greatest horrors are within ourselves." Oboler's series of anti-Fascist plays, produced quietly in the early 1940s, protested the worst extremes of that monster within.

Born Archibald Oboler. **Parents** Leo and Clara (Obeler) Oboler. **Marriage** Eleanor Helfand. **Children** Guy, David, Steven, Peter. **Education** Studied electrical engineering at University of Chicago. **Career** Playwright and author, 1934–87; writer, producer and director, MGM, 1940–73. **Radio** *Futuristic*, 1934; contributor to *Grand Hotel* radio programme, 1935; *Rich Kid*, 1936; (with M.E. Rickard) *Everything Happened to Him: The Story of Tex Rickard*, 1936; writer for *Lights Out* series, 1936–38; *Alter Ego*, 1938; *The Ugliest Man in the World*, 1938; *The Lonely Heart*, 1939; *Everyman's Theater* (series), 1940; *To the President* (series). **Films** *Escape*, 1940; *Bewitched*, 1945; *The Arnelo Affair*, 1946; *Five*, 1950; *Bwana Devil*, 1952; *The Bubble*, 1966; *Domo Arigato*, 1973. **Stage play** *Night of the Auk*, 1956. **Television** *Exploring the Kinsey Report* (documentary), 1961; *African Adventure* (radio-television series). **Offices and memberships** Member, Authors' League of America; past president, Radio Writers' Guild, western division. **Awards and honours** National award for best commercial dramatic play, *This Precious Freedom*, 1941; national award for best dramatic broadcast, *Johnny Quinn*, 13th Institute for Education by Radio, 1942; national award for best public service broadcast, 1942; first annual American Expeditionary Forces radio award, 1945; first award, Academy of Stereoscopic Arts and Sciences, 1952. **Publications** *Fourteen Radio Plays by Arch Oboler*, 1940; *Ivory Tower and Other Radio Plays*, 1940; *This Precious Freedom*, 1941; *Plays for Americans*, 1942; (editor, with S. Longstreet) *Free World Theater*, 1944; *The Oboler Omnibus*, 1945; *House on Fire*, 1969. **Cause of death** Heart failure, at age 77.

ELIZABETH POSTON

British Composer

***Born* Highfield, Hertfordshire, 24 October 1905**

***Died* Hertfordshire, England, 18 March 1987**

The night before Elizabeth Poston died, at the age of 81, she was sitting at her desk, as usual, composing music that was as good as the best of her work, and showing the characteristic charm that disguised her formidable technique.

She was a tall, elegant woman, handsome and engagingly stylish even when dressed for gardening or country walks. Her personality combined spirituality and hedonism in a most attractive way and it has been said of her that "in knowing how much of a suffragette to be, she contributed much to the notion that a woman could be a first-rate composer and remain intensely feminine".

As a small girl she was initiated into musical life, so it is said, by watching her father and George Bernard Shaw playing piano duets. Her favourite vantage point was under the grand piano where she could see them kicking each other's ankles to gain control of the sustaining pedal.

She studied at the Royal Academy of Music and on the Continent, and also studied piano with Harold Samuel. She first achieved recognition as a composer in 1925, when only in her late teens, through the publication of seven songs, including the well-known "Sweet Suffolk Owl". This is still regarded as one of the finest examples of an English part song. In 1928 she published five more songs which showed the beginnings of her mature personal style.

She won a Royal Academy prize for her violin sonata which was subsequently broadcast by the BBC at Savoy Hill. From 1931 to 1939 she spent much time abroad collecting folk songs, just as Vaughan-Williams, Bartók and Kodaly were doing. During the war she worked long hours in a senior administrative position in the BBC's European Music Service. This, in certain ways, included secret work for British Intelligence. Under Churchill's orders, music-related coding of highly classified information was broadcast overseas, with each piece of music carrying an encoded message. Poston never spoke openly about this period of her life.

She resigned from the BBC in 1945 and moved her folk song collecting operation to Canada for a couple of years. She then returned to London as one of the advisers to Douglas Cleverdon (q.v.) during the inception of the BBC's Third Programme. She had exactly the right background for this kind of work. Her musical skills, social advantages and literary tastes combined to make her invaluable to the service which was launched with her production of Milton's *Comus*. She remained at the BBC for a year and thereafter produced many important scores for radio in close collaboration with such writers as Dylan Thomas, C.S. Lewis and Terence Tiller (q.v.).

Poston produced several film scores, of which the best was probably that for *Howards End* (1970). She actually lived in the house after which the novel was named and enjoyed a close, lifelong friendship with its author E.M. Forster. Her extended choral works include *An English Kalendar* (1969) for female voices and harp, and *An English Day Book* (1971) for mixed voices and piano, both commissioned by the Farnham Festival. A *Concertino da Camera* (1950) for ancient instruments and a Trio (1958) for flute, clarinet and harp are her most significant chamber works.

She was versatile in her word settings and equally at home in a number of styles—Elizabethan, Augustan, Caroline or Victorian. She was emphatically a twentieth-century composer but one with a deep sense of cultural heritage. Her musical language belongs to the neo-classical tradition and lays great emphasis on clean craftsmanship and a sense of line.

Aside from composition itself, Poston involved herself in many para-musical activities, notably as president of the Society of Women Musicians from 1955 to 1961. She won particular respect as the editor of folk song, carol and hymn collections, for example, *The Cambridge Hymnal*, which she edited with David Holbrook in 1967. Her association with Peter Warlock made her a unique authority on the subject of that extremely complex man and his music.

Although her editorial work and her folk song and carol arrangements, such as her exquisite original miniature *Jesus Christ the Apple Tree*, have, for the most part, obscured her more substantial works, Poston's last years were happy and productive, and she enjoyed a considerable revival of interest in the more challenging parts of her output. She tended to lose interest in her creations once they had been heard and there is much of her music left to rediscover. Manuscripts and printed works scarcely even acknowledged to exist by Elizabeth Poston herself lie forgotten to this day in her Hertfordshire home.

Her last completed work *A Settled Rest* received its première at the Royal Albert Hall as part of the Women's World Day of Prayer centenary celebrations in spring 1987, but her plans for a collection of folk song arrangements, using hitherto unknown material from all the republics of the Soviet Union, unfortunately died with her.

Born Elizabeth Poston. **Education** Royal Academy of Music; studied piano with Harold Samuel; also studied on the Continent. **Career** Composer and arranger; made extensive collections of European folk songs, 1930–39; senior administrator, BBC European Service, 1939–45; collected folk songs in the US and Canada, 1945–47; adviser on the inception of BBC Third Programme, 1947. **Related activities** Worked for British Intelligence while at BBC European Service, 1939–45. **Offices and memberships** President, Society of Women Musicians, 1955–61. **Awards and honours** Royal Academy of Music prize for an early violin sonata.

Compositions "Sweet Suffolk Owl", one of seven part songs, 1925; five further part songs, 1928; film score for *Howards End*, 1950; *An English Kalendar*, for female voices and harp, 1950; *The Holy Child*, for chorus, vocal soloists and string orchestra, 1950; *Concertino da Camera on a Theme of Martin Peerson*, for ancient instruments, 1950; *The Nativity*, for chorus, vocal soloists and string orchestra/organ, 1951; Trio for flute, clarinet or viola and piano, 1958; *Peter Halfpenny's Tunes*, for recorder and piano, 1959; *Lullaby and Fiesta*, for piano, 1960; *Magnificat*, for four solo voices and organ, 1961; *Three Scottish Carols*, for chorus and strings/organ, 1969; *Harlow Concertante*, for string quartet and string orchestra, 1969; *An English Day Book*, for mixed voices and harp, 1971; Sonatina for cello and piano, 1972; *A Settled Rest*, choral; collaborated with David Jones, Terence Tiller, Dylan Thomas, C.S. Lewis and others to produce many radio and film scores. **Publications** *Penguin Book of American Folk Songs*, Harmondsworth, 1964; *Penguin Book of Christmas Carols*, Harmondsworth, 1965; (with David Holbrook) *The Cambridge Hymnal*, London, 1967; *Second Penguin Book of Christmas Carols*, Harmondsworth, 1970; *The Faber Book of French Folk Songs*, London, 1972. **Cause of death** Undisclosed, at age 81.

ROBERT PRESTON

American Actor

Born **Newton Highlands, Massachusetts, 4 June 1918**

Died **Santa Barbara, California, 21 March 1987**

Robert Preston remains something of a puzzle. He was a feisty, virile actor who was universally and consistently loved by audiences of stage and screen alike. His notices were uniformly superb, and throughout a career spanning 50 films and more than 100 plays, critics would often complain that they weren't seeing him in better parts. The versatile performer, best known for his swaggering, speed-talking Professor Harold Hill in *The Music Man*, in his own words, "played the best role in every B picture, and the second best role in A pictures". Many of those films were quite forgettable.

Preston never received the true fame he deserved. According to film critic Pauline Kael, "He has often been the best thing in a movie." The fault could well have been the blindness of the Hollywood casting machine.

For Robert Preston Meservey, whose father was a shipping clerk and whose mother worked in the record department of a Los Angeles music store, there seems to have been no other career choice but acting. He left high school in Hollywood at 16 and joined a Shakespearean group managed by Mrs Tyrone Power, mother of the actor. When the group failed, he found work at the Pasadena Community Theater, gaining two years' acting experience in 42 productions. His Harry Van, the hoofer in Robert Sherwood's *Idiot's Delight* was noticed by a talent scout; a Paramount Pictures contract resulted, and he remained for 12 years.

Being on the studio treadmill meant being typed; from the beginning Preston was cast as a "heavy". His first film—he was just 20—*King of Alcatraz* (1938), was not an auspicious beginning. Neither was his second. In the meantime, he had joined "18 Actors", a group organized by nine movie actors, including Dana Andrews and Victor Jory, and their wives. They performed over weekends and had a loyal subscriber audience of 1600. Preston loved to *act*—this was keeping his hand in.

Cecil B. DeMille liked Preston's performances in his films and signed him to a larger part in *Union Pacific*, as Barbara Stanwyck's husband. He turned in an excellent performance and worked with DeMille on several more pictures. At last, the industry began to perk up its head; the respected director William Wellman cast him as the third brother, alongside Gary Cooper and Ray Milland, in *Beau Geste* (1939). The chemistry between the threesome helped make the film a hit and brought Preston a measure of recognition, if not quite stardom.

A dozen forgettable films followed, including *Typhoon*, with Dorothy Lamour, in which he wore a version of her sarong. His inability to be immediately pigeon-holed into easily-manufactured characters by blinkered casting heads (they even played around with his hair, moustache and eyebrows) combined with indifferent scripts—only his performances were the redeeming factor.

After serving as a captain in the US Air Force for four years, Preston continued an industrious film career but made little of real merit. Two exceptions were Anthony Mann's *The Last Frontier* (1950) and Garson Kanin's *When I Grow Up* (1951), but the audience reaction was not overwhelming. Also in 1951 he made his Broadway début, replacing José Ferrer in his production of *Twentieth Century*, followed by *The Male Animal* and *Tender Trap*. Reviews were, again, laudatory, even by the most jaded columnist's standards. Theatre critic Walter Kerr remarked, "Robert Preston is his usual forthright self. Why doesn't someone write a play for his forthright self?" The versatile Preston played opposite actresses as varied as Celeste Holm, Uta Hagen and Margaret Sullavan, not only delivering invigorating and satisfying performances, but, in the words of one reviewer, "bringing out the best in whomever he played against".

Preston's more visible success led him to the early days of television; in 1951 he appeared in the series *Man Against Crime*, followed by *Anywhere, USA*, which ran from 1952 to 1954. But when Meredith Willson's *Music Man* opened on Broadway in December 1957, it was clear that a role had been tailor-made for Preston. Although he had studied singing for the part, it was his baritone semi-talking "We Got Trouble" song that clinched the audition. The story of the con man reformed by the love of a small-town librarian played for 1375 performances, winning him a Tony award in 1958. Preston's wicked glee was infectious, yet there was always enormous depth, even in his most charming characters.

Inexplicably, Warner Brothers wanted Cary Grant for the film version. He had declined, saying, "If you don't use Preston, I won't go to see it." The film was slightly clumsy, but Preston's silver-tongued dialogue is considered to be a high point of American musical history. He received an Oscar nomination in 1962. However, although he worked with some of the finest directors in the business—Henry Hathaway (*How the West Was Won*, 1963), Sidney Lumet (*Child's Play*, 1972) and others—both in film and on Broadway, he never reaped the rewards of stardom. His *S.O.B.* and, especially, *Victor/Victoria* performances with director Blake Edwards brought a second wind to his career; his earnest vitality saved even the silliest scripts. His ageing homosexual entertainer, Toddy, in the latter film has become a minor classic, partly because of the dignity he brought to what could have been a stereotype. Indeed, there was often a tragic underpinning to even the most witty of his characters, a kind of self-delusion that quietly shone through. Preston himself, a private and self-effacing man happily married for over 45 years, was fluent in dramatic literature and was often involved in groups performing Shakespeare, including one set up by Richard Burton. It was an ironic mistake that he was never able to demonstrate his formidable acting skill in that regard, professionally.

Born Robert Preston Meservey. **Father** Frank Meservey, a shipping clerk. **Marriage** Catherine Craig, an actress, 1941. **Education** Lincoln High School, Hollywood, California. **Military service** Captain, United States Air Force, in Europe, 1942–46. **Career** Actor, initially on the stage in Hollywood, later on Broadway and in films, 1938–84; on television from 1951; joined Shakespearean group managed by Mrs Tyrone Power; with Pasadena Community Theater, for two years; film début 1938; with 18 Actors theatre company, Hollywood; Broadway début, *Twentieth Century*, 1951. **Awards and honours** Tony award for *The Music Man*, 1958. **Stage** (includes) *Idiot's Delight*, 1938; *Twentieth Century*, 1951; *The Male Animal*, 1954; *The Tender Trap*, 1954; *His and Hers*, 1954; *The Magic and the Loss*, 1954; *Janus*, 1955; *The Hidden River*, 1957; *The Music Man*, 1957; *I Do! I Do!*, 1968; *Mack and Mabel*, 1974. **Films** *King of Alcatraz*, 1938; *Illegal Traffic*, 1938; *Disbarred*, 1939; *Union Pacific*, 1939; *Beau Geste*, 1939; *Typhoon*, 1940; *Moon Over Burma*, 1940; *Northwest Mounted Police*, 1940; *New York Town*, 1941; *Lady from Cheyenne*, 1941; *Night of January 16th*, 1941; *Parachute Battalion*, 1941; *Pacific Blackout*, 1942; *Reap the Wild Wind*, 1942; *This Gun for Hire*, 1942; *Wake Island*, 1942; *Star Spangled Rhythm*, 1942; *Night Plane from Chung-King*, 1943; *Wild Harvest*, 1947; *The Macomber Affair*, 1947; *Variety Girl*, 1947; *Whispering Smith*, 1948; *Blood on the Moon*, 1948; *The Big City*, 1949; *The Lady Gambles*, 1949; *Tulsa*, 1949; *The Sundowners*, 1950; *My Outlaw Brother*, 1951; *When I Grow Up*, 1951; *The Best of the Badmen*, 1951; *Face to Face*, 1952; *Cloudburst*, 1952; *The Last Frontier*, 1955; *The Dark at the Top of the Stairs*, 1960; *The Music Man*, 1962; *How the West Was Won*, 1963; *Island of Love*, 1963; *All the Way Home*, 1963; *Junior Bonner*, 1972; *Child's Play*, 1972; *Mame*, 1974; *Semi-Tough*, 1977; *S.O.B.*, 1981; *Victor/Victoria*, 1982; *The Last Starfighter*, 1984. **Television** (includes) *Man Against Crime* and *Anywhere, USA* (series), 1952–54; *My Father's House*, 1975; *The Chisholms*, 1980; *Rehearsal for Murder*, 1982; *The September Gun*, 1984; *Finnegan, Begin Again*, 1985. **Cause of death** Lung cancer, at age 68.

HAROLD ROSENTHAL

British Music Critic, Editor, Broadcaster and Archivist

Born **London, England, 30 September 1917**

Died **London, England, 19 March 1987**

Readers of *Opera* magazine will remember with affection the notice which used to appear each month: "The Editor of *Opera* requests readers to respect his privacy and *not* to telephone for information about performances, casts, etc. after office hours or during the weekend."

It is a remarkable fact that Harold Rosenthal spent 35 years as editor of *Opera* magazine, creating a unique information centre about the international opera world, whose resources he generously made available to casual enquirers on his telephone number—at all times except those stated in his courteous notice. A combination of efficiency, business sense and knowledge of opera-goers' tastes enabled him to keep the magazine buoyant, and through it he played a significant role in stimulating the new audience for opera that has been on the increase ever since the war years.

After serving as a non-combatant in the British Army during World War II, Rosenthal began his career as a teacher and became professionally involved with opera through regular correspondence with the Earl of Harewood, who founded *Opera* magazine in 1948. Associated with it from the beginning, Rosenthal took it over in 1953 and remained editor until his retirement in 1986, when he was made editor emeritus.

To his busy life as editor he soon added much writing, broadcasting and lecturing. He was also archivist of the Royal Opera House from 1950 to 1956, a post that enabled him to write his biggest book, *Two Centuries of Opera at Covent Garden* (1958). He also collaborated with John Warrack on *The Concise Oxford Dictionary of Opera*. His other books include *Sopranos of Today* (1956), and an autobiography, *My Mad World of Opera* (1982). He also edited *The Mapleson Memoirs* (1966) and a recent reprint of *Loewenberg's Annals of Opera* (1982).

Rosenthal's knowledge was encyclopedic and always wittily at the ready. Music critic Hilary Tangye remembers a conversation between Rosenthal and Tito Gobbi in which Gobbi asked for confirmation of facts about his career:

"Did I really do that?"
"Yes, Tito, you did."
"Of course, if you say so, Harold."

No job on the magazine was too small for Rosenthal. With the minimum of secretarial help he tackled the minutiae of its production from the morning room of his house in Muswell Hill. Many items of information for the "In the News" section were painstakingly typed out by his own hands.

As a reviewer he was always sensitive to the painful difficulties of any operatic performance, especially where young singers were concerned. He also fought against the élitist image associated with opera. "Not at all a champagne socialist," as Sir George Christie, chairman of Glyndebourne, said, "more a social democrat. He possessed a deep conviction that opera, exotically expensive though it was to produce, should be widely accessible. *Opera* the magazine, and opera the profession, were greatly enhanced and enriched by Rosenthal's input."

Born Harold David Rosenthal. **Parents** Israel Victor and Leah Samuels Rosenthal. **Marriage** Lillah Phyllis Weiner, 1944. **Children** One son and one daughter. **Education** City of London School; University College, London, BA, 1940; Institute of Education, London. **Military service** Non-combatant, British Army, World War II. **Career** Teacher; associated with magazine *Opera*, from 1948, assistant editor, 1950–53, editor 1953–86; also archivist, Royal Opera House, Covent Garden, 1950–56; London correspondent, *Musical America*, 1955–60; lecturer, writer and broadcaster; first publication *Soprano of Today*, 1956. **Related activities** Member of council and management committee, Friends of Covent Garden, 1962 onwards; editor, *Concise Dictionary of Opera*, 1964, 1979. **Offices and memberships** Patrons of Music Fund Committee, 1960–70; chairman, music section, Critics' Circle of Great Britain, 1965–67. **Awards and honours** Cavaliere Ufficiale, Order of Merit of the Republic of Italy, 1977; Officer, Order of the British Empire, 1983. **Publications** *Sopranos of Today*, 1956; *Two Centuries of Opera at Covent Garden*, 1958; (editor, with John Warrack) *The Concise Oxford Dictionary of Opera*, 1964, paperback edition, 1972, revised and enlarged edition, 1979; *Great Singers of Today*, 1966; (editor and annotator) *The Mapleson Memoirs*, 1966; *The Opera Bedside Book*, 1965; *Opera at Covent Garden*, 1967; *Covent Garden*, 1976; (editor) *Loewenberg's Annals of Opera 1597–1940*, third edition 1979; *My Mad World of Opera* (autobiography), 1982; *Annals of Opera 1940–80*, 1985. **Cause of death** Undisclosed, at age 69.

WALDO SALT

American Screenwriter

***Born* Chicago, Illinois, 18 October 1914**

***Died* Los Angeles, California, 7 March 1987**

"I think the major problem of the industry today is creative incompetence in the executive department. They no longer know or care about making film, they just know the wheeling, dealing and selling of a product. They try to apply business-school standards to an art form, computerized information to deal with the creative process and the content of pictures. I think we're too oriented toward moneymaking."

Waldo Salt's voice as recorded in a 1981 interview was, as we now know, a voice crying in the wilderness. It was the voice of a craftsman faced with the new order of machines, just like artists and painters had been crying out against the medium of film itself a few decades before Salt had started out in the business. All change is relative, but here he was pointing, perhaps, to a major one. After all, in a career spanning 40 years, Salt had seen a number of trends come and go. Indeed, his time in Hollywood can be seen as a microcosm of American film-making, ranging from romantic melodrama to light comedy, and from historical epics to the familiar modern-day star features. This change, this domination by computers and "business-school standards" Salt saw as something different, something he had never liked. It smacked of indirect censorship under the guise of commercialism. Perhaps it reminded him of the time when he was blacklisted for alleged communist sympathies; then too, outside forces had moved in to reorganize the industry according to non-artistic standards. It had cost Salt ten years of his film-writing career, even though his best work, the scripts for blockbusters such as *Midnight Cowboy* and *Coming Home*, were written well after the period in which he was banned from Hollywood.

Waldo Salt was born in Chicago in 1914, the son of a businessman father and an adoring mother who wanted him to go far in life. They had the means to send him to private school in Victoria, British Columbia. After a brief spell at San Raphael Military Academy in California, young Waldo went to Stanford University, where he graduated in 1934. A man of many parts, even at the age of 20, Salt briefly considered a musical career in the San Francisco Symphony Orchestra, but eventually he decided against it. This is how he got into films in 1936: "I had wanted to be a writer or an actor or director, and I was trying to get to Broadway. Going to Hollywood seemed to be the most direct way. I had studied theatre at Stanford and I had taught theatre and music for a year at Menlo Junior College. I was in Hollywood trying to get a job at something and the first one that came along was that of a junior writer at MGM, so I took it."

The first film he scripted was *Shopworn Angel* (1938), a romantic melodrama in the traditional mould, with James Stewart. This was not an original venture, in that the film had been made as a silent movie a few years earlier with Nancy Carroll and Gary Cooper; Salt rewrote it into a dialogue form as a sound picture. He did not have time to do anything else of note before he was drafted into the Office of War Information during World War II as a consultant on film. While there he wrote two semi-propaganda films designed to raise morale both at home and abroad: *Tonight We Raid Calais* and *Mr Winkle Goes to War*. The latter featured Edward G. Robinson as a bank clerk who decides to volunteer for the front and then, of course, becomes a hero. When asked what, if anything, he had learned from this period, Salt responded at length, providing fascinating insights into the war's impact on the film industry in general.

> As writers we had not paid as much attention to the documentary form in the 1930s as we began to in the 1940s...we were never particularly related to production or to the technical

> aspects of film in the early days. In the army and in the Office of War Information and the other places that were making documentary films around the war effort, writers were much more directly involved in production.

This broadened his knowledge of film-making, but there was a qualitative change too, for besides, he added, documentary film-making "took the writers out of the studios and put them on the streets....As romantic as most of the World War II films were, I think that the beginning of a realistic trend—not only in Italy, France and England, but also in the United States—came out of World War II."

For Salt, though, the pleasure of working in this newly-found genre did not last long. In 1947 he came under investigation by the House Un-American Activities Committee (the notorious HUAC) for alleged links with communists. When he refused to testify for the committee in 1951 he was sentenced *in absentia* and blacklisted. Thus, like so many of his friends and colleagues, Salt became a victim of McCarthyism. For some, he was well aware, it was a crushing blow from which they never recovered. Unlike actors and directors, it was easier for writers to find other work. Interviewed in the 1980s just after the Reagan election, Salt told of his feelings about those times: "Joseph McCarthy and the House Committee on Un-American Activities—those I'm bitter about...and probably even more so today because of the danger with a man like Reagan in the presidency. He has given indications that he is still going to continue his pretence that there never was a blacklist, which there was and which he participated in."

Nevertheless, Salt survived the 1950s in relative comfort. He spent some time in Europe writing for television, and even for films, under a pseudonym. Being banned from Hollywood also gave him the chance to return to his old love, music. He wrote the "folk opera" *Sandhog*, a musical play in three acts adapted from a short story by Theodore Dreiser, and had it produced on Broadway in 1954. By the early 1960s he was again working for MGM; he still had his best work before him.

Salt's first big hit was scored with the script for *Midnight Cowboy* (1969), adapted from the 1965 novel by James Leo Herlihy. It is a film about the New York underclass, a theme which by now has become something of a cliché but at that time had something new to say. Like all Salt's post-McCarthy scripts it (un-)covered part of the American Nightmare of destitution, crime, and urban collapse. Jon Voight and Dustin Hoffman came up with unforgettable portraits of a naïve country boy and a derelict hustler respectively, whose developing friendship forms the heart of the story. The *New Republic* called it "an unusually moving film", while the critic of *Newsweek* wrote that "the film's extraordinary staying power lies in its central relationship. The two strays truly touch and change...Their strange, tender connection is plainly love." Who could deny it? The final frame, where Hoffman's Ratso is dying in the arms of his friend on the bus to Florida, remains etched in the viewer's mind. In true Hollywood style the heartstrings are being pulled in a big way, but at least we are crying for something unusual: the lost dreams of two men on the underside of society, hardly the classic stuff of which weepies are made. Waldo Salt deservedly won an Oscar for his script.

But if there were hits (with others still to come), there were also misses. The aptly titled *The Gang that Couldn't Shoot Straight* (1972) was "a tasteless mess" according to the *New York Times* and "Waldo Salt's chaotic script turns Breslin's characters, which were already caricatures, into vicious racial stereotypes" said *Time*. Whatever next?

Salt countered quickly with *Serpico* (1973), co-authored with Norman Wexler after a book by Peter Maas. Al Pacino got the part of police detective Serpico, who uncovers large-scale corruption in the New York police. When he reports his findings to his superiors, they stonewall him; obviously, they too are involved in the bribe-taking and drug-trafficking that goes on. In the end Serpico exposes the scandal to the media and gets wounded in a shooting incident because his police colleagues do not protect him. He survives, but only to face a life of isolation. *Serpico* was another box-office hit, not only because it was a good story but also because its release coincided with the Watergate scandal and a national mood of disillusionment with the forces of law and order. America needed a hero and for a few weeks it had Frank Serpico. Even Pauline Kael, the usually acerbic queen of American film reviews, praised the movie for its "cynical, raw, but witty script". *Serpico* had its detractors too, of course. Some critics took issue with the ending of the film, which was rather bleaker than that of the novel on which it was based. They felt that Salt had concentrated too much on "Serpico's sense of isolation and futility rather than on the real Serpico's achievements (an immense shake-up in the New York Police department)".

After the success of *Serpico*, Salt took some time to script his new film, *Coming Home* (1978), about a paraplegic Vietnam veteran (Voight) who falls in love with another vet's wife (Jane Fonda). He spent about a year researching the story, talking to Vietnam veterans in hospitals and to their wives. As Salt himself saw it, the story was essentially about "two men finally coming together because they were both Vietnam veterans, that they would be able to talk to each other and understand each other, and they were unable to talk to or understand the families, friends, wives they came home to. That was a universal response from all the guys coming back that I talked to." *Coming Home* was a much-needed attempt to address another of America's silences—the trauma of Vietnam—but unfortunately the film did not work out in the way that Salt had meant it to. The love story between the two men and Fonda's character got in the way, so much so that the *New Republic* called it "a wobbly, sentimental triangle drama that could, essentially, have been about the war of 1812". *Coming Home*, though again a popular film at the box office, was an example of what Salt saw as his greatest problem as a screenwriter: "the contradiction between trying to deal with reality and the market....The writer must be concerned with the contents. I think the two things are almost always in contradiction."

However, there was also *The Day of the Locust* (1975), after Nathanael West's classic novel. Salt unequivocally regarded this film as his greatest achievement and it was no coincidence that the story concerns Hollywood, the film industry itself and what it does to people. Working on this material, Salt could use many of his own ideas about the conflicting demands of artistry and the market. *Newsweek* credited his achievement with the comment, "Waldo Salt's screenplay is essentially faithful to the original material and especially resourceful in locating visual equivalents for the inner reveries of West's characters." The man who said he admired film-makers like François Truffaut, John Schlesinger (who did *Midnight Cowboy*), Ingmar Bergman, Stanley Kubrick and Francis Ford Coppola, had finally scripted one to satisfy his own high standards.

Born Waldo Salt. **Parents** William Haslem, a business executive and artist, and Winifred (Porter) Salt. **Marriages** 1) Mary Davenport, 1942 (divorced); 2) Eve Merriam, an author, 1983. **Children** Two daughters, Jennifer and Deborah, by first marriage. **Education** Private school, Victoria, British Columbia; San Raphael Military Academy, California; Stanford University, California, 1934. **Military service** Civilian consultant, Office of War Information, 1942–45. **Career** Teacher, Menlo Junior College, California, 1935; screenwriter and lyricist, 1936 onwards; contract writer, MGM, 1936–42; first film as writer, *The Shopworn Angel*, 1938; investigated by House Un-American Activities Committee, 1947; blacklisted, 1951–62; wrote screenplays and television scripts in Europe under various pseudonyms, 1951–62. **Awards and honours** Writers' Guild Award nomination, for *Rachel and the Stranger*, 1948; best screenplay, British Society of Film and Television Arts, award from Organization Catholique Internationale du Cinéma, Academy Award for best screenplay, Academy of Motion Picture Arts and Sciences, all for *Midnight Cowboy*, 1969; Academy Award for best screenplay, Academy of Motion Picture Arts and Sciences for *Coming Home*, 1978; Writers' Guild Award for *Midnight Cowboy*, 1969, for *Serpico*, 1973, for *Coming Home*, 1978; Golden Globe Award nomination for best screenplay from Hollywood Foreign Press Association: for *Midnight Cowboy*, 1969, for *Coming Home*, 1978; Academy Award nomination for best screenplay for *Serpico*, 1973; Edgar Allan Poe Special Award, Mystery Writers of America Inc., for *Serpico*, 1973; Laurel Award, Writers' Guild of America. **Screenplays** *The Shopworn Angel*, 1938; (with John McClain) *The Wild Man of Borneo*, 1941; *Tonight We Raid Calais*, 1943; (with George Corey and Louis Solomon) *Mr Winkle Goes to War*, 1944; *Rachel and the Stranger* (also lyricist), 1948; *The Flame and the Arrow* (also dialogue director), 1950; *M* (author of additional dialogue only), 1951; *Taras Bulba*, 1962; (with Larry Markes and Michael Morris) *Wild and Wonderful*, 1963; (with Eliot Arnold) *Flight From Ashiya*, 1964; *Midnight Cowboy*, 1969; *The Gang that Couldn't Shoot Straight*, 1972; (with Norman Wexler) *Serpico*, 1973; *The Day of the Locust*, 1975; (with Nancy Dowd and Robert C. Jones) *Coming Home*, 1978. **Other** *Sandhog* (folk opera in three acts), produced on Broadway, 1954; *Davy Jones's Locker* (a marionette musical). **Cause of death** Cancer, at age 72.

RANDOLPH SCOTT

American Actor

Born **Orange County, Virginia, 23 January 1903**

Died **Los Angeles, California, 2 March 1987**

Strong, silent and leathery, armed with a rigid eye-for-an-eye morality, Randolph Scott's screen persona became for many the summation of the traditional western hero—tough, chivalrous, laconic and utterly predictable. It was what he did best, although it was not until he was "discovered" overnight in his late forties with some 20 years' film experience behind him that he completed the transition from competent, dependable Hollywood actor to one of the most dignified and expert exponents of the western genre.

Training as an engineer at the University of North Carolina was followed by a period as a straight stage actor before convalescence dictated a move west to the recuperative sunshine of California. Here he shared a flat with another Los Angeles aspirant, Archibald Leach (later to make a different name for himself as Cary Grant) and supported himself with menial jobs on the fringes of the film industry, including a spell as Gary Cooper's voice coach during the traumatic coming of sound. A chance meeting on a golf course with producer Howard Hughes led to a screen test and subsequent film début in *The Far Call* (1929). Scott's career sputtered fitfully over the following two decades. He worked in musicals and light comedies, although even in the early stages, the western quickly came to dominate his work. He appeared in supporting roles with Fred Astaire and Ginger Rogers (in *Follow the Fleet*, 1936), Mae West (in *Go West, Young Man*, also 1936) and, somewhat surprisingly, with Shirley Temple—twice (in *Rebecca of Sunnybrook Farm*, 1938, and *Susannah of the Mounties*, 1939). He was unlucky in working rarely with major directors; even when he did, it seemed to be in their least distinguished work, such as Fritz Lang's *Western Union*, Rouben Mamoulian's *High, Wide and Handsome,* and *Corvette K–225* produced by Howard Hawkes.

Wyatt Earp in the 1939 film *Frontier Marshal* marked the start of Scott's exclusive commitment to westerns, but it was not until the early 1950s that he found himself, for four lucrative years, in the top ten of most popular movie stars. This high-earning period, coupled with his enthusiastic subscription to the dictum, "Never let yourself be seen in public unless they pay for it", financed the flotation of an independent production company. Trading under the name "Ranown" in partnership with Harry Joe Brown, Scott went on to make a sequence of seven westerns which remain among the very best examples of the genre. Now nearly 50 years of age, he found a new affinity with the late middle-aged characters he portrayed under the expert direction of Budd Boetticher; *Seven Men from Now*, the first of the series has been described by Andre Bazin as "the most intelligent western I know of...and the most beautiful".

Retirement came in 1962, following Sam Peckinpah's *Ride the High Country* (considered by many to be the director's best film) which, appropriately enough, follows a pair of ageing gunslingers on their final mission. Astute business investments in oil and property had made Randolph Scott one of Hollywood's richest men, allowing him to fade into a comfortable and serene obscurity.

Some 12 years after Scott's retirement, the townsfolk in Mel Brooks's affectionate parody *Blazing Saddles* refuse to allow Black sheriff Cleavon Little 24 hours to clean up the town. "You would have given Randolph Scott 24 hours," he objects, whereupon the whole town bows its head for a moment of silent reverence. A suitable tribute to the man whose uncompromising dedication to the western raised it and him from B-movie status to international success.

Born George Randolph Scott. **Marriages** 1) Marianna du Pont Sommerville, 1936 (divorced, 1939); 2) Patricia Stillman, 1944. **Children** One son and one daughter. **Education** Georgia Institute of Technology, Atlanta; degree in engineering, University of North Carolina, Chapel Hill; studied acting, Pasadena Community Playhouse. **Military service** World War I. **Career** Started in film industry with series of menial jobs, including stuntman and voice coach for Gary Cooper; appeared occasionally on the stage; prolific film actor, mostly in westerns, 1928–62. **Related activities** Co-founder with Harry Joe Brown, Scott–Brown Productions, 1950–55 **Films** *Sharp Shooters*, 1928; *Dynamite*, 1929; *The Far Call*, 1929; *The Virginian*, 1929; *The Black Watch*, 1929; *The Women Men Marry*, 1931; *Sky Bride*, 1932; *Hot Saturday*, 1932; *A Successful Calamity*, 1932; *Island of Lost Souls*, 1933; *Wild Horse Mesa*, 1933; *Hello Everybody*, 1933; *Heritage of the Desert*, 1933; *Murders in the Zoo*, 1933; *Supernatural*, 1933; *Cocktail Hour*, 1933; *Man of the Forest*, 1933; *To the Last Man*, 1933; *Sunset Pass*, 1933; *Broken Dreams* 1933; *Thundering Herd*, 1933; *The Last Round-Up*, 1934; *Wagon Wheels*, 1934; *The Rocky Mountain Mystery* (*The Fighting Westerner*), 1935; *Roberta*, 1935; *Home on the Range*, 1935; *Village Tale*, 1935; *She*, 1935; *So Red the Rose*, 1935; *Follow the Fleet*, 1936; *A Sudden Death*, 1936; *The Last of the Mohicans*, 1936; *Go West, Young Man*, 1936; *High, Wide and Handsome*, 1937; *Rebecca of Sunnybrook Farm*, 1938; *Road to Reno*, 1938; *The Texans*, 1938; *Jesse James*, 1939; *Susannah of the Mounties*, 1939; *Coast Guard*, 1939; *Frontier Marshal*, 1939; *20,000 Men a Year*, 1939; *Virginia City*, 1940; *My Favourite Wife*, 1940; *When the Daltons Rode*, 1940; *Western Union*, 1941; *Belle Starr*, 1941; *Paris Calling*, 1941; *To the Shores of Tripoli*, 1942; *The Spoilers*, 1942; *Pittsburgh*, 1942; *The Desperadoes*, 1943; *Bombardier*, 1943; *Corvette K–225*, 1943; *Gung Ho!*, 1943; *Belle of the Yukon*, 1944; *China Sky*, 1945; *Captain Kidd*, 1945; *Abilene Town* (also, co-producer) 1946; *Badman's Territory*, 1946; *Home Sweet Homicide*, 1946; *Trail Street*, 1947; *Gunfighters*, 1947; *Christmas Eve* (*Sinner's Holiday*), 1947; *Albuquerque*, 1948; *Return of the Badmen*, 1948; *Coroner Creek*, 1948; *Canadian Pacific*, 1949; *The Walking Hills*, 1949; *The Doolins of Oklahoma*, 1949; *Fighting Man of the Plains*, 1949; *The Nevadan*, 1950; *Colt 45*, 1950; *The Cariboo Trail*, 1950; *Sugarfoot*, 1951; *Starlift*, 1951; *Santa Fe*, 1951; *Fort Worth*, 1951; *Man in the Saddle*, 1951; *Carson City* 1952; *Hangman's Knot*, 1952; *The Man Behind the Gun*, 1952; *The Stranger Wore a Gun*, 1953; *Thunder Over the Plains*, 1953; *Riding Shotgun*, 1954; *The Bounty Hunter*, 1954; *Rage at Dawn*, 1955; *Ten Wanted Men*, 1955; *Tall Man Riding*, 1955; *A Lawless Street*, 1955; *Seven Men from Now*, 1955; *Seventh Cavalry*, 1955; *The Tall T*, 1957; *Shoot-Out at Medicine Bend*, 1957; *Decision at Sundown*, 1957; *Buchanan Rides Alone*, 1958;

Ride Lonesome, 1958; *Westbound*, 1959; *Comanche Station*, 1960; *Ride the High Country*, 1962. **Cause of death** Heart disease, at age 84. **Further reading** George Fenin and William K. Everson, *The Western: From Silents to Cinerama*, New York, 1962; Kalton C. Lahue, *Riders of the Range*, Cranbury, New Jersey, 1973; James Robert Parish, *Great Western Stars*, New York, 1976.

JIM SKARDON

British Intelligence Officer

***Born* England, 15 March 1904**

***Died* Torquay, England, 9 March 1987**

Jim Skardon, OBE, was one of the most formidable and feared interrogators in the British Security Services for over 20 years. A quiet and unassuming man, he patiently extracted information from several of the most famous spies of the 1950s and 1960s, and uncovered several major espionage rings.

After an elementary education, Skardon secured a job as a clerk in the household of the Duke of Connaught. In 1925 he left this post to become a constable in the (London) Metropolitan Police Force. By 1940 he had risen to the rank of detective-sergeant and was one of a select group of CID officers seconded to the security service, MI5. In 1944 he was commissioned into the Intelligence Corps and posted to Supreme Headquarters Allied Expeditionary Force (SHAEF) in Europe. Here Skardon put his years of police experience to good use, tracking down a number of British citizens who had collaborated with the Axis Powers. According to his colleagues in SHAEF, Skardon was extremely successful in finding and interviewing scores of witnesses and collaborators. At the end of the war he was kept busy investigating several cases concerning war criminals and traitors. One of the most famous of these was that of William Joyce, commonly known to the British public as "Lord Haw-Haw", whose regular propaganda broadcasts on behalf of the Nazis had irritated and disgusted loyal British subjects throughout the war. After Joyce was arrested in Flensburg in 1945, Skardon prepared much of the case against him, and Joyce was eventually convicted and executed for treason.

In 1946 Skardon returned to Scotland Yard, this time as a detective inspector, but in the next year he accepted a transfer to the permanent staff of MI5, where he was to stay for the remainder of his career. His patient and subtle techniques brought him much success with one of his most celebrated cases, that of the Harwell research scientist, Dr Klaus Fuchs. The development of the British independent nuclear deterrent proved to be one of the most sensitive and delicate issues in the early post-war years and proved a major headache for the security forces. Fuchs, born in Frankfurt, a graduate of Leipzig and Kiel universities and a member of the German Communist Party, came to Britain in 1933, becoming a naturalized British citizen in 1942. A skilled scientist, he entered atomic research before being arrested in 1949 and charged under the 1911 Official Secrets Act with passing secret information to the Russians. Skardon was brought in to interrogate Fuchs, patiently probing his mind and answers day after day. After a month of subtle questioning Skardon was about to call a temporary halt to the proceedings when a friend suggested that Fuchs was covering up more than ever on some specific points. Skardon agreed and decided to concentrate on these points in particular; on 24 January 1950 he elicited a full confession from the scientist: "At this time I had complete confidence in Russian policy and I had no hesitation in giving all the information I had," Fuchs confessed.

Skardon had always held the British espionage service, MI6, in contemptuous distrust, and, following the revelations of the 1950s, was inclined to refer to its members as "the enemies". Indeed, Donald MacLean and Guy Burgess fled before Skardon was due to interrogate them, possibly because of this very fact. Their colleague and "fellow traveller" Kim Philby, who had access to the Fuchs file and was well aware of Skardon's skill, was briefly interviewed by Skardon and later confessed that it was he whom he most feared.

Skardon was then placed in charge of the Watcher Service, directing the surveillance operations on foreign spies and agents. In 1960 he was in command of the counter-intelligence force which broke the Portland spy ring. A certain Harry Houghton, a clerk at the Underwater Weapons Establishment, Portland, was suspected of passing military secrets to a Canadian, Gordon Lonsdale. Skardon set up a huge surveillance operation involving a large number of agents, cars and even helicopters, and eventually closed in on a bungalow in Ruislip owned by a Mr and Mrs Peter Kroger. Skardon employed all his tact and charm in persuading a neighbour to allow him and his men to use a room in their house to keep watch on the Krogers. Indeed, as the surveillance continued for some considerable time, it is a measure of Skardon's natural pleasantness and understanding that the intrusion was kept to an acceptable minimum. His patience paid off and all the participants in the espionage ring were arrested and convicted.

In the late 1960s Skardon retired with his wife to Torquay in Devon, where he spent much of his time in the peaceful activities of bowls, bridge and painting. He had begun his career as a simple bobby on the beat and, despite many changes of circumstance, retained many of the best aspects of the bobby throughout his working life. A soft and disarming exterior concealed a patient, yet razor-sharp and incisive mind capable of seizing upon the smallest detail. He was inspired by the belief that wrong-doers should not go unpunished, and was instrumental in securing the conviction of some of the most infamous traitors of the early post-war period.

Born William James Skardon. **Marriage** Georgia, 1926 (died, 1984). **Children** One son and one daughter. **Career** Clerk, in household of the Duke of Connaught; policeman, 1925; joined Metropolitan Police Force and promoted to detective, by 1940; seconded to security services, MI5, 1940; commissioned in the Intelligence Corps, 1944, at Supreme Headquarters Allied Expeditionary Force, Europe, 1944–46, interrogated William Joyce, "Lord Haw-Haw", 1945; detective inspector, Scotland Yard, 1946; joined permanent staff, MI5, 1947; interrogated Dr Klaus Fuchs, 1949–50; in charge of Watcher Service; in charge of counter-intelligence operation that broke Portland spy ring, 1960; retired late 1960s. **Cause of death** Undisclosed, at age 82.

BARONESS MARIA von TRAPP

Austrian Singer, Missionary and Author

***Born* Vienna, Austria, 26 January 1905**

***Died* Morrisville, Vermont, 28 March 1987**

Immortalized by Julie Andrews as the heroine of *The Sound of Music*, Maria von Trapp was a woman in whose real life the fairytale element was all too often offset by the harsh demands of everyday reality. Maria's marriage to Baron von Trapp, the success of the Trapp Family Singers and the family's romantic escape from Nazi-occupied Austria over the mountains to Italy did not automatically ensure the "happy ever after" ending the musical inevitably suggests. It was in combating the more prosaic difficulties the family encountered in their early and difficult years of exile that Maria von Trapp's truly heroic qualities were most in evidence.

Maria Kutschera, a 20-year-old postulant nun, first entered the story of the von Trapp family when she was sent by the mother superior in her Nonnberg Convent in Salzburg on a temporary assignment as governess to the widowed baron's seven children. An orphan herself, Maria became a devout Catholic at the age of 18 and, when the baron first proposed marriage, was torn between her love for him and his children and her wish to follow her vocation as a nun. It was, however, with the blessing of her mother superior that she finally married the baron in November 1927. Religion was always to remain one of the strongest forces in Maria's life.

In 1929 and 1931 two more daughters were born to the von Trapp family. At this time, too, they turned the large family home in Aigen into a guest house for students and clergymen, the baron having lost most of his fortune in the Depression. One of their guests, the Reverend Franz Wasner, heard the family singing some of the Tyrolean folk songs Maria had taught them and was so impressed that he became not only chaplain but also musical director to the family, widening their repertoire to include much of the religious and secular music of the Renaissance and Baroque. In August 1936 the family were heard by Lotte Lehmann, who invited them to appear at the Salzburg Festival. This appearance launched them on a professional career they had never sought to pursue and on their first European tour.

When the Nazis entered Austria, the baron, a much-decorated commander from World War I, was unwilling to cooperate with the new authorities, so the family decided to emigrate. With Father Wasner, and only a few possessions, they fled over the mountains to St Gorgen in Italy. In the autumn of 1938 they began their first American tour, only to have it cancelled half way through when their manager found out that Maria was, once again, pregnant.

The tenth von Trapp child, Johannes, was born early in 1939 but by then the family's visitors' visa had expired and they returned to Europe for a summer tour of Scandinavia. Back in the United States in the autumn the family attempted a second tour but it was ill-attended and seemed to spell failure for them in the US.

From this, the lowest point in their fortunes, the von Trapp family went on to become one of the most successful choirs in the United States. During the next 15 years they performed constantly, both in America and abroad, returning to Europe and to Salzburg in 1950, visiting Israel, New Zealand, Australia, South Africa and even the Hawaiian Islands. Their annual carol concerts in New York's Town Hall became a regular Christmas event. "Sing Weeks", introduced by Maria in 1944 at the Tyrolean farmhouse the family built in Vermont, developed into musical summer camps which brought young people together from all over the United States to sing and make music.

The family's success seems to have been due to the new professionalism that they brought to their American programme. Dressed in Austrian folk costume, the Trapp Family Singers presented sacred music and madrigals, as well as Austrian folk songs and yodels. Their programme also included ancient instruments like virginals, the recorder and the viola da gamba. Maria von Trapp acted as narrator and was always the driving force behind the family. "In this warm-hearted musician and mother, the group have their symbol and spokeswoman," wrote the *New York World Telegram and Sun* in December 1954. "Together they stand for good cheer and generosity, inborn refinement and easy hospitality."

After the death of her husband in 1947, Maria von Trapp kept all the family activities going alone—the upkeep of the Vermont house, "Cor Unum", and chapel, the concerts and summer camps, and the Trapp Family Relief Work for Austria. In May 1949 she published *The Story of the Trapp Family Singers*. That same year she also received a Papal decoration, and in 1956 was named "Catholic Mother of the Year" by the National Catholic Conference on Family Life. In 1955, when the group finally disbanded and the last of her children was almost grown up, Maria von Trapp turned her energy towards missionary work, visiting leper colonies and raising money for Catholic proselytizing in New Guinea and the Pacific Islands.

Of the musical that made her world famous, some reports say that Maria von Trapp received not a penny in royalties, having sold the film rights of her book to a German company some years earlier, and that she disliked Julie Andrews' portrayal of her. Others say that she only allowed the family story to be made into a musical when friends persuaded her that the royalties could be used for her missionary work. According to these sources, although Maria von Trapp claimed to have "very little business sense" and not to have made much money, the royalties she received from the stage, film and recorded versions of *The Sound of Music* made her half a million dollars.

Whatever the truth of this, it is clear from the story of her life that the show business element was always less important to Maria von Trapp than the religious. It is likely that the sincerity of her Catholic faith not only kept the family together through their early years in America but also gave their concerts a genuinely religious feeling, very different from the sentimental kitsch of the musical story.

Born Maria Augusta Kutschera. **Parents** Karl and Augusta (Rainer) Kutschera. **Marriage** Baron Georg von Trapp, 1927 (died, 1947). **Children** Rosemarie Erentrudis, Eleonore and Johannes, and seven stepchildren—Rupert, Agathe, Maria, Werner, Hedwig, Johanna, and Martina (deceased). **Education** State Teachers' College of Progressive Education, Vienna; St Mary's College, Notre Dame, Indiana, LLD, 1957; St Anselm's College, Manchester, New Hampshire, DMus, 1966; St Michael's College, Winooski, Vermont, 1971. **Emigration** Left Austria for US, 1938; naturalized, 1948. **Career** Postulant nun, Nonnberg Convent, Salzburg, 1925; governess to children of Baron von Trapp, Aigen, 1925–27; toured with Trapp Family Singers, 1938–56; author and lecturer, 1948 onwards. **Related activities** Manager, Trapp Family Lodge, 1942–67; founder, Trapp Family Austrian Relief Inc., 1947; missionary worker, 1952 onwards. **Awards and honours** Papal decoration, Bene Merenti medal, 1949; Catholic Writers' Guild St Francis de Sales Golden Book Award for best book of non-fiction, for *The Story of the Trapp Family Singers*, 1950; Lady of Holy Sepulchre Award, 1951; Austrian Gold Cross for meritorious service; named Catholic Mother of the Year by National Catholic Conference on Family Life, 1957; Austrian Honorary Cross 1st Class for Science and Art, 1967. **Publications** *The Story of the Trapp Family Singers*, 1948; *Around the Year with the Trapp Family*, 1951; *Yesterday, Today and Forever*, 1952; (with Ruth Murdoch) *A Family on Wheels*, 1959; *Maria*, 1972. **Cause of death** Gangrene of the small bowel and other ailments, at age 82.

PATRICK TROUGHTON

British Actor

***Born* London, England, 25 March 1920**

***Died* Columbus, Georgia, 28 March 1987**

It is fair to say that British theatre has for many years enjoyed a high reputation. A strong tradition has brought a solidity of performance—not in any unimaginative sense, but one which means that less conspicuous roles are played with thoroughness. Actors and actresses suggest sound characterizations, and by adding to the sum of the parts, distinguish a whole production. Patrick Troughton is a case in point—an actor of consistent, unshowy quality and, as it happened, one rewarded with a measure of stardom.

He was born in 1920 and educated at Mill Hill School in the north of London. He then trained at the Embassy School of Acting and, since this piece started with a large claim for the British, it must be owned that he won a scholarship to Leighton Rollin's Studio for Actors on Long Island, New York. During World War II he served in motor torpedo boats with coastal services, and when peace came he began work at the Bristol Old Vic, famous for its presentation of the classics. This grounding won him parts in Laurence Olivier's films of *Hamlet* and *Richard III*; in the latter Troughton was notable as Tyrell, the man who does Uncle Richard's dirty work in disposing of the princes in the Tower.

Although theatre was his first love, acting for the camera suited Troughton, and he moved early into the nascent British television scene. (While appearing in a production of *Robin Hood*, he noticed that a backdrop appeared upside-down. He could, he claimed, have played the scene standing on his head, but as Friar Tuck was also in it, he modestly forbore.) Throughout the 1950s he consolidated his reputation on the stage and the small screen. Good examples of his work came in Shaw's *Misalliance*, Galsworthy's *The Silver Box*, and Dickens' *David Copperfield*. A major break arrived in 1960, thanks to the felicitous discovery that he showed a marked resemblance to Saint Paul, or to be exact, a portrait of the itinerant idealogue on a marble fragment of the first century AD, found in Rome. Troughton got the title part in the ten-part series *Paul of Tarsus*.

It was a different kind of traveller who shot Troughton to eventual fame. Doctor Who, the apparently indestructible time-traveller, is now a cult figure on both sides of the Atlantic, and the Doctor has been impersonated by at least seven actors. Troughton became the second incumbent, in 1966, at a crucial period in the series' history. With the departure of William Hartnell, the BBC was considering its demise. It opted instead for new blood, and Troughton it was who established the tradition of Doctor Who's Protean reincarnations. In contrast to Hartnell's demi-senile hauteur, he gave us a cosmic hobo, dressed like Charlie Chaplin, down-mouthed like Buster Keaton, and one whose main strategy was creative confusion—when in doubt, run away. (One aficionado has counted that in "The Krotons", he ran away 14 times.) But like his spiritual ancestors in the silent films, he would return, scuttling, to confute the powerful, monstrous enemy. A critic has described the rhythm of these adventures as "confrontation–run–chase–chaos–conquest". Many early fans were appalled by this apparent diminution of their hero; but just as he played the recorder to get his head together, this Doctor charmed the viewers, revived an ailing series, and ensured that it was bound for glory.

Troughton's craftsmanship ensured him regular work. After leaving *Doctor Who* in 1969, he appeared on television in *The Six Wives of Henry VIII* and various classy standbys such as *Treasure Island*, *All Creatures Great and Small* and *The Famous Five*. On the big screen he was in

Scars of Dracula, *Sinbad and the Eye of the Tiger*, and provided a memorable Father Brennan in *The Omen*.

When not working, Troughton liked to dabble with oil paints; he did not call himself an artist, but would acknowledge praise for his skill as a copyist. Friends and relations might find themselves presented with a Corot, a Canaletto or a Constable, and he once proudly decorated the set of a play he was in with a rendition of Turner's "Fighting Temeraire". A daughter of his became an illustrator of children's books, and two of his six children followed him into the theatrical profession.

Although his success as Doctor Who enabled Patrick Troughton to display his extrovert side to the utmost, he consistently refused to be interviewed about it. "I believe," he said, "there's too much 'going behind the scenes' these days. It spoils what actors try and do!" Strength and unobtrusiveness generally marked his acting, of which there is no better example than his portrayal of Horatio, Hamlet's student friend. It is a difficult part to enlighten or enliven, as Horatio hangs in the gloomy prince's shadow and spends a lot of time having things explained to him; nevertheless Troughton made him emerge as a character of considerable force. Of course, he would not say how it was done.

Born Patrick George Troughton. **Marriages** Three; third wife, Shelagh. **Children** Four sons, two daughters, one stepson, one stepdaughter. **Education** Mill Hill School, London; Embassy School of Acting; scholarship to Leighton Rollin's Studio for Actors, Long Island, New York. **Military service** Coast forces, World War II. **Career** Actor on stage, film and television; initially Shakespearean actor, Bristol Old Vic; début as Dr Who, 1966. **Stage** (includes) *Eva Braun*, 1950; *The Viking Queen*, 1966. **Films** (include) *Hamlet*, 1948; *The Franchise Affair*, 1950; *Waterfront*, 1950; *Richard III*, 1955; *Scars of Dracula*, 1970; *The Omen*, 1976; *Sinbad and the Eye of the Tiger*, 1977. **Television** (includes) *Robin Hood*; *Paul of Tarsus*; *Misalliance*; *The Silver Box*; *David Copperfield*; *The Six Wives of Henry VIII*; *Jenny*; *Space 1999*; *The Famous Five*; *The Sweeney*; *Treasure Island*; *All Creatures Great and Small*; *Family at War*; *Dr Finlay's Casebook*; *Colditz*; *Dr Who*, 1966–69, also 1973, 1983, 1985. **Cause of death** Undisclosed, at age 67.

APRIL

CARLOS BAKER

American Critic, Editor and Novelist
***Born* Biddeford, Maine, 5 May 1909**
***Died* Princeton, New Jersey, 18 April 1987**

Carlos Baker was one of America's top academics. He taught English at Princeton University between 1938 and 1977 and wrote several important books about writers and their work. In addition, he is credited with three competent novels and two volumes of poetry. Baker made his mark primarily with a biography of Ernest Hemingway and an interpretive account of Shelley's poetry. Both have become indispensible in their own right, and both attest to Baker's capacity for intellectual coherence and scholastic restraint. At the same time, however, these two books are of widely different characters. *Shelley's Major Poetry* assigns value to the poet's life and work, making judgements about their relationship and nature. *Ernest Hemingway: A Life Story* focuses entirely on the facts concerning the novelist's life, content to draw no conclusions.

"Mr Baker commands genuine talents," wrote Irving Howe in *Harper's*. His objectivity, "sound and unpretentious style", and intelligent presentation were recognized by everyone. The Shelley book, for instance, is one of the few successful attempts to construct a solid foundation for studying this enigmatic poet. Conversely, Baker's rendering of Hemingway balances the man with his legendary persona well enough for readers to approach him without preconceptions. Not everyone approved of Baker's meticulous thoroughness, but all recognized its value. He understood the need to separate the activities of "criticism" and "interpretation", and did literature a great service by providing two examples of measured and balanced scholarship.

A major difficulty in the study of literature is that of definition. The two main disciplines in this study, criticism and interpretation, involve different methods, have different requirements and produce different results. Interpretation depends on determining the artist's conceptual foundations and explaining the artist's expression in those terms. It is, in a sense, an act of translation. Criticism, while avoiding matters purely of taste, looks outward from the text and centres on the value and significance of the artist's utterance. Interpretation asks questions which, ultimately, can be settled. Criticism is more personal, asking questions of a largely indefinite nature. Such was the position of E.D. Hirsch's *Validity in Interpretation*, which claims that the confusion of the two disciplines causes many distracting and pointless arguments. Baker's work demonstrates "the ways in which responsible criticism depends upon careful interpretation". He is careful to make his claims about Shelley's philosophy, psychology and ethics only after he has set down the poet's premises, aims and achievements. As a result, the reader can be certain of hearing Shelley's statements, as opposed to Baker's statements projected on to Shelley. If the interpretation is sound, then the criticism can be justified.

What Baker does reveal about Shelley helps to fix an image of the poet and his importance to end "these periodic jostlings and fluctuations" in the estimation of his career as a writer. *Shelley's Major Poetry* investigates his "developing thought as it bears upon and is reflected in the individual poems" written between 1812 and 1822. Baker portrays him as primarily philosophical and psychological, instead of a lyric poet. He makes this claim based on an analysis of the poems' structure, which shows that "though his medium was poetic" Shelley was not "deeply interested in the finer details of structure and texture...his laws were those of the philosopher...the seer, and the prophet, and it is to these laws...that he primarily conforms, both by preference and inner constitution".

Shelley was more stringently devoted to "a strong if unorthodox ethical bias" and a "set of aesthetic ideals" than to technical perfection. Without the burden of trying to explain the poetry as a causal factor in Shelley's development, Baker is able to see the move from belief to despair in the poet as the motivating force. His faith in love as the basis of self-realization and freedom never diminished, despite the shifting emphasis from general moral progress to individual action to the impossibility of growth and perfection. Moreover, Baker convincingly represents Shelley's belief in poetry as the embodiment of his ideals.

The Hemingway biography solves the problem of interpretation and criticism from the opposite direction. This book does not try to "prove" anything; it merely tries to set the record straight, so that the legend does not run away with history. If there is any thesis to the book, it is borrowed from his first study of Hemingway, which claims that Hemingway's fiction was rooted in an "obstinant devotion to the fact and its accompanying sensation". Rather than explain the author, as Baker did with the poet, he presents Hemingway by piecing together hundreds of recollections from acquaintances and Hemingway's own letters, papers and unpublished manuscripts. This earlier work, *Hemingway: The Writer as Artist*, was undertaken before the novelist's suicide in 1963, and his approval of it convinced his fourth wife, Mary, to appoint Baker as the official biographer. Like the Shelley work, Baker's task was to trace the author's development through his own words and actions. Unlike it, Baker's scope was much larger, his sources largely primary, and his conclusions left for the reader to make.

Baker was praised for giving a "full-length portrait" of the man, depicting both the "mythological figure" and the human being. He was never distracted from the business at hand by "political or psychological preconceptions", allowing him at times to be very dramatic in his straightforward description of "adventure, troubles, accidents and wives". This was a truly factual look at Hemingway's life and work, credited with "a superb job of research and organization. Its success," said Granville Hicks, "lies in the directness of its course".

Some criticism was directed at the book as well. Some felt the great canvas lacked dimension, that Baker's "ruthless objectivity" deprived his sketch of depth. The emphasis on the life experience as the context of the fiction, instead of engaging in biographical criticism, was seen as a poor decision by some. "As it stands," wrote James Toback, "Baker's dispassionate study is to biography what the *nouveau roman* is to prose fiction." These reservations to the contrary, the decision to order Hemingway's fiction in chronological terms make the *Life Story* complementary to *The Writer as Artist*. Again, Baker shows discernment in leaving the critical and imaginative tasks behind him as he wrote the biography. It is important to have, especially for one who is so much larger than life, an account that simply establishes the accuracy of the events in that life.

The biography is also a subtle tribute to Hemingway's maxim "to write truly, and having found out what is true, to project it in such a way that it becomes part of the experience of the person who reads it". The style and structure of Baker's opus mimics many of Hemingway's own techniques and moves in a manner similar to his novels. "Baker limits himself to a style purposefully declarative," wrote Lewis Leary in *Southern Atlantic Quarterly*. "His sentences may sometimes seem staccato, non-committal and repetitive in form...they seem to lull toward inattention. Hemingway himself might admire [it]." In trying to give the stage entirely to Hemingway and to avoid the temptation of critical comment, Baker even conforms the writing to his persona. Hemingway believed in Eliot's concept of the "objective correlative", in which the structure of poetry or prose must create the identity between fiction and reality; and it is a concept which Baker adopts in his biography.

Born Carlos Heard Baker. **Parents** Arthur E. and Edna (Heard) Baker. **Marriage** Dorothy Thomasson Scott, 1932. **Children** Diane, Elizabeth, Brian Arthur. **Education** Dartmouth College, Hanover, New Hampshire, BA, 1932; Harvard University, Cambridge, Massachusetts, MA, 1933; Princeton University, New Jersey, PhD, 1940. **Career** English teacher: Thornton Academy, Saco, Maine, 1933–34, Nichols School, Buffalo, New York, 1934–36; instructor, Princeton University, 1938–42, assistant professor, 1942–46, associate professor, 1946–51, professor of English, 1951–53, Woodrow Wilson Professor, 1954–77, professor emeritus, 1977 onwards; also novelist, poet, literary critic and editor. **Related activities** Chairman: department of English, Princeton University, 1952–58, 1974–75; Fulbright Lecturer in American literature, Oxford University, 1957–58; visiting professor, Centre Universitaire Mediterranéen, Nice, France, 1958. **Awards and honours** LittD, Dartmouth College, 1957; Guggenheim Fellowship, 1965–67; DHum, University of Maine, 1974; LHD, Monmouth College, 1977. **Offices and memberships** Modern Language Association of America; National Council of Teachers of English; College English Association; American Association of University Professors; Phi Beta Kappa; Century Association; Theta Delta Chi. **Publications** *Shadows in Stone* (poetry), Hanover, New Hampshire, 1930; *Shelley's Major Poetry: The Fabric of Vision*, Princeton, 1948; *Hemingway: The Writer as Artist*, Princeton, 1952, fourth edition, 1972; *A Friend in Power* (novel), New York and London, 1958; *The Land of Rumbelow: A Fable in the Form of a Novel* (novel), New York, 1963, London, 1964; *A Year and a Day* (poetry), Nashville, Tennessee, 1963; *Ernest Hemingway: A Life Story*, 1969; *The Gay Head Conspiracy: A Novel of Suspense* (novel), New York, 1973; *The Talisman and Other Stories* (short stories), New York, 1976. **Other** (editor) *The American Looks at the World*, New York, 1944; (editor, with Willard Thorpe and Merle Curti) *American Issues*, Philadelphia, 1941, revised edition, 1955; (editor) *The Prelude, with a Selection from the Shorter Poems and the Sonnets and the 1800 Preface to Lyrical Ballads* by Wordsworth, New York, 1948; (editor) *Selected Poetry and Prose* by Shelley, New York, 1951; (editor, with others) *The Major English Romantic Poets: A Symposium in Reappraisal*, Carbondale, 1957; (editor) *Joseph Andrews* by Henry Fielding, 1959; (editor) *Green Mansions* by William Henry Hudson, 1961; (editor) *Hemingway and His Critics: An International Anthology*, New York, 1961; (editor) *Ernest Hemingway: Critiques of Four Major Novels*, New York, 1962; (editor) *Poems and Selected Letters* by Keats, New York, 1962; (editor) *Coleridge: Poetry and Prose*, New York, 1965; (editor, with others) *Modern American Usage* by Wilson Follett, New York and London, 1966; (editor) *The Black Swan* by Thomas Mann, 1980; (editor) *Ernest Hemingway: Selected Letters 1917–1961*, New York and London, 1981. **Cause of death** Undisclosed, at age 77.

JOSEPHINE BELL

British Doctor and Novelist

***Born* Manchester, England, 8 December 1897**

***Died* Surrey, England, 24 April 1987**

"Doctor Turns to Crime". Such a headline conjures up all sorts of horrors. Images of acid-bath murderers and morphine addicts leap to mind—but Josephine Bell does not belong in their ranks. True, her main career was medicine, but her involvement in crime was a literary one, and her murders appear only on the printed page.

Born Doris Bell Collier, her father was a surgeon who died when she was only seven. The family moved to the south of England, and at the age of 19 she gained a place at Cambridge University's women's college, Newnham, to read medicine herself. After gaining her MB in 1922 she did her clinical training at London's University College Hospital. She qualified on time, in 1924, in spite of having met and married fellow doctor Norman Dyer Ball the previous year.

From 1927 onwards they practised together in Greenwich and central London, and had four children. Nine years later, in 1936, they moved to work in Guildford, Surrey, but Norman Ball was tragically killed in a car accident. As Dr Ball, Bell continued with her medical career, but took up writing, probably in order to cope with another devastatingly early and unexpected bereavement.

Her first novel, *Murder in Hospital*, was published the following year and included the central figures of her earlier books, Dr David Wintringham and the Scotland Yard Inspector, Steven Mitchell. Other regular characters included the barrister, Claude Warrington-Reeve and, later, another doctor, Henry Frost.

It has been said that Bell wrote far too much for any hope of becoming a classic writer, and that the failure to use a central, highly visible, continuing detective figure may also account for her failure to achieve a major position in the field of detective fiction. However, on these bases, even Agatha Christie could be held to have "failed". She too was prolific and employed a number of central figures, such as Hercule Poirot and Miss Marple, but sometimes she dispensed with the main detective figure entirely.

The fact is that Bell was far more interested in characterization than in plotting intricate puzzles, although she was more than capable of doing so when she chose. And, following the publication of her first seven crime novels, she produced her first mainstream novel, *The Bottom of the Well*, in 1940. Thereafter she alternated approximately one crime book with one mainstream work for several years, although her output went down during the latter days of World War II. This was probably the result of an additional workload in her practice, but also may be partly attributed to the shortage of paper in the UK which continued until well into the 1950s.

Bell's works fit a number of genres, although seldom is the fit exact. The early books are certainly detective works, but she rapidly moved towards the thriller and, in her non-crime novels, embraced a degree of romance. In addition, Gothic elements may be detected in *To Let, Furnished* (1952). At one point she moved to historical fiction and *Tudor Pilgrimage*, which came out in 1967, was very highly praised. A strong degree of social criticism is evident in her later books. *Such a Nice Client* (1977) contains a scathing attack on thoughtless social workers who have an over-simplistic approach.

Bell drew heavily on her own experiences for themes. Consistent throughout a great deal of her work is the young, idealistic, overworked and underpaid physician who is surrounded by hospital routine and personnel. Also consistent is a love affair involving a young career woman on whom the writing focuses, usually in the third person. After Bell bought her own five-ton yacht soon after the war, a nautical element crept into her writing.

Her criminals are usually evil, even when amateur. The strongest passion is hatred; sexual desire is portrayed as sordid and dangerous. But it is always her strong characterization that holds sway. *Death in Retirement*, which came out two years after her own retirement from medicine in 1954, centres on Dr Clayton, one of her most fascinating older women and beautifully drawn. This book obviously owed much to her personal experience and the fact that she had met such a wide range of people. This is also demonstrated in her ability to bring alive everyday domestic conflict, skilfully sketching the problems of living with tedious and boring family members whom one has not only to endure but also to care for. She never shied away from realism.

From the 1950s onwards her work was published in the United States, many of her earlier titles appearing under different ones, and she acquired a strong American following for her crime books which were, thereafter, published simultaneously in both countries.

Even in retirement Bell continued to mix medicine with writing. For eight further years, until 1962, she was a member of a hospital management board and continued her involvement with the Crime Writers' Association which she had co-founded in 1953 and for which, in 1961, she edited a valuable collection of essays called *Crime in Our Time*. The last of her output of over 60 books was *Wolf! Wolf!* which came out in 1979 when she was 82.

Bell's interest in crime writing never flagged and she continued to attend meetings of the Detection Club into late old age, never failing to express her opinions with vigour. This did not, however, conceal her fundamental kindness, warmth or concern for her fellow human beings and writers. Her voice remains a distinctive one and her craft a valuable example for any novelist.

Born Doris Bell Collier. **Pseudonym** Josephine Bell. **Father** Surgeon. **Marriage** Norman Dyer Ball, doctor, 1923 (died, 1936). **Children** Three daughters and one son. **Education** Godolphin School, Salisbury; Newnham College, Cambridge, 1916–19; University College Hospital, London, MB, BS, 1924. **Career** Practised medicine, 1927–54; began writing crime novels, 1937; later wrote mainstream novels and, in 1967, branched into historical fiction. **Offices and memberships** Co-founder, Crime Writers' Association, 1953; member, management committee, St Luke's Hospital, 1954–62; member, Detection Club. **Crime novels** (all London) *Murder in Hospital*, 1937; *Death on the Borough Council*, 1937; *Fall Over Cliff*, 1938, New York, 1956; *The Port of London Murders*, 1938, New York, 1958; *Death at Half-Term*, 1939, published as *Curtain Call for a Corpse*, New York, 1965; *From Natural Causes*, 1939; *All Is Vanity*, 1940; *Trouble at Wrekin Farm*, 1942; *Death at the Medical Board*, 1944, New York, 1964; *Death in Clairvoyance*, 1949; *The Summer School Mystery*, 1950; *To Let, Furnished*, 1952, published as *Stranger on a Cliff*, New York, 1964; *Bones in the Barrow*, 1953, New York, 1955; *Fires at Fairlawn*, 1954; *Death in Retirement*, London and New York, 1956; *The China Roundabout*, 1956, published as *Murder on the Merry-go-round*, New York, 1965; *Double Doom*, 1957, New York, 1958; *The Seeing Eye*, 1958; *The House Above the River*, 1959; *Easy Prey*, London and New York, 1959; *A Well-Known Face*, London and New York, 1960; *New People at the Hollies*, London and New York, 1961; *Adventure with Crime*, 1962; *A Flat Tyre in Fulham*, 1963, published as *Fiasco in Fulham*, New York, 1963, and as *Room for a Body*, New York, 1964; *The Hunter and the Trapped*, 1963; *The Upfold Witch*, London and New York, 1964; *No Escape*, 1965, New York, 1966; *Death on the Reserve*, London and New York, 1966; *The Catalyst*, 1966, New York, 1967; *Death of a Con Man*, London and Philadelphia, 1968; *The Fennister Affair*, 1969, New York, 1977; *The Wilberforce Legacy*, London and New York, 1969; *A Hydra with Six Heads*, 1970, New York, 1977; *A Hole in the Ground*, 1971, New York, 1973; *Death of a Poison-tongue*, 1972, New York, 1977; *A Pigeon Among the Cats*, 1974, New York, 1977; *Victim*, 1975,

New York, 1976; *The Touble in Hunter Ward*, 1976, New York, 1977; *Such a Nice Client*, 1977, published as *Stroke of Death*, New York, 1977; *A Swan Song Betrayed*, 1978, published as *Treachery in Type*, New York, 1979; *Wolf! Wolf!*, 1979. **Other novels** (all London) *The Bottom of the Well*, 1940; *Martin Croft*, 1941; *Alvina Foster*, 1943; *Compassionate Adventure*, 1946; *Total War at Haverington*, 1947; *Wonderful Mrs Marriott*, 1948; *The Whirlpool*, 1949; *Backing Winds*, 1951; *Cage-birds*, 1953; *Two Ways to Love*, 1954; *Hell's Pavement*, 1955; *The Convalescent*, 1960; *Safety First*, 1962; *The Alien*, 1964; *Tudor Pilgrimage*, 1967; *Jacobean Adventure*, 1969; *Over the Seas*, 1970; *The Dark and the Light*, 1971; *To Serve a Queen*, 1972; *In the King's Absence*, 1973; *A Question of Loyalties*, 1974. **Uncollected short stories** (all London unless otherwise stated) "The Case of the Faulty Drier", "Gale Warning", "Death in Ambrose Ward", "The Thimble River Murder" and "Death in a Cage" in *The Evening Standard Detective Book*, 1950; "The Packet Boat Murder" in *The Evening Standard Detective Book* second series, 1951; "The Sea Decides" in *Planned Departures*, edited by Elizabeth Ferrars, 1958; "Wash, Set and Murder" in *The Mystery Bedside Book*, edited by John Creasey, 1960; "Death in a Crystal" in *The Saint*, New York, 1960; "A Case of Fugue" in *Crime Writers' Choice*, edited by Roy Vickers, 1964; "Murder Delayed" in *Crimes Across the Sea*, edited by John Creasey, London and New York, 1964; "Experiment" in *The Saint*, New York, 1965; "The Commuters" in *John Creasey's Mystery Bedside Book*, edited by Herbert Harris, 1966; "The Unfinished Heart" in *John Creasey's Mystery Bedside Book 1974*, edited by Herbert Harris, 1973. **Edited works** *Crime in Our Time* (essays), London, 1961, New York, 1962. **Cause of death** Undisclosed, at age 89.

ERSKINE CALDWELL

American Novelist, Short Story Writer and Journalist

***Born* Moreland, Georgia, 17 December 1903**

***Died* Paradise Valley, Arizona, 11 April 1987**

A substantial number of readers think Erskine Caldwell is simply an author of sensational, torrid potboilers. For much of his career he had the dubious distinction of being the most-often banned and censored American writer, and has been called "the South's literary bad boy". He was never actually convicted on obscenity charges, and he managed to write 55 books throughout his career. These books, moreover, have been translated into 42 languages and boast sales of over 80 million copies. Despite this success, his lucid, unmannered description of the South's economic and moral putrescence alienated many contemporary readers for its social commentary and its vulgarity. Lately, the new generation of readers consider Caldwell a writer of tremendous skill and a literary artist of the highest calibre. Along with Thomas Wolfe, William Faulkner, Robert Penn Warren and Eudora Welty, Caldwell was a leading member of the famous "Southern literary renaissance", which produced such landmark fiction as *Look Homeward, Angel* and *Absalom! Absalom!*. Faulkner, in fact, listed Caldwell as one of the five greatest novelists of that generation. As a short story writer, critic and champion James Korges claims, "we would have to go back to Maupassant to find his equal".

One reason for this ambiguous reputation is that much of Caldwell's later fiction was sensational in proportion to its literary merit. But the quality and range of his earlier writing proves Caldwell's talents adequately. In addition to fiction, he also wrote biography and autobiography. He was able to balance strong feeling with objectivity in these, and was ambitious and eclectic in his choice of subjects. Satires, travelogues and polemics are also among his credits. With his second wife, Margaret Bourke-White, Caldwell produced *You Have Seen Their Faces*, a documentary which virtually reinvented the text-picture book and founded the "reportorial-photographic" school.

The first writing experience he received was as a journalist, and because of this the style, depth and dimension of his work eluded many reviewers at the time. Moreover, before anyone had a chance to appreciate Caldwell's contributions the freshness of his novels began to diminish. One of these contributions is the range of characters which we now so readily identify with the South. Today the persona of bigoted, superstitious and hopeless "white trash" is a familiar one, but the image was consolidated—if not created—by Caldwell. If he missed the mark later on, it is by the standards he created that the critics judge him. All writers suffer the whimsy of the fashionable intelligence, especially Southern writers. Caldwell has survived enough of them to prove his mettle. His best-known books, *Tobacco Road* and *God's Little Acre*, are legendary. At one point *Tobacco Road* was outselling the Bible in the heart of the Bible Belt. Clearly, Caldwell has a secure place in American literary history.

His intimate contact with the lower echelons of society shaped his life at an early age. He was the only child of an itinerant Presbyterian minister who travelled an area stretching "from Virginia to Florida, from the Atlantic to the Mississippi". This was among the most poorly paid professions at the time, and as a result Caldwell received just three years' formal schooling and two years of university education. His mother was responsible for most of his basic education, but the wandering was a great teacher, too. Years later Caldwell said, "You learned a lot living in small towns those days, before they became the smaller versions of the big towns." He began supporting himself at 14, becoming by turns a mill labourer, cotton picker, cook and salesman of "building lots...under three feet of water". He also spent some time running guns in Central America before returning to complete his high school education.

These experiences would form the raw material of his work. He decided to write professionally while at the University of Virginia in 1925. With his first wife (the first of four) he moved to Maine, where he wrote for seven years before he finally established himself with *Tobacco Road*. The picture he painted was neither pretty nor optimistic. Caldwell's characters, including Jeeter, Ellie May and Sister Bessie, Pearl and Tom commit acts of incest, adultery, prostitution, lechery, murder and religious hatred. The word that describes these figures and their condition is "depravity": they "ignore the civilization that contains them as completely as it ignores them". Caldwell's vision is essentially Machanean (i.e. Earth lies within the boundaries of hell), and slightly deterministic: Ty Ty Walden says in *God's Little Acre*, "God put us in the bodies of animals and tried to make us act like people." Korges suggests Caldwell's main concern in the novels is "tenacity in the spirits of men and women deserted by God and man...about the animal tug toward life that sustains men even in times of deprivation". That deprivation exists on all levels of Caldwell's storytelling. The conditions of life for the characters are frustration, loss and humiliation. It is a world where needs and passions are satisfied quickly or not at all.

Such universal themes symbolized by such a brutish and nasty setting as the poor South was bound to offend its audience. The general reaction to all his early work was either one of disgust at its content or amusement at its "burlesque-style" humour. Three years earlier when *Look Homeward, Angel* appeared, reviews resented how Wolfe "spat on the South". With *Tobacco Road* Caldwell was accused of "digging around in Southern muck [and] flinging it into the literary sky". Of course, what people failed to recognize in these and other cases, was that the South was merely the stage on which Caldwell's intensely human drama was set. Considering its widest implications, it was no more about Southern lower classes than *Moby-Dick* is about the proper method of whaling.

The Southern States do occupy a special place in the American spirit, without which it can neither be understood nor redeemed. Economically and politically destroyed by the Civil War, spiritually degraded by the Reconstruction, the South bears the mark of America's shame and self-hatred, and represents the defeat and frustration of its pastoral vision. Southern writers are forced into the roles of nurse and exorcist, and Southerners may loath their utterance the way Dorian Gray loathes his own portrait. Especially in this century they have tried to reclaim the South from its moribund state, from oblivion to greatness. So, they represent the grotesque and demonic; so are they often politically progressive, even Marxist. In all Caldwell's work, but more sharply in *Tobacco Road* and *God's Little Acre*, these traits are prominent. Running through his books is the struggle to recover family values and ties to the land. He often shows the power of these things in relation to life in the city, the symbolic position of the North in the American imagination, which he portrays as lacking any indelible relationships.

Tobacco Road barely survived publication, and was only a commercial success after Jack Kirkland put it on the stage. Another element of Caldwell's writing which contributed to its misreception is the comic irony of the narrative. Caldwell writes about insignificant people who act out our humanity, but are so far removed from the mainstream of humanity that their status is diametrically opposed to their significance. W.M. Frohock identifies this brand of humour as typically American:

> [This humour] is native to our earth and deep-rooted in our history. Its material is the man who has been left behind in the rush to develop our frontiers, the man who has stayed in one place, out of and away from the main current of our developing civilization, so largely untouched by what we think of as progress that his folk-ways and mores seem...quaint and a little exotic...

This type of humour has close ties with two great Southern writers of the nineteenth century—Bret Harte and Mark Twain. However, where much of their mirth had enthusiasm for life, much of Caldwell's has nothing but despair. In other ways Caldwell receives their inheritance, for Twain's view of human nature grew very dark and sour by the end of his life. Twain's gratitude to Adam for "bringing death into the world" would sympathize with Caldwell's rats who wait for Godot. The situation in Caldwell's *Trouble in July* is one example. It is about a lynching in which the Black man is accused by a White girl of raping her. The Whites form a vigilante group, the sheriff leaves town, and the girl belatedly reveals that the whole story was false. Not only does human dignity fail, but the law and institutions fail to protect us. "I don't know nothin' else to do," Jeeter says in *Tobacco Road*, "except wait for Him to take notice."

Taken together, Caldwell's main novels form a world as complete, though not as integrated, as Faulkner's mythical Yoknapatawpha County. But more than Faulkner, Caldwell created the first clear models of the Southerner. Walter Beacham in *Nation* acknowledges that "Caldwell's books became primers...for all the other Southern novels read in subsequent years. For at least a decade [his] characters became synonymous with the Southerner. [Caldwell] performed the vital service of unlocking fundamental mysteries of the South." However, according to Korges, as his career progressed, his novels were filled with "sensational plotting and trite characterization". The generally held view is that, having reached his pinnacle early on, and having presented a fictional world as comprehensive as, say, Thomas Hardy's, Caldwell repeated himself in the later works, tilling the same ground endlessly. Even though it was ground that he had broken, reviewers of the later works tended to feel that he "outgrew his usefulness, making a nuisance of himself by continuing to show us the obvious".

From a different angle, the sum of Caldwell's work provides a very dynamic portrait of the South. It is important to recall that he was producing important short fiction and journalistic work well into the 1960s. Korges advises reading him in groups, since he focuses on specific themes and character-types in different periods of his career. But if read in succession, the fiction and non-fiction accurately chronicle the growth and changing moods in the South in the first half of this century; as William Bradford Huie would later do within the time frame of the civil rights movement. Certainly, it is not unreasonable to place Erskine Caldwell at the headwaters of Southern cultural rejuvenation. The mass and variable quality of his work have sometimes confounded this contribution.

Born Erskine Preston Caldwell. **Parents** Ira Sylvester, a Presbyterian minister, and Caroline (Preston Bell) Caldwell. **Marriages** 1) Helen Lannigan, 1925 (divorced); 2) Margaret Bourke-White, 1939 (divorced, 1942); 3) June Johnson, 1942 (divorced, 1955); 4) Virginia Moffett Fletcher, 1957. **Children** Erskine Preston, Dabney Withers and Janet by first marriage; Jay Erskine by third marriage. **Education** Educated by mother, except for three years' formal schooling; Erskine College, Due West, South Carolina, 1920–21; University of Virginia, Charlottesville, 1922, 1925–26; University of Pennsylvania, Philadelphia, 1924. **Career** While writing first stories worked on a variety of jobs, including professional footballer, building lot salesman, mill labourer, cotton picker, cook, waiter, taxi driver, farmhand, cottonseed shoveller, stonemason's helper, soda jerk, bodyguard, stagehand in a burlesque theatre, boathand on vessel running guns to Central America; reporter, *Atlanta Journal*, Georgia, 1925; prolific writer of novels and short stories, 1930 onwards; first publication, *The Bastard*, 1930; screenwriter, Hollywood, 1930–34, 1942–43; foreign correspondent, radio correspondent, Mexico, Spain, Czechoslovakia, China, Russia, 1938–41; war correspondent in Russia for *Life* magazine, PM and Columbia Broadcasting System Inc., 1941; editor, *American Folkways* series, 1941–55. **Awards and honours** *Yale Review* Award for "Country Full of Swedes", 1933; honorary member, American Academy and Institute of Arts and Letters; Order of Cultural Merit, Poland, 1981; Order of Arts and Letters, France, 1983. **Offices and memberships** American Academy; Authors' League; American PEN; San Francisco Press Club; Phoenix Press Club. **Novels** *The Bastard*, New York, 1930; *Poor Fool*, New York, 1930; *Tobacco Road*, New York, 1932, London, 1933; *God's Little Acre*, New York and London, 1933; *Journeyman*, New York, 1935, London, 1938, revised edition, 1938; *Trouble in July*, New York and London, 1940; *All Night Long: A Novel of Guerrilla Warfare in Russia*, New York, 1942, London, 1943; *Tragic Ground*, New York, 1944, London, 1947; *A House in the Uplands*, New York, 1946, London, 1947; *The Sure Hand of God*, New York, 1947, London, 1949; *This Very Earth*, New York, 1948, London, 1949; *A Place Called Estherville*, New York, 1949, London, 1951; *Episode in Palmetto*, New York, 1950, London, 1951; *A Lamp for Nightfall*, New York and London, 1952; *Love and Money*, New York, 1954, London, 1955; *Gretta*, Boston, 1959, published as *Claudell*, London, 1959; *Jenny by Nature*, New York and London, 1961; *Close to Home*, New York and London, 1962; *The Bastard and Poor Fool*, London, 1963; *The Last Night of Summer*, New York and London, 1963; *Miss Mamma Aimee*, New York, 1967, London, 1968; *Summertime Island*, Cleveland, 1968, London, 1969; *The Weather Shelter*, Cleveland, 1969, London, 1970; *The Earnshaw Neighborhood*, Cleveland, 1971, London, 1972; *Annette*, New York, 1973, London, 1974. **Short stories** *American Earth*, New York, 1931, London, 1935, published as *A Swell-looking Girl*, New York, 1951; *Mama's Little Girl*, 1932; *A Message for Genevieve*, 1933; *We Are Living: Brief Stories*, New York, 1933, London, 1934; *Kneel to the Rising Sun and Other Stories*, New York, 1935, London, 1961; *The Sacrilege of Alan Kent*, Portland, Maine, 1936; *Southways*, New York, 1938, London, 1953; *Jackpot: The Short Stories of Erskine Caldwell*, New York, 1940, London, 1950, abridged edition published as *Midsummer Passion*, New York, 1948; *Georgia Boy*, New York, 1943, London, 1947; *A Day's Wooing and Other Stories*, New York, 1944; *Stories by Erskine Caldwell: 24 Representative Stories*, edited by Henry Seidel Canby, New York, 1944, also published as *The Pocket Book of Erskine Caldwell*, New York, 1947; *A Woman in the*

House, New York, 1949; *The Humorous Side of Erskine Caldwell*, edited by Robert Cantwell, New York, 1951, published as *Where the Girls Are Different and Other Stories*, New York, 1962; *The Courting of Susie Brown*, New York and London, 1952; *The Complete Stories*, New York, 1953; *Gulf Coast Stories*, Boston, 1956, London, 1957; *Certain Women*, Boston, 1957, London, 1958; *When You Think of Me*, Boston, 1959, London, 1960; *Men and Women: 22 Stories*, Boston, 1961, London, 1963. **Screenplays** *A Nation Dances* (documentary), 1943; *Volcano*, 1953. **Other** *In Defense of Myself*, 1930; *Tenant Farmer*, New York, 1935; *Some American People*, New York, 1935; *You Have Seen Their Faces*, with photographs by Margaret Bourke-White, New York, 1937; *North of the Danube*, with photographs by Margaret Bourke-White, New York, 1939; *Say! Is This the USA?*, with photographs by Margaret Bourke-White, New York, 1951; *All-Out on the Road to Smolensk*, New York, 1942, published as *Moscow Under Fire: A Wartime Diary, 1941*, London, 1942; *Russia at War*, with photographs by Margaret Bourke-White, New York and London, 1942; *The Caldwell Caravan: Novels and Stories*, Cleveland, 1946; *Call it Experience: The Years of Learning How to Write*, New York, 1951, London, 1952; *Molly Cottontail* (juvenile), Boston, 1958, London, 1959; *Around About America*, New York and London, 1964; *In Search of Bisco*, New York and London, 1965; *The Deer at Our House* (juvenile), New York and London, 1966; *In the Shadow of the Steeple*, London, 1966; *Writing in America*, New York, 1967; *Deep South: Memory and Observation*, New York, 1968; *Afternoons in Mid-America: Observations and Impressions*, New York, 1976. **Cause of death** Lung cancer, at age 83. **Further reading** Shields McIlwaine, *The Southern Poor White from Lubberland to Tobacco Road*, Norman, Oklahoma, 1939; James Korges, *Erskine Caldwell*, Minneapolis, 1969; William A. Sutton, *Black Like It Is/Was: Erskine Caldwell's Treatment of Racial Themes*, Metuchen, New Jersey, 1974.

TERRY CARR

American Science-Fiction Writer and Editor

***Born* Grants Pass, Oregon, 19 February 1937**

***Died* Oakland, California, 7 April 1987**

Terry Carr was never prolific as a science-fiction writer. Most of his career has been devoted to editing. He started out as an editor for Ace Books, where he founded the "Ace Science Fiction Specials" series. As a writer of fiction he tended to produce stories about alien creatures, but according to his own account "this [was] an outgrowth of my interest in communication between *all* kinds of people". He is responsible for some potboilers, like *Warlord of Kor*, as well as stories of definite literary merit, like "Ozymandias" and *Cirque*. Characteristic of Carr's style are humour and irony; and his ability to adapt materials from other sources demonstrated his versatility as a science-fiction professional.

Carr began his editorial career in the 1950s, when he worked on amateur magazines, including the award-winning *Fanac*. The 1950s was an especially rich period for science fiction, for it was then that other major writers and editors, among them Robert Silverberg, Ted White, Gregory Benford, Alfred Bester and Harlan Ellison, first gained prominence. Carr's most important collection is *Classic Science Fiction: The First Golden Age*, which combines significant work from the 1940s with excellent background notes. For this and other work, Carr earned the reputation of an "editor with impeccable taste".

Carr's writing career began in 1961. In the beginning his novels were of the sensational, pyrotechnic variety of science fiction. However, the short stories from that same period exhibit a far greater sophistication, polish and control over his materials. For example, "The Dance of the Changer and the Three" explores an alien culture by presenting one of its myths. "Ozymandias" is an interesting fusion of cryonics and Egyptian burial customs. Finally, "They Live on Levels" portrays both scene and character through the correspondence between two cultures.

Carr's Utopian novel, *Cirque*, shows the range of his imagination on a large scale. The city he describes is maintained by the literal rejection of filth. The crisis in the novel is grounded in the confrontation and acceptance of their behaviour and their nature. The plot is believable, despite the fact that it relies heavily on coincidence. It is a traditionally structured novel which explores the need for change, growth and acceptance; but it is also a religious parable on the power of love and "the transcendent experience".

Born Terry Gene Carr. **Pseudonym** Norman Edwards. **Marriages** 1) Miriam Dyches, 1959 (divorced, 1961); 2) Carol Newmark, 1961. **Education** City College of San Francisco, 1954–57, AA, 1957; University of California, Berkeley, 1957–59. **Career** Science-fiction/fantasy writer, editor and lecturer; associate editor, Scott Meredith Literary Agency, New York City, 1962–64; editor, Ace Books, New York City, 1964–71; freelance writer, editor and lecturer, 1971–87. **Related activities** Editor, *Science Fiction Writers' Association Bulletin*, 1967–68; co-editor, *Void* fanzine; editor, with Ron Ellik, *Fanac* fanzine. **Offices and memberships** Founder, Science Fiction Writers' of America Forum, 1967–68. **Awards and honours** Hugo Award for editing, 1959, for criticism, 1973. **Publications** *Warlord of Kor*, New York, 1963; (as Norman Edwards, with Ted White) *Invasion from 2500*, Derby, Connecticut, 1964; *Cirque*, Indianapolis, 1977, London, 1979; *The Light at the End of the Universe* (short stories), New York, 1976. **Edited works** (with Donald A. Wollheim) *World's Best Science Fiction*, seven volumes, New York, 1965–71, last four volumes, London, 1969–71, first four volumes published as *World's Best Science Fiction: First* [to *fourth*] *Series*, New York, 1970; *Science Fiction for People Who Hate Science Fiction*, New York, 1966; *New Worlds of Fantasy*, three volumes, New York, 1967–71, first volume published as *Step Outside Your Mind*, London, 1969; *The Others*, New York, 1968; *On Our Way to the Future*, New York, 1970; *Universe*, 17 volumes, New York, 1971–87, 13 volumes, London, 1975–86; *The Best Science Fiction of the Year*, nine volumes, New York, 1972–84, volumes 4–16, London, 1975–87; *The Side of Infinity*, New York, 1972; *An Exaltation of Stars*, New York, 1973; *Into the Unknown*, 1973; *Worlds Near and Far*, Nashville, 1974; *Fellowship of the Stars: Nine Science Fiction Stories*, New York, 1974; *Creatures from Beyond*, Nashville, 1975; *The Ides of Tomorrow* (juvenile), Boston, 1976; *Planets of Wonder: A Treasury of Space Opera* (juvenile), Nashville, 1976; *To Follow a Star* (juvenile), Nashville, 1977; *The Infinite Arena* (juvenile), Nashville, 1977; *Classic Science Fiction: The First Golden Age*, New York, 1978, London, 1979; *The Year's Finest Fantasy*, two volumes, New York, 1978–79; *The Best Science Fiction Novellas of the Year*, two volumes, New York, 1979–80; *Beyond Reality*, New York, 1979; *Dream's Edge: Science Fiction Stories about the Future of the Planet Earth*, San Francisco, 1980; (with Martin H. Greenberg) *A Treasury of Modern Fantasy*, New York, 1981; *Fantasy Annual 3–5*, New York, 1981–82; *The Best from Universe*, New York, 1984; (with Isaac Asimov and Martin H. Greenberg) *100 Great Fantasy Short Stories*, New York and London, 1984; *Terry Carr's Best Science Fiction of the Year*, New York, 1985. **Cause of death** Undisclosed, at age 50.

HENRI COCHET

French Tennis Player

Born **Villeurbanne, France, 14 December 1901**

Died **near Paris, France, 1 April 1987**

Henri Cochet was the smallest in stature of Les Mousquetaires—the foursome from France who were the dominant force in world tennis in the late 1920s and early 1930s. His finest hour on the court is almost universally recognized as being his win in the 1927 Wimbledon semi-finals, from which he went on to win the men's singles.

In the semi-final Cochet faced America's William "Big Bill" Tilden, a player who surpassed him in height, power, serving, and possibly, ego. It was the latter that allegedly led Tilden—after taking the match to 6–2, 6–4, 5–1—intentionally to lose a game to the Frenchman so that he could wrap up the semi-final while serving from the end of the court nearest the Royal Box.

Cochet, whose ability to anticipate shots was one of his strongest points in an otherwise unspectacular arsenal of shots, wrested the momentum from Tilden and used his wit to take the next 17 straight points and the set. Though small, Cochet had strength and endurance, fine reflexes and footwork, which he put to use in the next two sets by making his opponent run. While the exhausted Tilden dropped the three final sets 7–5, 6–4, 6–3, Cochet repeated the two-sets-down comeback in the final, against the "Bounding Basque" Jean Borotra (another of Les Mousquetaires) to win the first of his two Wimbledon titles.

As one of the famous French foursome—along with Borotra, René Lacoste and Jacques Brugnon—Cochet helped France to win its first ever Davis Cup in another edge-of-seat thriller, when he wrested it from the United States in 1927, in Philadelphia, in the fifth and deciding match against W.M. Johnston. France held on to the Davis Cup for a further four years as "The Four Musketeers" reached their zenith in international team competition.

Meanwhile, Cochet himself won both the United States and the French championships in 1928. And although he was never able to repeat his triumph in the US, he collected a total of five French singles titles during his outstanding career.

Cool, and completely self-confident, he occasionally lacked consistency, and sometimes lost to lower-ranked players. But he still possessed a certain genius on the court, and his quick-stepping footwork usually carried him to the right position. He also had the advantage of perfect balance, which meant dipping half volleys—the scourge of many players—rarely troubled him.

The son of an official at the Lyon Tennis Club, Henri Cochet was always close to the sport; and even at the age of 50 he was still displaying much of his former flair, as he won through to the final of the Hard Courts Championship at Bournemouth.

After World War II Cochet set up and ran a sporting goods store in Paris. He had turned professional in 1933, was reinstated as an amateur in 1945, and continued to give tennis lessons well into his seventies. In later life he also served as president of the International Lawn Tennis Club of France.

Born Henri Jean Cochet. **Parents** Gustave, secretary of Lyon Tennis Club, and Madame (Gailleton) Cochet. **Marriage** Jacqueline Saint-Pierre, 1942. **Children** Two daughters, Françoise and Cathérine, and one son, Christophe. **Education** Institution des Lazaristes, Lyon, France. **Career** Tennis player; first win, Aix-les-Bains, 1920; member, French Davis Cup team with René Lacoste, Jean Borotra, Jacques Brugnon, 1922–33; turned professional, 1933; reinstated as an amateur, 1945; owner and manager, Paris sports shop, post-war; continued to coach tennis until his seventies. **Related activities** Author of many books on tennis; also appeared in a film on the history of tennis. **Offices and memberships** President, International Lawn Tennis Club of France; United States Professional Tennis Association; Football-Club de Lyon; Tennis-Club de Lyon; Racing-Club de France; Tennis-Club de Paris; also belonged to tennis clubs around the world. **Awards and honours** Officer of the Legion of Honour; Officer of the National Order of Merit; commander of Sporting Merit; Gold Medal of Physical Education and Sport; also received honours from Syria, Tunisia, and Cambodia. **Major championships** French men's singles, 1922, 1926, 1928, 1930, 1932, runner-up, 1933; French men's doubles, 1927, 1930, 1932, runner-up, 1923–26, 1928–29; French mixed doubles, 1928–29, runner-up, 1923, 1925, 1930; Wimbledon men's singles, 1927, 1929, runner-up, 1928; Wimbledon men's doubles, 1926, 1928, runner-up, 1927, 1931; United States men's singles, 1928, runner-up, 1932; United States mixed doubles, 1927. **Publications** *Le tennis, sa technique et sa psychologie*; *Cochet parle aux jeunes*; (with Pierre Albarran) *Histoire du tennis*; (with J. Feuillet) *Tennis de A à Z*; (with J. Feuillet) *Tennis: du jeu mondain au sport athlétique*. **Cause of death** Undisclosed, at age 85.

HORST DASSLER

German Businessman and Sports Tycoon

***Born* Erlangen, West Germany, 12 March 1936**

***Died* Erlangen, West Germany, 9 April 1987**

The distinctive three stripes worn by millions of sportsmen and women on their shoes have become so familiar a sight throughout the world that the name of Adidas, whose logo it is, has become practically synonymous with sport itself. So closely, indeed, has Adidas been identified with quality in sports and leisure-wear, that even the Russians have coined the word "adidovsky" to denote something stylish and reliable. The man largely responsible for bringing the Adidas company to its present position as one of the world's largest and probably best-known sports equipment firms was Horst Dassler, son of the company's founder, Adolf Dassler. For someone whose career was cut short at the early age of 51, his achievement was considerable. In the words of the president of the International Olympic Committee, "Dassler's contribution to the development of sport...was exemplary".

His first contributions to sport were on the ice-hockey and soccer pitches and on the athletics track of his grammar school in Erlangen, where Dassler was able to develop the skills and interests instilled in him by his sports-minded family. His father had founded the Adidas company in 1920 and from an early age it seemed likely that the young Dassler would enter the business as soon as practicable. Little surprise, then, when he entered the Pirmasens College of Shoe Technology and picked up a specialist knowledge that was to stand him and his father's firm in good stead for many years. A dedicated and diligent devotee of the business, he quickly adapted to responsibility, and at only 20 years of age represented the company at the Melbourne Olympics, armed with a caseful of running shoes. By then, Adidas had already established an enviable reputation for itself; Jesse Owens had worn Adidas shoes at the Munich Olympics of 1936, but clearly the company still had a long way to go before the time when no less than eight out of every ten athletes would be wearing Adidas shoes—as happened at the Los Angeles Olympics in 1984. Horst Dassler, with his acute management expertise, his determination and energy, was instrumental in helping the company reach that peak.

In 1960 he founded Adidas (France) in Alsace, a new company in which he maintained a special interest. The many tributes which the French press and various public dignitaries paid to his memory on the occasion of his death bore witness to the close relationship Dassler enjoyed with the French sporting and business community. No less a figure than the then prime minister of France, Jacques Chirac, praised his "exceptional qualities, which brought him success worldwide", and went on to say that "Athletes of all levels were aware of the important technological progress which Dassler had made in the world of sport." Able to speak fluent French, English and Spanish, as well as his native German, he was dubbed "the foreign minister of Adidas", an apposite description in view of the great amount of ambassadorial work he did for the company.

A tireless and committed worker, Dassler inherited his father's fierce competitive streak, an attribute which, to some extent, Dassler senior had been forced to develop when his brother set up the rival firm Puma after a private dispute. Open-minded and upright though the son was, this tough, business mentality led to a "hard scale" approach which was reckoned by many in the international sporting bodies to be responsible for undermining the spirit of amateurism in sports. We do not have to remind ourselves of the extent to which current major sporting events are dictated to by the demands of "big money" advertising, and there is no doubt that Adidas has played a large part in that process.

After the death of Adolf Dassler in 1980, his widow, Käthe, took over the running of the company, and Horst Dassler returned to Germany with his wife and two children. He became company chairman in 1985 and soon managed to bring off the greatest coup of his career—the securing of marketing rights to the Olympic rings symbol, which earned Adidas 10 per cent on all sales connected with the symbol. Aggressive though he may have been in his methods, Dassler commanded the respect of his employees and the admiration of many in the sporting and political worlds. The West German football team manager, Franz Beckenbauer, the Olympic champions Edwin Moses and Daley Thompson, West German President Richard von Weizsäcker, FIFA secretary-general Josef Blatter, and Olympic Committee president Antonio Samaranch were just some of the many names with whom Dassler formed contacts.

During his brief lifetime Dassler received several awards; these included the Olympic Order of the IOC, the Distinguished Service Award of the United States, and the German Marketing Prize of 1985, the last awarded "for the unique and unusual way the brand has been built up worldwide". Dassler was also the first German to be awarded honorary membership of the Académie des Sports. None can dispute that Adidas is the world's number one sports equipment manufacturer—an enviable position largely achieved through the efforts of Horst Dassler. However, his contribution to sport goes beyond the purely commercial, for in his determination and enthusiasm he stands as an embodiment of the Olympic ideal itself. In the words of FIFA general secretary, Josef Blatter, "with his captivating personality, his dynamism, his enthusiasm and his entrepreneurial spirit, Horst Dassler has left his mark on modern sport".

Born Horst Dassler. **Parents** Adolf, company founder, and Käthe Dassler. **Marriage** Monika Schäfer, 1962. **Children** One daughter, Suzanne, one son, Adi. **Education** Primary school in Herzogenaurach; grammar schools in Ettal and Erlangen; studied business administration and shoe engineering at Pirmasens College of Shoe Technology. **Career** Joined family company, representing it at Olympic Games in Melbourne, 1956; founded Adidas-France, 1959; returned to company headquarters in Germany on death of his father, 1980; assumed control of company as chairman of managing board after death of mother, 1985. **Related activities** Chairman, endorsement committee, Sporting Goods Manufacturers' Association (SGMA); chairman, committee for international sports organizations of the World Federation of the Sporting Goods Industry (WFSGI). **Awards and honours** German junior javelin champion; Olympic Order of the International Olympic Committee; honorary member, Académie des Sports; Commandeur de l'Ordre du Mérite Sportif (Ivory Coast); Distinguished Service Award of the United States; golden SIS badge from West German President Richard von Weizsäcker, for services to safety in skiing; voted "Marketing Man of the Year" in *Horizont Advertising Age* magazine, 1986. **Cause of death** Cancer, at age 51.

JEAN-BAPTISTE DOUMENG

French Communist Financier
Born **Noë, France, 2 December 1919**
Died **Noë, France, 5 April 1987**

Jean-Baptiste Doumeng was something of an oddity in world political circles: a millionaire French communist dedicated to the overthrow of the Western democracies in which he lived and prospered. A mysterious man, known for unusual political observations, Doumeng maintained a healthy appetite for interviews and savvy public relations stunts. Much of his authorized life story, however, was heavily sanitized and offers few insights to the private man.

Doumeng was born shortly after World War I in a small town 20 miles south of Toulouse. The son of a poor tenant farmer, he displayed great interest during his youth in politics and society. He claimed to have sworn allegiance to the Communist Party at the age of 16 after watching his mother die of cancer without proper medical care. During World War II he ran supplies to the French Resistance, and afterwards developed a plan to ease food shortages. The centrepiece of this plan was Interagra, a company he founded in 1940, and through which he began trading overtures to the East.

His first major breakthrough in international trade occurred in 1952, when he was invited to the first post-war conference on East–West trade in Moscow. Doumeng forged numerous high-level contacts within the Soviet government, contacts which paid immediate dividends in preferential trading agreements for Interagra. He strongly criticized the Common Agricultural Policy of the European Economic Community, noting that it was bad for the farmers of his native Gascony. His sentiments notwithstanding, Doumeng made regular purchases of surplus EEC foodstocks for sale to the Soviet Union. These sales formed the basis of a growing personal fortune which earned Doumeng the nickname "Red Millionaire".

He was a personal friend of Josef Stalin, and later claimed to be the last living Frenchman to dine with the Soviet dictator. Exhibiting some talent with name-dropping, he also claimed to have begun a close personal friendship with Mikhail Gorbachev—and predicted his rise to power—fully 20 years before Gorbachev was elevated to the Soviet leadership.

Doumeng served as mayor of his native Noë from 1956 to 1976, and was a member of several agricultural unions and commissions. He was president of the Toulouse soccer team, kept a stable of thoroughbred horses, and even sponsored Jacques Esterel, the Paris fashion designer, whom he once discovered sketching at a café. Despite these élitist pursuits, Doumeng remained a blunt and outspoken figure in French politics. With his crude Gascon accent, he advocated communist causes while defending his wealth, once saying, "Communism will make everyone as rich as me."

A leading liaison with the Soviet leadership, particularly after France's withdrawal from NATO in 1966, Doumeng played a major role in grain sales to the Soviet Union after that country's spate of disastrous harvests during the 1970s. The grain deals netted Doumeng multi-million dollar commissions which, it was noted, were used to support his lavish lifestyle.

He caused a deep political shock in 1980, when he arranged a surprise summit meeting between French president Valéry Giscard d'Estaing and the Soviet leader Leonid Brezhnev on the outskirts of Warsaw. The meeting outraged political figures throughout the Quai d'Orsay—many of whom had not been informed—because France was still engaged in an official protest against the Soviet invasion of Afghanistan. Moreover, they believed that Giscard had forsaken their trust by enlisting the help of an "outsider".

Doumeng, however, was incensed over the summary termination of Interagra's profitable butter sales to the Soviet Union. Responding to European Community president Roy Jenkins's concern that Interagra's butter was cheaper in the Soviet Union than in France, Doumeng quipped, "I've got no time to play games with little boys like Jenkins." Such was his approach to diplomacy.

Defining his unique position in the era of détente, Doumeng warned that "if things go on like this, there can be a confrontation, even a military clash. But the more tension there is, the more I earn."

He spent his final years working to a lighter schedule from his villa in Noë. His role in French politics displaced somewhat after the Socialist victory in 1981, Doumeng witnessed the dismantling of many socialist reforms and the first steps toward a Soviet–American *rapprochement.*

Born Jean-Baptiste Doumeng. **Parents** Louis, a farmer, and Léontine (Berges) Doumeng. **Marriage** Denise Trinique, 1941. **Children** Two sons, Jean-Louis and Michel. **Education** École Primaire Communale de Noë, France. **Career** Shepherd; president, managing director and majority shareholder, Interagra, 1947 onwards. **Related activities** National treasurer, Confédération Générale Agricole, 1946–48; founding president, Union des Coopératives Agricoles du Sud-Ouest, 1946 onwards; administrator, Comptoir National d'Escompte de Paris, 1946–48; La Fédération des Exploitants Agricoles de la Haute-Garonne, secretary-general, 1946, vice-president, 1972 onwards; administrator, Comptoir Agricole Français et du Syndicat National des Coopératives Agricoles Exportatrices; president, Union Nationale des Caves Coopératives et du Bureau Économique du Comité Agricole de l'Alliance Coopérative Internationale; vice-president, Socopa. **Other activities** Communist mayor, Noë, 1959–76; counsellor, Carbonne district, 1970–76; council member, Coface, 1983 onwards; also, sponsor, fashion designer Jacques Esterel. **Offices and memberships** Communist Party, 1935–87; Association of Veterans of the Resistance; president, Toulouse football team. **Cause of death** Undisclosed, at age 67.

CHIEF LEABUA JONATHAN

Lesotho Prime Minister

***Born* Leribe, Basutoland, 30 October 1914**

***Died* Pretoria, South Africa, 5 April 1987**

The career of Chief Leabua Jonathan in many ways epitomizes the history of Black South African politicians, and particularly of small independent African states within the ambit of—and in the case of Chief Jonathan's country, Lesotho, completely surrounded by—South Africa.

Though born of a noble family—son of Chief Molapo and a great-grandson of Moshoeshoe I, the founder of the Basuto nation—Chief Jonathan's beginnings were simple enough in what was then the poor, neglected territory of Basutoland under the protection of the British. After a rudimentary education at a mission school in his native village, he followed the traditional path of Black southern Africans in going to South Africa to work in the Rand mines, but in Jonathan's case as a clerk and not underground. After four years he was recalled by his family to help administer the ward of a kinsman, Chief Jonathan Mathealira. The next 15 years gave him his grounding in tribal administration.

As president of the Basuto Courts, he came to the turning point of his career with his appointment in 1951 as assessor to the British judicial commissioner of Basutoland, Patrick Duncan. Duncan appreciated the latent talents of his Basuto adviser and encouraged him to enter politics. In 1956 Jonathan was elected to the district council of his birthplace, Leribe, and through it to the National Council; in the same year he was chosen as one of the four advisers to the Regent Paramount Chieftainess Mantsebo. Throughout the late 1950s he was elected to delegations to London seeking constitutional reform and moves towards representative government, and was a member of the Constitutional Review Committee which resulted in the granting of a new constitution in 1960. By this time Chief Jonathan was ready to enter active politics with a new modern party, the Basutoland National Party, which he founded in 1959. From the granting of responsible government in 1965, when his party defeated the rival Basutoland Congress Party, the chiefly inheritance came into its own. Chief Jonathan became prime minister on 5 July 1965 and his country became fully independent as Lesotho on 4 October the following year.

The fact that Chief Jonathan took on not only the premiership but also the portfolios of external affairs, defence and, three years later, internal security, development and planning, citizenship training and statistics was a foretaste of things to come. In the face of defeat at the first general elections after independence, in 1970, Jonathan suspended the constitution, declared a state of emergency and put King Moshoeshoe II under house arrest. Thereafter, for the next 15 years he ruled by decree, with the constitution in abeyance, until his overthrow by a military coup on 20 January 1986.

His downfall was less the result of a revolt against his authoritarian style of government (democracy was a fragile novelty in any case in Lesotho), but rather the inevitable outcome of his courageous and, in the event, foolhardy attempts to assert his independence of South Africa by his support of the exiled African National Congress. For most of his life Chief Jonathan had argued that his country's geographical situation dictated a policy of peaceful coexistence with its dominant neighbour on which it was almost entirely dependent. But accusations of being a South African puppet and of his country being little more than a tribal homeland led to his giving sanctuary to ANC guerrillas and to the opening of diplomatic relations with the Soviet Union and other communist countries in defiance of South Africa's anti-communist stance. By the end of 1985 South Africa decided to put a stop to the ANC attacks from Lesotho and imposed an economic blockade. Such tactics had always been a threat, and the coup which brought them to an end was the inevitable outcome.

Chief Jonathan bowed to the forces of *realpolitik* and thereafter remained under house arrest completely out of politics. His long tenure of power—21 years—was a remarkable achievement for a country whose very independence might seem anomalous. And his attempts to withstand South African bullying earned it considerable, and much needed, financial and development aid.

Born Leabua Jonathan. **Father** Jonathan Molapo, a chief of the Basuto nation. **Marriage** Manthli. **Children** Four daughters. **Education** Paris Evangelical Mission School, Leribe, 1924–30. **Career** Mining clerk, the Rand, South Africa, 1933–37; assistant administrator for ward of his uncle, Chief Jonathan Mathealira of Tsikoane, Basutoland (later Lesotho), 1937–50; appointed court president, 1938; president of Basuto Courts and assessor to judicial commissioner, 1950; entered politics, 1952; elected to Leribe district council, 1954, and as member for Leribe, Basutoland National Council, 1956; founded Basutoland National Party, 1959; member, Legislative Council, 1960–64; Basutoland National Party won general election, and though Jonathan was defeated in his constituency, a subsequent by-election allowed him to take his seat and he was sworn in as prime minister, 1965; also held posts as minister of: external affairs, 1965–71, defence, from 1965, civil service, 1965–68 and 1969–70, internal security, from 1968, development and planning, from 1968–74, citizenship, training and statistics, 1968–70; chief of electoral affairs, from 1971; when Basutoland National Party appeared to be losing general election of 1970, Jonathan suspended constitution, placed King Moshoeshoe II under house arrest, declared state of emergency and ruled by decree, 1970–86; deposed in military coup led by Chief Metsing Lekhanya, 1986. **Related activities** Member of delegation to London opposing appointment of South African A.G.T. Chaplin as resident commissioner of Basutoland, 1956; member of Chieftainship and Constitutional Review Committee to draft Basutoland constitution, 1956; member, Panel of 18, 1956–59; member, delegation to London demanding progress to self-government, 1958; delegate to Constitutional Conference, London, 1964. **Cause of death** Undisclosed, at age 73.

CLAUDE JUTRA

Canadian Film Director

***Born* Montreal, Canada, 11 March 1930**

***Died* Quebec, Canada, 19 April 1987**

Alzheimer's Disease, the crippling, degenerative mental illness, knows no boundaries of age, sex or nationality. Characterized most graphically by profound memory loss that amounts to near total erosion of personality, it is, as yet, incurable. Claude Jutra, the father of Canadian cinema, director, actor and qualified doctor was a victim of this disease, finally declared dead when his body was fished out of the St Lawrence River five months after his initial disappearance. He was 56.

A lifelong devotee of the cinema, Jutra was involved in film directing from the tender age of 17 when he worked on *Le Dément du Lac Jean Jeune* in collaboration with Michel Brault. The second product of their partnership, *Mouvement perpétuel*, went on to win a Canadian Film

Award for Best Amateur Film. His career was interrupted while he completed his medical studies at the University of Montreal, after which he went on to score a number of Canadian firsts: his *L'École de la peur* was the first original teleplay produced in the country, and his experimental feature *A tout prendre* marked the beginning of domestic feature film production.

Working in both French and English, Jutra articulates in his films a naïve, child-like innocence that speaks strongly of his own uncomplicated idealism. At the age of 20, smitten by the work of Charlie Chaplin, he wrote a fan letter to his idol for advice and encouragement. When at length the great man replied, Jutra displayed the three-line note with unbounded enthusiasm. A similar, rather jejune quality is evinced by his boyish love of electronic gadgetry which filled his Montreal apartment.

His best film, *Mon Oncle Antoine* (1971), follows the development of a young boy growing up in a Canadian mining village. The beauty of its photography and its sympathetic, fresh perspective led to eight Canadian Film Awards as well as Best Film and Best Screenplay at the Chicago Film Festival. Such foreign recognition of Jutra's work put Canadian film-making firmly on the international map. His *Kamouraska* not only constitutes Canada's first film epic but won the French Critics' Award at the 1972 Cannes Film Festival.

With *Dreamspeaker*, Jutra made his second foray into television, a medium he regarded as powerful, but ultimately short-lived. He said in an interview with *Cinéma Canada* that although "television has a wide audience and reaches a great number of people on all levels of society, it is forgotten. The impact is brief as it is intense." He strictly rejected any notion that television was an artistic compromise, however; he maintained that his approach was just as rigorous whether the final destination was theatre presentation or the small screen.

His untimely death deprived Canada of an enthusiast and a pioneer, a man in love with film and everything connected with it. It is testimony to his popularity and stature that the Directors' Guild of Canada and Les Réalisateurs du Québec have since combined to set up a bursary in his name to be awarded annually to one of the country's most promising young film directors.

Born Claude Jutra. **Education** University of Montreal, MD, 1952. **Career** Film director, 1947 onwards; directing début, as co-director with Michel Brault, 1947; author, first original Canadian-produced teleplay, *L'École de la peur*, 1953; intermittently with National Film Board, 1954–66; collaborator, with Norman McLaren (q.v.) on *A Chairy Tale*, 1957; with Jean Rouch in Niger Republic, early 1960s; founder, Films Cassiopée, 1961. **Awards and honours** (with Norman McLaren) First prize for experimental film, *A Chairy Tale*, Venice Film Festival, 1958; Best Film, Canadian Film Awards, for *A tout prendre*, 1964. **Films** (co-director) *Le Dément du Lac Jean Jeune*, 1947; (co-director, plus screenplay) *Mouvement perpétuel*, 1949; *Pierrot des bois* (screenplay), 1956; (co-director) *A Chairy Tale* (*Il était une chaise*) 1957; *Les Mains nettes*, 1958; *Anna la bonne*, 1959; *Felix Leclerc, troubadour*, 1959; *Fred Barry, comedien* (plus screenplay), 1959; *Le Niger—jeune république*, 1961; (co director) *La Lutte*, 1961; (co-director) *Québec—USA* (*L'Invasion pacifique/Visit to a Foreign Country*), 1962; (co-director) *Les Enfants du silence*, 1963; (co-director) *Petit discours de la méthode*, 1963; *A tout prendre* (*Take It All*), 1963; *Comment savoir* (*Knowing to Learn*), 1966; *Rouli-Roulant* (*The Devil's Toy*), 1966; *Wow*, 1969; *Au coeur de la ville*, 1969; *Marie-Christine*, 1970; *Mon Oncle Antoine*, 1971; *Kamouraska*, 1972; *Pour le meilleur et pour le pire*, 1975; *Pennies for My Chocolate* (for television), 1976; *Dream Speaker* (for television), 1976; *Surfacing*, 1978; (acting role) *Two Solitudes*, 1978; *By Design*, 1980. **Cause of death** Drowning, at age 56. **Further reading** Gilles Marsolais, *Le Cinéma canadien*, Paris, 1968; Jean Chabot, *Cinéastes du Québec 4: Claude Jutra*, Montreal, 1970; Eleanor Beattie, *A Handbook of Canadian Film*, Toronto, 1973.

CECIL KING

British Journalist and Newspaper Proprietor

***Born* London, England, 20 February 1901**

***Died* Dublin, Ireland, 17 April 1987**

Cecil Harmsworth King was one of the last of the old-style press barons of London's Fleet Street, the traditional home of the British press. He was born into a distinguished family, his father being a civil servant in India and, later, a professor of oriental languages. More importantly for his chosen career, he was a nephew of Lord Northcliffe, who founded popular journalism in Britain in the nineteenth century.

King was educated at Winchester public school and at Oxford University, where he gained an honours degree in history. He served his apprenticeship on the Scottish *Glasgow Record* and the national *Daily Mail* before joining the *Daily Mirror* in 1926. Within three years he became a director, and over the next 42 years he built the paper's circulation to a massive peak of five million, transforming it from a genteel right-wing daily into a radical, usually left-wing, brash, outspoken and breezy tabloid.

In 1951 he became chairman of the Mirror Group and from then on his empire seemed to grow almost exponentially as he bought out other newspaper and magazine houses such as Amalgamated Press and Odhams Press. The resulting conglomorate was named the International Publishing Corporation (IPC) and comprised 210 periodicals and 23 newspapers. These ranged from serious journals, such as *New Scientist*, to mass circulation women's weeklies like *Woman* and *Woman's Own*.

Despite his administrative responsibilities, King remained a newspaper man at heart throughout his career and made every effort to be as well informed as possible. He cultivated acquaintanceship with political leaders at home and abroad, and sought the friendship of those who had influence and who knew where influence lay. The political scene never ceased to fascinate him. He seldom failed to make his, mostly very well informed, opinions known—through his newspapers, his personal contacts and in his diaries, several of which were later published.

As early as 1940 the *Mirror*'s outspoken criticism of the British war effort so upset the government that it suspected a Nazi sympathizer might be pulling the strings. King's reply to Winston Churchill was that, "Differences of method are bound to arise, but if you consider we have gone beyond what should be permissible in wartime, we should, of course, meet your wishes in so far as we conscientiously can."

Although a supporter of the Labour movement in his paper, King later had several major differences with party policies, notable among which was Labour's reluctance to consider joining the European (Economic) Community. He first tangled with its (then) leader, the brilliant Hugh Gaitskell, in the late 1950s over the issues of defence and his opposition to Britain's application for EEC membership. This was an argument he continued to pursue with his successor, Harold Wilson, who later became prime minister. Another key issue in which King felt Wilson was failing in the 1960s was an effective prices and incomes policy: income growth was consistently way ahead of growth in productivity.

This interest in the country's financial management and difficulties was increased when King became a director of the Bank of England in 1965 and began to widen his perspective. Thus, although strongly pro-Labour in the 1964 election campaign, the *Mirror* was far more restrained when Wilson sought (and won) a further mandate from the electorate in 1966. Wilson subsequently wrote thanking King for the paper's support. King's reply was somewhat odd: "The more restrained support we gave you on this occasion was partly due to misgivings over the implementation of the prices and incomes policy, partly due to misgivings over your European attitude, and partly due to the wish *to avoid a landslide* which would leave you with an unwieldy majority and no effective opposition." (Emphasis added)

Among the many organs that came under King's control from Odhams was the *Daily Herald*, the official Labour party newspaper in which the Trades Union Council held an interest. King guaranteed to continue its publication for seven years even though there seemed little point in terms of editorial policy. Halfway through this period, when it had proved impossible to halt its falling circulation, he persuaded the TUC to part with its interest and changed the name and format. The result was the *Sun* which, with its rather prurient approach and page three pin-up girls, became a great success. It was ultimately sold to a rival group after King had left IPC in 1968.

The other side of King was an emotionally isolated man who had suffered painfully in childhood. In his autobiography, *Strictly Personal*, he revealed many family skeletons, particularly the lack of love he received from his mother. In addition, he revealed that his uncle, Lord Northcliffe, suffered severe mental illness in later life; both his brothers had been killed in World War I, one in action and the other on a torpedoed mail boat while returning to school; and his childhood sweetheart died from brain cancer at the tragically early age of 15. King movingly revealed that he only lost his feeling of self-hatred and his death wish in his sixties. However, although unable to deal comfortably with emotional situations, he was always without malice, fair and considerate to his employees.

It is interesting that it was the period leading up to the publication of *Strictly Personal*, when King was taking on an increasing number of activities outside IPC, that his colleagues began to feel he was overstepping the mark. In addition to his work at the Bank of England, he began to give many lectures and make frequent appearances on television. Concern was expressed about this diffusion of his energies. In fact, King was increasingly concerned about the failure, as he saw it, of the Wilson government. According to his diaries, he frequently discussed his concern with Wilson himself, his colleagues, and with prominent leaders of the Opposition, including the subsequent Tory prime minister, Edward Heath. For some time King had been mooting with friends and political figures the possibility of a national government. This he is said to have refined into a proposal for a coalition in which politicians would be supported by a group of high-level businessmen.

His long-time editor Hugh Cudlipp revealed in his book, *Walking on the Water*, published in 1976, that King had, in fact, gone much further. According to Cudlipp, King initiated a discussion with the late Lord Mountbatten about his fears for the future of Britain. This took place on 8 May 1968. Also present was Sir Solly (later Lord) Zuckerman. King laid out a scenario in which he foresaw the disintegration of the government, bloodshed on the streets and military involvement. He felt the British public would be looking towards a figure such as Mountbatten to take on the titular headship of a new administration. Would Mountbatten agree to such a role? Zuckerman apparently put an end to the discussion by stating that the proposal was "rank treachery" and King left. Later King claimed that the meeting had been initiated by Mountbatten and denied that a military coup had ever been envisaged.

There is no mention of this in *The Cecil King Diary 1965–70*, which had been published in 1972, four years prior to Cudlipp's book and long before the affair became national news in 1981. There are, however, two somewhat cryptic entries concerning Mountbatten in the volume. The first is an entry for 12 August 1967 where King writes that Cudlipp had met Mountbatten at a dinner a few weeks previously and goes on, "Hugh asked him if it had been suggested to him that our present style of government might be in for a change. He said it had. Hugh then asked if it had been suggested that he might have some part to play in such a new regime. Mountbatten said it had been suggested, but that he was far too old." The second entry regarding Mountbatten is dated 22 May 1969, nearly two years later. King records lunching with an eminent member of the Tory party with whom he discussed the Wilson government. King questioned, "Is there no venerated national figure outside politics who could bring our affairs to a head?" He continues, "We talked about Mountbatten and he left me, suggesting that Mountbatten or someone... should write a brief letter to *The Times* that would at least compel a change in the Labour Party leadership."

Whatever the full truth of this matter, on 10 May 1968 King published a signed editorial in the *Mirror* headed "Enough is enough", which called for Wilson to go. In order to do this he had to resign his cherished directorship at the Bank of England. Two days later the IPC board asked him to resign. King refused to do so and was sent a letter of dismissal.

According to his diary, this was a totally unexpected shock but he recovered quickly and continued with television appearances and writing for other newspapers, mostly for serious ones such as *The Times* and *Financial Times*.

King has been described as both an "autocratic press lord" and a "political eccentric". Both are true but these are only facets of his complex personality. He was also an immensely able, courageous and intelligent man whose primary concerns were the well-being of Britain and the continued improvement of its press.

Born Cecil Harmsworth King. **Parents** Sir Lucas White, civil servant and professor of oriental languages, and Geraldine Adelaide Hamilton (Harmsworth) King. **Marriage** Agnes Margaret Cooke, 1923 (divorced, 1962; died, 1985); Dame Ruth Railton, musician, 1962. **Children** Michael, Francis, Colin and Priscilla from first marriage; also adopted nephew's three children after fatal plane crash, 1950. **Education** Winchester College, 1919; Christ Church, Oxford, BA, 1922, MA, 1928. **Career** *Glasgow Record*, 1922; *London Daily Mail*, 1923–26; assistant advertising manager, Daily Mirror Newspapers Limited, 1926, director, 1929; director, *Sunday Pictorial*, 1935, deputy chairman, 1942, chairman, 1951–63; chairman, *Nigeria Daily Times*, *Sierra Leone Daily Mail* and West Africa Newspapers Limited, 1948–68; founder, *Ghana Graphic*, 1950; chairman, International Publishing Corporation, 1963–68; writer, 1968–87. **Offices and memberships** Board member, London Eye Hospital, 1931–38; chairman, Nigerian Printing and Publishing Company Limited, 1948–68; chairman, British Film Institute, 1948–52; director of realtors, 1953–59; director, Reuters, 1953–59; chairman, Fleetway Publications, 1959–61; director, finance committee, Church of England Children's Society; chairman, Newspaper Proprietors' Association, 1961–68; director, Bank of England, 1965–68; chairman, Wallpaper Manufacturers, 1965–67; part-time member, National Coal Board, 1966–69; member, Countryside Commission (formerly National Parks Commission) 1966–69; chairman, Butterworth and Company Limited, 1968; member, Society for Psychical Research. **Awards and honours** Gold badge for services to city of Warsaw, 1960; gold medal for services to the British newspaper trade; honorary DLitt, Boston University, 1974. **Publications** *The Future of the Press*, 1967; *Strictly Personal: Some Memoirs of Cecil H. King*, 1969; *With Malice Towards None: A War Diary*, 1970; *Without Fear or Favour* (essays), 1971; *The Cecil King Diary, 1965–1970*, 1972; *On Ireland*, 1973; *The Cecil King Diary, 1970–1974*, 1975; *Cecil King's Commonplace Book*, 1981. **Cause of death** Undisclosed, at age 86.

JOHN LEHMANN

British Editor, Poet and Biographer
***Born* Bourne End, Buckinghamshire, 2 June 1907**
***Died* London, England, 7 April 1987**

John Lehmann was born to be a man of letters. His father was R.C. Lehmann, best remembered for his editorship of *Punch*, a weekly magazine combining wit, satire and review in a gentle tradition definable as both literary and humorous rather than abrasive or brash.

He was the youngest child of the family and, after attending Eton, Britain's foremost independent school, went to Cambridge University. Like his older sister, Rosamond, he chose writing as his career, and published his first volume of verse in 1931, at the age of 24. Significantly, the publishers were Leonard and Virginia Woolf, with whom Lehmann later worked at the Hogarth Press.

After working abroad for a few years as a journalist, he commenced what emerged as the most important part of his career, as a publisher and editor. From 1935 onwards he was involved in the publication of work by new writers of his own selection. This was both with the Hogarth Press and later with his own press. He brought out *New Writing*, *Penguin New Writing*, *Daylight*, *New Writing and Daylight*, and later founded the *London Magazine*.

Lehmann's mission was to seek out new writers of excellence, both at home and abroad. He was publishing such eminent names as W.H. Auden, C. Day Lewis, Christopher Isherwood, Jean-Paul Sartre, Saul Bellow and Gore Vidal virtually before anyone else had recognized their abilities or potential. Even more importantly, he gave immense encouragement to writers in whom he believed but were suffering from a block. This was appreciated particularly in the United States. Julian Mitchell in the *New York Times Book Review* commented that, "A good editor must be eagle-eyed, poised to swoop up the smallest mouse of talent from the vast and turbulent plain of literature..." In Lehmann's case: "One whiff of talent and his head shoots forward, his eyes narrow to a penetrating blue, he listens, tense and still—then plummets for the prey.... There is scarcely a writer (of his generation)...who hasn't at one time or other been grateful for his passionate scrutiny."

Lawrence Graver, writing in the *New Republic*, explains Lehmann's effectiveness by invoking "a set of specific historical circumstances and a wide range of personal gifts", making special mention of his comfortable background and family. Or, as Mitchell put it, "Lehmann was born with a silver pencil between his fingers." And indeed his childhood was idyllic, Edwardian and advantaged.

As he grew towards adulthood, Europe was moving towards disaster. Lehmann, while valuing tradition and background, was well aware of the disturbances looming and of being brought up for a world that was likely to disappear. Yet he was able to reconcile these differences between his original expectations and the reality to be faced. As Graver said, "For many years [he] could defend *belles lettres* with the confidence of an eighteenth-century aristocrat, while at the same time printing incendiary works by a broad spectrum of modernist writers....[However], sensitivity and serviceable connections would have counted for little if [he] did not have a fundamental fitness for his job."

Lehmann was himself a prolific writer. He continued with poetry, his first love, throughout his life and also produced several novels. Sadly, however, he was personally unable to produce the quality of work he could recognize so readily in others and which he was so keen to foster. It has been said that his recognition of his own failure as an artist sometimes made him touchy and petulant in personal relationships, although he was unfailingly courteous and fair in professional life, having a knack of rejecting work in a way which let writers down gently and leaving them with their dignity intact.

His several volumes of autobiography and critical studies of other writers are of immense value. They chronicle people and events, especially in the legendary Bloomsbury Circle of writers and artists of the pre-war years.

Lehmann had a long working relationship with Virginia and Leonard Woolf which was only broken by disagreement over the publishing policy of what had become the Hogarth Press. He and Leonard Woolf had very different literary tastes. Lehmann, however, remained devoted to Virginia and his critical study, *Virginia Woolf and Her World*, was acclaimed as "brilliant" by the *New York Review of Books*. James Atlas, writing in the *New York Times Book Review*, said that Lehmann's "commentaries on the novels are dispassionate and lucid, based on a first-hand experience of how [Woolf] wrote them".

In his own poetry Lehmann constantly returned to that idyllic childhood in the countryside by the upper reaches of the Thames but, as Richard Eberhart (one of the first poets to be published by Lehmann) wrote sadly, he failed to invent "a new language or way of saying things, some inescapable idiom of his own, nor reached for mystery and strangeness in form or thought".

His overall contribution to literature has, in spite of that, been widely recognized. He has been honoured by Britain, Greece and France and, in the 1970s, was visiting professor at a number of universities in the United States.

Lehmann once commented that, had he had more time, he would have chosen to write more poetry but, when asked how he would like to be remembered, responded with characteristic modesty, "I cannot answer for posterity, but I hope my work as a literary editor will not be forgotten." Those who recall the grim years of material and intellectual impoverishment in the UK during World War II will never forget the enthusiasm generated by the appearance of those valued volumes of *Penguin New Writing*. They brought a breath of revitalizing cosmopolitan air into a society suffocated by the privations of austerity.

Born John Frederick Lehmann. **Parents** Rudolph Chambers, a writer, editor of *Punch* and member of parliament, and Alice Marie (Davis) Lehmann. **Education** King's Scholar, Eton College, Berkshire; Trinity College, Cambridge, BA. **Career** Poet, novelist, editor, 1928–87; general manager, Hogarth Press, London, 1931–32, 1938–46, partner, 1940–46; journalist in Vienna, 1932–36, in Soviet Transcaucasia, 1935–36; founder, managing director, John Lehmann Ltd, publishers, London, 1946–52; founding editor, *New Writing*, *Daylight*, *New Writing and Daylight*, *Penguin New Writing*, London, 1936–50, *Orpheus*, 1948–49, also the *London Magazine*, 1954–61. **Related activities** Advisory editor, the *Geographical Magazine*, London, 1940–45; editor, *New Soundings*, BBC Third Programme, 1952; chairman, British Council Editorial Advisory Panel, 1952–58; president, Alliance Française in Great Britain, 1955–64; member, Anglo-Greek Mixed Commission, 1962–68; president, Royal Literary Fund, 1966–67; visiting professor: University of Texas, Austin, 1970–71, State University of California, San Diego, 1970–71, University of California, Berkeley, 1974, Emory University, Atlanta, 1977. **Awards and honours** Officer, 1954, and Commander, Order of King George of the Hellenes, 1961; Officer, Legion of Honour, France, 1958; Grand Officer, Étoile Noir, 1960; Prix du Rayonnement Français, 1961; Foyle Prize, 1964; fellow, Royal Society of Literature; Commander, Order of the British Empire, 1964; Officer, Order of Arts and Letters, France, 1965; Queen's Silver Jubilee Medal, 1977; honorary DLitt, Birmingham, 1980. **Offices and memberships** Royal Society of Literature; PEN (association of Poets, Playwrights, Editors, Essayists and Novelists). **Verse** (published in London unless stated) *The Bud, Burial, Dawn, Grey Days, The Lover, The Mountain, Ruin, Gargoyles, Turn Not, Hesperides*, privately printed,

1928; *A Garden Revisited and Other Poems*, 1931; *The Noise of History*, 1934; *Forty Poems*, 1942; *The Sphere of Glass and Other Poems*, 1944; *The Age of the Dragon: Poems, 1930–1951*, 1951, New York, 1953; *The Secret Messages*, Stamford, Connecticut, 1958; *Christ the Hunter*, 1965; *Collected Poems, 1930–1963*, 1965; *Photograph*, 1971; *The Reader at Night and Other Poems*, Toronto, 1974. **Nonfiction** *Prometheus and the Bolsheviks*, London, 1937, New York, 1938; *Down River: A Danubian Study*, London, 1939; *New Writing in England*, New York, 1939; *New Writing in Europe*, London, reprinted, 1977; *The Open Night* (essays), London and New York, 1952; *Edith Sitwell*, London, 1952, revised edition, 1970; *A Nest of Tigers: The Sitwells in Their Times*, Boston, 1968, published as *A Nest of Tigers: Edith, Osbert and Sacheverell Sitwell in Their Times*, London, 1968; *Holborn: An Historical Portrait of a London Borough*, London, 1970; *Lewis Carroll and the Spirit of Nonsense*, Nottingham, 1974; *Virginia Woolf and Her World*, London, 1975, New York, 1965; *Edward Lear and His World*, New York, 1977; *Thrown to the Woolfs: Leonard and Virginia Woolf and the Hogarth Press*, London, 1978, New York, 1979; *Rupert Brooke: His Life and His Legend*, London, 1980, published as *The Strange Destiny of Rupert Brooke*, New York, 1981; *English Poets of the First World War*, London, 1982; *Three Literary Friendships: Byron and Shelley, Rimbaud and Verlaine, Robert Frost and Edward Thomas*, London, 1983, New York, 1984; *Christopher Isherwood: A Personal Memoir*, London, 1987, New York, 1988. **Novels** *Evil Was Abroad*, London, 1938; *In a Purely Pagan Sense*, London, 1976. **Autobiography** *The Whispering Gallery: Autobiography I*, London and New York, 1955; *I Am My Brother: Autobiography II*, London and New York, 1960; *The Ample Proposition: Autobiography III*, London, 1966; *In My Own Time: Memoirs of a Literary Life*, Boston, 1969. **"New Writing" anthologies** (as editor) *New Writing: Spring, 1936*, London, 1936; *New Writing: Autumn, 1936*, London, 1936; *New Writing: Spring, 1937*, New York, 1937; *New Writing: Fall, 1937*, New York, 1937; *New Writing: Spring, 1938*, 1938; (with Christopher Insherwood and Stephen Spender) *New Writing: Fall, 1938*, New York, 1938; (with Isherwood and Spender) *New Writing: Spring, 1939*, London, 1939; *New Writing: Christmas, 1938*, London, 1939; *The Penguin New Writing*, London, 1940, new edition, 1947, reprinted, 1977; *Folios of New Writing*, London, 1940–41; *New Writing and Daylight: Summer, 1942*, London, 1942; *New Writing and Daylight: Winter, 1942–43*, London, 1943; *New Writing and Daylight: Summer, 1943*, London, 1943, New York, 1944; *New Writing and Daylight: Winter, 1943–44*, London, 1944; *New Writing and Daylight: Autumn, 1944*, London and New York, 1945; *New Writing and Daylight, 1945*, London, 1945, New York, 1947; *Poems from New Writing, 1936–46*, London, 1946; *French Stories from New Writing*, London, 1947, published as *Modern French Stories*, 1948; *Best Stories from New Writing*, New York, 1951, published as *English Stories from New Writing*, London, 1951; *Pleasures of New Writing: An Anthology of Poems, Stories and Other Prose Pieces*, London, 1952, reprinted, 1977. **Other edited works** (with Denys Kilham Roberts and Gerald Gould) *The Year's Poetry: A Representative Selection*, London, 1934–36; (with T.A. Jackson and C. Day Lewis) Ralph Fox, *A Writer in Arms*, London, 1937; (with Stephen Spender) *Poems for Spain*, London, 1939; *Demetrios Capetanakis: A Greek Poet in England*, London, 1947, published as *Shores of Darkness: Poems and Essays*, 1949; *Shelley in Italy: An Anthology*, London, 1947; *Orpheus: A Symposium of the Arts*, Volume I, London, 1948, Volume II, London, 1949, reprinted, 1977; (with C. Day Lewis and contributor) *The Chatto Book of Modern Poetry, 1915–1955*, London, 1956, revised edition, 1959, reprinted 1978; *The Craft of Letters in England: A Symposium*, London, 1956, New York, 1957, reprinted, 1974; *Coming to London*, London, 1957, reprinted, 1971; (also author of introduction) *Italian Stories of Today*, London, 1959; Edith Sitwell, *Selected Poems*, London, 1965; (with Derek Parker) Edith Sitwell, *Selected Letters, 1919–1964*, London, 1970; (with Richard Basset) *Vienna: A Traveller's Companion*, 1988. **Contributor** *Poems of Today*, London, 1938; ed. Elizabeth Jennings, *An Anthology of Modern Verse, 1940–1960*, London, 1961; *Penguin Book of Contemporary Verse*, London, 1962;

eds Patricia Beer and others, *New Poems, 1963: A PEN Anthology*, London, 1963; ed. Robin Skelton, *Poetry of the Thirties*, London, 1964; ed. Brian Gardner, *Terrible Rain: The War Poets, 1939–1945*, London, 1966. **Cause of death** Undisclosed, at age 79.

PRIMO LEVI

Italian Novelist, Essayist and Poet
***Born* Turin, Italy, 31 July 1919**
***Died* Turin, Italy, 11 April 1987**

"I keep hearing the voice of a man struggling to retrieve the sense of what it means in the twentieth century to be, or become, a *Mensch*." This is how the literary critic Irving Howe described the work of Primo Levi, Europe's foremost literary interpreter of the Holocaust. Howe's statement is poignant because it draws on that peculiarly Yiddish idea of "what it is to be a *Mensch*"—with its paradoxical connotations of both saintliness and human failure—to characterize Levi as a Jew and a survivor of Auschwitz. What Howe wanted to say is: "This is what Levi is all about: how to preserve human dignity in the face of the hellish horrors man can inflict upon man."

By all accounts, Levi's work was remarkable in its refusal of hardline moral judgments or easy generalizations about race, religion and politics. His autobiographical accounts of Auschwitz and its aftermath have been universally praised for the human understanding that permeates them, avoiding both a tone of bitterness and the pathos of a camp-survivor's guilt. However, what such affirmations of Levi's humanism leave out of account is his supreme mastery of the art of writing-as-understatement, and the fact that he wrote in an ostensibly neutral voice, not out of some moral relativism, but in order to render daily life—and death—at Auschwitz all the more effectively to bring out the enormity of genocide in full. He wrote like the scientist that he was: to get at the real nature of things, to describe, to record, to analyse unsentimentally but relentlessly.

For Levi, writing itself was a matter of survival, and the preservation of human dignity more than just an abstract universal value: it was, in his view, the specific historical responsibility of the Jew who had witnessed, suffered—and lived.

Primo Levi's ancestors had been Spanish Jews who fled to Italy in the sixteenth century and settled there. Levi was born in 1919 in Turin, where his parents raised him as a Jew, though not in the religious tradition of Judaism. Levi soon distinguished himself as a quick learner. He attended the famous Liceo Massimo d'Azeglio, and from there, in 1939, he went straight on to university to read chemistry. Mussolini's race laws were not yet on the statute books so, although ostracized, Levi was not officially barred from studying and getting his qualification. By the time he graduated, however, in 1941, the situation had changed and it had become very difficult for Italian Jews to find work. Levi scratched a living by getting short-term jobs as an industrial chemist with employers who were willing to circumvent the law, but it was an insecure and increasingly marginal existence. After two years of travelling around begging for work and having to take whatever was on offer, Levi joined the Resistance.

In 1943 Allied forces had landed in Sicily, but the north of Italy was still occupied by the Germans. In the Piedmont and other regions pockets of resistance existed and small bands of partisans fought against the German's greater numbers and superior firing power. Levi headed one such unit, consisting of eleven poorly armed men. In December 1943 they were betrayed and captured by the German forces. Levi, together with 650 other Jews on that train, was deported to Auschwitz. Of this contingent, only 24 survived. Thanks to his previous training in physical survival techniques, his knowledge of industrial chemistry, which was valuable to the Germans, and the fact that he was ill when the Germans eventually had to flee Auschwitz (taking all the healthy prisoners with them), Levi escaped the fate of the vast majority of his fellow prisoners. But unlike even his fellow survivors, he lived in order to tell in measured, even tones the story of the Jewish resistance, of the camps, of systematic torture and humiliation, of murder, and of survival.

After his long and circuitous journey back from Auschwitz to Italy, Levi returned to his native Turin and to chemistry. He earned his living as an industrial chemist and took up writing; these were to be his twin careers for the next 30 years. In 1947 he published his first book, *Se questo e un uomo* (If This Is a Man), and married Lucia Morpurgo, with whom he raised two children, Lisa and Renzo. As well as being a devoted husband and father, Levi the chemist became a world expert on ceramic coatings for wire, while Levi the writer won numerous literary prizes and international critical acclaim. Still, the experience of Auschwitz never left him for a moment.

Much has been written about the horrors of the Nazi camps. Nevertheless, as Stuart Hughes has pointed out, Levi's "tone of moderation, of equanimity, punctuated by an occasional note of quiet humour" made *If This Is a Man* stand head and shoulders above the more lurid fiction and historiography of the camps. Alfred Werner entitled his review of the book "Amid suffering: the divine spark", with reference to Levi's refusal to draw the conclusion that man is "fundamentally brutal, egotistic and stupid in his conduct" when removed from the constraints of civilization. Another critic described Levi's first book as "the education of a rationalist in a place governed by absolute irrationality", a place where every sophisticated notion of humanity and culture is stripped down to its most basic elements. Levi understood the purpose of the camps not simply as machines for physical extermination, but also as instruments for the eradication of human values: "to annihilate us first as men in order to kill us more slowly afterwards".

Although *If This Is a Man* was extremely well received, its sequel, *La Tregua* (*The Reawakening*), followed after a long gap of 18 years, in 1965. In this book Levi recounted the story of his trek back from Auschwitz to Turin, which was a series of endless, senseless wanderings through Eastern Europe and the Soviet Union. Although the author/narrator never emerges clearly as a character, his fellow travellers stand out all the more vividly in the mind's eye with their hunger, their disillusionment, their vagabonding, boredom and inertia, but also with their compassion and their humour. Again, like *If This Is a Man*, *The Reawakening* is not a depressing book, despite dealing with extreme deprivation, fear and hopelessness. At the end there is a homecoming and a new beginning; *The Reawakening* traces first and foremost what one critic has aptly called "the struggle of the Holocaust's survivors to survive their own survival".

But Levi's two most famous books were still to come. In 1975 he published *Il sistema periodico* (*The Periodic Table*), which gained him international attention. Here chemistry and fiction were united in a collection of stories, each based on one of the elements in the periodic table—the chemist's bible. In them Levi attributed emotional values to elements such as iron and copper, which he said were "easy and direct, incapable of concealment", and turned them into the stuff of literature. One of the most chilling of these stories is "Vanadium", in which Levi, as narrator, recounts how a former camp official named Mueller contacts him after the war in a business capacity as representative of a paint manufacturer. The ex-Nazi, upon realizing with whom he is corresponding, suggests a reunion, as if they were old schoolfriends, claiming that he did not know Jews were being killed in the camps. He also claims to have read Levi's first book (on Auschwitz) and sees in it "an overcoming of Judaism, a fulfilment of the Christian precept to love one's enemies..."

Levi, in his usual style of objective reporting without frills, makes this a *vignette* of a particular brand of German post-war mentality in which crimes as well as suffering can go unrecognized and become totally dis-remembered. In the story Mueller dies unexpectedly at 60 years of age, eight days after the insolent request for a meeting with his ex-prisoner. Whether his sudden demise is fact or fiction, the suggestion is that Mueller met with *some* sort of justice, if only poetic.

The Periodic Table was followed in 1982 by *Se non ora, quando?* (*If Not Now, When?*), which was Levi's most outspoken and political book. With the intention of contributing to the debate surrounding the alleged Jewish "passivity" (on religious grounds) during the war, Levi—a lifelong agnostic—produced a vibrant account of the Jewish resistance in northern Italy in which he had taken part. The book was, on the one hand, a tribute to the many Jews who did fight back, and historical testimony on the other. "As a former partisan and deportee, I know very well that there are some political and psychological conditions in which resistance is possible, and others in which it is not," Levi wrote. The novel, for the first time in his *oeuvre*, represented a celebration of the positive emergence of a collective Jewish consciousness.

As a scientist, particularly one engaged in chemistry, Levi was wont to go to the heart of the matter and to "pry open the secrets of the universe"; so also, as a writer, did he use his experience and his skill with words to get to the hearts of men. He usually wrote his chapters "not in logical succession but in order of urgency" he said, only later to fuse them according to a carefully conceived literary plan. It was this, the combination of emotional urgency with considered design, that made his work so masterful a monument to suffering and survival alike.

Such harmony between inner and outer worlds did not exist for Levi personally. In the end, the man who survived war, imprisonment and the trauma of the Holocaust died after falling down the stairwell of the house where he had been born. He had lived there for most of his life, but it was as if the black hole at the heart of his existence had finally taken its toll.

Born Primo Levi. **Pseudonym** Damiana Malabaila. **Parents** Cesare, a civil engineer, and Ester (Luzzati) Levi. **Marriage** Lucia Morpurgo, a teacher, 1947. **Children** A daughter, Lisa, and a son, Renzo. **Education** Liceo Massimo d'Azeglio, Turin; University of Turin, BSc in chemistry, 1941. **Career** Industrial chemist, 1941–43; partisan in Italian Resistance, 1943; deported to Auschwitz concentration camp, Oswiecim, Poland, imprisoned, 1943–45; began writing novels, short stories, poems and essays, 1947; technical executive, SIVA, paints, enamels, synthetic resins, Settimo, Turin, 1948–74. **Awards and honours** Premio Campiello (Venice literary prize): for *La Tregua*, 1963, for *Se non ora, quando?*, 1982; Bagutta prize for *Storie naturali*; Premio Strega (Rome literary prize) for *La chiave a stella*, 1979; Premio Viareggio (Viareggio literary prize) for *Se non ora, quando?*, 1982. **Publications** *Se questo e un uomo*, Turin, 1947, eleventh edition, 1967, translated by Stuart Woolf and published as *If This Is a Man*, New York, 1959, London, 1960, published as *Survival in Auschwitz: The Nazi Assault on Humanity*, 1961, new edition, 1966, dramatic version in Italian, 1966; *La Tregua*, 1958, eighth edition, 1965, translated by Stuart Woolf and published as *The Reawakening*, Boston, 1965, published as *The Truce: A Survivor's Journey Home from Auschwitz*, England, 1965 and 1989; under pseudonym, *Storie naturali* (Natural History), Italy, 1967; (with Carlo Quartucci) *Intervista aziendale* (radio script), Italy, 1968; under pseudonym, *Vizio di forma*, Italy, 1971; *Il sistema periodico*, Italy, 1975, published as *The Periodic Table*, 1984; *L'osteria di Brema*, Italy, 1975; *Abruzzo forte e gentile*, Italy, 1976; *Shema: Collected Poems*, translated by Ruth Feldman and Brian Swann, 1976, revised edition as *Collected Poems*, 1988; *La chiave a stella*, Italy, 1978, translation published as *The Monkey's Wrench*, New York, 1986, and as *The Wrench*, London, 1987; *Se non ora, quando?*, Italy, 1982, translation published as *If Not Now, When?*, 1985; *Lilít* (short stories), 1981; editor, *La Ricerca della radice*, 1981; *Ad ora incerta* (poems), 1984; *L'Altrui mestiere* (essays); *Moments of Reprieve*, 1986; *I sommersi e i salvati*, translation published as *The Drowned and the Saved*, 1988; *Other People's Trades* (essays), 1989. **Cause of death** A fall, at age 67. **Further reading** Giuseppe Grassano, *Primo Levi* (in Italian), 1981.

ERVIN NYIREGYHAZI

Hungarian Pianist and Composer

Born **Budapest, Hungary, 19 January 1903**

Died **Los Angeles, California, 13 April 1987**

There can be few more extraordinary lives than that of the Hungarian pianist and composer, Ervin Nyiregyházi. A child prodigy and indisputably gifted musician, he would easily have ranked among the finest romantic pianists of this century had not nearly four decades of self-imposed obscurity deprived him of a dazzling musical career. Having lived half his life in a Los Angeles slum, and with no less than ten wives to his name, he is now known only to the keenest of musical specialists and to those lucky enough to hear the few recordings he made unexpectedly in the 1970s.

Nyiregyházi was in his artistic prime in the 1920s. Hailed as a genius in Europe for his performances of Liszt's Second Piano Concerto with the Berlin Philharmonic Orchestra under the great conductor Nikisch, he was also keenly received in the United States, where he made his début in 1920. Still only in his late teens, he played with a passion that excited his audience wherever he performed. His style was heavily romantic and highly individualistic—rich tonal colours, free tempos and bold phrasing were the hallmarks of his idiosyncratic playing; it defied categorization by music specialists.

Although the first 25 years of Nyiregyházi's life had shown promise of brilliance, the following years unravelled a decline in fortunes few people could imagine possible. His long period of "exile" on the West Coast of the US, without money, without friends, without even a piano, was the ultimate waste of a natural talent. To a sensation-seeking press, a brilliant East European pianist who forsakes his career for a life of drink, women and social oblivion, proved too much of a gift. He was constantly pursued by tabloid journalists hungry for a scandal.

As a six-year-old in Budapest, however, the wunderkind had already been playing the piano for some four years. Even at this early age, he displayed an astonishing grasp of musical technique, transposing at sight whole scores into remote keys, and memorizing large works with the greatest of ease. His photographic memory was even the subject of a scientific study entitled *The Psychology of a Musical Prodigy*, although its findings showed that Nyiregyházi was no more unusual than other similarly gifted musicians. His "tactile" memory was, nevertheless, something he retained throughout his life. "I never practised much after I was a young child," he once said. "I always memorized easily. That was enough. Practice was no good." Such unconventionality characterized everything he did.

With a father who was a professional tenor, and a mother who was an amateur pianist, it was said of Nyiregyházi that he "absorbed music by a kind of domestic osmosis". He entered the Budapest Academy of Music at the age of seven, moving with his family to Berlin in 1914. Here he became a student of the composer Ernst von Dohnányi and, more significantly, of Frederic Lamond, who had himself been a student of Franz Liszt. It was Lamond's influence that led to

Nyiregyházi's close association with Liszt's piano works, an association which was to last throughout his life. Individualist that he was, however, he was reluctant to recognize anyone as the arbiter of his musical style. Ignaz Paderewski and Ferruccio Busoni, both of them composers and pianists, were the only people who meant much to him—Paderewski for his similar "tonal ideal", and Busoni for the "monumentality" of his piano playing. Influenced or not, Nyiregyházi was always highly original in his musical approach; who else, for instance, would play repeats not indicated in the music, as he once did in a performance of the Liszt *Hungarian Rhapsody No. 3* simply because he "loved the melody"?

Nyiregyházi's fortunes began to decline in the early 1930s in the wake of personal problems after a divorce (the first of six). From New York he moved to Hollywood where he briefly made an unsatisfactory career as a studio pianist, but fell gradually into a state of dire poverty. Increasingly dependent on alcohol, he nevertheless continued to compose, leaving something in the order of 700 works by the time of his death. Characteristically, he never let anyone hear his compositions.

For approximately 40 years Nyiregyházi led the life of a down-and-out. So much more astonishing was it then, when, in 1973, a group of friends succeeded in persuading him to give a recital in a San Francisco church. Without music, and without even having practised seriously beforehand, he played Liszt's *St Francis Legends*, among the most difficult works in the piano repertoire. It was a sensational performance. An amateur recording of the concert led to recording contracts with Columbia Records, and to a two-year stipend from the Ford Foundation. Those who heard him were enthralled at this example of romanticism reborn, but Nyiregyházi did not return to the concert platform. Once again he retreated into relative obscurity. The performances he gave towards the end of his life were a potent reminder of what this exceptional pianist was capable of. They were an unlikely but welcome throw-back to the virtuosity he displayed in the early part of his career, to a talent which once moved the great Arnold Schoenberg to declare: "Such power of expression I have never heard before". Praise indeed for a man now largely forgotten.

Born Ervin Nyiregyházi. **Parents** Father a professional tenor, mother an amateur pianist. **Marriages** Ten, beginning with Mary Kelen, 1926 (divorced, 1927); five others ended in divorce, three in death; last wife, Doris. **Education** Budapest Academy of Music, under Albert Siklós, Leo Wiener and István Tomán, 1910–14; Berlin, under Ernst von Dohnányi and Frederic Lamond, 1914–19. **Emigration** Left Germany for USA, 1920. **Career** Concert pianist and composer; a "child prodigy", writing first compositions at age of four; début concert in Fiume at age six, 1909; German début playing Beethoven's Third Piano Concerto with Berlin Philharmonic, 1915; US début, Carnegie Hall, 1920; career faltered in early to mid-1920s; worked as studio pianist in Hollywood, late 1920s; made European tour, 1930; series of personal and professional setbacks resulted in his abandoning the piano (although continuing to compose in private), living in poverty in Los Angeles until 1973; played again in public, San Francisco, 1973; enthusiastic reception led to commission for a series of recordings for Columbia Records, 1970s. **Related activities** Composed 700 works by 1978, but all remained unheard. **Cause of death** Undisclosed, at age 84. **Further reading** Dr Géza Révész, *Psychologische Analyse eines musikalisch hervorragenden Kindes*, Leipzig, 1916, published in English as *The Psychology of a Musical Prodigy*, London, 1925.

BUDDY RICH

American Jazz Musician

***Born* Brooklyn, New York, 30 June 1917**

***Died* Los Angeles, California, 2 April 1987**

Buddy Rich was perhaps the greatest drummer who ever lived. Extremely dynamic, imaginative and unbelievably fast, Rich thrilled audiences and surprised his own band members with his powerful and disciplined style. He had an intense personality and a short temper, both of which helped him to preserve his unique philosophy of performance. "Your life's your own when you're off the stand," he would tell his sidemen, "but every night I own you for five hours. I kill myself every night and I expect you to wipe yourself out, too."

Rich was born in the Sheepshead Bay section of Brooklyn. His father, a soft-shoe dancer/ blackface comedian, and his mother, a singer, introduced Buddy to the vaudeville stage when he was only two years old. Dressed in a dollish sailor costume, and billed as "Baby Traps the Drum Wonder", the boy would beat out the rhythm for "Stars and Stripes Forever" on a small drum. Young Rich soon upstaged his parents and, after learning to dance, joined Raymond Hitchcock's Broadway show *Pinwheel.* At the age of six he toured the United States and Australia, and had been around the world. With only intermittent tutoring, Rich never made it beyond the sixth grade. Instead, he taught himself history, maths, literature—and to play the drums.

At the age of 15, Rich was making $1000 a week, second only to Jackie Coogan among highest-paid child stars. In his late teens he became seriously interested in jazz after hearing Tony Briglia, percussionist with Glen Gray's Casa Loma Orchestra, at the Colonnades Room of the Essex House in Manhattan. During the 1930s Rich studied other drummers, including William O'Neil Spencer, a brush specialist, Chick Webb, and Lou Watson, like Rich, also a singer. Later influences included Dave Tough, of the Woody Herman band, Sidney Catlett and Gene Krupa, whom he regarded as a great showman, and with whom he later staged monstrous drum battles. Fiercely independent, Rich developed his own style, as distinctive as any of his idols, but often unpopular with band leaders.

His first record date was with the Andrews Sisters, playing on their hit "Bei Mir Bist Du Schoen". At some time during 1937 Rich was invited to join Joe Marsala's band after sitting in for drummer Henry Adler for two sets. Slightly more than a year later he joined Bunny Berigan's band, and then Artie Shaw's group. Rich gave a new energy to the Shaw ensemble and, with the band, appeared in his first motion picture, *The Dancing Coed*, in 1939. Continuing to develop a witty stage personality in addition to his playing style, Rich made appearances on the Old Gold radio show with the humorist Robert Benchley. In the meantime, however, Rich's association with Shaw ended abruptly when the bandleader stormed off stage one night in New York, abandoning the orchestra, and left for Mexico.

Rich then began a two-year engagement with Tommy Dorsey's band (rooming with Frank Sinatra), and, with Dorsey, appeared in several more films. He also worked occasionally with Benny Carter. Despite being classified 3-A by his local draft board (because he was the sole support of his family), Rich enlisted with the US Marine Corps in 1942. He remained in the United States for the duration of the war, serving as a judo and combat rifleman instructor. The only Jew in his platoon, Rich became combative when told that Jews didn't know how to fight, or that Jews started the war. "After the first dozen beefs," he said, "I didn't hear any more talk like that."

Following his discharge in 1945, Rich, financed by Sinatra, formed his own big band. With star musicians such as Zoot Sims, Tony Scott and Al Cohn, the band enjoyed top billing at premier halls. Popular tastes, however, had changed, and jazz orchestras such as Rich's were soon forced to disband.

Joining Norman Granz's "Jazz at the Philharmonic", Rich played with such greats as Thelonius Monk, Charlie Parker, Dizzy Gillespie and Harry Edison. He spent a year with the Harry James orchestra but, beginning in 1954, took frequent leaves of absence, bored with being a mere sideman. He even appeared in a TV sitcom with Marge and Gower Champion. A few years later, leading his own band in the studio, Rich recorded particularly memorable versions of "Two O'Clock Jump" and Monk's "Straight, No Chaser", displaying unrivalled power, speed and skill. Playing with his own quintet in New Orleans in 1959, Rich suffered his first heart attack. Abandoning a one-year convalescence after only a month, Rich returned to the stage—this time as a singer. Popular demand, however, brought him back to the drums, and by 1960 he felt well enough to tour the Far East with a show sponsored by the US State Department.

He continued to be associated with the James orchestra until 1966, when he again formed his own big band. Known as the "Buddy Rich Big Band", or "Killer Force", and staffed with young and talented musicians, the band did much to revitalize the popularity of jazz. Rich gained even wider exposure in 1967, when his band appeared on the summer replacement for *The Jackie Gleason Show*. He was a regular guest on *The Tonight Show*, and began a close friendship with its host, Johnny Carson. Some of his best works were done during this period, and many became standards in his repertoire. The band continued to perform the "Channel One Suite", "West Side Story Medley" and the energetic "Machine" for many years.

The band performed from time to time with singers such as Tony Bennett, Mel Torme and Frank Sinatra, and played new arrangements of modern music, including "On Broadway", "Norwegian Wood" and "The Beat Goes On", featuring his daughter Kathy on the vocal. "This is her first time in front of an audience," he told the crowd. "She's only 12 years old and...she's drunk." In later years Kathy Rich assumed many of the managerial responsibilities of the band, permitting her father to keep up an exhaustive tour schedule.

Rich declared bankruptcy in 1968 after he was fined $2500 for tax evasion. His house and other belongings were later confiscated by the Federal government.

The band was dissolved in 1974, when Rich opened a New York nightclub called Buddy's Place. He performed there and at other clubs with a small ensemble, usually a septet. Emotionally addicted to the power of a big band, however, he formed a new 17-piece ensemble. A permanent fixture of the new Rich band was Steve Marcus, a brillo-haired, mild-mannered saxophonist who would play crazed and brilliant solos. Rich often humoured his audiences by glancing at his watch and making faces at Marcus during his solos, sometimes tilting a cymbal or otherwise gesturing that Marcus had lost his mind.

Self-described as a "very emotional man with the worst temper in the world", Rich continued to have problems with his health; he was hypertensive and had several heart attacks. He failed several times to quit smoking, but mellowed considerably after learning karate. Still, he demanded a busy schedule, playing one night at Carnegie Hall, and the next in a high school gymnasium in Iowa.

The life of a sideman in the Rich band was often nerve-wrecking. Band members spent most of their time on a bus, had to play often-difficult arrangements, and were given little warning about the next song. Usually, Rich would simply tap out a little rhythm on his high-hat, signifying the number of a certain chart. The entire band (with the exception of Marcus) scrambled through their sheet music, finding the correct piece literally as the song began. Rich was also known to fire under-performing band members on stage.

In 1983 he suffered yet another heart attack and underwent bypass surgery. His recovery was somewhat slower than in the past, but he nevertheless appeared to regain top form in 1985, when his band recorded *Live at Basin Street*. His final work, *Basin Street*, was released both as a three-album set and a video. To one who had never seen him in person, Rich appeared gruff and introverted, shouting at band members during songs. In fact, this was one of his many signatures as a band leader, encouraging the band and expressing satisfaction; he vocalized constantly, humming during drum solos. It was only after he finished a set that he took a microphone and addressed the audience.

Little more than a year later, in January 1987, Rich suffered an apparent stroke. While undergoing hospitalization, he was found to have a brain tumour. He was operated on and seemed to be recovering, when suddenly he suffered a seizure and then a heart attack. He died only a few months short of his seventieth birthday.

In an age of great drummers—Jack DeJohnette, Peter Erskine, Bill Bruford and Stewart Copeland—Rich was undeniably unique. Master of the left-handed drum roll, and capable of awesome solos, he performed hard-driving, inspiringly powerful big band jazz, not, as he put it, music for "tootsie tapping". Despite his being twice the age of most modern drummers, his dexterity never waned. The departure of Buddy Rich signalled not only an end to the works of a brilliant and prolific drummer, but the end of an era in jazz.

Born Bernard Rich. **Parents** Vaudeville artists known as Wilson and Rich. **Marriage** Marie, 1952. **Children** One daughter, Kathy. **Military service** Judo instructor and combat rifleman, US Marine Corps, 1942–44. **Career** Appeared with parents' act before second birthday; appeared in *Pinwheel* on Broadway at age of four; toured Australia and the USA at age of six; led own stage band by age eleven; played with Joe Marsala's band, 1937; with Bunny Berigan, 1938; Artie Shaw, 1939; Tommy Dorsey, 1939–42, 1944–45; Benny Carter, 1942; formed Buddy Rich Band, 1946; toured with "Jazz at the Philharmonic", appearing with Lester Young, Harry Edison, Oscar Peterson and Charlie Parker, among others, early 1950s; joined with Charlie Parker, Chubby Jackson and Marty Napoleon to form The Big Four, 1951; played with Harry James, 1953–54; toured Europe, 1957; TV actor, 1957–58; toured with his own quintet, 1958–59; played clubs in New York as a singer, 1960; played drums for a State Department sponsored tour of the Far East, 1960–61; played for Harry James, early 1960s; formed own big band, 1966–74; played with small groups in New York, mainly at own club; toured with band of young musicians, 1980s. **Related activities** Started own club, Buddy's Place, in New York, 1970s. **Awards and honours** *Metronome* magazine award, 1948; *Down Beat* magazine poll, 1941, 1942 and 1944; *Esquire* magazine gold award, 1947; *Down Beat* Critics' Poll award, 1953–54, 1968. **Recordings** A. Shaw, "Serenade to a Savage", Bb 10385, 1939; T. Dorsey, "The Minor Goes Muggin'", Victor 45-0002, 1945; (with Lester Young) "I Found a New Baby", Clef 11048, 1946; C. Parker, "Bloomdido", Mercury/Clef 11058, 1950; (with D. Gillespie) *Bird and Diz*, Mercury, 1950; (with L. Hampton and A. Tatum) *The Lionel Hampton–Art Tatum–Buddy Rich Trio*, Clef 709, 1955; *Buddy Rich vs. Max Roach*, Mercury 20448, 1959; *Swingin' New Big Band*, PJ 20113, 1966; *Lionel Hampton Presents Buddy Rich*, Who's Who in Jazz 21006, 1977; *Buddy and Sweets*, Verve; volumes 1, 4, 7, 8, 10 and 11, *Jazz at the Philharmonic*, Verve; other sessions with Roy Eldridge, Lionel Hampton, Count Basie and Tommy Dorsey. **Cause of death** Heart attack following operation on a brain tumour, at age 69. **Further reading** D. Meriwether Jr, *The Buddy Rich Orchestra and Small Groups*, New Jersey, 1974, revised as *We Don't Play Requests: A Musical Biography/Discography of Buddy Rich*, 1984; K. Strateman, *Buddy Rich and Gene Krupa: A Filmo-discography*, Germany, 1980; J. Nesbitt, *Inside Buddy Rich: A Study of the Master Drummer's Style and Technique*, New York, 1984.

DICK SHAWN

American Actor and Comedian

***Born* Buffalo, New York, 1 December 1924**

***Died* La Jolla, California, 17 April 1987**

In an acting career spanning nearly 40 years and encompassing numerous stage, screen and television roles, Dick Shawn is best remembered for his hilarious portrayal of a hippy Adolf Hitler in Mel Brooks's 1969 film *The Producers*. Though the film featured powerful performances by a host of distinguished actors, including Gene Wilder and Zero Mostel, and won Brooks an Oscar for best screenplay, it was Shawn who stole the show and made it an instant hit. For several decades, his idiosyncratic, self-deprecating comic style endeared him to audiences around the world.

Born Richard Schulefand in Buffalo, New York, and raised in nearby Lackawanna—the community he later described as the "organic source" of his comic vision—Shawn distinguished himself first as an athlete. Following high school, he studied at Miami University, heading for a career as a physical education instructor. He even pitched for a season with the Chicago White Sox before turning to the theatre. In 1948 he appeared on stage for the first time under the name of Richy Shawn in *For Heaven's Sake, Mother!* at New York's Belasco Theater. Discovering he was more adept at comedy than serious drama, he soon set his sights on cabaret work. But the real turning point came in 1953, when he appeared on stage at the Palace Theater as chief comedian in Betty Hutton's All-Star International variety show. His resounding success here launched him on his way.

In the 1950s Shawn concentrated on nightclub comedy, tirelessly developing and perfecting his lifelong speciality, the satiric monologue. During the 1960s he accepted a string of comic roles on Broadway, including those of Emile Magio in *The Egg*, Peter in *Peterpat*, and Byron Prong in *Fade Out–Fade In*. In 1964 he took over from Zero Mostel in *A Funny Thing Happened on the Way to the Forum*. Later he acted in a host of East Coast summer stock and repertory productions, and in 1977 appeared in his own one-man show, *The Second Greatest Entertainer in the Whole Wide World*, at New York's Promenade Theater. The show proved equally popular when it was revived in Beverly Hills eight years later.

Shawn's brand of humour, while powerful, was difficult to pigeon-hole. The script of *The Second Greatest Entertainer in the Whole Wide World*, which required him to portray an exhaustive range of characters, from a starving comedian to a fast-talking Las Vegas superstar, reflected this dilemma. "I've always been hard to classify," he told an interviewer in 1985. "I don't do mother-in-law or ugly girl jokes. In fact, I hardly tell jokes at all."

Although he first succeeded as a stage performer, it is as a comic film actor that Shawn gained his greatest popularity. Notable early pictures included *Wake Me When It's Over* (1960), *It's a Mad, Mad, Mad, Mad World* (1963), *A Very Special Favor* (1965), and *What Did You Do in the War, Daddy?* (1966). Then, in 1968, came *The Producers*, Mel Brooks's first feature film, and one of Shawn's most successful and challenging roles. Cast as a hippy actor with the initials L.S.D. who is commissioned to portray Hitler in a Broadway flop, Shawn delivered an uproarious and memorable performance. In 1979 he starred in another successful spoof, *Love at First Bite*. Over the years, he also appeared in a variety of TV series, including the popular drama *St Elsewhere* and Max Liebman's *TV Spectaculars*, playing both comic and serious roles. A final film, *Maid to Order*, was released just after his death.

In April 1987, while performing before an audience of some 500 people at the University of California at San Diego, Shawn fell suddenly to the stage, lying face down for several minutes in what the audience interpreted as a feigned stupor. He had been in the midst of delivering a monologue about nuclear war, in which all people but those present in the audience died. As he often threw himself to the ground at the end of his performances, forcing stagehands to carry him off stage—a ploy used to avoid curtain calls—observers' initial reaction was one of amusement. But then his son, watching from a balcony, called for help, and a doctor hurried to the stage to administer cardiac massage. The actor died in hospital shortly thereafter.

Born Richard Schulefand. **Children** Adam, Amy, Jenny and Wendy. **Education** University of Miami, Florida. **Career** Actor, comedian, international cabaret artist on stage, in films, on television; New York début under name Richy Shawn, playing Milton Rubin in *For Heaven's Sake! Mother*, 1948; Palladium début, 1954. **Other activities** Pitcher, Chicago White Sox baseball team, early 1950s. **Stage** (includes) *For Heaven's Sake! Mother*, 1948; *Betty Hutton and Her All-Star International Show*, 1953; *The Egg*, 1962; *A Funny Thing Happened on the Way to the Forum*, 1964; *Peterpat*, 1965; *Fade Out–Fade In*, 1965; *I'm Solomon*, 1968; *Room Service*, 1970; *Steambath*, 1970; *The Big House*, 1971; *Halloween*, 1972; *A Musical Jubilee*, 1975; *Stage at Bay*, 1976; *The World of Sholem Aleichem*, 1976; *Bananas and Drums*, 1976; *The Second Greatest Entertainer in the Whole Wide World* (one-man show), 1977. **Films** (include) *Wake Me When It's Over*, 1960; *It's a Mad, Mad, Mad, Mad World*, 1963; *A Very Special Favor*, 1965; *What Did You Do in the War, Daddy?* 1966; *Penelope*, 1966; *The Producers*, 1968; *Love at First Bite*, 1979; *Maid to Order*, 1987. **Television** (includes) *St Elsewhere*; *Max Liebman TV Spectaculars*. **Cause of death** Heart attack, at age 63.

JOHN SILKIN

British Politician

***Born* Balham, London, 18 March 1923**

***Died* Westminster, London, 26 April 1987**

The children of illustrious parents often carry a heavy burden of expectation, particularly if, as frequently happens, they enter the same profession to compete with the shadow of their successful forebear. It is especially hard when they fail to make a similar impact and suffer by invidious comparison with their predecessors.

John Silkin was a professional politician who had been brought up surrounded by legends of twentieth-century Labour history—Ramsay MacDonald, Herbert Morrison, Jimmy Maxton and even Bulganin, future president of the USSR, stayed with the Silkins at their home in southeast London, and played croquet with John's father, the first Baron Silkin of Dulwich. A veteran of the heady post-war reconstruction period which saw the foundation of the Welfare State, John's father, Lewis, was responsible for the Planning Act of 1947 which paved the way for the new towns.

It was fairly inevitable, therefore, that John Silkin should join the Labour Party at the beginning of World War II while still attending Dulwich College. He went on to the University College of Wales before serving in the Intelligence Corps with the Royal Navy on active service in the Indian Ocean. Towards the end of the war, he read law at Trinity Hall, Cambridge, before going into practice as a solicitor. (His brother, Sam, went to the Bar and later became attorney-general.)

John Silkin fought his first seat at the age of 27 when he contested Marylebone with very little hope of winning. He used the opportunity to develop his canvassing techniques, notably during the three hours he spent with one particular voter, actress Rosamund John. Two months later he married her, and promised not to make a habit of it in future election campaigns. His first real political success came in a 1963 by-election when he became MP for Deptford, southeast London, which he represented until his death.

A year later, the Labour victory under Harold Wilson in 1964 saw the start of an extremely promising three years for Silkin, at least in terms of the party structure—junior whip in 1964, deputy chief whip in 1966 and chief whip from 1966 to 1969. His ministerial appointments were less glamorous, but even so, by 1966 he had his own ministry in the shape of Public Buildings and Works. On Harold Wilson's return to power in 1974, following Edward Heath's administration, Silkin was appointed to full Cabinet rank with the Ministry of Planning. Here, he followed faithfully in his father's footsteps when he brought in legislation for the Community Land Act. It proved an expensive failure and resulted in a shortage of development land.

He was much more at ease in dealings with the EEC where, as anti-EEC minister for agriculture under James Callaghan in 1976, he had some tough battles to fight. He gained some popular success when he saved Britain's doorstep milk deliveries, in spite of fierce opposition from other member states. The often bullish nature of Community politics suited his style, earning him the epithet "fish-head" from his opposite number in the West German government when he refused to allow an EEC takeover of British fishing grounds.

The pinnacle of his political ambition was reached in the leadership contest of 1980 following James Callaghan's decision to step down after his defeat by Margaret Thatcher the previous year. He was unlucky when Michael Foot entered the competition as a late entrant and won; Silkin came in third.

From 1970 he had been a member of the left-aligned Tribune Group, and much of his energy was devoted from this time to the management of the party newspaper, *Tribune*, in a battle for control with the hard left. Silkin described himself as "driving from just left of centre", but encountered fierce opposition from his local party over his legal action against *Tribune* in 1983. It proved a sour and embittering fight, leading ultimately to his decision not to stand again at the following election, which actually happened just two months after his death.

John Silkin's political *curriculum vitae* could be described as worthy and respectable, but it lacks brilliance. His parliamentary career was sadly marred towards the end of his life by in-fighting and rear-guard action from opponents within his own constituency seeking to oust him from his seat. While his industry and commitment give the lie to accusations of "Campari socialism" (though not in the millionaire class, he nevertheless amassed considerable personal wealth), there is a sense in which he missed his time as a politician and was out-manoeuvred by history.

Born John Ernest Silkin. **Parents** Lewis, first Baron Silkin, member of parliament, and Rosa (Neft) Silkin. **Marriage** Rosamund John (Jones), an actress, 1950. **Children** One son, Rory Lewis. **Education** Dulwich College, London; University of Wales; Trinity Hall, Cambridge, BA, 1944, LLM (LLB, 1946), MA, 1949. **Military service** Lieutenant, Royal Navy Intelligence, 1941–46. **Career** Qualified as solicitor, 1950; partner in family firm, Lewis Silkin and Partners, 1950–64, 1970–74, 1979 onwards; unsuccessful Labour candidate: St Marylebone, 1950, West Woolwich, 1951, South Nottingham, 1959; member, St Marylebone Borough Council, 1962; member of parliament for Deptford, sponsored by the Transport and General Workers Union,

1963–74, of Lewisham, Deptford, 1974–83; junior whip, 1964; deputy chief whip, 1966; chief whip, 1966–69; deputy leader, House of Commons, 1968–69; minister of public building and works, 1969–70; minister for planning and local government, Department of the Environment, 1974–76; minister of agriculture, fisheries and food, 1976–79; opposition spokesman on industry, 1979–80, on defence and disarmament, 1981–83; shadow leader, House of Commons, 1980–83; contested Labour leadership against Peter Shore and Michael Foot, 1980. **Related activities** Member of several select committees of the House of Commons, including, Services Committee, New Parliamentary and Accommodation Committees, 1979, Privileges Committee, 1979; president, Parliamentarians for World Order, 1983 onwards; arbitrator, Dairy Trade Federation and Milk Marketing Board, 1984. **Other activities** Director, shareholder, Johnson Properties Limited, 1947–50, 1963–64, 1983 onwards, company secretary until 1950; director: Wayfegs Investments Limited, 1950–64, 1970–74, Tucker and Richardson Limited, 1955–63, 1960–64, Noble Motors Limited, up to 1957, Whitestream Estates Limited, from 1961; Pergamon Press, 1971–74, Tribune Publications Limited, 1982, Arena Limited and Arena Holdings Limited, from 1984; founder and chairman, Pontygwyndy Housing Association, Caerphilly, Wales, up to 1964; shareholder: Poltygwyndy Housing Association, Vincent Housing Association Limited, Central and Provincial Housing Trust Limited, Cranbrook Golf Club Limited. **Memberships** Tribune Group. **Awards and honours** Privy Counsellor, 1966; fellow, University College, Cardiff, 1981. **Cause of death** Heart attack, at age 64.

WILLI SMITH

American Fashion Designer

Born **Philadelphia, Pennsylvania, 29 February 1948**

Died **New York City, New York, 17 April 1987**

Trying to find any garment bearing the WilliWear label in a secondhand clothes shop, no matter how upmarket or designer-conscious, is hard work. The reason is not, as you might think, that WilliWear clothes are so exclusive and expensive that they would never end up on a secondhand rail. As Willi Smith, their designer, once said: "I don't design clothes for the Queen, but for the people who wave at her as she goes by." The answer then must be a different one, to do with the feel of the clothes themselves rather than the snob value of a designer label: WilliWear is simply so comfortable, stylish and fun to wear that no one wants to part with it once they own a few pieces. That is why WilliWear on the "one careful previous owner/good as new" circuit is impossible to find.

Willi Smith's premature death ended a career whose development had been rapid and smooth. It had not taken him long to establish his reputation as a popular designer and to secure the financial backing which enabled him to realize his creative talents to the full. He began studying fashion illustration at the Philadelphia Museum College of Art, where he graduated in 1964. He then won a scholarship to Parson's School of Design in New York—an essential move, not only because leaving his hometown for New York was an exciting thing to do in the mid-1960s, but also because it was necessary if he was going to be noticed as an up-and-coming designer. For although the "Philadelphia School" had a good reputation, yielding a crop of promising designers of whom many were, like Smith, young and Black, New York was the place to be for anyone with a serious ambition.

Everything went according to plan. Upon graduation from Parson's in 1968, Willi Smith immediately began freelance work as a knitwear designer. Never short of commissions, he was snapped up a year later by Digits, a sportswear firm for whom he did great things in dissolving the distinction between sports and leisure clothing. In this way he indirectly contributed to the enormous expansion of the consumer market for bright, comfortable, inexpensive clothes aimed at the health and fashion-conscious, who have money to spend but do not need clothes to convey their social status.

Smith's designs, needless to say, were a hit, and in 1976 he formed his own company, WilliWear Ltd, followed by WilliWear Men two years later. Although all his clothes bore the mark of saleability and comfort, his style of design changed gradually from the adventurous and fun to the more grown-up and serious. In his early career Smith had been the first to put plaids and stripes together and to mix and match patterns in a way that had hitherto been unheard of in men's fashion. By the mid-1980s, however, his collections showed a much more traditional, tailored line, although still with a characteristic tendency towards oversize and with the use of distinctly untraditional colours such as jade, green and coral. An example of one design like that was Edward A. Schlossberg's navy blue linen suit with silver tie, worn on the occasion of his wedding to Caroline Kennedy. It caused a controversy among the guests and a furore in the national press, much to Smith's pleasure. His PR man, Mark Bozek, later commented that the boss "took the business of having fun very seriously, and it showed in his clothes".

Perhaps it was also this serious business of having fun that induced Willi Smith to design 600 uniforms at the request of his friend, the artist Christo. Smith, sticking closely to his brief, made sure that all the workers who were to help Christo with his project of wrapping up the Pont Neuf in Paris would be suitably dressed for the occasion. After all, this was the world's capital of fashion—it was essential that the workers' outfits be colour-coordinated with the bridge.

Christo was not Smith's only artist-friend. As an art collector himself (mainly African, Oriental and contemporary American), Willi Smith counted many artists and performers among his acquaintance, moving as he did in the elegant, successful and demi-decadent circles of New York society. Still, unlike some of his friends, he did find time for work amid his social engagements. Probably the most successful of his generation of designers, he won the Coty American Fashion Critics' Award in 1983. He also lectured in fashion history and designed textiles and furniture for various companies other than his own. Of the latter, WilliWear in particular occasioned frequent travel, mostly to Asia, where many of the light cotton fabrics Smith liked to use in his designs were manufactured. India in particular inspired him, not only with the texture and delicacy of its fabrics but also culturally, with its colours and traditions. India was the mainstay of his creative imagination, and it was a bitter irony that the country which he loved so much also provided him during a month-long stay with shigella, a parasitic disease. Upon his return to New York, Willi Smith fell ill. Twenty-four hours after he had been admitted to the intensive care unit of Mount Sinai Hospital with pneumonia, he died, and a career which still promised so much was cut cruelly short.

Born William Donnell Smith. **Parents** Willie Lee and June Eileen (Bush) Smith. **Education** Studied fashion illustration, Philadelphia Museum College of Art, 1964; won scholarship to Parson's School of Design, New York, 1965–68. **Career** Fashion designer, 1969 onwards; freelance knitwear designer; sketcher, Bobbie Brooks, New York City, 1969; designer, sportswear firm, Digits, New York City, 1969–76; founder, designer and vice-president, own company, WilliWear Ltd, 1976, also of WilliWear Men, 1978 onwards; also designed for other companies, including McCall's, Kroll Associates, Bedford Stuyvesant Workshop. **Related**

activities Lecturer in fashion history, Fashion Institute, London; designed 600 uniforms for French artist, Christo, 1985. **Offices and memberships** League in Aid for Crippled Children; Bedford Stuyvesant Children's Association. **Awards and honours** Named Designer of the Year, International Mannequins, 1978; Coty Award nomination, 1979; Coty American Fashion Critics' Award, 1983. **Cause of death** Pneumonia complicated by shigellae organisms, at age 39.

MAXINE SULLIVAN

American Singer and Musician

Born **Homestead, Pennsylvania, 13 May 1911**

Died **New York City, New York, 7 April 1987**

One song, a very surprising song, transformed Maxine Sullivan from an unknown singer into a star. That song was "Loch Lomond", a Scottish air and an unlikely vehicle to stardom for a poor Black woman from Pennsylvania. Before that song, Sullivan had been making a small name for herself singing on radio stations in Pittsburgh, and by 1937 had made it to the Big Apple, where she sang in the intervals between shows at the Onyx Club. The arranger and bandleader Claude Thornhill heard her sing and put together arrangements of two Scottish songs—the other was "Annie Laurie"—as a feature for her to record. The song became a big seller, a feature about her appeared in the *New Yorker*, and Sullivan's career was made.

Maxine Sullivan was an unlikely star. A vocalist in the Swing Era was expected to swing a song with rhythmic attack. But Sullivan was precise, unfashionably low-key and controlled in her approach. When performing, she would sit motionless, her chin tilted slightly upwards, a quiet smile on her face, and deliver each song in what, in the 1950s, became known as a cool style. As she explained later, "I don't try to make a big production. If I sing two choruses, I sing the melody in the first. The second time around, I do a little improvising and an ending. And that's it." But that "it" had enough individuality to remake every song she touched.

At first, because of "Loch Lomond", she was typecast as a singer of folk and light-classical material, but in later life she broadened her scope to include the popular song repertoire of the 1920s and 1930s. She had had considerable experience of this genre, for she had appeared in two Hollywood musicals—*Going Places* (where she starred opposite Louis Armstrong) in 1937 and *St Louis Blues* in 1938—before making her Broadway début in *Swingin' the Dream*, a jazz version of *A Midsummer Night's Dream*, with Benny Goodman and again Armstrong, in the same year.

Meanwhile, she did not neglect her talents as a club singer, for until 1942 she sang regularly at the Onyx Club with her husband John Kirby's band, her pristine delivery a fine accompaniment to the light and airy chamber jazz of the group. She also starred for two years on a CBS radio programme and toured and recorded with Benny Carter's Orchestra in 1941. But when her marriage ended in 1942, she struck out on her own. Success continued to accompany her, for she sang with the likes of Benny Goodman, and for the rest of the 1940s she was a popular solo act in the various New York clubs.

Sullivan retired in the 1950s to bring up her family, earning her living as a teacher and a nurse and becoming active in community services in New York. Her club appearances were infrequent, although always with the very best musicians—Bobby Hackett, Charlie Shavers and Earl Hines among them. And then in 1958 she went back to full-time singing. Slowly at first, a lengthy residency at Washington's Blues Alley club in 1965 re-established her as one of the best jazz singers of her age. She worked regularly with Bob Wilber and the World's Greatest Jazz Band and delighted her growing audience with an album of *The Music of Hoagy Carmichael*, recorded with Wilber in the mid-1960s.

Approaching old age did not diminish her workload, and in 1979 she was given a Tony Award for her role in the musical *My Old Friend*, about growing old. She also celebrated her years with a more vocally emotional performance, notably on her 1986 album, *The Great Songs from the Cotton Club by Harold Arlen and Ted Koehler*, for which she was nominated for a Grammy, and on an album devoted to the music of Burton Lane. Live, she added to her vocal skills with performances on valve trombone and flugelhorn, only giving up the former in later life when it became too big for her to carry around!

At the time of her death, Maxine Sullivan was still hard at work, a frequent performer with a large jazz repertoire whose appearances packed clubs the world over. Unpretentious, often unassuming, Sullivan was an expressive singer whose sense of tone and rhythm had done so much to influence the early style of Ella Fitzgerald. Throughout her life, whatever material she chose to interpret, she never lost that quiet ability to make the song her own.

Born Marietta Williams. **Marriages** 1) John Kirby, 1938 (divorced); 2) Cliff Jackson, 1950 (died, 1970). **Children** One son and one daughter. **Career** Sang at various nightclubs, including the Onyx Club, New York; first attracted attention as member of Claude Thornhill band, popularized song "Loch Lomond", 1937; appeared in film musicals, *Going Places*, 1938, and *St Louis Blues*, 1939; performed on Broadway with Louis Armstrong and Benny Goodman in jazz version of *A Midsummer Night's Dream* called *Swingin' the Dream*, 1939; starred with husband John Kirby's band on radio series, *Flow Gently Sweet Rhythm*, 1940; embarked on solo career, 1942; trained as nurse and became active in community service in New York, mid-1950s, appearing infrequently at clubs and festivals; vocalist with *World's Greatest Jazz Band*, 1970s; continued singing career into 1980s. **Awards and honours** Tony Award for *My Old Friend* (TV musical), 1979; nomination for Grammy Award for *Songs from the Cotton Club* (album), 1986. **Films** (include) *Going Places*, 1938; *St Louis Blues*, 1939. **Stage** (includes) *Swingin' the Dream*, 1939; *Take a Giant Step*, 1953. **Radio** *Flow Gently Sweet Rhythm*, 1940. **Television** *My Old Friend* (musical), 1979. **Recordings** (include) "Loch Lomond", Voc/OK 3654, 1937; "Nice Work If You Can Get It", Voc/OK 3848, 1937; "St Louis Blues", Vic 25895, 1938; "When Your Lover Has Gone"/"My Ideal", Decca 18555, 1942; *The Complete Charlie Shavers with Maxine Sullivan*, Period 1113, 1956; *The Queen*, Kenneth 2052-5, 1981–85; *The Great Songs from the Cotton Club by Harold Arlen and Ted Koehler*, Milan 270, 1984; *Uptown*, Conc 288, 1985; *Looking for a Boy*, King; *Flow Gently Sweet Rhythm*, Period; *Shakespeare and Hyman*, Monmouth-Evergreen. **Cause of death** Undisclosed, at age 75. **Further reading** Arnold Shaw, *The Street that Never Slept: New York's Fabled 52nd Street*, New York, 1971, revised edition published as *52nd Street: The Street of Jazz*, 1977; D.J. Travis, *An Autobiography of Black Jazz*, Chicago, 1983.

GENERAL MAXWELL TAYLOR

American Soldier and Military Strategist
Born **Keytesville, Missouri, 26 August 1901**
Died **Washington, DC, 19 April 1987**

General Maxwell Taylor was a leading US paratroop commander in World War II, playing a major role in the Sicilian and Italian campaigns, the invasion of Normandy and the subsequent drive through Holland into Germany. He also served in Korea before being appointed military representative to President Kennedy. A distinguished scholar, he was a natural linguist, being fluent in French, Spanish, Japanese, Chinese, German and Italian.

Maxwell Davenport Taylor was the only child of John Earle and Pearle Maxwell. Inspired by his grandfather's stories of the US Civil War, it was his earliest ambition to attend the military academy, West Point. He was a prize scholar, excelling in classical and modern languages, and graduating from Northeast High School in Kansas City before he was 16. While making the arrangements to enter West Point, Taylor sat the entrance examinations for the Naval Academy but failed on account of his limited grasp of geography: "If the Strait of Malacca had been in Europe, I might have been an admiral instead of a general," as he later put it. He graduated from West Point in 1922 and was described in one undergraduate magazine as "one of the most learned members of the class".

Taylor's first commission was in the Corps of Engineers. In 1926 he transferred to the 10th Field Artillery, and the following year he was sent to France to improve his knowledge of the language. He returned to West Point as instructor of French and assistant professor of Spanish. Japanese was added to his repertoire following a period of service at the US embassy in Tokyo. While in Japan, Taylor wrote a detailed report on the Japanese Army which was subsequently used for instructive purposes following the attack on Pearl Harbor in December 1941.

Promotion was slow in the US Army in the inter-war years and it was not until 1940 that Taylor reached the rank of major, taking command of the 12th Field Artillery Battalion at Fort Sam Houston in Texas. The outbreak of war the following year found him as assistant secretary to the War Department General Staff in Washington, DC, but eager for a more active role, he arranged for his posting as chief of staff of the 82nd Infantry Division, one of the units chosen to become the nucleus of the US Airborne Divisions. On 4 December 1942 he was promoted to brigadier-general and became artillery commander of the 82nd Airborne Division. In March 1943 the 82nd went overseas and played a prominent role in the Sicilian and Italian campaigns, and in September of the same year Taylor undertook a personal action of which Eisenhower wrote, "The risks he ran were greater that I asked any other agent or emissary to undertake during the war. He carried weighty responsibilities and discharged them with unerring judgement, and at every minute was in imminent danger of discovery and death." The Italians, under Marshal Pietro Badoglio, had just surrendered to the Allies and Taylor, accompanied by Air Corps Colonel William Gardiner, landed by boat at Gaeta, well behind the German front line, to determine the feasibility of an airborne landing on Rome. Having travelled to Rome itself, undertaken personal reconnaissance and negotiations with the Italian authorities, Taylor decided against such an attack.

In March 1944 he took command of the 101st "Screaming Eagles" Airborne Division and two months later was promoted to major-general, to prepare his troops for their role in the forthcoming invasion. Indeed, in the early hours of 6 June 1944 Taylor became the first US general to fight in France in the war as he parachuted with his division into Normandy ahead of the main assault force. By September 1944 Taylor was again ahead of the front line, spearheading the airborne invasion of Holland as field commander of the US contribution to Operation Market Garden. Wounded in this difficult operation, "Mr Attack", as he had become known, returned to the US. While he was away the 101st, under its deputy commander Brigadier-General Antony McAuliffe, became encircled in Bastogne during the German Ardennes offensive in December 1944. Hurrying back to Europe, Taylor hurtled under fire through German lines in a jeep to assume command of his division. As a result of the 101st's famous defence of the town, the whole division was awarded a presidential citation, the first division to receive such an honour. Taylor remained with the division for the rest of the war, leading his troops into the very heart of Germany.

In September 1945 Taylor returned to the US to become the second youngest man ever to be appointed superintendent of West Point. In his three-year stay at the academy, Taylor radically overhauled the training course, giving greater weight to the liberal arts and social sciences, though allied to physical fitness. He also introduced special courses on military leadership, emphasizing the roles of character, human understanding, professional competence and devotion to the troops under the officer's command.

In 1949 he was appointed chief of staff of the US forces in Europe, before becoming the first commander of the American Military Government in Berlin in September of that year. After another spell in Washington as deputy chief of staff for operations, he succeeded General James Van Fleet as commander of the 8th Army in Korea in February 1953. There he took part in the bitter fighting in the months leading up to the armistice in July and afterwards organized the new army of the Republic of Korea and initiated the Armed Forces Assistance to Korea programme aimed at helping the Koreans rebuild their shattered nation. This programme became one of the main tasks of the 8th Army—one Taylor held to be very worthwhile—and by the time he left Korea some 1200 projects had been completed, with another 750 under way. At the end of 1954 he was transferred to command all ground forces in Japan before he took over from General John Hull in April 1955 as commander in chief of Far East Command with the rank of general.

A few months later Taylor was sworn in as chief of staff of the United States Army, replacing General Ridgway who had fallen foul of President Eisenhower by arguing for an expanded army capable of providing a strong alternative to the use of nuclear weapons. Unfortunately for Eisenhower, Taylor also rejected the nuclear threat argument and argued instead that "nothing we have discovered or...expect to discover will reduce the need for brave men to fight our battles". Taylor fought his corner well but the nuclear "massive retaliation" argument prevailed and when Eisenhower announced the army strength for 1960 would be 870,000 as against Taylor's call for a minimum of 925,000, Taylor felt compelled to resign, noting, "For four years I have struggled to modernize the army and my success was limited, so I decided I would do one thing for the country and withdraw an obsolescent general from inventory."

Upon retirement Taylor took up a number of commercial appointments but maintained his attack on the pro-nuclear lobby in *The Uncertain Trumpet* (1960) in which he again advocated the need for large conventional forces so as to provide a realistic alternative to nuclear war in times of emergency. Although he did not discount the use of nuclear weapons in appropriate circumstances, he often quoted Polybius who noted, "It is not the purpose of war to annihilate those who provoke it, but to cause them to mend their ways." Such views attracted the attention of then Senator J.F. Kennedy, who adopted similar arguments in his presidential campaign. Indeed, after his election, Kennedy invited Taylor to conduct an investigation into the role of the CIA in the Cuban fiasco of April 1961. He accepted the task and ultimately recommended a strict curbing of CIA covert activities.

On 1 July 1961 General Taylor took over the newly established post of military representative of the president to advise Kennedy on military aspects of international relations. Straight away, he headed a mission to South Vietnam to investigate the Communist threat and the possible deployment of US troops as a deterrent factor. By the autumn of 1962 Taylor was chairman of the Joint Chiefs of Staff and working closely with Robert McNamara, the defence secretary, with whom he was able to put into practice many of his firmly-held ideas. In June 1964 Taylor accepted a one-year tenure as ambassador to South Vietnam, at a time when the military situation was deteriorating rapidly despite the increasingly heavy counter-measures taken by the 75,000 US troops stationed there. These measures, which included the bombing of strategic targets in North Vietnam, failed to deter the Vietcong, and at the end of Taylor's time in office there were increasingly loud calls for stronger measures to be taken. Taylor, however, still did not retire completely, for he remained a member of the Foreign Intelligence Advisory Board until the time of his death. He also put his increasing spare time in retirement to good use, completing a number of books on international relations and strategy, including *Responsibility and Response* (1967) and *Precarious Security* (1976).

General Maxwell Taylor was a gifted man with a talent for command, politics and academic pursuits. He was not a "GI's General" in the mould of Patton or Bradley, but was widely respected for his tactical skill, bold leadership and devotion both to duty and the men under his command. An idealist with a sound grasp of the possible, he did much to influence US foreign and military policy in the early 1960s and beyond by advocating the need for strong conventional forces to provide a flexible and viable alternative to the use of nuclear weapons.

Born Maxwell Davenport Taylor. **Parents** John Earle Maxwell, attorney, and Pearle (Davenport) Taylor. **Marriage** Lydia Gardner (*née* Happer), 1925. **Children** John Maxwell and Thomas Happer. **Education** Northeast High School, Kansas City; Kansas City Junior College, 1917; US Military Academy, West Point, BS, 1922; Fort Humphreys Engineer School, Virginia, 1922–23; Field Artillery School, Fort Sill, Oklahoma, 1932–33; Command and General Staff School, Fort Leavenworth, Kansas, 1933–35. **Career** 2nd Lieutenant, Corps of Engineers; served with 17th Engineers, Camp Meade, Maryland; 3rd Engineers, Schofield Barracks, Hawaii; 6th Engineers, Camp Lewis, Washington; 10th Field Artillery, 1926; professor of French and assistant professor of Spanish, West Point Military Academy, 1927–32; promoted captain, 1935; attached to US embassy, Tokyo, 1935–39; assistant military attaché, Peking; attended Army War College, Washington, 1939; promoted to major, 1940; commanding officer, 12th Field Artillery Battalion, Fort Sam Houston, Texas, 1940; assistant secretary, War Department general staff, Washington, 1941; chief of staff, 82nd Infantry Division, Camp Claiborne, Louisiana, 1942; promoted to brigadier-general (temporary), 1942; artillery commander, 82nd Airborne Division, 1942; senior US member, Allied Control Commission in contact with Italian authorities; commanding officer, 101st Airborne Division, 1944; promoted to major-general (temporary), 1944; superintendent, US Military Academy, 1945; chief of staff, European Command Headquarters, Heidelberg, 1949; first US commander, Berlin, 1949; assistant chief of staff for operations, G3, department of army, 1951; deputy chief of staff, operations and administration of army, 1951; commanding general, 8th US Army in Korea, 1953; commander of all ground forces in Japan, Okinawa and Korea, at Camp Zama, Japan, 1954; commander-in-chief, Far East and United Nations Commands, 1955; chief of staff, US Army, 1955–59; retired from service, 1959; military representative of the president of the USA, 1961–62; chairman, joint chiefs of staff, US, 1962–64; American ambassador to South Vietnam, 1964–65; special consultant to president, 1965–69. **Related activities** President, Institute of Defense Analyses; member, Foreign Intelligence advisory board, 1965–. **Other activities** Director, Mexican Light and Power Company, 1959–60; president, Lincoln Center for the Performing Arts, 1961–. **Awards and honours** Silver Star, 1943 (Oak Leaf Cluster, 1944); Distinguished Service Cross, 1944; Distinguished Service Medal, 1945 (Oak Leaf Clusters 1954, 1959, 1964); Legion of Merit;

Bronze Star; Purple Heart; Croix de Guerre with palm; Belgian Cross of Grand Officer of the Order of Leopold; British Distinguished Service Order; Order of the Bath; Netherlands Militaire Willems Order; Military Order of Italy; Commander of the French Legion of Honour; honorary Knight Commander of the British Empire; honorary doctorates from New York University, Bowdoin College, University of Missouri, Williams College, Pennsylvania Military College, Trinity College and Yale University. **Publications** *The Uncertain Trumpet*, 1960; *Responsibility and Response*, 1967; *Swords and Plowshares*, 1972; *Precarious Security*, 1976. **Cause of death** Undisclosed, at age 85.

ANTONY TUDOR

British Dancer and Choreographer

Born **Finsbury, London, 4 April 1908**

Died **New York City, New York, 19 April 1987**

Antony Tudor probably did more than any other man this century to *change* the nature of ballet. The ghosts of Diaghilev, Ashton, Balanchine and company will probably rise up in horror at that claim, but Tudor brought to the ballet the psychology that Martha Graham took off her dancing shoes and contracted her spine in order to achieve. He found a *new* way of using the classical vocabulary to reveal the innermost thoughts of characters drawn from real life. Before Tudor the world of ballet was inhabited by the grand personalities of never-never land, whose chief concerns were to live happily ever after. As Tudor explained, "I don't know princes and princesses."

His background was certainly well away from castles and palaces. Tudor was raised in north London, the son of a shopkeeper. On leaving school, he went to work in a meat market. He held an initial interest in drama, but when he saw a dancer "flicking amid a golden pool of light" in a music hall, he was inspired to go to the ballet, where he watched performances by Pavlova and Diaghilev's visiting Ballets Russes. He began studying ballet with Madame Marie Rambert, Pearl Argyle and Harold Turner, while maintaining his position with a firm of real estate assessors. Two years later, recognizing Tudor's ambitions to choreograph, Rambert engaged him as a dancer, secretary, stage manager, pianist and odd-job man for her newly-founded Ballet Club.

His first choreographed work was *Cross-Garter'd* (1931), inspired by Shakespeare's *Twelfth Night*. It attracted praise from Léonide Massine who was the leading choreographer of the day. Over the next five years, Tudor's work as a dancer with the Vic-Wells Company, his staging for opera and his own ballet pieces inspired one critic to say that his work was "the most interesting yet on the British stage produced by an Englishman". His first abiding great work, *Le Jardin aux lilas* (Lilac Garden), came in 1937. One commentator has remarked that "no other choreographer in the half century since then has produced a more moving lyrical expression of deep feelings than this short work about lovers parted by a forced marriage".

Dark Elegies, his next piece, produced in 1937, was even more evocative as Tudor matured in his craft. Set to Mahler's "Kindertotenlieder", he demonstrated that equally powerful emotions (loss, regret) could also be dealt with in abstract dances. When the ballet was performed years later, after a major disaster, the truthfulness and power of Tudor's expression of grief for a group of lost children was captivating. He showed enormous technical fortitude in his choice of Mahler as composer, a point which is highlighted by the fact that it was nearly three decades before other choreographers tackled Mahler's ambitious scores.

After a fairly abortive attempt to form a company with Agnes de Mille in 1937, Tudor snapped up an offer from the fledgling American Ballet Theater in 1939 to become a founder member. From then on he spent most of the rest of his career in the US.

Lilac Garden and *Dark Elegies* won Tudor enormous approval from American audiences, while the critics fawned over his intellectual approach: "There is more than meets the eye in Tudor's ballets." During this first creative phase in America, the 1940s, Tudor choreographed three notable masterpieces. *Pillar of Fire* (1942), a study of a young girl's frustration, heralded Tudor's growing interest in human psychology. *Romeo and Juliet* (1943) showed his ability to sustain the narrative by "abandoning the erotic in favour of a tender lyricism". (Since Kenneth MacMillan's treatment, the eroticism of the young lovers has moved forcefully back centre-stage.) *Undertow* (1945) excited great controversy in that it dealt with issues usually considered anathema to the ballet: childbirth, murder, depravity, corruption... Tudor refused to provide programme notes for the piece, which left many critics complaining that it was "complex and confused". But for him it was an important function of the piece that each member of the audience should formulate an individual response to the work. "If audiences are to gain the fullest enjoyment," he once said, "they must be trained as well as the dancers to do some of the work." This remained a constant theme of his, which, interestingly enough, is nowadays held as the norm.

For most of the 1950s and early 1960s, Tudor devoted himself to teaching, although he did continue to produce works that were as gripping, if somewhat less startling, as his earlier pieces.

Since his youth, Tudor had always been an extremely charming, unassuming man. His thoughtful and contemplative personality developed into positive austerity when he moved into a Buddhist monastery in New York, having given away all his possessions. But that is not to denigrate his keen sense of humour, which dancers later often found sly and offbeat.

Although he, Frederick Ashton and, later, Kenneth MacMillan were giants among English choreographers, Tudor was largely ignored by his ungrateful mother country. Shortly before his death an honorary degree from Oxford University and a hasty Queen Elizabeth II Coronation Award from the Royal Academy of Dancing bestowed some degree of recognition, but the world of dance, however, remains eternally indebted to Tudor for rooting the ballet tradition within the twentieth-century psyche.

Born William Cook. **Father** Shopkeeper. **Education** Studied dance under Marie Rambert, Pearl Argyle, Margaret Craske and Harold Turner from 1928. **Emigration** Left England for US, 1938. **Career** Clerk, Smithfield Market, London; worked for firm of real estate assessors, 1930; dancer, director and choreographer, Ballet Rambert, 1930–38; worked with Sadler's-Wells Royal Ballet, 1931–36; choreographer, Royal Opera House, Covent Garden, 1935–38; staged dances for plays and musicals in London's West End and for BBC Television, 1937–39; founder, London Ballet, 1938; choreographer, American Ballet Theater, 1939–80, associate director, 1974–80, choreographer emeritus, 1980–87; set works for Royal Swedish Ballet, 1948–49, artistic director, 1963–64; choreographer, New York City Ballet, 1951–52; produced ballets in Japan, Greece, Canada and Australia. **Related activities** Head of faculty, Metropolitan Opera Ballet School, 1950 onwards, ballet director, 1957–63; dance teacher, Juilliard School, New York. **Awards and honours** DLitt, St Andrews University, 1970; Carina Ari Gold Medal, 1973; *Dance* magazine award, 1974; Creative Arts Medal, Brandeis University, 1976; Capezio Dance Award, 1986; Handel Medallion, 1986; Royal Academy of Dancing Queen Elizabeth II Coronation Award, 1986; honorary doctorate, Oxford University. **Ballets** (as dancer, include) *Façade*, 1931; *The Lord of Burleigh*, 1931; *Les Rendezvous*, 1933; *Le Carnaval*, 1933; *La Création du monde*, 1934; *Hommage aux belles Viennoises*, 1935; also danced a principal role in each of his own ballets until 1950. **Ballets** (as choreographer) *Cross-Garter'd*, 1931; *Mr Roll's Quadrilles*, 1932; *Constanza's Lament*, 1932; *Lysistrata*, 1932; *Adam and Eve*, 1932; *Pavanne pour une infante défunte*, 1933; *Atlanta of the East*, 1933; *Paramour*, 1934; *The Legend of Dick Whittington*, 1934; *The Planets*, 1934; *The Descent of Hebe*, 1935; *Le Jardin aux lilas*, 1936; *Dark Elegies*, 1937; *Suite of Airs*, 1937; *Gallant Assembly*, 1937; *Judgement of Paris*, 1938; *Soirée musicale*, 1938; *Gala Performance*, 1938; *Goya Pastoral*, 1940; *Time Table*, 1941; *Pillar of Fire*, 1942; *The Tragedy of Romeo and Juliet*, 1943; *Dim Lustre*, 1943; *Undertow*, 1945; *Shadow of the Wind*, 1948; *The Dear Departed*, 1949; *Nimbus*, 1950; *Lady of the Camellias*, 1951; *Les Mains gauches*, 1951; *Ronde du printemps*, 1951; *La Gloire*, 1952; *Trio con brio*, 1952; *Exercise Piece*, 1953; *Little Improvisations*, 1953; *Elizabethan Dances*, 1953; *Britannia Triumphs*, 1953; *Offenbach in the Underworld*, 1954; *La Leyenda de José*, 1958; *Hail and Farewell*, 1959; *A Choreographer Comments*, 1960; *Gradus ad Parnassus*, 1962; *Fandango*, 1963; *Echoes of Trumpets*, 1963; *Concerning Oracles*, 1966; *Shadowplay*, 1967; *Knight Errant*, 1968; *Divine Horseman*, 1969; *Continuo*, 1971; *Sunflowers*, 1971; *Cereus*, 1971; *The Leaves Are Fading*, 1975; *Tiller in the Fields*, 1978. **Theatre** *The Happy Hypocrite*, 1936; *To and Fro*, 1936; *Seven Intimate Dances*, 1938; *Johnson Over Jordan*, 1939; *Hollywood Pinafore*, 1945; *The Day Before Spring*, 1945. **Film** *In a Monastery Garden*, 1932. **Television** (all for the BBC) *Paleface*, 1937; *Hooey*, 1937; *Fugue for Four Cameras*, 1937; *After Supper*, 1937; *Dorset Garden*, 1937; *Boulter's Lock*, 1937; *Douanes*, 1937; *Excerpts from Relache*, 1937; *Siesta*, 1937; *Portsmouth Point*, 1937; *High Yellow*, 1937; *Full Moon*, 1937; *Tristan and Isolde*, Act II, 1938; *Wien*, 1938; *The Emperor Jones*, 1938; *Master Peter's Puppet Show*, 1938; *Cinderella*, 1938; *The Tempest*, 1939; *The Pilgrim's Progress*, 1939. **Cause of death** Undisclosed, at age 79.

HARRY WATT

British Documentary Film Director

***Born* Edinburgh, Scotland, 18 October 1906**

***Died* 2 April 1987**

The British documentary film movement of the 1930s and 1940s had a profound influence on the development of the industry as a whole. Fathered by John Grierson, the movement's birth and flowering under the guise of the Empire Marketing Board (EMB) and, later, the General Post Office (GPO) Film Unit led to the making of some of the best British factual and semi-factual films. Harry Watt, director of *London Can Take It*, *Target for Tonight* and *The Overlanders*, was lucky enough to be taken on by Grierson; inspired by his example, he made one of the most memorable and inventive documentaries of the past 50 years—*Night Mail*.

The son of a former Liberal MP, Watt was born in Edinburgh in the early years of this century. Restless and unsettled, he moved through a variety of jobs after leaving Edinburgh University without taking his degree. His experiences during sporadic work as anything from stevedore or factory worker to balloon-seller were later to prove useful in giving him a keen eye for the born naturalist actor among members of the general public. He was 25 before he joined the EMB and in fairy-tale style began by whitewashing the corridors. He served an apprenticeship by assisting American film-maker Robert Flaherty on films such as *Man of Aran* (in which his brief sea-going experience on the trip from Oban to Newfoundland in a small schooner came in handy), and the

March of Time series. With the demise of the EMB, he moved with its director, John Grierson, to the GPO Film Unit. It was here he learnt the art of directing, working under Cavalcanti.

It was only five years into his film career that he made the brilliantly original *Night Mail*, which follows an overnight mail train journey, combining the authenticity of actual postal workers with the poetry of W.H. Auden and the music of Benjamin Britten. Even today, it remains an impressive and formative influence on subsequent British films.

It was the advent of World War II that provided the film unit with its most fertile proving ground. Grierson's view that documentary could be an extremely valuable force for social inspiration, combining an educational role with involvement of everyday people in the working processes of their country, had obvious and powerful applications in a wartime situation. Taking his lead from this, Watt went on to experiment further with blurring the edges between hard fact and dramatized reality. In his preparation for *Target for Tonight*, Watt read over 3000 operational reports by pilots who had been involved in bombing raids on Germany. Filtering through the mass of information for the occasional personal touch Watt managed to put together a film where, with a modicum of characterization and dialogue, (though still using non-actors), historical events were given a dramatic dimension. This humanizing combination of fact and fiction became a standard form for British war documentaries used for morale-boosting purposes.

Using the expertise gained with the GPO, Watt went on to join Ealing Studios, where he turned his hand to feature-length work including the mini-epic *The Overlanders*. Based on a true story, it follows a huge cattle drive of some 100,000 animals across the dry-baked desert heart of Australia during the early days of Japanese involvement in World War II. His nascent enthusiasm for wildlife was fostered in another feature for Ealing, *Where No Vultures Fly*. Set in Kenya, it traces the everyday adventures of a game warden in one of the national parks and became one of the studio's most popular films.

Watt stayed with Ealing until his retirement following his and the studio's last feature, *The Siege of Pinchgut*. His memoirs, published in 1974 under the title *Don't Look at the Camera*, articulate his view of the documentary-maker's role as a "dramatic reporter" and reflect the down-to-earth good humour that enabled him to get the best out of the ordinary people he worked with in his films.

Born Harry Watt. **Father** Liberal member of parliament. **Education** Edinburgh Academy; Edinburgh University. **Career** Employed in a variety of jobs, including stevedore, factory worker, balloon-seller until 1931; became film director, mostly of documentaries, 1930s–1959; with Empire Marketing Board film unit under John Grierson, 1931; transferred to General Post Office Film Unit; assisted Robert Flaherty on first film, *Man of Aran*; made documentaries for Ministry of Information and Army Film Unit, 1939–42; joined Ealing Studios, 1942; film director: Australia, 1945–48, West Africa, 1951–53; television producer, Granada Television, 1955; with Ealing Studios, 1956–59. **Films** (as director) *Man of Aran*; (co-director) *BBC: Droitwich*, 1934; (co-director) *6:30 Collection*, 1934; (co-director) *Night Mail*, 1936; *The Saving of Bill Blewitt* (plus screenplay), 1936; (co-producer only) *Four Barriers*, 1937; (co-director) *Big Money*, 1937; *North Sea*, 1938; *Health in Industry*, 1938; (co-director) *The First Days*, 1939; *Squadron 992*, 1940; (co-director) *London Can Take It*, 1940; *The Front Line*, 1940; *Britain at Bay*, 1940; *Target for Tonight* (plus screenplay), 1941; *Christmas Under Fire*, 1941; *Dover Revisited*, 1942; *21 Miles*, 1942; *Nine Men* (plus screenplay), 1943; *Fiddlers Three* (plus screenplay), 1944; *The Overlanders* (plus screenplay), 1946; *Eureka Stockade* (*Massacre Hill*) (plus screenplay), 1949; *Where No Vultures Fly* (*Ivory Hunters*), 1951; *West of Zanzibar* (co-screenplay), 1954; *People Like Maria*, 1958; *The Siege of Pinchgut* (plus screenplay), 1959. **Publications** *Don't Look at the Camera* (autobiography), New York, 1974. **Cause of death** Undisclosed, at age 80. **Further reading** Forsyth Hardy, *Grierson on Documentary*,

London, 1946, New York, 1974; Paul Rotha, *Documentary Film*, 1966; Alan Lovell and Jim Hillier, *Studies in Documentary*, New York, 1972; Paul Rotha, *Documentary Diary*, 1973; Elizabeth Sussex, *The Rise and Fall of British Documentary: The Story of the Film Movement Founded by John Grierson*, Berkeley, California, 1975.

SIR GRAHAM WILSON

British Microbiologist

Born **Newcastle-upon-Tyne, England, 10 September 1895**

Died **London, England, 5 April 1987**

Sir Graham Wilson was world-famous as a microbiologist, but it was as co-author of the famous textbook known as "Topley and Wilson", and as the outstanding first director of the Public Health Laboratory Service, that he will be best remembered.

Graham Selby Wilson was educated at Epsom College, taking his degree at King's College, London University. Here his first interest in the biochemical aspects of physiology were awakened in 1912, especially the work of Abderhalden in Germany, so he decided a good knowledge of German would help his studies and he spent two holidays staying with German families. War began in 1914, so he had to qualify quickly. He studied pathology at Charing Cross Hospital, London, and won several coveted awards. It was here, too, that he first met Professor W.W. Topley. When Wilson solved a research problem Topley had set him, it led to his findings being published in the *Lancet*, the first of his many articles in that learned journal.

On qualifying in 1916, Wilson joined the Royal Army Medical Corps and served in it until 1920, the first two years being in India.

After the war, although offered more remunerative posts, he joined Professor Topley's Institute of Pathology and moved with it from Charing Cross Hospital to Manchester University, then back to the University of London in 1927, where he became reader in bacteriology. It was two years later that the first edition of *The Principles of Bacteriology and Immunity* was published. This work, the "bacteriologists' bible", was written with Topley, whom he knew for 25 years in all and for whom he had the greatest admiration. Wilson's knowledge of German was useful as the first edition was largely based on French and German bacteriology of the last quarter of the nineteenth century.

"Topley and Wilson" became the standard work for generations of students. With a succession of co-authors as it progressed, it reached its seventh edition (with Sir Ashley Miles) in 1984. In two substantial volumes, it is widely regarded as the finest reference book on bacteriology written in any language. Included in it are many personal judgements and stimulating ideas, which raise it above the more normal, comparatively tedious, sitting-on-the-fence reference works, but all available evidence is quoted and the reader is always left to draw his or her own conclusions.

In 1930 Wilson became the professor of bacteriology at the London School of Hygiene and Tropical Medicine, a branch of the University of London, and he held this post from 1930 to 1947. During this time, for a period of three years, he was also honorary physician to King George VI.

At the start of World War II a national laboratory service was planned as a defence against bacteriological warfare. This became the Public Health Laboratory Service and several people were nominated as director. Topley was committed elsewhere, and two other nominees were killed in an air raid, so it was unanimously decided to "send for Graham". Wilson, or "G.S." as he was known, was appointed and held the post until he retired in 1963.

His was the first guiding hand and inspiration behind the laboratory. His principal aim was to make it effective in studying epidemics and communicable diseases, and how best to identify, control and prevent them. He tried hard to make the service live up to Topley's initial ideals. "What would Topley have done in this situation?" was a question he often asked, and his answer was the guide to his behaviour.

Incorporated in the laboratory's methods was a freedom of strategy, tactics and action which allowed maximum efficiency. It was admired at home and abroad, and its method of studying epidemics was remarkably efficient because of its determined freedom from "committee-ridden bureaucracy". England and Wales provided a sufficiently compact area for such research, and Sir Graham attracted many fine scientists to the service. A stream of important publications resulted from their work.

His own research concentrated on tuberculosis, brucellosis and the hygiene of milk, but equally important was his success in stimulating the staff he recruited for the laboratories under his control (36 in 1948). He took a personal interest in all their work, visiting them regularly, by bicycle if possible. They soon acquired his confidence in the great importance of the service. Perhaps, in retrospect, his faith made him extend too much, for the laboratories grew to number 63 by 1969, and the resources were not adequate when spread so thinly, nor was his highly personal method of running the service as effective over so wide a range.

As a research collaborator he was outstanding, and he was also a superb editor. Friends and colleagues sometimes found him unpredictable in that he was innately shy, but capable of sudden openness. But he was not remote. He did have a stubborn streak, so that once persuaded to adopt a particular position, he was not easy to shift from it. In general, he had the air of an effective schoolmaster. But with it he was a perfectionist, scrupulously honest, but ruthless in the promotion of the Public Health Laboratory Service.

He received many honours, including his knighthood in 1962, and he was awarded a fellowship of the Royal Society in 1978. When he retired from the directorship of the laboratory at the age of 65, he returned to an honorary lecturership in bacteriology at the London School of Hygiene and Tropical Medicine. This he retained for another eleven years. Even after that he remained quietly studying at the school, updating "Topley and Wilson", carrying on voluminous correspondence and working on another book, this time a study of early bacteriologists.

Wilson was a keen cyclist nearly all his life, and celebrated his birthday with a 100-mile ride until well into his eighties. When a road accident forced him to give up his bicycle, he took to walking instead, and in his last years became equally keen on that. He loved fine wine and good food, was a very good gardener and a loyal and devoted member of the Church of England. A gentleman of unusual character and complete integrity.

Born Graham Selby Wilson. **Father** Clergyman. **Marriage** Mary Joyce Ayrton (died, 1976). **Children** Two sons. **Education** Epsom College; King's College, London; Charing Cross Hospital, London, MB, BS; MD, Diploma in Public Health, London. **Military service** Specialist in bacteriology Royal Army Medical Corps, 1916–20; captain, Royal Army Medical Corps, Special Reserve. **Career** Demonstrator in bacteriology, Charing Cross Hospital Medical School, 1919–20; lecturer in bacteriology, University of Manchester, 1923–27; reader in bacteriology, University of London, 1927–30; professor of bacteriology as applied to hygiene, London School of Hygiene and Tropical Medicine, 1930–47; William Julius Fellowship, University of London, 1939; director, Public Health Laboratory Service, 1941–63; honorary physician to King George VI, 1944–46; Milroy Lecturer, Royal College of Physicians, 1948;

honorary lecturer, Department of Bacteriology and Immunology, London School of Hygiene and Tropical Medicine, 1964–70. **Related activities** Member of several committees on tuberculosis, poliomyelitis and other infectious diseases. **Offices and memberships** Council member, Royal College of Physicians, 1938–40. **Awards and honours** Governors' Clinical Gold Medal, Charing Cross Hospital; Gold Medal, University of London; Weber-Parkes Prize, Royal College of Physicians, 1942; honorary fellow: American Public Health Association, 1953, Royal Society of Health, 1960, Royal College of Physicians, 1971, Royal Society of Medicine, 1971, Royal Society of Pathologists, 1972, London School of Hygiene and Tropical Medicine, 1976; Bisset Hawkins Medal, Royal College of Physicians, 1956; Marjory Stephenson Memorial Prize, 1959; Stewart Prize, 1960; knighted, 1962; Czechoslovak Medical Society, Jan Evangelista Purkyne, 1963; Buchanan Medal, Royal Society, 1967; Harben Gold Medal, 1970; Jenner Memorial Medal, 1975; LLD, Glasgow University; fellow, Royal Society, 1978. **Publications** (with Professor W.W.C. Topley and Sir Ashley Miles) *The Principles of Bacteriology and Immunity*, 1929, sixth edition, 1975, seventh edition (with Dr M.T. Parker), 1984; (with others) *The Bacteriological Grading of Milk*, 1935; *The Pasteurization of Milk*, 1942; *The Hazards of Immunization*, 1967; *The Brown Animal Sanatory Institution*, 1979; also contributed many articles on bacteriology to scientific periodicals. **Cause of death** Undisclosed, at age 91.

MAY

JAMES ANGLETON

American Intelligence Officer
***Born* Boise, Idaho, 1917**
***Died* Washington, DC, 11 May 1987**

James Jesus Angleton was one of the most important and controversial figures in the American intelligence "community" for 20 years. As founding director of the Central Intelligence Agency's counter-intelligence department, he was responsible for many complex operations designed to detect and expose "anti-American" agents and their activities, both at home and abroad. His single-minded pursuit of this task and his uncompromising methods excited considerable criticism from within the CIA and eventually led to his resignation, amid allegations of extravagance and even illegal activities.

His early life was spent in Europe as well as the US. Born in the Midwest in 1917 (the year of the Communist Revolution in Russia), he spent a lot of time either in England, attending Malvern College School, or in Italy, where his father worked for the National Cash Register Company. The culture and romance of the Old World encouraged the artistic side of his intellect. He roomed with the poet Reed Whittemore while at Yale, and the two of them founded a literary magazine. Writing and reading poetry remained a passion throughout his life, especially the complex, erudite work of T. S. Eliot and the unusual, awkward style of e.e. cummings. The dense, convoluted writings of James Joyce also fascinated him, causing some at the CIA to compare his department with the impenetrable world of Joyce's novels.

It was through a Yale professor that Angleton joined the Office of Strategic Services (OSS) during World War II. He directed agents operating against the Nazis and then went to Italy to help the Italians resist Russian-sponsored communists. He was given credit for preventing a communist rise to power in Italy, which made him a highly valued member of the new intelligence service that evolved out of the OSS in the post-war years—the CIA.

Back in the United States, his growing expertise in Soviet matters led him to specialize in KGB operations. The Soviet Union was now perceived as the main threat to American security and, therefore, the main object of attention for the CIA. Angleton believed that effective action required comprehensive knowledge. He built up a massive library of files on Soviet operations and agents, earning a reputation for his dogged, thorough enquiries.

In 1954 he was invited to set up a counter-intelligence department within the CIA. Amid a strong atmosphere of suspicion and fear of Russian intentions, he pursued Soviet agents in the

US and elsewhere. At the same time he used links forged at the time of the war to handle the CIA's delicate relationship with Mossad, the Israeli intelligence service. His wide powers and responsibilities provoked some bitter hostility from certain other high-ranking personnel at Langley.

Among the major episodes in which Angleton was involved were the acquisition of Khrushchev's secret denunciation of Stalin in 1956, the exposure of Kim Philby, the British journalist who spied for Russia, and the defections of Ivan Golitsin and Yuri Nosenko. The latter of these two Soviet agents was interrogated for more than three years. His denial that the KGB were behind President Kennedy's assassination in 1963 (as Angelton believed) raised doubts about Angleton's theories of vast KGB plots on a global scale. When Angleton put forward the suggestion that hostilities between Russia and China in the 1960s were a ruse designed to fool Western governments, this was taken as further proof of his paranoia.

Increasingly, Angleton's attention was directed inward, at American citizens and agents. In the "wilderness of mirrors" in which he operated it was possible to see plots and deceptions everywhere. He was one of the few senior figures who took seriously the allegations that Sir Roger Hollis, head of Britain's secret service, MI5, was a Soviet agent. He used his sweeping power at the CIA to remove anyone even remotely suspected of working for the Soviets, often without explanation of why they were under suspicion, thus arousing great resentment from his colleagues.

In the early 1970s matters began to come to a head. William Colby, a rival since the OSS days, became executive director of the CIA and challenged the established order. Angleton was charged with exceeding his authority in investigating anti-war activists and organizations in the US. His methods, especially the vast amounts of information he insisted on compiling, were held to be a waste of resources and of little use. One operation in particular, the opening of selected correspondence between people in the US and the Soviet Union, was condemned as illegal, violating a criminal law statute, although he considered it to be invaluable in his counter-intelligence work.

Angleton was criticized and rebuked without being removed, but in 1974, when Colby was made director of the CIA, he resigned. He retired from the agency amid a confused atmosphere of distrust and allegations of misconduct, especially during the Nixon administration. He did, however, receive the agency's highest award, the Distinguished Intelligence Medal, in recognition of his work. The nature of counter-intelligence had changed, but the foundations which James Angleton had laid in the 1950s and 1960s remained of the utmost significance.

Born James Jesus Angleton. **Marriage** Cicely d'Autremont. **Children** One son, Charles, and two daughters. **Education** Malvern College, England; Yale University, 1939–41. **Career** Joined Office of Strategic Services (forerunner of Central Intelligence Agency), directing agents in Italy operating against Germany, 1943; remained in Italy after war (as member of CIA after its founding in 1947) helping Italian counter-intelligence's work against Italian Communist Party; founder and director of counter-intelligence unit of CIA, 1954–74; resigned after public disclosure of his responsibility for massive CIA programme involving the opening of US private mail, 1974. **Awards and honours** Distinguished Intelligence Medal, 1975. **Cause of death** Lung cancer, at age 69.

JOHN I. H. BAUR

American Art Scholar and Curator

***Born* Woodbridge, Connecticut, 9 August 1909**

***Died* Manhattan, New York, 15 May 1987**

"He has never been bitten by the painting bug," a *New York Times* reporter once stated in a profile of John Baur. "In fact, he came close to failing a course in drawing at Yale." Add to those statements the fact that Baur graduated from Yale with a degree in English and intended to teach at a boys' school, and one wonders how it was that he came to be a leading scholar/curator in the field of American art.

The answer can be found in, of all odd factors, the American Depression. When Baur received his BA from Yale in 1932, there were no teaching jobs to be had. Thus, when Yale offered him an art history scholarship, he took it—even though prior to that time, his only experience with the subject had been an introductory art history course. Under the tutelage of two professors, however, Henri Focillon and Marcel Arbert, the young English student was soon engrossed in his second field of study and took his master's degree in art history in 1934. Two years of teaching followed, but by that time Baur's interests in lecturing had waned. In 1936 he took a position as curator of paintings and sculpture at the Brooklyn Museum in New York, where he began to specialize in the acquisition of American art. Just as his career had been determined by economics, so too was Baur's speciality: the Brooklyn's funds were modest at best and, at the time, American paintings were relatively inexpensive—Baur was able to purchase a Winslow Homer watercolour, for example, for around just $2000.

The war interrupted Baur's career for a short time in 1944, when he joined the army, yet his art interests remained unchanged. Before being discharged the following year, he helped organize an exhibition of soldiers' art at the National Gallery in Washington, DC.

Back at the Brooklyn, Baur's work continued in much the usual fashion, until several years later, when Library of Congress officials asked him to contribute some material for a series on American civilization. The subject matter was, of course, a survey of twentieth-century art, and the result was Baur's first book, *Revolution and Tradition in Modern American Art*. The work received good reviews; Alfred Frankenstein of the *Saturday Review of Literature* called it "a model of lucidity, simplicity, and comprehensiveness". While working on the book, Baur became associated with one of the leading authorities on American art, Lloyd Goodrich (q.v.), the associate director of the Whitney Museum of American Art, which was also located in New York City. By 1952 Baur himself had become a curator at the Whitney.

Established in 1930, the Whitney Museum was the country's first to be dedicated exclusively to American art. Initially, its goal had been to acquire American works from all centuries, but it was evident that this was not financially viable, so by 1949 the museum was concentrating on twentieth-century works. When John Baur joined it, the Whitney was located in a Greenwich Village brownstone; two years later, it moved to another site on West 54th Street, where the number of visitors rose from 70,000 to 270,000 annually. Not long afterwards it was clear that even larger premises had to be found. Baur, who had become associate director by 1958, was chosen to head the fund-raising campaign designed to build a museum suitable for the Whitney's needs. The drive, plan and construction of the new building lasted eight years, during which time Baur worked closely with the project's architects. The resulting five-storey "inverted ziggurat" of granite opened in 1966 and quickly became one of the most talked-about art buildings in the city. "Like Wright's Guggenheim or Stone's Huntington Hartford Museum," wrote Jane H. Kay of the *Christian Science Monitor*, "the Whitney sets itself off—at long last—as a place with an identity."

With its open, spacious galleries and its movable walls and lighting, the new Whitney provided an ideal setting for exhibitions. At its opening Baur stated that, while keeping to its primary purpose of focusing on living American artists, the Whitney would now be able to collect earlier works "...to provide," he said, "a kind of introduction and background" for contemporary movements. In addition to organizing the direction of its collections, Baur played a key role in developing many areas of the Whitney during the 1960s, including its educational and video and film programmes. Thus, it came as no surprise to anyone in the art world when he was appointed director of the Whitney in 1968, a post he retained until 1974.

The brown-haired, green-eyed curator was, by all accounts, a quiet man who shunned the limelight, yet he also possessed an aptitude for hard work, writing a number of volumes behind the scenes. Monographs on artists such as Eastman Johnson, John Quidor and William Zorach, and books such as *Nature in Abstraction* and *American Painting in the Nineteenth Century* were just some of his projects. He also edited books on art and was a regular contributor to art journals such as *Art in America* and *ArtNews*.

Unlike many of his colleagues in the field, John Baur was "not the sort of man who gets himself talked about" in as far as personal flamboyancy was concerned. He did, however, earn a great deal of respect, as Flora Whitney Biddle, chairman of the Whitney Museum, maintained: "He was a man of tremendous integrity and loyalty to the Whitney," she said, "and wonderful to work with. His great seriousness of purpose was accompanied by a delightful sense of humour. He was a very whole human being and had a rich life."

Born John Ireland Howe Baur. **Parents** Paul V.C., professor of archaeology, and Susan (Whiting) Baur. **Marriage** Louise Weld Chase, curator, 1938. **Children** Arthur, Susan and Jean. **Education** Yale University, BA, 1932, MA, 1934. **Military service** Infantry private, US Army, 1944; technical sergeant, Special Services, 1945. **Career** Supervisor of education, Brooklyn Museum, 1934–36; curator of paintings and sculpture, Brookyln Museum, 1936–52; curator, Whitney Museum of American Art, New York City, 1952–58, associate director, 1958–68, director, 1968–74, director emeritus, 1974–87. **Related activities** Visiting lecturer in American art, Yale University, 1950–51. **Offices and memberships** Member: Association of Art Museum Directors, Museums Council of New York City, Colby College Art Museum advisory board, Museum of American Folk Art advisory committee, editorial boards of the *Magazine of Art* and *Art in America*; trustee, Council of Arts, Westchester, 1968–69; chairman, Skowhegan School of Painting and Sculpture advisory committee; consulting director, Terra Museum of American Art, Chicago. **Publications** *John Quidor*, 1942; *Eastman Johnson*, 1946; *Theodore Robinson*, 1946; *Revolution and Tradition in Modern American Art*, 1951; *Loren MacIver and I. Rice Pereira*, 1953; *American Painting in the Nineteenth Century*, 1953; *ABC for Collectors of Contemporary Art*, 1954; *George Grosz*, 1954; (editor and contributor) *The New Decade: Thirty-five American Painters and Sculptors*, 1955; *Charles Burchfield*, 1956; *Bradley Walker Tomlin*, 1957; *Nature in Abstraction*, 1958; (editor and contributor) *New Art in America: Fifty Painters of the Twentieth Century*, 1958; (with Lloyd Goodrich) *Four American Expressionists: Doris Caesar, Chaim Gross, Karl Knaths and Abraham Rattner*, 1959; *William Zorach*, 1959; *Philip Evergood*, 1960; *Balcombe Greene*, 1961; (with Lloyd Goodrich) *American Art of Our Century*, 1961; *Bernard Reder*, 1961; contributor of numerous articles to journals, including *ArtNews, Art in America* and the *Magazine of Art*. **Cause of death** Heart failure, at age 77.

COLIN BLAKELY

British Actor

***Born* Bangor, Northern Ireland, 23 September 1930**

***Died* London, England, 7 May 1987**

Colin Blakely, in common with many great actors, had an unlikely background for the theatre and came to it by merest chance. He learned his art as he went.

He was born into a comfortable Ulster Protestant family and, as the eldest son, was destined to take over the family business, a sports shop. Indeed, after completing his education in Yorkshire and a year with the Slazenger sports firm, he returned to his homeland to do just that. For nine years he managed the Athletic Stores Ltd. in Belfast. However, he met, as young men tend to do, a girl he rather liked who was involved in an amateur operatic society. Blakely joined too as a means to pursuing her acquaintance and, shaking with fright, he performed the part of a singing waiter in *Annie Get Your Gun*. The relationship failed to prosper but the acting did. Within a year he was offered work with the Children's Touring Theatre company, so he quit the family firm and embarked on a career which never faltered.

Within a few months he was a member of the Group Theatre, Belfast, where he remained for two years and appeared in Dick McCardle's *Master of the House*. In 1959 he joined the English Stage Company (ESC) based at London's Royal Court Theatre in Sloane Square, which was then known as the home of the "angry young men" and where John Osborne's *Look Back in Anger* and *The Entertainer*, with Laurence Olivier, had recently been shown. Blakely counted himself fortunate to have had the right sort of looks and voice for the time. "They were looking for my kind of face," he said, adding, "My awkward provincial accent was considered not only allowable but desirable. It was the time of starkness and realism. Wesker and Arden were on the go. I looked like a rough fella who's fallen over a few times in his life. I was just lucky enough to come in at the right time."

His first performance for the ESC was in *Cock-a-Doodle-Dandy*. This was rapidly followed by parts in *Serjeant Musgrave's Dance*, *The Naming of Murderer's Rock* and *A Moon for the Misbegotten*. In 1961 he joined the Royal Shakespeare Company at Stratford where he played in *Richard III*, *As You Like It* and *Othello*. After returning to London he found himself in regular and constant work both at the Royal Court and then with the newly formed National Theatre Company at the Old Vic in Waterloo. Here he was given roles in *Hamlet*, *The Recruiting Officer* and the title role in *Philoctetes*. He stayed with the National until 1968, developing his stagecraft and his range—he was excellent in both comedy and serious roles.

The 1970s brought Blakely some of his best work and immense critical success. Now acknowledged as one of the leading actors of his generation, he was being offered very major parts. Back with the RSC he played in Pinter's *Old Times* followed, in 1972, by the ferocious challenge of *Titus Andronicus* in both Stratford and London. He played it with unrestrained force and it was an entire contrast to his next role—that of the mild husband of Claire Bloom's *Hedda Gabler*. This was followed by Captain Shotover in Shaw's *Heartbreak House* and continued with a run of West End plays by English writers, such as Alan Bennett and Alan Ayckbourn, and the American Arthur Miller.

The end of 1975 brought him possibly the most demanding part of his entire career. A play by an ex-journalist, Barry Collins, from the northern town of Halifax was put on at the Royal Court. It was a monologue called *Judgement* and involved Blakely being alone on stage for two and a half hours without an interval. He played a Russian officer, in prison at the end of World War II, the only survivor of a group reduced by cannibalism. The survivor is on trial for his life and the audience are the judges, witnessing a harrowing tale and being forced to examine their own capacities for mercy and understanding.

Discussing his approach to the role, Blakely admitted that the 27,000 words to be acted during the performance was a great test of sheer physical stamina. "I have to push myself through levels of exhaustion when the body weakens and the concentration goes," he said. "I take the audience with me. They get rattled and tired too. We're all in it together, a shared thing. It's a minefield of a play. My mouth dries up. I've put in two places where I can drink a glass of water. It's a bit unfair on the poor bloody audience, who can't even get out for a glass of gin!" *Judgement* was a *tour de force* and one of Blakely's finest performances.

He also worked in films and appeared regularly on television. One of his best remembered appearances was as Jesus Christ in Dennis Potter's *The Son of Man*. In this he portrayed Christ as a tough and real man, rather than a remote aesthete—although with Blakely it would have been difficult to do anything else. Looking, as he himself admitted, like a stevedore, he was nonetheless ready and capable of taking on the ultimate challenges acting has to offer.

In the theatre he continued working in such highly acclaimed plays as Shaffer's *Equus*, Ayckbourn's *Just Between Ourselves* and Bennett's *Enjoy*. His last performance, in 1986, was in *A Chorus of Disappointment*, which demonstrated that his sense of comedy was as great as ever, although his particular strength lay in parts needing authority and passion. He was confidently expected to become a major King Lear. Sadly, this was not to be. He had developed leukaemia and died within a few months of diagnosis. Blakely, however, had an immensely fulfilling and successful career and brought something new and unique to the British theatre. Those who were privileged to see him will long hold his work as a standard for comparison.

Born Colin George Edward Blakely. **Parents** Victor Charles and Dorothy Margaret Ashmore (Rodgers) Blakely. **Marriage** Margaret Whiting, an actress and singer, 1961. **Children** Three sons. **Education** Sedburgh School, Yorkshire, England. **Career** Tennis racket stringer, football stitcher, Slazenger's, Yorkshire; manager, Athletic Stores Ltd., Belfast, 1948–57; actor, 1958 onwards; associated with the English Stage Company, 1959, the Royal Shakespeare Company, 1961, 1971–73, and the National Theatre, 1963–65, 1965–68, 1975; also appeared on television and in films. **Offices and memberships** Equity Association; Screen Actors' Guild. **Stage** *Master of the House*, Ulster Group, Belfast, 1958; *Cock-a-Doodle-Dandy*, 1959; *The Bonfire*, 1958; *Serjeant Musgrave's Dance*, 1959; *The Naming of Murderer's Rock*, 1959, 1960; *Moon for the Misbegotten*, 1960; *Over the Bridge*, 1960; *Dreaming Bandsmen*, 1960; *Richard III*, 1961; *As You Like It*, 1961; *Othello*, 1961; *Box the Cox*, 1961; *The Fire-Raisers*, 1961; *A Midsummer Night's Dream*, 1962; *Hamlet*, 1963–65; *The Recruiting Officer*, 1963–65; *Andorra*, 1963–65; *Philoctetes*, 1963–65; *The Royal Hunt of the Sun*, 1963–65; *The Crucible* 1963–65; *Hobson's Choice*, 1963–65; *Mother Courage and Her Children*, 1963–65; *Love for Love*, 1963–65; *Juno and the Paycock*, 1965–68; *Oedipus Rex*, 1965–68; *Uncle Vanya*, 1970; *Old Times*, 1971; *Titus Andronicus*, 1972, 1973; *A Doll's House*, 1973; *The Illumination of Mr Shannon* (also director), 1973; *Cries from Casement*, 1973; *Section Nine*, 1973; *Heartbreak House*, 1975; *Judgement*, 1975; *Equus*, 1976; *Just Between Ourselves*, 1977; *Filumena*, 1977; *Semmelweiss*, 1978; *Enjoy*, 1980; *All My Sons*, 1981; *Lovers Dancing*, 1983; *One for the Road*, 1985; *Chorus of Disapproval*, 1986. **Major tours** Toured Moscow and Berlin with the National Theatre Company, 1965. **Films** *The Little World of Don Camillo*, 1952; *Saturday Night and Sunday Morning*, 1960; *This Sporting Life*, 1963; *Charlie Bubbles*, 1968; *Decline and Fall*, 1968; *The Private Life of Sherlock Holmes*, 1970; *The National Health*, 1973; *Murder on the Orient Express*, 1974; *It Shouldn't Happen to a Vet*, 1976; *The Pink Panther Strikes Again*, 1976; *Equus*, 1977; *Dogs of War*, 1980; *Nijinsky*, 1980; *Evil Under the Sun*, 1982. **Television** (includes) *When Silver Drinks*; *Son of Man*, 1969; *Donkey's*

Years; *Peer Gynt*; *Antony and Cleopatra*; *The Red Monarch*; *Landscape*, 1983; *The Father*, 1985; *The Dumb Waiter*, 1985; *Operation Julie*, 1985; *The Birthday Party*, 1986; *Drums Along Balmoral Drive*, 1986; *Paradise Postponed*, 1986. **Cause of death** Leukaemia, at age 56.

PAUL BUTTERFIELD

American Musician

***Born* Chicago, Illinois, 17 December 1942**

***Died* Los Angeles, California, 4 May 1987**

Paul Butterfield was a White American who made his name playing and singing an essentially Black form of American music, the blues. He was one of a number of young, college-educated enthusiasts who, in the mid-1960s, gained through the growing rock audience the mass acceptance for the blues that until then had been denied to the Black musicians who had created it. In doing so he and his contemporaries brought a new musical integrity to rock, as well as opening up new directions for the music to take.

Widely recognized in this new climate of musicianship as the finest blues harmonica player around, Butterfield was unusual in that he had "paid his dues" as a teenager in the late 1950s playing alongside the giants of the music, long before there existed rock critics to ask whether White men could sing the blues.

The blues, together with many of its most talented exponents, had made its way up from the rural South in the years immediately following World War II to settle in Chicago, where Paul Butterfield was born and raised. And his teen years coincided with the golden era of Chicago blues, a hard-edged, distinctly urban sound that he absorbed in the clubs and bars on the tough South Side of the city.

Young Paul had the great good fortune for an aspiring bluesman of being able to sit in with the leading blues musicians of the day, most notably Muddy Waters, then at his peak. The Waters' band featured Little Walter on harmonica ("mouth harp" in blues parlance), and it was his full-tilt style that Butterfield always credited as his greatest influence.

The Paul Butterfield Blues Band, formed in 1963, was the first of the White-American blues groups. Contemporary music-business wisdom still pigeonholed the blues as folk music, which was how the Butterfield band came to play the 1965 Newport Folk Festival in Rhode Island, breaking its taboo on electrically amplified music. This put Butterfield at centre stage for one of the most celebrated moments in pop music history: the band backed Bob Dylan on the day at Newport that the folk sage controversially "went electric" and crossed over into the rock camp.

Dylan's fateful step generated new artistic aspirations for rock, and the Butterfield band, with the talented Mike Bloomfield and Elvin Bishop on guitars, was ready to exploit them. It had signed with the independent Elektra record label, and from 1965 on cut a series of innovative albums.

At first Butterfield stuck with the Waters-influenced rhythm-and-blues sound which the group had been honing in the clubs of Chicago and New York, and which still sounded fresh to rock ears. The group then stayed ahead of the pack by incorporating new influences, notably from India on the *East–West* album, and then funkier soul sounds with the use of a Memphis-style horn section.

But it was other bands, picking up on these new ideas after Butterfield had discarded them, that seemed to be selling records. By the decade's end, both Bloomfield and Bishop had departed in search of the stardom that was now available to loud virtuoso guitarists. The band remained a popular concert attraction, playing both the 1967 Monterey Pop Festival in California and the massive Woodstock Festival in 1969, as well as touring continuously across the United States and Europe.

The music was moving on, however, and neither Butterfield's image nor his chosen instrument was suited to the era of the rock superstar. He finally dissolved the Blues Band in 1972, and the 1970s saw him engaged on a series of one-shot projects. These included the soundtrack for the movie *Steelyard Blues*, concert tours in various all-star line-ups, and occasional TV appearances alongside other blues veterans. After a bout of serious illness in 1980, he played and recorded only intermittently.

In 1969 Paul Butterfield had joined other blues-influenced rock musicians to play on Muddy Waters' *Fathers and Sons* album. It was a fitting tribute to his own roots, which were those of American music itself, and which he always sought to nourish.

Born Paul Butterfield. **Children** Two sons, Lee and Gabriel. **Education** Studied the flute, University of Chicago, *circa* 1960. **Career** Musician, playing flute, guitar, harmonica and piano, 1958–80; started by sitting in with Muddy Waters' group in local gigs, Chicago, 1958; leader, blues sextet, Butterfield Blues Band, with Elvin Bishop, Mike Bloomfield, Jerome Arnold, Sam Lay, later Billy Davenport, Mark Naftalin, 1964–72; recorded with own band, Elektra label, Chicago, 1965–68; Carnegie Hall début, 1968; recorded with Muddy Waters, Chess label, Chicago, 1969; freelanced, 1970s onwards; also leader, short-lived band, Better Days, early 1970s; recorded for Asylum label, Chicago, 1973; recorded with Better Days group, Warner Brothers-Bearsville label, Chicago, 1974–75; formed short-lived Danko-Butterfield Band with Rick Danko, late 1970s; performed rarely after serious illness, 1980–81. **Major appearances** Muddy Waters' group, Chicago, 1958; at Chicago clubs, including Blue Flame Club, Pepper's Lounge, 1015 Club, early to mid-1960s; at Big John's Club, Chicago, 1963; with Butterfield Blues Band, 1964; Sylvio's Lounge, Chicago, 1964; Big John's Club, Chicago, 1964–66; Turks Club, Chicago, 1964; The Village Gate, New York City, 1965; Cafe a-Go-Go, New York City, 1965; Mooncusser, Martha's Vineyard, Massachusetts, 1965; Club 47, Cambridge, Massachusetts, 1965; The Unicorn, Boston, Massachusetts, 1965; Town Hall, New York City, 1965; Butterfield Blues Band, Newport Folk Festival, Newport, Rhode Island, 1965; Whiskey a-Go-Go, Los Angeles, 1965–66; Chessmate, Detroit, 1966; Rheingold Central Park Music Festival, New York City, 1966–68; Monterey Jazz Festival, Monterey, California, 1966; International Pop Festival, Monterey, 1967; New Penelope, Montreal, Canada, 1967; La Cave, Cleveland, Ohio, 1967; Cheetah, Chicago, 1968; The Eagles, Seattle, 1968; Civic Auditorium, Santa Monica, California, 1968; Fillmore East, New York City, 1968–70; Carnegie Hall, New York City, 1968; Cafe a-Go-Go, New York City, 1968; Miami Pop Festival, Miami, Florida, 1968; Shrine Exposition Hall, Los Angeles, 1968; Kinetic Playground, Chicago, 1969; The Eagles, Seattle, 1969; toured Denmark, 1969; Fillmore West, San Francisco, 1969; Woodstock Music and Art Fair, Bethel, New York City, 1969; with Muddy Waters, Super Cosmic Joy-Scout Jamboree, Chicago, 1969; The Pavilion, New York City, 1969; with Janis Joplin, Madison Square Garden, New York City, 1969; Ravinia Park, Chicago, 1969; Civic Center, Baltimore, 1969; Auditorium Theater, Chicago, 1970; Lennie's, Boston, 1970; Washington University, St Louis, 1970; Festival for Peace, Shea Stadium, New York City, 1970; Midway Stadium, St Paul, Minnesota, 1971; Sunset Series Concert, Boston, 1972; Tulagi's Boulder, Colorado, 1973; Civic Center, Santa Monica, California, 1973; Cowtown Ballroom, Kansas City, 1973; with Better Days group, Capitol Theater, Passaic, New Jersey, 1973; on *Bonnie Raitt and Paul Butterfield*

Show, PBS-TV, 1974; on *Midnight Special*, NBC-TV, 1974; Winterland Auditorium, San Francisco, 1976; Jed's Inn, New Orleans, 1976; on *Saturday Night*, NBC-TV, 1977; with Foghat group, The Palladium, New York City, 1977; on *Don Kirshner's Rock Concert*, NBC-TV, 1978; toured with Levon Helm's RCO All-Stars, late 1970s. **Songs** "In My Own Dream", "Little Piece of Dying"; "You Can Run But You Can't Hide". **Films** *You Are What You Eat*, 1968; *Steelyard Blues* (recording only), 1973; *The Last Waltz*, 1978. **Recordings** (include) *The Paul Butterfield Blues Band*, 1965; *The Resurrection of Pigboy Crabshaw*, 1968; *Live*, 1970; *Golden Butter*, 1972. **Cause of death** Undisclosed, at age 44.

WILLIAM CASEY

American Lawyer and Public Servant

Born **New York City, New York, 13 March 1913**

Died **Washington, DC, 6 May 1987**

William (Bill) Casey was a survivor if ever there was one, holding various offices throughout his long career in Democrat and Republican administrations alike, though himself a supporter of the Republican Party, and reaching the zenith of his career as director of the Central Intelligence Agency with, uniquely for a holder of that position, a seat in the Reagan Cabinet. His last days as director were darkened by the Iran–Contra scandal, of which Casey denied all advance knowledge—an almost incredible assertion for a man in his position. But, throughout, Casey's career was a controversial one, and the brain tumour which killed him perhaps saved him—and the administration he served—from unwelcome disclosures.

Casey's early days followed the typical path of the American government official, from graduation at a minor university to night school in law while working by day—in his case as a New York City investigator. He was admitted to the New York Bar in 1938 and was already making his name as a corporation lawyer when the attack on Pearl Harbor brought the United States into World War II. He was soon commissioned into the US Naval Reserve and was then appointed assistant to William J. ("Wild Bill") Donovan, founder of the Office of Strategic Services—the forerunner of the CIA. From then on Casey had found his niche. For two years he worked in intelligence operations in Europe as head of the OSS's secret intelligence branch there, doing much to coordinate French Resistance forces in support of the Allied Normandy invasion. By the end of the war Casey knew a very great deal about clandestine warfare.

For a time he continued to employ his wide knowledge of Western Europe as an adviser to the Marshall Plan, but by the beginning of the 1950s he was back in legal practice in New York, as well as lecturing at New York University and writing several successful textbooks on law and economics. Casey specialized in tax law and amassed a considerable personal fortune. A staunch Roman Catholic, he worked in a voluntary capacity for several Catholic charities and was also a trustee of his old university.

Casey had always taken a keen interest in politics and ran unsuccessfully for Congress in 1966. As a stalwart Republican and a close associate, both professionally and politically, of Richard Nixon, he was inevitably drawn back into public service when Nixon became president. From 1969 to 1971 he was a member of the advisory council of the Arms Control and Disarmament Agency, and was also chairman of a nationwide citizens committee in support of the president's policy in Vietnam. In 1971 Nixon appointed him chairman of the Securities and Exchange Commission, a position which enabled him to exploit his financial and legal expertise to carry out a number of important reforms. A further year was spent as under-secretary of state for economic affairs, followed by two years as chairman of the Export–Import Bank. In 1976 he was appointed by President Ford to serve on his Foreign Intelligence Advisory Board, and throughout the Carter presidency he was a member of the Task Force on Equality and Venture Capital of the Small Business Administration.

Casey's skill in financial management and his ability to inspire confidence in colleagues led Ronald Reagan to appoint him as his campaign manager early in 1979, though the two men barely knew each other. Reagan's hunch paid off, and from then on the two worked closely together. Casey was rewarded for his campaign success by being appointed director of the CIA, with a seat in the Cabinet and thus an important influence on presidential policy. Despite what some of his younger CIA staff regarded as an old-fashioned approach, Casey raised the CIA to the peak of its influence on national policy—perhaps to too great an influence if its part in the Iran–Contra affair had ever been revealed. Casey inevitably carried this cloak-and-dagger reputation into the rest of his public dealings; he was an inveterate opponent of Congress whose influence he distrusted, despite his earlier attempt to join it. He managed to survive an investigation into his personal financial dealings, and Congress failed to find him "unfit to serve" in his CIA appointment. Throughout his term of office until his resignation through ill-health earlier in 1987, he was a close friend and confidant of President Reagan, whose presidential success undoubtedly owed much to his behind-the-scenes activity.

Born William Joseph Casey. **Parents** William Joseph and Blanche (La Vigne) Casey. **Marriage** Sophia Kurz, 1941. **Children** Bernadette. **Education** Fordham University, BS, 1934; St John's University Law School, New York City, LLB, 1937; Catholic University of America. **Military service** US Navy Reserve, World War II; attached to Office of Strategic Services (OSS) as assistant to director William J. Donovan, 1943; based in London and appointed head of OSS Secret Intelligence branch running agents into Germany and occupied Europe, 1943–45. **Career** Admitted to New York Bar, 1938 (and to Bars of US District Court for the Southern and Eastern Districts of New York, 1954, and District of Columbia, 1961); concentrated on corporation law; moved to Washington to work on war contracts, 1941–43; special counsel to US Senate small business committee, 1947–48; served as Marshall Plan adviser, 1948, before returning to private practice, specializing in tax law; lecturer on tax law: New York University, 1948–62, and Practicing Law Institute, 1950–62; partner, Hall, Casey, Dickler and Howley, New York, and Scribner, Hall, Casey, Thornburg and Thompson, Washington, 1957–71; chair, Securities and Exchange Commission, 1971–73; under-secretary of state for economic affairs, 1973; president, Export–Import Bank, 1974–75; counsel to New York City and Washington law firm, Rogers and Wells; member, Foreign Intelligence Advisory Board, 1976; member, Task Force on Equity and Venture Capital of the Small Business Administration, 1976–80; presidential campaign manager to Ronald Reagan, 1980; director, Central Intelligence Agency (CIA), 1981–87. **Other activities** Founder, Sophia and William Casey Foundation, grant-giving body to high school students. **Offices and memberships** Chair, board of editors of Research Institute of America, Washington, DC, 1938–49, and Institute for Business Planning, 1954–70; trustee, Fordham University, 1966–71; president and chair, Long Island Association of Commerce and Industry, 1968–71; member, General Advisory Committee on Arms Control and Disarmament, 1969–71; member, Presidential Task Force on International Development, 1969–70; president, International Rescue Committee, 1970–71; member, Advisory Committee, Notre Dame Law School; chair, Bishop's Committee for the Laity for Catholic Charities; member: American Bar Association; Nassau County Bar Association; Association of the Bar of the City of

New York. **Awards and honours** European Theater of Operations Bronze Star; William J. Donovan Award; honorary degrees: Fordham University, St John's University, New York Law School, Molloy College, Adelphi University, Polytechnic Institute of New York. **Publications** (with Jacob K. Lasser) *Tax Planning on Excess Profits*, 1951; (with Lasser) *Tax Sheltered Investments*, 1952; (with Lasser) *Tax Shelter for the Family*, 1953; (with Lasser) *Executive Pay Plans, 1952–53*, 1953; *Estate Planning Book*, 1956; *Lawyers' Desk Book*, 1965; *Forms of Business Agreements*, 1966; *How to Raise Money to Make Money*, 1966; *Accounting Desk Book*, 1967; *How to Build and Preserve Executive Wealth*, 1967; (with others) *How Federal Tax Angles Multiply Real Estate Profits*, 1968; *Encyclopedia of Mutual Fund Investment Planning for Security and Profit*, 1968; *Where and How the War Was Fought: An Armchair Tour of the American Revolution*, 1976. **Cause of death** Brain tumour, at age 74.

WILBUR COHEN

American Government Official

***Born* Milwaukee, Wisconsin, 10 June 1913**

***Died* Seoul, South Korea, 18 May 1987**

Wilbur Cohen did more to help the poor, the sick and the aged than almost any other American citizen. Whether working in government or universities, he exercised a profound effect upon the political scene by his grim determination to improve the social welfare of millions of Americans. He played a vital part in the formulation of every important piece of social legislation put forward by presidents Kennedy and Johnson under the "New Frontier" and "Great Society" label. But he will probably be remembered best for the leading role he played in the introduction of Medicare. His 25 years' experience of politics made him the government's chief strategist and expert in the social welfare field. He never abused that power or his wealth of knowledge, always keen to follow the democratic procedures and listen to the people who would be affected by new legislation. Cohen once said: "The day I have to give an order is the day I'm not an effective leader. When you can't persuade someone of something, you may still be the boss, but you're no longer the leader."

Born and raised in Milwaukee, the son of a Scottish-born store owner, Cohen always identified himself as a Jew although he once explained: "I am not an institutionalist with regard to religion. I have a strong belief that deeds are more important than words, although I believe all the Biblical injunctions that teach one to love his neighbour."

At school Cohen showed a flair for editing the school magazine, and at university, where he studied economics, he worked on the editorial board of the *Daily Cardinal*. When graduating, in 1934, Cohen named several people who had influenced his choice of career. One of these was Professor Edwin E. Witte who, in the year Cohen graduated, went to Washington to become executive director of President Franklin D. Roosevelt's Cabinet Committee on Economic Security. Cohen went with him as an assistant but he also worked with other pioneers of public welfare legislation and saw through the Social Security Act, which was passed in 1935. He went on to be the first employee of what became known as the Social Security Administration. During the 20 years that he worked there, first as technical adviser and then director of the bureau of research and statistics, he helped put into effect a mass of legislation to assist the sick, the blind, the aged and the permanently disabled; to widen benefits for domestics, farm-workers and the self-employed; and to help dependent children and children of the totally disabled. During the Korean War he introduced the idea of employers giving their workers health insurance benefits instead of wage increases. This led to the expansion of Blue Cross and other voluntary health insurance programmes.

By the time he withdrew from government in 1956 to become professor of public welfare administration at the University of Michigan, his skills, knowledge and determination were renowned. A former senator, Paul Douglas, once remarked that "A social security expert is a man with Wilbur Cohen's telephone number." While at Michigan University Cohen continued to act as adviser on government programmes and to testify before congressional committees. He was a great believer in academics and public officials meeting to discuss and formulate policies together; only then could legislation be sensible and effective.

His major work with the government in these years was concerned with the aged. Normally an amiable and gregarious man, he took on an almost religious zeal and an often aggressive manner when defending social welfare policies. A Democratic representative, Cecil R. King of California, called him: "One of those government officials ready to risk their reputations and their professions to do their duty as they see it."

Cohen was brought back to government by President John F. Kennedy who appointed him assistant secretary of health, education and welfare. This was a position he only narrowly achieved—by a margin of one vote—due to his reputation as a radical social reformer. The next four years were halcyon days for Cohen, who was able to put into effect around 65 major pieces of legislation involving civil rights, child welfare, mental health, aid to education, veterans' benefits, medical benefits for American Indians, consumer protection, and vocational training and rehabilitation. But the times were not yet liberal enough for his real passion, Medicare. This major piece of legislation, which he had worked towards for at least 15 years, only became a reality (as the Social Security Amendments Act) after President Lyndon Johnson's landslide victory in 1964. Another part of the act provided Medicaid through which people who are too poor to pay for health care can be financially helped from state and federal funds. Cohen always denied that this was "socialized medicine" which he thought was inappropriate for the United States. What he really wanted was the "establishment of a single, nationwide programme", believing that only through education and provision of better job opportunities could the enormously complex issue of poverty begin to be solved. "The cycle of poverty that is repeated from one generation to the next may ultimately be broken down through pre-school education, improved vocational training and instruction in family planning."

In April 1965 President Johnson appointed Cohen under-secretary of health, education and welfare, and when John Gardner resigned as secretary of the department in 1968 he recommended that Cohen take his place. When he was sworn into office President Johnson praised him for his "devotion to public service". Later he and Johnson completely reorganized federal health services and Cohen became principal federal official on health policy. Within a new interdepartmental health policy council he could assess the nation's health needs and propose policies.

With the end of President Johnson's term in office, Cohen returned to the University of Michigan as professor and dean of its School of Education. Here too he continued his tireless campaign for social justice. He was greatly disturbed by President Jimmy Carter's welfare cutbacks which he called "tragic, unsound, immoral, unjustified". To counter these measures he brought together a very effective coalition of organizations representing the elderly, workers, Blacks, the poor, students and the churches. This was named Save Our Society (SOS) and managed to block many of the proposed cutbacks.

Cohen spent much of his later life campaigning to improve conditions for the elderly. He never ceased this work, and even though he suffered two heart attacks, he continued to work a 60-hour week teaching, writing and lecturing. Indeed, on the night he died he was preparing a speech for a conference on "Ageing and Welfare for the Aged".

People will remember Cohen as an extraordinarily effective lobbyist and expert on social reforms. According to an article in the *Medical World News*, "Those who have worked with Cohen regard him as one of the most coolly efficient, pragmatic and persistent innovators Washington has ever seen...one who knows his way through the capital's jungle of politics and bureaucracy. And they have an abiding respect for the breadth and precision of his technical and sociological experiences." He has been called one of the major "action-intellectuals" who exercised enormous political influence.

Born Wilbur Joseph Cohen. **Parents** Aaron, store owner, and Bessie (Rubenstein) Cohen. **Marriage** Eloise Bittel, 1938. **Children** Christopher, Bruce, Stuart. **Education** University of Wisconsin, PhB, 1934. **Career** Research assistant, Cabinet Committee on Economic Security, 1934–35; technical adviser, US Social Security Administration, 1935–53; director, Division of Research and Statistics, 1953–56; professor of public welfare administration, University of Michigan, 1956–61; assistant secretary for legislation, US Department of Health, Education and Welfare, 1961–64, under-secretary, 1965–68, secretary, 1968; professor of education and dean of School of Education, 1969–79; Sid W. Richardson Professor of Public Affairs, Lyndon B. Johnson School of Public Affairs, University of Texas at Austin, 1980–83, professor of public affairs, 1983 onwards. **Related activities** Consultant on ageing to US Senate Committee on Labor and Public Welfare, 1956–57, 1959; consultant on ageing to United Nations, 1956–57; visiting professor, University of California at Los Angeles, 1957; chairman, advisory council of Retirement Advisors Incorporated, 1958–60, 1969–70; member, Advisory Council on Public Assistance, 1959; consultant, White House Conference on Ageing, 1959–60; member, house of delegates, Council on Social Work Education, 1959–62, 1974–76; chairman, President's Task Force on Health and Social Security, 1960; lecturer, Catholic University of America, 1961–62; vice-president, National Conference on Social Welfare, 1962, president 1969–70; chairman, President's Committee on Mental Retardation, 1968, President's Committee on Population and Family Planning, 1968, Advisory Committee on Highway Safety Research, 1969, Save Our Security, 1977 onwards; member, National Committee on Social Security, 1978–81; represented US government at international conferences on social security, social work and labour. **Other activities** Trustee, J.F. Kennedy Center for the Performing Arts, 1968; board of governors, Haifa University, 1971 onwards. **Offices and memberships** Member: Royal Society of Health of Great Britain, American Economic Association, American Association of Higher Education, Institute of Medicine of National Academy of Sciences, American Public Welfare Association (director, 1962–65, president, 1975–76), American Public Health Association, National Association of Social Workers, Industrial Relations Research Association (member of executive board, 1969–72); co-chairman, Institute of Gerontology, 1969. **Awards** John Lendrum Mitchell Award, University of Wisconsin, 1934; Distinguished Service Award, US Department of Health, Education and Welfare, 1956; Group Health Association Award, 1956; Florina Lasker Award, National Conference on Social Welfare, 1961; Terry Award, American Public Welfare Association, 1961; Blanche Ittelson Award, New York Social Work Recruiting Commission, 1962; awards from National Association of Social Workers, National Association for Mentally Retarded Children and Association of Physical Medicine, all 1965; Bronfman Public Health Prize, 1967; Rockefeller Public Service Award, 1967; Murray-Green Award, 1968; Wilbur Award, Golden Ring Council of Senior Citizens, 1968; Volunteers of America Annual Service Award, 1968; Forand Award, National Council of Senior Citizens, 1969; Jane Addams-Hull House Award, 1975; Merrill-Palmer Award, 1975; International Association for Social Security Award, 1979. **Honorary degrees** LHD: Adelphi College, 1962, State University, 1970,

Cleveland State University, 1970; LLD: University of Wisconsin, 1966, Yeshiva University, 1967, Brandeis University, 1968, Kenyon College, University of Detroit, 1969, Michigan State University, 1975; University of Louisville, DSS, 1969; Florida State University, DH, 1972; Central Michigan University; Eastern Michigan University; Northern Michigan University. **Publications** *Unemployment Insurance and Agricultural Labor in Great Britain*, 1940; (editor) *War and Post-War Security*, 1942; (editor, with William Haber) *Readings in Social Security*, 1948; *Retirement Policies Under Social Security*, 1957; (editor, with William Haber) *Social Security: Programs, Problems and Policies*, 1961; (with Sydney E. Bernard) *The Prevention and Reduction of Dependency*, 1961; (contributor) *Income and Welfare in the United States*, 1962; *The Program Against Poverty* (Sidney A. Teller lecture), 1964; (editor, with Sar A. Levitan and Robert J. Lampman) *Towards Freedom From Want*, 1968; *Health in America: The Role of the Federal Government in Bringing High Quality Health Care to All American People*, 1968; (author of introduction) *Toward a Social Report*, 1970; (with others) *Social Security: The First Thirty-five Years*, 1971; (with Milton Friedman) *Social Security: Universal or Selective?*, 1972; (contributor) *Welfare Reform: Why?*, 1976; (with Charles F. Westoff) *Demographic Dynamics in America*, 1977; (with W. Joseph Hefferman) *Welfare Reform: State and Federal Roles*, 1983; also author of other survey reports and government publications; contributor to *Encyclopaedia Britannica* and to social welfare, education and health journals. **Cause of death** Heart failure, at age 73.

GIOACHINO COLOMBO

Italian Racing Car Designer and Engineer
Born **Legnano, Italy, 1903**
Died **Italy, circa 10 May 1987**

Even to the uninitiated, the names Ferrari, Alfa-Romeo and Maserati conjure images of sleek, super-fast—and preferably red—racing cars. For an Italian to have designed a Grand Prix winner for one of these teams would have been sufficient reason to regard him as a national hero; to have designed winners for *all three* manufacturers would demand near canonization; such was the magnificent achievement of Gioachino Colombo.

Born in Legnano in Northern Italy, Colombo joined Alfa-Romeo in Milan in 1924 as a design draughtsman. Working initially as assistant to the great Vittorio Jano, his first task was to draw up many of the details of the Tipo P2—a car driven by the likes of Antonio Ascari and Guiseppe Campari—that was destined to become the dominant racer of the last two years of the 2-litre formula, 1924 and 1925, and which remained competitive until 1930, the same year that Achille Varzi rounded off the P2's career with a popular win on the famous Targa Florio circuit in Sicily.

Colombo's relationship with Jano was a close and fruitful one that was to last for over ten years. Indeed, this was possibly the most successful decade in the company's illustrious career, for it saw such legendary machines as the 1750 and 2300 sports cars, the Monza, and what turned out to be the supreme Grand Prix car of the traditional school, the Tipo B (or P3), flow from their design studio.

By 1934, however, a new threat to Alfa's supremacy was taking shape in the form of Mercedes Benz and Auto Union. The sheer speed and technological ingenuity of the German teams was to prove too much even for the vastly experienced Alfa-Romeo engineers. In 1938, in a last-ditch attempt to get on level terms with the Germans, the company built three cars for the new 3-litre formula. Equipped with straight-eight, 12- and 16- cylinder engines (308, 312 and 316), they made little impression, but in the meantime, at the behest of Enzo Ferrari (then in charge of Alfa's racing programme), the most successful of all Grand Prix Alfas was unwittingly being created.

Due to their inability to break the German grip on the Grand Prix circuits, Italian constructors were increasingly attracted by the 1.5-litre *voiturette* class of racing. Colombo was dispatched to Ferrari's workshop in Modena to design an Alfa-Romeo contender, and there the first Alfettas, Tipo 158, were built. Colombo's design was uncomplicated, elegant and well-balanced. Its engine was a straight-eight with a single supercharger, and although raced on ten occasions by the works team, the development programme outlined by Colombo was temporarily halted by the outbreak of World War II. While Colombo spent his time designing aero- and other engines that were destined for the war effort, the precious cars were moved from one secret hiding place to another, eventually spending the last two years of hostilities secreted in a barn in the village of Melzo.

With the resumption of peace, Colombo was somewhat shocked to hear that his services were no longer required by the Milanese hierarchy—a decision obviously influenced by his vociferous allegiance to Mussolini. Help was at hand, however, in the shape of Enzo Ferrari and his newly-established factory in Modena. Ferrari had long admired 12-cylinder engines and decided to build such cars; and, having worked with Gioachino Colombo on the two Alfa Bimotores of 1935 and the Alfetta of 1938, he offered him the position of designer in 1946. That same year Ferrari announced that he would embark on an ambitious programme of Grands Prix, sports, and road cars all powered by a V12 engine. In fact, this made sense, for it meant that with only minor modifications and (obviously) some detuning, the Grand Prix engine—as designed by Colombo—could be used for three types of car.

Many considered Ferrari's choice of engine audacious, presumptuous and even disastrous (given the pre-war potential of the Alfa 158), and they made their feelings known to Ferrari in no uncertain terms. He, however, swept their objections aside and was later to write: "Every engine has teething troubles at the beginning, but I never for once doubted that we would succeed, first and foremost because I had complete faith in the talents of its designer." Colombo produced a 1.5-litre V12, unusual at that time not only for its multiplicity of tiny cylinders, but in their use of greater bore than stroke. The car in which the engine was installed was designated Type 125.

Perhaps realizing that the decision to release Colombo was a rash one, it was not long before Alfa-Romeo poached him back to continue the development of the Tipo 158. In 1947 the 158 automatically became a Grand Prix racer under the new regulations. The car had won its first race (at Leghorn in 1938) as a *voiturette* and—albeit under the designation 159—it won its last race as a Grand Prix car 13 years later. As a Grand Prix car it had an unbroken run of 26 victories. Colombo remained with Alfa for barely two years before Enzo Ferrari lured him back to Modena again. There was thus a period—1950—when the only two real contenders for the World Championship, the 158/9 Alfa and the Ferrari Type 125, were from the pen of the same designer.

Towards the end of 1952, Colombo changed allegiance yet again—to Maserati. There he designed the A6GCM and the A6GCS sports cars, and in 1953 completely reworked the straight-six A6GCM engine in order to make it eligible for the new 2.5-litre Grand Prix formula which was to come into effect in 1954. The engine was installed in a much-improved chassis and was initially designated Type 6C–2500. This car became much more famous—indeed, immortal—as the Maserati 250F. Fangio won the first two Grands Prix of 1954 in the 250F, but his departure from the team was a considerable factor against Maserati winning another championship race in that season. The 250F was a no-nonsense Grand Prix car, classic in its proportions and workmanlike in its mechanical make-up. As a result, the model gained justifiable favour among leading independent entrants. In 1957 Fangio returned to lead the Maserati team, winning four Grands Prix and the Constructors' Championship for the marque.

It will come as no surprise to learn that Colombo did not stay too long at Maserati; in fact, he left before the 250F made its race début. The internal politics that are still a destructive force within Grand Prix racing inevitably took their toll on Colombo's patience. One can only assume that, like many brilliant designers, he was at his best working for himself rather than others, so he decided to set up his own design consultancy. Sadly, one of his first freelance commissions was the abortive Bugatti Type 251, with its transversely laid out straight-eight engine. It was also his last car design.

Although he was never to return to the sphere of Grand Prix racing—he spent his time thereafter working on Count Agusta's successful team of MV racing motorcycles—Gioachino Colombo's name will always be linked with those halcyon pre- and post-war years when Italian racing teams reigned supreme.

Born Gioachino Colombo. **Career** Design draughtsman, Alfa-Romeo, 1924; worked on Grand Prix sports cars, including the Tipo P2, the Monza and the Tipo B, 1920s–30s; also worked on Bimotores, 1935, and the Alfetta Tipo 158, 1938; joined Ferrari as designer, 1946; designed Type 125; returned to Alfa-Romeo to develop Tipo 158, 1947; returned to Ferrari and continued development of Type 125, 1948–52; moved to Maserati and designed A6GCM and A6GCS sports cars, 1952; created Type 6C-2500, later known as Maserati 250F, 1954; set up own design consultancy, but produced only the Bugatti Type 251, which proved unsuccessful, 1955; designed MV racing motorcycles for Count Agusta's team, 1955 onwards. **Cause of death** Undisclosed, at age 84.

CATHRYN DAMON

American Actress

***Born* Seattle, Washington, 11 September 1931**

***Died* Los Angeles, California, 4 May 1987**

To most people, Cathryn Damon was simply Mary Campbell, understanding wife and all-forgiving mother on the 1970s TV series *Soap*—a comic and controversial satire of daytime drama. In 1980 her performance won her an Emmy award as best actress in a comedy series.

But for Damon, a dedicated and driven professional, the role of Mary Campbell was merely a pleasant plateau in an enduring theatrical quest. After three seasons with *Soap*, she was eager to shake off a comfortable stereotype for new dramatic challenges. "Success on TV can be a double-edged sword," she told an interviewer in 1980. "The very thing that has brought you fame and fortune may be something you may not enjoy for a long time. You can feel trapped in one part. Variety is everything for an actor."

From the beginning, variety and professional discipline were important priorities for the strawberry-blonde, blue-eyed lady from Seattle. By the age of 16 she had decided on a career in dance, and moved to New York to study with the Ballet Repertory Company. She then spent two years as a soloist with the Metropolitan Opera Ballet, and from there turned her sights to Broadway. In later years, though her love of acting overtook her dancing ambitions, and successive film and TV contracts drew her west to Los Angeles, dance remained an absorbing passion, and New York her beloved adopted home.

At the height of her Broadway career, Damon appeared in a host of musical and dramatic productions. Among them were *Flora*, *The Red Menace*, *The Prisoner of Second Avenue*, *Foxy*, *The Last of the Red-Hot Lovers* and *Passion*. Off-Broadway shows included the revival of *The Boys from Syracuse*, *The Secret Life of Walter Mitty* and *Siamese Connections* at the New York Shakespeare Festival; *LA Under Siege* at the Buffalo Arena; and *The Dining Room* at the Kennedy Center in Washington, DC. She also played the starring role in the Pulitzer Prize-winning play *The Effect of Gamma Rays on Man-in-the-Moon Marigolds*, the part of Hester, the magistrate, in the Los Angeles Company production of *Equus*, and Miss Lucy in a recent revival of Tennessee Williams's *Sweet Bird of Youth*. During the summers she acted in travelling performances of Shaw, Chekhov and Shakespeare, ever striving to perfect her craft. Her last Broadway performance before beginning work with *Soap* was in André Serban's acclaimed production of *The Cherry Orchard* at Lincoln Center.

Even before the first episode of *Soap* was aired in 1977, ABC-TV received some 32,000 letters protesting its sensitive and controversial content. The 30-minute programme, a zany spoof which the network contended represented a major "revolution" in TV comedy, was peppered with references to adultery, incest and homosexuality, and rife with ludicrous and improbable occurrences. Burt Campbell, Mary's husband (played by actor Richard Mulligan), was once cloned by aliens from outer space. One son was embroiled in organized crime, and a second was an avowed bisexual. From 1977 until 1981, when the series ceased production, the valiant, long-suffering Mary Campbell smiled and fretted her way through situation after situation, gaining millions of sympathetic and loyal fans.

Though *Soap's* loosely structured format left room for endless variety in plot and situation, Damon soon longed for new challenges. Halfway through the filming of *Soap*, she was presented with one, in the form of her first film, *The Walls Came Tumbling Down*, produced by an all-female cast and crew. She embraced her controversial part with characteristic enthusiasm. "It is a heavy dramatic role dealing with abortion during the 1950s," she told an interviewer. "One of the reasons I took it was to get away from the 'understanding mother' image I have gained on *Soap*."

For Damon, moving from the small screen into feature films was the ultimate challenge. After the completion of *Soap*, she continued to appear in TV serials, including *Matlock*, *Mike Hammer*, *Murder, She Wrote* and *Webster*, but also featured in a handful of full-length motion pictures. In addition to playing a major part in the TV movie *Not in Front of the Children*, she appeared in two others, *How to Beat the High Cost of Living* and *She's Having a Baby*.

When asked in a 1980 interview why she had turned from TV to film work, Damon replied, "Why not? I have done everything else." Then, reflecting on the course of her career and her hopes for the future, added, "All I need now is for everything I have ever done to come together in one dream role. I guess I will always be a dancer at heart. Maybe I'll come full circle someday and be able to make a film about dancing. That would be the ultimate role for me."

Sadly, Cathryn Damon did not have time to develop her large-screen career, nor to appear in the dance film she had envisaged. But she did continue to dance in her spare time, combining this enduring interest with a number of other hobbies, including needlepoint, antique collecting, attending auctions and—though she was a compulsive dieter—gourmet cooking. She continued to work in film and television until her final illness incapacitated her.

Born Cathryn Damon. **Mother** Cathryn M. Springer. **Career** Dancer, Ballet Repertory Company; soloist, Metropolitain Opera Ballet; turned to acting, late 1940s; film début, 1946; Broadway début, 1954; star of TV series *Soap*, 1977–81. **Awards and honours** Emmy award for best actress in a comedy series, 1980. **Stage** (includes) *LA Under Siege*; *Siamese Connections*; *The Prodigal*; *By the Beautiful Sea*; *The Vamp*; *Shinbone Alley*; *A Family Affair*; *Come Summer*; *A Place for Polly*; *The Boys from Syracuse*; *Down by the River Where the Water Lilies Are Disfigured Every Day*; *L'Histoire du Soldat*; *The Effect of Gamma Rays on Man-in-the-Moon Marigolds*; *The Last of the Red Hot Lovers*; *Flora the Red Menace*; *Foxy*; *The Prisoner of Second Avenue*; *Sweet Bird of Youth*; *Equus*; *Criss-Crossing*; *Show Me Where the Good Times Are*; *Your Own Thing*; *The Secret Life of Walter Mitty*; *The Cherry Orchard*; *A View From the Bridge*; *The Dining Room*; *Passion*. **Films** (include) *The Walls Came Tumbling Down; How to Beat the High Cost of Living*, 1980; *She's Having a Baby*. **Television** (includes) *Not in Front of the Children*; *Matlock*; *The Love Boat*; *Murder, She Wrote*; *Mike Hammer*; *Webster*; *Soap*, 1977–81. **Cause of death** Cancer, at age 56.

RICHARD ELLMANN

American Critic, Biographer and Translator

***Born* Detroit, Michigan, 15 March 1918**

***Died* Oxford, England, 13 May 1987**

"The notion is sometimes advanced nowadays that a poet's development can be traced in terms of the literary tradition alone," Richard Ellmann says in his critical biography of W.B. Yeats. "But whether we would or not, we shall be driven to answer many questions which seem at first to be beyond the literary pale: what was his family like? where was he reared and educated? why did he form certain friendships and not others? what effect did his long frustrated love affair have upon him?" Ellmann was adamant that biographies avoid fashionable intellectual lenses for viewing writers. He considered them to be a distraction from seeing the person as a whole, and his method instead tried to combine the interpretive and the biographical. He was wholly successful at doing this, and the books he wrote on Yeats, James Joyce and Oscar Wilde are landmarks in the field of literary biography. *James Joyce* won him the National Book Award for 1960 and was called "one of the great literary biographies of this century". He was praised for his enthusiasm and exactness in writing. Anthony Burgess once remarked "his books...never fail to stimulate, instruct, amuse and...reawaken a sleeping belief in the glory of making literature".

Ellmann was something of a black sheep in his family. His father and two brothers went into the law, but he "made the eccentric choice of teaching English literature". As a senior at Yale University he learned about Yeats; and after receiving his degree in 1941 decided to pursue a dissertation on the Irish poet "even though Yeats...seemed at that time a subject suspiciously and brazenly modern". His work was interrupted by his war service, including the Seabees, the navy and the Office of Strategic Services. These assignments took him to London, and then to Dublin where he met Yeats's widow. She encouraged him to return after the war, and he spent 1946 and 1947 at Trinity College preparing *The Man and the Masks*.

This first work breaks with contemporary practice by bridging the purely critical and the factual biography. Ellmann does not search for one grand determining principle—the method of Edel,

Sartre, or Erikson. Instead he suggests that Yeats's poems must be "judged in terms of their private origins". The book was based on some 50,000 pages of unpublished manuscripts, an amount that would have overwhelmed most scholars. It is still regarded as an indispensable source for Yeats studies of any sort. As a follow-up, Ellmann focused more specifically "with his poetry more in its own terms". While he was Briggs-Copeland assistant professor of English composition at Harvard University he prepared *The Identity of Yeats*, which is "largely a work of explication of Yeats's 'dialectical' principle". According to *Contemporary Literary Critics*:

> The basic principle of Yeats's poetry, which Ellmann calls a principle of "affirmative capability", demands that "the more sharply we represent the contradictions of life, the more urgently we invoke a pattern of the reality which must transcend or include them". As for Yeats's significance now, Ellmann maintains that the principle of affirmation is "particularly suited to a time when there is no agreement over ultimate questions, when we are not even sure exactly what we think on matters that are so crucial and yet so obscure".

Ellmann finally concludes that Yeats's answer to those questions stands for "profane perfection of mankind", which he presents with "such power and richness that Eliot's religion...[seems] pale and infertile by comparison".

Out of his study of Yeats came the kernel of his ground-breaking work on Joyce. "One day in 1947," Ellmann recalled, "I asked Mrs Yeats in Dublin about the notorious first meeting of Yeats with Joyce, which occurred in 1902." Her recounting of their meeting led to an article on the relations of the two writers in 1951. The ensuing biography tried "to present his life with a little of the density of actual experience, yet always with at least covert reference to certain ruling passions and to his writing". The result was a narrative of over 300,000 words, 60 pages of references, and over 2000 citations of testimony. His work is still considered, 30 years after its publication, the essential biography of Joyce. Critic Frank Kermode opined that "it assembles a great mass of published and unpublished material....[Mr Ellmann] fixed Joyce's image for a generation."

Joyce's great contribution, according to the book, is his celebration of the "ordinary":

> Whether we know it or not, Joyce's court, like Dante's or Tolstoy's, is always in session. The initial and determining act of judgement in his work is the justification of the commonplace. Other writers had laboured tediously to portray it, but no one really knew what the commonplace was until Joyce had written....Joyce was the first to endow an urban man of no importance with heroic consequence....Bloom is a humble vessel elected to bear and transmit unimpeached the best qualities of the mind. Joyce's discovery, so humanistic that he would have been embarrassed to disclose it out of context, was that the ordinary is the extraordinary.

Among his other achievements is an interesting compilation of essays, edited with Charles Feidelson Jr, which traces the intellectual roots of twentieth-century literature, called *The Modern Tradition*. *Eminent Domain* studies with clarity, grace and wit the social and literary interactions between Yeats and a number of his eminent contemporaries. It is the kind of sophisticated literary history which Harold Bloom was to call for in *The Anxiety of Influence*. "As a young man," reads the article in *Literary Criticism*, "Yeats helped himself to what he needed from Oscar Wilde; later on, Pound, Eliot and Joyce took what they needed from Yeats. As Eliot puts it, rather more bluntly, lesser poets borrow, great poets steal—usually for purposes entirely their own."

Between 1970 and 1984 Ellmann was Goldsmiths' Professor of English literature at Oxford. During this time he researched and wrote, at considerable financial sacrifice, a popular biography of Wilde. He took up his post at Oxford to do the research, forcing him to relinquish his chair at

Yale. The book was completed, though not published, shortly before his death. It was very well received, though some complained that he was excessively credulous over certain myths surrounding Wilde's downfall and death.

Ellmann's work as a biographer, editor and translator has given English letters a rare contribution to this field. Sir William Hayton remembers him as a man with "a delightful personality and whose lectures were a unique experience".

Born Richard David Ellmann. **Parents** James I., a lawyer, and Jeanette (Barsook) Ellmann. **Marriage** Mary Donahue, a writer, 1949. **Children** Stephen, Maud, Lucy. **Education** Yale University, New Haven, Connecticut, BA, 1939, MA, 1941, PhD, 1947; Trinity College Dublin, BLitt, 1947. **Military service** US Navy and Office of Strategic Services, London, 1943–45. **Career** Instructor, Harvard University, Cambridge, Massachusetts, 1942–43, 1947–48, Briggs-Copeland assistant professor of English composition, 1948–51; Northwestern University, Evanstown, Illinois, professor of English, 1951–63, Franklin Bliss Snyder Professor, 1963–68; professor of English, Yale University, New Haven, Connecticut, 1968–70; Goldsmiths' Professor of English literature, from 1970; Oxford University, England, from 1970; fellow, New College, Oxford, from 1970; extraordinary fellow, Wolfson College, 1984. **Related activities** Frederick Ives Carpenter Visiting Professor, University of Chicago, 1959, 1968, 1975–77; visiting professor, Emory University, 1978–81, Woodruff Professor, 1982 onwards. **Other activities** Member, editorial committee, Publications of the Modern Language Association, 1968–73; member, United States/United Kingdom Educational Commission, 1970 onwards. **Awards and honours** Rockefeller Foundation Fellow in humanities, 1946–47; Guggenheim Fellow, 1950, 1957–58, 1970; grantee, American Philosophical Society and Modern Language Association of America, 1953; *Kenyon Review* Fellowship in criticism, 1955–56; fellow, Indiana University, School of Letters, 1956–60, senior fellow, 1967–71; National Book Award in non-fiction, Friends of Literature Award in biography for *James Joyce*, 1960; Thormond Monsen Award of Society of Midland Authors for *James Joyce*, 1960; American Scholar, 1968–74; fellow, Royal Society of Literature; fellow, American Academy and Institute; MA, Oxford University, 1970; DLitt: National University of Ireland, 1975, Emory University, 1979, Boston College, 1979, Northwestern University, 1980; research grant, National Endowment for the Humanities, 1977; PhD, University of Gothenburg, Sweden, 1978; fellow, British Academy, 1979; DHL, Rochester, 1981. **Publications** *Yeats: The Man and the Masks*, London, 1948, reprinted, 1978; *The Identity of Yeats*, Oxford, 1951, second edition, 1964; *James Joyce*, Oxford, 1959; (with E.D.H. Johnson and Alfred L. Bus) *Wilde and the Nineties: An Essay and an Exhibition*, ed. Charles Ryskamp, Princeton, 1967; *Eminent Domain: Yeats among Wilde, Joyce, Pound, Eliot and Auden*, Oxford, 1967; *Ulysses on the Liffey*, Oxford, 1972; *Golden Codgers: Biographical Speculations*, Oxford, 1973; *The Consciousness of Joyce*, Oxford, 1977; *James Joyce's Hundredth Birthday*, 1982; *Oscar Wilde at Oxford*, 1984; *W.B. Yeats's Second Puberty*, 1985; *Oscar Wilde*, 1987. **Edited works** *Selected Writing of Henri Michaux* (also translator), 1952; Stanislaus Joyce, *My Brother's Keeper: James Joyce's Early Years*, 1958; (with others) *English Masterpieces*, second edition, two volumes, 1958; Arthur Symons, *The Symbolist Movement in Literature*, 1958; (with Ellsworth Mason) *The Critical Writings of James Joyce*, 1959; *Edwardians and Late Victorians*, Columbia, 1961; James Joyce, *A Portrait of the Artist as a Young Man*, 1964; (with Charles Feidelson Jr) *The Modern Tradition: Backgrounds of Modern Literature*, Oxford, 1965; *Letters of James Joyce*, volumes II and III, 1966; James Joyce, *Giacomo Joyce*, 1968; James Joyce, *Ulysses*, London, 1969; Oscar Wilde, *The Artist as Critic: Critical Writings of Oscar Wilde*, New York, 1969; *Oscar Wilde: A Collection of Critical Essays*, 1969; (with Robert O'Clair) *Norton Anthology of Modern Poetry*, 1973; *Selected Letters of James Joyce*, 1975; *The New Oxford Book of American Verse*,

Oxford, 1976; (with Robert O'Clair) *Modern Poems: An Introduction to Poetry*, 1976; *Oscar Wilde, The Picture of Dorian Gray and Other Writings*, 1982. **Cause of death** Pneumonia arising from Lou Gehrig's disease, at age 69.

VICTOR FELDMAN

British Jazz Musician and Composer

Born **London, England, 7 April 1934**

Died **Los Angeles, California, 12 May 1987**

Victor Feldman was a trailblazer, one of the first British jazz musicians who managed to cross the Atlantic and make a successful living in the home of jazz. Once there, his own contribution to the music he loved was considerable.

Feldman was a child prodigy. He played the drums by the age of six and first appeared professionally with his two older brothers in the Feldman Trio at the age of seven. He was only eight when his uncle Max, also a drummer, got him a part in an Arthur Askey film (*King Arthur Was a Gentleman*) and barely ten when he played with the Glenn Miller Orchestra, at that time entertaining the American troops in Britain as they waited for D-Day. In his early teens he played in the big bands of Vic Lewis and Ted Heath, and he was only 15 when he toured Switzerland with Ralph Sharon in 1949.

Feldman was undoubtedly a child genius, and it was not long before he had mastered the drums and was looking for new inspiration elsewhere. He had started to learn the piano at the age of nine and he took up the vibes at the age of 14, studying at the London College of Music. His tutor was Carlo Krahmer, who later pointed out that, "I taught him how to play, not what to play", for Feldman was as precocious on vibes as he had been on drums. In 1954, at the age of 20, he was a member of Ronnie Scott's new nine-piece band, a powerhouse of the best of British jazz, but by this time Feldman had outgrown Britain. He decided to try his luck in America.

Feldman emigrated in September 1955 and within months he was playing with the best. A tour with bandleader Woody Herman in 1956–57 was followed by work with clarinettist Buddy DeFranco, a period studying arrangements with Marty Paich, and a two-year gig with the house band at the Lighthouse Club in Los Angeles. By this time he had made his home on the West Coast and only occasionally ventured out on tour, notably in 1960–61 with saxophonist Cannonball Adderley, whose quintet was attracting considerable commercial and artistic success, and in 1962, when he joined Benny Goodman on a US State Department tour of Russia. These tours, however, were the exceptions, for Feldman preferred the more settled life of the session musician, sitting in on numerous Los-Angeles-recorded albums throughout the 1960s.

This choice did not mean that Feldman was unwilling to play live, for in 1963 he got his biggest break. Miles Davis was playing a residency at San Francisco's Black Hawk club and was missing a pianist. Feldman sat in at short notice and was hired for a studio recording session as well. Miles recorded one of Feldman's compositions, "Seven Steps to Heaven", and made it the album's title track, although the version with Feldman was rejected in favour of one recorded later in New York with pianist Herbie Hancock.

Feldman's strengths lay not in being a full-time member of a band but in providing the right melody line or arrangement to the numerous studio sessions he played on. Such was his versatility that as music fashion changed, so did he, moving effortlessly into the field of jazz-rock in the 1970s and 1980s. His work with Steely Dan and Joni Mitchell was as good as any of his more mainstream jazz contributions.

Feldman died at the early age of 53, yet he had been playing professionally for 46 years. At one time in that long life, he had been a member of Peggy Lee's rhythm section alongside drummer Stan Levey. Levey almost wrote Feldman's epitaph in an interview he gave to a British journalist: "I'm not just saying this because I'm here in Britain...but Victor Feldman is one of the greatest things that ever happened to jazz. He is so talented on drums, piano and vibes. You must be proud of him."

Born Victor Stanley Feldman. **Education** London College of Music. **Emigration** Left England for the US, 1955. **Career** Percussionist from a very early age; played mainly piano and vibraphone, mid-1950s onwards; composer and arranger, 1959 onwards; toured and recorded with Cannonball Adderley, 1961–62; toured USSR with Benny Goodman's band, 1962; worked latterly with rock and jazz-rock artists, 1970–87. **Awards and honours** Five magazine awards as Britain's top vibraphone player; voted "New Star on Vibes", *Down Beat* critics' poll, 1958. **Compositions** (include) "Seven Steps to Heaven", recorded by Miles Davis, CS8851 Columbia, 1963. **Recordings** (include) Untitled, LAP5-6 Tempo, 1955; *Victor Feldman in London*, TAP8 Tempo, 1956; *The Arrival of Victor Feldman*, C3549 Cont, 1958; *Merry Olde Soul*, 9366 Riv, 1960–61; *Artful Dodger*, 38 Conc, 1977; *To Chopin with Love*, 8056 PAlt, 1983; *High Visibility*, 208 TBA, 1985; *Contemporary; Interlude*; also made numerous recordings with major jazz artists, including Milt Jackson, Art Tatum, Buddy Rich, Kenny Clarke, Duke Ellington and Miles Davis; percussionist on various rock artists' recordings, 1970–87. **Cause of death** Asthma attack, at age 53.

SIR HUGH FRASER

British Businessman

***Born* Scotland, 18 December 1936**

***Died* Mugdock, Scotland, 5 May 1987**

Sir Hugh Fraser, the British business tycoon, led an eventful business and personal life, dogged by the legacy of a dominantly successful father and the immense wealth he inherited from him. Renunciation of the barony bestowed on his father was his one real attempt to throw off this inheritance. Otherwise his father's shrewd and skilful accumulation of the vast drapery and household merchandising family firm into the House of Fraser, crowned by the renowned London store of Harrods, dominated his life, bringing him at the age of 30 the wealth and power which were to be his undoing.

After a conventional upper-class Scottish education, Hugh Fraser started work in one of his father's shops at the age of 17. This early "shop-floor" experience led many of his staff to expect great things of him. His imaginative approach led to lively changes in the somewhat staid image of the House of Fraser, and, a director by the age of 21 and chairman at 30, Fraser diversified the group's interests quite successfully to become the *Guardian*'s "Young Businessman of the Year" in 1973. From then on, however, his career began to go downhill. His negotiation of the sale of

House of Fraser to Boots Ltd. was blocked by the Monopolies and Mergers Commission. Three years later he was hauled over the coals by a Stock Exchange committee and the Department of Trade for his share dealings in his financial conglomerate Scottish and Universal Investments (SUITS), and later was found guilty in a court in Glasgow of improper dealings in shares and loans.

His proud inheritance dwindled. Large holdings in House of Fraser and SUITS passed to the Lonrho Group, to be followed by the group's long struggle for control of Harrods. At the same time Fraser's almost pathological passion for gambling involved him in losses reputedly of several million pounds. Despite setting up his own company, Allander Holdings, he was never again to be a company chairman.

"I think I've been a fool," he was reported to have said at the time of his Glasgow trial, "but I've learned a lot." But his premature success was to weigh against him; he did not learn his lessons in time. Two unsuccessful marriages drove him more and more to the gambling tables (or was it the other way round?). In any event, he died at a comparatively early age, a lonely and disillusioned man, his one solace his devotion to his family's charitable concerns, notable among them being his purchase of the island of Iona for the National Trust.

Born Hugh Fraser. **Parents** Baron Fraser of Allander and Kate Hutcheon (Lewis) Fraser. **Marriages** 1) Patricia Mary Bowie, 1962 (divorced, 1971); 2) Aileen Ross, an international showjumper, 1973 (divorced, 1982). **Children** Three daughters by first marriage. **Education** St Mary's, Melrose, Scotland; Kelvinside Academy, Scotland. **Career** Worked initially in one of father's department stores, at age of 17; director, House of Fraser, and Harrods Ltd., 1957; chairman: Harrods Ltd, 1966–81, House of Fraser, 1966–1986, Scottish Universal Investments, from 1966; chairman, Sir Hugh & Sir Group, 1982, joint managing director, 1985 onwards. **Related activities** Director: Allander Holdings Limited, Ettinger Brothers (Tailoring) Limited, Fras-air Limited, Glen Gordon Knitwear Limited, International Caledonian Assets Limited, Paisleys Limited, North Cape Textiles Limited, D & S Shirts Limited, Black Bear Limited, Twentieth Century Fashions Limited, Zucker Textiles Limited, Air Charter Scotland Limited, Hebridean Herbals Limited, Caird Retail Limited. **Other activities** Generous supporter of Scottish charities; bought island of Iona for the National Trust. **Offices and memberships** Scottish National Party, 1974 onwards. **Awards and honours** Named Young Businessman of the Year, the *Guardian* newspaper, 1973; honorary doctorate, Stirling University, 1985. **Cause of death** Lung cancer, at age 50.

HERMIONE GINGOLD

British Actress

***Born* London, England, 9 December 1897**

***Died* New York City, New York, 24 May 1987**

Towards the end of her long career, Hermione Gingold played a grandmother in Stephen Sondheim's operetta *A Little Night Music*, both on Broadway and in London's West End. The character, Madame Armfeldt, in her song "Liaisons", recalls a past crowded with incident, and laments the demise of style, skill and craft in the modern age. The words were Sondheim's, but

Hermione Gingold established her position as the high priestess of theatrical camp through her ability to bring an infinite degree of innuendo and *double-entendre* to such lyrics as:

> With a smile, and a will, but with more thought,
> I acquired a chateau extravagantly overstaffed...
> Too many people muddle sex with mere desire,
> And when emotion intervenes the nets descend.
> It should on no account perplex, or worse, inspire,
> It's but a pleasurable means
> To a measurable end...

In her prime, La Gingold (as she was known by camp followers) was one of the sharpest and least inhibited of revue artists and character actresses. A critic once described her as "less of a comedienne than a paroxysm". Her grand, flamboyant style, however, was not entirely the product of her fruitful imagination. Her father was an upper-middle-class Austrian and her mother was a similarly well-stationed Englishwoman. Her immediate lineage was to the courts of both Italy and Austria. Gingold firmly believed in Lady Bracknell's adage—"No woman should ever be quite accurate about her age. It looks so calculating."—and declined to give her year of birth in *Who's Who*. Suffice to say, she was born just before the turn of the century, and through her early study with a governess in France and private schooling in Britain, was on hand to witness the opulence and decadence of the last great years of the royal houses of Europe.

She trained for the theatre under Rosina Filippi and made her début at the age of eleven as a herald in one of Sir Herbert Beerbohm-Tree's productions. In 1912 she played Cassandra in William Poel's legendary production of *Troilus and Cressida* (Edith Evans played Cressida), and Jessica in 1914 in *The Merchant of Venice*, one of the Old Vic's earliest Shakespearean plays.

However, until 1932 she did not make any real impression on the theatrical scene; although she played very worthy parts, they were only intermittent. That season she played a series of roles at the old Gate Theatre, offering an indication of her particular talent for revue. In order to raise funds for the Gate in 1938, she played in *The Gate Revue* in which she scored an enormous personal success. In 1939 the show transferred to the Ambassadors' Theatre in the West End where Gingold went on to enjoy a phenomenal series of personal triumphs in intimate revues throughout the war years: *Sweet and Low*, *Sweeter and Lower* and *Sweetest and Lowest* firmly established her as a major star.

These were the days, however, when the prohibitive power of the Lord Chamberlain to defend and promote "public decency" was still absolute, and the limits within which he could be persuaded to waver were narrow. Hermione Gingold was, of course, a mistress of innuendo whose very appearance excited the blue pencil. In 1949 she appeared with Hermione Baddeley ("the Two Hermiones") in what Hugh Montgomery-Massingberd called "a spectacularly undisciplined revival of Noël Coward's drunken farce *Fallen Angels*...While Miss Baddeley spat bread pellets at the audience, Miss Gingold did unspeakably suggestive things with a table-napkin." Noël Coward was incensed at their antics, but could not put a stop to it because the "Gorgeous Gargoyles" (as Frank Marcus described them) had not changed a single word of the text. As Frederic Raphael recalled in the *Listener* magazine some 40 years later, "Fidelity was never so outrageous or so reluctantly forgiven."

Gingold was one of those spicy performers whose *risqué* repartee operated off-stage as well as on. She never took to the modern fashion of the sad clown, the artist who came to life only in performance. Her offerings were always meant to entertain, almost never infected with malice or spite. Thus, when it was said that a performance by Laurence Olivier had been a *tour de force*, she observed in her most lugubrious tones that Donald Wolfitt in the same role had been "forced to tour". Another classic "Gingold-ism" is the tale of her reply to a young aspiring playwright who had sought her opinion of his script: "My dear boy, in future I advise you never to write anything more ambitious than a grocery list."

In 1951 Gingold was introduced to American audiences in an intimate revue in Massachusetts. The show itself was not such a hit, but she received rave notices, after which John Murray offered her a role in his next Broadway production, which played in 1953. From then on she spent most of her time in the United States, appearing in films, television, straight plays and revues. Her films include *Around the World in 80 Days*, *The Music Man*, *Bell, Book and Candle*, and the outrageously over-hyped *Gigi*. Her performances of "malice in wonderland" meant that she frequently had problems finding a good play, or at least one that could hold her, although she did manage successful runs on Broadway and in the West End with *Oh Dad, Poor Dad, Mama's Hung You in the Closet, and I'm Feelin' So Sad*!

She returned to London in 1969 in what one critic described as a "mediocre extravaganza of espionage", a play called *Highly Confidential*. In 1972 she crashed the auditions for *A Little Night Music* and Harold Prince, the director, told her that she should not bother playing a woman of 74. "But Mr Prince," she replied, "I *am* 74," and went on to deliver the definitive Madame Armfeldt.

Her later successes included *Side by Side by Sondheim*, her touring one-woman show, and her appearances on British radio playing the character Druscilla Doom. Meanwhile, she also continued appearing in films and on television.

Hermione Gingold had what Hugh Montgomery-Massingberd calls "an endearingly individual approach to life". Her interior decoration ranged from an enormous china collection to objects she found by rummaging through other people's dustbins. On one occasion she found a complete set of the *Encyclopaedia Brittanica*, on another, an antique table. Her only comment on her activities was that "A lot of millionaires started in the junk business".

In 1945 Gingold produced a hilarious autobiography, *The World Is Square*, and later, *Sirens Should Be Seen and Not Heard*. She also wrote various articles and short stories. Reading some of her work offers a taste of her inimitable style and wit.

A lasting image of her is a speculative one. She once confessed to an interviewer that she enjoyed smoking little cigars in private and ate sweets "when trouble brews". The picture of *la grande dame* indulging in both these activities while waiting in the star's dressing-room, preparing to do battle with the censors, was probably larger in life than it is in imagination.

Born Hermione Ferdinanda Gingold. **Parents** James, a stockbroker, and Kate Frances (Walter) Gingold. **Marriages** 1) Michael Joseph, a publisher (divorced); 2) Eric Maschwitz, an author (divorced). **Children** Two sons, Leslie and Stephen, by first marriage. **Education** Taught by a governess in France; private schools, London; studied acting under Rosina Filippi. **Career** Revue artist and actress on stage, films, radio and television on both sides of the Atlantic; stage début, the herald in *Pinkie and the Fairies*, London, 1908; US début, *It's About Time*, Brattle Theater group, Cambridge, Massachusetts, 1951; New York début, *John Murray Anderson's Almanac*, Imperial, 1953. **Other activities** Author and columnist; member, board of governors, World Adoption International Fund. **Awards and honours** Donaldson Award for best Broadway actress for *Almanac*, 1954; Golden Globe Award from Hollywood Foreign Press Association for *Gigi*, 1958; citation and medal for promoting friendship and understanding between nations, United Nations. **Stage** *Merry Wives of Windsor*, 1909; *Troilus and Cressida*, 1912; *The Merchant of Venice*, 1914; *If*, 1921; *The Dippers*, 1922; *Little Lord Fauntleroy*, 1931–33; *From Morn to Midnight*, 1931–33; *One More River*, 1931–33; *Hotel Universe*, 1931–33; *I Hate Men*, 1931–33; *Mountebanks*, 1934; *This World of Ours*, 1935; *Spread it Abroad*, 1936; *Laura Garrett*, 1936; *In Theatre Street*, 1937; *The Gate Review*, 1939; *Swinging the Gate*, 1940; *Rise Above It*, 1941; *Sky High*, 1942; *Sweet and Low*, 1943; *Sweeter and Lower*, 1944; *Sweetest and Lowest*, 1946; *Slings and Arrows*, 1948; *Fumed Oak*, 1949; *Fallen Angels*, 1949; *It's About Time*,

1951; *The Sleeping Prince*, 1956; *Sticks and Stones*, US tour, 1956; *Fallen Angels*, US tour, 1957–58; *First Impressions*, 1959; *From A to Z*, 1960; *Abracadabra*, tour, 1960; *Milk and Honey*, 1962; *Oh Dad, Poor Dad...*, 1963; *Dumas and Son*, 1967; *Charley's Aunt*, 1968; *Highly Confidential*, 1969; *A Little Night Music*, 1975; *Side by Side by Sondheim*, 1978. **Films** (include) *Pickwick Papers*, 1952; *Our Girl Friday*, 1953; *The Cautious Amorist*; *Cosh Boy*; *Blackjack*; *Around the World in 80 Days*, 1956; *Gigi*, 1958; *Bell, Book, and Candle*, 1959; *The Naked Edge*, 1961; *The Music Man*, 1962; *Promise Her Anything*, 1966. **Radio** (includes) *Druscilla Doom*. **Television** (includes) *One Minute Please!*, 1954; *Omnibus*; *Person to Person*; *The Ed Sullivan Show*; *Jack Paar Show*; *The Tonight Show*; *Alfred Hitchcock Presents*; *This Is Your Life*. **Recordings** "La Gingold", 1956; "Life of the Party". **Publications** *Sketches and Monologues*, 1942; *The World Is Square* (autobiography), 1945; *My Own Unaided Works* (essays), 1952; *Abracadabra* (play), produced in summer stock, 1960; *Sirens Should Be Seen and Not Heard*, 1963; *How to Grow Old Disgracefully* (autobiography), 1989; columnist, "These I Have Loathed" in *Books of Today*. **Cause of death** Undisclosed, at age 89.

RITA HAYWORTH

American Actress

Born **New York City, New York, 17 October 1918**

Died **New York City, New York, 14 May 1987**

Rita Hayworth's most memorable film role was that of Gilda, in the film of the same name, which she made in 1946 at the pinnacle of her career. Everything before then was a build up, and almost everything that came later represented a steady decline. In *Gilda*, a steamy melodrama of murder, jealousy and corruption with George Macready and Glenn Ford, she danced her way through one of the best sequences of her life. Peeling her gloves from her arms she moved exotically and erotically through the number, "Put the Blame on Mame, Boys". The following year she was christened the great American Love Goddess by Winthrop Sargeant in *Life* magazine.

Few people saw past Hayworth's screen image, which was then earning her bosses at Columbia a great deal of money. In the mid-1940s her films were grossing $1 million a year at the box office. Sargeant himself said that it seemed incredible that at the centre of the industry which mushroomed around her image was "a rather likeable, simple and completely unaffected human being". Hayworth is reported to have commented once, "Every man I've known has fallen in love with Gilda and wakened with me." This may account for the fact that of her five marriages only the first lasted for more than five years. For Hayworth, as for most of the very greatest and most loved stars in Hollywood, she found success, but never a full sense of herself as an individual human being.

She was born Margarita Carmen Cansino, the daughter of an ex-Ziegfeld Follies girl and a Spanish dancer who had moved to the United States only a few years previously. With this lineage, the young Rita was destined for show business and, at the age of eight, appeared in her first film, *La Fiesta*, dancing with her family, The Dancing Cansinos.

Hayworth's father, Eduardo, obviously had a keen sense of the future of the movie industry. By 1927 he took the family to Los Angeles, where he taught dance and also directed dance sequences in films. Rita took acting and dancing lessons besides her regular school work and by the time she was 14 her father saw her potential. He took his daughter out of school, made her his partner and took her to Mexico where she made her stage début. They had an 18-month booking at the Foreign Club in Tijuana followed by seven months in the resort of Agua Caliente. They also performed on a California gambling boat. At 16 Hayworth, still working under the name of Margarita Cansino, was spotted and offered a supporting role in the rather disastrous 1935 Spencer Tracy movie, *Dante's Inferno*, made by the (then) Fox Film Corporation. This was followed up with a one-year contract and a lot of work in B-films playing a dark-haired Latin type. Fox did not renew the contract but she later signed with Columbia. The key movie which lifted her into the forefront of the public eye was Howard Hawks's *Only Angels Have Wings*, made in 1939. Hawks himself later commented, "I don't really think she knew how intensely sexy she seemed to others."

The Cansino into Hayworth transformation occurred after her first marriage in 1936, when she was 18, to a former auto salesman, Edward Judson. He began to revamp her image. Far from being a Latin type, he saw her as an all-American girl. He lightened the hair which her father had darkened and introduced her to Columbia. They completed the metamorphosis with a completely new make-up and electrolysis treatment to lift her hairline. The name was conjured from her own forename and her mother's maiden name.

For more than ten years Hayworth flourished in her twin roles—as the alluring and seductive *femme fatale* Gilda, and as the bright American dancer in many musicals. Like her cousin, Ginger Rogers, she was chosen to partner Fred Astaire in 1941 and 1942. Together they made *You'll Never Get Rich* and *You Were Never Lovelier*. Jeanine Basinger has written that "many felt that Hayworth, a natural dancer with great stamina and rhythm, was Astaire's best on-screen partner". The fact that her singing on screen was dubbed in no way detracted from her performance and success in the magical, musical fantasies which provided essential escapism, especially in Britain, during the drab and frightening years of the war and the subsequent years of austerity.

Hayworth was divorced from Judson in 1942. The following year she married Orson Welles and gave birth to a daughter, Rebecca. But the marriage didn't work out. Hayworth explained that "Orsie" was devoted to "Orsie" and she got tired of being a 25 per cent wife. In 1949 she scandalized Columbia and the whole of Hollywood by eloping with the rich playboy Aly Khan. The marriage lasted only four years but Hayworth always remembered him with affection and recalled that, "The world was magical when you were with him." She had a second daughter, Princess Yasmin, and returned to Hollywood, but she never recovered the acclaim and adulation of the previous decade. She briefly married the singer, Dick Haymes, but it lasted only two years, and tried to get back into films. But her own looks were fading fast and her performances were mostly of "fallen women". However, she did achieve some excellent reviews for her acting in *They Came to Cordura* (1959). Playing a dissolute and traitorous American, she looked "haggard, drawn and defeated" and gave the best performance of her career, according to *Variety*, which added, "If she shows only half the beauty she usually does, she displays twice the acting."

Hayworth herself felt that this marked a new phase in her life. Now a freelance, she was choosing her own roles. As she put it, "I looked at all the parts I had done and realized that, no matter how they were sliced, it was still Salome." Sadly though, it has to be acknowledged that she had lost her fame, her looks and her confidence simultaneously and, by the time she reached 40, she was a very middle-aged woman and totally deglamorized. When she married for the last time, in 1958, there was little publicity. She continued working for another 13 years, but landed mostly unworthy character parts in generally undistinguished films.

Her decline, which had begun when she married the Aly Khan at the age of 31, continued sadly and inexorably. She developed a serious alcohol problem which meant that in 1977 she was placed in the psychiatric ward of a California hospital and a court was asked to put her affairs in the hands of a public guardian. In another five years she had developed Alzheimer's disease, formerly known as senile dementia. At first sufferers become forgetful and behave inappropriately but, sooner or later, the deterioration becomes absolute. The outcome is complete loss of memory, total dependence and, eventually, death.

Rita Hayworth's life is one of Hollywood's saddest stories. She epitomized every ideal and every fantasy of womanhood and yet found no way of living as an "ordinary" woman. Unlike Monroe, she was fated to live more than half her life on a downswing, which was only ameliorated by the devoted support and care of her younger daughter.

Born Margarita Carmen Cansino. **Parents** Eduardo, a dancer, and Volga (Haworth), a "Ziegfeld Follies" girl, Cansino. **Marriages** 1) Edward C. Judson, a car salesman, 1936 (divorced, 1942); 2) Orson Welles, director and actor, 1943 (divorced, 1948); 3) Prince Aly Khan, 1949 (divorced, 1953); 4) Dick Haymes, a singer (divorced, 1955); 5) James Hill, a producer, 1958 (divorced, 1961). **Children** Rebecca, by second marriage, Princess Yasmin, by third marriage. **Education** Hamilton High School, Los Angeles; Carthay School, Los Angeles. **Career** Father's dance partner, 1927; professional stage début, Los Angeles, 1932; dancer with father, Foreign Club, Tijuana, Mexico, also on California gambling boat, 1934–35; film actress, 1935–72; juvenile film début, 1926; adult film début, 1935; on contract with Fox, 1935–36, with Columbia, from 1937; freelance actress on stage, from 1957–70s. **Films** *La Fiesta*, 1926; *Cruz diablo* (*The Devil's Cross*), 1934; *Under the Pampas Moon*, 1935; *Charlie Chan in Egypt*, 1935; *Dante's Inferno*, 1935; *Paddy O'Day*, 1935; *Piernas de seda* (*Silk Legs*), 1935; *Human Cargo*, 1936; *Meet Nero Wolfe*, 1936; *Rebellion* (*Lady from Frisco*), 1936; *A Message to Garcia*, 1936; *Trouble in Texas*, 1937; *Old Louisiana* (*Treason*), 1937; *Hit the saddle*, 1937; *Criminals of the Air*, 1937; *Girls Can Play*, 1937; *The Shadow* (*The Circus Shadow*), 1937; *The Game That Kills*, 1937; *Paid to Dance*, 1937; *Who Killed Gail Preston?*, 1938; *There's Always a Woman*, 1938; *Convicted*, 1938; *Juvenile Court*, 1938; *The Renegade Ranger*, 1938; *Homicide Bureau*, 1938; *The Lone Wolf Spy Hunt* (*The Lone Wolf's Daughter*), 1939; *Special Inspector* (*Across the Border*), 1939; *Only Angels Have Wings*, 1939; *Music in My Heart*, 1939; *Blondie on a Budget*, 1940; *Susan and God* (*The Gay Mrs Trexel*), 1940; *The Lady in Question*, 1940; *Angels Over Broadway*, 1940; *The Strawberry Blonde*, 1941; *Affectionately Yours*, 1941; *Blood and Sand*, 1941; *You'll Never Get Rich*, 1941; *My Gal Sal*, 1942; *Tales of Manhattan*, 1942; *You Were Never Lovelier*, 1942; *Show Business at War*, 1943; *Cover Girl*, 1944; *Tonight and Every Night*, 1945; *Gilda*, 1946; *Down to Earth*, 1947; *The Lady from Shanghai*, 1948; *The Loves of Carmen*, 1948; *Champagne Safari* (documentary of Hayworth and Khan wedding trip), 1951; *Affair in Trinidad*, 1952; *Salome*, 1953; *Miss Sadie Thompson*, 1953; *Fire Down Below*, 1957; *Pal Joey*, 1957; *Separate Tables*, 1958; *They Came to Cordura*, 1959; *The Story on Page One*, 1960; *The Happy Thieves*, 1962; *Circus World* (*The Magnificent Showman*), 1964; *The Money Trap*, 1966; *The Poppy Is Also a Flower* (*Danger Grows Wild*), 1966; *The Rover* (*L'Avventuriero*), 1967; *Sons of Satan* (*I Bastardi*, *I Gatti*, *The Cats*), 1971; *Road to Salina* (*Sur la route de Salina*, *La Route de Salina*), 1971; *The Naked Zoo* (*The Naked Lovers*, *The Hallucinators*), 1971; *The Wrath of God*, 1972; *Circle*, 1976. **Cause of death** Alzheimer's disease, at age 68. **Further reading** Marjorie Rosen, *Popcorn Venus*, New York, 1973; Gene Ringgold, *The Films of Rita Hayworth: The Legend and Career of a Love Goddess*, New Jersey, 1974; John Kobal, *Rita Hayworth: The Time, the Place and the Woman*, New York, 1978; Joe Morella and Edward Z. Epstein, *The Life of Rita Hayworth*, New York, 1983; Barbara Leaming, *If This Was Happiness*, New York and London, 1989.

JAMES G. HIRSCH

American Biologist

***Born* St Louis, Missouri, 31 October 1922**

***Died* New York City, New York, 25 May 1987**

When germs manage to invade, the body brings into action its own type of chemical warfare—the immune system. It was for his research on the part played by white blood cells in this immune reaction Dr Hirsch is best known.

James Gerald Hirsch graduated from Yale University in 1942, obtaining his medical degree from Columbia University four years later. For his internship he returned to Barnes Hospital in his birthplace, St Louis, Missouri. Here he also served as assistant resident, before becoming chief of medicine at the Warren Air Force Base Hospital in Cheyenne, Wyoming.

In 1950 he was awarded a research felloswhip to the Rockefeller Institute for Medical Research as a visiting investigator, and he stayed there, in Rockefeller University as it became, in increasingly important posts until appointed dean of graduate studies from 1972.

One of his early areas of research at Rockefeller concerned the treatment of tuberculosis sufferers. He showed that patients requiring chemotherapy did not have to be confined to bed, a discovery that altered the whole pattern of treatment in sanatoriums, and even allowed some patients to be cared for in their own homes.

But it was work on the white blood cells carried out by Dr Hirsch and his team that provided the greatest advances. His laboratory was described as "a nucleus for investigators who wished to understand the cell biology of the immune response. His studies set the groundwork for all that followed."

When infecting germs or bacteria penetrate the outer defences of the body, white blood cells muster to engulf and digest them. They also act as scavengers to clear away the remains of dead cells. Hirsch's particular interest was in how these white cells cooperate with other cells or systems in the general immune response.

During his 30 years' research, Dr Hirsch wrote more than 100 papers for scientific journals, also finding time to edit the *Journal of Experimental Medicine* and to be an associate editor of several other medical journals. He was much sought after for chairing medical discussions, for he was adept at tactfully reconciling the divergent views of others. At the same time he was able to express his own ideas in a quiet and impressive way. These skills and others he continued to use after retirement from Rockefeller University in 1981, for he became president of the Josiah Macy Jr Foundation, and in that position he started a new scheme enabling doctoral candidates to pursue research on human disease. At the same time he kept in contact with Rockefeller where he was an adjunct professor.

Hirsch was editor of the textbook *Bacterial and Mycotic Infections of Man*, but later widened his interest from simply medical matters to include the history of medicine and science. Sadly, and ironically, for a scientist who had had such success investigating cells, he contracted cancer in 1985, at a time when he was working on a scientific biography of Dr Paul Ehrlich, a turn-of-the-century pioneer in the fields of haemotology, immunology and chemotherapy. Unfortunately, the advance of the cancer attacking Hirsch's body was inexorable, and his own immune system failed to halt its progress.

Born James Gerald Hirsch. **Marriages** Two; second wife, Beate Kaleschke, a scientific technician. **Children** Henry and Ann by first marriage; Rebecca by second marriage. **Education** Yale University, Connecticut, BS, 1942; Columbia University, MD, 1946. **Military**

service Chief of medicine, Warren Air Force Base Hospital, Cheyenne, Wyoming, 1948–50. **Career** Barnes Hospital, St Louis, intern in internal medicine, 1946–47, resident, 1947–48; visiting investigator, Rockefeller Institute for Medical Research, now Rockefeller University, 1950–52, assistant pathologist and bacteriologist, 1952–53, associate and associate physician, respiratory diseases service, 1953–56, associate professor of medicine and microbiology and physician, 1956–60, professor of medicine and microbiology, head of cellular physiology and immunology laboratory, senior physician and dean of graduate studies, 1960–81, adjunct professor, 1981 onwards. **Related activities** Member, board of trustees, Trudeau Institute, 1966 onwards; president and member, board of trustees, Josiah Macy Jr Foundation, 1981 onwards; editor, *Journal of Experimental Medicine*, also of textbook, *Bacterial and Mycotic Infections of Man*; associate editor, various other medical journals; collaborator, with wife, on proposed biography of German scientist, Dr Paul Ehrlich; chairman: Class IV, National Academy of Sciences, 1977–80, Division of Medical Sciences, Assembly of Life Sciences, National Resources Council, 1979–81, Assembly of Life Sciences, 1981; president, Paul Ehrlich Foundation, 1981 onwards. **Offices and memberships** National Academy of Sciences; American Society of Microbiology; Society of Experimental Biology and Medicine; Association of American Physicians; American Society of Clinical Investigators. **Awards and honours** Doctor of Science, Rockefeller University, 1984. **Publications** (editor) *Bacterial and Mycotic Infections of Man*; also contributed many papers to learned journals. **Cause of death** Cancer, at age 64.

CHARLES LUDLAM

American Actor, Playwright and Director

Born **Floral Park, New York, 12 April 1943**

Died **New York City, New York, 28 May 1987**

In July 1987 close to 1000 members of New York's avant-garde theatrical community jammed the city's Second Avenue Theater to pay tribute to Charles Ludlam, one of the decade's most daring and prolific theatrical entrepreneurs. Actors from the Ridiculous Theatrical Company, the performing troupe he had founded and directed for almost 20 years, presented memorable scenes from several of his most influential plays, including *Der Ring Gott Farblonjett*, a bizarre Wagnerian travesty, *When Queens Collide*, an early satire of Marlowe, and *Houdini, a Piece of Pure Escapism*, an unfinished work in which Ludlam had hoped to star. The evening, aptly titled *Tabu Tableaux*, was described by the *New York Times* as having the "mournful exuberance of a New Orleans jazz festival"—a spirit which Ludlam, ever intrigued by life's reckless and ridiculous qualities, would surely have relished. He was just on the verge of bringing his wild and lunatic brand of stage entertainment out of Greenwich Village and into the mainstream theatrical world when Aids-linked pneumonia claimed his life.

Ludlam's ordinary appearance and quiet, mild manner belied his boundless creativity. His family background was equally conventional, offering no clue to his peculiar artistic genius. Raised in suburban Long Island, the second of three sons of a plasterer, young Charles was bored by other children and had little interest in ordinary games, sports and school activities. Then, at the age of six, he got lost at the Mineola state fair, and in his wanderings happened upon a Punch and Judy show. He was instantly entranced by the performance and soon set up his own basement puppet show with his mother and younger brother as the audience. "If I hadn't discovered the theatre early on, I most certainly would have become a juvenile delinquent," he commented later. He never lost his fascination with puppetry, and in 1975 earned a *Village Voice* Off-Broadway (Obie) Award for his highly acclaimed *Professor Bedlam's Educational Punch and Judy Show*. As a child, he was also influenced by the movies, as the family lived just opposite a cinema, and he and his mother attended every show.

Ludlam organized his first theatre group, which met over a liquor store in Northport, Long Island, while he was still in high school. Even then, the plays he presented were off-beat and iconoclastic, drawing from material as rarefied and sophisticated as Japanese *Noh* dramas and Russian symbolist works. His first exposure to professional theatre came soon afterwards, in the form of a summer apprenticeship at the Red Barn Theater in Newport, Rhode Island, arranged for him by an enthusiastic high school drama coach. By this time he had already established himself as a social and artistic rebel, wearing long hair and rejecting familiar concepts of order and decorum before it was fashionable to do so.

Though he entered Hofstra University in 1961 with a scholarship in acting, his professors persuaded him to concentrate on writing and directing instead, and filled his head with what he viewed as narrow and oppressive notions of what theatre was. "I realized they wanted me to behave in a civilized manner in a room, and not to do anything extraordinary," he remembered. "But everything I'm interested in is extraordinary." His artistic revelation came soon afterwards when he saw a Living Theater production of *The Connection*. "I suddenly realized what I wanted," he said. "Theatre could be an advanced, experimental influence on the whole culture, not just entertainment."

Following his graduation from Hofstra in 1965, Ludlam moved to Manhattan's Lower East Side to join the burgeoning underground film movement. Here he made a string of theatrical contacts, and soon formed an acting company—light-heartedly named The Playhouse of the Ridiculous—with director John Vaccaro and playwright Ronald Tavel. Ludlam made his New York stage début in 1966, in Tavel's *The Life of Lady Godiva*, presented in a rented loft on West 17th Street. Soon afterwards he appeared as Norma Desmond in a "Ridiculous" adaptation of the film *Sunset Boulevard*—the first in a long and colourful line of female impersonations.

The following year serious squabbles between Ludlam and Vaccaro led to a split in the theatrical troupe, and Ludlam left to form his own Ridiculous Theatrical Company, taking with him a handful of loyal actors. A month after Vaccaro presented Ludlam's *Conquest of the Universe* at the Bouwerie Lane Theater, Ludlam premièred his own version of the play, titled *When Queens Collide*. Until 1978, when it acquired a permanent home at One Sheridan Square, the Ridiculous Theatrical Company had no established venue, and moved from theatre to bar to loft for performances. Nevertheless, its productions attracted a devoted following.

Though Ludlam began with rambling, epic-style plays, such as *Turds in Hell* (1968) and *The Grand Tarot* (1969), he gradually moved towards more conventional productions, which gained him greater critical and popular acclaim. *Bluebeard*, performed in 1970, was the first of the company's productions to be widely reviewed. Yet even it defied classification. Critic Mel Gussow of the *New York Times* described it as "both a loving paean and a lunatic parody". Other notable Ridiculous productions of the period included a zany version of *Camille*, starring Ludlam as the tragic heroine, *Der Ring Gott Farblonjett*, a full-blown spoof of Wagnerian opera, and *The Ventriloquist's Wife*, a skilful take-off on a 1940s' British horror film. Later targets included psychoanalysis, the cult of superstardom, Gothic fiction, physical culturists and suburban life. In 1983 he delivered a stunning performance as Maria Callas in *Galas*, named among the year's best plays, and the following year produced *The Mystery of Irma Vep*, a comic *tour de force* in which he and actor Everett Quinton played all seven roles. The production won the Drama Desk Award for quick-change artistry. Then, in 1986, came *The Artificial Jungle*, a reckless comedy of murder and revenge combining elements of *Double Indemnity*, *The Postman Always Rings Twice* and *Little Shop of Horrors*.

At every turn Ludlam demonstrated his creative exuberance. While some of his plays were poorly received—critics used the words "camp" and "burlesque" to describe a number of early efforts—they never failed to shock and surprise, and, more often than not, provoke serious reflection. With the passing years, the company, which began its life as a mostly gay cult phenomenon, grew into a powerful and legitimate theatrical vehicle. In addition to delivering strong opinions about feminism, humanity and sexual identity (or lack thereof), Ludlam's work, wrote *Showbill*'s Gary M. Stern, emphasized a single important idea. "[He] urges people to free themselves from society's preconceived notions of what makes happiness, what determines morality and what is proper."

While he continued to write, direct and act in an endless stream of plays for The Ridiculous Theatrical Company, in his later years Ludlam reached out beyond the familiar New York theatre world to other realms, playing the title role in the American Ibsen Theater production of Hedda Gabler in 1984, and delivering a key performance in the feature film *The Big Easy* in 1987. That summer he had planned to direct a production of Shakespeare's *Titus Andronicus* for Joseph Papp's Free Shakespeare in the Park. He also lectured in drama and staged productions at a number of universities, winning fellowships from the Guggenheim, Rockefeller and Ford foundations, and grants from the National Endowment for the Arts. "His career was blossoming on so many fronts that he couldn't possibly have accomplished them all," said Steven Samuels, general manager of the Ridiculous, upon learning of Ludlam's death. Offstage, however, the flamboyant "Renaissance Man" of the avant-garde lived simply and quietly in a two-room flat in Greenwich Village with his long-time companion Everett Quinton, three canaries and four tropical fish.

Born Charles Ludlam. **Parents** Joseph William, a plasterer, and Marjorie (Braun) Ludlam. **Education** Scholarship to Hofstra University, Hempstead, New York, BA in dramatic literature, 1965. **Career** Involved with underground film movement; actor, director, playwright on stage and films, formed acting company with playwright Ronald Tavel; first production *Shower*, Coda Gallery, 1965; co-founder, The Playhouse of the Ridiculous, 1966; acting début, as Peeping Tom, 1966, appeared in many of his own plays; founder, Ridiculous Theatrical Company, New York, 1967 onwards; also performed outside own company in *Hedda Gabler*, 1984, and *The English Cat*, 1985. **Related activities** Drama teacher, University of Massachusetts, 1972; conducted workshop in "commedia dell'arte", University of Connecticut, 1974, 1975; lecturer: American University, Washington, DC, 1976, New York University, 1977, 1979; drama teacher, Carnegie-Mellon University, Pittsburgh, 1980; associate adjunct professor and playwright-in-residence, Yale University, 1982–83. **Awards and honours** *Village Voice* Off-Broadway (Obie) Award, 1969, 1970; Guggenheim Fellowship in playwriting, 1970; Obie Award with Lola Pashalinski, for roles in *Corn*, 1972; Obie Award for *Camille*, 1973; Special Obie Award for *Professor Bedlam's Educational Punch and Judy Show*, 1975; Obie Award for design in *Der Ring Gott Farblonjet*, 1977; National Endowment for the Arts Fellowship, 1981, 1984; Drama Desk Award for outstanding achievement in the theatre, 1981. **Publications** (plays) *When Queens Collide*, produced New York, 1967; *Big Hotel*, produced New York, 1967; *Conquest of the Universe*, produced New York, 1967; (with Bill Vehr) *Turds in Hell*, New York, 1970; *Bluebeard*, produced New York, London, 1971, published in *More Plays From Off-Off Broadway*, ed. Michael Smith, Indianapolis, 1972, revised edition, New York, 1975; *The Grand Tarot*, produced New York, 1972; *Eunuchs of the Forbidden City*, produced New York, 1972, published in *Scripts 6*, New York, 1972; *Corn* (also director), produced New York, 1972; *Camille: A Tear-Jerker* (also director), produced New York, 1973; *Stage Blood* (also director), produced New York, 1974;

Hot Ice (also director), produced New York, 1974; *The Mystery of Irma Vep*, 1984; *The Artificial Jungle*, 1984. **Film roles** (include) *Lupe*, 1966; *The Artificial Jungle*; *The Big Easy*, 1987. **Cause of death** Pneumonia complicated by Aids, at age 44.

CECIL MADDEN

British Television Producer

***Born* Mogador, Morocco, 29 November 1902**

***Died* London, England, 27 May 1987**

"It was one long mystery," Cecil Madden said of television's early days. "We hadn't even seen a picture; we hadn't seen what a camera looked like. Nobody knew anything about television—nothing."

As the man who produced the world's first television show for the BBC in 1936, Madden was actually making programmes before the accepted date of the medium's beginnings, 2 November 1936. "One of the key dates in the history of television is August 26," he said, "the day when all people involved in the new venture were summoned to Broadcasting House (the BBC's headquarters), where they were given November 2 as their official starting date." After this momentous meeting, Madden and his colleagues raced off to Alexandra Palace, the new location of the BBC's television facilities. "I'm not sure what I was expecting," Madden recalled, "but I took the lift to the third floor and found my office with my name in large letters on the door. It was bare of any furniture except for a telephone in the corner and, to my surprise, it was ringing." The call was a frantic plea from Sir Gerald Cock, television's first head of outside broadcasts: a radio show scheduled to air at Radio Olympia had proved a flop—the studio couldn't sell enough seats—and Cock thought that "this new thing television" could possibly save the day. "'Will you get your staff together and tell me by 5.00 today what you are going to do? You'll then have nine days to prepare something,' Cock told me," Madden stated. He came up with the goods, and *Here's Looking at You*, a half-hour production, was performed live 20 times over a ten-day period.

Such a story is typical of television's beginnings, yet Madden once remarked that he had not been afraid of dealing with the then-untested medium. "All we had to do," he explained, "was apply a bit of common sense and make the best use of the experience we had. I looked on it as a tremendous adventure." Madden, however, was a man used to such adventures. Born in Morocco in 1902, the son of a consulate official, he was already fluent in French and Spanish by the time he returned to England to enter Dover College. His first encounter with any form of show business came while he was working for Rio Tinto at a sulphur mine in Spain. Asked by the company to run a theatre, Madden complied by writing revues—in Spanish. Later he moved to London and turned his attention to playwriting. Finally, in 1932, he was invited by the BBC to produce a series of radio talks. For three years Madden ran the Radio Empire Service; then Gerald Cock told him about the "new animal"—television—and Madden immediately switched to the visual side of production. There he remained, barring the war years, until his retirement in 1964.

The early years of "the box" formed a series of adventures for Madden, not least because those in the world of radio were extremely jealous of the new method of broadcasting. "A lot of people at Broadcasting House wanted us to start small," Madden said in 1984, "to do only the occasional tiddly programme. I argued that we had to start as we meant to go on, which meant starting big. And that's what happened. With the press firmly behind us, we just went bowling along."

The process of "bowling along" initially comprised fewer than 20 broadcasting hours a week on a £1000 budget, but even so, Madden managed to produce a series of successful programmes during the next three years which included the likes of *Picture Parade* ("a magazine of topical and general interest") and *The Gossip Hour*, forerunner of the modern talk show. Standards for the early programming were also high; with a week's schedule including ballet, plays, talks and variety shows, "a play a day" became Cecil Madden's motto, and it was a motto he enforced—even if the drama were only 15 minutes long. Later on, Madden attracted "names" for his drama programmes: Agatha Christie, for example, wrote one of the first plays for television (*The Wasp's Nest*), and Bernard Shaw could often be found on the set, watching his plays being televised. Dramatic presentations served two purposes in those days: not only did they give the public quality viewing, they also provided the necessary breaks for such stars-to-be as Laurence Olivier, Constance Cummings and James Mason—despite the fact that television appearances paid far less then than radio spots did.

When World War II caused a cessation of television broadcasting, Madden returned to radio to produce a series of war programmes such as *Blitz Round-ups*, *Variety Bandbox* and the *American Eagle in Britain* show. When televisions were switched back on in 1946, however, Madden was taken out of actual production work. As chief planner of the service, he became largely responsible for conceiving programmes such as *This Is Your Life* and *What's My Line*—both of which were successfully translated on to American television screens—as well as theatre relays and solo performances. In 1950 he was placed in temporary charge of children's television, a move resulting in the transformation of a previously fragmented set of programmes for classics like *The Railway Children* and *Treasure Island*. In spite of large-scale public protest, Madden was removed from the post six months later and made assistant to the controller of television programmes. In the words of *The Times*, the move was certainly "less than he deserved", yet Madden remained in the post until his retirement.

As could be expected, his involvement with the world of entertainment did not end with his retirement from the BBC. The man responsible for discovering the Beverley Sisters and Petula Clark went on to found the British Film and Television Academy. At the time of his death, he was president of the British Puppet and Model Theatre Guild. A congenial colleague, and a fearless, imaginative practitioner, Cecil Madden gained and kept the respect of his peers throughout his career—a reputation which would probably have shocked John Reith, the BBC's "very dour man" who was responsible for interviewing and hiring Madden in the first place. "The only thing I think he really wanted to know was where my religious sympathies lay," Madden joked in an interview.

Born Cecil Charles Madden. **Parents** Archibald Maclean, a civil servant, and Cecilia Catherine (Moor) Madden. **Marriage** Muriel Emily Cochrane, 1932 (died, 1974). **Children** One son and one daughter. **Education** French lycées, Morocco; Spanish schools; Aldeburgh Lodge Preparatory School; Dover College. **Career** Author, playwright, radio and television producer; began writing plays while working for Rio Tinto mining company in Spain; wrote number of plays in London before joining BBC as producer of radio talks, 1933; moved to outside broadcasting, becoming senior producer in the Empire Service; first producer and programmes organizer for BBC television at Alexandra Palace, 1936; returned to radio work when television taken off air during World War II; appointed head of Overseas Entertainments Unit and made responsible for creation of all radio programmes for British and Allied forces abroad, 1940; in charge of production of Allied Expeditionary Forces' radio programmes, 1944–45; returned to television as programmes organizer, 1946; temporary head of children's television, 1950; assistant to controller of television programmes, 1951–64; in retirement, founded British Film and Television Academy. **Offices and memberships** President, British Puppet and Model Theatre Guild. **Awards and honours** Member, Order of the British Empire. **Books** (include) *Anywhere for a News Story*; *My Grimmest Nightmare*; *Living Dangerously*; *Not Long for This World*; plus a number of articles on technical aspects of the theatre. **Plays** *Little Angel*, 1927; *The Hero*, 1928; (from French of H.R. Lenormand) *The Equator*, 1928; (with X.Y. Stone) *Through the Veil*, 1930; (from E. Ugarte and J. Lopez Rubio) *Max and Mr Max*, 1931; (with Theodore Benson) *Prestige*, 1932; *Tonight We'll Dream*, 1933; (from Maxwell Anderson) *Saturday's Children*, 1934; *All's Well*, 1934; (from J. I. Luca de Tena) *The President's Double*, 1939; (with George Beardmore) *Chatterbox*, 1948; (with Macgregor Urquhart) *Loophole*, 1950; (with Vincent McConnor) *Chelsea Reach*, 1950; (with Macgregor Urquhart) *Silent Witness*, 1952; *A Touch of Magic*, 1955; (with Max Hart) *Investigation*, 1958; plus numerous revues (in French, Spanish and English), sketches, features, stories and talks for broadcasting. **Radio** Many serials, including *Blitz Round-ups*, *Variety Bandbox*, *Girl Friends of the Forces*, *The American Eagle in Britain*, *Allied Expeditionary Forces Programme*, *Merry Go Round*, all during World War II. **Television** (includes) *Here's Looking at You*, 1936; *Picture Page*, 1936; *Picture Parade* and *The Gossip Hour*, 1936–39; also largely responsible for *This Is Your Life*, *What's My Line* and *Children's Hour*, all post-war. **Cause of death** Undisclosed, at age 84.

TURK MURPHY

American Jazz Musician and Composer

Born **Palermo, California, 16 December 1915**

Died **San Francisco, California, 30 May 1987**

The one thing Turk Murphy *should* be remembered for is his championing of traditional New Orleans jazz in a period when modern jazz in the form of bebop was sweeping all before it. But the one thing Murphy *will* be remembered for is a quick arrangement he did of a song from a German opera written in the 1920s. It is an odd quirk of musical history that the man who helped keep the music of New Orleans alive in the 1940s was the same man who introduced "Mac the Knife" to the jazz repertoire in the 1950s.

Murphy's love of New Orleans jazz was genuine and heartfelt. After an apprenticeship in various cabaret bands playing trombone, an instrument he taught himself to play, Murphy joined Lu Watters' Yerba Buena Jazz Band in 1940. Trumpeter Bobby Hackett remarked that it was "certainly funny to hear those youngsters trying to play like old men", but Watters' band was a roaring success, and it became the foremost international band reviving the dormant music of New Orleans.

Murphy was to stay with Watters until the band folded in 1950. It was during this time that he perfected the characteristic "tailgate" style of trombone playing, a marching style made popular in New Orleans in the early 1900s and so called because when playing off the backs of wagons, as bands often did in those days, the trombonist had to stand on the wagon's tailgate in order to extend the instrument's slide. Murphy was not that special a soloist, but his ensemble playing was gutsy and robust, with plenty of humour, and he was also an efficient singer and composer.

With the demise of Watters' band, Murphy was well placed to lead a solo career, for he had been working with various combos since 1947. He formed his own revivalist band with many ex-Yerbas in the line-up and found plenty of work in New Orleans and New York, thanks to a successful recording contract with Columbia Records. In 1960 he opened his own club—Earthquake McGoon's—in San Francisco. There his band successfully mixed jazz classics from the 1920s with original compositions and well-known ballads, all played with a down-to-earth sense of fun. In later years foreign audiences were to hear this for themselves as his band toured and performed at various festivals overseas.

Murphy was one of the leading promoters of traditional jazz. He was a forthright and intelligent critic and wrote books and sleeve notes on his favourite music, despite the fact that, as he observed in 1956, "the music that I have been making for the past 15 years has been the subject of a concerted critical animosity almost unanimous in the music trade press". In 1986 he opened a traditional jazz museum in the Front Page in San Francisco, a testament to the longevity of trad jazz.

All the preceding achievements would have been quite enough to ensure fame for any man, but in 1955 Turk Murphy achieved immortality. In that year Louis Armstrong, himself benefiting from the New Orleans revivalist wave promoted by Murphy, approached him to arrange a few songs, one of which was "Mac the Knife", written by Kurt Weill for Bertolt Brecht's *Threepenny Opera* in 1928. Murphy took the operatic original and turned it into a jazz standard. It became a signature tune for Armstrong, a million-seller for Bobby Darin and a *pièce-de-résistance* for Ella Fitzgerald. It was a long way from New Orleans, but every bit as successful.

Born Melvin Edward Alton Murphy. **Military service** US Army, 1942–45. **Career** Trombonist and singer with Merle Howard Band; worked with Val Bender, Will Osborne and Mal Hallett as a trombonist and arranger, mid-1930s; played in Lu Watters' Yerba Buena jazz band, 1940; led his own band, 1947 onwards; played for Marty Marsala, 1951; popular band leader from mid-1950s; toured Australia and Europe with own band, 1974. **Related activities** Ran own clubs, Easy Street, 1957, and Earthquake McGoon's, San Francisco, 1960 onwards; opened Traditional Jazz Museum in the Front Page, San Francisco, 1986; composer of various pieces, including "Something for Annie" and "Ballad for Marie Brizzard". **Recordings** (singles) "Kansas City Man Blues"/"Shake That Thing", JM 31; "Brother Lowdown"/"Yellow Dog", JM 32; "Chimes Blues"/"When My Sugar Walks Down the Street", GTJ 3; "Papa Dip"/"Turk's Blues", GTJ 4; "Grandpa's Spells"/"All the Wrongs You've Done to Me", GTJ 8; "Struttin' with Some Barbecue"/"Waiting for the Robert E. Lee", GTJ 12; "Irish Black Bottom"/"Downtown Strutters' Ball", GTJ 17; "Sidewalk Blues", Co CL-6324, 1953; "Maryland, My Maryland," Co 40586, 1955; "Trombone Rag"/"Ragtime Dance", GTJ 18; "Canal Street Blues"/"Down by the Riverside", GTJ 40; "Minstrels of Annie Street"/"Hot Time in the Old Town", GTJ 62; (albums) *When the Saints Go Marching In*, Co CL-546; *Dancing Jazz*, Co CL-650; *New Orleans Jazz Festival*, Co CL-793; *New Orleans Shuffle*, Co CL-927; *Barrelhouse Jazz*, Co(10")CL-6257; *At the Roundtable*, Forum SF-9017; *At the Roundtable*, Roul SR-25076; *Let the Good Times Roll*, Vi 2501; *Music for Losers*, Verve 1013, 1957; *Turk Murphy at the Newport Jazz Festival 1957*, Verve 8232, 1957; *Turk Murphy*, GHB 93, 1972; (with Wally Rose) *Music of Jelly Roll Morton*, Co CL-559; (with Clancy Hayes) *Live at Earthquake McGoon's*, ABC-Para 591. **Cause of death** Undisclosed, at age 71. **Further reading** J. Goggin, *Turk Murphy: Just for the Record*, San Leandro, 1982.

GUNNAR MYRDAL

Swedish Economist

***Born* Gustafs Dalecarlia, Sweden, 6 December 1898**

***Died* Stockholm, Sweden, 17 May 1987**

You could be forgiven for thinking that Gunnar Myrdal was an American sociologist of liberal leanings, a high-up United Nations official who spoke out about population problems in the modern world, or a government minister who was the architect of Sweden as we know it—welfare state *par excellence*. If you thought any of these things, the correct answer is no, no and yes respectively, albeit with qualifications. Myrdal was a Swede who played a major role in both Swedish politics *and* in the development of the social sciences in the US. He also served as executive secretary to the United Nations Economic Commission for Europe, *and* wrote numerous scholarly books and reports in the fields of economic theory, social policy, demography and political economy. He was married and had a family, and to top it all, he was a Nobel Prize-winner.

Myrdal was born in 1898 in a tiny village where his father was employed in railway construction. He spent much of his youth here, in the peasant community of Gustafs, rather isolated from the rest of the world and especially from the centres of culture and education. It was for this reason that the family moved to Stockholm when Gunnar was older, so the book-mad boy could go to school and later to university. That the spirit of his early rural years had made an impression upon him which figured in his later intellectual development was something which Myrdal recognized very clearly. "By the accident of my upbringing and personal inclinations," he said, "my thinking was directly rooted in the englightenment philosophy, in Jeffersonian liberalism and in Swedish peasant democracy."

In 1923 young Myrdal received his law degree from Stockholm University. A year later he married a fellow student, Alva Reimer, who was to become the mainstay of his professional and personal life—collaborator and companion, as well as a diplomat, academic and politician in her own right. Together the Myrdals made a formidable team. They settled in Stockholm, where Gunnar had accepted a post as political economist at the university. Not content with this and his law practice, he went on studying (with sojourns in Britain and Germany) until, in 1927, he obtained his doctorate in economics. Soon after, he published his first book—a highly technical study on price theory.

A turning point came when in 1929 Myrdal was awarded a Rockefeller Fellowship to visit the United States. Arriving there on the day before the Wall Street crash, the freshly qualified doctor in economics witnessed both the actual event and its immediate consequences. He said later that his stay in America during this year (1929–30) had stimulated his interest in politics more than anything else. Pursuing this new interest, he travelled from the US to Geneva to work at the Institute of International Studies, before returning to Sweden in 1933. Back home he was asked to succeed his former professor in the chair of political economy at his alma mater. He was then just 35 years old.

A Swedish chapter opened. In 1934 he and his wife published a controversial study entitled *Crisis in the Population Question*, which not only advocated the right for people to determine the size of their families regardless of income (thus calling for a state-funded child support programme), but also argued that sex education and widespread availability of contraceptives were social necessities. This book, once the shockwaves had levelled out a bit, had a pervasive influence on social reform in Sweden.

The Myrdals did not just think up great ideas, however; both of them became actively involved in the Social Democratic Party in the mid-1930s. Gunnar Myrdal was elected to the Senate in 1934 and served on a number of important housing and population commissions. Slowly but steadily he was beginning to build a political career. Meanwhile, his international fame had also spread. In 1938 the Carnegie Corporation asked him to carry out a comprehensive survey of the situation of Black people in the United States. This was a daunting task by anybody's standards but Myrdal, characteristically undaunted, jumped to the challenge. The result was a two-volume classic: *An American Dilemma: The Negro Problem and Modern Democracy*. In its sheer bulk it was an unlikely bestseller but by 1962 it had already run to 26 reprints.

In *An American Dilemma* Myrdal stated unequivocally that modern America was labouring under a massive contradiction between what it promised all its citizens (constitutional rights and equality before the law) and what it actually delivered to Black people: discrimination and unequal treatment in virtually every area of life. After World War II, of course, this tension between promise and reality was to erupt in the protest movements of the 1950s and the race riots of the 1960s. Myrdal had seen it coming 20 years before, and it is no mere coincidence that his book was cited in the 1954 Brown *versus* Topeka Board of Education decision which made school segregation illegal—the first of a wave of civil rights legislative measures. Even then, Myrdal's work carried weight in the United States, even if his recommendations for social reform in the context of American politics and history perhaps sounded a little naïve.

After the German invasion of Norway and Denmark in 1940 Myrdal once more returned to Sweden to witness developments first hand. Sweden managed to stay out of the war by remaining neutral, but not without economic cost. It was Gunnar Myrdal's job to pull the post-war economy together when he was minister of commerce from 1945 to 1947. This was not a wholehearted success. Although he was respected as an independent thinker and a man of integrity during his term in government, his policies were not popular. He had to impose rationing and import restrictions because of a domestic currency crisis, and the Swedes were suspicious of his plan to set up trade on a grand scale with the Soviet Union, which they found "socialistic". In the event, Myrdal's proposed trade links with Russia were relegated to the wastepaper basket before they had even been seriously discussed because the United States came up with something much bigger and better: the Marshall Plan. Here Gunnar Myrdal's Cabinet career came to a full stop.

None the less, his interest in policy making continued, and in 1948 he took a job as executive secretary of the UN Commission for Europe, which was to last until 1957. His wife, meanwhile, had become ambassador to India and when he went to visit her there in 1953 the country made a deep impression on him. He was struck on the one hand by the profound deprivation and poverty he encountered, and on the other by widespread corruption and obstructive bureaucracy. He made up his mind there and then: the next few years of academic labour would be devoted to study of the Asian subcontinent. *Asian Drama: An Inquiry into the Poverty of Nations* in fact took more than ten years to complete. Polemically entitled against the free trade principles of Adam Smith's classic economic tract, *Asian Drama* attracted much attention for its critique of Western economists and of local ruling élites alike.

By the time this second of Myrdal's major works was published, he had already been holding the chair of international economy at Stockholm for eight years, and he was getting itchy feet. Moving with one of the most important issues of his day, he opted for the chairmanship of the International Peace Research Institute, where he worked from 1967 until his retirement in 1973. Of course, retirement made little difference to his punishing workload of writing, lecturing and travelling. In 1976 he caused a stir when he argued publicly that the Nobel Prize for economics should be abolished since it had been awarded to Milton Friedman (later monetarist adviser to

President Ronald Reagan). He obviously felt deeply offended that the Swedish Academy of Science had honoured Friedman in this way when only two years previously Myrdal and Friedrich von Hayek had won it for a body of thought diametrically opposed to Friedman's.

When dealing with a man of such substance, such versatility and longevity as Gunnar Myrdal, it is much easier to come to straightforward conclusions about the importance of his achievements than it is to get a grasp of the person. The reporter in *Time* who characterized Myrdal as "an apostle of thoroughgoing Swedish-style planning" took the easy way out and substituted the politics for the man, but he was not altogether wrong. For most of his life Myrdal held firmly to the belief that "human beings are good; we can improve conditions through reforms", a view that also says a lot about the person.

Unlike the later social democrats whose politics were influenced by the events of the 1960s, Myrdal's outlook was characterized by a conviction that social democracy should be administered through big state-governed institutions rather than work by popular participation or decentralized small-scale planning. On the other hand, in *An American Dilemma* and *Asian Drama* the strengths of his position are apparent: he could not and did not confine himself to economics or population matters, but ranged across the boundaries between economics and social science in order to make clear just how much need there was for planning on a world scale in the face of the strong blatantly exploiting the weak—White upon Black, West upon East.

Still, the disadvantages of Sweden's own systematized planning, in which he had played such a large part, were becoming increasingly apparent towards the end of Myrdal's life. In 1980 he is reputed to have said that "excessive taxation [was] turning the Swedes into a gang of hustlers" and that "the world is going to hell in every possible way". While statements such as these may in part be put down to the doom-laden perspective of a nuclear age, it may nevertheless be true to say that Myrdal died a disillusioned man. Signs that he was frustrated at the slow pace of change were apparent before. The planned follow-up report to *An American Dilemma*, for example, which he was to carry out in collaboration with Kenneth Clark, the noted Black American scholar, never came off; Myrdal felt that nothing much had changed since he had done his first survey. The United States, which had taught him so much and which he, as an outsider looking in, had come to know so well, was his particular target. In 1974 he said: "America is the one rich country with the biggest slums, the least democratic and least developed health system, and the most niggardly attitude towards its old people."

It is for statements like these that Myrdal has, deservedly, come to be considered one of the most influential foreign observers of the US. Regarding America very much as his second home, Myrdal could afford to make such blatantly critical judgements as if he were an insider. And yet his personal lifestyle could not be further removed from the American way: despite fame and fortune, Myrdal always maintained a simple standard of living which bordered on the frugal, indulging nothing other than his workaholism and his affection for his wife and family.

Born Karl Gunnar Myrdal. **Parents** Karl Adolf Petterson and Sofia (Matsdotter) Myrdal. **Marriage** Alva Reimer, a politician, diplomat and writer, 1924 (died, 1986). **Children** Jan Sissela Bok, Kaj Foelster. **Education** University of Stockholm, JD, 1923, Juris Doctor in Economics, 1927; studied in Germany and Britain, 1925–29; Rockefeller Fellow, USA, 1929–30. **Career** Lawyer, Sweden; teacher of political economy, University of Stockholm, 1927; associate professor, Postgraduate Institute of International Studies, Geneva, Switzerland, 1930–31; acting professor, University of Stockholm, 1931–32, Lars Hierta Professor of political economy and financial science, 1933–50, professor of international economy, 1960 onwards. **Related activities** Founder, Institute for International Economic Studies, 1961; visiting Robert Lazarus Professor of population studies, Ohio State University, 1967; visiting fellow, Center for Study of Democratic Institutions, Santa Barbara, California, 1973–73; distinguished professor, Graduate

School and University Center of the City University of New York, 1974–75; visiting professor: University of California, Irvine, spring, 1977, University of Wisconsin, Madison, autumn, 1977, Tom Slick Professor, Lyndon Baines Johnson School of Administration, University of Texas, 1978. **Other activities** Social Democrat member of Swedish Senate, 1935–38, 1944–47; director of study of American Negro problems for Carnegie Corporation of New York, 1938–42; minister of commerce, Swedish Cabinet, 1945–47; board member, Central Bank of Sweden; chairman, Post-war Planning Commission, 1945–47; member, government committees on housing, population, agriculture; executive secretary, United Nations Economic Commission for Europe, 1947–57; research director, Asian Study for Twentieth-Century Fund, 1957–68; chairman, Stockholm International Peace Research Institute, 1967–73. **Awards and honours** Carnegie grant, 1938; LLD: Harvard University, 1938, University of Leeds, 1957, Yale University, 1959, Brandeis University, Waltham, Massachusetts, 1962, Howard University, Washington, DC, 1962, University of Edinburgh, 1964, Swathmore College, Pennsylvania, 1964, Stockholm University, 1966, Sir George Williams University, Montreal, 1967, University of Michigan, 1967, Lehigh University, Bethlehem, Pennsylvania, 1967, Temple University, Philadelphia, 1968, Atlanta University, 1970, Helsinki University, 1971, University of Philippines, 1971, Gustavus Adolphus College, St Peter, Minnesota, 1971; DLitt: Fisk University, Nashville, Tennessee, 1947, Columbia University, New York, 1954, New School for Social Research, New York, 1956, Wayne State University, Detroit, 1963, Uppsala College, East Orange, New Jersey, 1969; JD, University of Nancy, 1950; DSoc Sc: University of Birmingham, 1961, University of Louisville, Kentucky, 1968; DD, Lincoln University, Pennsylvania, 1964; DPhil: Stockholm University, 1966, Oslo University, 1969; DCL, Temple University, 1968; DSoc, Jyvaeskylae University, Finland, 1969; co-recipient, with wife, West Germany's Peace Prize for literature and public service, 1970; DSc: Dartmouth College, Hanover, New Hampshire, 1971, Heriot-Watt University, Glasgow, Scotland, 1979; Seidman Award, Memphis, 1973; Nobel Prize for economics, 1974; Nitti Prize, 1976; Felix Newburgh Award, Sothonburg, 1977. **Memberships** Royal Swedish Academy of Sciences; Econometric Society; American Economic Association; Americans for Democratic Action; Hungarian Academy of Arts and Sciences; American Academy of Arts and Sciences; British Academy of Arts and Sciences. **Publications** *Prisbildningsproblemet och foranderligheten* (The Problem of Price Formation and Changeability), Uppsala, 1927; *Vetenskap och politik i nationalekonomien*, Stockholm, 1930, published as *The Political Element in the Development of Economic Theory*, London, 1953, Cambridge, Massachusetts, 1954; *Sveriges vag genom penningkrisen* (Sweden's Path Through the Monetary Crisis), Stockholm, 1931; *Wages, Cost of Living and National Income in Sweden 1860–1931*, London, 1933; *Bostadsfragan sasom socialt planlaggninsproblem under krisen och pa langre sikt* (The Question of Housing as a Social Planning Problem During the Crisis and in the Long Run), Stockholm, 1933; *Konjunktur och offentlig hushallning: En utrendning* (Conjuncture and Public Budgeting: An Explanation), Stockholm, 1933; *Undersokning rorande behovet av en utvidgning av bostadsstatistiken jamte vissa darmed forbundna bostadspolitiska fragor* (An Examination of the Need for an Enlarged Housing Statistics and Other Related Political Questions), Stockholm, 1933; *Finanspolitikens ekonomiska verkningar* (The Financial Policy's Economic Effects), Stockholm, 1934; *Kris i befolkningsfragan* (Crisis in the Population Question), Stockholm, 1934; *Befolkningsproblemet i Sverige: Radioforedrag den 27 Jan 1935* (The Population Problem in Sweden: Radio Lecture), Stockholm, 1935; *Samhallskrisen och socialvetenskaperna* (The Crisis in Society and the Social Sciences), Stockholm, 1935; *Vad galler striden i befolkningsfragan?* (What is the Controversy About in Regard to the Population Question?), Stockholm, 1936; *Jordbrukspolitiken under omlaggning* (The Agricultural Policy During Reorganization), Stockholm, 1938; *Monetary Equilibrium*, London, 1939, New York, 1962; *Population: A Problem for Democracy*, Cambridge, Massachusetts, 1940; *Kontakt med Amerika* (In Touch With America),

Stockholm, 1941; *Amerika mitt i varlden* (America in the Middle of the World), Stockholm, 1943; *An American Dilemma: The Negro Problem and Modern Democracy*, New York, 1944; *Economic Developments and Prospects in America*, Washington, 1944; *De internationella forhandlingarnai Washington om ekonomiska efterkrigsproblem* (The International Negotiations in Washington Regarding Post-war Economic Problems), Stockholm, 1944; *Varning for freds-optimism* (Warning Against Peace Optimism), Stockholm, 1944; *Psychological Impediments to Effective International Cooperation*, New York, 1952; *Realities and Illusion in Regard to Inter-Governmental Organizations*, London, 1955; *Development and Under-Development: A Note on the Mechanism of National and International Economic Inequality*, Cairo, 1956, revised edition as *Economic Theory and Under-Developed Regions*, London, 1957, as *Rich Lands and Poor: The Road to World Prosperity*, New York, 1958; *Varldsekonomin*, Stockholm, 1956, published as *An International Economy: Problems and Prospects*, New York, 1956; *Economic Nationalism and Internationalism*, Melbourne, 1957; *Value in Social Theory: A Selection of Essays on Methodology*, ed. Paul Streeton, London and New York, 1958; *Beyond the Welfare State: Economic Planning and Its International Implications*, London and New Haven, Connecticut, 1960; *Problemet Sverige hjalper* (The Problem Which Sweden Aids), Stockholm, 1961; *Vi och Vasteuropa* (We and Western Europe), Stockholm, 1962; *Challenge to Affluence*, London and New York, 1963; *Var onda varld* (Our Evil World), Stockholm, 1964; *USA och Vietnamkriget* (USA and the Vietnam War), Stockholm, 1967; *Objektivitetsproblemet i samhallsforskningen*, Stockholm, 1968, published as *Objectivity in Social Research*, New York, 1969, London, 1970; *Asian Drama: An Inquiry into the Poverty of Nations*, London and New York, 1968, abridged edition published as *An Approach to the Asian Drama: Methodological and Theoretical*, New York, 1970; *The Challenge of World Poverty: A World Anti-Poverty Programme in Outline*, New York, 1970; *Vi och Vasteuropa: Andra ronden* (We and Western Europe: Another Round), Stockholm, 1971; *Varldsfattigdomen* (World Poverty), Stockholm, 1972; *Against the Stream: Critical Essays on Economics*, New York, 1973, London, 1974; *Essays and Lectures*, ed. Mutsumi Okada, Kyoto, 1973; *Miljo och ekonomisk tillvaxt* (Environment and Economic Growth), Stockholm, 1976. **Cause of death** Undisclosed, at age 88. **Further reading** Herbert Aptheker, *The Negro Person in America: A Critique of Gunnar Myrdal's "The American Dilemma"*, New York, 1946; ed. Angus Maddison, *Myrdal's "Asian Drama": An Interdisciplinary Critique*, Liège, Belgium, 1971; R.A. Ul'ianovskii and V. Pavlov, *Asian Dilemma: A Soviet View and Myrdal's Concept*, Moscow, 1974; Harald Bohrn, *Gunnar Myrdal: A Bibliography 1919–1976*, Stockholm, 1976; Kerstin Assarsson-Rizzi and Harald Bohrn, *Gunnar Myrdal: A Bibliography 1919–1981*, New York, 1984.

NORMAN NICHOLSON

British Poet, Playwright and Critic

***Born* Millom, Cumberland, 8 January 1914**

***Died* Millom, Cumbria, 30 May 1987**

The Lakeland poet Norman Nicholson may not have been one of the best known of his generation of poets, but he may have been one of the happiest of them. In his poems there is little of the anguish and anger of so many of his contemporaries—rather more, perhaps, of joy and wonder. Nicholson himself spoke to Peter Orr of the BBC of his desire in writing, "to join in this exuberance which poetry is", comparing it to the desire of the musician to play the piano. "I enjoy being alive, you know," he said, "and writing poetry is part of it." Characteristically he also confessed to a certain pride in his profession, admitting that he liked people to know he was a poet.

Nicholson always said that his inspiration and his imagery came from the countryside of his birth—from the fells, dales, seashores, lakes and mining towns of his native Cumberland and, particularly, from the houses, streets and blast furnaces of the town of Millom where he spent almost all his life. In his teens his health broke down and he was sent south to Hampshire to convalesce. The enforced seclusion of these years destroyed his ambitions to become a university don; but they perhaps also strengthened his inner development as a poet.

Decisive also in Nicholson's development was his conversion to Christianity at the age of 22 and his discovery around the same time of the poetry of T.S. Eliot who, he said, set all the poets off "like a rocket" in the 1930s. Like Eliot's, much of Nicholson's early work was religious in theme—"nobbut God" remaining always the "pervasive presence" in his poems. It was only later, during the war, that he began consciously to write about the Lakes, scribbling while down a mine what he later called the "first Nicholson poem", "The Blackberry". Although he became very much a poet of locality, there was nothing provincial in Nicholson's work. Rather, he shared with Blake the ability "to see a world in a grain of sand". He felt that the pattern of life in a town like Millom "can be seen on a scale small enough for the mind to grasp it whole". His poems dwell often on this awareness of the underlying reality beyond the everyday world of local things. "Beneath the stone, the idea of a stone./ Beneath the idea, the love." In his most famous poem, "The Pot Geranium", Nicholson describes the way this small flower "contains the pattern, the prod and pulse of life, / Complete as the Nile or Niger".

Impermanence, another of Nicholson's recurring themes, was epitomized for him by the closure of the Millom ironworks, when "they shovelled my childhood/ On to a rubbish heap" and by his vision of the future disappearance of the town itself seeing, "The quick green turf push a green tarpaulin over /All that was mortal in five thousand lives." Musing on the Lancashire beach, he seemed almost to watch "The rocks crawl down the beach, / Taking a thousand years to move a yard."

By 1954 Nicholson had published four volumes of poetry, two little-known novels, three plays, of which two—*The Old Man of the Mountains* and *This Way to the Tomb*—were produced in London, an anthology of religious verse and editions of the poems of Cowper and Wordsworth. Between 1954 and 1964 he wrote few poems and, when he began again to write, his work had become less metaphysical, even more colloquial than before. In *A Local Habitation*, published in 1972, his poems are of lakes "bright as a sixpence", tides "unwrapping like a roll of oilcloth".

Although he felt a great affinity with Wordsworth, the other great poet of the Lakes, and with "the sense of his being here", Nicholson deliberately avoided Wordsworthian influences when writing about the countryside. Nor did he like Wordsworth's philosophy. However, he did admit that "the Wordsworthian element usually comes into my poetry when I am writing about the mines and the streets and the blast furnaces and things like that, because I can let it come in then".

"I think to have written poems," Nicholson said, "even if they are rather bad poems, is to have gone through a certain experience which, by sympathy, by intuition opens to you an enormous new realm of human expererience."

Born Norman Cornthwaite Nicholson. **Parents** Joseph, an outfitter, and Edith Nicholson. **Marriage** Yvonne Edith Gardener, a teacher, 1956 (died, 1982). **Education** Local schools, Millom, Cumberland, England. **Career** Poet, literary critic, novelist, playwright, lecturer and broadcaster; first verses published with poems of two other poets, *Selected Poems*, 1943; first "solo" publication, 1944. **Awards and honours** Fellow, Royal Society of Literature, 1945; Heinemann Award, for *Five Rivers*, 1945; MA: Manchester University, 1959, Open University, 1975; Cholmondeley Award, 1967; Northern Arts Association grant, 1969; Society of Authors' Travelling Award, 1972; Arts Council bursary, 1977; Queen's Gold Medal for poetry, 1977; honorary fellow, Manchester Polytechnic, 1979; Dlitt: University of Liverpool, 1980, University of Lancashire, 1984; Officer, Order of the British Empire, 1981. **Offices and membership** Royal Society of Literature; PEN (association of poets, playwrights, editors, essayists and novelists). **Verse** (with J.C.Hall and Keith Douglas) *Selected Poems*, London, 1943; *Five Rivers*, London, 1944, New York, 1945; *Rock Face*, London, 1948; *The Pot Geranium*, London, 1954; *Selected Poems*, London, 1966; *No Star on the Way Back: Ballads and Carols*, Manchester, 1967; *A Local Habitation*, London, 1972; *Hard of Hearing*, London, 1974; *Cloud on Black Combe*, Hitchin, Hertfordshire, 1975; *Stitch and Stone: A Cumbrian Landscape*, Sunderland, 1975; *The Shadow on Black Combe*, Ashington, Northumberland, 1978; *Sea to the West*, 1981; *Selected Poems 1940–1982*, London, 1982. **Plays** *The Old Man of the Mountains*, produced London, 1945, published London, 1946, revised edition, 1950; *Prophesy to the Wind: A Play in Four Scenes and a Prologue*, produced London, 1949, published London, 1950; *A Match for the Devil*, produced Edinburgh, 1953, published London, 1955; *Birth by Drowning*, produced Mirfield, Yorkshire, 1959, published London, 1960; *No Star on the Way* (television), 1963. **Novels** *The Fire of the Lord*, London, 1944, New York, 1946; *The Green Shore*, London, 1947. **Other** *Man and Literature*, London, 1943; *Cumberland and Westmorland*, London, 1949; *H.G. Wells*, London, 1950; *William Cowper*, London, 1951; *The Lakers: The Adventures of the First Tourists*, London, 1955; *Provincial Pleasures*, London, 1959; *William Cowper*, London, 1960; *Portrait of the Lakes*, London, 1963, revised edition published as *The Lakes*, 1977; *Enjoying It All* (BBC talks), London, 1964; *Greater Lakeland*, London, 1969; *Wednesday Early Closing* (autobiography), London, 1975; (with Gerda Mayer and Frank Flynn) *The Candy-Floss Tree* (juvenile), Oxford, 1984. **Edited works** *An Anthology of Religious Verse Designed for the Times*, London, 1942; *Wordsworth: An Introduction and Selection*, London and New York, 1949; *Poems* by William Cowper, London, 1951; *A Choice of Cowper's Verse*, London, 1975; *The Lake District: An Anthology*, London, 1977. **Cause of death** Undisclosed, at age 73. **Further reading** Kathleen Morgan, *Christian Themes in Contemporary Poets*, London, 1965; Philip Gardner, *Norman Nicholson*, New York, 1973.

JOHN H. NORTHROP

American Biochemist

***Born* Yonkers, New York, 5 July 1891**

***Died* Wickenberg, Arizona, 27 May 1987**

Enzymes are organic catalysts. These exist in the body, and it is because of their presence that some chemical changes essential for life can take place. However, just what they are, their chemical composition and whether they obey the laws of chemistry was a mystery until comparatively recently. It was for the light his work shed on this mystery that John H. Northrop was awarded a share of the Nobel Prize for Chemistry in 1946.

John Howard Northrop was attuned to a scientific environment from the moment he was born. His mother taught botany at Hunter College, New York, and his father was a member of the department of zoology at Columbia University. Indeed, it was at Columbia that the young Northrop gained his BS degree in 1912, his MA in 1913, and his doctorate in 1915. Apart from his academic work he was a member of the university fencing team which won the inter-collegiate championship in 1913.

With a travelling fellowship, he went to work for a year in the laboratory of the Rockefeller Institute for Medical Research under the biologist Jacques Loeb, studying the duration of life. The rest of his career was directed by this choice, for he was appointed an assistant at the institute immediately his fellowship expired, becoming an associate member in 1920, and a full member in 1924. From 1926 onwards he worked in the institute's Princeton Laboratories.

Only when the United States entered World War I was Northrop away from the institute; he served as a captain in the Chemical War Service of the US Army. During that time he studied fermentation, and his work led to a process for producing the acetone and ethyl alcohol used in the manufacture of war materials.

In 1920 he began his study of enzymes, the mysterious catalysts which are involved in the body's breathing, digestion and other life processes. Their chemical constitution was unknown. The first isolation of an enzyme in a chemical laboratory occurred in 1926, when James Sumner managed to prepare urease. Four years later Northrop managed to obtain a pure, cyrstalline form of pepsin, the enzyme which is part of the gastric juices and enables digestion to occur. He then demonstrated that it is a protein, thus resolving the question of the nature of enzymes.

Later, in collaboration with others, he isolated the pancreatic enzymes trypsin and chymotrypsin. Later still came the discovery of pepsinogen, which is the parent-substance, forming pepsin by reacting with hydrochloric acid in the stomach, and trypsinogen and chymotrypsinogen, the equivalent inactive parent-substances of trypsin and chymotrypsin. He developed the idea that all proteins, "whether they occur in meat, enzymes, viruses or antibodies", are derived from the same mother-substance, which he called proteinogen.

Using the same chemical methods, by 1938 he had isolated the first bacterial virus, or bacteriophage. Bacteriophages are part of the body's defence mechanism, living in the body and consuming bacteria. Northrop showed these to be nucleoproteins. He also studied bacteriophage action, and the conditions which govern their production.

Northrop published several scientific papers, and was co-author of *Crystalline Enzymes*, an important textbook. Many honours, visiting professorships and consultative posts came his way in recognition of his work, the most prestigious award being the 1946 Nobel Prize for Chemistry. He shared this with W.M. Stanley, his colleague at Princeton Laboratories, who had built on Northrop's work with enzymes in his study of viruses. The other half of the prize went to James Sumner who had isolated the first enzyme.

A keen sportsman, especially fond of shooting and fishing, Northrop lived to a grand old age, and left a body of work which had profound effects on medical practice.

Born John Howard Northrop. **Parents** John I., zoologist, and Alice Belle (Rich), botanist, Northrop. **Marriage** Louise Walker, 1917. **Children** Alice and John. **Education** Columbia University, BS, 1912, MA, 1913; Harvard University, MA, PhD, 1915. **Military service** Captain, Chemical Warfare Service, US Army, 1917–18. **Career** Assistant, Rockefeller Institute, New York, 1916, associate, 1917, associate member, 1920, member, 1924–56, life member, 1962; professor, University of California at Los Angeles, 1949–58; research biophysicist, Donner Laboratory, 1958–59. **Related activities** De Lamar lecturer, School of Hygiene and Public Health, Johns Hopkins University, 1937; Jesup lecturer, Columbia University, 1937–38; Hitchcock professor, University of California, 1939; Thayer lecturer, Johns Hopkins University,

1940; consultant, Office of Scientific Research and Development, 1941–45; visiting professor of bacteriology, University of California, 1949. **Offices and memberships** Member: National Academy of Sciences, American Association for the Advancement of Science, Society for Experimental Biology and Medicine, American Society of Biological Chemistry, American Chemical Society, American Academy of Arts and Science, Harvey Society, American Philosophical Society, Association of the New York Academy of Medicine, Society of General Physiologists, Halle Akademie der Naturforscher, Société Philomathique; trustee, Marine Biological Laboratory, Woods Hole, Massachusetts. **Awards and honours** W.B. Cutting Travelling Fellowship, Columbia University, 1915; Stevens Prize, Columbia College of Physicians and Surgeons, 1931; honorary DSc: Harvard, 1936, Columbia, 1937, Yale, 1937, Princeton, 1940, Rutgers, 1941; Charles Frederick Chandler Medal, Columbia University, 1937; honorary LLD, California, 1939; Daniel Giraud Elliot Medal for 1939, National Academy of Sciences, 1944; Nobel Prize for Chemistry, with W.M. Stanley and James B. Sumner, for contributions to the knowledge of enzymes, 1946; Certificate of Merit, United States, 1948; Lion Award, Columbia University, 1949; emeritus professor, University of California, 1959; Alexander Hamilton Award, Columbia University, 1961; emeritus professor, Rockefeller Institute, 1962; honorary fellow, Chemical Society, Royal Society of Chemistry; fellow, World Academy; Benjamin Franklin Fellow, Royal Society of Arts. **Publications** *Crystalline Enzymes*, 1939; (editor, contributor) *Journal of General Physiology*, *Experimental Biology Monographs and Funk and Wagnell's Encyclopaedia*; numerous papers on enzymes and aspects of physical chemistry. **Cause of death** Undisclosed, at age 95.

FREDERICK POTTLE

American Biographer and Literary Scholar

Born **Center Lovell, Maine, 3 August 1897**

Died **New Haven, Connecticut, 16 May 1987**

Anyone who knows about James Boswell knows about Professor Frederick Pottle. For over half a century, and in the course of over 30 publications, Professor Pottle re-established Boswell as a central literary figure of eighteenth-century England and confirmed himself as the pre-eminent authority on the Scottish biographer and man of letters. During this century a large mass of previously unavailable material by and about Boswell has been gathered and made public; nearly 35 more volumes of Boswell's journals have yet to be published. Pottle was the primary intellectual force behind these valuable contributions. The work he did at Yale University was so intensive that his workroom in the Sterling Library, where he presided over Yale's huge collection of Boswell papers, became known as the "Boswell Factory". In 1925 Pottle wrote that Boswell's biography of Samuel Johnson "has always been considered the greatest biography of all time", but he bemoaned the fact that "for the best part of a century people were content to read the work and ignore the author". Ironically, this was not his primary interest, though it became his most consuming one. With wit, finesse and expert scholarship, Pottle was able to play a major role in the development of Boswellian studies.

It is often the case that our lives are shaped by a combination of choice, circumstance and accident—and so it was with Pottle. Originally, he had intended to be "a poet and perhaps a writer of fiction". During World War I he recorded his time with the US medical forces and produced *Stretchers: The Story of a Hospital Unit on the Western Front.* Afterwards, he spent a brief period as a high school teacher of chemistry and history but soon enrolled in Yale's MA English programme, falling "deeply in love with scholarship". His master's and doctoral research on Boswell later appeared under the title *The Literary Career of James Boswell, Esq.* It was immediately hailed as the definitive biography. The style of presentation was greatly admired for its unobtrusiveness, and his command of the source material was also noteworthy. Before this book was actually published, Pottle had already been persuaded by Chauncey Brewster Tinker, with whom he studied at Yale, to write a bibliographic compilation of the Boswell papers then at the university. This resulted in the collaborative effort, *A New Portrait of James Boswell.*

Coincidentally, new opportunities were opening up in this area of study and Pottle came along at just the right time to seize them. An American collector named Colonel Ralph Isham had begun to publish his own extensive holdings of Boswell papers, which he had acquired from Malahide Castle near Dublin. When Isham's editor suddenly died after publication of a first volume, Pottle stepped in to carry on the work and develop the archives. This included retrieving the second collection of material, held in Fettercairn, Scotland, and arranging its transfer to Yale in 1949. The project was to become Pottle's life work; and even though he often had help, he scrupulously supervised every aspect of preparation, from typescript to proof.

Under Pottle's direction, 13 volumes of the "Yale Boswell Papers" were produced, along with four annotated volumes. The first of these, *Boswell's London Journal*, was the most popular, selling more than one million copies since 1950. (The spectacular sales of this volume so impressed the publishers that they dramatically overestimated the appeal of the subsequent volumes. After a number of excessive print-runs, they eventually regained their sense of proportion.) Another notable publication is Pottle's biography *James Boswell: The Early Years, 1740–1769*, which was presented as an analysis of his research on the subject. The book was widely acclaimed mainly, as *The Times* wrote, "because Boswell is so alive in it—furiously inconsistent, of astonishing and varying moods, sometimes hard to take or defend, but always vividly present".

Boswell himself was the melancholy, but immensely gifted son of Lord Auchinleck of Ayrshire. Boswell was a gentleman by standing and a lawyer by profession, and his captivating personality brought him into the company of some of the greatest men of his age: Johnson, Jean Jacques Rousseau and Voltaire. His unusual memory and literary talents enabled him to recreate the scenes and conversations he had with these people. Most importantly, he set down the *Life of Samuel Johnson* in 1791 from his own journals and diaries, as well as from Johnson's own papers. As Samuel Monk and Lawrence Lipking note, "The *Life* is a record not of Johnson alone but of literary England during the last half of the century. But Boswell wrote with his eye on the object and that object was Samuel Johnson, to whom every detail in the book is relevant, toward whom such eminent persons as Sir Joshua Reynolds, Edmund Burke, Oliver Goldsmith, Lord Chesterfield...always face." Therefore, Boswell's importance is his social genius and literary artistry. What has been revealed by Pottle's work has added new detail to the portrait not only of Boswell, but of eighteenth-century England.

Curiously, Pottle always regarded himself primarily as a scholar of the Romantic poets. His knowledge of Shelley, Wordsworth, Scott and Browning was impressive, though the published work could not compare with his other pursuit. Pottle joined Yale in 1925, becoming full professor in 1930, head of department in 1932, and Sterling Professor of English in 1944. He could often be seen on campus, a throwback to the older academic generation, with his wire-rimmed glasses, green eyeshade and bow tie. His longevity was also widely known, and J. Hillis Miller once jokingly remarked that he fully expected Pottle to be seated at the funerals of every colleague he worked with. Despite his fascination for Boswell, who was a "noisy, bouncy fellow",

Pottle was a pensive and quiet man. A fall in 1983 forced him to relinquish his full-time editorial duties. Later, because of ill-health, he was obliged to spend his final years in a convalescent home in New Haven.

As a tribute to his career and accomplishments, Pottle's colleagues and admirers dedicated a collection of essays to him in 1965, aptly called *From Sensibility to Romanticism*. His recognition by the Guggenheim Foundation and Glasgow University attests to the esteem in which his work is held and its value to British literary history.

Born Frederick Albert Pottle. **Parents** Fred Leroy and Annette Wardwell (Kemp) Pottle. **Marriage** Marion Isabel Starbird, 1920. **Children** One son, Christopher. **Education** Colby College, BA, 1917; Yale University, MA, 1921, PhD, 1925. **Military service** Private soldier, Evacuation Hospital No. 8, US Army Expeditionary Force, 1917–19. **Career** Assistant professor of English, University of New Hampshire, 1921–23; instructor, Yale University, 1925–26, assistant professor of English, 1926–30, professor of English, 1930–42, Emily Sanford Professor of English Literature, 1942–44; Sterling Professor of English, 1944–66; professor emeritus, 1966–87. **Related activities** Messenger lecturer, Cornell University; 1941; public orator, Yale University, 1942, 1946; fellow emeritus, Davenport College, Yale University; editor of the Boswell Papers; chair, editorial committee of Yale edition of *Private Papers of James Boswell*. **Other activities** Member, Joint Commission on Holy Matrimony of the Episcopal Church, 1940–46. **Offices and memberships** Trustee: Colby College, 1932–59, 1966–78 (honorary life trustee, 1978-87), General Theological Seminary, 1947–68; member: Chancellor Academy of American Poets, 1951–71, Provincial Utrechts Genootschap van Kunsten en Wetenschappen, 1953–87, American Academy of Arts and Sciences, 1957–87, American Philosophical Society, 1960–87; fellow, International Institute of Arts and Letters, 1958–87; president, Johnson Society, Lichfield, 1974; honorary member, Johnson Club; vice-president, Johnson Society, London; Modern Language Association of America; Medieval Academy of America; Guild of Scholars; American Association of University Professors; Phi Beta Kappa. **Awards and honours** John Addison Porter Prize, Yale University; LLD, University of Glasgow, 1936; LittD: Colby College, 1941, Rutgers University, 1951; Guggenheim Fellowships, 1945–46 and 1952–53; Wilbur Lucius Cross Medal, Yale University, 1967; William Clyde DeVane Medal, Yale University, 1969; Lewis Prize, American Philosophical Society, 1975; Distinguished Alumnus Award, Colby College, 1977; LHD, Northwestern University. **Publications** *Shelley and Browning: A Myth and Some Facts*, 1923, reprinted, 1965; (with C. B. Tinker) *A New Portrait of James Boswell*, 1927, reprinted, 1973; *The Literary Career of James Boswell*, 1929, reprinted, 1965; *Stretchers: The Story of a Hospital on the Western Front*, 1929; (with Marion S. Pottle) *The Private Papers of James Boswell: A Catalogue*, 1931; *The Private Papers of James Boswell*, volumes 7–18, 1931–34; (with C. H. Bennett) *Boswell's Journal of a Tour to the Hebrides, From the Original Manuscript*, 1936, revised edition, 1963; (with others) *Index to the Private Papers of James Boswell*, 1937; *Boswell and the Girl From Botany Bay*, 1937; *The Idiom of Poetry*, 1941, revised and enlarged edition, 1946, reprinted, 1963; *James Boswell: The Early Years, 1740–1769*, 1966. **Edited works** *Boswell's London Journal, 1762–63*, 1950; *Boswell in Holland, 1763–1764*, 1952; *Boswell on the Grand Tour: Germany and Switzerland, 1764*, 1953; (with Frank Brady) *Boswell on the Grand Tour: Italy, Corsica and France, 1765*, 1955; (with Frank Brady) *Boswell in Search of a Wife, 1766–69*, 1956; (with William K. Wimsatt) *Boswell for the Defence, 1769–74*, 1959; (with Charles Ryskamp) *Boswell: The Ominous Years, 1774–76*, 1963; (with Charles McC. Weis) *Boswell in Extremes, 1774–78*, 1970; (with Joseph W. Reed) *Boswell: Laird of Auchinleck, 1778–82*, 1977; *Boswell: The Applause of the Jury*, 1981; *Pride* *and Negligence: A History of the Boswell Papers*, 1982; also edited Yale Edition of *The Private Papers of James Boswell*, until 1983; contributed numerous articles to academic journals. **Cause of death** Undisclosed, at age 89.

ARTHUR M. SACKLER

American Psychiatrist, Businessman, Philanthropist and Art Collector
***Born* New York City, New York, 22 August 1913**
***Died* New York City, New York, 26 May 1987**

Arthur Sackler belonged to that rare breed of collector whose ancestry extends back to the Renaissance: a physician, patron, connoisseur and man of immense fortune, he combined the same qualities of learning, philanthropy and aesthetic judgement that might aptly describe a Medici duke of the fifteenth century.

Sackler's career presented a bewildering number of facets: acknowledged as an authority on biological psychiatry, as the first to use ultrasound in medical diagnosis, and for identifying histamine as a hormone, the fortune he amassed through his medical publishing and drug-company concerns enabled him to amass several highly important collections of art whose focus ranged from Chinese paintings and ceramics, to European terracottas and Impressionist paintings. He trained on a pre-medical course at New York University, and concurrently studied art history there and at the Cooper Union. To fund his studies he joined the William Douglas MacAdams medical advertising agency, eventually becoming its owner. The *Medical Tribune*, a bi-weekly newspaper first published by him in 1951, soon expanded into a worldwide organization, and he was editor in chief of the *Journal of Clinical and Experimental Psychopathology* from 1951 to 1962. His donations to the medical community were generous, and he established a research centre at the Brooklyn College of Pharmacy at Long Island University—the Laboratories for Therapeutic Research—with a contribution of $2 million. Several other universities, at home and abroad, also benefited from his philanthropy.

Within the arts his spectacular and consistent generosity is most evident. Few major American museums have not benefited from donations or loans from his collections, and Sackler once stated: "Great art doesn't belong to anybody. Never did. Never will." His policy of lending museums entire collections of works, such as the time in the 1960s when he deposited thousands of Chinese works of art at the Metropolitan Museum of Art in New York, at times led to controversy over their display. His eclectic tastes also led him to buy entire collections rather than single pieces, and in describing his approach he said, "I collect as a biologist. Really to understand a civilization, a society, you must have a large enough corpus of data."

His first interest had been in medieval painting and Impressionism, but he soon became fascinated by all facets of Chinese art, from ritual bronzes, jade carving and ceramics, to stone and wood sculpture. He was expertly advised in his acquisitions of Chinese paintings by the chairman of the Far Eastern department of the Metropolitan Museum, Wen Fong, and by specialist dealers. His close association with the Metropolitan Museum is witnessed by numerous endowments, principally the Sackler Wing, which houses the Temple of Dendur from Egypt, and the new Japanese galleries.

However, his benefaction was not confined to New York. At Harvard University in 1985 he donated the Arthur M. Sackler Museum, designed by the British architect, James Stirling, and just after his death, the Arthur M. Sackler Gallery opened at the Smithsonian Institution in Washington, its collection comprising some 1000 objects from his collection of Asian and Near Eastern art. Several other North American universities have works from the Sackler collections. Beijing University also enjoyed his patronage, with the establishment of the Sackler Museum for Chinese archaeology and a centre for Chinese studies in museology.

In latter years his tastes moved away from Oriental art, taking in pre-Columbian, American Indian, Graeco–Roman and twentieth-century American painting, eventually moving towards European art, and especially terracottas. His fascination for this medium was because it represented a "Western manifestation of the freedom of aesthetic expression I had found in so many of the paintings of China..." Furthermore, he stated in the introduction to a catalogue that, "They speak to me with an immediacy undimmed by time, with an intimacy unrestricted by technology, and with a personality as distinctive as what I see them to be—as individual as the *Fingerprints of the Artists*." The exhibition of terracottas from his collection illustrated the enormous breadth of his acquisitions, ranging from fifteenth-century reliefs of the *Nativity* to figures by the French nineteenth-century sculptor, Auguste Rodin.

If his change of aesthetic direction surprised some contemporaries, in his own mind Sackler, a man of affable and humorous spirit, with little concern for the intellectual arrogance of the art historical world, was able to counter this: "Why, I wondered, this sudden turn of aesthetic events in a life which had gone so far down the road of Oriental expressions? What a provincial thought that was, as though the neurosensory and neuromuscular systems of man in different parts of the world were so different in origin and its fundamental, intrinsic aesthetic so widely disparate." Clearly the words of a man secure in his convictions and of a man whose generosity has immeasurably enriched the collections of many public museums.

Born Arthur Mitchell Sackler. **Parents** Isaac and Sophie Sackler. **Marriages** 1) Else Jorgensen, 1935; 2) Marietta Lutze, 1949; 3) Jill? **Children** Two daughters, Carol and Elizabeth, by first marriage; one son and one daughter, Arthur and Denise, by second marriage. **Education** New York University, BS, 1933, MD, 1937; also studied art history at New York University and the Cooper Union. **Scientific career** House physician and paediatrician, Lincoln Hospital, New York City, 1937–39; resident psychiatrist, Creedmoor State Hospital, Queens Village, Long Island, 1944–46; founder and director of research, Creedmoor Institute of Psychobiological Studies, 1949–54; co-founder, Sackler School of Medicine, Tel-Aviv; research professor of psychiatry, New York Medical College, 1972. **Business career** Worked for William Douglas Adams advertising agency, while still a student, later became its principal owner; chairman, board of Medical Press Incorporated, 1954 onwards; president: Physicians News Service Incorporated, 1955 onwards, Medical Radio and Television Institutions Incorporated, 1955 onwards; director, Laboratories for Therapeutic Research, Brooklyn College of Pharmacy, Long Island University, 1957–83; founder, Medical Tribune Newspapers, 1960 onwards; also had interest in Purdue-Frederick drug company. **Related activities** Editor-in-chief, *Journal of Clinical and Experimental Psychopathology*, 1950–62; also contributed articles to many scientific journals; associate chairman, international committee for research, First International Congress of Psychiatry, 1950; benefactor to several scientific insitutions, 1957 onwards; chairman, international task force on world health manpower, 1969 onwards; chairman, National Committee to Save Our Schools' Health, 1971–72. **Other activities** Art collector and patron, 1940s onwards; member, advisory council, department of art history and archaeology, Columbia,

1961–74; founder, Sackler Laboratories of Art History and Archaeology, 1961; senior research associate in anthropology, Columbia, 1969–70. **Awards and honours** Award for advancement of medical communications, American Medical Association, 1969; achievement award, Heights Colleges Alumni Association, New York City, 1970; also awards for scientific exhibitions. **Offices and memberships** Trustee, New York Medical College, 1968–72; board of associates, Linus Pauling Institute of Science and Medicine, 1974 onwards; fellow: American Psychiatric Association, American Geriatrics Society, Royal Anthropological Institute of Great Britain and Ireland; member, International Association of Social Psychiatry, chairman, 1973 onwards; member: Gerontologists Society, American Association for the Advancement of Science, New York Academy of Sciences, United States committee, World Medical Association; board of governors, Chinese Art Society. **Endowments** Laboratory for therapeutic research, School of Pharmacy, University of Long Island, 1957; Arthur M. Sackler Sciences Center, Clark University, Worcester, Massachusetts; biomedical institutions at Tufts University and New York University; Sackler School of Medicine, Tel-Aviv University, Israel; Arthur M. Sackler Gallery, Princeton Museum; with brothers, Raymond and Mortimer, endowed Sackler Wing, Metropolitan Museum of Art, New York City; Sackler Gallery, Columbia University; special collections at Museum of American Indian Art; special loan collection, Brooklyn Museum; principal donor, works of art from Asia, Middle East and Mediterranean, Sackler Museum, Harvard, 1985; Arthur M. Sackler Museum, containing archaeological faculty, Beijing University, China, 1986; Arthur M. Sackler Gallery, Smithsonian Institution, Washington, 1988. **Publications** (co-author) *Great Physiodynamic Therapies*, 1956. **Cause of death** Heart attack, at age 73.

CHAUDHURY CHARAN SINGH

Indian Politician

Born **Noorpur, India, 23 December 1902**

Died **New Delhi, India, 29 May 1987**

Part of the legacy of British colonial rule in India is a chaotic, unstable political climate in which tactics and personality cults seem infinitely more important than ideology or policies. It is an exceedingly shrewd and astute politician who can successfully chart the treacherous waters of national politics within the vast subcontinent, where each general election involves nearly one twelfth of the world's population and a hugh range of ethnicity, religious belief and political opinion. Those who do make it to the premiership are constantly at risk from rival members of the uneasy coalitions which constitute the hallmark of Indian parliamentarianism.

Chaudhury Charan Singh, a Hindu born under the Raj in what is now known as Uttar Pradesh, attained the post of prime minister for a very brief period at the end of the 1970s. The son of a farmer, he never lost his emotional links with the countryside, even though he trained as a lawyer at Agra University. As a young advocate in Ghaziabad, he became active in the independence movement, where his involvement in demonstrations against the British led to a number of spells in prison. Far from damaging his subsequent governmental prospects, his career would have foundered badly had he not been able to point to evidence of anti-British activity, a *sine qua non* of post-war political credibility.

Abandoning his legal career in 1927 for full-time membership of the Congress Party, Charan Singh cut his political teeth before independence as a member of the State Assembly, and later rose to prominence with two terms as chief minister in the late 1960s. He identified himself early on as an opponent of Mrs Gandhi. A profoundly conservative man, Charan Singh maintained that the prevailing reliance on heavy industry as a solution for India's problems was misguided; he himself saw the way forward through a return to small-scale, family orientated, cottage-type industries. His distrust of urbanization and new technology once led Jawaharlal Nehru to dismiss him as "a man of the eighteenth century". As a representative of Jat Hindu farmers, Charan Singh's emphasis on agricultural solutions seems understandable enough.

Following his break with the Congress Party in 1969, he founded a number of new political groups. None of them prospered significantly, but his beliefs did not disallow him from making a number of alliances with a whole range of political opponents. Mrs Gandhi's fall from power in 1977 gave him an opportunity for success on a national scale and he led his Bharatiya Kranti (Indian Revolutionary) Party into coalition with the Janata Party, led by Morarji Desai. Following Desai's appointment as prime minister, Charan Singh was appointed home minister. In this post, he attempted to get rid of Mrs Gandhi by ordering her arrest on charges of corruption and abuse of power. This proved difficult to sustain and the charismatic former prime minister spent only one night in prison.

Charan Singh also served as finance minister before his constant criticism and numerous differences with Desai led to his expulsion from the Cabinet. However, Desai too found himself unable to remain in office, and the subsequent political vacuum was filled by Charan Singh in an unlikely coalition with his former opponent, Mrs Gandhi. It lasted only three weeks, when Mrs Gandhi withdrew her party's support, but Charan Singh remained as a nominal prime minister until elections in January 1980 returned Mrs Gandhi to the premiership.

Routed in that election, Charan Singh went on to form the Lok Dal Party, which sputtered on intermittently until it split into two factions following his stroke in 1985. He waited vainly for another chance of power and died an unhappy, disappointed man.

Born Chaudhury Charan Singh. **Marriage** Gyatri Devi. **Children** Five daughters and one son. **Education** Studied law at Agra University. **Career** Practised law in Ghaziabad before moving to Meerut, 1929; active in Indian independence movement, being imprisoned several times by British authorities in 1930s; elected to United Provinces (now Uttar Pradesh) State Assembly, 1937; held various offices in Uttar Pradesh State Government: parliamentary secretary in various departments, 1946–51, minister for justice and information, 1951–52, minister for revenue and agriculture, 1952, and for revenue and transport until 1959, minister for home affairs and agriculture, 1960, minister for agriculture and forests, 1962–65, and for local self-government, 1966–67; led political party Samyukta Vidhayak Dal, 1967; chief minister of Uttar Pradesh, 1967–68, 1970; founder and president, Bharatiya Kranti Dal (Indian Revolutionary Party), 1969–77; briefly jailed under Premier Gandhi's period of emergency rule, 1975–77; deputy chair, Janata Party, 1977–79; held various offices in Government of India: minister for home affairs, 1977–78, and for finance, 1979, joint deputy premier, 1979, prime minister and minister for home affairs, 1979–80; subsequently founded Lok Dal Party, which split and foundered after his incapacitation by a stroke in 1985. **Offices and memberships** Governor, International Monetary Fund, 1979. **Publications** (include) *Abolition of Zamindari*; *Cooperative Farming X-rayed*; *India's Poverty and Its Solution*; *Peasant Proprietorship or Land to the Workers*; *Prevention of Division of Holdings Below a Certain Minimum*; *India's Economic Policy: A Gandhian Blueprint*. **Cause of death** Undisclosed, at age 84.

WING COMMANDER ROBERT STANFORD-TUCK

British Fighter Pilot

***Born* England, 1 July 1916**

***Died* England, 5 May 1987**

Wing Commander Robert Stanford-Tuck, DSO, DFC, was one of the best known and most successful British pilots of World War II, despite being made a prisoner of war in January 1942. Even in captivity he maintained his indomitable spirit, making several attempts to escape. He finally succeeded in January 1945 and battled his way through enemy territory and harsh winter weather to the Russian lines.

Born the son of an army captain, who had served in the Queen's Royal West Surrey Regiment in World War I, Stanford-Tuck attended St Dunstan's College, Reading. Here he excelled as a gymnast, fencer, swimmer and boxer, besides being the school's best marksman—a product of his father's enthusiasm for firearms. Drawn to the sea in search of adventure, Stanford-Tuck joined the Merchant Navy as a sea cadet. After two and a half years of travelling the world, Stanford-Tuck was seduced by the lure of flying, and on 16 September 1935 reported to Uxbridge RAF Station to become an acting pilot officer (on probation). From there he was sent to Grantham Flying Training School where he proved to be far from "a natural" at flying. Indeed, he failed the course, but he persevered and eventually gained his wings in 1936.

In spite of his shaky start, Stanford-Tuck progressed steadily and became considered a skilful, if flashy, pilot. While flying Gladiators with 65 Squadron at Hornchurch in 1938, he was involved in an unavoidable mid-air collision in which the pilot of the other machine was killed and he himself was forced to bale out. Only a couple of months later he was involved in another mid-air collision, this time safely crash landing his damaged aircraft. Such experiences—together with a short-lived dismissal from the service for a minor road traffic offence—did much to curb his rash enthusiasm and introduced an element of precise calculation into his flying.

By the outbreak of war in September 1939, Stanford-Tuck was a relative veteran, with over 700 hours in his log book, including some flying time on Spitfires. Held back by Fighter Command, 65 Squadron saw very little action in the early months of the war, and it was not until May 1940, when he was posted to 92 Squadron based at Croydon, that he saw action for the first time.

On 10 May 1940 the German war machine unleashed itself against France and the Low Countries, meeting with immediate and devastating success. Flying Spitfires, 92 Squadron went into action for the first time on 23 May, and for Stanford-Tuck it was a memorable day. Flying over Dunkirk, the squadron was attacked by Me.109s and in the ensuing dogfight Stanford-Tuck latched on to the German leader's aircraft, caught him at the bottom of his dive and shot the aircraft out of the sky. In the following days he raised his personal tally to eight enemy fighters and earned a reputation for an indomitable fighting spirit, cool command, relentless aggression and consummate skill.

In September 1940 Stanford-Tuck was placed in command of a badly mauled and dispirited 257 Squadron flying Hurricane aircraft, the less glamorous workhorse of the Battle of Britain. Within a remarkably short period, Stanford-Tuck's bold and dashing leadership reinvigorated the squadron and welded it into a formidable, if battered, fighting force. By the end of the year, Stanford-Tuck's personal tally stood at 18 and his leadership and luck (on one occasion a bullet was deflected from his heart by a penny in his breast pocket) had become well-nigh legendary.

In July 1941 he was promoted to wing commander, taking charge of the famous Duxford Wing and leading them on the early "rhubarbs" over northern France. Later in the year he was sent to the United States to advise on combat and training techniques and was warmly welcomed everywhere as a charismatic fighter ace. Shortly after his return to operational flying in January 1942, Stanford-Tuck was shot down by anti-aircraft fire while leading a low level strafing attack over Boulogne. He was captured by German soldiers and, having just destroyed their vehicles and killed several of their comrades, expected a rough time. Instead he was treated with fairness and respect by all, and was even invited to dinner by Oberstleutnant Adolf Galland before he passed into captivity. The pair had met once before—as adversaries in the air—and had each shot down the other's wingman; "Even-Stevens", as Galland put it. Stanford-Tuck was sent to Stalag Luft III in Poland and was due to take part in the "Great Escape" led by his former 92 Squadron compatriot Roger Bushell. However, for no apparent reason he was suddenly transferred to another camp for two weeks. This chance movement may well have saved his life for 50 of the 76 escapers, including Bushell, were executed by the Gestapo. Following another unsuccessful attempt, Stanford-Tuck succeeded in escaping in the harsh winter conditions of January 1945. Trudging towards Russian lines by night with a fellow escapee, frostbitten and hungry, Stanford-Tuck had several close shaves with German troops. Despite speaking Russian (a legacy from his Russian childhood governess), he was unable to persuade the troops of their identity and instead was forced to fight the Germans for two weeks. Eventually he did make contact with the British Embassy in Moscow and, via Odessa, returned by sea to England, although too late to take any further part in the war. In the immediate post-war years, he held a number of Fighter Command appointments, both at home and abroad, before retiring in 1949 to farm mushrooms in Kent.

Robert Stanford-Tuck belonged to an élite band of almost legendary British fighter aces and can firmly take his place alongside the likes of Douglas Bader, Sailor Malan and Johnnie Johnson. At the end of the war, he was the eighth highest-scoring RAF pilot, with 29 confirmed victories, eight probably destroyed and six damaged—all achieved between May 1940 and January 1942. His exploits and determined leadership at a time of great peril inspired not only his fellow pilots but also the general public and earned him a DSO, three DFCs and an American DFC. Stanford-Tuck exemplified the best aspects of the spirit that maintained the British people in the dark days of 1940.

Born Robert Roland Stanford-Tuck. **Parents** Stanley Lewis and Ethel Constance Tuck. **Marriage** Joyce Ackerman, 1945 (died, 1985). **Children** Two sons. **Education** St Dunstan's Preparatory School and College, Reading, Berkshire, 1932. **Career** Held a couple of clerical posts before becoming a cadet in the Merchant Navy with Lamport and Holt; joined Royal Air Force, 1935; acting pilot officer, No. 3 Flying Training School, Grantham, Lincolnshire; received his wings, 1936; served with 65 Fighter Squadron, 1936–39; flight-lieutenant, 92 F Squadron, May 1940; commander, 257 Burma Fighter Squadron, September 1940–July 1941; wing commander, Duxford Wing, July 1941; visited United States as adviser on combat and training techniques, 1941; wing commander flying, Biggin Hill Wing, late 1941; taken prisoner, 1942; escaped from Stalag Luft III, 1945; after war held Fighter Command appointments in UK and overseas; retired, 1948; subsequently farmed mushrooms in Kent. **Awards and honours** Companion of the Distinguished Service Order, 1940; Distinguished Flying Cross (two bars), 1946; American Distinguished Flying Cross, 1946. **Cause of death** Undisclosed, at age 70. **Further reading** L. Forrester, *Fly For Your Life*, London, 1956.

PHYLLIS TATE

British Composer

Born **Gerrard's Cross, Buckinghamshire, 6 April 1911**

Died **London, England, 29 May 1987**

Phyllis Tate was a representative of the first generation of musicians which, stimulated by the talent, perseverence and fortitude of Dame Ethyl Smythe, managed to produce several outstanding women composers asserting their creativity on equal terms in a heavily male-dominated world.

Her most ambitious work was an opera, *The Lodger*, written in 1960. It stands apart from her other compositions, which largely reflect the twentieth-century preoccupation with chamber music, using small, unusual combinations of instruments and the voice. These experiments with texture and sonority often resulted in fascinating and highly individual effects.

Phyllis Margaret Duncan Tate was born in the staunchly middle-class Home Counties, the daughter of an architect. Her first musical experiences were with a banjo, which she was given at the age of 12 and on which she began to write foxtrots and other types of light music. One day Herbert Farjeon heard her play, thought she was talented and decided to teach her himself, at the Royal Academy of Music, where she also studied the piano and timpani.

While at the academy she wrote an operetta called *The Policeman's Serenade* to a libretto by A. P. Herbert. It was performed by students to considerable acclaim, but she later withdrew it, along with many of her other juvenilia, including a cello concerto of 1934 which Dame Ethyl Smythe had heard and admired.

After college, Tate took a job at Oxford University Press, where she worked for Hubert Foss in the music department. He encouraged her by putting on concerts of her music, and during the war years she began to acquire more confidence in her writing. The first work to meet her own satisfaction was a saxophone concerto of 1944. It was her nocturne (1946) that brought her music to the attention of the public. It showed her original gift for instrumentation, in this case, bass clarinets, string quartet, double bass and celeste. Her sonata for clarinet and cello of the following year is another example of her taste for unusual instrumental combinations and still enjoys the popular success it achieved at the ISCM festival in 1952.

Her opera *The Lodger*, to a libretto by David Franklin, tells the Jack the Ripper story in a graphic, direct way, and was produced to critical acclaim in 1960. It is a rare example of a successful musical thriller whose effectiveness is grounded on psychological understanding and an authentic social atmosphere. It was followed by a modest number of other works, notably the Secular Requiem of 1967. In 1978 Charles Causley's narrative poem based on the story of St Martha, who is still celebrated at Tarrascon for offering her assailant, a dragon, love and kindness instead of a sword, inspired Tate to write a setting. One reviewer referred to it as "plain and direct, often conversational in tone, yet enlivened by much wit and poetry, with an individuality that lifts it far above the general run of custom-made cantatas".

Tate was not a prolific composer but always a pragmatic one, which meant that she wrote very successfully for children, who appreciated her simple, tonal language, as found in her suite *Street Sounds*. A larger work, *Invasion*, was written for the Coventry Schools Festival. These works as much as any reveal her desire to be a communicator.

Her later works, such as *Rainbow and the Cuckoo* (1975) for oboe and string trio, and the *Lyric Suite* for piano duet (1974), aimed for a sparser texture. She accepted the challenge of paring down her style but referred to it as "self-inflicted torture". Tate always kept an open mind about sonority and quite later in life attended evening classes in African drumming. Her music has been described as bristling with "abrasive dissonances and asymmetrical rhythms, [while retaining] its classical purity"; it remains popular with players and listeners alike.

Born Phyllis Margaret Duncan Tate. **Parents** Duncan, architect, and Annie S. (Holl) Tate. **Marriage** Alan Frank, music scholar and publisher, 1935. **Children** One son and one daughter. **Education** Royal Academy of Music, London, 1928–32. **Career** Worked in music department of Oxford University Press prior to World War II, before turning to composition full-time. **Awards and honours** Fellow of the Royal Academy of Music, 1964. **Compositions** *The Policeman's Serenade*, operetta; cello concerto, 1933; *Valse Lointaine*, for small orchestra, 1933, *Prelude, Interlude and Postlude*, for chamber orchestra, 1942; saxophone concerto, 1944; *Nocturne for Four Voices*, for mezzo-soprano, tenor, baritone and instruments, 1945; nocturne for bass clarinets, string quartet, double bass and celeste, 1947; sonata for clarinet and cello, 1947; string quartet, 1952; choral scene from *The Bacchae* of Euripides, double chorus, 1953; *Occasional Overture*, 1955; *The Lady of Shalott*, cantata for tenor, viola, percussion, two pianos and celeste, 1956; *Air and Variations*, for violin, clarinet and piano, 1958; *London Fields*, 1958; *Sonatina No. 2*, piano, 1959; *The Lodger*, opera, 1960; *Dark Pilgrimage*, television opera, 1963; *A Victorian Garland*, for soprano, contralto, horn and piano, 1965; Seven Lincolnshire Folk Songs for chorus and instruments, 1966; *Gravestones*, for Cleo Laine, 1966; *Secular Requiem*, for chorus and orchestra, 1967; *Christmas Ale*, for soloists, chorus and orchestra, 1967; *Apparitions* ballad sequence for tenor, harmonica, string quartet and piano, 1968; *Twice in a Blue Moon*, fantasy operetta, 1968; Gaelic Ballads, for violin and piano, 1968; (arranger) Three Northumbrian Coastal Ballads, for baritone and instruments, 1969; *Illustrations*, brass band, 1969; *To Words by Joseph Beaumont*, for two sopranos, alto and piano, 1970; *Variegations*, solo viola, 1971; *Serenade to Christmas*, for mezzo-soprano, chorus and orchestra, 1972; Two Ballads, for violin and guitar, 1972; *Lyric Suite*, for two pianos, 1973; *Explorations Around a Troubadour Song*, piano, 1973; *The Rainbow and the Cuckoo*, for oboe, violin, viola and cello, 1974; *Sonatina Pastorale*, for harmonica and harpsichord, 1974; *Songs of Sundrie Kindes*, for tenor and lute, 1976; *Songs Without Words*, orchestra, 1976; *Scenes from Kipling*, for baritone and piano, 1976; *St Martha and the Dragon*, for narrator, soloists, chorus and orchestra, 1976; *Seasonal Sequence*, for viola and piano, 1977; *Panorama*, for strings, 1977; *All the World's a Stage*, for chorus and orchestra, 1977; *Compassion*, for chorus and organ/orchestra, 1978; Three Pieces for Solo Clarinet, 1979; *The Ballad of Reading Gaol*, for baritone, organ and cello, 1980; *Movements*, string quartet, 1980; *Prelude, Aria, Interlude and Finale*, for clarinet and piano, 1981; also composed many small choral pieces, songs and other works for schools and young people, including *Street Sounds*, *The Story of Lieutenant Cockatoo*, *A Pride of Lions*, *Scarecrow*, *Invasion* and *Solar*. **Cause of death** Undisclosed, at age 76.

JUNE

ELIZABETH ACKROYD

British Civil Servant

***Born* England, 13 August 1910**

***Died* London, England, 28 June 1987**

Dame Elizabeth Ackroyd was a formidable campaigner for the rights of the consumer; she was one of those noble people who enrich the lives of the rest of us by their tireless efforts to wrest justice for the underdog, be he client, customer or patient, from the arms of government, industry and the health service. She was widely liked and respected by her colleagues and opponents alike. Friends described her as "a tough, nice lady" and as "one of the most formidable women I have ever met". Trained by Oxford and the Civil Service in the art of committee warfare, she was not one to lose a battle or concede a case lightly.

Sadly, when people talk of Betty Ackroyd, they are more likely to mention the things she failed to achieve than to list her successes—maybe because these were what mattered most to her. She regretted, in particular, her failure to stop banks closing on Saturdays and to get ten shillings rather than the pound adopted as the new unit of currency in the decimalized system. The long battle she fought with Prime Minister Edward Heath to prevent the abolition of the government-funded Consumer Council, which she directed for seven years until her retirement in 1971, was probably the defeat that galled her most.

Ackroyd's early jobs in the Civil Service included the directorship of the Steel and Power Division of the Economic Commission for Europe, and membership of the UK delegation to the High Authority of the European Coal and Steel Community. It was, however, as director of the newly established Consumer Council that she found her public voice and her final direction.

Nothing in Elizabeth Ackroyd's busy "post retirement" career ever gave her the power and influence she wielded at the Consumer Council, where she was known for a time as "Public Protector No. 1". But as vice-president of the Consumers' Association, chairman of the Patients' Association, member of the Post Office Users' National Council, the South Eastern Electricity Consumers' Council, the Cinematograph Films Council, the Westminster Police Consultative Committee and the Pedestrians' Association, she continued to fight many of the same battles with undiminished vigour.

Elizabeth Ackroyd never married. She had what seems to have been an unlikely interest in horse-racing and was herself a racehorse owner. The sociologist Michael Young, her "friend and enemy" at the National Suggestions Centre, remembered Betty Ackroyd as "generous, lighthearted and always humorous with a deep crackly sunny laugh that made me think of beaches in classical Greece".

Born Dorothy Elizabeth Ackroyd. **Father** Major Charles Harris Ackroyd. **Education** St Hugh's College, Oxford, MA, BLitt. **Career** Civil servant, 1940–71: Ministry of Supply, 1940–42, 1946–49, 1951–52, under-secretary, 1952, Ministry of Production, 1942–45, Board of Trade, 1945–46, 1955–61, Ministry of Trade, 1961–63, director, Consumer Council, 1963–71. **Related activities** Commonwealth Fund fellowship, 1949–50; director, Steel and Power Division, Economic Commission for Europe, 1950–51; member, UK delegation to High Authority of European Coal and Steel Community, 1952–55. **Offices and memberships** Vice-president, Consumers' Association, 1970 onwards; Post Office Users' National Council, 1970–84; Bedford College Council, 1970–85; member, Cinematograph Films Council, 1970–85, chairman, 1981–85; president, Patients' Association, 1971–78, chairman, 1978 onwards; honorary treasurer, Pedestrians' Association for Road Safety, 1971; chairman: South East Electricity Consultative Council, 1972–84, Bloodstock and Racehorse Industries Confederation Limited, 1977–78; governor, Birkbeck College, 1973 onwards; Waltham Forest Community Health Council, 1974 onwards; Horserace Totalizer Board, 1975–84; council member, Royal Society of Arts, 1975–81; vice-chairman, London Voluntary Service Council, 1977 onwards; independent member, Council for the Securities Industry, 1978–83; executive committee, National Council for Voluntary Organizations, 1980 onwards. **Awards and honours** Dame Commander Order of the British Empire, 1970. **Cause of death** Undisclosed, at age 76.

MARGUERITE de ANGELI

American Illustrator and Children's Writer

***Born* Lapeer, Michigan, 14 March 1889**

***Died* Philadelphia, Pennsylvania, 16 June 1987**

Educated at schools in Lapeer and Philadelphia, Marguerite Lofft was a professional singer, with a rich contralto voice, from 1904 to 1921. Her interest in drawing, however, eventually dictated a new career as an illustrator. She drew for various magazines and other people's books for some time, then, in 1935, embarked upon a series of picture-story books for six-year-olds. *Ted and Nina Go to the Grocery Store* (1935) and *Ted and Nina Have a Happy Rainy Day* (1936) and others have domestic themes and settings. So too do some of this author's stories designed for older children, which are also often sparked off by specific events in her own family life. *Copper-toed Boots* (1938), for example, was stimulated by her father's childhood in Lapeer, while *Fiddlestrings* (1974) is a fictionalized account of the life of her husband, John de Angeli, whom she married in 1910.

De Angeli tackles more sweeping themes in her historical novels, and in stories about ethnic groups in American society. Her most atmospheric historical books are *The Door in the Wall* and *Black Fox of Lorne*, both of which were first published in 1959. The former is set in the England of Edward III, a place and period which fascinated her, and which she uses to excellent effect as she recreates brooding but impressive castles and claustrophobic communities which contrast with the openness and freshness of early England's "green and pleasant land". *Black Fox of*

Lorne has a colourful Viking backgound: it focuses on two brothers who avenge the treacherous murder of their father. The hero of *The Door in the Wall*, like the leading characters in her ethnic stories, tackles problems which are applicable to most societies, however far they may be separated by time and space: Robin has to accept his handicap, but manages to overcome all manner of other hardships, just as Hannah, the small heroine of *Thee, Hannah!* (1962) has painfully to accept her drab Quaker bonnet and its meaning, but to wear it proudly.

Marguerite de Angeli's own childhood memories illuminate her pictures, and the particular becomes universal in her illustrations to the *Book of Nursery and Mother Goose Rhymes*, which she edited in 1954, and which, like her *Yonnie Wondernose* (1944), became a Caldecott honour book. She was awarded the Newbery Medal for *The Door in the Wall.* In 1963 she became the first recipient of the Drexel Award for children's literature, and in 1968 the Catholic Library Association awarded her the Regina Medal for a "lifetime of devotion to literature for children".

Born Marguerite Lofft. **Parents** S.C. and Ruby (Tuttle) Lofft. **Marriage** John de Angeli, 1910 (died, 1969). **Children** Four sons and one daughter. **Education** Schools in Lapeer, Michigan, and Philadelphia, Pennsylvania. **Career** Professional singer, 1904–21; magazine and book illustrator, particularly of children's books, 1924 onwards; became author, sometimes illustrating own books, 1935 onwards. **Awards and honours** American Library Association Newbery Medal for *The Door in the Wall*, 1950; *Yonnie Wondernose* and *Book of Nursery and Mother Goose Rhymes* named Caldecott honour books, 1954; *Black Fox of Lorne* named an honour book, 1956; Drexel Award for children's literature, Massachusetts Institute of Technology, 1963; Catholic Library Association Regina Medal, 1968; Lapeer Public Library dedicated to her, 1981. **Novels** (all published in New York, unless stated) *Ted and Nina Go to the Grocery Store*, 1935; *Ted and Nina Have a Happy Rainy Day*, 1936; *Henner's Lydia*, 1936, Kingswood, Surrey, England, 1965; *Petite Suzanne*, 1937; *Copper-toed Boots*, 1938, Kingswood, Surrey, 1965; *Skippack School*, 1939, Kingswood, Surrey, 1964; *A Summer Day with Ted and Nina*, 1940; *Thee, Hannah!*, 1940, Kingswood, Surrey, 1962; *Elin's Amerika*, 1941, Kingswood, Surrey, 1964; *Up the Hill*, 1942; *Yonnie Wondernose*, 1944; *Turkey for Christmas*, Philadelphia, 1944; *Bright April*, 1946; *Jared's Island*, 1947; *The Door in the Wall*, 1949, Kingswood, Surrey, 1959; *Just Like David*, 1951; *Black Fox of Lorne*, 1956, Kingswood, Surrey, 1959; *The Ted and Nina Storybook*, 1965; *Fiddlestrings*, 1974; *The Lion in the Box*, 1976; *Whistle for the Crossing*, 1977. **Other** (editor) *Book of Nursery and Mother Goose Rhymes*, 1954; (editor) *The Old Testament*, 1960; *A Pocket Full of Posies: A Merry Mother Goose*, 1961; (editor) *A Book of Favorite Hymns*, 1963; (with others) *Libraries and Reading: Their Importance in the Lives of Famous Americans*, ed. Donald H. Hunt, Philadelphia, 1964; *The Goose Girl*, 1964; *Butter at the Old Price: The Autobiography of Marguerite de Angeli*, 1971. **Illustrator** *The New Moon* by Cornelia Meigs, 1924; *Meggy MacIntosh* by Elizabeth Janet Gray, 1930; *A Candle in the Mist* by Florence Crannell Means, 1931; *The Christmas Nightingale* by Eric Kelly, 1932; *The Covered Bridge* by Cornelia Meigs, 1936; *Joan Wanted a Kitty* by Jane Brown Gemmil, 1937; *Alice-All-by-Herself* by Elizabeth Coatsworth, 1937; *Red Sky Over Rome* by Anne D. Kyle, 1938; *The Princess and the Gypsy* by Jean Rosmer, 1938; *Prayers and Graces for Little Children* ed. Quail Hawkins, 1941; *They Loved to Laugh* by Kathryn Worth, 1942; *In and Out: Verses* by Tom Robinson, 1943; *The Empty Barn* by Arthur C. de Angeli, 1966; *The Door in the Wall: A Play* by Arthur C. de Angeli, 1968. **Cause of death** Undisclosed, at age 98. **Further reading** B. Miller, *Illustrators of Children's Books*, 1947, 1958, 1968; B. Miller and E. Fields (eds), *Newbery Medal Books: 1922–1955*, 1955; M. Hoffman and E. Samuels, *Authors and Illustrators of Children's Books*, 1972; L. Hopkins, *More Books by More People*, 1974.

FRED ASTAIRE

American Dancer and Actor

***Born* Omaha, Nebraska, 10 May 1899**

***Died* Los Angeles, California, 22 June 1987**

For generations of film-goers the phrase "top hat, white tie and tails" conjures up one image—the slender figure of Fred Astaire, immaculate in evening dress, tap dancing his way across the floor with elegance and wit in a seemingly effortless routine.

Astaire was born Frederick Austerlitz, the son of an Austrian army officer who had emigrated to America and married a local schoolteacher. Austerlitz senior, who changed the family name to Astaire, would often say that there were only two kinds of Austrians—rascals and musicians. From his love of the theatre and music it is clear he belonged to the latter group, and Astaire and his elder sister, Adele, were raised in that tradition, attending dancing school from their earliest years.

They were soon appearing in vaudeville, and initially it was Adele who led the way in the partnership with Astaire tagging along behind. An agent's report in 1908 stated "the girl seems to have talent but the boy can do nothing", while a newspaper review in Washington, DC, in 1914 comments, "one of the best brother-and-sister acts seen here in a long time is given by Fred and Adele Astaire. The girl is superior to the boy." Interestingly, Adele herself was more perceptive and always maintained that Fred had been the more talented and inventive of the pair.

The Astaires' first Broadway performances were in the musicals *Over the Top* (1917) and *The Passing Show* (1918), which marked their graduation from vaudeville. Although some of their Broadway shows, notably *The Love Letter* (1921) and *The Bunch and Judy* (1923), were spectacular flops in themselves, the Astaires were always singled out for enthusiastic reviews and their careers flourished.

The year 1924 was to mark a watershed both for Astaire's career and for American musicals in general. George and Ira Gershwin were commissioned to write *Lady Be Good* especially for the brother and sister act. This was to be their first great success and it established the Astaires as stars. The show ran for 330 performances on Broadway and received rave reviews. It then transferred to London, where it was equally well received. The distinguished actress Hermione Baddeley, commenting on the London performance, wrote, "The Astaires were like automatons. They were magic, covering the stage with this terribly smooth, gorgeous rhythm bringing the best of American choreography together—we couldn't believe they were quite human."

Interestingly, the plot of *Lady Be Good* had one of the weakest storylines of all time, to the extent that the Astaires nearly backed out of performing in it. However, it was the music of George Gershwin and the lyrics of his brother Ira that raised the musical to great heights. This was the first time that the brothers had worked together on a musical comedy and it marked the coming of age of their talents, as it did of the Astaires. It was in this show that Astaire had a solo number for the first time, which was received with great enthusiasm and finally established him as the equal of his sister.

The Astaires went from strength to strength over the next years with such hits as *Funny Face* (1927) and *The Bandwagon* (1931). However, in 1932 Adele married into the English aristocracy and the partnership came to an end. Knowing that *The Bandwagon* would be their last show together, the Astaires pulled out all the stops and it was rated as one of the best Broadway musicals of all time. Astaire went on to do one more musical, *Gay Divorce* (1932), which included one of Cole Porter's most famous songs, "Night and Day", before deciding to try his luck in Hollywood where the advent of talking pictures had given the musical great popularity.

Astaire's first significant film performance was in *Flying Down to Rio* (1933) in which he partnered a little-known dancer called Ginger Rogers. Although by no means top of the bill, they stole the show, and the great partnership, which was to last for eight films, was born. From the beginning it was clear that Astaire and Rogers, who were soon known universally as Fred and Ginger, had created something very special. They were ideally suited in grace, versatility and temperament, and they broke new ground by working out all their dance variations on set with the camera in mind. In this way they created a new art form of film-dance. The result was that the audience was able to identify with the ideal romantic couple on screen and dance away with them in their imaginations. Indeed, the dance-hall business boomed in the 1930s, a phenomenon which has been attributed to the influence of the famous partnership. As critic Benny Green wrote in his biography of Astaire, "Every man wanted to woo every lady by dancing at, with, or round her."

Astaire and Rogers danced from hit to hit with such films as *Follow the Fleet* and *Swing Time*, both 1936, and *Shall We Dance* (1937). Perhaps the pinnacle of their perfection was reached in the 1935 film *Top Hat*. This film, with words and music by Irving Berlin, contains many of the songs which Astaire has made indubitably his own, such as "Isn't This a Lovely Day", "Cheek to Cheek" and, of course, "Top Hat, White Tie and Tails".

In 1939 the magical partnership broke up when Rogers decided to concentrate on straight acting. Astaire began to consider retirement but never quite got round to it, and over the next years made several films with different partners. However, it was not until 1945, in the film *Ziegfeld Follies*, which was to prove one of his biggest successes, that Astaire hit top form again. For the next ten years he made a string of films and, if he never quite recaptured the magic of his partnership with Rogers, he had some huge successes, notably *Daddy Long Legs* (1955) with Leslie Caron, *Funny Face* (1957) with Audrey Hepburn and *Silk Stockings* (1957) with Cyd Charisse.

Silk Stockings marked the end of Astaire's musical films. However, his career was by no means at an end. He appeared in a series of acclaimed television spectaculars where he danced with a new partner, Barrie Chase. He also took on a series of straight acting roles, notably in *On the Beach* (1959), where he played a convincing scientist in a nuclear drama, and *The Towering Inferno* (1975), for which he was nominated for an Oscar. Astaire introduced the hugely popular MGM compilation films *That's Entertainment Part 1* (1974) and *Part 2* (1976), which told the story of the studios' musicals. By this time he had become a legend, enchanting generation after generation of film-goers. Arlene Croce, one of Astaire's most perceptive critics, wrote that with him "dancing was transformed into a vehicle of serious emotion between a man and a woman. It never happened in movies again."

Born Frederick Austerlitz. **Parents** Frederick E. and Ann (Geilus) Austerlitz; name legally changed to Astaire. **Marriages** 1) Phyllis Livingston Potter, 1933 (died, 1954); 2) Robyn Smith, a jockey, 1980. **Children** Fred and Ava from first marriage; Peter Potter (stepson). **Education** Alvienne School of the Dance, New York; Ned Wayburn Studio of Stage Dancing. **Career** Formed dancing partnership with sister Adele, while still a child; toured vaudeville circuits together, 1908 onwards; appeared on Broadway and in London, 1917–32; New York début, *Over the Top*, 44th Street Roof Theater, 1917; London début, *Stop Flirting*, Shaftesbury Theatre, 1923; partnership with sister ended, 1931; in films from 1931, initially as singer/dancer, later as dramatic actor; film début, 1931; first dramatic film role, *On the Beach*, 1959. **Awards and honours** Honorary Academy Award for contributions to film, 1949; Emmy Award for Outstanding Performance in a Variety or Musical Programme or Series, for *Astaire Time*, 1960–61; Best Supporting Actor, British Academy, for *The Towering Inferno*, 1975; Emmy Award for

Outstanding Lead Actor in a Special, for *A Family Upside Down*, 1978; Life Achievement Award, American Film Institute, 1981. **Stage** (includes) *Over the Top*, 1917; *The Passing Show of 1918*, 1918; *The Love Letter*, 1921; *For Goodness Sake*, 1922; *The Bunch and Judy*, 1923; *Stop Flirting*, 1923; *Lady, Be Good!*, 1924; *Funny Face*, 1927, 1928; *Smiles*, 1930; *The Bandwagon*, 1931; *Gay Divorce*, 1932, 1933. **Films** *Municipal Bandwagon* (short), 1931; *Dancing Lady*, 1933; *Flying Down to Rio*, 1933; *The Gay Divorcee*, 1934; *Roberta*, 1934; *Top Hat*, 1934; *Follow the Fleet*, 1936; *Swing Time*, 1936; *Shall We Dance?*, 1937; *A Damsel in Distress*, 1937; *Carefree*, 1938; *The Story of Vernon and Irene Castle*, 1939; *Broadway Melody of 1940*, 1940; *Second Chorus*, 1940; *You'll Never Get Rich*, 1941; *Holiday Inn*, 1942; *You Were Never Lovelier*, 1942; *The Sky's the Limit*, 1943; *Yolanda and the Thief*, 1945; *Ziegfeld Follies*, 1946; *Blue Skies*, 1946; *Easter Parade*, 1948; *The Barkleys of Broadway*, 1949; *Three Little Words*, 1950; *Let's Dance*, 1950; *Royal Wedding* (*Wedding Bells*), 1951; *The Belle of New York*, 1952; *The Bandwagon*, 1953; *Deep in My Heart*, 1954; *Daddy Long Legs*, 1955; *Funny Face*, 1957; *Silk Stockings*, 1957; *On the Beach*, 1959; *The Pleasure of His Company*, 1961; *The Notorious Landlady*, 1962; *Paris When It Sizzles*, 1964; *Finian's Rainbow*, 1968; *Midas Run (A Run on Gold)*, 1969; *The Over-the-Hill Gang Rides Again* (for television), 1970; *Imagine*, 1973; *The Towering Inferno*, 1974; *That's Entertainment Part 1*, 1974; *That's Entertainment Part 2*, 1976; *Un Taxi mauve* (*The Purple Taxi*), 1977; *The Amazing Dobermans*, 1977; *A Family Upside Down* (for television), 1978; *Battleship Gallactica* (for television), 1978; *The Man in the Santa Claus Suit* (for television), 1980; *Ghost Story*, 1981. **Television** (includes) *General Electric Theater*: *Imp on a Cobweb Leash*, 1958; *Man on a Bicycle*, 1959; *An Evening with Fred Astaire*, 1958; *Another Evening with Fred Astaire*, 1959; *Astaire Time*, 1960; *Fred Astaire's Alcoa Première Theater*: *Mr Easy*, 1962; *Guest in the House*, 1962; *Mr Lucifer*, 1962; *Blues for a Hanging*, 1962, also host, 1961–63; *Bob Hope's Chrysler Theater*, 1964; *Think Pretty*, 1964; *Dr Kildare*, 1965; host and entertainer, *Hollywood Palace*, 1965–66; *The Fred Astaire Show*, 1968; *It Takes a Thief*, 1969–70; *Santa Claus Is Coming to Town*, voice only, 1971; *'S Wonderful, 'S Marvelous, 'S Gershwin*, 1972; *Fred Astaire, Change Partners and Dance*, 1980. **Publications** *Steps in Time*, New York, 1959, revised edition, 1981. **Cause of death** Undisclosed, at age 88. **Further reading** John Springer, *All Talking, All Singing, All Dancing*, New York, 1966; Howard Thompson, *Fred Astaire: A Pictorial Treasury of His Films*, New York, 1970; John Kobal, *Gotta Sing, Gotta Dance*, New York, 1970; Alfons Hackl, *Fred Astaire and His Work*, Vienna, 1970; Stanley Green, *Ring Bells! Sing Songs!*, New York, 1971; Lawrence B. Thomas, *The MGM Years*, New York, 1972; Arlene Croce, *The Fred Astaire and Ginger Rogers Book*, New York, 1972; Stanley Green and Burt Goldblatt, *Starring Fred Astaire*, New York, 1973; *The Fred Astaire Story: His Life, His Films, His Friends*, London, 1975; Stephen Harvey, *Fred Astaire*, New York, 1975; Michael Freedland, *Fred Astaire*, London, 1976, reissued, 1989; Benny Green, *Fred Astaire*, London, 1979; Alain Lacombe and Claude Rocle, *De Broadway à Hollywood*, Paris, 1980; Gilles Cèbé, *Fred Astaire*, Paris, 1981; *Astaire, Rogers and the Hollywood Song*, London, 1983; Bob Thomas, *Astaire: The Man, the Dancer*, New York, 1984; Tim Satchell, *Astaire*, London, 1988; Bill Adler, *Fred Astaire: A Wonderful Life*, London, 1988.

ERROL BARROW

Barbadian Lawyer and Politician

Born **St Lucy, Barbados, 21 January 1920**

Died **Bridgetown, Barbados, 1 June 1987**

Errol Barrow, resourceful and energetic prime minister of the island of Barbados from 1961 to 1976, played a leading role in his country's achievement of independence from Britain, in building and maintaining its ties with Western hemisphere countries, and in attracting investment and tourism, which helped reduce economic dependence on the sugar crop and on Great Britain. He also worked to alleviate domestic problems of overpopulation and unemployment and for closer cooperation among Caribbean islands. Once described as "the only active volcano in Barbados", he had a strong physical presence as well as a volatile and forceful personality, and always took great delight in new machines or ideas which he felt could benefit his country's development.

Densely populated Barbados, the most easterly of the Caribbean islands, with an area of 166 square miles and a population with African or racially mixed roots, had an elected legislature from 1639 and had become fully self-governing in 1961, but it was only on 30 November 1966 that the island finally ended some 340 years as a British colony and became fully independent, taking its place as the twenty-sixth member nation of the British Commonwealth. The Duke of Kent attended the ceremony as representative of the British Crown and presented the instruments of government to Errol Barrow, who was the first man to assume the office of prime minister of independent Barbados. He also became minister of external affairs and minister of finance and planning. The independence celebrations, timed to take place between the cricket season and the tourist season, included steel bands, calypso singing and dancing in the streets. The guest list, from which Cuba and Haiti were noticeably absent, included 80 invited representatives. On taking office, Barrow stressed that his country wished to enjoy good relations with the democratic nations of the Western hemisphere.

At the time of independence, Barrow was leader of the Democratic Labour Party, which he had co-founded in 1955 when he broke away from Sir Grantley Adams's Barbados Labour Party to form a party with more radical reform policies. He was a politician in touch with the needs and difficulties of ordinary Barbadians and had the gift of expressing himself in clear and straightforward language, doing much to break down any remaining barriers of racial segregation and discrimination, while also helping to avoid racially-based conflict during the years when "Black power" had its greatest influence. As prime minister, he also helped to create a climate of stability and prosperity on the financial front by shrewdly encouraging foreign investors and by opening up Barbados's tourist potential with its all-year-round warm climate and delightful beaches.

Errol Watson Barrow, one of five children, was the son of the Reverend Reginald Grant Barrow, an Anglican clergyman and headmaster. His mother, Ruth (O'Neal), was the daughter of a wealthy sugar mill and plantation owner. The young Barrow attended the Primary Danish School on St Croix, Virgin Islands, returning to Barbados to study at Wesley Hall Boys' School and at Combermere. In 1934 he entered Harrison College, the island's leading boys' school, where he won the Island Scholarship in classics. On graduating in 1939, he did a year of teaching.

During World War II he served with distinction, joining the British Royal Air Force in 1940, training in Canada as a flying officer and navigator and assigned to England for the invasion of Europe. He flew over 50 operational missions, including action in the battles of Bastogne and

Arnhem, and becoming attached to the British Air Ministry in 1947. As a flying officer, even peace-time service had its dangers, including a forced landing on a frozen lake in the Soviet zone of Germany while personal navigator to the commander-in-chief of the British forces in Germany in 1946, and a crash landing on the North Sea coast of England while flying from Hamburg to London. These were years Barrow looked back on with affection.

In 1947, his RAF service completed, he enrolled at the London School of Economics and Political Science, simultaneously reading law at Lincoln's Inn. He passed his Bar examinations in 1949 and gained his economics degree a year later, which was an unusual achievement at the time. Returning home, his court appearances in Trinidad, St Lucia and Antigua, and his work as legal counsel to the Antigua Labour Union and the St Kitts–Nevis Trade Union, soon made his law practice well known in the British West Indies

Errol Barrow was first elected to the House of Assembly, the lower house of the colonial legislature, on 20 December 1951 at a time when universal adult suffrage first came into being following the Representation of the People Act in 1950. In 1956 he and his Democratic Labour Party, formed only the year before, suffered a defeat, winning only four out of 24 seats in the House. However, victory in a by-election in 1958 brought him back, and his party gained strength, mainly through working-class support, winning half the seats in the 1961 general election, following which Barrow became premier. By then, Sir Grantley Adams had become less of a force in domestic politics through becoming prime minister of the Federation of the West Indies, which may have contributed to Barrow's success. The Federation failed in 1962, as did a subsequent attempt to create a smaller federation of the "little eight", and although Barrow favoured pan-Caribbean unity, he turned his attention to preparation for the island's independence and its place in the Commonwealth and in the Western hemisphere. His government published its independence proposals in August 1965, and they were approved by the House of Assembly the following year.

As well as achieving independence in 1966, Barbados also became the 122nd member of the United Nations. The year following it became the first Commonwealth nation to join the Organization of American States. After three successive election victories, Barrow's years as prime minister came to an end in 1976, when the Barbados Labour Party was returned to power under the leadership of Tom Adams, son of Sir Grantley Adams. Barrow's downfall was partly due to the electorate mistrusting his party's links with business interests. Following the death of Tom Adams, Barrow had a brief return to power in 1986, promising to reduce taxation, especially for the low paid, but he died the following year.

As a younger man, Barrow's energies found an outlet in such active hobbies as flying, sailing, fishing, driving, skin-diving, tennis and photography. He seemed to become quieter and more restrained in later years, which lent him a more distinguished air. In 1945 he married Carolyn Plaskett of Montclair, New Jersey, whom he met in Canada. Like himself, she was the child of a church minister. They had two children, but the couple lived apart in later years. An efficient and resourceful man, Barrow attracted both friends and enemies. To those who were "a patriot for me", he showed great loyalty, bestowing promotions and protection, but to those he distrusted, he displayed a more petty, suspicious and vengeful side to his nature.

Despite his "workaholic" itinerary, Barrow found time to publish two books, and his diligent efforts on behalf of Barbados won him international recognition. This was probably best summed up in a 1967 Head of State Award "for outstanding service to the country".

Born Errol Walton Barrow. **Parents** Reginald Grant, Anglican Bishop of Barbados, and Ruth (O'Neal) Barrow. **Marriage** Carolyn Plaskett, 1945 (separated). **Children** One daughter, Lesley, and one son, David O'Neal. **Education** Primary Danish School, St Croix; Wesley Hall Boys' School, Barbados; Combermere School, Barbados, 1931–34; Harrison College, Barbados,

1934–39; London School of Economics, BSc, 1950; also studied law at Lincoln's Inn, London, passing Bar examinations, 1949. **Military service** Pilot officer, then flying officer, Royal Air Force, 1940–47. **Career** Barrister and politician; called to Barbados Bar, 1950, running law practice and becoming legal counsel to Antigua Labour Union and St Kitts–Nevis Trade Union; elected as member of Barbados Labour Party to House of Assembly, 1951; with others, founded Democratic Labour Party, 1955; served as parliamentary leader of party until he lost seat in House of Assembly, 1956; returned to House of Assembly, 1958; chair, Democratic Labour Party, 1958–76; minister of finance, 1961–76; premier, 1961–66; prime minister of independent Barbados, 1966–76, 1986–87; also minister of external affairs, 1966–72, and of finance and planning. **Offices and memberships** Privy Counsellor, 1969; Queen's Counsel, 1979; Democratic Labour Party (Barbados); freeman, Guild of Air Pilots and Air Navigators; life member, National Association for the Advancement of Colored People (USA). **Awards and honours** Honorary LLD, McGill University, Canada, 1966; Lions International Head of State Award, 1967. **Publications** *What Canada Can Do for the West Indies*, 1964; *Democracy and Development*, 1979. **Cause of death** Undisclosed, at age 67.

ARTHUR BURNS

American Banker and Economist

***Born* Stanislau, Austria, 27 April 1904**

***Died* Baltimore, Maryland, 26 June 1987**

Dr Arthur Burns enjoyed the good fortune of a successful career in both the academic world, as a long-standing professor of economics at Columbia University, and in the real world of finance and diplomacy, as chairman of the US Federal Reserve System and as US ambassador to the Federal Republic of Germany. In addition, he was blessed with a long and happy marriage and family life.

Burns's life was the archetypal American success story. The son of poor Austro-Hungarian immigrants who arrived in the US shortly before World War I, when he was still a child, he was able to profit from a good American education, most particularly when he won a scholarship to Columbia University, New York. Burns worked his way through college, taking jobs as a waiter, shoe salesman, house painter (like his father), postal clerk and seaman, and from time to time contributing business articles to the *New York Herald Tribune*. On graduation, he was torn between the possibilities of careers in architecture, law and economics, but the deciding influence was his association with Wesley C. Mitchell, the founder of the National Bureau of Economic Research (NBER), where Burns worked as a researcher in the 1930s. Mitchell's influence on him was crucial, and their early work together in analysing business cycles and leading economic indicators was to provide much of the basis for the economic plans of the leading OECD nations. A conservative economist—though less so than his most famous pupil, Milton Friedman—Burns was deeply opposed to the Keynesian philosophy of public expenditure as the way out of recession. Instead, he advocated the good housekeeping and careful management which was ultimately to reach its apogee in the school of monetarism.

Columbia University was to remain Burns's spiritual home. After a period at Rutgers, he returned to Columbia as professor of economics in 1944, and from 1959 to 1969 was John Bates Clark Professor there, and thereafter professor emeritus.

In March 1953 President Eisenhower named him as his chief economic adviser, an appointment which some regarded as dangerously ideological in view of his anti-Keynesian reputation. Burns immediately revived the former practice of a presidential Council of Economic Advisers, of which he was made chairman. His earlier experience of analysing business cycles led him to predict that the tight money policy of the time would inevitably bring on a recession; he urged tax cuts and easier credit policies which brought the boom of the mid-1950s. By this time Burns had retired from the government and returned to Columbia and the NBER, but he continued to advise the president unofficially. He urged an end to the excessive taxes and the stop-go monetary and fiscal policies of the second Eisenhower administration, and in March 1960 warned Vice-President Nixon that unless steps were taken to curb the recession, the Republicans would lose the election.

In 1961 Burns became the only Republican member of President Kennedy's Advisory Committee on Labor-Management Policy. In this capacity he recommended training programmes for unskilled workers and technical assistance for small companies in order to boost industrial activity. Once again he urged reforms of the taxation system, which he saw as "a legacy of the Great Depression", in order to provide more investment capital and hence more jobs. His hesitation about government spending was dominated throughout his career by his dread of inflation. In the middle of President Johnson's term of office Burns again urged annual tax cuts as the necessary stimulus to the economy. "The savings of some become the borrowings of others. Capital that might otherwise remain idle is put to productive use." In 1968 he became economic adviser to his old friend Richard Nixon, and shortly after his inauguration Nixon put him in a new Cabinet post as counsellor to the president.

Within months Burns was nominated by President Nixon to succeed William McChesney Martin as chairman of the Federal Reserve System—an appointment hailed by the Democratic vice-chairman of the Congressional Joint Economic Committee as "the best President Nixon ever made". Burns was now able to put his long-standing ideas of national good housekeeping into practice. Money supply became the prime focus of attention, though Burns did not hesitate to attend to such seeming details as streamlining procedures, delegating responsibility and replacing the Fed's fleet of limousines with more economical vehicles. During his eight years in office he had to face two potential major economic crises: the rescue from bankruptcy first of Penn Central Railroad, and then of New York City. In both cases Burns assured the larger banks that the "Fed" would live up to its role as lender of last resort and relieve the threat to liquidity.

Burns's influence was also felt on areas other than monetary policy; it ranged over the whole field of the budget, energy and labour policy. Early on he recommended an incomes policy as an antidote to inflation; later he urged President Ford to use the federal government to reduce unemployment, even at the cost of letting the money supply rise. The inflation which inevitably followed—according to his own theory—then forced him to raise interest rates with the inevitable consequent recession.

Despite this departure from his own economic doctrines, Burns's replacement at the Fed when Jimmy Carter became president caused a fall of the dollar which shook the new administration. Burns, meanwhile, returned to academic life; he became distinguished scholar at the American Enterprise Institute (AEI) and professorial lecturer at Georgetown University. The return of a Republican administration in 1980 brought him back into public life, this time as ambassador to Bonn. Again, he faced a period of crisis with much anti-American feeling against the deployment of cruise and Pershing missiles in Europe. Burns was absolutely the right man for the job. His time at the Fed had earned him the respect of all Europe's political leaders, and the agreement he was able to negotiate with the West German foreign minister did much to allay the tensions within NATO.

After four years in Bonn, Burns returned to the AEI to resume his academic writing programme. Having been, during his time at the Fed, one of the most powerful men in the United States, Burns may still prove, by his prolific writings, to remain one of the most powerful. At the same time, he may also have been one of the most friendly and approachable, with his relaxed pipe-smoking appearance, looking for all the world, as one reporter described him, like "a small-town druggist circa 1910".

Born Arthur Frank Burnzeig. **Parents** Nathan and Sarah (Juran) Burns. **Marriage** Helen Bernstein, 1930. **Children** Two sons, David and Joseph. **Education** Columbia University, BA, MA, 1925, PhD, 1934. **Emigration** Left Austria (now part of Ukrainian Soviet Socialist Republic) for US while still a child. **Career** Economics lecturer, Columbia University, 1926–27; instructor, Rutgers University, New Brunswick, 1927–30, assistant professor, 1930–33, associate professor, 1933–43, professor of economics, 1943–44; professor, Columbia University, New York, 1944–59, John Bates Clark Professor of economics, 1959–69; counsellor to the president, 1969–70; chairman, Federal Reserve System, 1970–78; distinguished scholar in residence, American Enterprise Institute, 1978–81; American ambassador, Federal Republic of Germany, 1981–85. **Related activities** Research associate, National Bureau of Economic Research, New York, 1930–31, member of research staff, 1933–69, director of research, 1945–53, member, board of directors, 1945 onwards, president, 1957–69, chairman, 1967–68, honorary chairman, 1969–87; visiting professor: Columbia University, 1941–44, Stanford University, 1968; alternate governor, International Monetary Fund, 1973–78; distinguished professorial lecturer, Georgetown University, 1978–81. **Other activities** Member, US Railway Emergency Board, 1942; chairman: President's Council of Economic Advisers, 1953–56, President's Advisory Board on Economic Growth and Stability, 1953–56, Cabinet Committee on Small Business, 1956; member: Advisory Council on Social Security Financing, 1957–58, Temporary State Commission on Economic Expansion, New York, 1959–60, President's Advisory Committee on Labor-Management Policy, 1961–66, Governor's Committee on Minimum Wage, New York, 1964; director: Nation Wide Securities Company, 1957–68, Calvin Bullock Company, 1957–68, 1978–81, Dividend Shares Incorporated, 1958–68; consultant, Lazard Frères, 1978–81; Trilateral Commission, 1978–81. **Memberships** Board member, Academy of Political Science, 1957–68, president, 1962–68; distinguished fellow, American Economic Association, president, 1959; fellow: American Statistical Association, Econometric Society, American Academy of Arts and Sciences; correspondent, American Philosophical Society, Council on Foreign Relations, Institut de Science Économique Appliquée. **Awards and honours** Gilder Fellow, Columbia University, 1926–27; Alexander Hamilton Medal, Columbia University, 1969; Distinguished Public Service Award, Tax Foundation Incorporated, 1969; Mugungwha Decoration, Korean Government, 1970; *Finance* magazine's Star of Achievement, 1971; fellow, Jewish Theological Seminary of America, 1971; Award of Excellence, Columbia University, 1974; Jefferson Award, American Institute of Public Service, 1976; Alexander Hamilton Award, US Treasury, 1976; commander, French Legion of Honour, 1977; Japanese Order of the Rising Sun, First Class, 1978; German Grand Cross Order of Merit, 1978; Frank E. Seidman Distinguished Award for Political Economy, 1978; Francis Boyer Award, American Enterprise Institute Public Policy Research, 1978; Charles Waldo Haskins Award, New York University, 1983; honorary degrees from over 40 universities and colleges, including University of Chicago, Rikkyo University, Tokyo, University of Pennsylvania, Dartmouth College and Columbia University. **Publications** *Production Trends in the United States Since 1870*, 1934; (with W.C. Mitchell) *Measuring Business Cycles*, 1946; *Economic Research and the Keynesian Thinking of Our Times*, 1946; *New*

Facts in Business Cycles, 1950; *The Instability of Consumer Spending*, 1952; *Business Cycle Research and the Needs of Our Times*, 1953; *Frontiers of Economic Knowledge*, 1954; *Prosperity Without Inflation*, 1958; *The Management of Prosperity*, 1966; (with P.A. Samuelson) *Full Employment, Guideposts and Economic Stability*, 1967; (with Jacob K. Javits and Charles J. Hitch) *The Defense Sector and the American Economy*, 1968; *The Business Cycle in a Changing World*, 1969; *Reflections of an Economic Policy Maker*, 1978. **Cause of death** Undisclosed, at age 83.

VERA CASPARY

American Novelist and Screenwriter

***Born* Chicago, Illinois, 13 November 1904**

***Died* New York City, New York, 13 June 1987**

"To be a writer you must have a point of view in what you experience. You need to keep an ear and an eye always at the keyhole, without malice. After you have observed, and listened at keyholes, all you need is a will of iron."

Vera Caspary's counsel to aspiring writers was peculiarly appropriate to her own chosen genre, that of crime fiction. Her words conjure up an image of her eavesdropping outside a door, or with her ear pressed tightly to the wall so as not to miss a word of a vile plot being hatched; then watch her withdrawing to the writing table to create a new novel or screenplay. In this way, or in the less fanciful manner of sheer hard work, Vera Caspary wrote more than 17 novels and as many film scripts, plus a musical (*Les Girls*) and her autobiography, *The Secrets of Grown-ups*. And these were only part of the total output—not counting advertisements and other hack work—in a writing career which spanned more than 60 years and covered the best part of the twentieth century.

Born in Chicago, the youngest of three children, Vera Caspary was educated in local public schools but, money being tight, she left school at 17 to start earning her own keep. She began as a stenographer, but was soon promoted to copywriter in a Chicago advertising agency. Not knowing anything more but that she wanted to write, the job was a godsend: here she learned to be concise and to the point, having to sell everything from cold cream to milking machines in equally alluring prose. That advertising was the best possible training for a relatively uneducated young writer proved to be true in Caspary's case, as it was with so many other American writers, and soon Chicago became too small for her. New York, centre of the publishing industry, beckoned, and she moved there to pursue the dual career of editor of *Dance* magazine and freelance writer. Things went according to plan and by 1927 she was able to drop the editorship and devote all her time to freelance writing. She was just 23 years old.

Caspary did not, however, begin as a crime writer. *The White Girl* (1929), her first novel, is about the predicament of an Afro-American woman from the South who is light-skinned enough to pass for white and does so, in order to make a life in Chicago. Although the theme of the light-skinned mulatto travelling North was familiar enough in the Black literature of the day, Caspary's treatment was unusual because of her passionate feeling for the problems of an inauthentic existence. The *New York World* called the novel "vivid, harsh and realistic".

Themes of migration and displacement obviously interested Caspary a great deal at this time, for in her fourth novel, *Thicker Than Water* (1932), she returned to it in a tale of a Portuguese–Jewish family in Chicago for whom time-honoured traditions and religious observances gradually lose their significance as the pressures of conforming to American life increase. This was one of the few novels in which Caspary used autobiographical material; as a fabulist through and through, she tended to keep her private life out of her books (at least until the appearance of her autobiography in 1979).

During the 1930s Caspary continued writing and publishing, earning enough to keep herself in moderate comfort, but the real breakthrough in her career did not occur until 1942 with the publication of *Laura*, her first venture into crime fiction. The story concerned a policeman-detective who falls in love with the victim during investigation. The story is told from various different angles to great effect; *Laura* has been described as a critique of the American Dream because of this ambiguous perspective which is highlighted by the novel's double climax. *Laura* was immediately recognized as "something quite different from the run-of-the-mill detective story, done with a novel twist and much skill", as reviewer Will Cuppy wrote in the *New York Herald Tribune Book Review*. Another critic said it was "a difficult book to classify; it carries a triple threat as a mystery, a love story and a character study". These were to be characteristics of all Vera Caspary's subsequent mystery novels: they were as much studies of personality as tales of crime and punishment, as much psychological thrillers as fast-moving plots.

Despite popular follow-ups, such as *Bedelia* (1944) and *Stranger Than Truth* (1946), *Laura*—first published in serial form, then as a book—remained the most successful of Caspary's works in this genre. Its popularity was no doubt boosted when it was made into a feature film, directed by Otto Preminger, which became something of a cult classic. In addition, *Laura* toured New England as a play in 1946, reaching Broadway a year later. Clearly the novels of this period were the stuff that films are made of. Caspary had begun writing drama in the early 1930s, usually in collaboration with other writers, but during the 1940s she produced numerous other screenplays, of which *Bedelia* (1946), *Letter to Three Wives* (1949), *Three Husbands* (1950) and the musical *Les Girls* (1954) are probably the best known. In 1949 she also married into the business when she tied the knot with Isadore Goldsmith, a film producer whom she had met on the set of one of her projects. She married relatively late in life and lost her husband early: when he died in 1964, she was just 60 years old. Loyal to the memory of their 15 years together, she never remarried.

The style of Vera Caspary's work has often been described as "taut and gritty", devoid of sentimentality and moral judgement. Undoubtedly one of her greatest strengths was an unfailing ear for dialogue—that ear famously pressed to the wall—which, of course, also made her writing so uniquely suited to adaptation for the big screen. As far as content goes, it has been noted by many, and acknowledged by herself, just how well she depicted twentieth-century American life during a time of great social change. In a review of her autobiography, *The Secrets of Grown-ups*, one critic described Caspary's life as "a Baedeker of the twentieth century" and drew attention to the fact that Caspary started writing as an independent woman in an unliberated era, subsequently chronicling world wars, the Depression, glamorous and romantic Hollywood, the effects of McCarthyism, and the carelessly rich lifestyle of Broadway people and the New York publishing world. The *New York Times Book Review* concluded that "despite the coy title, this is a lively, tough account of how a woman born into a conservative Jewish family broke conventions by plunging into the world of journalism and screenwriting at a time when women's liberation was still a faint rumble from the underground".

Caspary used what might be seen as feminist themes well before their time had come. The eponymous heroine of *Evvie* (1960) and the narrator, Louise Goodman, consider themselves emancipated women whose friendship is the only constant factor in the insecure world of prohibition-era Chicago. When Evvie gets killed, Louise's attempt to come to terms with herself, her friend and with Evvie's mystery lover becomes central to the novel, as much a quest for personal identity as a search for the killer. Here Caspary clearly anticipated the modern feminist detective novels, which often combine personal crises in the persona of the detective with more conventional themes such as murder and false identity.

It was no mere coincidence then, that Vera Caspary spoke of writing as a matter of "iron will"—keyhole fieldwork being no more than preparation. After all, she herself had had to carve out a space for her writing which did not previously exist, a space in which her own and subsequent modern-day female crime fiction has been able to flourish.

Born Vera Caspary. **Parents** Paul, a department store buyer, and Julia (Cohen) Caspary. **Marriage** Isadore Goldsmith, a film producer, 1949 (died, 1964). **Education** Chicago public schools. **Career** Stenographer, then copywriter, Chicago advertising agency; director, correspondence course school; editor of *Dance* magazine and freelance writer, New York, 1925–27; full-time author of novels, thrillers, screenplays, 1929–87. **Awards and honours** Awards from Screenwriters' Guild, for *A Letter to Three Wives* and *Les Girls*. **Memberships** Authors' Guild; Authors' League of America; Dramatists' Guild; Writers' Guild of America West. **Crime novels** *Laura*, Boston, 1943, London, 1944; *Bedelia*, Boston and London, 1945; *The Murder in the Stork Club*, New York, 1946, published as *The Lady in Mink*, London, 1946; *Stranger Than Truth*, New York, 1946, London, 1947; *The Weeping and the Laughter*, Boston, 1950, published as *The Death Wish*, London, 1951; *Thelma*, Boston, 1952, London, 1953; *False Face*, London, 1954; *The Husband*, New York and London, 1957; *Evvie*, New York and London, 1960; *A Chosen Sparrow*, New York and London, 1964; *The Man Who Loved His Wife*, New York and London, 1966; *The Rosecrest Cell*, New York, 1967, London, 1968; *Final Portrait*, London, 1971; *Ruth*, New York, 1972; *Elizabeth X*, London, 1978, published as *The Secret of Elizabeth*, New York, 1979. **Other novels** *The White Girl*, New York, 1929; *Ladies and Gents*, New York, 1929; *Music in the Street*, New York, 1930; *Thicker Than Water*, New York, 1932; *The Dreamers*, New York, 1975. **Plays** (with Winifred Lenihan) *Blind Mice*, produced New York, 1930; (with Samuel Ornitz) *Geraniums in My Window*, produced New York, 1934; (with George Sklar) *Laura*, produced London, 1945, New York, 1947; *Wedding in Paris*, produced London, 1954, published in New York, 1956. **Screenplays** (with Jane Storm and Oscar M. Sheridan) *Such Women Are Dangerous*, 1934; *I'll Love You Always*, 1935; (with Preston Sturges) *Easy Living*, 1937; (with Bertram Millhauser and Eddie Welch) *Scandal Street*, 1938; (with others) *Service Deluxe*, 1938; (with others) *Sing Dance, Plenty Hot*, 1940; (with others) *Lady from Louisiana*, 1941; (with Edmund L. Hartmann and Art Arthur) *Lady Bodyguard*, 1942; (with Rose Franken and William Brown Meloney) *Claudia and David*, 1946; (with others) *Bedelia*, 1946; (with Walter Bullock and Edward Eliscu) *Out of the Blue*, 1947; (with Joseph L. Mankiewicz) *A Letter to Three Wives*, 1949; (with Edward Eliscu) *Three Husbands*, 1950; (with Abraham Polonsky) *I Can Get It for You Wholesale*, 1951; (with Charles Hoffman) *The Blue Gardenia*, 1953; (with Albert Hackett and Frances Goodrich) *Give a Girl a Break*, 1954; (with John Patrick) *Les Girls*, 1957; (with Valentine Davies and Hal Kanter) *Bachelor in Paradise*, 1961. **Other** *The Secrets of Grown-ups* (autobiography), New York, 1979. **Cause of death** Undisclosed, at age 87.

JACKIE GLEASON

American Actor

***Born* Brooklyn, New York, 26 February 1916**

***Died* Fort Lauderdale, Florida, 24 June 1987**

To millions of the television viewing public, Jackie Gleason was known as "Mr Saturday Night", due to the enormous popularity of his television shows. As wide in the waist as in ego, the blustery comedian was loved for a variety of characters he created in his *Cavalcade of Stars* which ran from 1950 to 1952, one of which developed into *The Honeymooners*' Ralph Kramden, others which populated *The Jackie Gleason Show*. All three series, with their broad humour, dominated TV ratings for a total of 13 years, making Gleason a major figure in television's "Golden Age".

Gleason's own deprived background may have had something to do with the excesses he enjoyed throughout his successful career, in everything from food to money to personality. Growing up in a succession of tenements in one of Brooklyn's toughest neighbourhoods, he became a "big guy on the block", both street-smart and funny, to stay ahead. His father, an insurance auditor who sold candy to fellow employees for extra income, walked out when Gleason was eight. An older brother died not long after. His mother made change in the subways to make ends meet, but they barely did. Gleason's education stopped at the eighth grade, after which he did little of note but frequent pool halls and sweet shops, by his own account. When his mother died, Gleason was 19. "That night, after my mother was buried, I went out on my own with only 39 cents in my pocket...Some kid asked me where I was going. I told him I was going to the big time," he remembered. That was Manhattan, where he spent the next few years being a very amateur boxer, a bouncer, an MC in small shows and doing comedy routines in burlesque halls. In one of those fairytale twists of fate, film mogul Jack Warner caught his act at Club 18 and signed him to a contract.

Those few years in Hollywood netted a series of miscast film roles, from gangster to blue-eyed Arab, in *Navy Blues* (1941), *Larceny, Inc.* (1942) and *Springtime in the Rockies* (1942), all quite forgettable. Gleason also performed in some of the smaller nightclubs around town, doing improvisation and impersonation comedy routines. He fared better back in New York. His Broadway début in a musical comedy, *Keep Off the Grass* (1940), went unnoticed; however, he impressed critics more favourably in *Follow the Girls* (1944) and *Hellzapoppin'* (1945). The shows were not particularly noteworthy, but Gleason's personality was.

In 1949 young television beckoned. Gleason's first show, *The Life of Riley*, concerning a blue-collar family, lasted for a season. (It later became a series with William Bendix in the lead role.) It established Gleason as the king—and a surprisingly creative one—of the big gesture, the explosive buffoon who was frequently misunderstood, the larger-than-life entertainer. In *Cavalcade of Stars*, a splendid variety show which ran from 1950 to 1952, Gleason developed such characters as suave-but-smashed playboy and sot Reggie Van Gleason III, the sensitively done Poor Soul, constantly in trouble from efforts to help others (a role in which many critics believed Gleason's pathos rivalled that of Chaplin), Joe the Bartender with his three-cent philosophic monologues, and Charlie Brattan, the loudmouth. All were sides of Gleason himself. "All my characters are psychologically constructed. Each is consistent...I give each one a saving grace, a touch of sympathy," he said, explaining the success of his creations.

By now his catchphrases—"And awaaaay we go!" and "How sweet it is!"—were everyday vocabulary to his fans. *The Jackie Gleason Show* (1952–55), which created characters such as Crazy Guggenheim, one of his best loved, and Fats Fogarty, earned him *TV Guide*'s "Best

Comedian of the Year" award in 1955. Later that year came *The Honeymooners*, in the biggest financial deal in TV history. It was the ironically-titled situation comedy about, again, a blue-collar Brooklyn couple who constantly fought. It quickly established itself as a classic; today, repeats are shown continually by local networks across America. It was loud, stagey (shot with two stationary cameras), and somewhat rough: early live television characteristics. His Ralph Kramden was a bus driver, while best friend and simple soul Ed Norton was a sewer worker. The show gave co-star Art Carney, as Norton, his first rung of stardom. In one of the show's more famous sketches, Norton's innocent humour is illustrated as he endeavours to teach his domineering buddy the rudiments of golf: "First you must address the ball," he says, leaning over to gaze at it with club in hand. "Hello, ball!" Audrey Meadows starred as Alice, the long-suffering, wise-cracking Mrs Kramden, and Joyce Randolph as Norton's wife. *Time* magazine described Gleason's persona as "a big bassett hound who had just eaten W.C. Fields". Certainly *The Honeymooners* has indirectly been of great influence on succeeding sitcoms for decades afterward. Gleason, a workaholic, attended to nearly every aspect of the production himself, and sometimes had to be given oxygen on the set. He was notorious at CBS for ignoring scriptwriters, and dismissing rehearsals. But his performances were flawless. In 1959 he was elected to the TV Hall of Fame.

Gleason's weight constantly fluctuated between 185 and 285 pounds—usually the latter. His reputation was that of a man who was explosive, mischievous, egotistical, generous to his friends, best centre-stage but shy with strangers. It was inevitable that his talents would extend to other media. He recorded six albums of mood music, entitled *Music for Lovers Only*, which were highly successful. Films followed. *The Hustler* (1961), starring Paul Newman, established Gleason as a serious actor. He portrayed Minnesota Fats, a pool shark who plays for 31 straight hours to defend his reputation as the best player alive. In actual fact, Gleason played professional-quality pool. He received his only Oscar nomination and superb notices. Later that year he starred with Anthony Quinn as a double-dealing manager of an ageing boxer in *Requiem for a Heavyweight*, again to excellent reviews. *Gigot*, his own project that remained dear to his heart, was an underestimated, delicate film in which Gleason played a Parisian mute. He wrote the script and scored the music, while Gene Kelly directed. It did poorly at the box office, a fact which Gleason felt keenly for years. A brief series of unimpressive light comedies followed, including *Papa's Delicate Condition*, about a decent man with drinking problems (1963), and *Don't Drink the Water* six years later. His caricature of a Southern sheriff in *Smokey and the Bandit*, parts I, II and III, in 1977, 1980 and 1983 established a comeback, although a mild one. In 1978 Gleason's national tour of a hit play, *Sly Fox*, was cut short by his heart condition, a result of excessive fondness for good food and good liquor, as well as constant dieting. In *Sting II*, in 1983, his portrayal of the Big Con, Fargo Gondorff, produced a glimmer of his previous genius; however, after the last *Bandit* film, Gleason wisely refrained from participating in an indifferent industry.

Gleason married three times, and used his talents in areas not generally known of by the public, including inventing children's games and designing jewellery and clothes. He also had developed a knowledgeable interest in psychic phenomena and was a talented hypnotist.

Born Herbert John Gleason. **Parents** Herbert, an insurance clerk, and Mae (Kelly) Gleason. **Marriages** 1) Genevieve Halford, 1936 (divorced, 1971); 2) Beverley McKittrick, 1971 (divorced, 1974); 3) Marylin Taylor. **Children** Two daughters, Geraldine and Linda, from first marriage. **Education** Public Grade School 73, Brooklyn, New York, 1931; also briefly attended Bushwick High School and John Adams High School, New York. **Career** Master of ceremonies, Folly Theater, Brooklyn, 1932; worked and toured in a variety of jobs on fringes of entertainment world, including a barker in carnivals on Eastern seaboard, master of ceremonies at Pennsylvania and New Jersey resorts, bouncer at Miami Club, Newark, New Jersey, and occasional disc jockey, 1935–38; cabaret artist, Club 18 and Leon and Eddie's, New York City, 1938; full-time actor on Broadway, in films and television, 1940 onwards. **Related activities** Recording artist, record cover designer and conductor, making 38 recordings with own orchestra. **Awards and honours** "Best Comedian of the Year", *TV Guide*, 1952; Tony Award for best Broadway actor in *Take Me Along*, 1959; elected to Television Hall of Fame, 1985. **Stage** (includes) *Keep Off the Grass*, 1940; *Follow the Girls on Broadway*, 1945; *Hellzapoppin'*; *Artists and Models*; *The Laugh Maker*, 1953; *Take Me Along*; *Sly Fox*, 1978. **Films** *Navy Blues*, 1941; *Springtime in the Rockies*, 1942; *The Desert Hawk*, 1950; *The Hustler*, 1961; *Gigot*, 1962; *Requiem for a Heavyweight*, 1962; *Soldier in the Rain*, 1963; *The Time of Your Life*, 1963; *Papa's Delicate Condition*, 1963; *Skidoo*, 1968; *How to Commit a Marriage*, 1969; *Don't Drink the Water*, 1969; *How Do I Love Thee?*, 1970; *Mr Billion*, 1977; *Smokey and the Bandit*, 1977; *Smokey and the Bandit II*, 1980; *The Toy*, 1982; *Sting II*, 1983; *Smokey and the Bandit III*, 1983. **Television** (includes) *Life of Riley*, 1949–50; *Cavalcade of Stars*, 1950–52; *The Jackie Gleason Show*, 1952–55, 1957–59, 1966–70; *The Honeymooners*, 1955–56. **Cause of death** Undisclosed, at age 71. **Further reading** Jim Bishop, *The Golden Ham: A Candid Biography of Jackie Gleason*, New York, 1956.

SIR EDOUARD GRUNDY

British Electronics Expert

***Born* England, 29 September 1908**

***Died* England, 15 June 1987**

During World War II German night-time bombers were directed to their targets by radio beams. The man who interfered with the beams so that most of the bombs fell away from their targets, was Edouard Grundy.

Educated at St Paul's School in London, Grundy subsequently attended the Royal Air Force College at Cranwell where he gained his commission in 1928. For a short while afterwards he served with a small squadron stationed on the Chinese side of the border with Hong Kong, before spending two years with 403 Flight of the Fleet Air Arm.

Having shown considerable aptitude for electronics, he was sent on a year's course to develop his skills. Then, after a time at RAF North Weald, he joined the Royal New Zealand Air Force on exchange, which is where he was based when World War II started in 1939.

Night-time raids by Luftwaffe bombers caused enormous damage to British cities during the Blitz, and their accuracy was thanks to a beam-apparatus called *knickebein*. After the fall of France the Germans built a row of transmitting stations on the Channel coast, and the first two of these started operating at Dieppe and Cherbourg on 23 August 1940. Their beams were trained on Birmingham, the major industrial city in the Midlands.

Grundy was put in charge of a team to counter this threat, and what Sir Winston Churchill designated as the Battle of the Beams began. It played a crucial part in the war, similar to the efforts to counter the magnetic mine. Grundy's team installed its own jamming stations to bend the beams and, after a very short period of initial problems, they succeeded in bending them during the crucial months of September and October 1940.

Their success was entirely unexpected on the German side. Goering boasted to Hitler that there was no way the beams could be disturbed. Nevertheless, four-fifths of the bombs were directed away from their target areas, and one pilot was so confused that he landed in Devon thinking he was in France.

The Germans refined the system into the "X apparatus" which used two beams, and the mass raid on Coventry on the night of 14/15 November 1940 was directed by this. Nevertheless, the British team led by Grundy managed to counteract that, as they did with the further variation which was known as the "Y apparatus". Very soon after each innovation was introduced, the bitter comments passing from the bomber pilots to their home stations showed how their faith in the system had been shattered by the countermeasures.

After a time as officer commanding 80(S) Wing, working on radio countermeasures, Grundy served with the Northwest African, Mediterranean and Middle East commands for the remainder of the war, and in 1945 returned to become commandant of the Empire Radio School. That year he married his first wife, Lucia le Sueur.

His promotion and progress upwards continued. After a spell as deputy director of policy with the Air Ministry, from 1949 to 1951 he helped in an advisory capacity to rebuild the Royal Norwegian Air Force, for which he was honoured by Norway. After a short time with the Supreme HQ Allied Powers Europe, he was senior air staff officer with the British Joint Services Mission in Washington, DC, and then chairman of the NATO Military Agency for Standardization for three years. His next appointment was air officer in charge of administration for the Far East Air Force.

His final active post in the services, from 1962 to 1966, was as controller of guided weapons and electronics at the Ministry of Aviation. The British programme of guided weapon development at Woomera, Australia, was under his direction, and he also controlled research, development and supply of all guided weapons and ballistic missiles, including Skybolt and Polaris. Space technology was an additional responsibility. In 1963 he was knighted for his services.

On leaving the Royal Air Force, Grundy turned to industry, becoming managing director of Royston Ltd. who made the Midas airborne data recorders known as "black boxes". Two years later, in 1968, he moved to be chairman of Short Brothers & Harland in Belfast, and he was there eight years until his complete retirement. During that time the company developed the highly successful Blowpipe missile and the SD3-30 "commuter" airliner, while the sales of Skyvan increased enormously. Also during that period his first wife died, and he remarried two years later.

Tall and energetic, Grundy was a formidable man, always busy and enthusiastic. Fishing and sailing were his recreations, and he was an entertaining and amusing public speaker, frequently asked to lecture on electronics.

Born Edouard Michael FitzFrederick Grundy. **Parents** Frederick and Osca Marah (Ewart) Grundy. **Marriages** 1) Lucia le Sueur (née Corder), 1945 (died, 1973); 2) Marie-Louise Holder, 1975. **Children** Three sons and one daughter (deceased), from first marriage; one stepson. **Education** St Paul's School, London; Royal Air Force College, Cranwell. **Career** Commissioned 56(F) Squadron, 1928; 403 Flight, Fleet Air Arm, 1929–31; attended signals specialist course, 1932; Royal Air Force North Weald, 1933–36; on exchange duties, Royal New Zealand Air Force Headquarters, 1937–40; officer commanding 80(S) Wing, 1941–42; chief signals officer, Northwest African Air Force, 1942–45; chief signals officer, Mediterranean Allied Tactical Air Forces, 1943–45; chief signals officer, Royal Air Force, Middle East, 1944–45; commandant, Empire Radio School, 1945–46; deputy director, air staff policy, Air Ministry, 1947–49; air adviser, Royal Norwegian Air Force, 1949–51; deputy chief signals officer, Supreme Headquarters Allied Powers Europe, 1951–52; staff member, Imperial Defence College, 1953;

senior air staff officer, British Joint Services Mission, United States, 1954–55; chairman, Military Agency for Standardization, North Atlantic Treaty Organization, 1955–58; air officer in charge of administration, Far East Air Force, 1958–61; commandant-general, Royal Air Force Regiment, 1961–62; controller, guided weapons and electronics, Ministry of Aviation, 1962–66; retired from Royal Air Force, 1966; managing director, Royston Instruments Limited, 1966; chairman, Short Brothers & Harland, Belfast, 1968–76. **Offices and memberships** Engineering Industries' Council, 1975 onwards; president, Society of British Aerospace Companies, 1975–76. **Awards and honours** Fellow, Royal Aeronautical Society; officer, Order of the British Empire, 1942; chevalier, Royal Norwegian Order of St Olaf, 1953; Companion of the Order of Bath, 1960; Knight Commander Order of the British Empire, 1963. **Cause of death** Undisclosed, at age 78.

RALPH GULDAHL

American Golfer

***Born* Dallas, Texas, 1912**

***Died* 11 June 1987**

Ralph Guldahl is remembered in the world of professional golf as the tall Texan who dominated the United States circuit during the 1930s, but who faded almost entirely from the scene as early as one decade later. His own explanation—that he "never did have a tremendous desire to win"—concealed the fact that he had achieved the remarkable feat of winning the United States Open twice in succession, in 1937 and 1938. But while others refer to Guldahl as a great player who woke up one morning to discover his swing had deserted him in his sleep, Guldahl always maintained that it was not his swing that he lost—rather, his interest in the game.

Born in Dallas in 1912, Guldahl grew to over 6 feet tall, and used this Texan attribute of size to full effect during his professional career. Almost entirely self-taught (and noted for the habit of combing his thick, curly hair after every shot), Guldahl's explosive back swing and sledgehammer down stroke might have appeared unorthodox, but as early as the age of 19, it was helping him to become one of the youngest players ever to win a tournament on the pro tour.

Having turned professional during the middle of a tournament in 1930, he first came to the fore when he finished as runner-up in the 1933 US Open, when all that separated him from the winner was a missed 4-foot putt on the last hole.

But Guldahl preferred a club job and time with his family; and after the birth of his son in 1935, he left the professional tour altogether for a full 18 months. That rest, nevertheless, seemed to prepare him for his finest years in the sport. In a short 1936 season he won $8600—which compared favourably with the $9000 collected by the season's highest earner, Horton Smith. He was also awarded the Radix Trophy for the year's low stroke average, of 71.65.

It was in 1937, however, that Guldahl truly "arrived". He finished second in the Masters, won the US Open, and was included in the American Ryder Cup team which travelled to Britain. To win the US Open, Guldahl found he needed to par his way in to tie the lead with Sam Snead. His only alarm came at the fifteenth when he found his ball resting against a cigar butt in a bunker. But he played the ball to within 6 feet of the pin, holed the putt, and went on to record a new US Open record of 281.

Guldahl again finished as runner-up in the 1938 Masters, and then returned to the Open to retain his title in style, scoring a final round of 69 to put himself at the top of the leader board after starting the day four behind Dick Metz and Emory Zimmerman.

His domination of the domestic game continued in 1939 with victory in the Masters, and a place in the Ryder Cup team; and yet the brightest star on the American circuit was about to burn itself out. He featured strongly in the 1940 US Open and was included, for the last time, in an American Ryder Cup team in 1941. But he played only sporadically during the 1940s, and his spell at the very top of the sport was probably too short to earn him the kind of recognition he truly deserved. He never, for example, became a household name in Europe, and in the absence of the television coverage the sport enjoys today, too few people were allowed the opportunity of seeing Ralph Guldahl play. However, 40 years after his third consecutive Ryder Cup appearance, Guldahl was finally nominated to the World Golf Hall of Fame.

Born Ralph Guldahl. **Marriage** Maydelle. **Children** One son. **Career** Professional golfer, 1930–35; one of youngest golfers to win a professional tour, 1931; unofficially credited with eleven US tour wins; member, Ryder Cup team, 1937, 1939, 1941. **Awards and honours** Nominated to World Golf Hall of Fame, 1981. **Major championships** Western Open, USA, 1936–38; Radix Trophy, USA, 1936; US Open, 1937, 1938, runner-up, 1933; US Masters, 1939, runner-up, 1937, 1938; Canadian Open Championship, runner-up, 1939. **Cause of death** Undisclosed, at age 75.

WALTER HELLER

American Economist

***Born* Buffalo, New York, 27 August 1915**

***Died* St Paul, Minnesota, 15 June 1987**

Professor Walter Wolfgang Heller once described himself as "one of those fortunate individuals who has been able to realize his youthful professional ambitions, namely a combined career of teaching, research and public service". Fortunate indeed! No wonder he was such a pleasant, happy character.

Walter Heller was born in Buffalo, New York, and educated at Oberlin College, obtaining a PhD in economics from the University of Wisconsin. During World War II he worked as a fiscal economist in the US Treasury Department, but in 1946 returned to academic life to take up a teaching post at the University of Minnesota, which he retained until his retirement in 1986. He supplemented his academic teaching by continuing as a fiscal consultant with the Treasury and the Minnesota Department of Taxation. From 1955 to 1960 he was also an economic adviser to the governor of Minnesota.

Heller had early established himself as something of a taxation authority, and he had been at the University of Minnesota only a year when he was recalled to public service to act as chief of finance to the military government in the US zone of Germany, soon to be united with the British and French zones following the currency reforms of 1948. The economic success of the post-war West Germany owes much to Heller. He fundamentally reformed the German tax structure (his early research had been mainly on federal and state income taxation and fiscal relations) and laid the basis for the fiscal stability of the new Federal Republic.

It was not surprising, therefore, that he should be chosen by President Kennedy to chair his Council of Economic Advisers to usher in the "new economics" of the 1960s. Heller's Keynesian economics were seen as the basis for realizing Kennedy's promise to "get the country moving", and Heller remained to see out the first Democratic term under President Johnson and to implement the tax cuts he had persuaded President Kennedy to adopt to promote economic expansion. As chairman of an OECD Group of Fiscal Experts he continued to apply his Keynesian theories to practical policy, arguing that to prevent recession, governments needed to abandon their preoccupation with balanced budgets. In this, of course, he came up against the orthodoxy of such monetarists as Milton Friedman, with whom his *Dialogue*, published in 1969, argued that such theories "work only in heaven".

Once returned to academic life, Heller continued to contribute to debate on economic policy, most notably with his so-called "Heller Plan" to restore a portion of income-tax revenues to the states unconditionally, in contrast to most federal grants-in-aid. The plan was first proposed in 1960; President Nixon finally signed into law a revenue-sharing bill in 1972. Heller was also interested in fiscal policy in Third World countries, particularly in the field of agricultural taxation. He served as tax adviser to King Hussein and the government of Jordan in the late 1950s. His quiet humour and charm of manner disguised formidable powers of persuasion which made him an able advocate and an inspiring teacher.

Born Walter Wolfgang Heller. **Parents** Ernst and Gertrude (Warmburg) Heller. **Marriage** Emily Karen Johnson, 1938 (died, 1985). **Children** Walter Perrin, Eric Johnson and Kaaren Louise. **Education** Oberlin College, BA, 1935; University of Wisconsin, MA, 1938, PhD, 1941. **Career** Instructor, University of Wisconsin, Madison, 1941–42; fiscal economist, US Treasury Department, 1942–46; associate professor, University of Minnesota, Minneapolis, 1946–50, professor, 1950-67, chair of department, 1957–60, Regents' professor of economics, 1967–86. **Related activities** Visiting professor: Universities of Wisconsin, Washington and Harvard; chief of internal finance, US Military Government in Germany, 1947–48; member, Economic Cooperation Administration Mission on German Fiscal Problems, 1951; fiscal adviser to governor of Minnesota, 1955–60; director, National Bureau of Economic Research, from 1960, chair, 1971–74, 1982–83; tax adviser to King Hussein and Royal Commission of Jordan, 1960; member, Minnesota State Council on Economic Education, from 1961; chair, President's Council of Economic Advisers, 1961–64, consultant, from 1974; consultant, Executive Office of the President, 1965–69, 1974–77; member, US Treasury Committee on Internal Monetary Arrangements, 1965–69; member, Minnesota State Planning Board, 1965–71; chair, Group of Fiscal Experts, Organization for Economic Cooperation and Development, 1966–68; member, board of contributors, *Wall Street Journal*, from 1973; member, Federal Energy Office Advisory Panel, from 1974; member, US Congressional Budget Office, from 1975; member, Banco del Lavoro advisory board, Rome, 1984–87; occasional consultant to United Nations, Minnesota Department of Taxation, Brookings Institution and US Census Bureau. **Other activities** Various business directorships, including International Multifoods Inc., National City Bank of Minneapolis, Northwestern National Life Insurance Co., Commercial Credit Co. **Offices and memberships** Fellow, American Academy of Arts and Sciences, 1963–87; American Economic Association (vice-president, 1967–68, president, 1974, distinguished fellow, 1975); American Finance Association; National Tax Association for Evolutionary Economics; fellow, American Philosophical Society, 1975–87; American Council on Germany; Phi Beta Kappa; Beta Gamma Sigma; Alpha Kappa Psi; trusteeships: Oberlin College, from 1966, College Retirement Equities Fund, 1968–72, General Growth Properties Inc. **Awards and honours** Ford Foundation

Fellowship, 1965–66; Carnegie Fellowship, 1967–68; US Treasury Distinguished Service Award, 1968; honorary degrees: Oberlin, 1964, Kenyon, 1965, Ripon, 1967, Coe, 1967, Long Island, 1968, Wisconsin, 1969, Roosevelt, 1976, Loyola, 1979. **Publications** (contributor) *Financing the War*, 1941; (contributor) *Germany and the Future of Europe*, ed. H.J. Morgenthau, 1951; (contributor) *Limits of Taxable Capacity*, 1953; (editor, with Francis M. Boddy and Carl L. Nelson) *Savings in the Modern Economy*, 1953; (with C. Penniman) *State Income Tax Administration*, 1959; (contributor) *The Hidden Force*, ed. F. Goodwin and others, 1962; (contributor) *The Economists of the New Frontier*, eds. B.H. Wilkens and C.B. Friday, 1963; *New Dimensions of Political Economy*, 1966; (with R. Ruggles and others) *Revenue Sharing and the City*, 1968; (editor) *Perspectives on Economic Growth*, 1968; (contributor) *To Heal and to Build*, ed. J. MacGregor Burns, 1968; (with M. Friedman) *Monetary vs. Fiscal Policy: A Dialogue with Milton Friedman*, 1969; *Economic Growth and Environmental Quality: Collision or Co-Existence?*, 1973; *The Economy: Old Myths and New Realities*, 1976; also contributed to *Encyclopaedia Britannica*, academic journals and government publications. **Cause of death** Undisclosed, at age 71.

JOHN HEWITT

Irish Poet

***Born* Belfast, Northern Ireland, 28 October 1907**

***Died* Belfast, Northern Ireland, 27 June 1987**

John Hewitt was one of Ireland's best known and most respected poets. Although he spent most of his working years involved in other branches of the arts, poetry remained his great love and the tool with which he expressed his deepest feelings about his homeland and the conflicts that have repeatedly beset it in recent centuries.

Both his parents were involved in education, so it was probably inevitable that Hewitt would early develop a respect for literature and learning. After gaining a degree in general studies at Queen's University, Belfast, he joined the staff of the Belfast Museum and Art Gallery, rising to become deputy director during his 27 years there. He then moved to England to take on the directorship of the Herbert Art Gallery and Museum at Coventry, a post he retained until 1972, when he retired and returned to his native city in the early years of the current "troubles". Without going too deeply into the "Irish question", there seems little doubt that partitioning any country for the benefit of dissenting inhabitants has little chance of lasting success, whether it be in Asia, the Middle East or Ireland. And Hewitt's work has always reflected the dichotomy that ensues when trying to reconcile the desire for harmony with the individual experience and understanding of the past, as demonstrated in his poem, "The Glens":

> I fear their creed as we have always feared
> the lifted hand between the mind and truth.
> I know their savage history of wrong
> and would at moments lend an eager voice,
> if voice avail, to set that tally straight.

Hewitt's work had been published in periodicals throughout his adult life but it was only in 1968 when the London firm of MacGibbon and Kee published his *Collected Poems 1932–1967* that his work became known to a wider audience and justified his reputation as mentor to many young Irish poets.

Hewitt used his work to bring the images and complexities of Northern Ireland life and its polarities alive. In his poems the Protestant planter met the indigenous Catholic, the urban scene was juxtaposed with the rural, his vision always Protestant, although he professed himself a humanist. Neil Corcoran, reviewing Hewitt's work in 1980 for the *Times Literary Supplement*, said that his "persistent theme is the search for self-definition among conflicting traditions, the desire to locate a cultural and poetic 'homestead' where the native land has been eroded by dispossession and colonization".

Hewitt himself commented, "My poetry is a quest for identity as an individual, as an Irishman of settler stock [and] as a twentieth-century man." Retirement gave him the opportunity for an explosion of work: in the 1970s and early 1980s he produced seven volumes of poetry, found time to edit a collection of verse by eighteenth- and nineteenth-century poets in his homeland, and to bring out a study of art in Ulster. He also gave unstintingly of his time and energy in a commitment to further the development of all the arts in Belfast when a lesser man might have kept his head down and not bothered. His kindness and generosity were tempered with humour and, at times, asperity.

Hewitt's work is best summed up by the critic Terence Brown:

> Hewitt's poetry has a strength and integrity of purpose that can occasionally suggest limitations of range and depth but that remind us of human continuities and moral courage in the midst of historical flux and the permanencies of nature. His lifelong attachment to the local has been a strong-minded celebration of man the maker in his society, family and tribe. The scrupulous care of his art is a reflection of his faith in human making, while its moments of calm lyricism are his testimony to the fundamentally benign realities of man's life.

Ireland's senior poet is gone but his influence remains with those whom he inspired and whose talent he fostered. As one of them once commented, he was the "Daddy" of them all.

Born John Harold Hewitt. **Pseudonym** John Howard. **Parents** Robert Telford and Elinor (Robinson) Hewitt, a teacher. **Marriage** Roberta Black, 1934 (died, 1975). **Education** Methodist College, Belfast, Northern Ireland, 1924; Queens University, Belfast, BA, 1930, MA, 1951. **Career** Art assistant, Belfast Museum and Art Gallery, rising to deputy director, 1930–57; art director, Herbert Gallery and Museum, Coventry, England, 1957–72. **Other activities** Poet and literary critic; member, arts advisory committee, Arts Council of Northern Ireland, 1943–56; editor, *Lagan* magazine, Lisburn, County Antrim, 1945–46; contributor of essays, sometimes under pseudonym, to periodicals; poetry editor, *Threshold* magazine, Belfast, 1957–61; member, literature advisory committee, Arts Council of Northern Ireland, 1971–81; writer-in-residence, Queen's University, Belfast, 1976–79. **Awards and honours** DLitt: New University of Ulster, Coleraine, 1974, Queens University, Belfast, 1983; Irish–American Cultural Institute Prize, 1983; freeman, City of Belfast, 1983. **Offices and memberships** Irish Academy of Letters, 1960; Arts Council of Northern Ireland; William Morris Society; trustee, Lyric Players' Theatre, Belfast; fellow, Museums' Association. **Verse** *Conacre*, privately printed, 1943; *No Rebel Word*, London, 1948; *Tesserae*, Belfast, 1967; *Collected Poems 1932–1967*, London, 1968; *The Day of the Corncrake: Poems of the Nine Glens*, Belfast, 1969; *The Planter and the Gael*, Belfast, 1970; *An Ulster Reckoning*, privately printed, 1971; *Out of My Time: Poems 1967–1974*, Belfast, 1974; *Time Enough: Poems New and Revised*, Belfast, 1976; *The Rain Dance: Poems New and Revised*, Belfast, 1978; *Kites in Spring: A Belfast Boyhood*, Belfast, 1980; *The Selected John Hewitt*, ed. Alan Warner, Belfast, 1981; *Mosaic*, Belfast, 1981; *Loose Ends*, Belfast, 1983; also contributor to *The Oxford Book of Twentieth-Century English Verse*, ed. P. Larkin, Oxford,

1973, *The Faber Book of Irish Verse*, ed. J. Montague, London, 1974. **Play** *The Bloody Brae*, produced Belfast, 1957, published in *Threshold*, autumn 1957. **Other** *Coventry: The Tradition of Change and Continuity*, Coventry, 1966; *Colin Middleton*, Northern Ireland, 1976; *Art in Ulster I: Paintings, Drawings, Prints and Sculpture*, Belfast, 1977; *John Luke (1906–1975)*, Belfast, 1978. **Edited works** (with Sam H. Bell and Nesca A. Robb) *The Arts in Ulster: A Symposium*, London, 1951; *Poems of William Allingham*, Dublin, 1967; *Rhyming Weavers and Other Country Poets of Antrim and Down*, Belfast, 1974. **Cause of death** Undisclosed, at age 77. **Further reading** Heinz Kosok, *Studies in Anglo-Irish Literature*, Bonn, West Germany, 1983.

DICK HOWSER

American Baseball Manager
***Born* Miami, Florida, 14 May 1937**
***Died* Kansas City, Missouri, 18 June 1987**

Dick Howser was generally regarded as one of the best baseball managers of his era, although his managerial career was cut short by a brain tumour and lasted only seven years. He was a paradigm "baseball man" who participated in major league baseball as a player, coach and manager.

Howser attended Florida State University in his native state, where he was twice an All-American selection and set a school record with a .422 batting average in the 1956 season. After getting his BS from Florida State, he signed a professional baseball contract and spent three years in the minor league system of the Kansas City Athletics. He made it to the major leagues in 1961, playing a full season as the Athletics' shortstop. He hit for a .280 average that year and earned the *Sporting News* "Rookie of the Year" award as the American League's outstanding first-year player.

His playing career never lived up to this initial promise. He spent eight seasons as a major-league player, but his subsequent performance never matched the level of his 1961 campaign and he played for a sequence of distinctly mediocre clubs. Early in the 1963 season the Athletics traded Howser to the Cleveland Indians, where he assumed a part-time role as shortstop. He was the Indians' starting shortstop in 1964, playing the full season and maintaining respectable (but not outstanding) batting and fielding averages. In 1965 Howser's playing career took a downturn and he was relegated to part-time duty at shortstop and second base, a status he retained on the 1966 Cleveland team.

After the 1966 season the Indians traded Howser to the New York Yankees, once the most powerful team in baseball from the 1920s to the early 1960s, but by 1967 they had fallen on hard times. The Yankee team Howser joined lost consistently, and he had a limited role as a part-time infielder. He finished his playing career in 1968, ending with a lifetime batting average of .248, 617 hits, 16 home runs and 165 runs batted in.

In 1969, at the age of 31, he joined the Yankee coaching staff and participated in the re-emergence of the Yankees in the 1970s. New York won three consecutive American League pennants between 1976 and 1978, and World Series championships in 1977 and 1978 while Howser was a Yankee coach. He left the Yankees after the 1978 season to manage the Florida State University baseball team, but returned to the major leagues in 1980 when George

Steinbrenner, the Yankees' controversial owner, hired him to manage the team. Steinbrenner's decision was surprising, since Howser's previous managing experience consisted of one year at college level and a one-game stint as interim manager of the Yankees in 1978. Under Howser the 1980 Yankees had a highly successful season and won 103 games—the most by an American League team since 1970. As is his custom, Steinbrenner did not hesitate to criticize his manager during the course of the season, despite the team's success. When the Kansas City Royals eliminated the Yankees from the pennant play-off in three straight games, Howser was dismissed.

He returned as a manager in the major leagues midway through the 1981 season, when he was hired by the Kansas City Royals, the team which had bested him in the 1980 play-off but was convinced of his managerial ability. The 1981 season was shortened by a players' strike, resulting in a complicated split-season arrangement where winners of the "pre-strike" portion of the season played for divisional titles against winners of the "post-strike" season. Howser's Royals won the second part of their season but were eliminated in three straight games by the Oakland Athletics, giving Howser a 0–6 record as a manager in post-season play.

Continuing as manager of the Royals, Howser led his team on to win the Western Division of the American League in 1984, facing the Detroit Tigers in the play-off for the American League pennant. Once again, the team lost in three straight games, leaving Howser with an unenviable record of no wins and nine losses in play-off competition. Despite his failures in post-season play, he was well-respected among baseball managers and was credited with a fine understanding of baseball strategy, the ability to motivate his players and a superior ability to evaluate players' talent. In 1985 he took the Royals to the American League play-offs for the second year running, where the team faced the Toronto Blue Jays and lost the first two games. The play-off format had been switched from a "best of five" to a "best of seven" series for the 1985 season, so these opening two losses did not leave Howser in the dire straits he had faced the previous year. Nevertheless, his play-off record stood at 0–11 and he had long since established a record for futility in post-season baseball. Miraculously, the Royals rallied to beat Toronto in a tense seven-game play-off for the American League pennant and Howser advanced to the World Series.

The 1985 World Series pitted the St Louis Cardinals against the Kansas City Royals, with St Louis being heavily favoured to win the "best of seven" series for the championship. Things began grimly for Howser's team, as they lost the first two games in their home stadium and faced the seemingly impossible task of mounting a comeback in St Louis. Good pitching and timely hitting enabled the Royals to win two of the three games played in St Louis, and the series returned to Kansas City with the Cardinals holding a 3–2 edge. The sixth game of the 1985 World Series was a close and controversial affair, with the Royals winning 2–1 by scoring two runs in the bottom of the last inning on a disputed umpiring call. The seventh and deciding game of the 1985 World Series was an 11–0 rout for Kansas City. Thus, Howser reached the pinnacle of managerial success, winning a championship against great odds.

Aged 49 when he masterminded the championship win, Howser was still considered young among major league baseball managers. At the start of the 1986 season he had established very impressive credentials as a manager and it was assumed that he had many successful years before him. None of his teams had ever finished worse than second place and many thought that he would win several championships before he retired.

However, midway through the 1986 season he was diagnosed with a brain tumour. Ironically, the diagnosis came on the eve of the annual All-Star game in which Howser was supposed to manage a select team of the best American League players in an exhibition game against the best of the National League. He resigned his position as manager of the Royals and devoted his efforts to combating his cancer. The lure of baseball remained strong, however, and when offered the chance to manage the Kansas City team in the 1987 season, he accepted. Unfortunately, he soon discovered that the job was too demanding and resigned in February, after only one day of his team's spring training. He faced the final months of his illness with courage and fortitude, earning in sickness, as in health, his reputation as a "supreme battler".

Born Richard Alton Howser. **Marriage** Nancy. **Children** Twin daughters, Jan and Jill. **Education** Florida State University, BS in education. **Career** Baseball player for three seasons with the minors before joining Kansas City Athletics, 1961; also played for Kansas City franchise; member, American League All-Star team, 1961, 1963; with Cleveland Indians, 1963–66; with New York Yankees, 1967–68; baseball coach, New York Yankees, 1969–78, manager, 1980; baseball coach, Florida State University, Tallahassee, 1979; manager, Kansas City Royals, 1981–87. **Other activities** Investor in real estate, publishing and bowling. **Awards and honours** Named American League's "Rookie of the Year", *Sporting News*, 1961; Florida State University's baseball stadium renamed after Howser, 1986. **Cause of death** Cancer, at age 51.

RASHID KARAMI

Lebanese Politician

***Born* Tripoli, Lebanon, 30 December 1921**

***Died* Beirut, Lebanon, 1 June 1987**

Rashid Karami spent his life at the centre of the tortuous political stage of his troubled native land. The republic of Lebanon has a population of one and a half million people, approximately 54 per cent Christian and 44 per cent Muslim. Until 1918 it was part of the Ottoman Empire; after that it was administered by France under a League of Nations mandate. In World War II the Free French Government declared the country an independent republic, and the constitution drawn up in 1943 stipulated that the president must always be Christian and the prime minister Muslim.

Karami was born into a family with a tradition of political leadership. His father, a Sunni (Orthodox) Muslim, was not only Grand Mufti (Muslim spiritual leader) of Lebanon, but had helped to draw up the constitution of 1943 and served as prime minister in 1945. Rashid Karami was educated in Tripoli, the second largest city in Lebanon, and then went on to study law at Cairo University, graduating in 1947. He practised law for two years in Beirut before spending a year in France and Britain.

When his father died in 1950, Rashid Karami became head of the family and entered politics. In 1951 he was elected to the Lebanese Parliament as a deputy for Tripoli, and was immediately appointed minister for justice. In 1953 he became minister of national economy and social affairs, and two years later (at the age of 34) was appointed prime minister and minister of the interior—the youngest premier in the history of the Lebanon. However, he resigned after only seven months in office because his policies were unpopular with the Chamber of Deputies. (As a good son of Tripoli, he supported the movement for a union with Syria, whereas the Chamber of Deputies favoured closer economic ties with Iraq.)

Sami Solh subsequently became prime minister (for the sixth time) and pursued pro-Western policies. In 1957 he made a pact with the United States, who agreed to provide equipment for the Lebanese army as part of the Eisenhower doctrine of mutual defence against communism. This policy won an overwhelming vote of confidence in the Chamber of Deputies, but Karami resigned his seat in protest, believing that Lebanon's interests lay with Egypt and Syria and in "positive neutrality" not in alignment with the West in the Cold War struggle.

In February 1958 Syria and Egypt merged to form the United Arab Republic (UAR), a move that led to severe divisions in Lebanon. Solh, supported by President Camille Chamoun, was accused of attempting to manipulate the constitution to favour a pro-Western coalition, and even though he denied it, Arab nationalists who supported the UAR were greatly alarmed. Riots broke out in Beirut and Tripoli, and citizens forcibly opposed government orders to take down portraits of Abdul Nasser, leader of the UAR. Karami assumed leadership of this anti-government movement, which spread rapidly across the country and lasted 140 days. Solh's foreign minister accused the UAR of "massive interference in Lebanon's affairs". In June the United Nations organization agreed to station observers in Lebanon. They reported that there was "no massive infiltration" but that there were some Syrian volunteers among the rebel forces.

In 1968 a coup overthrew the pro-Western regime in Iraq. President Chamoun, fearing that the same might happen in the Lebanon, called on the United States for support. In response, American marines and paratroopers were sent in. In July the Chamber of Deputies elected the army chief-of-staff, General Fuad Shehab, as president to succeed Chamoun, and the new president named the rebel leader Karami to be his prime minister in an attempt to reconcile the factions in Lebanon.

Karami chose a Cabinet of eight Christians, three Muslims and one Druse. He pledged himself to maintain the independence and territorial integrity of Lebanon and to practise a policy of "positive neutrality". Karami accepted a large grant of aid from the US "without strings", but at the same time he kept the door open to aid from the USSR.

The Christian Phalange Party supporters of ex-President Chamoun violently opposed Karami. There were riots and deaths in Beirut and a general strike was called. Karami threatened to appoint a military government but was not able to do so. He formed a compromise Cabinet, including the Phalange leader Pierre Gemayel as deputy premier, but this compromise failed to work. When Karami asked for and gained emergency powers to disarm the civilian population, the Phalangists left the Chamber in protest.

Between 1959 and 1969 Karami served as prime minister five times. He tried to modernize Lebanon, to build up trade with Iraq and Egypt, and to maintain a balance between support of Nasser and friendship with the West. He arranged for Lebanon to join the Arab Development Bank and urged greater Arab participation in oil refining and marketing. He resigned in 1969 when a pro-Palestinian demonstration was put down with great brutality.

When full-scale civil war broke out in Lebanon in 1975, President Suleiman Franjieh asked Karami to lead a government of "national salvation". He accepted, but when Franjieh lost his position the following year, Karami too fell from power. Ten years later, when President Gemayel rejected a Syrian-backed peace initiative for Lebanon, Karami joined with other Muslim leaders in refusing to cooperate or deal with the Christian Phalangists. This brought about a complete paralysis of the administration.

Although an adroit politician, adept at exploiting the powers available to him under the constitution, Radhid Karami lacked the statesmanship which might have been able to bring peace in his own land. He was killed in a bomb explosion in Beirut, having been prime minister of his country a total of ten times.

Born Rashid Abdul Hamid Karami. **Father** Abdel-Hamid Karami, Grand Mufti of Lebanon, and prime minister, 1945. **Education** Graduated in law, Fuad-al-Awal University, Cairo, 1947. **Career** Lawyer, 1947–49; elected to parliament, 1951; justice minister, 1951; minister of national economy and social affairs, 1954–55; prime minister and minister of the interior, 1955–56; prime minister, 1958–60; minister of finance, economy, defence and information, 1958–59; minister of finance and defence, 1959–60; prime minister and minister of finance, 1961–64; prime minister, 1965–66, 1966–68, 1969–70; prime minister, minister of finance, defence and information, 1975–76; prime minister, 1984–87. **Cause of death** Bomb explosion, at age 65.

SAMMY KAYE

American Bandleader

Born **Lakewood, Ohio, 13 March 1913**

Died **Ridgewood, New Jersey, 2 June 1987**

If one person can be held to personify the difference between critical and commercial success, it was the big band leader Sammy Kaye. Throughout the 1930s, it was fashionable to knock his band for its bland repertoire of "mickey-mouse music" executed by magnificently trained but entirely unoriginal musicians who performed on the bandstand with long faces and a complete lack of showmanship. Yet Kaye found work for his band right through to the 1980s, long outlasting his more critically favoured peers, and he retired a rich man with a string of more than 100 chart successes behind him.

Part of the problem was Kaye's slogan. "Swing and Sway with Sammy Kaye" was only half true, for his band rarely swung at all. Instead, it played music for "dancing and romance", popularizing such songs as "The Old Lamplighter" and "Harbor Lights". With a reedy ensemble sound designed to sooth, not agitate or excite, the band played sweet, smooch music to accompany millions of people dancing cheek to cheek throughout World War II. One song of Kaye's was a direct result of this war: on 7 December 1941 Kaye and his band were performing on his long-running NBC network show, *Sunday Serenade*, when the announcer, Ben Grauer, broke in to announce the Japanese attack on Pearl Harbor. After the show, Kaye returned home to write "Remember Pearl Harbor", which became an immediate hit.

The commercial success of the band owed much to Kaye's astute direction. As critic George T. Simon has noted,

> Kaye always kept his ear attuned to the times and to the dancers. He was adept at setting ideal tempos for dancing, at mixing his selections to get the most out of sets, at pacing each set so that there would never be a lull between numbers, at fronting his band with grace and charm, and at supplying satisfying sounds for those unable to appreciate and/or comprehend what the more musical bands were playing.

Not that Kaye was immune to outside influences. At the height of the Swing Era, in 1941, he hired such notable swing musicians as Roy Eldridge, Gene Krupa and Teddy Wilson to play at his "Afternoon at Meadowbrook" series of concerts, and later hired Milt Bruckner, Lionel Hampton's arranger, to contribute a few scores to the band's repertoire. Close attention to his music would also have revealed that, as Kaye himself noted, "...we were really more versatile than many people realized". In the 1950s he even allowed the band to play dance arrangements that swung a little and sold as well, if not better than, his earlier work. But such pieces were the exceptions that largely proved the rule.

Critics always scoffed at Kaye's seemingly undemanding music, but one of his musicians, Marty Oscard, noted that "Sammy knew just what he wanted and he worked like a dog to get it". Those who did "get" it were the musicians, who endured gruelling rehearsals to perfect the band's sound. So harsh was Kaye in his dictatorial control of his musicians—during one rehearsal he barked out orders at them while wearing a silk dressing gown and waving a long cigarette-holder around—that almost the entire band once left Kaye to start up on their own. They failed, for Kaye had a highly developed business acumen; he paid his band above the going rate, had them travel first class, and was much more open to new ideas than his reputation might have suggested.

For such a strong-willed man, Kaye was surprisingly aware of his own limitations. He was no instrumental virtuoso, although his clarinet and alto saxophone playing were perfectly acceptable, and he rarely played in public. Indeed, he hired few musicians for their soloing, as opposed to ensemble, abilities, preferring instead to use singers rather than instrumentalists to front the band. By 1941 the band sported six such singers, notably Don Cornell, who sang such hits as "Careless Hands" and "Room Full of Roses". His singers were almost all men; indeed, it was rumoured that he had once fired a woman singer because she was taller than he and distracted audience attention from the leader!

Kaye was also fond of gimmicks, inviting members of the audience to come up on stage and conduct the band for themselves. "So You Want to Lead a Band" might sound like a corny idea, but it delighted the audience, whose applause decided the winner. Bottles of champagne and Sammy Kaye batons were the prizes. Another successful gimmick was his marketing of a book of poems. *The Sunday Serenade Book of Poems* annually sold more than 100,000 copies during the 1940s.

Kaye's career might sound like the quintessential American success story, a reward for hard work and continually pleasing the punter, but Kaye was, in fact, a first-generation Czech who took elocution lessons in his youth to hide his accent. He was born in a suburb of Cleveland and attended Ohio University, where he studied civil engineering. But while at university, he became increasingly involved in music and, after graduation in 1933, he opened a venue on campus known as the Varsity Inn. He set up a big band as one of the opening attractions, and with the band went on to gain national recognition in 1937 through a broadcast coast-to-coast on NBC from the Cleveland Country Club. By the time the band made its New York début at the Commodore Hotel in 1938, it was already well known throughout the United States, thanks to its first hit, "Rosalie", released in 1937.

For 50 years the Kaye band plied its trade with great success. Radio and television shows, numerous recording sessions and national tours established it as a national institution, playing at the inaugurations of both presidents Nixon and Reagan. By the time Kaye retired, he was a successful businessman who had invested the profits from his band in publishing, bowling alleys and other ventures. For such a critically dismissed musician, Kaye had done well for himself.

Born Samuel Kaye. **Parents** Samuel and Mary (Zarnocay) Kaye. **Marriage** Ruth Knox Elden, 1940 (divorced, 1956). **Education** Track scholarship, Ohio University, BS, civil engineering, 1933. **Career** Bandleader, Sammy Kaye Orchestra, 1933 onwards; also, songwriter; appeared on films, television and radio; recorded with Columbia Records and Victor Records; first major broadcast from Cleveland Country Club on NBC, 1935; first major hit, "Rosalie", 1937; New York début, Commodore Hotel, 1938. **Recordings** (include) "Rosalie"; "Love Walked In"; "All Ashore"; "Hurry Home"; "Penny Serenade"; "Dream Valley"; "Daddy"; "Remember Pearl Harbor"; "I Left My Heart at the Stage Door Canteen"; "Chickery Chick"; "I'm a Big Girl Now"; "The Gypsy"; "That's My Desire"; "Serenade of the Bells"; "Careless Hands"; "Room Full of Roses"; "The Four Winds and the Seven Seas"; "It Isn't Fair"; "Harbor Lights"; "Walkin' to Missouri". **Television** Own show, *Sunday Serenade*, NBC. **Cause of death** Cancer, at age 77.

FULTON MACKAY

British Actor

***Born* Paisley, Renfrewshire, 12 August 1922**

***Died* England, 6 June 1987**

Fulton Mackay was one of Britain's leading character actors. Although he became best known through the television programme *Porridge*, in which he played the prison warder, he had a very full acting career on the stage. He played leading roles with the Royal Shakespeare Company, the National Theatre, the Royal Court Theatre and most major repertory companies, as well as appearing in several films. And, although he was best known as an actor, he also wrote plays for television and radio, and was a very gifted painter.

Mackay's mother died young and his father was away in the army, so he was brought up in Clydebank by a widowed aunt. He attended Clydebank High School and although he had no contact with the theatre said he always instinctively knew that he would be an actor. He first worked as a quantity surveyor "but that was only to try and be reasonable", he once said. In 1941 he volunteered for the air force, but was rejected owing to a perforated eardrum. Instead, he joined the Black Watch and stayed in the army for five years, spending much of that time in India.

After the war he began his acting career in earnest. He was accepted by RADA (the Royal Academy of Dramatic Art) in London, later claiming that he applied because he read on the back of a packet of cigarettes that Charles Laughton was a former student. In a profession with a high unemployment rate, Mackay was never short of work. Director and author Bill Bryden explained why: "He is not just a very fine actor but he has a wide range. He can do everything from Ibsen to light comedy. His work is distinguished and reliable. If he accepts a piece of work he will try to mine it for the best that's in it."

Perhaps the inheritance of a Scottish Calvinist work ethic also contributed to his success. It certainly drove him to work to perfection and for every minute of the day. Only after giving his all did he think he deserved to relax over a drink in the evening.

After leaving RADA Mackay worked with several repertory companies before going to the Citizens' Theatre in Glasgow. "That was my instinctive home," he once said. "When I got there I knew I was in the right place." The Citizens' gave him the opportunity to act a great variety of roles and, occasionally, to direct. In 1960, two years after leaving the company, he played his first notable part in London—Oscar in *Naked Islands*. By 1962 he had joined the Old Vic Company for a year, where his parts included the Preacher and Solveig's Father in *Peer Gynt*, Salerio in *The Merchant of Venice*, and Dapper in *The Alchemist*. He went on to play at the Royal Court and the 69 Theatre Company in Manchester. In 1969 he became director of the Scottish Actors' Company for whom he directed *The Wild Duck* at that year's Edinburgh Festival. He also played Wangel in *The Lady From the Sea* and was excellent in the role of the cunning tramp in *The Caretaker* at the Shaw Theatre, London. By the late 1970s he had also acted with the Royal Shakespeare Company and won much praise for his part as Squeers in *Nicholas Nickleby*.

Although Mackay lived most of his working life in London, he always kept close links with Scotland and was delighted to be asked to join the board of the new Scottish Theatre Company by its director Ewan Hopper. Here he acted and helped to formulate company policy. Hopper is reported as saying, "Fulton was one of the first people I approached to be on the board. He has a long association with the theatre in Scotland and I was keen to get actors on the board. I wanted the groundwork laid by people who knew what they're talking about, and Fulton, apart from being knowledgeable about theatre, is very astute and doesn't let any nonsense pass. He doesn't take any easy routes. He demands the highest quality and expects the greatest effort from everybody." The company was backed by the Scottish Arts Council and aimed to stage Scottish plays, something of which Mackay approved: "People act and communicate better in their own tongue."

Fulton Mackay held many awards but could never be persuaded to talk about any of them, except one: a small tin figure marked "Warder of the Year" which was given to him by Ronnie Barker who played prisoner to his warder in the extremely funny and popular television series *Porridge*. Mackay was well aware that, despite all his other acting achievements, it was for his role as thin-lipped, humourless Mr Mackay that he would be best remembered by the public. Maybe some would also remember him for his appearances in other series such as *Special Branch* and *The Foundation*, and the controversial programme about ex-convict Jimmy Boyle, *A Sense of Freedom*. He also ventured into films, among them *Gumshoe*, a brilliant satire on a detective played by Albert Finney, and *Local Hero* with Burt Lancaster.

Always an intensely private man, Mackay wrote several television and radio plays using the pseudonym Aeneas MacBride. He was also a very talented painter, though he was typically modest about his work. "I find I can put paints together, but I can't really understand what I'm doing," he once said. "When I'm on stage acting I know what I'm doing and I understand all the forces which are at work. That doesn't happen when I paint. But putting colour on canvas comes quite naturally and I enjoy it...Painting is like fishing. Either you catch something, or you don't." Perhaps more to the point, painting was a medium through which he could let his emotions overcome his intellect.

Although Mackay and his wife had no children, he did a lot of good work for the Child and Family Trust, a Glasgow charity. This was just one more facet of a proud and private man, who was a wonderfully versatile and creative actor.

Born Fulton Mackay. **Pseudonym** Aeneas MacBride. **Parents** William and Agnes (McDermid) Mackay. **Marriage** Sheila Manahan, an actress. **Education** Clydebank High School, Glasgow, Scotland; Royal Academy of Dramatic Arts, London, 1946. **Military service** Black Watch regiment, British Army, 1941–46. **Career** Quantity surveyor until 1941; actor, 1947 onwards; stage début, on tour in Liverpool and Leeds, 1947; London début, as walk-on angel, Strand, 1947; début, Edinburgh Festival, 1948; in repertory, Citizens' Theatre, Glasgow, 1949–51, 1953–58; with Old Vic Company, London, 1962–63; début as director, *The Wild Duck*, for the Scottish Actors' Company, 1969; at the National Theatre, 1977–78; with the Royal Shakespeare Company, 1978–79. **Related activities** Director, Scottish Theatre Company, from 1981. **Other activities** Television scriptwriter under pseudonym; plays include *Diamond's Progress*, *Girl with Flowers in Her Hair*, *Dalhousie's Luck*. **Awards and honours** Officer, Order of the British Emprie. **Offices and memberships** Child and Family Trust, Glasgow. **Stage** *The Thrie Estates*, 1950; *Naked Island*, 1960; *The Lower Depths*, 1962; *Peer Gynt*, 1962–63; *The Merchant of Venice*, 1962–63; *The Alchemist*, 1962–63; *Justice Is a Woman*, 1966; *In Celebration*, 1969; *Peer Gynt*, 1969; *The Wild Duck*, also director, 1969; *The Lady from the Sea*, 1971; *The Douglas Cause*, 1971; *Willie Rough*, 1972, 1973; *The Thrie Estates*, 1973; *The Man with a Flower in His Mouth*, 1973; *The Caretaker*, 1976; *Old Movies*, 1977; *The Passion*, 1978; *Balmoral*, 1978; *The Hang of the Gaol*, 1978; *Anna Christie*, 1979; *Nicholas Nickleby*, 1984; *Die Fledermaus*, 1986. **Films** (include) *Gumshoe*, 1971; *Porridge*, 1979; *Local Hero*, 1983. **Television** (includes) *Special Branch*; *Porridge*; *The Foundation*. **Cause of death** Undisclosed, at age 64.

BRUCE MARSHALL

British Novelist

***Born* Edinburgh, Scotland, 24 June 1899**

***Died* Antibes, France, 18 June 1987**

Bruce Marshall was a prolific novelist whose books covered a wide range of topics: religious themes, espionage, thrillers, historical novels and satire. Inevitably, he reached a wide reading public, but he never achieved the stature that some critics felt he deserved.

Educated at Edinburgh Academy and Glenalmond College, he went to St Andrews University to read classical studies, but his career was interrupted by World War I. Forsaking his degree, he joined the army and served in the Royal Irish Fusiliers. Shortly before the armistice, he was wounded and taken prisoner, subsequently losing a leg because of poor treatment. He eventually returned to Edinburgh University, where he gained a degree in commerce and an MA, and later qualified as a chartered accountant.

Between the wars Marshall lived in Paris, working as an accountant. During this time he began writing, using many of his own experiences as background for his novels. One of his first books, which was better received in the US than in Britain, was called *Father Malachy's Miracle* (1931). It was set in Presbyterian Scotland and was the first of several novels with a religious theme. Although a Catholic convert, Marshall was not above criticizing the Church he loved. In *The Thread of Scarlet* (1959) he dealt with priestly ambition, and *The Bishop* (1970) tackled the thorny problems of birth control and celibacy. Neither were especially successful in terms of sales, but Marshall considered them to be among his best works.

Returning to England in 1940, Marshall joined the army for a second time. At first he was assigned to the Pay Corps, but later transferred to Intelligence. After the war he served on the Allied Control Commission in Austria dealing with displaced persons. Two novels were inspired by this brush with bureaucracy—*The Red Danube* (1947), later made into a film, and *A Girl From Lübeck* (1962), a satire on international red tape. However, one of his best known post-war novels is *George Brown's Schooldays* (1946), an update of the nineteenth-century classic *Tom Brown's Schooldays*, which bluntly describes the savagery and homosexuality still prevalent in British public schools.

Acclaim eventually arrived with the publication of *The White Rabbit*, an unsparing account of the experiences of Wing Commander F.F.E. Yeo-Thomas, a British agent in France during World War II. Captured while helping to reorganize a section of the French Resistance movement, Yeo-Thomas suffered appalling torture at the hands of the Gestapo. Marshall's knowledge of France and his work in war-time intelligence made him eminently suited to write this book, and it is tribute to his skill that it is as compelling as it is shocking.

Considered by some to have been seriously underestimated, Marshall was often compared unfavourably with another well-known convert to Catholicism—Graham Greene. However, to make comparisons on the basis of a shared faith is to do injustice to both writers. Marshall's novels have been accused of shallow plots and imperfect characterization, but they were never intended to be more than light dramatizations for the man in the street. Perhaps, in his attempt to make serious issues accessible, Marshall erred on the side of superficiality, but in so doing he acquired legions of avid readers, one of whom described him thus: "Bruce Marshall is full of mockery; he succumbs sometimes to merely carnal or spiritual comedy, but he is never morbid or mean...he relishes the farce and the terror of man."

Born Bruce Marshall. **Father** Claude Niven Marshall. **Marriage** Phyllis Clark, 1928. **Children** One daughter. **Education** Edinburgh Academy, 1906–09; Trinity College, Glenalmond, 1909–15; St Andrews University, 1916–17; Edinburgh University, 1922–25, MA, 1924, BCom, 1925; qualified as accountant, 1926. **Military service** Royal Irish Fusiliers, 1918–20; Royal Army Pay Corps and Intelligence, 1940–46. **Career** Chartered accountant, Peat Marwick Mitchell Ltd., Paris, 1926–40; writer of thrillers, short stories, satires and novels, 1919–87. **Awards and honours** Wlodimierz Petrzak Prize, Warsaw, 1959. **Novels** *This Sorry Scheme*, London, 1924, New York, 1926; *Teacup Terrace*, London, 1926; *The Stooping Venus*, London and New York, 1926; *The Other Mary*, London, 1927; *And There Were Giants*, London, 1927; *The Little Friend*, London, 1928, New York, 1929; *High Brows: An Extravaganza of Manners—Mostly Bad*, London, 1929; *The Rough House: A Possibility*, London, 1930; *Children of This Earth*, New York, 1930; *Father Malachy's Miracle*, London and New York, 1931, revised edition, 1947; *Prayer for the Living*, London and New York, 1934; *The Uncertain Glory*, London, 1935; *Canon to Right of Them*, London, 1936; *Luckypenny*, London, 1937, New York, 1938; *Delilah Upside Down: A Tract with a Thrill*, London, 1941; *Yellow Tapers for Paris: A Dirge*, London, 1943, Boston, 1946; *All Glorious Within*, London, 1944, published as *The World, The Flesh and Father Smith*, Boston, 1945; *George Brown's Schooldays*, London, 1946; *The Red Danube*, London, 1946, published as *Vespers in Vienna*, Boston, 1947; *To Every Man a Penny*, Boston, 1949, published as *Every Man a Penny*, London, 1950; *The Fair Bride*, London and Boston, 1953; *Only Fade Away*, London and Boston, 1954; *Girl in May*, London and Boston, 1956; *The Bank Audit*, London, 1958, published as *The Accounting*, Boston, 1958; *A Thread of Scarlet*, London, 1959, published as *Satan and Cardinal Campbell*, Boston, 1959; *The Divided Lady*, London and Boston, 1960; *A Girl from Lübeck*, London and Boston, 1962; *The Month of the Falling Leaves*, London and New York, 1963; *Father Hilary's Holiday*, London and New York, 1965; *The Bishop*, London and New York, 1970; *The Black Oxen*, London, 1972; *Urban the Ninth*, London, 1973; *Operation Iscariot*, London, 1974; *Marx the First*, 1975; *Peter the Second*, London, 1976; *The Yellow Streak*, London, 1977; *Prayer for a Concubine*, London, 1978; *Flutter in the Dovecote*, London, 1986; *A Foot in the Grave*, London, 1987; *An Account of Capers*, London, 1987. **Short stories** *As a Thief in the Night and Other Stories*, Amersham, Buckinghamshire and London, 1919. **Other** *The White Rabbit*, London, 1952, Boston, 1953; *Thoughts of My Cats*, London and Boston, 1954. **Cause of death** Undisclosed, at age 87.

GERALDINE PAGE

American Actress

Born **Kirksville, Missouri, 22 November 1924**

Died **New York City, New York, 13 June 1987**

Geraldine Page's life story reads like a 1950s' film treatment of the archetypal actor's success story: rigorous training followed by hard years of poverty, peanut butter sandwiches and dead-end, part-time jobs until the proverbial big break rockets her name to above the title in a Broadway play. It is testament to Page's dedication and commitment to the ideals of acting as laid down by the American Method school that, unlike many real-life colleagues, she refused to make the Faustian deal with Hollywood and insisted on the stage remaining the primary forum for her exploration of her craft.

The child of a medical household, Page grew up in Missouri before the family moved to Chicago. A lengthy debate with her father following her performance in an amateur production of *Excuse My Dust* convinced him of the seriousness of his 17-year-old daughter's desire to act. An honourable man, the doctor kept his promise to send her to the Goodman Theater Dramatic School in Chicago. After graduation, unemployed and desperate for experience, she formed her own company at Lake Zurich, outside Chicago, where she appeared in four summer seasons. The winters were spent shivering in New York where she paid the rent with a succession of casual jobs—clerical work, hat-check girl, theatre usher, book sales assistant and even negligée model in a dress shop.

It was not until the early 1950s that Page struck lucky with an off-Broadway production of Tennessee Williams's *Summer and Smoke* at the Circle-in-the-Square Theater in Greenwich Village. The repressed spinster Alma Winemiller became one of her favourite parts and won considerable critical acclaim. "Great", "astounding" and "magical" were the kind of epithets that spelt success, particularly when the reviewers could congratulate themselves on an "overnight discovery". (Page had spent some eight years working as a professional actress since graduating from Goodman and was at this stage nearly 30 years old.)

Her success as Alma led to her Hollywood film début, a bit-part in the entirely undistinguished *Taxi*. Twenty-first billing in that soon became top for her first Broadway hit, *Midsummer*. In this she played the part of an idealistic heroine, a role that needed charm, pathos and superlative technique to bring it off. She succeeded and her career was set.

Page's demonstrated affinity with Tennessee Williams characters led to a number of roles in that writer's plays. She specialized in slightly odd, spinsterish neurotics whose shyness and vulnerability she captured exceptionally well. This ability transferred well to the screen and led to a number of parts in films, such as *Toys in the Attic*, *Dear Heart* and *You're a Big Boy Now*. The eccentricity could be pushed to extremes for ostensibly sweet psychopaths in *The Beguiled* and *Whatever Happened to Aunt Alice?* More recently, Woody Allen cast her as the self-pitying, overbearing mother of *Interiors*.

Page kept up with her professional training and took classes with Uta Hagen for a number of years. A leading exponent of the Method school, Hagen taught the value of linking together spontaneity, observation and technical rigour to achieve dramatic truth. The lessons learnt there enabled Page to avoid the typecasting that films seemed to wish to thrust upon her and she went on to play an impressive range of stage roles in plays by writers as diverse as Terence Rattigan, Anton Chekhov, Alan Ayckbourn and, again, her beloved Tennessee Williams.

For many years it seemed that, no matter how lauded her stage work and no matter how many other, lesser television and film awards she won, the cinema industry's ultimate accolade, the Oscar, would be denied her. She was nominated a record seven times before winning on the eighth time round in 1986 for the part of Carrie Watts in *The Trip to Bountiful*.

Modestly listing her recreation as "studying acting", Geraldine Page demonstrated her lifelong belief that acting is a craft to be worked at. Her mentor, Uta Hagen, says in her book, *Respect for Acting*, that "for a would-be actor, the prerequisite is *talent*", which she goes on to define as "an amalgam of high sensitivity, easy vulnerability, high sensory equipment, a vivid imagination, as well as a grip on reality, and the desire to communicate one's own experience and sensations, to make oneself heard and seen". Geraldine Page fulfilled all these conditions without compromise and died in harness during a Broadway revival of Noel Coward's *Blithe Spirit*—final testament to her considerable versatility.

Born Geraldine Sue Page. **Parents** Leon Elwin, an osteopathic physician and surgeon, and Edna Pearl (Maize) Page. **Marriages** 1) Alexander Schneider, violinist (divorced); 2) Rip Torn, actor and director. **Children** One daughter, Angelica, and twin sons, Anthony and Johnny. **Education** Goodman Theater School, Chicago, 1942–45; also trained under Sophia Swanstrom Young, Chicago, 1940, and Uta Hagen, 1949–56, Mira Rostova, 1950, and Alice Hermes, all in New York City. **Career** Stage début in *Excuse My Dust*, Englewood Methodist Church, Chicago, 1940; undertook summer stock productions at Lake Zurich Summer Playhouse, Illinois, 1945–48, Woodstock Winter Playhouse, Illinois, 1947–49, and Shadylane Summer Playhouse, 1950–51; off-Broadway stage work while working for International Thread Company, early 1950s; Broadway début in *Midsummer*, Vanderbilt Theater, 1953; Hollywood film début in *Hondo*, 1953; subsequent career divided between stage, film, television and radio work. **Offices and memberships** Actors' Equity Association; Screen Actors' Guild; American Federation of Television and Radio Artists; Actors' Studio; Phi Beta Kappa. **Awards and honours** Academy Award nomination as Best Supporting Actress for *Hondo*, 1953; Donaldson Award, *Theater World* Award and co-winner of *Variety* New York Drama Critics' Poll, for *Midsummer*, 1953; winner, *Variety* New York Drama Critics' Poll for *Sweet Bird of Youth*, 1959; Sarah Siddons Award for *Sweet Bird of Youth*, 1960; *Who's Who of American Women* Award as outstanding woman of the year in the theatre, 1960; *Cue* magazine Best Actress Award, 1961; Academy Award nomination as Best Actress for *Summer and Smoke*, 1961; (all for *Sweet Bird of Youth*) Cinema Nuovo Gold Plaque, Venice, 1961, National Board of Review of Motion Pictures Award, 1961, Golden Globe Award, 1962, Academy Award nomination as Best Actress, 1962 and Donatello Award, 1963; Golden Globe Award for *Dear Heart*, 1964; Emmy Best Actress Awards for *A Christmas Memory*, 1967, and *The Thanksgiving Visitor*, 1969; British Academy of Film and Television Arts Award for *Interiors*, 1979; Academy Award as Best Actress for *A Trip to Bountiful*, 1986. **Films** *Out of the Night*, Chicago,1947; *Taxi*, 1953; *Hondo*, 1953; *Summer and Smoke*, 1961; *Sweet Bird of Youth*, 1962; *Toys in the Attic*, 1963; *Dear Heart*, 1964; *The Three Sisters*, 1965; *Monday's Child*, 1966; *You're a Big Boy Now*, 1966; *The Happiest Millionaire*, 1967; *Trilogy*, 1969; *Whatever Happened to Aunt Alice?*, 1969; *The Beguiled*, 1971; *J.W. Coop*, 1972; *Pete 'n' Tillie*, 1972; *Happy As the Grass Was Green* (*Hazel's People*), 1974; *The Day of the Locust*, 1974; *The Abbess of Crewe*, 1976; voice in *The Rescuers* (animation), 1977; *Nasty Habits*, 1977; *Interiors*, 1978; *Honky Tonk Freeway*, 1980; *Harry's War*, 1980; *I'm Dancing as Fast as I Can*, 1982; *The Pope of Greenwich Village*, 1984; *The Bride*, 1985; *White Nights*, 1985; *A Trip to Bountiful*, 1986; *Native Son*, 1986; *My Little Girl*, 1987. **Stage** (all in New York City, unless stated) *Excuse My Dust*, Chicago, 1940; *Seven Mirrors*, 1945; *Yerma*, 1951–52; *Summer and Smoke*, 1951–52; *Midsummer*, 1953; *The Immoralist*, 1954; *The Rainmaker*, 1954, and on tour, 1955; *The Innkeepers*, 1956; *Desire Under the Elms*, Chicago, 1956; *A Month in the Country*, Chicago, 1956; *The Immoralist*, Chicago, 1956; *Separate Tables*, 1957; *Sweet Bird of Youth*, 1959; *The Umbrella*, Philadelphia, 1962; *Strange Interlude*, 1963; *The Three Sisters*, 1964; *P.S. I Love You*, 1964; *The Great Indoors*, 1966; *White Lies*, 1967; *Black Comedy*, 1967; *Angela*, 1969; *The Marriage Proposal*, Philadelphia, 1971; *Marriage and Money*, on tour, 1971; *The Boor*, Philadelphia, 1971; *Look Away*, 1973, 1974; *The Little Foxes*, Philadelphia, 1974; *Absurd Person Singular*, 1974; *A Streetcar Named Desire*, Lake Forest, 1976; *Creditors*, 1977; *Slightly Delayed*, on tour, 1979; *Mixed Couples*, 1980; *Clothes for a Summer Hotel*, 1980; *Agnes of God*, 1982, 1983–85; *Blithe Spirit*, 1987; *Papa Is All*. **Television** *Easter Story*, 1946; *The Turn of the Screw*, 1955; *Barefoot in Athens*, 1966; *A Christmas Memory*, 1966; *A Thanksgiving Visitor*, 1966; *Montserrat*, 1971; *Look Homeward Angel*, 1972; *Live Again, Die Again*, 1974; *Something for Joey*, 1977; *The Parade*, 1984; episodic appearances in *Goodyear Playhouse*, *Omnibus*, *Studio One*, *Kraft Television Theater*, *US Steel Hour*, *Robert Montgomery Presents*, *Philco Playhouse*,

Windows, *Sunday Showcase*, *The Long Hot Summer*, *The Name of the Game*, *Night Gallery*, *Medical Center*, *Ghost Story*. **Radio** (includes) *Liliom, The Glass Menagerie* and *Summer and Smoke* for the Theater Guild of the Air. **Cause of death** Undisclosed, at age 62.

FRANÇOIS PERROUX

French Economist

***Born* Lyons, France, 19 December 1903**

***Died* Paris, France, 2 June 1987**

François Perroux was one of the outstanding French economists of his generation and his influence was widely regarded both nationally and internationally as comparable only with that of Keynes. He received honorary degrees from a number of universities not only in Europe but also in North and South America, and was a member of many scientific institutions throughout Europe as well as in his own country.

Perroux was born and educated at Lyons and his first teaching post was at his own university of Lyons. From the mid-1930s his main interest outside his professional economic studies was the problem of the rise of National Socialism in Germany, and in 1936 he published *Les Mythes Hitlériens*. In 1944, with the liberation of France, he founded the Institute of Applied Economic Science (later the Institute of Sciences and Applied Economic Mathematics). He was a strong supporter of the Marshall Plan for post-war Europe, which he saw as introducing a revolution in thinking on international relations. His book *Le Plan Marshall ou l'Europe nécessaire au monde* in many ways heralded later developments within NATO and the European Economic Community.

From 1955 to 1976 Perroux held the chair of analysis of social and economic data at the Collège de France, and for most of the time was also in charge of the Institute for the Study of Economic and Social Development. It was during this period that he developed his major economic theories, in particular his theories of planning and general equilibrium.

Perroux was in great demand as a lecturer outside his own country, being fluent in English, Spanish, Italian and German, as well as French. After the war he was the first French economist to be invited to Harvard and to the London School of Economics and he travelled extensively throughout the latter part of his long academic career.

Born François Perroux. **Education** University of Lyons, Licence et Diplôme d'Études Supérieures des Lettres, 1924, Doctorat de Sciences Économiques, 1932. **Career** Professor, Collège de France, 1925–75, honorary professor, 1976–87; professor, University of Lyons, 1926–28; professor, École des Haute Études, Sorbonne, University of Paris, 1938–55; founder and president, Institute of Applied Mathematical and Economic Science, 1944–87; chair of analysis of social and economic data, Collège de France, 1955–76; head, Institute for Study of Economic and Social Development, Paris, 1960–69. **Related activities** National Council for Public Services, 1945; Higher Council on Accounting, 1947; president, International Congress on Accounting, 1948; Ways and Means Subcommittee; Budget and Accounts Commission; Economic and Social Council. **Other activities** Co-director, European Society for Culture, Venice, 1956; International Council of Social Sciences, 1960; frequent lecturer in France and abroad. **Awards and honours** Grand Croix de l'Ordre National du Mérite; commander, Legion of

Honour; commander, Palmes Acadèmiques; fellow in economic science, University of Paris, 1928; honorary doctorates from: Sao Paulo, 1936, Coimbra, Portugal, 1937, Liège, 1955, Frankfurt, 1957, Lisbon, 1960, Cordoba, 1963, Montevideo, 1963, Georgetown, Washington, 1963, ICA, Peru, 1964, Lima, 1964, Chile, 1967, Barranquilla, Colombia, 1967, Bogota, 1968, Quebec, 1968, Barcelona, 1969, Bucharest, 1969, Ottawa, 1974; corresponding fellow, British Academy, 1961; honorary member, American Economic Association, 1962; Gold Medal of C.C. Soderstrom, Royal Academy of Sciences, Stockholm, 1971. **Offices and memberships** International Council of Social Sciences, 1960; foreign member, Accademia Nazionale dei Lincei, 1960; Centre National du Recherche Scientifique, 1963; associate member, Académie de Bruxelles; member, Royal Academy, Barcelona. **Publications** (include) *Le Problème du profit*, 1926; *Les Mythes Hitlériens*, 1936; *La Valeur*, 1943; *Le Plan Marshall, ou l'Europe nécessaire au monde*, 1946; *Les Comptes de la nation*, 1949; *Théorie générale du progrès économique*, 1956–57; *L'économie du XXème siècle*, 1961; *Les Techniques quantitatives de la planification*, 1965; *Pouvoir et économie*, 1975; *Unités activés et mathématiques nouvelles: Revision de la théorie de l'équilibre générale*, 1975; *A Basic Concept of Development: Basic Trends*, 1983. **Cause of death** Undisclosed, at age 83.

SIR WALTER SALOMON

British Banker

***Born* Hamburg, Germany, 16 April 1906**

***Died* London, England, 16 June 1987**

Sir Walter Salomon was a highly successful banker, universally respected for the integrity and independence of his professional life and views. In private he enjoyed, like most successful bankers, many of the good things of this world, with a fine house in central London, a score of golf and yacht club memberships and a list of hobbies which included skiing, art, bridge and snooker.

Salomon prided himself on his old-fashioned views on banking. He constantly stressed the importance of personal responsibility, and referred to himself as a practitioner of "the dying craft of personal banking". Indeed, he always said that he would prefer his own "merchant bank", Rea Brothers, to be known as a "private bank". "Private banking has been and remains," he wrote, "a bastion of individualism and private enterprise." He deplored the development of limited liability companies and warned against the mergers of the 1960s on the grounds of morality and efficiency. "My proposition," he explained, "is the larger the size, the more the remoteness; the more the remoteness, the less the personal involvement; the less the personal involvement, the smaller the profit." A well-run bank, to Salomon, was one run on grounds of strict moral probity—anything else would be inefficient and liable to lose money.

Inflation was another of Salomon's bugbears. Having lived through the terrible inflation of the Weimar Republic after World War I, Salomon spoke from his own experience when he blamed the monetary instability of those days for the rise of Nazism in Germany. And it was Nazism which eventually forced him to leave his native Hamburg in 1937 and seek exile and a new start in London. In an essay entitled "The Scourge of Inflation", Salomon argued that all inflation is caused by governments whose prime duty is, he believed, to ensure a sound currency. Political stability, he maintained, can only exist alongside monetary stability.

Individual liberty and the existence of an "Awkward Squad" prepared to challenge the discretionary powers of ministers and their bureaucrats in Britain was also of pre-eminent importance to Salomon. To this end he himself engaged in a three-year battle with HM Customs and Excise to get back a little less than £16 duty he had been wrongly charged on an imported camera. He also proudly claimed to be the man responsible for changing the racial categories listed by immigration officials at US airports. At four in the morning at Philadelphia Airport he had argued the point for several hours with officials unprepared to accept his own classification of himself as "human" and his unwillingness to choose among his own German/Canadian/French/British parentage, before finally fixing on the compromise of "white". For a man who had grappled with the Nazis and with the unwelcoming City of London in his youth, taking on the Civil Service must have seemed positively simple.

Sir Walter Salomon devoted considerable energy to putting the principles he preached into practice both in and out of his bank. In 1963 he founded the Young Enterprise Movement to give teenagers a chance to test at first hand their own entrepreneurial capacities. He was also a vice-president of the Cambridge Settlement, a member of the Hudson Club and of the wildlife protection 1001 Club. So much was banking in his blood that he delighted in the definition provided by his eight-year-old son of a "free country" as one that allowed its citizens to take out more than £50 in foreign exchange.

Born Walter Hans Salomon. **Parents** Henry, a banker, and Rena (Oppenheimer) Salomon. **Marriage** Kate Oppenheimer, 1935. **Children** One son and one daughter. **Emigration** Left Germany for England, 1937. **Education** Oberreal, Eppendorf, Hamburg; Hamburg University. **Career** Started work as an office boy in a bank in Germany, at age of 16; bank manager at age 21; moved to England and founded own merchant bank in Finsbury Square, City of London, 1937; chairman, Rea Brothers, 1950–84, president, 1984 onwards; chairman, Canal-Randolph Corporation. **Related activities** Adviser to British companies abroad. **Other activities** Founder and life president, Young Enterprise, 1963 onwards; author, lecturer on economic and financial affairs. **Offices and memberships** Council of British Bankers' Association; member of Baltic Exchange, 1957; member of Lloyd's, 1958; vice-president, Cambridge Settlement; Luso–Brazilian Council; Anglo–Portuguese Society; 1001 Club (World Wildlife), 1973; Hudson Institute, 1976. **Awards and honours** Fellow, Institute of Banking, 1964; freeman, City of London; commander, Southern Cross of Brazil, 1971; master, Pattenmakers' Company, 1977–78; Officer's Cross (1st Class) of the Order of Merit of the Federal Republic of Germany, 1979; knighted, 1982. **Publications** *One Man's View*, 1973; (with others) *Fair Warning* (essays), 1983. **Cause of death** Undisclosed, at age 81.

ANDRÉS SEGOVIA

Spanish Guitarist

***Born* Linares, Spain, 21 February 1893**

***Died* Madrid, Spain, 2 June 1987**

"The guitar has been my mistress, my wife, my child, my life."

When Andrés Segovia first played in public over three-quarters of a century ago, the guitar was reviled as an instrument of peasant café music. The pioneering achievement of his long life in music was to establish the guitar's popularity and high profile on the modern concert platform, to develop and refine the instrument's technique, to expand its repertoire, to establish academic traditions of guitar study and to nurture the international careers of his more famous pupils, who included Julian Bream, John Williams, Alirio Diaz and Oscar Ghilyia. Respected as one of the finest of all international soloists, he was playing to capacity audiences until well after his ninetieth birthday.

Segovia was first drawn to the sound of the guitar at the age of six, when he met a travelling flamenco player. Four years later his family moved from his birthplace, Linares, to Granada. Here he bought his first guitar and began the lifelong task of teaching himself to play, remaining self-taught apart from a few lessons with Miguel Llobet. He once said: "I wanted to play the guitar but I was told by my family that it was not respectable and had no present and no future. My father broke two or three guitars to stop me practising." In those days the instrument was a vital part of Spanish popular culture but not considered a serious instrument for study. "I said to myself, 'How is it possible that such a beautiful instrument has no serious music composed for it?'," he recalled, "and I set out to extract the guitar from the noisy and disreputable folkloric amusements and make it well known to the 'philharmonic public'."

Segovia was a pioneer almost completely without mentor or guide. He had to discover for himself the technique and history of the guitar. Some indigenous sense confirmed him in the belief that somewhere a repertoire for such a noble instrument must exist. Much of his subsequent career was to be spent discovering the riches of the guitar repertoire from the sixteenth century onwards. With the help of friends he began to collect nineteenth-century works and became aware of the possibilities of transcription. His progress was rapid, and at the age of 16 he gave his first recital at the Centro Artistico in Granada. The success and novelty of the occasion was such that he was convinced to indulge his consuming interest and make the guitar his career.

Concerts in Córdoba and Seville followed, and in 1913 he made his début in Madrid playing at the Ateneo. These were years that tested Segovia's determination, both to acquire greater artistry *and* to persuade concert managers and the public to listen to the guitar. His first international tour in 1919 took him to South America. He also persuaded Spanish composers to write for him, encouraging Frederico Moreno Torroba with the words, "Pretend you are writing for a violin with six strings and I will do the rest".

Segovia's Paris début in 1924 set a seal on his international reputation. The recital, which included a work written for him by Roussel, entitled simply *Segovia*, was attended by many distinguished musicians. Two years later he was commanded to appear before the Queen of Spain. Searching for an appropriate compliment, she told him, "Young man, you play like a music box." Segovia had the tact to reply, "Your Majesty, I have yet to reach such perfection."

His international engagements grew massively. Between 1924 and 1925 he played in Switzerland, Germany and Austria; in 1926 came débuts in the Soviet Union and Britain. In 1927 he performed for the first time in Scandinavia, and in 1928 he made a triumphant tour of the USA. In 1929 came his first performances in Japan. In Paris, in 1935, with some opposition from the critics, he premièred his transcription of J.S. Bach's *Chaconne* from the Partita No. 2 for Violin—a vital landmark in the guitar's history. The following year Segovia left Spain at the beginning of the Civil War, destined to remain in exile from Fascism for 16 years. During World War II he lived in Montevideo and New York.

All the time he was attempting to persuade composers of the possibilities of his "miniature orchestra". Those who wrote works for him included the Spanish composers, Turinia and Roderigo, the Mexican, Ponce, the Italian composer, Castelnuovo Tedesco, the Brazilian, Villa Lobos, the Pole, Tansman, and many others.

His recitals thus gradually evolved their traditional format—a blend of old music from the medieval Spanish vihuelists (the vihuela was an early type of guitar) and lutenists, transcriptions of later music from composers such as Bach, Handel, Scarlatti, Purcell, Mendelssohn, Grieg and so on, juxtaposed with new music often dedicated to or commissioned by himself. The concerts usually ended with music by Spaniards such as Granados or Albeniz. This variety of music, and Segovia's combination of restraint and expressive freedom in performance endeared him to audiences worldwide.

From 1939 he began to introduce the guitar concerto to the concert hall. Concertos were dedicated to him by Castelnuovo Tedesco, Ponce (*Concierto del Sur*), Villa Lobos and Roderigo (*Fantasia para un gentilhombre*). He was one of the first classical guitarists to enter a gramophone recording studio. In 1929 he cut his first "78" for EMI and went on to make more than 40 records.

Segovia made significant refinements to guitar technique, especially for the right hand, using the fingertips and nails subtly to give a wide range of colours. His style in performance was romantic, elegant, distinctive and unostentatious. His ingenious transcriptions and careful editing of commissioned works gave generations of musicians a unique source of technical insight and recital material. One of Segovia's aims was to see the guitar established as an instrument of study in conservatoires throughout the world. This took many years to achieve, but by 1960 almost every major conservatoire of music offered tuition in the classical guitar—a direct result of Segovia's advocacy.

He was a generously spirited teacher and took great pride in teaching. He participated for many years in summer schools in Siena, Santiago di Compostela and Berkeley, California, as well as holding master classes far and wide. "There are two million guitar students in Japan alone!" he once said, comically horrified by the figure. He also set examples in life. "He does nothing to excess," said a friend. "He eats, drinks, reads, looks at and listens to only the best. He does not even practise the guitar to excess, just two and a half hours in the morning and two and a half in the afternoon. The most important word to associate with Segovia is civilized."

He never sought popularity and on occasion expressed his disapproval of those musicians who do. Humility towards the music was the key. This did not prevent his becoming one of the twentieth-century's most popular performers, filling the world's largest concert halls until well after his ninetieth birthday. In 1976 he published the first part of his autobiography, *The Guitar and Myself*, covering the years 1893 to 1920, and he continued to work on further chapters of the projected four-volume work.

His achievements were formally honoured by many countries and institutions. He received the Albert Schweitzer Award in 1981, and in the same year was awarded the title Marquis of Salobreña by King Juan Carlos.

Born Andrés Segovia Torres. **Marriages** Three; third wife, Emilia, guitarist, 1962. **Children** Two sons, one daughter. **Education** Studied guitar briefly with Miguel Llobet. **Emigration** Left Spain, 1936; lived in Montevideo and New York during World War II; returned to Spain,

1952. **Career** Began learning guitar at age of ten; made début as guitarist at the Centro Artistico, Granada, at the age of 16; played in Madrid at the Ateneo, 1912, Barcelona, 1916; toured South America, 1919; Paris début, 1924; subsequently played throughout Europe; made Soviet and British débuts, 1927, US début at Town Hall, New York, 1928; continued to make concert appearances throughout his lifetime, appearing in 1984 in celebration of the 75th anniversary of his concert début. **Related activities** Adapted and transcribed works by Bach, Haydn, Mozart and others for guitar; pioneered guitar as a concert instrument; taught widely, giving classes at summer schools at the Accademia Musicale Chigiana, Siena, Santiago de Compostela, and Berkeley, California. **Memberships** Spanish Royal Academy of Fine Arts, 1978. **Awards and honours** Grand Cross of Isabel la Católica; Gold Medal of the Royal Philharmonic Society; Order of Alfonso X el Sabio; Cavalier Grand Cross of the Order of Merit of the Italian Republic; Order of the Rising Sun of Japan; Spanish Gold Medal for Meritorious Work, 1967; honorary DMus, Oxon, 1972; Albert Schweitzer Award, 1981; Ernst von Siemens Prize, 1985; created Marquis of Salobreña by King Juan Carlos, 1981. **Publications** *Andrés Segovia: An Autobiography of the Years 1893–1920*, translated by W.F. O'Brien, New York, 1976; (with George Mendoza) *Segovia: My Book of the Guitar*, 1979. **Recordings** Over 40 recordings of guitar works. **Cause of death** Undisclosed, at age 94. **Further reading** B. Gavoty, *Andrés Segovia*, Geneva, 1955; V. Bobri, *The Segovia Technique*, New York, 1972; R.C. Purcell, *Andrés Segovia: Contributions to the World of the Guitar*, California, 1973; ed. G. Clinton, *Andrés Segovia*, London, 1978; G. Wade, *Segovia: A Celebration of the Man and His Music*, London, 1983; A. Kozinn, *Andrés Segovia*, 1984.

SIR BILLY SNEDDEN

Australian Politician and Lawyer

Born **Perth, Australia, 31 December 1926**

Died **Melbourne, Australia, 27 June 1987**

It is rare for a politician to be remembered with fondness by allies and opponents alike, but Sir Billy Snedden is such a rarity. Even odder is that his political career was not especially brilliant or memorable. His fame and popularity stemmed from his years as Speaker of the Australian House of Representatives—a role for which his qualities of calmness, honesty and, above all, fair play, ideally suited him.

He was born the son of a Scottish stonemason who died when the boy was aged nine. Young Billy might well have followed his father into the honourable craft of stonemasonry had it not been for World War II. His period of service with the Australian Armed Forces entitled him to an ex-service grant, so on demobilization he enrolled at Perth University to study law. His endeavours paid off when he was admitted to the Bar of Western Australia in 1951, and some 13 years later he was appointed to the Supreme Court of Victoria.

Meanwhile, however, political ambitions superseded legal ones, and Snedden entered parliament in 1955 as the representative for Bruce, Victoria. There followed eight years of diligent service on behalf of his constituents, and he was eventually rewarded with his first government post in 1963 when Sir Robert Menzies, the Liberal prime minister, appointed him attorney-general. Three years later he became minister of immigration, concurrently holding the post of leader of the House, until he became treasurer in 1971.

After the death of Sir Robert Menzies in 1966, the Liberal Party went through a difficult time, and it was Snedden who did much to hold it together. In 1972, when the Liberals lost the election, he became leader of the party, and thus leader of the Opposition. In this role he had to face the redoubtable Labour prime minister, Gough Whitlam, across the dispatch box—a formidable undertaking for anyone, but particularly so for such a courteous and thoughtful man as Snedden. At last, he seemed to have landed a job that was beyond him, frequently finding himself bested by Whitlam's rhetoric and wit.

When the Liberal Party lost a second election in 1974, Snedden was replaced as leader by Malcolm Fraser, a stronger and much more abrasive man. In a rare display of ego, Snedden refused to serve under him and retired to the back benches.

After two years "in the wilderness", Snedden was offered the post of Speaker, and at last he found the niche for which he was tailor-made. He believed passionately in parliamentary democracy and strove to bring the Australian Speakership closer to the Westminster model. (In the British House of Commons at Westminster the Speaker, although an elected MP, must be completely neutral. He or she presides over debates, keeps order in the chamber and makes sure that members have equal opportunities to be heard, being particularly careful about the rights of minorities.) In a break with previous Australian practice, Snedden raised the position of Speaker above party loyalties and made it free of partisanship.

In 1979 he led an Australian delegation of MPs from both Houses to visit the French Parliament, the European Parliament and the European Commission. This greatly increased goodwill among these various institutions and demonstrated Snedden's skill in building bridges—a skill that had not served him well in the cut and thrust of his earlier political career.

Snedden served as Speaker for seven years, resigning in 1983. During this time his valuable contribution to politics was recognized with a knighthood from the Queen—an honour, which, much to his delight, was bestowed on him at Balmoral in Scotland.

There is a saying, "It takes one to know one", so the tribute from Viscount Tonypandy, one of the greatest British Speakers is no mean accolade: "Sir Billy was a giant among Speakers. His natural courtesy, his infectious sense of humour and his deep faith in parliamentary democracy combined to earn for him a special place in the respect and affection of Speakers throughout the Commonwealth."

Born William Mackie Snedden. **Father** A. Snedden, a Scottish stonemason. **Marriage** Joy, 1950. **Children** Two sons and two daughters. **Education** University of Western Australia, Perth, LLB. **Military service** Australian Armed Forces, World War II. **Career** Admitted to the Bar of Western Australia, 1951; migration officer, England, 1952–53; admitted to the Bar of the Supreme Court, Victoria, Australia, 1955; Federal Member of Parliament for Bruce, Victoria, 1955–83; attorney-general, 1963–66; Queen's Counsel, 1964; minister for immigration, 1966–69; leader of the House, 1966-71; minister for labour and national service, 1969–71; treasurer, 1971–72; deputy leader, Liberal Party, 1971–72; leader, Liberal Party in Opposition, 1972–74; returned to back benches, 1974–76; Speaker, House of Representatives, 1976–83. **Related activities** Chairman, Standing Committee of Conference of Commonwealth Speakers and Presiding Officers, 1978–81; leader, Australian parliamentary delegation to France, the European Parliament and Commission of European Communities, 1979. **Offices and memberships** National Patron, Young Liberal Movement, 1980–82; president, Melbourne Football Club, 1981 onwards; councillor, Melbourne Scots. **Awards and honours** Privy Counsellor, 1971; Knight Commander, Order of St Michael and St George, 1978. **Cause of death** Undisclosed, at age 60.

KID THOMAS

American Jazz Musician

***Born* Reserve, Louisiana, 3 February 1896**

***Died* New Orleans, Louisiana, 16 June 1987**

One by one, the keepers of the New Orleans jazz flame are passing away. These are the musicians who learnt New Orleans jazz—the first and for many the foremost style of jazz—in the early years of this century, and who remained true to it despite its decline in popularity and eclipse by newer styles as the years wore on. Many of them lived through several revivals and even more downturns, yet they continued to play the music they loved with a freshness that belied the age of both music and musician. The death of Kid Thomas at the age of 91 extinguishes one of the authentic flames.

For many people, Kid Thomas Valentine (he rarely used his surname) epitomized the enduring vitality of New Orleans music, for he was a professional trumpeter long before Louis Armstrong came to dominate trumpet-playing in the mid-1920s. Thomas was born some 30 miles up-river from New Orleans in a musical town—the family of clarinettist Edmond Hall lived there—and to a musical family. His father kept all the instruments for, and was a member of, the Pickwick Brass Band, so Thomas had plenty of opportunity to make music. He began to play a trumpet seriously at the age of ten, and became a Pickwick member at 14, by which time he was proficient on cornet. By 1914 Thomas was playing in a band with Edmond Hall and his brothers, before moving down the River Mississippi to the town of Algiers, opposite New Orleans, in 1922. The following year he joined the band of banjoist Elton Theodore and took lessons from Professor Manual Manetta, a famous teacher.

While in Algiers, Thomas got involved in a "cutting" contest with fellow townsman Henry "Red" Allen. The two bands played a contest to determine who was the best. First prize, a leather briefcase, went to Allen, but Thomas thought that his band had gone down better with the audience and asked a policeman to confirm this. The result was reversed but this unsporting gesture harmed Thomas's reputation. Allen went on to achieve great success while Thomas was left to struggle for himself.

Throughout the 1920s and 1930s Thomas found a variety of gigs in and around New Orleans, taking over the leadership of Theodore's band in 1925 and renaming it the Algiers Stompers. When times were hard, he found work with the Southern Pacific Railroad or as a house-painter, but most of the time he was kept busy as a musician. He struck up an association with the dance-hall proprietor Specks Rodriguez, and played for him at various venues in Louisiana, notably the Moulin Rouge in Marrero, where he performed well into the 1950s. Yet it was not until 1951 that this fine musician made his first recording, with a pick-up band. He was to record frequently for the rest of his life, often with clarinettist George Lewis, one of the most important figures in the post-war revival of New Orleans jazz. Lewis remarked, "Thomas just plays the chords, but he's up there all the time, or he's doing something underneath, even just one or two notes you know what he's doing. He has the right idea of this type of music."

It was that right idea that made Thomas a natural choice when the Preservation Hall opened in New Orleans in 1961 and started to hire local musicians to play the local music. Thomas became a regular performer at this centrepiece of New Orleans jazz, playing and touring with his own Algiers Stompers and as a member of the hall's own band well into his eighties. His style was individual, a "mercurial mix of growls, note clusters and just plain sounds", to quote British critic and fellow trumpeter and admirer, Digby Fairweather. He could be elliptical and impressionistic in his playing, stating the melody sparsely and with many subtleties of tone and timbre before exploding in a searing, wide-vibrato passage that would roar out through the ensemble with robust vitality, yet he was always massively rhythmical in every note he played. On slower numbers, he used a harmon mute and played with great poignancy.

This subtle yet forthright approach made Thomas an eloquent musician, well able to drive a band through any number. For those who heard him play, his sound was unforgettable, his very presence on the bandstand a reminder that not all the glories of New Orleans jazz were in the past.

Born Thomas Valentine. **Father** Brass band player. **Career** Started to play the trumpet at age 10; member, Pickwick Brass Band, at age 14; with Edmond Hall and family formed own band, at age 18; first professional appearance with Jack Carey's band, 1915; became full-time jazz trumpeter and bandleader in and around New Orleans, occasionally supplementing income by working for Southern Pacific Railroad or as a house-painter; bandleader, Elton Theodore's band, 1925; worked for dance-hall owner, Specks Rodriguez, at venues such as the Moulin Rouge, Marrero, 1940–1950s; first recording, 1951; first appeared at Preservation Hall with own band, Algiers Stompers, also known as the Preservation Hall Jazz Band, 1961; regular appearances until mid-1980s; international concert tours include Scandinavia and the Soviet Union. **Recordings** *Kid Thomas' Algiers Stompers*, AM 642, 1951; *Kid Thomas at the Moulin Rouge*, Center 14, 1956; *Kid Thomas Valentine's Creole Jazz Band*, 77LA9, 1959; *Jim Robinson and his New Orleans Band* (as sideman), Center 8, 1964; *Original Jass Band and Kid Thomas' Jazz Band in Scandinavia*, Rarities 16, 1964, 1971; *Kid Thomas at Kohlman's Tavern*, La Croix 4-5, 1968; "Just a close walk with thee", 1971; *Kid Thomas 1981*, Lulu White's Black Label 033, 1981. **Cause of death** Undisclosed, at age 91.

GRACE THORNTON

British Diplomat

Born **Northamptonshire, England, 27 June 1913**

Died **London, England, 23 June 1987**

Dr Grace Thornton enjoyed a very distinguished career in the British diplomatic service. Working in a world that was, and still is, dominated by men, she said she experienced few problems or much opposition. Once she had demonstrated her unquestionable abilities and commitment to the service, men accepted her on equal terms. As she once said: "They soon learned we didn't lose the keys or get seduced by South Americans."

Clara Grace Thornton was an only child. She was educated at Kettering High School and went on to Newnham College, Cambridge, where she earned a doctorate in early Icelandic studies. From an early age she was drawn to Scandinavia and listed the region as one of her recreations in *Who's Who*. Like many people, her career was interrupted by the war, during which she worked for the Ministry of Information and spent some time with the famous Bletchley code-breakers.

Her first diplomatic posting came in 1945, when she was appointed press attaché to the Copenhagen embassy. Only three years later, at the age of 34, she took on a job considered at the time to be one of the most responsible diplomatic posts of its kind—vice-consul in Reykjavik.

Such was her success in this position that a year later she was given the job of chargé d'affaires. No woman had ever held such a responsible position, especially one that was regarded as the first step to becoming an ambassador. Sadly, although her work was impeccable, she never did receive an embassy of her own. Perhaps there was more male hostility towards her than she realized.

After a short spell back at the Foreign Office, where she worked in the American department, she returned to Copenhagen in 1954. This time she worked as first secretary and consul. She stayed in this post for six years before moving on to the Brussels embassy, where she was first secretary and information officer.

Moving on again in 1962, Thornton was appointed consul-general in the much more troubled environment of Djakarta. Civil unrest was rife and she became very concerned about the safety of civilians, some of whom were British nationals trapped at the Shell oilfields in eastern Borneo. She flew to the area with a letter from the Indonesian Government and the authority of the British ambassador to take whatever action she felt necessary. On arrival, she immediately evacuated 166 civilians, arranging a flight to Djakarta where the RAF took them on to the safety of Singapore. Many of Thornton's personal belongings had to be left behind in the Djakarta embassy and one of the evacuees only left after he had defiantly played the bagpipes while the Indonesians took over the embassy. Characteristically, Thornton would take no credit for getting so many people out to safety.

Her last posting abroad was in 1965 when she was appointed consul-general in Lisbon. While here, some Danish friends gave her a copy of Hans Christian Andersen's account of his visit to Portugal in 1866. She began to translate it into English, and the book was published in 1972. Next, she translated Andersen's *A Visit to Spain, 1862*, and her last translation, from the Dutch, was *A Visit to Germany, Italy and Malta, 1840–41*, published in 1985.

Thornton ended her career in the diplomatic service with three years at the Foreign Office in London. She retired in 1973 but immediately took on the very demanding job of secretary to the Women's National Commission. Attached to the Cabinet Office, this organization works to explain the female point of view and impress it upon a very male-orientated world. During her time there, Thornton lobbied to extend the commission's work to international issues.

Grace Thornton was always calm, even in the most tense situations. She was never afraid of being outspoken, and often intimidated people with an expression that her housekeeper called her "frightening the horses look". In her spare time she loved to listen to music and to embroider. Cats were her constant companions.

Born Clara Grace Thornton. **Parents** Arthur Augustus, a jeweller, and Clara Maud (Hines) Thornton. **Education** Kettering High School, Northamptonshire; Newnham College, Cambridge, MA, PhD in early Icelandic studies, 1939. **Career** Ministry of Information, 1940–45; press attaché, Copenhagen embassy, 1945–48; vice-consul, Reykjavik embassy, 1948–51, chargé d'affaires, 1949–50; American department of the Foreign Office, 1951–54; first secretary and consul, Copenhagen embassy, 1954–60; first secretary and information officer, Brussels embassy, 1960–62; first secretary and consul, Djakarta embassy, 1962–64, consul-general, 1963–64; consul-general, Lisbon embassy, 1965–70; head of consular department, Foreign and Commonwealth Office, 1970–73; secretary, Women's National Commission, Cabinet Office, 1973–78. **Related activities** Alternate United Kingdom delegate, United Nations Status of Women Commission, 1978. **Other activities** Author and editor; translator of several books by Hans Christian Andersen; associate fellow, Newnham College, Cambridge, 1972–81. **Offices and memberships** President: London Association of University Women, 1974–78, Associates of Newnham College, 1975–78, Newnham Roll, 1982–84, vice-president, 1980–82; governor, Great Britain/Eastern Europe Centre, from 1981. **Awards and honours** Danish Freedom Medal, 1945; Order of Dannebrog, 1957; lieutenant, Royal Victorian Order, 1957; officer, Order of the British Empire,

1959; commander, Order of the British Empire, 1964; honorary fellow, Newnham College, Cambridge, 1982; Order of Icelandic Falcon, 1983. **Publications** *Conversation Piece*, 1979, second edition, 1985; *Notes on No. 2 Audley Square*, 1980; (editor) *Take Your Hare When it is Cased* (recipes), 1980. **Translations** *A Visit to Portugal, 1866*, 1972; *A Visit to Spain, 1862*, 1975; *A Visit to Germany, Italy and Malta, 1840–41*, 1985. **Cause of death** Undisclosed, at age 73.

JULY

AIR VICE-MARSHAL EDWARD ADDISON

British Airman and Electronics Expert
Born **Cambridge, England, 4 October 1898**
Died **Surrey, England, 4 July 1987**

Edward Barker Addison was a man of wide-ranging abilities and interests. He joined the Royal Flying Corps as a mechanic in 1915 and, when the Royal Air Force was formed in 1918, gained a commission. After World War I he went to Cambridge University to read natural sciences but chose to return to a career with the RAF and was recommissioned. Although he learned to fly, his career was mainly devoted to technical and, later, electronic matters.

He spent three years in India on routine squadron maintenance work before returning to Europe for further study. In 1927 he gained a diploma in engineering at the École Supérieure d'Électricité in Paris, after which he specialized in electronics. It was after serving as a signals officer with a squadron of torpedo bombers in the Far East that he made his first notable contribution to the developing difficulties of World War II in Britain. Returning to the UK in 1940, at the age of 42, he became involved in what was dubbed the "Battle of the Beams".

The Germans possessed a system of guidance by radio beam to assist them in night bombing raids. At first their existence was only suspected from the precision of the night bombing, but examination of documents from planes shot down produced the name *Knickebein*. Subsequent questioning of prisoners brought admissions of knowledge of *Knickebein*, and some blind flying by an expert tracked down the first beam to be discovered which crossed the British coast over East Anglia, travelled westerly towards Derby and, if projected backwards, led to the town of Cleves on the Continent. Derby and Cleves were mentioned in the documents naming *Knickebein*. Rapidly more beams were discovered and it was found they enabled a formation of German aircraft to be positioned over any target in Britain within an accuracy of 400 yards.

A new unit was rapidly set up under the command of Air Vice-Marshal Addison. Christened No. 80 Wing, its purpose was to transmit signals on the same frequency as the beams and thus jam them. Receivers were installed on the radar masts and, as a beam was discovered, it was possible to plot its intersection with another and thus predict where the next raid would occur. Fighter Command could then be alerted to intercept. Simultaneously the jamming crews confused the beams as much as possible. As the Germans increasingly found the beams unreliable, being led to unload their bombs in places they could do little harm, more experienced British flyers were taking the risk of night flying and thus the tables began, slowly, to turn.

Addison's most valuable contribution to the war effort came in 1943, however, when he took over the command of the famous 100 Group which had been formed to support the night bombing of enemy targets in Europe, at that time forcefully contested by the formidable night fighter defences of the Nazi regime. The group expanded rapidly and the Mosquito and Beaufighter squadrons involved attacked German fighter planes, jammed their radio and radar, and thoroughly confused their opponents as to the destinations of Bomber Command's nightly bombing expeditions to Germany. The Mosquito, in particular, became greatly feared by the courageous German fighter plane pilots and by the controllers on the ground.

Very soon 100 Group obtained vital back-up from the American Flying Fortresses, the huge B–17 bombers that became such a feature of the British countryside in the 1940s. These massive planes had the capacity to carry the increasingly sophisticated and heavy electronic equipment required and they could fly at 28,000 feet. They also enabled 100 Group to carry out vastly improved fake raids, which involved either the use of electronic equipment or the dropping of tinsel strips, known as "window", to add to the general confusion of the enemy. It has been said that only the superb fighting qualities of the Luftwaffe allowed its pilots to stay in the battle when faced with such technical superiority. But their losses were large. By the end of the war, 100 Group numbered 253 aircraft and its long-range fighters claimed a total of 257 enemy planes destroyed against the group's own losses of only 67.

Addison remained with the RAF until his retirement in 1955, after which he held a number of directorships with electronics companies. It is, however, for his formative work in 100 Group that he will best be remembered. His leadership played a vital role in lessening the threat of German night fighters to the work of Bomber Command. It also speeded the end of the war in Europe and proved to be the precursor of today's electronic warfare.

Born Edward Barker Addison. **Marriage** Marie-Blanche Marguerite Rosain, 1926. **Children** One son, one daughter. **Education** Sidney Sussex College, Cambridge, 1918–21, BA, 1921, MA, 1926; diploma in engineering, l'École Supérieure d'Électricité, Paris, 1927. **Career** Mechanic, Royal Flying Corps, 1915–1918; commissioned, Royal Air Force, 1918, recommissioned, 1921; stationed in India, 1923–26; signals officer, Far East, 1928–40; commanded No. 80 Wing in the "Battle of the Beams", 1940; appointed air officer commanding 100 Group, 1943; assistant chief of air staff (Signals), 1950–52; senior air staff officer, Flying Training Command; retired, 1955. **Related activities** Chartered engineer; director and divisional manager, Redifon Limited, 1956–63; director, Intercontinental Technical Services Limited, 1964–72; consultant, Vocational Guidance Association, 1966–72. **Offices and memberships** Associate member, Institute of Electrical Engineers, 1933, member, 1941, fellow 1966. **Awards and honours** Officer, Order of the British Empire, 1938; Commander, Order of the British Empire, 1942; Companion of the Order of the Bath, 1945; Commander, United States Legion of Merit, 1947. **Cause of death** Undisclosed, at age 88.

MALCOLM BALDRIGE

American Businessman and Political Aide
***Born* Omaha, Nebraska, 4 October 1922**
***Died* Walnut Creek, California, 26 July 1987**

Malcolm Baldrige, who died in office as President Reagan's commerce secretary, was a staunch defender of free trade, despite the inevitable pressures in recent years to protect American industry. He was also a model businessman whose success was translated to the political sphere.

Baldrige was a Midwesterner and a lifelong participant in rodeos and steer-roping, an enthusiasm which was to cost him his life. He inherited a political background from his father, who sat in the Nebraska legislature, and in 1930 was elected for a single term as member of the US House of Representatives.

As a boy Baldrige worked as a ranch hand and mill worker. He majored in English at Yale, primarily because he was not yet certain what he wanted to do for a career, and gained his BA in 1944. After graduation he saw active service in the Pacific in the field artillery of the 27th Infantry Division. He left the army in 1946 with the rank of captain.

His meteoric business career began in 1947, as a foundry manager for the Eastern Malleable Iron Company in Connecticut. By 1951 he was managing director of one of the company divisions, becoming vice-president in 1957, and president in 1960. Two years later he was head-hunted by the ailing Scovill Manufacturing Company in Waterbury, Connecticut, and joined them as executive vice-president. In the course of turning around this brass mill and making it one of the most vibrant firms in the country, Baldrige became president and chief executive in 1963, and chairman of the board in 1969.

Baldrige concentrated first on paring down Scovill's luxuriant growth of administrators and ornamental vice-presidents, and largely did away with decision-making by committee. The new Scovill style, he explained in 1968, was "based on individual responsibility...extended as far down the line as possible". He also diversified the company's activities almost beyond recognition. Within a short time Scovill was moving into aluminium, household appliances, door and window frames, sewing accessories, Yale locks, electronic security devices, tyre valves and many other items. By 1980 Scovill ran 81 plants in the US and abroad, had an annual revenue of some $950 million, and employed 15,000 people. Baldrige himself was a much sought-after adviser for other firms, and held numerous directorships, American and foreign.

In addition to his business career, Baldrige involved himself to a commendable extent in civic affairs, playing a role in the local Easter Seal Society and the Red Cross, joining the National Association for the Advancement of Colored People, and promoting low-cost housing and job and recreational opportunities for the disadvantaged.

A politically active Republican from the early 1960s, Baldrige was a delegate to successive National Conventions from 1964 onwards. He acted as Connecticut chairman in the campaign to elect the Nixon–Agnew ticket in 1968 and helped George Bush to one of his few primary wins against Ronald Reagan in 1980. The later emergence of a Reagan–Bush ticket in the 1980 presidential campaign made Baldrige's political elevation almost certain. Nevertheless, the story persists that, when President-Elect Reagan was deliberating on whom to appoint as commerce secretary, the news that Baldrige was "out roping" was the decisive factor in his favour.

As commerce secretary, Baldrige confronted a different sort of empire from his business imperium, and one notoriously less amenable to his streamlining techniques. The Department of

Commerce in 1981 had a budget of $2.8 billion and employed some 48,000 people. Baldrige, however, in his first year in office managed to cut departmental expenditure by 40 per cent.

His principal concern in the Reagan administration was to reduce international trade barriers and promote a policy of free trade wherever possible. This was seen as a vital requirement for cutting the already alarming American trade deficit. In pursuit of this goal Baldrige headed trade missions to countries around the world, trying to persuade foreign governments from the Soviet bloc to West Africa and the Far East to open their markets to US manufactures. A key instrument in this on the American side was the Export Trading Company Act of 1982, which made it easier for small firms to contemplate exporting.

There was always an implicit paradox in Baldrige's position, however, in that his period in office coincided with a growing demand in the United States itself for protection against foreign goods. In particular, the resentment of the auto industry, and public opinion generally, at the booming Japanese share of the home market, complicated Baldrige's task. He deplored legislation by Congress against foreign imports, and yet early in 1987 ended by calling for a certain measure of tariff protection against Japanese electronics.

In an administration notorious for its ways with words, under a chief world-famous for woolly thinking, Baldrige was a notable opponent of Haigspeak and bureaucratese. As he put it, "The only reason I can see for talking that kind of talk was a subconscious urge to cover oneself."

Baldrige's passion for rodeo and steer-roping won him numerous awards, and in 1984 he was elected to the Cowboy Hall of Fame. Unlike that of his political boss, his cowboy status was not a cinematic pose, and for this very reason it had fatal consequences. He died of injuries sustained when his horse fell on him while roping steers in California.

Born Howard Malcolm Baldrige. **Parents** Howard Malcolm, lawyer and former US Congressman, and Regina (Connell) Baldrige. **Marriage** Margaret Trowbridge Murray, 1951. **Children** Megan Brewster and Mary Trowbridge. **Education** Hotchkiss School, Connecticut; Yale University, BA, 1944. **Military service** US Army, rising to captain, 1943–46. **Business career** Foundry superintendent, Eastern Malleable Iron Co., 1946, managing director, Frazer and Jones division, 1951–57, vice-president, 1957–60, president, 1960–62; executive vice-president, Scovill Manufacturing Co., 1962–63, president and chief executive officer, 1963–69, chair and chief executive officer, 1969–81; numerous other business interests included directorships with AMF Inc., New York, Connecticut Mutual Life Insurance Co., Bendix Corp., IBM Inc., Uniroyal Inc. and Southwest Brazing and Macron Farms. **Political career** Delegate to Republican National Conventions, 1964, 1968, 1972 and 1976; chair, Connecticut Scranton for President Committee, 1964; delegate to Connecticut Constitutional Convention, 1965; appointed to Connecticut State Budget and Finance Committees, 1966 (chair of latter, 1969–72); member: advisory committee on labour for the Connecticut State Republican Central Committee, 1967, Connecticut Citizens' Commission on the State Legislature, 1968, Connecticut State Republican Platform Committee, 1968, National Republican Finance Committee, 1969; co-chair, Connecticut United Citizens for Nixon–Agnew, 1968; chair, Connecticut Bush for President Committee; national vice-chair, Business for Reagan–Bush Committee; US secretary of commerce, 1981–87. **Other activities** Rodeo steer-roper; director of Professional Rodeo Cowboys' Association; advisory board member, Rodeo Information Foundation, winning many awards on professional rodeo circuit, ranking fifth nationally in 1970. **Offices and memberships** Member: Business Council, Council on Foreign Relations, International Chamber of Commerce, Citizens' Research Foundation, Connecticut Business and Industry Association, Yale University Development Committee, National Association for the Advancement of Colored People, Connecticut Governor's Committee on the Status of Women; chair and trustee: Greater Waterbury Chamber of Commerce, Waterbury Non-Profit Development Corporation, St Margaret's School Annual

Fund-Raising, Waterbury Mayor's Citizens' Advisory Committee; chair: Waterbury YMCA Development Fund, Central Valley Drug Help Drive, Waterbury Red Cross Drive, 1968, Connecticut Resources Recovery Board, 1973–75, Yale University National Business Gifts Committee, 1976–79; incorporator, Waterbury Easter Seal Society; trustee: Waterbury Hospital, Swiss Reinsurance Company. **Awards and honours** National Secretaries' Association's International Boss of the Year, 1967; Professional Rodeo Cowboys' Association's Man of the Year, 1981; elected to Cowboy Hall of Fame, 1984. **Cause of death** Riding accident, at age 64.

ALFIE BASS

British Actor

Born **London, England, 8 April 1921**

Died **London, England, 15 July 1987**

The cheerful face of Alfie Bass was very familiar to British television audiences in the 1950s and 1960s. Most people knew him as "Bootsie" from the television series in which he played a Cockney army conscript, but Bass was a versatile actor, skilled at both comedy and pathos, and seemed just as much at home playing Shakespeare or the milkman Tevye in the musical *Fiddler on the Roof*. His talents were enriched by his Cockney and Jewish roots and the fertile soil of British working-class humour.

He was a short, stocky, likeable man with a big grin and an air of infectious enjoyment about him. The television series which made him a household name was *The Army Game*, first shown in 1957, in which Alfie Bass as Bootsie and Bill Fraser (q.v.) as Snudge played two conscripts in a platoon mainly concerned with avoiding danger and responsibility. Like its US counterpart, *Sergeant Bilko*, the series focused on behind-the-scenes intrigue, comradeship and bureaucratic muddles. Bootsie particularly avoided wearing regulation footwear and is remembered for his catchphrase, "Never mind, eh?", with which he would attempt to pacify or cheer up members of Hut 29 in all adversity. So popular were the two characters played by Bass and Fraser that they were able to transfer to fictional civilian life in a spin-off series, *Bootsie and Snudge*, without losing their faithful fans.

Barry Took, the British screenwriter and producer has said, "All successful comedies have some trap in which people must exist—like marriage." Though out of the army in *Bootsie and Snudge*, Bass and Fraser still found themselves "trapped" in an enclosed, class-divided and largely male world by working "below stairs" in a gentleman's club. As in many single-sex comedy duos, their relationship was like that of husband and wife in its emotional bond.

Alfie Bass did not start his career as an actor. Born the youngest of ten children to immigrant Russian parents who had escaped from Jewish persecution, the young Alfie started in his father's trade of cabinet-making after leaving elementary school. This skill came in useful when he joined the amateur Unity Theatre, where, as well as acting, he was put to work making sets and scenery. His only previous acting experience had been in local boys' club amateur dramatics. Being unemployed and on the dole, he appeared in various Unity productions, making his début in 1939 as Izzie in *Plant in the Sun* with the great Black singer Paul Robeson. He also toured all over the country with the Unity Theatre, receiving just a shilling a week allowance from the company.

Early in his working life he had attended union meetings with an elderly shop steward friend, whom he remembered with gratitude. This, combined with his experience of growing up in a large family in the East End and his early struggles to make his way, gave him a strong fellow-feeling and respect for the British working-class man. He was always concerned, and often involved in, the social and political events of his day, such as the historic battle in London's Cable Street when Oswald Mosley's Fascists were prevented from marching through the East End. He was also involved in anti-H Bomb demonstrations and was strongly opposed to racial discrimination.

Alfie Bass also took his acting seriously and was respected by directors for his approach to roles. A natural comedian, he realized that comedy was a complex matter, saying it was more than a talent for slapstick and funny hats. "Laughter should arise from natural situations, because the roots of comedy are in reality....The foibles of man can be both tragic and comic—and good comedy should also have an element of sadness about it."

Bass drew warm tributes for a season of Shakespeare plays performed at Stratford-on-Avon in 1948. His roles included Gurney in *King John*, Launcelot Gobbo in *The Merchant of Venice*, Second Gravedigger in *Hamlet*, Grumio in *The Taming of the Shrew* and Autolycus in *The Winter's Tale*.

At the beginning of World War II Bass had been turned down by the Royal Air Force, so he worked in an engineering factory while continuing with the Unity Theatre. He was later called up into the Middlesex Regiment as a dispatch rider. He appeared in concert party work and took part in Army Film Unit documentaries.

Early stage successes included the title role in *Buster* by Ted Willis at the Arts Theatre Club in 1943, and later that year opposite Alistair Sim in James Bridie's *Mr Bolfry* in the role of Glen, remembered as a Cockney soldier expressing frankly his opinion of Scottish Highland weather. In 1945 he played Abel Drugger in Jonson's *The Alchemist* and Og the leprechaun in the American musical *Finian's Rainbow* in 1947. In 1953 he played in Wolf Mankowitz's *The Bespoke Overcoat*, appearing in the film version in 1969. During the rest of the 1950s he spent more and more time on TV and film work.

Bass made more than 30 films, including *The Lavender Hill Mob*, directed by Charles Crichton (1951), in which he played Shortie Fisher. This was a hugely successful Ealing comedy, also starring Sidney James, Stanley Holloway and Alec Guinness who steal a million pounds in gold bars, melt them down into gold souvenirs of the Eiffel Tower and smuggle them into France. This was considered one of the very best Ealing comedies and won the British equivalent of an Oscar as best film of 1951. Other film appearances included *The Millionairess* (1961), *Help!*, the 1965 Beatles film, *Alfie* (1966), *Up the Junction* (1968), *The Revenge of the Pink Panther* (1978) and *Death on the Nile* (1978). His many television appearances included *Till Death Us Do Part*, *Robin Hood*, the department store comedy series *Are You Being Served?*, and the role of Puck in Shakespeare's *A Midsummer Night's Dream*. Bass returned to stage work later, taking over from Topol in the role of Tevye the milkman in the musical *Fiddler on the Roof* (1968). He also played Eccles in a revival of Robertson's *Caste* (1972) at Greenwich, followed by two appearances in pantomime in *Cinderella* and *Jack and the Beanstalk*.

Although Alfie Bass's unmistakable face was known to almost every person in Britain, he did not see fame as a great virtue, telling a newspaper journalist, "Instead of interviewing people like me, you ought to try interviewing some of the folk who are doing an important job of work, day in and day out, without the sort of recognition which is attached to television stars...teachers or shop stewards, who every day in the factory are helping their mates." However, he sometimes enjoyed his fame too, pretending to a policeman once that he was a relative of the then prime minister, Harold Macmillan, so as to be allowed through a cordon at a Ban-the-Bomb demonstration. The policeman, recognizing him, laughed and let him through.

Apart from his meticulous pride in his work and his enjoyment of being an actor of the people, Bass was motivated by an idealistic belief, formed at the Unity Theatre in his earliest acting days, that "...true art, by truthfully interpreting life, can move people to work for the betterment of society". He demonstrated this by always retaining his interest in social issues and by doing charitable work for spastic children and boys' clubs.

Born Alfred Bass. **Parents** Jacob, a cabinet-maker, and Ada (Miller) Bass. **Marriage** Beryl Margaret Bryson. **Children** One son and one daughter. **Military service** Dispatch rider, Middlesex Regiment, World War II. **Career** Cabinet-maker; began acting in amateur dramatics at local boys' clubs; joined amateur company, Unity Theatre, Kings Cross, London, making début as Izzie (opposite Paul Robeson) in *Plant in the Sun*, 1939; rejected by RAF at outbreak of war, continued at Unity while working in engineering factory; acted in concert parties and Army Film Unit documentaries after conscription into Middlesex Regiment; much stage, television and film work after the war; first came to national attention in the TV series *The Army Game*, followed by spin-off series *Bootsie and Snudge*; subsequently became well known for playing a wide range of stage and television characters. **Other activities** Politically active since his teens in trade union, anti-Fascist and nuclear disarmament campaigns; involved in charitable work for boys' clubs and children with disabilities. **Stage** (all in London, unless stated) *Plant in the Sun*, 1939; *Buster*, 1943; *Mr Bolfry*, 1943; *The Alchemist*, Liverpool, 1945; *Alice in Thunderland*, 1945; *Those Were the Days*, 1947; *He Who Gets Slapped*, 1947; *Headlights on A5*, 1947; *Finian's Rainbow*, 1947; *King John*, *The Merchant of Venice*, *Hamlet*, *The Taming of the Shrew*, *The Winter's Tale*, all in repertory at Stratford-on-Avon, 1948; *The Golden Door*, 1949; *The Gentle People*, 1949; *Trelawny of the Wells*, 1952; *Starched Aprons*, 1953; *The Bespoke Overcoat*, 1953; *The World of Sholom Aleichem*, 1955; *The Punch Revue*, 1955; *The Silver Whistle*, 1956; *Fiddler on the Roof*, 1968; *Caste*, 1972; *Cinderella*, 1973; *Jack and the Beanstalk*, 1974. **Films** (include) *Johnny Frenchman*, 1945; *Holiday Camp*, 1947; *The Hasty Heart*, 1949; *The Monkey's Paw*, 1949; *Pool of London*, 1950; *The Galloping Major*, 1950; *The Lavender Hill Mob*, 1951; *Brandy for the Parson*, 1954; *Svengali*, 1955; *A Kid for Two Farthings*, 1956; *Make Me an Offer*, 1956; *The Angel Who Pawned Her Harp*, 1956; *A Child in the House*, 1957; *A Tale of Two Cities*, 1958; *The Night My Number Came Up*, 1959; *I Only Arsked*, 1959; *The Millionairess*, 1961; *The Magnificent Seven Deadly Sins*, 1962; *Help!*, 1965; *A Funny Thing Happened on the Way to the Forum*, 1966; *Alfie*, 1966; *The Fearless Vampire Killers*, 1967; *It Always Rains on Sunday*, 1968; *Up the Junction*, 1968; *The Fixer*, 1968; *A Challenge for Robin Hood*, 1969; *The Bespoke Overcoat*, 1969; *The Revenge of the Pink Panther*, 1978; *High Rise Donkey*, 1978; *Death on the Nile*, 1978; *Moonraker*, 1979; *Dick Turpin*, 1980 (unreleased). **Television** (includes) *The Army Game*; *Bootsie and Snudge*; *Till Death Us Do Part*; *Danger UXB*; *Star Maidens*; *Our Mutual Friend*; *Robin Hood*; *Are You Being Served?*; *A Midsummer Night's Dream*. **Cause of death** Heart attack, at age 66. **Further reading** Jeffrey Richards and Anthony Aldgate, *Best of British: Cinema and Society, 1930–70*, London, 1983; David Quinlan, *British Sound Films: The Studio Years, 1928–59*, London, 1984; Francis Wheen, *Television: A History*, London, 1985; Bruce Crowther and Mike Pinfold, *Bring Me Laughter: Four Decades of TV Comedy*, London, 1987.

MICHAEL BENNETT

American Dancer, Choreographer, Director and Producer

***Born* Buffalo, New York, 8 April 1943**

***Died* Tucson, Arizona, 2 July 1987**

The world of musical theatre became a much poorer place with the death of Michael Bennett; the loss is as real as it is heartfelt. It is impossible to mention his name without saying, in the same breath, that this was the man who masterminded *A Chorus Line*, the longest-running musical in Broadway's history, More than ten years after its creation, the show remains one of the most iconoclastic and innovative pieces of modern theatre, the embodiment of Bennett's eclectic, freewheeling style. He drew on his own experiences as a chorus dancer for the show, which won nine Tony awards and the 1976 Pulitzer Prize for Drama, a rare honour for a musical.

Bennett's own dance career started during his childhood when he would dance at weddings and bar mitzvahs. He began his stage career as a dancer, but became an overnight sensation when he choreographed his first Broadway show, *A Joyful Noise*, aged only 23. It ran for only a week, but it won him a Tony award. In the decade following his début, he choreographed or directed (occasionally both), one or two shows a season. His collaborations with Harold Prince and Stephen Sondheim on *Company* (1970) and *Follies* (1971), permanently altered the Broadway landscape. Stanley Green, in his "bible" of the business, *The World of Musical Comedy*, has noted that, "Though the story was originally written as a play without songs, *Company* developed into a tightly coordinated 'conceptual' musical, utilizing music and dance not only as a part of the action, but also to comment on the actions and characters." He applauds the collaborators for having created a "seemingly seamless production that was almost as much a revue with a theme as it was a book musical". When, in 1975, *A Chorus Line* opened at the Shubert Theater, Bennett had already achieved in ten years what few even approached in a lifetime: five Tonys.

A Chorus Line began life as an experimental offering on one of Joe Papp's stages. The source material was provided by some 30 hours of tape-recorded discussions that Bennett held in 1974 with a group of dancers. Performed without scenery, except a mirrored rear wall, and, but for one scene, with the entire cast in practice clothes, the show followed a group of hopefuls through an audition to selection. There is the barest of plots; the show consists largely of a series of vignettes that allows each applicant to give some of his or her history and dreams. This format did not lead to the dull, self-indulgent treatment which the piece might have suffered in less able hands. Gerald Bordman, writing in his book *American Musical Comedy—From Adonis to Dreamgirls*, perhaps provides the most illustrative reaction: "The lyrics were hardly June-moon, touching on homosexuality, suicide and similar delicate subjects, and occasionally resorting to offensive expressions. Nonetheless, as a piece of theatre, as a metaphor in stage terms for the frightening battle for acceptance, *A Chorus Line* was spellbinding."

Some fifteen years later, the show remains vivid and truthful, surely the litmus test of any work of art. Unfortunately, at the time of writing, the show can only run on Broadway until various legal problems that arose upon Bennett's death can be resolved, and open the way for other productions.

The decade following *A Chorus Line* was not quite as starry as the one preceding it. There were three new musicals: *Ballroom* (1978) was a critical and box-office flop, but *Dreamgirls* (1981) delivered what *Company* and *A Chorus Line* had promised. It was another groundbreaking, popular work, running for more than 1500 performances, its theme being the rise, fall and afermath of a 1960s "girlie" group. Although it was vigorously denied that the show was based on the lives of Diana Ross and the Supremes, the protest seems a little too vigorous given the obvious parallels. One of the great devices of the show was a huge, show-stopping solo at the end of act one, an emotional and musical outpouring that made an instant star of the singer, 17-year-old Jennifer Holliday.

In 1977 Bennett had bought a building to house the ultimate musical theatre incubator: a place outside the Broadway hot-house where writers, composers, choreographers, designers, singers, dancers and actors could develop and test material without prohibitively expensive public try-outs. Christan Pye, an aspiring musician who worked in the building, recalls the tremendous atmosphere of the place, overflowing with such varied and weighty talent, and the comings and goings of the heavyweights among performing artists. Here, Bennett began to develop his next musical, *Scandal*—but after more than a year of intense work with company and writers, he shut down the project. "A number of very dear friends of mine got very greedy," he said at the time, but other factors also affected his decision. The abrupt end came as a shock to the company who still carry an unbridled enthusiasm for the piece.

In 1986 came the equally shocking news that Bennettt had sold his workshop building—a development that seemed to support many of the rumours circulating about the dubious state of Bennett's physical and artistic health. Jeremy Gerard, writing in the *New York Times*, voiced his opinion that, "For 20 years Mr Bennett had exerted nearly unparalleled influence on the musical theatre; now one of Broadway's most prodigious talents seems intent on closing out an era of the musical theatre defined chiefly by his own art." Bennett's defence was, "I've found that I can do my work anywhere." He insisted that the days of the workshop were dead. "The truth is, it runs in cycles. Every ten years, we find a new way to do shows. So now we'll find another."

Bernard Jacobs, president of the Shubert Organization, who had a long association as a producer with Bennett, perhaps shed the most accurate light when he observed, "The real tragedy is that Michael is sick and does not perceive that he will be working in the forseeable future."

Although his output of original material was slight after *Dreamgirls*, Bennett still made his influence felt on the musical theatre stage. He became one of the most respected show doctors on Broadway, sitting in on the productions of *My One and Only*, *Sunday in the Park with George*, and the disastrous beauty pageant musical, *Smile*. He was due to direct *Chess* in London in 1985, but pulled out because of ill health.

At the time of his death, Bennett was still enormously frustrated by the competitive and isolated working atmosphere that created bumbling shows ("What Broadway community?"). The whole premise of workshops had been the supportive, cooperative atmosphere and mode of working they engender. He would receive some comfort, though, from the fact that his influence, his development of style and craft still live on in the theatre, not least through the work of his long-standing assistant Bob Avian. In a business renowned for its backstabbing as much as its glamour, Michael Bennett was universally esteemed. In the words of one colleague he was simply "the best".

Born Michael Bennett. **Career** Choreographer, producer and director; began stage career as dancer; choreographic Broadway début, *A Joyful Noise*, Mark Hellinger Theater, 1966; subsequently associated with many hit shows, including *Promises, Promises*, 1968, *Company*, 1970, *God's Favorite*, 1974, and *A Chorus Line*, 1975. **Awards and honours** Tony awards for: *A Joyful Noise*, 1966, *Follies*, 1971 (two awards), *Seesaw*, 1973, *A Chorus Line*, 1975 (nine awards), *Ballroom*, 1978; Pulitzer Prize for Drama, for *A Chorus Line*, 1975. **Principal shows** (as director, choreographer and/or producer) *A Joyful Noise*, 1966; *Henry, Sweet Henry*, 1967;

Promises, Promises, 1968; *Coco*, 1969; *Company*, 1970; *Follies*, 1971; *Twigs*, 1971; *Seesaw*, 1973; *God's Favorite*, 1974; *A Chorus Line*, 1975; *Ballroom*, 1978; *Dreamgirls*, 1981; *Scandal*, 1985 (unstaged). **Cause of death** Undisclosed, at age 44.

JIM BISHOP

American Journalist and Author

Born **Jersey City, New Jersey, 21 November 1907**

Died **Delray Beach, Florida, 26 July 1987**

Jim Bishop was a man with an overwhelming desire to become a writer, who took nearly half a century to find his unique "day" book formula and success.

He was born James Alonzo Bishop into an Irish–Catholic family and, as the eldest, used to spend his evenings watching his policeman father compiling reports on surveillance and arrests. This was the inspiration that led him to major in shorthand and typing and, at the age of 18, quit his $52-a-week job as a milkman for a paltry $12-a-week copy boy position on the *New York Daily News*. After a year spent mostly running out for sauerkraut juice for hungover reporters, he progressed to cub reporter and, at 21, had achieved a reporting job on the *New York Daily Mirror*. A couple of years later he became assistant to Mark Hellinger on his daily Broadway column and it was here Bishop was really able to polish his technique, before moving on to rewriting and features.

In his mid-thirties he left newspapers for the post of associate editor of *Colliers'* magazine, subsequently becoming its war editor. This was followed by a spell with *Liberty* magazine, after which he moved into publishing. He had begun writing books in 1945 during his time as executive editor with *Liberty*, but the early ones, which included a biography of Hellinger and his work, were not particularly successful. He realized, however, that an interest in the events leading up to Abraham Lincoln's assassination, and which he had been pursuing as a hobby since his early days in journalism, had the makings of a book. His research was packed into a series of notebooks, each one dedicated to one of Lincoln's 24 last hours. He literally retraced the steps of Lincoln and Booth during that fateful day and within six months his perseverance paid off. *The Day Lincoln Was Shot* detailed in journalistic fashion the minute-by-minute events leading up to the president's death. It rapidly became a best seller and was selected by both the Book-of-the-Month Club and the Reader's Digest Book Club. David Donald, in the *New York Herald Tribune Book Review*, praised it as "good reading and good history...a book which has all the suspense of a high-grade thriller...By his acute awareness of dramatic structure, by his skilful use of direct quotations from the assassination trials, and by his careful and colorful descriptions, Mr Bishop has managed to give to this familiar story an immediacy which is almost painful."

Bishop, now 48, had found his *métier* at last. He was immediately sought after for features and, as a direct result, begged by comedian Jackie Gleason (q.v.) to write his biography. Bishop was doubtful. He told Gleason that if he did so the book would have to be the truth as he saw it. Gleason accepted and the book was duly written. An immediate success, *The Golden Ham* won a Benjamin Franklin Magazine Award from the University of Illinois and excerpts were published in *Life* magazine. However, as Bishop had feared, Gleason was unhappy about the candour and a rift developed between them.

His new-found success brought Bishop his long and lucrative contract with Hearst's King Features Syndicate. In 1957 he signed to write three features a week, which appeared under the title *Jim Bishop: Reporter* in over 200 newspapers for the next 26 years. He said his primary interest in the column was to "write stories about little people...each one, I hope, with a thought-provoking moral".

With his strong faith and involvement with the Catholic press, morality obviously played a major part in Bishop's life, and his follow-up "day" book reflects this. *The Day Christ Died* came out in 1957, and although some eyebrows were raised at Bishop's lack of Biblical scholarship and his Catholic bias in interpretation, it was, nonetheless, recognized as a valuable contribution to the reading of unsophisticated Christians. He followed up with a number of other books, including *The Day Christ Was Born* but had to wait seven years for his next real success with the formula.

After researching an article for *Good Housekeeping* magazine about a typical day of President Kennedy, he was invited by the president to turn it into a "day" book and permitted to spend four days at the White House to gather material. *A Day in the Life of President Kennedy* was completed ten days prior to Kennedy's own assassination and approved by him without revision. Jacqueline Kennedy later asked for 60 small alterations which Bishop acceded to. Despite this apparently good relationship between Bishop and the Kennedys, considerable differences arose when Jacqueline Kennedy learned he was planning to write *The Day Kennedy Was Shot*. In 1966 Bishop said he had received two letters from her asking him to cease working on it. His request that she not stand in the "doorway of history" went unheeded. She replied that "none of the people connected with November 22 will speak to anyone but Mr [William] Manchester [writer of *Death of a President*]—that is my wish and it is theirs also".

Bishop was not deterred. The next year he visited the White House again to research for *A Day in the Life of President Johnson* (1967), and by utilizing the personal help of the president, his own research and the Warren Commission Report, the Kennedy book appeared in 1968 and was received with as much favour as the Manchester version.

Bishop's writing style was terse and modelled on that of Ernest Hemingway, whom he admired greatly. He freely admitted to reading a few pages before sitting down at his typewriter in the hope that some of the Hemingway "magic" would rub off on him. He never rewrote his own words, saying that newspaper training had taught him to produce his best effort first time around. He believed the first flush of inspiration to be the best.

For Bishop it usually was.

Born James Alonzo Bishop. **Parents** John Michael, a policeman, and Jenny Josephine (Tier) Bishop. **Marriages** 1) Elinor Dunning, 1930 (died, 1957); 2) Elizabeth Jane Stone, 1961. **Children** Virginia Lee and Gayle Peggy from first marriage; Karen and Kathleen from second marriage. **Education** St Patrick's Parish School, New Jersey; Drake's Secretarial College, 1923. **Career** Milk deliveryman, New Jersey, 1928; copy boy, *New York Daily News*, 1928, cub reporter, 1929; reporter, *New York Daily Mirror*, 1930, assistant to columnist Mark Hellinger, 1932–34, rewrite man and feature writer, 1934–43; associate editor, *Colliers'* magazine, 1943–44, war editor, 1944–45; executive editor, *Liberty* magazine, 1945–47; director, literature department, Music Corporation of America, 1947–49; founding editor, Gold Medal Books, 1949–51; executive editor, *Catholic Digest*, 1954; founding editor, *Catholic Digest* Book Club, 1954–55; columnist, King Features Syndicate, writing three columns a week to appear in as many as 200 newspapers, 1957–83. **Other activities** President of Royalty Productions, radio and television production company; scriptwriter for TV documentary, *The Valley of the Fallen*, 1962. **Awards and honours** Catholic Institute of the Press Award, 1956; Banshees' Silver Award, 1956; Northwestern University Award, 1956; National Association of Independent Schools Award for

The Day Lincoln Was Shot, 1956; University of Illinois Benjamin Franklin magazine award for *The Golden Ham: A Candid Biography of Jackie Gleason*, 1956; honorary DLitt: St Bonaventure University, 1958, Belmont Abbey College, 1968. **Publications** *The Glass Crutch: The Biographical Novel of William Wynne Wister*, 1945; *The Mark Hellinger Story: A Biography of Broadway and Hollywood*, 1952; (with Le Roy E. McWilliams) *Parish Priest*, 1953; *The Day Lincoln Was Shot*, 1955; *The Golden Ham: A Candid Biography of Jackie Gleason*, 1956; *Fighting Father Duffy* (for children), 1956; *The Day Christ Died*, 1957; *Go With God*, 1958; *The Day Christ Was Born: A Reverential Reconstruction*, 1960; *Some of My Very Best*, 1960; *The Murder Trial of Judge Peel*, 1962; *Honeymoon Diary*, 1963; *A Day in the Life of President Kennedy*, 1964; *Jim Bishop, Reporter*, 1966; *A Day in the Life of President Johnson*, 1967; *The Day Kennedy Was Shot*, 1968; *The Days of Martin Luther King Jr*, 1971; *FDR's Last Year*, 1974; plus contributions to numerous magazines and journals. **Television** Commentator, weekly TV series *Byline—Jim Bishop*, WABC-TV, 1961–62; presenter, *Findings: A Minority Report*, WNEW-TV, 1966. **Cause of death** Respiratory failure, at age 79.

JAMES BURNHAM

American Political Philosopher

***Born* Chicago, Illinois, 22 November 1905**

***Died* Kent, Connecticut, 28 July 1987**

In a lifetime of vigorous political debate, James Burnham veered from committed socialist to ardent conservative. Along the way he produced a string of important works and helped found two influential political journals—the *Symposium* and the *National Review*. But he is best remembered for his book *The Managerial Revolution*, a provocative analysis of modern bureaucracy published in 1941. In it he offers a controversial new view of modern political organization, wherein both capitalism and socialism give way to a new form of totalitarian despotism headed by a powerful managerial and technocratic class. Reviewer Ordway Tead described it as a book "worth reading...not for the conclusions it imparts but for the disturbance to habitual thought patterns which it will engender". Burnham was, without question, one of the crowning figures in American post-war political thought.

Burnham's early radicalism may have had something to do with his childhood environment—a reaction, perhaps, against economic privilege and the capitalist system which had engendered it. He was raised in Chicago, the son of a British-born business executive who went on to become vice-president of the Burlington Railroad. Academic achievement came easily to him, and in 1927 he graduated as Latin salutatorian (first scholar of his class at Princeton University. He then studied at Balliol College, Oxford, and received his second Bachelor of Arts degree two years later. In 1930 he joined the faculty at New York University, taking time out to finish a philosophy MA at Oxford in 1932. From then on he served as professor of philosophy at NYU's Washington Square College. In 1930 he founded the critical journal the *Symposium* with philosopher Philip E. Wheelwright, and acted as co-editor until 1933. He and Wheelwright also collaborated on another project in 1932: an ambitious college textbook entitled *Introduction to Philosophical Analysis*, described by one commentator as a "full, right-minded book", which despite some shortcomings, was written "in the spirit of modernity...alive, rapid, colloquial".

Throughout the 1930s Burnham became increasingly involved with the socialist movement. He joined the political group known as the Trotskyists, or the Fourth Internationalists, in 1933, and until 1940 made frequent contributions to radical publications. At one point he even served as co-editor of the *New International*, the political organ of the American Trotskyists, and in 1937 wrote and circulated a pamphlet entitled *People's Front: The New Betrayal*, condemning the communist vision of a "people's front" against Fascism. Yet, even then, his scepticism was apparent. He was heard to comment, somewhat disdainfully, that the "official names of the group changed frequently", adding that the changes themselves would "hardly be intelligible without a supplementary history of radical politics during those years". By 1939 he was embroiled in an angry polemical battle with Trotsky himself—still alive in Mexico—and the following year his disillusionment led him to make a definitive break with the organization. "The basic reason for the break," he commented later, "was my conclusion that Marxist politics in practice lead not to their alleged goal of democratic socialism but to one or another form of totalitarian despotism."

Though Burnham once commented that his break with the Trotskyists had left him with "no politics", he soon became a champion of conservative causes, launching a whole new career of right-wing political prophecy. After World War II he directed his attention to what he viewed as the Soviet Union's drive for world domination, and between 1947 and 1964 produced three books exploring the idea, which he saw as an encouraging development, and condemning the Western liberal response to it. One book, *Suicide of the West*, offers an exhaustive historical criticism of liberalism, beginning with Locke and ending with Arthur Schlesinger Jr.

But Burnham's crowning literary achievement was unquestionably *The Managerial Revolution*. Some critics condemned its tone—according to one, it revealed "the Olympian defeatism of a doctrinaire radical gone sour"—while others praised it for its thoroughness and originality: "...one of the best recent books on political and social trends" and probably "the bible of the next generation of neo-Marxists". As a measure of its value, Ralph Thomson of the *New York Times* devoted two entire days to reviewing it. A number of Burnham's predictions—his warning of an inevitable US–Soviet confrontation, for example—have been borne out by recent events.

In the mid-1950s Burnham left his teaching post at NYU and joined forces with William F. Buckley Jr to found the *National Review*, the renowned journal of American conservatism. He remained a member of the magazine's editorial board, continuing to contribute articles, reviews and commentaries, until his death. In 1983 he was awarded the Presidential Medal of Freedom.

While he spent his working hours pondering historical trends and analysing contemporary political developments, Burnham escaped to the countryside at every opportunity. Together with his wife and children, he spent his leisure time doing simple, rustic chores. Cultivating vegetables and growing flowers were among his favourite hobbies.

Born James Burnham. **Parents** Claude George, executive vice-president of Burlington Railroad, and Mary May (Gillis) Burnham. **Marriage** Marcia Lightner, 1934 (deceased). **Children** One daughter, Marcia (deceased), James Bernard, and one other son. **Education** Princeton University, BA, 1927; Balliol College, Oxford, BA, 1929. **Career** Lecturer in philosophy, Washington Square College, New York University, professor of philosophy, 1932–54. **Related activities** Co-founder and co-editor with Philip E. Wheelwright, the *Symposium*, 1930–33; editor, the *New International*; contributor, *Partisan Review*, 1933–40; co-founder with William Buckley Jr, the *National Review*, 1955. **Awards and honours** Latin salutatorian, Princeton University, 1927; Presidential Medal of Freedom, 1983. **Memberships** Trotskyist movement, 1933–40. **Publications** (with Philip E. Wheelwright) *A Critical Introduction to Philosophy*, 1932; (pamphlet) *People's Front: The New Betrayal*, 1937; (contributor) *Whose Revolution?*, 1941; *The Managerial Revolution*, 1941, revised 1972; *The Machiavellians*, 1943; *The Struggle for the World*, 1947; (co-author) *The Case for De Gaulle*, 1948; *The Coming Defeat of Communism*, 1950;

Containment or Liberation?, 1953; *The Web of Subversion*, 1954; *Congress and the American Tradition*, 1959; *Suicide of the West*, 1964; *The War We Are In*, 1967. **Cause of death** Undisclosed, at age 81.

LIONEL CHEVRIER

Canadian Politician

***Born* Cornwall, Ontario, 2 April 1903**

***Died* Montreal, Quebec, 8 July 1987**

Lionel Chevrier will be best remembered as the man who created the St Lawrence Seaway. Like those who forged the Suez and Panama canals, he significantly altered the geography and trading pattern of the globe.

Chevrier was born to French–Canadian parents. His father was mayor of his home town during World War I, and his mother was a member of a prominent Canadian family. While still at elementary school, Chevrier often accompanied his father on trips to the United States. Little did he guess that links between the US and Canada were to become a life-long obsession.

His higher education began at the University of Ottawa, where, in 1924, he gained both a BA and PhB, having also won medals for chemistry and debating. Aside from academic commitments, he also managed to captain the university football and hockey teams. He went on to receive a law degree from Osgoode Hall in Toronto and was admitted to the Ontario Bar in 1928. After working for 18 months in a Toronto law firm, Chevrier returned to Cornwall, where he set up the general law partnership of Chevrier and Latchford, which was later to become Chevrier, Latchford and Fitzpatrick. By 1938 he had been named a King's Counsel.

Chevrier's political career began in 1935, when he stood as a Liberal candidate and was elected to the House of Commons to represent the constituency of Stormont, Ontario. He was to be re-elected eight times. A popular man, speaking English and French fluently, he was seen as a fine example of the country's bi-cultural tradition. His career really took off during World War II. By 1940 he was deputy-chief government whip, and two years later was chairman of the Special Parliamentary Subcommittee on War Expenditures. A year later he was named as parliamentary assistant to the minister of munitions and supply, and in 1945 was nominated to the Privy Council.

It was also in 1945 that he assumed his most important appointment—as minister of transport. Chevrier held this post for nine years and it was a very considerable portfolio. He was responsible for the supervision of harbours, canals, railways, shipping, civil aviation, radio and meteorology and, by 1948, the operation of telegraph and telephone services. But, most of his time was spent developing the plans for the great St Lawrence Seaway. The enormous complex of canals and lift-locks which enables ocean-going ships to sail to the Great Lakes and into the industrial heartland of North America was thought about for at least 100 years. Chevrier was to put the thoughts into practice. He had a passionate belief in the project, and stressed its importance from both the economic and industrial points of view: "Without construction of the seaway, the large deposits of high-grade iron ore in Labrador cannot move economically and expeditiously to the Great Lakes steel centres...you would find within the Montreal area 6,000,000 horsepower of electrical energy...when this power is fully developed, I would venture the opinion that this will be one of the richest areas on the North American continent".

From the beginning, Chevrier talked of a joint Canadian–American project but the United States Congress did not immediately welcome involvement, so in 1952 Canada passed legislation to embark on the project alone. Even when the US did become involved, it was only on the development of the hydroelectric project, which left Canada to undertake the river-deepening work alone. For this reason US ships were eventually obliged to pay a toll for use of the waterway. Meanwhile, the project was riddled with controversy; Chevrier was blamed for exceeding the budget and many other associated problems. Despite these adversities, the waterway eventually had its grand opening in 1959, presided over by Queen Elizabeth II and President Eisenhower.

In 1954 Chevrier left politics temporarily to become the first president of the St Lawrence Seaway Authority. Three years later he returned to a Cabinet post, but soon after the Liberals lost office to the Conservatives for the first time in 22 years. For the next six years, along with a group of ex-Liberal ministers known as the Four Horsemen, he did his best to filibuster and bend all the rules in an effort to harass the Conservative administration. When the Liberals regained power in 1963, Chevrier became minister of justice, a post he held for one year before taking up a diplomatic post in London. Three years later he served as commissioner-general for state visits at Expo 67, the world fair in Montreal.

Chevrier travelled widely, representing his country at many overseas meetings and often heading delegations. In a political career that was diligent, if unexceptional, his greatest triumph was undoubtedly overseeing the construction of the St Lawrence Seaway—a magnificent memorial by anyone's standards.

Born Lionel Chevrier. **Parents** Joseph Elphège and Malvina (de Repentigny) Chevrier. **Marriage** Lucienne Brûlé, 1932. **Children** Three sons, Robert, Jean and Bernard, and three daughters, Lucie, Adèle and Marie. **Education** Cornwall College Institute, 1917; Ottawa University, BA, 1924, PhB; Osgoode Hall, Toronto, LLB, 1928. **Career** Called to Bar, Ontario, 1928; MP for Stormont, Canada, 1935–54; King's Counsel, 1938; deputy-chief government whip, 1940; minister of transport, 1945–54; president, St Lawrence Seaway Authority, 1954–57; called to Bar, Quebec, 1957; MP for Montreal–Laurier, 1957–64; minister of justice, 1963–64; high commissioner, London, 1964–67; commissioner-general for state visits, Expo 67, Montreal. **Related activities** Chairman, special parliamentary subcommittee on war expenditures, 1942; parliamentary assistant to the minister of munitions and supply, 1943; delegate, Bretton Woods Conference, 1945; privy counsellor, 1945; chairman, Canadian delegation, UN general assembly, Paris, 1948; president, Privy Council, Canada, 1957; commander-general for state visits to Canada, 1967; chairman, Canadian economic mission to francophone Africa, 1968; chairman, mission to study Canadian consular posts in USA, 1968; chairman, seminar to study river navigation for Unitar, Buenos Aires, 1970. **Offices and memberships** Secretary, board of trade, Cornwall, Ontario, 1928–32; member, sessional committee on railways and shipping, 1945 onwards. **Awards and honours** Honorary LLD: Ottawa, 1946, Laval, 1952, Queen's, 1956, Concordia, 1984; honorary colonel, Stormont, Dundas and Glengarry Highlanders, 1949; honorary DCL, Bishops', 1964; Companion of the Order of Canada, 1967; president, alumni association of Ottawa University; Knight of Columbus. **Publications** *The St Lawrence Seaway*, 1959. **Cause of death** Undisclosed, at age 84.

J. RIVES CHILDS

American Biographer and Diplomat

***Born* Lynchburg, Virginia, 6 February 1893**

***Died* Richmond, Virginia, 15 July 1987**

James Rives Childs combined the roles of scholar and emissary in his long and eventful life. He was, at different times, an officer in military intelligence, a reporter for Associated Press, a member of the Foreign Service, and a writer on subjects as varied as Middle Eastern affairs and the life of Casanova.

Childs's early working life was spent as a reporter for the *Baltimore American* newspaper. He soon gave up this job to study at Harvard University, where he gained an MA in 1915. When the United States became involved in World War I, he joined the army and was put in charge of the American section working on the deciphering of German codes, which involved close co-operation with colleagues from Britain and France. His diplomatic skills were further nurtured at the Paris Peace Conference after the war, and in special diplomatic missions to Yugoslavia and Russia. It was in the latter country that he met his future wife Georgina.

Childs returned to journalism for a brief spell as the Washington correspondent for Associated Press, but the lure of exotic places and diplomatic missions drew him back to the service of his country. He joined the Foreign Service of the State Department in 1923 and was assigned to the Near and Middle Eastern embassies and consulates. He served in Jerusalem, Cairo, Tangier and Tehran, as well as being the US ambassador in Saudi Arabia, Yemen and, finally, in Ethiopia. He retired in 1953, writing a fascinating book about his years as a diplomat, entitled *Farewell to Foreign Service: Thirty Years in the Near East*. An earlier book, *American Foreign Service* (1948), was an informative and entertaining account of the activities and traditions of the diplomatic corps. Childs tended to be descriptive rather than analytical in his treatment of complicated issues, although he was not without his own strong opinions, especially on the formation of the state of Israel and the partition of Palestine. He was completely opposed to this solution to the Arab–Jewish conflict, having come to sympathize with the Arab viewpoint after so many years of close contact with their society and their politics.

On his retirement, Childs devoted a greater proportion of his time to a fascinating subject—the life and works of Giovanni Giacomo Casanova. There can be no doubt that part of his attraction to this dissolute adventurer lay in a certain similarity in their experiences. Casanova was a widely travelled Venetian musician who served as both diplomat and spy. His adventures were far more exotic than those of Childs, however, which made his autobiography, *History of My Life*, one of the most exciting of all literary works. Childs wrote four books on Casanova and spent many hours researching into the authenticity of the stories which he told. His efforts were encyclopedic in their nature, but marked by a tendency to believe all he found in Casanova's rather exaggerated writings. He visited several cities and plotted the precise details of his subject's amorous adventures, cataloguing them with the precision which one would expect of a former codebreaker. Given this background, the biography is heavily biased in Casanova's favour. It ignores the dubious morals of the world's most famous bachelor and gigolo, preferring to see him as a serious scholar and even a potential philosopher, a view which cannot bear up to the closest scrutiny.

Childs was never one to hide his own opinions from the public; he wrote with sincerity and an exactitude based upon careful research. His own life was colourful and, in no small way, comparable to that of his favourite historical figure. He can hardly be refused a certain licence in his appreciation of a kindred spirit.

Born James Rives Childs. **Pseudonym** Henry Filmer. **Marriage** Georgina, *circa* 1920 (died, *circa* 1970). **Education** Randolph-Macon College; Harvard University, MA 1915. **Military service** Wireless intelligence and decipherer, US Army, 1917. **Career** Reporter, *Baltimore American*, 1911–14; Washington correspondent, Associated Press, 1918–23; consular service, US State Department, serving in Jerusalem and Israel, 1920s; US ambassador to Saudi Arabia, Yemen and Ethiopia, 1930s–53. **Other activities** After war, attended Paris Peace Conference and served with relief missions to Yugoslavia and Russia; authority on Casanova; editor, *Casanova's Gleanings*, magazine of Casanova Society. **Offices and memberships** President, International Casanova Society. **Publications** (some under pseudonym) *American Foreign Service*, 1948; *Casanova: A Biography Based on New Documents*; *Diplomatic and Literary Quests*; *Collector's Quest*: *The Correspondence of Henry Miller and J. Rives Childs, 1947–1965*, 1968; *Farewell to Foreign Service: Thirty Years in the Near East*; *Vignettes, or Autobiographical Fragments*. **Cause of death** Cardiac-pulmonary infection, at age 94.

ABU SAYEED CHOWDHURY

Bangladeshi Politician

***Born* Negbari, India, 31 January 1921**

***Died* London, England, 31 July 1987**

Abu Sayeed Chowdhury was the first president of the People's Republic of Bangladesh. Appointed to office on 12 January 1972, he was unanimously elected for a further five-year term under the new constitution of Bangladesh in April 1973. Eight months later he had resigned and become his country's special representative in Geneva. Here he worked to coordinate aid for Bangladesh, led countless delegations to the various UN agencies and headed goodwill missions to countries like Egypt, Japan, Turkey, Syria, Lebanon and Algeria. Chowdhury returned to Bangladesh and to politics for a brief spell in 1975 when he became foreign minister in President Ahmed's short-lived government.

Chowdhury finally left Bangladesh and found exile in London after the military coup of November 1975, which left his country under army rule. Here, he became honorary fellow of the Open University and, in 1978, a member of the UN Commission on the Prevention of Discrimination and the Protection of Minorities. In 1985 he was made chairman of the UN Commission of Human Rights.

The political career of Abu Sayeed Chowdhury accurately reflects the troubled times of his country. Born the son of a former speaker of the East Pakistan Provincial Assembly, he was educated at Calcutta University and called to the Bar at Lincoln's Inn in London in 1947. Thereafter, he practised as a barrister in Dacca and in the Pakistan Supreme Court. He became a judge of the Dacca High Court and vice-chancellor of Dacca University.

When the troubles that were to lead to the secession of East Pakistan and the formation of the state of Bangladesh erupted into civil war in March 1971, Chowdhury was in Geneva for a meeting of the UN Commission on Human Rights, as representative for Pakistan. He immediately announced his support for "Bangla Desh" (Free Bengal), saying that after the bloody suppression of the autonomist movement he could never return to a country where his own professors and students had been murdered, and appointing himself ambassador-at-large for the new state. For the rest of the year Chowdhury headed Bangladesh missions in London and New York.

Chowdhury's enthusiasm for the new state of Bangladesh did not long survive his return home. His belief that the country, however economically poor and undeveloped, should aspire to a democratic future was not in tune with the autocratic ambitions of Bangladesh's new prime minister and leader, Sheikh Mujibur Rahman. Not only did the sheikh abolish all political parties, but he also pushed through the National Assembly a series of amendments allocating himself almost unlimited power. Chowdhury resigned the presidency and became Bangladesh's special representative in Geneva, where he coordinated foreign aid for his country.

When Sheikh Mujib was assassinated two years later, Chowdhury returned to Bangladesh, becoming foreign minister under President Ahmed. Unfortunately, within three months Ahmed was toppled in another coup, and Chowdhury returned to England. For the remainder of his life he worked for the UN, where he devoted himself to the cause of human rights—thus keeping faith with his principles to the very end.

Born Abu Sayeed Chowdhury. **Father** Abdul Hamid Chowdhury, formerly speaker, East Pakistan Provincial Assembly. **Marriage** Khurshid Chowdhury, 1948. **Children** Two sons, one daughter. **Education** Presidency College; Calcutta University, MA, BL. **Career** Called to Bar at Lincoln's Inn, 1947; practised as barrister, Pakistan Supreme Court, Dacca; advocate-general, East Pakistan, 1960; judge, Dacca High Court, 1961–72; ambassador-at-large and High Commissioner in UK, 1971; head of missions, London and New York, 1971–72; president, Bangladesh, 1972–73; minister of foreign affairs, also of shipping and ports, 1975; member, United Nations subcommission on Prevention of Discrimination and Protection of Minorities, 1978–84; chairman, UN Commission on Human Rights, 1985–86. **Related activities** Member, Pakistan delegation to general assembly of United Nations, 1959; member, Constitutional Commission, 1960–61; chairman, Central Board for Development of Bengali, 1963–68; leader, Pakistan delegation to World Assembly of Judges and fourth world conference on world peace through law, 1969; vice-chancellor, Dacca University, 1969–72; member, United Nations Human Rights Commission, 1971, 1982, 1986–87; chancellor, all Bangladesh Universities, 1972–73; special representative of Bangladesh, Geneva, 1973–75; leader, Bangladesh delegations: conference on humanitarian law, Geneva, 1974–75, chairman, human resources committee, conferences on law of the sea, Caracas, 1974, Geneva, 1975, general conference of International Atomic Energy Agency, Vienna, 1974, non-aligned Foreign Ministers' Conference, Lima, 1975, United Nations Foreign Ministers' Conference, Jeddah, 1975; leader, goodwill missions to Saudi Arabia, Egypt, Syria, Lebanon and Algeria, 1974, Turkey, 1975, Japan, 1984; visiting professor, Franklin Pierce Law Center, USA, 1983; chairman, United Nations working group on slavery practices. **Offices and memberships** General secretary, Presidency College Union, 1941–42; president, UK branch of All-India Muslim Students' Federation, 1946. **Awards and honours** Honorary Deshikottama Viswabharati (Shantiniketan), 1972; honorary LLD, Calcutta, 1972; honorary research fellow, Open University, 1977. **Cause of death** Undisclosed, at age 66.

PATIENCE COLLIER

British Actress

***Born* London, England, 19 August 1910**

***Died* London, England, 13 July 1987**

Throughout her long and distinguished career Patience Collier commanded enormous respect and admiration in the acting profession, not only as a colleague who operated on the highest level of professional integrity, but also as an artist of uncommon versatility and imagination. In 1954, at the Lyric Theatre in Hammersmith, London, tradition has it that she created a definitive Charlotta Ivanova in John Gielgud's legendary production of *The Cherry Orchard*, no small feat in an age when Western theatre still basks in a reverent glow of the Chekhov–Stanislavsky legacy.

The trademark of Collier's work lay in the clarity and detail which she brought to her characters. Blessed with superb vocal range and crisp diction, her distinctive talent was in creating minutely-observed characters, both comic and tragic. As one newspaper obituary noted, "she was a penetrating observer and a cruelly accurate mimic". She also had such a brilliant turn of phrase that she could transform an account of a bus ride into the funniest story one had ever heard.

Her privileged early life no doubt fostered her innate sense of style, grace and social confidence. Her parents were wealthy Austrians who had her educated and "finished" at some of the finest schools in Europe. This culminated in her training at the Royal Academy of Dramatic Art in London, where she won Lady Tree's Elocution Award. Collier made her début in the autumn following her graduation in 1932, in Theodore Komisarjevsky's production of *Versailles* at the Kingsway Theatre in London, although it was characteristic of her ability that she played *five* parts.

From then until 1950 she played in numerous repertory productions and established herself as an outstanding radio actress. After her sensational success with *The Cherry Orchard* in 1954, she was rarely off the stage and worked with practically *everybody* (Noel Coward, Peter Brook, John Gielgud, *et al*) doing practically *everything*: works by Brendan Behan, John Mortimer, Shakespeare, and so on.

She became more widely known by the public from 1961 when she began her distinguished association with the Royal Shakespeare Company, playing an extraordinarily wide variety of parts. The *Independent*'s obituary fondly recalls how "she stole the show as the almost wordless Edna in Albee's *A Delicate Balance*, provoked gales of laughter in *The Government Inspector*, glittered as the Duchess in *The Revenger's Tragedy*, and offered a chilling Regan in *King Lear*".

Patience Collier began working in films from 1968 and will probably be especially remembered for her portrayal of the sour Mrs Poulteney in *The French Lieutenant's Woman* (1981). Television, however, was responsible for her biggest popular success—as Katerina in *Who Pays the Ferryman?*. The small screen naturally took her to an even wider audience, and her last full-length play for this medium was *The House on Kirov Street* by Chekhov, thus neatly bringing her full circle.

When she played Charlotta for the third and final time, it was on the stage at the National Theatre for Sir Peter Hall. Some 30 years after her original triumph, her performance was once again a rich, truthful portrayal. Few people guessed, as she performed Charlotta's little dance, that her legs were weak from a long and painful illness and had barely been able to carry her to the theatre. But by the absolute and rigorous standards of Patience Collier, it was but a small hazard in a life dedicated to perfection.

Born René Ritcher. **Parents** Paul and Eva (Spitzel) Ritcher. **Marriage** Henry Collier, doctor (died, 1985). **Children** One son, two daughters. **Education** Spaldings, Queen's Gate; St Monica's, Tadworth; Villa St Monique, Auteuil, Paris; Royal Academy of Dramatic Art, 1930–32. **Career** Stage début in five small roles in Komisarjevsky's production of *Versailles*, Kingsway Theatre, London, 1932; provincial repertory and much radio work until the 1950s; returned to London theatre in *The Velvet Moss*, 1950; joined Royal Shakespeare Company, 1961, playing in London and at Stratford-upon-Avon, becoming associate artist of the company, 1967; subsequently rarely absent from the major stages; entered films, 1968; also made a number of television appearances. **Stage** (all in London, unless stated) *Versailles*, 1932; *Well Gentlemen*, Cambridge, 1932; *Josephine*, 1934; *Roulette*, 1935; *The Velvet Moss*, 1950; *The Cherry Orchard*, 1954; *My Three Angels*, 1955; *The Power and the Glory*, 1956; *The Family Reunion*, 1956; *Nude With Violin*, 1956; *Living for Pleasure*, 1958; *The Sea Shell*, tour, 1959; *The Hostage*, New York, 1960; *'Tis Pity She's a Whore*, 1961; (the following with the Royal Shakespeare Company in London and at Stratford-upon-Avon) *The Cherry Orchard*, 1961; *The Caucasian Chalk Circle*, 1962; *Cymbeline*, 1962; *King Lear*, 1962; *The Comedy of Errors*, 1962; *The Physicists*, 1963; *King Lear*, Paris, 1963; *The Beggar's Opera*, 1963; *Richard II*, 1964; *Henry IV, Parts I and II*, 1964; *Henry V*, 1964; *The Governor's Lady*, 1965; *Henry V*, 1965; *Squire Puntila and His Servant Matti*, 1965; *The Government Inspector*, 1966; *Tango*, 1966; *The Meteor*, 1966; *The Revenger's Tragedy*, 1966; *The Judge*, Cambridge, 1967; (RSC Aldwych Season) *A Delicate Balance*, *Bartholomew Fair*, *The Silver Tassie*, *The Revenger's Tragedy*, 1969–70; *Awake and Sing*, Hampstead, 1971; *All Over*, 1972; *The Hostage*, 1972; *The Old Ones*, 1972; *The House of Bernarda Alba*, 1973; *A Month in the Country*, Chichester, 1974; *Heartbreak House*, 1975; *The Devil's Disciple*, 1976; *Ivanov*, 1976; *Brand*, 1978; *The Cherry Orchard*, 1978. **Films** (include) *Every Home Should Have One*, 1970; *Perfect Friday*, 1970; *The Countess Dracula*, 1970; *The French Lieutenant's Woman*, 1981. **Radio** (includes) *Jane Eyre*. **Television** (includes) *Who Pays the Ferryman?*; *David Copperfield*; *The House on Kirov Street*; *Nanny*. **Cause of death** Undisclosed, at age 76.

GERARDO DIEGO

Spanish Poet and Literary Critic
***Born* Santander, Spain, 3 October 1896**
***Died* Madrid, Spain, 8 July 1987**

Gerardo Diego was a man of many talents—a professor of literature, poet, anthologist and critic, as well as a pianist and musicologist. He was a member of the Spanish Academy and a holder of the Great Cross of King Alfonso X.

A northerner, he attended the Jesuit College of Deusto in Bilbao, going on to study at the universities of Salamanca and Madrid, and graduating in romance philology in 1916. He became a professor of literature and taught in Soria, Gijón, Santander and Madrid. In the 1920s he began to give recitals of Spanish music, performing throughout Europe and in Asia and Latin-America. He later collaborated on a work of musicology, *Diez años de música en España* (Ten Years of Music in Spain), published in 1949, and also gave lectures on this subject.

Diego's literary career began in 1918 when he won a prize in a literary contest sponsored by the periodical *La Revista General*. In 1925 he was awarded the National Prize for Literature, together with the poet Rafael Alberti, for his verse collection *Versos humanos*. While never considered quite on a par with his contemporaries of the so-called "Generation of '27"—Alberti, Lorca and Guillén—he was nevertheless a supreme technician, being the master of the sonnet and responsible for reviving the ten-line *décima*, associated with the baroque period, as a contemporary form.

As a poet he cleaved to no one particular form, preferring to use a variety of styles, and this was evident in *Carmen*, the literary magazine he edited. The main body of the publication was given over to poetry evincing the *culto* or refined and elegant manner of writing, while its supplement *Lola* accommodated verse in a simple style, in part to poke fun at those poets who in his view took themselves too seriously. His own poetry ranged from that of the "Ultraist" movement, heavily influenced by Dadaism, Cubism and Surrealism, and as exemplified by *Imagen* (1922), through the *creacionista* in *Manual de espumas* (1924), written following his meeting with Huidobro, the French-based Chilean poet who wrote mainly in French and believed that art should be autonomous, to the calm lyricism of *Versos humanos* (1925); and from the neo-gongorist—homage to the Generation of '27's seventeenth-century mentor Luis de Góngora—in *Fábula de equis y zeda* (Fable of X and Z, 1926–7, published in 1932) to the religious poetry of *Angeles de Compostela* (1940). He also wrote sonnets dedicated to his favourite composers, from Beethoven and Schumann to Fauré and Debussy, and poems about bullfighting, *La suerte y la muerte* (Fortune and Death, 1963). A common element to all his poetry is its supreme artistry and use of poetic language rather than its forceful emotion or message.

Diego is perhaps best known for his influential anthology of his contemporaries' work, *Poesía española contemporánea*, which was first published in 1932 and subsequently expanded and revised in 1949 and again ten years later. He also produced an anthology in 1927 for the *Revista de Occidente* which commemorated the 300th anniversary of the death of Góngora, entitled *Antología poética en honor de Góngora desde Lope de Vega a Rubén Darío*.

For many years Diego was understandably ignored by those who were opposed to General Franco's 40-year dictatorship of Spain. He had backed the Nationalist cause in the civil war of 1936–39 because of his catholicism and innate political conservatism. This alienated him from his many contemporaries who had backed the Republic and risked death at the hands of the Nationalists—the fate of Lorca and Hernández—or were forced into exile, like Alberti. During the long years of Spain's isolation and cultural stagnation, Diego helped to keep alive the flame of its literary traditions, and it is perhaps on this that his reputation will rest.

Born Gerardo Diego Cendoya. **Education** Jesuit schools at Deusto and Bilbao; University of Salamanca; University of Madrid, PhD, 1916. **Career** Poet, anthologist and critic; professor of literature, Soria, Gijón, Santander and Madrid. **Related activities** Edited literary periodicals, *Carmen* and *Lola*; travelled widely on cultural missions and lectured in France, the Philippines and Latin-America. **Other activities** Musician and musicologist. **Awards and honours** National Prize of Literature, 1924 (shared), 1956; City of Barcelona Prize, 1958. **Poetry** *Iniciales*, 1918; *Romancero de la novia*, 1920, rewritten, 1944; *Imagen*, 1922; *Manual de espumas*, 1924; *Versos humanos*, 1925; *Vía Crucis*, 1931; *Fábula de equis y zeda*, 1932; *Soria*, 1933, augmented, 1948; *Angeles de Compostela*, 1940; *Glosa sobre Villamediana*, 1940; *Primera antología*, 1941; *Poemas adrede*, 1943; *Alondra de verdad*, 1943; *La sorpresa*, 1944; *Poemas*, 1948; *Hasta siempre*, 1949; *La luna en el desierto y otros poemas*, 1949; *Limbo*, 1951; *Variación*, 1952; *Biografía incompleta*, 1953; *Amazona*, 1955; *Paisaje con figuras*, 1956; *Egloga de Antonio Bienvenida*, 1956; *Amor solo*, 1958; *La suerte o la muerte*, 1963. **Other** (editor) *Antología poética en honor de Góngora desde Lope de Vega a Rubén Darío* (anthology), Madrid, 1927; (editor) *Poesía española contemporánea, 1915–1931*, 1932, revised 1949, 1959; (collaborator) *Diez años de música en*

España, 1949. **Cause of death** Undisclosed, at age 90. **Further reading** G. de Torre, *Literaturas europeas de vanguardia*, Madrid, 1927; D. Alonso, *Ensayos sobre poesía española*, Madrid, 1946; A. Del Río, *Historia de la literatura española*, New York, 1948.

CHARLES STARK DRAPER

American Aeronautical Engineer

***Born* Windsor, Missouri, 2 October 1902**

***Died* Cambridge, Massachusetts, 25 July 1987**

In World War II guns in US battleships were able to shoot down kamikaze attacks even in rough seas; after the war nuclear submarines were enabled to sail for months and know exactly where they were; later still the Apollo astronauts were guided with pinpoint accuracy to and from the moon. In all these cases the inertial guidance system devised by Dr Draper and his team lay at the heart of success. Indeed, his navigation systems are today in all missiles and in virtually all submarines and aircraft.

Charles Stark Draper gained his BA degree in psychology in 1922, after study at the universities of Missouri and Stanford, and it was only then that he decided to change to electrochemistry, enrolling at the Massachusetts Institute of Technology. There he gained his BS in electrochemical engineering in 1926, his MS in 1928, and finally his ScD in physics in 1938. That same year also marked his marriage to another engineer, by which time he had been an assistant professor in aeronautical engineering at MIT for three years. In 1939 he was a full professor.

Guidance systems were Draper's big interest, and he based his research on gyroscopes. These spinning discs tend to continue indefinitely in the same place and rotating along the same axis, and a force is required to make them move in any way. They were the core of his innovations.

In his 34 years as director of the MIT Instrumentation Laboratory, there were some remarkable advances. His early improvements in the design and use of gyroscopes led to improved fire-control and director systems. Rolling ships provided a particular problem, especially when attacked by air. Draper devised rate-measuring gyros which could offset errors in the observer's line of sighting caused by ship movements. Corrections for range, wind and ballistics also entered the system semi-automatically. Draper ignored previous methods and fundamentally simplified the gunsight system. The most dramatic demonstration of its effectiveness came in 1942, when the USS *South Dakota* was able to shoot down 32 kamikaze pilots.

His next application of gyroscopes was to navigation. By measuring the forces on a group of gyroscopes it is possible to compute which way a vehicle is moving and how far it has gone; no external information such as radio signals or star sightings are required. During development Draper tested the equipment by using it in his own private plane, much to the consternation of his MIT supervisors. On a test flight from Boston to Los Angeles he landed within ten miles of his intended destination—a remarkable achievement at the time.

By 1954 the MIT Instrumentation Laboratory, under his aegis, had completed the first ship's inertial navigation system (SINS), and in 1956 his group rapidly completed its contract with the Navy Special Projects Office for development of an inertial guidance system for Polaris. Further work led to inertial guidance systems for missiles, and then the guidance methods that led to the success of the Apollo moon landings.

Awards and honours in plenty came his way, and he found time to serve on many committees and to be consultant engineer for many aeronautical manufacturers and instrument makers. He enjoyed sports cars and gliding, and, with others, found time to write the three-volume *Instrument Engineering*, published between 1952 and 1955.

In 1973, long after the age most men retire, he left MIT to found the Charles Stark Draper Laboratory in Cambridge, Massachusetts, for the development of precision engineering equipment. It was there that his innovative contributions to science and technology eventually came to an end.

Born Charles Stark Draper. **Parents** Charles A. and Martha Draper Ditmeyer. **Marriage** Ivy Hurd Willard, an engineer, 1938. **Children** Three sons, one daughter. **Education** Stanford University, BA in psychology, 1922; Massachusetts Institute of Technology, BS in electrochemical engineering, 1926, MS, 1928, ScD in physics, 1938. **Career** Aeronautical engineer; assistant professor, Massachusetts Institute of Technology, department of aeronautical engineering, 1935–38, associate professor, 1938–39, professor, 1939–71; director, MIT Instrumentation Laboratory, 1935–69; head, department of aeronautics and astronautics, 1951–66; vice-director and president, Charles Stark Draper Laboratory, 1970–87. **Related activities** Research and development on fire control, flight control and inertial guidance systems for US Air Force and Navy; consulting engineer to many aeronautical companies and instrument manufacturers; member, several advisory groups connected with military services. **Offices and memberships** President, International Academy of Astronautics; honorary fellow: American Institute of Aeronautical Sciences, British Institute of Mechanical Engineers, British Interplanetary Society, Royal Aeronautical Society; honorary life member, Instrument Society of America; honorary member: German Society for Guidance and Navigation, British Institute of Navigation, and numerous other societies; foreign member, Académie des Sciences, 1978–87. **Awards and honours** Sylvanus Albert Reed Award from Institute of Aeronautical Sciences, 1945, honorary fellowship, 1958, Louis W. Hill Space Transportation Award, 1962; Medal of Merit (presidential citation), 1946, Exceptional Civilian Service Award (Department of Air Force), 1951, 1968, 1969; Navy Distinguished Public Service Award, 1956, 1960; Holley Medal from American Society of Mechanical Engineers, 1957; elected to National Academy of Sciences, 1958; William Proctor Prize of the Scientific Research Society of America, 1959; Potts Medal Award, Franklin Institute, 1960; named one of *Time* magazine's "Men of the Year", 1960; elected to National Academy of Engineering, 1965; National Medal of Science, 1965; honorary degree, Eidgenössische Technische Hochschule, Switzerland; Guggenheim Medal of the United Engineering Trusts, 1967; National Aeronautics and Space Administration Public Service Award, Apollo Achievement Award, 1969; Founder's Medal, National Academy of Engineering, 1969; Founder's Medal of the National Academy of Engineering, 1970; Rufus Oldenburger Medal of the American Society of Mechanical Engineers, 1971; Distinguished Civilian Service Medal, Department of Defence; honorary degree, University of Portland, Oregon, and many other national awards. **Publications** (with Walter Wrigley and John Hovorks) *Inertial Guidance*, 1960; (with Walter McKay and Sidney Lees) *Instrument Engineering*, three volumes, 1952, 1953, 1955. **Cause of death** Pneumonia, at age 85.

RICHARD EGAN

American Actor
***Born* San Francisco, California, 29 July 1921**
***Died* Santa Monica, California, 20 July 1987**

When Richard Egan arrived in Hollywood at the age of 28, he must have been one of the most academic actors to appear on screen. He had a BA from San Francisco University, a master's degree in theatre history and dramatic literature from Stanford University, and had pursued post-graduate theatre research at Northwestern University. In addition, he had "rugged good looks" and "spectacular pectoral development". Little wonder he was chosen for immediate stardom. Critics billed him as the obvious successor to Clark Gable—the archetypal hero figure.

The reality, however, turned out differently. Egan's first film, *The Damned Don't Cry* (1950) was not, despite a distinguished cast which included Joan Crawford, a success. There followed a series of action films, including *One Minute to Zero*, *The Hunters* and Elvis Presley's *Love Me Tender*, which fared a little better. In 1962 Egan scored something of a hit in the costume drama *The 300 Spartans* in which he played Leonidas. However, the majority of his 30-odd films were unmemorable, and few of them were made after 1971.

Egan explained his failure in terms of his own strong moral principles, claiming that he refused to accept parts that would "embarrass my kids". He would remain off the screen, he said, as long as the present trend for nudity and explicit sex predominated. "There are other sides to life. There is some place where man is trying to succeed, to do right, to live right." With his five children all baptized by his brother, a Jesuit priest, it is certainly possible to see Egan as a man living according to his own principles, unswayed by the chance of cheap glamour and easy fame.

Gilbert Adair, writing Egan's obituary in the London *Independent*, was less charitable. Why, he asked, should an actor who today is almost forgotten and whose main appearances for the last two decades had been confined to guest roles on television, merit remembrance? Egan, to him, was a star totally lacking in anything resembling star quality, "...in whose performances no thematic consistency could be detected, whose histrionic range ran the gamut from adequacy to competence, whose physical allure was unmatched by any comparable spiritual intensity". Perhaps he simply failed to find parts that would bring out his talents.

Whatever the reason for his unmemorable, even mediocre work, Egan is of interest, if only for the light his career sheds on the old Hollywood practice of making its actors into salaried employees, of giving them, in effect, tenure for life. Until the early 1960s stardom was conferred as a permanent gift—a far cry from the fleeting, ephemeral quality we know today. Richard Egan was simply a lucky beneficiary.

Born Richard Egan. **Marriage** Patricia Hardy, actress, 1958. **Children** Four daughters, one son. **Education** San Francisco University, BA, 1942; Stanford University, MA; postgraduate work at Northwestern University. **Military service** Judo instructor in US Army, World War II. **Career** Briefly employed as an instructor in public speaking before turning to Hollywood, 1949; film actor, 1950–1971; mainly TV actor, 1970s onwards. **Films** *The Damned Don't Cry*, 1950; *Undercover Girl*, 1950; *The Killer That Stalked New York*, 1950; *Bright Victory*, 1951; *Split Second*, 1952; *One Minute to Zero*, 1952; *Demetrius and the Gladiators*, 1954; *Wicked Woman*, 1954; *Gog*, 1954; *Underwater*, 1955; *Untamed*, 1955; *Violent Saturday*, 1955; *The View From Pompey's Head*, 1955; *Seven Cities of Gold*, 1955; *The Revolt of Mamie Stover*, 1956; *Love Me Tender*, 1956; *Tension at Table Rock*, 1956; *The Voice in the Mirror*, 1958; *These Thousand Hills*, 1958; *The Hunters*, 1958; *A Summer Place*, 1959; *Pollyanna*, 1960; *Esther and the King*, 1960; *The*

300 Spartans, 1962; *The Destructors*, 1966; *Chubasco*, 1968; *The Big Cube*, 1969; *Up Front*; *Khyber Patrol*; *The Lion of Sparta*; *Heavens Above*; *Valley of Mystery*. **Stage** Occasional roles, including a tour of the comedy *No Hard Feelings*. **Television** Roles in series such as *The Streets of San Francisco*, *Police Story*, *Empire*, *Redigo* and *Capitol*; TV movies include *Throw Out the Anchor* and *Shootout in a One Dog Town*. **Cause of death** Prostate cancer, at age 65.

POLLY ELWES

British Television Broadcaster

***Born* London, England, 29 February 1928**

***Died* Berkshire, England, 15 July 1987**

Polly Elwes was one of the most versatile and memorable women to appear in the early days of British television. Having trained as an actress at London's Central School of Speech Training and Dramatic Art, she joined a repertory company and subsequently worked in London's West End for 18 months. The theatre, however, was not to be her true *métier*.

Undaunted, she turned to television, and in the developing BBC of the 1950s quickly carved a niche for herself as an actress in televised drama and as an announcer. In 1950 she was voted "Best Female Television Personality", but Polly Elwes was determined to make her mark as more than a personality. A leap year baby herself, she put forward a suggestion for a programme about this odd phenomenon. It was accepted and she produced an excellent programme around the topic in 1956. As she had had the foresight to invite a number of producers in radio and television to watch it, offers of more work began to come in rapidly.

First, she was recruited to compère *Woman's Hour*, a very long-running radio magazine programme broadcast every weekday afternoon. Donald Baverstock, one of the key men in pioneering the *Tonight* programme, which was televised in the early evening during the previously empty slot of 6–7 p.m., asked her to join the team as a roving reporter. Among her many assignments was a trip to a bleak Scottish monastery to ask the monks what had prompted their vocation, and to Britain's wettest village to enquire how its inhabitants coped with the damp. Despite the quirkiness of these interviews, they did lead to more serious opportunities. In 1959 she joined the team of *Panorama*, the weighty current affairs programme, and that same year covered the general election.

Her versatility combined with her elfin charm and quick mind brought her invitations for shows such as *What's My Line?* where celebrities had to guess individuals' occupations from a piece of mime, *Face the Music*, where panellists had to guess pieces of (mostly) classical music and which requires a keen knowledge of the subject, and *Juke Box Jury*, a dearly-loved programme of younger viewers, in which an invited panel voted on whether newly released popular records would be "hits" (ping of the bell) or "misses" (resounding raspberry). She also worked in a number of radio programmes.

As a presenter she was equally at ease with subjects such as beauty, motoring and teaching deaf people new methods of communication. However, her efforts were not always applauded. One television critic asked plaintively, "Why [does she feel] compelled to talk like a friendly Brown Owl, advising very dim members of her pack?"

Polly Elwes came from a very distinguished family. Her father was a high court judge, her grandfather a celebrated tenor, and one of her uncles a fashionable portrait painter. With such a background it was perhaps inevitable that she became a performer herself.

She was 32 when she married, her husband being an equally well-known face in television: Peter Dimmock, the sports commentator. She gave up working when she began a family and accompanied her husband to New York in 1977 when he took up a post with ABC. But when she returned in later years she found herself still popular and in demand.

Polly Elwes was also a woman of immense courage. The last eleven years of her life were marred by lengthy fights against bone cancer. Yet she never lost hope, her sense of fun, or her zest for life. As Cliff Michelmore, the host of *Tonight*, later remarked, she was always the "lovely Polly Elwes".

Born Mary Freya Elwes. **Father** Sir Richard Elwes, a high court judge. **Marriage** Peter Dimmock, broadcaster, 1960. **Children** Three daughters. **Education** Poles Convent, Ware; Central School of Speech Training and Dramatic Art. **Career** Stage manager and actress, Windsor Theatre Royal repertory company; appeared in *For Better For Worse*, Comedy Theatre, London; dubbed skaters in *Aladdin on Ice*, Wembley; appeared in television plays, *Until the Morning* and *Party Manners*. **Radio** Broadcaster on *Roundabout* and *Home This Afternoon*; presenter, *Woman's Hour*. **Television** Reporter, *Tonight*, 1957–59; presenter, *Panorama*, 1959–61; panellist on *What's My Line?*, *Juke Box Jury* and *Face the Music*. **Awards and honours** Best Female Television Personality, 1950. **Cause of death** Bone cancer, at age 59.

GILBERTO FREYRE

Brazilian Anthropologist, Writer and Politician

Born **Recife, Brazil, 15 March 1900**

Died **Recife, Brazil, 18 July 1987**

Gilberto Freyre has been acknowledged as the most influential Brazilian intellectual of this century. This influence derived from his ability to weld together his varied interests—in literature, politics, sociology and, above all, social anthropology—under the influence of Franz Boas, the founding father of cultural anthropology in the United States.

Coming from a privileged Catholic family, Freyre was thought to be retarded in his early childhood. Against the wishes of the family, his father sent him to the local American Protestant school after a period of little success with private tutors. Here Freyre discovered his passion for literature. By the age of eleven he was writing poetry, and by the time he left at 17 he had become proficient in both French and English. Gaining a first degree in political and social science at Baylor University in Texas, he subsequently went to Columbia to read for his master's degree in social anthropology. It was here he met Boas, who was to remain a lifelong mentor. Boas (whose students also included such well-known names as Alfred Kroeber, Melville Herskovits, Paul Radin, Ruth Benedict and Margaret Mead) had split with the European Durkheimian approach in the 1890s, arguing for historical particularism or cultural relativism: namely that each and every culture has to be viewed in its own context and explained in terms of its own history.

This is precisely the approach Freyre used in writing about Brazil's development for his dissertation and which he took home after a further year spent travelling in Europe.

Subsequently he expanded his dissertation and eventually published it some ten years later as *Casa-grande e senzala*, later translated as *The Masters and the Slaves*. It covered the period of Brazilian history during the sixteenth and seventeenth centuries and argued strongly and forcefully that the racial mix of Portuguese slave-owners, their imported African slaves and the indigenous Amerindian population had produced not an inferior mongrel race, as was then felt to be the case, but one which was ideally suited, both mentally and physically, to the Brazilian climate and way of life. Although flawed by anthropological and sociological misconceptions, it was hailed, nonetheless, as his seminal work. The flaws really relate to the methods employed in both anthropological and sociological research, both of which involve the collection of "live" data. Although Freyre utilized every possible source, including recipes and etiqette manuals, it is clear that the major part of his material must have derived from the records of the land- and slave-owning aristocracy—of which he was himself a descendant. Amerindians and African slaves would have left few literary legacies.

However, this book, together with its later companion volume, *Sobrados e mucambos* (*The Mansions and the Shanties*), covering the transition from rural to urban society in the nineteenth century, proved a catalyst insofar as it gave all Brazilians a sense of national identity and of belonging together. It also proved the launch-pad for Freyre's political career.

Having previously worked as secretary to the governor of Pernambuco and spent two years as professor of sociology at the Escola Normal de Pernambuco, in 1934 Freyre organized the first Afro–Brazilian Congress. He was greatly concerned at the rise of Nazism in Europe and, as a result of this and his opposition to the Brazilian dictator, Vargas, spent a brief period in prison. He kept a low profile politically after his release, concentrating on writing and his academic work. From 1935 to 1938 he was professor of sociology at the University of Brazil, where he also inaugurated a department of anthropology. Simultaneously, he also held advisory posts with the government department dealing with historical documents and the national geography council.

The year 1941 brought both sorrow and joy for Freyre: sorrow because Boas, to whom he had been so close, died; joy because of his marriage. In 1946 he was able to resume his political career, thanks to the forced resignation of Vargas the previous year. Freyre served as a member of parliament until 1950 and became a delegate to the developing United Nations, where he also served on the race relations committee.

He was in his sixties when he turned to fiction for the first time. His first novel, *Doã Sinhá e o filho padre*, subsequently translated as *Mother and Son*, was the story of a latent homosexual, pushed into the priesthood by a dominating mother during the sweeping social, religious and political changes of late nineteenth-century Brazil. Freyre himself called it a "semi" novel. It is possible, however, that even the fictional theme had a basis in his personal reality and own family life when we recall it was his father who defied family feeling and gave him the opportunity of so much self-development. Although some critics felt the narrative too frail for the context, others found it a subtle psychological work, one describing it as "...delicate, immensely touching [and] generous in its comprehension of sexual ambivalence".

Freyre, who continued to write, lecture and gain recognition with doctorates from universities in the Americas and Europe until well into his eighties, was, first and foremost, an ardent Brazilian who determined to use his immense energy and ability to counteract the prevailing self-destructive intellectual thinking of his youth with something much more positive and forward-looking. It was anthropology and Boas that showed him a method he could utilize, and Freyre, in his turn, could be called the founding father of modern Brazil, his influence reaching out through all the spheres of his life—academic, political, literary and diplomatic.

It is considered impossible for anthropologists to look clearly at their own society because they cannot be objective about it. There are too many matters that *go* without saying because they *come* without saying. These are the aspects every member within a culture takes for granted. As an anthropologist Freyre attempted the impossible. As a politician and Brazilian he achieved it: he gave his compatriots a full sense of their own culture and nation.

Born Gilberto de Mello Freyre. **Parents** Alfredo, a teacher and judge, and Francisca (de Mello) Freyre. **Marriage** Maria Magdalena Guedes Pereira, 1941. **Children** One daughter and one son. **Education** American Colégio Gilreath, Recife; Baylor University, Waco, Texas, BA, 1921; Columbia University, New York, MA, 1922. **Career** Travelled for a year after graduation, returning to Brazil to become a leader of the modernist movement, 1923; private secretary to governor of Pernambuco, Recife, 1927–30; professor of sociology, State School of Recife, 1928; director, *A Provincia* newspaper, 1928–30; visiting professor, Stanford University, California, 1931; organizer, first Afro–Brazilian Congress, 1934; imprisoned for political activities, 1934; professor of sociology, faculty of law, Recife, 1935; founding professor of social anthropology, University of Brazil, Rio de Janeiro, 1935–38; lectured in Europe and USA, 1938–39; representative to National Assembly, 1946, and to House of Deputies, 1947–50; Brazilian delegate to United Nations General Assembly, 1949 and 1964; founder, Joaquim Nabuco Institute, Recife, 1949; supervisor, Northeast Brazil Social and Educational Research Centre, from 1957; lectured worldwide. **Related activities** Technical adviser to government department responsible for care of historical documents, 1937; adviser to the national geography council, 1938; member, United Nations committee on race relations in South Africa, 1954; director, *Diogène* and *Cahiers Internationaux de Sociologie*, Paris. **Offices and memberships** Academy of Letters of Sao Paulo, 1961; Brazilian Academy of Letters, 1962; Royal Anthropological Institute; American Academy of Arts and Sciences. **Awards and honours** Felippe d'Oliviera Award, 1934; honorary PhD: Columbia University, New York, 1954, University of Coimbra, 1962, University of Paris, University of Sussex and University of Münster, 1965; Anisfield–Wolf Award, 1957; Machado de Assis Prize, 1963; Aspen Award, 1967; La Madonnina International Literary Prize, Italy, 1969; Knight Commander, Order of the British Empire, 1971; José Vasconcelos Gold Medal, Mexico, 1974. **Novels** *Doã Sinhá e o filho padre*, Rio de Janeiro, 1964, published as *Mother and Son*, New York, 1967; *O outro amor do Dr Paulo*, Rio de Janeiro,1977. **Verse** *Talvez poesía*, Rio de Janeiro, 1962; *Gilberto poeta: algumas confissoes*, Recife, 1980; *Poesía reunida*, Recife, 1980. **Non-fiction** (all published in Rio Janeiro, unless stated) *Casa-grande e senzala*, 1933, revised edition, 2 vols, 1943, published as *The Masters and the Slaves: A Study in the Development of Brazilian Civilization*, New York, 1946, London, 1947, revised edition, New York, 1956 and 1964; *Guia prático, histórico e sentimental de cidade do Recife*, Recife, 1934, revised edition, 1942, 1961, 1968; *Artigos de jornal*, Recife, 1935; *Sobrados e mucambos*, Sao Paulo, 1936, revised edition, 1951, 1961, published as *The Mansions and the Shanties: The Making of Modern Brazil*, New York, 1963; *Mucambos de Nordesta*, 1937, revised edition, Recife; *Nordeste*, 1937, revised edition, 1951, 1961; *Olinda: 2º guia prático, histórico e sentimental de cidade brazileira*, 1939, revised edition, 1944, 1960, 1968; *Açúcar*, 1939; *Um engenheiro francês no Brasil*, 1940, revised edition, 2 vols, 1960; *O Mundo que o português criou*, 1940; *Região e tradição*, 1941; *Uma cultura ameaçada*, 1942; *Ingleses*, 1942; *Problemas brasileiros de antropología*, 1943, revised edition, 1954; *Na Bahia em 1943*, 1944; *Perfil de Euclydes e outros perfis*, 1944; *Sociologia*, 2 vols, 1945, revised edition, 1957, 1962; *Brazil: An Introduction*, New York, 1945, revised edition published as *New World in the Tropics: The Culture of Modern Brazil*, 1959; *Ingleses no Brasil*, 1948; *Quase politica*, 1950, revised edition, 1966; *Aventura e rotina*, 1953; *Um brasileiro em terras portuguêsas*, 1953; *Assombraçoes do Recife velho*, 1955, revised edition, 1970; *Integração portuguesa nos trópicos*, Lisbon, 1958, published as *Portuguese Integration in the Tropics*, Lisbon, 1961; *A propósito de frades*, Salvador, 1959; *A propósito de Morão, Rosa e Pimenta*, Recife, 1959; *Orden e progresso*, 2 vols, 1959, published as *Order and Progress: Brazil from Monarchy to Republic*, edited and translated by R.W. Horton, New York,

1970; *Brasis, Brasil e Brasilia*, Lisbon, 1960, revised edition, 1968; *O Luso e o trópico*, Lisbon, 1961, published as *The Portuguese and the Tropics*, Lisbon, 1961; *Vida, forma e côr*, 1962; *Home, cultura e trópico*, Recife, 1962; *O escravo nos anúncios de jornais brasileiros do século XIX*, Recife, 1963, revised edition, São Paulo, 1979; *Retalhos de jornais velhos*, 1964; *O Recife, sim! Recife, não!, São Paulo*, 1967; *Sociologia da medicina*, Lisbon, 1967; *Como e porque sou e não sou sociólogo*, Brasilia, 1968; *Contribução apra uma sociologia da biografia*, Lisbon, 2 vols, 1968; *Oliveira Lima, Don Quixote gordo*, Recife, 1968; *A casa brasileira*, 1971; *Nós e a Europa germânica*, 1971; *A condição humana e outros temas*, edited by M.E.D. Collier, 1972; *Além do apenas moderno*, 1973; *The Gilberto Freyre Reader*, New York, 1974; *A presença do acúcar na formação brasileira*, 1975; *Tempo morto e outros tempos: Trechos de um diário de adolescência e primeira mocidade 1915–1930*, 1975; *O brasileiro entre os outros hispanos*, 1975; *Alhos e bugalhos*, 1978; *Cartas do próprio punho sobre pessoas e coisas do Brasil e do estrangeiro*, edited by S. Rabello, 1978; *Prefácios desgarrados*, edited by E. Nery da Fonseca, 2 vols, 1978; *Heróis e viloes no romance brasileiro*, São Paulo, 1979; *Oh de casa!*, Recife, 1979; *Tempo de aprendiz*, edited by J.A. Gonsalves de Mello, São Paulo, 1979; *Arte, cienca e trópico*, São Paulo, 1980; *Pessoas, coisas e animais*, 1981; *Insurgências e ressurgeñcias atuais: Cruzamentos de sins e naos num mundo em transicão*, 1983; *Médicos, doentes e contextos sociais*, 1983. **Cause of death** Undisclosed, at age 87. **Further reading** Diogo de Melo Menezes, *Freyre*, Rio de Janeiro, 1944; Diogo de Melo Menezes, *Freyre: Sua ciencia, sua filosofia, sua arte*, Rio de Janeiro, 1962.

PAUL FROMM

American Music Patron

***Born* Kitzingen, Germany, 28 September 1906**

***Died* Chicago, Illinois, 4 July 1987**

"He had a total commitment as our champion. He believed in us and dared us to believe in ourselves. He was the Esterhazy of the twentieth century." So said the composer Ralph Shapey about the distinguished music patron Paul Fromm.

Fromm was a fifth-generation member of a family of vintners, who emigrated to the USA in 1938 and settled in Chicago where he founded the Great Lakes Wine Company in 1940. He became a US citizen in 1944 but was well known for the strong German accent he never lost. He became one of the great music philanthropists of the twentieth century, particularly through the Fromm Foundation (now at Harvard University), which he established in 1952 to promote the composition and performance of contemporary music and to re-establish the composer in his rightful position at the centre of musical life.

Paul Fromm was born into a prosperous family in 1906, and was a cousin of Erich Fromm the psychoanalyst and author. Fromm played the piano as a child and attended the festivals of contemporary music at Donaueschingen. His first encounter with Stravinsky's *Rite of Spring* in 1927, as he put it, "made a twentieth-century man of me".

Fromm never abandoned his principle that great art was a rarefied experience and that his nurturing should be devoted to work that really needed it. "We must realize that great art does not belong to everybody," he wrote in the *New York Times* in 1978. "It never did and never will. It is up to us to create the stimulants to cultural development and to foster an environment that is friendly to cultural pursuits. We can do this best by not trying to bring serious art to more people but by educating a more knowledgeable and more devoted body of art patrons. We must look to them as a nucleus from which a healthy culture can grow."

Fromm served as overseer of the Boston Symphony Orchestra and leader of several Chicago charities. He received numerous awards for his services to contemporary music, including the George Peabody Medal, the American Music Center Award and honorary doctorates from the New England Conservatory and the University of Cincinnati.

The Fromm Foundation has commissioned more than 150 works from young and relatively unknown composers, and also from established ones. It has sought to provide the best possible conditions for the performance of contemporary music, provided subsidies for recordings, sponsored radio programmes and seminars for composers and critics, and for some years supported the periodical *Perspectives of New Music*. In 1956 the foundation began to sponsor concerts of contemporary music at Berkshire Music Center which were expanded into a contemporary music festival in 1964. In an attempt to broaden its sponsorship policy, the foundation ceased its support of the festival in 1983 and re-directed its funds to reach more diverse schools of music composition. The foundation sponsored conferences and concerts at the Aspen Music Festival from 1985. The first series of concerts there reflected Fromm's breadth of vision in its title "Musical Pluralism in the 1980s".

At the time of writing, nearly 200 composers have received commissions, and their names read like an honour roll of twentieth-century American classical music. Among works sponsored over the years by the foundation are *Circles* by Luciano Berio, *Double Concerto* by Elliott Carter, George Crumb's *Music for a Summer Evening*, Ginastera's *Cantata per America Magica*, Oliver Knussen's *Flute Concerto*, Martinu's *Piano Concerto No. 4* and Roger Sessions's *Concertino*.

Fromm was a modest man who once described himself as "a footnote in musical history". He was the first to admit that he relied heavily upon advisers such as Milton Babbit and Elliott Carter. Through all the shifts of musical fashion, he retained his commitment to and faith in the vitality of twentieth-century music. In 1979 he wrote, "I am convinced that our century will eventually prove to be one of the great musical centuries. If we choose to ignore what is happening in our midst, then it is our great loss."

Born Paul Fromm. **Parents** Max, a vintner, and Matilde (Maier) Fromm. **Marriage** Erika Oppenheimer, a psychologist, 1938. **Children** One daughter, Joan. **Emigration** Left Germany for USA, 1938; naturalized, 1944. **Career** Founder and president, Geeting and Fromm Inc., wine importers, Chicago, 1939–87, Great Lakes Wine Company, 1940–87; founder, Fromm Music Foundation, Harvard University, 1952, director, 1952–87. **Related activities** Member: visiting committee of humanities and music, University of Chicago, visiting committee of music department, Harvard University, board of overseers, Boston Symphony Orchestra, board of directors, Orchestral Association. **Other activities** Member: citizens' committee, University of Illinois, board, Institute of Psychoanalysis, Chicago, advisory council, Princeton University. **Awards and honours** Honorary degrees: New England Conservatory, Boston, 1967, University of Cincinnati, 1974; Golden Baton Award, American Symphony Orchestra League; Jesse L. Rosenberger Medal, University of Chicago; George Peabody Medal, Peabody Institute; American Musical Center Award. **Cause of death** Series of heart attacks, at age 80.

TAWFIQ al-HAKIM

Egyptian Novelist

Born **Alexandria, Egypt, 9 October 1898**

Died **Cairo, Egypt, 26 July 1987**

Tawfiq al-Hakim was Egypt's major playwright, representing in his plays the Egyptian revivalism of the 1920s when the discovery of the tomb of Tutankhamun and a new, liberal constitution encouraged such revivalism. The two works that portrayed this reawakening were *The Return of the Soul* and *The People of the Cave*, the latter based on the biblical tale of the seven sleepers of Ephesus. Hakim's output was enormous, rivalling that of Galsworthy or of Shaw with whom he has sometimes been compared in his tackling of Egypt's social issues.

Hakim was strongly influenced by French literary genres. After studying law in Egypt, he had continued his studies in France and married a Frenchwoman. His first meeting with her is charmingly described in "Devant son guichet", a short story in which a young man asks the girl selling tickets for a "place" at the Paris Odéon but soon reveals that the place he wants is in the girl's heart rather than in the theatre's stalls.

In Paris he fell under the spell of theatre, particularly that of Ibsen, Shaw and Pirandello. When he returned to Cairo in 1928, determined to become a writer, he adopted the French beret and bohemian Left Bank manners. In contrast with his Paris days, he soon became a public prosecutor in the provinces and was to draw on his legal experiences to write his best-known novel outside Egypt, *The Maze of Justice*, which was published in 1937.

The Return of the Soul, a two-volume romance and his first novel, was set during the 1919 uprising for Egyptian independence under the leadership of the Wafd Party. Its heroes are literate but lower-class Egyptians, and for the first time in Arabic literature Hakim, eager to communicate with a popular readership, used colloquial rather than classical Arabic for his dialogue.

Hakim's first major play, *Muhammad*, depicted the life of the Prophet on an epic scale although, given Islam's condemnation of any figurative representation of the Prophet, it could be read but not acted. However, to have written the play at all was a bold gesture, given the sensitivity of the subject.

The publication of *The People of the Cave* in 1933 was considered a landmark in Arabic literature. Based on the Qur'anic story of the people of the cave, a variant on the Christian legend of the seven sleepers of Ephesus, Hakim follows the Qur'anic rendering in which there were only three sleepers, the fourth being the dog Qitmir. After they awake from their three centuries'-long sleep, they begin to realize that the world is not really theirs and that they are the "property of history", and they soon begin to decay. The loyal lover Pariska accompanies her decaying Mishliniyya in much the same way that Aida accompanies her Radames to the grave. The theme is time, and otherworldliness is indicated by telling touches, such as the shunning of Qitmir by the other dogs. The story is also a parable on the resurrection of Egypt after a long period of decay.

Hakim supported Nasser's revolution of 1952, having decried the corrupt years of King Farouk. After the founding in 1956 of the Higher Council for the patronization of arts, letters and sciences, Hakim headed its committee on the theatre for many years. However, by the 1970s, the period of President Sadat's open-door policy and the new wealth that came with it, Hakim became disillusioned, and by the late 1970s his writing was provoking the ire of the Muslim fundamentalists. After the 1973 war with Israel, he had led the movement which concentrated on

Egyptian rather than pan-Arab nationalism, reflecting his own recall of pharaonic tradition in the 1920s and 1930s. In 1977 to 1978 he initiated a debate around Egypt's new "neutrality", following the peace agreement signed with Israel. The debate was between the old-style Egyptian nationalists and the militant Islamic fundamentalists.

Hakim has described his works as spiritual, reformist and diverse. The variety of his output was, indeed, impressive. It includes plays, novels, short stories, political commentaries and published interviews and correspondence. Although much of his writing concentrated on Egyptian themes, plays such as *Oedipus* and *Pygmalion* are derivative.

Born Husayn Tawfiq Isma'il Ahmad al-Hakim. **Marriage** One, 1946 (died, 1977). **Children** One son (died, 1978), and one daughter. **Education** Damanhur infant school; Muhammad Ali Secondary School, Cairo; University of Cairo law school, 1921–25; Sorbonne, Paris, 1925–28. **Career** Lawyer, playwright and novelist; apprentice public prosecutor, Alexandria, 1928–29; public prosecutor in small towns, 1929–34; director, Investigation Bureau, Ministry of Education, 1934–39; director, Social Guidance, Ministry of Social Affairs, 1939–43; full-time writer, 1943–87. **Related activities** Associate on newspapers, *Akhbar al-Yawm* and *Al-Ahram*; director-general, Egyptian National Library, 1951; member, Egyptian Higher Council of Arts, Literature and Social Sciences, 1956–59, 1960–87; Egyptian representative, UNESCO, Paris, 1959–60; president, Nadi al-Qissa, 1974. **Memberships** Academy of the Arabic Language, 1954. **Awards and honours** Cordon of the Arab Republic of Egypt, 1958; state literature prize, 1961. **Fiction** *Awdat al-Ruh* (The Return of the Spirit), 1933; *Ahl al-Fann* (Artistes), 1934; (with Taha Husayn) *Al-Qasr al-Mashur* (The Enchanted Castle), 1936; *Yawmiyat Na'ib fi al-Aryaf*, 1937, translated as *The Maze of Justice*, 1947; *Tarikh Hayat Ma'ida* (Biography of a Stomach), 1938, reissued as *Malik at-Tufayliyin* (King of the Moochers), 1946, reissued as *Ash'ab, Amir at-Tufayliyin* (Ash'ab, Prince of Moochers), 1963; *'Usfur min ash-Sharq*, 1938, translated as *A Bird from the East*, Beirut, 1966; *'Ahd ash-Shaytan* (Pact with Satan), 1938, reissued as *Madrasa ash-Shaytan* (Satan's School), 1955; *Raqisa al-Ma'bad* (The Temple Dancer), 1939; *Ar-Ribat al-Muqaddas* (The Sacred Bond), 1944; *Qisas* (Stories), two volumes, 1949; *'Adala wa Fann* (Justice and Art), 1953; reissued as *Ana wa'l-Qanun wal 'Fann* (The Law, Art and I), 1973; *Arini Allah* (Show Me God), 1953; *Min Dhikrayat al-Fann wa'l-Qada'* (Memories of Art and Justice), 1953; *Madrasa al-Mughaffalin* (School for Fools), 1953; *Laylat az-Zifaf* (Wedding Night), 1966; *Al-Amira al-Bayda aw Bayad an-Nahar* (Snow White), 1978. **Plays** (all in Cairo or London unless stated) *Ahl al-Kahf*, 1933, in English as *The People of the Cave*, 1971; *Shahrazad*, 1934, as *Shahrazad*, 1981; *Muhammad*, 1936; *Masrahiyat* (plays), two volumes, 1937; *Nahr al-Junun*, 1937, as *The River of Madness*, New York, 1963; *Praxagora*, 1939; *Nashid al-Anshad* (The Song of Songs), 1940; *Pygmalion* (translation), 1942; *Sulayman al-Hakim*, 1943, as *The Wisdom of Solomon*, 1981; *Shajarat al-Hukm* (The Rulership Tree), 1945; *Al-Malik Udib*, 1949; as *King Oedipus*, 1981; *Masrah al-Mujtama* (The Theatre of Society), 1950; *Al-Aydi an-Na'ima*, 1954, as *Tender Hands*, 1981; *Isis*, 1955; *Al-Masrah al-Munawwa'* (The Diverse Theatre), 1956; *As-Safqa* (The Deal), 1956; *Rihla ila al-Ghad* (Voyage to Tomorrow), 1957, as *Al-'Alam al-Majhul* (The Unknown World), Beirut, 1973, as *Voyage to Tomorrow*, 1981; *La'bat al-Mawt* (Death Game), 1957; *Ashwak as-Salam* (The Thorns of Peace), 1957; *As-Sultan al-Ha'ir*, 1960, as *The Tree Climber*, 1966; *At-Ta'am li-Kull Fam* (Food for the Millions), 1963, as *Samira wa Hamdi*, Beirut, 1973, as *Food for the Millions*, 1981; *Rihla ar-Rabi' wa-l-Kharif* (Spring and Autumn Journeys), 1964, as *Ma'a az-Zaman* (Over the Years), 1973; *Shams an-Nahar*, 1965, *Shams wa Qamar*, Beirut, 1973, as *Princess Sunshine*, 1981; *Al-Warta*, 1966, as *Incrimination*, 1981; *Bank al-Qalaq* (Anxiety Bank), 1966; *Masir Sarsar*, 1966, as *Fate of a Cockroach*, 1973; *Majlis al-'Adl* (Council of Justice), 1972; *Fate of a Cockroach and Other Plays*, 1973; *Al-Hubb* (Love), 1973; *Ad-Dunya Riwaya Hazaliya* (Life Is a Farce), Beirut, 1974; *Al-Hamir* (Donkeys), 1975; *Plays, Prefaces and*

Postscripts, two volumes, Washington, DC, 1981–84; *Ashab as-Sa'ada az-Zawjiwa* (Happily Married), 1981; *Imsik Harami* (Catch a Thief), 1981; *Ah...Law 'Arifa ash-Shabab* (Oh...If Only Youth Knew), 1981; *'Imarat al-Mu'allim Kanduz* (The Building of Master Kanduz), 1981. **Other** *Tahta Shams al-Fikr* (By the Light of the Sun of Thought), 1938; *Himar al-Hakim* (Al-Hakim's Ass), 1940; *Sultan az-Zalam* (The Reign of Darkness), 1941; *Taht al-Misbah al-Akhdar* (By the Light of the Green Lamp), 1941; *Min al-Burj al-'Aji* (From the Ivory Tower), 1941; *Zahrat al-'Umr* (The Flower of Life), 1943; *Himari Qala li* (My Donkey Told Me), 1945; *Fann al-Adab* (The Art of Literature), 1952; *'Asa al-Hakim* (Al-Hakim's Staff), 1954; *Ta'ammulat fi as-Siyasa* (Reflections on Politics), 1954; *At-Ta'aduliya* (The Art of Balance), 1955; *Adab al-Hayat* (The Literature of Life), 1959; *Sijn al-'Umr* (The Prison of Life), 1964; *Qalibuna al-Masrahi* (Our Theatrical Form), 1967; *Qult...dhat Yawm* (I Said One Day), 1970; *Tawfiq al-Hakim yatahaddath* (Tawfiq Al-Hakim Discusses), 1971; *Thawrat ash-Shabab* (Revolt of the Young), 1971; *Ahadith ma'a Tawfiq al-Hakim min sana 1951–1971* (Conversations with Tawfiq al-Hakim), edited by Salah Tahir, 1971; *Rahib bayna Nisa'* (A Monk Among Women), 1972; *Rihla bayna 'Asrayn* (Journey Between Two Ages), 1972; *Himari wa'Asaya wa'l-Akharun* (My Donkey and Stick and the Others), 1972; *Hadith ma'a al-Kawbab* (Conversations with the Planet), Beirut, 1974; *'Awdat al-Wa'y* (Return of Consciousness), Beirut, 1974; *Safahat min at-Tarikh al-Adabi min Waqi' Rasa'il wa-Watha'iq* (Pages from Literary History: Selected Letters and Documents), 1975; *Bayn al-Fikr wa'l-Fann* (Between Thought and Art), Beirut, 1976; *Ta'am al-Fann wa'r-Ruh wa'l-Aql* (Food for Art, Spirit and Intellect), 1977; *Malamih Dakhiliya* (Inner Features), 1982; *Equilibrium and Islam*, 1983; *The Return of Consciousness*, 1985–86. **Cause of death** Undisclosed, at age 88. **Further reading** Richard Long, *Tawfiq al-Hakim, Playwright of Egypt*, London, 1979.

JOHN HAMMOND

American Music Impresario, Journalist and Record Producer
Born **New York City, New York, 15 December 1910**
Died **New York City, New York, 10 July 1987**

Photographs of the young John Henry Hammond make him look like a youth of today. If unsurprising, since the whirligig of fashion has come round again to crisp hair, collar and tie, the coincidence is an indicator of his deeper strengths. He never bothered to change his own style, but used his intelligence, taste, energy and money to promote music and race relations.

Hammond had a comfortable start in life. His father was a banker, railroad executive and lawyer, and his mother was a Vanderbilt. Home was a mansion on East 91st Street, and summers were spent at the family estate at Mount Kisko. Early influences were firmly White Anglo-Saxon Protestant, conservative and dutiful. He described his early self as "...an inheritor of the guilt and therefore the obligations of wealth", and for a while considered entering the ministry. Music, though, was his first and abiding passion, from Rachmaninov to the Original Dixieland Jazzband, "...but the rhythm and creative ingenuity of the jazz players excited me the most. It was not long before I discovered that most of them—certainly all those I liked best—were Black."

Meanwhile, his expensive education had taken him to the exclusive Hotchkiss School in Lakeville, Connecticut. Returning to New York City for weekly violin lessons, he took the opportunity of a little fashionable slumming at such venues as the Harlem Alhambra, where he heard Bessie Smith. He also took to dangerous literature, like the communist *New Masses*, and to philosophy classes on a Sunday. Clearly, the rot had set in. After graduating from Hotchkiss in the summer of 1929, he worked as an apprentice newsman in Maine on the *Portland Evening News*, so broadening his education in journalism, trade unionism, and the civil rights movement. That autumn he entered Yale, and early in 1931, to paternal dismay, he dropped out.

Hammond had his name removed from the Social Register and moved into a modest Greenwich Village apartment. Now 21, he entered the jazz scene as a critic and columnist, contributing to such publications as *Down Beat* magazine, the *Brooklyn Daily Eagle* and the British music paper *Melody Maker*. With his earnings and an annual allowance from family trust funds, he began to subsidize and promote the recording of jazz musicians. In 1932 he acquired the Public Theater on Manhattan's Lower East Side, and began to stage concerts there, featuring notably his early protégé, Fletcher Henderson. That same year he worked as a disc jockey on a New York radio station and furthered the then uncommon practice of featuring racially-mixed bands. In 1933 he became the US recording representative for the British Columbia and Parlophone labels. He befriended an obscure young clarinettist from Chicago, Benny Goodman, and recorded him with a 17-year-old he had discovered in a Harlem speakeasy. "I decided that night that she was the best jazz singer I had ever heard," he said, characteristically forthright. "She" was Billie Holiday. Hammond produced some of her most memorable records, including "A Fine Romance" and "I'll Get By".

On another visit to Chicago, Hammond dug out the young Black pianist Teddy Wilson. Teaming him with Goodman and the drummer Gene Krupa, he organized the Benny Goodman Trio—the first racially integrated jazz group to play publicly for a paying audience. Hammond added the vibra-harpist Lionel Hampton, discovered in downtown Los Angeles, and by 1937, Goodman was being hailed as the "King of Swing".

Twiddling the knobs on his car radio, in the constant search for something worth listening to, Hammond hit a broadcast from the Reno Club, Kansas City, and was "blown away" by a nine-piece band led by one Count Basie. He hurried over and talked the Count into visiting New York, recorded him in October 1933, and brought more strong Black current into the musical mainstream.

Although Hammond had limited success in producing the plays *Little Old Boy* (1933) and *Jaywalker* (1934), he realized a dream with the "Spirituals to Swing" concert at Carnegie Hall in December 1938. Running to plan, it brought together the elements of Black music from early beginnings to contemporary jazz. Sonny Terry, Big Bill Broonzy, Benny Goodman, Sidney Bechet and Sister Rosetta Tharpe, among many others, appeared to resounding acclaim. There was a follow-up the next year featuring Count Basie and another Hammond discovery, the electric guitarist Charlie Christian. It was, according to Hammond, "Very professional and not half so exciting". In 1940 he supervised the recording of *Contrasts*, which Benny Goodman had commissioned from Béla Bartók, and in 1943 he toured the United States to find a Black cast for the Broadway production of *Carmen Jones*.

There was much else too that concerned Hammond during all this time. In the early 1930s he accompanied Edmund Wilson and others to Kentucky in the support of striking miners. In 1933 he went to Alabama to report on the celebrated Scottsboro case, in which nine young Black men were accused of rape, and covered its further proceedings two years later for *New Republic*. He joined the board of directors of the National Association for the Advancement of Colored People (NAACP) in 1935 and stayed with it until 1967, when he resigned in protest against its refusal to take a stand against United States involvement in Vietnam.

Hammond spent World War II with the army's Information and Education Department, getting musicians to entertain the troops. After the war he became less involved with current jazz: "Bop lacked the swing I believe essential to great jazz playing...it defied the jazz verities without improving on them." He resigned from Columbia in 1946, chopped and changed labels, and, until 1952, concentrated on classical music with Mercury Records. From 1953 to 1958 though, he did produce pioneering, high-fidelity records with some of his trusted jazz artists. He also became a lecturer at New York University, and though the baleful eye of Joseph McCarthy inevitably turned his way, no evidence of "subversive activity" was found against him.

In 1959 he returned to Columbia as a staff producer, signed up Pete Seeger, and in 1960 "the most dynamic jazz voice since Billie Holiday"—Aretha Franklin. The next year he identified a back-up guitarist and harmonica player as a "superlative artist...with an acuity of vision of American life". Hammond's colleagues did not share his enthusiasm. He struggled long to keep his find on the label and, eventually, "Hammond's Folly" came good. It was Bob Dylan.

Leonard Cohen joined the roster in 1962, Bruce Springsteen in 1973. By 1975 Hammond was past Columbia's statutory retirement age, but the company kept him on as an independent. He and his wife formed the Snum Music Corporation and in 1975 introduced the young Polish jazz pianist Adam Makowitz. Throughout the 1970s accrued honours made Hammond into the elder statesman. The Newport Jazz Festival, Rutgers Institute of Jazz Studies, Yale University's school of music and New York City's Northside Center for Child Development all called on his expertise. If he was ever bothered about it, he was eventually, finally reassured that The Establishment loved him when in 1979 he was named as head of a commission to make selections for the White House record library.

Despite several heart attacks in the last decade of his life, Hammond persisted with a "compulsion to see, read and hear everything as soon as possible". His reactions were omniverous and intense, his record collection numbered in tens of thousands and he was, by the by, an accomplished violinist. Nat Hentoff's comment in the *Village Voice* is a fitting epitaph: "No non-musician has had anywhere near as fundamental effect on jazz as Hammond, with his big, quick ears and his stubborn zeal in proselytizing his discoveries....'No player can be taught to swing,' says Hammond. And no layman can be taught how to listen like Hammond."

Born John Henry Hammond. **Pseudonym** Henry Johnson. **Parents** John Henry, banker and lawyer, and Emily Vanderbilt (Sloane) Hammond. **Marriage** 1) Jemison McBride, 1941 (divorced, 1948); 2) Esmé O'Brien Sarnoff, 1949. **Children** John Paul, Douglas (died in infancy), Jason. **Education** Private schools in New York, including The Froebel League, St Bernard's School and Browning School; Hotchkiss School, Connecticut, 1924–29; Yale University, 1929–31. **Military service** Information and Education Department, US Army, 1943–46. **Career** Played viola in string quartets, 1928–29; apprentice newspaperman with the *Portland Evening News*, Maine, 1929; recorded and promoted jazz concerts, 1931–32; announcer, programme producer and disc jockey, WEVD radio station, New York, 1932; American recording representative, UK Columbia and Parlophone Company, 1933–36; sales manager, Columbia Masterworks, 1937; associate recording director, Columbia Records, 1939–42, 1946; board of directors, Keystone Records, 1946, president, 1947; recording director, Majestic Records, 1947; vice-president, Mercury Records, 1947–52; producer and director of popular music, Vanguard Records, 1953–58; producer, Columbia Records, 1958–76, director of talent acquisition, 1963, vice-president in charge of talent acquisition, 1973; independent record producer, 1976–87; board chairman, Hammond Music Enterprises, 1982–87. **Related activities** Correspondent, *Gramophone*, 1931–33, *Melody Maker*, 1933–37; music critic, *Brooklyn Daily Eagle*, 1933–35; co-founder, Henry Hammond Incorporated, 1933; produced plays *Little Old Boy*, 1933, and *Jaywalker*, 1934; associate editor, *Melody News*, 1934–35; columnist, *Down Beat*, 1934–41; recording director for Irving Mills, 1934; supervised recordings for Victor, Okeh, Vocalion-Brunswick and other labels, 1935–38; correspondent, *Rhythm*, 1937–39; promoted "Spirituals to Swing" concerts, 1938, 1939, 1967; co-publisher and co-editor, *Music and Rhythm*,

1942–43; casting director, Broadway production of *Carmen Jones*, 1943; lecturer, New York University, 1953–56; board member, Newport Jazz Festival, 1956–70; music editor, *Gentry*, 1956–57; contributor, *Hi-Fi Music at Home*, 1958; consultant, Columbia Records, 1976–87. **Other activities** Wrote for *New York Daily Compass*, 1950–52, *New York Times*, 1953–54, *New York Herald Tribune*, 1955–56, *Saturday Review*, 1958–59, *Nation*, *New Republic*, and *New Masses*, under the pseudonym Henry Johnson. **Offices and memberships** Member, executive board, National Association for the Advancement of Colored People, 1935–67; past president, East Coast chapter, National Academy of Recording Arts and Sciences; vice-president, Newport Jazz Festival; member: board of directors, Rutgers University's Institute of Jazz Studies, Horizon Press, Crisis Publishing Company, Professional Children's School and Northside Center for Child Development, New York City. **Awards and honours** Grammy award for Columbia reissue of Bessie Smith library, 1971; certificate of merit, Yale University School of Music, 1973. **Publications** (with Irving Townsend) *John Hammond on Record* (autobiography), 1977. **Cause of death** Undisclosed, at age 76.

McDONALD HOBLEY

British Actor and Television Presenter

Born **Port Stanley, Falkland Islands, July 1917**

Died **Bournemouth, England, 30 July 1987**

Born in the Falkland Islands, where his father was chaplain of Port Stanley Cathedral, Dennys Jack Valentine McDonald-Hobley came to England to complete his education. After studying at Brighton College he joined the Brighton Theatre Royal repertory company. Before signing on in the army on the outbreak of war in 1939, he had appeared in the musical comedy *No, No, Nanette* on Brighton's West Pier and toured Britain for a year in J.B. Priestley's *Time and the Conways*.

His pre-war acting experience took McDonald Hobley straight into the world of troop entertainment in Southeast Asia, where he served as a captain in the Royal Artillery. Here he attracted the attention of Lord Mountbatten who seconded him to the Southeast Asia Command (SEAC) radio station newly established in Ceylon.

Back home, against stiff competition from 281 other applicants, McDonald Hobley won the coveted job of television presenter: "I thought it would be a good idea to get into it and meet the six producers, and they would get to know me by my first name and I would thereby get employed as an actor when I left TV after six months," was how he later explained this move. But, in fact, it was to be another 20 years before McDonald Hobley finally left television and went back to theatre.

Television, as it re-opened on 7 June 1946 to cover the Victory Parade in London, was a very different animal from the beast we know today. Broadcasting lasted from 8.30 until 10.30 each evening, with the presenters appearing in dinner jackets. Autocues did not exist and all scripts had to be memorized in advance. Television saw itself "as a theatre in the living room for which formalities had to be observed".

As television's first post-war producer, McDonald Hobley's face and name soon became universally well known. He himself told with some amusement a tale of being out with Laurence Olivier and finding that *his* was the autograph everyone wanted. In 1954 he was voted Television

Personality of the Year, and in 1956 lured away to the newly-launched independent ATV company at a vast salary increase—from £25 to £100 a week. For the BBC he had, by this time, covered all the great events of the decade, from the Queen's Coronation to the launch of Eurovision. He had appeared as a sports commentator, chat show host, interviewer and panel game compère.

Independent television was, however, to be a disappointment. Chairing the progamme *Yakity-Yak* was but the first of a number of silly assignments that eventually tried McDonald Hobley's patience to the limit. Feeling that he was forced endlessly to make a fool of himself in essentially mindless programmes, Hobley finally quit in 1967. "There used to be a gag," he said in explanation, "that went 'If the show is wobbly send for Hobley'."

On stage McDonald Hobley had a number of small successes; he appeared in the West End in *No Sex Please—We're British*, toured in *Not Now, Darling*, *Side by Side by Sondheim* and, as one of Denis Thatcher's drinking buddies, in *Anyone for Denis*. At the Thorndike Theatre in 1984 he played the grumpy professor in *On Golden Pond*, and in 1987 took the lead role in *Forty Years On*.

McDonald Hobley seems to have been one of those rare people who remain, or appear to remain, largely unaffected by public acclaim. His easy, relaxed manner was the same both on and off the television screen. Sylvia Peters, Hobley's fellow presenter at the BBC, testified to the sincerity of his charm. She also recalled with admiration the cool way in which he would sit on his script, and the unruffled way he would refer to it if he should "dry up" in front of the cameras. Dismissing his own fame, McDonald Hobley himself assured one newspaper interviewer that, "if you pick your nose often enough on TV, and often if you pick your nose badly, you will become a TV personality".

Born Dennys Jack Valentine McDonald-Hobley. **Father** Naval chaplain, Port Stanley, Falkland Islands. **Marriages** First two ended in divorce; third to Pauline Garner, actress. **Education** In South America and at Brighton College. **Military service** Captain, Royal Artillery during World War II, including work for forces radio station in Ceylon. **Career** Actor, television announcer and personality; began in repertory at Brighton Theatre Royal; toured in J.B. Priestley's *Time and the Conways*; continuity announcer, BBC, 1946–56; commentator, ATV television, 1956–59; chairman, *Yakity-Yak*, ITV; chairman, *Does the Team Think?*, BBC Radio, 1958–1976; many other television roles; returned to stage, 1967. **Awards and honours** TV Personality of the Year, 1954. **Stage** Toured in plays, musicals and pantomimes in the UK and abroad, including *No, No, Nanette*, *Time and the Conways*, *Not Now Darling*, *Side by Side by Sondheim*, *No Sex Please—We're British*, *The Dresser*, *She Stoops to Conquer*, *Twelfth Night*, *On Golden Pond*, *Forty Years On*. **Cause of death** Undisclosed, at age 70.

R.J. HOPPER

British Historian and Archaeologist
***Born* Cardiff, Wales, 13 August 1910**
***Died* Sheffield, England, 3 July 1987**

Robert John Hopper was a leading figure in the study of ancient history in the post-war period. During his many years at Sheffield University he was responsible for the development of his subject from an off-shoot of classics and archaeology into a separate discipline, attracting many keen students to the steel city's university. He was educated at Mount Radford School in Exeter and read classics at Swansea University before going to Gonville and Caius College, Cambridge, on a Welsh Studentship. It was at Cambridge that he developed his interest in classical Greek archaeology and history, receiving a PhD for his thesis on the foreign trade of classical Athens, part of which he researched while a fellow of the British School of archaeology in Athens.

He travelled widely in Greece and the Near East before taking up a post as lecturer in classics at the University of Wales in Aberystwyth. He married in 1939, to another former student of the British School, and looked set for a long career. World War II, however, interrupted his plans. From 1941 to 1945 Hopper was a serving soldier in the Royal Welch Fusiliers, attached to the Intelligence Corps. He rose to the rank of company sergeant major, serving in British Guiana, Italy and Austria.

After the war he returned to Aberystwyth but did not stay long. In 1947 he succeeded A.M. Woodward as sole lecturer in ancient history at Sheffield. Here, he was required to teach Greek and Roman history to a growing number of students, a task he undertook with considerable zest and skill. He earned great respect for his subject within the university, enabling him to expand his department, especially during his time as dean of the Faculty of Arts. The changes he made reflected both his own increasing expertise in ancient history and a general move away from the traditional classics department of British universities, with their emphasis on Greek and Latin language and literature, towards schools of ancient history and archaeology. Ancient history offered a more comprehensive approach to the study of classical civilizations, due in no small way to the stimulus provided by the work of two Jewish scholars who established themselves in England in the 1950s and changed the face of ancient history. Arnaldo Momigliano (q.v.) in London and Moses Finley in Cambridge encouraged ancient historians away from their traditional concern with political élites and made them look at the cultural, social and economic ideas and institutions which supported them.

Hopper's work proceeded in this new direction from an early stage. He studied the social and political institutions of the Athenians, and then proceeded to examine their economic context. His work on the Athenian silver mines at Laurion combined the disciplines of geology, metallurgy, archaeology, epigraphy and philology. It led to a fuller appreciation of the workings and significance of the mines which financed Athens' fleet of triremes, victorious against the Persians at the battle of Salamis. After this he continued to work on trade and manufacture in Attica. The Laurion study was published at length in the *Annual* of the British School at Athens. Hopper served twice as editor of this important periodical and devoted a great deal of time and effort to his position as trustee of the school. He was also a regular contributor to the *Classical Review*, assessing a wide variety of new books. In 1964 he published a re-edited version of J.C. Stobart's *The Glory That Was Greece*. It was a highly successful revision of the 50-year-old classic and became a best seller both in Britain and the United States.

Towards the end of his university career a lighter burden of teaching and other duties left him free to complete several major books. *The Acropolis* (1971) was a general study which gave due weight to the neglected pre-classical period. This was also the subject of his book *The Early Greeks*, an excellent introduction to the Greeks before the "classical" period. Both books demonstrated his ability to convey the results of scholarly research in clear, plain language for a general readership. His latest, and most widely read book, *Trade and Industry in Classical Greece*, was the result of many years' study of the economic life of Athens and the other major Greek cities. It immediately became a definitive work and made a fitting culmination to his distinguished career.

Born Robert John Hopper. **Parents** Robert and Alice Hopper. **Marriage** Henriette Kiernan, 1939. **Education** Mount Radford School, Exeter; University of Wales, Swansea; Gonville and Caius College, Cambridge, PhD. **Military service** Royal Welch Fusiliers and Intelligence Corps, 1941–45. **Career** Historian of the ancient world; Macmillan Student of British School, Athens, 1935–37; lecturer, University College of Wales, Aberystwyth, 1938–41, 1945–57; lecturer, University of Sheffield, 1947–55, professor, 1955–75, professor emeritus, 1975–87, dean, Faculty of Arts, 1967–70. **Related activities** Trustee and editor of *Annual*, British School of Archaeology, Athens, for two years. **Awards and honours** Fellow: University of Wales (in Athens and Rome), 1936–38, Royal Numismatic Society, 1949, Society of Antiquaries, 1951. **Publications** (editor) John Clarke Stobart, *The Glory That Was Greece: A Survey of Hellenic Culture and Civilization*, fourth edition, London, 1971; *The Acropolis*, London, 1971; *The Early Greeks*, London, 1976, New York, 1977; *Trade and Industry in Classical Greece*, London, 1979; frequent contributor to *Classical Review*. **Cause of death** Undisclosed, at age 76.

TRAVIS JACKSON

American Baseball Player

Born **Waldo, Arkansas, 2 November 1903**

Died **Waldo, Arkansas, 27 July 1987**

The words "gritty" and "determined" could have been invented specifically to describe baseball players like Travis "Stonewall" Jackson who, despite being plagued by recurrent knee injuries ever since his college days, excelled at shortstop, became a favourite of the fans, and finally—in 1982—was inducted to the Hall of Fame.

Born in Waldo, Arkansas, in 1903, Jackson starred on the Ouachita College baseball team, where he first picked up the knee injury which was to trouble him for the rest of his playing days. He began his professional career in 1921 with the Little Rock Travelers of the Southern Association. Its manager, Norman "Kid" Elberfield, arranged for the New York Giants' manager, John McGraw, to see Jackson play; and 60 years later, Jackson himself recalled how fortunate he was to make the Major Leagues: "I guess I set a world record for errors. I had a pretty good arm, see, but I didn't have much control," joked Jackson. "The people in the first-base and right-field bleachers knew me. When the ball was hit to me they scattered. 'Watch out! He's got it again'!" But McGraw, who earned his pick of the Little Rock squad by loaning the

Travelers a player for the 1922 season, stuck by his original selection and was quickly vindicated once Jackson got his arm under control.

Jackson went hitless in his two appearances at the plate in his initial game with the Giants, but was soon pulling his weight with the bat. A great bunter, he also possessed a surprisingly powerful swing and finished his career with a total of 135 home runs—several of them dramatic, game-winning blows. He hit over .300 six times, recorded a career high of .339 in 1930, and ended his career with a .291 average.

But it was in the field, at shortstop, that Jackson truly earned his niche in baseball history. He became the Giants' regular shortstop in 1924, and, despite reinjuring his knee the following season, played with no other Major League team in a career that was to last 15 years. Jackson possessed a powerful arm and great range, and—for most of his career—was considered the best player at his position in the National League. Not surprisingly, the Giants' fans loved the 5 foot 10-inch, 163-pound shortstop who captained their team in 1936. And in 1982—exactly 60 years after he had entered the Major League—the man they nicknamed "Stonewall", or "Stoney", was finally named to baseball's Hall of Fame.

A further injury in 1932 foreshadowed the end of Jackson's career and his knee problems forced him to shift to third base for the 1935 and 1936 seasons. He retired from playing at the end of the 1936 season and managed a Giants' farm team in Jersey City until 1938, when he became the Giants' coach. Tuberculosis sidelined him for five years, but he returned as the Giants' coach in 1947, and before retiring in 1961, he managed eleven other minor league clubs—mostly in the Milwaukee Braves' farm system.

Travis Jackson is nevertheless best remembered for his work at shortstop, and writer Arnold Hano painted a clear picture of this popular, workmanlike player when he wrote: "All through his career, one picture remains vivid, and that is the lean, dark-haired young man gliding to his right and rifling out runners at first."

Born Travis Calvin Jackson. **Marriage** Mary Blackman, 1928. **Children** Dorothy Fincher and William Travis Jackson. **Education** Ouachita Baptist College. **Career** Baseball player; shortstop: Little Rock Travelers, Southern Association, 1921, New York Giants, National League, 1922–36; manager, Giants AAA farm team, Jersey City, New Jersey, 1937–38; coach, New York Giants, 1938–40, 1947–48; managed eleven other minor league clubs, mostly in Milwaukee Braves farm system, including Jackson, Mississippi, 1946, Tampa, Florida, 1949, Owensboro, Kentucky, 1950, Bluefield, West Virginia, and Hartford, Connecticut, 1951, Appleton, Wisconsin, 1952–53, Lawton, Oklahoma, 1954–57, Midland, Texas, 1958, Eau Claire, Wisconsin, 1959, Quad-City, 1960; retired 1961. **Career statistics** Played 1656 games, four World Series; batted .291; 1768 hits, 291 doubles, 135 home runs, 921 runs batted in. **Awards and honours** Elected, National Baseball Hall of Fame, 1983. **Cause of death** Alzheimer's disease, at age 83.

JACOB KAPLAN

American Financier and Philanthropist

***Born* Lowell, Massachusetts, 23 December 1891**

***Died* New York City, New York, 18 July 1987**

Jacob Merrill Kaplan exemplified the American dream. He was the poor boy who fought his way up the economic ladder with vigour, yet became a man of compassion, never forgetting his origins nor what it felt like to be poor and in need—of food, of education, of material and non-material opportunities. He knew that while man needs bread, bread alone is insufficient. He also knew that people cannot exist in isolation. They have to be supportive of each other.

Kaplan's childhood was one of poverty but, from an early age, he found a way to contribute to the family budget—by peddling soap in the streets of Boston. He attended public schools in the city but left at the age of 16 to go to Latin America, where he founded the beginnings of his fortune. Little has been written about how he got his start but his entrepreneurial abilities took him into the molasses industry and, by the age of 19, he was helping sugar planters to organize themselves into cooperatives which, of course, enabled them to maximize profits with minimal capital outlay. Within ten years he had joined the Oldetyme Molasses Company, later serving as president. He continued as president following a merger with Dunbar Molasses until the company was sold in 1928.

After a number of other financial ventures, he joined the Welch Grape Juice Company, where he translated his cooperative ideas into use by the grape growers. In the 1940s he took over the company, following his reorganization of it, and headed it for the following 19 years.

Although the origins of his fortune derived from his work in Latin America, the bulk came from the Juice Company and enabled him, in 1947, to establish the J.M. Kaplan Fund. In the early years, at least, the massive revenue emanating from the fund was devoted to making New York, a city so greatly loved by Kaplan throughout his life, a better place in which to live and work.

Inventiveness and diversity were the hallmarks of his philanthropy throughout his life. The fund supported not only the arts but also humanitarian causes, such as civil liberties, human rights, legal defence, education, environmental and housing projects. Donations could be outright funding or "seed money" enabling, say, musicians to commission works from chosen composers, or for the New York Botanical Garden to save a grove of virgin hemlock from extinction in the Bronx. Money was channelled into improvements in city parks, into vital youth programmes, into the Fund for Free Expression, into the Straphangers and went towards saving Carnegie Hall from demolition.

Funding was found for a housing development for artists, for the 42nd Local Development Corporation, for the New School's Center for New York Affairs, for a synagogue, for the Coalition for the Homeless, for a women and children's refuge in Brooklyn, and for non-profit-making book shops. More money went, over the years, into campaigning work: for better public transport facilities, for preservation and rebuilding programmes, for waterfront reclamation, and for many other urban amenities. The money was always directed to the improvement of the quality of life for everyone, and to helping those in need, regardless of age or background.

In 1986, utilizing the techniques he had developed with the sugar planters in Latin America, Kaplan initiated a massive $1 million nationwide fund to promote housing cooperatives for elderly people living in areas where funding for such housing was not forthcoming from public or private sources. This may have been prompted by the realization of his own good fortune in terms of both finance and sound health, and also the knowledge that public housing provision for the elderly in the US is patchy, to say the least. In response to questions of doubt as to their viability, he responded, "If they are efficient, there's no reason why [they] cannot work," adding, as he had doubtless done throughout his life, "I'll help."

Kaplan's ideas and ideals were enthusiastically supported by his family and his daughter took over the presidency of the fund as he entered his ninetieth decade. But his interest and enthusiasm never left him and, looking a little like an older David Niven, many mornings saw him walking jauntily to the fund's Madison Avenue office from his Manhattan apartment—taking in an inexpensive breakfast at the General Motors Building on his way.

He remained alert until the end. Only the year before his death—still upright and twinkling with an avuncular smile—he told people, "I still believe there is a meaning to human existence but I do not know anyone who can prove the answer. I still wonder the purpose and destiny [of humanity]."

He may not have been able to answer the question in words but there is no doubt that he answered it in the manner of his life, nor that New York owes him a tremendous debt of thanks. His legacy to the city lives on.

Born Jacob Merrill Kaplan. **Parents** David and Fanny Kaplan. **Marriage** Alice Manheim, 1925. **Children** Elizabeth, Mary Ellen and one other daughter; one son, Richard. **Education** Public schools around Boston. **Career** Began working as an organizer on sugar plantations, 1910; president, Dunbar Molasses and of Oldetyme Molasses Company prior to merger with Dunbar, 1920–28; president, Jemkap Incorporated, 1930–87; organizer, president and owner, Welch Grape Juice Company, 1940–58. **Related activities** President and chairman, Hearn Department Stores, 1932–36. **Other activities** Founder and trustee, J.M. Kaplan Fund Incorporated, 1947–87, providing support mainly for New York-based organizations, including NAACP Legal Defense and Education Fund, Municipal Art Society and Parks Council, New York Landmarks Conservancy, Natural Resources Defense Council, South Bronx 2000 Local Development Corporation, Fund for Free Expression, Straphangers, Westbeth Artists' Housing, 42nd Local Development Corporation, New School's Center for New York City Affairs, Eldrich Street Synagogue, Carnegie Hall, National Coalition for the Homeless, and the Chips Center for women and children in Brooklyn; founded the Kaplan Cooperative Fund, to promote cooperative housing for the elderly. **Offices and memberships** Trustee, Freedom House; past chairman of board of trustees, New School. **Cause of death** Undisclosed, at age 95.

JACK LESCOULIE

American Television Personality

***Born* Sacramento, California, 1912**

***Died* Memphis, Tennessee, 22 July 1987**

When *Today*, NBC-TV's popular morning interview programme, first went on the air in January 1952, Jack Lescoulie spoke its opening words. Dubbed "the saver" for his uncanny ability to enliven flagging interviews with injections of quick wit and wisdom, he remained with the show for nearly 15 years, serving as co-host first with commentator Dave Garroway and then with

Hugh Downs. His popularity was such that when he left the programme in 1961 to anchor a children's educational series, thousands of *Today* viewers wrote in to protest his absence. He rejoined the show the following year.

Born in Sacramento, Lescoulie launched his show business career at the age of seven, when he appeared in his parents' vaudeville act in Los Angeles. After finishing high school, he remained on the West Coast, taking up an announcer's job at KGFJ Radio and studying acting at the Pasadena Playhouse. Before abandoning the theatre world for broadcasting, he appeared in a handful of plays—some of which he accompanied to Broadway—and acted in a series of movie westerns entitled *The Three Mesquiteers*. One of his oddest Broadway assignments—anticipating the lighthearted antics of his NBC days—involved standing offstage and delivering an elephant's bellow.

Following World War II service as an Army Air Force combat reporter in Italy, Lescoulie returned to New York and soon joined forces with actor Gene Rayburn to create the *Jack and Gene Show*, an early-morning programme broadcast on WOR Radio. He had his first brush with television in 1949, when he was offered a starring role in an ABC dramatic anthology, and went on to work as a producer with CBS-TV in the early 1950s. Then, in 1952, NBC launched *Today*, and he was asked to serve as the programme's co-host alongside Dave Garroway. For more than nine years the dynamic team covered sports, light news and features, capturing the loyalty and admiration of millions of American viewers. Lescoulie's blond good looks and pleasant humour earned him a reputation as the all-American boy, and he frequently found himself performing silly tasks that endeared him to the audience. These included wrestling a walrus, interviewing a penguin and engaging in a rigorous breakfast-eating marathon.

Despite his commitments with *Today*, Lescoulie made time for a host of other television projects in the 1950s. In addition to making a string of commercials for Milton Berle, he announced for *The Jackie Gleason Show*, acted as host of an NBC sports-interview series called *Meet the Champions*, and in 1958, served as co-host of the *Brains and Brawn* quiz programme. In 1957, when NBC introduced an experimental late-night entry to replace the *Tonight* show—called *Tonight: America After Dark*—he agreed to host it.

When *Today* went live in 1961, Lescoulie resigned his long-standing morning job and accepted a position as co-host of the *1,2,3—Go!* children's series with then-schoolboy Richard Thomas. Then came the deluge of viewers' letters, convincing him to return to *Today* the following year. Teamed this time with Hugh Downs, Lescoulie remained there until 1967, still specializing in humorous stunts and lively commentary. His next post, with Avco Broadcasting in Cincinnati, allowed him to escape the hubbub of New York and at the same time to participate in a wide variety of broadcasting projects. These ranged from making commercial voice-overs to substituting for vacationing talk-show hosts to anchoring the company's annual radio and TV broadcasts from the Ohio State Fair. His last television appearance was on the *Today* show's 35th anniversary special, six months before cancer claimed his life.

Born Jack Lescoulie. **Parents** Vaudeville performers. **Marriage** Virginia. **Children** One daughter, Linda Ann, and one son, John Philip. **Military service** Army Air Force combat reporter in Italy, World War II. **Career** Actor and broadcaster; studied acting at Pasadena Playhouse; acted briefly on Broadway; appeared in series of movie westerns, *The Three Mesquiteers*; after war service performed on radio in New York with Gene Rayburn in *The Jack and Gene Show*; appeared in dramatic anthology for ABC, 1949; CBS producer, 1950–51; co-host (with Dave Garroway and later, Hugh Downs) *The Today Show*, NBC, 1952–61, 1962–67; host, *Meet the Champions*, NBC; host, *Tonight: America After Dark*, NBC, 1957; co-host, *Brains and Brawn*, NBC, 1958; host, *1,2,3—Go* (children's programme), NBC, 1961–62; joined Avco

Broadcasting, Ohio, 1967; many other appearances and commercial voice-overs. **Related activities** Announcer for Jackie Gleason; commercials for Milton Berle. **Cause of death** Colon cancer, at age 75.

JOSEPH E. LEVINE

American Film Producer

Born **Boston, Massachusetts, 9 September 1905**

Died **Greenwich, Connecticut, 31 July 1987**

Levine was often called the last of the movie moguls. He was actually the first of a kind, for when the traditional Hollywood studio system died out with the emergence of television, a new breed of independents entered—with the pioneer, Joseph E. Levine. He was a master showman, who knew more about the art of promotion than anyone in the business.

Levine was born into poverty, and his youth was often shadowed by anti-Semitism, a background which nearly all the Hollywood studio heads had shared. His father died when Levine was four. He quit school at 14 and went to work selling papers and shining shoes. This was followed by a stint as a driving instructor, then he sold religious artefacts to followers of a Harlem evangelist, "Daddy" Grace, worked in a garment factory, ran a dress shop with his brother and was a restaurant operator. In the late 1920s he borrowed $4000 and bought the Lincoln Arts Theater. His first venture into films was in 1945, when he co-produced *Gaslight Follies*, a compilation of silent film clips released under his own Embassy Pictures name. Like his previous purchase, which was a batch of B westerns, this did not make a great profit; however, a decade later, his purchase of a sex hygiene film, *Body Beautiful*, did. With the profits he bought a small cinema where he offered an irresistible double bill: Julien Duvivier's classic *Un Carnet de Bal* plus *How to Undress in Front of Your Husband*. He bought up for next to nothing foreign-made epics with sex, horror and plenty of spectacle, had them dubbed into English, and with flair, energy and money, *promoted*. He bought *Godzilla*, for example, for $12,000 (1956), promoted it with a borrowed $400,000, and the film then grossed $1 million at the box office.

Levine was teaching the Hollywood machine how to sell its product, and nobody liked him for it, although he was secretly admired. In 1959 he offered the Italian "sand, spear and beefcake" epic *Hercules*, starring the California weightlifter Steve Reeves. It was rejected by every major studio. Levine loved "the glowing and vivid colors", bought the American rights for $150,000, and spent nearly double that for publicity. The film made more than $10 million. More Bible-theme epics, such as *Sodom and Gomorrah*, came and conquered—then Levine switched to Italy. His production in the US of *Two Women*, which earned Sophia Loren the first Oscar for a foreign actress in a foreign-language film, revolutionized the "art film" business. While the story of two women displaced from their home in a small, war-torn town did big business in the art houses, Levine launched a campaign for Loren within the industry itself. It worked; in fact, it is possible that Loren would never have received her Oscar otherwise. His purchase of *Boccaccio '70*, Fellini's *8½*, *Marriage Italian Style* and many other films revitalized the Italian film industry, earning Levine not only several Italian medals but, in 1964, a private audience with the Pope. In addition, his production relationship with Italy's Carlo Ponti resulted in a score of other classic films released by Embassy, from Jean-Luc Godard's *Contempt* and Claude Chabrol's *Landru*, to Vittorio De Sica's *Sunflower* and Ingmar Bergman's *Devil's Wanton*.

Levine released other countries' films as well, including Germany's *Bimbo the Great* (not a huge success), Czechoslovakia's *The Fabulous World of Jules Verne*, and many others, releasing and co-producing with other major companies like Warner Brothers and 20th Century-Fox. Other major successes back home were *The Carpetbaggers* (1964), *Zulu* (1965), De Sica's charming *Woman Times Seven* (1966) and *Darling*, the most important British film of 1965, which earned an Oscar for Julie Christie.

Levine had a gift for spotting talent in directors and actors alike. He rescued Mike Nichols from off-Broadway obscurity and had him direct *The Graduate*, both Nichols' and Levine's greatest success. (Nichols had never directed a film before.) He also found talent in an unknown stage manager named Dustin Hoffman to play the lead role, and insisted on using Anne Bancroft when other people, including the director, wanted a foreign actress for the worldly-wise Mrs Robinson. Another of Levine's "finds" was Mel Brooks, who had not been able to attract backers for *The Producers* (1967). According to Levine, "He was a very funny kind of guy—kind of a nut." Levine's fruitful partnership with Richard Attenborough, who, until then, had directed only *Oh! What a Lovely War* and *Young Winston* (both hardly money-spinners), produced the monumental *A Bridge Too Far* (1977). It took two and a half years to make at a cost of $25 million to cinematize. The film used 146 locations, all under Levine's eye. As usual, he reserved the right to the final cut; that eye was unerring, and only Nichols was allowed to get away with the final. Levine paid several stars small fortunes to appear for only a few minutes on screen; for the amount of money he was putting into *Bridge's* promotion, the credits list on the advertising had to be splendid.

Levine also built the Festival and Lincoln Arts Cinema in New York and became a major shareholder in Paramount Pictures. He maintained that his biggest error of judgement was in 1967, when he sold Embassy Pictures to the Avco Corporation of America (for $40 million), although he remained chief executive/president of Avco. During this time, he produced his favourite film ("a wonderful success, both spiritually and financially"), *The Lion in Winter*, starring Peter O'Toole and Katharine Hepburn. However, Levine was basically a loner; after six years of being Avco–Embassy's head, he left to set up his own independent company. Among his most successful productions for this new concern were *Soldier Blue* (1970) and *Night Porter* (1975) with Dirk Bogarde and Charlotte Rampling.

It must be noted that Levine was also capable of producing losers, among them *Generation*, *Stiletto*, *Don't Drink the Water*, *C.C. and Company*, *Day of the Dolphin* and others. But he always argued forcefully that if a film had a good, solid story, established actors and an international flavour, it had a good chance of being successful. He produced or presented over 500 films in his career, so it can be said that his formula was generally sound.

Privately, rather a mild and shy man, Levine loved Impressionist paintings and collected a fine series of them, as well as a good number of walking sticks. He freely gave of his time and talents to many humanitarian projects. Forever optimistic and enthusiastic, he was loyal to friends and employees, and received countless awards from the cinema industry. "It's all an art form," Levine once said of his producing acumen. "Someone's got to have instinct...I had confidence in my judgements."

Born Joseph Edward Levine. **Father** Russian immigrant tailor. **Marriage** Rosalie Harrison, singer, 1939. **Children** Tricia and Richard. **Career** Newspaper seller; shoeshine boy; garment factory worker; salesman; café manager; first entered film business through buying New England rights to group of B westerns for $4000, also buying the Lincoln Theater, late 1930s; became small-scale film exhibitor, owning seven cinemas, including three drive-ins; became involved in distribution, early 1940s; first production (with Maxwell Finn), *Gaslight Follies*, 1945; area sub-distributor for American–International Pictures, early 1950s; established own company, Embassy Pictures, with *Godzilla: King of the Monsters*, 1956; went on to distribute and produce scores of films; sold Embassy Pictures to Avco Corporation, 1967, remaining chief executive officer of the new Avco–Embassy company; resigned to form Joseph E. Levine Presents, 1972. **Awards and honours** Numerous awards from theatre owners' associations; six honorary degrees, including Emmerson College, 1968; Harvard Business School Communications, Arts and Entertainments Club "Man of the Year", 1978. **Films** Over 500 as producer and/or distributor, including: *Body Beautiful*, early 1940s; *Open City*, early 1940s; *Paisan*, early 1940s; *The Bicycle Thief*, early 1940s; *Gaslight Follies*, 1945; *Night Is My Future*, 1948 (released, 1962); *The Devil's Wanton*, 1949 (released, 1962); *Love Is Better Than Ever/Light Fantastic*, 1951; *Godzilla: King of the Monsters*, 1956; *Attila*, 1958; *Jack the Ripper*, 1958; *Hercules*, 1959; *Hercules Unchained*, 1960; *The Hellfire Club*, 1960; *Fury at Smuggler's Bay*, 1960; *What a Carve Up!*, 1961; *Two Women*, 1961; *Salvatore Giuliano*, 1961; *Bimbo the Great*, 1961; *The Fabulous World of Jules Verne*, 1961; *The Wonders of Aladdin*, 1961; *Morgan the Pirate*, 1961; *The Thief of Baghdad*, 1961; *Boccaccio '70*, 1962; *Divorce Italian Style*, 1962; *Sodom and Gomorrah*, 1962; *Landru*, 1962; *The Conjugal Bed*, 1962; *The Sky Above, the Mud Below* (documentary), 1962; *Boy's Night Out*, 1962; *The Easy Life*, 1963; *8½*, 1963; *A Face in the Rain*, 1963; *Yesterday, Today and Tomorrow*, 1963; *The Carpetbaggers*, 1964; *The Empty Canvas*, 1964; *A House Is Not a Home*, 1964; *Where Love Has Gone*, 1964; *Darling*, 1965; *The Tenth Victim*, 1965; *Zulu*, 1965; *Dingaka*, 1965; *The Sands of the Kalahari*, 1965; *Harlow*, 1965; *Nevada Smith*, 1966; *The Idol*, 1966; *The Spy With a Cold Nose*, 1966; *The Oscar*, 1966; *The Caper of the Golden Bulls*, 1966; *Woman Times Seven*, 1967; *The Producers*, 1967; *The Graduate*, 1967; *Robbery*, 1967; *The Lion in Winter*, 1968; *Romeo and Juliet*, 1968; *Baby Love*, 1968; *A Nice Girl Like Me*, 1969; *Stiletto*, 1969; *Generation*, 1969; *The Man Who Had Power Over Women*, 1970; *The People Next Door*, 1970; *Macho Callahan*, 1970; *Promise at Dawn*, 1970; *Soldier Blue*, 1970; *The Adventurers*, 1970; *Carnal Knowledge*, 1971; *Arruza*, 1972; *Thumb Tripping*, 1972; *They Call Me Trinity*, 1972; *The Ruling Class*, 1972; *The Day of the Dolphin*, 1973; *Paper Tiger*, 1975; *The Night Porter*, 1975; *Casanova '70*, 1976; *A Bridge too Far*, 1977; *Magic*, 1978; *Tattoo*, 1981; also produced: *The Ape Woman*, *Contempt*, *Sunflower*, *Only One New York*, *The Second Best Secret Agent in the Whole Wide World*, *Strangers in the City*, *And Now My Love*, *Santa Claus Conquers the Martians*, *Git!*, *A Man Called Adam*, *Don't Drink the Water*, *C.C. and Company*. **Cause of death** Undisclosed, at age 81.

HOWARD McGHEE

American Jazz Musician

Born **Tulsa, Oklahoma, 6 March 1918**

Died **New York City, New York, 17 July 1987**

For many Swing Era musicians, the advent of bop in the mid-1940s was a nightmare, an alien sound transplanted right into the core of jazz and rapidly taking over its whole body. Yet for trumpeter Howard McGhee, the new music was simply "a relief...to hear somebody doing something different". That relief, however, was not without its considerable personal problems.

Although born in Tulsa, Oklahoma, McGhee moved north to Detroit with his family when he was still a child. His half-brother, a guitarist, turned him on to music, and it was at the famous Cass Technical High School that he learned to play clarinet, tenor saxophone and piano, giving him a wide-ranging musical education that was to stand him in good stead in later life. He quit school at the age of 15 and played tenor with a band touring his old home state of Oklahoma, but a year later, back in Detroit, he heard Louis Armstrong play at the Greystone Ballroom and he was immediately hooked on the trumpet.

To start with, his technique was shaky, and his first engagement in 1935 lasted only three months before he was asked to leave the band. But after intensive practice with local bands, McGhee re-emerged in 1941 in a top-flight outfit, playing with Lionel Hampton's band. He soon joined Andy Kirk as principal soloist, as well as providing compositions and arrangements for the band, before working with Charlie Barnett, Kirk again, Georgie Auld, Count Basie and then Coleman Hawkins, with whom he went to the West Coast in 1944. By this time, McGhee was a major soloist and stylist in his own right, with a steady swing and an authoritative and rhythmic, sometimes riff-based, approach that alternated with a vein of pure lyricism.

While the preceding list of engagements might suggest a trumpeter firmly in the swing tradition, McGhee was also alive to the new music of bop. For while in New York in 1942, he had participated in the many jam sessions at Minton's Playhouse and Monroe's Uptown House that gave birth to the new style. McGhee was thus well placed to bridge the stylistic divide between old and new, as can be seen on the Andy Kirk number "McGhee Special", recorded in 1942, where his trumpet playing harks back to the playing of Armstrong and Roy Eldridge, but also makes more than a nod towards the developing bop style of his contemporary, Dizzy Gillespie. Between 1945 and 1947 he led his own group in Los Angeles, that for a time included Charlie Parker. Eventful sessions with Parker in 1946 and 1947—one of which, "Lover Man", was originally issued under McGhee's name—and Coleman Hawkins, and touring with the Just Jazz and the Jazz at the Philharmonic packages put McGhee in the forefront of modern jazz. He took his own group to the 1948 Paris Jazz Festival and was deservedly named "Trumpeter of the Year" by *Down Beat* magazine in 1949, for by this time he was one of the most recorded and most highly regarded musicians of the bop era.

One session, recorded in 1949, typifies the distance McGhee had travelled and also the limits of that journey. "Double Talk" features McGhee with fellow trumpeter Fats Navarro, a colleague from Andy Kirk's band. There is considerable creative friction between Navarro's total bebop style and McGhee's bravura transitional approach that is, to quote critic Chris Sheridan, "bebop informed by smoke from earlier fires".

In 1950 McGhee looked to be at the top of his profession, but then things went terribly wrong. He took a big band on the road at a time when big bands were bad business and lost $18,000. Further problems then arose, complicated by his increasing drug addiction, and by 1952 McGhee had almost dropped out of sight. In the seven years to 1959, he recorded less than in 1945 alone.

Lesser men would have gone under. McGhee had already had a tough life, losing an eye in a childhood accident, which is why he always wore dark glasses, and like many Black musicians he had suffered considerable prejudice, as when his wife was beaten up and he was framed on a dope charge because she was White. Yet he fought back. He played frequently during the 1960s, having a second and more successful stab at putting together a big band in 1966, and even worked with Duke Ellington for a short time in 1965. He became a regular on the festival circuit and worked in a group with J.J. Johnson and Sonny Stitt which toured Europe. Yet his recovery was fragile, and his confidence largely gone. In later years his tone was thinner, almost brittle, although it remained as agile as ever, facets that could be traced back to his early playing on the clarinet. His final records, notably a session with saxophonist Teddy Edwards, are rather poignant, for they lack the consistency of his earlier work.

At his best, McGhee was "a fat-toned, brilliantly flighted bebop soloist with a romantic heart" who managed a compromise between the rhythmic approach of the swing era and the long lines of bebop. He thus ensured that the modern jazz trumpet retained its singing quality and melodic majesty. As critic Nat Hentoff remarked, McGhee was "a unique example of a jazzman who spanned several stylistic eras, adapting himself to each one while retaining an intensely personal tone and conception".

Born Howard B. McGhee. **Education** Cass Technical High School, Detroit. **Career** Played clarinet and tenor saxophone before taking up trumpet, 1935; played with local mid- and northwest bands, 1935–41; joined Lionel Hampton, 1941; principal soloist, composer and arranger, Andy Kirk band, 1941–42; jam sessions, Minton's Playhouse and Monroe's Uptown House, 1942; Charlie Barnet band, 1942–43; Andy Kirk band, 1943–44; Count Basie band, 1944; Georgie Auld band, 1944; Coleman Hawkins band, 1945; Jazz at the Philharmonic tour, 1947–49; Paris jazz festival, 1948; inactive, 1950–60; participated in many tours and jazz festivals, 1960 onwards; formed own band, 1966. **Awards and honours** Trumpeter of the Year, *Down Beat* readers' poll, 1949. **Recordings** (as leader, include) "Bebop", Dial 1007, 1946; "Dialated Pupils"/"Midnight at Minton's", Dial 1011, 1946; "Dorothy"/"Night Mist", Dial 1027, 1947; "Double Talk", BN 557, 1948; *The Howard McGhee Sextet with Milt Jackson*, Savoy 12026, 1948; (with T. Edwards) *Together Again*, Cont 7588, 1961; *Cookin' Time*, Zim 2004, 1966. **Recordings** (as sideman, include) (with Andy Kirk) "McGhee Special", Decca 4405, 1942; (with Coleman Hawkins) "Sportsman's Hop"/"Ready for Love", Asch 3533, 1945; "Too Much of a Good Thing"/"Bean Soup", Cap 15855, 1945; Jazz at the Philharmonic: "How High the Moon", Asch 4531-2, 1945; (with Lester Young) "Jammin' with Lester", Ala 128, 1946; (with Charlie Parker) "Lover Man", Dial 1007, 1947; "Relaxin' at Camarillo", Dial 1012, 1947; *Dixieland vs. Birdland*, MGM; one track with Coleman Hawkins in *History of Jazz*, Cap; *Jazz: South Pacific*, Reg; *Jazztime, USA*, Bruns; *Jingles All the Way*, Lib. **Cause of death** Undisclosed, at age 69.

DON McMAHON

American Baseball Player

***Born* Brooklyn, New York, 1930**

***Died* Los Angeles, California, 22 July 1987**

Former All Star pitcher Don McMahon used to joke: "When I go, bury me out on the mound. Dig a hole out there and put me in it." The irony of it is that he almost got his way.

McMahon suffered a heart attack on the pitchers' mound at Dodger Stadium, Los Angeles, doing what he loved to do. As a small boy in Brooklyn, for 18 years as a professional in the Major Leagues, and for almost ten more years as a pitching coach, McMahon had loved throwing a baseball. He collapsed while pitching batting practice to the Dodgers' pitchers; and, despite being rushed to hospital, he died, aged 57.

As a schoolboy in Brooklyn, McMahon pitched for Erasmus Hall High where he was joined on the team by Al Davis—himself, later to become the owner of the Los Angeles Raiders. "Don was like an artist who leaves behind the work he did," said Davis. "He wasn't in it for profit or glory. He played baseball because he had a dream."

It was Davis who helped McMahon to get his job as a scout, coach and "eye in the sky" (someone who sits in the press box and charts where the hits go) with the Dodgers. The story goes that Davis was in a Los Angeles restaurant when Tom Lasorda, the manager of the Dodgers, came over to say hello. "Have you got a job?" asked Davis. "For who?" responded Lasorda who, on being told it was for Don McMahon, instantly added, "Don McMahon? I love that guy. Tell him to call me in the morning."

That was in 1985: less than two years after McMahon had undergone a quintuple heart bypass operation. The doctor had advised him if he could live without pitching batting practice there would be no need for surgery. The prospect of never being able to pitch again, however, was just too much for McMahon, and he opted for the surgery instead.

Even when he sat in an easy chair at home with his wife, Darlene, MacMahon would have a baseball in his hand. The eldest of his four sons—and one of six children—Jack McMahon revealed, "He'd rub it along the seams, and flip it up into the air. He always loved to have a baseball in his hand."

At 6 feet 2 inches and 215 pounds, McMahon became known as a fine relief pitcher in his Major League playing days, after joining the Milwaukee Braves in 1957 as a 27-year-old rookie. A fastball-curveball pitcher, he was still challenging batters in the Major League 18 years later; and his 874 appearances placed him (at that time) fourth on the all-time list. In all, he played with seven big league teams and achieved an earned run average of 2.96 and 153 saves. Highlights of an illustrious professional career included his selection to the All Star team, and his pitching appearances in three World Series.

On the night Don McMahon died, he had been throwing batting practice to the Dodgers' pitchers for almost 15 minutes. He was rushed to hospital where, still in his cleats, he was pronounced dead. Tough, highly competitive, but extremely likeable, McMahon left a big impression on the game. He may not have had his wish granted to be buried under the pitchers' mound. But Jack McMahon later revealed that they did at least bury his father with a baseball in his hand.

Born Donald John McMahon. **Marriage** Darlene. **Children** Four sons and two daughters. **Education** Erasmus Hall High School, Brooklyn. **Career** Baseball pitcher; seven major league teams in 18 years, including Milwaukee Braves, retired, 1974; pitching coach, Minnesota Twins, Cleveland Indians; special scout, Los Angeles Dodgers, 1985–87. **Career statistics** Pitched in 874 games, three World Series; won 90; lost 68; earned run average, 2.96; 153 saves. **Other activities** Sporting-goods salesman, 1984. **Cause of death** Heart attack, at age 57.

CARMELITA MARACCI

American Dancer, Choreographer and Ballet Teacher

***Born* Montevideo, Uruguay, 1911**

***Died* Hollywood, California, 26 July 1987**

Carmelita Maracci has been described as "one of the great dance figures of our time". She arrived in the United States at an early age and trained in classical ballet in Los Angeles, but she was also heavily influenced by the dance traditions of her native Uruguay and she studied Spanish dance with the famous teacher Hyppolito Mora. Maracci made her first professional appearances as a classical ballet dancer with a touring company directed by Alexis Kosloff. Soon after this début she began to experiment with her own choreography, mixing classical ballet and Spanish dance to create a new and highly individual dance style.

Maracci gave the first performance of her own work in Los Angeles in 1930. This was a great success and she was encouraged to choreograph several more works. She formed a group which toured the United States performing a repertory of her own dances, and she made her New York début in 1937. Here her work attracted favourable attention. John Martin, dance critic of the *New York Times*, wrote, "Here is a mistress of ballet technique and style who never dances ballet, of Spanish dance who never does Spanish dances. Both styles are merely materials out of which she fashions an act that is altogether personal, purely subjective in its creative approach, and utterly unique."

Maracci's output was prolific and in the period 1930–45 she produced almost 30 works which were performed by her company. However, the late 1940s brought some setbacks. Maracci had a disagreement with the powerful impresario Sol Hurok and she ceased to appear under his auspices. She continued to choreograph new works but the cool reception given to *Circo de España* (1951), a suite of dances which she had created for Ballet Theater, was discouraging and she decided to turn to teaching.

Maracci proved admirably suited to this new role and it is her teaching above all which proved to be a lasting influence in the world of dance. Among her most illustrious pupils was Cynthia Gregory, principal dancer of American Ballet Theater. Maracci became her chief teacher and Gregory, recalling Maracci's unorthodox approach, described her as teaching "on pointe and wearing pink tights, puffing on a cigarette, flicking it out of the window and dashing off a fast, furious set of pirouettes".

Over the years Maracci's other pupils included the great classical dancer Erik Bruhn, choreographers Jerome Robbins, Agnes de Mille and Gerald Arpino, and Leslie Caron, Geraldine and Charles Chaplin from the world of show business. Although she began to suffer from arthritis in later years, Maracci continued to teach in her highly idiosyncratic way until 1985. The dance writer Donna Perlmutter, who was also one of her pupils, wrote, "every class of hers was really a performance. She lived in a world of people who came to sit at her feet—and stand at the barre but be imaginative."

Unusually for a dancer, Maracci had very wide interests. In her classes she stimulated discussions on a range of subjects, including politics and philosophy, as well as other branches of the arts. During her last illness she continued to teach by gathering her students at her bedside to talk of the art and history of dance. Her enthusiasm—so inspirational to young dancers—will be sorely missed.

Born Carmelita Maracci. **Marriage** Lee Freeson. **Education** Studied ballet with Luigi Albertieri and Enrico Zanfretta; studied Spanish dance with Hyppolito Mora. **Emigration** Settled in United States as a child, although some dispute her Uruguayan origins. **Career** Ballet instructor and choreographer; toured United States performing own dances, 1930s; New York début, 1937; predominantly a teacher, 1951 onwards; students included Cynthia Gregory, principal dancer, American Ballet Theater, Geraldine and Charles Chaplin, Erik Bruhn, Jerome Robbins, Agnes de Mille, Donald Saddler, Gerald Arpino and Christine Sarry. **Works choreographed** *Pièce en forme de habañera*, 1932; *Reflets dans l'eau*, 1932; *Dance of the Shadow of Evil*, 1932; *Étude satyrique*, 1932; *Dance with Green Gloves*, 1932; *Form in Sound and Movement*, 1935; *Carlotta Grisi: In Retrospect*, 1935; *Cante hondos*, 1935; *Farucca*, 1935; *Primitive Study*, 1935; *Spain Cries Out*, 1937; *Tango Introspective*, 1937; *Live for the One Who Bore You*, 1937; *Two Caprices*, 1937; *Pavana*, 1941; *Another Goyescas*, 1941; *Madrigal*, 1941; *Jota and Synthesis*, 1941; *Romanza*,

1941; *Zambra*, 1941; *Flamenco*, 1941; *Sonata*, 1945; *Gavotte Vivace*, 1945; *Suite of Moments Musicales*, 1945; *The Nightingale and the Maidens in Raw España*, 1945; *Suite in D Minor*, 1950; *E Minor Suite*, 1950; *Les Adieux*, 1950; *Rondo, Opus 28*, 1950; *Chaconne*, 1950; *Sonata in A Flat Major*, 1950; *Klavierstucke*, 1950; *Circo de España*, 1951. **Cause of death** Undisclosed, at age 75.

EDWARD MIDDLEDITCH

British Artist

***Born* Chelmsford Essex, 23 March 1923**

***Died* Chelmsford, Essex, 29 July 1987**

Edward Middleditch appeared at the forefront of British painting in the early 1950s. He, together with fellow artists Jack Smith, Derrick Greaves and John Bratby, were seen to herald a new social realism and were dubbed the "Kitchen Sink Painters" by the art critic David Sylvester in 1954. Of these four very distinct talents, Middleditch perhaps most suffers from this misnomer. Later in life he was quoted as saying with exasperation: "I never painted a kitchen sink in my life!" Indeed, he painted few interiors and even fewer human subjects. However, early exceptions are "Portrait of a Woman" (1951), "Baby" (1952), "Butcher" (2 versions, 1952), and "Crowd at Earl's Court" (1954). Overall his work shows nature and landscape to be his major source of inspiration.

Middleditch spent his childhood in Nottingham, an area bordering on the industrial heartland of Britain. However, it was the rural country of Essex, his birthplace, to which he returned in later life, and this area, together with its neighbour Suffolk, provided many subjects for his paintings and drawings. His youthful artistic ambitions were halted by World War II, when he served in the army from 1942 until 1947, and was awarded the Military Cross.

It was not until 1948 that he began his training—first at the Regent Street Polytechnic, then at the renowned Royal College of Art, where he met Smith, Greaves and Bratby among other near contemporaries. However, Middleditch was the only artist of that era to have fought in the war; it was a subject to which he never referred again.

In keeping with the post-war mood in Britain, Middleditch displayed a note of seriousness and sense of purpose in his work, avoiding any kind of cleverness or virtuosity, which was evident in the paintings of fellow artists Greaves, Smith and Bratby. They tended to concentrate on scenes of everyday life, depicting the most mundane incidents in very ordinary interiors. Middleditch applied his sense of commitment to a wide range of subjects where nature and "things" predominate. Even in his very evocative "Crowd at Earl's Court", where the people form a dark, drab mass walking across a West London road, it is the swirling puddles and evening light on the stark pavement that fill the canvas.

Middleditch tended to approach his subject with a sense of detachment, yet emotion and expression are not totally hidden. In, for example, "Sleep" (1954), where a woman's head and hands are just visible above swathes of sheet and blanket which dominate the composition, he shows tenderness, not only for the sleeping woman, but also, more noticeably, for the simple beauty of sleep itself. Also from the mid-1950s, "Sheffield Weir" (1954) is one of Middleditch's most memorable and haunting works, revealing his lifelong fascination for water (particularly rivers and ponds, sometimes the sea), and for the stark solidity of mass stripped of detail—in this case, buildings and rocks above the powerful waters of the weir. His palette is muted, sombre and restrained; even in the later works where his colours are much lighter, they are never too bright. His technique, based on skilled draughtsmanship, is strong and distinctive.

The year 1954 also saw Middleditch's first one-man show at the Beaux Arts Gallery in London. Others followed, including important groups shows. In 1956 Middleditch, together with Bratby, Greaves and Smith, was chosen to represent his country at the XXVIII Biennale in Venice where he showed only landscapes. In the same year he exhibited at the Pittsburgh International. Thus, by his mid-thirties, Middleditch had become recognized and collected by public institutions and private collectors alike. Helen Lessore, owner of the Beaux Arts Gallery in London, and highly instrumental in Middleditch's success, said after his death that he was "purely a poet of appearances". Others refer to his poetic qualities; for example, Alan Bowness (former director of London's Tate Gallery) described him as the "poet among the painters", when reviewing the 1956 Biennale. In the late 1950s Middleditch turned largely to painting still lifes, finding miraculous and dramatic effects and unusual combinations, as in "Flowers, Chairs and Bedsprings" (1956) and "Sunflowers in Electric Light" (1955/6).

Like many other artists, Middleditch supplemented his income with teaching. However, he was also very committed to his students' development, letting them find their own vision, rather than steering them towards any fashions or trends. He was not interested in theory or dogma and said, "If you could talk about art, there would be no need to do it". After teaching at Chelsea Art School, he went to Norwich Art School and soon brought this institution into the forefront of art teaching.

Meanwhile, Middleditch had discovered a new source of inspiration in the landscape of Ronda in Spain. His drawings of this period (the early 1960s) are some of his most sensitive and "poetic". It is not mere coincidence that the artist David Brumberg worked in the same area 30 years earlier; there are definite affinities and both artists reveal the magic of this stark landscape. Middleditch always had a high respect for drawing; if not satisfied with a painting he might destroy it, but he would keep the preparatory drawing: "...a good drawing has a degree of finality and authority about it which painting cannot have".

For an artist interested in form and mass, his later preoccupation with flowers, particularly roses and carnations, and fields of oats or wheat, seems somewhat contradictory, yet he captures the subtle beauty of flowers and fields without any sentimentality or sweetness. The many works he exhibited at London's Royal Academy during the 1970s revealed his preoccupation with series, such as "Cornfields" and "Reflections". By this stage he had totally abandoned the dramatic perspectives of the 1950s and adopted an unerring preference for the plane, emphasizing the canvas's two-dimensionality. Despite the seemingly calm atmosphere of these later works, Middleditch never lost that brooding lonely quality first seen in the 1950s.

Considering Middleditch's early prominence in the art world, it is sad that his later achievements, although not always outstanding, have been largely overlooked. His own modesty and shyness of the art establishment contributed to this neglect, and perhaps because of the "Kitchen Sink" years, he took a number of different courses, always hoping to find the vision that would sustain him. He never fitted neatly into any category, and as one critic said, "In Middleditch there is no charm—only a private ecstasy".

Born Edward Middleditch. **Parents** Charles Henry, a craftsman, and Esme (Buckley) Middleditch. **Marriage** Jean Kathleen Whitehouse, an engraver (died, 1949). **Children** One daughter, Emily. **Education** Mundella School, Nottingham; King Edward VI Grammar School, Chelmsford; Regent Street Polytechnic Art School, early 1948; Royal College of Art, 1948–52. **Military service** Conscripted into army and served in France, Germany, India, West Africa,

1942–47; commissioned, Middlesex Regiment, 1944. **Career** Part-time teacher: Colchester School of Art, Langford Grove near Barcombe Mills, Sussex, 1955, Chelsea School of Art, 1958–63, Regent Street Polytechnic, 1960; head of fine art department, Norwich School of Art, 1964–85; Keeper of the Royal Academy Schools, Burlington House, London, 1985–86. **Awards and honours** Military Cross, 1945; associate, Royal College of Art, 1951; second prize, Daily Express Young Artists' Exhibition, 1955; Gulbenkian Foundation Scholarship, 1962; Arts Council of Great Britain bursary, 1964; Arts Council of Northern Ireland bursary, 1968; Royal Academician, 1973 (associate, 1968). **Individual exhibitions** Beaux Arts Gallery, London, 1954, 1956, 1958, 1960, 1961, 1962; The New Art Centre, London, 1969, 1971, 1974; Radlett Gallery, London, 1975. **Group exhibitions** Royal Academy Summer Exhibition, London, 1949–50; *Artists of Fame and Promise*, Leicester Galleries, London, 1951; *Young Contemporaries*, RBA Galleries, London, 1952; *Eight Young Contemporaries*, Institute of Contemporary Art, London, 1952; *Looking Forward: An Exhibition of British Realists*, Whitechapel Art Gallery, London, 1952; *Some Rising Painters*, Roland, Browse & Delbanco, London, 1954; *British Painting*, Whitechapel Art Gallery, London, 1954; *Giovani Pittori*, Galleria Nazionale d'Arte Moderna, Rome, 1955; Daily Express Young Artists' Exhibition, London, 1955; Pittsburgh International Exhibition, Pittsburgh, 1955; *Contemporary English Painting and Sculpture*, Leeds, 1955; Heffers' Bookshop, Cambridge, 1955; *Quattro Giovani Pittori Inglesi*, XXVIII Venice Biennale, 1956; Royal Academy Summer Exhibition, London, 1956–57; *Six Young Painters*, Arts Council of Great Britain, London, 1957; *British Painting 1950–57*, Arts Council of Great Britain, London, 1957; Pittsburgh International Exhibition, Pittsburgh, 1958; *16 Paintings by 16 Painters: Aspects of Realism*, AIA Gallery, London, 1959; *The Graven Image*, Whitechapel Art Gallery, London, 1959; *British Painting 1700–1960*, British Council, Moscow, 1960; *Younger British Painters*, Austria, 1960; *Critics' Selection*, Arthur Tooth & Sons, London, 1960; *British Painting Today and Yesterday*, London, 1961; Roland, Browse & Delbanco, London, 1966; *Painters in East Anglia*, Arts Council of Great Britain travelling exhibition, 1966; *Drawing Towards Painting 2*, Arts Council of Great Britain, 1967; *Helen Lessore and Beaux Arts Gallery*, Marlborough Fine Art, London, 1968; Royal Academy Summer Exhibition, 1968–72; *The English Landscape Tradition in the 20th Century*, Camden Arts Centre, London, 1969; *Works on Paper*, Bear Lane Gallery, Oxford, 1970; Fischer Fine Art, London, 1972; *Landscape Painting*, Serpentine Gallery, London, 1973; *British Painting '74*, Hayward Gallery, London, 1974; Royal Academy Summer Exhibition, London, 1976–79; *British Painting 1952–1977*, Royal Academy, London, 1977; *Books and Folios*, Arts Council of Great Britain touring exhibition, 1981; Royal Academy Summer Exhibition, London, 1981–84; *A Happy Eye*, Norwich School of Art Gallery, Norwich, 1983; *The Forgotten Fifties*, Sheffield City Art Galleries and tour, Sheffield, 1984; *Rocks and Flesh*, Norwich School of Art Gallery and tour, Norwich, 1985; *A Paradise Lost*, Barbican Art Gallery, London, 1987; Castle Museum, Norwich, 1987; Serpentine Gallery, London, 1988. **Collections** Tate Gallery, London; Arts Council, London; Victoria & Albert Museum, London; Contemporary Art Society, London; Manchester City Art Gallery, Manchester; Ferens Art Gallery, Hull; National Gallery of Victoria, Melbourne; National Gallery of South Australia; National Gallery of Canada; Chrysler Art Museum, Massachusetts; Toledo Museum of Art, Ohio. **Cause of death** Undisclosed, at age 64.

HALLAM MOVIUS

American Archaeologist and Anthropologist

***Born* Newton, Massachusetts, 28 November 1907**

***Died* Cambridge, Massachusetts, July 1987**

Professor Hallam Movius was one of the world's leading authorities on the Stone Age in Ireland and France. Indeed, he brought a new type of professionalism to archaeological fieldwork.

Movius was Massachusetts-born and very much a Harvard man; apart from fieldwork, he spent his entire academic career there, progressing from BA (1930) to MA (1932) to PhD (1937) with the single-mindedness that characterized all his later work. He was also a member of faculty at the university from 1930 until his retirement.

Movius's practical research in the 1930s included digs in Czechoslovakia and other sites in central Europe, in Palestine, and in Burma and Java. In the Far East, his research into fossil remains made it possible to estimate for the first time the antiquity of human life in the region. Movius concentrated on the faunal sequence, the rhythm with which the bones of mammals hunted by early man, such as elephants, horses and cattle, accumulated at the foot of mountain ranges in the intervals between glacial periods. He was able to show that this process took place in Asia in much the same way as it had in Europe, and at much the same time.

Movius's Asian work also did much to confirm the existence throughout most of Asia of a Pleistocene civilization based on what he termed "choppers" or chopping tools rather than hand-axes. Hand-axes were the dominant tool of the Pleistocene period in Europe, Africa and southern India, whereas the chopping tool culture, in the light of Movius's findings, appears to have evolved independently in the Far East.

Prior to World War II, however, Movius's most important research took place in Ireland from 1932 to 1936. This earned him his doctorate and was later published to much acclaim as *The Irish Stone Age* (1942).

On the basis of half a dozen sites, mainly in Northern Ireland, Movius concluded that Stone Age cultures in Ireland were heavily dependent on their natural surroundings. In a post-glacial climate, which Movius likened to living on today's Baffin Island in the shadow of the Greenland icecap, it was vital to be near a source of flint for making tools. The earliest arrivals in Ireland, from southern France and the north Iberian Peninsula, found flint in abundance in what are now Counties Antrim and Down. Movius called this indigenous culture Larnian, after his principal site at Larne in Antrim. The Larnian culture was a hunting and food-gathering one, and in the second half of the third millenium BC was eventually overtaken by the first rudiments of agriculture.

In the post-war period Movius did more fieldwork in eastern and south-western France, a task doubly congenial because of the French background of his Australian wife, Nancy Champion de Crespigny, whom he had married in 1936. The French fieldwork gave rise to the long-running excavation of a cave shelter near Pataud in the Dordogne, the so-called Abri Pataud. Between 1958 and 1973, Movius's annual supervision of this site brought a formidable breadth of knowledge to the work, and the site became famous as a training ground for colleagues and students from around the world, not least because of the "almost military discipline" which Movius insisted on.

The Abri Pataud dated from the Upper Palaeolithic period or late Stone Age, between 33,000 and 10,000 BC. It was in the most densely populated area of Stone Age France, and hence one of the richest in the cave paintings and sculpture, elaborate tools and burial sites of the period.

Movius's familiarity with stratigraphy—determining the precise sequence of deposits—was obviously important here. He was also a proponent of the radiocarbon dating of remains. The results of the Abri Pataud excavations were published in the late 1980s—the culmination of many years' dedication and collaboration.

When not out in the field, Movius was quietly scaling the heights of his profession at Harvard. From 1950 to 1957 he was curator of the Peabody Museum, and then a full professor of anthropology until 1977, when he retired gracefully at the age of 70, having contributed to greatly improved standards in Stone Age research.

Born Hallam Leonard Movius Jr. **Parents** Hallam Leonard and Alice Lee (West) Movius. **Marriage** Nancy Champion de Crespigny, 1936. **Children** One son, Geoffrey Hallam, and one daughter, Alice Vierville. **Education** Harvard University, AB, 1930, MA, 1932, PhD, 1937. **Career** Faculty member, Harvard University, 1930–50, associate professor, 1950–57, professor of anthropology, 1957–77; curator, palaeolithic archaeology, Peabody Museum, 1950–77. **Related activities** Field expeditions: Czechoslovakia, 1930, Central Europe, 1931, Palestine, 1932, Ireland, 1932–36, Burma and Java, 1937–38, Eastern France, 1948, Western Europe, 1949, 1953, 1954–55; field director, Abri Pataud, south-western France, 1958–73. **Offices and memberships** Fellow: American Academy of Arts and Sciences, Society of Antiquaries, London, American Anthropological Association, Geological Society of America: member, National Academy of Sciences; honorary member: Schweizerischen Gesellschaft für Urgeschicte, Société Préhistorique de l'Ariège, Instituto Italiano di Prehistoria e Protostoria; corresponding member, Deutsches Archaologisches Institut, Prehistoric Society of England, Department of Archaeology, Government of India, Musée Nationale d'Histoire Naturelle. **Awards and honours** Viking Fund medallist in archaeology, 1949; honorary doctorate, University of Bordeaux, France, 1961; Chevalier, Ordre des Arts et des Lettres, France. **Publications** *The Irish Stone Age*, 1942. **Cause of death** Undisclosed, at age 80.

NATHAN PERLMUTTER

American Civil Rights Activist

***Born* New York City, New York, 2 March 1923**

***Died* New York City, New York, 12 July 1987**

When, just a month before his death, Nathan Perlmutter was awarded the Presidential Medal of Freedom, President Reagan said in his speech that Perlmutter had "made it his life's work to champion human dignity". He was referring to Perlmutter's work for the Anti-Defamation League of B'nai B'rith, the most powerful voice of American Jewry. Nathan Perlmutter, a blunt-spoken lawyer from Brooklyn, devoted the best part of his life to the vigorous defence of the interests of Israel in US foreign policy and became, through vociferous public exposure of anti-Semitism, the foremost civil rights spokesman for American Jews.

Nathan Perlmutter was born in 1923, the child of Polish immigrants in Williamsburg, Brooklyn. After the stockmarket crash of 1929 which launched the Depression, the Perlmutters left New York to find work elsewhere. Like many small craftsmen, Perlmutter senior had to relinquish his trade of tailoring during the poverty-stricken 1930s since there was no money to be earned among the poor—which now included many previously well-to-do people. He found work as a labourer for the Works Projects Administration, part of Roosevelt's New Deal, while his wife sold ices from a pushcart.

Economically, things got better with the start of World War II. In 1941, just 18 years old, Nathan Perlmutter volunteered for the US Marine Corps and served in China. Two years later he married Ruthann Osofsky, and enrolled at Georgetown and Villanova universities. He then went to graduate school in New York where he received his law degree in 1949. Upon qualifying as a lawyer, Perlmutter took up a post with the Anti-Defamation League as civil rights and human relations education executive, working in Denver, Colorado, from 1949 to 1952 and in Detroit the year after. This was followed by three years in New York and finally a move to Miami, Florida, where Perlmutter, his wife and their young family settled down for eight years. By this time, the mid-1960s and the heyday of civil rights activity (albeit mostly Black civil rights), Nathan Perlmutter was one of the most experienced fieldworkers in the organization. He felt it was time for a change. When the American–Jewish Committee offered him a job as associate national director, this was promotion indeed. He worked in that capacity from 1965 until 1969, when he became vice-president of Brandeis University in Waltham, Massachusetts. After dutifully serving a four-year term in a job which did not excite him, Perlmutter finally returned to the Anti-Defamation League in 1973.

Although initially appointed as assistant national director, he soon found himself in the driving seat, overseeing not only national headquarters in Manhattan but also 31 regional offices in the US, and with additional responsibility for overseas bureaux in Jerusalem, Rome and Paris, plus a liaison branch in Latin America. But this was not just an administrative job: Perlmutter was frequently called upon to respond to political events in the Middle East, as well as at home. During the 1970s and 1980s he became increasingly concerned about what he saw as diminishing support for Israel in the Western world, and in the United States in particular, a lack of support which he equated with anti-Semitism. At the same time, there were reasons for concern about racism at home: when confronted with the results of a survey showing an increase in the frequency of anti-Semitic attacks, Perlmutter commented that the findings "suggest that there is a high quotient of anti-Semitism and anti-Jewish hostility which still exists just beneath the surface of American life." The particularly thorny issue of purported Black hostility to Jews came to the fore repeatedly in the mid-1980s, when both Louis Farrakhan (leader of the Black Muslims) and Jesse Jackson, who was just about to launch his Rainbow Alliance, made public pronouncements critical of Israel and the American–Jewish establishment. Perlmutter, as was his custom, did not mince words. "By providing Farrakhan with a bullhorn for his ravings, the press is magnifying his significance," he said. He adopted a similar attitude in relation to Jackson: "Jews speak for their dignity against his anti-Semitic statements and somehow that becomes 'arrogant' and 'contemptuous',"—words Jackson himself had used when he contended in an interview that Jewish leaders were trying to make him an outcast. From Jackson, at least, Perlmutter got a "candid and welcome" apology.

In 1985 Perlmutter was diagnosed as suffering from lung cancer, possibly the result of inveterate cigar-smoking, even though he had quit several years before. Knowing that he was a dying man, Perlmutter kept a journal for some weeks, of which a part was published in the *New York Times* under the title "Diary of a Cancer Patient". In it he described how he had put his life in the balance and found it had been well spent: "My mind is smiling at what I feel I've accomplished. I married the prettiest girl in the neighbourhood. I made it to Marine infantry officer, wrote a few books and became director of ADL."

The few books included one on horse-racing, which he loved, and one volume of autobiographical essays. As a publicist he was a frequent contributor to such cultural and political journals as the *Nation*, *Frontier*, *Commentary* and, of course, *National Jewish Monthly*. He described his politics as "variable", but in relation to Israel he was clearly on the right hand of the spectrum of Jewish–American opinion. Perlmutter, however, did not exclusively concern himself with the civil rights of Jews. Soon after his death Ed Koch, the flamboyant mayor of New York, added another achievement to Perlmutter's own list: "[He] had the deepest commitment to justice for everyone without regard to ethnicity, religion or gender that I've ever encountered."

Born Nathan Perlmutter. **Parents** Hyman, tailor, and Bella (Finkelstein) Perlmutter. **Marriage** Ruthann Osofsky, 1943. **Children** Nina and Dean. **Education** Georgetown University, 1942–43; Villanova College, 1943–44; New York University, LLB, 1949. **Military service** US Marine Corps, 1943–46; discharged with the rank of second lieutenant. **Career** Assistant director, Anti-Defamation League of B'nai B'rith, Denver, 1949–52, regional director, Michigan, 1952–53, assistant director, community service division, New York, 1953–56, regional director, Florida, 1956–64, director, New York City, 1964–65, regional director, New York, 1973–79, assistant national director, national director, 1979–87; associate national director, American Jewish Committee, New York, 1965–69; vice-president for development, Brandeis University, 1969–73. **Related activities** Director, American Jewish World Service; member, board of advisers, Jewish Institute for National Security Affairs. **Memberships** New York Bar, International League for the Rights of Man, American Civil Liberties Union, National Association of Intergroup Relations Officials. **Awards and honours** Presidential Medal of Freedom, 1987. **Publications** *How to Win Money at the Races*, 1964; *A Bias of Reflections: Confessions of an Incipient Old Jew*, 1972; (with Ruthann Perlmutter) *The Real Anti-Semitism*, 1982; contributor of articles to *Frontier*, *Nation*, *Progressive*, *New Leader*, *Commentary*, *National Jewish Monthly*, *Florida Historical Quarterly*, *Midstream*. **Cause of death** Lung cancer, at age 64.

LADY RAMA RAU

Indian Women's Rights Activist

***Born* Hubli, India, 10 May 1893**

***Died* Bombay, India, 19 July 1987**

Lady Rama Rau once wrote in an article for *Atlantic Monthly*:

> The women of India showed their political awareness and power in India's first free election, for which they turned out in record numbers to vote with their men—though not necessarily for the same candidates. At the moment they are conducting a great fight against orthodoxy and conservatism by demanding that the ancient Hindu laws governing marriage, divorce and inheritance be overhauled and made more equitable. Many thousands of women have now taken jobs of one sort or another, ranging from government service to positions as salesgirls in shops, or hostesses on planes. India has women in its foreign service all the way up to the rank of ambassador. There are women in Parliament and in the Cabinet. There are women lobbyists, women on the National Planning Commission, women presidents of colleges. Almost all of them owe their jobs, their power and their position to the rights that the Indian women's movement has established for them through 25 years of work.

Perhaps to our surprise, this was written not in the feminist 1970s or 1980s, but in 1954 when Lady Rama Rau was touring the United States in order to further understanding between East and

West. Nor did she make any mention of her own formidable contribution to the changes in Indian women's lives which had come about since Independence and which in 40 years of unstinting commitment to the plight of women had earned her the title of the "Indian Margaret Sanger". Like that other social worker and birth control activist, Lady Rama Rau's life project was to free women from the blight of compulsive childbearing through education and self-help. By the time she died at the age of 94, it was evident that her efforts had not been in vain: a whole generation of self-determined Indian women had grown up to take over a vibrant Indian women's movement, which Lady Rau herself had helped found in the early years of this century.

Lady Rama Rau was born Dhanvanthi Handoo in 1893 in a small village in southwest India, where her father held a civil service position with the government-run railways and her mother was a freelance journalist with an interest in women's rights. Young Dhanvanthi's life was unconventional from the start: to begin with, her parents sent her to school rather than having her educated at home as was the custom for Indian girls, and she soon established herself as the star pupil in Hubli. But the unconventional turned into the unseemly when she went to Madras University to study English. This was a break with tradition indeed, especially for a woman of her caste. The men at Madras University taunted her daily with the accusation that she was a "traitor" to her caste and did not belong there; initially it was only because of her parents' unconditional support that she was able to withstand the pressure from her peers to return home and be a "good girl".

Instead of confining herself in the time-honoured way to home and husband, she soon developed other interests at college alongside her normal studies. The Irish suffragette Margaret Cousins and the social reformer Sarojini Naidu both inspired her to take part in the struggle for women's independence. Again, Dhanvanthi's own situation became a touchstone for her beliefs: should she or should she not accept a post as lecturer in English which was offered her on graduation in 1917? She consulted her parents whose authority and judgement she deeply respected, and got the go-ahead. From 1917 until the time of her—again unconventional—civil registered marriage to a man from a different state, (Sir) Benegal Rama Rau, she was a pioneer of the Indian women's movement, as well as a noted academic. She knew how to persuade people of the need for change, and she also knew that organizing women is different; militant rhetoric about women's rights would not stretch very far. "We held drawing-room meetings and it was a contest between the squalling babies on the floor and the speaker. One never knew who would win the contest," she said later.

During the 1920s Lady Rama Rau was primarily engaged in what might be called a campaign of consciousness-raising on the need for a good education for girls, social and legal reform, health information and facilities, and women's participation in public life. She was instrumental in getting the Sarda Act of 1930 passed, which raised the legal age of marriage for girls to 14 and effectively made child-marriages illegal. When she moved to England with her diplomat husband in 1929, she quickly made contact with the British women's movement and met Margaret Sanger, who convinced her of the importance of birth control to improve the lot of the poor. Upon return to India in 1938, Lady Rama Rau decided to take action and she toured the country with two British friends, Dr Helen Wright and a Mrs Seligman, who provided the money to dispense information and contraception free of charge to all who needed and wanted it—especially those who lived in isolated rural areas. All three women maintained the firm belief that government coercion would do no good at all—only persuasion and actual provision would prove effective in the long run. However, this work was cut short in 1943 when the Bijapur famine required Lady Rama Rau, as president of the Bombay Women's Committee, to put all her energies into famine relief. At this time she was also vice-president of the All-India Women's Conference, an office which she held from 1939 until 1947, when she became president of the organization.

After World War II Lady Rama Rau moved once more, this time to the United States, where her husband served as ambassador. In Washington she quickly familiarized herself with the workings of the United Nations and came to realize that overpopulation was not just the problem of a developing nation like India, but of the whole world. In 1949 she founded the Family Planning Association of India, becoming its first president, and in 1953 the International Planned Parenthood Federation, to which she devoted most of her energy before retiring 20 years later at the age of 80. There had been many changes in the lot of Indian women during her lifetime—not a few of them thanks to her.

> When I was young, girls were betrothed at nine and married at 14; a bride went to live in her mother-in-law's house and wasn't supposed to play a musical instrument, or eat with her husband, or go out alone...most young brides, even those from the best of families, couldn't read or write...from as far back as I can remember, I knew that I wanted—if I could—to break those terrible bonds.

Whether Lady Rama Rau ever succeeded in playing a musical instrument is not known, but during her long life she certainly relished having broken all the other taboos.

Born Dhanvanthi Handoo. **Parents** Rup Krishna, civil servant, and Bhagvati (Shah) Handoo. **Marriage** Benegal Rama Rau, 1919 (died, 1969). **Children** Two daughters, Premila and Santha. **Education** Presidency College, University of Madras, MA, 1917. **Career** Lecturer in English, Queen Mary's College, University of Madras, 1917–19; secretary, All India Child Marriage Abolition League, 1927–28; board member, International Alliance of Women for Suffrage and Equal Citizenship, 1932–38; vice-president, All India Women's Conference, 1939–46, president, 1946–47; president, Bombay branch, All India Women's Conference, 1946; founder and president, Family Planning Association of India, 1949–63. **Related activities** Member, Advisory Panel on Health, National Planning Commission; president, Bombay Women's Committee for Famine Relief, 1943, International Planned Parenthood Federation, 1953; member, Family Planning Programmes and Research Committee, Indian Ministry of Health, 1953; chair, Social and Moral Hygiene Enquiry Committee, 1955; member, Central Social Welfare Board, 1956–61, Consultative Committee of Planning Commission for Third Five-Year Plan (Health), 1961, major committee on women's rights, Indian Five-Year Plan; head of Bombay Women's Association; founder, Bombay children's orthopaedic hospital; lecturer on family planning, women's rights and related subjects. **Memberships** Women's Indian Association, 1917, International Council of Women, International Federation of University Women. **Awards and honours** Mahaden Parmanand Prize, Sattianathan Gold Medal and Griggs Gold Medal, all from University of Madras; Kaiser-I-Hind Gold Medal, 1938; citation, Barnard College, 1953; bicentenary medallion, Columbia University, 1953; honorary DHL, Bard College, New York, 1953; Lasker Award, 1955; Padma Bhusan Award, 1959. **Publications** (with daughter Santha) *An Inheritance*, 1977. **Cause of death** Undisclosed, at age 94.

BENGT STRÖMGREN

Danish Astrophysicist

***Born* Göteborg, Sweden, 21 January 1908**

***Died* Copenhagen, Denmark, 4 July 1987**

Bengt Strömgren's great achievement was to explain the constitution of the clouds of luminous gas in space, and his name is preserved in the Strömgren sphere which forms part of that explanation.

Bengt Georg Daniel Strömgren was born in Stockholm and his family was Swedish. There is nothing surprising in his becoming an astronomer, for his father was one before him, and it was because Eli Strömgren became director of the Royal Copenhagen Observatory that the family moved to Denmark. At Copenhagen University young Bengt Strömgren gained his MS degree in 1927, and his PhD in 1929.

In 1931 he was married, and the same year he and his father produced their first textbook on astronomy. Two years later he became a lecturer at Copenhagen University, and in 1936 began a long connection with Chicago University when he was appointed assistant and associate professor. He was a full professor back at Copenhagen from 1938 to 1940 when he succeeded his father as director of the Royal Copenhagen Observatory.

During this time Strömgren was already studying luminous gases in space. Since the eighteenth century it had been thought that the luminous gas found between stars must be energized by nearby stars, but how that happened had not been understood. Strömgren began attempts to explain the observed shapes, sizes, luminosities and internal characteristics of these strange areas.

After the war he held a variety of positions in the United States, continuing with his work on luminous gases. To explain their appearance and characteristics he suggested that a uniformly dense cloud of hydrogen and dust was exposed to radiation from a very hot star. The hydrogen gas within a certain distance, which could be calculated and came to be known as the Strömgren sphere, would be ionized by this radiation and split into protons and electrons, but in a narrow band outside it the protons and electrons would recombine into hydrogen atoms. The immense outer volume of non-luminous hydrogen gas would therefore absorb the visible radiation lines of the hydrogen spectrum, but would emit in other parts of the electromagnetic spectrum, especially the 21-centimetre radio band.

Although Strömgren's equations were approximate, ignoring various complicating factors, they were found to apply accurately to varying nebular regions and explained the sharply defined regions observed in these clouds. For a star whose surface temperature was about 30,000°C, the radius of the Strömgren sphere had a diameter of about 500 light-years, while a cooler, fainter star with a surface temperature of about 10,000°C ionized hydrogen in a sphere of diameter of only about 1.5 light-years.

His theory also helped analysis of overlapping interstellar clouds in a galaxy and could also be used to estimate size, distance and luminosity of nebular matter. In addition, it could be applied to the ionization of helium clouds, as well as hydrogen.

In 1951 Strömgren was made director of both the Yerkes Observatory in Wisconsin and the McDonald Observatory in Texas. He helped redesign the equipment for more precise observations, and it was while in these posts that he carried out an extensive investigation of stellar spectra using photoelectric techniques. Previously the classification of stellar spectra had been largely guesswork. His determinations of the abundance of hydrogen, helium and other elements in space are still considered accurate.

In 1957 he left his post with these observatories, as well as his professorship in Chicago, to join the Institute of Advanced Studies in Princeton, New Jersey, where, among other innovations, he devised a new method for fixing the ages and distances of stars. He was there for ten years, before returning once more to the University of Copenhagen to be professor of astrophysics.

Born Bengt Georg Daniel Strömgren. **Parents** Svante Elis, astronomer, and Hedvig (Lidforss) Strömgren. **Marriage** Sigrid Caja Hartz, 1931. **Children** One son and two daughters. **Education** University of Copenhagen, MS, 1927, PhD, 1929. **Career** Lecturer, University of Copenhagen, 1933, professor, 1938–40; director of observatory, 1940; assistant professor, University of Chicago, 1936–37, associate professor, 1937–38, visiting professor, 1946–48; professor and director, Yerkes and McDonald Observatories, 1951–57; member, Institute of Advanced Study, Princeton, 1957–67. **Offices and memberships** Member: Royal Danish Academy of Sciences and Letters, Danish Academy of Technical Sciences, American Academy of Arts and Sciences, Royal Astronomical Society; associate member: Société Royale des Sciences de Liège, American Astronomical Society; honorary member: Academy Coimbra, Royal Swedish Academy of Sciences, Physiographic Society, Koninklijke Nederlandse Akademie van Wetenschappen; general secretary, International Astronomical Unions, 1948; executive committee member, International Council of Scientific Unions, 1948. **Awards and honours** Augustinus Prize, 1950; Bruce Medal, Astronomical Society of the Pacific, 1959; gold medal, Royal Astronomical Society, 1962. **Publications** (with Elis Strömgren) *Laerobog i Astronomi*, 1931; (with Elis Strömgren) *Lehrbuch der Astronomie*, 1933; editor, *Handbuch der Experimentalphysik*, vol. 26, 1937. **Cause of death** Undisclosed, at age 79.

LORD TREND

British Civil Servant

***Born* London, England, 2 January 1914**

***Died* London, England, 21 July 1987**

Burke St John Trend (created a life peer in 1974) was a perfect example of the very highest in the traditions of the British Civil Service, while at the same time being by no means the dry-as-dust official such a description could conjure up, but a warm and friendly person, whose sense of humour spared him from the pomposities of his position and made him a useful channel for colleagues to the Cabinet over whose workings he presided.

Burke Trend followed the classic education of the English professional class—public school and Oxford where he obtained a first in Greats, the traditional subject of the English intellectual generalist. There was never any question of what his career would be. He entered the administrative class of the Home Civil Service in 1936, opting first for the Board of Education. He was spotted early on as a high-flyer, however, and transferred to the Treasury a year later. He was henceforth to remain at the centre of government, either in the Treasury or the Cabinet Office.

In the first two years of World War II Trend became assistant private secretary to the chancellor of the exchequer, first Sir John Simon and then Sir Kingsley Wood. At the end of the war he returned as principal private secretary to the chancellor, first to Hugh Dalton and then to

Sir Stafford Cripps, and he worked in this important position during the first critical years of peacetime when the Treasury was trying to deal not only with the problems of re-establishing the international economic and financial system on the new Bretton Woods footing, but also with the Labour Government's policy of nationalizations and Keynesian economics. Trend's clear mind and honest non-partisan approach were invaluable here. In 1949 he was made under-secretary in charge of the core Home Finance Division. Four years later he moved to the new Central Economic Planning Staff until the then chancellor, R.A. Butler, left to become Lord Privy Seal taking Trend with him to head that office.

At about the same time Trend became deputy secretary to the Cabinet with a great deal of responsibility for the day-to-day running of Cabinet affairs. This experience was to stand him in good stead when, after a two-year stint as second secretary (in effect permanent secretary) and deputy head of the Civil Service, he succeeded Sir Norman Brook as secretary to the Cabinet at the end of 1962. Here he was to remain for the rest of his Civil Service career, serving four prime ministers: Harold Macmillan, Sir Alec Douglas-Home, Harold Wilson and Edward Heath.

Trend was the master of the government machine, understanding and meticulously observing the minutiae of the relations between Crown and Government, Cabinet and committees, Cabinet and Parliament. No wonder he was made a privy counsellor at the end of his service! Some ministers were to resent this mastery. Richard Crossman saw him as the manipulator of Cabinet minutes who held back the Wilson Government from its more radical policies. Harold Wilson, who came to respect his fair-mindedness, described him as "feline". Edward Heath regretted his arm's length neutrality towards government policy and tried to draw him into a more executive form of advice. But Trend was too well trained to abandon the olympian stance of setting out the options and leaving the politicians to make—and live with—the choices. Manipulate he might, but influence, never! Trend was always ready to welcome new approaches to the working of the Civil Service, as his own report on the service and his policy analyses for the Cabinet showed, but he was always sensitive to the constitutional niceties of his position, a sensitivity which was heightened by his close partnership with the new permanent secretary to the Treasury, Sir William Armstrong. Together they dominated the other departments of state for a decade.

Trend was also sensitive to the wider implications of British policy. Throughout the attempts during the 1960s at British membership of the European Economic Community, he remained aware of the paramount importance of the special relationship with the United States. He was held in very high regard by Dr Kissinger and was thus of great value to the Foreign Office on many occasions; similarly, with the relationship with the Commonwealth, where Britain's European preoccupations were to prove even more traumatic. It was not for nothing that he was asked to become president of the Royal Commonwealth Society in 1982.

On his retirement in 1973 Trend became rector of Lincoln College, Oxford—not his own college as an undergraduate, but one for which he developed a warm affection. He carried out a number of improvements to the college buildings, and it was under his regime that the college became co-educational. He also took an active part in university life, acting as pro-vice-chancellor and chairman of the Appointments Committee. Other important public offices he undertook included chairman of the Trustees of the British Museum and of the Nuffield Foundation.

One interesting sideline came early in his retirement. As a principal in the Treasury, he had been given responsibility for detailed work on the secret service and later became accounting officer for the secret vote. In this capacity he looked after the terms and conditions of the secret services, for whose work he came to have a high respect. In 1974–75 he was asked to conduct an investigation into whether the former head of MI5, Sir Richard Hollis, had acted as a spy for the Soviet Union. Trend's scrupulous examination of the files never enabled him to reach a firm conclusion either way. This finding from such a man as Trend should have closed the matter once and for all.

Born Burke St John Trend. **Parents** Walter St John Trend and Marion (Tyers) Trend. **Marriage** Patricia Charlotte Shaw, 1949. **Children** Two sons and one daughter. **Education** Whitgift School, Croydon; Merton College, Oxford, first class honours degree in moderations, 1934, literae humaniores (classics), 1936. **Career** Joined Civil Service, 1936; Home Civil Service, administrative class, 1936; Ministry of Education, 1936; transferred to Treasury, 1937; assistant private secretary to chancellor of exchequer, 1939–41, principal private secretary to chancellor of exchequer, 1945–49, under-secretary, 1949–55; transferred to office of Lord Privy Seal, 1955–56; transferred to Cabinet, deputy secretary, 1956–59; third secretary, Treasury, 1959–60, second secretary, 1960–62; secretary to Cabinet, 1963–73. **Other activities** Pro-vice-chancellor, Merton College, 1975–83. **Offices and memberships** Member, British Museum Trustees, 1973–79, chairman, 1979; member, Nuffield Foundation Managing Trustees, 1973–80, chairman, 1980; member, Advisory Council on Public Records, 1974–82; president, Royal Commonwealth Society, 1982; High Bailiff of Westminster and Searcher of the Sanctuary, 1983–87; member: Governing Body, Westminster School, Cheltenham College council. **Awards and honours** Commander of the Royal Victorian Order, 1953; Companion of the Order of the Bath, 1955; Knight Commander of the Order of the Bath, 1962; honorary fellow, Merton College, Oxford, 1964; Knight Grand Cross of the Order of the Bath, 1968; honorary DCL, Oxford University, 1969; privy counsellor, 1972; created baron, 1973; rector, Lincoln College, Oxford, 1973–83, honorary fellow, 1983; honorary LLD, St Andrews University, 1974; honorary DLitt, Loughborough University, 1984. **Cause of death** Undisclosed, at age 73.

PHILIP VERNON

British Psychologist

***Born* England, 6 June 1905**

***Died* Calgary, Canada, 28 July 1987**

Professor Philip Vernon was one of Britain's most well known and popular psychologists. He was a man of great honesty and fairness, and although a strong critic, he was well respected by a wide audience. This would please Vernon, as it was always his aim to make his work accessible to those beyond scientific circles.

After attending Oundle School, Vernon went on to St John's College, Cambridge, where he graduated with first class honours. The excellence of his academic work won him several scholarships, including one to study his other abiding interest—sacred music. Thus began a career which led him to become one of the leading members of the London school of psychological thought, following in the footsteps of such eminent psychologists as Charles Spearman and Cyril Burt, and their Victorian predecessors, Sir Francis Galton and Karl Pearson. What distinguished this school from others was its concentration on statistical analysis of mental test data which was mostly conducted through correlations and factor analysis. In the field of intelligence and personality, this school had many pioneers, and Vernon was its most critical and non-partisan member.

While on a scholarship to Harvard, and aged only 28, Vernon co-wrote a book called *Studies in Expressive Movement*, which showed such originality and thoroughness that it won him international recognition. Following a scholarship at his alma mater, St John's College, he worked as a psychologist at the Maudsley Hospital Child Guidance Clinic in London, and as head of the psychology department at the Jordanhill Training Centre for teachers in Glasgow. This was followed by nearly a decade as head of the psychology department at Glasgow University.

The years 1942 to 1945 found him as psychological adviser to the Admiralty and the War Office, advising on personnel selection and recruitment tests. The results of his work here were written up with those of J.B. Parry, who worked for the Air Force Psychology Group, and published as *Personnel Selection in the British Forces* in 1949. Apart from his distinguished professional qualifications, Vernon's "unfailing good humour, honesty and knowledge" were valuable assets in persuading the military to see the importance of scientific testing.

Moving back to London in 1949, Vernon became professor of educational psychology at the Institute of Education, and in 1964 professor of psychology. However, health problems and increasing disenchantment with the lack of research opportunities in Britain combined to persuade him to up sticks and move to Canada, where he spent the last ten years of his life as professor of educational psychology at the University of Calgary.

Throughout his career, Vernon was a prolific author who wrote a great deal about intelligence and achievement, latterly in relation to Orientals and Eskimos. In the sensitive areas of racial differences and the nature/nurture debate, he was always "transparently honest in his attempt to let the facts speak for themselves and not impose any ideological constraints on them". When assessing other people's work he was "unrivalled for accuracy, fairness and modesty". In the words of the *Times* obituary, "he was a good psychologist, and what is more, he was a good man".

Born Philip Ewart Vernon. **Father** Horace Middleton Vernon. **Marriages** 1) Annie C. Gray, 1938 (deceased); 2) Dorothy Anne Fairley Lawson, a psychologist, 1947. **Children** One son, Philip, from second marriage. **Education** Oundle School; St John's College, Cambridge University, MA, first class honours in both National Science Tripos, Part I, 1926, and Moral Science Tripos, Part II, 1927; Yale University; Harvard University. **Career** Psychologist to London County Council at Maudsley Hospital Child Guidance Clinic, 1933–35; head of psychology department, Jordanhill Training Centre, Glasgow, 1935–38; head of psychology department, University of Glasgow, 1938–47; professor of educational psychology, University of London, Institute of Education, 1949–64, professor of psychology, 1964–68; professor of educational psychology, University of Calgary, 1968–78; emeritus professor: University of Calgary, University of London, 1978–87. **Related activities** Psychological research adviser to Admiralty and War Office, 1942–45; numerous international educational consultancies and lecture tours for British Council, 1953–68; visiting professor: Princeton University and Educational Testing Service, 1957, Teachers' College, Sydney, 1977. **Offices and memberships** President: Psychological section, British Association for the Advancement of Science, 1952, British Psychological Association, 1954–55. **Awards and honours** John Stewart of Rannoch Scholarship in Sacred Music, 1925; Strathcona Research Studentship, 1927–29; Laura Spelman Rockefeller Fellowship in Social Sciences, 1929–31; fellowship, St John's College, Cambridge, 1930–33; Pinsent-Darwin Studentship in mental pathology, 1933–35; fellow, Center for Advanced Studies in Behavioral Sciences, Stanford University, 1961–62; Government of Alberta Achievement Award, 1972; visiting fellow, Canada Council, 1975; honorary LLD, University of Calgary, 1980. **Publications** (with Gordon W. Allport) *Studies in Expressive Movement*, 1933;

The Measurement of Abilities, 1940, second edition, 1956; (with J.B. Parry) *Personnel Selection in the British Forces*, 1949; *The Structure of Human Abilities*, 1950, second edition, 1961; *Personality Tests and Assessments*, 1953; *Secondary School Selection*, 1957; *Intelligence and Attainment Tests*, 1960; *Personality Assessment: A Critical Survey*, 1963; *Intelligence and Cultural Environment*, 1969; *Readings in Creativity*, 1971; (with G. Adamson and Dorothy F. Vernon) *Psychology and Education of Gifted Children*, 1977; *Intelligence: Heredity and Environment*, 1979; *Abilities and Achievements of Orientals in North America*, 1982; numerous papers in British and American psychological journals. **Cause of death** Undisclosed, at age 82.

DICK WELLSTOOD

American Jazz Musician

Born **Greenwich, Connecticut, 25 November 1927**

Died **Palo Alto, California, 24 July 1987**

Jazz has always had a very ambiguous attitude to its past, not least because the headlong rush towards the sound of the new constantly relegates the old to the sidelines. But one man who consistently ignored that urge and successfully combined the old with the new was the pianist Dick Wellstood. For him, jazz history was jazz present, and almost every style of jazz was at his fingertips.

Wellstood was essentially a stride pianist who used that boisterous style as a basis for his improvisations. He learned to play piano in Boston and New York in the early 1940s, a period when the stride piano of James P. Johnson, Willie "The Lion" Smith and others was at the height of its popularity, and soon became a proficient stride and boogie-woogie pianist. He made his first public appearance in New York's Paddock Lounge in 1945, and a year later he was playing dixieland with Bob Wilber's Wildcats. In 1947 he was playing and recording with the great Sidney Bechet in Chicago. By this time, exposure to jazz in its two major cities meant that Wellstood had listened at first hand to all those pianists—notably Art Tatum and the bop pianist Bud Powell—who were to influence him most.

Throughout the 1950s, Wellstood worked with an impressive array of stars, including Roy Eldridge, Charlie Shavers, and Bechet again, and played with numerous bands. In New York he was house pianist at the Metropole and then Nick's Club, and in the 1960s he worked frequently as soloist, or as an accompanist to a large number of established swing or dixieland stars, notably Henry "Red" Allen, Coleman Hawkins, Ben Webster and Wild Bill Davidson. For two years he toured with Gene Krupa's quartet, visiting South America (1965) and Israel (1966). By this time, Wellstood was well established in his own right and recorded a number of solo albums that did much to widen his reputation as a proficient and astute improviser.

As with many jazz musicians, the later 1960s were lean times, for rock music was diminishing the opportunities for live work. Wellstood was scathing about this new music. "All this electric junk's really beaten the shit out of acoustic music," he told *Crescendo* in an interview in the mid-1970s, and at one time he was forced to work with Paul Hoffman's society orchestra, hardly at the cutting edge of jazz! However, Wellstood refused to compromise, and managed to combine live solo performances on the concert, club and festival circuit with sleeve-note writing. But in 1985 he was forced to leave music in order to earn some real money, and for ten months he worked in a law firm. Wellstood had qualified as a lawyer from Columbia University Law School in 1958, although he had never practised. Law to him was the last resort, and while "the firm liked my work and I could have stayed there...I realized that all those years in music had ruined me for something like the law". This was not his first break with music, for in the early 1950s he had almost been lost to jazz entirely, racing cycles and hoping for Olympic selection. Luckily for music, he was unsuccessful.

In his piano playing Wellstood remained his own master. Energetic and virtuosic in his approach, his mastery of harmony allowed to him include such bop pieces in his repertory as John Coltrane's "Giant Steps", the ultimate in complex chord progressions. Whatever he played, his wit, knowledge and command of the keyboard allowed him to swing the most unlikely material, for Wellstood loved to revive tunes everyone else had forgotten. Most he played in medium-to-fast tempos, fleshing out the tune with left-hand figures that rarely strayed too far from the deepest end of the keyboard. He would often turn a piece into a stride attack, and was fond of bringing out the ragtime roots in works by such as Ellington. Few pianists had his command of jazz history, and every tune he played he found something interesting to say about it. Wellstood was truly irreplaceable.

Born Richard McQueen Wellstood. **Marriages** Two; second to Diane McClumpha. **Children** Four daughters by first marriage. **Education** Studied piano, Boston and New York; graduated Columbia University Law School, 1958. **Career** Jazz pianist; professional début, Jimmy Ryan's in Bob Wilber's combo, 1946; played with Bob Wilber, 1946–50, Jimmy Archey, 1950–52, Roy Eldridge, 1953, Conrad Janis, 1953–60, Gene Krupa, 1965–57; also pursued solo career; played occasionally with Sidney Bechet, Rex Stewart, J. Windhurst, Red Allen, Ben Webster, Coleman Hawkins, Wild Bill Davison, Vic Dickenson and Buster Bailey; regular performer at Newport and JVC Jazz Festivals. **Other activities** Practised law, 1985. **Recordings** (include) (as soloist) *Alone*, Jigy JCE73, 1970–71; *From Ragtime On*, Chi 109, 1971; *At the Cookery*, Chi 139, 1975; "Giant Steps" on *Piano Giants*, Swingtime 8202, 1980; (as leader) *From Dixie to Swing*, Classic Editions 10, *ca.*1972; (with P. Ind) *Some Hefty Cats!*, Hefty Jazz 100, 1977; (as sideman) Sidney Bechet, "Polka Dot Stomp"/"Kansas City Man Blues", Col 38319, 1947; R. Eldridge, *Swing Goes Dixie*, Verve 1010, 1956; Joe Venuti and Zoot Sims, *Joe and Zoot*, Chi 128, 1974. **Cause of death** Heart failure, at age 59.

DAME LESLIE WHATELEY

British Director of Women's Military Service

***Born* London, England, 28 January 1899**

***Died* Wiltshire, England, 4 July 1987**

Born into a distinguished army family at the end of the last century, Dame Leslie Whateley followed the family tradition of giving her life to public service. Her father, Colonel Evelyn Wood, had begun his army career with the Ashanti Expedition to Africa four years earlier, and her grandfather, Field Marshal Sir Evelyn Wood, had been awarded a VC.

However, the young Leslie Violet Lucy Evelyn Mary Wood, as she was initially, was not educated with a military career in mind. As was suitable for a girl of her time, she was sent to convent schools in Sussex and London, leaving by the time she was 16 to assist her grandfather in writing his memoirs, later published as *Winnowed Memories*. Subsequently she worked as secretary to a number of District Nursing Associations. In 1922 she married and had her only child, a son.

It was in 1938, at the time of the Munich Crisis, when she was 39, that she decided to join the newly-formed Auxiliary Territorial Service (ATS) as a subaltern at Finsbury Barracks, situated in a less than inspiring inner-London area. The ATS was originally intended to be precisely what its name implied: an auxiliary force of women volunteers to back up and assist the army. However, it rapidly became apparent that women were capable of very much more than was previously considered possible, or even probable. Leslie Whateley was making rapid movement upwards and within three years had become deputy director. Two years later she was the overall director and her organizational abilities had been well recognized by the War Office.

Having been classified for just four different types of war work, women actually became proficient in over 100 capacities. The types of work ranged from the unsurprising office, mess, switchboard and cookhouse duties, to the more traditional male jobs, such as welding, driving, examining ammunition and camouflage. They also grew to encompass the totally new field of radar and field communications. Many saw active service abroad and over 3000 women qualified for the Africa Star. Others were in the front line at home. The ATS manned vital anti-aircraft gun emplacements in London's dockland (a prime target for enemy bombing). They were expected to keep the generators running, which included being able to strip them down and service them, as well as to watch the radar for hostile approaches.

Women were not conscripted but recruited through the Ministry of Labour. One recruit had registered with the Labour Exchange in 1942 but was not permitted by her family to pursue her ambition for active service for two more years. As the war in Europe was coming to a very clear ending, No. 230873 Second Subaltern Elizabeth Alexandra Mary Windsor started with the No. 1 Mechanical Transport Training Centre. Later to become Queen Elizabeth II, she was soon driving heavy vehicles and chauffeuring her commandant to base every morning. According to a 1983 biography, it was quite normal to find the heir presumptive to the British Throne "emerging from beneath a lorry with grease all over her hands, or talking sparking-plugs throughout dinner". The ATS was a tremendous force in bringing women from immensely varied backgrounds into close contact, and giving them an insight into each other's lives—something unimaginable in the very class-ridden society of pre-war Britain.

Leslie Whateley, as she became on her second marriage in 1939, was made a Commander of the British Empire in 1943 and a Dame Commander in 1946 on her retirement from the ATS. During her leadership, members of her "army" numbered over a quarter of a million and they served not only at home but in France, Africa, Canada, Germany, the West Indies, Palestine, Egypt, Italy and the USA. Her help in training and equipping French women volunteers earned her nomination to the Legion of Honour, and her advice on the enlargement and management of women in military service in the USA brought her the Order of Merit.

It might be thought that, now aged 47, Dame Leslie would have eased herself back into a comfortable upper-middle-class retirement in England, enjoying her leisure pursuits of golf and gardening. But, once she had written her own war memoirs, *As Thoughts Survive*, she was ready to tackle something new. In her early fifties she took on the directorship of the World Bureau of Girl Guides, which involved her in a formidable programme of travel throughout the world. Her primary interest lay in Asia where she felt the guiding movement had much to offer in terms of alleviating juvenile delinquency and in fostering positive attitudes towards voluntary work with orphans and the homeless.

Leaving this onerous position at the age of 65, she still had energy and commitment for the welfare of others. She became the administrator of voluntary services at Queen Mary's Hospital in Roehampton, on the southern fringes of London. This post involved organizing amenities for patients which lie outside the province of medical or nursing staff.

She finally stopped working in 1974 when she had reached her mid-seventies, thus epitomizing a typically British middle-class way of life, with a lengthy history of service to her country and to those less fortunate than herself.

Dame Leslie Whateley has left the Western world one tremendous legacy. Prior to the last war women had no traditional place in any of the armed services. Thanks to her pioneering work in what has been renamed the Women's Royal Army Corps, it is now accepted that women have a full and vital role to play in all of them.

Born Leslie Violet Lucy Evelyn Mary Wood. **Parents** Colonel Evelyn F.M. and Ada Lilian (Hutton) Wood. **Marriages** 1) W.J. Balfour, 1922; 2) H. Raymond Whateley, squadron leader, Royal Air Force Volunteer Reserve, 1939. **Children** One son from first marriage. **Education** Convents of the Holy Child, St Leonards-on-Sea, Essex, and Cavendish Square, London. **Military service** Deputy director, Auxiliary Territorial Service, 1938–46, 1941–43, director, 1943–46, retired 1946. **Career** Private secretary, 1915–22; secretary to several District Nursing Associations and Village Institutes, 1922–38; director, World Bureau of Girl Guides/Girl Scouts, 1951–64; administrator of voluntary services, Queen Mary's Hospital, Roehampton, 1965–74. **Awards and honours** Commander of the Order of the British Empire, 1943; Chevalier, Legion of Honour, 1945; Dame Commander Order of the British Empire, 1946; United States Order of Merit, 1946; honorary colonel, 688 Battalion Heavy Anti-Aircraft Regiment Royal Artillery (Territorial Army), 1948–53; Territorial Efficiency Decoration, 1951. **Publications** *As Thoughts Survive*, 1949; *Yesterday, Today and Tomorrow*, 1974. **Cause of death** Undisclosed, at age 88.

HUGH WHEELER

British/American Novelist and Playwright
***Born* Northwood, Middlesex, 19 March 1912**
***Died* Monterey, Massachusetts, 26 July 1987**

Hugh Wheeler was one of those unusually lucky or gifted people able to live by his pen. "I've never done a day's other work," he once said, "never been hired by anyone." His published output ran to some 40 novels, almost as many short stories, 15 plays, six screenplays and the scripts of at least three musicals. "One of my ridiculous efforts," Wheeler confessed, "was to try to write in every medium, which I've somewhat self-consciously done." During his early years as a novelist his lifestyle generally included six months travelling each year; later in life he would usually spend the winter in the Caribbean. Like many successful writers, Wheeler's working timetable was rigid. He got up early and wrote every day between six and eleven. He never took a holiday, saying that he was able to fit any holiday activity easily into his working life.

Wheeler himself appeared to ascribe chance a large role in the drama of his life. He had always wanted to be an American, then "just happened" to discover that because he had fought in the US Army during the war, he was eligible for US citizenship. Similarly, he had always wanted to be a writer and "just happened" to meet the crime writer Wilson Webb in 1933 when Webb was looking for a replacement collaborator on his Q. Patrick series and Wheeler was fresh out of university and looking for a job. Later, when Wheeler tired of crime writing, it "just happened" that all his close friends were theatre people, which made it quite natural for him to turn his talents to playwriting.

Wheeler's collaboration with Wilson Webb lasted until 1952. Together they produced an astonishing number of books under three pseudonyms: Q. Patrick, Patrick Quentin and Jonathan Stagge. When Webb finally retired, Wheeler went on to write another four books alone. At the beginning of his career as a crime writer, he claimed that his own reading tastes were nearer to Proust. His talents were, however, ideally suited to the job. The books won praise from the critics, the *New York Times* describing Patrick Quentin as "one of the truly great plotters in the field of suspense", and the British critic Francis Iles opining that, "he's the number one of American crime novelists". Perhaps even more telling was that, in 1984, almost all Wheeler's books were still in print, including some that were 50 years old.

When, in the 1960s, Wheeler turned to the theatre, two of his plays—*Big Fish, Little Fish* and *Look: We've Come Through!*—appeared on Broadway, as did his later *We Have Always Lived in the Castle*. Wheeler won the New York Drama Critics' Circle Award four times, and went on to write the scripts for a number of successful films, including *Cabaret* and *Travels With My Aunt*. The musicals he worked on in collaboration with Hal Prince and Stephen Sondheim included *A Little Night Music*, *Sweeney Todd* and *Candide*—all of them adding to what Hal Prince described as Wheeler's "considerable reputation". Despite his belief in chance, there was no doubt by the time he died that Hugh Wheeler's reputation was based not only on good fortune but also on considerable and versatile talent.

Born Hugh Callingham Wheeler. **Pseudonyms** Q. Patrick; Patrick Quentin; Jonathan Stagge. **Parents** Harold, a civil servant, and Florence (Scammell) Wheeler. **Education** University of London, BA, 1932. **Emigration** Left England for USA, 1933; naturalized, 1942. **Military service** US Army Medical Corps, World War II. **Career** Writer, principally of detective novels and short stories (with Richard Wilson Webb until 1952); also playwright, screenwriter and librettist. **Awards and honours** Mystery Writers' of America Edgar Allan Poe Award, 1962, 1973; Tony Award for *A Little Night Music*, 1973, for *Candide*, 1974, and for *Sweeney Todd*, 1979; New York Drama Critics' Circle Award, 1973, 1976, 1979; Vernon-Rice Award, 1973; Drama Desk Award, 1973, 1974, 1979; Outer Critics' Award, 1979; Hull-Wariner Award, 1981. **Novels as Patrick Quentin** (all published in New York and London, unless stated) *A Puzzle for Fools*, 1936; *Puzzle for Players*, 1938, 1939; *Puzzle for Puppets*, 1944; *Puzzle for Wantons*, 1945, 1946, reissued as *Slay the Loose Ladies*, New York, 1948; *Puzzle for Fiends*, 1946, 1947, reissued as *Love Is a Deadly Weapon*, New York, 1949; *Puzzle for Pilgrims*, 1947, 1948, reissued as *The Fate of the Immodest Blonde*, New York, 1950; *Run to Death*, 1948; *The Follower*, 1950; *Black Widow*, New York, 1952, published as *Fatal Woman*, London, 1953; *My Son, the Murderer*, New York, 1954, published as *The Wife of Ronald Sheldon*, London, 1954; *The Man With Two Wives*, 1955; *The Man in the Net*, 1956; *Suspicious Circumstances*, 1957; *Shadow of Guilt*, 1959; *The Green-eyed Monster*, 1960; *Family Skeletons*, 1965. **Novels as Q. Patrick** *The Grindle Nightmare*, New York, 1935, published as *Darker Grows the Valley*, London, 1936; *Death Goes to School*, 1936; *Death for Dear Clara*, 1937; *The File on Fenton and Farr*, 1937, 1938; *The File on Claudia Cragge*, 1938; *Death and the Maiden*, 1939; *Return to the Scene*, New York, 1941, published as *Death in Bermuda*, London, 1941; *Danger Next Door*, London, 1952. **Novels as Jonathan Stagge** *Murder Gone to Earth*, London, 1936, published as *The Dogs Do Bark*, New York, 1937; *Murder or Mercy*, London, 1937, published as *Murder by Prescription*, New York, 1938; *The Stars Spell Death*, New York, 1939, published as *Murder in the Stars*, London, 1940; *Turn of the Table*, New York, 1940, published as *Funeral for Five*, London, 1940; *The Yellow Taxi*, New York, 1942, published as *Call a Hearse*, London, 1942; *The Scarlet Circle*, New York,

1943, published as *Light From a Lantern*, London, 1943; *Death My Darling Daughters*, New York, 1945, published as *Death and the Dear Girls*, London, 1946; *Death's Old Sweet Song*, 1946, 1947; *The Three Fears*, 1949. **Short stories as Q. Patrick** *The Ordeal of Mrs Snow and Other Stories* (collection), London, 1961, New York, 1962; "Murder on New Year's Eve", *American Magazine*, Springfield, Ohio, October 1937; "Another Man's Poison", *American Magazine*, Springfield, Ohio, January 1940; "Witness for the Prosecution", *Ellery Queen's Mystery Magazine*, New York, July 1946; "The Plaster Cat", *Mystery Book*, New York, July 1946; "White Carnations", *Best Detective Stories of the Year* 1946, edited by David Coxe Cooke, New York, 1946; "This Way Out", *Mystery Book*, New York, March 1947; "Little Boy Lost", *Ellery Queen's Mystery Magazine*, New York, October, 1947; "The Corpse in the Closet", *Ellery Queen's Mystery Magazine*, New York, January 1948; "Farewell Performance", *Ellery Queen's Mystery Magazine*, New York, January 1948; "The Jack of Diamonds", *Ellery Queen's Mystery Magazine*, New York, February 1949; "The Lord Seest Me", *Ellery Queen's Mystery Magazine*, New York, July 1949; "Murder in One Scene", *Best Detective Stories of the Year 1949*, edited by David Coxe Cooke, New York, 1949; "Girl Overboard", *Four and Twenty Bloodhounds*, edited by Anthony Boucher, New York, 1950, London, 1951; "Another Man's Poison", *Ellery Queen's Mystery Magazine*, New York, January 1951; "Death Fright" *American Magazine*, Springfield, Ohio, January 1951; "Who Killed the Mermaid?", *Ellery Queen's Mystery Magazine*, New York, February 1951; "Town Blonde, Country Blonde", *Ellery Queen's Mystery Magazine*, New York, August 1951; "All the Way to the Moon", *Ellery Queen's Awards, 6th Series*, Boston and London, 1951; "This Looks Like Murder", *Ellery Queen's Mystery Magazine*, New York, March 1952; "The Pigeon Woman", *Ellery Queen's Mystery Magazine*, New York, July 1952; "Death on the Riviera", *Ellery Queen's Mystery Magazine*, New York, September 1952; "Death on Saturday Night", *Ellery Queen's Mystery Magazine*, New York, January 1953; "Woman of Ice", *Ellery Queen's Mystery Magazine*, New York, February 1953; "The Laughing Man", *American Magazine*, Springfield, Ohio, March 1953; "The Hated Woman", *The Saint*, New York, August 1953; "The Red Balloon", *Weird Tales*, Chicago, November 1953; "The Glamorous Opening", *Ellery Queen's Mystery Magazine*, New York, January 1954; "Death and Canasta", *Ellery Queen's Mystery Magazine*, New York, April 1954; "The Predestined", *Weird Tales*, Chicago, May 1954; "Death Before Breakfast", *Crime for Two*, edited by Frances and Richard Lockridge, Philadelphia, 1955, and London, 1957; "On the Day of the Rose Show", *Ellery Queen's Mystery Magazine*, New York, March 1956; "Going, Going, Gone!", *Ellery Queen's Mystery Magazine*, New York, October, 1956; "Murder in the Alps", "*This Week's" Stories of Mystery and Suspense*, edited by Stewart Beach, New York, 1957; "Lioness vs. Panther", *Ellery Queen's Mystery Magazine*, New York, July 1958. **Short stories as Patrick Quentin** "This Will Kill You", *The Edgar Winners*, edited by Bill Pronzini, New York, 1980. **Plays** (with date and location of first production) *Big Fish, Little Fish*, New York, 1961, London, 1962; *Look! We've Come Through!*, New York, 1961; *Rich Little Rich Girl*, adapted from play by Miguel Mihura and Alvaro deLaiglesia, Philadelphia, 1964; *We Have Always Lived in the Castle*, adapted from novel by Shirley Jackson, New York, 1966; (with Leonard B. Stern) *The Snoop Sisters* (for television), 1972; *A Little Night Music*, music and lyrics by Stephen Sondheim, adapted from film by Ingmar Bergman, New York, 1973, London, 1975; (with Joseph Stein) *Irene*, adapted by Harry Rigby from play by James Montgomery, music by Harry Tierney, lyrics by Joseph McCarthy, New York, 1973, London, 1976; *Candide*, music by Leonard Bernstein, lyrics by Richard Wilbur, adapted from novel by Voltaire, New York, 1973; *Truckload*, music by Louis St Louis, lyrics by Wes Harris, New York, 1975; (with John Weidmann) *Pacific Overtures*, music and lyrics by Stephen Sondheim, New York, 1976; *Sweeney Todd, the Demon Barber of Fleet Street*, music and lyrics by Stephen Sondheim, adapted from play by C.G. Bond, New York, 1979, London, 1980; *Silverlake*, adapted from libretto by Georg Kaiser, music by Kurt Weil, New York, 1980; *The*

Student Prince, adapted from libretto by Dorothy Donelly, music by Sigmund Romberg, New York, 1980. **Screenplays** (with Peter Viertel) *Five Miles to Midnight*, 1962; *Something for Everyone*, 1969; *Cabaret*, 1972; (with Jay Presson Allen) *Travels With My Aunt*, 1973; *A Little Night Music*, 1977; *Nijinsky*, 1980. **Other** "Who'd Do It?", *Chimera*, New Jersey, Summer 1947; (as Hugh Wheeler) *The Crippled Muse* (novel), London, 1951, New York, 1952; (as Q. Patrick) *The Girl on the Gallows*, reportage, New York, 1954. **Cause of death** Undisclosed, at age 75.

AUGUST

I.W. ABEL

American Labour Leader
***Born* Magnolia, Ohio, 11 August 1908**
***Died* Malvern, Ohio, 10 August 1987**

"He was a visionary who recognized decades before the notion became fashionable, that workers, employers and the public each have a stake in the others' well-being." Thus Lynn Williams, president of the steelworkers' union, said of Iorwith Wilbur "Abe" Abel, the man who helped found the labour union, the United Steelworkers of America. As is often the case, this "visionary" had good reason for his ideals: during the 1920s Abel went to work for the steel industry at a time when employees were considered only so much fodder. The Depression reinforced his convictions and it was not long before unionism became Abe Abel's *raison d'être*.

The son of a blacksmith/clayworker and of a coalminer's daughter of Welsh descent, Abel's educational expectations in turn-of-the-century Ohio were not very high. He attended the local elementary schools and went briefly to the Canton Actual Business College, but by the age of 17, he was working for the American Steel and Tin Works in Canton, not far from where he was born. His first job was as an iron moulder, but soon he took shifts at various iron and steel companies in Canton. "Back in those days," he recalled, "you just moved around pretty much at will. There were times, depending on the work, when we'd make $12 or $14 a day, hourly scale about 75 cents." While such wages were not terribly bad for the 1920s, job security was virtually non-existent, and with the advent of the Depression, wages followed the same route. Abel was reduced to firing a kiln in a bricklaying works for 16 cents an hour, 12 hours a day, seven days a week. The hardship proved to be a turning point: "That miserable job helped straighten out my social thinking," Abel declared, "and pointed me in the direction I was to travel the rest of my life." As time would show, that direction was as a union leader, a calling often fraught with tragedy.

In 1936 ten organizers for the steelworkers' union movement were gunned down by police in Chicago when they opened fire on a Memorial Day rally. It was after this incident that Abel, now working at the Tinker Company in Canton, joined the infant union's organizing committee and helped found Local Union 1123; he remained a dues-payer in the local for the rest of his life. During this period Abel came under the influence of Philip Murray, founder and president of the

Steelworkers' Organizing Committee. Murray appointed Abel as head of the committee staff; then in 1942, when the union came into formal existence, Murray became national president and Abel was chosen as the director of the Canton district. Throughout the war years, Abel remained active on many fronts, serving as a panel member of the War Labor Board and as a member of the Political Action Committee of the Congress of Industrial Organization (CIO).

In 1952 Philip Murray died, and the first heyday of the union almost died with him. Abel ran for the post of national secretary-treasurer and won; for the next 12 years he served under the new president, David J. McDonald. It was not long before Abel had cause for concern. Under McDonald the union became rife with discontent throughout the country and went through three major strikes. While McDonald continued what Abel termed "tuxedo unionism" (i.e. a smart appearance with nothing underneath), Abel himself travelled around the nation listening to the various grievances McDonald chose to ignore. By 1965 Abel had amassed a loyal following, enough to allow him to challenge McDonald for the presidency and beat him by 10,000 votes. He went on to be elected as a vice-president of the American Federation of Labor (AFL)–CIO.

Abel's primary goal, however, was to rebuild the steelworkers' union membership and resolve some of the tensions which had built up for over a decade. His policies were well presented and unpretentious. Under his leadership the union's membership rose dramatically, a strike fund of over $85 million was compiled, and a no-strike agreement to end production and stockpiling swings was reached. A shy man in public, Abel had a talent for listening to both union men and employers, which soon won him the respect of both. He was calm and understanding, two factors which were indispensable at the bargaining table, and he was never quick to use militant action.

"Collective bargaining is pretty much of a crisis business," he explained. "You have to have patience and you have to be tolerant. A strike is an important action and a prerogative for labour, but, like every other right, it's got to be exercised with good judgment. It's an act of last resort, pretty much like getting involved in a war."

Abel did not believe that negotiation should be confined to the bargaining table. He campaigned in Washington, DC, for legislation to improve health and safety conditions on the job and for pension guarantees for employees. He also served as a member of the US delegation to the United Nations. The grandfatherly labour leader made history in 1973, when he signed the Experimental Negotiating Agreement with Big Steel—an act with which the union pledged not to strike during the 1974 contract talks, with both sides agreeing to submit irreconcilable differences to arbitration. As it happened, the 1974 talks gave steelworkers a $2 an hour wage increase over three years, as well as the right to strike over plant conditions—a right which had previously been denied them. The main achievement, however, was the end of the so-called "boom-bust" cycle caused by stockpiling. Unfortunately, the arrangement ceased when the steel industry fell into recession during the late 1970s, an almost predictable turn of events considering Abel retired in 1977.

Even in his retirement, the former labour leader still actively monitored union affairs. In 1986 he said that he believed attitudes towards organized labour had deteriorated in recent years, mainly because the new generation did not remember the struggle for rights which had been present at its beginnings. "Some of it is fear," Abel remarked. "Some of it is concern with what is happening, industry shutting down plants and laying off many people. Then you've got the younger element. They think we've always had good wages because employers believed in paying good wages. They think they get benefits like we have and holidays, vacation, medical insurance and all that because employers want to give them that."

White-haired and stocky with a preference for conservative dark suits, in his latter years Abel more closely resembled a church deacon than the determined steelworker who in one year alone led 42 wildcat strikes. His dedication to the cause of labour relations never wavered, and generations of workers to come will benefit from his endeavours.

Born Iorwith Wilbur Abel. **Parents** John Franklin, a blacksmith and clay worker, and Mary Ann (Jones) Abel. **Marriages** 1) Bernice N. Joseph, 1930 (died, 1982); 2) Martha L. Turvey. **Children** Two daughters, Karen and Linda, from first marriage. **Education** Local elementary schools; Magnolia High School, Ohio; Canton Actual Business College, Ohio. **Career** Steel worker and labour leader; moulder, American Sheet and Tin Plate Company, 1925–33; also worked for Canton Malleable Iron Company, Timkin Roller Bearing Company, Colonial Foundry, Canton, and as a brickyard worker, 1933–37; organized Canton local branch, United Steelworkers of America, 1936, staff, 1937–77, elected director, Canton–Massillon district, 1942, secretary-treasurer of national organization, 1953–65, president, 1965–77, retired, 1977. **Related activities** Member, War Manpower Commission and War Labor Board, World War II; American Federation of Labor–Congress of Industrial Organizations: elected vice-president and executive council member, 1965, president, industrial union department, 1968; appointed to pay board, National Stabilization Program, 1971, resigned, 1972. **Other activities** Alternate delegate, United States delegation to United Nations, 1967; National Advisory Commission on Civil Disorders: Democrat, nominated Hubert Humphrey for president, national convention, 1968. **Cause of death** Cancer, at age 78.

CARLOS DRUMMOND de ANDRADE

Brazilian Poet

***Born* Itabira, Brazil, 31 October 1902**

***Died* Rio de Janeiro, Brazil, 17 August 1987**

Carlos Drummond de Andrade was, by general consent, one of the major Portuguese language poets of the century. Yet his deceptively simple work has been poorly served outside his native language by inadequate translations; and his own retiring personality helped keep his international reputation a modest one.

Drummond de Andrade, his father a local landowner and his mother of Scottish descent, was born at Itabira in the mining state of Minas Gerais, some 300 miles to the north of Rio de Janeiro. Minas Gerais is a region of stark contrasts, where the living conditions, at least for the poor, are harsh, and where religion plays an important role in daily life.

The young Drummond de Andrade was country bred and showed an early interest in literature. When aged 16 he was sent to a Jesuit college at nearby Nova Friburgo, but he rebelled against what he considered the excessive discipline of the Jesuits, and was eventually expelled.

In 1920 the family moved to Belo Horizonte, capital of Minas Gerais. Here young Drummond de Andrade's horizons improved; he was soon actively involved in the literary café society of the province, winning a competition with an early short story, and making contact with many of the leading figures in Brazilian art and literature. In 1921 he began studying pharmacy at the University of Minas Gerais but, although he graduated four years later, he never took up pharmacy as a career. The call of literary controversy was too great. Instead, he helped start up the Modernist periodical *A Revista* (The Review), and to make ends meet got a job teaching geography and Portuguese back in Itabira. This led to a living in journalism, first as contributor, then eventually as chief editor of the *Diário de Minas* (Minas Daily), then on the official state newspaper, *Minas Gerais*, where he worked from 1930 to 1932.

In the meantime Drummond de Andrade was beginning to make his mark as a poet. To be young and literary in the Brazil of the 1920s was to be a Modernist, committed to a sometimes shocking extravagance of expression. Drummond de Andrade was clearly part of this movement, but like all great artists took from it only what he needed.

In the first issue of *A Revista* he described the modern artist as "shunning all abstract theories in order to pursue reality with unblemished hands". For him, as he later explained, this meant giving voice to Brazilian nationalism, however primitive, in an attempt to avoid foreign models. This was demonstrated in his first volume of poems, *Alguma Poesia* (Some Poetry), published in 1930, which emphasized local, provincial experience. His verse was remarkably unadorned, involving a flat relation of the visible and the matter of fact, and considerable repetition.

His second volume, *Brejo das Almas* (Swamp of Souls, 1934), was altogether more sombre, making clear the poet's own rather despondent attitude to human experience. For Drummond de Andrade the essential elements of modern man's predicament were his isolation (something the poet felt keenly himself, despite being by then happily married and a father), and the impossibility of overcoming most of the obstacles in his way. This cultural pessimism can only have been reinforced by the depressing march of world affairs in the 1930s, as well as the almost insuperable problems of Brazil itself.

In 1934 Drummond de Andrade moved to Rio de Janeiro, where he had been appointed personal adviser to the minister of education. He eventually secured a job as archivist in the same ministry, but in 1945 moved to the Office of National Historical and Artistic Heritage, where he headed the history section, a position he kept until his retirement in 1967. He also did editorial work for the Rio *Correio da Manhã* (Morning Mail).

During these years Drummond de Andrade's output continued to grow, reflecting the tremendous variety of his poetic talent, by turns pessimistic, humorous, elegiac, and at all times richly evocative of Brazilian life and conditions. Among his numerous collections, *Sentimento do Mundo* (Grief of the World, 1940) reflected the poet's sense of horror and despondency at the spectacle of world war, as did *Poesias* (Poems, 1942), and *A Rosa do Pove* (The Rose of the People, 1945). One of his most famous poems, "José", has ever since been taken as a classic symbol of Brazilian problems:

> Key in hand, you'd like to open the door—
> there's no door;
> you'd like to drown in the sea,
> but the sea's dried up.

Drummond de Andrade's general outlook became a little more relaxed as he grew older, and it is clear that he lost his belief in socialism and, indeed, in any form of political activism, as a remedy for human problems. His last volume of verse, *Lição de Coisas* (The Lesson of Things), came out in 1962, but he continued to produce critical essays, short stories and translations of French and Spanish authors. Translations of his own work have appeared in most European languages, including English, but the quality of these has often been uneven.

Born Carlos Drummond de Andrade. **Parents** Carlos de Paula Andrade, landowner, and Julieta Augusta (Drummond) de Andrade. **Marriage** Dolores Morais, 1925. **Children** One daughter, Maria Julieta. **Education** Entered Jesuit Colégio Anchieta at Nova Friburgo, 1918, expelled, 1920; studied pharmacy, University of Minas Gerais, 1921–25. **Career** Poet, journalist, critic and short story writer; taught geography and Portuguese, Ginásio Sul-Americano, Itabira, and helped found literary journal, *A Revista*, 1926; joined staff, *Diário de Minas* (Minas Daily), becoming chief editor, 1925–30; editorial staff, *Minas Gerais* (official state newspaper), 1930–32; personal adviser to minister of education, Rio de Janeiro, 1934–45; head, history section, Office of the National Historical and Artistic Heritage, 1945–62; historian, *Correio da Manhã* (Morning Mail), 1954–62; retired, 1962. **Awards and honours** Literary prize for short story "Joquim do Telhado" (Roof-top Joaquin), 1922. **Publications** *Alguma Poesia* (Some Poetry), 1930; *Brejo das Almas* (Swamp of Souls), 1934; *Sentimento do Mundo* (Grief of the World), 1940; *Poesias*, 1942; *A Rosa do Pove* (The Rose of the People), 1945; *Poesia até Agora* (Poetry to Date), 1948; *Claro Enigma* (Bright Enigma), 1951; *Fazendeiro do Ar* (Planter of Air), 1954; *Lição de Coisas* (The Lesson of Things), 1962; *Obra Completa* (Complete Works), 1964; *In the Middle of the Road*, translated by John Nist, 1965; and numerous essays, short stories and short prose works. **Cause of death** Undisclosed, at age 84. **Further reading** M. de Andrade, *Aspectos da Litertura Brasileira*, 1959; H. Martins, *A Riman na Poesia de Carlos Drummond de Andrade*, 1968; G.M. Teles, *Drummond*, 1970; A. Brasil, *Carlos Drummond de Andrade*, 1971; E. de Moraes, *Drummond, rima, Itabira, mundo: ensaio*, 1972; A.R. de Sant'Anna, *Drummond*, 1972.

GEORGIOS ATHANASIADIS-NOVAS

Greek Politician and Poet

***Born* Nafpaktos, Greece, 9 February 1893**

***Died* Athens, Greece, 10 August 1987**

Like Disraeli, Georgios Athanasiadis-Novas led a distinguished life in both the literary and the political arena. In the former he published seven collections of poetry, two of short stories, and a novel, and he was chairman of the prestigious Athens Academy. In politics he held a variety of positions, rising right to the top, albeit to remain there for a short time only: he was prime minister of Greece for 33 days.

Born in Nafpaktos, a port on the Gulf of Corinth, he read law at Athens University and qualified in 1917. He soon decided to become a journalist rather than a lawyer, and from 1919 to 1922 he was a war correspondent, covering the Asia Minor campaign, which culminated in the crushing defeat of the Greek Army and a massive population exchange.

Athanasiadis-Novas began writing at a young age, and in 1920 had his first collection of poetry published, entitled *Proino Xekinima* (Morning Start). Although he enjoyed literary success throughout his life, this and his second collection, *Agapi ston Epakto* (Love in Epaktos), brought him the greatest acclaim, and certainly established him as one of Greece's foremost poets. His work was pastoral, imbued with a provincial freshness, not least because in style he was a devoted follower of Kostis Palamas (1859–1943), the lyric poet who dominated the Greek literary scene for over half a century during a period of great intellectual ferment. Athanasiadis-Novas, who always wrote under the pseudonym of George Athanas (presumably because his real name hardly trips off the tongue), was one of the last Greek poets of what might be called the Palamas circle. His strict observation of orthodox rhyme and versification systems give his work a rather dated feel today. His later works include *Prasino Kapello* (Green Hat), *Deka Erotes* (Ten Love Stories), *Aploikes Psiches* (Simple Souls), *Tragoudia ton Vounon* (Mountain Songs), *Evdokia* (Good Will) and *Monokontilies* (Pencil Strokes).

His political career took off when he was elected a member of parliament for his home town of Nafpaktos in 1926, representing the Free-Thinkers Party. When the latter collapsed in 1928 he joined the Progressive Party, and was re-elected as a deputy in 1932 and 1936.

In 1935 he married Maria Bulgari, daughter of the famous Greek jeweller based in Rome. They did not have any children, and despite his longevity she survived him.

He lived abroad for several periods of his life, including during the Metaxas dictatorship (1936–40), mostly in Italy, where he felt particularly at home. He returned to Nafpaktos during the German occupation of Greece (1940–44), but when the Communists burnt his ancestral home to the ground, destroying, among other things, his precious library and some unpublished manuscripts, he fled to Italy again.

Athanasiadis-Novas joined the Liberal Party in 1949 and was re-elected to parliament the following year. He served as minister of the interior, of education, of industry and as minister in charge of the prime minister's office. It was during this period, in 1955, that he became a member of the Athens Academy.

In 1961 Prime Minister George Papandreou's Centre Union Party absorbed the Liberals, and in 1964 Athanasiadis-Novas became speaker, or president, of the Chamber of Deputies when Papandreou won a decisive election victory.

King Constantine and Prime Minister Papandreou came to blows, irreversibly. Athanasiadis-Novas was one of a number of Centre Union dissidents who supported the king, and on 15 July 1965 Constantine chose him as his prime minister. In a radio broadcast, Athanasiadis-Novas told the Greek people that the king had asked him to form a government exclusively from the majority Centre Union Party in order to restore "normal political conditions"; he added that his appointment was "intended to underline the king's firm determination to cooperate with the parliamentary majority and to respect the spirit and the letter of our constitutional regime". He took the education portfolio too.

He immediately allied himself still further with the monarchy by alleging that Papandreou had concealed three vital letters that he had received from the king.

Things quickly turned sourer still when pro-Papandreou demonstrations took place in Crete and Athens. By 21 July the police were using tear gas to disperse thousands of demonstrators in Athens who were calling for the dismissal of the Athanasiadis-Novas government. The violence escalated, a student was killed (the trouble began outside the university), and many civilians and police were wounded. The Communists played a leading part in the protests.

Public order was eventually restored, but inevitably Athanasiadis-Novas's government failed to win a vote of confidence (although he only lost by 167 votes to 131), and on 5 August he resigned after a three-day debate characterized by much Greek-style uproar in the chamber, and more demonstrations by Papandreou supporters outside.

The left-wing Centre Union leader Elias Tsirimokos then formed a Cabinet, of which Athanasiadis-Novas was appointed deputy prime minister. This regime did not last long either, and in September Athanasiadis-Novas became deputy premier of the Stefanopoulos government, which hung on with a tiny majority for 17 months.

But political stability was not to return to Greece for a long time. In 1967 the hated military regime of the colonels put a stop to all this democratic coming and going, and Athanasiadis-Novas withdrew from political life, living in quiet retirement with his wife until his death at the age of 94.

Born Georgios Athanasiadis-Novas. **Pseudonym** George Athanas. **Parents** Themistoklis and Evdokia Athanasiadis-Novas. **Marriage** Maria S. Bulgari, 1935. **Education** Athens University. **Career** Poet and politician; journalist and lawyer; joined Free-Thinkers Party, 1926;

member of parliament, 1926–39, 1951, 1956, 1958, 1961, 1963, 1964; joined Progressive Party, 1928; minister of interior, 1945; minister of education, 1945, 1950–51; joined Liberal Party, 1949; minister of industry, 1951–52; minister in charge of prime minister's office, 1951–52, 1963; joined Centre Union Party, 1961; president, Chamber of Deputies, 1964–65; prime minister, July–August, 1965; deputy prime minister, 1965–66. **Offices and memberships** Member, Athens Academy, 1955, chairman, 1964. **Publications** (as George Athanas) *Proino Xekinima* (Morning Start); *Agapi ston Epakto* (Love in Epaktos); *Prasino Kapello* (Green Hat); *Deka Erotes* (Ten Love Stories); *Aploikes Psiches* (Simple Souls); *Drosseri Kaimi* (Happy Trouble); *Tragoudia ton Vounon* (Mountain Songs); *Evdokia* (Good Will); *Vathies Rizes* (Deep Roots); *Timia Dora* (Honest Gifts); *Astegnoto Dakri* (Tears That Do Not Dry); *Enos ke Thrinos* (Praise and Lament); *Monokontilies* (Pencil Strokes). **Cause of death** Undisclosed, at age 94.

CLARENCE BROWN

American Film Director

Born **Clinton, Massachusetts, 10 May 1890**

Died **Santa Monica, California, 17 August 1987**

For many years, Clarence Brown's reputation has rested on the eight films in which he directed Greta Garbo. Fortunately, this somewhat restricted view of his work has in recent decades expanded to his other films of note. His versatility in handling any genre, his meticulous and smooth execution, and his facility for drawing the best from his performers (particularly women) are three major reasons why Brown became the number one director for Metro-Goldwyn-Mayer. They are also reasons, among others, why he is so respected by film historians.

The others are wrapped around his complete devotion to his work. That single-mindedness was demonstrated the first time the young Brown saw a film in the making. The engineering graduate was fixing and selling cars in 1915 when he saw the cameras roll at Fort Lee, New Jersey, the major studio, in those days. "I was absolutely fascinated," he remembered. "I thought, 'I could do that'." He sold his business and went to Hollywood, where he met and apprenticed himself to Maurice Tournier, a major name at Universal Studios. He remained with him for seven years, and often acknowledged his debt to his mentor. "He taught me everything there is to know about making movies: composition...and the most important thing of all, tempo."

Brown graduated from assistant to editor, then, when Tournier fell ill, co-director. Their first film together was *The Last of the Mohicans* (1920). His *Signal Tower* (1924) illustrated an excellent command of cutting; like David Lean, Brown would create a superb film because he knew the anatomy of the art from the inside out. United Artists, impressed by what they had seen, signed Brown to make *The Eagle* (1925), with Rudolf Valentino, and Brown's name was made. He then signed with Metro-Goldwyn-Mayer, where he remained until 1952. (He has the distinction of being the only director there with whom Louis B. Mayer never quarrelled.) A second turning point came a year later with *Flesh and the Devil*, starring the (comparatively) new Garbo, the experienced John Gilbert and Swedish import Lars Hanson, who was already considered a brilliant actor and matinée idol in Scandinavia. His talents were to be wasted in Hollywood, but not by Brown, who proved to be his best director (apart from Victor Sjöström—Seastrom in the US). The assignment was difficult, partly because the storyline was threadbare and melodramatic, and partly because in the beginning Gilbert regarded his co-star as temperamental, while she did not seem to regard him at all. However, Brown had a certain renown, like George Cukor, for being "a woman's director"; his tact in smoothing frayed tempers helped ensure good performances, imbuing Garbo's with a subtlety not achieved before. The film was a hit, and the chemistry between Garbo and Gilbert that was to fuel the gossip columns later, shone through. Brown directed them again in *Woman of Affairs* (1929).

The title "A film by Clarence Brown" was a commonplace and popular attribute throughout the 1920s, as the audiences recognized the role of the director to be almost as important as the star. This kind of appreciation was not to reappear until the 1960s. Fortunately, the trend has remained.

Garbo's first talking picture, *Anna Christie* (1930), was directed by Brown, who helped establish her as a woman of strong sexuality. With dialogue, he not only made her appear both tragic and comical, but he also sidestepped the traps which were often lurking for people with heavy accents. (Vilma Banky and Anna Sten, for example, did not survive their dialogue.) *Romance* (1930), *Inspiration* (1931), *Anna Karenina* (1935) and *Conquest* (also known as *Marie Walewska*, 1938) followed. The combination of Brown's and Garbo's names ensured success, and he became her favourite director. "Greta's main thing was her shyness," Brown said. "A stranger on the set would upset her. I would never do anything aggressive with Garbo; nobody ever knew what directions I gave her because we'd always go behind a set and talk very quietly about the scene." Brown's sensitivity also brought out the best in Joan Crawford, with whom he made five pictures, including *Chained* and *Gorgeous Hussy*, Clark Gable (*Romance*), Spencer Tracy (*Edison the Man*), Jean Harlow (*Wife vs. Secretary*), James Stewart and Hedy Lamarr (*Come Live With Me*) and Elizabeth Taylor (*National Velvet* and *White Cliffs of Dover*).

Brown's filming of *Ah! Wilderness* in 1935 marked the beginning of his love for nostalgic American themes. Eugene O'Neill's gentle study of small town life bloomed under Brown's camera. Like John Ford, Brown had a feeling for the American landscape, which he handled with both affection and power. His love for intelligent scripts produced *The Human Comedy* in 1943, William Saroyan's story about the home front. Here Brown introduced touches of expressionism and surrealism in a transition scene of cosy streets turned into child's nightmare. *The Yearling* (1947) and *Intruder in the Dust* (1950), concerning Southern racial prejudice, followed. ("I went through the Atlanta Race Riots in 1906. I saw 25 Negroes murdered by a goddamned mob of White men. That's why I made the film.")

Brown controlled every detail of his films, from lighting to the scoring. He was an *auteur*, for there was a very distinctive "Brown" stamp. Some of his sound films in the 1940s were considered touching but perhaps slightly old-fashioned. His "human" stories were full of deeply-felt emotions and reflective sentimentality. The lush visual effects learned in his silent film days were not always appreciated by his contemporaries as realism became more popular during that decade. *Plymouth Adventure* (1952) with Spencer Tracy was his last film. He turned to producing and, in 1971, founded the Clarence Brown Theater for Performing Arts at the University of Tennessee in Knoxville.

Brown made more than 50 films between 1920 and 1952. They were full of cinematic imagination, taste and energy with a dynamic visual style. No one could develop atmosphere like Brown. He was also among the very first to shoot on location, then record voice and effects in the studio afterwards. He also specialized in capturing primal fears, and feelings of disorientation and loss. His greatest gift was letting his camera eye quietly observe small private moments, but never making itself "known", nor reflecting back on its own presence—something like the man *behind* the camera eye.

"I think that silent pictures were more of an art than talkies ever have been. No matter how you manage it, talkies have dialogue, and dialogue belongs to the stage; too many people let the dialogue do their thinking for them. Silents were...subtler, I guess."

Born Clarence Brown. **Father** Cotton mill manager, Knoxville, Tennessee. **Marriages** 1) Mona Maris, actress; 2) Alice Joyce, actress; 3) Marian Ruth Spies, secretary. **Education** University of Tennessee, graduated in mechanical and electrical engineering, 1910. **Military service** Flying cadet, US Army, World War I. **Career** Worked for Moline Automobile Company, 1909–11; car salesman, Stevens Duryea Company, 1911–13; founded Brown Motor Car Company, Birmingham, Alabama, 1913; moved to New York to become assistant to film director Maurice Tourneur, becoming editor and co-director, 1914–21; independent director, 1921–23; signed with Universal, 1923; contracted to MGM, 1924–52; producer, 1953. **Related activities** Helped found Clarence Brown Theater for the Performing Arts, University of Tennessee. **Films** (with Maurice Tourneur) *The Great Redeemer*, 1920; (with Maurice Tourneur) *The Last of the Mohicans*, 1920; (with Maurice Tourneur) *The Foolish Matrons*, 1921; *The Light in the Dark*, 1922; *Don't Marry for Money*, 1923; *The Acquittal*, 1923; *The Signal Tower*, 1924; *Butterfly*, 1924; *Smouldering Fires*, 1924; *The Goose Woman*, 1925; *The Eagle*, 1925; *Kiki*, 1926; *The Flesh and the Devil*, 1927; *A Woman of Affairs*, 1928; *The Trail of '98*, 1929; *Wonder of Women*, 1929; *Navy Blues*, 1929; *Anna Christie*, 1930; *Romance*, 1930; *Inspiration*, 1931; *A Free Soul*, 1931; *Possessed*, 1931; *Emma*, 1932; *Letty Lynton*, 1932; *The Son-Daughter*, 1932; *Looking Forward*, 1933; *Night Flight*, 1933; *Sadie McKie*, 1934; *Chained*, 1934; *Anna Karenina*, 1935; *Ah! Wilderness*, 1935; *Wife vs. Secretary*, 1936; *The Gorgeous Hussy*, 1936; *Conquest*, 1937; *Of Human Hearts*, 1938; *Idiot's Delight*, 1939; *The Rains Came*, 1939; *Edison the Man*, 1940; *Come Live With Me*, 1941; *They Met in Bombay*, 1941; *The Human Comedy*, 1943; *The White Cliffs of Dover*, 1944; *National Velvet*, 1944; (producer/director) *The Yearling*, 1946; *Song of Love*, 1947; *Intruder in the Dust*, 1949; (producer only) *The Secret Garden*, 1949; *To Please a Lady*, 1950; *Angels in the Outfield*, 1951; (episode) *It's a Big Country*, 1951; *When in Rome*, 1952; *Plymouth Adventure*, 1952; (producer only) *Never Let Me Go*, 1953. **Cause of death** Undisclosed, at age 97. **Further reading** Kevin Brownlow, *The Parade's Gone By*, London, 1968.

DOUGLAS BYNG

British Actor and Entertainer

***Born* Nottingham, England, 17 March 1893**

***Died* Northwood, Middlesex, 24 August 1987**

Douglas Byng earned himself the title "High Priest of Camp" for his own wonderfully outrageous comedy songs and for his female impersonations in an amazing variety of characters, usually invented by himself. He was also one of the greatest pantomime dames of all time, that popular transvestite figure without which no British pantomime would be complete. He made his début as a dame in 1924, playing Eliza the Cook in *Dick Whittington*. He scored great success with his song "Oriental Emma of the Harem", which became the hit of the show, and went on to perform in 27 Christmas pantomimes in the course of his career.

Byng made his professional début in a concert party at Hastings in 1914. By 1917 he was appearing at the Gaiety Theatre in London, and from 1922 to 1924 he played twice nightly in variety theatres with Harry Day's revue *Crystal*. Indeed, reviews provided a steady source of work between the wars. The great impresario Charles B. Cochran employed him in 1925 for *On with the Dance*, a revue for which Noël Coward wrote the music, lyrics and sketches and which helped establish Coward's supremacy on the London revue scene. In one memorable sketch, "Oranges and Lemons", Douglas Byng and Ernest Thesiger played two spinsters preparing for bed in their Bloomsbury hotel on New Year's Eve. The other highlight was Alice Delysia singing "Poor Little Rich Girl".

Byng starred in all the Cochran revues at the Pavilion between 1925 and 1931. At the same time, he was also making his way in the cabaret world. After shows at the Pavilion he would often go on to the Chez Henri club in Covent Garden, singing topical duets with Lance Lister and sending up popular sister acts of the time, such as Bettie and Babs, and Lorna and Toots Pounds. Byng and Lister became known as "The Cabaret Boys" and Byng himself described them as "the first slightly *queer* number of the lot". As a solo cabaret act, he became famous for such comic songs as "The Pest of Budapest", "Mrs Lot", "Sex Appeal Sarah", "Boadicea", "Milly the Messy Old Mermaid" and "The Lass Who Leaned Against the Tower of Pisa". Other venues included the Café de Paris, the Café Anglais and the Monseigneur, all popular and fashionable pre-war London nightspots.

He made his New York cabaret début in 1931, billed as "London's most important and expensive cabaret star", and at the Monte Cristo in Paris in 1934 he was described as "l'acteur extraordinaire anglais". In his cabaret work, he used a good deal of *double entendre* and *risqué* jokes, but had so much style that he usually avoided giving offence, preferring subtle allusion to explicit bluntness. There were sometimes fears that he was not a suitable pantomime dame for the eyes and ears of children, but he knew where to draw the line, often performing this role with great dignity.

The wit and elegance of Byng resisted typecasting and he wrote much of his own material, also designing many of his outrageously extravagant costumes, for which he could draw on his earlier training as a costume designer. At the Alhambra in the 1930s he presented a one-man pantomime, *Hop o' My Thumb*, first appearing on a trapeze bar, singing "I'm Doris, the Goddess of Wind" as he descended, and following this with monologues such as "I'm a Tree", "Whistler's Mother's Mum" and "The Girl Who Went and Found It at the Astor". In *Hi Diddle-Diddle* at the Comedy in 1934 he played Policewoman Pellet of Piccadilly, gossiping happily to another policewoman while crimes are committed almost before their eyes. Other famous roles in his wide range included Boadicea, "Queen of the Obsceni" ("O, those ru-id Druids"), in *How D'You Do?*, Charlot's revue at the Comedy in 1933, and as the butler singing Cole Porter's "Miss Otis Regrets", announcing "she is unable to lunch today".

By 1931 live light entertainment was hitting hard times. The advent of cinema "talkies", wireless and, later, television, took their toll, despite desperate efforts to revive live shows with novelty, spectacle and non-stop entertainment, most famously at the Windmill Theatre. During the war years, however, live entertainment flourished again. Byng worked in musicals, variety and cabaret and entertained troops at home and in India and Burma with his song "Blackout Bella". During the Blitz, before the famous Café de Paris in London's West End was bombed, he was billed as "Dougie Byng, Bawdy but British".

After World War II, with the further decline of revue, not to be revived until *Beyond the Fringe* in 1961, Byng acted in the Feydeau farce *Hotel Paradiso* and was the sole member of the cast to remain through both the London and New York runs, and then for its filming. He played the stammering and foot-stamping Monsieur Martin and hoped the film version would make him rich and famous. Although this was not to be, Alec Guinness, who had acted in the original London run ten years earlier and who joined Byng in Paris for the making of the film, recalled Byng's reception there: "The first-night theatre audience greeted his entrance with the loudest and warmest welcome I have ever heard. He was greatly chuffed by it and said to me afterwards with some wonderment in his voice, 'They remembered me!'. But those who saw him in cabaret and revue in his heyday couldn't possibly forget him."

In 1967, at the age of 74, Byng starred in the British television series *Before the Fringe*, performing many of the songs he made famous in revue, much to the delight of his former fans. He then retired, though not completely, as he would occasionally get "back into harness" in a double act with fellow veteran Billy Milton. At this time he lived in an elegant mansion flat on the Brighton seafront, which he found both "breezy and salty". Eventually, he moved to Denville Hall, the actors' charitable trust home, where he was kindly looked after but always hankered for theatre gossip of the days he had known and lamented the passing of their particular kind of innocence. Alec Guinness recalled: "His grande dame's lavatorial instruction, 'Don't leave your fan on the seat', was one of my adolescent catch-phrases. I reminded him of it last Christmas, when I visited him at the actors' home…'Oh, *that*!' he said. 'It shocked some people, you know. Nowadays they are all unshockable. I don't know what the world is coming to. Time for people like me to go.'"

In 1970, Byng published his refreshingly unpretentious memoirs, entitled *As You Were*. Towards the end of his life he had a pleasant surprise when the BBC, which in earlier times had found him too shocking to broadcast, put together a programme about his life on the occasion of his ninetieth birthday.

A week before he died, Byng was talking to a friend about funerals, and with characteristic spirit said, "I don't care *what* they do with me or my box. The only sort of box I'm interested in is a full box at Daly's or the Gaiety." He had also composed his own epitaph:

So here you are, old Douglas,
A derelict at last.
Before your eyes what visions rise
Of your vermilion past.
Mad revelry beneath the stars,
Hot clasping by the lake.
You need not sigh, you can't deny
You've had your bit of cake.

Born Douglas Byng. **Education** Waverley School, Nottingham; Stanley House, Cliftonville. **Career** After early work as theatrical costume designer, made stage début in concert party at Hastings, 1914; on tour in shows, including *The Girl in the Taxi* and *The Cinema Star*, 1914–16; understudy in *Theodore & Co.,* London, 1916; West End début, Gaiety Theatre, 1917; work in comedies and farces (including first pantomime appearance as the Grand Vizier in *Aladdin*, London Palladium, 1921) followed by touring variety with Harry Day's revue *Crystal*, 1922–24; first dame role in *Dick Whittington and his Cat*, New Oxford Theatre, 1924; featured in most Cochran revues at London Pavilion, 1925–30; also moved into cabaret with Lance Lister as "The Cabaret Boys" at the Chez Henri club; appeared in New York, 1931 and at Monte Carlo; presented one-man pantomime, *Hop o' My Thumb*, Alhambra, London, 1931; continued in cabaret and revue at London venues, including the Café de Paris, the Café Anglais, the Monseigneur and the Comedy throughout the 1930s and 1940s; also played to troops in Britain and Far East during World War II; post-war, moved into straight theatre and farce, including New York and London runs and subsequent filming of Feydeau's farce *L'Hôtel de Libre Exchange* (filmed as *Hotel Paradiso*); also occasional television appearances, notably in series *Before the Fringe*. **Publications** *As You Were* (memoirs), 1970. **Shows** (all in London, unless stated, include) *The Girl in the Taxi*, tour, 1914–16; *The Cinema Star*, tour, 1914–16; *Theodore and Co.*, 1916; *Aladdin*, 1921; *Dick Whittington and his Cat*, 1924; *On with the Dance*, 1920s; *One Damn Thing After Another*, 1920s; *This Year of Grace*, 1920s; *The Cabaret Boys*, 1920s; *Hop o' My Thumb*, 1931; *Hi Diddle-Diddle*, 1934; *Before the Fringe*, television, 1960s; *Hotel Paradiso*,

New York, London and film. **Songs/monologues** (include) "Sex Appeal Sarah"; "Milly the Messy Mermaid"; "The Lass Who Leaned Against the Tower of Pisa"; "The Girl Who Made Them Pay in Peyton Place"; "Playboy Club Bunny"; "Blackout Bella"; "Oriental Emma of the Harem"; "Oranges and Lemons"; "I'm Doris the Goddess of Wind"; "I'm a Tree"; "Whistler's Mother's Mum"; "The Girl Who Went and Found It at the Astor". **Cause of death** Undisclosed, at age 94. **Further reading** Raymond Mander and Joe Mitchenson, *Revue: A Story in Pictures*, London, 1971; Roy Busby, *British Music Hall—An Illustrated Who's Who From 1850 to the Present Day*, London, 1976.

CAMILLE CHAMOUN

Lebanese Politician and Statesman

***Born* Chouf district, Lebanon, 3 April 1900**

***Died* Beirut, Lebanon, 7 August 1987**

Camille Chamoun was one of the most important Lebanese personalities of the twentieth century. Prime minister of his country for only six years, he held considerable influence in Lebanese politics for virtually all his adult life. His advocacy of expanded contacts and cooperation with the West—during a period in which Arab nationalism was on the rise—won him many enemies. He is remembered, however, as one of the Middle East's wisest statesmen; a man who dedicated his career to the unity and integrity of Lebanon.

Chamoun was born into a distinguished Maronite Christian family in the Chouf district of present-day Lebanon which, at that time, was administered by Ottoman Turkey as part of Syria. He studied at French missionary schools until the age of 18, when the League of Nations awarded the northern Levantine possessions of Ottoman Turkey to France. In 1920 the French partitioned the region into the culturally homogeneous nation of Syria, and Lebanon, consisting of a myriad of Christian and Muslim nations.

Chamoun continued his studies at the French Collège des Frères, and in 1922 graduated from the law school of the Jesuit University of St Joseph. He qualified as a lawyer and was called to the Lebanese Bar in 1924. He spent the next ten years engaged in private practice, while experimenting with journalism and politics.

In 1934 Chamoun was elected to the chamber of deputies, where he demonstrated great skill as a speaker. He became editor of the Arabic-language daily *Saut-el Ahrar* (Voice of Freedom) and, despite the powerlessness of the parliament in which he served, emerged as a champion for Lebanese independence from France. He was appointed to the largely ceremonial post of minister of finances in 1938.

The war in Europe created great opportunities for Chamoun, who took advantage of the fall of France in 1940. Control of Lebanon fell to the government of Vichy France, whose troops and representatives were expelled from both Lebanon and Syria by British and Free French forces in 1941. In spite of the French Mandate, Lebanon declared independence from France on 26 November of that year. The Free French, claiming authority over Lebanon and Syria, refused to recognize the declaration but, under British pressure, promised to grant independence eventually to both countries.

In 1943, with France still under German occupation, free elections were held in Lebanon. A government was elected—in which Chamoun served as interior minister—and declared the immediate termination of the French Mandate over Lebanon. Not yet willing to grant independence, and sensing British meddling in French affairs, the head of the Free French arrested most of the Lebanese government, including Chamoun, and interned them at a remote camp. British pressure on General de Gaulle eventually won their release and return to office.

Most of the powers of state were transferred to the Lebanese government on 1 January 1944. A year later Chamoun was named minister to London. He was immensely popular in England, where, with his able and attractive Anglo–Lebanese wife Zelpha, he enjoyed great success advancing the causes of his country. In 1946 he won an agreement for the simultaneous withdrawal of all French and British troops from Lebanon, thereby achieving formal independence. With the election of a new government in 1947, Chamoun returned to Lebanon and again assumed the position of interior minister.

Chamoun remained active in government and was elected president in 1952. As a Maronite Christian, however, he was opposed by Muslim factions under the leadership of Kamal Jumblat and Saeb Salam. Chamoun worked hard to preserve harmony within Lebanon and strongly urged his countrymen to pursue association with the West. But the Muslims he sought to persuade drew considerable support from the Egyptian leader Gamal Abdel Nasser. Nasser, considered the spiritual pillar of Arab nationalism, deeply resented Chamoun's advocacy of non-intervention during the 1956 Suez Crisis. Eager to destroy Chamoun and end Christian domination of the Lebanese government, he revealed a scheme by the Lebanese president to amend the national constitution and extend his term. Further discredited by Egyptian propaganda, Chamoun faced an insurrection in 1957 which the following year degenerated into all-out civil war.

After the failure of United Nations observers to halt the flow of arms from Syria, Chamoun requested an invasion by American forces. President Eisenhower responded immediately, and on 15 July 1958 several thousand American troops landed at Beirut. The American State Department, however, concluded that peace could only be maintained by Chamoun's resignation. He was replaced by General Chehab, a compromise candidate, and retired to his home in the Chouf mountains.

In retirement, Chamoun remained largely in the background, coordinating Maronite support in various governments. After a prolonged depression brought on by the death of his wife after a long illness, Chamoun became active again in Lebanese politics. He was incensed by the presence of the Palestine Liberation Organization in his country and blamed it for inciting unusual bitterness between Christian and Muslim factions in Lebanon. The hostilities erupted into civil war again in March 1975 and prompted an invasion by Syrian troops in November of the following year.

Meanwhile, Chamoun had established a Maronite stronghold in the northern port of Jounieh. Subsequent terrorist attacks carried out against Israel by the PLO led to a punitive invasion of southern Lebanon by Israeli troops in 1979. Upon withdrawal, the Israelis turned over command posts to Christian militias allied with Chamoun, whose military power had reached a new high.

Chamoun refused to compromise in delicate power-sharing arrangements, plunging the government into political stalemate. The deadlock was broken on 7 July 1980, when Chamoun's forces were defeated by the rival Maronite Phalangist movement under Bashir Gemayel. In spite of this, Chamoun remained the head of an umbrella organization of Christian groups called the Lebanese Front.

A second, larger Israeli invasion during 1982 ousted the PLO from Lebanon and bolstered the power of Christian forces. During the occupation, Gemayel, who had just been elected president, was assassinated. Days later, Israeli forces revealed a massacre of Palestinians in three refugee camps by Christian forces. A multinational peacekeeping force was brought into Beirut to support the faltering government, but was forced to withdraw after numerous terrorist attacks, including one which destroyed the American compound.

Chamoun attended reconciliation conferences at Geneva and Lausanne during 1983 and 1984, and reluctantly accepted Syrian terms for the formation of a new government under Amin Gemayel, brother of the slain president. The government, formed in August 1984, included leaders of many rival Christian and Muslim groups. Chamoun served as minister of finance, housing and cooperatives until his death three years later.

In spite of his uncompromising dedication to maintaining Maronite ascendancy in government, Chamoun was above all dedicated to the unity of Lebanon. He believed that the disintegration of his country could be prevented only through the benign leadership of Maronites. He blamed the strife in Lebanon on external factors—the "proxy wars" fought in Lebanon between Syria, Iran, Israel and the Palestinians—which destroyed the mutual respect and balance of power between various Lebanese factions. Camille Chamoun was, perhaps, Lebanon's last true voice of moderation and reconciliation.

Born Camille Bey Chamoun. **Marriage** Zelpha (died, *circa* 1975). **Education** Collège des Frères, Beirut; law school, University of St Joseph, Beirut, graduated, 1922. **Career** Called to Lebanese Bar, 1924; elected to Chamber of Deputies, 1934; minister of finance, 1938; minister of interior, 1943–44; minister to allied governments, London, 1944; president, Lebanese Republic, 1952–58; leader, Liberal Nationalist Party, 1958–86; deputy prime minister and minister of the interior, posts, telephones, telecommunications, power and electricity, 1975–76; minister of foreign affairs, 1976; minister of defence, 1976; minister of finance, housing and cooperatives, 1984–87. **Related activities** Editor, *Saut-el Ahrar* (Voice of Freedom) newspaper; delegation head, International Civil Aviation Conference, Chicago, 1944; delegate, UNESCO Conference and United Nations Preparatory Committee, 1945; delegate, United Nations General Assembly, London and New York, 1946; Lebanese representative, United Nations Interim Committee, 1948; attended "national reconciliation conferences", Geneva and Lausanne, 1983–84. **Cause of death** Heart attack, at age 87.

SHEILA van DAMM

British Rally Driver and Theatre Manager

***Born* London, England, 17 January 1922**

***Died* Sussex, England, 23 August 1987**

To many who lived through the London Blitz, the words "Windmill Girl" were synonymous with long-legged young ladies who appeared daily in nude tableaux in a little theatre in London's West End. It must therefore have come as something of a shock to the staid organizers of the 1950 MCC *Daily Express* Rally to find the very same words emblazoned on the side of a Sunbeam Talbot. The entry listed the driver of the car as being a certain Miss S. van Damm, and on closer inspection the gentlemen were no doubt relieved to find a portly and, mercifully, clothed young lady seated behind the wheel. Such were the events that surrounded the competition début of Sheila van Damm, Britain's leading woman driver in motor rallies, and one of the best-liked personalities of the 1950s.

It is fair to say that most people take up rallying because they like cars, toil away at club events for years, and dream of a possible works drive in the future. Sheila van Damm had no interest at all in cars and scarcely knew what a rally was when her father persuaded the Rootes Group to enter his youngest daughter in one of their works cars. Vivian van Damm (irreverently known as "Old VD" in the showbiz world) had sponsored speedway racing in the 1920s before taking over the management of the Windmill Theatre. For him, his daughter's entry was no more than a blatant publicity stunt; but not for her—Sheila van Damm won third prize in the ladies' section, and from having started near the top she simply went up from there.

On the strength of her first performance she was invited to join the all-women crew of a Hillman Minx in the 1951 Monte Carlo Rally. The same year, driving her own Hillman, she won the ladies' prize in the RAC Rally of Great Britain. This was the last time in which she competed as a private entrant, for under the watchful eye of competition chief Norman Garrard she drove cars on behalf of the Rootes Group. Having served as a WAAF driver during the war, and then qualified as a pilot, Sheila van Damm was a fast learner, and for all her bubbling sense of fun, she took her rallying seriously, and in more than five years as a Rootes driver, never once did she fail to finish an event.

Her first important success was in the 1952 Motor Cycling Club (MCC) Rally, when she won the ladies' prize in a Sunbeam Talbot. In the Monte Carlo Rally of 1953, however, a puncture in the mountains put her out of the running. Success was to follow in what was to be the most serious test of her driving abilities to date. For the gruelling Alpine Rally she was entered with Anne Hall; they won the Coupé des Dames but more importantly they took home one of the coveted Coupé des Alpes for finishing the rally without loss of marks. In all events Sheila van Damm's determination shone through and was often a good substitute for mechanical knowledge—notably on the 1954 Austrian Alpine when her car was delayed with what she thought was a faulty dynamo. Opening the bonnet, she struck the offending article a hefty blow with a hammer, only to find a loose wire which she fixed with Elastoplast. Once back on her way, she went on to win her class.

The Great American Mountain Rally of 1953 saw her teamed for the first time with a male co-driver. One can only speculate as to how this partnership fared; a previous and inexperienced co-driver had remarked after her first and last rally with van Damm, "That woman is so tough, if you threw a brick at her it would bounce off". Van Damm was greatly amused by this, but it was true that she would frequently yell at her co-drivers, usually because she was so involved in keeping the car on the road. She had a reputation for taking the lion's share of the driving, often to her co-driver's annoyance, and always insisted on tackling the "tricky" bits—no doubt because, while still fairly new to the sport, she was badly frightened on an earlier Monte Carlo Rally when driven fast on ice by the more experienced Nancy Mitchell.

In 1954 Sheila van Damm covered 14,000 miles of competition motoring. Along the way she won the Coupé des Dames in the Tulip Rally and, by winning the ladies' prize in the Viking Rally in Norway, she set the seal on her first Ladies' European Touring Championship. She was to share the championship the following year with Anne Hall, but of more personal importance, she finally took the Coupé des Dames in the Monte Carlo Rally—the trophy that she had tried in vain to win since 1951.

In between rallies Sheila van Damm was occupied with her father's business, and it was because of her mounting commitment to the Windmill Theatre that she felt obliged, in late 1955, to ask Sir William Rootes to release her from her contract. At Rootes's request she competed in the 1956 Monte Carlo Rally but without success. Having officially retired from rallying (although she reserved the option of driving occasionally for fun), she took up motor racing for the first time. Sharing a Sunbeam Rapier with Peter Harper, she won her class in the 1956 Mille Miglia, characteristically the toughest event in the calendar.

On her father's death in 1960, Sheila van Damm inherited the Windmill Theatre. Originally a cinema, it had been converted to a theatre in 1931, its first production being Michael Barrington's *Inquest.* Attendances for legitimate theatre being low, the theatre began to stage continuous variety, entitled *Revudeville*, with performances running from 2.30 to 11 p.m. This change of policy pulled in the crowds and the Windmill Girls became a famous feature of London life. The theatre also became a noted training ground for young comedians, among them Peter Sellers, Harry Secombe and Tony Hancock. The Windmill was the only West End theatre to remain open during the war and became renowned under its slogan "We Never Closed".

Soho in the early 1960s saw the rapid growth of strip shows and seedy cinemas. Audiences dwindled at the theatre, its rather innocent brand of pornography unsuited to the blatant prurience of its surroundings, and it was to Sheila van Damm's chagrin that she carved out yet another niche for herself when she finally closed down the Windmill in 1964.

After retiring to Sussex, she worked tirelessly to help the handicapped, living with her sister Nona and helping to run their farm and stables. Gone were the days that she described as "screaming up and down mountains on very bad roads"; Sheila van Damm was content to confine her driving to country lanes.

Born Sheila van Damm. **Father** Vivian van Damm, director, Windmill Theatre. **Military service** Driver, Women's Auxiliary Air Force, World War II; pilot, Royal Air Force Volunteer Reserve. **Career** Rally driver, chiefly for the Rootes Group; third prize, ladies' section, MCC Car Rally; Monte Carlo Rally, 1951–56, Coupé des Dames, 1955; (as a private entrant) ladies' prize for closed cars under 1500 cc, RAC Rally, 1951; ladies' prize, MCC Rally, 1952; Coupé des Dames and Coupé des Alpes prizes, Alpine Rally, 1953–54; Great American Road Rally, 1953; Coupé des Dames prize, Tulip Rally, 1954; ladies' prize, Viking Rally; Norway, winner, Women's European Touring Championship, 1954, (with Anne Hall) 1955; winner of class, Mille Miglia race, 1956; retired from rally racing, 1956. **Other activities** Managed Windmill Theatre, London, until its closure, 1960–64. **Offices and memberships** President, Doghouse Club. **Awards and honours** Honorary colonel, Warwickshire and Worcestershire battalion of the Women's Royal Army Corps (Territorial Army). **Publications** *No Excuses* (autobiography), 1957. **Cause of death** Undisclosed, at age 65.

GENERAL IRA C. EAKER

American Air Force Commander

***Born* Field Creek, Texas, 13 April 1896**

***Died* Andrews Air Force Base, Maryland, 6 August 1987**

In a distinguished military career, General Ira Eaker is best remembered as a brilliant World War II commander. During this period he commanded the US Army Air Force in the British Isles and, later, the Allied Forces in the Mediterranean. He was thoroughly educated in most aspects of flying, as well as being renowned for his bravery, imagination and decisiveness. He also had a particular gift for cooperation, which proved vital during his postings in Europe. These characteristics won him numerous honours and many admirers.

Eaker was born in rural Texas and graduated from the Southeastern State Teachers' College in Durant, Oklahoma, in 1917. In that same year he was commissioned a second lieutenant in the infantry section of the Officers' Reserve Corps and stationed with the 64th Infantry in El Paso, Texas. He was 21 years old and the United States had just entered World War I. Shortly after his commission, he was placed on detached service to receive flying instruction at Austin and Kelly

Fields, then moved on to the 84th Infantry of the Regular Army at Rockwell Field, California. During the next ten years or so he continued his education at various postings. He studied at the University of the Philippines, law at Columbia University, and journalism at the University of Southern California.

Eaker was quite a daredevil, and in his early thirties undertook experiments and "stunts" in flying, often accompanied by his colleague and "friendly rival", Major-General James H. Doolittle, who was leader of the US raid on Tokyo early in 1942. Both men were trained in aeronautics and very well knew the risks they were taking. In their constant competition to set new records, it was Eaker who, in 1929, managed to establish a world record for flying endurance when he stayed airborne for 150 hours, 40 minutes and 15 seconds. This was achieved thanks to Eaker's invention of a new mid-air refuelling system. He was also probably the first person to succeed in the technique of "blind flying", when he flew 3000 miles across the United States in a pursuit plane using only his instruments.

On one occasion, however, Eaker's sense of adventure brought him into conflict with the flying authorities. A desire to come to grips with the practical aspects of dive bombing led him to dive his aeroplane down to within 100 feet of houses around Oakland airport; he was subsequently charged with "violating air traffic rules".

None the less, by this time his flying knowledge and expertise were considerable. He went on to develop organizational skills, which proved immensely valuable during later years. The first opportunity to put them to good use was when he was placed in charge of the enormous Hoover Airfield at Washington. Subsequently, soon after the US entered World War II, he was able to use them in Great Britain when he took over the 8th USAAF Bomber Command stationed in East Anglia. In replying to the official welcoming committee, his response was characteristically unassuming: "I have nothing to say until we have done something. When we have gone I hope you will be glad that we came."

For a long time Eaker had held the belief that bombers could be decisive in a war. Within five months of his new command he was ready to act on this theory. In August 1942 he launched his first all American raid (on the marshalling yards and engine sheds at Rouen) with 12 B–17 Flying Fortresses and a fighter escort made up of Spitfires. Simultaneous diversionary attacks were made by other Fortresses. All the bombs struck their target, and every bomber returned safely. In recognition of his role in this successful raid, Eaker was awarded the Silver Star. By December he was given permanent command of the 8th Air Force and had control over its entire bombing operation in Europe. His British allies had only praise for him:

> The Royal Air Force could have asked for no more loyal or encouraging a comrade, for not only did he prove himself cooperative in all directions, but he took every suitable occasion to pay the highest tributes to the RAF. Set only on securing maximum of common effort, he deprecated comparisons between the two air forces, maintaining that each was superlative in its way.

Eaker's expertise was also acknowledged by those in non-military positions. When Churchill and Roosevelt decided to call a halt to mass daylight bombing, Eaker persuaded them to let it continue. Working with the RAF under Air Chief Marshal Sir Arthur Harris, he proved that mass daylight raids *without* fighter escort over heavily fortified enemy industrial targets were possible and practical. Repeated heavy raids by the US Air Force by day, and the Royal Air Force by night materially reduced Germany's power to carry on the war and were widely credited with greatly reducing later invasion losses. For his services in this command, Eaker was awarded the Legion of Merit and the Distinguished Service Medal.

In January 1944 he was moved from Britain to the Mediterranean as air commander-in-chief of the Allied air forces under the supreme command of General Sir Henry Maitland Wilson. Here he directed both the tactical and strategic air force raids in support of ground operations in Italy and Yugoslavia and against oil and rail targets in Austria and Southern Germany. And it was here that he saw the final collapse of Germany.

Although totally committed to his military role, Eaker still found time to write several books in collaboration with General Henry Harley Arnold; these included *The Flying Game* and *Winged Warfare*, both published before his involvement in the war, and *Army Flyer*, published in 1942. On retirement in 1947 he became vice-president of the Hughes Tool Company and later of Douglas Aircraft. He was founding president of the US Strategic Institute and for many years wrote a syndicated weekly newspaper column which examined matters concerning national security.

Eaker was a handsome man, "dark and swarthy in complexion", with very earnest eyes. He was a skilful and brave pilot, and a brilliant commander. The defeat of Germany owed much to such men.

Born Ira Clarence Eaker. **Parents** Young Yancy and Dona Lee (Graham) Eaker. **Marriage** Ruth Huff Apperson, 1931. **Education** Southeastern State Teachers' College, Durant, Oklahoma, 1917; University of the Philippines, 1920–21; Columbia University, 1922–23; University of Southern California, AB, 1932–33. **Career** Second lieutenant of infantry, Officers' Reserve Corps, 1917; Army Air Corps, 1917; 84th Infantry, Regular Army, 1917; promoted to first lieutenant, 1918; promoted to captain, 1920; commanding officer, Manila air depot, Philippines, 1921; executive assistant to chief of air service, 1923–26; executive officer to assistant secretary of war, 1927–28; operations and line maintenance officer, Bolling Field, Washington DC, 1928–32; commander, 34th Pursuit Squadron and 17th Attack Group, 1933–35; promoted to major, 1935; served in office of chief of Air Corps, 1937–40; promoted to lieutenant-colonel, 1940; commander, 20th Pursuit Group, 1941; promoted to colonel (temporary), 1941; promoted to brigadier-general (temporary), 1941; commander, 8th Bomber Command, England, 1942; promoted to major-general (temporary), 1942; commander, 8th Air Force, 1942; promoted to lieutenant-general (temporary), 1943; promoted to brigadier-general, 1943; commander, US Army Air Forces, UK, 1943; air commander-in-chief, Mediterranean Allied air forces, 1944; deputy commander, Army Air Forces and chief of air staff, 1945–47. **Related activities** Author, syndicated weekly column on matters concerning national security, 1962 onwards. **Other activities** Vice-president, Hughes Tool Company, 1947–57; vice-president, Douglas Aircraft, 1957–61; founding president, US Strategic Institute. **Awards and honours** Distinguished Flying Cross, 1927, oak leaf cluster added on establishing a new world flight endurance record, 1929; Silver Star, 1942; honorary Knight of the British Empire, 1943; Legion of Merit, 1943; Call Alumni Achievement Trophy, 1943; US Army Distinguished Service Medal, 1944 (subsequently with two oak leaf clusters); Air Medal, 1945; US Navy Distinguished Service Medal, 1945; honorary Knight Commander of the Order of the Bath, 1945; Wright Brothers Trophy, 1977; Special Congressional Gold Medal, 1979; USAF Distinguished Service Medal for exceptionally meritorious service, 1957–81, 1981; Chilean Order of Merit; Peruvian Order of the Sun of Peru; Venezuelan Order of the Liberator; grand official order, Brazilian Order of the Southern Cross; Bolivian Order of the Condor of the Andes; Yugoslav Partisan Star, 1st class; grand officer, French Legion of Honour; Croix de Guerre, with palm; grand master, Italian Order of Saints Maurice and Lazarus; Brazilian Order of Aeronautical Merit; Polish Military Order of the Gold Cross of Merit. **Publications** (all with General Henry Harley Arnold, include) *This Flying Game*, 1936; *Winged Warfare*, 1940; *Army Flyer*, 1942. **Cause of death** Undisclosed, at age 91.

RUDOLF HESS

German Soldier and War Criminal

***Born* Alexandria, Egypt, 26 April 1894**

***Died* Berlin, West Germany, 17 August 1987**

Rudolf Hess was closely involved with Adolf Hitler from the early days of the National Socialist movement in Germany. Yet his role was primarily that of a party apparatchik and, above all, Hitler's most loyal assistant, rather than as a force in his own right. His active career ended with a bizarre solo flight to Scotland in 1941, in a bid to induce Britain to make a separate peace. Condemned to life imprisonment at Nuremberg, Hess achieved renown as the world's oldest and loneliest prisoner, committing suicide in Spandau at the age of 93.

It is significant that, like many other prominent Nazis, from Hitler down, Hess was a "marginalized" German, being born in Egypt, the son of a Bavarian export merchant, and spending his first 14 years there. Being brought up outside the Reich only seems to have made Hess's nationalism the stronger.

At 14 Hess was sent to school at Bad Godesberg, near Bonn; at 17 he enrolled in a commercial course prior to entering his father's business. He spent some time in French Switzerland (his mother came from a Swiss farming family) and Hamburg, before returning to Alexandria. In August 1914, at the start of World War I, Hess was again in Hamburg. He immediately enlisted in the 1st Company of the 16th Bavarian Infantry Regiment, the same regiment in which Hitler was to serve throughout the war, although the two did not meet at this stage.

The war was a formative experience for Hess, as for so many other leading Nazis. Hitler, for example, was to make great play, in his political speeches, of his pride in having been a *Frontschwein*, one of the "poor bloody infantry", and there is no doubt that ex-servicemen, in the post-war period, considered themselves to be a class apart. Hitler articulated the frustrations of men such as Hess, who felt that their sacrifices at the front had been rewarded with a shameful defeat.

Hess was wounded at Verdun in 1916, later writing a poem about his experiences in this protracted conflict on the western front. He was commissioned as a lieutenant the same year, and served in the campaign against Romania and on the eastern front. In the last months of the war he gained admission to the German Air Force, winning his wings as a scouting pilot.

The Hess family business was ruined by the war, and after the armistice in 1918 Hess gravitated to Munich, where he became a student at the university. He studied "geo-politics" under his former brigade commander, Professor Karl Haushofer, whose theories on the Germans as a master race, and their need for *Lebensraum* (room for expansion) were characteristic of the radical nationalism then in vogue in right-wing circles.

Hess also entered the ultra-nationalist and anti-Semitic Thule Society, which involved him in plotting against the short-lived Bavarian Councils' Republic in the spring of 1919. At one point he was lucky to escape arrest and summary execution; on 1 May, by one account, he was wounded in the fighting which retook Munich and toppled the Councils' Republic.

Already, in January 1919, the Thule Society had helped found the German Workers' Party under Anton Drexler, devoted to creating a mass movement which would be both working class and strongly nationalist. Hitler joined this party in September 1919, and by the beginning of 1920 was its leading propagandist and star orator, changing the name to National Socialist German Workers' Party (NSDAP). It was in the course of 1920 that Hess first heard Hitler at a public meeting. The effect on the essentially simple-mined Hess was catatonic. According to one witness he could only stammer, "The man, the man..."; later, he was to describe Hitler as "pure reason in human form". Henceforward, Hess was to serve Hitler with blind and unconditional loyalty. Indeed his virtually religious faith in Hitler was to contribute substantially to the subsequent cult of the *Führer* (leader).

Hess soon made himself Hitler's right-hand man, as the latter consolidated his hold on the Nazi Party. In February 1921 Hess organized a Nazi branch among the students of Munich University. In the summer of 1921 he helped orchestrate the chorus within the party to make Hitler "first chairman with dictatorial powers". In November 1923 Hess was involved in the planning of Hitler's abortive "Beer Hall *Putsch*" to seize control of Munich and, from there, to effect a change of government in Berlin. Hess was in charge of arresting the Bavarian prime minister on 8 November, but the *coup* collapsed the next day.

Such was Hess's devotion to Hitler that, although he had succeeded in escaping to Austria, he voluntarily returned to Munich to share Hitler's imprisonment at Landsberg. It was during Hitler's nine-month sojourn in prison that *Mein Kampf* was written, or rather dictated largely to Hess, whose geo-political ideas found full expression in Hitler's annexationist fantasies.

Once out of prison, Hess continued as Hitler's private secretary, writing speeches and pamphlets, and dealing with the administration of the growing Nazi movement. In 1926 he was appointed secretary of the party's new "Reich directorate". In December 1932, with Germany in chaos and the Nazis on the threshold of power, Hitler made Hess chief of the political wing of the party, the counterpart to Erich Röhm's command of the Storm-troopers (SA), the paramilitary wing. With Hitler, Hess had the final say in all important political and propaganda decisions.

Hess's subordination even extended, in 1927, to marrying at Hitler's behest. It was said that Ilse Proehl, his bride, was suggested to him by the *Führer*. She herself was known to say that Hess "belonged" to Hitler.

With the Nazi accession to power in January 1933, Hitler reinforced the initially small party representation in the Cabinet by formally appointing Hess as his deputy. In February 1934, long after total power had been conferred on Hitler by the Enabling Act of March 1933, a new cabinet council was created. Hess became minister without portfolio, empowered to sit in on all Cabinet meetings and coordinate action between different ministries in the name of the party, a symbol of the close connection between party and state in the new regime.

Throughout the dark years of Nazi rule Hess never hesitated in his backing for Hitler. He led the public apologias for the "Night of the Long Knives" in July 1934, when Röhm and the SA leadership were brutally murdered at Hitler's command. He fully supported the anti-Jewish policies and the series of international aggressions which led to World War II. It is interesting, however, that Hitler never entrusted him with real ministerial responsibilities. Hess's value was as an adjutant and mouthpiece, the "brown mouse", as he was called.

The war saw a marked decline in Hess's prominence within the regime, again because Hitler probably recognized that Hess had neither the ability nor the will to be a wartime heavyweight. Instead, Hermann Goering was nominated Hitler's immediate successor. Even Hess's personal influence with Hitler diminished with the appointment of Martin Bormann as the *Führer*'s private secretary.

It was this sidelining which seems to have determined Hess on his crackbrained mission to Britain. On 10 May 1941 he took off in a long-range Messerschmitt across the North Sea and parachuted into Scotland, breaking an ankle in the process. His purpose, as he eventually explained to the bemused British authorities, was to enlist the support of the Duke of Hamilton for a negotiated peace between Germany and Britain. (Hess was convinced the Duke possessed high-level contacts which would facilitate this goal.)

Hess appears to have believed that he still knew Hitler's mind better than anyone else, and that an accommodation with Britain, whereby Germany allowed the British to retain their empire, in return for Germany's lost colonies and the assurance of European hegemony, was what the

Führer wanted. In fact Hitler, to whom the news of Hess's defection came as a complete surprise, had no real interest in a peace with Britain. Hess was interned for the duration of the war.

At the Nuremberg trials, and despite considerable doubts as to his sanity, Hess was convicted of conspiracy and crimes against peace, and sentenced to life imprisonment. (He was acquitted of charges of war crimes and crimes against humanity.) The convictions, like the sentence, were essentially the product of a trade-off between the British, American and French judges, on the one hand, and the Soviet judge on the other, since the Soviets started by demanding the death penalty and only accepted the compromise of life imprisonment as, in their view, the lesser of two evils.

Hess was to remain in Spandau Prison, under four-power surveillance, for the rest of his life. For reasons which have never been clarified, the Soviets maintained their veto on Hess's release, even after his only remaining fellow prisoners, Albert Speer and Hjalmar Schacht, were set free in 1966. Many influential voices, including those of former enemies, were raised in favour of clemency, but in vain.

The circumstances of Hess's death remain ambiguous. According to the prison authorities he was found hanging by an electrical cord, and the four-power inquest returned a verdict of suicide. The Hess family were not convinced, and mounted a private enquiry which, however, came to no firm conclusions.

Hess belonged to the type of what has been called the "passive totalitarian man", the person for whom the charismatic leader is essential for political motivation, and who subordinates himself gladly to such an authority. His sense of burning faith in Hitler never left him. As he said at Nuremberg, "It was given me to work many years of my life under the greatest son whom my people have brought forth in their thousand-year history."

Born Walter Richard Rudolf Hess. **Parents** Fritz H., businessman, and Klara (Münch) Hess. **Marriage** Ilse Proehl, 1927. **Children** One son, Wolf. **Education** In Alexandria, Egypt, to 1908; high school in Godesberg on the Rhine, 1909–11; began commercial course, 1911; Munich University. **Military service** Enlisted, 16th Bavarian Regiment, World War I; wounded, Verdun 1916; fought in Romania as lieutenant; pilot and lieutenant, German Air Force, flew with scouting flight "35". **Career** Private secretary to Professor Dr Karl Haushofer, director of Institute of Geo-Politics, Munich University; joined nationalist and anti-Semitic Thulesgesellschaft (Thule Society), 1919; heard Hitler speak and became early member of Nazi Party, 1921; appointed Hitler's bodyguard, 1921; orchestrated kidnapping of Bavarian premier and the minister of home affairs, 1923; arrested and imprisoned with Hitler, Landsberg Prison, where *Mein Kampf* was dictated to him, 1924–25; private secretary to Hitler, 1925–32; head, Politische Zentralkommission (Political Control Commission), Nazi Party, 1932; appointed deputy *Führer*, 1933; cabinet minister without portfolio, 1934; chairman, committee on party publications, 1934; second-in-command, Storm-troopers (SA), 1934; signed Nuremberg Laws (for persecution of Jews), 1935; superintendent, Auslandsdeutsch Bewengung (foreign branch of Nazi party), 1936; made many speeches on behalf of war effort, 1939–41; flew to Britain to try to negotiate separate peace, 1941; prisoner-of-war, Mytchett Place, Hampshire, England, 1941–45; tried as a war criminal, Nuremberg; found guilty and sentenced to life imprisonment, Spandau Prison, 1946–87. **Cause of death** Suicide, at age 93. **Further reading** Joseph Bernard Hutton, *Hess: The Man and His Mission*, 1970; James Douglas-Hamilton, *Motive for a Mission: The Story Behind Hess's Flight to Britain*, 1971; Roger Manvell, *Hess: A Biography*, 1971; Eugene K. Bird, *The Loneliest Man in the World: The Inside Story of the 30-year Imprisonment of Rudolf Hess*, 1974; Hugh Thomas, *The Murder of Rudolf Hess*, 1979, reissued as *Hess: A Tale of Two*

Murders, 1988; Peter Allan, *The Crown and the Swastika: Hitler, Hess and the Duke of Windsor*, 1983; Wolf Rudiger Hess, *My Father Rudolf Hess*, 1986; David Irving, *Hess: The Missing Years, 1941–45*, 1987; Wulf Schwarzwaller, *Rudolf Hess: The Deputy*, 1988.

JOHN HUSTON

American Film Director, Actor and Screenwriter

***Born* Nevada, Missouri, 5 August 1906**

***Died* Newport, Rhode Island, 28 August 1987**

John Marcellus Huston was indisputably one of the most talented film-makers of his generation, and his influence in the film world was, for decades, a strong one. Yet his career was as full of contradictions as his character. His works were frequently "off-beat" and adventurous (within the confines of commercial film) and uneven: when they worked, they were brilliant, but like the children's rhyme, when they didn't, they were horrid. Some critics praised him from the very first, some considered him overrated, while others vacillated between respect and loathing. Everyone has strong opinions about Huston.

Perhaps one of the difficulties he poses is that his films cannot be categorized. There are Huston subjects and a certain Huston tone, but he was never an *auteur*—nor would he admit to the thought—in the sense of having consistent themes and styles running through his work. What was constant was his battle with the Hollywood studio system, yet many of his finest films were made within those boundaries; his professional freedom did not always guarantee good quality.

The Maltese Falcon, *The Treasure of the Sierra Madre*, *The African Queen*, *The Misfits, The Man Who Would Be King* and a dozen other films are classics—and were so when they were made. Hindsight analysis only adds a patina and, often, an intellectual interpretation that Huston probably would have laughed at. Then again, he might not; Huston was full of contradictions.

The son of respected actor Walter, Huston's own childhood was no model of consistency, nor even of stability. His parents divorced when he was six. A sickly child, he was diagnosed as having an enlarged heart and kidney disease (he spent time in a sanatorium earlier for chest trouble), and was taken to California by his mother to recover. That he did, becoming the amateur lightweight boxing champion of the state two years later. The next period was a restless one. He became a competent horseman and was made an honorary member of the Mexican Cavalry in 1925. When he was 24, he moved to New York and performed in *The Triumph of the Egg* at the Provincetown Playhouse and, having decided to try journalism, became a reporter for the *New York Daily Graphic*. He moved back to Hollywood in 1930, where his father was cast in his first picture, and Huston worked on scripts for William Wyler, including *A House Divided* (1931) and *Murders in the Rue Morgue* (1932). In 1932 he had a brief and fruitless spell doing the same thing for Gaumont-British in London. The following year he went to Paris to study painting, often doing portraits on street corners. By 1934 he was back in New York editing *Midweek Pictorial* and dabbling in acting.

Huston's wandering ended in 1936 when he returned to Hollywood, screenwriting for Warner Brothers and working—often uncredited—on *Jezebel*, *Dr Ehrlich's Magic Bullet*, *Sergeant York* and *High Sierra*. (He was to continue to write many of his own scripts when he began directing in 1944.) He directed his father in 1939 on Broadway in *Passage to Bali*, but the play did poorly. However, in 1941 he made an outstanding film début when he directed *The Maltese Falcon*, starring Humphrey Bogart, Mary Astor, Peter Lorre and, in his first film at age 61, Sydney Greenstreet. Ironically, Huston had to beg permission repeatedly of the studio heads as the story had been filmed three times previously, none with any remarkable degree of success. His next film, *Across the Pacific* (1942) failed, but *In This Our Life* with Bette Davis, the same year, was considered quite competent, and did better at the box office.

Huston joined the US Army film unit, reaching the rank of major, and made several excellent documentaries—so good that the War Department branded the first, *Battle of San Pietro*, "anti-war" and kept it on the shelf for years; later, with "judicious" cuts, it was reduced to a training film. His second, *Let There Be Light*, illustrated shell-shock so powerfully that the army refused to screen it. (They relented only in 1980.)

After the war, Huston worked on several screenplays, including *Three Strangers* (1946) and, uncredited, *The Killers*. In 1947 he helped establish the committee for the First Amendment to counter the House Un-American Activities Committee's witch-hunt "investigations", protesting in Washington along with other morally outraged actors and writers. (Huston was to move to Ireland in 1952 after fighting several more years of one of the most shameful chapters in US history.)

In 1948 Huston's *Treasure of the Sierra Madre*, in which he directed his father and Bogart, received Oscars for both direction and script. A classic study of self-destructive greed, it is, according to Pauline Kael, "one of the strongest of American movies". Three Americans who are stranded in Mexico prospect for gold, strike it lucky, then, in the words of writer/director/cameo actor Huston, "I just look on and let them stew in their own juices." Curiously, it did poorly at the box office, as audiences were not willing to accept Bogart in anything but his *Casablanca* stereotype. Huston directed *Key Largo* the same year, with Bogart and a young Lauren Bacall—"You'll do, kid," Bogart is reputed to have told his young co-star when he discovered she had been cast. In this film, which did much better at the box office, Bogart portrays a major in a seedy Florida Keys hotel who, disillusioned with the value of fighting, is forced into action against gangsters who try to take over the place.

Huston's *We Were Strangers* (1949) was, to him and the critics, a more personal film, a "message" political story set in 1920s' Cuba. A string of wildly uneven films followed: *Asphalt Jungle* (1950) with more atmosphere and character than usual in his action scenes, as gangsters cause their own downfall. The thriller included a sterling performance from his old friend, Sam Jaffe, as well as the superb veteran actor James Whitmore, and a young Marilyn Monroe in a bit part. The film inspired a "crime seen from the inside" series. In *The African Queen* (1951) Huston produced one of the films for which he is best known—which also happens to be one of the best loved. The inspired casting which combined Katharine Hepburn and Humphrey Bogart created a film encompassing several genres—a love story, comedy, adventure tale—all of them handled with charm. The comedy which, as Huston wrote, was not present in C.S. Forester's novel nor James Agee's script, grew out of the two actors' relationship. Hepburn later wrote in her book *The Making of the African Queen*, that filming was going poorly until Huston suggested that she play her Rosie while thinking of Eleanor Roosevelt. After that, everything flowed smoothly, and the chemistry between Hepburn, Bogart and Huston has never been matched in Hollywood. Much of the dialogue was even improvised.

The year 1951 did not continue well, however. When *Red Badge of Courage*, the Civil War classic with Audie Murphy, was butchered by the studio and died at the box office, Huston grew disillusioned and did not work in the US for the next six years. The idiocy of the blacklist combined with the studio system drove him to Ireland. (He received his citizenship in 1964 and was given an honorary degree from Trinity in 1970. Later, he sold his home in Galway and moved to Mexico.) Huston's interest in Irish film, ignored by much of the world, was strong; however, it remained a project that needed more attention than his time could permit. When the writer of this essay wrote to him regarding plans to bring Irish film programmes to the US through a doctoral project, he expressed enthusiasm and offered to meet; sadly, he fell ill in Mexico and the project went unrealized.

In 1953 Huston directed *Moulin Rouge*, with José Ferrer playing Toulouse-Lautrec. It failed, despite interesting colour photography, and marked a return to his brand of pessimism and his exploration of man's futility. His 1954 film *Beat the Devil* was a parody of *The Maltese Falcon*, to a degree, reuniting Bogart and Lorre, with Robert Morley taking the Greenstreet part. It remains one of his more colourful, complex and curious films, with a zany humour that prompted Truman Capote to pronounce: "I have a suspicion that John wasn't too clear about it." Bogart was more blunt: "Only the phonies think it's funny. It's a mess." *The Barbarian and the Geisha* (1958) was a disaster, while *The Unforgiven* (1960), his first western, was characteristically used for a wider comment on racism—until the producers removed the sting. It too failed. In 1961 Huston collaborated with Arthur Miller on *The Misfits*, a story concerning cowboys who hunted wild horses for dog food. It proved to be an unlucky film, and both Clark Gable's and Marilyn Monroe's last. It was plagued by delays caused by Monroe's depressions, and filming conditions were believed to be responsible for Gable's heart attack after shooting was completed. At a cost of $4 million, it was one of the most expensive black and white films made up until that time. The performances, including Montgomery Clift's, were astounding, however.

In the early 1960s Huston's career lost momentum. He directed a string of films which were mediocre—some even poor. His heavy bio-pic *Freud* (1963) was badly cut on initial release and denounced, while *The List of Adrian Messenger* (1963) was a slight but amusing whodunnit with a who's who of actors, heavily disguised, including George C. Scott, Burt Lancaster, Tony Curtis, Frank Sinatra and Kirk Douglas. *The Bible* (1965) was a dreary plod, enlivened only by Huston's own role as Noah and his narration; his rich, grainy voice was superb. The slump continued until *Fat City* (1972), a study of two struggling boxers which showed a personal commitment. It was his first American film in 20 years—a commercial failure, but the critics loved it.

The Man Who Would Be King (1975) was an adventure fantasy with Michael Caine and Sean Connery, made with great affection. The story of two men who decide to conquer a barbarous land, it was both comic and exhilarating; many considered it to be Huston's comeback. *Wise Blood*, another reasonable success, followed in 1979.

By 1980 Huston, aged 74, was the oldest American director still working. His television film, *Escape to Victory* (1981), concerning prisoners planning a breakout during a football match against their Nazi captors, was respected, gaining good reviews. He had directed virtually every film genre possible, from western to gangster, romance to bio-pic, thriller to adventure. *Annie* (1981) was his first musical; it received mixed reviews, but made good box-office returns. *Prizzi's Honor* (1985) with Jack Nicholson, daughter Anjelica and Kathleen Turner brought the laurel wreath back, as it was hailed by critics and public alike, being reminiscent of the Huston insouciance with which he often thumbed his nose at society. *The Dead* (1987), based on a James Joyce short story, was a family affair; Huston directed it from a wheelchair, son Tony wrote the script, and Anjelica played a leading role. It proved to be a superb final tribute. He died two months after filming was completed.

Huston was also a performer, acting in his own, as well as other directors' films—*Treasure of the Sierra Madre*, *The Cardinal*, *Myra Breckenridge*, *Chinatown* and others—developing into an excellent character actor.

On a personal level he was difficult to categorize, and he no doubt revelled in that fact. He was a hell-raiser, yet demanding upon himself. Erudite and philosophical, he was poorly educated;

stubborn, sensitive and essentially a loner, he was married five times. He was intellectually sophisticated and enormously popular.

His coolly objective, shrewd camera observed, as film writer Richard Schickel wrote, "the slow, the mad and the merely mistaken. He set aside their better natures in order to embrace their greediest impulses...and sometimes adventures put the light of self-transcendence in their eyes. That wicked gleam was always in Huston's glance, too." According to Pauline Kael, "Huston finds a grisly humour in the self-deceptions of ruthless people chasing rainbows; that might almost be his comic notion of man's life on earth. He earns esteem by not sentimentalizing that quest. Yet his inability to show affection for characters who live on different terms shows how much the rogues mean to him."

Huston was never indulgent with poetry but he remained respectful. He also displayed an interest in relating film to painting; every film reflected a strong awareness of the moving portrait and his use of colour was sensitive. His shots were arranged like canvasses. One important theme was the effect of the individual ego upon a group, another was like Sam Spade: the obsessed professional, proud and dedicated, to whom women were threats or temptresses or his obsession. Bogart, who appeared in more of his films than any other actor, personified this. Love is often unfulfilled, and when reciprocated, is often doomed by circumstances; generally, male and female relationships are bleak things.

Huston's themes also invariably encompass choices—between illusion and reality, the practical and fantastic; certainly the religious fantasy is, in Huston's world, a dangerous one (*Night of the Iguana*, *The Bible*, *Wise Blood*). Man's ability to find solace and sense in animals and nature remain important, as does an unpredictable world governed by either a whimsical god, or none at all. Huston's characters were often weak, not salvaged by even the best intentions, and doomed if given to too much thought or feeling. Both the ignorant and the arrogant were pathetic, but the heroic sacrificed all for self-understanding, independence and isolation, typified by Lautrec and Freud, two people with whom Huston felt an affinity. His tough marine in *Heaven Knows, Mr Allison* and the ambassador in *The Barbarian and the Geisha* are two other examples.

Huston's ideal heroes were ironically close to what others thought of him, as expressed by James Agee: "A natural-born authoritarian, individualistic, libertarian anarchist...he operates largely by instinct."

Born John Marcellus Huston. **Parents** Walter, actor, and Rhea (Gore), writer and reporter, Huston. **Marriages** 1) Dorothy Jeanne Harvey, 1926 (divorced, 1933); 2) Leslie Black, 1937 (divorced, 1944); 3) Evelyn Keyes, 1946 (divorced, 1950); 4) Enrica Soma, 1950 (died, 1969); 5) Celeste Shane, 1972 (divorced, 1977). **Children** Pablo Albarran (adopted), from third marriage; Walter Anthony, Anjelica and Allegra (adopted), from fourth marriage; one son, Daniel, from liaison with Zoë Sallis. **Education** Parochial and public schools, Los Angeles; Lincoln High School, Los Angeles; Art Students' League, Los Angeles. **Emigration** Left US for Ireland, 1955; naturalized, 1964; left Ireland for Mexico, 1972. **Military service** Mexican Cavalry, rising to rank of lieutenant, 1925–27; documentary film-maker, US Army Signal Corps, Army Pictorial Service, rising to rank of major, 1942–45. **Career** Professional boxer, California, early 1920s; moved to New York, appearing in *Triumph of the Egg* and *Ruint*, 1924–25; reporter, *Daily Graphic*, New York, late 1920s; writer for MGM, California and Gaumont-British, England; first film roles, 1929; studied art in Paris, early 1930s; editor, *Midweek Pictorial*, New York, 1934; resumed acting career, 1935; writer, Warner Brothers Studios, Hollywood, from 1936, director, 1941–42, 1945–48; independent producer, forming Horizon Productions with Sam Spiegel, 1948; continued to direct films for major studios; formed John Huston Productions, 1952; career appeared to flag in 1960s, but regained momentum, 1970s–87. **Related activities** Some stage direction on Broadway, including *A Passage to Bali*, 1939, *In Time* *to Come*, 1940, and *No Exit*, 1947; directed Richard Bennet's opera, *The Mines of Sulphur*, Milan, 1963; appearances and narration on television, from mid-1960s. **Offices and memberships** Fellow, British Academy of Film and Television Arts, 1980. **Awards and honours** New York Drama Critics' Circle Award for *In Time to Come*, 1939; Academy Awards for best director and best screenplay for *Treasure of the Sierra Madre*, 1949; New York Film Critics' Award for best director for *Treasure of the Sierra Madre*, 1949; One World Award for *Treasure of the Sierra Madre*, 1949; Screen Directors' Guild Award for *The Asphalt Jungle*, 1950; Academy Award nomination for *The Asphalt Jungle*, 1950; Academy Award nomination for screenplay of *The African Queen*, 1951; New York Film Critics' Award for best director of the year for *Moby Dick*, 1956; National Board of Review of Motion Pictures Award, 1956; Academy Award nomination for screenplay of *Freud*, 1962; Screen Writers' Guild Silver Laurel Award for *Night of the Iguana*, 1963; Directors' Guild Silver Award for *Night of the Iguana*, 1964; Martin Buber Award for *The Bible*, 1966; David di Donatello Award for *The Bible*, 1966; Motion Pictures Exhibitors' International Laurel Award for *Reflections in a Golden Eye*, 1968; honorary DLitt, Trinity College, Dublin, 1970; Cannes International Film Festival Special Award, 1984. **Publications** *Frankie and Johnny*, New York, 1930; *In Time to Come* in *The Best Plays of 1941–1942*, ed. Burns Mantle, New York, 1942; *Juarez* in *20 Best Film Plays*, eds Gassner and Nichols, New York, 1943; *Let There Be Light* in *Film: Book 2* by Robert Hughes, New York, 1962; *An Open Book* (memoirs), New York, 1980, London, 1988; plus numerous articles and interviews in film journals. **Film scripts** *A House Divided*, 1931; *Murders in the Rue Morgue*, 1932; *It Started in Paris*, 1935; *Death Drives Through*, 1935; *Jezebel*, 1938; *The Amazing Dr Clitterhouse*, 1938; *Juarez*, 1939; *The Story of Dr Ehrlich's Magic Bullet* (*Dr Ehrlich's Magic Bullet*), 1940; *High Sierra*, 1941; *Sergeant York*, 1941; *The Killers*, 1946; *The Stranger*, 1946; *Three Strangers*, 1946. **Films directed** *The Maltese Falcon*, 1941; *In This Our Life*, 1942; *Across the Pacific*, 1942; *Report from the Aleutians* (army documentary), 1943; *Tunisian Victory*, 1943; *The Battle of San Pietro* (army documentary), 1945; *Let There Be Light* (army documentary), 1946; (part only, uncredited) *A Miracle Can Happen* (*On Our Merry Way*), 1946; *The Treasure of the Sierra Madre*, 1948; *Key Largo*, 1948; *We Were Strangers*, 1949; *The Asphalt Jungle*, 1950; *The Red Badge of Courage*, 1951; *The African Queen*, 1952; *Moulin Rouge*, 1953; *Beat the Devil*, 1954; *Moby Dick*, 1956; *Heaven Knows, Mr Allison*, 1957; (part only, completed by King Vidor) *A Farewell to Arms*, 1957; *The Barbarian and the Geisha*, 1958; *The Roots of Heaven*, 1958; *The Unforgiven*, 1960; *The Misfits*, 1961; *Freud* (*Freud: The Secret Passion*), 1963; *The List of Adrian Messenger*, 1963; *The Night of the Iguana*, 1964; *La bibbia* (*The Bible*), 1965; *Casino Royale*, 1967; *Reflections in a Golden Eye*, 1967; *Sinful Davey*, 1969; *A Walk With Love and Death*, 1969; *The Kremlin Letter*, 1970; *The Last Run*, 1971; *Fat City*, 1972; *The Life and Times of Judge Roy Bean*, 1972; *The Mackintosh Man*, 1973; *The Man Who Would Be King*, 1975; *Independence*, 1976; *Wise Blood*, 1979; *Phobia*, 1980; *Victory* (*Escape to Victory*), 1981; *Annie*, 1982; *Under the Volcano*, 1984; *Prizzi's Honor*, 1985; *The Dead*, 1987. **Film roles** (include) *The Shakedown*, 1929; *Hell's Heroes*, 1929; *The Storm*, 1930; *The Treasure of the Sierra Madre*, 1948; *We Were Strangers*, 1949; *The Cardinal*, 1963; *The Directors*, 1963; *The List of Adrian Messenger*, 1963; *La bibbia* (*The Bible*), 1965; *Casino Royale*, 1967; *Candy*, 1968; *The Rocky Road to Dublin*, 1968; *De Sade*, 1969; *A Walk With Love and Death*, 1969; *The Kremlin Letter*, 1970; *Myra Breckenridge*, 1970; *The Bridge in the Jungle*, 1971; *The Deserter*, 1971; *Man in the Wilderness*, 1971; *The Life and Times of Judge Roy Bean*, 1972; *Battle for the Planet of the Apes*, 1974; *Chinatown*, 1974; *Breakout*, 1975; *The Wind and the Lion*, 1975; *Sherlock Holmes in New York*, 1976; *Tentacles*, 1977; *Il grande attaco* (*La battaglia di Mareth/The Biggest Battle*), 1977; *El triangulo diabolico de las Bermudas* (*Il triangulo delle Bermude/Triangle: The Bermuda Mystery/The Mystery of the Bermuda Triangle*), 1977; *Angela*, 1977; *Il visitatore* (*The Visitor*), 1978; *Jaguar Lives*, 1979; *Winter Kills*, 1979; *Wise Blood*, 1979; *Head On*, 1980; *Agee*, 1980; (narrator)

To the Western World, 1981; (narrator) *Cannery Row*, 1982; *Lovesick*, 1983. **Cause of death** Complications of emphysema, at age 81. **Further reading** Paul Davay, *John Huston*, Paris, 1957; Jean-Claude Alais, *John Huston*, Paris, 1960; William Nolan, *John Huston, King Rebel*, Los Angeles, 1965; Robert Benayoun, *John Huston*, Paris, 1966; Riccardo Cechinni, *John Huston*, 1969; *Romano Tozzi, John Huston: A Picture History of His Films*, New York, 1971; Axel Madsen, *John Huston*, New York, 1978; Stuart Kaminsky, *John Huston: Maker of Magic*, London, 1978; plus many articles (see *The International Dictionary of Films and Filmmakers*, vol. 2, Chicago, 1984).

LEON H. KEYSERLING

American Economist

***Born* Charleston, South Carolina, 22 January 1908**

***Died* Washington, DC, 9 August 1987**

Perhaps the most influential economist to serve in the Truman administration, Leon Keyserling remained consistently dedicated to a liberal approach to government economic policy throughout his more than 50 years as a public servant and writer. Described as "brilliant" and "immensely forceful", he is credited with maintaining President Truman's advocacy of New Deal policies during a period in which conservatives held considerable influence in Washington. He contributed greatly to the transition of America's war economy to peacetime and in many ways helped to determine the shape of the United States' post-war economic boom.

Leon Keyserling was born in Beaufort, near Charleston, in 1908. After graduation from high school at the age of 16, he attended Columbia University, where he completed a liberal arts curriculum. He studied law at Harvard University, was admitted to the New York Bar at the age of 23 and, shortly thereafter, made a name for himself when he conducted an investigation for the General Education Board.

After a brief period of teaching economics at Columbia, Keyserling, like many young intellectuals, was drawn by the new Roosevelt administration to Washington, DC, with the intention of serving in government. He joined the legal staff of the Agricultural Adjustment Act in May 1933, but left after only a few months to take a position as legislative assistant to Senator Robert F. Wagner of New York. In this capacity, he helped to draft a series of New Deal social programmes, including the National Industrial Recovery Act of 1933, the Railway Retirement Act of 1934, the Social Security Act of 1935 and the National Labor Relations Act (also called the "Wagner Act").

Keyserling served in a number of other capacities under Senator Wagner, working to secure federal assistance for low-income housing and the establishment of the United States Housing Authority (USHA). He left Wagner's staff in 1937 to serve as general counsel for the USHA under its administrator, Nathan Straus. The agency was later placed under the authority of the War Department, where Keyserling won praise from, among others, Senator Truman, for raising productivity while placating the unions. In 1941 he was named commissioner of the Public Housing Authority, and later succeeded Straus as head of the USHA. As a result of the war, these agencies were merged into the National Housing Agency, in which Keyserling was appointed general counsel.

In 1944, while planning for post-war housing needs of several million war workers, Keyserling won the Pabst Award for proposed solutions to the question of post-war employment. He advocated a system under which standard free-market mechanisms would be suspended in favour of broad, pro-active government/labour efforts aimed specifically at job creation. Many of these ideas formed the basis for subsequent legislation, including the Employment Act of 1946.

Harry Truman, who succeeded Roosevelt as president in 1944, appointed Keyserling to his newly-formed Council of Economic Advisers, serving with Edwin G. Nourse and John D. Clark. In this position, Keyserling enjoyed considerably greater influence over national economic affairs, being considered a "non-political New Dealer, unconnected with pre-Truman White House economic planners".

The council advocated price controls and moderation in labour issues in order to keep inflation low and to avoid crippling strikes in essential sectors of the economy. These "Fair Deal" policies were not popular in Washington, and sparked opposition from conservative elements within Truman's own Democratic Party. Keyserling, however, was adamant about the correctness of his view and demonstrated exceptional diplomatic capabilities in maintaining support for his programme. He was made chairman of the council in 1949, and served in that post until Truman left office in January 1953.

After leaving public office, Keyserling returned to private practice as a lawyer and consultant. He testified on behalf of union organizations and became a prolific writer on economic issues pertaining to employment and labour issues. His clients included virtually every public employee labour organization in New York City, and the governments of France, India and Israel.

Keyserling had numerous works published during the 1960s and 1970s, and returned to public service briefly during the Carter administration, when he helped to draft the Full Employment and Balanced Growth Act of 1978. This effort, however, was largely undercut by exogenous inflationary economic factors related to oil price rises, and unfortunately was never fully appreciated. In one of his last works he warned of spiralling deficit spending in Reagan administration economic policies, and outlined in precise terms how inflation, unemployment and the federal budget deficit could be simultaneously arrested.

A portly man with wire-rimmed glasses, and known for his partiality to bright neckties, Keyserling carried the label of "New Dealer" throughout his career. He advocated strong government intervention in the economy and, were it not for his apolitical demeanour, could have been targeted as a socialist. However, he must be given credit for formulating the basic post-war economic policies which kept inflation low, minimized unemployment and stimulated unprecedented economic growth.

Born Leon Hyman Keyserling. **Parents** William and Jennie (Hyman) Keyserling. **Marriage** Mary Dublin, economist, 1940. **Education** Columbia University, AB, 1928; Harvard Law School, LLB, 1931; admitted to New York Bar, 1931; postgraduate in economics, Columbia University, 1931–33. **Career** Assistant, department of economics, Columbia University, 1932–33; attorney, Agricultural Adjustment Administration, 1933; secretary and legislative assistant to US Senator Robert F. Wagner, 1933–37; general counsel, US Housing Authority, 1937–38, deputy administrator and general counsel, 1938–42, acting administrator, 1941–42; acting commissioner, Federal Public Housing Agency, 1942; general counsel, National Housing Agency, 1942–46; vice-chairman, Council of Economic Advisers, 1946–50, chairman, 1950–53; consultant, economist and practising attorney to various national firms, organizations and individuals in the US; economic consultant to governments of France, India, Israel and Puerto Rico, 1953–71. **Related activities** Expert, US Senate Committee on banking and currency, 1935–37; consultant New York State Constitutional Convention, 1938; de facto member, Cabinet and National Security Council; consultant to various members of US Senate and House of

Representatives, 1942–46, 1953 onwards; voluntary public service to US economy and policies, 1971 onwards; editor of board, US Center of Presidency, 1980–87. **Offices and memberships** Founder and president, Conference on Economic Progress, 1954; president, National Committee for Labor, Israel, 1969–73; member: American Economic Association, American Political Science Association, American Bar Association. **Awards and honours** Phi Beta Kappa, 1928; Pabst Award, 1944; Man of Year Award, American Jewish Congress; honorary DBusSci, Bryant College, 1965; honorary faculty member, Industrial College of Armed Forces, 1966; honorary LHD, University of Missouri, 1978; Congressional Award, Centenary of Fiorello H. LaGuardia, 1983; Special Award, Industrial College of Armed Forces, 1983; National Center for Full Employment Award, 1986; named to National Housing Center Hall of Fame, 1986. **Publications** (with Rexford G. Tugwell) *Redirecting Education*, 1934; *Toward Full Employment and Full Production*, 1954; *Inflation—Cause and Cure*, 1959; *The Federal Budget and the General Welfare*, 1959; (with Benjamin A. Javits) *The Peace by Investment Corporation*, 1961; *Key Policies for Full Employment*, 1962; *Poverty and Deprivation in the US*, 1962; *Taxes and the Public Interest*, 1963; *Two Top Priority Programs to Reduce Unemployment*, 1963; *The Toll of Rising Interest Rates*, 1964; *Progress or Poverty*, 1964; *Agriculture and the Public Interest*, 1965; *The Move Toward Railroad Mergers*, 1965; *The Role of Wages in a Great Society*, 1966; *A Freedom Budget for All Americans*, 1966; *Goals for Teachers' Salaries in Our Public Schools*, 1967; *Achieving Nationwide Educational Excellence*, 1968; *Israel's Economic Progress*, 1968; *Taxation of Whom and for What?*, 1969; *More Growth with Less Inflation or More Inflation without Growth?*, 1970; *Wages, Prices and Profits*, 1971; *The Coming Crisis in Housing*, 1972; *The Scarcity School of Economics*, 1973; *Full Employment Without Inflation*, 1975; *"Liberal" and "Conservative" National Economic Policies and Their Consequences, 1919–79*, 1979; *Money, Credit and Interest Rates: Their Gross Mismanagement by the Federal Reserve System*, 1980; *The Economics of Discrimination*, 1981; *How to Cut Unemployment by 4 per cent and End Inflation and Deficits by 1987*, 1983; *The Current Significance of the New Deal*, 1984; *Why Have Economists Learned So Little from US Economic Experience?*, 1985; co-author of numerous publications and reports from the Council of Economic Advisers, 1946–53; author of numerous articles. **Cause of death** Undisclosed, at age 79.

NOBUSUKE KISHI

Japanese Politician

Born **Yamaguchi Prefecture, Japan, 13 November 1896**

Died **Tokyo, Japan, 7 August 1987**

The political career of Nobusuke Kishi coincided with some of the most momentous years in modern Japanese history, and he more than once played a controversial role at the centre of events. A former minister in General Hideki Tōjō's cabinet during World War II, Kishi endured imprisonment under the US occupation, was instrumental in the unification of post-war Japan's political Right through the foundation of the Liberal-Democratic Party, and held the position of party leader and prime minister from 1957 until 1960, when he was forced to resign.

Kishi was born Nobusuke Satō, one of ten children (younger brother Eisaku Satō would also become prime minister), the change of name being due to adoption by a paternal uncle. As an outstanding law graduate of Tokyo Imperial University, he made what by Japanese standards was rapid progress through the ranks of the civil service: at the age of 40 he became a vice-minister in the industrial department of the government of Manchuria, promoting industrialization there and in north China following Japan's seizure of those regions.

Returning to Japan three years later as vice-minister of commerce and industry responsible for wartime economic reorganization, Kishi suffered a setback when industry resisted his efforts to impose total government control, and he resigned. By 1941, however, he was back, this time as minister, and when Tōjō formed his first war cabinet later that year, Kishi, now state minister and vice-minister of munitions, displayed formidable ability in mobilizing the economy for the war effort, meanwhile winning a seat in the House of Representatives.

But, not surprisingly, under Tōjō militarists carried more weight than technocrats, and from 1943 onwards Kishi increasingly found himself at odds with the general's policy of war at all costs. Forced to resign in 1944 after the fall of Saipan, whose loss for Kishi signalled inevitable defeat for Japan, he effectively brought down the Tōjō government, showing notable nerve in making his criticisms public in the press.

After Japan's surrender, Kishi was arrested as a class A war criminal by the American occupation authorities, but he was never brought to trial and was released in 1948. Purged from public service, he re-established himself in business before the restoration of Japanese sovereignty and concomitant amnesty of 1952 enabled him to resume his political career and he was elected to the reformed Diet on the Liberal ticket.

When Prime Minister Shigeru Yoshida named Kishi to the chair of the Committee to Investigate the Constitution, perhaps hoping to sideline both the man and the investigation, he could not have dreamed that within two years his minion would successfully have organized the new, rival Democratic Party and organized his overthrow. Leader of the new party, Ichiro Hatoyama, was elected premier and soon faced the thorny problem of pushing the 1955 budget through a largely hostile Diet. Kishi once more demonstrated his considerable political agility with a successful rallying call for conservative unification.

The new unity was consolidated by the end of the year with the formal creation of the merged Liberal-Democratic party, with Hatoyama at the helm and Kishi as secretary-general. When ill-health forced retirement on both Hatoyama and then his successor Tanzan Ishibashi, under whose brief premiership Kishi served as foreign minister, he was the natural choice for party leader and prime minister, which he duly became in February 1957. It was less than a decade since his release from prison.

If Kishi's three-year term as prime minister was a turbulent one, this was in part because unlike many who have acceded to that position in Japan he was not afraid to court controversy. An arch-conservative—opponents would say reactionary—he brought to the forefront many of the issues that have served as touchstones for Japan's right wing ever since: restoration of military strength, maintenance of close security ties with the United States while questioning the "alien", US-imposed post-war constitution (more particularly its prohibition of the "potential to make war"), emphasis on law and order and so-called traditional values, and minimal relations with communist neighbours (Kishi opposed recognition of China to the end).

While Kishi has been seen as the architect of Japan's economic resurgence, the project closest to his heart—and the one which indirectly proved to be his downfall—was that to revise the US–Japan security treaty, ostensibly with a view to putting the relationship between the two nations on an equal basis and restoring Japan's independent diplomacy. In 1957 he visited Washington, DC, for talks with US president Dwight D. Eisenhower, and he returned in January 1960 to sign a revised treaty. It should have been the high point of his career. But not all Japanese were as convinced of the virtues of such a treaty, and opposition to it was both militant and widespread. When Kishi pushed its ratification through the Diet while opposition parties were boycotting the session, and then proceeded to order the police to enter the building in force and eject protesting

Socialist members, the result was large-scale demonstrations against him. A visit by Eisenhower had to be cancelled, and a chastened Kishi resigned.

Kishi was undoubtedly a man of authoritarian instincts who often seemed to be hankering after the more "authentic" nation of his younger days. Yet it was he who made a start on reopening relations with the countries of Southeast Asia that had suffered so much at the hands of that same Japan. In 1957 he visited nine such nations to offer reparations and economic cooperation as well as, to each in turn, a public apology for Japan's treatment of them, in what was termed "the statesmanship of the humble heart".

Nevertheless, it was not often humility that guided Kishi in his political conduct; in the wake of his resignation, as the crisis he provoked in 1960 gradually subsided, consensus was restored to its position among the primary virtues in democratic Japan. Kishi himself remained politically active, while the party for whose creation he was largely responsible continued to dominate the Japanese scene until the end of his life.

Born Nobusuke Satō. **Father** Hidesuke Satō, sake (rice-wine) manufacturer. **Marriage** Yoshiko Kishi. **Children** One son, Nobukazu, and one daughter, Yoko. **Education** Graduated from College of Law, Tokyo Imperial University, 1920. **Career** Clerk, Ministry of Agriculture and Commerce, 1920; chief of industrial administration section, Industrial Affairs Bureau, 1932; secretary, Ministry of Foreign Affairs, 1933; chief of archives section, Ministry of Commerce and Industry, 1933; secretary, temporary industrial rationalization bureau and director, Industrial Affairs Bureau, 1935–36; head of reorganization of Manchuria and North China industries, 1936; director, Patent Bureau and assistant director, General Affairs Bureau, 1937–39; vice-minister of commerce and industry, 1939–41; minister of commerce and industry, 1941–42; member, House of Representatives, 1942, 1953, 1955; state minister and minister of munitions, 1942; minister of state without portfolio, 1943–44; imprisoned as class A war criminal, 1944–47; purged from public service, 1947; chairman, Committee to Investigate the Constitution, 1953; secretary-general, Democratic Party, 1953–55; secretary-general, Liberal-Democrats, 1955–56; chairman, Railway Construction Council, 1955; minister of foreign affairs, 1956; acting premier, 1956; prime minister, 1957–60; president, Liberal-Democrats, 1957–60. **Related activities** Chairman, board of directors, Toyo Pulp Manufacturing Company, 1949; organizer, Japan Reconstruction League, 1952–53. **Cause of death** Undisclosed, at age 90.

UYS KRIGE

South African Poet, Playwright and Short Story Writer

Born **Swellendam, Cape Province, 4 February 1910**

Died **Onrust, Cape Province, 10 August 1987**

Uys Krige was an Afrikaner writer who did much to bridge the English/Afrikaans language barrier in South Africa. He was, perhaps, unique in his ability to write with equal fluency in both languages. He enriched the cultural heritage of his own people by translating into Afrikaans some English and Spanish classics, including Lorca's *Yerma* and Shakespeare's *Twelfth Night*. To the English-speaking world he brought his own interpretations of the Afrikaans culture and way of life in the stories he wrote in English.

Krige was a lyrical, poetic writer whose inspiration came from within the Afrikaner traditions in which he grew up. In his work he explored the nature of this tradition, its European ancestry, its roots in the soil of South Africa, and its strongly-held Calvinist beliefs. One of his stories, "The Coffin", describes the life of a lonely Afrikaner patriarch awaiting death, his coffin stored in the attic above his house. Another, "The Dream", is full of his own nostalgic memories of childhood in South Africa. His finest achievement—a play that was successful in both South Africa and the US—was *The Two Lamps*, which examines the conflict inherent in a father/son relationship.

It was after the war, in which Krige worked as a war correspondent in Europe and was captured and imprisoned in Italy, that he began to write in English as well as Afrikaans. *The Way Out* was an autobiographical account of his escape from prisoner-of-war camp in Italy and described the emotional side of wartime suffering and heroism. It was also in English that Krige produced one of his few stories dealing with Black characters. In "Death of a Zulu" he describes a single, lonely, wartime death in the desert, and it is tribute to his skill that the story presents a universal truth—not one bounded by considerations of race or colour.

Though he began life as a journalist, working before the war as a reporter on the *Rand Daily Mail* and freelancing in France and Spain, Krige avoided politics in his work. The real racial issues of South Africa, the conflicts between White and Black in that country, are not his theme. In this, perhaps, lay his strength. Krige wrote about the country and the people he knew and, in so doing, perhaps gave a picture of the ordinary Afrikaner that was more accurate, less prejudiced than many, that had at least a human face.

Born Uys Krige **Marriage** Lydia Pindeque, 1937. **Children** Two. **Education** Paul Roos Gymnasium; studied law, Stellenbosch University, 1927–29. **Career** Reporter, *Rand Daily Mail*, Johannesburg, 1931; freelance journalist, France and Spain, 1931–36; correspondent, *Die Suiderstem*, Cape Town, 1936; broadcaster, Bureau of Information, 1939; war correspondent in Egypt and Abyssinia, World War II; prisoner of war, Italy, 1941–43; founding editor, *Vandag* (Today) newspaper, Johannesburg, 1949. **Awards and honours** French government bursary, 1952; honorary doctorate, University of Natal, 1958; Carnegie grant, 1959; Hertzog Prize for poetry, 1974, for drama, 1985. **Plays** *Binnenshuis* (adapted from Maeterlinck), 1931; *Magdalena Retief* (in Afrikaans), Cape Town, 1938, revised edition, 1948; *Die Wit Muur* (The White Wall), Cape Town, 1940; *All Paaie Gaan na Rome* (All Roads Go to Rome), Cape Town, 1949; (adapted from a story by Sannie Uys) *Die Twee Lampe* (The Two Lamps), Johannesburg, 1951; *Die Ryk Weduwee* (The Rich Widow), Johannesburg, 1953; *Die Goue Kring* (The Golden Circle), Cape Town, 1956; *The Sniper and Other One-Act Plays*, Cape Town, 1962; *Yerma* (in Afrikaans, adapted from Lorca), Cape Town, 1963; *The Two Lamps* and *The Big Shots*, Cape Town, 1964; (adapted from Shakespeare) *Twaalfde Nag* (Twelfth Night), Transvaal, 1965; *Muur van die Dood* (Wall of Death), Cape Town, 1968; *Die Grootkanonne* (The Big Shots), Johannesburg, 1969; *Die Ongeskrewe Stuk* (The Unwritten Play), Johannesburg, 1970; *Die Huis van Bernarda Alba* (adapted from Lorca), Cape Town, 1980; *Vier Eenbedrywe*, Pretoria, 1980; *Die Wit Muur en ader Eenbedrywe*, Pretoria, 1983; *Die Lewe is Alleen Draaglik as Mens bietjie Dronk is* (Life Is Bearable Only While One Is a Little Drunk), Cape Town, 1985; *Die Apie* (The Little Monkey) (TV play), 1985. **Verse** *Kentering* (Turning Point), Pretoria, 1935; *Rooidag* (Daybreak), Pretoria, 1940: *Ooclogsgedigte*, Pretoria, 1942; *Die Einde van die Pad* (The End of the Road), Pretoria, 1947; *Hart Sonder Hawe* (Heart without Haven), Cape Town, 1949; *Vir die Luit en die Kitaar* (For the Lute and the Guitar), Johannesburg, 1950; *Ballade van die Groot Begeer* (Ballad of the Great Desiring), Cape Town, 1960; *Gedigte 1927–1940* (Poems), Pretoria, 1961; *Eluard en die Surrealisme*, Cape Town, 1962; *Vooraand* (Eve), 1964; *Versamelde Gedigte* (Collected Poems), Cape Town, 1985. **Short stories** *Die Palmboom* (The Palm Tree), Pretoria, 1940; *The Dream and the Desert*, London, 1953, Boston, 1954; (with others) *Rooi*, Cape Town,

1965; *Orphan of the Desert*, Cape Town, 1967. **Other** (with Conrad Norton) *Vanguard of Victory: A Short Review of the South African Victories in East Africa 1940–1941,* Pretoria, 1941: *The Way Out: Italian Intermezzo* (autobiography), London, 1946, revised edition, Cape Town, 1955: *Sol y Sombra* (in Afrikaans), Pretoria, 1948, revised edition, Pretoria, 1955; *Ver in die Wereld* (Far in the world), Johannesburg, 1951; *Sout van die Aarde* (Salt of the Earth), Cape Town, 1961. **Edited works** *Poems of Roy Campbell*, Cape Town, 1960; *Olive Schreiner: A Selection*, Cape Town and London, 1968, New York, 1969; (with Jack Cope) *The Penguin Book of South African Verse*, London, 1968; (translator and editor) *Spaans–Amerikaanse Keuse* (Spanish–American Verse), Cape Town, 1969. **Cause of death** Undisclosed, at age 77. **Further reading** Christina Van Heyningen and Jacques Berthoud, *Uys Krige*, New York, 1966.

JOSEPH P. LASH

American Author and Journalist

***Born* New York City, New York, 2 December 1909**

***Died* Boston, Massachusetts, 22 August 1987**

It could be deemed unfair to state that, but for Eleanor Roosevelt, the name of Joseph P. Lash would have remained unknown to millions of American readers. Yet when one considers the fact that of his ten biographical works, six are primarily concerned with the “First Lady of the World” and a seventh deals in part with her husband, such an assertion does not seem far off the mark. Neither does it mean that Lash was found lacking as a writer, for despite the fact that Mrs Roosevelt provided tailor-made subject matter, one does not win the Pulitzer Prize and the National Book Award for biography simply by riding along on the skirts of the famous. When *Eleanor and Franklin* appeared in 1971, critics went wild in their praise and enthusiasm. Richard Rovere classed it as “exemplary biography...perfectly shaped and splendidly written from start to finish”. Yet one cannot help but wonder what shape Lash’s career would have taken had he not encountered Eleanor Roosevelt in 1939, on a train bound for Washington, DC.

Given his political beliefs and outspoken radicalism, Lash seemed destined to come into contact with Mrs Roosevelt. Born in New York City in 1909, he was the eldest son of two Jewish–Russian emigrés. When his father died, young Lash was nine years old; he quickly became “...part of the street. There were Irish and Hungarian kids, and a few Jewish kids like myself. I was the smallest guy in the group. It wasn’t the easiest life.” Despite his disadvantaged beginnings, Joe Lash managed to obtain a university education, first at New York’s City College, then at Columbia University, where he received his MA in English literature in 1932. Degrees did not mean much during the Depression, however, and when the graduate found himself among the countless number of out-of-work academics, he quickly became heavily involved in the Association of Unemployed College Alumni and Professional People. As chairman of the association, he campaigned for government aid programmes to alleviate unemployment—hardly surprising since the young intellectual had been a member of the Socialist Party since 1929.

Steeped in the political consciousness of the times, Lash became, in his own words, “swept up by the revolution”, and when a group of Socialist and Communist youth organizations merged to form the American Student Union (ASU) at Columbia in 1935, he lost no time in adding his voice to the already-militant association. For the next four years he served as the ASU’s national secretary, co-authoring with James A. Wechsler (the director of publications) a history of the peace and student activist movements called *War, Our Heritage*, published in 1936. Lash's radicalism grew during his involvement with the ASU, and he was almost ready to join the Communist Party as a statement of his beliefs, when the announcement of the Nazi–Soviet Pact stopped him in his tracks. Conflicts within the ASU added to Lash's frustration and general disillusionment, and in late 1939 he was summoned to Washington to testify before the House Committee on Un-American Activities on Communist influence in American youth organizations. It was on his train journey to the capital that the man, once described as "the Tom Hayden or Mark Rudd of his generation", first encountered Eleanor Roosevelt. The then first lady boarded the train at Pennsylvania Station and counselled Lash and his friends to "be cool and responsive to the committee". She also lent her moral support to the ASU by appearing before the committee herself the following day. Thus began the friendship between Lash and the first lady, a relationship which lasted until Mrs Roosevelt's death in 1962.

It was not a relationship without its problems, however. Joseph Lash began to work for FDR's third-term presidential campaign in 1940, serving as director of the Youth Division for the Democratic National Committee, and afterwards as the general-secretary of the International Student Service. Both positions necessitated close contact with Eleanor Roosevelt, and the two friends worked long hours together, planning youth leadership institutes and other projects. Soon, Communist Party members were criticizing Lash as the "bought and paid for elder statesman of the student movement", while conservatives pegged him as one of Eleanor Roosevelt's "unsavoury radical favourites". Lash took the criticism in his stride; no doubt it was this close working relationship with Eleanor Roosevelt which allowed him to write so accurately of the woman in later years.

Lash served in the army during World War II. After his discharge, he continued his political activism, eventually working with Eleanor Roosevelt again when the two helped found the controversial Americans for Democratic Action (ADA) group, a non-communist liberal organization. Lash remained with the ADA as its New York director until 1948, when he assisted Elliott Roosevelt in editing two volumes of FDR's letters. Finally, in 1950, Lash's journalistic career began in earnest when he joined the *New York Post*, working first as the paper's United Nations correspondent and later as the assistant editor of its editorial page. It was through his involvement at the UN that Lash came to the attention of Secretary-General Dag Hammarskjold, who eventually authorized him to write an impersonal biography. *Dag Hammarskjold: Custodian of the Brushfire Peace* was published in 1961, and although some critics praised it ("interpretive reporting at its best" was the *New Republic* magazine's comment), others objected that Lash glossed over his subject's failures—hardly fair, considering that Hammarskjold had insisted that the biography be confined to his professional career.

The following year, Eleanor Roosevelt died, and Joseph Lash decided to write a short biography on his own terms. *Eleanor Roosevelt, A Friend's Memoir* appeared in 1964, the first of Lash's Eleanor-cycle of books. The reviews on this work were more favourable in the main; Lash had contained his own feelings well and rarely slipped into sentimentality, plus the book was lent some poignant touches by the memories of Lash's wife Trude Pratt, who had also been a close friend of the former first lady. No one was surprised, then, to hear that Franklin Roosevelt Jr chose Lash to write his mother's definitive biography. The task allowed Lash sole access to Eleanor Roosevelt's files in the Franklin D. Roosevelt Library in Hyde Park, New York. Here, starting in 1966, Lash spent the better part of three years sorting through the mounds of papers. Next, he shut himself away in an old house near the Hudson River to condense the material into some kind of readable format. The result was the 765-page *Eleanor and Franklin: The Story of Their Relationship Based on Eleanor Roosevelt's Private Papers*, and its 368-page sequel, *Eleanor: The Years Alone*.

It was the former work which set Lash on his literary pedestal. *Eleanor and Franklin* took the public and the critics by storm, prompting Richard Rovere to write:

> The prose is lucid, spare and never obtrusive. It is clear from the outset that this is the work of a close friend and admirer, but Lash can nowhere be faulted for sycophancy or indulgence...His portraits of turn-of-the-century life in the Hudson Valley, of early twentieth-century New York, and of Washington during the years of the two world wars are superb. So are his renderings of the dozens of characters who moved in and out of the Roosevelts' lives. But his focus is always sharply on his subject...[This] is biography in the Grand Manner.

In addition to the National Book Award and the Pulitzer Prize, *Eleanor and Franklin* also won for its author the Francis Parkman Prize of the Society of American Historians. The book would later be made into a television mini-series.

Its sequel, dealing with Mrs Roosevelt's life after the death of FDR, received a somewhat cooler reception from many critics, although it was well-received in the main, partly due, it has to be admitted, to the hype which surrounded its parent volume. But having established himself as *the* authority on the Roosevelts, Lash had no cause for concern, and he moved on to other projects, including *Roosevelt and Churchill*, a book which examined the policies of the American and British leaders during the war years, and *Love, Eleanor—Eleanor Roosevelt and Her Friends* (collected letters). The latter confronted the rumours of Mrs Roosevelt's alleged lesbian affair, as well as those of an alleged affair between Mrs Roosevelt and Lash himself. A second volume of collected letters followed, as did a centenary portrait of Lash's obsession. In between Roosevelt pursuits, however, the author had turned his attention briefly to another subject—a study of the relationship between Helen Keller and Anne Sullivan, which resulted in *Helen and Teacher* in 1980. As with the Roosevelt sagas, this work was also highly acclaimed.

The man behind the biographies was described as resembling an Old Testament prophet: brown eyes, black hair and beard. Throughout his lifetime, Joseph Lash retained his concern for politics, continuing his affiliation with Americans for Democratic Action, and joining the Tilden Democratic Club in New York. Whatever one's feelings about the style of his writing (once described as "pedestrian at best"), one has to admit that Joseph P. Lash succeeded by blending "a journalist's interest...with a scholar's intellect". It was no doubt these very qualities which attracted Eleanor Roosevelt to him (and vice-versa) in the first place.

Born Joseph P. Lash. **Parents** Samuel, a storekeeper, and Mary (Avchin) Lash. **Marriages** 1) Name unknown, 1935 (divorced, 1940); 2) Trude von Adam Wenzel Pratt, director of Citizens' Committee for Children, 1944. **Children** One son, Jonathan. **Education** De Witt Clinton High School, New York City, 1923–27; College of the City of New York, BA, 1931; Columbia University, MA, 1932. **Military service** Second lieutenant, US Army, and awarded Air Medal, 1942–45. **Career** Editor, *Student Outlook*, 1933–35; national secretary, American Student Union, 1936–39; general-secretary, International Student Service, 1940–42; secretary, Americans for Democratic Action, New York City branch, 1946–48; assistant to Elliot Roosevelt, 1948–50; UN Correspondent, *New York Post*, 1950–61, assistant editor of editorial page, 1961–66; freelance writer, 1966–87. **Offices and memberships** Member, American Socialist Party, 1929–37; chair, Association of Unemployed College Alumni and Professional People, early 1930s; secretary, Student League for Industrial Democracy, 1932–35; cabinet member, American Youth Congress, late 1930s; director of youth division, Democratic National Committee, 1940; consultant to youth division, Office of Civilian Defense, early 1940s; member: Union for Democratic Action, 1945–46, Tilden Democratic Club, New York City, Americans for Democratic Action, American Civil Liberties Union, American Veterans' Association, UN

Correspondents' Association, PEN (society of Poets, Playwrights, Editors, Essayists and Novelists); Authors' League, Society of American Historians. **Awards and honours** Pulitzer Prize and National Book Award for biography *Eleanor and Franklin: The Story of Their Relationship Based on Eleanor Roosevelt's Private Papers*, 1972; Samuel E. Morrison Award for history for *Roosevelt and Churchill: A Study of Their Relationship*, 1978; Robert Kennedy Book Award nomination and American Library Association notable book citation for *Helen and Teacher: The Story of Helen Keller and Anne Sullivan Macy*, 1980. **Publications** (with James A. Wechsler) *War, Our Heritage*, 1936; *Dag Hammarskjold: Custodian of the Brushfire Peace*, 1961; *Eleanor Roosevelt: A Friend's Memoir*, 1965; *Eleanor and Franklin: The Story of Their Relationship Based on Eleanor Roosevelt's Private Papers*, 1971; *Eleanor: The Years Alone*, 1972; *From the Diaries of Felix Frankfurter*, 1975; *Roosevelt and Churchill: A Study of Their Relationship*, 1976; *Helen and Teacher: The Story of Helen Keller and Anne Sullivan Macy*, 1980; (collected letters, vol. 1) *Love Eleanor: Eleanor Roosevelt and Her Friends*, 1982; (collected letters, vol. 2) *A World of Love: Eleanor Roosevelt and Her Friends, 1943–62*, 1984; *Life Was Meant to Be Lived: A Centenary Portrait of Eleanor Roosevelt*, 1984. **Cause of death** Heart ailment, at age 77.

WADE H. McCREE Jr

American Judge and Solicitor General

Born **Des Moines, Iowa, 3 July 1920**

Died **Detroit, Michigan, 30 August 1987**

The senior Wade Hampton McCree was said to have been the first Black man to own a pharmacy in the state of Iowa, and to have been one of the first Negro narcotics inspectors to work for the Federal Food and Drug Administration (FDA)—no small achievement in the United States of the early twentieth century. It is hardly surprising, then, that his son should tally up his own string of firsts: Wade McCree Jr was the first Negro to be elected to a judgeship in the state of Michigan, the first to serve as a circuit judge in Wayne County, and, much later in his career, the first Black Federal judge to preside in the South, albeit during a colleague's absence. McCree was, more importantly, the second Black man to be appointed as a federal district judge and the second Negro solicitor general in United States history. Throughout his career, Wade McCree was known as a highly articulate and careful—if sometimes overly zealous—judge, whose life was devoted to two purposes: judicial fairness and breaking the barriers of racial prejudice.

McCree's childhood was spent variously in Iowa, Hawaii, Chicago and Boston, due to his father's work for the FDA. Young Wade graduated from Boston's Latin School and went on to study at Fisk University. From there he entered the Harvard Law School, where his classmates included Kingman Brewster Jr, who became president of Yale University, Elliot L. Richardson, later secretary of commerce, and William T. Coleman Jr, future secretary of transportation. After obtaining his degree from Harvard in 1944, McCree's career was interrupted by World War II; he served in the infantry as a battalion staff officer in three Italian campaigns. It was 1948 before he was admitted to the Michigan Bar.

While searching for a job, Wade McCree encountered racial prejudice first-hand, the type of bigotry he was to fight throughout his career. He approached one of Detroit's more glamorous law firms for a job; the company happened to be an all-White organization and the secretary was more than taken aback by the colour of McCree's skin—despite the fact that he presented a letter of recommendation from Harvard. "She thought that at best I had found the letter," McCree recalled in 1977, "and that at worst I had stolen it." Needless to say, the young Black lawyer was not taken on by that particular firm, but he nonetheless found work: McCree practised in Detroit from 1948 to 1952, when he was appointed commissioner for the Michigan Workmen's Compensation; after that, his rise to prominence began. First he served as Wayne County's circuit judge until 1961, and during that year President Kennedy appointed him district judge for Michigan's Eastern District, a position he held until 1966. President Lyndon Johnson then promoted McCree to the United States Court of Appeals for the Sixth Circuit, an area which covered Michigan, Ohio, Kentucky and Tennessee. Finally, President Carter appointed him to the post of solicitor general in 1977, a job McCree held until 1981, and one which he described as being "the most exciting lawyer's job in the nation".

McCree had already come face to face with the wrong type of "excitement" in his judicial experiences. Earlier in his role as an appeal judge, a White client had asked that McCree be replaced by a White judge because the case pitted a White man against a Black. McCree replied that he would step down only if a mulatto could be found to take his place. "That was one hell of an assumption," he said of the plea. "The ultimate of arrogance is achieved when a White person thinks another White person can make a judgement without being influenced by race, and a Black person cannot."

McCree himself, however, would later be accused of the same type of colour-blindness. During his career as solicitor general, in which his duties were to represent the administration and the Justice Department before the Supreme Court, McCree was called upon to devise the Carter administration's stance on the controversial Bakke case of the 1970s. Allan Bakke, a White Californian, had applied for entrance to medical school at the University of California at Davis. His application, he alleged, had been turned down in favour of less-qualified minority applicants—an argument which resulted in the phrase "reverse-discrimination". McCree countered by saying that race could indeed be used as a factor in a university's policy of seeking a diverse student body, but the Supreme Court found that, in Bakke's case, the medical school *had* gone too far, violating the US Constitution and working against Bakke. After the case ended, some of McCree's colleagues said that the Black judge had found it difficult and extremely painful to reconcile his zeal for civil rights with the other legal implications of the case, yet for the duration of his post, McCree enjoyed the respect and goodwill of the Supreme Court justices, who admired his character and sound judgement.

Wade McCree resigned as solicitor general in 1981 to join the University of Michigan Law School, where he remained until the end of his life. One of his colleagues there, Dean Lee C. Bollinger, described Wade McCree as "one of the great figures in law of his time...He was very distinguished as a judge, and as a solicitor general and as a professsor. Few people can match the genuine significance of his career."

Born Wade Hampton McCree Jr. **Parents** Wade Hampton, pharmacist, later narcotics inspector, Federal Food and Drug Administration, and Lulu H. (Harper) McCree. **Marriage** Dores B. McCrary, professional librarian, 1946. **Children** Two daughters, Kathleen and Karen, and one son, Wade Hampton III. **Education** Boston Latin School; Fisk University, AB, 1941; Harvard Law School, LLB, 1944. **Military service** Captain, Army of the United States Infantry, European Theatre of Operations. **Career** Admitted to Michigan Bar, 1948; practised law, Detroit, 1948–52; commissioner, Michigan Workmen's Compensation Commission, 1952–54; circuit judge, Wayne County, Michigan, 1954–61; United States district judge, Michigan Eastern District, 1961–66; United States Court of Appeals judge for the Sixth Circuit, 1966–77; United States solicitor general, 1977–81; faculty member, University of Michigan Law School, 1981–87.

Related activities Member, law faculty, Salzburg Seminar American Studies, 1969; member, visiting committee, Wayne State University Law School and Harvard Law School; vice-president, United Fund, Detroit; member, Commission on Private Philanthropy and Public Needs; executive board, Detroit Area Council of Boy Scouts of America; member, national council of advisers, University of Mid-Am; vice-chairman, board of trustees, Fisk University, Nashville; board of directors: Federal Judicial Center, Metropolitan Hospital, Henry Ford Hospital, Founders' Society, Detroit Institute of Arts; board of overseers, Harvard University. **Offices and memberships** Member: American Bar Association, advisory board of editors of journal, commission on standards of judicial administration, Michigan Bar Association, Detroit Bar Association, Institute on Judicial Administration, American Law Institute, Seminar Society, Detroit, Phi Beta Kappa. **Awards and honours** Fellow, American Bar Association; honorary LLD: Wayne State University, 1964, Tuskegee Institute, 1965, Detroit College of Law, 1967, University of Detroit, 1968, Harvard University, 1969, Michigan State University, 1971, University of Michigan, 1971, Oakland University, 1974; honorary DLitt, Centre College, Danville, Kentucky. **Cause of death** Bone marrow cancer, at age 67.

LEE MARVIN

American Actor

Born **New York City, New York, 19 February 1924**

Died **Tucson, Arizona, 29 August 1987**

The most important influence on Lee Marvin, both personally and for his work, derived from his experiences in the Pacific during World War II. These not only enabled him to bring the total cold reality of violence and horror to the screen, but also to re-enact violence in a strikingly cold-blooded way. It was this that gripped his audiences and made him one of the screen's greatest tough guys of all time.

Marvin was born into one of the oldest families in the United States. His childhood was sheltered and his education somewhat disturbed by expulsion from several schools at which he had been less than happy. Eventually the war gave him the opportunity to quit and he joined the US Marine Corps. His father, a one time US Smallbore Champion, gave him his personal automatic, a Colt .45, which he had bought from the exclusive firm of Abercrombie and Fitch. "It was," recalled Marvin, "the civilian model which is rather better finished than the standard government issue." Even more important, he learned from his father the best technique to fire the difficult-to-handle weapon. Marvin described the gun as a "real coke-burner. It's not an attacking weapon, more of a defensive one. I wouldn't use it unless the target is going to get powder burns on him. It's strictly short range. But the slug is big, very heavy. When he gets hit, he stays hit." All of which sounds like a Marvin role and not the real man. Yet it is very much part of the man, Lee Marvin:

> One time in the Pacific, after we'd hit the beach, I'm crawling around, and look up and see there's this wrapee [a Japanese] right in front of me. So I pull out the .45 from under my arm, and I've got it primed and with the safety off just as it's coming up, and I get him right in the chest and that's that. Later on I realize I've hit him with my old man's gun, so I crawl back to get some kind of memento. And the guy's got lots of gold in his teeth. So I get out my knife and use the handle to knock a few of the teeth out to take back. Unfortunately they fall back

into the guy's throat. By this stage rigor mortis has set in, so I can't force the guy's jaw open. I go away and think about this, then come back later only to find someone else had beaten me to it. Cut the guy's throat wide open, and taken the teeth for himself.

It is important to realize that this was not a particularly sadistic or unusual occurrence. It was a perfectly normal and common aspect of behaviour towards the Japanese in that time and place. It demonstrates clearly, however, the theatre of war in which Marvin learned the beginnings of the craft he later brought to the screen—one in which gratuitous violence was a part of everyday life, and in which anyone might cut open the throat of a corpse to obtain a few bits of gold as a keepsake. This background helps greatly in understanding Marvin's minimalist approach in reproducing violence in his screen roles. He was being (in part) himself.

Marvin's war ended at Saipan in 1944. His company stormed a beach, was caught in Japanese crossfire, and 241 of his companions were killed. Marvin was one of six survivors. He fell to the ground. "There are just two prominent parts of your body in view to the enemy when you flatten out," he remembered, "your head and your ass. If you present one, you get killed. If you raise the other, you get shot in the ass. I got shot in the ass." This left Marvin with a massive wound at the base of the spine which earned him over a year's hospitalization and surgery, a Purple Heart, and a lifetime disability pension of $40 a week. After a number of odd jobs, he became a plumber's apprentice but his interest in acting gradually took over and in 1950, by the age of 26, he had gained experience in summer stock and appeared in *Billy Budd* on Broadway. He then waited three days at the open casting session held by Henry Hathaway for *You're in the Navy Now*, forced his way in and got himself a role paying $175 a week.

He appeared in three other films in 1951, and five more the following year, mostly being cast as a hired assassin in western and gangster films. The following year brought him to the public attention in a major way. His six films in 1953 included *The Caine Mutiny* and *The Big Heat*, the latter directed by Fritz Lang. This was remarkable for the scene in which he threw scalding coffee in the face of the character played by Gloria Grahame. One critic has said, "This early, shocking role displayed a vicious side to Marvin's screen personality which continued to simmer just under the surface, and occasionally erupt, throughout his career."

Over the next four years he appeared in a total of 14 other movies, but it was a three-year spell in television, starring as a Chicago detective in over 100 episodes of *M Squad*, which took him back to Hollywood as a leading actor. The early 1960s brought such roles as Liberty Valance in *The Man Who Shot Liberty Valance* and, in 1965, the film which made him a leading star and brought him his only Oscar, *Cat Ballou*. The part of Tim Strawn had been hawked around Hollywood for some time and turned down by everyone of note. Marvin described himself as "the lone man on the totem pole". Although the film itself was not highly rated and the comedy has not stood the test of time, Marvin greatly enjoyed the role and the change from playing the heavy. It did not last long, however. After making *The Professionals* in 1966, he followed on with, possibly, the best known film of his career, *The Dirty Dozen*, in which he played a convict turned commando. This was succeeded by *Point Blank* in which he played an avenging gangster, and *Hell in the Pacific* in which he and Toshiro Mifune starred as World War II survivors stranded on a remote island.

Then came a complete departure. Now mellowing, Marvin took on the part of Ben Rumson in the musical *Paint Your Wagon* and produced what is possibly the most unexpected hit single of the century with his meandering and gravelly interpretation of "I Was Born Under a Wandering Star".

His career is said to have faltered in the 1970s, but it is equally probable that Marvin no longer felt the need to drive himself so hard and was also taking time off to pursue his favourite hobby, deep-sea fishing. In *The Big Red One*, another war movie, which he made in 1978, he was still utilizing his own experiences and, together with Sam Fuller, trained the younger actors in warcraft. Marvin recalled one scene in the film where he passed a dead German and "put a couple of rounds in him and just [kept] on going on the patrol". Sam Fuller rather fancied this bit of business but, despite his own war experiences, failed to do it to Marvin's exacting requirements. Said Marvin, "If you passed a dead Jap, you'd stick your bayonet in him and leave it there, just to let the next guy in line know that he's not playing possum." When Fuller came up and put two rounds in the body Marvin pulled him up for looking at the corpse. "That's wrong," he told Fuller. "What you do is fire by instinct, but keep your eyes firmly fixed up, because if there's a guy up there on the ridge, he's going to nail you. Fire on instinct, and keep your eyes on the next guy."

Something similar happened eleven years earlier when making *Point Blank*. He told the director, John Boorman, that he felt the sound of gunshot was usually too small. Everyone except the sound recordist was sent home and Marvin produced his own .44 Magnum, which he just happened to have on him at the time, and blasted away at an armour-plated door with live ammunition. So great was the blast that flakes of plaster fell from the ceiling. This effect was actually used later in the film when the character played by Marvin was shot in his cell.

In 1979 Marvin was at the centre of a famous legal battle in which his former mistress, Michelle Triola, sued him for what became known as "palimony", claiming half his earnings for the six years they had lived together—some $1.75 million. The court ruled that there had been no contract between them and awarded her only $104,000, but this case made legal history by establishing the right of co-habitees to seek support when a relationship ended.

Another side-effect of this case was that it added fuel to the popular stories of Lee Marvin as a hard drinking hell-raiser. While there was certainly some truth to this part of his reputation, it by no means accounted for the whole man. His first marriage, to Betty Edeling, lasted 13 years and they had four children. Two more marriages and at least one live-in lover followed, but the man always enjoyed family life. In his later years he happily entertained grandchildren and his mother-in-law at his spacious home in Tucson, where he pursued a keen interest in the local geology and natural history on which he could converse knowledgeably. His favourite fishing grounds were off the Great Barrier Reef of Australia and, it is worth noting, he turned down the film *Jaws* because he felt it maligned sharks! It was his ambition always to get as far away from it all as possible. Once, in the Australian back of beyond, he met what looked like an ageing female hippy, with two children playing in the dust. They were introduced and after a pause she asked him what he did. Marvin confessed to being an actor. There was an even longer pause, during which he wondered if she had recognized him and was pretending not to. Then she enquired, "What's a fuckin' actor?" Marvin finishes the story, "And then I know I'm really home and dry. This is about as far from anywhere as I can possibly get."

Acting, Marvin acknowledged, had been his salvation. It enabled him to work out, and through, the horrors that happened to him in the Pacific. It was probably as good a therapy as any analysis and gave the world a macho screen figure that is unlikely ever to be bettered. Marvin's star may well have wandered a little but he never let it dim.

Born Lee Marvin. **Parents** Lamont W., advertising executive, and Courtenay D., fashion writer, Marvin. **Marriages** 1) Betty Edeling, 1952 (divorced, 1965); 2) Unknown; 3) Pamela Freely, 1970. **Children** four, from first marriage. **Education** Various state schools; American Theater Wing, New York. **Military service** Scout sniper, US Marines, World War II (wounded and hospitalized, 1944). **Career** Odd jobs, then plumber's apprentice, Woodstock; began acting career in summer stock productions; stage début in *Roadside*, Woodstock, 1947; film début, *You're in the Navy Now*, 1951; Broadway début, *Billy Budd*, 1951; gained film reputation for playing villains, 1950s; in *M Squad*, NBC TV, 1957–60; subsequently starred in many major films. **Awards and honours** Academy Award as Best Actor for *Cat Ballou*, 1965; Berlin Film Festival Award for *Cat Ballou*, 1965; British Academy Award as Best Foreign Actor for *The Killers* and *Cat Ballou*, 1965; Spanish Silver Film Award, 1970. **Films** *You're in the Navy Now*, 1951; *Down Among the Sheltering Palms*, 1951; *Diplomatic Courier*, 1951; *The Duel at Silver Creek*, 1951; *We're Not Married*, 1952; *Hangman's Knot*, 1952; *Seminole*, 1952; *The Glory Brigade*, 1952; *Eight Iron Men*, 1952; *Gun Fury*, 1953; *The Stranger Wore a Gun*, 1953; *The Wild One*, 1953; *The Big Heat*, 1953; *The Caine Mutiny*, 1953; *Gorilla at Large*, 1953; *The Raid*, 1954; *A Life in the Balance*, 1954; *Bad Day at Black Rock*, 1954; *Not as a Stranger*, 1954; *Violent Saturday*, 1955; *I Died a Thousand Times*, 1955; *Pete Kelly's Blues*, 1955; *Shack Out on 101*, 1955; *Pillar of the Sky*, 1955; *Seven Men from Now*, 1955; *The Rack*, 1955; *Attack!*, 1956; *Raintree County*, 1956; *The Missouri Traveller*, 1957; *The Commancheros*, 1961; *The Man Who Shot Liberty Valance*, 1961; *Donovan's Reef*, 1962; (for TV) *Sergeant Ryker*, 1963; *The Killers*, 1963; *Ship of Fools*, 1964; *Cat Ballou*, 1964; *The Professionals*, 1965; *The Dirty Dozen*, 1966; *Point Blank*, 1967; *Hell in the Pacific*, 1968; *Tonight Let's All Make Love in London*, 1968; *Paint Your Wagon*, 1968; *Monte Walsh*, 1969; *Pocket Money*, 1971; *Prime Cut*, 1971; *The Emperor of the North Pole* (*Emperor of the North*), 1972; *The Iceman Cometh*, 1973; *The Spikes Gang*, 1973; *The Klansman*, 1974; *Shout at the Devil*, 1975; *The Great Scout and Cathouse Thursday*, 1976; *Avalanche Express*, 1978; *The Big Red One*, 1978; *Death Hunt*, 1980; *Gorky Park*, 1982; *Canicule* (*Dog Day*), 1983; (for TV) *The Dirty Dozen: The Next Mission*, 1985. **Television** *Rebound*, 1952; *The Doctor*, 1952; *Center Stage*, 1954; *M Squad*, 1957–60; *People Need People*, 1961; *Treasury Men in Action*; *TV Readers' Digest*; *Kraft Suspense Theater*. **Recordings** "I Was Born Under a Wandering Star", 1968. **Cause of death** Heart attack, at age 63. **Further reading** Donald Zee, *Marvin: The Story of Lee Marvin*, London, 1979.

GEORGE MIKES

Hungarian Humorist

Born **Siklós, Hungary, 15 February 1912**

Died **London, England, 30 August 1987**

One hoary definition of a Hungarian is somebody who enters a revolving door behind you and exits ahead. This generates two ideas about George Mikes. Firstly, how astute was he? Did he really nail the British, or did they, sentimental, over-embrace the notion of themselves being mocked by a quaint foreigner? Secondly, how useful are national stereotypes anyway, especially as they became his stock in trade? A Magyar answer might be, "Don't expect answers here; this is *The Annual Obituary*, not *The Cambridge Quarterly*."

George Mikes was born into a non-practising Jewish family, undertaking his early education at the Cistercian Gymnasium in Pécs. In 1922 the family moved to the capital, Budapest, and he entered the university there. At the age of 17 he became a Roman Catholic. His stepfather was a doctor and his real father a lawyer; Mikes chose to study for the latter profession, though the hint of a literary career emerged as he became the university's theatre critic on various Budapest newspapers. After graduation, he worked as London correspondent for those papers until 1938. Then the German Army marched into Austria and Mikes, with many others, considered exile.

The decision was made for him when one of his papers sent him to London to cover the crisis precipitated by Hitler's invasion of Czechoslovakia. The assignment was for two weeks; in fact, he made England his home. In Siklós, many of his friends and relatives in the Jewish community were murdered.

During the war, Mikes worked for the Hungarian Service of the BBC, and wrote on a freelance basis. His early work was notable for *The Epic of Lofoten*, a "remarkable document" recording the experiences of young Norwegians evacuated from Nazi invasion by the Royal Navy. The book, which established Mikes in the eyes of the British as a humorist, appeared immediately after the war, in 1946. It was published by a fellow-Hungarian, André Deutsch, whom Mikes remembered as "my brother's little friend". *How to Be an Alien* was intended to be caustic, according to its author, "to hit hard at all things the British held dear: chapters on tea, cricket and sex—the shortest in the book, of course". *The Times* wrinkled its nose—"Rather funny"—and fulfilled his implicit prophecy by ascribing him to the wrong race: "Worth reading for its own peculiar brand of Slav humour".

That apart, British readers clasped him to their hearts and kept him there. Mikes had discovered How to Be Successful. He became prolific. Dispatched by Deutsch, he directed his alien eye at the Israelis (*Milk and Honey*, 1950), the French (*Little Cabbages*, 1955), the Italians (*Italy for Beginners*, 1956), then the Swiss, Jamaicans, Australians and Japanese—all of which, says a critic, "demonstrates his talent for getting at national character via the apparently innocent and light side". Which is indeed the case, but Mikes did not find his quizzical posture infinitely sustainable. By 1970 he was accused of giving "facts, not insights...setting out to update the picture of Japan with the air of one earnestly explaining the mechanics of a wheelbarrow, it is perhaps inevitable that Mikes should be a bit of a bore." Another reviewer, discussing an earlier book, reached a similar conclusion, and added what may be the nub: "Most funny writers get very furious indeed at travelling about on a Joke Special."

Mikes averaged about one book per year. As a measure of reassurance from the nation he had set out to scathe, the Duke of Bedford, no less, suggested that they write something in collaboration. The fruits of this union were *A Book of Snobs*, and *How to Run a Stately Home*. Mikes was modest about the nature of the collaboration, but insisted that it was a process superior to ghost writing. In 1970 he produced a sort of manifesto—*Humour in Memoriam*—in which he guyed long-headed theories about the phenomenon, claimed that nobody wanted written humour any more, that "all humorists are sad, melancholy people", and rounded off with some good jokes. (Readers who remember the Six-Day War might like the one about the Russian adviser to the Arabs, who tells them as they retreat ever further, "Don't worry, wait till the snows come.")

The Mikes output was not all aimed at mirth. *The Hungarian Revolution* describes the events leading to the 1956 uprising, and *A Study of Infamy* is an analysis of AVO, the Hungarian political police system. In 1970, when Mikes returned to Hungary to make a film for BBC Television, the authorities "asked him to leave", which he and the whole crew did, in protest. Into the middle-of-the-road, middlebrow *Punch* magazine, Mikes slipped an early, sardonic warning about Romania's President Ceaucescu, whose larger domestic depradations subsequently became international news.

By the time he published *How to Be Seventy*, on his birthday in 1982, Mikes had long been a naturalized British subject. He avoided overstatement, eschewed the display of emotion, and doted on cats. He had also become a club man, favouring the Hurlingham, where he played tennis and sponsored the Mikes Cup, and the Garrick, where he could no doubt sit and observe his adoptive countrymen. To all appearances, he had actively or passively chosen to imitate the objects of his erstwhile derision. Others remained strongly aware of the Budapest *bel esprit*, the man in the figurative corner for whom "face values are no values at all".

Born George Mikes. **Parents** Alfred, lawyer, and Margit Alice (Gál) Mikes. **Marriage** Isobel Gerson, 1941 (divorced); Lea Hanak, 1948. **Children** Martin Alfred, from first marriage; Judith Pamela, from second marriage. **Education** University of Budapest, LLD, 1933. **Emigration** Left Hungary for England, 1938. **Career** Theatre critic, Budapest, 1931–38; London correspondent for Budapest newspapers, 1938–41; worked for BBC Hungarian Service, 1941–51. **Other activities** Governor, London Oratory School, 1978 onwards. **Offices** President, PEN in Exile, 1973–80. **Publications** *The Epic of Lofoten*, 1941; *Darlan: A Study*, 1943; *We Were There to Escape: The True Story of a Yugoslav Officer*, 1945; *Pont ugye mint az angolok* (songs and verses), 1945; *How to Be an Alien: A Handbook for Beginners and More Advanced Pupils*, 1946; *How to Scrape Skies: The United States Explored, Rediscovered and Explained*, 1948, published in US as *How to Be a Swell Guy: The United States Explored, Rediscovered and Explained*, 1959; *Wisdom for Others*, 1950; *Milk and Honey: Israel Explored*, 1950; *Talicska: Humoreszkek, esszek, sohajtasok*, 1950; *Down With Everybody! A Cautionary Tale for Children Over Twenty-one, and Other Stories*, 1951; *Shakespeare and Myself*, 1952; *Über Alles: Germany Explored*, 1953; *Eight Humorists*, 1954; *Leap Through the Curtain: The Story of Nora Kovach and Istvan Rabovsky*, 1955; *Little Cabbages*, 1955; *Italy for Beginners*, 1956; *The Hungarian Revolution*, 1957; *East Is East*, 1958; *A Study in Infamy: The Operations of the Hungarian Secret Police*, 1959; *How to Be Inimitable: Coming of Age in England*, 1961; *As Others See You*, 1961; *Tango: A Solo Across South America*, 1961; *The Best of Mikes*, 1962; *Switzerland for Beginners*, 1962; *Mortal Passion*, 1963; *How to Unite Nations*, 1963; (editor) *Prison: A Symposium*, 1963; *How to Be an Alien: In Britain, France, Italy, Germany, Switzerland, Israel, Japan*, 1964; (with John R. R. Bedford) *The Duke of Bedford's Book of Snobs*, 1965, published as *The Book of Snobs*, 1966; *Eureka! Rummaging in Greece*, 1965; (editor) *Germany Laughs at Herself: German Cartoons Since 1848*, Stuttgart, 1965; *How to Be Affluent*, 1966; *Not By Sun Alone*, 1967; *Boomerang: Australia Rediscovered*, 1968; *Coat of Many Colors: Israel*, published in UK as *The Prophet Motive: Israel Today and Tomorrow*, 1969; *Humour in Memoriam*, 1970; *The Land of the Rising Yen: Japan*, 1970; *Laughing Matter*, 1971; *Any Souvenirs?*, 1972; (with John R. R. Bedford) *How to Run a Stately Home*, 1972; *The Spy Who Died of Boredom*, 1973; *Charlie*, 1976; *How to Be Decadent*, 1977; *Tsi-Tsa, the Biography of a Cat*, 1978; *English Humour for Beginners*, 1980; *How to Be Seventy* (autobiography), 1982; *The Virgin and the Bull* (play), 1982; *How to Be Poor*, 1983; *Arthur Koestler, the Story of a Friendship*, 1983; *How to Be a Guru*, 1984; *How to Be a Brit*, 1984; contributor to *Observer*, *Encounter*, *Times Literary Supplement* and other periodicals. **Cause of death** Undisclosed, at age 75.

POLA NEGRI

Polish-American Actress

***Born* Lipna, Poland, 31 December 1894**

***Died* San Antonio, Texas, 1 August 1987**

In the movies, the 1920s and 1930s were the age of the "vamp", and the champion vamp was Pola Negri. Her origins were exotic, her heyday spectacular, and her age suitably mysterious In an autobiography sweetly entitled *Memoirs of a Star*, she wrote that she was born in 1899—other sources say three to five years earlier—in Lipna, Poland. Her name was then Barbara Apollonia Chalupiec. She was from a family of impoverished nobility and her father, a Slovak immigrant, was imprisoned by the Tsarists for revolutionary activity. Mother went to work as a cook and managed to maintain a one-room slum apartment in Warsaw; the child went to the Imperial Ballet School at St Petersburg, Russia. Tuberculosis ended a brief dancing career, but after a cure, she returned to Warsaw and entered the Imperial Academy of Dramatic Art.

By the age of 17 she had become Pola Negri (Pola from her own name, Negri from an admired Italian poet) and was one of Poland's leading actresses. Her first movie was a two-reeler entitled *Slaves of Sin*. In 1918 she went to Berlin, to appear in Max Reinhardt's pantomimic *Sumurun*, and was quickly appropriated by the emerging German cinema, most significantly by the brilliant young director Ernst Lubitsch. Critics generally agree that she was at her best under his tutelage, in films like *Carmen* (1918) and *Madame Dubarry* (1919) "...to which she brought not only expressiveness and beauty, but an unusual depth of character, so that she showed up stage actors for their artifice". *Madame Dubarry*, retitled *Passion*, was released in the United States. Negri's "vital and uninhibited" portrayal of its French courtesan heroine impressed the Hollywood studios, and a Paramount contract brought her there in 1922.

She walked straight into a heavyweight vamping contest with Gloria Swanson. No doubt the studio connived at and profited from the feud, but the Paramount bosses were politic enough to put a continent between their warring divas. Miss Swanson was transferred to the Astoria Studios, while Madame Negri, as she now preferred to be called, was installed in Hollywood. The green-eyed madame initially had a huge following and made some good films, peaking with a brilliant comic performance in *Paradise*, under Lubitsch's direction again, and then *Lily of the Dust* and *Shadows of Paris*, the work of Herbert Brenan. Gradually, her popularity dissipated. If her talent was mishandled so that it sank beneath the weight of coiffure, gowns and jewellery (the "grooming process"), her personality was unfortunately collusive. Says Rodney Ackland: "She had a blind and uncritical admiration of her own genius in the blaze of which her sense of humour evaporated like a dewdrop on a million-watt arc lamp." Moreover, she was openly, unwisely disdainful of the American cinema as beneath her artistic pedigree. During the second half of the 1920s, she had made a dozen films, of which *Hotel Imperial* is rated as "a pinnacle of silent-screen dramatics", but by 1928 her Hollywood career was effectively over. Paramount strove in vain to find a suitable vehicle for its expensive investment, and had now to contend with the arrival of the "talkies". Pola Negri's first one, *A Woman Commands*, is thought to be a good performance wasted on a poor film, or a shoddy affair, depending on which critics you read.

In 1931 she appeared in a one-act play at the London Coliseum where one critic observed, "...if her acting lacks greatness, it at least reaches a sufficiently inspiring level of sincerity and competence". She made one film in France—*Fanatisme*—before returning to Germany in 1935. Here her career revived. A café singer in *Mazurka*, a cocaine addict in *Tango Notturno* and the title role in *Madame Bovary* were not departures from type, but the films were strong and she was able to show a new restraint. World War II broke out, and she returned to the United States, to make *Hi, Diddle Diddle*, but Pola Negri had been forgotten. It was not until 1963 that she reappeared on the American screen, in a Walt Disney thriller, *The Moon Spinners*. And that was it.

But vamps were expected to supplement their public with off-screen entertainment, and Pola Negri was good value for money. Firstly, there was the affair with Charlie Chaplin. He claimed to be the reluctant conquest, she claimed to have rejected his tearful proposal of marriage. Then there was Rudolph Valentino, who spread rose petals on the bed and wept because he was losing his hair. Nevertheless, Madame Negri sped from filming *Hotel Imperial* to collapse, black-swathed, at his funeral, then to take his body back by train to California. There were dozens of stops along the way so that other Valentino-worshippers could pay tribute. If these were stunts, they did not prop up her ailing box-office receipts, and were greeted with some scorn. There were husbands, too. In 1919 she had married Count Eugene Domski, and divorced him a year later.

Less than a year after Valentino's death came Serge Mdivani, an impecunious Georgian nobleman who met his death on the polo field, but not before being divorced in 1931. Adolf Hitler was rumoured to have been charmed. Certainly, the *Führer*'s office intervened to deny the "serious accusation" that Pola Negri was of Jewish descent. Asked about his contribution to her revived career, she said, "There have been many important men in my life—Valentino, for example." Hitler's response to the comparison has not been discovered.

Pola Negri finished her days in a San Antonio apartment, with a couple of servants. Her fortune, once flamboyantly displayed, had included one million dollars' worth of diamonds and pearls, bought cut-rate from the Hapsburgs and Hohenzollerns who could no longer afford them. Most of her wealth disappeared in the 1929 stockmarket crash. Turbans, high boots and painted toenails were among her innovations, and in the pre-talkie days, that and the rest of her colourful, mysterious style cut a serious deal of ice. The Hollywood films have frozen her into a succession of heavy, silly attitudes, but she was an actress with talent. How much did she conspire to obscure it?

Born Barbara Apollonia Chalupiec. **Marriages** 1) Count Popper (died); 2) Count Eugene Domski, 1919 (divorced, 1921); 3) Prince Serge Mdivani, 1927 (divorced, 1931). **Education** Boarding school of Countess Platen, Warsaw; Imperial Ballet School, St Petersburg; Imperial Academy of Dramatic Art, Warsaw. **Emigration** Left Poland for Germany, 1917; left Germany for USA, 1923. **Career** Stage début in Hauptmann's *Hannele*, Warsaw, 1913; first film role, *Niewolnica Zmyslow*, 1914; moved to Germany and quickly gained prominence in the German film industry, 1917–23; signed to Paramount in Hollywood and made US film début in *Bella Donna*, 1923; career peaked mid-1920s; thereafter declined with advent of sound in late 1920s; made *The Woman He Scorned* in England, 1929; London stage début, 1931; returned to USA to make *A Woman Commands*, 1932; made films in France, 1934, and Germany, 1935–39; spent early war years in France but returned to USA to make *Hi, Diddle Diddle*, 1943; then retired, appearing in just one cameo role in *The Moon Spinners*, 1964. **Publications** *Memoirs of a Star*, New York, 1970; *La Vie et la rêve au cinéma*, Paris, no date. **Films** *Niewolnica Zmyslow*, 1914; *Pokoj no. 13*, 1915; *Bestia*, 1915; *Czarna Ksiazka*, 1915; *Jego Ostatni Czyn*, 1916; *Zona*, 1916; *Studenci*, 1916; *Arabella*, 1916; *Küsse, die man in Dunkeln stiehlt*, 1917; *Nicht lange täuschte mich das Glück*, 1917; *Rosen, die der Sturm entblättert*, 1917; *Zügelloses Blut*, 1917; *Die toten Augen*, 1917; *Der gelbe Schein*, 1918; *Wenn das Herz in Hass erglüht*, 1918; *Mania*, 1918; *Die Augen der Mummie Ma*, 1918; *Carmen*, 1918; *Das Karussell des Lebens*, 1919; *Kreuziget sie!*, 1919; *Madame Dubarry*, 1919; *Camille*, 1919; *Comptesse Doddy*, 1919; *Geschlossene Kette*, 1920; *Medea*, 1920; *Das Martyrium*, 1920; *Die Marchesa d'Arminiani*, 1920; *Sumurun*, 1920; *Vendetta*, 1920; *Die Bergkatze*, 1921; *Sappho*, 1921; *Die Damme in Glashaus*, 1921; *Arme Violetta*, 1921; *Die Flamme* (*Montmartre*), 1922; *Bella Donna*, 1923; *The Cheat*, 1923; *Hollywood*, 1923; *The Spanish Dancer*, 1923; *Shadows of Paris*, 1924; *Men*, 1924; *Lily of the Dust*, 1924; *Forbidden Paradise*, 1924; *East of Suez*, 1925; *The Charmer*, 1925; *Flower of Night*, 1925; *A Woman of the World*, 1925; *The Crown of Lies*, 1926; *Good and Naughty*, 1926; *Hotel Imperial*, 1927; *Barbed Wire*, 1927; *The Woman on Trial*, 1927; *Three Sinners*, 1928; *The Secret Hour*, 1928; *Loves of an Actress*, 1928; *The Woman from Moscow*, 1928; *Are Women to Blame?*, 1928; *The Woman He Scorned*, 1929; *Street of Abandoned Children*, 1929; *A Woman Commands*, 1931; *Fanatisme*, 1934; *Mazurka*, 1935; *Moskau–Shanghai*, 1936; *Madame Bovary*, 1937; *Rudolph Valentino*, 1938; *Die Nacht der Entscheidung*, 1938; *Tango Notturno*, 1938; *Die fromme Lüge*, 1938; *Hi, Diddle Diddle*, 1943; *The Moon Spinners*, 1964. **Stage** (includes) *Hannele*, Warsaw, 1913; *Sumurun*, Berlin, 1917; *Farewell to Love*, London, 1931. **Cause of death** Pneumonia, at *circa* age 91. **Further reading** Marjorie Rosen, *Popcorn Venus*, New York, 1973.

CARDINAL PATRICK O'BOYLE

American Clergyman

***Born* Scranton, Pennsylvania, 18 July 1896**

***Died* Washington, DC, 10 August 1987**

Cardinal Patrick O'Boyle enjoyed a mixed reputation in the Church and in the city of Washington whose first Catholic archbishop he was from 1948 until his retirement in 1973. On the one hand he was known and respected for his lifelong commitment to the fight for racial and social equality; on the other for the staunch and old-fashioned conservatism of his views on all matters pertaining to Catholic doctrine. It was this which earned him the name of "orthodox strongman".

Desegregating the Catholic schools of Washington was, perhaps, the new archbishop's most long-lasting reform. Three years before the Supreme Court's historic decision barring segregation in the nation's public schools, and only two years after his own enthronement as archbishop, Patrick O'Boyle had Black and White children being educated together in parochial schools throughout the District of Columbia.

Father O'Boyle was known for his social work long before he became archbishop. After training as a priest, he had enrolled for a postgraduate degree in social work. Then, during the 1930s, he worked for the childcare department of the Catholic Charities of New York and, during the war, for the National Catholic War Relief Services, sending aid and support to the war-torn countries of Europe and North Africa. No doubt his own background as the son of impoverished Irish immigrant parents, and his own need, as a child, to work after school to help support his widowed mother, only increased his personal wish to help the poor and needy and to see justice done for them.

Although, as archbishop, Patrick O'Boyle continued to work among the underprivileged and to support schemes to aid the inner city poor and the migrant farmworkers, he later fell foul of the more radical elements in the civil rights movement who distrusted his caution and his unwillingness to nail the Church's colours more wholeheartedly to theirs. People began to accuse him of "lingering paternalism" and of "believing more in charity than in changing institutions". James Gibbons, president of the Washington Lay Association, went one step further, describing the archbishop to the *New York Times* magazine as a "fraud" who had not "done one thing for the Negro in Washington since he desegregated the schools", and whose "liberal image is as phony as a three-dollar bill".

Nonetheless, honours continued to be showered on Patrick O'Boyle. In 1948 he became spiritual director of the Society of St Vincent de Paul and in 1955 received the highest award possible for a Roman Catholic—the George Meany Lattare Medal. When, in 1967, Pope Paul VI made him a cardinal, O'Boyle interpreted this honour as an "expression of the Holy Father's gratitude not only to priests, religious and devoted laity of the Washington archdiocese, but also to the many clergy and laymen of other faiths who have laboured beside us in attacking problems of racial and social injustice which are of common concern".

It was in the year after he became cardinal, the year of the controversial papal encyclical *Humanae Vitae*, that Patrick O'Boyle blundered into the debate that was to dominate the rest of his working life: the question of clerical authority. The issue around which it bubbled was contraception. Troubled, as was the Pope himself, by many of the reformist views aired during the Vatican II Council, Cardinal O'Boyle was one of those churchmen who most heartily welcomed *Humanae Vitae*'s restatement of the traditional ban on all uses of artificial contraception by practising Catholics. Unlike many bishops in the US and Europe who encouraged priests to follow their own consciences when hearing confessions and counselling parishioners, Cardinal O'Boyle chose to regard *Humanae Vitae* as an *ex cathedra* statement and ordered his own flock to follow it "without equivocation, ambiguity or dissimulation".

To the opposition which arose in the Catholic University and among the clergy, Cardinal O'Boyle responded by disciplining some 40 rebel priests. The strength of feelings aroused may be estimated from the fact that, when the cardinal preached a sermon in the cathedral justifying his actions, half the congregation walked out. Those who were left, on the other hand, gave him a standing ovation. The cardinal himself appeared bewildered. Pilloried in the press as "a cross between Genghis Khan, King Lear and a neurotic Irish priest", O'Boyle sadly told another reporter that he had no idea he had so many enemies. He did not, however, give any indication of regretting for a moment the firm stand he had taken.

"Stand in the faith" was the motto Patrick O'Boyle chose for himself when consecrated archbishop. It remained the one he lived by. The faith, for him, meant strict Church authority, the retention of Latin in the Mass, the care of the poor and the needy. It did not include such "flagrant violations of the liturgy" as the 1960s "folk masses". Nor was there much room in it for the workings of the individual Catholic conscience. A close friend who once described this short, grey-haired priest with the twinkling eyes and the Irish accent as a man of "simple tastes and complex humanity" probably came the closest of all to the truth.

Cardinal O'Boyle spent the last 14 years of his life in retirement in Washington, careful not to interfere in the work of his successors.

Born Patrick Aloysius O'Boyle. **Parents** Michael, a steelworker, and Mary (Muldoon) O'Boyle. **Education** St Thomas's College, now Scranton University, 1917; St Joseph's Seminary, Yonkers, New York, 1921; New York School of Social Work, 1931. **Career** Worked briefly as an office boy; ordained Roman Catholic priest, 1921; parish priest, St Columba's Church, 1921–26; executive director, Catholic Guardian Society, 1926–31; teacher, Fordham University School of Social Services; executive director, National Catholic War Relief Services; executive director and special consultant, Catholic Charities, New York, 1947 onwards; consecrated archbishop, diocese of Washington, 1948; elevated to cardinal, 1967; retired 1973. **Related activities** Chancellor, Catholic University of America; executive director, Immaculate Virgin Mission, Staten Island; organizer and chairman, Interreligious Committee on Race Relations, 1963; head of interfaith convocation for early enactment of Civil Rights Bill, Georgetown University, 1966; assigned to Roman Curia, the administrative organ of the Roman Catholic Church, 1967. **Offices and memberships** Spiritual director, Society of St Vincent de Paul, 1948 onwards; elected to administrative board, National Catholic Welfare Conference; member, Vatican Ecumenical Council Commission for seminaries, universities and Catholic schools, 1962. **Awards and honours** George Meany Lattare Medal, 1955. **Cause of death** Pneumonia following surgery on a broken hip, at age 91.

CLARA PELLER

American Television Personality

***Born* Russia, 1901**

***Died* Chicago, Illinois, 11 August 1987**

In these confusing times, when everything is either a commercial or looks like one, where political events are dramatized on television before they are concluded in real life, and where the photo-opportunity replaces the confrontation, it is difficult to say whether Walter Mondale secured Clara Peller's place in history, or whether it was the other way around. Her megaphonic rendition of, "Where's the beef?" on behalf of Wendy's hamburgers not only boosted the food chain's sales by 32 per cent, but found its way into Johnny Carson's monologues and Mondale's jabs in the 1984 presidential campaign. For a while the phrase enjoyed an almost ubiquitous presence in American conversation, earning Peller a tidy sum beside. Perhaps it is not so astonishing that what was essentially a bad joke became a national motto, when organizations like Amnesty and Greenpeace have their own lines of merchandise and Watergate criminals sell everything from books to ice-cream. As a sarcastic footnote to the whole episode, talk show host David Letterman suggested that the next fad-phrase should be "They pelted us with rocks and garbage."

Peller's precise age is not known. She was born in Russia sometime in 1901 and soon afterwards moved with her parents to Chicago. For 35 years she worked as a local manicurist and beautician, moving into commercials in 1970. Her diminutive stature (4 feet 10 inches) and her ascerbic persona helped her get steady, if undistinguished, work. It was with the 1984 Wendy's spot that she gained instant celebrity status.

The 1980s witnessed the emergence of a new variety of commercial signalling a new self-awareness in the "genre". Instead of projecting outward the images of people and lifestyles which were supposedly desirable, these new models looked inward at that very imagery of commercialism. Directed by such notable film-makers as Ridley Scott, they began to function as an alter-ego of the standard product. They used stylized misfits to sell things, dead-pan humour and movements that seemed either drugged or robotic. Their appeal lay in an almost Kafkaesque sense of humour—oppressed people unable to make any non-functional movement, incapable of behaving normally, staring numbly at conveyor belts, or looking vacantly at the boss. The spots evoked a desire to possess the thing that inspired such identifiable, if lunatic, submission.

The Wendy's commercial is one such darkly amusing, consumerist, propagandist advertisement. It features Peller, filmed at such an acute angle that she almost vanishes in the back of the picture tube, staring up at the pontifically placed camera, intoning her famous words. Between them is an unappetizing burger, whose beef patty is no larger than a coin. Peller looks like an octogenarian two-year-old, struggling to be seen and heard over the counter. To stand even that tall she had to perch on a wooden crate; moreover, her hearing was so poor that a production assistant had to crouch behind her to cue her line. The room·is devoid of shape and colour, carrying the implication that the burger is the only object worth possessing and in turn justifying Peller's anger at its small size, even though McDonalds alone has sold over 100 billion just like it.

What is startling is not that it caught the attention of so many, but that it could be so emblematic and adaptable. Mondale used it successfully to rebuke fellow-contender Gary Hart at the Democratic National Convention in Chicago that year. The commercial led to licensing deals for "Where's the beef?" T-shirts, coffee mugs and beach towels; and it seemed to take on the hue of a general cry of complaint and dissatisfaction. Obviously, it did not improve Mondale's fortunes much, but the method caught on. George Bush's successful run at the presidency depended heavily on stock phrases taken from the media, such as "read my lips" and "make my day". Peller's importance in American political dialogue may be vindicated yet.

The sums associated with the commercial are also, in an incidental way, part of its interest. Wendy's claim Peller made $500,000 from the broadcasts, even though she was only paid $317.40 per day for the first spot. "I made some money," Peller admitted, "but Wendy's made millions out of me." Their annual sales for 1984, from 2850 restaurants worldwide, was $2 billion. The following year they terminated her contract when she appeared in a commercial for Prego spaghetti sauce for which the slogan was, "I found it. I really found it."

However, perhaps Peller's spit in the skillet of stardom is most significant for the way it highlights the bankruptcy of mass culture. If the only common experience a nation has of itself, legitimized by political patronage and incorporation, is created in the name of selling fast food, one could easily wonder what kind of nation allows this to happen. Does it react with horrified delight to whatever can express the vanity of that nation's achievement, and then buy whatever it has to sell? Whatever the conclusion, it was at least able to provide Peller with a decent pension.

Born Clara Peller. **Children** Two daughters. **Emigration** Left Russia for the US as a child. **Career** Manicurist and beautician in Chicago for 35 years; actress in television commercials, best known for Wendy's "Where's the beef?" hamburger campaign, 1984. **Cause of death** Undisclosed, at age 86.

VINCENT PERSICHETTI

American Composer and Teacher

***Born* Philadelphia, Pennsylvania, 6 June 1915**

***Died* Philadelphia, Pennsylvania, 16 August 1987**

Vincent Persichetti was a remarkable man who managed to combine a career as a sculptor with that of composer and teacher of composition theory. His influence is evident from the success of his pupils, who included the controversial jazz composer and pianist Thelonious Monk, the pop musician Frank Zappa and the modern minimalist composer Philip Glass.

Persichetti was a versatile musician from childhood and became proficient on the piano, organ, double-bass and tuba. He also began composition and theory studies at an early age. His professional performing career began at the age of eleven, and he became a church organist at 15. Later, as a student of Russell King Miller, he took composition lessons at the Combs College of Music, and on graduating in 1935 immediately became head of its composition and theory department. At that time he was also studying conducting with Fritz Reiner at the Curtis Institute of Music, and piano with Olga Samaroff at the Philadelphia Conservatory. He also took some composition lessons with Roy Harris at the Colorado College. From 1941 to 1947 he was head of the theory and composition department of the Philadelphia Conservatory.

From 1947 he taught at the Juilliard School of Music, and in 1963 became chairman of the composition department. Meanwhile, stepping outside his teaching role, he became director of music publishing with Elkan Vogel Ltd. and found time to write a book entitled *Twentieth-century Harmony: Creative Aspects and Practices*. For his services to music, Persichetti received many awards, including two Guggenheim fellowships. He was also in demand as a composer, and his orchestral commissions included works for the Philadelphia Orchestra, the St Louis Symphony Orchestra, the Louisville Symphony Orchestra and the Koussevitsky Foundation.

Persichetti's music is remarkable for its polyphonic skill, stylistic versatility, and for fusing the apparently irreconcilable idioms of classicism, romanticism and modernism, while sustaining a sense of line almost italianate in its singing quality. He did not ally himself to any school and his music explores all combinations of modal, polyphonic, tonal or atonal structures. A virtuoso pianist he has contributed an important corpus of piano works to the repertoire, while his song settings favoured American poets—Dickinson, Cummings, Frost, Sandburg, Teasdale and Whitman. His output extended to some 150 compositions in all, including nine symphonies, four string quartets, 12 piano sonatas, choral works, band music and an opera called *Sybil*. Many of his works were premièred by the Philadelphia Orchestra.

Born Vincent Persichetti. **Parents** Vincent R. and Martha (Buch) Persichetti. **Marriage** Dorothea Flanagan, 1941. **Children** One daughter, Lauren, and one son, Garth. **Education** Combs College of Music, BMus, 1935; Curtis Istitute of Music, diploma in conducting, 1939; Philadelphia Conservatory, MMus, 1940, DMus, 1945. **Career** Head of theory and composition department, 1936, Combs College of Music; head of theory and composition department, 1941–47, Philadelphia Conservatory; joined faculty, Juilliard School of Music, New York, 1947, composition department chairman, 1963, literature and materials department chairman, 1970. **Related activities** Director of music publishing, Elkan-Vogel Ltd., 1952; adviser, Ford Foundation, 1964; commissioned to write works for many organizations, including Juilliard Music Foundation, 1948, Martha Graham Company, 1949, Louisville Orchestra, 1950, Samaroff Foundation, 1952, Koussevitzky Foundation, 1955, St Louis Symphony, 1959, Naumburg Foundation, 1960, Lincoln Center, 1962. **Other activities** Sculptor in marble, granite and wood. **Offices and memberships** Music Educators' National Convention, 1964–87; director, American Society of Composers, Authors and Publishers; director, Philadelphia Art Alliance. **Awards and honours** Juilliard Publishing Award, 1943; Blue Network Award, 1945; grantee, National Institute of Arts and Letters, 1948; Italian Government Medal, 1958; Guggenheim Fellow, 1959, 1969, 1973; citation, American Bandmasters' Association, 1964. **Publications** (with F. R. Schreiber) *William Schuman*, New York, 1954; *Twentieth-century Harmony: Creative Aspects and Practices*, New York, 1961. **Operas** *Parable XX*, in two acts, 1976; *Sibyl*, 1984. **Orchestral compositions** Symphonies: No. 1, 1942, No. 2, 1942, No. 3, 1946, No. 4, 1951, No. 5 *Symphony for Strings*, 1953, No. 6 *Symphony for Band*, 1956, No. 7, 1958, No. 8, 1967, No. 9, 1970; Concertino for piano and orchestra, 1941; *Dance Overture*, 1942; *Fables*, for narrator and orchestra, 1943; *The Hollow Men*, for trumpet and stringsorchestra, 1944; *Divertimento*, for band, 1950; *Fairy Tale*, for orchestra, 1950; concerto for piano, four hands, 1952; *Pageant*, for band, 1953; piano concerto, 1962; *Introit*, for strings, 1964; *Masquerade*, for band, 1965; *Night Dances*, for orchestra, 1972; concerto for English horn and string orchestra, 1977; a series of works, each entitled *Serenade*: No. 1, for ten wind instruments, 1929, No. 2, for piano, 1929, No. 3, for violin, cello and piano, 1941, No. 4, for violin and piano, 1945, No. 5, for orchestra, 1950, No. 6, for trombone, viola and cello, 1950, No. 7, for piano, 1952, No. 8, for piano, four hands, 1954, No. 9, for soprano and alto recorders, 1956, No. 10, for flute and harp, 1957, No. 11, for band, 1960, No. 12, for solo tuba, 1961, No. 13, for two clarinets, 1963, No. 14, for solo oboe, 1984; a series of works, each entitled *Parable*: I for solo flute, 1965, II for bass quintet, 1968, III for solo oboe, 1968, IV for solo bassoon, 1969, V for carillon, 1969, VI for organ, 1971, VII for solo harp, 1971, VIII for solo horn, 1972, IX for band, 1972, X (actually his string quartet No. 4), 1972, XI for solo alto saxophone, 1972, XII for solo piccolo, 1973, XIII for solo clarinet, 1973, XIV for solo trumpet, 1973, XV for solo English horn, 1973, XVI for solo viola, 1974, XVII for solo double bass, 1974, XVIII for solo trombone, 1975, XIX for piano,

1975, XX, an opera in two acts, 1976, XXI for solo guitar, 1978, XXII for solo tuba, 1981, XXIII for violin, cello and piano, 1981, XXIV for harpsichord, 1982; four string quartets, 1939, 1944, 1959, 1972; 12 piano sonatas, 1939–80; six piano sonatinas, 1950–54; eight harpsichord sonatas, 1951–84. **Chamber music** Suite for violin and cello, 1940; sonata for solo violin, 1940; concertato for piano and string quartet, 1940; sonatine for organ, pedals alone, 1940; *Fantasy*, for violin and piano, 1941; *Pastoral*, for woodwind quintet, 1943; *Vocalise*, for cello and piano, 1945; *King Lear*, septet for woodwind quintet, timpani and piano, 1948; sonata for solo cello, 1952; quintet for piano and strings, 1954; *Little Recorder Book*, 1956; *Infanta Marina*, for viola and piano, 1960; *Shimah B'koli* (Psalm 130), for organ, 1962; *Masques*, for violin and piano, 1965; *Do Not Go Gentle*, for organ, pedals alone, 1974; *Auden Variations for Organ*, 1977; *Reflective Keyboard Studies*, 1978; *Little Mirror Book for Piano*, 1978; *Four Arabesques for Piano*, 1978; *Three Toccatinas for Piano*, 1979; *Mirror Études for Piano*, 1979; *Dryden Liturgical Suite for Organ*, 1980; *Song of David*, for organ, 1981; *Little Harpsichord Book*, 1983. **Choral works** (include) *Proverb*, for mixed chorus, 1948; *Hymns and Responses for the Church Year*, 1955; *Song of Peace*, for male chorus and piano, 1959; *Mass for Mixed Chorus*, a cappella, 1960; *Stabat Mater*, for chorus and orchestra, 1963; *Te Deum*, for chorus and orchestra, 1963; *Spring Cantata*, for women's chorus and piano, 1963; *Winter Cantata*, for women's chorus, flute and marimba, 1964; *Celebrations*, for chorus and wind ensemble, 1966; *The Pleiades*, for chorus, trumpet and orchestra, 1967; *The Creation*, for soprano, alto, tenor, baritone, chorus and orchestra, 1969; *Flower Songs* (Cantata No. 6), for mixed chorus and string orchestra, 1983; also composed a number of songs, including the major cycle for soprano and piano entitled *Harmonium*, after poems of Wallace Stevens, 1951. **Cause of death** Undisclosed, at age 72.

DIDIER PIRONI

French Grand Prix Driver

***Born* France, 1952**

***Died* English Channel, 23 August 1987**

The year 1980 was one that French followers of Grand Prix racing greeted with great anticipation: at long last, after years of disappointment, a Frenchman driving a French car looked capable of winning regularly. In terms of sheer speed the driver in question was being rated with the Canadian Gilles Villeneuve, and spoken of as a future world champion. His name was Didier Pironi.

Having learned his craft in France's motor-racing school system, Pironi rapidly became one of its outstanding pupils. The successes he achieved in the national Formule Renault had drawn favourable comments, and in 1977 he raced in the highly competitive Formula 2 category—then the penultimate rung on the ladder to Formula 1. Almost from the beginning of his professional career, Pironi had received personal backing from Elf, the giant French petroleum concern, and when, in 1978, Ken Tyrrell's Elf-sponsored Grand Prix team needed a replacement for Ronnie Peterson, Pironi was the automatic choice.

His stay with the British-based team lasted for a frustrating two seasons. Indeed, his only major success was with the Renault sports car team in the 1978 Le Mans 24-hour race where he shared an emotional victory with Jean-Pierre Jaussaud. After the World Championship-winning years with Jackie Stewart, Tyrrell had gone into decline, and the cars, as raced by Pironi and team-mate Patric Depailler, were rarely competitive. Through no fault of his own, Pironi was to gain something of a reputation as a car-wrecker, so frequent were the mechanical failures that he suffered. Undeterred, he soldiered on, content that the knowledge gained would come in useful when, hopefully, he would drive a competitive car. Fortunately, he did not have to wait long.

For 1980, Pironi joined Guy Ligier's Gitanes-backed team, and at last he had a car that was worthy of his abilities. Right from the start of the season, he was quicker than his more experienced team-mate Jacques Lafitte, and it was not long before he took the chequered flag in the Belgian Grand Prix to record his first win in the major league. It was a faultless drive and, as if to emphasize his challenge to the frontrunners, he followed it with a scintillating lap at Monte Carlo to claim pole position for the Monaco Grand Prix. The twisting streets of Monaco make for one of the most demanding circuits in the world and to win at Monte Carlo is to join the exalted ranks of the Grand Prix greats. Sadly, this was not to be for Pironi, for after leading comfortably for 54 laps, he overcorrected a slide at the famous Casino Square and the car hit the barriers: his race was over.

Didier Pironi could not be described as a typical Frenchman. He felt no nationalist pride in racing the blue Ligiers; he went racing simply for his own satisfaction, and as the season wore on it became apparent to observers that all was not well between the talented driver and some members of his team. By the time of the French Grand Prix, Guy Ligier and team manager Gerard Ducarouge were treating him with disdain. Pironi, they felt, was showing dangerous signs of independence, and it was rumoured that his contract would not be renewed for 1981. Unmoved by the internal politics of the team, Pironi finished second to Alan Jones in the French race and then moved on to the British Grand Prix, held that year at the scenic Brands Hatch circuit in Kent. He repeated his impressive Monaco form in practice, claiming pole position by a substantial margin, and then led the race from the start, only to rush into the pits to replace a broken wheel. Rejoining in twenty-first position he drove an inspired race, taking the Ligier through the field to fourth place and breaking the lap record countless times in the process. Towards the end, he suddenly pulled off and stopped out on the circuit. Another wheel had broken and a tyre was flat. As at Monaco, he was no doubt deeply disappointed but he did not show it; he simply stepped from the car with no exhibition of temper or emotion, and with hardly a backward glance, walked casually into the pits.

Despite their misgivings, the Ligier team decided that they would retain Pironi for the 1981 season after all. But the man himself had other ideas, as did Enzo Ferrari. At the Italian Grand Prix the Old Man formally announced that Pironi was to join regular driver Gilles Villeneuve in the Italian team. To many Frenchmen this was seen to be an act of treachery and, as might be imagined, the atmosphere in the Ligier pits at Monza was very tense indeed.

The Pironi–Villeneuve partnership worked well from the start—the two Italian cars always to the fore of the field. But as Pironi's confidence in the Ferrari developed, so did his ambition, and it was not long before there was an intense rivalry between the two drivers. This was best illustrated in the San Marino Grand Prix of 1982. After an epic struggle between the dominant red cars, team manager Mauro Forghieri decided that, as team leader, Villeneuve should take the chequered flag. As the two Ferraris sped past the pits in the closing stages of the race the drivers were instructed to hold their positions. Pironi was having nothing of this and passed Villeneuve on the run-in to the flag. The two never spoke again and a fortnight later Villeneuve was killed in Belgium.

Despite the controversial victory, Pironi's season had been marked by a series of serious accidents: he was lucky to escape unharmed from a testing crash at the Paul Ricard Circuit in France, and again on the starting grid in Canada, where his Ferrari stalled and was hit from behind by Ricardo Piletti, who was killed by the impact. The appalling accident that occurred during practice for the German Grand Prix was, however, to destroy his career. After being trapped in his car and suffering crippling leg injuries, he was to undergo more than 30 operations over the next three years, during which he had 50 pins inserted in his legs and was highly fortunate not to lose his right foot. Throughout his long recovery, Enzo Ferrari loyally maintained that there would always be a car waiting for him at Maranello. Pironi, however, was more realistic, and resigned himself to the fact that his Formula 1 days were over.

Following his convalescence, Pironi turned his attentions to powerboats and developed a thriving business in St Tropez. Although handicapped by his weakened legs, he saw in the sport an opportunity to get back behind the driver's wheel and, by suitably adapting his boats, he embarked on a new career. Tragically, it was to be short-lived, for while competing in a race off the south coast of England, his powerboat overturned, killing him and two members of his crew.

Although he won only three of the 70 Grands Prix in which he competed, Didier Pironi was leading the World Championship at the time of the German crash and looked destined to become the first Frenchman to claim the sport's ultimate honour. Therefore, it was with some irony that Alain Prost, whose car Pironi hit, was to achieve this goal three years later.

Born Didier Pironi. **Career** Formule Renault driver, mid-1970s; Formula 2 driver, 1977; joined Ken Tyrrell's Elf-sponsored team, 1978–80, Ligier, 1980, Ferrari, 1981–82; entered 70 Grands Prix, winning Belgian Grand Prix, 1980, San Marino Grand Prix, 1982; serious injuries led to retirement from motor racing, 1982; turned to speed-boat racing, 1987. **Cause of death** Powerboat accident during competition, at age 35.

BAYARD RUSTIN

American Civil Rights Activist

***Born* Westchester, Pennsylvania, 17 March 1910**

***Died* Washington, DC, 24 August 1987**

Important people, those who are pivotal to the process of social change and who embody the spirit of an era, often find themselves in the same place at the same time. This is how Maya Angelou, the noted Black poet, activist, entertainer and autobiographer, approached her first meeting with Martin Luther King's right hand in his civil rights organization, the Southern Christian Leadership Conference:

> The SCLC offices were on 125th Street and Eighth Avenue in the centre of Harlem. I had telephoned and made an appointment to speak to Bayard Rustin. When I walked up the dusty stairs to the second floor, I rehearsed the speech I had tried out on John Killens...John had told me that Bayard Rustin had led protest marches in the United States during the forties, worked to better the condition of the Untouchables in India, and was a member of the War Resisters' League.

As it turned out, civil rights was to be Bayard Rustin's major contribution in the cause of a lifetime's devotion to humanitarian issues.

With Dr King and Malcolm X, Bayard Rustin found himself in the mid- to late 1960s at the heart of the Black struggle in the United States. While Malcolm X, as leader of the Black Muslims, spoke of "White devils" and confrontation, King and Rustin preached reconciliation and argued for action by non-violent means. The association between the two men began in 1955, when King invited Rustin down to Montgomery, Alabama, to organize the bus boycott there which was to make history as the beginning of a major non-violent desegregation drive in the Southern US. Rustin at this time began to make plans for a civil rights organization which could coordinate campaigns such as these, and the SCLC was founded in the same year. With King as the preacher and charismatic speaker, and Rustin as organizer behind the scenes, they made an effective team working side by side for seven years.

By the early 1960s, Rustin had established himself in his New York headquarters as Northern coordinator of SCLC. From there he organized numerous civil rights demonstrations and fund-raising events, notably the demonstrations held in 1960 to put pressure on the Republican and Democratic conventions which were being held to nominate the parties' presidential candidates.

However, Rustin's greatest achievement, one that will go down in the history books as the watershed of post-war civil rights activism, was the "March on Washington for Jobs and Freedom" which he conceived and organized in 1963. On 28 August some 250,000 Americans, Black and White, marched, sang, chanted and demonstrated that peaceful biracial protest was possible. Writers like James Baldwin, entertainers such as Josephine Baker and Harry Belafonte, folk-singers Odetta, Bob Dylan and Joan Baez, actors like Marlon Brando, and the great gospel singer Mahalia Jackson were there; the largest single mobilization of trade unionists was present; and Martin Luther King's historic speech "I Have a Dream" brought tears to the eyes of onlookers and those in the rest of the world who saw the event relayed on television. The march had taken months of planning and energy to persuade disparate groups to take part and passed joyously without a single incident of violence, just as Rustin, King, the Student Nonviolent Coordinating Committee and the American Federation of Labor/Congress of Industrial Organizations had envisaged it. Time was on their side: by 1964 the toughest desegregation legislation in US history was passed, followed a year later by the Voting Rights Act.

Bayard Rustin was born in Westchester, Pennsylvania, in 1910 as an illegitimate child. Raised by his grandparents, he grew up a Quaker with a lifelong commitment to pacifism and moral justice. At school he was a good student and able sportsman. When, on one occasion, he travelled with his football team to a nearby town and was physically thrown out of a restaurant which would not serve Blacks, he vowed never to accept segregation. After graduation in 1928, he spent a few years travelling around doing odd jobs and periodically taking classes in history and literature. Like many young educated Blacks in the 1930s, he joined the Young Communist League in 1936, which brought him to Harlem as an organizer and enabled him to take further studies at City College in New York. He earned his living as a nightclub singer at the Café Society, where he was popular: "He was really very good, you know," said George Houser, who knew him in those days. "If he'd wanted it that way, he could have been a Belafonte." But Rustin had other ambitions.

By 1941 he had become disillusioned with the Communist Party and joined the Fellowship of Reconciliation, a religious organization which espoused non-violence as the means of effecting change. Rustin set up a branch of the Congress for Racial Equality (CORE) in New York as part of his work for the fellowship, which spanned 12 years. The year 1941 also marked his meeting with A. Philip Randolph, president of the Sleeping Car Porters' Union, who had plans to organize a march on Washington to protest against Black unemployment. Rustin became involved as youth organizer, but the march was eventually called off after President Roosevelt issued an executive order banning discrimination in employment with government defence contracts. Eventually, of course, the march was held on the wider agenda of Black civil rights in 1963, with 20 years of mounting Black anger and frustration in between.

In those 20 years, Bayard Rustin was actively involved in one historic movement after another, and in several not so well known but equally worthwhile causes. In 1942 he concerned himself with the plight of Japanese–Americans who, after Pearl Harbor, had been placed in work camps on the West Coast, automatically labelled as collaborators. A year later he began a three-year prison sentence as a conscientious objector to army service in World War II. At this point the plot thickened. Upon release, he assumed the chairmanship of the Free India Committee and, at the invitation of the Congress Party, spent six months in India studying Gandhian non-violence. (Gandhi's tactics later became the inspiration for the form of non-violent struggle chosen by Southern Blacks in the US.)

This sojourn abroad was followed in the early 1950s by a trip to West Africa, as founder of the American Committee on Africa. Here, Rustin met Kwame Nkrumah and other leaders of African independence. Again, he was in the right place at the right time, forging links between American protest and African resistance at the centre of world developments which were to change the post-war political map irrevocably.

In the meantime, Rustin had been active on the home front too. In 1947 he had helped to organize the first "freedom ride" into the South. He was arrested in North Carolina and served three weeks' hard labour on a chain gang. When his experience, as recounted in an article for the *Baltimore Afro-American*, hit the national papers, North Carolina began an investigation which led to the abolition of chain gangs—one of the traditional instruments of racial oppression. Rustin went on to protest against racial discrimination in the armed forces, which again proved successful when, in 1948, an executive order issued by Truman made discrimination in the army illegal; young Black men and women have been entering the US Army in increasing numbers ever since.

His protest about the army did not mean that Rustin had changed his pacifist stance. In the immediate post-war years he became convinced that nuclear weaponry, as used for the first time in World War II, had altered the complexion of human existence to such an extent that it had to be a primary focus of social protest. In 1953 he therefore accepted a post with the War Resisters' League, a pacifist group with whom he travelled first to Britain in 1958 to help organize the first march of the Campaign for Nuclear Disarmament, then to the Sahara in 1960 to protest against French nuclear tests, and finally to Europe as an advance organizer for the San Francisco-to-Moscow peace walk. Hardly pausing to catch his breath, Rustin returned to the US early in 1961 to resume his civil rights activities, which were to culminate in the 1963 march on Washington and a New York school boycott in 1964, the largest civil rights demonstration of any kind up to that time which was supported by almost half of all the city's schoolchildren.

However, in that same year and in that same place—Harlem—the tide of civil rights changed with the eruption of violent riots during the summer. Rustin was dismayed by the sight of broken glass, cars on fire and bloodied faces on 125th Street. He still believed that non-violence was the only answer, and that racial hatred would only disappear when people came to understand each other through moral persuasion and non-violent example, which—he believed—were beneficial to all. But a generation gap had opened up: younger Blacks found more dignity in fighting in the streets than in sacrificing themselves willingly to police clubs in sit-down protests, and they taunted Rustin with accusations of "Uncle Tom-ism". In typical fashion, he responded: "I'm prepared to be a Tom if it's the only way I can save women and children from being shot down in the street." But sadly, a couple of years later even he had to admit that rioting, whatever its moral and physical costs, had forced the authorities to grant the demands of urban Blacks more quickly and more effectively than years of peaceful petitioning. It was a bitter pill to swallow. "We are in a society," he said, "where young people—particularly young Negroes—are being systematically taught that unless they resort to violence there is no future for them." Rustin realized, although he would never be convinced of the justice of violence, that the days of non-violent protest had passed and those of militant resistance had been ushered in with the ghetto riots of 1964. He, the pallbearer of non-violence, had to move on.

From 1964 he was director of the A. Phillip Randolph Institute, where he devoted himself to the development and promotion of a comprehensive ten year plan that would combat poverty and social deprivation in the urban centres, create real employment and restructure the educational system. "A Freedom Budget for All Americans", with great foresight as to future social, economic and environmental developments, included ways of coping with the problems of new technology, pollution of water and air, urban decay, unemployment and the resulting poverty—without raising taxes. Rustin firmly believed in a programme of economic change that would benefit all: Blacks, Whites, Jews, rich, poor, young and old alike. Despite ridicule from younger, more radical groups like the Black Panthers and the Nationalists who thought him lacking in political realism, Rustin was not naïve. Convinced that violence was a short-term reaction, not a long-term solution for social injustice, he advocated political power as the means to achieve large-scale change. He did not believe that any Black movement or the Black people could do it alone. "We need allies," he said. "The future of the Negro struggle depends on whether the contradictions of this society can be resolved by a coalition of progressive forces which becomes the *effective* political majority in the United States. I speak of the coalition which staged the march on Washington...Negroes, trade unionists, liberals and religious groups." Some 20 years later, Jesse Jackson's Rainbow Coalition was attempting to be just that, but when the plan for a new march on Washington was mooted in 1983, Rustin was equivocal. Once he had said about himself, "I believe in social dislocation and creative trouble". This time, not believing that the worsened economic situation of the early 1980s would allow a peaceful demonstration to pass without incident as it had 20 years before, Rustin withheld his wholehearted support for fear of uncreative, destructive violence. It emphasized his estrangement from younger Black activists, with whom he had also disagreed about job and college admission quotas. In the hardened climate of 1983, Rustin's political style was seen truly to belong to the early 1960s, with King and SCLC and Black and White students together sitting down at lunch counters to force desegregation. But whereas King, by virtue of his untimely death, became a martyr, Rustin was doomed to be an anachronism. Maya Angelou, so overawed by Bayard Rustin at first, saw the direction of events probably before anyone else did. Soon to take his place as SCLC coordinator, she saw his disillusionment even in the still-heady days of 1965:

> I looked at Bayard. His long, handsome face was lined and his eyes appeared troubled. Oh, he was sick. He had to be sick to leave an organization he loved so dearly and had worked for so diligently...."I'm going for a short rest." Distance was already in Bayard's voice, confirming my assessment. "And I'll be joining A. Philip Randolph and the Sleeping Car Porters." His face said he was already there.

Angelou did not write about Rustin other than in his public role, and neither did many others. But a few things are known about his personal life. Work was it, more or less, but if that sounds too virtuous it is worth mentioning that although he might work 18 hours a day one week, it was quite usual for him not to show up at all the next. He smoked ferociously and his apartment was filled with German religious sculpture which he collected. And to say that for seven years he was Martin Luther King's "right hand" is to be ironic; when, as a child at school, Rustin had been forced to use his right hand, he experienced difficulty in writing, reading and eventually also speaking. In the end a psychiatrist had to intervene to permit him to revert to his natural left-handedness. Quite fitting, really, for a lifelong Black socialist compelled to live in White capitalist America.

Born Bayard Rustin. **Parents** Janifer and Julia (Davis) Rustin. **Education** Wilberforce University, 1930–31; Cheney State College, 1931–33; City College, New York, 1933–35. **Career** Nightclub singer, 1938–41; race relations director, Fellowship of Reconciliation, 1941–53;

executive secretary, War Resisters' League, 1953–55; special assistant to Martin Luther King Jr, 1955–60; executive director, A. Philip Randolph Institute, New York, 1964 onwards. **Related activities** Chairman, Leadership Conference on Civil Rights and Recruitment and Training Program; field secretary, Congress for Racial Equality, 1941; chairman, Free India Committee, 1945 onwards; director, Committee Against Discrimination in the Armed Forces, 1947; organizer: bus boycott, Montgomery, Alabama, 1955, Aldermaston ban-the-bomb march, England, 1958, first New York City school boycott, 1963, "March on Washington for Jobs and Freedom", 1963; Ratner lecturer, Columbia University, 1974; co-chairman, Social Democrats of the USA; co-founder, Committee to Support South African Resistance, later the American Committee on Africa; editor, *Liberation*. **Offices and memberships** Member: Young Communist League, 1936–41, National Association for the Advancement of Colored People, 1964 onwards, Society of Friends, Omega Psi; board of directors: Notre Dame University, Metropolitan Applied Research Center, League for Industrial Democracy. **Awards and honours** Man of the Year award, Pittsburgh chapter, National Association for the Advancement of Colored People, 1964; Eleanor Roosevelt Award, Trade Union Leadership Council, 1966; Liberty Bell Award, Howard University Law School, 1967; LLD, New School for Social Research, 1968; LittD, Montclair State College, 1968; John Dewey Award, United Federation of Teachers, 1968; Family of Man Award, National Council of Churches, 1969; John F. Kennedy Award, National Council of Jewish Women, 1971; LLD, Brown University, 1972; Lyndon Johnson Award, Urban League, 1974; honorary degrees from Columbia University and Clark College. **Publications** *Down the Line: The Collected Writings of Bayard Rustin*, 1971; contributor of numerous articles to periodicals. **Cause of death** Heart attack, following surgery for a ruptured appendix, at age 77.

PETER SCHIDLOF

Austrian Violist

***Born* Vienna, Austria, 9 July 1922**

***Died* Sunderland, England, 16 August 1987**

Peter Schidlof, OBE, was the viola player with the celebrated Amadeus Quartet for nearly 40 years until his death at the age of 65. A virtuoso who could easily have pursued a solo career, he was the bedrock of the quartet and earned from the other three the soubriquet "eagle ears" because he was a stickler for accuracy. At the time of Schidlof's death, Martin Lovett, the cellist, spoke for his two colleagues, Norbert Brainin and Sigmund Nissel, when he said: "He is simply irreplaceable."

Schidlof was born into an Austrian–Jewish family which was forced into exile by Hitler's invasion of Austria in 1938. He won a music scholarship to Blundells School in Devon, but when war broke out the following year he suddenly acquired the status of enemy alien and found himself in an internment camp. It was there that he met Brainin and Nissel who had also fled Austro–Fascism. A fellow internee has told the story of the miserable journey to the camp in a sealed train.

> Morale was below zero point. Peter's initiative changed all that. He took his violin out of its case—mercifully he had been allowed to keep it—and began to play in the corridors of the train the most sentimental and touching music. It is almost impossible to describe the feeling

which his masterly playing evoked. He lifted the gloom that had descended on us and restored our self-confidence.

After the war the three compatriots studied with Max Rostal who persuaded Schidlof to switch from violin to viola. On Rostal's advice, they teamed up with the British cellist Martin Lovett and formed what was at first called the Brainin Quartet. In 1948 they renamed themselves the Amadeus Quartet in homage to Mozart and immediately became affectionately known as the Wolf Gang. Imogen Holst gave them £100 so that they could make their début at the Wigmore Hall in January that year. A professional string quartet was a relatively rare thing in Britain in those days and they played the concert to a packed and appreciative audience, little knowing it was to be the first of more than 4000 concerts.

They quickly became established as the leading quartet in Britain. Tours in Europe soon followed and they appeared at many leading festivals, including Edinburgh and Salzburg. In the 1960s and 1970s the quartet toured regularly, in the USA and Germany particularly. From 1966 to 1968 they were the resident quartet at the University of York and all received honorary doctorates. They preferred to concentrate on the classical composers—Mozart, Haydn, Beethoven and Schubert—but did not neglect the modern repertoire, playing quartets by Bartók, Tippett and other twentieth-century composers such as Benjamin Britten, who wrote his third string quartet for them in 1975. They played it to him privately shortly before his death.

The Amadeus Quartet's gramophone recordings are an almost comprehensive covering of their repertoire—first the quartets of Haydn, Mozart and Schubert, and in later years Beethoven and Brahms.

It is difficult to assess Schidlof's contribution to the quartet's success as an individual—and maybe that in itself is testimony to his supreme sensitivity as an ensemble player. His playing was warm, intuitive and rich in tone and he acquitted himself on many occasions as a fine soloist. He was much in demand for performances of Berlioz's symphonic poem featuring the viola—*Harold in Italy*—and he and Brainin were famous for their interpretation of Mozart's *Sinfonia Concertante* (K. 365). Undoubtedly, his penetrating musical insights and knowledge of a wide repertoire outside the chamber music field combined with his cultivated, attractive personality were an important part of the quartet's chemistry.

The quartet played their last concert in Cheltenham in the summer of 1987. It was a fitting programme: two works by Beethoven and one by Britten, symbolic of their roots in Central Europe and of the depth of their commitment to their adopted country. Their swan-song was Beethoven's E flat quartet, Opus 74.

The cellist William Pleeth, who often joined the quartet for performances of the Schubert *Quintet*, remembers Peter Schidlof for two things. One was his passion for shoes, the other was "the nervous energy that still rings in my ears. 'Come, boys come—let's go! Come.' He itched to get on to the platform and play—like waiting for the off at some great event."

Born Peter Schidlof. **Marriage** Margit Ullgren, 1952. **Children** One daughter. **Education** Blundells School, Devon, England. **Emigration** Left Austria for England, 1938; private music studies with Max Rostal, 1940s. **Career** Violinist and violist with Amadeus Quartet, 1947–87. **Related activities** Professor of music, Cologne High School, Germany. **Offices and memberships** Member: Incorporated Society of Musicians, Royal Society of Arts and Commerce, Royal Academy of Music (honorary); fellow, Royal Society of Arts. **Awards and honours** Honorary doctorate, York University, 1968; officer, Order of the British Empire, 1970; Gross Verdienstkreuz, German Federal Republic, 1973; Ehrenkreuz fur Kunst und Wissenschaft, Austria, 1974; honorary DMus, University of London, 1983. **Recordings** Most of the chamber music for string quartets, chiefly the works of Mozart, Haydn, Schubert, Beethoven and Brahms. **Cause of death** Heart attack, at age 65.

JEAN SCHLUMBERGER

French Jewellery Designer

***Born* Mulhouse, France, 1907**

***Died* Paris, France, 29 August 1987**

Jean Schlumberger's early career will always be associated with his time as a designer for Elsa Schiaparelli, whose colour trademark "Shocking Pink" was wittily combined with eccentric and Surrealist designs that enjoyed huge success during the 1930s. Schlumberger's ingenious mounting of Dresden ceramic flowers, found in the Paris flea market, as clips and brooches had first attracted Schiaparelli, and she later invited him to design buttons and costume jewellery for her. This professional association continued for the next 30 years.

The son of an established Alsatian textile manufacturer, Schlumberger's education in Switzerland did not equip him for his eventual career. Despite his talent as a draughtsman, he had been actively discouraged from undertaking a formal artistic training, and during the 1920s was sent to Berlin to enter banking, rapidly abandoning that career for one in publishing.

Finally escaping to Paris, he began to design jewellery before entering the French Army. After seeing active service during World War II, when he was evacuated from Dunkirk, he emigrated to New York and remained there for the rest of his career. He worked briefly as a designer for the fashion house Chez Ninon, and in 1946 opened a jewellery salon with his business partner, Nicolas Bongard. During this decade he produced the designs which mark his style: flowers, jellyfish, shells, birds and his hallmark, the starfish. Setting the precious gems in intricate settings of interwoven bands and coils of platinum, gold and richly coloured enamels, his work has been compared to a twentieth-century Cellini and in the league of Fabergé. Animal and plant forms assume fanciful and amorphic shapes, and describing his approach he once stated, "I try to make everything look as if it were growing, uneven, at random, organic, in motion."

In 1956 Schlumberger was invited by Walter Hoving, chairman of the renowned New York firm of Tiffany and Co., to join as a designer and as vice-president. There he enjoyed the luxury of his own mezzanine showroom. The following year he undertook one of his most prestigious commissions, for the setting of the Tiffany diamond, the largest canary diamond in the world. Discovered in 1871 and weighing some 128.51 carats, Schlumberger designed a diamond ribbon necklace and clip around the stone.

Despite enormous popularity with American millionairesses (clients included the Duchess of Windsor, Daisy Fellowes, Bunny Mellon and Françoise de la Renta), Schlumberger is poorly represented in French museums, although throughout his career in New York he continued to keep a design studio in Paris. His only work in a French public collection is the sword of the academician, Marcel Achard, in the Musée Carnavalet in Paris. However, shortly after his death his reputation improved dramatically, with works fetching three times the expected sum at auction, an ironic and belated recognition of his consummate skills as a designer of jewellery combining the elegance of Renaissance jewels with the fantasy of the Surrealists. His designs were produced in editions of no more than ten examples; in some cases designs were unique. Given the fickle nature of collectors and museums, Schlumberger will doubtless enjoy a revival of interest, and perhaps it is better that it should occur posthumously; such attention might have been unwelcome to a man who by nature was reticent and shy of publicity.

Born Jean Schlumberger. **Education** Switzerland. **Emigration** Left France for US, 1940. **Military service** French Army, World War II; survived Dunkirk; served with Free French forces in England and the Middle East under General de Gaulle. **Career** Worked briefly in banking and publishing; began to design jewellery for fashion designer Elsa Schiaparelli, Paris, *circa* 1932; clothes designer, Chez Ninon, New York, 1945; (with Nicolas Bongard) opened jewellery salon, New York, 1946; designer and vice-president, Tiffany & Company, New York, 1956 onwards. **Awards and honours** Chevalier of the National Order of Merit, 1977. **Cause of death** Undisclosed, at age 80.

JESSE UNRUH

American Politician

***Born* Newton, Kansas, 30 September 1922**

***Died* Marina del Ray, California, 4 August 1987**

Jesse Unruh was one of the United States' great politicians. His direct experience of poverty in the early part of his life was to influence all his dealings in the state of California where he was Democratic party leader. The enormous power he held was nearly always used to benefit the poor and the homeless, or to fight for civil rights, better education and welfare. Through his considerable parliamentary skills and liberal convictions he became the best-known state legislator in the US.

Unruh's strong sense of social justice was born out of his own impoverished upbringing. His father was an illiterate sharecropper descended from German Mennonites who fled Prussia to avoid military conscription. Jesse was the youngest of five children, all brought up in a strict religious atmosphere—a mixture of Mennonite heritage and Presbyterian practice. Set against the backdrop of the Depression, the family might have stepped from the pages of John Steinbeck's novel, *The Grapes of Wrath*. But life was very real and hard for the Unruh family, who travelled from farm to farm in the Dust Bowl years, finally making a home in a two-room shack on a sharecropping plot in Swenson, Texas.

Jesse Unruh once recalled: "The central realism of our youth was economic...only the toughest, the most ruthless, would survive and succeed." Unruh must have had some of these characteristics because he was the only one of the family to go beyond elementary school, and on graduating in 1939 he won a year's scholarship to Wayland Baptist College in Plainview, Texas. However, his childhood experiences were to affect him for the rest of his life. Addressing students at the University of California in Los Angeles in 1968, he said: "Our flower children of the thirties died in the hobo camps, the drafty barns and the welfare lines, and those memories haunt and motivate us just as much as...Vietnam obsesses you". But the past did not make him politically narrow-minded, and later that year he also spoke out publicly against the Vietnam War.

While serving in the US Naval Air Corps during World War II, Unruh took the opportunity to continue his self-education. Stationed in the lonely Aleutian Islands as a sheet metal worker, he spent hours reading, and writing essays and short stories. It was from the snappily titled *30 Days to a More Powerful Vocabulary* that he remembers learning the definition of "liberal", and from reading *USA* by Jon Dos Passos that his social conscience became even more deeply stirred. The inequalities and injustices of his childhood followed him here too. Drunkenness was common among the men, but officers were treated more leniently than enlisted men, and Whites more leniently than Blacks.

After the war, his experiences and observations of inequality led him towards the idea of joining the Communist Party, but he never actually became a member. With the financial help available to war veterans, Unruh went to the University of Southern California where he majored in journalism and political science. Here he participated in communist activities, but withdrew in 1948 when the communists took a hard line against all supporters of the Marshall Plan. He preferred to devote himself to working for the re-election of Helen Gahagan Douglas, a Marshall Plan supporter and US Representative for California. Subsequently, he also worked for Harry S. Truman.

Obtaining his BA in 1948, Unruh worked for a rail freight company over the next three years while studying for an MA. It was in 1950 that he embarked on his career in politics. He stood twice as candidate for the California State Assembly, winning the seat in 1954. From that time forward he was single-minded in his attempts to equalize a deeply meritocratic society. Although a liberal who wanted to introduce much pro-labour and anti-poverty legislation, he was also a pragmatist, conscious of just how far his electorate would tolerate left-wing reforms. Fortunately, when he first came to office the times were liberal and the Democrats' popularity was high. Rapidly building a power base, he rose ever higher in the Assembly, and by 1959 was chairman of the Ways and Means Committee, which held the purse strings. Unruh's policies proved popular; funds from the party faithful came rolling in and Unruh was able to use his sizeable bloc of votes to promote a great deal of liberal legislation.

In 1958 he managed the campaign to get Edmund (Pat) Brown elected as governor and it was this campaign that won the Democrats their first majority in the California Assembly for 14 years. At around the same time Unruh sensed the potential of a rising young politician—John F. Kennedy. The two men became good friends, and Unruh became a loyal member of the presidential campaign, remaining liaison man for all of California when Kennedy reached the White House. Later, Unruh was the first politician of national stature to publicly support Robert F. Kennedy in his bid for the presidency.

Unruh's own power base was further enhanced in 1961 when he was elected speaker of the Assembly. This enabled him to appoint all chairmen and members of the Assembly's 20 committees and have final approval of their bills. It was in this capacity that he really displayed his parliamentary and fund-raising skills and, incidentally, his often aggressive manner. His leadership greatly increased the power of the Assembly, which became "a model of legislative professionalism with a well-trained, well-paid, full-time staff, a staff internal programme and a programme of university seminars for the legislators". He had a strong belief in the "constitutional inimicality" between the legislature and the executive branches of government and fought hard for the power of the former over the latter—a battle often fought with Governor Brown.

By now Unruh was a heavyweight politician in every sense. Sometimes weighing as much as 290 pounds, his critics called him "Big Daddy", and his ruthlessness was legendary. One observer in 1965 noted: "All of his sophistication, all of his energy and all of his lust for power has been turned by Jesse Unruh to the State Assembly...If there is any monument to this ambitious man, it is the Assembly. There is no legislative body quite like it anywhere."

Despite his imposing physical presence, Unruh had one major drawback as a politician: poor charisma. A report in the *New York Times* magazine noted that Unruh spoke "with a faint lisp, which troubles the friends who wish he had the TV charisma to match his intellect and parliamentary skill". Maybe this deficiency contributed to his unsuccessful bid for the governorship of California in 1970. (Ronald Reagan pipped him to the post.) Or maybe he lost because of the growing conservatism among the Californian electorate.

It was in Reagan's years as governor that Unruh changed his image. He lost weight, toned down his aggressive attitude towards the former governor Pat Brown, and acted with "deference and care" towards Reagan. One newspaper reported: "In his day-to-day duelling with Reagan,

Unruh moves like a chess player, adroit and quiet, seeing the whole game even when his back is turned...[He] is brusque, tense and exact." Others described him as "on the surface...reticent, taut, wary and unsentimental" and known for his "self-control and equanimity", even when dealing with Reagan with whom he radically disagreed and kept up a steady and persistent opposition. But a friend of Unruh's saw a further change in Unruh after the assassination of President Kennedy in June 1968: "There is a fatalism now about his own career; Jesse is less driven, more reflective [and] as a statesman more mature".

Unruh described himself as a "chronic problem solver", claiming to be "less concerned with ideologies than solutions". His modernization of the California State Assembly stands as testimony to this claim.

Born Jesse Marvin Unruh. **Parents** Isaac P., sharecropper, and Nettie Laura (Kessler) Unruh. **Marriage** Virginia June Lemon, physical education teacher, 1943. **Children** Bruce, Bradley, Robert, Randall, Linda Lu. **Education** Wayland Baptist College, Plainview, Texas, 1939–40; University of Southern California, BA, 1948, MA, 1949. **Military service** US Naval Air Corps, 1942–45. **Career** Sheet metal worker, Douglas Aircraft, Los Angeles, 1940–42; worked for a railway freight company, 1949; district staff director, federal census, 1950; worked for Pacific Car Demurrage Bureau, 1950–54; member for Inglewood, Los Angeles, of California State Assembly, 1954–70; unsuccessful Democratic candidate for governor of California, 1970; state treasurer of California, 1970–87. **Related activities** Member, California Central Democratic Committee, 1954 onwards; chairman, Committee of Finance and Insurance, 1957–59; manager, California Democratic gubernatorial campaign, 1958; chairman, Ways and Means Committee, 1959–61; Southern California manager, John F. Kennedy presidential campaign, 1960; speaker of Assembly, 1961–68; Southern California co-chairman, gubernatorial campaign, 1962; statewide coordinator assembly, congressional campaigns, 1962; president, National Conference of State Legislative Leaders, 1966; member, Advisory Commission on Intergovernmental Relations, 1967–70; chairman, Robert F. Kennedy's California presidential campaign, 1968; Democratic leader of Assembly, 1968–70; chairman, California delegation, Democratic National Convention, 1968. **Other activities** Consultant professor of political science, Eagleton Institute of Politics, Rutgers University, 1965 onwards; visiting professor of political science, San Fernando Valley State College, 1970; visiting professor, University of Southern California School of Law, 1971–72. **Offices and memberships** Board of regents, University of Southern California, 1961–68; trustee, California State Colleges, 1961–68; co-chairman, Seminar of Young Legislators, Carnegie Corporation Chubb Fellow at Yale, 1962; trustee, Institute for American Universities Citizens' Conference on State Legislatures, 1968 onwards. **Awards and honours** Alumnus of the Year, University of Southern California, 1963; honorary LLD, University of Southern California, 1967. **Cause of death** Prostate cancer, at age 64.

CHARLES WESLEY

American Educator and Historian

***Born* Louisville, Kentucky, 2 December 1891**

***Died* Washington, DC, 16 August 1987**

When the revised edition of Charles Wesley's *The Collapse of the Confederacy* was published in 1937, reviewers agreed that the author had succeeded in providing a fair examination of the internal disintegration which led to the South's downfall. "In general," A.B. Miller commented in *The Annals of the American Academy of Political and Social Science*, "Wesley had done his modest share toward shattering the illusion...that the Southern states presented a single, devoted front to their foe." When one considers that the author was a Black man and that the first version of the book appeared in the early 1920s, however, Wesley's "share" of such an analysis should be called anything but modest.

Long before the civil rights movement of the 1960s drew the world's attention to the Black cause in its explosive fashion, this Yale scholar, historian and author had been quietly advocating fair treatment for Negroes—not only for those living in the modern world, but also for the way their forbears had been treated in terms of historical fact. "The Negro in the United States," Wesley wrote, "must be viewed without blind prejudice, and his contributions to American life and history should be included with those of other people." A just assertion, yet Wesley went one step further: "When this is done," he continued, "without doubt some Negroes will appear inferior to some Whites and some Whites will appear inferior to some Negroes. Any other position is contrary to the facts and their logical interpretation." Given statements like these, it hardly seems surprising that Charles Wesley was considered to have personally broken the ground in the writing of Black history.

He was born in Louisville, Kentucky, in December 1891. After gaining his BA at Fisk University in Nashville, Tennessee, Wesley, because of his outstanding grades, was awarded a graduate fellowship at Yale, where he received his MA in 1913. This was followed by a year at the Guilde Internationale in Paris, then a stint at the Howard University Law School in Washington, DC, and finally by a doctoral degree from Harvard University (1925). As with most scholars and educators, Wesley's teaching career had begun immediately after the completion of his master's degree in history: he became an instructor at Howard University and remained there for the next 29 years, serving as a professor, dean of the college of liberal arts, and eventually as dean of the graduate school. Wesley left Howard in 1942 to take up the post of president at Ohio's Wilberforce University for five years; afterwards he left to help establish the Central State University (also in Wilberforce), where he remained until his retirement from education in 1965.

Charles Wesley's teaching career has been described as "a study in devotion to a cause", the main cause being that of an honest, objective approach to history in general and to Black history in particular. "History," he said, "is an expanding concept embracing the ways *all* people have lived throughout the ages." Because the Black participation in that concept had long been ignored or mythologized, Wesley's best-known works were naturally centred around the historical perspective of the Negro.

His first book, *Negro Labor in the United States, 1850–1925*, traced the history of the Black labour force from Southern slavery to its migration to the industrial Northern states. As with most of Wesley's works, this one was well received; the *New York Times* described it as a "valuable contribution to the economic history of the country", while other reviewers lauded its "clearness of statement and marshalling of pertinent facts". His interest in the labour force led Wesley to write several magazine articles on the subject, but his next book was concerned with ecclesiastical matters: *Richard Allen, Apostle of Freedom* appeared in 1935 as a study of the Black Methodist minister who organized the first Negro church in the United States. This concern with religious subjects was not a new one to the author, for by the time the book was written, Charles Wesley had been the pastor of the Ebenezer and Campbell African Methodist Episcopal Church in Washington, DC, for 17 years.

Other Wesley works ranged from *A History of Alpha Phi Alpha* (a Negro fraternity), a collection of essays on Negro history entitled *Neglected History*, and even a *Manual of Research and Thesis Writing*. Throughout his career as an educator, Wesley also contributed numerous scholarly articles to magazines and newspapers, and eventually served as the editor of the eleven-volume *International Library of Negro Life and History*. Just before his death at the age of 95, he was still preparing two more books for publication.

His energy in writing, teaching and scholarship seemed to permeate all facets of his life; at the age of 82, for example, he came out of retirement to become the first director of the Afro-American Historical and Cultural Museum in Philadelphia. Music, tennis and golf were among his favourite hobbies, and he was both a Mason and a member of the Society of Odd Fellows.

As one of the most eminent Black scholars in the US, Wesley's stance on the treatment of history remained steadfast throughout his lifetime. "It should not be a part story but a whole one," he stated in an interview, "written honestly and objectively. It should include both White and Black. It must be devoid of racial or colour superiority or inferiority." Certainly it is clear from his numerous books and writings, from his honorary degrees, fellowships and awards, and finally from his outstanding reputation in all circles of scholarship that Charles Harris Wesley never once wavered from that belief.

Born Charles Harris Wesley. **Parents** Charles Snowden and Matilda (Harris) Wesley. **Marriage** 1) Louise Johnson, 1915 (died, 1973); 2) Dorothy B. Porter, 1978. **Children** Two daughters, Louise Johnson (deceased) and Charlotte Harris, from first marriage; one stepdaughter, Constance, from second marriage. **Education** Fisk University, BA, 1911; Yale University, MA, 1913; Guilde Internationale, Paris, 1914; Howard University Law School, 1915–16; Harvard University, PhD, 1925. **Career** Instructor in teaching history, Howard University, Washington, 1913, history instructor, 1914–18, assistant professor, 1918–19, associate professor, 1919–20, professor of history and head of history department, 1921–42; president, Wilberforce University, Ohio, 1942–47; president, Central State University, Wilberforce, Ohio, 1947–65, president emeritus, 1965–87. **Related activities** President, Inter-University Council in Ohio, 1955–56. **Other activities** Education secretary, Young Men's Christian Association, 1919–20, overseas secretary, 1920–21; executive director, Afro-American Bicentennial Historical and Cultural Museum, Philadelphia, 1975–76. **Offices and memberships** Member: American Antiquarian Society, American Historical Association, American Association of School Administrators, American Association of University Professors, National Council for Social Studies, National Historical Society, National Education Association, Society for the Advancement of Education, Black Academy of Arts and Letters, Southern Historical Association, Freemasons, Phi Beta Kappa, Alpha Phi Alpha (general president, 1931–64, historian, 1940–80), Ohio College Association (member of executive committee, 1947–49, 1960–61, 1964–65, chairman, resolutions committee, 1951–53, president, 1963–64), Association of Ohio College Presidents and Deans (president 1954–55); fellow, American Geographical Society. **Awards and honours** DD, Wilberforce University, 1928; Guggenheim Fellowship, 1930–31; LLD: Allen University, 1932, Virginia State College, 1943, Morris Brown University, 1944, Paul Quinn College, 1946, Campbell College, 1946, Morgan State College, 1961, University of Cincinnati, 1964, Tuskegee Institute, 1968, Howard University, 1970; Social Science Research Council Grant, 1936–37; EdD, Central State College, 1965; LHD, Berea University, 1971; awards from Kentucky

Education Association, Phi Beta Kappa, and Xenia Chamber of Commerce. **Publications** *The Collapse of the Confederacy*, Washington, 1922; *Negro Labor in the United States, 1850–1925: A Study in American Economic History*, 1927; *The History of Alpha Phi Alpha: A Development in Negro College Life*, 1929, 8th edition published as *The History of Alpha Phi Alpha: A Development in College Life*, 1957; *Richard Allen: Apostle of Freedom*, 1935; (editor) *The Negro in the Americas*, 1940; *A Manual of Research and Thesis Writing for Graduate Students*, 1941; *History of Sigma Pi Phi, First of the Negro–American Greek-Letter Fraternities*, 1954; *History of the Improved Benevolent and Protective Order of Elks of the World, 1898–1954*, 1955; (with Carter G. Woodson) *Negro Makers of History*, 5th edition, 1958, 6th edition, 1968; (with Carter G. Woodson) *The Story of the Negro Retold*, 4th edition, 1959; *The History of the Prince Hall Grand Lodge of Free and Accepted Masons of the State of Ohio, 1849–1960: An Epoch in American Paternalism*, 1961; *Ohio Negroes in the Civil War*, 1962; (with Carter G. Woodson) *The Negro in Our History*, 10th edition, 1962, 12th edition, 1972; *Neglected History: Essays in Negro History by a College President, Charles H. Wesley*, 1965; (with Patricia W. Romero) *Negro Americans in the Civil War: From Slavery to Citizenship*, 1967; *In Freedom's Footsteps: From the African Background to the Civil War*, 1968; *Negro Citizenship in the United States: The Fourteenth Amendment and the Negro-American; Its Concepts and Developments, 1868–1968*, 1968; *The Quest for Equality: From Civil War to Civil Rights*, 1968; (editor and author of introduction) *The Mis-Education of the Negro*, 1969; *The Fifteenth Amendment and Black America, 1870–1970*, 1970; (reviser with Thelma D. Perry) *Sadie Iola Daniel, Women Builders*, 1970; *Prince Hall: Life and Legacy*, 1977; *Henry Arthur Callis: Life and Legacy*, 1977; (editor) *The International Library of Negro Life and History*, eleven volumes, 1966–67; contributor of articles to magazines and newspapers. **Cause of death** Pneumonia, at age 95.

GEORG WITTIG

German Chemist

***Born* Berlin, Germany, 16 June 1897**

***Died* Heidelberg, West Germany, 26 August 1987**

Fond of painting, music, hiking and mountain climbing, Professor Georg Wittig also won the Nobel Prize for Chemistry in 1979. As one of the world's leading chemists of this century, it is somewhat surprising that he did not concern himself with the practical side of the science. Instead of discovering new substances, he spent his lifetime in the exploration of the fundamental mechanics of the chemical process itself.

Born in Berlin during 1897, the son of a professor, the young Wittig attended the high school in Kassel before entering the University of Marburg, where he took his degree. There he served as a lecturer for six years until 1932, when he left to become the director of the Technische Hochschule in Braunschweig, not far from the present East/West border. Eventually his career took him back into the university system, first at the University of Braunschweig, then at Freiburg in the Black Forest region, then at Tübingen. Finally, Wittig settled in Heidelberg, where he lectured as professor emeritus until 1967, at the same time directing the Institute of Organic Chemistry there.

During his teaching years, Wittig had not been idle: his *Textbook of Stereo-chemistry* had been published as early as 1930. By 1953, however, he was renowned throughout the scientific community for his investigations into the rearrangement reaction which was to bear his name. The Wittig Reaction, which is the process of regulating the regrouping of atoms in a molecule, opened up a hitherto unknown area of organic chemistry. By causing phosphorus ylides to react with ketones and aldehydes (thus forming alkenes), the Wittig Reaction made possible the introduction of double bonds between carbon molecules in specific locations. This in turn led to the synthesis of various pharmaceuticals and other complicated organic substances, such as Vitamin A, derivatives of Vitamin D, and prostaglandin, the hormone found in mammalian tissues.

It was his work in this area that earned Georg Wittig the Nobel Prize for Chemistry, which he shared with Professor Herbert Brown of Purdue University, Indiana, in 1979. Not surprisingly, Wittig was also the recipient of numerous other awards for his scientific work, including the German Ordens Grosses Verdienstkreuz—the Award of Highest Service—in 1980.

Born Georg Wittig. **Parents** Gustav, professor, and Martha (Dombrowski) Wittig. **Marriage** Waltraut Ernst, 1930 (died, 1978). **Children** Two daughters. **Education** Wilhelms-Gymnasium, Kassel; Marburg University, PhD, 1923. **Career** Lecturer, Marburg University, 1926–32; division director, Technische Hochschule, Braunschweig, 1932–37; professor, Universities of Braunschweig, Freiburg and Tübingen, 1937–56; professor, Heidelberg University, 1956–67, emeritus, 1967–87. **Offices and memberships** Member: Academy of Sciences, Munich and Heidelberg, Académie Française, Societa Quimica del Peru, Leopoldina Halle; honorary member: Swiss Chemical Association, New York Academy of the Sciences, Chemical Society, London, Société Chimique de France; honorary doctorates from the Sorbonne and Hamburg University. **Awards and honours** Adolf von Baeyer Medal, Society of German Chemists, 1953; Silver Medal, University of Helsinki, 1957; Dannie Heineman Award, Göttinger Academy of Sciences, 1965; Otto Hahn Prize, Germany, 1967; Silver Medal, City of Paris, 1969; Paul Karrer Medal, University of Zurich, 1972; Medal of the Bruylants Chair, University of Leuwen, 1972; Roger Adams Award, American Chemical Society, 1973; Karl Ziegler Prize, Society of German Chemists, 1975; Nobel Prize for Chemistry, 1979; Ordens Grosses Verdienstkreuz, 1980. **Publications** *Textbook of Stereo-chemistry*, 1930; also wrote numerous articles on metallorganic, ylid and carbanion chemistry for learned journals. **Cause of death** Undisclosed, at age 90.

ALASTAIR WORDEN

British Life Scientist

***Born* Lancashire, England, 23 April 1916**

***Died* Hemingford Abbots, Cambridgeshire, 10 August 1987**

Professor Alastair Worden was founder of both the Huntingdon Research Centre and the Cantab Group. A remarkable innovator as well as a brilliant and dedicated scientist, his life's work was tempered and motivated by his love of people and animals.

Alastair Norman Worden was a doctor's son, and because of his early interest in animals he took a veterinary qualification at the Royal Veterinary College in 1938, before continuing to Cambridge where he obtained a degree in the natural sciences tripos. Having graduated, he joined the remarkable research team in the Lister Institute of Preventive Medicine at Cambridge, under Professor Gowland Hopkins. Vitamins, the essential organic components for the maintenance of health and growth, had recently been discovered, and the team were identifying further members of the B group. Much of Worden's work was with laboratory animals.

When aged only 28, he was appointed professor of animal health at the University of Wales at Aberystwyth, a post he held five years. While there he was chosen to edit the handbook on *The Care and Management of Laboratory Animals* for the Universities Federation for Animal Welfare, and this became the standard work on the subject.

With quite remarkable courage, in 1950 he resigned his university chair, and with the help of family and friends he purchased Cromwell House in the High Street of Huntingdon, Cambridgeshire. (This was the birthplace of Oliver Cromwell [1599–1658], who led the Parliamentarians in the English civil war and eventually became head of state.) Laboratories were constructed in the house, and the first animal accommodation was at the bottom of the garden. Here, in 1951, Worden established the Nutritional Research Centre, employing only five other scientists. It was advertised as a consulting practice, using animals for experiments, and at first work was very hard to obtain. Worden persisted doggedly, using his charm and influence, and eventually the contracts came. The workload enjoyed a particular boost after the publication of Rachel Carson's book on pesticides, *The Silent Spring*, and the well-publicized tragedy of the thalidomide babies; both contributed to a new awareness that chemically active substances needed thorough testing and control. Regulations were enacted that made it mandatory for testing to be done by an independent laboratory, and the Huntingdon Research Centre was one of the very few in the world. Work poured in, and Worden and his small group of enthusiasts found themselves working for famous international companies producing the data required by governments of many countries.

This was the beginning of "contract research", and it now involves thousands of scientists from educational establishments such as universities and polytechnics, as well as independent laboratories. To cope with its share of the work, Worden's centre had to expand. Moving to buildings on a former 100-acre farm site, the name was changed to the Huntingdon Research Centre. From its humble beginnings, it became a company listed on the stock exchange, employing almost 1000 people, with a laboratory in the US and units in France and Germany.

Worden presided over this expansion for 26 years, until he resigned in 1978. Apart from his work there, he was very involved in other committees and groups in Britain and abroad, earning many honours and awards, including the visiting professorship of toxicology at Bath University from 1973. Nevertheless, throughout his time at the centre, even with these outside involvements, he presided with a firm but caring hand over all its activities. To his colleagues he was a leader who always tempered his firmness with kindness and patience. In addition, for all work involving animals he insisted that they should be humanely treated, and he agreed to their use only in essential experiments.

On retirement from the centre, he fulfilled a lifelong ambition by enrolling as a student at Addenbrooke's Hospital in Cambridge to qualify in human medicine. This he achieved at the age of 65. What would he do next? Such an energetic, stimulating, original workaholic could not just retire. Instead he founded the Cantab Group. Working with a number of distinguished scientists and researchers from Huntingdon, he became involved in the development and evaluation of medicinal and veterinary products and industrial chemicals. Soon, this venture too began to expand beyond the confines of Huntingdon; a clinical pharmacology unit was set up at Hinchinbrooke Hospital, and units were established in Sheffield and Japan. Worden was involved with the work of the group until his sudden death.

Apart from his prodigious laboratory workload, Worden also wrote prolifically. His publications included *Laboratory Animals*, *Animal Health, Production and Pasture* and *Animals and Alternatives in Research*. Outside his work, he found time for recreation, and had a strong interest in cricket and rugby. History and natural history also fascinated him, and he was an enthusiastic traveller.

In spite of his great achievements, Worden was a modest, unassuming man, surprisingly inconspicuous in a formal gathering. He died as he would have wished, quietly at home while still very active.

Born Alastair Norman Worden. **Parents** Dr C. Norman and Elizabeth Worden. **Marriages** 1) Agnes Marshall Murray, 1942; 2) Mrs Dorothy Mary (Peel) Jensen, 1950. **Children** One son, Blair, from first marriage; two sons, Robert and Mark, and one daughter, Sarah, from second marriage. **Education** Queen Elizabeth's School, Barnet; St John's College and School of Clinical Medicine, Cambridge, MA, MB, BChir, PhD; Royal Veterinary, Birkbeck and University Colleges, London, DVetMed, DSc. **Career** Research student, Lister Institute of Preventive Medicine, Cambridge University, 1938–41, research officer, 1941–45; Milford research professor and joint head, biochemistry department, University of Wales, 1945–50; founder and chairman, Huntingdon Research Centre, 1951–78; founder, Cantab Group (Cambridge Applied Nutrition, Toxicology and Biosciences), 1981. **Related activities** Agricultural Research Council Technical Committee on Calf and Pig Diseases, 1944; Joint Agricultural Research Council Agricultural Improvement Council Committee on Grassland Improvement Station, 1946; Animal Husbandry and Welfare Committee, Zoological Society, London, 1954, honorary research associate, 1979; Agricultural Research Council Research (Frazer) Committee on Toxic Chemicals, 1961; Ministry of Agriculture, Fisheries and Food British Agrochemicals Joint Medical Panel, 1961; Japan Pharmacological Society, 1970; fellow and coordinator of environmental studies, Wolfson College, Cambridge University, 1971–83, emeritus, 1983–87, council member, 1974–78; chairman, Institute of Food Technologists, 1973–74; professor of toxicology, University of Bath, 1973–85; expert in pharmacology and toxicology, Ministry of Public Health, France, 1974; Asociación Medica Argentina, 1974; Royal Society Study Group on Long-term Toxic Effects, 1975–78; secretary, Fund for the Replacement of Animals in Medical Experiments, Toxicity Committee, 1979; professor of toxicology, University of Surrey, adviser to department of biochemistry, 1985–87. **Other activities** Member, Papworth–Huntingdon Hospital Management Committee, 1970–74. **Offices and memberships** Governor, Taverham Hall Educational Trust, 1968; trustee, Lucy Cavendish College, Cambridge, 1975; trustee, Cambridge University Veterinary School, 1981; president: Huntingdonshire Branch, Historical Association, Huntingdonshire Fauna and Flora Society, 1965, Bedfordshire and Huntingdonshire Naturalist Trust, Huntingdonshire Football League, Huntingdonshire County Cricket Club, Football Association, and Referees' Association; chairman, Mammal Society of the British Isles, 1953–54; life member: Cambridge University Cricket Club, Cambridge University Rugby Union Football Club, Blackpool Football Club; member, Worshipful Society of Apothecaries, 1971; freeman, City of London, 1974. **Awards and honours** Doctor of Veterinary Medicine, Zurich; fellow: Royal College of Pathologists, Royal College of Veterinary Surgeons, American Academy of Veterinary and Comparative Toxicology, Royal Society of Chemists, Institute of Biology, Linnean Society, Royal College of Surgeons of England, British Institute of Regulatory Affairs; licentiate, Society of Apothecaries; chartered chemist. **Publications** *Laboratory Animals*, 1947; (with Harry V. Thompson) *The Rabbit*, 1956; *Animal Health, Production and Pasture*, 1964; *Animals and Alternatives in Research*, 1983; numerous papers on nutrition, biochemistry and toxicology. **Cause of death** Heart failure, at age 71.

SEPTEMBER

EDGAR ANSTEY

British Film Director, Producer and Critic
***Born* Watford, Hertfordshire, 16 February 1907**
***Died* Hampstead Garden Suburb, London, 26 September 1987**

Edgar Anstey played a leading part in the development of the British documentary film, generally regarded as Britain's greatest contribution to the development of world cinema. He was one of a young and talented group of early documentary-makers, including Stuart Legg, Basil Wright, Arthur Elton, Harry Watt, John Taylor and Humphrey Jennings, which was dominated by the forceful personality of John Grierson, the "founding father" of the British documentary, as he called himself. They were mainly middle-class, well-educated young men with a social conscience, who came together in the heady days of the early 1930s with a perhaps naïve belief in the truth and objectivity of documentary film. As Rachael Low comments in her book *Documentary and Educational Films of the 1930s*, "It was a time of great interest in the power of the press, radio and film; in fact, the power of what were later to be called the mass media was beginning to be realized and to be used to popularize everything from Fascism to Ovaltine. The word 'propaganda' had not yet acquired the sinister overtones of falsification and indoctrination which it was soon to have."

Some of these films mixed education and the arts in an exciting way, using the verse of W.H. Auden and the music of Benjamin Britten. It has also been suggested that the social and welfare reforms of the post-war British government owed something to the influence of these films. Anstey himself, always idealistic, believed strongly that through film, the ordinary man in the street could learn to understand the changing world he lived in and rise to its challenges.

Two much-praised early films, which expressed Anstey's talents and his social concerns, were *Housing Problems* (1935), co-directed with Arthur Elton and sponsored by the British Commercial Gas Association, and *Enough to Eat* (1936), sponsored by the Gas Light and Coke Co. The first focused on the plight of slum-dwellers in the East End of London and broke new ground by allowing people to speak in their own words and in their own surroundings. One woman, indicating her appalling housing conditions says: "It gets on yer nerves. I'll tell yer, I'm fed up." This is such a usual documentary style more than 50 years on that it is difficult to realize how original it was and what an impact it made at the time.

Enough to Eat, relating malnutrition and social class, an unfamiliar idea at the time, took Anstey into a more verbal style of direct interviews with the pictures acting rather as a background illustration to the words, which carried the bulk of the message. It was narrated by Julian Huxley and was one of the films described as "using the camera as a reporter", a popular phrase at the time. According to Rachael Low, it also firmly established "the sponsorship of films unrelated to the commercial interests of the backer".

The early British documentary film movement was given coherence by two men—Sir Stephen Tallents, an eminent civil servant and secretary of the Empire Marketing Board (EMB), and John Grierson, film-maker, a small Scotsman trained in the social sciences who had spent time in the United States in the early 1920s, where he had been influenced by Russian silent films, such as Eisenstein's *Battleship Potemkin*. Grierson was also influenced by Robert Flaherty, an early pioneer of documentary film. Tallents and Grierson set up the Empire Marketing Board's film unit, whose first film *Drifters* (1929), a beautiful study of the North Sea herring fleet, was a great success and a prototype for films to follow. The film unit blossomed into a movement and Edgar Anstey joined them in 1931.

Anstey first made his mark by his skilful editing of *Industrial Britain* (1933) about the country's transition from a workforce of small craftsmen to one of modern industry, and showing that even in the latter, some of the old crafts were still needed. The film contained sequences shot by various film-makers, including glass-blowing shot by the talented Robert Flaherty, who was in Britain on a visit.

Granton Trawler (1934), commissioned by the Empire Marketing Board, was partly filmed by Grierson, who, according to one account, was seasick while filming and allowed the camera to fall. Turning adversity to advantage, Anstey used the falling camera to create severe storm-like effects at sea. Alberto Cavalcanti, a Brazilian who had joined the group from the French film industry, produced the sound for the film, and went on to be an innovator in the sound field.

At about this time, the EMB Film Unit was transformed into the GPO (General Post Office) Film Unit. For the GPO, with the assistance of Harry Watt, Anstey directed *6.30 Collection* (1934), an interesting film about one of London's postal sorting offices.

In 1934 Anstey became an independent film-maker, but after the success of *Housing Problems* and *Enough to Eat*, he devoted himself mainly to producing. However, he did encourage new talent in both directors and technicians, and continued to do so throughout his life. After completing these two films, he joined the London office of "The March of Time", the American news documentary service, as its London director of productions, and later worked for them in New York as foreign editor. "The March of Time" style was racier and more dramatic than the EMB/GPO productions, often using actors for interviews in the studio and for reconstructions of events. Unlike the more educational and thought-provoking approach of the British films, "March of Time" aimed more at opening up controversy. Anstey's first two items for this service were on malnutrition and army recruits, and on problems in the British coal industry.

It had already been ruled inappropriate for the GPO Film Unit, as an official unit, to be making films for all comers, whether other official or commercial organizations, and that it was unfair competition for the film industry. Others from the original close-knit group had, like Anstey, already extended their skills to producing as well as directing, and larger firms were starting to see the possibilities of prestige publicity through being film sponsors. Shell-Mex BP sought the advice of Grierson and Anstey, who together set up the Shell Film Unit in 1933. Their first production was *Airport* (1934), a two-reel film of a day at Croydon Airport, then one of the busiest in the world. In the early 1940s Anstey worked as producer in charge of the Shell Film Unit, which came to be respected throughout the world for its science and technology films.

During the war, Anstey, like many other film-makers, found himself producing propaganda films for the Ministry of Information. He also made some for the Ministry of Agriculture, encouraging more intensive cultivation of land on farms and in urban gardens. Among his films at that time were *A Day in the Factory*, *How to File*, *Fire-guard*, *Young Farmers* and *The Crown of the Year*. When the war was over, he did no film-making for some years, working as film critic on the *Spectator* magazine and becoming known to radio audiences through his regular contributions to the BBC programme *The Critics*.

In 1949 Edgar Anstey married Daphne Lilly, a Canadian film-maker with whom he had a son and a daughter. In the same year he became a member of the Films Council and film officer to the British Transport Commission, a job which he held until 1974 and in which he came into his own, using his various talents and experience to organize an enterprising and successful documentary unit, British Transport Films. The unit made many prize-winning films, including *Journey into Spring* (1957), a lyrical film about naturalist Gilbert White's picturesque Hampshire village of Selborne, *Between the Tides* (1958), a study of coastal marine life, and *Terminus* (1961), a day at London's Waterloo station, directed by the young John Schlesinger and perhaps influenced by his friendship with English poet John Betjeman, who was so fond of the older English railway stations. The film won an award at the Venice Festival, while *Wild Wings* (1965) won an Oscar.

Anstey served on many bodies connected with film. He was chairman of the British Film Academy in 1956 and again of its successor, the British Academy of Film and Television Arts, in 1967; he led British cultural delegations to the Soviet Union, and was for ten years governor of the British Film Institute. In later years he particularly encouraged scientific film work, and both he and Arthur Elton took active part in the Scientific Film Association, formed in 1943. Later they set up the International Scientific Film Association, where Anstey was regarded with affection and respect by both East and West.

For many years he was chairman of the committee which advised the British Productivity Council on its film-making, and in the 1970s he expressed regret that film-makers had not shown a visionary understanding of the dangerous future of a society based on competitive consumption, nor been able to put over the message clearly before it was too late to change. He wrote: "...both with the council and in my responsibility for films for a number of nationalized industries, I did not sufficiently emphasize the need for job satisfaction and a sense of community service....Those of us who concentrated our film-making in the public sector of the economy were moving ahead of history, but our call to public service never matched the siren song of the market place."

Edgar Anstey was a versatile, far-seeing man, dedicated to public service and social change and always disturbed by society's cultural divisions, such as the rigid compartments of work, leisure and home, and the split between science and the arts. He himself embodied a unifying of the two disciplines, showing in his work the aesthetic skills of the artist and, as one of the very few documentary-makers to be scientifically trained, a profound wish to spread scientific understanding of the world and its technology. He felt the most powerful tool to this end was to dramatize the issues through film, and thereby appeal to people's imagination in the realm of music and poetry. His distinguished and varied career bears witness to his great commitment to his aims.

Born Edgar Harold Macfarlane Anstey. **Parents** Percy Edgar Macfarlane and Kate Anstey. **Marriage** Daphne Lilly, film-maker, 1949. **Children** One son and one daughter. **Education** Watford Grammar School, Hertfordshire. **Career** Joined Empire Marketing Board (EMB) Film Unit and began long association with pioneer documentary film-maker John Grierson, 1931; directed films for EMB, 1931–34; independent film producer and co-founder, Shell Film Unit, 1934–36; joined US news documentary series "The March of Time" as London director of productions, then as foreign editor in New York, 1936–38; joined board of directors, Film Centre, 1940; producer in charge of Shell Film Unit, 1940–45; produced numerous wartime films for ministries and British Armed Forces, 1940–45; film planning and production for BOAC, Venezuelan oil industry and the Colonial Office, 1946–49; organizer and producer-in-charge, British Transport Films, 1949–74. **Related activities** Film critic, the *Spectator*, London, 1946–49; member of Cinematograph Films Council, 1947–49; regular contributor to *The Critics*, BBC radio programme; chair, British Film Academy, 1956, and with Society of Film and Television Arts, 1967; president, International Scientific Film Association, 1961–63; council member, Royal College of Art, 1963–74, senior fellow, 1970; led British cultural delegations to USSR, 1964 and 1966; governor, British Film Institute, 1965–75; chair, British Industrial and Scientific Film Association, 1969–70, president, 1974–81; chair, Children's Film Foundation Production Committee, 1981–83; adjunct professor, Temple University, from 1982. **Awards and honours** British Film Academy Award and Venice Award for *Journey into Spring*, 1957; Venice Award for *Between the Tides*, 1958; British Film Academy Award and Venice Award for *Terminus*, 1961; US Academy Award (Oscar) for *Wild Wings*, 1965; officer, Order of the British Empire, 1969; honorary fellow, British Kinematograph Society, 1974. **Publications** *The Development of Film Technique in Britain (Experiment in the Film)*, 1948. **Films** (include) *Waters* and *Eskimo Village*, both early 1930s; (editor) *Industrial Britain*, 1933; *Granton Trawler*, 1934; *6.30 Collection*, 1934; *Housing Problems*, 1935; *Enough to Eat? (Nutrition)*, 1936; *Airport*, mid-1930s; *A Day in a Factory*, *How to File*, *Fire-guard*, *Young Farmers* and *The Crown of the Year*, all during war years; *Journey into Spring*, 1957; *Between the Tides*, 1958; *Terminus*, 1961; *Wild Wings*, 1965. **Cause of death** Undisclosed, at age 80. **Further reading** Rachael Low, *Documentary and Educational Films of the 1930s: The History of the British Film, 1929–39*, London, 1979; Rachael Low, *Films of Comment and Persuasion of the 1930s*, London, 1979.

MARY ASTOR

American Actress

Born **Quincy, Illinois, 3 May 1906**

Died **Los Angeles, California, 25 September 1987**

Hollywood wasted much of Mary Astor's talent. Although the silken-voiced actress is best known for her portrayals as the generous-hearted, elegant ex-patriate in *Dodsworth* and the treacherous Brigid O'Shaughnessy in *The Maltese Falcon*, her talents were varied and enormous. Unfortunately, the studios typecast her—first, as the sweet heroine, then as the cool, contained screen bitch—rarely giving her the opportunity to display her breadth of talent. But the over-riding image Astor always conveyed to her admirers was that of highly intelligent elegance. Her portrayals were never less than skilful, so that she could draw attention away from the biggest stars or the most threadbare scripts.

Astor's career would possibly have attained a higher profile had her own life not been dogged by personal misfortune, which included three divorces (the first husband died in a plane crash after less than two years of marriage), depression and alcoholism, as well as scandal, when one of her diaries, produced during a custody fight, highlighted her romance with playwright George S. Kaufman. Astor was an excellent writer, narrating her life in a decidedly unglossy fashion in two autobiographies. She also wrote half a dozen novels, most of which gathered good reviews.

It is curious that Astor's career, spanning 40 years and over 100 films, plus TV, theatre and radio, began through no desire of hers. Born Lucile Langhanke, she was the daughter of German immigrant parents who were determined to see their daughter a star. (They were to sue her for non-support in 1934, feeling the $75,000 house she bought them was not enough.) Her father entered her in various beauty contests in an effort not only to groom her for posterity, but her family for prosperity.

Although Lucile got a screen test after being spotted at a beauty contest, the director, D.W. Griffith, recognized the problem of a "walking cash register" father, who would interfere with his actress's development, so he turned her down. However, in 1920 she signed a six-month contract with Famous Players-Lasky in New York, received her new name, and the family moved to Los Angeles. Her first role, a tiny part in *Sentimental Tommy*, ended up on the cutting-room floor. Her second was shelved. However, her part in a two-reeler, *The Beggar Maid*, made after her contract had expired, showed off her luminous beauty, if not an astounding acting ability.

More two-reelers followed, most of little interest, according to Astor ("Thrillers, Canadian Mounties and that sort of thing,"), until she got her first feature film, *John Smith*, by the Selznick brothers—and another contract. In 1923 John Barrymore saw a picture of the 17-year-old Astor in a magazine and was instantly taken with her, casting her opposite him in *Beau Brummel*. He was quite willing to extend the casting to a more personal, fervent role, and by all accounts, she would have liked nothing better. However, her overbearing mama, who saw the need to protect her investment from the great actor's reputation, put an end to any developments behind the camera, much to Barrymore's annoyance. There seems to be no doubt that he was genuinely smitten with Astor, but rumours of a great romance remained just that—rumours.

Since Astor had no voice regarding either role or script—a common situation at that time for everyone but a tiny handful of stars—she was, in her words, "kept on a treadmill of trash" doing "pulp magazine stories"—the sweet heroine in a string of forgettable melodramas. Two of her more likeable films of that time are *Don Q, Son of Zorro* (1925) opposite Douglas Fairbanks and *Don Juan* (1926) with Barrymore, one of the first pictures with synchronized music. By then Astor was considered to be one of the loveliest actresses in Hollywood.

She jumped at the chance to portray a more interesting and substantial role as a gun moll in *Dressed to Kill* (1928) and impressed the critics. Surprisingly, however, she failed a Movietone sound test when the "talkies" arrived and was out of work for ten months. The turning point came when she appeared on stage with Edward Everett Horton in *Among the Married*, a comedy-drama. Her shrewd delivery and natural timing with dialogue ensured that she was flooded with scripts from the studios that had previously shown her a cold shoulder.

Among her best films in the early 1930s were *Holiday* (1930), a sharp talkie which influenced the Cukor remake, *Red Dust* (1932), with Jean Harlow and Clark Gable, and two thrillers with Edward G. Robinson. Sweet heroine had turned tough cookie in half a decade. However, much of her talent was still buried in a string of B pictures with B directors (apart from William Wellman, Michael Curtiz and Robert Florey, who were given inferior scripts).

Her personal life became frayed. She had been left a widow at 25, survived a parental lawsuit, and her second husband was granted custody of their child. When she sued for custody, he used her diary (she maintained that it was forged) which contained a record of alleged romances with film celebrities. Some pages of her admittedly genuine diary came to the public eye the same way, and gave the press a field day about her romance with the then-married George S. Kaufman.

Fortunately, her movie-rating zoomed skyward; audiences stood and cheered when she came on screen during *Dodsworth* (1936)—her personal favourite—with Walter Huston. She gave one of her finest performances, and better films followed, including *The Prisoner of Zenda* (1937), John Ford's *Hurricane* and *Brigham Young* by Henry Hathaway, both in 1940. Astor made a rare stage appearance in Noël Coward's *Tonight at 8:30* and Jamer Thurber's *Male Animal*. She also became a hostess of a radio show, and did dramatic radio work in between. In 1941 her portrayal of a neurotic concert pianist opposite Bette Davis in *The Great Lie* won her an Oscar as best supporting actress. That was followed by *The Maltese Falcon* (1941), directed by John Huston. It became the classic private-eye thriller. She teamed again with Huston and Bogart in *Across the Pacific* (1942) and had a guest spot later that year in Huston's *In This Our Life*.

Until 1949 the quality of her films—not her performances—declined, yet ironically, she worked with other excellent directors, including Preston Sturges, Jules Dassin, Vincente Minnelli, Fred Zinnemann and Mervyn Leroy. Better films included *Palm Beach Story* (1942) and *Little Women* (1949). Although she was only in her thirties, her career had reached a kind of peak. It now began to decline—again, through inept studio handling. However, the process was undoubtedly hastened by further strains in her personal life, shadowed by depression. She was typecast in "motherly" roles, playing Kathryn Grayson's in *Thousands Cheer* (1943), Elizabeth Taylor's in *Cynthia* (1947), Judy Garland's in *Meet Me in St Louis* (1944) and several stars' in *Little Women*. However, a small role as a whore in Zinnemann's *Act of Violence* (1944) proved once again that she could conquer any challenging role given to her.

In 1949 her mental and physical health collapsed, and she entered a sanatorium for alcoholism. She made only one film in the next seven years. During the 1950s she performed on television, in plays and drama series, later doing cameos in embarrassing pictures, such as *Return to Peyton Place* (1961) and *Hush, Hush Sweet Charlotte* (1964). She retired from acting in 1964, finding happiness and probably more satisfaction from her other activities. Her autobiographies were begun as a kind of therapy yet she had become an accomplished author; indeed, writing became more important than her acting. She also organized the Screen Actors' Guild, learned to fly and studied painting and sculpture. All in all, a "happy ending" to a life that had, at times, been as melodramatic as one of her films.

Born Lucile Vasconcellos Langhanke. **Parents** Otto Ludwig Wilhelm and Helen (Vasconcellos) Langhanke. **Marriages** 1) Kenneth Hawks, film director, 1928 (killed in plane crash, 1930); 2) Franklyn Thorpe, gynaecologist, 1931 (divorced, 1935); 3) Manuel del Campo, 1937 (divorced, 1942); 4) Thomas G. Wheelock, 1945 (divorced, 1955). **Children** One daughter, Marylyn, from second marriage; one son, Antonio, from third marriage. **Education** Kenwood-Loring School for Girls, Chicago. **Career** Adopted name of Mary Astor and signed six-month contract with Famous Players-Lasky, New York, 1920; film début, *Bullets or Ballots*, 1921; appeared in two-reelers for independent film company, 1921–23; re-signed with Famous Players-Lasky, 1923; first starring role opposite John Barrymore in *Beau Brummel*; signed with Fox, 1928; contract not renewed on introduction of sound pictures, 1929; undertook freelance and stage work; signed to RKO, 1931; subsequent personal problems, including being sued by her parents for non-support, 1934, and a sex scandal arising from a custody battle over daughter with second husband, 1936, affected career, though she began to gain better film roles; signed to Columbia, mid-1930s; Broadway début, mid-1940s; alcoholism followed by alleged suicide attempt, 1951; turned to writing while making occasional film, stage and television appearances from 1959. **Other activities** Learnt to fly and worked for the Civil Air Patrol at start of World War II. **Offices and memberships** Screen Actors' Guild; American Red Cross. **Awards and honours** Academy Award as best supporting actress for *The Great Lie*, 1941. **Publications** (all published in New York) *My Story* (autobiography), 1959; *The Incredible Charlie Carewe* (novel), 1960; *The Image of Kate* (novel), 1962; *The O'Connors* (novel), 1964; *Goodbye Darling, Be Happy* (novel), 1965; *A Place Called Saturday* (novel), 1969; *A Life on Film* (autobiography), 1971; *My Friends Have Blue Eyes* (juvenile), n.d. **Films** *Bullets or Ballots*, 1921; *The Beggar Maid*, 1921; *Brother of the Bear*, 1921; *The Lady o' the Pines*, 1921; *The Bashful Suitor*, 1921; *The Young Painter*, 1922; *Hope*, 1922; *The Scarecrow*, 1922; *The Angelus*, 1922; *John Smith*, 1922; *The Man Who Played God*, 1922; *The Rapids*, 1922; *The Bright Shawl*, 1923; *Hollywood*, 1923; *To the Ladies*, 1923; *The Marriage-maker*, 1923; *Puritan Passions*, 1923; *Second Fiddle*, 1923;

Success, 1923; *Woman-proof*, 1923; *Beau Brummel*, 1924; *The Fighting American*, 1924; *The Fighting Coward*, 1924; *Inez from Hollywood (The Good Bad Girl)*, 1924; *The Price of a Party*, 1924; *Unguarded Woman*, 1924; *Don Q, Son of Zorro*, 1925; *Enticement*, 1925; *Oh, Doctor!*, 1925; *The Pace That Thrills*, 1925; *Playing With Souls*, 1925; *Scarlet Saint*, 1925; *Don Juan*, 1926; *Forever After*, 1926; *High Steppers*, 1926; *The Wise Guy*, 1926; *No Place to Go*, 1927; *Rose of the Golden West*, 1927; *The Rough Riders*, 1927; *The Sea Tiger*, 1927; *The Sunset Derby*, 1927; *Two Arabian Knights*, 1927; *Dressed to Kill*, 1928; *Dry Martini*, 1928; *Heart to Heart*, 1928; *Romance of the Underworld*, 1928; *Sailors' Wives*, 1928; *Three-Ring Marriage*, 1928; *New Year's Eve*, 1929; *The Woman From Hell*, 1929; *Ladies Love Brutes*, 1930; *The Runaway Bride*, 1930; *The Lash (Adios)*, 1930; *The Royal Bed (The Queen's Husband)*, 1930; *Steel Highway (Other Men's Women)*, 1931; *Behind Office Doors*, 1931; *The Sin Ship*, 1931; *White Shoulders*, 1931; *Smart Woman*, 1931; *Men of Chance*, 1931; *The Lost Squadron*, 1932; *Those We Love*, 1932; *A Successful Calamity*, 1932; *Red Dust*, 1932; *The Little Giant*, 1933; *Jennie Gerhardt*, 1933; *The World Changes*, 1933; *The Kennel Murder Case*, 1933; *Convention City*, 1933; *Easy to Love*, 1934; *Upperworld*, 1934; *Return of the Terror*, 1934; *The Man with Two Faces*, 1934; *The Case of the Howling Dog*, 1934; *The Hollywood Gad-about*, 1934; *I Am a Thief*, 1935; *Straight From the Heart*, 1935; *Red Hot Tyres (Racing Luck)*, 1935; *Dinkey*, 1935; *Page Miss Glory*, 1935; *Man of Iron*, 1935; *The Murder of Dr Harrigan*, 1936; *And So They Were Married*, 1936; *Trapped by Television (Caught by Television)*, 1936; *Dodsworth*, 1936; *Lady from Nowhere*, 1936; *The Prisoner of Zenda*, 1937; *The Hurricane*, 1937; *No Time to Marry*, 1938; *Paradise for Three (Romance for Three)*, 1938; *There's Always a Woman*, 1938; *Woman Against Woman*, 1938; *Listen, Darling*, 1938; *Midnight*, 1939; *Turnabout*, 1940; *Brigham Young—Frontiersman (Brigham Young)*, 1940; *The Great Lie*, 1941; *The Maltese Falcon*, 1941; *In This Our Life*, 1942; *Across the Pacific*, 1942; *The Palm Beach Story*, 1942; *Thousands Cheer*, 1943; *Young Ideas*, 1943; *Meet Me in St Louis*, 1944; *Blonde Fever*, 1944; *Claudia and David*, 1946; *Desert Fury*, 1947; *Cynthia* (*The Rich Full Life*), 1947; *Fiesta*, 1947; *Cass Timberlane*, 1947; *Act of Violence*, 1948; *Little Women*, 1949; *Any Number Can Play*, 1949; *The Power and the Prize*, 1956; *A Kiss Before Dying*, 1956; *The Devil's Hairpin*, 1957; *This Happy Feeling*, 1958; *Stranger in My Arms*, 1959; *Return to Peyton Place*, 1961; *Youngblood Hawke*, 1964; *Hush...Hush, Sweet Charlotte*, 1964. **Stage** (includes) *Among the Married*, 1929; *Tonight at 8.30*; *Male Animal*; *Many Happy Returns*; *Time of the Cuckoo*; *The Starcross Story*, 1954; *Don Juan in Hell*. **Radio** (includes) hostess, *Hollywood Showcase*, 1930–40s. **Television** (includes) *Studio One*; *Producer's Showcase*; *US Steel Hour*, 1950s. **Cause of death** Emphysema, at age 81. **Further reading** David Shipman, *The Great Movie Stars: The Golden Years*, 1979.

PATRICK BASHFORD

Zimbabwean Politician

Born **London, England, 9 October 1915**

Died **Harare, Zimbabwe, 9 September 1987**

Patrick Bashford had an unusual background for a man destined to become one of the founders of a political party which was to play such a vital role in achieving Rhodesia's legitimate independence, but he had, as he described it, "a bee in his bonnet about racial discrimination, which he hated with an almost pathological intensity".

He was born and grew up in London's East End and left England for South Africa at the age of 21, moving on to Rhodesia two years later, where he worked as a builder and carpenter before being called up for war service. After the war he turned to farming and in 1950, when he was 35, bought some bushland in the Karoi area, which he turned into a highly successful tobacco farm.

At this time there was a steady influx of White settlers from both England and South Africa but the majority of the White population failed to appreciate the rapidly changing attitude of all Africans to White domination. Those in urban areas were becoming vociferous about their lack of political power. However, the majority of the White settlers were reluctant to accept the full implications of apartheid as practised in South Africa.

In 1953 Southern Rhodesia, Northern Rhodesia and Nyasaland formed a federation. This had been mooted before the war and was put into practice for economic reasons; there were strong business links between the three countries. However, African opposition was always strong because of the belief that this would mean perpetual White domination. The benefits derived from federation were considered a secondary matter. However, the federation was dissolved after ten years, following the election of a less progressive government in Southern Rhodesia, headed by Sir Edgar Whitehead.

Nyasaland and Northern Rhodesia became the independent countries of Malawi and Zambia, leaving Southern Rhodesia as a British colony with a government demanding dominion status. Eventually, after lengthy discussion with Britain, a new constitution was proposed in 1961 which allowed minority African representation. African political leaders rejected it as being inadequate, and the following year found that their principal political party, the Zimbabwe African People's Union (ZAPU) had been banned and its leaders placed "under restriction". The United Nations tried to intervene but Britain rejected this, steadfastly maintaining that Rhodesia, as a British colony, was beyond UN competence. The governing United Federal Party pledged an end to racialism, which probably accounted for their defeat in the December election. The right-wing Rhodesia Front, led by Winston Field, took office.

Over the next two years Field and the British government held discussions regarding independence, taking the 1961 constitution as a base. However, the talks broke down over the issue of a time limit for majority rule; the Rhodesian government insisted that this be left open and, in 1964, Field was replaced by Ian Smith whose subsequent victory in the May election swept all opposition away.

Smith failed to reach agreement with Britain and, in 1965, issued his Unilateral Declaration of Independence (UDI). Britain declared the Smith regime illegal and Rhodesia to be in a state of rebellion against the Crown. Strong sanctions were imposed, including a total embargo on trade.

During Ian Smith's second meeting with Prime Minister Harold Wilson to discuss a settlement, Bashford's influence on liberal opinion became clear. A group of younger settlers formed the multi-racial Centre Party and Bashford was chosen by consent to lead it. Although handicapped in terms of credibility by being predominantly White, the party rapidly began to appeal to many sections of the Black population and fought vigorously for a negative vote in the 1969 referendum for a constitution validating White power. This brought Bashford considerable personal abuse from his fellow farmers. He was subjected to a poison pen letter campaign and, on one occasion, entered his office to find it daubed with swastikas. But he refused to be intimidated, declined a personal guard for himself and his family, and continued campaigning. The Centre Party subsequently gained 30 per cent of the White vote and had seven successful Black candidates in the 1970 election.

The following years were very difficult in Rhodesia. There was widespread guerrilla warfare, an increase in White military forces, censorship and considerable repression of anyone who opposed the Smith regime. Eventually, however, Smith began to make some concessions urged on by the Centre Party and backed up by world opinion. Even the United States became involved. When Henry Kissinger made his first visit to Africa as secretary of state in 1976, he announced that the US was willing to help bring about majority rule in Rhodesia in any possible way, barring military aid. It was his meeting with Kissinger and discussions with the South African premier that led Smith to announce that his government would agree to majority rule within two years, but there was still a long way to go. In fact, it took a further two years for an interim government to be set up. Independence was granted four years later in 1980.

Bashford himself never sat in parliament but gave unstinting support and encouragement from the sidelines, continuing as a vehement campaigner against all forms of White supremacist legislation.

His last years were not all he might have wished. Tragically, his only son was run down by a car while manning a road block during conscription service with the police. Following this bereavement, Bashford suffered a stroke which left him with permanent disabilities. He nevertheless found the time and energy to write his autobiography and to lodge a further volume of memoirs with the Zimbabwe archives.

Diana Flynn, a fellow co-founder of the Centre Party, has written, "When we first launched the Centre Group, we looked around for an outspoken, fearless person to lead us. Pat had always spoken his mind on the question of man's inhumanity to man, and when he was approached he did not hesitate." As Flynn adds, "He was a caring and courageous man."

Born Thomas Henry Patrick Bashford. **Marriage** Margaret Horsfield, 1940. **Children** One son (deceased) and four daughters. **Education** Shooter's Hill School, London; Woolwich Polytechnic, London. **Emigration** Left England for South Africa, 1935; settled in Southern Rhodesia (later Zimbabwe), 1937. **Military service** Enlisted, 1940–45. **Career** Builder and carpenter, 1935–40; farm manager, 1945–50; managing director, St Brendan's Farm (Private) Ltd, 1950–87; founder, Rhodesia Centre Party, 1968, party president, 1970–74. **Related activities** Secretary, National Industrial Council, Building Industry, 1945–47; assistant secretary, National Building and Housing Board, 1947–49. **Offices and memberships** Founder/member, National Affairs Association, 1945–73. **Cause of death** After-effects of stroke, at age 72.

BILL BOWES

British Cricketer

***Born* Elland, Yorkshire, 25 July 1908**

***Died* England, *circa* 7 September 1987**

Gentle reader, this was written at a grave moment for English cricket. The summer game has hit rock bottom. There is no grimmer humiliation. Australia has just beaten us resoundingly, several times, here in England. Therefore, it is fitting that we "...as 'twere with a defeated joy, With an auspicious and a dropping eye," remember one who smote Australians long ago. When England was Top Cricketing Nation. Sometimes.

William Eric Bowes was born in Elland, near the industrial town of Leeds in the county of Yorkshire, in 1908. He came to cricket by answering an advertisement 20 years later. Marylebone

Cricket Club (headquarters, Lords cricket ground, London) was, for the first time, seeking to establish a ground-staff of young professionals, and Bill Bowes became one of them. He aspired to fast bowling, and he looked an unpromising candidate for this athletic trade, being tall, bony and bespectacled, but he left no one in any doubt about his ability. In his first year with MCC he did the hat trick—dismissing three batsmen with three consecutive balls—against Cambridge University. The following year he was loaned back to his country, and by 1930 had a regular place in a mighty Yorkshire team. Yorkshire generally takes its cricket very seriously, and during the 1930s, most opposition flew like chaff before it. Bowes spearheaded Yorkshire's bowling attack during these years of county championship success and regularly took 100 wickets a season. In 1935, in a match against Northamptonshire, he took 16 wickets with only 35 runs scored against him. The experts say that he was not genuinely fast. This is not strictly to the point, as he obviously did the business. Thanks to his height, and the fact that he kept his bowling arm very straight, he could precipitate the ball to great effect, getting a steep rearing bounce which would test the batsman's nerve and technique.

As predicated earlier, Bill Bowes' most spectacular moments came against the Australians. He was a member of the MCC team which toured Australia in 1932–33—the notorious "Bodyline Tour". Bodyline was a stratagem much favoured by the team's captain Douglas Jardine, for whom the politest epithet is Spartan. The idea was not to knock over the batsman's wicket, but to bowl hard and fast at his person. He would then (went the theory) be forced into unscientific defence, and deflect the ball to a long cordon of fieldsmen poised to catch it. The actual result in this case was some serious injuries and a storm of ill-feeling, during which ungentlemanly telegrams flew between the game's mandarins in Australia and London.

Bowes was not implicated, though he had employed the controversial tactic back in England. He played in only one international match on the tour, but during it he enjoyed the most glorious of moments. The Australian star was the batsman Donald Bradman, one of cricket's all-time greats. Naturally, when he came out to face the bespectacled Bowes, all expected him to devastate as usual. He took a slow, careful walk out to the wicket, allowing his eyes to grow accustomed to the light. Bowes ran up to bowl. Bradman signalled that he wasn't ready. For want of something to do, Bowes fondly recalled, he moved one of his fieldsmen and ran in again. The batsman held up play once more. In the hiatus, Bowes moved another fieldsman, and then it occurred to him. He had got the truth by accident. Bradman was by now expecting the fierce, rising ball that would tempt him to give away a catch. When Bowes finally delivered, he slowed it down, kept it straight and bowled the master straight out. In 1934 the Australians were in England and wreaking revenge. On 18 August Bradman was again at the wicket, and on his way to 244 swift runs. At 6.16 p.m. Bowes at last got him again, with the high bouncer he had been expecting on the other side of the world.

During World War II, Bowes was taken prisoner by the Italians. He returned as an England bowler immediately after the war, but never enjoyed full health. By 1947 he had retired as a player and become cricket correspondent first for the *Yorkshire Evening News*, and then the *Yorkshire Evening Post*. He also returned to Australia as a cricket reporter and was esteemed "a delightful press-box companion"—popular, philosophical and humorous. His autobiography, *Express Deliveries*, appeared in 1949—and he did not employ a ghostwriter.

All told, Bowes took 1639 wickets in first class cricket, conceding an average of 16.76 runs for each of them. He never did anything of note as a batsman, and comments on his fielding are such as "moderate" or "merely jovial". Well, there should always be room for the jovial. In leisure time he was a member of the Magic Circle, the brotherhood of conjurers. Armchair cricketers, such as this writer, may be cheered to know that Bill Bowes' pipe-smoker's wheeze "could be heard a long way off".

Born William Eric Bowes. **Military service** Commissioned officer; prisoner of war, Italy. **Career** First class cricketer, 1928–47; 1529 runs (average 8.58 per innings), 1638 wickets (16.75), played for Marylebone Cricket Club and Yorkshire County Cricket; played in 15 test matches, 28 runs (4.66), 66 wickets (22.33) and two catches. **Related activities** Cricket correspondent, *Yorkshire Evening News* and *Yorkshire Evening Post.* **Offices and memberships** Member, Magic Circle. **Publications** *Express Deliveries* (autobiography), 1949. **Cause of death** Undisclosed, at age 79.

GENERAL J. LAWTON COLLINS

American Soldier
Born **New Orleans, Louisiana, 1 May 1896**
Died **Washington, DC, 12 September 1987**

One of the most successful American generals of World War II, "Lightnin' Joe" Collins commanded in the Far East and the campaign in northern Europe. Later he was US Army chief of staff during the Korean War. He was renowned not only for the speed and forcefulness of his attack, but also for the readiness with which he exposed himself to the same hazards as the troops under his command.

Collins was born one of eleven children to an Irish immigrant father who himself, at age 16, had joined the Union Army in the American Civil War. After a year at the State University of Louisiana, Collins went on to the US Military Academy at West Point in 1913. Graduating with a BS degree in 1917, he was commissioned as a second lieutenant in the 22nd Infantry, stationed at Fort Hamilton, New York.

Collins missed active service in World War I, as his regiment was not sent overseas until May 1919, when it formed part of the Allied army of occupation in western Germany. His promotion, however, was rapid. It was while attached to the army of occupation that he spent some months in command of a battalion at Coblenz; and by June 1920 he was assistant chief of staff in the Plans and Training Division.

Returning to the United States in 1921, Collins spent much of the inter-war period exercising what was an obvious flair for both learning and training. He was an instructor at his old academy, West Point, from 1921 to 1925, taught at the Infantry School from 1927 to 1931, and at the Army War College from 1938 to 1940. In between these appointments Collins studied infantry tactics and field artillery himself, attended staff college, and saw a tour of duty in the Philippines as assistant chief of staff for military intelligence.

By 1940 he was assistant secretary to the general staff of the War Department in Washington, and in June 1941 chief of staff to VII Corps. When, in December 1941, a shocked United States found itself the victim of Japan's surprise attack on Pearl Harbor, it was Collins who was sent out to reorganize the defences of Hawaii.

In May 1942 he was given his first active command, which was to show his brilliance as a general in the field. The 25th Infantry Division (codename "Lightning") was originally employed in the defence of Hawaii. In December 1942, it was dispatched under Collins, as part of XIV Corps, to take Guadalcanal in the Solomon Islands from the Japanese. The struggle for Guadalcanal had already been raging since August 1942, a savage seesaw on land, in the air and at sea. Here Collins proved his tactical virtuosity, deploying his division with a speed and talent for surprising the enemy that earned him the nickname of "Lightnin' Joe". He also proved he was a leader from the front and not from the rear, constantly joining his men under fire in a way that compelled their admiration. Guadalcanal fell in January 1943. Collins and the 25th Division spent the rest of 1943 as part of the American advance through the Solomons, taking New Georgia and Vella Lavella.

Collins was obviously a man who could get results, and in recognition of this he was transferred at the end of 1943 to the European theatre, where the gigantic build-up for the Normandy landings was already under way. He received command of VII Corps, and spent the next six months using his experience in island warfare to train his troops in how to cope with the dense *bocage* of the Norman countryside.

The target of VII Corps on D-Day (6 June) was "Utah" Beach on the extreme west of the attack front, one of the most strongly defended sectors. Nevertheless, Collins's customary drive led the corps across the Cotentin Peninsula by 20 June, and captured Cherbourg by the 26th. VII Corps then headed the break-out from the Allied bridgehead in the neighbourhood of St Lô.

In the subsequent campaign across northern Europe into Germany, VII Corps fought its way through Belgium to Aachen, which it captured in mid-October 1944. During the Ardennes counter-offensive by the Germans, at the end of the year, Collins was given the task of building up the reserve for a counter-attack, but his units were in fact deployed piecemeal in the desperate effort to stem the German attack. After this temporary setback, the Allied advance continued. VII Corps took Cologne in March 1945, and Paderborn on 1 April. At the time of the German surrender, Collins and his men were already on the Elbe and had linked up with the Russians.

After the war, Collins's career as the indispensable man of the US Army continued. He held a succession of senior staff appointments, including a spell as head of the Public Information Section of the War Department from 1945 to 1946.

From 1949 to 1953 Collins was chief of staff, US Army. He was thus the senior army officer throughout the Korean War, and as a member of the Joint Chiefs of Staff had responsibility for directing the operations of General MacArthur, the commander-in-chief in the Far East. When MacArthur's insistence on total victory in Korea was followed by his dismissal in April 1951 at the hands of President Truman, public uproar ensued. Collins was firmly associated with the repudiation by the Joint Chiefs of Staff of MacArthur's strategy which, they claimed before Congress, "would involve us in the wrong war, at the wrong place, at the wrong time, and with the wrong enemy".

Collins also emerged from the Korean War a member of the so-called "Never Again Club" of senior army officers. This influential group vowed it would never again commit troops in an Asian theatre of war without a government commitment to bomb enemy cities and supply lines from the air. Some of the implications of this stance became apparent during Collins's last public appointment, as the US representative in the NATO Standing Group and Military Committee from 1953 to 1956. In this capacity he spent six months in Vietnam as a military adviser with ambassadorial status. In the wake of the French withdrawal from Vietnam and the country's partition in 1954, the Collins mission was to train the South Vietnamese army to defend South Vietnam without any American troop presence. In the event, the only lasting lesson South Vietnamese commanders appear to have learned was to rely utterly upon American troops and (the bitter legacy of the "Never Again Club") American bombers.

Collins retired in 1956, and spent the rest of his active life as a director in private business, and as voluntary chairman of a variety of educational and charitable concerns.

Born Joseph Lawton Collins. **Parents** Jeremiah Bernard and Catherine (Lawton) Collins. **Marriage** Gladys Easterbrook, 1921. **Children** Gladys May, Nancy Katherine and Joseph Easterbrook. **Education** Louisiana State University, 1912–13; United States Military Academy,

West Point, BS, 1917; graduated, Infantry School, Fort Benning, Georgia, 1926, advanced course, Field Artillery School, Fort Sill, Oklahoma, 1927; Command and General Staff School, 1931–33, Army Industrial College, 1936–37, Army War College, 1937–38. **Career** Commissioned second lieutenant, United States Army, 1917; assigned 22nd Infantry, Fort Hamilton, New York, 1917; commanded 18th Infantry battalion, Coblenz, Germany, also serving at Montabaur and Selters, Germany, 1919–20; assistant chief of staff, Plans and Training Division, American forces, Germany, 1920–21; instructor, West Point, 1921–25; instructor, Infantry School, Fort Benning, 1927–31; served with 23rd Brigade (Philippine Scouts), later assistant chief of staff, Military Intelligence, Philippines, 1933–36; instructor, Army War College, 1938–40; assigned to office of the secretary, War Department General Staff, 1940–41; chief of staff, VII Corps, Birmingham, Alabama, 1941–42; chief of staff, Hawaiian Department, 1942; commanding general, 25th Infantry Division, 1942–44; commander, VII Corps, 1944–45; deputy commanding general and chief of staff, Army Ground Forces, Washington; chief, Public Information, War Department, 1945–56; deputy and vice chief of staff, United States Army, 1946–49, chief of staff, 1949–53; United States representative, NATO, Military Committee and Standing Group, 1953–55; special representative of United States in Vietnam, with personal rank of ambassador, 1955–56; retired, 1956. **Other activities** Director and vice-chairman, President's Committee for Hungarian Refugee Relief, 1956–57; chairman, board of directors, Foreign Student Service Council of Greater Washington, Incorporated, 1957–58; vice-chairman, board of directors, Pfizer International and subsidiaries, 1957–69, consultant from 1969; chairman, advisory committee, Washington office, Institute of International Education; member, executive committee, National Catholic Community Service; general chairman, fundraising committee for the extension of the Catholic Chapel of the Most Holy Trinity, United States Military Academy. **Offices and memberships** Trustee, Institute of International Education, Incorporated, New York City, 1957–65. **Awards and honours** Distinguished Service Medal with three Oak Leaf Clusters; Silver Star with Oak Leaf Cluster, Legion of Merit with Oak Leaf Cluster; Navy Gold Star; Bronze Star; Companion of the Order of the Bath; two Order of Suvorov, second class (Soviet Union); Croix de Guerre Palm; Grand Officer of the Legion of Honour (France); Grand Officer, Order of Leopold II; Croix de Guerre with Palm (Belgium), 1940; Grand Cross, Royal Order of George I (Greece); Grand Officer, Orden de Boyaca (Columbia); Taekuk Distinguished Military Service Medal with Gold Star (Republic of Korea); Laetare Medal, 1950; Cardinal Gibbons Medal, Catholic University, 1955; honorary LLD: Tulane University, 1953, Georgetown University, 1956. **Cause of death** Heart attack, at age 91.

SIR WILLIAM COOK

British Civil Servant

Born **Wiltshire, England, 10 April 1905**

Died **London, England, 16 September 1987**

The life of Sir William Cook has been described as one of hydrogen bombs and nuclear reactors. To a certain extent this is true, but to accept it as the whole truth would be to disregard his vital contribution to defence systems in many fields, including Europe and the USA.

He joined the Civil Service at the age of 23 following his graduation from Bristol University, and joined the Research Department based at Woolwich, which was then administered by the War Office. At that time, 1928, armaments work generally had a low profile, although the branch Cook entered—ballistics—was considered important. Within a few years, fears of a further war gained credence and he was given more responsibility as the need for rearmament became apparent. He was one of the first people in Britain to appreciate the role of the rocket in weapons systems and, during World War II, his work involved research into its development under the aegis of the Ministry of Supply. Following the war, he was involved in investigating the development of the V1 and V2 rockets in Germany, which had brought such fear to Londoners during the last months of the war, and appreciated only too clearly the outcome of marrying rocket systems with nuclear weapons. At that time the only two atomic bombs used in war had been dropped by aeroplane.

Cook was made director of the new research and development establishment for rockets, again under the Ministry of Supply, but, within a couple of years, it became clear that the government could not be persuaded to maintain the type of effort Cook felt essential for Britain. The decision to slow down British rocket development and rely on the Americans left him disheartened and precipitated his move to the Admiralty, where he was appointed director of physical research. He rapidly mastered what was an entirely new field of work, involving a totally different element, but his abilities and influence led to the development of considerable advances in underwater warfare. In 1950, at the age of 45, he became chief of the Royal Naval Scientific Service, which he headed with skill and understanding for four years. He gained the full confidence of both the service and his naval colleagues. His decision to move into the field of nuclear energy in 1954 was felt as a great loss.

He became deputy director of the Aldermaston research centre into nuclear power. At this time Britain was developing its own hydrogen bomb and, in the remarkably short span of three years (plus a great deal of hard work on his own part in mastering all the technical aspects of the work), the British weapons were ready to undergo what proved successful testing in Australia, and Cook earned a knighthood. It cannot, however, have been altogether a happy period for him because, although his work had borne fruit, there was a considerable public outcry, particularly among younger people, against the development of nuclear weapons. London saw many demonstrations against the bomb and the Campaign for Nuclear Disarmament (CND) came into being with its long Easter marches beginning at Aldermaston on Good Friday and culminating with a massive rally in London on Easter Monday.

At this point in his career, Sir William, now 53, turned his attention to the civil aspects of nuclear power. He joined the UK Atomic Energy Authority at a time of rapid expansion. The major part of his work involved the application of knowledge gained from the building of reactors for military use to the economic production of electricity on a massive scale. Prior to this time, electricity had primarily relied on fossil fuels, mainly coal, which was obviously going to run out within a very few years. He was responsible for the development of the reactors used in the first British Nuclear Power Programme and continued the development of the advanced gas-cooled reactor which was subsequently to form part of the second programme. He also initiated investigation into the development of the steam-generating heavy-water system. Before he could take this work further, however, he was invited back into the field of defence.

In 1964 he became deputy chief scientific adviser in the reorganized Ministry of Defence. His wide experience enabled him to advise on the many difficult decisions to be made about different projects. He was held in such high regard that in 1967 he was appointed chief adviser (Projects), and it was in this position that he had overall responsibility for new weapons systems. Accompanied only by an embassy defence attaché and a counsellor for defence supply, he held talks in Bonn late in 1967 with senior representatives of the German Ministry of Defence and the

Luftwaffe. These and subsequent talks led to the project, later named Tornado, to develop the joint Anglo/German/Italian multi-role combat aircraft.

Although he retired from full-time work in 1970, at the age of 65, Cook continued as a consultant to the ministry and also began an assessment, for the government, of prospects for the RB–211 engine which had been developed by Rolls-Royce to power the American Lockheed Tristar jet. He joined the board of the newly formed Rolls-Royce (1971) Ltd and contributed greatly to the company's renewed development, both in the UK and in collaboration with European partners.

Cook has been described as a man of small stature but huge energies. His dedication to his scientific work and to his country was absolute. His contribution towards maintaining the balance of power in the world and in working for closer links between European countries should not be undervalued.

Born William Richard Joseph Cook. **Father** John Cook. **Marriages** 1) Grace Purnell, 1929; 2) Gladys Allen, 1939. **Children** One daughter from first marriage; one son and one daughter from second marriage. **Education** Trowbridge High School; Bristol University. **Career** Entered civil service, 1928; various scientific posts in research establishments of War Office and Ministry of Supply, 1928–47; director, Physical Research, Admiralty, 1947–50; chief, Royal Navy Scientific Service, 1950–54; deputy director, Atomic Weapons Research Establishment, Aldermaston, 1954–58; member, Atomic Energy Authority, for engineering and production, 1958–59, for development and engineering, 1959–61, for reactors, 1961–64; deputy chief scientific adviser, Ministry of Defence, 1964–67; chief adviser for projects and research, Ministry of Defence, 1968–70; retired from civil service, 1970. **Related activities** Director: Buck and Hickman Limited, 1970–83, Rolls-Royce (1971) Limited, 1971–76, GEC-Marconi Electronics Limited, 1972–79; chairman, Marconi International Marine Company, 1971–75; board member: Rolls-Royce Turbomeca Limited, Rolls-Royce Turbo-Union Limited; consultant: Ministry of Defence, British Telecom. **Awards and honours** Companion of the Order of the Bath, 1951; knighted, 1958; fellow, Royal Society, 1962; honorary DSc: Strathclyde, 1967, Bath, 1975; Knight Commander of the Order of the Bath, 1970; fellow, Institute of Physics; fellow, Institute of Nuclear Engineers. **Cause of death** Undisclosed, at age 82.

LADY DIANA DELAMERE

British Socialite

***Born* England, 1911**

***Died* Soysambu, Kenya, 3 September 1987**

The unsolved murder of a lover, four marriages, sex, drink, aristocracy, Africa and a *ménage à trois* in old age—such is the stuff that films are made of. Lady Diana Delamere died around the time that "her" film, *White Mischief*, was released for the entertainment of Europe's cinema audiences. Based on the novel by James Fox, which in turn was inspired by some facts and much fiction of Lady Delamere's life, *White Mischief* brought the story of aristocratic murder in the wilds of Kenya to the silver screen. More than just a whodunnit, the film also aimed to portray the decadence of British colonial life, the fermentation of sex and violence that so often goes with moral and political bankruptcy.

Admittedly, it was a good story. The central event of *White Mischief* is the murder, on 24 January 1941, of the 22nd Earl of Erroll in his Buick a few miles outside Nairobi, Kenya. Erroll was not only military secretary of East Africa Command, but also a notorious womanizer, whose romantic and sexual exploits with Diana Caldwell were a flaunted, public secret. Diana at this time was a married woman, and the film shows through a mist of mysterious manipulations how her husband, "Jock" Delves Broughton, was brought to trial for Erroll's murder. At the same time, more than a hint of suspicion is cast upon Diana who appears to reside, as film creatures do, at the heart of a veritable web of secrecy and intrigue.

But this is how the story goes. Real life followed the plot only up to a point. Jock Broughton was acquitted and the crime remained unsolved. Diana had a life after Erroll, in which she became rather more of an interesting person than the film would seem to suggest, and less of a cliché.

Diana Caldwell was already married (to a pianist) when she met Sir Delves Broughton during the London Blitz. It is not clear whether it was romantic adventure or sheer force of circumstance that made them flee Britain together, but in any case they landed up in Kenya where, as soon as Diana obtained her divorce, they got married. Romantic bliss did not last, however, and as soon as Erroll came on the scene, Diana was lost. A torrid love-affair developed between them, and a few less-than-chivalric confrontations between lover and husband ensued. A few days later Erroll was found dead. The rest is film history, until after Jock Broughton's acquittal. Under miserable circumstances and obviously much disturbed by the events in Kenya, Broughton returned to England. A year later he committed suicide in a Liverpool hotel. Ostensibly, then, Diana *femme fatale* was connected with the death of two men. But who, we might ask, or what, had been really responsible?

Broughton, Diana, Erroll and the friends who witnessed the events in Kenya in the 1940s were all part of a largely aristocratic set residing in "Happy Valley", a colonial paradise in the so-called White Highlands of Kenya. Drugs, drink, and sexual licence were reputed to be endemic among these wealthy settlers who, unfettered by the constraints of war which suffocated Britain, lived the good life while it lasted. But here again it is difficult to disentangle myth from reality, for it is also known that despite this reputation for "decadence" Diana Caldwell was addicted to all sports—from hunting to fishing to flying—and had a genuine love for Kenya, its landscape and its people. This is also evidenced by the fact that in 1943 she married Gilbert Colville, a landowner, cattle-rancher and recognized expert on the Masai whom most of the Happy Valley crowd dismissed as having "gone native". However, Diana and he had many Kenyan interests in common, and neither were prone to soul-searching about the contradictory nature of their position as White Britons in Kenya. To complicate matters further for the political analyst, it must also be recorded that the couple supported Kenyan independence long before it actually came about. Although this stance did not enhance their popularity among fellow Whites in the British community, it may well explain why they were left in peace when Kenya came into existence as an independent nation.

By the time this happened, however, Diana was divorced from Colville and married to the Lord Delamere, her last husband. Contrary to popular expectations (based on the acrimonious separations of the past which had resulted in such death and destruction), Diana and her new husband remained close friends with Gilbert Colville. For most of the year the three lived together in the affluent seclusion of Soysambu, maintaining a happy *ménage à trois*. Only during the winter season did Colville desert them for an even quieter place, in order to avoid Lady Diana's numerous guests from Britain who would come over to Kenya to bask in the warmth.

By all accounts, Lady Delamere was an adventurous woman with a lust for life and love. She was also a great hostess and warm friend to the many who visited her beloved corner of Kenya. Whether she was a murderess too is a question perhaps best left to the imagination. She was buried next to her third and fourth husbands, both of whom predeceased her some years earlier. Positioned between two men once more, Lady Delamere's final resting place seems the ironic mirror-image of the scandal which had been at the centre of her life, except that on that occasion, subsequently known as "white mischief", she had been the only one who survived.

Born Diana Caldwell. **Father** Seymour Caldwell. **Marriages** 1) Vernon Motion (divorced); 2) Sir Henry John Delves Broughton, 1940 (committed suicide, 1942); 3) Gilbert de Préville Colville, 1943 (divorced, 1955); 4) Lord Delamere, 1955 (died, 1979). **Emigration** Settled in Kenya, 1940. **Cause of death** Undisclosed, at age 76. **Further reading** James Fox, *White Mischief*, 1982.

SIR WILLIAM DICKSON

British Air Marshal

Born **England, 24 September 1898**

Died **England, 12 September 1987**

Sir William Dickson was an airman of wide experience, who saw active service in both world wars. He was the first chief of the defence staff, an amalgam of all three services, in the late 1950s.

Dickson happened to be a direct descendant of the illicit union of Lord Nelson and Lady Hamilton; his maternal grandfather was the son of Horatia Nelson, the naval hero's only child. More than one observer remarked Dickson's resemblance to his ancestor: he was small, kindly, magnetic and seemingly impervious to fear. As Lord Trenchard, father of the Royal Air Force, told Dickson's fiancée, her future husband was "brave as a lion and clever as a monkey".

After school in Sussex, Dickson completed his education at Haileybury College, and entered the Royal Naval Air Service in 1916. He spent his first year of the war flying patrols in the North Sea and the English Channel. In 1917, flying a Sopwith Pup, he participated in the first landings on the prototype aircraft carrier, HMS *Furious*. This led to the first ever bombing raid conducted from a carrier, when Dickson and six other Sopwith Camel pilots from *Furious* bombarded the German Zeppelin base at Tondern in Schleswig-Holstein. The raid was successful but costly, Dickson's being one of the few aircraft to return to *Furious*.

After the war, in 1919, Dickson transferred to a permanent commission in the Royal Air Force but continued to do naval flying work, including experimental deck landings. From 1921 to 1922 he tested aircraft for the Royal Aircraft Establishment, then a motorcycle accident in 1923 led to an enforced three years of deskwork for the Air Ministry. Here he gained experience of both the operational and intelligence aspects of air power.

From 1927 to the outbreak of World War II Dickson combined practical flying service with staff work. He commanded a succession of fighter squadrons, attended Andover Staff College, served in India from 1929 to 1930, and worked for the Imperial Defence College.

For the first two years of the war he was in the Directorate of Plans, in the chief of air staff's department, becoming director himself in 1941. Between 1942 and 1943 he returned to flying service, commanding 9 and 10 Groups in Fighter Command, then briefly leading 83 Group in preparation for the Normandy landings. Shortly before D-Day, however, Dickson was sent to take overall command of the Desert Air Force, by that time operating over Italy. This put him in charge of air support for the Allied advance up the Italian Peninsula in 1944–45.

In the post-war period Dickson's rise through the upper echelons of the service was steady. After a spell on the air staff, he became air commander-in-chief for the Mediterranean and Middle East during the difficult period following the creation of Israel. Further senior staff appointments in Britain followed, including a time as chairman of the Chiefs of Staffs Committee from 1956 to 1959, a post overtaken by the new job of chief of the defence staff in 1958. This post was the creation of the Macmillan government, and marked the first unitary staff organization for all the armed forces.

Dickson retired in 1959, leaving behind a reputation for honesty in decision-making (typified by dropping the excessively expensive Supermarine Swift fighter), and for realistic appraisal of priorities, such as admitting the reduced need for air resources in an age of nuclear missiles.

Born William Forster Dickson. **Parents** C.C. Forster, Chancery Registrar, and Agnes (Nelson) Dickson. **Marriage** Patricia Marguerite Allen, 1932. **Children** Two daughters (one deceased). **Education** Bowden House, Seaford, Sussex; Haileybury College, Hertfordshire. **Career** Royal Naval Air Service, 1916–18; transferred to Royal Air Force, 1918, permanently commissioned, 1918; employed on naval flying work, 1919–21; test pilot, Royal Aircraft Establishment, 1921–22; Air Ministry, 1923–26; 56 (Fighter) Squadron, 1926–27; Royal Air Force Staff College, Andover, 1927–28; posted to India, 1929, served on Northwest Frontier, 1929–30, and at Royal Air Force headquarters, New Delhi; commanded Royal Air Force station, Hawkinge, and 25 (Fighter) Squadron, 1935–36; staff director, Staff College, 1936–38; Imperial Defence College, 1939; director of plans, Air Ministry, 1941–42; commanded 9 and 10 Groups, Fighter Command, 1942–43; commanded 83 Group in Tactical Air Force, 1943–44; commanded Desert Air Force, 1944; assistant chief of air staff (Policy), Air Ministry, 1945–46; vice-chief of air staff, Air Council, Air Ministry, 1946–48; commander-in-chief, Middle East Air Force, 1948–50; member for supply and organization, Air Council, 1950–52; chief of air staff, 1953–56; chairman, Chiefs of Staff Committee, 1956–59; chief of defence staff, 1958–59; retired, 1959. **Offices and memberships** Ex-services Mental Welfare Society, 1960–76; president, Royal Central Asian Society, 1961–65; Haileybury Society, 1962; Forces Help Society and Lord Roberts Workshops, 1974–81. **Awards and honours** Companion of the Distinguished Service Order, 1918; Air Force Cross, 1922; Companion of the Order of the Bath, 1942; officer, Order of the British Empire, 1934; Russian Order of Suvorov, 1944; United States Legion of Merit; Commander of the Order of the British Empire, 1945; Knight Commander of the Order of the British Empire, 1946; Knight Commander of the Order of the Bath, 1952; Knight Grand Cross of the Order of the Bath, 1953; master, The Glass Seller's Company, 1964. **Cause of death** Undisclosed, at age 88.

MORTON FELDMAN

American Composer

***Born* New York City, New York, 12 January 1926**

***Died* Buffalo, New York, 3 September 1987**

Morton Feldman was an experimental composer who was one of the leading lights of his generation of American avant-garde composers. He was closely associated with John Cage, and can be called the forerunner of the minimalist movement since he pioneered the use of hypnotic repetition to create atmospheric, timeless music 20 years before Phillip Glass, Michael Nyman and Steve Reich were given credit for its invention.

Feldman's compositions were atmospheric, marked by extremely low dynamic levels and slow formal evolution in which silence is often as important as sound. His main interest was in different textures and combinations of timbres, usually played very softly. Feldman's music has proved to be exceedingly demanding for the musician. Some of the pieces are a stamina test, lasting as long as four and a half hours, and he often calls for notes to be sounded without any noticeable attack or fluctuation. This insistence on pure tones has been a defining feature of his music.

Feldman studied the piano with Vera Maurina-Press and had composition lessons with Wallingford Riegger in 1941 and Stefan Wolpe in 1944. He later claimed that encountering the abstract expressionist movement in painting in the late 1940s influenced him more than any musician, with the possible exception of Webern and Varèse. These abstract painters, together with the composer and musical philosopher, John Cage (whom Feldman met in 1940), and the avant-garde composers Brown, Wolff and Tudor, combined to provide the right environment for Feldman's experiments.

Among his innovations was the concept of indeterminacy, which he first used in *Projections I–IV* (1950–51) for different instrumental combinations. In such works he adopted similar titles to the abstract expressionist painters, often borrowed from the world of science. The indeterminacy was indicated by a form of graphic notation which replaced the conventional system of notes on a musical staff. It indicated only an approximation of the instrumentation and notes to be played in a musical "action", specifying the instrumental range and the number of notes per time-unit but on precise notes or durations.

Feldman sometimes transcribed these pieces into normal staff notation for practical performance purposes, which was an indication that the new method had its drawbacks. In fact, Feldman abandoned graphic notation altogether during 1953 to 1958, feeling that he had exhausted the possibilities of such imprecision, but the return to conventional staff notation proved equally restrictive; he still considered flexibility essential to the musical expression and the problem with conventional notation was that he always ended up with a fixed piece.

He solved the problem eventually by abolishing rhythmic notation while retaining control over pitch, only writing note heads and general tempo markings. *Last Pieces* for piano (1963) uses this method. Feldman also evolved another solution, which was simple but more experimental: a single part was given to a number of players to produce "a series of reverberations from an identical sound source". In practice, in a work such as *Piece for Four Pianos* (1957), the source becomes muddied and the result is highly complex polyphony, the structure heavily reliant on repetition. Another solution was to retain most aspects of notation but leave the note lengths relatively free for the player to choose. This was tried in the *Durations* series (1960–62), a group of works showing Feldman's mastery of instrumentation; the individual lines are clearly distinguished and yet the whole blends perfectly.

Around 1970, having finally found the way to create fully composed works that did justice to his tranquil, non-rhetorical sound world, Feldman abandoned graphic notation altogether. Conventional notation now gave him what he wanted. As the musicologist William Bland has written, "Aural satisfaction seems to be the sole arbiter in all Feldman composes—the intention being to 'wash' a period of time with a general hue."

Born Morton Feldman. **Education** Studied piano with Vera Maurina-Press and composition with Wallingford Riegger, 1941, Stefan Wolpe, 1944. **Career** Composer, strongly influenced by abstract expressionism of modern painting, 1940s–87. **Compositions** *Illusions*, 1950; *Projections I–IV*, 1950–51; *Intersections I*, for orchestra, 1951, *II* and *III*, for piano, 1952, 1953, *IV*, for cello, 1953; *Marginal Intersection*, for orchestra, 1951; *Four Songs to e.e. cummings*, for soprano, cello and piano, 1951; *Extensions I*, for violin and piano, 1951, *III*, for piano, 1952, *IV*, for three pianos, 1952–53, *V*, for two cellos; *Intermissions I–VI*, 1951–53; *Intersection*, for tape, 1951; *Structures*, for string quartet, 1951; *Piano Pieces*, 1952, 1955, 1956, 1963, 1964, 1977; *Two Pieces*, for two pianos, 1954; *Three Pieces*, for string quartet, 1954–56; *Piece*, for four pianos, 1957; *Two Pianos*, for two pianos, 1957; *Two Instruments*, for cello and horn, 1958; *Atlantis*, for orchestra, 1958; *Last Pieces*, for piano, 1959; *Trio*, for three pianos, 1959; *Trio*, for two pianos and cello, 1959; *Ixion* (*Summerspace*), for ten instruments or two pianos (ballet), 1960; *Durations I–V*, 1960–61; *The Swallows of Salangan*, for chorus and 23 instruments (cantata), 1960; *Out of "Last Pieces"*, for orchestra, 1960–61; *Journey to the End of the Night*, for soprano and four wind instruments, 1960; *Structures*, for orchestra, 1960–62; *Intervals*, for baritone and instruments, 1961; *Two Pieces*, for clarinet and string quartet; *Philip Guston*, for small orchestra, 1962; *For Franz Kline*, for soprano, violin, cello, horn, chimes and piano, 1962; *The Straits of Magellan*, for seven instruments, 1963; *De Kooning*, for piano, violin, cello, horn and percussion, 1963; *Four Instruments*, for violin, cello, glockenspiel and piano, 1963; *Chorus and Instruments I–II*, 1963, 1967; *Vertical Thoughts I–V*, for different instrumental combinations, 1963; *The O'Hara Songs*, 1963; *Numbers*, for nine instruments, 1964; *Rabbi Akiba*, for soprano and ten instruments, 1964; *The King of Denmark*, for percussion, 1965; *Christian Wolff at Cambridge*, for chorus a capella, 1965; *Two Pieces*, for three pianos, 1966; *First Principles*, for large instrumental ensemble, 1966–67; *In Search of an Orchestration*, for orchestra, 1967; *False Relationships and the Extended Ending*, for violin, cello, trombone, three pianos and chimes, 1968; *On Time and the Instrumental Factor*, for orchestra, 1969; *Between Categories*, for two pianos, two chimes, two violins and two cellos, 1969; *Madame Press Died Last Week at Ninety*, for chamber ensemble, 1970; *The Viola in My Life I*, for solo viola and six instrumentalists, *II*, for solo viola and seven instrumentalists, *III*, for viola and piano, *IV*, for viola and orchestra, 1970–71; *Pianos and Voices*, for five voices, 1971; *Three Clarinets, Cello and Piano*, 1971; *Chorus and Orchestra I–II*, 1971–72; *I Met Heine on the Rue Fürstenberg*, for voice and six instrumentalists, 1971; *The Rothko Chapel*, for solo viola, chorus and percussion, 1971; *Cello and Orchestra*, 1971–72; *Voice and Instruments I*, for soprano and chamber orchestra, 1972, *II*, for voice, clarinet, cello and double bass, 1974; *Voices and Instruments I*, for chorus and nine instrumentalists, *II*, for three voices, flute, two cellos and double bass, 1972; *For Frank O'Hara*, for seven instrumentalists, 1973; *String Quartet and Orchestra*, 1973; *Voices and Cello*, for two voices and cello, 1973; *Instruments I*, for five instruments, *II*, for nine instrumentalists, 1974–75; *Piano and Orchestra*, 1975; *Four Instruments*, for piano quartet, 1975; *Oboe and Orchestra*, 1976; *Orchestra*, 1976; *Voice, Violin and Piano*, 1976; *Routine Investigations*, for oboe, trumpet, piano, viola, cello and double bass, 1976; *Elemental Procedures*, for chorus and orchestra, 1976; *The Spring of Chosroes*, for violin and piano, 1977; *Neither*, monodrama after an original text by Samuel Beckett, for soprano and orchestra, 1977; *Only*, 1977; *Flute and Orchestra*, 1977–78; *Why Patterns*, 1978. **Cause of death** Pancreatic cancer, at age 61.

HENRY FORD II

American Businessman and Industrialist

Born **Detroit, Michigan, 4 September 1917**

Died **Detroit, Michigan, 29 September 1987**

He never received a university degree, had little mechanical ability, and by the time he joined the family business, he possessed no relevant business experience. Yet within a year he was elected vice-president, rising to executive vice-president four months later; it was only a matter of time before he took control of the company. After one decade, Henry Ford II had turned a multi-million dollar loss-maker into a company which netted $15 million a month. Although his methods were decidedly different, the successor and namesake of the man who founded America's Ford Motor Company followed in his grandfather's footsteps. One established an empire; the other ensured its survival.

The eldest son of Edsel Bryant and Eleanor (Clay) Ford, Henry Ford II showed no hint of his amazing managerial skills and shrewd business sense in early life. He spent a childhood somewhat sheltered from the outside world; together with his brothers and sisters, the young automotive heir was kept well away from the public eye—and from kidnappers' clutches. He was an average, indifferent student who preferred athletics to books, a characteristic which he carried over to his university days at Yale where he managed the Yale crew. Although the young Ford remained at that institution for the requisite four years, he never earned his degree; his senior thesis was rejected after it was revealed that it had been ghostwritten, and Henry Ford could not be bothered to write another one.

After this unpromising start, Ford took a job as a mechanic at his family's plant at Dearborn, Michigan, with the idea of learning about the automobile business from the ground up. However, it soon became evident that Henry Ford's mechanical ability was virtually nil, and that he was in no hurry to advance himself within the company. Thus, when World War II broke out, the young Ford seemed glad to enlist in the navy, where he rose from ensign to lieutenant. In 1943, however, Edsel Ford died suddenly at the age of 50, leaving the Ford Motor Company without a visible head. Secretary of the Navy Frank Knox decided that Henry Ford could best serve his country by returning to the business. Thus, at age 26, Ford found himself learning about the industry once more—this time, from the top down.

There was much more to Knox's decision than simple compassion. The government had just signed a contract with the firm to manufacture thousands of planes for the war effort, and there were rumours that Ford Motor Company was in serious financial trouble. Those rumours, young Henry soon learned, were not without foundation.

Ford's grandfather had kept a tight hold over the company, despite his advanced age, and that control consisted in large part of relying on an ex-prizefighter named Harry Bennett. As the eldest Ford grew more indecisive—especially after suffering two strokes—Bennett's power in the company increased, to the extent that he eventually dominated the employees by means of a Gestapo-like secret police force. Management had been neglected for megalomania, so that by the time Henry Ford II came into the company, its output had dropped from controlling 40 per cent of US car sales to less than 20 per cent, and its profits had shrunk from $80,000,000 in 1929 to just $6,000,000 in 1941. Through the influence of his mother and grandmother (both major shareholders), young Ford rose to the presidency of the company. His first act was to fire Harry Bennett and his supporters.

As if the company were not in enough trouble, more trials were added in the form of union disputes. Fortunately, however, Ford developed and maintained good relations with the workers' union officials, negotiated with them, and agreed to a 15 per cent wage increase in return for a union guarantee against illegal strike action. "If we can solve the problem of human relations in industry," the new industrialist said, "I believe we can make as much progress toward lower costs during the next ten years as we made during the past quarter century through the development of the machinery of mass production." His beliefs paid off. While his employees stayed on their jobs with their new and higher wages, those at rival General Motors walked out on strike.

Next, Ford began completely to reorganize the ailing company itself. He decentralized managerial responsibility in all its departments, and promoted many men within the firm. He also brought in important new talent from the outside, including the so-called "whizz kids"—a group of ex-air force officers who could apply military management techniques to private business. Another strategy implemented by Ford was to divest the company of many numerous side-businesses gathered by his grandfather. The focus of the Ford Company, he felt, should first and foremost be directed on automobiles, yet while Ford cut down on diversification, he also expanded the company's car automotive works both at home and abroad.

In what at least one journalist has termed "a mixture of luck and judgement", Ford's policies turned the tide. By 1950 the once-ailing company was netting $265,000,000, and by 1953 it had become the second most profitable name in the automotive industry, a position it held for more than two decades. The only major setback came with the introduction of the Edsel, a new car Ford pushed into production in memory of his father, despite warnings from some of his executives. Yet even when the Edsel proved a flop, Ford shouldered all the blame for its failure and kept going, and the company produced machines such as the highly successful Falcon, the sporty Mustang, the Maverick and the Pinto—all mainly the creation of Lee Iacocca, who worked for Ford for a number of years. In the meantime, the company's Lincoln–Mercury division was challenging General Motor's Buick, Oldsmobile and Pontiac market.

In addition to his corporate success, Henry Ford II was also making himself known outside the company. While he strongly opposed what he saw as politically motivated legislation against the industry, and waged open warfare with certain "gold-digging" environmentalists, he also welcomed the serious trend towards greater safety and pollution consciousness, i.e. what he considered as "legitimate" attempts to safeguard both the roads and the environment.

Ford's energy did not stop even there. As a trustee of the Ford Foundation, a philanthropic organization established by his grandfather, he became extremely active in international and civic affairs, giving aid to private universities and medical centres, among other worthy causes. Ford was especially concerned with political and social affairs. Following the violent Watts riots in Los Angeles in 1966, he warned: "The greatest danger to a civilized nation is the man who has no stake in it and nothing to lose by rejecting all that civilization stands for." He was a firm believer in equal opportunity ("the most urgent task our nation faces"), and put his advice into practice by ordering the Ford Motor Company to hire illiterate Black workers, some of them ex-convicts, in 1967. Not surprisingly, President Lyndon Johnson named him chairman of the National Alliance of Businessmen in 1968, to help coordinate industry and government in finding jobs for the unemployed.

One of the richest men in the US, the one-time reluctant schoolboy had turned into a hardworking industrial leader. Ford often put in ten-hour days, and occasionally stayed at his office overnight. He was a great internationalist with a love of travel, dancing and history—the latter certainly did not coincide with his grandfather's maxim that "history is bunk". Another outside interest was his art collection, which contained works by Van Gogh, Degas, Matisse and Cézanne. He also had a passion for hunting.

Because of his charitable efforts, his leadership and contributions to the national community (including the urban renewal plan for Detroit's Renaissance Center), Henry Ford received an honorary doctor of laws degree from Yale in 1972, as well as the Presidential Medal of Freedom in 1969. It seemed that the only arena in which he was something less than successful was his personal life: he divorced twice and married a third time in 1980.

Born Henry Ford II. **Parents** Edsel Bryant, president, Ford Motor Company, and Eleanor (Clay) Ford. **Marriages** 1) Anne McDonnell, 1940 (divorced, 1964); 2) Mrs Maria Christina Vettore Austin, 1965 (divorced, 1980); 3) Kathleen DuRoss, 1980. **Children** Charlotte, Anne and Edsel Bryant II, from first marriage. **Education** Hotchkiss School, Connecticut; Detroit University School; Yale University, 1936–40. **Military service** Commissioned ensign, United States Navy, 1941; promoted to lieutenant; resigned, 1943. **Career** Mechanic, Ford Motor Company, 1938–41, employee, River Range plant, Michigan, 1940–41, executive vice-president, 1944, president, 1945–60, chief executive officer, 1945–79, chairman of the board, 1960–80, retired, 1982. **Related activities** Alternate delegate, United Nations General Assembly, 1953; director and vice-chairman, Sotheby's Holdings, Incorporated; director, Manufacturers' Trust Company of Florida; chairman, board of trustees, Henry Ford Health Corporation; trustee, The Ford Foundation, 1943–76; member, Business Council, 1947–87; chairman, National Alliance of Businessmen, 1968; chairman, National Center for Voluntary Action, 1970–72. **Offices and memberships** Member: Society of Automotive Engineers, Engineering Society of Detroit, Rackham Engineering Foundation, Traffic Safety Association of Detroit, Detroit Board of Commerce. **Awards and honours** Presidential Medal of Freedom, 1969; honorary LLD, Yale University, 1972. **Publications** *The Human Environment and Business*, 1970. **Cause of death** Undisclosed, at age 70. **Further reading** Booton Herndon, *Ford*, 1969; Peter Collier and David Horowitz, *The Fords: An American Epic*, 1988.

WOLFGANG FORTNER

German Composer

Born **Leipzig, Germany, 12 October 1907**

Died **Germany, 12 September 1987**

Of all the twentieth-century German composers, Wolfgang Fortner perhaps best represented the German musical tradition of Bach. Born in Bach's own town of Leipzig, he grew up in the Lutheran church tradition of which Bach's sacred music had formed so great a part. Its influence on Fortner lasted throughout his life, even during his *rapprochement* with 12-tone serialism in the years after the war. It was against this background that he held a position in the musical life of Germany comparable to that held by the guru of twentieth-century French music, Olivier Messiaen.

Fortner's links with the tradition of Baroque polyphony were confirmed when, in the mid-1920s, he went to study composition with Hermann Grabner at the Leipzig Conservatory. Grabner had been a student of Max Reger, whose organ music emanated intellectually and emotionally from the polyphonic traditions of Bach. No surprise, then, that Fortner's first instrument while at the conservatory was the same as that of both Bach and Grabner—the organ. But his earliest compositions were sacred choral works, settings of biblical texts which bore witness to his Protestant upbringing. Such works remained a key element of his creative output for the rest of his working life.

Having started composing at the age of eleven, in 1927 Fortner moved from the Leipzig Conservatory to Leipzig University, where he studied musicology under Theodor Kroyer. He was to spend much of the rest of his life in academic circles, first as a student, but soon as a teacher, a lecturer, and later as a highly respected professor of music. His pupils included such notable figures of German contemporary music as Hans Werner Henze. His professional life took him to a variety of locations inside Germany, as well as to other parts of Europe and the US. In 1931 he was appointed as teacher of composition at the Heidelberg Institute of Church Music, rising to professor of composition at the German State Academy of Music at Detmold in 1954. After a time as lecturer of music at the Academy of Arts in West Berlin, he became professor of music at the State High School of Music in Freiburg, where he tutored and lectured for some 15 years.

Always a vigorous supporter of contemporary musical activities, Fortner founded the Heidelberg Chamber Orchestra in 1935 and helped set up the series of Musica Viva concerts in Heidelberg, Freiburg and Munich. His contribution to the German contemporary music scene cannot be undervalued.

Fortner's music was largely characterized by an emphasis on complex contrapuntal structures and adherence to a clear basic tonality. If Bach was the main influence on his compositional style, he was not the only one. From Hindemith and Stravinsky Fortner developed his own neo-classical style, combining contrapuntal textures with striking rhythmic structures, and earning for himself the distinction in some critics' eyes as "the most learned and skilful artist in musical form after Hindemith". In all his works, the opposition of Romantic spontaneity and technical mastery was always apparent.

Disclaiming as worthless the music he wrote during the Nazi period, he moved stylistically closer to the Viennese Atonal School of 12-tone serialism in the years after the war. His only symphony, written in 1947 in response to the spiritual paucity of the war years, used "rhythmic cell" devices, concentrating on colour and harmonic consistency, and was the first example of Fortner's new musical style.

An intelligent and passionate man, Fortner had a keen understanding of the interrelationship between music and poetry. He exploited this to the full in his several works for the stage. His first ballet, *The White Rose*, based on Oscar Wilde's *Birthday of the Infanta*, appeared in 1949, followed in 1953 by a television opera entitled *The Forest*. This was followed in 1957 and 1962 by two operas based on works by the Spanish poet Lorca—*Blood Wedding* and *Don Perlimplin*, the latter regarded by many as Fortner's most beautiful score. In his portrayal of Elizabeth and Mary in his opera *Elisabeth Tudor*, he found a vehicle for the expression of the opposition between emotional passion and intellectual sobriety, something which is characteristic of so much of his music, while in *That Time*, a musical drama after Beckett, scored for silent actor, female narrator, soprano, mezzo, baritone, guitar, harpsichord and live electronic accompaniment, he displayed his lasting penchant for musical experimentation and modernity.

Fortner was a prolific composer who consistently showed an attachment to "the intellectualism of music". Among his orchestral works were concertos for organ, piano, violin, viola and harpsichord, and a number of smaller scale symphonic works, in addition to his one major symphony. His chamber works show a special affinity for the flute, although it was to choral works that he devoted most attention. Several times a prize-winner for his compositions, Fortner, throughout his life, did great credit to the German musical scene. As Sibelius once wrote: "If any composer has truly portrayed the destiny of his time in his work, that composer is Wolfgang Fortner."

Born Wolfgang Fortner. **Education** Leipzig Conservatory; Leipzig University, 1927–31. **Career** Teacher of composition and music, Heidelberg Institute of Sacred Music, 1931–53; professor of composition, Northwest German Music Academy, Detmold, 1954–57; professor, Freiburg State High School for Music, 1957–73. **Related activities** Taught 12-note composition at Darmstadt summer schools, 1946 onwards; lecturer, Academy of Arts, West Berlin, 1954 onwards; founder, Musica Viva concerts, Heidelberg, 1935; director, Musica Viva concerts, Munich, 1964 onwards. **Offices and memberships** President, German section, International Society for Contemporary Music, 1957; head of music section, Berlin Academy of Arts; member, Bavarian Academy of Fine Arts. **Awards and honours** Schreker Prize, Berlin, 1948; Spohr Prize, Brunswick, 1953; North Rhine–Westphalia Große Kunstpreis, 1955; Bach Prize, Hamburg, 1960. **Opera compositions** *Bluthochzeit*, 1956; *Corinna*, 1958; *In Seinem Garten liebt Don Perlimplin Belisa*, 1962; *Elisabeth Tudor*, 1971; *That Time (Damals)*, 1977. **Ballet compositions** *Die Weiße Rose*, 1949; *Die Witwe von Ephesus*, 1952; *Carmen*, 1970. **Orchestral compositions** *Suite*, 1930; concerto for organ and string orchestra, 1932; concerto for string orchestra, 1933; concertino for viola and small orchestra, 1934; harpsichord concerto, 1935; *Capriccio und Finale*, 1939; *Ernste Musik*, 1940; piano concerto, 1942; *Streichermusik II*, 1944; violin concerto, 1946; symphony, 1947; *Phantasie über die Tonfolge B-A-C-H*, for two pianos, nine solo instruments and orchestra, 1950; cello concerto, 1951; *Mouvements*, for piano and orchestra, 1953; *La Cecchina*, 1954; *Impromptus*, 1957; Bläsermusik, 1957; *Ballet Blanc*, for two solo violins and string orchestra, 1958; *Aulodie*, for oboe and orchestra, 1960; *Triplum*, for orchestra and three obbligato pianos, 1966; *Immagini*, 1967; *Marginalien*, 1969; *Zyklus*, for cello, winds, harp and percussion, 1969; *Prolegomena*, 1973; *Prismen*, for flute, oboe, clarinet, harp, percussion and orchestra, 1974; *Triptychon: Hymnus I*, for six brasses, 1977; *Improvisation*, for large orchestra, 1977; *Hymnus II*, for 18-voice string orchestra, 1977; *Variationen*, 1979. **Vocal compositions** *Die Entschlafenden*; *Glaubenslied*; *Grenzen der Menschheit*, cantata, 1930; *Lied der Welt*, 1931; *Drei Geistliche Gesänge*, 1932; *Eine Deutsche Liedmesse*, 1934; *Vier Gesänge*, for alto, baritone and piano, 1934; *Nuptiae Catulli*, for tenor, chamber chorus and chamber orchestra, 1937; *Herr, bleibe bei uns*, for mezzo-soprano, baritone, organ/harpsichord and optional string trio, 1944; *Shakespeare Songs*, for mezzo-soprano, baritone and piano, 1946; *An die Nachgeborenen*, cantata, 1947; *Zwei Exerzitien aus der Hauspostille*, for three female voices and 15 instruments, 1948; *Mitte des Lebens*, cantata for soprano and 15 instruments, 1951; *Arie*, for mezzo-soprano, flute, viola and chamber orchestra, 1951; *Isaaks Opferung*, for three soloists and 40 instruments, 1952; *The Creation*, for voice and orchestra, 1954; *Chant de Naissance*, cantata for soprano, chorus, solo violin, strings, winds, percussion and harp, 1958; *Berceuse Royale*, for soprano, solo violin and string orchestra, 1958, revised for soprano and seven instruments, 1975; *Prélude und Elegie*, 1959; *Impromptus*, for soprano and orchestra, 1959; *Der 100 Psalm*, for chorus, three horns, two trumpets and two trombones, 1962; *Die Pfingstgeschichte nach Lukas*, for tenor, chorus, eleven instruments, or chamber orchestra and organ, 1963; *Fragment Maria,* chamber cantata, 1969; *Drei Gedichte von Michelangelo*, for bass-baritone and orchestra, 1972; "*Versuch eines Agon um...?*", for seven singers and orchestra, 1973; *Gladbacher Te Deum*, for baritone, chorus, tape and orchestra, 1973; *Machaut Balladen*, for voice and orchestra, 1973; *Petrarca-Sonette*, 1979; various other choruses and songs. **Chamber music** Four string quartets, 1929, 1938, 1948, 1975; Suite for solo cello, 1932; violin sonata, 1945; Serenade for flute, oboe and bassoon, 1945; flute sonata, 1947; cello sonata, 1948; string trio, 1952; *Six Madrigals*, for violins and cellos, 1954; *New-Delhi-Musik*, for flute, violin, cello and harpsichord, 1959; *Five Bagatelles*, for wind quintet, 1960; *Zyklus*, for cello and piano, 1964; *Theme and Variations*, for solo cello, 1975; *Neun Inventionen und ein Anhang*, for two flutes, 1976. **Piano compositions** Sonatina, 1935; *Kammermusik*, 1944; *Seven Elegies*, 1950; *Epigramme*, 1964. **Organ compositions** *Toccata and Fugue*, 1930; *Preamble and Fugue*, 1935; *Intermezzi*, 1962. **Cause of death** Undisclosed, at age 79. **Further reading** H. Lindlar, ed., *Wolfgang Fortner*, Rodenkirchen, 1960.

BOB FOSSE

American Choreographer, Dancer and Director
Born **Chicago, Illinois, 23 June 1927**
Died **Washington, DC, 23 September 1987**

"It's showtime, folks!"

Joe Gideon, Bob Fosse's cinematic *alter ego* in the film *All That Jazz* (1979), ritualistically struggles daily through this personal rallying cry in front of his shaving mirror. We are taken inside the heart of the man whose energy and very existence are fuelled by the need to create. There lies a glimpse of what it must have been like to be Bob Fosse.

In any age, at any time, Bob Fosse would shine. This acclaimed, yet highly controversial dancer, choreographer, director, innovator, author, having triumphed equally on stage, in film and on television, was a pure product of the musical. Fosse's particular stamp was in creating dances and, conversely, perspectives, that were characterized by unusual jerky movements, sexual suggestiveness and well-rehearsed precision—a universal theme of artists trying to represent/project what it is like to be alive in the twentieth century. Typically, he downplayed his artistry, defining musical theatre as "an evening in the theatre when everybody has a good time—even in the crying scenes". His personal litmus test was: "Screw art! Does it work?"

Bob Fosse was stagestruck from a very early age, having inherited the bug from his father, an ex-vaudeville singer turned salesman. He began taking classes in a small neighbourhood dance school and started dancing professionally while still in high school. At 15 he was given his first choreographic assignment—providing the staging for a number in a nightclub, in which girls manoeuvred ostrich feather fans to Cole Porter's *That Old Black Magic*. After graduation, as his contribution to the war effort, he performed with Pacific entertainment units for the US Navy until 1947. This was followed by stints as a chorus dancer in the national tours of *Call Me Mister* (1948) and *Make Mine Manhattan* (1948–49). His Broadway début came in 1950 in a revue called *Dance Me a Song*. He went on to understudy Harold Lang in the title role of a 1952 revival of *Pal Joey*, and then took over the part on tour.

The following year, Fosse landed a contract with MGM and moved to Hollywood. In his first film *Give a Girl a Break*, he provided a spectacular closing by executing a backward somersault. He tried the move many times in rehearsal, but only performed it successfully (and perfectly) at the actual moment of filming.

When he had arrived in Hollywood, Fosse was hoping to take over where Mickey Rooney had left off—the brash, energetic, idealistic, "horse-powered college kid", full of ambitious dreams. However, by the time he had played his third role in *Kiss Me Kate*, he had become, frankly, a bit-part actor. As he later told an interviewer: "I decided to get the hell out of there and take a try at Broadway, so I asked for a release from my contract. This they gave me—rather quickly as I remember. It still stings me a little that they gave me an 'out' so easily." As he was only a contract player at the time, and therefore not privy to all the political machinations of the studio, he was not aware that the Hollywood musical was on its last legs.

When he returned to Broadway, Jerome Robbins recommended him to the director George Abbott, who took him on to choreograph *The Pajama Game*. The show was an enormous success for which Fosse won huge praise and his first Tony award for best choreography. The same team produced *Damn Yankees* the following year for which Fosse won another Tony. Even more significantly, it heralded the beginning of his successful collaboration with the show's star, Gwen Verdon.

For the next 12 years, up until 1966, Fosse shuttled between Hollywood and New York, confining his film work to choreography, while extending his stage work to direction as well as choreography (known as doing "double duty"). His talent really began to develop in the vehicles he helped create for Gwen Verdon, whom he had married in 1960. *New Girl in Town* and *Redhead* were actually of little merit, apart from Fosse's choreography and Verdon's dancing, but they became notable successes, none the less. Fosse choreographed two undisputed hits in 1961 and 1962: *How to Succeed in Business Without Really Trying* won more awards than any musical in Broadway history, while *Little Me* won him his fourth Tony award (for co-direction and choreography). Meanwhile, he took the lead role in the New York revival of *Pal Joey*, recreating the part he had first played ten years earlier. The critics were adoring ("...the best lead in *Pal Joey* I have ever seen..."), and his ego was given a much-needed boost.

In 1966 Fosse hit full stride with *Sweet Charity*, which ran for over a year and a half on Broadway. Walter Terry called the musical a "Bob Fosse Show" in which the director/choreographer "co-starred with Miss Verdon" even though he never set foot on the stage. The show was essentially a Cinderella story except that the Prince got cold feet at the altar. The only happy element in the ending was that Charity's unquenchable optimism would help her survive. However, as John Kobal observed in his book *Gotta Sing, Gotta Dance*, the power of the piece as a contemporary work "lay in the energy behind the telling of the story and in the brilliantly choreographed dances. Fosse offers us an overabundance of fabulous solos, *pas de deux*, electrifying threesomes and spectacular production numbers which come hot on the heels of one another for a chorus drilled to stop on cracks and tap on dimes, to grab audiences by the throat and shake them out of their mollycoddled state."

Fosse signed up with Universal Pictures to direct and choreograph a screen version with a budget of $10 million. Not only did the film mark his début as a film director, but he also became the first person since Busby Berkeley to be assigned complete control over direction and choreography for a Hollywood film. On its release, the film was universally panned. Critics thought the star, Shirley MacLaine, woefully miscast, and one described the work as "a platinum clinker designed to send audiences flying to the safety of their television sets". Fosse suddenly became "out" in Hollywood—shunned at parties and cold-shouldered on the pavement. In an interview some ten years later, he revealed his contempt for the system and his ambivalent attitude towards his profession: "I hate show business and I love it. I love working with actors and dancers and writers and designers. But I hate the bullshit—the Beverly Hills homes with swimming pools, [the] Mercedes, [the] Gucci bags..." (*Charity*, however, remains critic-proof within show business. It was, after all, the sight of Paula Kelly, Shirley MacLaine and Chita

Rivera doing *grands jêtés* across the rooftops of Manhattan that inspired a generation to enrol in dance classes.)

Fosse retreated to Broadway, but salvation beyond his wildest dreams was soon to come. After several directors had turned it down, he was offered the job of directing and choreographing *Cabaret*. Starring Liza Minnelli as a waif adrift in Weimar Germany, with Joel Grey as an androgynous master of ceremonies, the film broke new ground in movie musicals. No longer were the musical numbers "integrated" into the narrative with people singing to each other; all performances were logically grounded, occurring where they might be expected—on a stage, for example. The "integration" took place in the sense that each performance was a comment on the narrative action.

In *Cabaret* Fosse distilled his perspective on movement; the film amplifies the isolated and exaggerated forms of human motion that embody his famous style. He taught us all the proper use for bowler hats, high-backed chairs and fishnet stockings. Indeed, this writer remembers a dance teacher once chiding a class for sloppiness by reminding it that Fosse "got six girls to blink at the same time and made a mint". With hindsight, Fosse's contribution seems obvious: he showed that on stage, choreography is presented by the performers, so that what the audience sees is "the routine"; in film "you see everything within a frame". Camera angle and camera image become more important choreographically than the dancing, so the routine itself is subordinated. That is why the viewer responds emotionally to the dance, and does not just sit back and admire, say, pretty boys in pastel shirts dancing through rubble in New York, or fun-lovin' folk outoors having yet another good time.

Cabaret was ground-breaking too in that the material was hard and unsentimental. The dancers were fat fraüleins, not leggy ballerinas. Pauline Kael, writing in the *New Yorker* in 1972 said that "...until now, there has never been a diamond-hard big American musical..." John Kobal commented, "It sounds good, it looks good, but the meaning is terrible. That is new. That is powerful. That is the artist, through his art, pulling the blinkers off our eyes."

The film won nine Oscars, including one for Fosse's direction, which helped to make 1972 a high point for him. He also won two Tony awards for the direction and choreography of the Broadway show *Pippin* and an Emmy award for his television special, *Liza With a Z*—the only triple crown in show business history.

However, Fosse was under no illusion about his change of fortune with *Cabaret*. If, in spite of its merits, it had not earned its millions, he knew he would have been reviled and dismissed as a failure. This perception preserved him from the corrupt self-aggrandizing posture that people usually affect after financial success.

In 1975, while Fosse was rehearsing the stage musical *Chicago*, which he wrote with Fred Ebb, he had a severe heart attack, an experience that inspired his 1979 film *All That Jazz*. It attracted much comment for the fact that many of the gory details surrounding a cardiac arrest were included, so much so that the film's merits tended to be overshadowed by magazine features speculating on how much longer its director was likely to live.

Here, Fosse expanded on his concepts of "believability..., integrated commentary" and visual fragmentation of performance via camera angle. "I don't think there is any such thing as a realistic musical. As soon as people start to sing to each other, you've already gone beyond realism in the usual sense...." So, in *All That Jazz*, the musical numbers are either in an audition/rehearsal situation, or are hallucinations, obviously separated from the narrative, but still logically grounded within it.

Fosse's later work, especially the stage show *Dancin'*, tended to be pure displays of dance virtuosity. But he constantly expanded his choreographic ideas, always the dance first. This love for his work inspired enormous affection in all those with whom he worked. His individual approach to dance/direction, the fact that the unique talents of each performer were highlighted and employed meant that recasting his shows was a perennial problem. But it also meant too that he inspired a fierce loyalty in all who worked for him.

Fosse died of a second heart attack the day that his revival of *Sweet Charity* opened in Washington, DC. His energy, obsessions and relentless dedication to commercial dance have indelibly left their mark on the art.

Born Robert Louis Fosse. **Marriages** 1) Mary Ann Niles, dancer (divorced); 2) Joan McCracken, musical comedy actress (divorced); 3) Gwen Verdon, dancer (divorced). **Children** One daughter, Nicole Providence, from third marriage. **Education** Amundsen High School, Chicago; American Theater Wing, New York, 1947. **Military service** US Navy entertainment units, 1945–47. **Career** In dance team, *The Riff Brothers*, with Charles Grass, appearing in burlesque and vaudeville, 1940–42; nightclub master of ceremonies, 1942; chorus dancer, touring companies, 1948–50; Broadway dancing début, 1950; dancer in nightclubs and television shows, 1951–52; moved to Hollywood and signed with MGM, 1953; returned to New York and made Broadway début as choreographer, 1954; choreographer, Broadway and Hollywood, late 1950s; Broadway début as choreographer/director, 1959; first film as director, 1968; last project, Washington stage revival of his 1966 Broadway show and 1968 film, *Sweet Charity*, 1987. **Awards and honours** Ten Tony Awards for stage work, including: *The Pajama Game*, 1955; *Damn Yankees*, 1956; *Cabaret*, 1973; *Pippin*, 1973; Academy Award as Best Director for *Cabaret*, 1973; British Academy Award as Best Director for *Cabaret*, 1973; Emmy Television Award for *Liza With a Z*, 1973; plus various Academy Award nominations for films he was associated with, including nine for *All That Jazz*, 1979. **Films** (as choreographer) *My Sister Eileen*, 1955; *The Pajama Game*, 1957; *Damn Yankees (What Lola Wants)*, 1958; (as director/choreographer) *Sweet Charity*, 1968; *Cabaret*, 1973; (director only) *Lenny*, 1974; (choreographer of "Snake in the Grass" number only) *The Little Prince*, 1974; *All That Jazz*, 1979; (director only) *Star 80*, 1983. **Film roles** *The Affairs of Dobie Gillis*, 1953; *Kiss Me Kate*, 1953; *Give a Girl a Break*, 1953; *My Sister Eileen*, 1955; (dancer in "Who's Got the Pain" number) *Damn Yankees*, 1958; *The Little Prince*, 1974; *Thieves*, 1976. **Stage** (including as dancer) *Dance Me a Song*, 1950; (as choreographer) *The Pajama Game*, 1955; *Damn Yankees*, 1956; (as director/choreographer) *Redhead*, 1959; *Sweet Charity*, 1966; *Dancin'*, n.d.; *Chicago*, 1973; *Big Deal*, n.d. **Television** (including as dancer) *Show of Shows*, 1951-52; *Toni Review*, 1951–52; *Hit Parade*, 1951–52; *The Wonderful World of Entertainment*, 1958; *The Seasons of Youth*, 1961; (as director/choreographer) *Liza With a Z*, 1973. **Cause of death** Heart attack, at age 60.

BILL FRASER

British Actor

***Born* Perth, Scotland, 5 September 1908**

***Died* London, England, 5 September 1987**

Bill Fraser, one of Britain's best known character actors, began with a career in banking but hated, as he put it, counting other people's money, and eventually persuaded his parents to allow him to attempt his heart's desire—a career as an actor.

His beginning, however, was not auspicious. After a period of semi-starvation and sleeping rough in London he made his first professional appearance (aged 23) at the south coast resort of Broadstairs in Kent playing a detective. He then went to India with a touring company but the company collapsed. Fraser, undeterred, returned to England. From the beginning he had been looking for a theatre where he could launch his own repertory company and, comparatively quickly, found the ideal venue in another seaside town. After a hard struggle he was able to take over a cinema and the Worthing Repertory Company, based at the Connaught Theatre, took off in 1933. Recalling those years towards the end of his life, Fraser said they had been "gloriously happy and productive. That was when I learnt everything about my business—and I'm not sure a small weekly repertory company might not do well if revived today."

The company was halted by the outbreak of war in 1939 and, following a brief spell in revue in London's West End, Fraser joined the Royal Air Force, serving as a signals officer. Following demobilization in 1946 he moved back to West End revue, then into supporting roles in a number of straight plays, and followed up with two years' directing a summer show at coastal resorts. This was, more importantly, also the time that he achieved national acclaim in television, playing Sergeant Major Snudge in a situation comedy called *The Army Game*. Such was the success of this series that another was created. *Bootsie and Snudge*, co-starring another *Army Game* character played by the late Alfie Bass (q.v.), traced the two men's return to civilian life. The programmes took over Fraser's career for a decade and left him anxious about being typecast thereafter. They also wove themselves into the hearts and minds of the British population, becoming compulsory and compulsive viewing for everyone. His catch phrase, "'Ave no fear, Snudge is 'ere," can still be heard today—with variations on the name.

There were some months without work following the second series but Fraser counted himself fortunate to be given parts in two good films, followed by five seasons at the Chichester Festival Theatre in Sussex where he played in the classics such as Shakespeare and Shaw. It was then inevitable that he would go on to the Royal Shakespeare Company, and 1969 brought him the part of Sir Toby Belch at Stratford. Then came an offer from the National Theatre Company, spearheaded by Lord Olivier, and over the following two years Fraser played in Shaw and Goldsmith, at the Old Vic theatre in London.

He was seldom out of the theatre for the rest of his life, almost always in classic productions of such widely varying playwrights as Maugham, Ibsen and Chekhov. One of his dearest wishes was to see a repertory theatre established which would stage the works of Shaw all year round. He continued to appear in television, although in supporting roles. He was a judge in the situation comedy series on the legal profession, *Rumpole of the Bailey*, and a splendid Mr Micawber in the BBC serialization of *David Copperfield*. Fraser was also particularly proud of his work in the BBC serial, *Flesh and Blood*. He was filming, almost to the end of his life, two comedy series based on Sue Townsend's creation of Adrian Mole, a very average teenage boy whose main concerns are the (not very) dissolute behaviour of his mother, his spots, his dog and his passion for a girl named Pandora.

As late as 1986 Fraser was still working in West End theatre, this time as the wandering photographer in J.B. Priestley's *When We Are Married*, at the Whitehall. This brought the chance of work on Broadway but, as he said, "At the age of 78 I'm not sure that I'm not too old to go chasing off over there, but we'll see." Sadly, it was not to be.

Fraser's work in the theatre could well have been overshadowed by his television fame but his inherent professionalism, integrity and generosity ensured that the respect accorded him by his colleagues and the critics was ultimately shared by the theatre-going public as a whole.

Born William Fraser. **Parents** Alexander and Betty (Scott) Fraser. **Marriage** Pamela Cundell, actress, 1981. **Children** One stepdaughter. **Education** Strathallan School. **Military service** Signals officer, Royal Air Force, 1941–45. **Career** Worked in bank, Perth, Scotland; stage début in *The Fourth Wall*, Broadstairs, 1931; toured India with R.B. Salisbury's company, 1932; founded and ran Worthing Repertory Company, 1933–39; film début, 1938; London stage début in revue, *New Faces*, 1941; found national fame through TV series *The Army Game* and *Bootsie and Snudge*, 1950s–60s; directed coastal resort summer shows, 1956–58; joined Royal Shakespeare Company, 1969; appeared and starred in stage and television productions all over UK. **Awards and honours** Acting award for role in *The Cherry Orchard*, London, 1967. **Publications** (contributor) *Minding My Own Business* (guide to shop owners), 1960. **Stage** (all produced in London, unless stated, include) *The Fourth Wall*, Broadstairs, 1931; *The Outsider*, 1932; *New Faces* (revue), 1940–41; *Between Ourselves* (revue), 1946; *Four, Five, Six*, 1948; *The Schoolmistress*, 1950; *Touch and Go* (revue), 1950; *Albertine by Moonlight*, 1956; (director) *Between Ourselves* (seaside summer review), 1956–58; *Schweyk in the Second World War*, 1963; *The Subtopians*, 1964; *The Clandestine Marriage*, Chichester Festival, 1966; *The Cherry Orchard*, Chichester Festival, 1966; *Macbeth*, Chichester Festival, 1966; *The Farmer's Wife*, Chichester, 1967; *The Beaux Stratagem*, Chichester, 1967; *An Italian Straw Hat*, Chichester, 1967; *Heartbreak House*, Chichester and London, 1967; *Ring Round the Moon*, 1968; *Twelfth Night*, Stratford, 1969; *King Henry VIII*, Stratford, 1969; *Mrs Warren's Profession*, 1970; *The Captain of Köpernick*, 1971; *King George in Tyger*, 1971; *The Good-natured Man*, 1973; *Misalliance*, 1974; *Something's Burning*, 1974; *An Inspector Calls* (tour), 1974; *An Enemy of the People*, Chichester Festival, 1975; *The Fool*, 1975; *Monsieur Perrichon's Travels*, Chichester, 1976; *Twelfth Night*, Chichester, 1976; *The Circle*, Chichester and London, 1976; *Trelawny of the Wells*, n.d.; *Uncle Vanya*, 1982; *When We Are Married*, 1986. **Films** (include) *A Home of Your Own*, 1965; *Captain Nemo*, 1969; *All the Way Up*, 1970; *The Eye of the Needle*, 1981; *Wagner*; several *Carry On* productions. **Television** (includes) *The Army Game*; *Bootsie and Snudge*; *Rumpole of the Bailey*; *Comedians*; *Flesh and Blood*; *David Copperfield*; *The Secret Diary of Adrian Mole*. **Cause of death** Undisclosed, at age 79.

MAXWELL FRY

British Architect

***Born* Wallasey, Cheshire, 2 August 1899**

***Died* Barnard Castle, Co. Durham, 3 September 1987**

Maxwell Fry came to be, in his later years, one of the saint-like figures of British architecture. As a young man he was a product of the extraordinary flowering of design talent fostered by the Liverpool School of Architecture. Initially, his reputation was founded on a rather small number of modernist houses and some blocks of fixed-rent flats. Perhaps more influential than any of these buildings was the fact that he was, for two years during the 1930s, in partnership with Walter Gropius. Fry also devoted a great deal of time to the Royal Institute of British Architects (RIBA) and the Modern Architectural ReSearch group (MARS).

In the early chapters of his charming, if somewhat muddled, book *Autobiographical Sketches* (1975), Fry gives an almost classic account of childhood beset by a weak constitution, illness and bullying at school. Like many sensitive children, he sought refuge from the insensitivity of others in painting and drawing. He also recorded his own dismal lack of academic success with amusing candour.

Fry's progress to higher education was interrupted by the urgent demands of conscription for World War I. He served from 1917 to the armistice in the Liverpool Regiment, seeing action in France. His pre-war plan to become an architect had met with the direct opposition of his father, so on demobilization in 1919, Fry worked for a time as a lowly clerk for his father's company in Liverpool. He later took a similar job for another firm in a different district, simply, it seems, to get away from his family.

At last, financially independent, albeit rather precariously, he was able to enter the School of Architecture at Liverpool University. "The school was famous on account of its director, the inimitable and notorious Charles Reilly." Fry recalled how he, as a newly arrived student, drew a caricature of Reilly "...as a winged cherub on a cloudlet blowing his own trumpet; he recognized himself with glee and loved me ever after." Reilly's partiality was later shown in a practical way when Fry was among a select band of students chosen to spend six months working in the US during their fourth year of study. In his 1938 autobiography, *Scaffolding in the Sky*, Reilly revealed that he had negotiated a minimum wage of $35 per week for his students, adding, "Some, like Maxwell Fry, with overtime, made that up to $60"—no small sum in the 1920s.

Upon arrival at the New York firm of Carrere and Hastings, Fry was set (with no supervision) to draw out a full-scale detail of a window. When he completed the task two days later, his boss said approvingly, "Bully for you, Christopher Wren!" This became, Fry said, his sobriquet for the rest of his stay.

Graduating from Liverpool with first-class honours in 1924, Fry made for London clutching two letters of recommendation from Professor Reilly. One of these letters was addressed to Stanley Davenport Adshead (1868–1946), "...who turned out to be disarmingly unconventional. He drove an old car from which he had removed most of the dashboard instruments as being superfluous for a man of simple tastes and for convenience he carried the door handle in his pocket." Adshead had no work to offer, but Fry acted on his advice: "If all else fails, try Tommy Adams."

Fry went to see the expatriate Scots architect and town planner; the two got on pretty well, and, after a three-year period when he worked as chief engineer for the Southern Railway, Fry was offered a partnership in the practice.

The firm of Adams, Thompson and Fry produced several housing estates in the "Garden City" manner during the mid- to late twenties, some of which were preponderantly the responsibility of the young Max Fry. They were part of the "Homes for heroes" campaign, advocated by popular newspapers after World War I. Kemsley Garden village, near Sittingbourne in Kent, is one of the estates designed by Fry. In common with other Modern Movement architects, he later tended to deny, or at least belittle, these early, conventionally-styled buildings, though the planning he learned with Adams was to be of value to him all his working life.

The energetic editor and architect, Christian Barman [1898–1980], who had been at the Liverpool School of Architecture just before Fry, saw some of Fry's drawings of London streets and published them in the *Builder*. This sort of exposure naturally led to his name becoming known more widely among the architectural fraternity.

Fry had established links with the Royal Institute of British Architects (RIBA) on first arriving in London. Through his subsequent work for them and, perhaps, the good offices of Reilly, Fry got to know all the important figures in the architectural establishment of the time. It was a period of endless meetings, plans and proclamations. Fry was a member of the English delegation to the *Congrès Internationaux d'Architecture Moderne* (CIAM) and a founder member of the MARS group—the members of which were labelled "Martians" by George Bernard Shaw, when he wrote a preface to their exhibition catalogue.

The influence of those architects and theorists he mixed with converted Fry wholeheartedly to the Modern Movement. The first fruit of this conversion was probably the showroom he built in 1933 for the Westminster Electricity Supply Corporation. This was the first of his designs that he was later prepared to acknowlege.

Other modern buildings followed: the Sun House in Hampstead, Kensal House and Sassoon House, both low-rent blocks of flats, brought sensible modern planning and hygienic facilities within the reach of working people.

In 1934 the RIBA held an exhibition under the title *International Architecture 1924–34*. Fry was the secretary to the exhibition committee, which was, by and large, composed of Modern Movement architects. Needless to say, the architecture on display was consistent and uniform in its adherence to the modernist canon.

In 1975 Fry wrote about the pre-war days: "It is quite possible for a young architect to become an acceptable member of his profession, to sit on committees of his institute and to be kindly treated by his superiors, and yet to be entirely desperate." He was referring, as usual, to his finances, which were straitened by the high cost of living in London and his recent marriage.

After Hitler became Reichschancellor in 1933, heroic efforts were made by the Modern Movement élite in England to get refugee designers safely out of Nazi Germany. Partnerships with British architects were arranged as the RIBA would not permit foreign architects to practise alone. Walter Gropius, former head of the Bauhaus, arrived in 1934 and was taken into partnership by Fry.

The Village College at Impington was the finest achievement of the partnership of Fry and Gropius. Impington is the most architecturally distinguished of the village colleges built around Cambridge during the late 1930s and early 1940s. Low, intimate-scale buildings are cleverly disposed in a parkland of trees and grass in a way that never strikes a discordant note. The celebrated architectural critic, Sir Nikolaus Pevsner—also a refugee from the Nazis—enthused over Impington in his *Buildings of England*: "One of the best buildings of its date in the country, if not *the* best."

The idealism and limited successes of the 1930s, rather than the semi-desperation of reality, are captured in a book Fry wrote during World War II. *Fine Building* was published in 1944 and dedicated to Jane Drew, his second wife, with whom he also entered into a professional partnership.

Fine Building deals with the planning and architecture of a better Britain. Ranging over town planning, traffic congestion, the design of schools and low-rent flats, with examples from Fry's own practice, the book presents a strictly Modern Movement point of view. It was written and published in a hurry, Fry said long after, in case he should be killed in the war without passing on his ideas.

Fry also published other books, usually in partnership with Jane Drew. Perhaps the best-known of their collaborations are the books dealing with building in the Tropics. These sprang directly from Fry's experiences in World War II, when he served with the Royal Engineers in Africa. His wartime work in Nigeria and Ghana led to his being retained as a consultant, and to a subsequent commission for the design of University College, Ibadan.

Another prestigious assignment came from Le Corbusier, who called in Fry and Drew as members of his team to work on the new city of Chandigarh, India, in 1951. They stayed in India for three years, becoming involved with the housing zones, planning layouts and devising standard house-types.

After entering his sixties, Maxwell Fry rather retired from active designing, although his practice continued to thrive as Fry, Drew, Knight and Creamer. Their work may be said to have lost the *élan* that characterized the earlier designs of Fry. He perhaps never regained the high point of his work in partnership with Gropius.

Born Edwin Maxwell Fry. **Parents** Ambrose Fry and Lydia Thompson. **Marriages** 1) Ethel Speakman, 1927 (divorced, 1942); 2) Jane B. Drew, architect, 1942. **Children** Ann. **Education** Liverpool Institute, 1910–17; School of Architecture, University of Liverpool, BArch, 1923. **Military service** Lieutenant, King's Regiment, 1918–20; Department of Fortifications and Works, Royal Engineers, London, 1939–42; staff captain/major; deputy commandant, Gold Coast, West Africa, 1942–44. **Career** Assistant to architects Adams and Thompson, London, 1925–27; chief assistant, Southern Railway Architects' Department, London, 1927–30; partner, Adams, Thompson and Fry, London, 1930–34; partner, Gropius and Fry, London, 1934–36; continued alone, 1936–39; town planning adviser to resident minister, West Africa, 1944–46; founding partner, Fry, Drew and Partners, London, 1946–73; founding partner, Fry, Drew, Knight and Creamer, from 1973 to retirement. **Related activities** Senior architect for new capital, Chandigarh, Punjab, India, 1951–54. **Offices and memberships** Fellow, Royal Institute of British Architects (vice-president, 1961–62); fellow, Royal Town Planning Institute; member, Royal Fine Art Commission; corresponding member, Académie Flamande, 1956; honorary fellow, American Institute of Architects, 1963; Royal Society of Arts; professor of Architecture, Royal Academy. **Awards and honours** Commander of the Order of the British Empire, 1953; Royal Gold Medal for Architecture, Royal Institute of British Architects, 1964; honorary LLD, University of Ibadan, Nigeria, 1966. **Works** Showroom for Westminster Electricity Supply Corporation, Victoria Street, London (demolished), 1933; "Little Winch" (house), Chipperfield, Hertfordshire, 1934; The Sun House, Frognal Way, Hampstead, London, 1935; R.E. Sassoon House, St Mary's Road, Peckham, London, 1935; Apartments, St Leonard's Hill, Windsor, Berkshire (project; with Walter Gropius) 1935; Kensal House, Ladbroke Grove, London, 1936; House, 66 Old Church Street, Chelsea, London (with Walter Gropius), 1936; Impington Village College, Cambridgeshire (with Walter Gropius), 1936; The Wood House, Skipbourne, near Sevenoaks, Kent (with Walter Gropius), 1936; Papworth Sanatorium School, Cambridgeshire (project; with Walter Gropius), 1936; Histon School, Cambridgeshire (with Walter Gropius), 1936; London Film Productions Worshops, Denham, Hertfordshire (with Walter Gropius), 1936; Donaldson House, Sussex (with Walter Gropius), 1936; "Miramonte" (house), Coombe, near Kingston, Surrey, 1937; Electricity showrooms, Regent Street, London, 1938; Flats, Ladbroke Grove, London, 1938; Homerton College Nursery School, Cambridge, 1940; Cecil House (girls' hostel), Gower Street, London, 1940; Aburi School and College, Ghana, 1946; Adisadel College, Ghana (with Jane Drew), 1946; Accra Community College, Ghana, 1946; Amedzofe Teacher Training College, Togoland (with Jane Drew), 1946; Broadcasting House, Nigerian Broadcasting Company, Kaduna, 1948; The Tea Centre, London, 1949; Passfields (flats), Lewisham, London (with Jane Drew), 1950; Cooperative Bank of Western Nigeria, Ibadan, 1950; Ashanti Secondary School for Boys, Kumasi, Ghana, 1950; Royal Exchange Assurance Company Ltd, Ibadan, Nigeria, 1950; Waterloo Bridge Entrance and Harbour Bar, *South Bank Exhibition*, Festival of Britain, London (with Jane Drew), 1951; Flats, Whitefoot Lane, Lewisham, London (with Jane Drew), 1953; Flats, Bromley Road, Lewisham, London, 1953; Oriental Insurance Company Office Block, Calcutta, 1954; New Capital City, Chandigarh, India (with Jane Drew, Le Corbusier, and Pierre Jeanneret), 1955; Teacher Training Centre, Wudil, Nigeria, 1958; Women's Teachers Training College, Kano, Nigeria, 1958; University College, Ibadan, Nigeria (with Jane Drew), 1959; Holy Cross School, Lagos, Nigeria, 1960; St Matthias School, Lagos, Nigeria, 1960; St Patrick's School, Lagos, Nigeria, 1960; College of Engineering, and Veterinary Science Buildings, University of Liverpool, 1960; Dow Agro Chemicals Ltd Plant and Offices, King's Lynn, Norfolk, 1960; British Petroleum Company Offices, Lagos, Nigeria, 1961; Housing, Lagos, Nigeria, 1961; Offices for Longmans Green, publishers, Lagos, Nigeria, 1961; Wates Ltd Head Office, Norbury, London; Plan for the University of Sheffield, Yorkshire, 1963; Isle of Thorns College, Chelwood Gate, Sussex, 1964; Chelwood House, Gloucester Square, London, 1965; Legislative Asembly, Port Louis, Mauritius, 1966; Kingston House, Hull, 1967; Macintosh Square Development, Gibraltar, 1967; Mid-Glamorgan Crematorium, 1969; Redevelopment of Hatfield Old Town, Hertfordshire, 1972; Garage, Old Hatfield, Hertfordshire, 1972; Shop Block A, Hatfield, Hertfordshire, 1972; A1 Trunk Road Development Study, 1973; Flats, Portchester Terrace, London, 1974; Breakspear Crematorium, Northwood, London, 1975; Institute of Education, Le Reduit, Mauritius, 1977. **Publications** (all published in London) (with John Gloag) *The Need for Planning Town and Countryside*, 1933; *English Town Hall Architecture*, 1934; *Fine Building*, 1944; (with Jane B. Drew) *Architecture for Children*, 1944, revised edition as *Architecture and the Environment*, 1976; (with Jane B. Drew and Harry L. Ford) *Village Housing in the Tropics*, 1947; (with Jane B. Drew) *Tropical Architecture in the Humid Zone*, 1956; (with Jane B. Drew) *Tropical Architecture in the Dry and Humid Zones*, 1964; *The Bauhaus and the Modern Movement*, 1968; *Art in the Machine Age*, 1969; *Maxwell Fry: Autobiographical Sketches*, 1975; plus articles in the *Architects' Journal, RIBA Journal*, *Building, Contemporary Review*, and other professional publications. **Exhibitions** One-man show, Drian Gallery, 1974. **Cause of death** Undisclosed, at age 88. **Further reading** Stephen Hitchins (editor), *Fry, Drew, Knight, Creamer: Architecture*, London, 1978.

EINAR GERHARDSEN

Norwegian Politician

***Born* Oslo, Norway, 10 May 1897**

***Died* Oslo, Norway, 19 September 1987**

In 1945, just after the Nazis surrendered and Norway was freed from German occupation, King Haakon asked Einar Gerhardsen, then chairman of the country's Labour Party and former mayor of the city of Oslo, to form a coalition government committed to a full and effective programme of post-war reconstruction. When the Labour Party won the general election in October, Gerhardsen, a humble, quiet man often called the "Ernest Bevin of Norway", became the country's youngest prime minister, and, as head of two Labour administrations, helped guide the war-scarred nation through a difficult and important period of economic recovery and diplomatic development. In addition to helping maintain Norway's strongly pro-Western foreign policy, he played a major role in the formation of the welfare state, and remained a leading light in Norwegian Labour politics for more than 50 years.

For Gerhardsen, Labour politics was a way of life. His father was a labourer and an active member of the Social Democratic Party, and from his earliest years, Einar was encouraged to participate in labour activities. At the age of 17 he took a job as a road worker for Oslo's Office of Roads, and remained in the post for eight years, organizing, and then chairing, a Road Repairers' Union aimed at improving roadmen's working conditions. Earlier he had served as chairman of a Labour youth organization. Until 1919, when he accepted the position of secretary of the Union of Norwegian Municipal Workers, he continued to work on the roads. Thereafter, politics took over his life. By 1925 he had become secretary of the Oslo Labour Party, and remained in the post for a full ten years. During this period, he also served as a member of Oslo's Town Council, and in 1935 became secretary of the Norwegian Labour Party. When he was not participating in politics, he was studying the subject as an academic discipline, working diligently to provide himself with a thorough background in history and political philosophy. His efforts paid off in the form of a Conrad Mohr academic scholarship, which allowed him to spend six months studying socialism in Austria and Bavaria.

When the Germans invaded Norway in April 1940, Gerhardsen was serving as Oslo's mayor. Such was his determination that, although he was forced out of the capital along with the king and other government officials, Gerhardsen refused to leave the country, and returned to Oslo surreptitiously a few months later, intending to resume his post as mayor. However, the Germans dismissed him from office a day later and he returned to his work as a city road labourer. But this time his road mending was more than a means of earning a living. He became a member of the secret Central Committee and used his lowly trade as a cover for organizing a major resistance against the occupying forces.

By 1941, however, the Germans had recognized Gerhardsen's aims. He was immediately arrested, jailed and sent away to the Sachsenhausen concentration camp in Germany. But even here, Gerhardsen was undeterred, and quickly rose to a position of prominence among the Norwegian prisoners. He might have remained there longer, but for the fierce British Mosquito raids on the Oslo Gestapo headquarters in 1944. In hopes that the former mayor's presence in the city would help guard against further raids, the Germans returned him to Oslo and housed him in their new headquarters. When the RAF bombers had moved on to other targets, Gerhardsen was sent to a second camp, at Grini, from which he was liberated in May 1945, after the Nazis surrendered. He was reinstated as Oslo's mayor the following day, and then elected Labour Party chairman. When Labour emerged victorious in the autumn election, Gerhardsen was named prime minister and quickly converted the interim coalition government into a full-fledged Labour administration.

Under Gerhardsen's direction, the new Norwegian government worked tirelessly to reconstruct the country's war-damaged cities and heal its social and economic ills. Gerhardsen himself served as the driving force behind the all-parties agreement which led to the development of an old-age pension scheme, free hospital care and unemployment benefits. He also made important moves in foreign policy. In 1949, despite Russian disapproval and initial reservations of his own, he resolved to bring Norway into NATO. At first the Russians had viewed the Atlantic pact as an unfriendly alliance directed against them. They felt that since Norway shared a common frontier with the Soviet Union, it should participate in a non-aggressive pact similar to that arranged for the USSR's other northwestern neighbours. Gerhardsen rejected the Russian pact as unnecessary, noting that both countries were members of the United Nations and affirming that Norway would take no part in an aggressive policy or grant bases for foreign military powers on Norwegian soil. But by 1964 he had become staunchly pro-Western in outlook, resisting strong pressure from Soviet leader Nikita Khrushchev to weaken Norwegian ties with the Western allies.

In 1951, worn out by the rigours of office, Gerhardsen handed the reins of power to his best friend, and spent four years in the much less demanding post of speaker of the House. He returned to the premiership in 1955 and remained in the position for ten more years. Then, in 1965, the Norwegian Labour Party, in power for 20 years, suffered a decisive defeat, and Gerhardsen stepped down as prime minister. He continued to serve as a member of parliament until his retirement from politics in 1972.

Though Einar Gerhardsen became one of Norway's most influential politicians, highly respected in all political circles, he never forgot his humble origins. He began his working life as a road labourer, and the problems of the average man remained a constant preoccupation. Gerhardsen's wife, Werna, spent her youth as an active Labour Party campaigner, and the family inhabited a simple, state-owned apartment in Oslo. And once, while on an official government visit to Britain, the Norwegian prime minister made an especially unusual request: to go down the shaft of a working coal mine to experience the harsh conditions for himself.

Born Einar Gerhardsen. **Parents** Gerhard, labourer, and Emma (Hansen) Olsen. **Marriage** Werna Julie Karen Christie, 1932 (died, 1970). **Children** One daughter and two sons. **Education** Self-taught; awarded Conrad Mohr Scholarship to study socialism in Austria and Bavaria, 1928. **Career** Road worker, Oslo, 1914–22; chair, Road Repairers' Union, 1919; secretary, Union of Norwegian Municipal Workers, 1922–23; secretary, Oslo Labour Party, 1925–35; member, Oslo Town Council, 1932–45; secretary, Norwegian Labour Party, 1934–45; mayor of Oslo, 1940; dismissed from office by German occupation forces, 1940; returned to road labouring while joining Norwegian resistance organization, Home Front Leadership; arrested by Germans and placed in Sachsenhausen concentration camp, 1941; brought back to Oslo and imprisoned in Gestapo HQ to deter RAF raids, 1944; removed to Grini concentration camp before being liberated, 1945; reinstalled as mayor of Oslo, 1945; chair, Norwegian Labour Party, 1945–65; leader, Norwegian Labour Party in parliament, 1951–55; prime minister of Norway, 1945–51, 1955–63, 1963–65; continued as member of parliament, 1965–72. **Cause of death** Undisclosed, at age 90.

LORNE GREENE

Canadian Actor

***Born* Ottawa, Canada, 12 February 1915**

***Died* Santa Monica, California, 11 September 1987**

Lorne Greene's chief claim to fame was as the father, Ben Cartwright, in the hugely popular television western *Bonanza*.

Greene was born in Ottawa, the only surviving child of Jewish immigrants from what was then imperial Russia. His relationship with his parents was happy and uncomplicated. Indeed, Greene himself admitted to modelling the character of Ben Cartwright on his own father, who ran a small business as a maker of orthopaedic boots and shoes.

Greene enrolled at Queen's University in Kingston, Ontario, in 1932, intending to train as a chemical engineer. However, he soon found himself increasingly involved in drama, both as actor and director, and changed his speciality to languages (French and German), in order to have more time for acting.

He received his BA in 1937, and the same year moved to New York to study drama seriously, having won a fellowship at the Neighborhood Playhouse School of the Theater. Returning to Canada in 1939, Greene wound up as a radio journalist. On the strength of his impressive baritone, the Canadian Broadcasting Corporation hired him to read their national news programme. For the first few years of World War II Greene's broadcasts made him known as the "Voice of Canada". Later in the war he saw service with the Royal Canadian Air Force.

After the war Greene settled in Toronto, where he founded the Academy of Radio Arts and a repertory company, the Jupiter Theater Inc., working with the latter as actor and director in some 50 productions. This period saw some television roles, but mainly in commercials and documentaries.

On a trip to New York in 1953, Greene attracted the notice of Fletcher Meckle, producer of CBS's *Studio One*. This led to a number of radio play roles, notably in an adaptation of George Orwell's *1984*, in which Greene's portrayal of the thought police supremo, O'Brien, was described as "superb, alternately friendly, understanding and deadly sinister".

Between 1953 and 1958 a number of Broadway theatre performances followed, as well as a season with the Stratford, Ontario, Shakespeare Festival, but not all Greene's appearances won praise. His Brutus in *Julius Caesar*, for instance, was frankly voted "dull", with Brutus's death "hardly more than the collapse of a ponderous career".

Greene's first film opportunity was as the apostle Peter in *The Silver Chalice* (1954), and throughout the 1950s he continued to appear in a succession of more or less forgettable films, perhaps most memorably as the prosecuting attorney in *Peyton Place* (1957).

Television provided Greene with steadier employment. His big break came in 1959 with his performance in an episode of the western series *Wagon Train*. The producer, David Dortort, recognized Greene as the ideal actor for his projected *Bonanza* series, which revolved around the relationship of a father and his three sons in the nineteenth-century American west.

Bonanza, which was to be shot in colour, was partly intended by the National Broadcasting Corporation as a vehicle for marketing colour television sets on behalf of RCA. NBC were also influenced (however ridiculous this may seem today) by psychological studies which claimed that young American males were in thrall to "Momism", an excessive identification with their mothers. This was supposed to have led to defections by US soldiers in Korea, and NBC conceived it their patriotic duty to offer viewers, in Greene's own words, "a strong father-and-son relationship".

The character of Ben Cartwright in the series was a stern but loving patriarch and landowner, who read the Bible but was not above putting the occasional judgemental bullet through a bad guy. Greene played up the "loving" side of his role considerably more than had originally been intended, since he saw Cartwright as a father "who commands respect through the force of his own personality".

The Ponderosa ranch and its characters quickly became the standard viewing fare of the American public, especially after being rescheduled in their second year to avoid clashing with another hardy perennial, *Perry Mason*. By 1964 *Bonanza* had the highest ratings of all programmes on the air. It ran from 1959 to 1973, and at its peak in the mid-1960s was broadcast to as many as 400 million people in 80 different countries. President Johnson reputedly did not dare make television announcements of his own at the same time for fear of being ignored.

The show was praised by Congress for its high standards, meaning it was considered clean family entertainment; but not everyone thought *Bonanza* wonderful. One critic derided it for its "interpersonal dramas dear to the hearts of soap-opera fans", and others found it cloyingly sentimental. Also, like many of the "family" shows of the 1950s and 1960s, it turned a blind eye to sex, but was liberally dosed with violence.

Greene became one of the most well-known faces in the world. His fan-mail showed the extent to which, like that other television patriarch Walter Cronkite, he had become a father-figure to millions. In the process Greene also became a multi-millionaire, not only from the series but from innumerable appearances at rodeos, fund-raising affairs and the like. Inevitably, he developed some signs of identifying strongly with his role in private life, even building a replica "Ponderosa" for himself in Arizona.

When *Bonanza* finally folded in 1973, Greene continued to find roles on television in such series as *Battlestar Galactica* and *Roots*, as well as in films like *Earthquake* and *Tidal Wave*. At the time of his death he was contracted to recreate the character of Ben Cartwright in a made-for-television film, *Bonanza: The Next Generation*.

Born Lorne Greene. **Parents** Daniel, orthopaedic shoe-maker, and Dora Greene. **Marriages** 1) Rita Hands, 1940 (divorced, 1960); 2) Nancy Deale, 1961. **Children** Twins, Belinda and Charles, from first marriage; Gillian, from second marriage. **Education** Queen's University, Ontario, BA, 1937; Neighborhood Playhouse School of the Theater, New York City; Martha Graham School of Contemporary Dance. **Military service** Royal Canadian Air Force, World War II. **Career** Newscaster, Canadian Broadcasting Corporation, 1939–early 1940s; returned to radio in Toronto after war and founded Academy of Radio Arts; founder, director and actor, Jupiter Theater Inc; occasional television work in plays, commercials and narrating documentaries; American television début in "Arietta", *Studio One*, 1953; Broadway début, *The Prescott Proposals*, 1953; film début, *The Silver Chalice*, 1954; spent remainder of 1950s moving between stage, film and television engagements; became internationally known as Ben Cartwright in television western series, *Bonanza*, 1959–73; subsequently appeared in numerous television series, single programmes and films. **Related activities** Hundreds of personal appearances on the strength of *Bonanza* role, principally at rodeos, setting an attendance record at the San Francisco Cow Palace in 1965; master of ceremonies, Canadian Royal Variety Performance for Queen Elizabeth II, 1964; introduced *London Palladium Show*, May 1966. **Other activities** Programme supervisor, advertising agency. **Offices and memberships** Actors' Equity Association; Screen Actors' Guild; American Federation of Television and Radio Artists; vice-chair, American Horse Protection Association; former chair, National Wildlife Foundation; director, Pritikin Research Center; former chair, American Freedom from Hunger Foundation. **Awards and honours** National Broadcasting Company Award for announcing, 1942; *Radio and Television Mirror* Award as most popular television star; Variety Club of America Heart Award; California Teachers' Association John Swett Award; Foreign Press Association Award for best performance by an actor; honorary doctorate of law, Queen's University, Ontario, 1969; Order of Canada Award, 1971; Tournament of Roses Parade Grand Marshal Award, 1981; honorary doctorate of Humane Letters, Missouri Valley College, 1981. **Films** *The Silver Chalice*, 1954; *Tight Spot*, 1955; *Autumn Leaves*, 1956; *The Hard Man*, 1957; *Peyton Place*, 1957; *Last of the Fast Guns*, 1958; *Gift of Love*, 1958; *The Buccaneer*, 1959; *The Trap*, 1959; *Earthquake*, 1974; *Tidal Wave*; (narrator) *Heidi's Song*, 1982. **Stage** (all Broadway, unless stated, includes) *The Prescott Proposals*, 1953; *Speaking of Murder*, 1956; *Edwin Booth*, 1958; also appeared in *Merchant of Venice* and *Julius Caesar* with the New Play Society, Canada, the Earl Grey Players,

Toronto, and at the Stratford Shakespeare Festival, Canada. **Television** (includes) "Journey to Nowhere", *Philip Morris Playhouse*, 1953; *Bonanza*, 1959–73; *Destiny of a Spy*, 1969; *The Harness*, 1971; *Griff*, 1973–74; (narrator) *Lorne Greene's Last of the Wild*, 1974–79; *Man on the Outside*, 1975; *Nevada Smith*, 1975; *The Moneychangers*, 1976; *Roots*, 1977; *The Bastard*, 1978; *Battlestar Galactica*, 1978–80; *Code Red*, 1980–81; plus (no dates available) *Star Stage*; *Actuality Specials*; "How the West Was Won", *Kraft Music Hall*; *Andy Williams Show*; *Johnny Cash Show*; *Sonny and Cher Show*; *1984*, *Studio One*; (narrator) *Tribute to John F. Kennedy*; *Lorne Greene's American West*; *Christmas Special with United Nations Children's Chorus*; *Lewis and Clark Expedition*; *Big Cats, Little Cats*; *Wonderful World of Horses*; *Swing Out, Sweet Land*; *Celebration*; *The Barnum and Bailey Special*; *SST: Death Flight*; *The Trial of Lee Harvey Oswald*. **Recordings** *Welcome to the Ponderosa*; (narrator) *Peter and the Wolf*; "Ringo"; "Destiny"; "Five Card Stud". **Cause of death** Heart attack following surgery for a perforated ulcer, at age 72.

SIR WILLIAM HALEY

British Editor and Television Administrator

***Born* Jersey, Channel Islands, 24 May 1901**

***Died* Jersey, Channel Islands, 6 September 1987**

Only the highest standards of integrity and sheer hard work would satisfy a man like Sir William Haley, director general of the British Broadcasting Corporation from 1943 to 1952 and editor of *The Times* from 1952 to 1966. As he told his *Times* colleagues in his farewell speech at the end of 1967, "There is no half-way house between honesty and dishonesty. There are things which are bad and false and ugly and no amount of argument will make them good or true or beautiful. It is time these things were said, and time for the press to say them."

These sterling qualities Haley inherited from his Yorkshire-bred father who had moved to the Channel Islands before he was born. Haley was true to his inheritance. Born and educated in Jersey, it was to Jersey that he returned in his retirement to take part in local affairs as a commissioner of income tax and chairman of the Jersey Arts Council. But throughout his working life he was at the centre of public affairs and had as much influence as any man of his generation on the direction of the British media.

Haley began and ended his career at *The Times* and in the process, as Lord Beaverbrook put it, he changed *The Times* into a real newspaper. He came in through the recognized channel for promising young journalists—as a shorthand-typist/telephonist in 1919. Here he met his wife who was also working on the newspaper. As dispatches came through from the Continent on his telephone, Haley saw the wastefulness of the procedure and did not hesitate to put up a suggestion for better coordination. As a result the young Haleys were sent off to Brussels to reorganize the system. While there, Haley sent back a weekly newsletter on Continental events to the *Manchester Evening News*, and in 1922 moved north to join that paper. The young man's organizing skill soon led to his becoming chief sub-editor, and by 1930 managing editor and director. With the outbreak of World War II he took over as joint managing director of Manchester Guardian and Evening News Ltd and was also a director of the Press Association and

Reuters, in which capacity he undertook special wartime missions to the United States and Australia.

In 1943 there came a major new move to the BBC in the newly-created post of editor-in-chief. A year later Haley was appointed director general at a critical time in the BBC's history when wartime reporting had led to an unprecedented extension of government influence and interference in the corporation's affairs. Haley was unshakeable in his defence of the BBC's autonomy from undue official control, fortunately helped by his good relationship with the then minister of information, Brendan Bracken. Haley's time at the BBC was to see important new developments—the creation of the Third Programme, which deepened the corporation's cultural influence, and the setting up of the rival Independent Television companies.

In 1952 Haley returned to his first love—newspapers—and to his first paper, *The Times*. He was appointed to succeed William Casey as editor—again at a difficult time when, apart from anything else, there was a chronic shortage of newsprint. Haley and his manager fought bravely to get paper rationing ended. He was determined to change the Thunderer's portentous image and to make it a "balanced, interesting and entertaining paper for intelligent readers of all ages and classes", to quote his own words. He widened the scope of the features pages even to the extent of covering women's topics—an unprecedented step! He gave more importance to the paper's arts coverage and, as "Oliver Edwards", contributed a regular weekly book article. He introduced cartoons. And in 1966 he shook the Establishment by moving the news to the front page. (Until that time, the front page had been devoted to advertising and the personal columns.) Haley's attention to detail covered every aspect of the paper. Though rationing the number of leading articles from his own pen, he did not hesitate to speak out in his own incisive style on issues on which he felt strongly, and he kept a vigilant watch on the contributions of all his staff, in whose appointments he took a close personal interest.

Towards the end of his time at *The Times*, the changes in ownership and business and financial matters occupied him more and more. In 1965 he became chief executive and director of the Times Publishing Company, and with the formation of Times Newspapers Ltd. at the beginning of 1967, under the Thomson Organization, he was appointed chairman. The then newly appointed editor, William Rees-Mogg, reported on Haley's scrupulous care during the period of his chairmanship to respect his editorial independence—a carefulness which only a man of Haley's integrity could have maintained. The new regime was also scrupulous in acknowledging its debt to Haley—especially in the staff he handed on. Haley himself took off for Chicago in 1968 to become editor-in-chief of the *Encyclopaedia Britannica*. Perhaps in his intense preoccupation with British journalism he had failed to realize how far the direction of this great undertaking had been taken out of British hands. In any event, the new venture was a failure and Haley left within a few months to return to his native island.

Born William John Haley. **Parents** Frank and Marie (Sangan) Haley. **Marriage** Edith Susie Gibbons, 1921. **Children** Two sons and two daughters. **Education** Victoria College, Jersey, Channel Islands. **Military service** Wireless operator, Merchant Navy, World War I. **Career** Worked for *The Times*, 1921; reporter, *Manchester Evening News*, 1922, sub-editor, 1922–25, chief sub-editor then news editor, 1925–30, managing editor, 1930–39; secretary of the board, Manchester Guardian and Evening News Ltd, 1930–39, joint managing director, 1939–43; director, Press Association, 1939–43; director, Reuters, 1939–43; editor-in-chief, British Broadcasting Corporation, 1943, director-general, 1944–52; editor, *The Times*, 1952–66; director and chief executive, The Times Publishing Co. Ltd, 1965–66; chair, Times Newspapers Ltd, 1967; editor-in-chief, *Encyclopaedia Britannica*, 1968–69. **Other activities** Commissioner of appeal for income tax, Jersey, 1971–83. **Offices and memberships** Fellow, Royal Society of Literature; president, National Book League, 1955–62; chair, Jersey Arts Council, 1976–77. **Awards and**

honours Knight Commander, Order of St Michael and St George, 1946; Chevalier, Legion of Honour, 1948; Grand Officer, Order of Orange Nassau, 1950; honorary LLD: Cambridge, 1951, Dartmouth, New Hampshire, 1957, London, 1963, St Andrews, 1965; honorary fellow, Jesus College, Cambridge, 1956. **Cause of death** Undisclosed, at age 86.

WALI MIANGUL JAHAN ZEB

Pakistani Potentate and Head of State

Born **Swat, West Pakistan**

Died **Swat, West Pakistan, 14 September 1987**

Without disrespect to you, the reader, or to the subject of this essay, let us start with a confession. The present writer had thought that Swat belonged to the imagination of Edward Lear, and that its relation to reality was no stronger than that of the Bong tree, or the runcible spoon. So, you may or may not be surprised to hear that this is not the case.

In fact, Swat is (or rather was, as will become clear) a territory along what the British used to call with some thrill and trepidation, the North West Frontier—a border country of mountains, valleys and rivers. Bloody campaigns were fought hereabouts. When Pakistan was created in 1947, Swat willingly acceded to it. Swat state then began a little over 100 miles northeast of the ancient city of Peshawar, and ended 200 miles south of Pakistan's border with the USSR. Its area was about 4000 square miles—approximately 80 in length and 50 in width. This was so until its absorption in 1969, when the last traditional ruler—or Wali—stepped down. He was Major General Miangul Jahan Zeb.

He became wali in 1949, when his father abdicated two years after the union with Pakistan. Over the next 20 years, Jahan Zeb exercised a conscientious and progressive rule, ushering in what is now viewed as having been "The Golden Age of Swat". Under his energetic and passionate supervision, schools, hospitals and roads were built. The nature of his inherited regime was autocratic, and it is both bemusing and exhausting to contemplate its responsibilities. For a start, Swat did not contain one specimen of the type known to us as a practising lawyer. The wali heard all cases—up to 80 a day—and his judgement was final. Jahan Zeb also took it upon himself to deal with affairs of state personally; all his subjects, at least theoretically, had his ear. They had only to send in their cards to procure an audience. In fairness, it must be added here that there is no obvious record of what happened if they did not possess a card, or did not know what a card was. When not interviewing individuals, the wali would address himself to files and was known to get through hundreds in a day. In the larger sphere, he kept aloof from Pakistan's politics, though he could maintain lines of communication through members of his family who sat in that country's assemblies.

In dress and manner the wali was a "confirmed and unabashed Anglophile". Unlike the majority of his countrymen, he went clean-shaven, and unlike them he could afford to sport felt hats, ties and English suits. He was, moreover, addicted to English cuisine (you might think that last phrase a contradiction in terms)—and liked to round off a meal with apple pudding. Altogether, he subjected his personality to a rigorous and unbending schedule.

The mountains within Swat state kept their snowcaps all year round. On their slopes, below the conifers and in the valleys grew many fruit trees—walnuts, apples, citrus fruits, apricots and peaches. To join these, Jahan Zeb brought olive trees, imported from Italy and tended with care. When he handed his state, with offices, land and transport, to Pakistan, the olives were indiscriminately cut down. It is an image of Swat's decline. Lootings, kidnappings and murder have become more regular occurrences. If the video cassette recorder has become more common property, so has the rifle. As a newspaper obituary sadly recorded, with Jahan Zeb's death "...in an age of pygmies, a giant has passed away".

Born Miangul Jahan Zeb. **Father** Badshah Sahib, Wali of Swat to 1949. **Career** Ruler of Swat, in the northwest corner of Pakistan, 1949–69; presided over "Golden Age of Swat", administering all affairs of state and making the region the envy of the rest of Pakistan. **Cause of death** Undisclosed.

LOUIS KENTNER

Hungarian/British Pianist

Born **Karwin, Silesia, 19 July 1905**

Died **London, England, 22 September 1987**

Louis Kentner was widely known and respected as a pianist and teacher but was admired above all as an interpreter of a composer who shared his Hungarian origins—Franz Liszt. Kentner's exhaustive studies of Liszt's music and his own fine intellect and command of piano technique brought him worldwide recognition.

Louis Philip Kentner was born in 1905 in what was then part of the Austro–Hungarian Empire, and which is now known as Czechoslovakia. At the age of six he began studies at the Liszt Ferenc Academy in Budapest, where he remained until 1922. During that time he studied composition with the great Hungarian composer and pioneer of music education, Zoltan Kodály.

He first came to the notice of the public in 1916 for his performances of Chopin at the academy. He made his professional début at the age of 16 and began the life of a touring virtuoso, visiting all the European countries and also giving concerts in the United States, although he did not make his New York début until 1956. His Chopin and Liszt interpretations made his name, winning him the Chopin Prize in Warsaw and the Liszt Prize in Budapest, but he also championed a more recent Hungarian composer, Bartók, giving the première of the *Piano Concerto No. 2* in 1933 under Otto Klemperer in Budapest. In 1945, the year of Bartók's death, Kentner gave the first British performance of the third piano concerto and, with his wife, Ilona Kabos, of the two-piano concerto. He also premièred Bartók's posthumously revived *Scherzo, Opus 2* .

Kentner became a naturalized British subject in 1945, after living in England for nine years and contributing his own personal war effort of giving many troop concerts. The British audiences took him to their hearts for his interpretations of the Mozart concertos, and because he gave complete cycles—a rare approach in those days—such as the whole of Bach's "48" and the complete Beethoven and Schubert sonatas. Hungarian pianists of his generation had usually been solidly trained in the German classics as this music was an essential part of their Austro–Hungarian heritage.

Kentner did not confine his exploration of new music to Bartók. He also took an interest in the work of his contemporaries, Tippett and Rawsthorne. William Walton wrote a violin sonata in

1950 for Kentner and his brother-in-law Yehudi Menuhin, with whom he kept up a duo partnership for many years, touring widely, including a trip to India in 1954. With Menuhin, Kentner indulged his love of chamber music and they occasionally expanded themselves into a trio with Cassado.

He was also a committed teacher who took great care over points of interpretation, and was almost equally careful in dispensing good, practical advice to pianists on the brink of a professional career.

Above all, Louis Kentner was a Liszt interpreter to the end and contributed many valuable articles to Lisztian musicology, especially to the Liszt Symposium in 1967. In recognition of that fact, he was made president of the Liszt Society and took a prominent part in the organization of the Liszt Festival in London during 1977.

Kentner was also a composer from a very early age and his output includes a serenade for orchestra, a divertimento for chamber orchestra, a string quintet, two string quartets, three sonatinas and other short piano pieces, together with a number of songs. In 1970 he was made honorary fellow of the Royal Academy of Music, and in 1978 a CBE. In 1985 he successfully returned to the concert platform for his eightieth birthday celebrations.

Born Lajos Philip Kentner. **Parents** Julius and Gisela Kentner. **Marriages** 1) Ilona Kabos, 1931 (divorced, 1945); 2) Grisela Gould, 1946. **Education** Royal Academy of Music, Budapest, under Arnold Szeleky, Leo Weiner and Zoltan Kodály, 1911–22. **Emigration** Left Hungary for England, 1935; naturalized, 1946. **Career** Concert pianist and composer; first attracted attention for playing of Liszt, Budapest Royal Academy of Music, 1916; official début, Budapest, 1920; toured Europe and USA; gave first Hungarian performance of Bartók's *Piano Concerto No. 2*, 1933; subsequently specialized in both Liszt's and Bartók's music; after settling in England also became known for championing work of living British composers, including Tippett, Rawsthorne and Walton; gave numerous troop concerts during World War II; gave European première of Bartók's Third Piano Concerto, London, 1946; premièred many of Kodály and Weiner's piano works; toured Europe, South Africa, Far East, New Zealand, Australia, South America, USA (six tours) and USSR (three tours); formed chamber music duo with Yehudi Menuhin, and trio with Menuhin and Cassado; made many recordings; last performance, 1985. **Related activities** Helped organize London Liszt Festival, 1977. **Offices and memberships** President, Liszt Society, from 1965; European Piano Teachers' Association, from 1978. **Awards and honours** Chopin Prize, Warsaw; Liszt Prize, Budapest; honorary member, Royal Academy of Music (British), 1970; Commander of the Order of the British Empire, 1978. **Compositions** (include) A serenade for orchestra, a divertimento for chamber orchestra, a string quintet, three sonatinas, some small piano pieces and a number of songs. **Publications** *Three Sonatinas for Piano*, 1939; *Liszt Symposium* (two essays), 1967; *The Piano*, 1976. **Cause of death** Undisclosed, at age 82.

MERVYN LEROY

American Film Director and Producer

***Born* San Francisco, California, 15 October 1900**

***Died* Beverly Hills, California, 13 September 1987**

For nearly four decades, Mervyn LeRoy was one of Hollywood's most successful film directors and producers. "Out of 75 films I made," he once said, "not one ever lost money." The complete studio professional, he turned out polished works and was completely fluent in whatever genre he decided to tackle, be it the gangster film (*Little Caesar*), the literary classic (*Little Women*), the war film (*Thirty Seconds Over Tokyo*) or the comedy (*Marx Brothers at the Circus*).

Like several other studio moguls of his generation, LeRoy's start in life was rather less than promising. When he was five, his mother left his father to marry another man. At six he saw the Great San Francisco Earthquake destroy his father's business. Thereafter, his father remained dispirited and bowed by the demands of a motherless, hungry family; he died when Mervyn was 14.

LeRoy made his acting début at the age of 12, as a newspaper boy in a stage act. (He had been selling them on street corners for the previous two years.) He entered amateur talent contests, winning one for his impersonation of Charlie Chaplin, and this helped him up the rungs of the vaudeville ladder. For seven years he toured the major national circuits, learning the importance of audience response, honing an instinct for what appealed to the entertainment-seeking masses. When his cousin Jessie L. Lasky, who was already making his own name in the film business, found him a job, LeRoy moved to Hollywood and worked in the wardrobe department, then as comedy gag writer, a bit actor and assistant cameraman.

The first film he directed, *No Place to Go* (1927), a comedy with Mary Astor (q.v.), demonstrated a quick command of formula film-making, surprising given his lack of experience. He made nine more films which were forgettable farces, but proved himself to be not only fast but adaptable, two very crucial qualities for the contract director. His first big success, *Little Caesar*, with Edward G. Robinson, was in 1930. As a result of his taut handling of the rise and fall of a hoodlum, a series of gangster films was launched by nearly all the major studios, not just Warner Brothers. His next big success, *I Am a Fugitive From a Chain Gang* (1932) with Paul Muni, about an innocent man brutalized by the abuses of the penal system, led to a major campaign for reform. *They Won't Forget* (1937) was an indictment of the lynch law. (It also introduced Lana Turner. "She had sex, beauty and heart. There wasn't much else to see.")

LeRoy maintained that he had no interest in either cultivating politics, or a message. He just made good films with a good plot. "Exposé films were the rule. We were able to combine our social exposé with entertainment," he said. In 1933 he also directed *Gold Diggers of 1933* with a cynical Ginger Rogers, *Tugboat Annie*, a character comedy, and *Hard to Handle*, with James Cagney. In 1938 he left Warner Brothers for Metro-Goldwyn-Mayer, who promised larger budgets and greater freedom. He produced *The Wizard of Oz* (1939), securing a certain star's future by insisting on 16-year-old Judy Garland instead of having Shirley Temple on loan (or even Deanna Durbin) as the studio wanted. He also insisted on keeping in E.Y. Harburg's song, "Somewhere Over the Rainbow", to the lyricist's gratitude and, eventually, the public's.

Here LeRoy's career took a turn, as his tough style of social realism (apart from *Oz*) changed to the lushness of melodrama, bio-pic and costume drama. He told his stories using average resources with surprisingly little fuss, compared with his contemporaries. He was less interested in content, but chose his projects because "they had a good solid story and the quality I call 'heart'". Vivien Leigh considered his *Waterloo Bridge* (1940) the best film she ever made. According to Greer Garson, the star of *Random Harvest* (1942), LeRoy's last-minute instructions to his actors summed up his whole approach, not only to film-making but to his life in general: "Now, let's have a nice scene with a lotta feeling." He was liked by actors and studio administration, partly because of his tact, partly because of his enthusiasm. His bio-pic *Madame Curie* and the war film *Thirty Seconds Over Tokyo* were two of the biggest successes of 1944. LeRoy also used his gift for talent-spotting, launching the careers of Clark Gable, Melvyn Douglas, Loretta Young and Jane Wyman.

In World War II he made short, public service documentaries for the government on such subjects as dealing with bombs and putting out fires, to prepare Americans for the possibility of attack. He received his only Oscar in 1945 for a ten-minute short on the theme of racial intolerance—*The House I Live In*, with Frank Sinatra. It was the first film made under the aegis of LeRoy's own production company. His lack of political involvement meant an untroubled career, which was, unfortunately, not true of many of his cohorts in the industry who were damaged by the 1930s Anti-Nazi League or, especially, the fanatical Un-American Activities hearings in the decade after the war.

In 1951 LeRoy produced film's counter-attack to the onslaught of television: the three-hour blockbuster *Quo Vadis*. Back at Warners in 1954 (replacing John Ford who became ill), his films generally turned more serious, with a few exceptions such as *Rose Marie* (1954) and *Mr Roberts*, the following year, with Henry Fonda and James Cagney. A few years later he fought successfully to curb studio influence in the Academy Awards by persuading the officials to allow the academy, not the studio, to choose the category of actor (best or supporting). He also tried to have the Oscar votes made public, feeling that secret balloting was undemocratic.

According to film writer Tony Rayns, LeRoy's "major successes look like anonymous summations of his studio's house style". Certainly, LeRoy was no *auteur*; there is no specific personal stamp upon his works. However, he had an affinity for certain subjects. His protagonists were often isolated and vulnerable. From *I Am a Fugitive* to *Gypsy*, many of his characters unsuccessfully endeavour to fight through society's expectations, only to find themselves face to face with their own inadequacies, inability to adapt and their own confusion with their surroundings.

His dislike of the "new" Hollywood increased as the studio system broke down. According to Rayns, "His last films...are scattered and uncertain, as if he were shadow-boxing with the tastes of an audience he no longer knew how to exploit." The last term Rayns uses is unnecessarily harsh because LeRoy also rightly scorned film producers who are merely money men, and who not only know little about what makes a good film, but do not even pretend to give credence to creativity. The touch LeRoy had was the common one, which, in the end, made millions of people delighted with what they saw on the screen.

Born Mervyn LeRoy. **Parents** Harry, department-store owner, and Edna (Armer) LeRoy. **Marriages** 1) Edna Murphy, film actress, late 1920s (divorced); 2) Doris Warner, 1933 (divorced, 1944); 3) Katherine Spiegel, 1946. **Children** One son, Warner, one daughter, Linda, and two stepdaughters, Rita and Eugenia, all from second marriage. **Career** Newsboy, 1910–12; film début, as newsboy, in *Barbara Fritchie*, 1912; minor roles and work as extra in films; appeared in vaudeville as "The Singing Newsboy" and then the "Boy Tenor of this Generation", 1912–15; formed act with Clyde Cooper, "Leroy and Cooper: Two Kids and a Piano", 1917–19; worked in film industry, folding costumes, 1919; juvenile film roles, 1919–24; gag writer and comedy construction specialist for director Alfred E. Green, 1924–27; first film as director, *No Place to Go*, 1927; directed number of films for First National and Warners, 1927–38; signed to MGM as producer/director, 1938; formed own production company, 1944; ultimately connected with the making of 75 films. **Other activities** Racehorse breeder; co-founder and president of Hollywood Park race track. **Awards and honours** Special Academy Award for *The House I Live In*, 1945; Victoire du Cinéma Français for *Quo Vadis*, 1954; Irving Thalberg Academy Award, 1976. **Publications** (with Alyce Canfield) *It Takes More Than Talent*, New York, 1953; (with Dick Kleiner) *Mervyn LeRoy: Take One*, New York, 1974. **Films** (as gag writer) *In Hollywood with Potash and Perlmutter (So This Is Hollywood)*, 1924; *Sally*, 1925; *The Desert Flower*, 1925; *The Pace That Thrills*, 1925; *We Moderns*, 1925; *Irene*, 1926; *Ella Cinders*, 1926; *It Must Be Love*, 1926; *Twinkletoes*, 1926; *Orchids and Ermines*, 1926. **Films directed** *No Place to Go*, 1927; *Flying Romeos*, 1928; *Harold Teen*, 1928; *Oh, Kay!*, 1928; *Naughty Baby* (*Reckless Rosie*), 1929; *Hot Stuff*, 1929; *Broadway Babies* (*Broadway Daddies*), 1929; *Little Johnny Jones*, 1929; *Playing Around*, 1930; *Showgirl in Hollywood*, 1930; *Numbered Men*, 1930; *Top Speed*, 1930; *Little Caesar*, 1930; *Too Young to Marry*, 1930; *Broad-minded*, 1930; *Five Star Final* (*One Fatal Hour*), 1930; *Tonight or Never*, 1930; *High Pressure*, 1932; *Heart of New York*, 1932; *Two Seconds*, 1932; *Big City Blues*, 1932; *Three on a Match*, 1932; *I Am a Fugitive from a Chain Gang*, 1932; *The Dark Horse*, 1932; *Hard to Handle*, 1933; *Tugboat Annie*, 1933; *Elmer the Great*, 1933; *Gold Diggers of 1933*, 1933; *The World Changes*, 1933; *Heat Lightning*, 1934; *Hi, Nellie!*, 1934; *Happiness Ahead*, 1934; *Oil for the Lamps of China*, 1935; *Page Miss Glory*, 1935; *I Found Stella Parish*, 1935; *Sweet Adeline*, 1935; *Anthony Adverse*, 1936; *Three Men on a Horse*, 1936; *The King and the Chorus Girl*, 1937; *They Won't Forget*, 1937; (producer only) *The Great Garrick*, 1937; *Fools for Scandal*, 1938; (producer only) *Stand Up and Fight*, 1938; (producer only) *Dramatic School*, 1938; (producer only) *At the Circus*, 1938; (producer only) *The Wizard of Oz*, 1939; *Waterloo Bridge*, 1940; (and producer) *Escape*, 1940; (and producer) *Blossoms in the Dust*, 1941; *Unholy Partners*, 1941; *Johnny Eager*, 1941; *Random Harvest*, 1942; *Madame Curie*, 1944; *Thirty Seconds Over Tokyo*, 1945; (producer only) *The House I Live In*, 1945; *Without Reservations*, 1946; *Desire Me*, 1947; *Homecoming*, 1948; (and producer) *Little Women*, 1949; *Any Number Can Play*, 1949; *The Great Sinner*, 1949; *East Side, West Side*, 1950; *Quo Vadis?*, 1950; *Lovely to Look at*, 1952; *Million Dollar Mermaid* (*The One-piece Bathing Suit*), 1952; *Latin Lovers*, 1953; *Rose Marie*, 1954; *Strange Lady in Town*, 1955; (co-director only) *Mr Roberts*, 1955; *The Bad Seed*, 1956; *Toward the Unknown* (*The Brink of Hell*), 1956; *No Time for Sergeants*, 1958; *Home Before Dark*, 1958; *The FBI Story*, 1959; *Wake Me When It's Over*, 1960; *The Devil at Four o'Clock*, 1961; *A Majority of One*, 1961; *Gypsy*, 1962; *Mary, Mary*, 1963; *Moment to Moment*, 1965; (with Wayne and Kellog) *The Green Berets*, 1968. **Film roles** (include) *Double Speed*, 1920; *The Ghost Breakers*, 1921; *Little Johnny Jones*, 1923; *Going Up*, 1923; *The Call of the Canyon*, 1923; *Broadway After Dark*, 1924; *The Chorus Lady*, 1924. **Cause of death** Alzheimer's disease, at age 86.

LORD MANCROFT

British Politician, Businessman and Writer

Born **Norwich, Norfolk, 27 July 1914**

Died **London, England, 14 September 1987**

The second Baron Mancroft was a man of many parts, academically bright at school and performing well in many fields—in the law, local and national politics, business and writing—and yet never really coming to the top in any of them, almost too gifted and versatile a spirit to make a lasting mark anywhere. Son of a dominant and intense legal father, the son showed many-sided talents at Winchester, where he not only shone apparently without effort on the academic side but was also good at games and proficient in music. This same academic ease continued at Christ Church, Oxford, where he became involved in student politics with the University Conservative Association but where his chief claim to fame was a passion for hunting. Good-looking to boot, the dashing young Mancroft came down from Oxford, the world his oyster, and being called to the Bar in 1938 seemed set for a brilliant legal career.

World War II intervened. Mancroft was commissioned in the Territorial Army in 1938 and served throughout the war in the Royal Artillery (TA), being awarded the MBE and the Croix de Guerre. By the time he returned to the Bar in 1945 he had succeeded his father as the second baron and had become interested in local politics in London. A member of the House of Lords, and a lord-in-waiting to the queen from 1952 to 1954, he joined the Churchill government in 1954 as parliamentary under-secretary for the Home Department, continuing under Anthony Eden, and then in the first six months of 1957 becoming parliamentary secretary to the Ministry of Defence in the Macmillan government. Thereafter, for about 15 months until October 1958, he was minister without portfolio and a leading government figure in the Lords, where his wit and eloquence contributed greatly to enliven the debates.

Perhaps it was the prospect of being perpetually confined to the periphery of politics by his membership of the upper chamber and so excluded from the real action which unsettled him, or perhaps some chance opportunity via his Jewish connections to dabble in "pastures new". In any event, he suddenly resigned from office to become a director of Great Universal Stores Ltd, and later chairman of Global of London, deputy chairman of Burberrys Ltd., and from 1966 to 1971 deputy chairman of the Cunard Steamship Company. The hurly-burly of the business world seemed to appeal to him, though as a practising Jew he sometimes fell foul of Arab interests, as when in 1963 he was obliged to resign from the board of the Norwich Union insurance company. Business offered him a new variety of public interests. He was chairman of the London Tourist Board from 1963 to 1973, president of the Institute of Marketing (1959–63), chairman of the Horserace Totalizator Board (1972–76) and then of the Greyhound Racing Board from 1977 to 1985. For four years (1967–70) he was chairman of the British National Export Council–USA, and here again he pulled no punches in his denunciation of Britain's failure to take advantage of the vast potential of the US market.

In short, Mancroft did not hesitate to speak his mind on a number of issues on which post-war Britain was tending to become complacent and to take the line of least resistance. He also outlined his restless and enquiring ideas in a series of hooks, among them *A Chinaman in My Bath*, *Bees in Some Bonnets* and a collection of his essays from *Punch* entitled *Booking the Cooks*.

Born Stormont Manuel Samuel Mancroft. **Parents** First baron and Phoebe (Fletcher) Mancroft. **Marriage** Diana Elizabeth (Lloyd) Quarry, 1951. **Children** One son, Benjamin Lloyd Stormont Mancroft, and two daughters. **Education** Winchester; Christ Church, Oxford, MA, 1938. **Military service** Commissioned Territorial Army, 1938; Royal Artillery (Territorial Army), 1939–46, rising to lieutenant-colonel; rejoined Territorial Army, 1947–55. **Career** Called to Bar, Inner Temple, 1938; member, St Marylebone Borough Council, 1947–53; lord-in-waiting to the queen, 1952–54; parliamentary under-secretary, Home Office, 1954–57; parliamentary secretary, Ministry of Defence, 1957; minister without portfolio, 1957–58; director, Great Universal Stores, London, 1958–66; deputy chairman, Cunard Line, London, 1966–71; chairman, Horserace Totalizator Board, 1972–76; chairman, British Greyhound Racing Board, 1977–85. **Related activities** President, Institute of Marketing, 1959–63; member, board of directors, Norwich Union, resigned 1963; president, London Tourist Board, 1963–73; chairman, Global of London Limited; deputy chairman, Burberrys Limited, 1966–71; member, Council of Industrial Design; president, Restaurateurs' Association of Great Britain; chairman, British National Export Council, 1967–70; member, Council on Tribunals, 1972–80. **Offices and memberships** President, St Marylebone Conservative Association, 1961–67. **Awards and honours** Member, Order of the British Empire, 1945; Croix de Guerre; Territorial Efficiency Decoration, 1950; Knight Commander, Order of the British Empire, 1959; honorary colonel commandant, Royal Artillery, 1970–80. **Publications** *Booking the Cooks*, 1969; *A Chinaman in My Bath*, 1974; *Bees in Some Bonnets*, 1979. **Cause of death** Undisclosed, at age 73.

RICHARD MARQUAND

British Film Director

***Born* Cardiff, Wales, 22 September 1937**

***Died* Tunbridge Wells, Kent, 4 September 1987**

Hollywood blockbusters of recent years have relied heavily on American writers, technology and know-how. Breaking into this tightly knit community is no easy task, especially for non-Americans. However, this is just what Richard Marquand did achieve, and he went on to become Britain's most successful film-maker in the US.

Marquand was born into an intellectual and political family, his father being a university professor and a Labour member of parliament. His elder brother, David, followed in these footsteps (although in the reverse order), but Richard, it seems, had ambitions in neither direction: "I never wanted to enter politics. I went to Emmanuel School, and then to university in France where I discovered sex, and since then I haven't looked back." From France he went to King's College, Cambridge, where he joined the drama society, Footlights, and acted with the likes of Peter Cook, Eleanor Bron, Derek Jacobi and Trevor Nunn. This was in the 1950s, the days of real optimism, when everything seemed possible. On graduating, he did his national service with the RAF in Hong Kong, a place he enjoyed so much that he stayed on after demobilization. "It was fantastic....I became a television star and read the news and did interviews and commercials for watches....People used to stop me in the street. Lovely it was." (Note the Welsh roots betrayed in that last sentence.)

When he returned to London, Marquand almost became a newsreader for ITN, but he turned down the job as he was much more interested in making his own programmes. Luckily for him, he joined the BBC documentary department in the 1960s at a time when it was under the innovative leadership of Sir Hugh Greene (q.v.). Here he was teamed with the late James Cameron, one of the century's finest journalists. Together they made several very distinctive films under the series title "Cameron's Country". However, recognition for Marquand only began to materialize when he went freelance and directed dramas and documentaries. Two films in the series "Search for the Nile" won him Emmy Awards, and at last he had his *entrée* to film-making in the US.

His first feature film was a horror movie called *The Legacy* (1979), which turned out to be horrific in more ways than one. Marquand found the experience a "waking nightmare....The crew and producer were the most disloyal people I had ever met. They used to do things like removing the filter from the camera because they'd been rung up in the night by Universal telling them to remove it. I would wake up screaming with fear and loathing." Like many bad experiences, however, some good was to come of it. In this case, Marquand was to learn three important things about directing: not to drink, to employ his own film crew, and to maintain a "stubborn, dogged attitude".

His next big film was *Eye of the Needle* (1981), which starred Donald Sutherland and was based on the best-selling book by Ken Follett. The film was moderately successful but, more importantly, it brought Marquand into contact with the highly successful film-maker George Lucas. Liking what he saw in the rough-cut, Lucas arranged to meet Marquand. The two men got on well, having much to share in the way of horrific directing experiences. Nothing came of this meeting immediately, but Marquand pursued the contact by visiting Lucas every time he went to California, and learned more about his working methods in the process.

From the mid-1970s Marquand's career really took off, but the effort did not always come easily. Curiously, he claimed that the difficulty of making films was not the actual filming, but getting geared up to do it: "It's as though you've had an Olympic gold...and four years later you've got to run the same distance again. I love making films, but it's getting the body into peak performance to do it which is the drag."

Despite this, Marquand never appears to have lacked energy or enthusiasm. While working on his film *The Birth of the Beatles* (1980), he spoke with tremendous excitement about the making of it. In recreating the early years of the group, he took infinite care to get everything as close to reality as possible. The actors who played John Lennon and Brian Epstein were old hands from the West End show *John, Paul, George, Ringo and Bert*, and the music was pre-recorded by an American group who specialized in recreating Beatle sounds "right down to the mistakes". Even the extras for the club and concert scenes were "authentic", being real schoolchilren who "became hysterical just like they used to do for the real thing". Pete Best, the sacked Beatles' drummer, acted as adviser on the film and Marquand later expressed his admiration for Best's total recall and lack of bitterness—"...there was never a trace of acrimony in anything he said. He never criticized or blamed anyone."

In 1983, two years after they had first met, George Lucas picked Richard Marquand from a lengthy shortlist to direct *Return of the Jedi*. This second sequel to the fantastically popular *Star Wars* managed to maintain the series' brilliant use of special effects, but was roundly panned for almost everything else. Pauline Kael called it "an impersonal and rather junky piece of movie-making", while another critic likened it to a "mindlessly tedious video game in the sky". Given the fickleness of Hollywood, it could have been the end of Richard Marquand, but it wasn't.

His next major film was the highly praised *Jagged Edge* (1985), a gripping whodunnit starring Glenn Close and Beau Bridges. The story concerns a lawyer, played by Close, who falls for the client she is defending on an apparently unjust murder charge. In it Marquand creates constant uncertainty about the alleged murderer, manipulating the audience between absolute confidence in his innocence and complete conviction of his guilt. The film was scripted by Joe Ezterhas, a writer for *Rolling Stone* magazine; Marquand recalled: "He was a reporter with a social conscience...[who had] done a lot of work with female litigation lawyers...he sent me an early draft of *Jagged Edge* and it really took me by storm. I could really see that as a thriller it was rock hard. There was no way it was written beside the pool in Bel Air."

On the personal front, Marquand had made what the newspapers described as a "dynastic marriage" when, in 1960, he had married the daughter of Attorney-General Elwyn Jones. "We had our reception on the terrace of the Houses of Parliament." This marriage produced two children and lasted ten years. A decade later he married again, this time to a member of the film world, and two more children were born.

While Marquand's career had its ups and downs, there is little doubt that, but for his early demise, he would have gone on to make many more successful films. Perhaps it is of some consolation that his short life was creative and that he got so much enjoyment from it: "Here I am in my middle years getting enormous pleasure and self-satisfaction out of a very menial job—the sort of job where all I do is go about shouting at people, telling them where to stand and what to do. Yet for me the whole thing is magic."

Born Richard Marquand. **Parents** Hilary A., member of parliament and university professor, and Rachel E. (Rees) Marquand. **Marriages** 1) Josephine Jones, 1960 (divorced, 1970); 2) Carol Bell, film director, 1981. **Children** Hannah Rachel and James Elwyn from first marriage; Sam Adair and Molly Joyce from second marriage. **Education** Emmanuel School, London; Université d'Aix, Marseilles, 1955; King's College, Cambridge, BA, 1959, MA, 1963. **Military service** Special Services, Royal Air Force, Hong Kong, 1959–61. **Career** Television presenter, Hong Kong, 1961–62; film-maker, BBC documentary department, 1962–79; freelance film and television director, 1979–87. **Offices and memberships** United Kingdom Association of Cinematic and Television Technicians; Directors' Guild of America. **Awards and honours** Emmy Awards for "The Search for the Nile" series, 1975, and *Big Henry*, 1977. **Films** *The Legacy*, 1979; *The Birth of the Beatles*, 1980; *Eye of the Needle*, 1981; *Return of the Jedi*, 1983; *Until September*, 1984; *Jagged Edge*, 1985; *Capa*, 1986; *Hearts of Fire*, 1987. **Television** (documentaries, include) *One Pair of Eyes*; "Cameron Country" series; *Brendan Behan* (profile for *Omnibus*); "The Search for the Nile" series, 1975; *Big Henry*, 1977. **Cause of death** Stroke, at age 49.

QUINN MARTIN

American Producer and Scriptwriter

***Born* New York City, New York, 22 May 1922**

***Died* Rancho Santa Fe, California, 6 September 1987**

In one of the few interviews ever given by Quinn Martin, the man known as the godfather of television crime dramas presented the facts as he saw them. "I know I am the best scriptwriter in television," he said simply. "I understand what people want to watch." From any other producer, such statements might have appeared as the height of arrogance, but for Martin's assertions, the facts speak for themselves. His company, QM Productions, churned out more than 2000 hours of television programmes, which included such long-running series as *The Fugitive*, *The Untouchables*, *Cannon*, *The FBI*, *Barnaby Jones* and *The Streets of San Francisco*. His 16 network series and numerous made-for-television movies earned Martin several Emmy awards and countless fans on both sides of the Atlantic; at least 1600 episodes of his productions and over 30 television movies have been viewed by the British public alone.

A very private man, Martin was rarely photographed and almost never interviewed, so few details are known about his personal life. Born in New York, he grew up in Los Angeles, where his father obtained a job as a film producer and editor. Young Martin graduated from Fairfax High School, served for five years in the army during World War II, then graduated from the University of California at Berkeley in 1949. His first job was as a film editor with Metro-

Goldwyn-Mayer. Soon he took to writing scripts, and for several years he worked as a writer and head of post-production at various companies, including Desilu Productions, the company established by actors Desi Arnaz and Lucille Ball. It was at Desilu that Martin had his first taste of producing when he worked on the *Jane Wyman Show*. From there he quickly moved into the type of production that later became his hallmark: in 1959, still at Desilu, he produced a two-hour television movie which told the story of FBI agent Eliot Ness. Starring Robert Stack, *The Untouchables* proved so popular that Martin turned it into a series which ran for four years and won him six Emmy awards. Despite its popularity, however, *The Untouchables* was one of several so-called "action features" denounced by Congress in 1961 as being excessively violent.

Undeterred (Martin had formed his own company the previous year), the new king of crime dramas began producing other series in the same vein: *The Fugitive*, starring David Janssen, *The FBI*, starring Efrem Zimbalist Jr, and the less-successful *The Invaders*, starring Roy Thinnes. *The FBI* created enormous publicity when its principal actors were cleared by the real FBI before they were allowed to play agency members and their families. The final episode of *The Fugitive* in 1967 drew the highest rating of any television episode up to that time; only when J.R.'s attacker was revealed on *Dallas* 13 years later was that rating surpassed.

Series followed successful series in Martin's career, and his audible credit—"This has been a Quinn Martin Production"—could be heard at the end of all his programmes. In addition, Martin produced a popular feature film entitled *The Mephisto Waltz*. As well as his television activities, Martin served as an adjunct professor of drama at Warren College of the University of California at San Diego, and held positions as president of both the La Jolla Playhouse, a well-established regional theatre, and the Del Mar Fair Board. In 1979 he sold QM Productions to Taft Broadcasting and retired to Rancho Santa Fe; evidently, he had done what he set out to do in the world of television.

In a rare interview given in London during 1973, Martin disclosed a little about his working methods. While writing, he said that he usually woke at 5 a.m., relegating sleep to no more than four hours a night. "I've probably been carrying the idea around in my head for months," he said of a new project. "I can clear the presentation for a new series with about 12 days' hard work. If it's a cop series, I always like to have a good guy in the police system, as well as a guy who'll break the rules. It's the same if it's a medical series: you can't destroy systems which people like and trust by making out everyone to be all bad. It's also important to capture the mood of people."

As his success shows, Martin was adept at gauging that mood by creating heroes who were human as well as tough. His heroes, however, were often far less trouble to the producer than the actors who played them. William Conrad, for example, the rotund actor who played the lead in *Cannon*, was fine, Martin said, until "his head became as big as his belly. It's always something you have to fight against," the producer continued. "The actor is speaking the words created by me. I don't usually step on his turf—this is one of the reasons I don't normally do interviews—and I don't expect him to step on mine."

Privacy was something Martin respected, both for his actors (if they desired it) and for himself. "I don't play the Hollywood game," he stated. "I'm not seen at the so-called 'in places'. That's for the people I write for." It is ironic, then, that the man who hid from public view should go down in media history as "Mr TV".

Born Martin Cohn. **Father** Martin G. Cohn, film editor and producer. **Marriage** Mariane (Muffet) Martin, 1961. **Children** Jill, Cliff and Michael. **Education** Fairfax High School; University of California, Berkeley, BA, 1949. **Military service** US Army Air Corps, World War II. **Career** Apprentice editor at MGM; film editor, writer and head of post-production at various studios, including Universal, 1950–54; writer and producer of Desilu Productions' *Jane Wyman Show*, *The Desilu Playhouse* and *The Untouchables*, 1957–59; founder, president and chief executive officer, QM Productions, producing action series, 1960–79; sold QM Productions to Taft Broadcasting, 1979; chairman of board, Quinn Martin Films; president, Quinn Martin Communications Group, 1982–87. **Related activities** Adjunct professor of drama, Warren College, University of California; endowed chair of drama, 1983. **Offices and memberships** President, Del Mar (California) Fair Board, with jurisdiction over Del Mar Race Track, 1983–84; president, La Jolla Playhouse, California, 1985–86; trustee, Buckley School, North Hollywood, California. **Awards and honours** Various Quinn Martin productions have won television industry awards, including six Emmys for *The Untouchables*. **Productions** *The Jane Wyman Show*, 1957; *The Desilu Playhouse*, 1958; *The Untouchables*, 1959–63; *The Fugitive*, 1960–67; *The FBI*; *The Invaders*; *The Streets of San Francisco*; *Barnaby Jones*; *Cannon*, *The Manhunter*; *Most Wanted*; *Tales of the Unexpected*; *12 O'clock High*; also made a number of television films, and one feature film, *The Mephisto Waltz*, 1971. **Cause of death** Heart attack, at age 65.

ARNALDO MOMIGLIANO

Italian Historian

Born **Caraglio, Italy, 4 September 1908**

Died **London, England, 1 September 1987**

Arnaldo Momigliano was one of the most influential historians of the twentieth century, and one of the greatest scholars of any time. His most outstanding qualities were the breadth of his learning, his creative originality and his clarity of mind. These qualities were evident to all who knew him or studied under him, and they live on in his published work. He was a historian of immense range and versatility; although his research was concentrated on the ancient world, it covered all periods of Greek, Roman and Jewish history, and sought to uncover the classical roots of modern Western civilization. His principal interests lay in the general field of the history of ideas: ancient religions (especially Judaism and Christianity), issues of political, religious and intellectual liberty, the interaction of ancient cultures, and the relationship between history and biography. He also devoted himself to the study of historiography and the development of historical method from classical antiquity to the present day, fields in which his learning was unrivalled and in which he was recognized as the leading authority.

The number of his publications runs well into four figures, including over 700 major books, articles and reviews. The most important of his essays (the form which he preferred above all) are published in a series of collected volumes, of which eight have so far appeared, and a ninth is in preparation. Selections of his essays include *Studies in Historiography* (1966), *Essays in Ancient and Modern Historiography* (1977), and *On Pagans, Jews and Christians* (1987). Of his books, the most important is probably *Alien Wisdom: The Limits of Hellenization* (1975), a study of the interaction of Greek and non-Greek cultures. His profound analysis of the Greeks' failure to understand foreign cultures contains an important lesson for Western civilization in the modern world.

Momigliano was born and brought up in Piedmont, a member of a prominent local family of Jewish intellectuals. Details of his early life are hard to come by, but we know that he had an orthodox Jewish upbringing and was educated at home by private tutors. As with many Italian intellectuals, his development was precocious. He entered the University of Turin when he was barely 17, began publishing articles before he was 20, and had more than 30 major publications to his name by the age of 22, including his first book, on the Maccabees (this was, incidentally, also the subject of his last major article, written from a hospital bed in Chicago in the summer of 1987).

In 1929 he moved to Rome and took up a post at the university in 1932. Meanwhile, he worked for the *Enciclopedia Italiana*, for which he wrote over 230 articles. Although this was an official publication, most of those whom it employed had no sympathy for Fascism and looked rather to the philosopher Benedetto Croce, the leader of the anti-Fascist intelligentsia, for intellectual inspiration and moral guidance. Momigliano became closely associated with Croce, whom he had first met while a student in Turin, and was deeply influenced by him.

In 1936 he returned to Turin as professor of Roman history. Turin University was a centre of anti-Fascism, but at this time life in Italy was becoming increasingly difficult and dangerous for anti-Fascists, and in particular for Jews. In September 1938 Momigliano fell victim to Mussolini's decree dismissing all Jewish professors and teachers. A year later he fled to England with his wife and daughter and took up residence in Oxford, where he did research for several years, assisted by a grant from the Rockefeller Foundation. Meanwhile, the war claimed the lives of many of his family and friends, including both his parents, who were murdered in a Nazi concentration camp in 1943.

After the war he chose to stay in England, although he retained his Italian citizenship until the end of his life. In 1951 he moved to London, to the chair of ancient history at University College, where he taught until his retirement in 1975. London remained his home until his death, although he travelled widely in Europe and the US. He spent much of his time in Italy, making frequent visits to Turin, where he had been reinstated in 1945 and was permitted by the Italian Foreign Ministry to retain his chair *in absentia*, and to Pisa where, in 1964, he was given a special chair at the Scuola Normale Superiore. After his retirement he was also Alexander White visiting professor at the University of Chicago.

In England his relationship with the academic establishment was ambivalent. In formal terms his distinction was recognized; he was one of the few scholars to be awarded honorary doctorates by both Oxford and Cambridge, and after his retirement he held visiting fellowships at All Souls (Oxford) and Peterhouse (Cambridge). None the less, Momigliano always remained something of an outsider, and in general was as suspicious of Oxbridge dons as they were of him. Moreover, he never concealed his lack of sympathy with the methods of contemporary English historiography. As a follower of Croce, he did not find much to attract him in an approach which shunned ideas and concentrated on the detailed analysis of political élites. In the 1930s this kind of history was made fashionable by Sir Lewis Namier, who, according to Momigliano, "had persuaded the English that the history of ideas was an un-British activity". In ancient history the chief exponent of this trend was Sir Ronald Syme, whose school still dominates the subject in Britain, and whose long-running public debates with Momigliano form an important chapter in the history of modern historiography.

At University College, London, however, with its freethinking tradition and informal atmosphere, Momigliano felt at ease and was able to teach and research in his own way. The nearby Warburg Institute (which had moved to London from Germany in the 1930s) was also a source of inspiration. "When I arrived in Oxford in 1939," he once wrote, "it was enough to mention the word 'idea' to be given the address of the Warburg Institute." At the Warburg he did much of his reading and ran a memorable weekly seminar. He attracted a dazzling array of speakers to these occasions, but most of those who attended came principally to hear Momigliano's interventions. As a rule he would begin the discussion after a paper by raising "a couple of small points", and then proceed to deliver a 20-minute lecture which invariably hit the nail on the head.

Momigliano had a colourful and engaging personality, a sparkling sense of humour and a mischievous twinkle in his eye. His jokes and anecdotes were hilarious, but often had a serious purpose behind them; and many of his most important insights were expressed, both verbally and in writing, as jokes. With his squashed hat and dishevelled black suit, bulging pockets and huge bunches of keys, he appeared a strikingly eccentric figure; and no one who saw it ever forgot the string bag in which he carried his books. But the impression of a chaotic and absent-minded professor was misleading; in fact, he was a man who organized his life with great care, and showed extraordinary professionalism and efficiency in his scholarly work. His disciplined personal regime meant that he was never too busy to answer personal letters or to talk to friends, colleagues or pupils. He loved to talk, and to do so while walking was his favourite pastime. He was immensely generous with his time, especially to younger scholars, whose company he always enjoyed. Those who benefited from his friendship, advice and instruction were completely devoted to him.

To the end of his life Momigliano showed great physical and intellectual energy. After his retirement he continued to travel widely (though not until 1985 did he feel able to visit Germany), and divided his time between England, Italy and the United States. He received countless international honours and awards, including more than a dozen honorary degrees from universities in Europe and the US. He was made an honorary knight of the British Empire in 1974.

Born Arnaldo Dante Momigliano. **Parents** Riccardo and Ilda (Levi) Momigliano. **Marriage** Gemma Segre, 1932. **Children** One daughter, Anna Laura. **Education** Taught at home by tutors; University of Turin, DLitt; University of Rome. **Emigration** Left Italy for England, 1938. **Career** Professor of Greek history, University of Rome, 1932–36; professor of Roman history, University of Turin, 1936–38: dismissed by Mussolini on racial grounds; research work in Oxford, 1939–47; supernumerary professor of Roman history, University of Turin, 1945–64; lecturer in ancient history, University of Bristol, 1947–49, reader in ancient history, 1949–51; professor of ancient history, University of London, 1951–75. **Related activities** Co-editor, *Rivista Storica Italiana*, 1948–87; Alexander White visiting professor, University of Chicago, 1957, 1975–1987; supernumerary professor of Roman history, Scuola Normale Superiore, Pisa, 1964–87; Sather Professor in classics, University of California, 1961–62; J.H. Gray Lecturer, University of Cambridge, 1963; Wingate Lecturer, Hebrew University of Jerusalem, 1964; visiting professor and Lauro de Bossis Lecturer, Harvard University, 1964–65; C.N. Jackson Lecturer, Harvard University, 1968; Jerome Lecturer, Michigan University, 1971–72; visiting scholar, Harvard, 1972; Trevelyan Lecturer, Cambridge University, 1973; Flexner Lecturer, Bryn Mawr, 1974; Grinfield Lecturer on the Septuagint, Oxford, 1978–82; Efroymson Lecturer, Hebrew Union College, Cincinnati, 1978; Gauss Lecturer, Princeton, 1979; Lurcy Professor, University of Chicago, 1982; visiting fellow: Peterhouse, Cambridge, 1983–85, Princeton University, 1984; visiting professor, École Normale Supèrieure, Paris, 1984. **Offices and memberships** Corresponding member, German Archaeological Institute, 1935; Accademia dei Lincei, 1961 (corresponding member, 1947–61); honorary member, American Historical Association, 1964; president, Society for Promotion of Roman Studies, 1965–68; Arcadia, 1967; Accademia delle Scienze di Torino, 1968; Instituto di Studi Romani, 1970 (corresponding member, 1954–70); Instituto Studi Etruschi, 1973; foreign member: Royal Dutch Academy, American Philosophical Society, American Academy of Arts and Sciences, Institut de France. **Awards and honours** Premio Cantoni, University of Florence, 1932; fellow, British Academy, 1954; Premio Feltrinelli for historical research (Accademia dei Lincei Award), 1960; Knight Commander Order of the British Empire, 1974; honorary MA, Oxford; honorary DLitt: Bristol, 1959, Edinburgh, 1964, Oxford, 1970, Cambridge, 1971, London, 1975, Chicago, 1976,

Leiden, 1977, Urbino, 1978; honorary DHL: Columbia, 1974, Brandeis, 1977, Hebrew Union College, 1980, Bard College, 1983, Yale, 1985; honorary DPhil: Hebrew University, 1974, Tel-Aviv University, 1981; Marburg University, 1986; honorary fellow: Warburg Institute, 1975; University College London, 1976; Kaplun Prize for historical research, Hebrew University, 1975; Gold Medal, Italian Ministry of Education, 1977; Kenyon Medal, British Academy, 1981; Premio Sila, 1985. **Publications** *La composizione della Storia de Tucidide*, 1930; *Prime linee di storia della tradizione maccabaica*, 1931 (second edition, 1968); *Claudius*, 1934 (second edition, 1961); *Filippo il Macedone*, 1934; *La storiographia sull' impero romano*, 1936; *Contributo alla storia degli studi classici*, 1955; *Secondo contributo alla storia degli studi classici*, 1960; *Terzo contributo alla storia degli studi classici*, 1966; *Studies in Historiography*, 1966; *Paganism and Christianity in the Fourth Century*, 1968; *Quarto contributo alla storia degli studi classici*, 1969; *The Development of Greek Biography*, 1971 (translated into Italian and Japanese); *Introduzione bibliographica alla storia greca fino a Socrate*, 1975; *Quinto contributo alla storia degli studi classici*, 1975; *Alien Wisdom: The Limits of Hellenization*, 1975 (second edition, 1978, translated into Italian, German and French); *Essays on Historiography*, 1977; *Sesto contributo alla storia degli studi classici*, 1981; *La storiographia greca*, 1982 (translated into Spanish, 1984); *Problèmes d'historiographie ancienne et moderne*, 1983; *New Paths of Classicism in the Nineteenth Century*, 1983; (editor) *Aspetti di Hermann Usener filologo della religione*, 1983; (editor) *Aspetti dell'opera di G. Dumézil*, 1983; *Sui fondamenti della storia antica*, 1984; *Settimo contributo alla storia degli studi classici*, 1984; *Ottavo contributo alla storia degli studi classici*, 1987; (contributor) *Cambridge Ancient History*, *Journal of Roman Studies*, *History and Theory*, *Journal of the Warburg Institute*, *Daedalus*, *Enciclopedia Italiana*, *Encyclopaedia Britannica* and *Encyclopedia Judaica*. **Cause of death** Heart failure, at age 78.

HOWARD MOSS

American Poet, Critic, Playwright and Editor

Born **New York City, New York, 22 January 1922**

Died **New York City, New York, 16 September 1987**

Howard Moss was an American man-of-letters whose range of talent and accomplishment exhibited a Renaissance intelligence. "Without people like Howard Moss," writes David Ray, "we could, indeed, have no literary culture." As poetry editor for the *New Yorker* from 1950, he discovered and championed the talents of several influential poets, including Richard Wilbur and Elizabeth Bishop. As a poet himself, he was at the front line of new developments in American verse, producing a steady stream of poems between 1946 and 1985. They expressed "quiet, structured power" and could be deftly visual and musical. His plays have largely been well-received in production. As a critic and editor he possessed the "sensitive and keen mind" which allowed him to recognize and explore new trends, shown by his advocacy of the then-unfashionable Paul Blackburn in the 1960s. His "distrust of theses and theories about writing" gave him an eclectic approach to his critical work. Despite the quality of his work, suggests Harold Bloom, he was always "too quiet and almost quietistic to attract really wide attention". Yet his work has a devoted following, and anyone familiar with his writing appreciates the skill, wisdom and craftsmanship it displays.

Moss was raised in a middle-class environment in New York City, but he said, "two facts made my life somewhat different from most people's: my father [a Lithuanian immigrant] brought his mother and father over from the 'old country'....I was really under the care of my grandparents, who were of another flavour unmistakably". Though he was born and raised in New York, he grew up "in two places at once". Though he often felt separated from the metropolis (his home was actually in one of New York's coastal suburbs), the only extended period he spent elsewhere was at the University of Michigan.

The experience and training he acquired as a young man ideally suited his editorial ambitions. This included being a copy boy at *Time* magazine, and then becoming its book reviewer—"An embarrassing step forward," he recalled. "The colleagues with whom I distributed paper clips one week distributed them to me the next." He was an English instructor at Vassar College for two years, then fiction editor of *Junior Bazaar* for a year before coming to the *New Yorker* in 1948. Two years later he advanced to poetry editor, where he remained until his death.

On the writing side, he turned to poetry and drama in college, having written short stories and verse since grammar school. His first play, *The Folding Green*, was produced when he was 26 years old, and his first book, *The Wound and the Weather*, at 24. It met with a rather tepid reception, but after that, his work and reputation steadily improved. His fourth volume, a selection of old and new poems confirmed him in the eyes of Thom Gunn as a talent "superior to that of most of his generation". The poems in *Finding Them Lost*, the subsequent collection, made one reviewer say that the absence of "the urgent infantilism [and] imperativeness" brought him "very close to being a French poet in English". His calm, off-hand approach to subject matter appears in this excerpt from "The Restaurant Window":

A time-lapse camera might do it justice,
This street outside the restaurant window,
Feeling hurrying by one side
And thought on the other.
Gradually night sponges up vision,
A moment so made up of other moments
No one can tell one famous variation
From another. Soon they will become the theme.
It is then that the power of form is felt
(Could it have been, all along, the subject matter?)
Connecting everything, the ginko's gesture
And the ginko, even permitting
The streetlamp turning on every evening
Its one small circle of illumination....

Moss's critical works share the same readability and lack of pretension. He wrote an ambitious study of Proust's *Remembrance of Things Past*, which organized the novel around four metaphysical concepts: gardens, windows, parties and steeples. The usefulness of this framework was not clear to everyone, but his insights to Proust's novel met with general approval. One of the notable aspects of this part of his work has to be the variety of his method. A disciple of no particular "school" of thought, his analyses ranged from new criticism to reader-response to formalism.

Moss's poetry continued to refine the ease and vividness for which it had become known. By the time *Selected Poems* was published in 1971, he had mastered technique and sought to "concentrate on what is harder". John Hollander wrote that he "pierces even deeper the patterns...of love, idleness, hope and regret". He was often compared to W.H. Auden, Wallace Stevens and—not always flatteringly—to Yeats. Moss worked towards and achieved an understanding of the vital role of art and fantasy. His skill at writing poetry produced some excellent verse, but it was the excitement and awe with which he infused them that was the stuff of artistry:

> Exiled from exile, you will always bear
> Two sacred marks of the interior:
> Memory and art. How early it grows dark!
> They say the snow will bury us this year.

Born Howard Moss. **Parents** David Leonard and Sonya (Schrag) Moss. **Education** University of Michigan, 1939–40; Harvard University, 1942; University of Wisconsin, BA, 1943; graduate study, Columbia University, 1946. **Career** Copy boy, *Time* magazine, New York City, 1943, book reviewer, 1944; instructor, Vassar College, Poughkeepsie, New York, 1945–46; fiction editor, *Junior Bazaar*, 1947; staff member, *New Yorker*, New York City, 1948–50, poetry editor 1950–87. **Related activities** Hurst Professor, Washington University, 1972; adjunct professor: Barrington College, 1976, Columbia University, 1977, University of California, Irvine, 1979, University of Houston, 1980. **Offices and memberships** American Academy and Institute of Arts and Letters; judge, National Book Awards, 1957, 1964. **Awards and honours** Janet Sewell Davis Award, *Poetry*, 1944; Brandeis University Creative Arts Award, 1962, 1983; Avery Hopwood Award, 1963; American Academy and Institute of Arts and Letters Award, 1968; Ingram Merrill Foundation Grant, 1972; (co-winner) National Book Award for Poetry for *Selected Poems*, 1972; National Endowment for the Arts Award, 1984. **Verse** (all published in New York, unless stated) *The Wound and the Weather*, 1946; *The Toy Fair*, 1954; *A Swimmer in the Air*, 1957; *A Winter Come, a Summer Gone: Poems, 1946–1960*, 1960; *Finding Them Lost and Other Poems*, New York and London, 1965; *Second Nature*, 1968; *Selected Poems*, 1971; *Chekhov*, 1972; *Travel: A Window*, 1973; *Buried City*, 1975; *A Swim Off the Rocks: Light Verse*, 1976; *Tigers and Other Lilies* (for children), 1977; *Notes from the Castle*, 1979; *Rules of Sleep*, 1984; *New Selected Poems*, 1985. **Plays** *The Folding Green*, produced Cambridge, Massachusetts, 1954, published New York, 1964; *The Oedipus Mah-jong Scandal*, produced New York, 1968; *The Palace at 4 a.m.*, produced East Hampton, New York, 1972; *Two Plays: The Palace at 4 a.m. and the Folding Green*, New York, 1980. **Other** (all published in New York, unless stated) (editor) *Keats*, 1952; *The Magic Lantern of Marcel Proust*, New York, 1962, London, 1963; (editor) *The Nonsense Books of Edward Lear*, 1964; *Writing Against Time: Critical Essays and Reviews*, 1969; (editor) *The Poet's Story*, New York, 1973, London, 1974; *Instant Lives* (satire), 1974; (editor), *New York: Poems*, 1980; *Whatever Is Moving* (essays), Boston, 1981; (translator) *The Cemetery by the Sea* by Paul Valéry, 1985; *Minor Movements* (essays), 1986. **Cause of death** Heart attack, at age 65.

VIKTOR NEKRASOV

Soviet Writer

***Born* Kiev, Russia, 17 June 1911**

***Died* Paris, France, 3 September 1987**

Of all his better known compatriots now living in the West, perhaps the Soviet writer Víktor Nekrásov least deserved the title of dissident. His literary works are relatively mild in their level of anti-Soviet criticism, reflecting the universal difficulties of a post-war, post-Stalin society rather than any single staunchly political viewpoint. As an exile in Paris, Nekrásov was never an outspoken critic of the Soviet regime, preferring to remain separate from those other high-profile Soviet dissidents such as Alexander Solzhenitsyn. He conducted himself with admirable generosity towards his opponents, preserving that independence of mind which was always his characteristic trait. It is ironic that Nekrásov died at a time when, under Gorbachev's political and cultural *perestroika*, the exile of so creative a writer would be practically unthinkable. Rumour has it that at the time of his death the question was going about, not *if* Nekrásov would be given leave to return to the USSR, but *when*.

Nekrásov was by no means a prolific writer—something he himself confessed when he wrote, "In the 20 years I have devoted to literature I have not written a great deal: three novels, 15 stories, three travel essays, some film scenarios, and articles on art and architecture." But for his three novels—*Frontline Stalingrad* (1946), *In His Home Town* (1954) and *Kira Georgievna* (1961)—his mark on the Russian literary scene would doubtless have been negligible. His first and best known novel, *Frontline Stalingrad*, won him immediate renown and established him on his career as a writer. Praised as one of Russia's greatest wartime novels and compared in its time to *All Quiet on the Western Front*, it neither attacks the wartime politics of Josef Stalin, nor adulates the Red Army's accomplishments with that jingoistic bravado which came to characterize so much of the literature written about the war. Instead, Nekrásov recalls his wartime experiences as a lieutenant in the Engineers to depict the Battle of Stalingrad as seen and lived through by the ordinary soldiers. His dispassionate treatment of the theme is reflected in a simplicity and directness of narrative, while the theme itself concentrates not on the heroism of fearless soldiers, but on the everyday hardships of life in the Russian trenches and on the comradeship and bravery of ordinary men united in common cause. Despite what many saw as an "unpatriotic approach", Nekrásov won the Stalin Prize for the novel.

The apparent ease with which he wrote *Frontline Stalingrad* belied his background and training. Brought up in Lausanne by his mother, a medical graduate, Nekrásov spent his childhood in Switzerland, then Paris. (The influence of French culture on his life remained strong right to the end. After World War I, he returned to Kiev, enrolling as a student at the Institute of Civil Engineering. But architecture, not engineering, was Nekrásov's passion; his ambition was to become the Soviet equivalent of Le Corbusier, to which end he left the Institute of Railway Engineering and enrolled at the Construction Institute of Kiev. Soon he began to develop other artistic aspirations, and taking the actor-director Stanislavsky as his model, spent four years touring the USSR as an actor, stage-designer and assistant director. He never lost his interest in architecture, however, but continued to write articles for architectural journals. The outbreak of war put an end to his stage career, when he joined up as an officer in the Engineers. Having fought unscathed right the way through the Battle of Stalingrad, he was severely wounded in Lublin in Poland in 1944, and spent the last year of the war convalescing. It was while lying in hospital that he began his first and most famous novel, and with it, his writing career.

His other two novels, *In His Home Town* and *Kira Georgievna*, deal with the theme of homecoming—a war veteran in the first, and a returnee from a Stalin labour camp in the second. Linked as they are with such universal issues as creativity and art, they both explore the disillusion felt by those who experience unfulfilled expectations and who are forced to reassess their priorities. Hardly anti-Soviet in character, they nevertheless fell foul of the authorities because of their emphasis on individual rather than corporate experience. Of *Kira Georgievna*, for example, the staunchly pro-Soviet writer and critic Fadeyev wrote, "The central characters are almost isolated from public life. Reality is examined by the author through the prism of their personal difficulties."

But it was not so much these novels as Nekrásov's growing disillusionment with the Soviet regime that led to his eventual denunciation by Khrushchev. On tours of Europe and the USA in 1957, 1960 and 1962, Nekrásov had the opportunity to experience life in the West, forming impressions and thoughts which he subsequently set down in a book entitled *Both Sides of the Ocean*. The candid comparisons between West and East which appeared in the book were unwelcome to the authorities, who accused him of unpatriotic "bourgeois objectivity", and of being too approving of the West. Increasingly, Nekrásov spoke out against the State, against the Soviet invasion of Czechoslovakia in 1968, against Soviet policy against the Jews and the Ukrainians.

Exasperated by his refusal to knuckle under, the authorities permitted Nekrásov to leave the USSR in 1974, whereupon he was stripped of his Soviet citizenship. He went to Paris where he was joined by his wife and son two years later. Together they lived a life of relative quiet, participants in the cultural life of the French capital, and away from the politics of anti-Soviet propaganda. Editor of the émigré journal *Kontinent* for several years, Nekrásov maintained a lively interest in literature until the time of his death. Those who knew him, either through his books or personally, praised him for his honesty and dignity. As one commentator wrote, "Nekrásov is a heavy-handed writer and traveller who saw only the most obvious things. The personality that comes through his book, however, is charming and open." Such was the verdict of those who made his acquaintance.

Born Víktor Platónovich Nekrásov. **Parents** Both doctors. **Children** One son. **Education** Institute of Civil Engineering, Kiev, 1930–33; Construction Institute, Kiev, 1933–36; Kiev acting academy, 1936–37. **Emigration** Left USSR for France, 1974; stripped of Soviet citizenship by USSR. **Military service** Lieutenant, Soviet Army Engineers, World War II; saw service at the Siege of Stalingrad, wounded and demobilized, 1944. **Career** Worked as architect, 1938; actor, assistant director and set designer, 1939–41; first novel published, winning Stalin Prize, 1947; published various books and articles on architecture, painting, film and literature, throughout the 1950s and 1960s while also active as scriptwriter, 1957–65; official criticisms of writing built up throughout career; account of visit to USA published, 1962; attacked by Khrushchev for "unpatriotic bourgeois objectivity" and threatened with expulsion from Communist Party and Writers' Union; reprimanded by party, 1969; expelled, 1973; manuscripts confiscated and given permission to emigrate, 1974; acting editor-in-chief, *Kontinent* journal, Paris, 1975–82. **Related activities** Supported individual dissidents and movements; actively opposed Soviet invasion of Czechoslovakia, 1968; participated in protests on Jewish and Ukrainian issues. **Memberships** Communist Party of the Soviet Union, 1944–72; Writers' Union. **Awards and honours** Stalin Prize (second class), 1947. **Publications** (include) *Vokopakh Stalingrada*, 1947, translated by David Floyd as *Frontline Stalingrad*, 1962; *Vrodnam gorode* (*In His Home Town*), 1954; *Pervoe znakomstvo: Iz zarubezhnykh vpetchatlenii* (First Acquaintance), 1958; *Sudak*, 1960; *Vasya Konakov: Rasskazy* (stories), 1961; *Kira Georgievna*, 1961, translated into English under same title, 1962; *Izbrannye proizvedeniya*, 1962; *Povesti, rasskazy, putevye zametki*, 1962; *Po obye* *storony okeana*, 1962, translated by Elias Kulukundis as *Both Sides of the Ocean*, 1964; *Vtoraya noch'* (stories), 1965; *Vzadannon raione*, 1965; *Mesyats vo Frantsii* (A Month in France), 1967; *Puteshestviya v raznykh izmereniyakh* (reports), 1967; *V zhizni i v pis'makh* (essays), 1971; *Zapiski zevaki* (Notes of an Idler), 1976; *Vzgljad i necto* (Views and Something More), 1977; *Po obe storony steny* (On Both Sides of the [Berlin] Wall), 1978; *Iz dal'nikh stranstvij vozvratjas* (On Returning From Foreign Lands), 1979–81; *Stalingrad*, Frankfurt, 1981; *Saperlipopet, ili Esli by da kaby, da vo rtu rosli griby* (memoirs), London, 1983; *Malen'kaja pecalnaja povest* (A Sad Little Story), 1985, London, 1986. **Cause of death** Cancer, at age 76.

JACO PASTORIUS

American Musician and Composer

***Born* Norristown, Pennsylvania, 1 December 1951**

***Died* Fort Lauderdale, Florida, 21 September 1987**

Jaco Pastorius is considered to have been the most influential bass guitarist since Jimmy Blanton, who first introduced bass as a lead instrument while playing with Duke Ellington during the early 1940s. Pastorius had a unique approach to the instrument, making frequent use of chords, harmonics, percussive sounds, and sudden bursts of speed and volume, but above all concentrating on the quality and texture of each note he played. A self-taught musician, he developed new methods which have been universally imitated. The originality and feeling of his compositions have been compared with those of Charlie Mingus, Toshiko Akiyoshi and Gil Evans.

Pastorius was born in 1951 near Philadelphia, the son of a jazz singer and drummer and his Finnish wife. After his parents separated in 1959, the young Jaco moved to Fort Lauderdale with his mother and two brothers. An athletic and naturally talented child, he learned to play piano, guitar and saxophone, but took a particular interest in the drums.

During his teens he worked as a drummer for the Las Olas Brass, but was asked to leave when the band found a better drummer. Eager to remain in the band, he switched to playing bass and worked very hard, playing every night for weeks on end.

In 1968 he purchased what would become his trademark—an abused 1962 Fender Jazz Bass, which cost $90. The original owner had attempted to make it into a fretless bass by pulling out each of the metal frets with pliers. This left deep gouges on the fingerboard and an uneven playing surface. A resourceful repairman, Pastorius filled the gouges with wood putty and finished the playing surface with six coats of epoxy varnish.

While working as house bassist at the nightclub Bachelors III, Pastorius wrote band arrangements for the Ira Sullivan and Peter Graves orchestras. During this period, he wrote several songs, including the local band standard "Domingo", using only a toy piano.

Already prominent on the Florida scene, Pastorius travelled to New York, where he worked briefly with Lou Ralls and his friend Pat Metheny. But while touring with Wayne Cochran and the CC Riders, he tired of life on the road and returned to Fort Lauderdale. He spent the next year engaged in serious practice, and taught music at the University of Miami, using Nicholas Smolensky's *Thesaurus of Melodic Scales and Patterns* and Hannon's *Virtuoso Pianist* for bass instruction.

In 1975 his wife, then a waitress at Bachelors III, told a visiting band member (drummer Bobby Colomby of Blood, Sweat & Tears) that she was "married to a bass player who's the greatest in the world". Colomby asked to hear him and was stunned by the performance, describing it as "absolutely amazing". He took his find back to New York, and Pastorius played with Blood, Sweat & Tears and Metheny while also working on a solo album.

While back in Florida, he was asked to lend equipment to Alphonso Johnson, then the bassist for the jazz group Weather Report. He attended the band's concert and afterwards introduced himself to its co-founders Joe Zawinul and Wayne Shorter, saying, as Zawinul recalls, "I'm Jaco Pastorius and I'm the greatest bass player in the world." The two were greatly impressed by Pastorius's recordings, and later invited him to replace Johnson in the group.

The solo album, *Jaco Pastorius*, released in 1976, featured a startling rendition of Charlie Parker's "Donna Lee" and a beautifully textured bass solo called "Portrait of Tracy". Other compositions introduced melodic and rhythmic concepts as revolutionary to bassists as any work since Blanton or his contemporary Paul Chambers.

The addition of Pastorius to Weather Report greatly changed that group's style and audience. Concert-goers were enthralled by his commanding stage presence; he was a brightly dressed and physically animated performer who bounded across the stage, sometimes leaving it completely. His soulful and energetic style attracted a younger, more commercial element to Weather Report, particularly after the group's 1977 album *Heavy Weather*, which featured the hit "Birdland". Pastorius's compositions "Teentown" and "Havona" showcased rapid and melodic "punk jazz" bass-lines which demonstrated even greater mobility for the bass as a lead instrument.

Pastorius collaborated with several leading musicians, including Al Di Meola, Herbie Hancock, David Sanborn, John McLaughlin and the German trombonist Albert Mangellsdorf. He was a highly visible performer on recordings by Joni Mitchell, providing a new sense of strength and lyricism to her music. The formula remained successful through four albums and a major tour, for which Pastorius assembled a band which included Metheny, Don Alias and Mike Brecker.

Divorced from his first wife in 1978, Pastorius married Ingrid Horn Müller the following year. And, while he had previously shunned drugs of all forms, complaining that they impeded his playing, he began to abuse alcohol. This caused a sudden change in his character which occasionally affected his performance in the band.

Weather Report, however, was changed again by the addition of the drummer Peter Erskine. Pastorius and Erskine formed a solid and highly disciplined rhythm section capable of frenzied energy levels. As a quartet, Weather Report embarked on a world tour that took them to such places as Brazil, Japan, Cuba, Australia and Costa Rica. Recordings of the tour were later released on the album *8.30*, which won a Grammy Award for best jazz album of 1980. The album showcased Pastorius several times, most notably on the powerful bass solo "Slang", in which he borrowed liberally from Jimi Hendrix's "Third Stone From the Sun" and ends wryly with a cliché from "The Sound of Music".

Pastorius was highly suspicious of record executives, and disaffected many by refusing to fit their "mould". Despite an increased preoccupation with drinking, Jaco continued to make strong musical statements on Weather Report's 1981 *Night Passage* album. For the fourth year in a row, he won *Down Beat* magazine's award for best bassist.

Later that year he and Erskine left Weather Report to pursue their own projects. Pastorius began work on a second album, entitled *Word of Mouth*, which like his first album, featured several guest musicians, including Erskine, Hubert Laws, Jack DeJohnette and the Belgian harmonica player Toots Thielemans. The album opens with an extraordinary version of Bach's "Chromatic Fantasy" (performed as a bass solo), flows into a bass and harmonica version of Paul

McCartney's "Blackbird", and then into a pyrotechnic bass solo. The album also features a waltz performed by a jazz orchestra and an abstract improvisation called "Crisis". Pastorius's music had become increasingly complex and diverse—qualities neither understood nor welcomed by commercial critics.

In 1982 he formed a 21-piece big band, which featured Erskine, Thielemans, Peter Graves, Randy Brecker and steel drum player Othello Molineaux. Unable to win backing from his record company, Warner Brothers, Pastorius, at his own expense, led the band on a tour of Europe and Japan. The band, however, was soon distracted by his personal problems. He was forced to retire temporarily after falling from a hotel window and severely damaging his shoulder; and to add to his woes, his bass (for which had once been offered $80,000) was broken during shipping.

Erskine noticed increasingly bizarre behaviour in Pastorius, and at the end of the tour consulted his father, a psychiatrist, who suggested that Pastorius might be suffering from some form of chemical imbalance. Several attempts by friends and family to have him hospitalized ultimately failed. As his condition worsened, wild mood swings and outrageous stunts, followed by belligerence, intransigence and severe depression caused great friction in his personal and professional lives.

Leaving several recording projects unfinished, Pastorius moved to New York in 1984, where he was seen living as a vagrant, sleeping on park benches. Guitarist Mike Stern, a close friend who had overcome substance abuse, tried but failed to help him. In an unusually sad episode, Pastorius was committed to Bellevue Hospital, where it was learned he was manic depressive and drug dependent. His addictions developed from a condition, probably congenital, in which euphoria became his only means of escaping a feeling of paranoia. He was prescribed Tegretol, but later abandoned the medication because it affected his playing. Subsequently, he frequently came into conflict with the law for violent or obnoxious behaviour. In a 1985 video instruction package, in which he appeared with bassist Jerry Jemmott, Pastorius was visibly troubled.

In 1986 he began to rebuild his life. He went back on his medication and remained, for the most part, free from drugs and out of trouble. He worked out regularly and recorded for the first time in three years with Stern, guitarist Bireli Lagrene and the drummer Brian Melvin. Eager to get his "Florida sound" back, he returned to Fort Lauderdale in 1987. It was, perhaps, a fatal decision, as he spent most of his time with hard-drinking street people.

On 11 September that year, Pastorius attended a concert by Carlos Santana near Miami. Ironically, he climbed on stage during a bass solo by Alphonso Johnson and was expelled from the theatre. He later turned up at the Midnight Bottle Club, where he started an altercation. After kicking the door, he was chased down and severely beaten by the club's bouncer Luc Havan. Unrecognized, he was admitted to Broward General Medical Center with internal bleeding and a fractured skull. Eventually, he was identified by the doctor who had delivered his children. While in hospital, Pastorius suffered a stroke. Nine days later, with friends and family by his side, he died. Havan was convicted of manslaughter, and served only nine months.

At a memorial gathering after his funeral, Pat Metheny noted the great influence Pastorius had over popular style; his contributions were routinely incorporated by other bassists, including Marcus Miller, Victor Bailey and Mark Egan, and he was revered by such venerable bassists as Jack Bruce, Jeff Berlin and Stanley Clarke, all of whom he had befriended and played with in later years.

A fearless and raw, but still vulnerable and insecure man, Pastorius was tremendously misunderstood; he was once dismissed as a frustrated guitarist who aspired to become "the Jimi Hendrix of the bass". In fact, he will be remembered as the catalyst that propelled Weather Report to fame, and as a highly imaginative composer and stylist, who reinvented the instrument through a new melodic, more expressive approach. He demanded to be heard, and as part of his legacy, laid to rest the notion that bassists had to be unassertive, secondary members of an ensemble. His distinctive, growling low notes, profound improvisations, and senses of rhythm and coloration will influence musicians for decades. And while his rhythm and blues-based "Florida sound" will continue to invite imitation, Jaco Pastorius will remain the standard by which all other electric bassists are measured.

Born John Francis Pastorius III. **Parents** Jack, jazz drummer and singer, and Stephanie (Haapala) Pastorius. **Marriages** 1) Tracy Lee, 1970 (divorced, 1978); 2) Ingrid Horn Müller, 1979 (divorced, 1985). **Children** Mary and John from first marriage; Julius and Felix from second marriage. **Education** Northeast High School, Fort Lauderdale. **Career** Drummer with Las Olas Brass during early teens; switched to playing bass guitar; house bassist, Bachelors III nightclub, Florida; "discovered" by Bobby Colomby, drummer with Blood, Sweat & Tears, subsequently returning with him to New York; worked briefly with Lou Ralls and Pat Metheny; toured with Wayne Cochran and the CC Riders; took year out to study and teach, University of Miami; played with Blood, Sweat & Tears and Pat Metheny, New York, 1975; replaced Alphonso Johnson in jazz group Weather Report; made world tour, leaving group in late 1981; collaborated with many musicians, including Al Di Meola, Herbie Hancock, David Sanborn, John McLaughlin, Albert Mangellsdorf and Joni Mitchell; formed own band, Word of Mouth, with Metheny, Don Alias and Mike Brecker, 1980–83; formed 21-piece band, featuring Erskine, Thielemans, Peter Graves, Randy Brecker and Othello Molineaux, and embarked on tour of Europe and Japan; forced to retire temporarily through shoulder injury; suffered severe depression which resulted in a period of living rough in New York followed by hospitalization at Bellevue; returned to Florida and made recordings with Mike Stern, Bireli Lagrene and Brian Melvin; career brought to an end by severe beating at nightclub near Miami. **Related activities** Performed on film *Shadows and Light* with Joni Mitchell, 1980; collaborated on instructional video with Jerry Jemmott, 1985. **Awards and honours** Grammy Award (with Weather Report) for *8.30*, best jazz album of 1980; *Down Beat* magazine award for best bassist, 1979, 1980, 1981, 1982; elected to *Guitar Player* magazine's Hall of Fame; Maretti Award (Fort Lauderdale). **Recordings** (include) *Party Down Little Beaver*, 1974; *Jaco* (solo album), 1974; Ira Sullivan, *Ira Sullivan*, 1975; Tom Scott, *Tom Scott in LA*, 1975; Ian Hunter, *All American Alien Boy*, 1975; Pat Metheny, *Bright Size Life*, 1976; *Jaco Pastorius* (solo album), 1976; *Flora Purim*, 1976; Weather Report, *Black Market*, 1976; Al Di Meola, *Land of the Midnight Sun*, 1976; Joni Mitchell, *Hejira*, 1976; Albert Mangellsdorf, *Trilogue*, 1977; Weather Report, *Heavy Weather*, 1977; Joni Mitchell, *Don Juan's Reckless Daughter*, 1977; Weather Report, *Mr Gone*, 1978; Joni Mitchell, *Mingus*, 1979; Weather Report, *8.30*, 1980; Joni Mitchell, *Shadows and Light*, 1980; Contributor, *Havana Jam I*, 1980; Herbie Hancock, *Mr Hands*, 1980; Weather Report, *Night Passage*, 1981; Contributor, *Havana Jam II*, 1981; *Word of Mouth* (solo album), 1981; Weather Report, *Weather Report*, 1982; *Twins*, 1983; *Invitation* (solo album), 1983; Randy Bernsen, *Music for People, Planets and Washing Machines*, 1985; Brian Melvin, *Brian Melvin*, 1986; Mike Stern, *Upside Down*, 1986; Bireli Lagrene, *Stuttgart Aria*, 1987; Brian Melvin, *Nightfood*, 1988. **Compositions** (include) "Domingo"; "Portrait of Tracy"; "Teentown"; "Havona"; "Slang"; "Crisis". **Cause of death** Injuries from a severe beating, at age 35.

MARGARET MANN PHILLIPS

British Translator, Historian and Literary Scholar

***Born* Kimberworth, Yorkshire, 23 January 1906**

***Died* Teddington, Middlesex, 18 September 1987**

Margaret Mann Phillips was one of the foremost authorities on the works of Desiderus Erasmus, the Dutch scholar who was the leading light of the Renaissance in Northern Europe. She was a translator, an editor and a commentator of great skill and learning whose work continues to be beneficial to students and scholars at all levels.

She was the daughter of a clergyman in York; her father's parish comprised much of the poorer quarters of the city, and she had the opportunity to see the best and the worst of life within its medieval walls. Her early life left a deep, lasting impression and inspired her to write poetry and prose from an early age. *Outgoings*, a collection of her poems, was published in 1936, and *Within the City Wall*, her (autobiographical) story of a young girl's life in York at the end of World War I, was published in 1943. A theme common to both was the dream and the fear of leaving the enclosed city.

The young Margaret Mann realized that dream by going to university and marrying to bring up a family of her own. Her husband was Charles Phillips, an archaeologist who is best known as the excavator of the Sutton Hoo burial ship. After his death in 1985 it was left to her to oversee the publication of his autobiography, *My Life in Archaeology*.

Phillips' own academic career was highly successful. She attended Somerville College, Oxford, and was awarded a first class degree in French. This was followed by a period of study and teaching in France, at the University of Paris. The result of this was her first major scholarly work, *Erasme et les débuts de la réforme française*, a doctoral thesis which won the prestigious Prix Bordin of the Académie de Belles Lettres in 1934. She was appointed to a lectureship at Newnham College, Cambridge, in the same year and elected to a college fellowship two years later. She taught at Cambridge until 1945, eventually resigning to devote more time to her family. However, she continued to research and publish, including an introductory work entitled *Erasmus and the Northern Renaissance*. This excellent book quickly became required reading for anyone with an interest in the subject. It is a mark of the book's quality that even now, in its third edition, it remains the best introduction to Erasmus in English.

The humanist scholar from Rotterdam exercised a tremendous influence over the development of Western literature and thought. He was typical of the learned men of his time in concentrating on the great works of classical Greece and Rome. He recognized the value of pagan ideas and philosophy (as contained in the works of Aristotle, Plutarch, Cicero and many others) as a supplement to the received wisdom of the Catholic Church. Like his English friend Sir Thomas More, Erasmus saw a continuity of thought and expression from pre-Christian to Christian values, arguing that even those deprived of the light of Christ were still striving towards the same goal as the Christian fathers. It was a stance which brought him into conflict with the Church of his day, but in the long term his work broadened knowledge and understanding of the classics and of Christianity to a remarkable degree.

Phillips was similarly devoted to the cause of knowledge. She taught French and Latin literature of the Renaissance at King's College, London, with great enthusiasm and skill, becoming reader in French in 1964. She published work on several literary figures, including Thomas More, Margaret of Navarre and Montaigne, although Erasmus remained her main concern. In her major work, *The Adages of Erasmus: A Study with Translations* (1964), she combined careful textual study with a broad range of illuminating comments on the adages in their classical and Renaissance contexts. She was an obvious choice to contribute to "The Collected Works of Erasmus", a series published in Toronto, for which she edited and translated his polemical dialogue, *Against the Barbarians* (1978).

After her retirement, Phillips continued to study and teach in London, at University College and the Warburg Institute. She was one of a group of brilliant scholars, including John Hale, Peter Brown and Arnaldo Momigliano who made London into a leading centre for the study of the classical tradition. In 1979 Oxford University awarded her a DLitt in recognition of her outstanding contribution to scholarship.

Born Margaret Mann. **Parents** Francis Arthur, clergyman, and Martha Hannah (Haigh) Mann. **Marriage** Charles William Phillips, archaeologist, 1940 (died, 1985). **Children** John and Penelope. **Education** York College for Girls; Somerville College, Oxford, BA, 1927, MA, 1931; Sorbonne, University of Paris, doctorate d'Université, 1934. **Career** Lecturer in English, University of Bordeaux, 1929–30; assistant lecturer in French, University of Manchester, 1934–36; fellow and director of studies in modern languages, Newnham College, Cambridge, 1936–45; lecturer in French, King's College, University of London, 1959–60, reader in French, 1964–68; honorary lecturer: University College, London, from 1971, Warburg Institute. **Offices and memberships** Member: advisory committee, "The Collected Works of Erasmus", Toronto, Modern Humanities Research Association, British Federation of University Women, Society of French Studies, Society of Renaissance Studies, Teilhard de Chardin Society. **Awards and honours** Prix Bordin of Académie de Belles Lettres for *Erasme et les débuts de la réforme française*; medal, Collège de France, 1969; honorary DLitt, Oxford University, 1979. **Publications** *Erasme et les débuts de la réforme française*, Paris, 1933; *Outgoing*, 1936; *Within the City Wall* (autobiography), Cambridge, 1943; *Erasmus and the Northern Renaissance*, 1945; second edition, 1965; (contributor) *Courants réligieux et humanisme*, Paris, 1959; (editor and translator) *The Adages of Erasmus*, Cambridge, 1964; *Erasmus and His Times*, Cambridge, 1967; (contributor) *Luther, Erasmus and the Reformation*, 1969; (contributor) *Erasmus*, London, 1970; (translator) *Antibarbari* (*Against the Barbarians*), volume 23 of "The Collected Works of Erasmus", Toronto, 1978; many articles in scholarly periodicals in England and France. **Cause of death** Undisclosed, at age 81.

AL READ

British Comedian

***Born* Manchester, England, 3 March 1909**

***Died* Yorkshire, England, 9 September 1987**

Al Read was probably one of the very last of the truly great radio comedians. His humour was based on his piercing observations of ordinary people in ordinary situations and he would preface his monologues with such knowing phrases as, "*You* know, *you've* met 'em," whereupon he would launch into a sketch in which he played all the parts.

He was born into a sausage and pie manufacturing family and went into the business, becoming a director at the age of 23. The business prospered and it was by the merest chance that Read was "discovered" at the age of 40. A BBC radio producer happened to be attending a golf club social evening at which Read performed one of his amateur turns. The producer was so impressed he invited him to try his hand at radio and he was offered a spot on the weekly music hall programme, *Variety Bandbox*. Read was an instant success and became the resident comedian on the programme. This was soon followed by the offer of his own weekly half-hour show, *Such Is Life*.

It is perhaps difficult to appreciate the impact of this both for Read and for the British public, but one has to remember that in the early 1950s there were only three radio stations, all run by the BBC, which operated a national network with only a few regional variations. Anyone who sought pop music had to listen to the varying signal of Radio Luxemburg which was usually only audible after dark. Television was in its infancy, the BBC operating only a fairly new single channel which was limited in its transmission area. Thus the BBC's Light Programme, as it was then known, was the primary source of entertainment for the majority of people in the UK. Read's popularity was instantaneous and up to 35 million listeners tuned in each week to hear his observations on life.

His routines involved familiar everyday situations such as the problems inherent in obtaining the services of a decorator to do up a spare bedroom; an awkward customer in a pub; a motorist being humiliated by a garage mechanic; a plumber undermining a householder's confidence with gloomy prognostications of what might happen once he commenced work—"I suppose you *know*..."; an uncooperative attendant in a car park and know-alls of every type. These he presented without any costumes or settings, just an ordinary man in the street who could tell you confidentially about the trials of the woman trying to park her car, the garage proprietor of doubtful temper and the Manchester housewife who hinted at unmentionable skeletons in assorted family cupboards with the simple words, "There was enough said at our Billy's wedding."

It has been said that an appreciation of Read's humour depended on how far his audience was acquainted with life "north of Watford", which is a British semi-joke indicating that any life existing much more than ten miles north of central London is probably only a semi-life. This actually detracts from the shrewdness of Read's observation of human frailties. It may be uniquely British but anyone who could understand the northern accent and was vaguely acquainted with the life of ordinary people could appreciate the universality of the characters he enshrined in his gallery of life situations. Awkward customers and doom and gloom merchants cross all social situations and classes.

Read's popularity brought him stage success in London's West End, a number of appearances in the *Royal Variety Show*—an annual show performed for members of the Royal Family to raise money for charity—and many bookings on the northern club circuit. He did, with reluctance, try television but it was not his medium. As with others, such as the late and greatly loved Tony Hancock, it seemed that the more complex technicalities of television prevented him achieving a rapport with his audience. If it had been solely a matter of not leaving enough to the imagination of the audience, as has been claimed, Read would never have had the lasting impact he achieved in the theatre and clubs.

Read never let his success interefere with his hobbies. He was a keen hunter and, when travelling the club circuits, always took his beloved horses, Quorn and Copper Monarch, along in a British Rail horse-box. He also enjoyed golf and owned several race horses with such names as "You'll be lucky" which was one of his catch-phrases.

Those who were fortunate to have heard Read in his heyday will always retain the memory of his unique voice and phrasing of his smiling words such as "Right monkey" (pronounced "Rart mounki") or the equally memorable, "You'll be lucky" ("Yurll bi looki"). He was truly a very great comic in a medium which is, sadly, no longer the province of such men.

Born Alfred Read. **Marriages** 1) Joyce Entwistle, 1938 (divorced, 1967); 2) Elizabeth Allen, 1967. **Children** Two sons and one daughter from first marriage. **Career** Joined family meat pie and sausage firm, 1924, director, 1932, president to 1960; regular amateur performer; BBC radio début, 1950; resident comedian, *Variety Bandbox*, BBC Radio, 1950; *The Al Read Show*, BBC Radio, 1951; *Such is Life*; *What a Life*; many appearances on radio, television, summer seasons, pantomime and West End shows, including several seasons in music-hall revue, Adelphi Theatre, London, and in several Royal Variety Shows. **Publications** *It's All in the Book* (autobiography), 1985. **Cause of death** Undisclosed, at age 78.

LORD RHODES

British Politician and Businessman

***Born* Saddleworth, Lancashire, 12 August 1895**

***Died* Oldham, Lancashire, 11 September 1987**

From rags to riches may be one kind of saga, but from Lancashire mill-hand to member of the House of Lords and Knight of the Garter—the most prestigious and exclusive of the English orders of chivalry—is a career very seldom achieved, and then only by very exceptional personalities. Such a man was Hervey Rhodes, the son of workers in the cotton mills of Saddleworth in the northwest of England and himself a mill-hand at the age of 12 after the most rudimentary of educations supplemented by evening classes at Huddersfield Technical College. Rhodes introduced himself to the head of the College of Arms on his appointment as a life peer in 1964 as "Hervey of Jack's of Bill's of Jack's of Joe's of John's of Thomas's of Dean Head", and this summed up the man and his Lancashire pedigree back to the seventeenth century. He was a Lancashire man through and through—and proud of it!

Rhodes fought throughout World War I, serving in the King's Own Royal Lancs and surviving the horrors of the trenches. He was commissioned in 1917 and transferred to the Royal Flying Corps on the Western Front, in which he survived a serious injury which crippled him and required daily dressing for the rest of his life. But even this the resourceful Rhodes turned to good use. He put his compensation into a woollen textile business which he built up during the 1920s with careful attention to the betterment of the life of his mill-hands.

He entered local politics in his native district in 1938 and continued as an active member of the Home Guard in World War II. The general election of 1945 saw his first attempt to enter national politics, standing as Labour candidate for Royton, an election which he only just lost. At a by-election later the same year he was returned for Ashton-under-Lyne, a constituency which he continued to represent until he was elevated to the House of Lords 17 years later. During this time he was parliamentary private secretary to the Ministry of Pensions from 1948 to 1951, and parliamentary secretary to the Board of Trade from 1950 to 1951 and again from 1964 to 1967. He had particularly active contacts with China, leading parliamentary delegations in 1978, 1979, 1981 and 1983, and he had a great deal to do with setting up the queen's visit to China in 1986. He was also a major instigator of the government's funding of Hong Kong's railway system.

Rhodes was indefatigable in his efforts to promote British trade interests throughout the world. He was internationally renowned for his practical knowledge of the textile industry and was willing to risk his own career prospects for the interests of his fellow Lancastrians—as when he sent a telegram in 1951 to the then foreign secretary, Herbert Morrison, protesting against a cotton enterprise being negotiated in Sudan, a foolhardy move for a junior minister to make but one which he managed to survive. He was also very active in public life in the northwest and was lord lieutenant of Lancashire from 1968 to 1971. In 1972 he received the ultimate honour of being made a Knight of the Garter. Typical of the man was his immediate reaction to the official news of his award: "You must be joking." He also received honorary degrees from Bradford and Manchester universities and was a keen patron of music and the arts in the north and a close friend of L.S. Lowry, the painter of the mill scenes of his family background.

Born Hervey Rhodes. **Parents** John Eastwood and Eliza Ann Rhodes, handloom weavers. **Marriage** Ann Bradbury, 1925 (died, 1983). **Children** Two daughters. **Education** Greenfield, St Mary's Elementary School; Huddersfield Technical College; evening classes. **Military service** King's Own Royal Lancashires, 1914–17, commissioned, 1917; transferred to Royal Flying Corps, 1917, shot down, 1918, hospitalized, 1918–21. **Career** Woollen mill-hand, 1907–14; founded woollen manufacturing business, 1921; member of parliament (Labour), Ashton-under-Lyne, 1945–64; parliamentary private secretary to Ministry of Pensions, 1948–51; parliamentary secretary, Board of Trade, 1950–51, 1964–67; led all-party delegations to China, 1978, 1979, 1981, 1983. **Other activities** Served on local authority; chairman, Urban District Council, 1944–45; commanded 36th West Riding Battalion Home Guard; lord lieutenant of Lancashire, 1968–71. **Offices and memberships** Chairman, Saddleworth War Charities; president: Saddleworth Festival of the Arts, 1957, SELCARE, 1971, North West Arts, 1972. **Awards and honours** Distinguished Flying Cross and Bar, 1918; created baron, 1964; freedom of the borough: Ashton-under-Lyne, 1965, Saddleworth, Yorkshire, 1966; honorary DTech, Bradford, 1966; Knight of the Most Venerable Order of the Hospital of St John of Jerusalem, 1968; Privy Counsellor, 1969; honorary LLD, Manchester, 1971; Knight of the Order of the Garter, 1972; deputy lieutenant Lancashire, 1971; fellow, Huddersfield Polytechnic, 1976; honorary member, Royal Northern College of Music, 1982. **Cause of death** Undisclosed, at age 92.

DAN ROWAN

American Comedian

***Born* Beggs, Oklahoma, 2 July 1922**

***Died* Englewood, Florida, 22 September 1987**

In 1968 a zany comedy programme called *Rowan and Martin's Laugh-In* soared to the top of the Nielsen ratings, ending its first season with four Emmy Awards and an estimated 40 million TV viewers. Reflecting on the show's instant and enormous success, a *Variety* critic wrote, "Not the least of it is Dan Rowan's authoritative anchoring of the comedy".

The fast and frenetic *Laugh-In* series, co-hosted by straight-man Rowan and his loony sidekick Dick Martin, introduced a new and revolutionary brand of comedy, dependent on sharp one-liners, running gags and cutting cameos laced with seering social commentary to small-screen viewers. For six seasons, while Martin joked his way through Vietnam, Watergate and Flower Power, the more serious, socially conscious Rowan waged a quiet moral and political protest. Despite reproval from NBC executives, he insisted on wearing a peace emblem during filming, and throughout the programme's madcap life, presented a warm and reassuring face of sanity and equilibrium.

Born in Oklahoma, the only child of carnival workers, Dan Rowan was orphaned at an early age and spent most of his youth at a children's home in Pueblo, Colorado. But despite his rough beginnings, he excelled in high school track and football, and also served as president of his class. When he graduated in 1940, he headed for Hollywood, where he soon found employment in Paramount's mail-room, and then as a junior writer. Following World War II service with the Fifth Air Force, he returned to Hollywood, and was soon combining evening acting classes with a job in foreign car sales. Then, in 1952, a comedian friend introduced him to Dick Martin, a struggling radio writer working as a bartender. This casual meeting marked the beginning of a professional partnership that was to last more than 20 years and earn them both millions of dollars.

In no time Rowan and Martin devised a nightclub comedy act, with Rowan the eternal straight-man and Martin the buffoon. For three years they struggled along on the small-club circuit in Los Angeles, until a favourable plug in Walter Winchell's syndicated newspaper column brought them a wave of new and better engagements. They were also offered an exclusive contract with NBC-TV, and appeared together on the *Ed Sullivan Show* in 1960, but, finding the contract hindered more than it helped, continued to focus their energies on nightclub work. Around the same time they starred in an amusing but commercially unsuccessful western spoof, *Once Upon a Horse*, and released an album of their most popular nightclub routines. Rowan had already won *Variety*'s praise as an "unusually able straight-man".

But Rowan and Martin's biggest break came in the summer of 1966, when they replaced the vacationing Dean Martin on NBC's most popular prime-time variety programme. The traditional comedy hour they presented attracted a larger audience than any show that summer, and the network immediately offered the pair their own situation comedy or variety hour. What Rowan and Martin had in mind, however, was something completely different—an innovative "cartoon humour" show free from lengthy monologues, elaborate staging and set musical numbers.

Though the old guard at NBC distrusted the new proposal, former TV executive Ed Friendly approached it with overwhelming enthusiasm and soon joined forces with independent producer George Schlatter, who had been struggling unsuccessfully for three years to promote a similar type of free-form comedy programme. Together with Rowan and Martin and a team of ten writers, they created a hip, fast-moving format designed for a sophisticated and demanding American TV audience. The pilot programme was broadcast as an NBC special in September 1967, and in January, when it was introduced into the regular weekly schedule, the new series, *Rowan and Martin's Laugh-In*, became an instant sensation. *Laugh-In* "impresses as one of the freshest comic inspirations to come down the pike in a long time", critics wrote, adding, "The producers have at last found a format to suit the veteran nitery comics of Rowan and Martin".

Produced at the NBC studios in "Beautiful Downtown Burbank", the *Laugh-In* programme relied on a strong resident cast of comedians, all skilled in improvisation, and a string of famous guests. Figures as influential and important as Billy Graham, John Wayne and Richard Nixon (before his election to the presidency) made cameo appearances, uttering silly catch phrases such as "Sock it to me" and "You bet your bippy"—*Laugh-In*'s powerful and enduring linguistic legacy. But despite its often subversive humour, the programme itself had no political bias, and whenever possible, Rowan introduced socially conscious material into the script. "We don't set out to offend anybody, but if you're so concerned about the possibility of offending somebody, you can end up doing nothing," he told the *New York Times*.

The depth of Rowan's political and social consciousness was once revealed in his choice of props for a skit satirizing the president's campaign platform. The scene required two manila folders—a bulging file on Vietnam, and a near-empty one on Poverty. "I don't know if there will be ten people in this country who will notice the difference in the size of the folders," he said. "It's just a comment of mine on that situation. Maybe it's cynical, but the facts are that a lot of people are tired of spending money on that war, and that a lot of folks in this country are in dire straits." Both on the stage and off, Rowan's serious-mindedness contrasted sharply with Martin's fecklessness, though the two remained trusted friends.

When *Laugh-In* finished filming in January 1973, many of its regular comics—among them Goldie Hawn, Lily Tomlin and Arte Shaw—went on to become successful stars in their own right. But Rowan, who had often confessed that one of his favourite pastimes was "getting in a boat and sailing out beyond the sight of land", moved to Forida with his family, and as the years passed became increasingly reclusive. Never at home with the glamour and glitz of Hollywood, he also became increasingly content. "I have reached that stage in life when I just want to be left alone to do nothing," he said. When he died, most of the people in his small, coastal town were surprised to learn that the tall, moustachioed comedian from *Laugh-In* —a household name for an entire generation—had even lived there.

Born Daniel Hale Rowan. **Parents** John and Clella (Hale) Rowan, carnival workers. **Marriages** 1) Phyllis Mathis, 1946 (divorced, 1960); 2) Adriana van Ballegooyen, model, 1963; 3) Joanna. **Children** One son, Thomas Patrick, and two daughters, Maryann and Christie, from first marriage. **Education** Central High School, Pueblo, Colorado; extension courses in acting and other subjects, University of California and University of Southern California, late 1940s. **Military service** Fighter pilot in New Guinea with US Fifth Air Force, World War II. **Career** Worked in mail-room and as junior writer, Paramount Pictures, 1940–41; part-owner of car dealership, Los Angeles, while studying acting, late 1940s; introduced to future partner, Dick Martin, and formed nightclub comedy act, 1952; starred (with Martin) in unsuccessful film, *Once Upon a Horse*, 1958; signed television contract, later cancelled, with NBC TV, 1958; first television appearance, CBS TV's *Ed Sullivan Show*, 1960; continued nightclub engagements throughout 1960s; filled in for Dean Martin on NBC TV, winning highest show ratings, 1966; formed production company with NBC executive Ed Friendly and independent producer George Schlatter to create comedy television show, 1966; pilot of *Rowan and Martin's Laugh-In* shown on NBC TV, 1967; subsequent series ran for six seasons, 1968–73; released spoof horror film, *The Maltese Bippy*, 1969; withdrew from public appearances after *Laugh-In* ended, 1973. **Awards and honours** Emmy Awards for *Rowan and Martin's Laugh-In*, 1968, 1969. **Films** *Once Upon a Horse*, 1958; *The Maltese Bippy*, 1969. **Recordings** *Rowan and Martin at Work*, 1960. **Publication** *Dan Rowan and John D. MacDonald: A Friendship*, New York, 1986. **Cause of death** Lymphatic cancer, at age 65.

LORD SOAMES

British Politician and Statesman

***Born* Sussex, England, 12 October 1920**

***Died* Hampshire, England, 16 September 1987**

Christopher Soames was of that breed of politician whose skills are more at home in the delicate world of diplomacy than in the hurly-burly of electoral point-scoring. Although at one stage he might have hoped to crown his career by becoming leader of the British Conservative Party, in the event it was in Africa, overseeing Zimbabwe's transition to independence, that he made a lasting mark.

Soames followed the traditional path mapped out for the non-academic upper-class Englishman, being educated at exclusive Eton College and the Royal Military College, Sandhurst, before being commissioned as a second lieutenant in the élite Coldstream Guards regiment at the outbreak of World War II.

Promoted to captain, he saw active service in the Middle East, but this was curtailed in the Western Desert, Egypt, by a mine that shattered his right leg. As liaison officer with General Charles de Gaulle's Free French movement in North Africa, Italy and Normandy, France, he was awarded France's highest military honour, the Croix de Guerre, and the war's end saw him in the post of assistant military attaché at the British embassy in Paris.

Having married the daughter of Conservative Party leader and wartime prime minister Winston Churchill, Soames now not surprisingly contemplated a parliamentary career. In the 1950 general election he won the county town constituency of Bedford, 50 miles from London, from the governing Labour Party, holding the seat at the following year's election, which brought the Conservatives back to power.

The ageing Churchill was once again premier, and Soames became his parliamentary private secretary. This essentially junior position unexpectedly took on extra importance when the prime minister suffered a severe stroke in 1953. With magisterial British discretion, it was decided that the public should not be informed that the head of its government was incapacitated, and Soames was thus thrust into an influential position, controlling the flow of ministers who wished to see his mentor and effectively acting as prime ministerial mouthpiece within the corridors of power. It was a role that brought to the fore both his diplomatic and his political skills and established his reputation in the party.

Two years later, with Churchill finally in retirement, Soames became a junior minister under Anthony Eden, subsequently rising in Harold Macmillan's administration to minister of agriculture. Soames now came into his own: he played an important part in the negotiations to take the country into the European Economic Community.

Britain's long-established pattern of trade with its former colonies seemed at odds with the community's complex system of internal subsidies and external barriers, but thanks in part to Soames's mastery of his subject, real progress was made. Although de Gaulle, now French president, distrustful of British intentions, vetoed the application to join the community, Soames's own status was enhanced, both at home and abroad.

The Labour Party's return to power in 1964 saw Soames become Conservative spokesman on defence, and when new party leader Edward Heath, a fellow partisan of Britain's role in the new Europe, gave him responsibility for foreign affairs, his place in a future Conservative cabinet seemed assured.

But Soames lost his parliamentary seat in Labour's landslide 1966 election victory, and suddenly his career seemed to have reached a dead end. It was rescued by Labour foreign secretary George Brown, who appointed him ambassador in Paris. The posting was ideal for Soames, who enthusiastically promoted Britain's European cause. De Gaulle was still resolutely opposed to British membership, however, and London's leak of its version of an interview between the two men only served to push his hostility to new heights. But the general's days in power were numbered, and with his dramatic retirement in the wake of the mass student and industrial unrest of 1968, Soames and Britain swiftly established good relations with the new regime of Georges Pompidou.

Soames stayed on in Paris after the 1970 election of the Heath government to play his part in finally securing European Community membership. When he did step down, it was as a grand officer of the Legion of Honour, awarded in recognition of his services to Anglo–French relations.

He moved on to serve a four-year term within the Community itself, as a vice-president of its Commission for the European Communities with responsibility for external relations, having to deal notably with the challenge to European stability posed by the oil embargo that followed the Middle East conflict of 1973.

Back in Britain, Soames sought a return to parliament, but a prolonged bout of ill-health put paid to his hopes of finding a winnable seat in the House of Commons. In the event, it was in the House of Lords that he was to sit, as a life peer, and with the election of Margaret Thatcher's Conservative government in 1979 he was appointed leader of the House and minister responsible for the Civil Service.

Within a year he was embarking on his most exacting assignment, as final governor of Britain's last African possession. Representatives of the White minority in Rhodesia, encouraged by neighbouring South Africa, had unilaterally declared the colony independent in 1965 with the aim of preventing Black majority rule. Liberation groups had fought a bloody war of attrition against the rebel regime all through the 1970s. Now a negotiated but precarious settlement had been reached in London whereby elections would be held on a universal suffrage leading to independence and majority rule for the new state of Zimbabwe. With a ceasefire in place, the governor had to hold the delicate balance between the communities, help rebuild a divided land and ensure the elections were free and fair.

It was acknowledged by all that Soames, bringing all his skill and experience to the task, achieved this in masterly fashion, earning praise notably from Zimbabwe's first prime minister, Robert Mugabe, who offered him citizenship of the new nation.

It was ironic, then, that just a year after his return in triumph to London, Soames's career should end in acrimony when he was made to carry the can for a wave of government employee strikes and dropped from the Thatcher cabinet in an altercation that could, it was said, be heard all over Downing Street.

Soames's Conservatism was of a different brand from Thatcher's and belonged perhaps to another era altogether. Personal integrity, commitment to public service and, not least, an ability to enjoy the good things in life were the qualities most associated with him, and if he never quite realized his full potential, they ensured that he would be remembered with genuine affection as well as respect.

Born Arthur Christopher John Soames. **Marriage** Mary Churchill, daughter of Winston Churchill, 1947. **Children** Three sons and two daughters. **Education** Eton College, Berkshire; Royal Military College, Sandhurst. **Military service** Second lieutenant, Coldstream Guards, 1939, promoted to captain, 1942; served in Middle East, Italy and France; assistant military attaché, British Embassy, Paris, 1946–47. **Career** Member of parliament for Bedford, 1950–66; parliamentary private secretary to the prime minister, 1952–55; parliamentary under-secretary of state, Air Ministry, 1955–57; parliamentary and financial secretary, Admiralty, 1957–58; secretary of state for war, 1958–60; minister of agriculture, fisheries and food, 1960–64; ambassador to France, 1968–72; vice-president, commission of the European communities, 1973–77; governor, Southern Rhodesia, 1979–80; lord president of the council, leader of the House of Lords, minister responsible for the Civil Service, 1979–81. **Other activities** Director: Decca Limited, 1964–68, James Hole and Company, Limited, 1964–68, N.M. Rothschild and Sons Limited, 1977–79, National Westminster Bank Limited, 1978–79; chairman, ICL (UK) Limited, 1984. **Offices and memberships** President, Royal Agricultural Society of England, 1973. **Awards and honours** Croix de Guerre (France), 1942; Commander of the Order of the British Empire, 1955; privy counsellor, 1958; Knight Grand Cross of the Order of St Michael and

St George, 1972; Knight Grand Cross of the Royal Victorian Order, 1972; grand officer, Legion of Honour (France), 1972; Medal of the City of Paris, 1972; Grand Cross of St Olave (Norway), 1974; honorary LLD, St Andrews, 1974; created Baron Soames of Fletching in the County of East Sussex, life peer, 1978; companion of honour, 1980; honorary DCL, Oxford University, 1981. **Cause of death** Cancer, at age 66.

MICHAEL STEWART

American Librettist and Lyricist

Born **New York City, New York, 1 August 1924**

Died **New York City, New York, 20 September 1987**

Pick a musical, any musical, your favourite—now a short test: who wrote the music? the lyrics? directed it? choreographed it? starred in it? And the librettist, the book writer—who was it?

Chances are you were easily defeated by the last question. It is a sad fact of musical theatre that the book-writer is the first to be blamed if the show flops, the last to receive any credit if it succeeds. Michael Stewart was a librettist of the highest calibre who wrote a number of classics of musical theatre, but remained largely unknown outside the business. The popular story, as told by Stewart himself, is that he decided to write for the theatre when, as a ten-year-old, he had gone with his family to see Ethel Merman in the Cole Porter musical *Anything Goes*. Such an inspiration is easily understandable, as that particular show is glued together with frothy, slight material that passes as a "book" in what is essentially a vehicle for some good tunes.

Stewart's ambitions took him to the Yale School of Drama. While there, in 1951, he contributed sketches and lyrics to *Razzle Dazzle*, a revue staged in-the-round at the Edison Theater. After graduation in 1953, he supplied material to three notable Broadway revues: *The Shoestring Revue* (1955), *The Littlest Revue* and *Shoestring '57*. He was in very good company when he went on to write for Sid Caesar's television series, *Caesar's Hour*—his fellow contributors included Neil Simon and Mel Brooks.

In 1954 he met the composer Charles Strouse and the lyricist Lee Adams and they collaborated on the show that eventually opened on Broadway in 1960 with the title *Bye Bye Birdie*. With Gower Champion directing a cast that included Dick van Dyke, Chita Rivera and Paul Lynde, the show captured the spirit of the rock 'n' roll generation, the newly-discovered teenager, hypnotized by the gyrating Elvis Presley. Michael Stewart won a Tony Award for his contribution, as did Champion, Strouse and Adams for theirs.

From *Bye Bye Birdie* onwards, Stewart was widely considered to be Broadway's most successful writer of musical comedy books. In 1964 he adapted Thornton Wilder's *The Matchmaker* into *Hello, Dolly!*, once more collaborating with Gower Champion, but this time with Jerry Herman writing the music. The noted critic Mark Steyn, writing in the *Independent* at the time of Stewart's death, considers *Dolly* to have "one of the most expert books of any show, a model two-act musical. For a musical comedy libretto, it was stylistically consistent with the rest of the production, a minor breakthrough. If ever our universities and drama schools get around to a serious consideration of musical theatre, Stewart's *Dolly* libretto would be on the curriculum."

In an article in the *New York Times* in 1979, Stewart commented: "I don't know why any bright person would want to be a musical book-writer. You're scorned by critics, you get no recognition from the public the money isn't that good either. I feel I've written two classic American musicals, *Birdie* and *Dolly*, but both books got terrible reviews." However, one of the great ironies of Stewart's career is the fact that the libretto he wrote for *Mack and Mabel* in 1974, again in collaboration with Jerry Herman, received ecstatic critical response, but the public just would not go to see it, so it survived only 65 performances. A cult has grown up around the show, the members of which constantly press for it to be revived on Broadway and/or in London's West End. Although a concert version has been staged at the Theatre Royal in Drury Lane, London, rumours still abound about a possible revival.

It was due partly to this frustration at the ill-perceived notions of librettists that led Stewart to diversify into lyric-writing. *I Love My Wife* (1977) and *Barnum* (1980) are not particularly outstanding for Stewart's lyrics, but he did prove himself to be an immensely able, competent craftsman.

However, his book-writing still shone, most notably in *42nd Street*, although producer David Merrick only credited Stewart and his partner, Mark Bramble, with writing "lead-ins and crossovers" rather than the book for the musical. An attempt at a sequel to *Bye Bye Birdie* in 1981—*Bring Back Birdie*—was a disappointment, although an off-Broadway run of *Elizabeth and Essex*, based on the life of Queen Elizabeth I, was a big hit.

At the time of his death, Stewart was collaborating on a new musical, once again with Cy Coleman and Mark Bramble, of which it is rumoured that production will continue. The final tribute to him is best expressed by the composer Jule Styne, who, on hearing of his death, said: "He was an extremely talented and knowledgeable man of the theatre. He was one of the great musical theatre writers and his string of hits showed that."

Born Michael Rubin. **Mother** Kate Rubin. **Education** Queens College, New York; Yale School of Drama, MFA, 1953. **Career** Sketch and lyric writer for *Razzle Dazzle* revue, Edison Theater, 1951; supplied material to off-Broadway shows *The Shoestring Revue*, *The Littlest Revue*, *Shoestring '57*, 1955–57; comedy writer on Sid Caesar's *Your Show of Shows* (television), 1957; turned to writing libretti for musical comedies; later diversified into writing lyrics, becoming one of the most successful musical authors of the modern Broadway period. **Awards and honours** Tony Award for best book of a musical, *Bye Bye Birdie*, 1960, and *Hello Dolly!*, 1964; New York Drama Critics' Circle Award, *Carnival*, 1961. **Works** (as librettist or lyricist, include) *Bye Bye Birdie*, 1960; *Carnival*, 1961; *Hello, Dolly*, 1964; *George M.*, 1968; *Mack and Mabel*, 1974; *I Love My Wife*, 1977; *The Grand Tour*, 1979; *Barnum*, 1980; *42nd Street*, 1980; *Bring Back Birdie*, 1981; *Elizabeth and Essex*, 1984; *Harrigan 'n' Hart*, 1985; *Treasure Island*, Edmonton, Canada, 1986. **Cause of death** Pneumonia following surgery for a perforated colon, at age 63.

LEE THEODORE

American Dancer and Choreographer

***Born* Newark, New Jersey, 13 April 1933**

***Died* New York City, New York, 3 September 1987**

Lee Theodore once told an interviewer that "theatre dance is the way the American dancer expresses his culture, his understanding of the time". It was this earnestly-held belief in the importance and vitality of commercial dance that fuelled her enthusiasm and dedication in promoting show dancing among her contemporaries and students.

Her biggest claim to fame as a dancer is that she was the original "Anybodys", the tomboy member of the Jets gang in *West Side Story* in 1957, a performance that has been imitated in every revival of the piece. The show provided her great Broadway break, coming eight years after her graduation from the New York High School of the Performing Arts (immortalized in the film *Fame*). It certainly developed Theodore's dancing, singing and acting talent to well above Broadway standard.

As well as *West Side Story*, she also appeared in *Gentlemen Prefer Blondes*, *The King and I*, *Damn Yankees* and *Tenderloin*. It seemed inevitable that she should move into choreography, and this she did in the Broadway musicals *Baker Street*, *Apple Tree* and *Flora, the Red Menace*. She also choreographed television variety shows for many of the stars of the 1950s and 1960s.

The high point of her career was when she made her directorial début with a 1968 revival of *West Side Story*, for which she was chosen by Jerome Robbins, the creator and choreographer supremo of the show. She considered her work with great innovators, like Robbins, to be the touchstone of American theatre dance, the apprentice system whereby the techniques and craftsmanship of one generation were passed on to another. "I had the privilege of working as a dancer and assistant with what I call the masters, people like Jerome Robbins, Danny Daniels, Don Saddler, Jack Cole...I would be teaching at universities around the country and the kids wouldn't know who Jack Cole or Agnes de Mille were. Their work is a part of our history and I began to feel it would be lost to this generation." Wanting to provide young dancers with similar opportunities, in 1975 she founded the American Dance Machine, a company devoted to the preservation of Broadway choreography of the past, as well as providing training facilities for show dancers.

Initially the company attracted some controversy as there were those who felt that theatre dance did not belong to the concert stage. Several choreographers, including Gower Champion, Agnes de Mille and Michael Kidd, felt that as dances were created for a commercial setting, they would not stand up on their own. The idea of presenting "numbers" outside a show's setting certainly goes against the tide of recent musical theatre history, where the goal is complete integration of action, song and dance. By presenting the dances as a separate entity, Theodore offered a direct challenge to these received ideas. But the calibre of her work was such that the opposition soon withered. As Theodore observed: "Gower Champion felt that way, but when he saw the company he changed his mind." Agnes de Mille and Michael Kidd were also converts and de Mille went on to become an active supporter of the company.

At the time of her death Lee Theodore was working on her last ballet, *Dance Timecapsule*, described by her husband as a "sort of...compendium of everything she had learned". During her lifetime she had received several awards for the energy and generosity with which she shared "everything she had learned", but she still remains one of the great unsung heroines of the dance, fit to be added to the list of "masters of the theatre".

Born Lee Becker. **Parents** Zena and Gayna (Klasner) Becker. **Marriage** Paris Theodore, 1962. **Children** Two sons, Saïd and Ali. **Education** High School of the Performing Arts, New York, 1949. **Career** Dancer on stage and in films, 1950s onwards; founder/director, Jazz Ballet Theater, 1961–63; founder/director, American Dance Machine, New York, 1975–87. **Related activities** Guest instructor: American Theater Association, Society of Stage Directors and Choreographers, Lincoln Center Library of the Performing Arts. **Offices and memberships** Member: President's Music Commission, 1962, National Educational Association, New York State Choreographers' Association, Society of Stage Directors and Choreographers, Actors' Equity Association, American Guild of Musical Artists, American Federation of Television and Radio Artists. **Awards and honours** Tony Award nomination for choreography, *The Apple Tree*, 1967; *Dance* magazine, Award, 1982; Dance Educators' of America trophy, 1982. **Stage** (as performer) *The King and I*; *Gentlemen Prefer Blondes*; *Tenderloin*; *Damn Yankees*; *West Side Story*; guest artist: New York City Ballet, Donald McKayle Company. **Choreographed works** *Baker Street*; *Flora, the Red Menace*; *The Apple Tree*; International Jazz Festival, Washington, 1962; *The Song of Norway* (film), 1970; various television programmes, including *Kraft Music Hall*, *Perry Como Show*, *Ed Sullivan Show*, *Sid Caesar Show*, *Steve Allen Show*. **Cause of death** Undisclosed, at age 54.

REAR-ADMIRAL AMÉRICO TOMÁS

Portuguese Statesman

Born **Lisbon, Portugal, 19 November 1894**

Died **Cascais, Portugal, 18 September 1987**

Américo Tomás was the president of Portugal for the better part of two decades. Yet his death was little lamented by his compatriots. The reason, of course, is that throughout his career in public life, Portugal was a dictatorship, and when a new generation of radical military officers swept to power in 1974's revolution of the flowers, Tomás was deposed, interned in Madeira and then exiled to Brazil. Perhaps most humiliatingly of all, he was expelled from the navy in which he had served for 60 years.

Tomás had enlisted at the outbreak of World War I and graduated top of his year from the Lisbon Naval Academy, seeing active service on troop convoys and being promoted to second lieutenant before the war was out. He was then transferred to the hydrographical surveying vessel *Cinco de Outubro*, where he spent 16 years charting Portuguese coastal waters, rising to the rank of lieutenant-captain and assuming command in the process.

Like many of his military contemporaries, Tomás was an enthusiastic partisan of the Fascist-style "new state" established by the 1932 constitution that followed the military coup of 1926. Devised by Dr António de Oliveira Salazar, it gave virtually unlimited executive power to the prime minister, who, in this instance and for the next 36 years, was the sinister Salazar himself. Tomás could thus safely be confided the post of special assistant to the navy minister, having by now advanced to the rank of commander, and he progressed via the presidency of the merchant marine board to become the minister himself in 1944.

Portugal, like her neighbour Spain, declined to enter World War II alongside their German, Italian and Japanese counterparts—and if anything favouring the Allies—the dictatorship remained undisturbed by the defeat of the Axis powers. Tomás could carry through his ambitious plan of 1945 to modernize and expand the Portuguese merchant fleet.

Promoted to the rank of rear-admiral in 1951, he remained navy minister through most of the 1950s. With Portugal now a member of NATO, he was able to modernize the country's naval establishment and its naval training system.

At a time when Tomás was contemplating retirement, Salazar unexpectedly made him the ruling party's candidate for president in the election of 1958. Given the perfunctory nature of Portuguese democracy (no opposition candidate had been permitted to run since 1928), this was tantamount to being offered the presidency itself, actually a job of little consequence beside that of premier.

Amid well-documented accusations of ballot-rigging from opposition candidate General Humberto Delgado, whose campaign was severely curtailed by the authorities, Tomás duly became president. Delgado nevertheless officially managed 22 per cent of the poll, a shock that prompted Salazar to repress all political opposition and replace popular elections for president with an electoral college comprising government trusties. Under this less risky system, Tomás was re-elected in 1965 and 1972.

Virtually the sole power vested in the president under the Salazar constitution was that of appointing the prime minister, which in 1958 and 1965 meant, of course, the formality of renewing the mandate of the constitution's architect. This is not to say that Tomás was a mere figurehead, however. His bland exterior masked a genuine dedication to the order he served.

When, in 1968, Salazar fell seriously ill, Tomás did not hesitate to exercise his prerogative and dismiss him, turning to Dr Marcello Caetano, a regime stalwart who nevertheless occasionally needed reminding that there was to be no deviation from the course long since set for Portugal, no matter who was at the helm.

This applied as much to Portugal's overseas possessions, to which Tomás paid frequent visits, as it did at home. The twin jewels in Portugal's crown were its southern African colonies of Angola and Mozambique. It was something of a paradox that one of Europe's most poverty-stricken and economically backward nations should have an empire to its name. Many of Portugal's young, middle-ranking military officers, committed by Lisbon to fighting a bloody colonial war against dedicated and well-equipped freedom fighters, were beginning to draw the logical conclusions. Coming home from their tours of duty in Africa influenced by the liberationist ideologies of those they had been detailed to repress, they plotted the revolution that liberated their own people from half a century of oppression, brought the colonies their overdue independence, and incidentally put an ignominious end to the career of Américo Tomás.

While Tomás spent much of that career in the background, allowing other names to be more closely associated with an unsavoury period in Portugal's history, his was a baleful influence. That he was permitted to return home after just four years in exile to live out his final years in peace showed that Portugal was now governed with a humanity notably lacking during his years of power.

Born Américo Deus Rodrigues Tomás. **Parents** António Rodrigues and Maria da Assunção (Marques) Tomás. **Marriage** Gertrudes Ribeiro da Costa, 1922. **Children** Maria Natália and Maria Madalena. **Education** Naval Academy, Lisbon, 1914–16. **Career** Served aboard cruiser, *Vasco da Gama*, escorting troop ships, 1916–17; promoted to second lieutenant, served on auxiliary cruiser *Pedro Nunes*, destroyers *Douro* and *Tejo* and commanded training ship *Guarda Marinha Janeiro*, protecting fishing vessels, 1918–19; responsible for charting coastal waters at Marine Ministry's Coastal Hydrographic Mission, 1919–20; transferred to survey ship *Cinco de Outubro*, 1920–35; made first lieutenant, 1922; lieutenant-captain, commander of *Cinco de Outubro* and chief of Coastal Hydrographic Mission, 1931; departmental head to minister of navy, 1936; president, Merchant Marine National Board, 1940; promoted to highest level captain (capitão de mar e guerra), 1941; minister of navy, 1944–58; promoted to rear-admiral, 1951; president of Portugal, 1958–74; ousted by 1974 revolution and held in Madeira before being expelled from the navy and exiled to Brazil; allowed to return on condition he took no part in politics, 1978; occupied remaining years compiling his memoirs. **Related activities** Active supporter of Estado Novo (New State) right-wing dictatorial regime established under influence of Italian Fascism, 1932. **Awards and honours** Visconde de Lançada Award for highest marks at Naval Academy, Lisbon, 1916. **Cause of death** Undisclosed, at age 92.

PETER TOSH

Jamaican Musician

***Born* Westmoreland, Jamaica, 19 October 1944**

***Died* St Andrew, Jamaica, 11 September 1987**

Peter Tosh's short life saw the birth, rapid development and international success of reggae music. For a while, he was one of its lions, as a founder member of the legendary Wailers. His violent death might have been prefigured in one of their turbulent, rousing creations.

He was born Winston Hubert McIntosh in 1944, at Westmoreland, on the Caribbean island of Jamaica. It was then still a British colony, with a largely rural economy. During the 1950s, though, the population became increasingly urbanized and its culture received a sharp blast of rhythm and blues, imported on record from the United States. The bruising, electrified music of the American urban Blacks became immensely popular, and elided with the local "mento" style and its propensity for social comment. The amplified result, early in the 1960s, was ska. By this time the young Tosh had developed a baritone voice and played piano, guitar and organ. With Bob Marley and Neville "Bunny" Livingstone, he founded the Wailing Wailers in 1963. At the same time, he was running a solo career as Peter Mackingtosh, Peter Macintosh, Peter Tosh and, most often, Peter Touch. He released numerous singles in Jamaica, often backed by Marley and Livingstone. Meanwhile, the island continued to develop its music. Ska slowed down into rock steady by 1965, then in 1969 arrived the loping beat and defiant posture of reggae.

Peter Tosh, with the Wailers, became prime exponents of the new form. The songs dealt often with injustice, poverty and unemployment. Tosh himself revealed a rather despairing attitude on two of his compositions, "400 Years" and "Stop That Train", which appeared on the album *Catch a Fire*. The Wailers could now attract more sophisticated record production than reggae had previously been able to use. With solid commercial backing, their commanding performances brought reggae to an international audience. London followed Kingston, Jamaica, in its enthusiasm for the music. In both capitals, the Wailers' next album, *Burnin'*, spoke forcibly to the condition of young Blacks. Battle cries like "Get Up, Stand Up" and the protest "I Shot the Sheriff", where Tosh blended powerfully with Bob Marley, told of oppression ideological and material, and gun law.

In 1973 Tosh quit the Wailers. He felt that Bob Marley and his ululating, percussive voice were usurping too much space. How much of the quarrel was principle or how much naked resentment is not clear. However, if he had a point to prove, Tosh succeeded—at least temporarily. Two solo albums released in the mid-1970s are described as "tough, memorable reggae combining the roots tradition with a strong international appeal". They are *Legalize It*—the theme song being his hymn to marijuana—and *Equal Rights*, which contains the notably double-tracked "Stepping Razor". In 1978 some 30,000 people attended a Peter Tosh concert in Kingston. One of them was Prime Minister Michael Manley. Tosh treated him to a huge display of marijuana ingestion, and a 30-minute harangue on his refusal to "legalize it". Later that year, Tosh was arrested at his studio and taken to a police station, where he was given a near-fatal beating before being released.

Also in 1978 he signed for the Rolling Stones label. The three resulting albums *Bush Doctor* (1978), *Mystic Man* (1979) and *Wanted Dread or Alive* (1982) mark a downturn. Critical opinion is generally united in the idea that the music is an unconvincing hybrid, destroying credibility with the reggae audience, and failing to cross him successfully into a rock one. Nevertheless, Tosh was guaranteed some cachet when he recorded a duet—"(You Got to Walk and) Don't Look Back"—with Mick Jagger. It may be uncharitable to consider what vicarious glory the ageing Rolling Stone felt in return for this comfortable association with the danger man. Tosh toured the United States with the Rolling Stones, opening the show with his Word Sound and Power band. In 1982 he toured there with a newer reggae hero, Jimmy Cliff. *Mama Africa*, Tosh's 1983 album, did little for his musical prestige; it rather sadly featured an over-produced reggae version of Chuck Berry's "Johnny B. Goode".

Tosh was killed at his home in a Kingston suburb, together with another man. Five others were wounded. The motive is thought to have been robbery; gunmen broke in on Tosh and demanded the money they assumed he had to hand after a recent tour of the United States. He refused and was shot. As is evident from his career and some of his songs, Peter Tosh inhabited a hard world; "Mark of the Beast", recorded in 1975, is a testimony to his relations with the Jamaican police. His best was called "excellent, pure reggae", and his ex-adversary Michael Manley eulogized him as a man who "gave to Jamaica and the world an unforgettable library of musical works which will be played and sung by many generations of people".

Born Winston Hubert McIntosh. **Pseudonyms** Peter Mackingtosh, Peter Macintosh, Peter Touch. **Career** Reggae artist; (with Bob Marley) founded the Wailers, 1963, left, 1973; pursued solo career, 1973–87. **Awards and honours** Grammy Award nomination for best reggae recording, "Captured Live", 1985. **Recordings** (with Mick Jagger) "(You Got to Walk and) Don't Look Back"; (with Wailers) "Stir It Up", "I Shot the Sheriff", "Get Up, Stand Up", *Catch a Fire*, 1973; (solo) "Mark of the Beast", *Equal Rights*, 1977, *Bush Doctor*, 1978, *Mystic Man*, 1979, *Wanted Dread or Alive*, 1982, *Mama Africa*, 1983, "Captured Live", 1985, *No Nuclear War*, 1987. **Cause of death** Shot during an armed robbery at his home, at age 42.

EMLYN WILLIAMS

British Actor and Playwright

***Born* Mostyn, North Wales, 26 November 1905**

***Died* London, England, 25 September 1987**

"A mind like a cut-throat razor and a tongue to match," was Richard Burton's succinct assessment of his early mentor and benefactor, the man who gave him his first professional theatre job, introduced him to his first wife, and wrote a part especially for him for his film début—Emlyn Williams.

They had much in common—humble origins, steely determination, ready wit combined with the rugged egotism that constitutes the hallmark of success, and a deep-rooted Welshness that enabled both men to tap the innate artistry of the Celtic spirit. Unlike his protégé, however, whose ambivalence towards the stage led him off into the realms of filmic mediocrity and colossal wealth, Williams was primarily a man of the theatre, although his 60-year *oeuvre* encompasses all media, both as creator and practitioner. His writing output was prodigious—a total of 32 plays, nine screenplays, four television plays, a radio play and two volumes of autobiography.

An impressive achievement for anyone, but particularly a miner's son born the year before the National Strike into a tiny North Wales mining community. He would in all probability have passed unnoticed into the massed ranks of anonymous coal cutters had it not been for the influence of Sarah Grace Cook. A teacher of acute perception and formidable drive, she spotted the young Williams's talent and potential and guided him from the Holywell County School to an open scholarship to read French at Christ Church College, Oxford.

Oxford before the war was an extremely fertile proving ground for actors, and it was here that Williams abandoned the teaching career that would have given him job security, social status and a pension in favour of a notoriously treacherous profession where work was intermittent, morality dubious and success, if it ever came, proverbially fickle. In near-traditional style, it was a favourable notice from one of the century's most influential critics for his performance in a production by the Oxford University Dramatic Society (OUDS) that sealed his decision. James Agate's "I think I spy an actor in Mr G.E. Williams, who gave the small part of Morton very well indeed," was the catalyst that sent the young Welshman down to London after taking his MA to carve out a career for himself in the theatre.

Williams was lucky. Student work under the direction of J.B. Fagan led to his first professional job in the latter's Savoy Theatre production of *And So to Bed* (1927), a small part that nevertheless took him across the Atlantic for the Broadway transfer. The following year saw him for the first time, at the age of 23, in his own play, *Glamour*, which, though minor and unsuccessful, has some of the ingredients which anticipate his best theatrical work—Wales, the theatre and a central role written for Emlyn Williams.

His most successful plays, *The Corn Is Green* and *The Druid's Rest*, both draw on his own boyhood experience to feed a closely observed, humorous realism and an elegiac Celtic lyricism that has drawn comparisons with the work of Irish playwrights Sean O'Casey and J.M. Synge. His other major hit, *Night Must Fall*, exploits the thriller convention to achieve a brooding suspense that also stems from the atavistic menace in the heart of the Welsh character. His theatrical style dated fast after the explosion in the British theatre of the late 1950s, and the Angry Young Man effectively put an end to his playwriting output.

Williams was an accomplished performer, at his best a virtuoso, and his stage portrayals of Charles Dickens and Dylan Thomas became part of his stock-in-trade, taking him around the world with their many popular revivals. Film work kept him reasonably busy up to the end of the 1960s, by which time he had turned his attention to autobiography and later, at the age of 75, his first novel, *Headlong*.

He commanded enormous respect both from the theatrical establishment and fellow practitioners, including luminaries such as Elizabeth Taylor. This in spite of his heated denunciation of Richard Burton's future wife at the time of the *Cleopatra* scandal: "Look at her," he said, mistakenly assuming she was out of earshot, "she walks like a chorus girl!" It was only later, good humour restored, that Williams's own wife Molly reminded him that he himself had married a chorus girl.

In true trouper tradition, Williams was still breaking new ground until very nearly the end of his life, appearing in television plays as late as 1983. While his own stage works may now be of chiefly historical interest, he had considerable influence on the British theatre scene for nearly three decades. As he himself might have said—not bad for a boy from the valleys.

Born George Emlyn Williams. **Parents** Richard, greengrocer, and Mary (Williams) Williams. **Marriage** Molly O'Shann, 1935 (died, 1971). **Children** Two sons. **Education** Holywell County School, Flintshire; St Julien's, Geneva; Christ Church College, Oxford, MA. **Career** Began acting while at university; first play, *Full Moon*, performed by Oxford University Dramatic Society; professional stage début in *And So to Bed*, London and New York, 1927; film début, 1932; thereafter achieved growing recognition and success as actor, playwright and director. **Awards and honours** New York Drama Critics' Circle Award, 1941; honorary LLD, University College of North Wales, Bangor, 1949; Commander of the Order of the British Empire, 1962. **Plays** *Vigil* (produced, 1925), in *The Second Book of One-Act Plays*, 1954; *Full Moon* (produced, 1927); *Glamour* (produced, 1928); *A Murder Has Been Arranged: A Ghost Story* (produced, 1930), 1930; *Port Said* (produced, 1931, revised version as *Vessels Departing*, produced, 1933); *The Late Christopher Bean*, from a play by Sidney Howard based on play by René Fauchois (produced, 1933), 1933; *Josephine*, from a work by Hermann Bahr (produced, 1934); *Spring 1600* (produced, 1934, revised version produced, 1945), 1946; *Night Must Fall* (produced, 1935), 1935; *He Was Born Gay: A Romance* (produced, 1937), 1937; *The Corn Is Green* (produced, 1938), 1938; *The Light of Heart* (produced, 1940), 1940; *The Morning Star* (produced, 1941), 1942; *Yesterday's Magic* (produced, 1942); *Pen Don* (produced, 1943); *A Month in the Country*, from a play by Turgenev (produced 1943, revised version produced 1956), 1957; *The Druid's Rest* (produced, 1944), 1944; *The Wind of Heaven* (produced, 1945), 1945; *Thinking Aloud: A Dramatic Sketch* (produced, 1945), 1946; *Trespass: A Ghost Story* (produced, 1947), 1947; *Pepper and Sand: A Duologue* (radio broadcast, 1947), 1948; *Dear Evelyn*, from a play by Hagar Wilde and Dale Eunson (produced, 1948); *Every Picture Tells a Story* (television, shown 1949); *Accolade* (produced, 1950), 1951; *Emlyn Williams as Charles Dickens*, from writings of Dickens (produced, 1951), revised as *Readings from Dickens*, 1953; *Bleak House*, reading from Dickens (produced, 1952); *Someone Waiting* (produced, 1953), 1954; *In Town Tonight* (television, shown, 1954); *A Boy Growing Up*, reading from works of Dylan Thomas (produced, 1955), revised as *Dylan Thomas Growing Up* (produced, 1977); *Beth* (produced, 1958), 1959; *The Master Builder*, from a play by Ibsen (produced, 1964), 1967; *A Blue Movie of My Own True Love* (television, shown, 1968); *The Power of Dawn* (television, shown, 1975); *Saki*, reading from works by Saki (produced, 1977). **Screenplays** *Friday the Thirteenth*, 1933; (with Marjorie Gaffney) *Evergreen*, 1934; (with A.R. Rawlinson and Edwin Greenwood) *The Man Who Knew Too Much*, 1934; (with Richard Benson) *The Divine Spark*, 1935; *Broken Blossoms*, 1936; (with others) *Dead Men Tell No Tales*, 1938; (with others) *The Citadel*, 1938, published in *Foremost Films of 1938*, ed. Frank Vreeland, 1939; *This England*, 1941; (and director) *The Last Days of Dolwyn*, 1949. **Other publications** *George: An Early Autobiography*, 1961; *Beyond Belief: A Chronicle of Murder and Detection*, 1967; *Emlyn: An Early Autobiography, 1927–35,* 1973; (editor) *Short Stories* by Saki, 1978. **Stage roles** (all in London, unless stated, include) *And So to Bed*, London and New York, 1927; *The Pocket-Money Husband*, 1928; *Glamour*, 1928; *The Case of the Frightened Lady*, London and New York, 1931–32; *Port Said*, 1933; *Night Must Fall*, London and New York, 1935–36; *He Was Born Gay*, 1937; season with the Old Vic, performing in *Richard III*, *Measure for Measure* and *Ghosts*, 1937–38; *The Corn Is Green*, 1938–40; *The Light of the Heart*, 1940; *The Morning Star*, 1941; *A Month in the Country*, 1943; *The Druid's Rest*, 1944; *The Wind of Heaven*, 1945; *The Winslow Boy*, 1946;

Trespass, 1947; *Montserrat*, New York, 1949; first series of Dickens' readings, New York, 1952; *The Wild Duck*, 1955; *Growing Up*, as Dylan Thomas, 1955, 1958, 1980, New York, 1957; season at Stratford-upon-Avon, 1956; *Shadow of Heroes*, 1958; *Three*, 1961; *Daughter of Silence*, New York, 1961; *A Man For All Seasons*, New York, 1962; *The Deputy*, New York, 1964; world tour as Dickens, 1964–65, London, 1965, 1975; *A Month in the Country*, Cambridge, 1965; *Forty Years On*, 1969. **Film roles** (include) *The Case of the Frightened Lady*, 1932; *David Copperfield*; 1934; *Jamaica Inn*, 1939; *The Stars Look Down*, 1939; *You Will Remember*, 1940; *Major Barbara*, 1941; *This England*, 1941; *Hatter's Castle*, 1941; *The Last Days of Dolwyn*, 1949; *Another's Man's Poison*, 1951; *Ivanhoe*, 1952. **Cause of death** Undisclosed, at age 81. **Further reading** Richard Findlater, *Williams: An Illustrated Study of His Work with a List of His Appearances on Stage and Screen* (includes bibliography), 1957.

OCTOBER

JEAN ANOUILH

French Playwright

***Born* Bordeaux, France, 23 June 1910**

***Died* Lausanne, Switzerland, 3 October 1987**

"It's scandalous to think that I earn my livelihood by amusing myself as much as I do." This is Jean Anouilh speaking in the 1950s, at the height of his fame. At the time, he had several of his plays running concurrently in London and Paris, he had just married his second wife, Nicole Lançon, and was, by all accounts, a happy man. Now an old hand in the theatre, he boasted that it only took him about a month to write a play. Workwise he could get by with three months a year in Paris, the rest of his time being spent at his country house in Brittany or skiing in the French Alps. Contemplating this lifestyle, it is hard to believe that we are talking about one of the major French playwrights of this century, a man who became renowned for his no-hope view of human existence. Describing himself as a "comic misanthrope", with echoes of Molière whom he greatly admired, Anouilh countered criticism that his work was too cynical with the statement "My work is a fairy tale compared to reality".

Jean Anouilh was born in a small village near Bordeaux in 1910. He came into contact with the theatre at an early age because his mother, a violinist, played regularly at the local casino where, as a boy, Anouilh was often allowed to stay up and watch the operettas. He took up playwriting almost as soon as he could hold a pen, completing his first full-length drama at the age of 16. Around this time the family moved to Paris, where young Jean went to the École Colbert and later to the Sorbonne to study law. It soon became evident that this had not been a good idea. Anouilh was bored to tears by the dry-as-dust discipline of legal study, and he dropped out after only a year and a half. Money had to be earned, however, so he got himself a job with an advertising company. Here, at least, he felt he was in a useful trade: "For three years I wrote copy for products ranging from noodles to automobiles. I consider advertising a great school for playwriting. The precision, conciseness and agility of expression necessary in writing advertisements helped me enormously," he recalled later.

Trying to raise his meagre income by selling comedy ideas to film producers, Anouilh managed to keep his hand in with theatrical work. But his early plays, like *L'Hermine* (*The Ermine*, 1932) and *Le Bal des voleurs* (*Thieves' Carnival*, 1938), were largely about the fear of poverty, albeit in a comic vein. *Y'avait un prisonnier* (There was a Prisoner, 1935) alleviated this problem somewhat, when Anouilh sold the film rights for it to Metro-Goldwyn-Mayer. That the film was never made did not seem to bother Anouilh much; "...overnight I had a new car and enough money to keep us going for two years", and that was what mattered.

With his early plays Anouilh managed to score a modest success. *Le Bal des voleurs* was considered "enchantingly comic stage entertainment" and *Le Voyageur sans bagage* (*The Traveller Without Luggage*, 1937), about an amnesiac war veteran who goes to seek his family and, upon finding the truth, rejects his past and starts anew, was described in the press as "a troubling study of the mystery of personality presented with satiric wryness, vigorous observation and philosophic weight".

But Anouilh did not gain serious critical attention until the staging of his first wartime play *Eurydice* in 1941. This, and a reworking of the classical Greek story *Antigone*, which was produced a year later, established Anouilh as a writer of tragedy. Both Orpheus and Antigone here are tragic protagonists for whom death is preferable to a life of intolerable moral compromise: idealism wins out over realism but at the cost of life itself. Both plays were staged in modern dress and with the accoutrements of modern daily life; it was this, said the critics, which lent the plays an air of universality, of real tragedy as opposed to mere historical spectacle. In Britain also both plays were produced to great acclaim. *Antigone* played at the Old Vic in 1949, with Vivien Leigh in the title role and Laurence Olivier as the Chorus, while *Eurydice* was staged under the title *Point of Departure*, with Dirk Bogarde, Mai Zetterling and Hugh Griffiths at the Hammersmith Lyric in 1950.

Another success of the 1940s was the rather more lighthearted *L'Invitation au château* (1947) which centred on the classic comedy theme of what you can do with identical twins. Translated by Christopher Fry as *Ring Round the Moon* (1950), the play attracted large audiences in Britain and France in the immediate post-war years. During the rest of the decade Anouilh wrote some plays about the theatre, using the device of plays within plays, as in *Colombe* (1951) and *La Répétition* (*The Rehearsal*, 1950), a preoccupation which again surfaced much later in *Dear Antoine* (1969) and *Director of the Opera* (1973).

He himself devised a classification for his plays, dividing them up into *pièces noires* (black plays, or tragedies), *pièces roses* (pink ones, or comedies), *pièces brillantes* ("shimmering" plays, executed and received with ease and elegance) and—undoubtedly the most interesting category—*pièces grinçantes* (plays which set your teeth on edge). Of the latter, his *Pauvre Bitos* (*Poor Bitos*, 1956) is a good example, since it is an awkward play in which Anouilh takes a swipe at political theatre. He lets both Left and Right come off badly, but without offering any alternative apart from a rather unpleasant and cowardly cynicism. The play expresses most problematically what has been identified in Anouilh as right-wing sympathies, resulting in a mocking provocation of the French Left, not only of his fellow playwrights (like Sartre and Camus) but especially of the French Resistance in World War II. Proudly proclaiming that he had nothing to do with any resistance during the war, Anouilh once said that he had spent the years under German occupation watching carefully with a telescope from a top floor flat to see when the food lorry was going to arrive at the grocer's. This, in the view of many, was no mere cynicism, but stupidity masquerading as self-effacing "honesty".

After the first wave of notoriety achieved with the classical tragedies, Anouilh experienced a second in the early 1950s with a new category of historical plays which he called *pièces costumées*. His reworking of the story of Joan of Arc became *L'Alouette* (*The Lark*, 1952), a re-run of the idealist/realist dilemma he had treated in *Antigone*, but in a more optimistic vein. Here, also, it became obvious how political a supposedly mainstream, "apolitical" writer can be, for his representation of the Inquisition in *L'Alouette* was widely taken to mean an attack on the totalitarian Left. Another historical drama, *Becket, ou L'Honneur de Dieu* (*Becket, or the Honour of God*, 1958) was very popular in Britain, where distinguished actors like Richard Burton, Anthony Quinn, Laurence Olivier, Christopher Plummer and Peter O'Toole vied for the honour of playing one of the major parts, Becket or Henry.

The critical reception of Anouilh's plays has varied enormously, but there does seem to be a consensus about his place in the modern French theatre. Unlike his literary contemporaries, Anouilh was not a social critic and he had less than cordial relations with most of his colleagues since in 1945 he had—unsurprisingly—failed to find support for his defence of a German collaborator. He did, however—despite a later satire on avant-garde drama in *L'Hurluberlu* (*The Fighting Cock*, 1959)—come out in support of Ionesco's early plays and the theatre of the absurd, but it was quite obvious that his own work had little in common with the avant-garde. Anouilh's brand of innovation and his significance lie instead in the re-working of important themes in the history of drama, using Sophocles, Euripides, Molière, Shaw, Strindberg and Eliot for source material. Tragedy, undoubtedly, was his *métier*, due to a world view which could admit to few shades in human nature other than black or pink, not in the sense of good or evil but of heroic and common. The hero, in the true tradition of tragedy, can, within this philosophy, no more escape death than the common man can represent anything other than banality: they belong to essentially different species and thus change is not possible. It is from this that Anouilh's reputation of "nihilism" derives, and it must also be this aspect which might explain why Anouilh has never become important to the American theatre. Many of his plays were produced on Broadway in the 1950s, but none of them ever took off. The reaction to *Mademoiselle Colombe* in 1954 may be regarded as typical. *Time* called it "an amorality play", while the reviewer from the *Herald Tribune* probably put his finger on it when he wrote: "It may be that we can tolerate Monsieur Anouilh's moral ambivalence only at the fringes....Or it may be that there is something fundamental in the author's flyspeck philosophy which is ineradicably alien to us." Undoubtedly, Anouilh's static perception of the human condition was the thing that was alien to the American public and to the American spirit at large.

Anouilh as tragedist and Anouilh as comedy writer highlighted, albeit in divergent ways, the absurdity of existence. In this sense he was certainly in tune with the times and with his contemporaries, however much he differed with Ionesco and Adamov, the "proper" writers of the absurd. As one perceptive critic has observed, Anouilh, though not a moralist or an ideologue, nevertheless had many things in common with people like Camus and Sartre—notably a concern with such questions as what is fate? what is soul? what is truth? identity? the nature of reality?—really the questions posed by existentialism. In theatrical technique and in the conclusions he reached Anouilh stood apart from his colleagues, it is true, but their themes were perhaps more similar than he would have liked to admit.

Jean Anouilh was indeed a master of the theatre in the sense that from a very young age he had learned to manipulate its props and its people to greatest effect. He had the reputation of being a tremendous craftsman who knew the tricks of the trade inside out. His dialogues, for instance, are still so popular with actors for their fluency and effectiveness that no one ever feels moved to change any of them. This technical facility, however, began to wear thin in Anouilh's later years and he could no longer impress the public with formulas which had not significantly changed in decades. Having made his mark in the 1940s and 1950s, Anouilh did not really renew himself in any major way. "He just keeps grinding out one play after another," a critic said. We may speculate about the reasons why: writer's block (though he was still prolific in a mechanical way), or perhaps the fear of poverty still haunted him after 30 years of living by the pen. Or perhaps it was simply the opposite: the "scandalous" pleasure of earning a living by "amusing myself as much as I do".

Born Jean Marie Lucien Pierre Anouilh. **Parents** François, a tailor, and Marie-Magdaleine, a violinist (Soulue) Anouilh. **Marriages** 1) Monelle Valentin, 1931 (divorced); 2) Nicole Lançon, 1953. **Children** One daughter, Catherine, from first marriage; two daughters and one son from second marriage. **Education** École Colbert, Bordeaux; Collège Chaptal; Université de Paris à la Sorbonne, 1931–33. **Military service** French Army, 1930s. **Career** Publicity and gag writer for films, advertising copywriter for Publicité Damour, Paris, early 1930s; secretary to Louis Jouvet, Comédie des Champs-Élysées, Paris, 1931–32; assistant to director Georges Pitoeff; full-time playwright, mid-1930s–87; also directed occasional films. **Awards and honours** Grand Prix du Cinéma Français, 1949; Tony Award (USA), 1955; New York Drama Critics' Circle Award, 1957; Cino del Duca Prize, 1970; French Drama Critics' Award, 1970; Paris Critics' Prize, 1971. **Plays** *L'Hermine* (produced Paris, 1932), Paris, 1934, as *The Ermine* (produced Nottingham, 1955), in *Plays of the Year 13*, London, 1956, and in *Five Plays*, 1958; *Mandarine* (produced Paris, 1933; *Y'avait un prisonnier* (produced Paris, 1935), in *La Petite Illustration*, May 1935; *Le Voyageur sans bagage* (produced Paris, 1937), in *Pièces noires*, 1942, as *The Traveller Without Luggage* (produced London 1959, New York, 1964), London, 1959, in *Seven Plays*, 1967; *La Sauvage* (produced Paris 1938), Paris, 1938, as *The Restless Heart* (produced London 1957), London, 1957, in *Five Plays*, 1958; *Le Bal des voleurs* (produced Paris 1938), Paris, 1938, as *Thieves Carnival* (produced London, 1952, New York, 1955), London and New York, 1952; *Léocadia* (produced Paris, 1940), in *Pièces roses*, 1942, as *Time Remembered* (produced London 1954, New York, 1957), London, 1955, New York, 1958; *Marie-Jeanne, ou La Fille du peuple* (produced Paris, 1940); *Le Rendezvous de Senlis* (produced Paris, 1941), in *Pièces roses*, 1942, as *Dinner with the Family* (produced London, 1957, New York, 1961) London, 1958; *Eurydice* (produced Paris, 1942), in *Pièces roses*, 1942, (as *Eurydice* produced Hollywood, 1948, as *Point of Departure* produced London, 1950), published as *Point of Departure*, London, 1951, as *Legend of Lovers* (produced New York, 1951), New York, 1952; *Pièces roses*, Paris, 1942, augmented edition, Paris, 1958; *Pièces noires*, Paris, 1942; *Antigone* (produced Paris, 1944), Paris, 1946; translated as *Antigone* (produced New York, 1946, London, 1949), New York, 1946, London, 1957; *Roméo et Jeannette* (produced Paris, 1946), in *Nouvelles pièces noires*, 1946 (as *Fading Mansions* produced London 1949, as *Jeannette* produced New York, 1960), published as *Romeo and Jeannette* in *Five Plays*, 1958; *Nouvelles pièces noires*, Paris, 1946; *Médée* (produced Paris, 1953), in *Nouvelles pièces noires*, Paris, 1946, as *Medea* (produced London, 1956, New York, 1972), in *Plays of the Year 15*, London, 1956, in *Seven Plays*, 1967; *L'Invitation au château* (produced Paris, 1947), Paris, 1948, as *Ring Around the Moon* (produced London and New York, 1950), London and New York, 1950, *Ardèle ou La Marguerite*, with *Episode de la vie d'un auteur* (produced Paris, 1948), Paris, 1949, (as *Cry of the Peacock*, produced New York, 1950, as *Ardele* produced London, 1951), published as *Ardele*, London, 1951, in *Five Plays*, 1958; (with Jean Arenche) *Humulus le muet* (produced Paris, 1948), *Grenobles*, n.d., as *Humulus the Great* (produced New York, 1976); *La Répétition, ou L'Amour puni* (produced Paris, 1950), Geneva, 1950, as *The Rehearsal* (produced Edinburgh, 1957, London 1961, New York 1963), in *Five Plays*, 1958, published separately, London, 1961; *Monsieur Vincent*, Munich, 1951; *Colombe* (produced Paris, 1951), in *Pièces brillantes*, 1951, as *Colombe* (produced London, 1951, New York, 1954), London, 1952, New York, 1954, revised version, Paris, 1961; *Pièces brillantes*, Paris, 1951; *Cécile, ou L'École des pères* (produced Paris, 1954), in *Pièces brillantes*, 1951, as *Cécile*, or *The School for Fathers* in *Seven Plays*, 1967; *La Valse des toréadors* (produced Paris, 1952), Paris, 1952, as *The Waltz of the Toreadors* (produced London, 1956, New York, 1957), London, 1956, New York, 1957; *Trois comédies*, Paris, 1952; *La Nuit des rois* (produced Paris, 1961), in *Trois comédies*, Paris, 1952; (with Georges Neveux) *Le Loup*, Paris, 1953; *L'Alouette* (produced Paris, 1953), Paris, 1953, as *The Lark* (produced London and New York, 1955), London, 1955, New York, 1956; *Ornifle, ou Le Courant d'air* (produced Paris, 1955), Paris, 1956, translated as *Ornifle*, New York, 1970, London, 1971, as *It's Later Than You Think*, Chicago, 1970; (with Claude Vincent) *Il est important d'être aimé* (produced Paris, 1964), in *L'Avant-scène 101*, 1955; *Pauvre Bitos, ou Le Diner de tètes* (produced Paris, 1956), in *Pièces grinçantes*, 1956, as *Poor Bitos* (produced London, 1963, New York, 1964), New York and London, 1964; *Pièces grinçantes*, Paris, 1956; *Five Plays*, New York, 1958; *L'Hurluberlu, ou Le Réactionnaire amoreux* (produced Paris, 1959), Paris, 1959, as *The Fighting Cock* (produced New York, 1959, Chichester and London, 1966), New York, 1960, London, 1967; *Becket, ou L'Honneur de Dieu* (produced Paris, 1959), Paris, 1959, as *Becket, or The Honour of God* (produced New York, 1960, London 1961), New York, 1960, London, 1961; *Madam de...* (produced London, 1959), London, 1959; (with Roland Laudenback) *La Petite Molière* (produced Paris, 1959), in *L'Avant-scène*, December 1959; *Le Songe du critique* (produced Paris, 1960), in *L'Avant-scène 143*, 1959; *Pièces costumées*, Paris, 1960; *La Foire d'empoigne* (produced Paris, 1962), in *Pièces costumées*, Paris, 1960, as *Catch as Catch Can* in *Seven Plays*, 1967; *Tartuffe* (produced Paris, 1960), in *L'Avant-scène*, May 1961; *La Grotte* (produced Paris, 1961), Paris, 1961, as *The Cavern* (produced London, 1965, Cincinnati, 1967, New York, 1968), New York, 1966; *Victor, ou Les Enfants au pouvoir* (produced Paris, 1962), in *L'Avant-scène*, November 1962; (with Nicole Anouilh) *L'Amant complaisant* (produced Paris, 1962), Paris, 1962; *L'Orchestre* (produced Paris, 1962), Paris, 1970, as *The Orchestra* (produced New York, 1969), in *Seven Plays*, 1967, published separately, London, 1975; *Richard III* (produced Paris, 1964), Paris, n.d.; *L'Ordalie, ou La Petite Catherine de Heilbronn* (produced Paris, 1966), in *L'Avant-scène*, January 1967; *Seven Plays*, New York, 1967; *Le Boulanger, la boulangère et le petit mitron* (produced Paris, 1968), Paris, 1969, as *The Baker, the Baker's Wife and the Baker's Boy* (produced Newcastle-upon-Tyne, 1972); *Théâtre complet*, 9 vols, Paris, 1968; *Cher Antoine, ou L'Amour raté* (produced Paris, 1969), Paris, 1969, as *Dear Antoine, or The Love That Failed* (produced Chichester, 1971, Cambridge, Massachusetts, 1973), London and New York, 1971; *Le Théâtre, ou La Vie comme elle est* (produced Paris, 1970?); *Ne réveillez pas madame* (produced Paris, 1970), Paris, 1970; *Les Poissons rouges, ou Mon Père, ce héros* (produced Paris, 1970), Paris, 1970; *Nouvelles pièces grinçantes*, Paris, 1970; *Tu étais si gentil quand tu étais petit* (produced Paris, 1971), Paris, 1972, as *You Were So Sweet* (produced London, 1974); *Le Directeur de l'opéra* (produced Paris, 1973), Paris, 1972; as *The Director of the Opera* (produced Chichester, 1973), London, 1973; *Piéces baroques*, Paris, 1974; *L'Arrestation* (produced Paris, 1975), Paris, 1975, as *The Arrest* (produced Billingham, Durham, 1976); (television) *Le Jeune Homme et le lion*, 1976; *Chers Zoizeaux* (produced Paris, 1976), Paris, 1977; *Pièces secrètes*, Paris, 1977; *Vive Henri IV*, Paris, 1977; *La Culotte* (produced Paris, 1978), Paris, 1978; (television) *La Belle vie*, 1979; *La Belle vie, suivi de Episode de la vie d'un auteur*, Paris, 1980; *Le Nombril*, Paris, 1981; *Number One*, London, 1984; *Five Plays*, 1987. **Screenplays** (with Jean Aurenche) *Les Dégourdis de la onzième*, 1936; (with Jean Aurenche) *Vous n'avez rien à declarer*, 1937; (with Jean Aurenche) *Les Otages*, 1939; *Cavalcade d'amour*, 1939; (with Jean Aurenche) *Le Voyageur sans bagage*, 1944; (with Jean Bernard Luc) *Monsieur Vincent*, 1947; (with Julien Duvivier and Guy Morgan) *Anna Karenina*, 1948; (with Jean Bernard Luc) *Pattes blanches*, 1949; *Caroline chérie*, 1951; (with Monelle Valentin) *Deux sous de violettes*, 1951; *Le Rideau rouge*, 1952; *Le Chevalier de la nuit*, 1953; *La Mort de belle* (*The Passion of Slow Fire*), 1961; *La Ronde* (*Circle of Love*), 1964; *Time for Loving*, 1972. **Other** *Les Demoiselles de la nuit* (ballet scenario), 1948; (with Georges Neveux) *Le Loup* (ballet scenario), 1953; (with Pierre Imbourg and André Warnod) *Michel-Marie Poulain*, Paris, 1953; *Fables*, Paris, 1962. **Cause of death** Heart attack, at age 77. **Further reading** Marguerite Archer, *Anouilh*, New York, 1951; Edward O. Marsh, *Anouilh: Poet of Pierrot and Pantaloon*, London and New York, 1953; Leonard C. Pronko, *The World of Anouilh*, Berkeley, 1961; John Harvey, *Anouilh: A Study in Theatrics*, New Haven, 1964; Philip Thody, *Anouilh*, Edinburgh, 1968; Alba della Fazia, *Anouilh*, New York, 1969;

Kathleen White, *Anouilh: An Annotated Bibliography*, New Jersey, 1973; Lewis W. Falb, *Anouilh*, New York, 1977; H.G. McIntyre, *The Theatre of Anouilh*, London and New York, 1981; W.D. Howarth, *Anouilh: Antigone*, London, 1983.

ALFRED BESTER

American Science-fiction Writer

Born **New York City, New York, 18 December 1913**

Died **Doylestown, Pennsylvania, *circa* 20 October 1987**

True to the old adage, the influence of Alfred Bester's work is inversely proportional to its size. Along with such acknowledged masters as Arthur C. Clarke, Robert Heinlein and Isaac Asimov, Alfred Bester is one of the few who belong in the circle of major science-fiction writers. His output was not large by any standards, but he was one of the first modern science-fiction writers to raise the genre to a literary level. He was able to achieve exciting variations in form by adapting other genres to the science-fiction mode. At his best, he could raise it to a level of art; and even his disappointments were not failures.

Bester was a master storyteller, his plots moved along at breakneck speeds, and his characters achieved mythic stature from the momentum of events. Indeed, the passion-driven, obsessed, archetypal character in science fiction is sometimes called "Besterian". The proof of Bester's importance lies in the influence he had on major science-fiction authors such as John Brunner, Robert Silverberg and Kurt Vonnegut. Bester's significance bears also on the evolution of the novel in this century, insofar as his manipulation of text and his intellectual foundations anticipate such central figures as William S. Burroughs and the absurdist novelists. The value of Bester's work is summed up by the *Washington Post*'s Peter Nicholls, who said, "As a writer of science fiction, Bester has never been prolific, merely revolutionary".

By the time he published his first book in 1953, a satirical novel called *Who He?*, Bester had completed an unusual apprenticeship. In 1938, three years after receiving his BA from the University of Pennsylvania, Bester began writing short stories, radio scripts for *Charlie Chan* and *The Shadow*, and comic book scenarios for *Superman* and *Batman*. The demands of this type of composition gave him a strong sense of action and the discipline to develop the fantastically woven plots of his novels. His work is always full of incident and complication, moving ahead until it runs out of steam or hits the guardrail. His intellectual interest in psychology and literature merged with this training to produce a fine example of the "pyrotechnic" style of science fiction: an episodic manner of narrative, linear in its presentation of conflicts and resolutions, replete with heavily drawn characters and action. Bester devoted much more attention to characterization than most other writers in this genre, producing elaborate case studies into the motivations of good and evil, dignity, conquest and love.

Bester's first important novel, *The Demolished Man* (1953), illustrates his ability to weave high symbolism with heavy action. It is similar to his shorter fiction, on a larger scale. However, it presents "a more heterogeneous picture of culture than was usual for 1950s' science fiction", writes Robert Froese. On the surface it is a detective story: a corporate mogul named Ben Reich murders a rival whom he believes is out to destroy his empire. What makes this event so extraordinary is that in the twenty-fourth century a select group of telepaths, known as Espers, can prevent such crimes by detecting criminal intentions before the act can take place. The book opens with Reich performing what was supposed to be impossible. Esper prefect Lincoln Powell sets out to discover the felon and bring him to justice. In the course of his pursuit we learn about the characters of the two men, who are actually two sides of the Besterian vision of human nature.

These psychological overtones not only give dimension to the characters, they force the reader to identify with them. Both are driven men, both ostensibly in pursuit of good or evil, but both Reich and Powell are flawed. Bester gives the reader insights into Reich's genuine fear of the "Man with No Face", whom he believes is his rival, but whom the reader begins to suspect is the dark forces within Reich himself. Bester also shows the reader the faults in Powell's character and how he breaks the Esper ethical code in order to trap Reich. By the end of the novel, when Powell performs "Mass Cathexis" to flush out the criminal, the reader perceives the unity of the two characters. They are part of an unbreakable duality, reinforced by the image of the Mass Cathexis in which Powell wakes up from the procedure to find Reich in his arms, curled up into a tight foetal ball. This symmetry of Reich and Powell is central to the theme of the novel.

Much more could be said about the book, such as Bester's skill at rendering dialogue and at portraying female characters. Suffice it to say that they are still exceptional qualities to find in a science-fiction novel, and ones that were acknowledged by *The Demolished Man* being awarded the first Hugo Award for best novel of the year. Bester's next work, *The Stars My Destination* (1957), succeeds and improves on the earlier work. As before, it deals with the incomplete psyche that starts in a position of weakness and is then reborn with genuinely superior dimensions of capacity and understanding. It concerns a man named Gully Foyle—timid, insignificant, left to die by his crew—who saves himself to seek revenge on his former crew members. Revenge is his sole motive as he gains great power, wealth and understanding, but when he is finally powerful enough to destroy his enemies he discovers that his values no longer make sense to him. Gradually, he learns that until he masters his inner self he will be a victim of his obsession. In the course of the novel he is profoundly transformed from a man of rage to a man of love.

Here again, Bester is able to weave and adapt other sources to the science-fiction genre. Most obvious of these is Alexandre Dumas's *The Count of Monte Cristo* (1844–45). Bester applied the unjust sentence and imprisonment, the escape, the secret treasure and the guise of a socialite which the protagonist uses to beguile his opponents. Bester employed devices like epiphanaic passages, stream-of-consciousness, interior monologues, varied points of view, and typographic experiment, which were simply not in most writers' repertoire at that time. There are elements of William Blake's poem "The Tyger", which Bester converts into horrible facial tattoos on Foyle that are visible only when he is enraged. The "fearful symmetry" of which Blake speaks appears in *The Stars My Destination* as the tiger and the Burning Man. Foyle fears this image as Reich fears the Man with No Face, but Foyle discovers that it is an image not of hatred but compassion. As Powell affirms: "...there is nothing in man but love and faith, courage and kindness, generosity and sacrifice. All else is only the barrier of your blindness."

One of the barriers which Bester most often assaults is the culture of regimentation. He continually mocks the conformist mentality encouraged by modern society. One hilarious example of this is the group of "Mr Prestos" in *The Stars My Destination*, who have deformed their bodies in order to better use the products sold by the big corporations. His novels are filled with such "freaks, monsters, and grotesques", who are almost allegorical representations of the crippling effects of our age. They provide an ideal counterpoint to the scope and dynamism of the main characters. The subcultures which Reich, Powell, and Foyle pass through, and the aberrations they encounter, present a very Dantean vision of human failings and serve a straightforward didactic purpose for the reader. Bester himself considered writing a "therapy" for him. He once said, "The mature science-fiction author doesn't merely tell a story about Brick

Malloy versus the Giant Yeastmen from Gethsemane. He makes a statement [of] himself, the dimension and depth of the man." In one sense, then, Bester is merely confronting the conflicting elements in his own psyche. In another he finds the universal in the particular, which is the essence of his therapy. It is evident in the novels that the reading is a therapy, too.

Surprisingly, not much was heard from Alfred Bester after these *tours de force* were published. The next book, *The Computer Connection*, came 19 years later and was something of a disappointment. To be sure, it had all the great themes, twisted personalities and typographical eccentricities, but it lacked the integration of all these elements that occurred in the first two novels. *Golem*^{100}, published five years later, was no less disappointing, but far more interesting. Bester had been developing the manuscript for several years. It was to be a "visio-narrative", which contained "pages of pure graphics and scenes written in full [musical] score...to convey deep unconscious images". Not surprisingly, it was not until 1980 that the manuscript could actually be printed. The production problems were overcome, but the book met with scepticism by readers and critics alike. Nevertheless, it stands as one of the most ambitious projects ever attempted in science fiction.

The best tribute to Bester is the continuing interest he attracts. Today, the greater part of science fiction is hopelessly dated, and its visions of the space age naïve and childish. Bester's tales of human transformation, good and bad, fill them with faith in and hope for the future. His belief in man's potential emerges at every twist of plot, as the final sentences from one of his short stories makes clear: "Stephen Krane smiled up at the stars, stars that were sprinkled evenly across the sky. Stars that had not yet formed into the familiar constellations, and would not for another hundred million years."

Born Alfred Bester. **Parents** James J., a shoe merchant, and Belle (Silverman) Bester. **Marriage** Rolly Goulko, advertising executive, 1936. **Education** University of Pennsylvania, BA, 1935. **Career** Freelance writer, 1940s–1950s; editor, various popular magazines, mid 1950s–early 1970s; senior editor, *Holiday* magazine, early 1970s; radio and television writer; full-time writer from about 1972. **Related activities** Author of comic scenarios, including *Batman* and *Superman*, 1940s; book reviewer, *Fantasy and Science Fiction*, New York, 1960–62. **Memberships** Science Fiction Writers of America. **Awards and honours** Science Fiction Writers' of America Hugo Award for Best Novel, for *The Demolished Man*, 1953. **Novels** (all science fiction, unless stated) *The Demolished Man*, Chicago and London, 1953, new edition edited by Lester Del Rey, 1975; *Who He?*, (satire) New York, 1953; reissued as *The Rat Race*, New York, 1956, London, 1984; *Tiger! Tiger!*, London, 1956, published as *The Stars My Destination*, New York, 1957; *The Computer Connection*, New York, 1975, published as *Extro*, London, 1975; *Golem*^{100}, New York and London, 1980; *The Deceivers*, New York, 1981, London, 1984. **Short story collections** *Starburst*, New York, 1958, London, 1968; *The Dark Side of the Earth*, New York, 1964, London, 1969; *An Alfred Bester Omnibus*, London, 1967; *The Light Fantastic*, vol 1, New York, 1976, London, 1977; *Star Light, Star Bright*, vol 2, New York, 1976, London, 1978, published in one volume as *Starlight: The Great Short Fiction of Alfred Bester*, New York, 1976. **Other** *The Life and Death of a Satellite* (non-fiction), Boston, 1966, London, 1967; author of English libretti for Verdi's *La Traviata* and Mussorgsky's *The Fair at Sorochinsk*; contributor to magazines and journals, including *Holiday*, *Show*, *Venture* and *Rogue*. **Radio scripts** (include) *Charlie Chan* and *The Shadow*, 1940s. **Cause of death** Undisclosed, at age 74. **Further reading** Carolyn Wender, *Alfred Bester*, Washington, 1982.

CATHERINE BRAMWELL-BOOTH

British Commissioner of the Salvation Army

***Born* London, England, 20 July 1883**

***Died* Berkshire, England, 4 October 1987**

Catherine Bramwell-Booth's life can only be fully understood by looking at the origins and work of the Salvation Army and its founding family into which she was born, the first child of the first child of William and Catherine Booth.

William Booth had been ordained a minister of the Methodist Church but in 1865 had left to work as an evangelist and founded the Christian Mission. Both he and his wife, the first Catherine in the family, preached all over the country and, in 1878, the movement was renamed the Salvation Army with the primary aim of saving souls and bringing them to Jesus. With its brash approach of "Why should the devil have all the best tunes?" and outspoken songs such as, "The devil and me we can't agree/I hate him and he hates me," the movement brought horror to the hearts of those practising orthodox Christianity. The Salvationists were seen as unseemly and unspeakably vulgar. As the biographer, Mary Batchelor, wrote,

> Anglicans were accustomed to well-bred clergy who were Oxford or Cambridge educated, but William recognized no such requirements...and allowed women as well as men to preach. Any Tom, Dick or Harry could stand up at the street corner and preach, provided he had experienced "conversion", even though he might be—and sometimes was—a prize fighter or a chimney sweep....William Booth might encourage his officers to tell a man, once converted, to beat the drum and not his wife, but to many middle-class churchgoers, the whole noisy business was distasteful, even blasphemous.

The Army was reviled in the press and officers were likely to be attacked on the streets; many were seriously injured. Others appeared before lay magistrates who were often the publicans whose income had dropped somewhat when their former customers joined the movement and renounced drink. They gave the Salvationists a hard time. The Riot Act was read frequently.

Despite middle-class outrage and her father's disapproval, a young woman called Florence Soper, who had heard Catherine Booth speak, decided that this was the religion for her. When she saw an advertisement for a companion to accompany one of Catherine Booth's daughters to France, she applied for the post. Not only did she get the post, but she also (eventually) gained her father's approval. Later she was wooed and won by General Booth's eldest son, Bramwell. Their daughter was Catherine Bramwell Booth.

Two days before her first birthday, Catherine was carried to the East End of London where her mother, Florence, was to begin her first major job with the Army—that of helping women and, in particular, very young girls, out of a life of prostitution and into safety. Florence felt herself inadequate to the work but her determination carried her through and it was her efforts that started the Army's massive social work movement which was instrumental in ending the sale of children for immoral purposes and in having the age of consent raised to 16.

Catherine, who had been given to God at birth, was constantly encouraged to rededicate herself to Jesus. She was educated by her mother, who continued with her work of superintending the developing social work with "fallen" women while bearing six more children at two-year intervals. From an early age, however, Catherine also had a great deal of responsiblity. In Florence's absence, she took on the role of mother for her younger siblings and, always anxious to please her father, fitted in daily visits to the general, her grandfather, who was now a widower. With such a background it was inevitable that, despite many internal doubts and torments, she should become an officer herself. Florence herself wrote of Catherine, "I have been fortunate indeed in having as leader of my flock one who resembled her father in heart and mind as well as likeness, and who even from her tenderest years has been my right hand."

Becoming an officer meant, for Catherine, not only embracing a life of service, poverty and abstention but also one of chastity. An officer in the Salvation Army can only marry a fellow officer but there was no one of similar standing to the Booth girls who were, in their time, akin to royalty, so they all remained unmarried. When General Booth died on 20 August 1912, his body rested for three days in a Salvation Army Hall while 65,000 people paid homage to their great leader. Wreaths were received from King George V and Queen Mary, from Queen Alexandra, the German Kaiser and the American ambassador. Catherine's grandfather was a figure of world renown, her father, Bramwell, had been designated his successor and she was seen as the heir apparent.

Following her own training, Catherine worked both in the front line in the UK and in training new cadets, but once her father took over as general, Catherine began to travel with him. In 1913 she went to Scandanavia and Russia, where she preached at secret meetings in rooms heavily shuttered and curtained to prevent any sounds escaping to the street below. World War I handicapped her European work for a few years but by the time it was ending she was once again on her way, this time to assist in the distribution of milk to the starving children of Berlin. She was now international secretary for European affairs and spent the next six years travelling in Europe. However, a major illness in 1922 forced her to rest for over three years and it was not until 1926 that she regained sufficient health and strength to return to work, this time as a full colonel in the post held by her mother—leader of Women's Social Work. This was now a very big part of the Army and Catherine was responsible for over 600 officers throughout the British Isles. There were homes for women and girls at all stages of life, including prisoners and vagrants. The work also involved district maternity care and what is now the work of probation officers—assisting young women in trouble with the law and ex-prisoners.

Now Commissioner Booth, she managed to combine overall administration without losing touch with grass roots' feeling, or with the difficulties experienced by her officers in the field. She always managed to answer her enormous mail with a personal note attached to the end of the typewritten letters and to visit the homes regularly. She was also a great advocate of mixed "eventide" homes, believing that women took more care of themselves and men were more considerate and polite when they were together.

Early in 1929 Catherine's ailing father was forced by the High Council of the Army to relinquish his position and an "outsider" (General Higgins) was elected to succeed him. This change in the method of selecting the general was later enshrined in an Act of Parliament. No longer was leadership of the Army the exclusive province of the Booth family. This may have been a change for the ultimate good of the now massive and ever expanding organization, but it brought great sorrow to Catherine and, she believed, hastened her father's death. He died later that year. In 1930 Catherine was granted a two-year furlough to write his biography and, to ensure his name lived on, changed her own to Bramwell-Booth.

She continued with social work and, following World War II, was once again involved with refugees, until her enforced retirement in 1948, something she bitterly resented. However, her life and vitality continued and her greatest fame came to her many years later. In her nineties she began to appear in television chat shows and rapidly became a hit with both the interviewers and the audience. Her many years of public speaking and, no doubt, dealing with hecklers, had ingrained in her the art of performing. She was quick-witted and witty. When one of her hosts commented inadvisedly, "My money is on you reaching a hundred," her response was instantaneous: "I hope that doesn't mean to say you're a gambling man." In another show with her two younger sisters, just before her hundredth birthday, the then famous Russell Harty leaned forward and began to say, "Now then, you are..." whereupon Catherine innocently enquired, "And who are you?" It brought the house down.

In another interview, when Malcolm Muggeridge, the well-known journalist and a devout Christian, talked to her about his being "well content to move on...to the heavenly future", she disagreed strongly. In his foreword to her biography, Muggeridge recalled that Catherine Bramwell-Booth insisted that "despite everything, mortality was well worth while at any age...Heaven no doubt has much to recommend it, but there was no need to expedite getting there."

As Muggeridge concluded, "Commissioner Catherine remains an inexhaustible subject—a great Christian on her own terms; a great pilgrim going through many of John Bunyan's hazards. Surely she will reach the Celestial City, with all the trumpets sounding for her."

Born Catherine Booth; adopted surname Bramwell-Booth in memory of her father, 1929. **Parents** Bramwell, leader of the Salvation Army, and Florence, Army officer, (Soper) Booth. **Career** Officer, Salvation Army, 1903; trained cadets at International Training College, 1907–17; International Secretary for Europe, 1917; promoted to colonel in command of Women's Social Work in Great Britain and Ireland, 1926; appointed commissioner, 1927; International Secretary for Europe, 1946–48; retired, 1948; commissioner of the Salvation Army. **Related activities** Accompanied her father to Russia and Scandinavia, preaching at secret meetings, 1913; worked in Berlin, distributing milk to starving children, 1918–19; worked with refugees, World War II. **Other activities** Frequent appearances on TV chat shows between ages of 90 and 100. **Awards and honours** Companion of the Order of the British Empire, 1971; Order of the Founder, Salvation Army, 1983; Best Speaker Award, Guild of Professional Toastmasters, 1978. **Publications** *Messages to the Messengers*; *A Few Lines*; *Bramwell Booth* (biography), 1933; (compiler) *Bramwell Booth Speaks*, 1947; *Verse*, 1947; *Catherine Booth, the Story of Her Loves*, 1970; *Fighting for the King* (poems), 1983; (with Ted Harrison) *Commissioner Catherine*, 1983. **Cause of death** Undisclosed, at age 104. **Further reading** Mary Batchelor, *Catherine Bramwell-Booth*, 1986.

JOSEPH CAMPBELL

American Writer, Editor and Educator

***Born* New York City, New York, 26 March 1904**

***Died* Honolulu, Hawaii, 31 October 1987**

For Joseph Campbell, one of this century's best-known mythologists and seminal scholars, this was an exciting time to be alive. He did not see the advent of modern life destroying our spiritual sensibilities, nor alienating us from our environment. On the contrary, he saw this period as the beginning of a fundamental change in human experience, the like of which has not been seen since the development of stable agricultural civilizations thousands of years ago. This new order of experience and relationship to the "deep principles" of human understanding have been developing for centuries, but are now perceivable in this age of scientific research and power-driven machines. The old foundations of our world culture, based on the opposition of matter and spirit, our subjection to superior beings and forces, and the archetypes of fall and redemption, cosmic floods and heroic journeys is giving way to a mythology based on actual individuals' lives. To recognize and accept this challenge was the inspiration behind Campbell's work—work commended for its insight, graceful narration and scholarship.

Campbell proposed that myths answer four basic human needs: they create a psychological harmony in the individual, protect and mediate the relationships between the individual and society, likewise explain man's place in the universe, and finally, answer the eternal questions about life and being. Every culture has its myths, and all myths perform these four functions. From his earliest readings, Campbell was continually impressed by the recurring themes in such legends: creation, fire-stealing, death and resurrection, virgin births and mythic heroic quests. He was troubled and challenged by the similarities between the tales of such diverse peoples as American Indians, ancient Hindus and modern Europeans. This, especially, made him question the nature of his own Roman Catholic heritage. Despite their commonality, all faiths hold themselves up as unique. To understand their common foundations and claims to truth-value, Campbell investigated everything from Zuni to Greek mythology, and from Arthurian narratives to the work of Picasso, Freud and Joyce. His discoveries have moved and influenced millions of people through such works as Richard Adams's *Watership Down* and George Lucas's *Star Wars*. Throughout his career, Campbell tried to show that myth is "the pictorial vocabulary of communication from the source zones of our energies to rational consciousness".

Campbell's interest in folklore and mythology began when he was a boy in New Rochelle, New York. He was fascinated with Buffalo Bill's Wild West Show, which exhibited cowboys, sharpshooters and "Indians right off the plains". The Campbell family lived next to a public library, where he read all he could about American Indian lore, especially Morgan's *League of the Iroquois*, and the works of Franz Boas. While in Canterbury prep school (in Connecticut), he read the latest work on the people of the Pacific, so that by the time he entered Dartmouth College he was "light years" ahead of his classmates.

"My serious studies," he recalled, "were not resumed until one year after graduation from Columbia," where he completed his first degree. Campbell had entered a master's programme at New York's Columbia University to study medieval literature. While preparing a thesis on Malory's *Le Morte d'Arthur*, "I realized...that many motifs in the Arthurian legends resembled themes that I could recall from my American Indian studies. From that first moment," he wrote, "the problem of the mythological archetypes has been the *primum mobile* of all my research."

The world began to open up for Campbell at this point, as these recurrent themes began to appear in everything he encountered. In 1927 Columbia awarded him a two-year Proudfit Fellowship, which sent him to Paris and then Munich. His intention was to study Old French and Provençal, but soon he discovered Sanskrit and Indo-European philology. His odyssey led him from French to *Ulysses*, from Sanskrit to Freud, Jung, Mann, Goethe and Hinduism, and from these to Picasso and Matisse. Much to his wonderment, he found "a constant requirement in the human psyche for a centring and a harmonization". More importantly, he saw in the work of twentieth-century artists, poets and philosophers that our cultural evolution has transformed the nature of this search for harmony. Our vision has shifted from the archetypal heroes, who are in all ways superior to us, to the modern heroes, who search not for the Grail, but for the courage "to credit their own senses, honour their own decisions, name their own virtues, and claim their own vision of truth".

The profundity of this discovery led him far away from his doctoral studies, and upon his return to the US he decided to assimilate this new perspective. Of course, the recent Wall Street crash had something to do with this decision as well, and for the next three years he "learned to live on nothing, and...did little else but read and take notes". During this hegera, Campbell spent time in Woodstock, New York and in Carmel, California, on the rocky northern coast that was home to several writers and poets. He read voraciously, adding Spengler, Schopenhauer and Nietzsche to his store of learning. He even managed to sell a short story, which enabled him to continue his research after one year of teaching at his old prep school. By the end of 1934 he was teaching comparative mythology at Sarah Lawrence College in Bronxville, New York, and after so many years of exploration, his efforts began to bear fruit.

In the 1940s Campbell prepared commentaries to *The Complete Grimms' Fairy Tales* and an essay for *Where the Two Came to Their Father*, a comparative analysis of Navaho heroes. He was then appointed editor of the papers of the late Indologist Heinrich Zimmer, with whom Campbell had a close personal friendship. Beginning in 1946, and continuing for the next 12 years, Campbell prepared an important body of Zimmer's work on Indian/Asian civilization.

Though he would not write a book on his own for another decade, Campbell's writing career dates back to 1939. Prior to that, he "tried short stories for a while when I returned from Europe, but contracted an allergy to the popular press". Then his Columbia friend Henry Morton Robinson persuaded Campbell to write a "key" to *Finnegans Wake*, which had recently been published. Campbell had long been a fan of Joyce—since his days in Paris. He met Sylvia Beach of the Shakespeare and Company Book Shop in Paris, where *Ulysses* was published and where the day's great writers would congregate. He had the privilege of seeing the work-in-progress publication of *Finnegans Wake*, and after studying the published version with Robinson became certain that it provided the key to Joyce's entire achievement and to his own vision.

He called the novel "a mighty allegory of the fall and resurrection of mankind", and a "complete and permanent record of our age". Campbell's and Robinson's companion piece, *A Skeleton Key to Finnegans Wake*, took five years to prepare. It was embraced by critics as a valuable diviner to Joyce's often-difficult text, but the manuscript was not accepted for publication until it received T.S. Eliot's personal recommendation.

Campbell's childhood concern over "the truths disguised...under the figures of religion and mythology" is the backdrop of his first solo work, *The Hero with a Thousand Faces*. His herculean ambition was always to show that "everything...is a function of myth", and in *The Hero* he tries to absorb everything in American Indian, ancient Greek, Hindu, Buddhist, Mayan, Biblical, Nordic, Arthurian and other legends into a "monomyth". He describes the hero's descent from the real world to the underworld, where the hero confronts his own deepest self and discovers the true identity of himself, society and the universe. It is a rite of passage which Campbell believes every individual must perform, regardless of the circumstances. The goal of the heroic journey is not rapture, but mastery of both physical and psychic realms. The Shaman dreams of his own destruction and returns to the waking world with the power to heal the sick. The Bodhisattva sees nirvana but returns to the sensual world to guide others. The hero, and humanity, struggles to achieve a radical understanding of his or her own condition.

Campbell's view that modern-day individuals can take the heroic path even as they "stand...on the corner...waiting for the traffic light to change" clearly bears the imprint of Joyce on Campbell's thought. Similarly, in his introduction to *The Hero* the stated goal was to expose and encourage "those forces that are working in the present world for unification...in the sense of mutual human understanding". And, like *Finnegans Wake*, reviews expressed their puzzlement at this "fascinating and maddening book". Now, however, it is a classic introductory text in American colleges and universities.

After this impressive work, it is remarkable that the bulk of Campbell's accomplishments still lay ahead of him. The work which particularly distinguishes Campbell, and the work for which *The Hero* is but a primer, is the monumental four-volume series *The Masks of God*. Appearing between 1959 and 1968, it is an effort to weave together all the mythic types of the world from the dawn of man. And as before, the guiding force behind his plan is the interest in the present stage of human history; that is, the basic change taking place. The first volume, *Primitive Mythology*, identifies the essential factors of human existence. The cycles of night and day, the polarity of gender, human growth and the natural seasons form the rudiments of mythology in the palaeolithic and neolithic symbolism. Such a symbolism is characteristic of hunting and planting societies; or, the civilization we have had for nearly all our history. Volumes II and III compare and contrast oriental and occidental traditions. Campbell's consideration of Hindu, Buddhist, Taoist and Confucian philosophies holds up the Asian notion of the transcendent and immanent God as being more integrated than the Western experience of God and the rational agent. In Volume III he traces the history of Western mythology from its Mesopotamian origins to its Judaeo-Christian and Islamic legacy, reviewing the consequences of the death of the earth-mother traditions on its development.

The grand finale to *The Masks of God* is *Creative Mythology*, which entwines all Campbell's conclusions and intepretations of our mythological heritage. We are, he claims, coming to the end of a "monumental stage" of history—one that has been with us for the past 5000 years. Our intellectual, personal, social and spiritual life is no longer guided by the paradigms born in the nomadic tribes and agricultural cities of 5000 years ago. Further, Campbell points to the fourteenth century as the beginning of this new, transitional period. Then, people like Peter Abelard began to sense the possibility of the individual's own transcendent essence. The emphasis on experience over authority marked the continuation of this process through to our present "world culture", offering the hope of "future against past, individual quest and the sharp cut of 'proof' into the grip of 'faith'". All that we have done in the past centuries is predicated on this integral psychological shift.

To blend together the combined experience of 30,000 years and form "the lineaments of a new science...of man's gods and heroes" is a tremendous task. So it is not surprising that many reviewers were daunted and confused by the result. One criticism was that the narrative "shifted...uneasily between the popular-poetic and the scholarly-scientific", making clarity rather elusive. But a work so ambitious and erudite as this could become nothing other than a focal point for all subsequent study in a handful of fields.

In the year he retired from Sarah Lawrence, Campbell finished editing *Myths, Dreams and Religion*, which focuses more specifically on his thoughts of the future. Campbell believed that eventually, though now we seem culturally impoverished, new myths will replace the old. The symbols of the split atom and the exploration of space may provide the new vocabulary that will connect us to the "unity in the universe and a unity in [ourselves]".

Campbell's incredibly active and varied career continued in his retirement and pursued several new directions. Before his death he was able to complete two instalments of *The Historical Atlas of World Mythology*, which opens characteristically with an "Outline on Everything". His influence has been noted time after time by admirers and students. Film-maker George Lucas once said that "if it hadn't been for him, it's possible that I would still be trying to write *Star Wars* today". A film treatment was done on Campbell's life and work in 1987, and in 1988 some 23 hours of his interviews were prepared by the Public Broadcasting Service. Even at the age of 80, Campbell felt that he was only at the beginning of a journey, and perhaps this is what helped keep him so active and enthusiastic. "I'm 80," he said, "but you've got to live as though there were no time limit."

Born Joseph Campbell. **Parents** Charles William, hosiery importer and wholesaler, and Josephine (Lynch) Campbell. **Marriage** Jean Erdman, dancer and choreographer, 1938. **Education** Canterbury School, New Milford, Connecticut, 1921; Dartmouth College, 1921–22; Columbia University, AB, 1925, MA, 1927; University of Paris, 1927–28; University of Munich, 1928–29. **Career** Teacher, Canterbury School, 1932–33; faculty member, department of literature, Sarah Lawrence College, Bronxville, 1934–72; lecturer, Foreign Service Institute, Department of State, Washington, 1956–73, Columbia, 1959. **Other activities** Co-founder with wife, Foundation for the Open Eye, sponsoring lectures and theatre in New York City, 1972. **Offices and memberships** President, Creative Film Foundation, 1954–63; trustee, Bollingen Film Foundation, 1960–69; member, National Institute of Arts and Letters; director, Society for Arts, Religion and Contemporary Culture; president, American Society for the Study of Religion, 1972–75. **Awards and honours** Proudfit Fellowship, 1927–28; Distinguished Scholar Award, Hofstra University, 1973. **Publications** (with Jeff King and Maud Oakes) *Where the Two Came to Their Father: A Navaho War Ceremonial*, 1943; *Grimms' Folk Tales: Folkloristic Commentary*, 1944; (with Henry Morton Robinson) *A Skeleton Key to Finnegans Wake*, 1944; (contributor) *James Joyce: Two Decades of Criticism*, 1948; (translator, with Swami Nikhilananda) *The Gospel of Sri Ramakrishna*, 1951; *The Masks of God: Vol. I, Primitive Mythology*, 1964, *Vol. II, Oriental Mythology*, 1962, *Vol. III, Occidental Mythology*, 1964, *Vol. IV, Creative Mythology*, 1967; *The Flight of the Wild Gander: Exploration in the Mythical Dimension*, 1969; *Myths to Live By*, 1972; *The Mythic Image*, 1975; *The Historical Atlas of World Mythology: Vol I, The Way of the Animal Powers*, 1984; *The Inner Reaches of Outer Space*, 1986. **Edited works** *Myths and Symbols in Indian Art and Civilization* by Heinrich Zimmer, 1946; *The King and the Corpse* by Heinrich Zimmer, 1948; *Philosophies of India* by Heinrich Zimmer, 1951; *The Viking Portable Arabian Nights*, 1952; *Papers from the Eranos Yearbooks*, Vols.I–VI, including *Spirit and Nature*, 1954, *Spiritual Disciplines*, 1960, *The Mystic Vision*, 1969; *The Art of Indian Asia* by Heinrich Zimmer, 1955; *Myths, Dreams and Religion*, 1970; *The Portable Jung*, 1972; *My Life and Lives: The Story of a Tibetan Incarnation* by Rato K. Losang, 1977; also contributed articles to numerous journals. **Cause of death** Undisclosed, at age 83.

MADELEINE CARROLL

British/American Actress

***Born* West Bromwich, Warwickshire, 26 February 1906**

***Died* Marbella, Spain, 2 October 1987**

British-born film star Madeleine Carroll was famous for her cool, blonde beauty. She was every thinking man's dream girl of the 1930s—lovely, frail but brave and true. Her best remembered British film is Alfred Hitchcock's *The 39 Steps* (1935), in which she played Pamela, one of his early, glacial, beautiful heroines, opposite the gifted British actor, Robert Donat. Her fame increased with her subsequent Hollywood pictures, including the spectacular and sumptuous *The Prisoner of Zenda* (1937), in which she played Princess Flavia opposite Ronald Colman as an Englishman on holiday in a small Balkan country who finds himself substituting for the real king at his coronation. The couple fall in love but nobly sacrifice love to duty. With Gary Cooper she appeared in the exciting adventure story *The General Died at Dawn* (1936) and in the spy comedy *My Favorite Blonde* (1942) she was described as "a perfect foil" for Bob Hope, with whom she co-starred.

Carroll's first Hitchcock film, *The 39 Steps*, was based on John Buchan's novel and in it Hitchcock began to develop his reputation for building mood and attention to detail. The story concerns a young Canadian named Hannay (Robert Donat) who chases a spy ring responsible for stabbing a woman to death in his London flat, and who, in turn, is chased by the police in the belief that he is the murderer. The film is exciting and fast-moving, full of hair-raising moments and narrow escapes, and remains Hitchcock's most popular British film. At a deeper level, the film concerns the struggle between order and chaos and, in order to avoid being trapped in either, the growth of spirit and flexibility, as portrayed by the male and female leads. Madeleine Carroll's Pamela, a pretty woman grown cynical about men's predictably amorous intentions, meets Hannay on a train and turns him over to the police. The couple subsequently find themselves handcuffed together as Hannay drags the unwilling Pamela in pursuit of the spies. In such inconvenient proximity, their feelings towards each other develop and in one of the film's most famous scenes, full of what was then considered daring eroticism, Donat helps Carroll to take off her wet stockings.

Madeleine Carroll made a second Hitchcock film the following year, playing Elsa in *Secret Agent* (1936), the "wife" assigned to a British intelligence agent named Ashenden, in reality a famous writer called Edgar Brodie, played by the young John Gielgud. Eventually the couple fall in love and decide to quit spying. Ashenden/Brodie has been assigned to go to neutral Switzerland to find and kill a spy but an innocent man is killed by mistake with the real spy meeting his death only accidentally in a train crash later. This disturbing film, less of a box-office success than *The 39 Steps* and based on Somerset Maugham's adventure stories about World War I, challenges conventional assumptions about purity and heroism in war, while showing the dangers and self-deceptions inherent in neutrality. One of the film's most gripping scenes involves a chase through the Swiss chocolate factory in which the enemy German spies have their headquarters.

Carroll was born Marie Madeleine Bernadette O'Carroll in West Bromwich, part of the industrial Midlands; her mother was French, while her father was of Irish descent. She gained a BA honours degree in French at Birmingham University, appearing in college dramatic productions and turning down the offer of a stage contract, partly because of parental pressure. She did postgraduate studies in Paris and then taught at a girls' school in Hove, near Brighton, abandoning her teaching career for the less secure life of an aspiring actress in London. Success did not come easily, but in 1927 she landed a small part as Jeanne in *The Lash* at the Winter Gardens Theatre, with which she then toured. On returning to London, Carroll modelled hats for a time before joining a touring company headed by Sir Seymour Hicks, who gave her private coaching and allowed her to leave his company after touring with *Mr What's His Name* to accept a part in a London play. At this time she had her first screen test and was chosen from 150 applicants for the leading part in *The Guns of Loos* (1928), a British film about World War I, which led to more stage and film offers.

Her stage roles included Pauline Sanger in *The Constant Nymph* (1928), Arabella Allen in *Mr Pickwick* (1929), Phyl in John van Druten's *After All* (1931) and, her last performance on the English stage, as Julia Chertsey in *Duet in Floodlight* (1935). Among her early films were the silent *What Money Can Buy* (1928) and *The Crooked Billet* (1929), while her first "talkie" was *The American Prisoner* (1929). This was followed by the role for Laura Simmons in *Young Woodley* (1930) and Lucille de Choisigne in *Madame Guillotine* (1931). Carroll was to transport her career to Hollywood in 1936, but in the early 1930s she married her first husband, an English army officer, Captain Philip Astley, and became one of Britain's most popular female film stars, gradually assuming a sleeker and blonder image and rivalled in popularity at home only by the much-loved Gracie Fields. However, her status as a film star was not yet on the scale of American actresses' and she was often dissatisfied with the quality of some of the British films she appeared in. This led to her retirement from the screen, but she continued to act regularly on the stage. However, Gaumont-British subsequently offered her a generous contract—reportedly £650 a week—and gave her leading parts in two of the better British films of 1933: *Sleeping Car*, with Ivor Novello, and *I Was a Spy*, in which she played a Belgian woman who spied for the British and sabotaged German communications. The latter was very popular in Britain, due less to her acting than to her striking beauty and obvious sincerity. Following this success, she went to Hollywood for John Ford's *The World Moves On* (1934), one of the many films at that time with an anti-war message but regarded as one of Ford's worst, described by one critic as "talky, preachy and pompous" and showing little affinity between Ford and his actors. Carroll then returned to England to make the equally unsuccessful *The Dictator* (1935), Clive Brook's first British film after a long spell in Hollywood.

It had been reported that Carroll, having had a taste of Hollywood, found British studios less efficient, so in 1936, following her Hitchcock films, Alexander Korda sold her contract to Hollywood, to be shared by Walter Wanger and 20th Century-Fox. Her first film there was *The Case Against Mrs Ames* (1936), followed in the same year by the more successful and interesting *The General Died at Dawn*. From this time until the United States entered World War II, Carroll's fame and popularity grew through her appearances in no less than 16 Hollywood pictures, mostly historical adventures, romances and light comedies. She had success with two 20th Century-Fox productions—*Lloyds of London* (1936), a historical saga with Tyrone Power, and a musical with Dick Powell, *On the Avenue* (1937), in which Alice Faye did the singing and dancing. Then came the immensely popular *Prisoner of Zenda*, with Ronald Colman, *Blockade* (1938) with Henry Fonda, and three consecutive films with Fred MacMurray—*Café Society* and *Honeymoon in Bali* (both 1939), and *Virginia* (1941). She received much praise for her performance opposite Louis Hayward in *My Son, My Son* (1940), showing that beauty was not her only asset. However, she had less scope with *Safari* (1940), starring Douglas Fairbanks Jr, and with deMille's *Northwest Mounted Police* (1940). In the latter and in *Bahama Passage* (1942), in which she co-starred with second husband Sterling Hayden, it was agreed that she looked more stunning than ever in colour but that the films had few other merits. *Bahama Passage* audiences reportedly burst out laughing when Carroll invited Hayden to make love and he replied, "No, let's fish". Carroll co-starred with Bob Hope in *My Favorite Blonde* (1942), described by the *New York Herald Tribune* as a "superior screen comedy" of "great, good fun". During these years, she also took part in radio programmes, including *Madeleine Carroll Reads* (1942) in which she read extracts from favourite books.

After completing her filming commitments, Carroll showed a compassionate and committed side to her character by devoting herself to war efforts under another name to avoid publicity. When her nineteen-year-old sister was killed in a 1940 London bombing raid, she had said: "The personal loss drove home the full meaning of the hideous fate that had closed in on the people of Europe." Already, in 1940, she had converted her French home near Paris into an orphanage, returning to the United States just before the surrender of France to German forces and helping to set up the Committee for the Care of European Children. She took the unpaid post of entertainment director of the United Seamen's Service in New York City and for 18 months organized entertainment and benefits for those "forgotten warriors" of the war. She joined the American Red Cross in 1943 and during the following war years, nursed the wounded from the Allied fronts in Italian hospitals and on French hospital trains. At the end of the war she aided rehabilitation of those returning from the horrors of concentration camps and in 1948 was one of 59 men and women on the United States Committee for the United Nations Appeal for Children. In recognition of her work, Carroll, who had become a US citizen in 1943, received the French Legion of Honour and the United States Medal of Freedom.

Carroll's marriage to Sterling Hayden ended in 1945 and the following year she married Henri Lavorel, producer of films for the United Nations, who had served in the French Resistance. Together they made four documentary films, including *Children's Republic*, set in a French school, and *The Eternal Fight*, made for the United Nations about the work of the World Health

Organization. The pair spoke of forming a company to make films "to promote a better understanding between the peoples of the world" but nothing came of this and the couple were divorced in 1949 after only three years of marriage.

Carroll returned to films in 1947 in the British *White Cradle Inn*, co-starring Michael Rennie. She made a late American stage début in 1948 in a Broadway production of Fay Kanin's *Goodbye My Fancy*, in which she played a liberal congresswoman, Agatha Reed, who forces a college president to allow a documentary on the horrors of war to be shown on campus. The play itself had a mixed reception but Carroll's acting received excellent reviews. Brooks Atkinson in the *New York Times* wrote: "Miss Carroll looks lovely in her own right and gives a shining performance that is lucid and charming and that has strength of character in spite of its personal modesty." John Lardner of the *New York Star* described her as "a performer virtually matchless today for her combination of honesty, intelligence and sheer scenic zing". Carroll had felt the need to return to acting on the stage before a live audience and made only a few more films, including *Don't Trust Your Husband* (1948), teaming up again with Fred MacMurray, and *The Fan* (1949), an unsuccessful version of Oscar Wilde's play, in which she played Mrs Erlynne. In 1964 she appeared for a time in *Beekman Place* before its pre-Broadway run.

In between acting commitments, she did some work for UNESCO and was married for a fourth time, in 1950, to *Life* magazine publisher, Andrew Heiskell. The couple were divorced after 15 years of marriage. Her later years were divided between London, Paris and Marbella in southern Spain, where she had a beautiful villa in the hills outside the city and where she became a virtual recluse in the last five years of her life, following the death of her only daughter.

Madeline Carroll was 5 feet 4 inches tall, with blue eyes, ash-blonde hair and fine bone structure. In 1937 one critic voted her the most beautiful woman in the world, while another discribed her as "fragile and feminine as a Dresden shepherdess". Although her beauty was memorable, the same could not be said of all her films. She often had undemanding roles in mediocre productions, but she was more than a pretty face; her intelligence as well as her beauty came over powerfully on the screen and she was also admired for the refreshing lack of affectation and posturing in her acting.

Born Marie Madeleine Bernadette O'Carroll. **Parents** John and Hélène (de Rosière Tuaillon) O'Carroll. **Marriages** 1) Philip Astley, British Army officer, 1931 (divorced, 1939); 2) Sterling Hayden, actor, 1942 (divorced, 1945); 3) Henri Lavorel, producer, 1946 (divorced, 1949); 4) Andrew Heiskell, publisher, 1950 (divorced, 1965). **Children** One daughter (died, 1982). **Education** Birmingham University, BA in French. **Emigration** Left England for USA, 1936; naturalized, 1943. **Career** French teacher, girls' school, Sussex; stage début, 1927; film début, 1928; appeared in various British films, 1928–35; brought to attention of US audiences in Hitchcock's *The 39 Steps*, 1935; moved to US and signed to Paramount, 1936; featured in 16 Hollywood productions before World War II; during the war, worked in France with refugee orphans before the French surrender, subsequently returning to US to organize war work, including post of entertainments director, United Seamen's Service, New York; joined US Red Cross as hospital worker, assigned to 17th General Hospital, Italy, 1943; worked on hospital trains in France, 1944–45; aided concentration camp returnee rehabilitation, 1945–46; formed own film company with third husband, producing documentary films for the United Nations; returned to US, playing in just three more films after the war; appeared in Broadway play, 1948; last film role, 1949; attempted stage comeback, 1964; subsequently retired to Marbella, Spain. **Offices and memberships** Member, United States Committee for the United Nations Appeal for Children, 1948. **Awards and honours** Legion of Honour (France); United States Medal of Freedom. **Films** *The Guns of Loos*, 1928; *What Money Can Buy*, 1928; *The First Born*, 1928; *The Crooked Billet*, 1929; *The American Prisoner*, 1929; *Atlantic*, 1929; *The "W"*

Plan, 1930; *Young Woodley*, 1930; *French Leave*, 1930; *Escape*, 1930; *The School for Scandal*, 1930; *Kissing Cup's Race*, 1930; *Madame Guillotine*, 1931; *Fascination*, 1931; *The Written Law*, 1931; *Sleeping Car*, 1933; *I Was a Spy*, 1933; *The World Moves On*, 1934; *The Dictator (The Love Affair of the Dictator/The Loves of a Dictator/For Love of a Queen)*, 1935; *The 39 Steps*, 1935; *The Story of Papworth* (charity appeal), 1936; *The Secret Agent*, 1936; *The Case Against Mrs Ames*, 1936; *The General Died at Dawn*, 1936; *Lloyds of London*, 1936; *On the Avenue*, 1937; *It's All Yours*, 1937; *The Prisoner of Zenda*, 1937; *Blockade*, 1938; *Café Society*, 1939; *Honeymoon in Bali (Husbands or Lovers)*, 1939; *My Son, My Son*, 1940; *Northwest Mounted Police*, 1940; *Virginia*, 1941; *One Night in Lisbon*, 1941; *Bahama Passage*, 1941; *My Favorite Blonde*, 1942; *La Petite République*, 1946; *White Cradle Inn (High Fury)*, 1947; *Don't Trust Your Husband (An Innocent Affair)*, 1948; *The Fan (Lady Windermere's Fan)*, 1949. **Stage** (all produced in England, unless stated, include) *The Lash*, 1928; *The Constant Nymph*, 1928; *Mr What's His Name*, 1929; *Mr Pickwick*, 1929; *Beau Geste*, 1929; *The Roof*, 1930; *French Leave*, 1930; *Enchantment*, 1930; *Dance With No Music*, 1930; *The Tot Cart*, 1930; *After All*, 1931; *Little Catherine*, 1931; *Pleasure Cruise*, 1932; *Veronica*, 1933; *Duet in Floodlight*, 1935; *Goodbye, My Fancy*, Broadway, 1948. **Radio** (includes) *Madeleine Carroll Reads*, 1942; *Cavalcade*; *Beloved Enemy*; *Romance*; *There's Always Juliet*. **Cause of death** Cancer, at age 81. **Further reading** David Shipman, *The Great Movie Stars—the Golden Years*, London, 1970, revised edition, 1979; Maurice Yacowar, *Hitchcock's British Films*, London, 1977; Ken Wlaschin, *The World's Great Movie Stars and Their Films*, London, 1979.

DOUGLAS CLEVERDON

British Publisher and Radio Producer
Born **Bristol, England, 17 January 1903**
Died **London, England, 1 October 1987**

Although an author himself, Douglas Cleverdon will chiefly be remembered for his services to those artists and poets whose work he published or produced on the radio. Friendships with him were long-lasting. Those with whom his name is most often linked are the Bloomsbury artist Roger Fry, the engraver Eric Gill, Gill's colleague, the Welsh poet and artist David Jones, and that most Welsh of all poets, Dylan Thomas. Theirs are the names that tend to occur and recur throughout Cleverdon's long and successful career.

Roger Fry gave Cleverdon many of the books that enabled him to open an antiquarian bookshop in Bristol when he came down from Oxford University in 1926. He also painted the bookshop sign. Eric Gill did the lettering for the sign and it was Gill's *Art of Love* and *Engravings* that were among the first books Cleverdon published in those early years. Another was an edition, in 1929, of *The Ancient Mariner*, with copper engravings by David Jones.

Although Cleverdon's early lists earned him admiration and respect, and established his reputation among booksellers, they did not always bring in enough money to live on. To keep himself solvent after the slump of 1929, Cleverdon used to supplement his income with freelance radio acting in Bristol. It was this that led to the second stage of his career—in broadcasting.

In 1939 Cleverdon got a six months' contract with the BBC to work on the *Children's Hour* programme, which led to 30 years' employment as a features producer. He worked in Bristol until 1943 and then in London until his retirement in 1969. After that, Cleverdon returned to publishing with the Clover Hill Press, while continuing also to do freelance producing with the BBC. Most of his work was with the newly established Third Programme, but he also did a spell in Burma as a war correspondent in 1945 and was one of those responsible for setting up the very successful *Brains Trust* programme.

With the BBC, Cleverdon continued to exercise his magic on those whose work he most admired—nursing Dylan Thomas through the first radio and stage productions of *Under Milk Wood*, coaxing from David Jones the full text of his long prose poem about war, *In Parenthesis*, and his later *Anathemata*. For his productions of *Under Milk Wood* and of Jacob Bronowski's *The Fate of Violence* Cleverdon won the Halea Prize. Other programmes which people still remember included the work of the poets Ted Hughes and Stevie Smith, the essayist and caricaturist Max Beerbohm, and the composer Elizabeth Poston (q.v.)—programmes which have been described as a "radio library of masterpieces".

When Douglas Cleverdon returned to publishing in the 1960s he reissued earlier editions of Gill's engravings and of *The Ancient Mariner*, published a new edition of David Jones's *Engravings*, a work on *The Growth of Milk Wood* and an edition of Theocritus's *Six Idyllia*. The friend and colleague who wrote Cleverdon's obituary in the London *Times* described him as someone who "suggested the virtues as well as the complexities" of the Victorian era. "Pickwickian in aspect, in enthusiasm, in warmth and in loyalty to friends, he had Sam Weller's shrewdness, perceptive wit and his eye to the main chance."

Born Thomas Douglas James Cleverdon. **Parents** Thomas Silcox and Louisa (James) Cleverdon. **Marriage** Elinor Nest Lewis, 1944. **Children** Julia, Lewis and Francis; one son deceased. **Education** Bristol Grammar School; Jesus College, Oxford. **Career** Bookseller and publisher of fine printing, Bristol, 1926–39; freelance actor and writer for BBC West Region, 1935–39; joined BBC, producing *Children's Hour*, 1939; West Regional features producer, 1939–43; features producer, London, 1943–1969; publisher, Clover Hill Press, 1964–87. **Other activities** Directed first stage productions of *Under Milk Wood*, Edinburgh, London, 1955, New York, 1957; organized poetry festival, Stratford-upon-Avon, 1966–70; organized Cheltenham Festival of Literature, 1971; compiled exhibition of paintings, engravings and writings of David Jones, National Book League, 1972. **Offices and memberships** President, Private Libraries Association, 1978–80. **Awards and honours** Halea Prize for first radio productions of *Under Milk Wood* by Dylan Thomas and *The Faces of Violence* by Jacob Bronowski. **Publications** *Engravings by Eric Gill*, 1929; *The Growth of Milk Wood*, 1969; (compiled with Nicolas Barker) *Stanley Morrison, 1989–1967*, 1969; (author of introduction) *Six Idyllia* by Theocritus, 1971; (editor and author of introduction) *Under Milk Wood: A Play for Voices* by Dylan Thomas, 1972; *Verlaine, Femmes/Hombres*, 1972; *The Engravings of David Jones: A Survey*, 1981. **Radio** Devised and co-produced *Brains Trust*, BBC, 1941; BBC war correspondent, Burma, 1945; subsequently worked on Third Programme, including radio works by Max Beerbohm, Jacob Bronowski, Bill Naughton, George Barker, David Gascoyne, Ted Hughes, David Jones, Stevie Smith, Henry Reed, Dylan Thomas, Peter Racine Fricker, Elizabeth Poston, Humphrey Searle and many others. **Cause of death** Undisclosed, at age 84.

ALBERT CRARY

American Geophysicist and Explorer
***Born* Pierrepont, New York, 25 July 1911**
***Died* Washington, DC, 29 October 1987**

Few men these days leave their names permanently on maps or in the books of records, but Dr Albert Crary, a distinguished geophysicist, Arctic explorer and scientific administrator is immortalized in both ways. His name is to be seen on the maps of Antarctica, and he was the first man to stand on both the North and the South Poles.

Albert Paddock Crary trained as an earth scientist at St Lawrence and Lehigh universities, and then worked with commercial companies as an exploration geophysicist. This was a rapidly expanding field, and offered him a distinguished, successful and lucrative career, but he deliberately changed course as he was determined to take part in scientific projects in the polar regions. Accordingly, in 1946 he joined the US Air Force Research Center.

In 1952, when air reconnaissance flights reported that large icebergs seemed to drift round the North Pole, Crary led a small party which set up a station on an "ice-island" called T–3. He spent a whole year there, including a trip to the Pole, initiating long-term geophysical studies which made great contributions to knowledge of the ice and ocean. This knowledge was invaluable for later submarine navigation in polar waters.

For the US effort in International Geophysical Year Crary was the clear choice to be chief scientist in the Antarctic. He excelled in the job. The harshness of the elements and the strain of living in uncomfortable conditions in close quarters test leaders to the utmost. His strength, unflappability and care for his men earned him the greatest respect of all who were with him.

He led trips in a Sno-Cat from the base at Little America V in 1956–58, and from McMurdo Station in 1960–61, completing thorough geophysical surveys of the Ross Ice Shelf and the route to the South Pole. In fact, he reached the South Pole in February 1961. The three major trips he led during those years covered 3400 miles through some of the world's most inhospitable terrain, and the data gained then, and on other traverses, unfolded a remarkable portrait of the bitter continent. In particular, his report on the ice shelf survey and his paper on fjord formation in the region were regarded as models of their kind.

Crary's fine leadership qualities and skilful planning were invaluable. The perpetual daylight of the polar summers gives scope for extended work but is extremely exhausting. Crary insisted on a fixed routine. "Let's take one day at a time," he would say, though what he meant by a day was working from 8 a.m. to midnight.

He had stamina and courage, as well as strength and mental alertness, and he needed them all on the occasion he fell into the sea off high ice cliffs. Somehow he managed to claw himself up on to an iceberg, and then ran on the spot for two hours to repel frostbite until he was rescued by helicopter.

He married in 1968, when he had settled back in the United States. His great achievements were recognized in medals and awards, and he became a distinguished scientific administrator with the National Science Foundation in Washington. Apart from this, his name lives on in the Crary Mountains and Crary Ice Rise on the continent he came to know so well.

Born Albert Paddock Crary. **Children** One son. **Education** St Lawrence University, BS, 1931; Lehigh University, MS, 1933. **Career** Geophysicist, Independent Exploration Company, 1935–41; project scientist, Woods Hole Oceanographic Institute, 1941–42; exploratory geophysicist, United Geophysics Company, 1942–46; project scientist, US Air Force Cambridge Research

Center, 1946–60; chief scientist, Official Antarctic Programme, National Science Foundation, 1960–67, deputy director, 1967–69, director, Division of Environmental Science, 1969–75, director, Division of Earth Science, 1976; resident associate, Haverford College, 1979–82. **Related activities** Deputy chief scientist, US National Committee, International Geophysical Year, Antarctic Programme, National Academy of Science, 1956–58. **Memberships** American Association for the Advancement of Science; American Geophysical Union; American Geographic Society. **Awards and honours** Vega Medal, Swedish Society of Anthropology and Geography; Cullum Medal, American Geographic Society, 1959; honorary PhD, St Lawrence University, 1959; Patrons' Medal, Royal Geographic Society, 1963; distinguished Service Award: US Civil Administration, US Navy, and US Air Force. **Cause of death** Undisclosed, at age 79.

JOHN N. FINDLAY

South African Philosopher

Born **Pretoria, South Africa, 25 November 1903**

Died **Boston, Massachusetts, 8 October 1987**

Professor John Findlay is acknowledged as one of the most original philosophers of the twentieth century. Throughout his life he studied all the main branches of European and American philosophy and, unusually for a Westerner, he also explored Indian, Chinese and Japanese thought in considerable depth. Findlay could, therefore, distil his theories from an exceptionally wide range of knowledge.

He was born and brought up in South Africa where his father was an attorney. After graduating from high school in Pretoria, he entered Transvaal University College, gaining a bachelor of arts degree in 1922. He continued with his studies at the university and two years later was awarded a masters degree. Findlay then won a Rhodes Scholarship to Balliol College, Oxford, where he studied humanities, gaining a first in 1924. He moved on to study in Austria at the University of Graz where, in 1933, he received a doctorate. Following this, Findlay travelled to New Zealand and was appointed professor of philosophy at the University of Otago, Dunedin, in 1934. He remained in this post for ten years before returning to his native South Africa to take up an appointment as professor of philosophy at the University of Natal, Durban.

In 1946 Findlay again visited England and was appointed professor of philosophy at Durham University, taking up a similar post at King's College, London, two years later. During the last two years of this appointment, 1964–66, Findlay was also Gifford Lecturer at St Andrews University, Scotland.

In the mid-1960s Findlay moved to the US, spending a year at the University of Texas, before being appointed Clark Professor of moral philosophy and metaphysics at Yale in 1967. His final appointment was as Borden Parker Bowne Professor at the University of Boston in 1972.

Findlay began publishing his work in 1933 with *Meinong's Theory of Objects and Values*, a book that was to be reprinted 30 years later. It was during his period at the University of London that Findlay began to write prolifically. He was a regular contributor to *Contemporary British Philosophy*, and in 1958 published *Re-examination*, which aroused considerable interest and provoked a reappraisal of its subject in Britain and the US.

Findlay's next book, *Values and Intentions* (1961), was a landmark work. In it he described his own philosophical beliefs which he had constructed from his studies over the previous 25 years. Findlay had come to believe that the modern schools of philosophy had crucially failed to explore the relationship between human behaviour and moral values. He attributed this failure to the enormous influence of G.E. Moore and Bertrand Russell who had launched a concerted attack on idealism in 1903. Findlay considered that philosophy had lost its way since that time, and this belief is implicit in all his works. His views were never fashionable but this does not appear to have troubled him in the slightest. Indeed, a *Times Literary Supplement* reviewer wrote of him, "he was clearly resolved to be unfashionable on the grand scale".

Findlay was a man of great learning whose wisdom was leavened by charm and vivacity. He was, and will continue to be, an inspiration to many generations of students.

Born John Niemeyer Findlay. **Parents** John H.L., an attorney, and Elizabeth (Niemeyer) Findlay. **Marriage** Aileen May Davidson, 1941. **Children** Paul H.D. and Rachel Clare. **Education** Transvaal University College, BA, 1922, MA, 1924; Balliol College, Oxford, BA, 1926, MA, 1930; University of Graz, Austria, PhD, 1933. **Emigration** Lived in England, 1948–66; settled in US, 1966. **Career** Lecturer in philosophy, Transvaal University College, 1927–33; professor of philosophy, University of Otago, New Zealand, 1934–44; professor of philosophy, Rhodes University College, South Africa, 1945; professor of philosophy, Natal University College, 1946–48; professor of philosophy, King's College, Durham University, 1948–51; university professor of philosophy, King's College, London, 1951–66; professor of philosophy, University of Texas, 1966–67; Clark professor of moral philosophy and metaphysics, Yale University 1967–72; professor of philosophy, Boston University, from 1972; Borden Parker Bowne professor of philosophy, from 1978. **Related activities** Gifford Lecturer, University of St Andrews, 1964–66. **Offices and memberships** Aristotelian Society (president, 1955–56, then vice-president); fellow, British Academy, 1956; fellow, King's College, London, 1970; fellow, American Academy of Arts and Sciences, 1978. **Publications** *Meinong's Theory of Objects and Values*, 1933, new edition, 1963; (contributor) *Clarity Is Not Enough*, 1953; (contributor) *Contemporary British Philosophy*, 1956; *Hegel: A Re-Examination*, 1958; *Values and Intentions*, 1961; *Language, Mind and Value*, 1963; *The Discipline of the Cave*, 1965; (editor) *Studies in Philosophy*, 1966; *The Transcendence of the Cave*, 1967; (translator) *Husserl, Logische Unterschungen*, 1969; *Axiological Ethics*, 1970; *Ascent to the Absolute: Metaphysical Lectures and Papers*, 1970; *Plato's Written and Unwritten Doctrines*, 1974; *Plato and Platonism*, 1978; *Kant and the Transcendental Object*, 1981; *Wittgenstein: A Critique*, 1984; plus numerous articles in academic journals, including *Mind*, *Philosophy*, *Philosophy and Phenomenological Research*, *Proceedings of the Aristotelian Society*. **Cause of death** Undisclosed, at age 83. **Further reading** Cohen, Martin and Westphal (eds), *Studies in the Philosophy of J.N. Findlay*, 1985.

MAXWELL FINLAND

American Medical Researcher

***Born* Russia, 15 March 1902**

***Died* Boston, Massachusetts, 25 October 1987**

For more than 50 years Dr Maxwell Finland worked at Harvard Medical School and Boston City Hospital, and he became an international authority on the study of infectious diseases and their treatment.

He was born in Russia, but he lived there for only four years before being taken to the United States by his parents. He went to school in Boston, and then studied at Harvard where he gained his BS degree in 1922, and his MD in 1926. His life's work, like his education, was to be bounded by Harvard and Boston.

His first, short-lived post was as assistant resident at Boston Sanatorium, from where he went as medical house officer to Boston City Hospital. Already he was interested in the bacteria which cause pneumonia, and by using penicillin and sulfadiazine for treating patients, he managed to cut the mortality rate to one-third. At the same time, he held a teaching fellowship at Harvard Medical School, and through the years he progressed upwards through increasingly important posts at the Medical School and the City Hospital. In 1963 he was made the George Richard Minot professor of medicine, and in 1968, when he retired from this and his other posts at Boston City Hospital and the Thorndike Memorial Laboratory, he was made George Richard Minot professor emeritus of medicine. At the same time the Maxwell Finland Professorship of clinical pharmacology was established in his honour.

During his working life he wrote or helped write 800 scientific papers. He also served on the editorial board of many influential journals, including *Applied Microbiology*, *Antimicrobiological Agents and Chemotherapy* and the *Journal of Infectious Diseases*.

Apart from his pioneering treatment of pneumonia, his research into respiratory diseases caused by exposure to noxious gases was of prime importance. Perhaps as important was his thorough testing of drugs as they came on the market. As early as 1952 he campaigned against their misuse and overuse, pointing out that they could actually increase the number of infections as the bacteria developed new, resistant strains.

In addition to his academic posts and his work as a physician, Dr Finland served on a number of national committees. He received many awards for his work, including being made an honorary citizen of Panama. A life-long bachelor, he gave much of the money he received in awards to Harvard Medical School, and he also persuaded drug companies and other concerns to donate money. In fact, he probably helped to add more than £6 million to the school's endowment.

Born Maxwell Finland. **Parents** Frank and Rebecca (Povza) Finland. **Education** Wendell Phillips School, Boston; English High School, Boston; Harvard, BS, 1922, MD, 1926. **Emigration** Left Russia for the US, 1906; naturalized, 1925. **Career** Assistant resident, Boston Sanatorium, 1926–27; medical house officer, Boston City Hospital, 1927–28, resident physician for pneumonia and medical service, 1928–29, junior visiting physician, 1938, chief IV Medical Service, Harvard, 1939–62, director, II and IV Medical Service, Harvard, 1963–68, head, department of medicine, 1963–68, honorary physician from 1972; Harvard Medical School: Charles Follen Folson teaching fellow in hygiene, 1928–29, assistant, 1929–32, Francis Weld Peabody Fellow, 1932–37, instructor, 1935–37, associate, 1937–40, assistant professor, 1940–46, associate professor, 1946–62, professor of medicine, 1962–63, George Richard Minot professor of medicine, 1963–68, emeritus, 1969–87. **Related activities** Assistant resident, Thorndike Memorial Laboratory, 1929–32, assistant physician, 1932–41, associate physician, 1941–50, associate laboratory director, 1950–63, director, 1963–68; visiting physician, Pondville Hospital, 1933–69; epidemiologist, Boston City Hospital, 1968–72. **Other activities** Consultant, Veterans' Administration, 1945–73, member, clinical investigators committee, department of medicine and surgery, 1955–69, chairman, 1964–69, distinguished physician, from 1973; member, sub-committee on infectious diseases, National Research Council, 1946–54, chairman, 1955–59; associate member, commission on acute respiratory diseases, Armed Forces Epidemiological Board, 1950–67, member 1967–72; chairman, committee for Lederle Medical Faculty awards, 1952–68; member, bacteriological and mycological study section, National Institute of Health, 1958–63; member, advisory committee on influenza research, United States Public Health Service, 1959–63; member, drug research board, National Academy of Sciences-National Research Council, 1964–71; member, editorial board: *New England Journal of Medicine*, 1945–68, *Applied Microbiology*, 1964–74, *Anti-microbiological Agents and Chemotherapy*, 1960–71, *Journal of Infectious Diseases*, 1969–72, *Journal of the American Medical Association*, from 1973, *Journal of Clinical Microbiology*, from 1974. **Offices and memberships** Master, American College of Physicians; fellow, American Association for the Advancement of Science; member: Association of American Physicians (emeritus, 1978;) Massachusetts Medical Society, American Medical Association, Society of Experimental Biology and Medicine, American Society for Clinical Investigation (councillor, 1942–45, vice-president, 1947–48), American Board of Internal Medicine, Infectious Diseases Society of America (president, 1963–64), American Association of Immunologists, Society of American Bacteriologists, American Academy of Arts and Sciences, New York Academy of Sciences, American Epidemiological Society (councillor, 1957–60, vice-president, 1961–62), National Academy of Sciences, Harvard Medical Alumni Association (president, 1971–72), Association of Clinical Pathologists (London); corresponding member: Sigma Xi, Alpha Omega Alpha. **Awards and honours** Charles V. Chapin Award, City of Providence, 1960; Bristol Award, Infectious Diseases Society of America, 1966; Modern Medicine Award, 1969; honorary citizen, City of Panama, 1970; John Phillips' Memorial Award, American College of Physicians, 1971; Oscar B. Hunter Memorial Award, American Society of Clinical Pharmacology and Therapeutics, 1971; Sheen Award, American Medical Association, 1971; honorary DSc, Western Reserve University, 1964; Kober Medallist, American College of Physicians, 1978; honorary DHL, Thomas Jefferson University, 1978; outstanding contribution award in field of antibiotic research, Bristol Meyers Company, International Division, 1981. **Publications** Contributor of articles, editorials and reviews to many scientific journals and medical text books; editor and co-editor on numerous books on infectious diseases. **Cause of death** Undisclosed, at age 85.

RAYMOND FRANCIS

British Actor

***Born* London, England, 6 October 1911**

***Died* Sussex, England, 24 October 1987**

Raymond Francis was part of an acting generation that is rapidly dying out in Britain. He learned his craft the hard way, in local repertory companies in the 1930s. Ironically, it was television, which ultimately made him a household name and face, that was instrumental in the dying of "rep". That Francis was saddened by this must go without saying—he claimed that those early years were the happiest of his career.

After a six-year break for army service during World War II, Francis returned to the theatre with enthusiasm, this time in London's West End, where he continued to work for most of the rest of his life, allowing for his excursions into movies and, of course, television. He appeared as Jackie, a supporting role in Terence Rattigan's *The Deep Blue Sea* in 1950, and also in J.B. Priestley's *Mr Kettle and Mr Moon*.

During the 1950s he made such memorable and typically British films of the times as *Carrington VC*, *Reach for the Sky* and *Carve Her Name with Pride*; perhaps even more importantly, he also made his début in television. His first role was as the amateur detective, Dr Watson, in a BBC production of *Sherlock Holmes*.

It is important to recall the circumstances of the development of television in the United Kingdom. Although some experimental and limited transmissions were tried out in the 1930s, it was not until June 1946 that government permission was given to the BBC to start up a proper service. At first it was limited to one channel only and that was in the London area. It was 14 years before the service was available throughout the UK, and it was only in 1955 that a "commercial" service began, achieving coverage of most of the country by the end of the decade. It was thus that Francis, known as a thoroughly competent and professional actor, was offered parts in full-length dramas for the BBC and came to be seen in an adaptation of *The Deep Blue Sea* and in *The Devil's Disciple*. It was Independent Television, however, that made him one of the earliest TV stars.

Viability for the independent companies lay in wooing viewers from the BBC which, for nine full years, had had a monopoly. Programmes had to be similar in approach (the rules of what was permissible were strict) but offer something fresh. One of the BBC's most successful weekly series was *Dixon of Dock Green*, which was centred around the daily work of an upright, honest and kindly London "bobby" in the East End. ITV's tailored response was *Murder Bag*, a half-hour weekly series in which Francis played Lockhart, an urbane, snuff-taking detective, who always got his man. Over the years, Lockhart was gradually promoted, rising to detective chief superintendent, and the spot lengthened to one hour under the new title of *No Hiding Place*. The public loved it so much that the original plans to end the series had to be postponed. It ultimately ended in 1966. It was a triumph for Francis personally—he and Lockhart maturing together. It was also very much a product of its time, presenting wholesome and straightforward stories which gave the police an image of being always honest, loyal and invariably successful.

In spite of his experience, Francis became a victim of his own success in the role and found himself typecast for television thereafter. He seldom appeared on the small screen again but moved back to the theatre, once more in supporting roles. In time, though, he was offered better parts, and later starred in a Francis Durbridge thriller, *The Gentle Hook*. He also worked in a number of more serious plays at the Shaw Theatre and the Royal Court, the latter reknowned for its policy of producing experimental and, occasionally, very controversial work.

Off-stage Francis was a private and family man. He lived quietly out of the public eye and enjoyed simple, typically English pleasures such as watching cricket and gardening. Despite poor health in his later years, he continued to act, but he rarely escaped the murder/mystery genre. One of his last roles was in the *Miss Marple* series—a predictable end, perhaps, to his career.

Born Raymond Francis. **Marriage** Margaret. **Children** Caroline, Frances and Clive. **Military service** British Army, 1939–45. **Career** Much provincial repertory and London stage work before World War II; various roles in West End theatre and British films from 1950s; first played detective-inspector Tom Lockhart in television series *Murder Bag*, mid-1950s; became household name in same part in *No Hiding Place*, ITV, 1959–67; subsequent typecasting as policeman hindered later career, but eventually returned in starring and supporting roles on stage and television. **Films** (include) *Carrington VC*, 1954; *Reach for the Sky*, 1956; *Carve Her Name with Pride*, 1958. **Stage** (all in London, includes) *The Deep Blue Sea*, 1952; *Mr Kettle and Mr Moon*, 1955; *The Gentle Hook*, 1974; plus various productions at the Shaw and Royal Court theatres, 1972. **Television** (includes) *Laburnum Grove*; *The Devil's Disciple*; *The Deep Blue Sea*; *Murder Bag*; *No Hiding Place*, 1959–67; *The Drummonds*; *Me and My Girl*; *Miss Marple*. **Cause of death** Undisclosed, at age 76.

HANS GÁL

Austrian Composer and Musicologist

***Born* Vienna, Austria, 5 August 1890**

***Died* Edinburgh, Scotland, 7 October 1987**

Hans Gál was a distinguished composer and musicologist who lived for nearly a century, spending the first half of his long life in his native Austria and the second half in Scotland. After leaving Vienna in 1938 as a refugee of Austro-Fascism, Gál settled in Edinburgh where, as well as continuing to teach and write music, he was very involved with the Edinburgh Festival, which he helped found.

Gál, who was of Hungarian extraction, was born in Brunn, near Vienna. He was largely self-taught as a composer, until he studied at the University of Vienna with Eusebius Mandyczewski, who had been a close friend of Brahms. Gál and Mandyczewski were later to combine on the editorship of *The Complete Brahms Edition*. During his five years in Vienna, Gál also studied music history with Guido Adler. By the time of his graduation he had established a reputation as an innovative musicologist, already had several major musical works to his credit and had been awarded the State Prize for composition.

In Serbia and Italy, on war service, he took every possible opportunity to absorb foreign influences. Then, after the war, in 1919, he was appointed music theory lecturer at Vienna University. He wrote three operas of which the most successful was *Die Heilige Ente*—"a play with gods and humans". It enjoyed considerable success at its first performance in 1923, which was repeated in Düsseldorf, Berlin, Prague, Weimar, Karlsruhe and many other cities. He also won an international reputation through some of his orchestral and chamber works.

After winning the Columbia Schubert Centenary Prize for his Sinfonietta in 1928, Gál was appointed director of the Mainz Municipal Academy of Music but was forced to relinquish the post when Hitler rose to power, and performances of his music were forbidden. He went home to Austria where he became conductor of the Wiener Madrigal-Vereinigung and the Wiener Konzert-Orchester.

Gál was forced to emigrate shortly before the anschluss of 1938. A meeting with Donald Tovey diverted him from his original intention of making his home in the US, and he set off for Scotland instead, where, after a period of internment, he secured a post as lecturer in Edinburgh University's music department, which he retained until his retirement in 1965. Gál remained in Edinburgh for the rest of his life, composing, teaching, writing about music and giving occasional performances on the piano. He wrote several important works of musical criticism, including *The Golden Age of Vienna* (1948), *Johannes Brahms* (1961), *Richard Wagner* (1963) and *Giuseppe Verdi* (1975).

Hans Gál's music is neither well known nor widely performed but its champions recommend it for its fine craftsmanship, its old-world lyrical grace and a wit that bordered on craftiness. His style remained firmly opposed to the second Viennese School of Schoenberg and his disciples, although the opportunity to come under its influence had been there in the early part of Gál's career. His musical roots were nearer to Brahms and Strauss, and it was in the classical tradition of those composers that he continued to work. In his later works Gál favoured chamber music combinations, although he did continue to write orchestral works. In all, he produced a work for every year of his life—a tireless flow of warm-toned pieces elegant in their musical argument.

His friends have said of Gál that he was the most charming of men and much loved for his kindness and ability to communicate his considerable knowledge both with levity and infectious enthusiasm.

Born Hans Gál. **Education** Studied music under Eusebius Mandyczewski and Guido Adler, Vienna University, 1908–13. **Emigration** Left Austria for Scotland, 1938. **Military service** Austrian Army, World War I. **Career** Lecturer in music theory, Vienna University, 1919–29, composing three operas and winning an international reputation with orchestral and chamber compositions in that time; director, Hochschüle für Musik and the Conservatory, Mainz, 1929–33; rise of Hitler saw works banned; returned to Austria, becoming conductor of Wiener Madrigal-Vereinigung and Wiener Konzert-Orchester, 1934–38; left Austria before anschluss, settling in Scotland, 1938; interned by British authorities on outbreak of World War II; lecturer, Edinburgh University, 1945–65; remained in Edinburgh, helping found Edinburgh Festival and continuing to compose, conduct, teach, write and perform as pianist, 1965–87. **Awards and honours** State Prize for Composition, Vienna, 1913; Columbia Schubert Centenary Prize, 1928. **Publications** *The Golden Age of Vienna*, London, 1948; *Johannes Brahms*, Frankfurt, 1961, published in English, 1964; *Richard Wagner*, Frankfurt, 1963; (editor) *The Musician's World: Great Composers in their Letters*, London, 1965, published in German, 1966; *Franz Schubert, oder die Melodie*, Frankfurt, 1970, published in Hungarian, 1973, in English, 1974; *Giuseppe Verdi*, 1975; *Schumann: Orchestral Music*, 1979; *Brahms: Letters*, 1979. **Operas** *Der Arzt der Sobeide*, opus 4, Breslau, 1919; *Die heilige Ente*, opus 15, Düsseldorf, 1923; *Das Lied der Nacht*, opus 23, Breslau, 1926; *Der Zauberspiegel*, opus 38, Breslau, 1930; *Die beiden Klaas*, opus 42, 1933. **Orchestral works** *Overture to a Puppet Play*, opus 20, 1923; Symphony No. 1 (Sinfonietta), opus 30, 1928; Ballet Suite, opus 36, 1930; Violin Concerto, opus 39, 1933; Concertino, opus 43, 1934; *A Pickwickian Overture*, opus 45, 1939; Serenade, opus 46, 1937; *Liliburlero: Improvisations on a Martial Melody*, opus 48, 1946; Concertino, opus 52, 1939; Symphony No. 2, opus 53, 1949; Concertino, opus 55, 1948; Piano Concerto, opus 57, 1947; Symphony No. 3, opus 62, 1952; Cello Concerto, opus 67, 1944; *Meanders*, opus 69, suite, 1955;

Idyllikon, opus 79, suite, 1959; Concertino, opus 87, 1965; *Triptych*, opus 100, 1970; Symphony No. 4, (Sinfonia concertante), 1975. **Choral works** *Von ewiger Freude*, opus 1, 1913; *Von Bäumlein, das andere Blätter hat gewolt*, opus 2, 1914; *Fantasies*, opus 5, 1914; Three Partsongs, opus 11, 1913; Three Partsongs, opus 12, 1914; *Kinderverse*, opus 14, 1921; *Motet*, opus 19, 1922; *Herbstlieder*, opus 25, 1926; *Requiem für Mignon*, opus 26, 1923; *Epigramme*, opus 27, 1926; Three Partsongs, opus 31, 1928; Five Serious Songs, opus 32, 1929; Drei Porträtsstudien, opus 34, 1929; Three Partsongs, opus 37, 1930; Drei Idyllen, opus 40, 1931; Eight German Folksongs, 1931; *Nachtmusik*, opus 44, 1933; *Summer Idylls*, opus 47, 1936; *De Profundis*, opus 50, 1948; Five Partsongs, opus 51, 1949; Four Partsongs, opus 61, 1953; Two Partsongs, opus 63, 1954; *Lebenskreise*, opus 70, 1955; *Songs of Youth*, opus 75, 1959; *A Clarion Call*, opus 76, 1959; *Of a Summer Day*, opus 77, 1952; Six Partsongs, opus 91, 1967. **Chamber and instrumental works** (for 3–8 instruments) Variations on a Viennese "Heurigen" Melody, opus 9, 1914; Five Intermezzi, opus 10, 1914; Piano Quartet, opus 13, 1915; String Quartet, opus 16, 1916; Piano Trio, opus 18, 1923; Divertimento, opus 22, 1924; String Qaurtet No. 2, opus 35, 1929; String Trio, opus 41, 1931; Little Suite, opus 49a, 1948; Little Trio, opus 49b, 1948; Suite, opus 59/2, 1952; Divertimento, opus 68/3, 1957; Quartettino, opus 78, 1960; Concertino, opus 82, 1961; Trio Serenade, opus 88, 1966; *Huyton Suite*, opus 92, 1940; Serenade, opus 93, 1941; Trio, opus 94, 1941; String Quartet No. 3, opus 95, 1969; Sonata, opus 96, 1941; Trio, opus 97, 1950; String Quartet No. 4, opus 98, 1971; (for two instruments) Suite, opus 6, 1920; Sonata, opus 17, 1921; Suite, opus 56, 1950; Sonatina, opus 59/1, 1952; Suite, opus 68/1, 1956; Six Three-part Inventions, opus 68/2, 1957; Three Sonatinas, opus 71, 1956; Divertimento, opus 80, 1968; Sonata, opus 84, 1964; Sonata, opus 85, 1964; Sonata, opus 89, 1953; Divertimento, opus 90/1, 1962; Divertimento, opus 90/2, 1968; Divertimento, opus 90/3, 1969; Sonata, opus 101, 1942; Suite, opus 102a, 1949; Suite, opus 102b, 1949. **Keyboard and songs** Four Serbian Dances, opus 3, 1916; Three Sketches, opus 7, 1916; Sonata, opus 28, 1927; *Weisen aus Alt-Wien*, 1934; 24 Preludes, opus 83, 1960; Organ: Toccata, opus 29, 1928; Songs: Two Songs, opus 21, 1922; Three Songs, opus 33, 1928. **Cause of death** Undisclosed, at age 97. **Further reading** W. Waldstein, *Hans Gál*, Vienna, 1965.

ROGER LANCELYN GREEN

British Author, Critic and Biographer

Born **Norwich, England, 2 November 1918**

Died **Wirral, England, 8 October 1987**

Anyone wishing to explore children's literature of the nineteenth and twentieth century and the mythology of several cultures could do no better than to study the works of Roger Lancelyn Green. His output, as fiction-writer, editor, biographer, compiler and re-teller of tales was both prolific and distinguished.

His passion for books began in childhood when, because of ill-health, he missed a great deal of conventional schooling. Fortunate enough, however, to grow up in a large house filled with books, he was able to explore in depth a wide range of literature. When his health recovered, his education took place at Dane Court School in Surrey and at Liverpool College. He then went to Merton College, Oxford. Significantly, he made the works of Andrew Lang, the eminent

Victorian re-teller of myths, legends and fairy-tales, the subject of his bachelor of literature degree. Green was later to follow in Lang's footsteps as a compiler and presenter of stories of this nature, achieving classic status with his versions of *The Adventures of Robin Hood, Heroes of Greece and Troy*, *King Arthur and his Knights of the Round Table*. Collections of Norse, Egyptian and other legends, of folk and fairy tales and stories from Shakespeare followed. Arguably, Green's most memorable contribution to the study of literature is his *Tellers of Tales*, an evocative and perceptive commentary on a vast range of fiction and writers. First published in 1946, it has been reprinted and updated several times; it deals with popular fiction, as well as classic literature for children. *Tellers of Tales* not only whets juvenile appetites for almost every kind of story but is a splendid read in itself, which, apart from some inadequacies in the section on school stories, can hardly be faulted.

Despite Green's fascination with books, he did not start out as a writer. On leaving Oxford he taught for a brief period, and also, despite being shy and having a slight stammer, briefly pursued a theatrical career. It was playing the part of the pirate Noodler in Barrie's *Peter Pan* in London and on tour in 1942–43 that awakened his fascination with the character who never grew up, and ultimately inspired his definitive history of the play—*Fifty Years of Peter Pan* (1954).

After a short spell as an antiquarian bookseller in Oxford, Green became deputy librarian at Merton College from 1945 to 1950. He married June Burdett in 1948, and two years afterwards they took up residence in Green's ancestral home in Northern England in the Wirral, Merseyside. This return to his childhood roots seems to have triggered off his eight published novels for children. The first four of these are closely connected with the expansiveness of his early family life; the four later stories derive from the deep feeling for Greek mythology that he had cherished since childhood.

Commenting in *Twentieth-Century Children's Writers* about the first four books (all of which were published in the early 1950s), Green says: "My intention...was to write exciting adventure stories set against a background of the way of life on a country estate in the 1920s and 1930s—a way of life that had almost passed away even as I wrote." He concedes that these might have been "out of date". In the 1980s, however, these well-crafted novels have acquired a satisfying period flavour; perhaps it is time for two more which he wrote for the set, which were never published, to find their way into print.

Green's works of fiction were overshadowed by the excellence of his books of literary comment, his collections of legends, and the literary biographies for which he is celebrated. His account of the life and work of Andrew Lang in 1946 was followed by studies of A.E.W. Mason, J.M. Barrie, Mrs Molesworth, Rudyard Kipling, Lewis Carroll and C.S. Lewis. His connections with the two last-named writers are particularly interesting. Green's own reserve with grown-ups, and rapport with children (as well as his slight speech impediment) gave him an affinity with Carroll. As well as writing his biography, he edited *The Diaries of Lewis Carroll* (1953), revised Williams and Madden's 1931 work, *The Lewis Carroll Handbook* (1962) and assisted Morton Cohen with the editing of *The Letters of Lewis Carroll*. Green was a long-standing friend of C.S. Lewis, and, as well as admiring his contributions to religious thought and literature, he immediately and enthusiastically recognized the brilliance of Lewis's first fictional work for children—*The Lion, the Witch and the Wardrobe*—and encouraged him to publish it.

Green's feeling for popular, as well as classical, fiction found happy expression in his contribution to the Sherlock Holmes canon. He privately published "*Holmes, This Is Amazing*" in 1975, and frequently wrote for the *Sherlock Holmes Journal* (which he edited from 1957 to 1979).

Although battling with severe illness for several years at the end of his life, Green never lost his enthusiasm for books and writers. He leaves a legacy that will inform and entertain generations to come.

Born Roger Gilbert Lancelyn Green. **Parents** Gilbert Arthur Lancelyn, major in Royal Field Artillery, and Helena Mary Phyllis (Sealy) Green. **Marriage** June Burdett, 1948. **Children** Scirard Roger Lancelyn, Priscilla June Lancelyn and Richard Gordon Lancelyn. **Education** Dane Court School, Surrey; Liverpool College; Merton College, Oxford, BA, 1940, MA, 1944, BLitt, 1944. **Career** Actor, Oxford Repertory Theatre and London, 1942–45; antiquarian bookseller, Oxford, 1943; deputy librarian, Merton College, Oxford, 1945–50; William Noble research fellow in English literature, Liverpool University, 1950–52, member of university council, 1964–70; writer and editor, mainly of children's literature. **Related activities** Andrew Lang Lecturer, University of St Andrews, 1968–69; editor, *Kipling Journal*, 1957–79. **Other activities** Director, Lancelyn Court Ltd; hereditary lord of the manors of Poulton-Lancelyn and Lower Bebington. **Offices and memberships** National Book League; editor and committee member, Kipling Society; William Morris Society; Dickens Fellowship; R.L. Stevenson Club; Society of Authors and Dramatists; Players' Theatre Club; Arts Theatre Club; Sherlock Holmes Society; Oxford University Dramatic Society (secretary, 1945). **Awards and honours** Mythopeoic Society Award (USA), 1975; Scout Association Chief Scout's Medal, 1976; Knight of Mark Twain, 1978; honorary DLitt, Liverpool University, 1981. **Children's fiction** (all published in London, unless stated) *The Wonderful Stranger: A Holiday Romance*, 1950; *The Luck of the Lynns*, 1952; *The Secret of Rusticoker*, 1953; *The Theft of the Golden Cat*, 1955; *Mystery at Mycenae: An Adventure Story of Ancient Greece*, 1957, New York, 1959; *The Land Beyond the North*, New York, 1959; *The Land of the Lord High Tiger*, 1958; *The Luck of Troy*, 1961. **Edited works** (all published in London and New York, unless stated) *Modern Fairy Stories*, 1955; *The Book of Nonsense*, 1956; *Fairy Stories*, London, 1957; *Tales of Make-Believe*, 1960; *The Book of Verse for Children*, London, 1962; *Ten Tales of Detection*, 1967; Rudyard Kipling, *Stories and Poems*, London, 1970; *Thirteen Uncanny Tales*, 1970; *The Hamish Hamilton Book of Dragons*, London, 1970, published as *A Cavalcade of Dragons*, New York, 1970; Lewis Carroll, *Alice's Adventures in Wonderland, and Through the Looking-Glass and What Alice Found There*, 1971; Edgar Allan Poe, *Tales of Terror and Fantasy: Ten Stories from "Tales of Mystery and Imagination"*, London, 1971; *Ten Tales of Adventure*, London, 1972; *The Hamish Hamilton Book of Magicians*, London, 1973, published as *A Cavalcade of Magicians*, New York, 1973, published as *A Book of Magicians*, London, 1977; *Strange Adventures in Time*, 1974; *The Hamish Hamilton Book of Other Worlds*, London, 1976, published as *The Beaver Book of Other Worlds*, London, 1978. **Retellings** (all published in London, unless stated) *The Sleeping Beauty and Other Tales*, Leicester, 1947; *Beauty and the Beast and Other Tales*, Leicester, 1948; *The Story of Lewis Carroll*, 1949, New York, 1950; *King Arthur and His Knights of the Round Table*, 1953; *The Adventures of Robin Hood*, 1956; *Old Greek Fairy Tales*, 1958, New York, 1969; *Tales of the Greek Heroes*, 1958; *The Tale of Troy: Retold from the Ancient Authors*, 1958; *Heroes of Greece and Troy*, 1960, New York, 1961, revised edition, London, 1973; *The Saga of Asgard: Retold from the Old Norse Poems and Tales*, 1960, reissued as *Myths of the Norsemen*, 1962; *The True Book About Ancient Greece*, 1960; *Ancient Greece*, 1962, New York, 1969; *Once, Long Ago: Folk and Fairy Tales of the World*, New York, 1962, published as *My Book of Favourite Fairy Tales*, London, 1969; *Authors and Places: A Literary Pilgrimage*, 1963, New York, 1964; *Ancient Egypt*, 1963, New York, 1964; *Tales of the Greeks and Trojans*, 1964; *Tales from Shakespeare: The Comedies and Tragedies and Romances*, 2 vols, 1964–65, New York, 1965; *Tales the Muses Told: Ancient Greek Myths*, London and New York, 1965; *A Book of Myths*, London and New York, 1965; *Myths from Many Lands*, 1965; *Folk Tales of the World*, London and Boston, 1966; *Sir Lancelot of the Lake*, 1966; *Stories of Ancient Greece*, 1967; *Tales of Ancient Egypt*, 1967 and New York, 1968; *Jason and the Golden Fleece*, 1968; *The Tale of Ancient Israel*, London and New York, 1969; *The Tale of Ancient Thebes*, London and New York, 1977. **Adult publications** *The Lost July and Other Poems* (verse), London, 1945;

(translator) *The Searching Satyrs* by Sophocles, Leicester, 1946; *Tellers of Tales*, Leicester, 1946, revised editions, 1953, London and New York, 1965, London, 1969; *Andrew Lang: A Critical Biography with a Short Title Bibliography of the Works of Andrew Lang*, Leicester, 1946; *The Singing Rose and Other Poems* (verse), Leicester, 1947; *From the World's End: A Fantasy*, Leicester, 1948, New York, 1971; *Poulton-Lancelyn: The Story of an Ancestral Home*, Oxford, 1948; *A.E.W. Mason: The Adventures of a Story Teller*, London, 1952; (editor) *The Dairies of Lewis Carroll*, 2 vols, London, 1953, New York, 1954; *Fifty Years of Peter Pan*, London, 1954; *Into Other Worlds: Space-Flight in Fiction from Lucian to Lewis*, London, 1957, New York, 1957; (translator) *Two Satyr Plays: Euripides' Cyclops and Sophocles' Ichneutai*, London, 1957; (editor) *A Century of Humorous Verse, 1850–1950*, London and New York, 1959; *Lewis Carroll*, London, 1960, New York, 1962; *J.M. Barrie*, London, 1960, New York, 1961; (editor) *The Readers' Guide to Rudyard Kipling's Work*, Canterbury, 1961; *Mrs Molesworth*, London, 1961, New York, 1964; (editor) J.M. Barrie, *Plays and Stories*, London and New York, 1962; *Andrew Lang*, London and New York, 1962; *The Lewis Carroll Handbook, Being a New Version of a Handbook of the Literature of the Rev. C.L. Dodgson*, London, 1962, revised edition, London and New York, 1970; *C.S. Lewis*, London and New York, 1963, revised edition in *Three Bodley Head Monographs,* 1969; *Kipling and the Children*, London, 1965; (editor) *The Works of Lewis Carroll*, London, 1965; (editor) *Kipling: The Critical Heritage*, London and New York, 1971; (with Walter Hooper) *C.S. Lewis: A Biography*, London and New York, 1974; "*Holmes, This Is Amazing*": *Essays in Unorthodox Research*, privately printed, 1975. **Cause of death** Undisclosed, at age 68.

JEAN HÉLION

French Artist

Born **Couterne, Normandy, 21 April 1904**

Died **Paris, France, 28 October 1987**

To many critics of the modern art world, Jean Hélion appeared to be something of a schizophrenic. At first devoting himself to the non-figurative abstract style that was in tune with the French movements of the 1930s, after more than a decade he made a sudden shift to naturalism. In 1983 Hélion himself put it this way: "For ten years [1929–1939], I devoted myself entirely to abstract painting, until I found that it had transformed my vision of the world: the unknown world, so well hidden behind practical notions and conventions. Then I could not resist trying to decode reality with renewed rhythms, sequences and qualities. At the intersection of painting, experience and imagination I wonder and wander."

Some critics, like Sheldon Williams, however, viewed the artist's switch in styles in a slightly different light. "It is as if Jean Hélion had severed his roots and gone to another planet," Williams wrote. Indeed, when the hard-edged, luminescent canvasses which had caused art writers of the 1930s to cry "Oh, Hélion! Oh, Headlights!" gave way to crowded scenes of new, vivid colours, many of Hélion's abstract admirers fell away. Even so, as Williams points out, "probably an equal proportion of his admirers stayed faithful to him". The reasons behind the division in artistic application will never be known for certain. It is curious, nonetheless, that Hélion's changes in approach to art coincided with another sharp division in his personal life—his experiences as a prisoner of war during World War II. Another factor in his choice of style may have been his early professional training.

Born in Normandy in 1904, Hélion trained as an engineer in Lille before going to Paris in 1922 to study architecture. His first job was as an architect's draftsman, but while in Paris, he came under the influence of Cubism; Piet Mondrian is said to have been his mentor. Hélion, however, soon abandoned the style of his master and began to use curved and broken lines in his own work of the 1930s. With Theo van Doesburg, Otto Carlsund and Leo Tutundjian, Hélion founded the short-lived Art Concrèt group, which sought to achieve impersonalized "scientific" standards in art. Characteristics such as these logical, mechanized theories led critics like Anatole Jakovski to draw comparisons between Hélion's work and architecture. In his *Supplément au Dictionnaire Biographique des Artistes Contemporains*, Jakovski wrote that Hélion's non-objective style was "born through a process of abstraction both scientific and experimental. For a long time, with passion and obstinacy, he drew and painted lemons, heads, bottles. One day the bottles, the heads and the lemons disappeared from the canvas, leaving behind in their places amazing rhythmical structures."

The Art Concrèt movement lasted for around a year, when it was renamed Abstract-Creation. Under this heading, Hélion and his contemporaries practised their own form of creating colour-objects until roughly 1936. Not all the world was thrilled with the results. *Art News* had this to say concerning a 1936 exhibition of Hélion's paintings in New York City: "Untitled, impersonal, they convey their significance obliquely. They add no warmth to the room—their contribution is their cool and esoteric presence...Unless one is initiated to the particular symbols of the painter's subconscious, the amount of enjoyment to be found in the work is limited."

Nonetheless, Hélion's reputation was such that he was able to remain a full-time painter until 1940. At that time, the artist left his adopted US homeland, his American wife and their newborn son, and went back to the country of his birth to fight the Nazis.

"I was not sent to war," Hélion wrote in his book *They Shall Not Have Me*. "It came to me in Mézières en Drouais, a charming village west of Paris, where for months I crawled upon the hills, ducked under blank shots, dug model trenches and absorbed soporific chapters from the infantry sergeant's handbook, very peacefully." The war, however, soon came for Hélion. Along with 2000 other soldiers, the artist was captured by the Germans and force-marched some 162 miles in six days, fortified by nothing more than one meagre plate of soup. For the survivors, the phrase "they shall not have me" became the motto which sustained them throughout the march and during the long months of subsequent captivity. After more than a year of torment, Hélion began to make preparations for his escape. In the spring of 1942, masquerading as a Flemish worker, he fled from Stettin to Berlin, then crossed Germany to Cologne, finally crossing into Belgium and travelling on to Paris. Eventually he returned to the United States, where he began to write an account of his horrific experiences. *They Shall Not Have Me* was the result of his labours, a story which *Time* magazine said ranked "with the escape of Casanova from the Leads, or Peter Kropotkin from the fortress of Peter and Paul". Hélion himself simply stated that "escaping is really all a matter of keeping your nerve, distracting attention at the crucial moment".

While writing his narrative, the artist took up his brushes once again and the following year he mounted a retrospective exhibition at the Art of This Century Gallery in New York. His style had altered by this time. Although still classified as "mechanical" ("painted with logic, sensibility, and taste", wrote a *New York World-Herald* critic), Hélion's work had already taken on a figurative quality. New colours emerged—cuprous pinks and cerulean blues—and both the canvasses and the layers of paint became increasingly crowded. Finally it was official: Hélion had returned to naturalism, a decision which dismayed many of his followers, but one which did nothing to harm his reputation. From 1950 to 1980, he showed his work in 23 individual exhibitions in Paris, London, Rome, Brussels and New York, among other world cultural centres. During the 1970s and 1980s interest in his painting revived, especially in the new works which depicted the artist as a young man in the company of various nudes of glowing colours.

Hélion had returned to Paris in 1946, and remained in France until his death. Among other awards, he received the Grand Prix de la Ville de Paris in 1979, and the Grand Prix National des Arts in 1983. Unfortunately, during the 1980s Hélion began to lose his sight; in spite of this, he remained undaunted and turned his creative energy to writing by dictation, producing many lectures on his theories of the reality of art. He also dictated instructions for paintings he himself would never be able to paint.

"Stocky, open-faced, and likeable," were adjectives applied to Hélion. According to one commentator, he was a remarkable man, as well as an artist of repute: "If many more artists as resourceful, ingenious, courageous, gifted with such prowess of leadership as Jean Hélion could be found, it might be well for the world if they were entrusted with governments and armies."

As ever, it seems that an artist creates more than mere captured images of colour.

Born Jean Hélion. **Parents** Louis and Marguerite (Bernier) Hélion. **Marriages** 1) Pegeen Vail, *circa* 1937 (divorced); 2) Jacqueline Ventadour, 1963. **Children** Fabrice, David and Nicolas from first marriage; Jean Jacques and Louis from second marriage. **Education** École Auguste-Janvier, Amiens, 1912–18; Institut Industriel du Nord, Lille, 1920–21; École des Arts Décoratifs, Paris, 1922; Académie Adler, Paris, 1925–26. **Emigration** Left France for USA, 1936; returned to France permanently, 1946. **Military service** French Army, 1927; re-enlisted, 1940; prisoner of war, Pomerania, 1940–42; escaped and fled to USA, 1942. **Career** Pharmacist's assistant, Bagnoles-de-l'Orne, 1918–19; architect's assistant, Paris, 1921–24; first paintings produced, Paris, 1922; maths teacher, Paris, 1924–25; full-time painter, Paris, 1925–36, Virginia, USA, 1934–40, Virginia and New York, 1942–46 Paris, 1946–73, Bigeonnette, France, 1973–87. **Related activities** Founder member, Art Concrèt group, Paris, 1929–34 (renamed Abstraction-Creation group, 1930); costume and set designer for French television production of *King Lear*, 1964. **Awards and honours** Grand Prix de la Ville de Paris, 1979; honorary member, American Academy of Arts and Letters, 1979; Grand Prix National des Arts, France, 1983; Chevalier, Legion of Honour, France, 1984; Commander, Ordre des Arts et Lettres, France, 1985. **Publications** *Book Upon Captivity and Escape: They Shall Not Have Me*, New York, 1943; *Kaleidoscope*, Paris, 1975; *Journal d'un peintre: carnets 1929–84*, Marseilles, 1984; contributor to *Pyrenees Review*, 1929, *L'Art Concrèt* review, 1930, and *Abstraction-Creation* review, 1932–34; also to *Burlington Magazine* and *Axis* magazine. **Individual exhibitions** Galerie Pierre, Paris, 1932, 1938; Gallery John Becker, New York, 1932, 1933; Galerie Cahiers d'Art, Paris, 1936, 1956, 1958, 1961; Valentine Gallery, New York, 1936; Putzel Gallery, Hollywood, 1936; San Francisco Museum of Art, 1937, 1943; Arts Club of Chicago, 1937, 1943; Grand Rapids Museum, Michigan, 1938; Arts Club of Lynchburg, Virginia, 1939; The Whyte Gallery, Washington, 1939; Georgette Passedoit Gallery, New York, 1940; Virginia Museum of Fine Arts, Richmond, 1942; Art of This Century, New York, 1943; Bennington College, Vermont, 1943; Stendahl Gallery, Los Angeles, 1943; Paul Rosenburg Gallery, New York, 1944, 1945; Hollins College, Virginia, 1944; Museum of Fine Arts, Baltimore, 1945; Caresse Crosby Gallery, Washington, 1945; Galerie Renou et Colle, Paris, 1947; Hanover Gallery, London, 1951; Sala digli Specchi, Venice, 1951; Galleria del Milione, Milan, 1951; Feigl Gallery, New York, 1951; Galleria San Marco, Rome 1951; Chez Mayo, Paris, 1953; *Peintures 1929–39*, Galerie Louis Carré, Paris, 1962; *Paintings by Jean Hélion 1928–64*, Gallery of Modern Art, New York, 1964; Galerie Yvon Lambert, Paris, 1964; Leicester Galleries, London, 1965; Galerie René Andrieu, Toulouse, 1965, 1972; Galerie du Dragon, Paris, 1966; Willard Gallery, New York, 1967; Galerie Arcanes, Brussels, 1967; Galleria Mutina, Modena, 1968; Galleria Il Fante di Spade, Rome, 1968; Galerie Verrière, Lyon, 1969; Galleria Eunomia, Milan, 1969; *Cent*

Tableaux 1928–70, Centre National d'Art Contemporain, Paris (and French tour), 1970; Maisons des Jeunes et de la Culture, Paris, 1970; Galerie Weiller, Paris, 1971; Galerie Henriette Gomes, Paris, 1971; *Oeuvres Récentes*, Galerie Saint-Germain, Paris, 1973; Musée Tavet, Pointoise, France, 1974; Galerie Chauvelin, Paris, 1974; Galerie Saint-Germain, Paris, 1975; Galerie Karl Flinker, Paris, 1975, 1978, as *Les Années 50*, 1980, 1981, 1983, 1984; Maison de la Culture, Saint-Étienne, France, 1975; Galerie der Spiegel, Cologne, 1975; Spencer Samuels Gallery, New York, 1976; Musée de l'Abbaye Sainte-Croix, Les Sables d'Olonne, France, 1977; Galerie du Centre, Paris, 1977; Musée d'Art Moderne de la Ville, Paris, 1977, retrospective, 1984; Galerie Sapone, Nice, 1978; Musée Ingres, Montaban, France, 1978; *Bilder und Zeichnungen*, Galerie Thomas Borgmann, Cologne, 1979; Galerie Michael Hasenclever, Munich, 1979; Athens Gallery, Athens, 1979 *Peintures et Dessins 1929–79*, Musée d'Art et Industrie, Saint-Étienne, France, 1979; Musée d'Art Moderne, Strasbourg, 1979; Centre Georges Pompidou, Paris (and French tour), 1980; *Bilder und Zeichungen 1929–80*, Galerie Poll, West Berlin, 1980, 1984; Museum of Art, Peking (and Chinese tour), 1980; Musée des Beaux-Arts, Rennes, 1980; Galleria Fonte d'Abisso, Modena, 1981; *Paintings and Drawings from the Years 1939–60*, Robert Millar Gallery, New York, 1981; Musée de Caen, France, 1981; Musée de la Bouère, Liège, Belgium, 1981; Kunstverein, Wolfsburg, West Germany, 1981; Galerie Academia, Austria, 1981; Galerie Bronda, Helsinki, 1981; Musée d'Etat, Luxembourg, 1982; (retrospective) Städtische Galerie im Lenbachhaus, Munich, 1984; Rachel Adler Gallery, New York, 1985; Peggy Guggenheim Collection, Venice, 1986; Louis Carré et Compagnie, Paris, 1987; Aarhus Kunstmuseum, Denmark, 1987; Albemarle Gallery, London, 1987. **Group exhibitions** *Mercedes–Benz Show*, Paris, 1971; *European Paintings in the 1970s*, Los Angeles County Museum (and US tour), 1975; *Biennale*, Venice, 1976; *Peinture Aujourd-hui*, Maison de la Culture, Fontenay-sous-Bois, France, 1976; *20th-Century Art*, Centre Georges Pompidou, Paris (and Japanese tour), 1980; *A New Spirit in Painting*, Royal Academy of Arts, London, 1981; *Panorama de l'Art Français 1960–1980*, Vienna, 1982; *Painting in France*, at Biennale, Venice, 1984; *Colour Since Matisse*, at Edinburgh Festival, Scotland, 1985. **Collections** Centre Georges Pompidou, Paris; Musée d'Art Moderne de la Ville, Paris; Musée d'Art et Industrie, Saint-Étienne, France; Pinacothek, Munich; Tate Gallery, London; Museum of Modern Art, New York; Guggenheim Museum, New York; Museum of Fine Arts, Philadelphia; Museum of Fine Arts, Boston; Art Institute of Chicago. **Cause of death** Undisclosed, at age 83. **Further reading** Anatole Jakovzki, *Arp, Calder, Hélion, Miró, Seligman*, 1933; Herbert Read (editor), *Jean Hélion: A Coat of Many Colours*, London, 1952; Pierre Bruguiére, *Hélion*, Paris, 1970; René Micha, *Jean Hélion*, Paris, 1979; plus numerous exhibition catalogues.

WOODY HERMAN

American Musician and Bandleader

***Born* Milwaukee, Wisconsin, 16 May 1913**

***Died* Los Angeles, California, 29 October 1987**

With the death of Woody Herman, the big band era finally came to a close. He was the last of the working leaders, and only Charlie Barnet and Artie Shaw survived him in retirement. Herman's achievements are numerous, not the least of which was his ability to organize and maintain a band over long periods of time, while continually updating its sound. Few other bandleaders achieved a similar level of success yet remained so well-liked in the process.

Herman was born in Milwaukee and, encouraged by his parents, was working in vaudeville at the age of six, billed as "The Boy Wonder" for an act that saw him tap dance and sing. He soon learned to play alto saxophone and then the clarinet, both bought out of his own earnings, and after playing with various bands in Chicago, he toured Texas with Joe Lichter's band in the late 1920s. Herman tried to form his own band in 1933, but the attempt was unsuccessful, so he worked with a couple of bands before securing a place with the Isham Jones Juniors, for whom he sang and played clarinet and saxophone. With this band, he made his first recordings for Decca. But the band was far from stable, or successful, and when Jones decided to stop touring in 1936, the leading musicians formed a cooperative under Herman's name. Thus was born The Band That Played the Blues, a slightly misleading title that might more aptly have been applied to Count Basie's band, for Herman's outfit also included popular songs and non-jazz instrumentals in its swing and blues repertoire.

Success was slow to come, despite the band making its Manhattan début at the Roseland Ballroom in January 1937. Although recording extensively for Decca, it was only in April 1939 that the band struck lucky with a recording of the "Woodchopper's Ball". The record eventually sold more than a million copies and remained the most requested piece in the Herman repertoire. Spurred on by this success, and the increasing number of engagements it had brought, Herman started to raise the standards of the band, influenced by the sound of the Ellington, Lunceford and Basie bands. Bass player Chubby Jackson joined in 1943, and arranger Neil Hefti, tenor saxophonist Flip Phillips and trombonist Bill Harris in 1944, all first-rate performers who together created an internationally famous band renowned for the force and originality of its sound. Under the name of Herman's Herd, this was the first of many Herds, its trademark an astute blend of driving rhythms and brightly melodic turns of phrase powered by an enthusiastic, exciting frontline. With drummer Dave Tough as both dependable timekeeper and star soloist, the First Herd was one of the most spectacular big bands of all time.

The success of the First Herd was such that Igor Stravinsky wrote *Ebony Concerto* for the band, which was performed at the Carnegie Hall in March 1946. Recordings for Columbia sold well, the band appeared in several films, had its own radio show and won major polls in 1945 and 1946. But the economics of the post-war years were against big bands and Herman decided to call it a day in December 1946. He retired to the house in Hollywood he had bought from Humphrey Bogart and worked as a disc jockey, making a few records with scratch bands. Within six months he was bored, and was back with the Second Herd.

This new incarnation lasted until 1949, but in its brief existence it achieved considerable fame for its four-saxophone line-up of three light-sounding tenors and a baritone, played respectively by Stan Getz, Zoot Sims, Herbie Steward and Serge Chaloff. Nicknamed the Four Brothers after an arrangement written for them by Jimmy Guiffre, the four integrated bebop into the big band format, the Second Herd producing a smooth, close-formation ensemble sound that was much imitated but rarely matched by other bands. With trumpeter Red Rodney and composer Shorty Rogers in the Second Herd, the links with bebop were clear, while Ralph Burns's feature for Getz, "Early Autumn", brought the saxophonist's cool lyricism immediate fame.

Once again, economics forced the Herd to disband, and in 1949 Herman took a small band to Cuba for a series of engagements. In 1950 he formed the Third Herd, which lasted until 1958, with a Fourth Herd emerging in 1961. This incarnation lasted well into the 1980s, but since later Herds took regular annual breaks, non-numerical, occasional Herds—such as the Anglo-American Herd that toured England in 1959, the Singing Herd and finally the Thundering Herd, which played both the fortieth and fiftieth anniversary celebrations of the band—have all made their appearance. All are distinguished by their arrangements, notably those of Guiffre and

Burns, and although to some extent less creative than their illustrious predecessors, these later Herds displayed a consistently high level of musicianship, for Herman was as astute at picking good, young musicians as he was at selecting and edting arrangements for them to play. What was remarkable about Herman was that he never got into a rut, maintaining high standards despite changing personnel while also overseeing a gradual but inevitable sylistic evolution as jazz itself evolved. throughout a lengthy career, Herman kept the loyalty of his musicians and fans alike; he was tough when required but universally liked and respected as a bandleader.

In the early 1960s Herman widened his scope by taking up the soprano saxophone, on which he sounded as smooth as on alto, in contrast to his spikey, sharp-toned delivery on clarinet. He started to include various jazz-rock players in his group, featured an electric piano and, ever alive to what his peers were doing, used material by Thelonius Monk, Charlie Mingus and Herbie Hancock. In the 1970s a new generation of players introduced him to John Coltrane's work, for Herman was free from the sectarianism of much of jazz and was open-minded in his choice of material. Yet every night, he would answer requests for "Woodchopper's Ball" and make it and the band sound as fresh and lively as their predecessors had done in the 1930s.

Circumstances, however, forced Herman to continue long after he might otherwise have retired. During the 1960s, one of his managers gambled away the money Herman had set aside for tax. The US Inland Revenue Service finally caught up with Herman, who found himself having to pay a back-tax debt of $1.6 million. From being a moderately well-off man, he was now virtually penniless. Forced to sell his house at auction for far less than it was worth, he was unable to afford the rent to stay there, and was bailed out after an appeal by a local Los Angeles radio station. His health gave out, and with five-figure medical bills to pay, friends and musicians from all over the world contributed money. The US Congress considered a bill to relieve the tax debt on Herman, but it was too late, and Herman died a pauper, hounded to his death by overwork and worry over his debts. It was a sad end to a distinguished career.

Born Woodrow Charles Herman. **Parents** Otto C., singer and pianist, and Myrtle (Barth) Herman. **Marriage** Charlotte Neste, 1936. **Children** Ingrid. **Education** St John's Cathedral Preparatory School; Marquette University, Milwaukee (one term only). **Career** As a child, stage dancer, singer and saxophonist; began playing in Chicago with Tom Gerun, Harry Sosnik, Gus Arnheim and Joe Moss bands, 1930–33; played tenor sax and clarinet and sang with the Isham Jones Juniors, making first recordings on Decca, 1934–36; used leading members of now disbanded Isham Jones band to form own orchestra, making its début at Roseland Ballroom, Brooklyn, 1936; recording career began to take off with success of "The Woodchoppers Ball", 1939; with changing personnel, band grew to international fame by mid-1940s as first of succession of Herman bands known as Herman's Herds that toured almost without a break until 1980s; First Herd disbanded, 1946; reformed as the Second Herd, featuring Stan Getz and Zoot Sims, 1947–49; formed smaller band, among others, to tour Cuba, 1949; formed Third Herd, early 1950s, making several European tours and touring South America under the auspices of US State Department, 1958; formed the Anglo–American Herd, 1959, and the Swinging Herd, 1962; by late 1960s was including pop and jazz-rock players in his bands; toured widely in 1970s; held club residency, New Orleans, early 1980s; subsequently worked on West Coast of America before holding residency at St Regis Hotel, New York, 1985; formed final band, 1986. **Awards and honours** Best Swing Band, *Down Beat* popularity poll, 1945; *Billboard* Award, 1946; *Metronome* poll winner, 1946; *Esquire* Silver Award, 1946, 1947. **Films** (include) *What's Cookin'?*; *Winter Time*; *Quota Girl*; *Summer Holiday*; *Sensations of 1945*; Earl Carroll's *Vanities*. **Radio** Own show as The Woody Herman Herd, mid-1940s. **Recordings** (include) "The Woodchopper's Ball", Decca 2440, 1939; "Blue Flame", Decca 3643, 1941; "Apple Honey", Columbia 36803, 1945; "Caldonia", Columbia 36789, 1945; *At Carnegie Hall*, MGM

30601-8, 1946; *Ebony Concerto*, Columbia 7479M, 1946; "Lady McGowan's Dream", Columbia 38365-6, 1946; "Summer Sequence", Columbia 38365-7, 1946–47; "Four Brothers", Columbia 38304, 1947; "Lemon Drop", Cap 15365, 1948; "Early Autumn", Cap 57616, 1948; "Blues in Advance/Terrissita", Mars 100, 1952; *Woody Herman's New Big Band at the Monterey Jazz Festival*, Atlantic 1328, 1959; *Encore: 1963*, Phi 600092, 1963; *Light My Fire*, Cadet 819, 1968; *Woody and Friends at the Monterey Jazz Festival*, Conc 170, 1979. **Cause of death** Heart disease and emphysema, at age 74. **Further reading** E. Edwards Jr, *Woody Herman and His Orchestra: A Discography*, Denmark, 1961, California, 1965; J.A. Treichel, *Keeper of the Flame: Woody Herman and the Second Herd, 1947–49*, Florida, 1978; C. Garrod, *Woody Herman and His Orchestra, 1936–47* (volume 1), Florida, 1985, *1948–57* (volume 2), Florida, 1986; S. Voce, *Woody Herman*, London, 1986.

MARIA IVOGÜN

Hungarian Opera Singer

***Born* Budapest, Hungary, 18 November 1891**

***Died* 7 October 1987**

The role of Zerbinetta in Richard Strauss's opera *Ariadne Auf Naxos*, is an Everest for coloratura sopranos. A wordless, virtuoso aria in Act Two, in which Zerbinetta thinks back over her love-life, provides a wonderful opportunity for a display of dazzling vocal technique. For Richard Strauss there was only one real interpreter of the role and that was the legendary soprano Maria Ivogün. Although she did not create Zerbinetta, she was, in his words, "simply unique and without rival". The matchless beauty of her voice, together with her secure technique, natural musicality and personal charm fitted her perfectly for the role. Strauss made a point of ensuring Ivogün was his Zerbinetta every time *Ariadne* was produced.

Maria Ivogün was the daughter of a military officer and a singer. Her real name was Ilse Kempner, but she took her mother's name, von Günther, and compressed it into the stage name I(lse)vo(n) Gün(ther). She studied singing in Vienna with Irene Schlemmer-Ambros, then moved to Munich where she took lessons with Hanny Schöner.

Bruno Walter engaged Ivogün for the Bavarian State Opera, Munich, in 1913, after attending her audition for the Vienna State Opera, which did not accept her. She made a successful début in *La Bohème* as Mimi, and with that role launched a career in Munich that was to last until 1925. During these years, as well as performing Mimi and Zerbinetta, Ivogün sang the roles of Queen of the Night, Zerlina, Gilda and Constanze, and attracted an enthusiastic audience for her interpretations.

In 1917 she created the part of Ighino in Pfitzner's opera *Palestrina*, and two years later sang the title role in Pfitzner's *Christelflein*. In these and other operas she frequently partnered the Munich tenor Karl Erb, to whom she was married from 1921 to 1932.

In 1922 she went on a concert tour of the USA which was successful, although she made only isolated appearances in Chicago and New York (without appearing at the Metropolitan Opera House) and failed to set herself up as a credible opposition to the leading American coloratura soprano of the day—Galli Curci. At that period Ivogün also made appearances in London, making her Covent Garden début with Zerbinetta in 1924, and also singing in Italy at La Scala, Milan, and at the Salzburg Festival in 1925.

In 1925 she moved to the Berlin City Opera. Here she began to explore heavier roles, such as Manon, and took leading roles in several now-forgotten contemporary works. She retired from the stage in 1932, married her accompanist Michael Raucheisen, and confined herself to *Lieder* recitals which won her much respect. Ivogün also became a committed voice teacher. From 1948 to 1950 she taught at the Vienna Academy and from 1950 to 1958 was on the faculty of the Berlin Hochschüle für Musik, where her pupils included Elisabeth Schwarzkopf and Rita Streich.

The majority of her records are pre-electric (1916–25) but well convey the purity of her voice. A smaller group made for HMV by the electrical process in 1932 include a performance of the Zerbinetta aria that justifies Richard Strauss's praise.

Born Ilse Kempner. **Parents** Father, a military officer, mother, Ida (von Günther) Kempner, singer. **Marriages** 1) Karl Erb, tenor, 1921 (divorced, 1932); 2) Michael Raucheisen, accompanist, 1932. **Education** Studied voice with Amalie Schlemmer-Ambros, Vienna, then Hanny Schöner, Munich. **Career** Professional singing début as Mimi in *La Bohème*, Bavarian State Opera, Munich, 1913; remained with this company until 1925; during this time made various appearances at Covent Garden, London, La Scala, Milan, Salzburg Festival, and concerts in Chicago and New York; joined Städtische Oper, Berlin, 1925–34; retired from stage, 1932; gave *Lieder* recitals and became voice teacher, 1932 onwards; taught at Vienna Academy of Music, 1948–50, Berlin Hochschüle für Musik, 1950–58. **Recordings** Many from the pre-electric period, 1916–25; a few made for HMV, 1932. **Cause of death** Undisclosed, at age 95.

WILLIS JACKSON

American Jazz Musician

***Born* Miami, Florida, 25 April 1928**

***Died* New York City, New York, 25 October 1987**

With one impassioned saxophone solo recorded in 1948, Willis Jackson not only made his name as a musician, but gained a lifelong nickname too. The piece of music was "Gator Tail", written by Jackson and recorded by the Cootie Williams Sextet. It featured a typical Jackson solo—vivid, eloquent and hard-driving—and after it became a hit record, Willis Jackson gloried in the nickname of "Gator". The record's success in 1949 enabled him to start up his own band the following year, working regularly in and around New York. In the studio his robust sound graced many jazz, r'n'b and rock'n'roll records, while live, he was always in demand for his danceable brand of rhythmic jazz.

Jackson was born in Miami and while still in his teens played with local bands in whose ranks were the up-and-coming jazz stars of the 1950s—Fats Navarro, Blue Mitchell, Cannonball Adderley and others. He studied theory and harmony at the Florida Agricultural and Mechanical University and, preferring to finish his education, turned down offers to join the bands of both Lionel Hampton and Andy Kirk. Once graduated, he joined the Cootie Williams Sextet (sometimes augmented to a septet or octet) in 1948 and stayed sporadically with that essentially r'n'b-flavoured outfit until 1955, combining that commitment with leading his own bands.

Jackson's bands were often marked out for their unusual instrumentation, for he backed up his saxophone with organ, bass and drums. His was probably the first group to sport such a line-up, and it won him many followers, particularly when the organist was Jack McDuff. Together they played a gritty, driving jazz that found immense popularity among young audiences. Jackson's success as a solo artist meant that he played with the best—Charlie Parker, Dizzy Gillespie and others—and in later life he worked regularly in clubs and nightspots in and around New York, often accompanied by all-star groups of sidemen. For many years he played at the West End Café near Columbia University in New York, where he worked with George Kelly, an old friend from Miami, in a band called Two Tenor Boogie. As before, he recorded prolifically.

Jackson's later life was marred by illness, in particular diabetes, and his robust sound lost some of its edge. He thus increasingly turned to ballads, for which he had designed a modified saxophone, called, not surprisingly, the Gator horn. His death, after complications caused by heart surgery, removes one of the leading stylists of the big-toned, driving school of tenor saxophone.

Born Willis Jackson. **Marriage** 1) Ruth Brown, rhythm and blues singer; 2) Ann. **Children** Leon and Ronald. **Education** Florida Agricultural and Mechanical University. **Career** Played tenor saxophone in local bands, 1946–48; joined Cootie Williams' band, 1948–55; toured with own band, forming close association with organist Jack McDuff, from 1950; played regularly at Club Harlem, Atlantic City, from 1963; toured France, 1979–80; played with George Kelly in band called Two Tenor Boogie, New York, from 1981. **Related activities** Worked regularly recording and playing as side-man with Charlie Parker and Dizzy Gillespie; designed a modified saxophone, the Gator horn, for playing ballads. **Recordings** (include) "Gator Tail" (also composed), Mer. 8131, 1948, "Thunderbird", Prst. 7232, 1962. **Cause of death** Complications after heart surgery, at age 59.

SIR HENRY JONES

British Engineer and Industrialist

***Born* Paddington, London, 13 July 1906**

***Died* Aylesbury, Buckinghamshire, 9 October 1987**

Sir Henry Jones, chairman of the UK Gas Council from 1960 to 1972, came from a distinguished line of gas men. His great-grandfather first lighted a London street in the nineteenth century; his grandfather, a civil engineer, established a well-known firm of consulting gas and civil engineers and in 1917 became president of the Institution of Civil Engineers, and his father was director of a number of gas concerns, including the South Metropolitan Gas Company, of which he became chairman. The young Henry, however, educated at Harrow and Pembroke College, Cambridge, where he obtained a first-class degree in the mechanical science tripos, was not destined to follow in the family tradition. By the time he graduated, gas appeared to be on the decline in the face of competition from electricity and the incipient competition from the increasing discoveries of oil.

Nevertheless, the young Henry Jones was inevitably drawn into the service of gas. He became a student at the Institution of Civil Engineers and his paper entered for the Miller Prize, which he won in 1929, was on the subject of "Long Distance Gas Transmissions". From then on he was hooked. He became articled to the well-known gas consulting engineer, Sir George Evetts, and moved on to the Watford and St Albans Gas Company, the Wandsworth and District Gas Company, the South Metropolitan, the South Suburban and other companies where he was either a director or deputy chairman, often under his father. The latter exercised a strong influence on his only son—after all, he had taken him with him, when he was only a young lad, to see the damage after the Silvertown explosion in the East End of London in 1917. Frank Jones instilled in his son the importance of good financial control and marketing, as well as good engineering, and much of Henry's later success in his control of the rejuvenated nationalized industry in the 1960s was due to his father's tutoring in the pre-eminence of cost control in gas management.

Prior to his military service during World War II—from which he emerged with the rank of brigadier—Jones had been engaged not only in the design and construction of gasworks plant, but also in rating and valuation matters and in merging many of the very small gas companies scattered around the country into more viable larger entities. Among other things, he drew up plans for gas grids for Scotland and South Yorkshire. This was to be a good preparation for the Labour Government's nationalization of the industry in 1949. Jones became chairman of the East Midlands Gas Board, as well as a member of the central authority, the Gas Council, and three years later he was back in London as the council's deputy chairman.

The outlook for the industry in the 1950s was far from bright. The coal industry, also nationalized, regarded gas as its captive market to the extent of raising its prices to almost untenable levels, while at the same time the complex purification processes demanded high capital and labour input. Competition from electricity, which did not need such high-quality coking coal, and from oil, was growing. It was only through the enlightened and imaginative approach of engineers like Jones, who were prepared to experiment with fuels other than coal and to improve marketing techniques, that gas's market share was preserved—and ultimately enlarged through the introduction of domestic gas central heating. Jones's appointment as chairman of the Gas Council also coincided with the first experiments in bringing in shipments of liquid methane, first from the Gulf of Mexico and then from Algeria, a fuel which could produce twice the amount of energy as coal. In the second year of his chairmanship Jones went out to Algeria to inspect the natural gas field at Hassi R'Mel and was resolute in his stand against the outcries from the threatened British coal industry. In any case, the outcry was in vain, for the discovery of huge reserves of natural gas beneath the North Sea revolutionized the prospects for the gas industry. By the time Jones retired in 1972, the national programme of conversion from town to natural gas was well under way, and gas had become the favourite form of domestic heating and cooking.

None of this would have worked, however, without the national transmission system which was set up under Henry Jones's chairmanship. His earlier study for the Miller Prize stood him in good stead. Transmission lines were almost doubled from 74,000 miles at the time of nationalization to 127,000 miles by 1973. The industry's management structure was also rationalized. The 12 area boards were replaced by regional managers chosen by the central authority, and the chairman's particular attention to the recruitment of top and middle management established a forward-looking and progressive industry able to seize and capitalize on the natural gas bonanza.

After his retirement from the Gas Council, Sir Henry (he was knighted in 1965) became more active on the World Energy Conference, becoming its vice-chairman for three years. He also joined the boards of Benzene Marketing Company and Benzole Producers Ltd, and was chairman of both from 1972 to 1977. He served as a member of a Royal Commission on Standards of Conduct in Public Life. His prime interest, however, was always the Institution of Gas Engineers, of which he became president in 1957. He was an engineer first and foremost, and he delivered one of the Institution's Centenary Addresses in 1963, received its Birmingham

Medal the following year and became an honorary fellow in 1970. During his later years he extended his interest to global energy matters, being a member of the advisory committee of Energy International NV, for which he wrote a number of papers. His own unflagging energy was an appropriate, not to say vital, asset in his work. Little wonder he was described as "a man who looked forward to Monday mornings".

Born Henry Frank Harding Jones. **Parents** Frank Harding Jones, civil engineer, and Gertrude Octavia (Kimber) Jones. **Marriage** Elizabeth Angela Langton, 1934. **Children** Richard Harding, John Harding, Antony Harding, and Priscilla Mary McDougall. **Education** Harrow School; Pembroke College, Cambridge, first class degree, mechanical science tripos, 1927. **Military service** Essex Regiment, 1939–45; staff, France and Belgium, 1939–40, India and Burma, 1942–45; promoted to lieutenant-colonel, 1943, colonel, 1945, brigadier, 1945. **Career** Articled to engineer Sir George Evetts of H.E. Jones & Son, 1927; consultant to gas industry to 1939; deputy chairman: Watford and St Albans Gas Company, Wandsworth and District Gas Company; director: South Metropolitan, South Suburban and other gas companies; chairman, East Midlands Gas Board, 1949–52; deputy chairman, Gas Council, 1952–60, chairman, 1960–71; chairman, British National Committee, 1968–71; vice-chairman, International Executive Council, World Energy Conference, 1970–73, honorary vice-chairman from 1973. **Related activities** Chairman: Benzene Marketing Company, 1972–77, Benzole Producers Limited, 1972–77. **Offices and memberships** Member, Royal Commission on Standards of Conduct in Public Life, 1974–76; chairman, Economic Development Committee for Chemical Industry, 1972–75. **Awards and honours** Liveryman, Clothworkers' Company, 1928, master, 1972–73; Miller Prize, Institution of Civil Engineers, 1929, fellow; member, Order of the British Empire, 1943; knighted, 1956; honorary fellow, Institution of Gas Engineers, president, 1956–57; fellow, Royal Society of Arts, 1964; Knight Commander Order of the British Empire, 1965; honorary LLD, Leeds, 1967; honorary DSc: Leicester, 1970, Salford, 1971; Knight Grand Cross Order of the British Empire, 1972; honorary fellow, Clare College, Cambridge, 1973; fellow, Fellowship of Engineering, 1976; fellow, Institution of Chemical Engineers. **Cause of death** Undisclosed, age 81.

ANDREI KOLMOGOROV

Soviet Mathematician

Born **Tambov, Russia, 25 April 1903**

Died **Moscow, USSR, 20 October 1987**

Andrei Kolmogorov made fundamental advances in many branches of modern mathematics, but he will probably be best remembered for his work on probability theory, which promoted the subject to be an integral part of analysis. His influence on countless pupils and disciples worldwide has been immense.

He was born in Tambov, about 250 miles southeast of Moscow, and at 17 was enrolled at Moscow University. Here he worked on the theory of the functions of real variables, and before he was 19 he completed a study in the theory of operations on sets, which was published some years later. He obtained his degree in 1925, and remained at the university as an instructor and research associate. This was when his great interest in probability theory began.

Probability theory was a subject on which considerable work had been done, but haphazardly and disconnectedly. Kolmogorov's important work, *General Theory of Measure and Probability Theory*, was published in 1929. In 1931 he was made a professor, and in 1933 a director of the Institute of Mathematics at the university. Also in 1933 he expanded his book into *Foundations of the Calculus of Probability* and it was published in German. The English translation did not appear until 1950. Not only did it lay down a clear basis for the subject, codifying the work of others, but it added many beautiful theories of his own making. Included among them was the famous Strong Law of Large Numbers, and the two systems of partial differential equations, describing transition probabilities controlling a Markov process, which bear his name. They have applications in Brownian movement and diffusion.

The book provided the first axiomatic presentation of the theory of probability, and his system is still the most widespread logical scheme. It also led to the study of random systems dispersed in space or developing in time, and thence to his idea of a filtration of sigma-algebras representing the progressive swelling of the corpus of available information. This is the foundation of the modern theory of random processes, and a vital contribution to control theory, as well as Kolmogorov's synthesis of information and ergodic theory. Other applications were found in many branches of physics, chemistry, civil engineering and biology.

Kolmogorov also refined the concept of the algorithm, one of the crucial ideas behind mathematical logic-calculus. It has important applications in cybernetics and programmed instructions, and he also used it to work out the theory of conveying information along communication channels. Following this work, he studied Markov chains in depth, and the ensuing work on dynamic systems was the starting point for numerous studies by other mathematicians.

Topology was another branch advanced by Kolmogorov, including the conception of the homological ring, and the formation of the duality law on equivalent representations of certain mathematical properties. His articles, *On Topological Group Formulation of Geometry* and *On Formulation of Projective Geometry*, both came out in the 1930s, as well as others on the areas of functional analysis and the optimum approximation of functions.

World War II was a highly creative time for Kolmogorov. Of practical importance, he applied his equations on predictability and randomness to develop techniques for planes to land on the heaving decks of aircraft carriers in rough seas. He also developed, independently of Wiener, the theory of the smoothness and prediction of stationary time-theories, and he also constructed pathological examples which are still being studied. In addition, he published his two papers on the theory of turbulent fluid flow, putting into precise mathematical form the structure of the small-scale components of turbulent motion. This had many applications, for instance in the study of what happens in the wake of jet aircraft. His two papers were translated into English in 1941 and made their way to British libraries during the war.

The breadth of Kolmogorov's interests was wide, and he worked on examples from many branches of science. He and his pupils wrote about subjects as diverse as crystal growth, the geometry of the interactions of plants, "birth and death" processes, and genetics, this last study leading to a clash with Lysenko whose erroneous ideas had official backing from the Kremlin. He even attempted to analyse some aspects of Russian poetry, and his lectures on Pushkin were especially memorable.

Working in the USSR, Kolmogorov enjoyed a better association with those involved with practical problems than was the case for mathematicians in the West, but at the same time he was working in isolation from Western knowledge for much of his life, for travel by Western scientists was not allowed, nor was there other contact. When, in the 1970s, the beginnings of the revolutionary study now called "Chaos" was exciting scientists in the West, and the two sides met at occasional conferences, the Americans were astonished to find that they were in some cases rediscovering what Kolmogorov and his colleagues had worked out many years before. As contact with the West increased, and knowledge could flow in both directions, he gained the affection and admiration of a worldwide band of followers, particularly those interested in probability theory.

Kolmogorov's unselfish devotion to the development of talent in others was remarkable. He worked tirelessly to improve the standard of mathematics teaching in secondary schools, and in the establishment of special schools for young, unusually gifted mathematicians. He enjoyed the company of young people, and guided them in developing their ideas. His *dacha* near Moscow attracted many outstanding mathematicians, and one of them said it was just like the mathematical institute in the Black Forest called Oberwolfach "except that Kolmogorov buys all the drinks".

He is widely mourned by those who knew him, but he will not be forgotten when they die as well. Such were his achievements, his name is enshrined in several branches of mathematics.

Born Andrei Kolmogorov. **Education** Graduated from Moscow University, 1925. **Career** Mathematician, Moscow University, 1925, professor, 1931–34, head of the university, 1934–37, chair of theory of probability, 1937 onwards. **Offices and memberships** Member, USSR Academy of Sciences, 1939–87, chairman, committee on mathematical education. **Publications** *Foundations of the Calculus of Probabilities*, 1933; and many other articles and books. **Cause of death** Undisclosed, at age 84.

ALFRED LANDON

American Politician

Born **West Middlesex, Pennsylvania, 9 September 1887**

Died **Topeka, Kansas, 12 October 1987**

The fact that Alf Landon lived to be 100 years old is just about as important as his other claim to fame: that of being the unfortunate Republican candidate defeated by Franklin Delano Roosevelt in the 1936 US presidential election. Nonetheless, because the little "lamb-faced" governor of Kansas took his pummelling in good grace, he remained something of a celebrity—at least within the Republican Party he represented.

Born in Pennsylvania, the son of an oil prospector, Alfred Mossman Landon was 17 years old when his family moved to Independence, Ohio, to take advantage of the new oil fields just being discovered in the area. Landon was an indifferent student at school, but became firmly involved in campus politics when he studied law at the University of Kansas. After graduating in 1908, he was not inclined towards the subject of his studies and instead joined a bank in his hometown as a book-keeper, remaining there for four years. While working in the bank, Landon did not remain idle; by investing part of his earnings in oil-drilling ventures, he had soon saved enough to form his own company with three other men. Through careful planning and shrewd investment, he was soon a rich man; thoughts of the bank and of law were left far behind.

At the same time as he was amassing his fortune, Landon had become involved in politics, and found he had the same knack for it in the public world as he had possessed in college. He served as secretary to the governor of Kansas in 1922, and soon became much respected as an adviser on political tactics. By 1928 he was elected chairman of the Republican State Central Committee, and by 1931 he himself was running for the office of governor in Kansas. With his friendly, common-sense, man-of-the-people approach ("I'm Alf Landon" had become his catch-phrase), he was the only Republican governor to be elected west of the Mississippi River during 1932, and the only Republican governor anywhere in the United States by 1934. During his term in office, he spoke out against the Democrats' New Deal policy which was sweeping the nation at the time, yet his second inaugural speech could almost have been written by Roosevelt himself. "America bids fair to join the procession of nations of the world in their march toward a new social and economic philosophy," Landon said. "Some say this will lead to socialism, some communism, others fascism. For myself I am convinced that the ultimate goal will be a modified form of individual rights and ownership of property, out of which will come a wider spread of prosperity and opportunity for a fuller, richer life." Such words as these led Landon to be called a "progressive" by members of his own party, but whatever the classification, he was the only possible candidate the Republicans dared to put up against Roosevelt for the presidential election of 1936.

"Life, liberty, and Landon" became the slogan of the nominee many called the "poor man's Coolidge". With a sunflower in his buttonhole and a Midwest twang, Alf Landon fought an honest, forthright campaign. As more than one newspaper has noted, however, "no man on earth could have beaten Roosevelt in 1936". Landon carried only two states—Vermont and Maine—although he did manage to gain 16 million votes to FDR's 27 million—a respectable showing for anyone competing against a legend.

After his defeat, the affable politician made no further attempts to run for any public office. Instead, he returned to his business, adding radio equipment to his oil-rig interests. In the 1940s he served as a delegate to three Republican National Conventions, and it was his popularity as a "grand old man" of the Grand Old Party that helped one of his daughters win an election to the United States senate in latter years. Republican office-holders—Ronald Reagan included—often made a pilgrimage to Landon's house on his birthday, to see the man whose name made history for just one year: 1936.

Born Alfred Mossman Landon. **Parents** John Manuel, oil prospector and promoter, and Anne (Mossman) Landon. **Marriages** 1) Margaret Fleming, 1915 (died, 1918); 2) Theo Cobb, 1930. **Children** One daughter, Margaret Anne, from first marriage; one son and one daughter from second marriage. **Education** Marietta Academy, Ohio; University of Kansas, LLB, 1908. **Military service** Lieutenant, US Army Chemical Warfare Division, 1918. **Career** Bookkeeper, Independence Bank, Kansas, 1908–12; founding president, A.M. Landon and Co., oil producers, from 1912; chairman, Republican Party State Central Committee, 1928; governor of Kansas, 1933–37; unsuccessful Republican candidate for US presidency, 1936; abandoned politics and resumed business interests, 1936 onwards. **Offices and memberships** Delegate, Pan–American Conference, Peru, 1938; leader of Kansas delegation and member of Platform and Foreign Trade Committees, Republican National Convention, 1944; member, Phi Gamma Delta. **Awards and honours** Honorary LHD, Kansas State, 1968; honorary LLD, Emporia College, 1969; Distinguished Citizenship Awards: Washburn University, 1967, Baker University, 1975. **Cause of death** Respiratory ailments, at age 100.

HERMANN LANG

German Grand Prix Driver
***Born* Stuttgart, West Germany, 6 April 1909**
***Died* Stuttgart, West Germany, 19 October 1987**

Although the history of Grand Prix motor-racing now covers over 80 years, and contains many dramatic phases, the period between 1934 and 1939 could scarcely be equalled for prolonged drama, sheer spectacle and significant technical achievement. The year 1934 marked the serious return to the major circuits of the famous Mercedes-Benz concern after several years during which their racing efforts, though effective, were restricted by economic constraints. The same year also marked the début of a sensational rival protagonist, the rear-engined 16-cylinder Auto Union, enabling Germany to mount a double challenge to the established teams of Alfa-Romeo, Maserati and Bugatti. The result was an epic series of struggles that eventually developed into a straight Mercedes-Benz versus Auto Union fight for Grand Prix supremacy, fought by the world's greatest drivers.

The Hermann Lang story is the stuff from which *Boy's Own* adventures are made. Born near Stuttgart of simple country folk, he was apprenticed as a motor-cycle mechanic in 1923. A keen and enthusiastic worker, he persuaded his foreman to let him work on his own machine after hours and it was not long before the young Hermann had his first taste of circuit racing. He rapidly gained a reputation as a fearless rider, and in due course rode for the works Standard team. Between 1929 and 1931 he was their leading side-car rider, becoming German hill-climb champion in 1931.

When the Depression hit Germany, Lang became unemployed. Eventually, after months of seeking work, he found a job driving a diesel train in a gravel pit. Every day his journey to work took him past the Daimler-Benz factory and the sight of the magnificent cars fired his imagination. Through persistence he eventually found a position in the Mercedes test department, putting the works engines through their paces on the dynamometer. Lang's rise from lowly mechanic to works driver for the Mercedes organization was an object lesson in discipline, sheer hard work and unwavering determination.

It was in 1933 that Daimler-Benz made their decision to return to Grand Prix racing. Hitler had come to power at the end of January, and his genuine enthusiasm for motor-racing (and an infinitely more sinister ambition for overall German supremacy in Europe) led him to offer an annual grant of 450,000 marks (about £40,000/$100,000) to any German concern building a Grand Prix contender. When Auto Union also took up the challenge, it was decided that the grant be shared between them, with the added incentive of cash bonuses for finishing first, second or third in eligible races. The resultant 225,000 marks was scarcely a tenth of what Mercedes would actually spend on Grands Prix in just one season, but their racing and development costs were allowed as a sales and publicity expense "item" in their lucrative contracts with the German government for supplying diesel and aero engines.

Although there was a shortage of German drivers in the mid-1930s, it seemed most unlikely that the board of directors would look to one of their lowlier employees to fill the breach. However, Lang had made such a good impression of himself as a mechanic, that from testing production cars he was promoted to the hallowed racing preparation department and, on occasion, allowed to drive the racing cars up to the circuit. By chance, his foreman heard that

Lang had racing experience and put his name forward to team manager Alfred Neubauer as a team "cadet".

In 1935 Lang became a reserve driver, the Mercedes front-line team including Caracciola, Fagioli and von Brauchitsch. For German enthusiasts the big event of the year was the Eifelrennen meeting held at the famous Nürburgring. Some 300,000 spectators would regularly occupy the mountainous course in order to catch a glimpse of the Silver Arrows, as the Mercedes team had become known. Manfred von Brauchitsch, always at his best at the "Ring", had recorded fastest lap in practice and stormed away from the start, only to retire three laps from the end. Caracciola then took the lead but came increasingly under pressure from Auto Union's new recruit Bernd Rosemayer. An epic battle ensued, with the Mercedes finishing less than two seconds ahead of the Auto Union. Sheer experience had won the race, but to Rosemayer went the fastest lap, and a new star had arrived. It was evident that another was on his way, for Mercedes' new driver, Hermann Lang, finished fifth, in this, his very first race, not far behind Fagioli, the old master, who did much to teach him the complex craft of motor-racing.

With such a wealth of talent in the established drivers, Lang was fortunate to drive on three further occasions that year: a sixth place in the Swiss Grand Prix at Bremgarten sandwiched by two retirements did not discourage him, and when he was not racing he continued his duties as a race mechanic with enthusiasm.

No doubt remembering his promising début, Neubauer entered Lang for the 1936 Eifelrennen. Twenty-two laps of the Nürburgring meant a gruelling 316-mile race lasting almost four hours, but von Brauchitsch put on a show from the very start. He led on completion of lap one, closely followed by Rosemayer and Lang, the "baby" of the Mercedes team, surprisingly ahead of Caracciola. As the race progressed, one problem after another was to befall the Mercedes team: Brauchitsch pitted after hitting a bank, Caracciola, lying third, fell back with fuel-feed problems and Fagioli was also trailing. Consequently, the works' hopes centred on the young Lang, who actually led on lap seven when Rosemayer stopped for fuel and tyres. Lap eight, and Caracciola retired his ailing car. A lap later Lang pulled into the pits in agony, having broken his little finger against the cockpit side during an over-enthusiastic gear change. Caracciola took over his car and when Brauchitsch came in, the spare driver, Zehender, eagerly prepared himself to take over at the wheel. Lang, his finger now bound and splinted, had other ideas. He made his way quickly to the car and was signalled into the cockpit by Neubauer, eventually to finish seventh.

For 1937 Mercedes-Benz rewarded Lang with a permanent place in the team and he was quick (in more ways than one) to show his gratitude. The first Grand Prix of the season was at Tripoli, and there the Silver Arrows were confronted with an entry that included no less than five Auto Unions and six Alfa-Romeos. After a frantic start, Lang maintained a position in the leading bunch and by three-quarter distance had fought his way to the front. He held on to the lead, hounded home by four Auto Unions, and averaged a staggering 134.25 mph to record his first Grand Prix win.

The next race was an extraordinary affair that produced specially designed streamlined cars from both Mercedes and Auto Union, and also what will probably remain the biggest race-day attendance—380,000—for a European Grand Prix. The Berlin authorities planned a new link road to an exhibition hall at the city end of the Avus high speed circuit, and this necessitated a new North Curve. A special 43-degree "wall of death" banked corner was therefore constructed, promising to raise even further the already frighteningly high lap speeds. The Avus race was to be run in two seven-lap heats and an eight-lap, 96-mile final. Caracciola and von Brauchitsch raised Mercedes' hopes by winning the heats, but it was Hermann Lang who led the field home in the final at an *average* speed of 162.61 mph! After receiving his victory laurels from Huhnlein, German minister of sport, one of the first to congratulate him in the winner's podium was propaganda minister, Goebbels.

A new lap record in the Belgian Grand Prix, where he was timed on one stretch of the Spa circuit at 195 mph, confirmed Lang as one of the fastest drivers of his time, but victory eluded him for the remainder of the season: indeed, he was lucky to survive the year.

The main feature of the old Masaryk circuit at Brno, scene of that year's Czechoslovakian Grand Prix, were solid kilometre stones that marked the edge of the road. Lang, having made a promising start to the race, entered a corner that had loose pebbles and earth scattered over it by another car. His Mercedes slid outwards and hit one of the markers, overturning the car and hitting a group of spectators seated in a forbidden area by the trackside: two were killed instantly and a dozen more seriously injured. Poor Lang was held responsible by the local authorities, the case going before three courts and dragging on for four years before he was cleared from blame.

The following season, 1938, saw the introduction of a new set of regulations that were intended not only as a chance for the French and Italian teams to get on a par with the might of Germany, but also as an effort to reduce the ferocious speeds that had been witnessed the previous year. After early season problems with the new 3-litre supercharged W154, Hermann Lang and Mercedes were quickly into their stride with a crushing 1–2–3 victory at Tripoli in May, Lang leading the way home. By early August the team had gathered at Livorno, Italy, for the Coppa Ciano. Following Caracciola's retirement, Lang led from von Brauchitsch, who kept trying to pass him but could not succeed—much to the aristocrat's annoyance. While making a desperate attempt to overtake on a corner, von Brauchitsch slid off the track where, despite his protests, several excited spectators pushed him back on to the road. He then drove like a man possessed and overtook Lang when the latter had to pit for fresh tyres. Brauchitsch took the chequered flag, only to be disqualified later for receiving outside assistance and Lang was pronounced the winner after all.

A week later came the Pescara race for the Coppa Acerbo. If luck was on Lang's side at Livorno it deserted him here. On lap four his engine exploded, a fragment severing the main fuel line, and the car caught fire. His overalls were burning as he frantically stopped the car, leaping from the cockpit in an effort to find sand or water to extinguish the blazing Mercedes. With over 50 gallons of high-octane fuel on board, nothing could save it from being reduced to a pile of ashes. On returning to the pits, the bitterly disappointed Lang was warmly greeted by team manager Neubauer, unconcerned about the total loss of a highly expensive racing car. "We can always make another racing car, but not another Lang," he said.

The year 1939 was to see the end of an era. What with Hitler's invasion of Czechoslovakia, it was difficult to disassociate Grand Prix racing on the German scale from power politics, yet the cars remained fascinating for their technical brilliance and shattering performance, and their drivers for their courage and tremendous skill. For Hermann Lang, the year was to see him dominate the Grand Prix season. The former racing mechanic could certainly drive quickly, but he did it with his head, having the technical ability to extract the very best from his car, although his success was not so popular with his German team-mates. Von Brauchitsch disliked being eclipsed by a former mechanic, while Caracciola, as team leader, complained at the Nürburgring (the scene of Lang's third consecutive 1939 win) that he was given an inferior car. British team-mate Richard Seaman was to sum up the feelings in the camp by saying, "Their whole wrath is, of course, directed against poor Lang, with whom they are now starting to include Seaman, apparently for the sole reason that we are younger and have our share of success." He went on to add, "Quite apart from his driving, he is a good fellow and not a sulky child like the others."

Tragically, the friendship between the two ended at the very next race when Seaman lost his life in the Belgian Grand Prix. Seeing Seaman trapped in his blazing car "like a stone statue" (to quote from his book *Grand Prix Driver*), Lang wanted to pull out of the race, but Neubauer bade him continue to a reluctant, joyless victory.

Lang retired from the German Grand Prix but bounced back to lead an impressive Mercedes 1–2–3 in the Swiss. The victory clinched the title of European Champion for him and, as he also won two hill-climbs at Vienna and Grosslockner, he became European Mountain Champion—an extraordinary achievement.

One can only imagine the success that Lang would have achieved had not the war interrupted his career. Judging by his return to racing in 1946—marked by a win at the Ruhestein hill-climb—it was apparent that none of his form had been lost to the intervening years. Although Mercedes-Benz were not allowed to compete again in international racing until 1950, their real return was in 1952 with the 300SL "Gullwing" sports car, when Lang took a second place at Berne, won the prestigious Le Mans 24-hour race, and then led a Mercedes 1–2–3–4 at the sports car Grand Prix at the Nürburgring. His last major achievement was a brilliant second place to his team-mate Karl Kling in the Carrera Pan-America in Mexico, one of the toughest long-distance races ever. His retirement from the sport came in 1954 after the Grand Prix of Europe held at the Nürburgring. There he drove one of the four works Mercedes but had the bad luck, while lying second to Fangio, to spin off and retire. It was a quiet end to a brilliant racing career.

Hermann Lang's love affair with Mercedes did not end there, for he continued as a service inspector for the engine and chassis areas of Daimler-Benz throughout Germany, finally retiring in 1974. The company always treated him as a star, with celebrations for his fortieth anniversary with the organization, and for his seventy-fifth birthday. And, no doubt remembering the loyalty and remarkable career of their former mechanic, the board of directors took great pleasure in allowing Lang to "keep his hand in" by giving demonstration runs in the historic Silver Arrows—a task that he was thrilled to carry out well into his seventies.

Of the countless thousands that bore witness to the feats of the pre-war racers, sadly few survive. Therefore, let this writer leave the last words to the photographer, George Monkhouse, who was present at the 1937 British Grand Prix: "Nothing I can say will give any idea of the reaction this amazing start produced in the spectators, who had never heard, smelt or seen anything like it in their lives....Hardly had they recovered their breath when Lang shot the crest of Starkey's Straight in a cloud of white dust at 170 mph, the rest of the silver cars at his heels. Grand Prix racing had really come to Britain at last!"

Born Hermann Lang. **Marriage** Lydia. **Children** Peter. **Career** Apprenticed to motor-cycle mechanic, 1923; entered various motor-cycle racing events, 1923–31, including Tour of Württemberg, circuit events, Solitude, near Stuttgart; raced for Standard motor-cycles, becoming their leading side-car rider, 1929–31; German hill-climb champion, 1931; fractured skull, 1931; drove diesel train in gravel pit; joined Daimler-Benz test department, 1934, reserve driver for Mercedes, 1935; finished fifth in first race at Nürburgring; full time driver for Mercedes, 1936–39, 1946–54; service inspector, 1954–74. **Major wins** Tripoli Grand Prix, 1937, 1938, 1939; Avus-rennen, Berlin, 1937; Coppa Ciano, Livorno, 1938; Belgian Grand Prix, Spa, 1939; Pau Grand Prix, France, 1939; Swiss Grand Prix, Berne, 1939; Eiffelrennen, Nürburgring, 1939; European Champion, 1939; Ruhestein hill climb, 1946; first place (with Reiss), Le Mans 24-hours, 1952; Sports Car Grand Prix, Nürburgring, 1952. **Publications** *Grand Prix Driver* (autobiography), Somerset, 1953. **Cause of death** Undisclosed, at age 77.

PHILIP LEVINE

American Medical Researcher

***Born* Kletsk, Russia, 10 August 1900**

***Died* New York City, New York, 18 October 1987**

Dr Philip Levine's life work was the study of human blood, and he was one of the great pioneers in the subject. The crucial part he played in the discovery of the Rhesus factor in blood was probably his greatest achievement. This not only made blood transfusions safer, but it also cut the rate of infant mortality.

Philip Levine was born in pre-Revolutionary Russia, emigrating to the United States with his family when he was only eight. They settled in Brooklyn, New York, where the young Philip attended Brooklyn Boys' High School. From there he went to the City College of New York, to which he won a scholarship in 1916. After the US entered the war in 1917, he served as an infantry private in the Students' Army Training Corps, which later made him eligible for an ex-serviceman's grant and helped pay his fees at Cornell University Medical School.

Some of his research for his higher degrees had been into allergies, and his instructor, Professor Coca, sent him as an assistant to Karl Landsteiner at the Rockefeller Institute of Medical Research. Here he studied the relationship between human and chimpanzee blood, and also the susceptibility of blood to introduced foreign material, such as proteins.

In 1901 Karl Landsteiner had first classified blood by the proteins it contains, group A containing the protein labelled A in the outer membranes of red cells, group B protein B, group O containing neither, and group AB both. Landsteiner had demonstrated that group A opposed the introduction of group B proteins, with red cells being destroyed and clots forming, and vice versa, while group O opposed both proteins and group AB neither. His work had shown how some transfusions up to that time had been beneficial but others fatal, and his grouping led to success in nearly every case. He was awarded the Nobel Prize in 1930 for this advance.

Levine was fascinated by Landsteiner's conviction that human blood was individual, so he continued under him working on the same lines, and it was during his seven years at the institute that he discovered three new blood groups—M, N and P.

In 1932 Levine became an instructor at the University of Wisconsin, where he investigated the substances in human and animal intestines which destroy disease bacteria. He still retained his interest in blood grouping, and sponsored a law granting Wisconsin courts the power to order blood tests in cases of disputed paternity. He also studied the distribution of blood factors M and N among tribes of Blackfoot Indians.

The year 1935 saw his return to the East Coast, when he worked as a bacteriologist and immunologist at Beth Israel Hospital in Newark, New Jersey. Here he sponsored a similar blood test law to Wisconsin's and was given charge of the blood bank. He was particularly interested in the way red cells were destroyed after transfusions, even though the blood groups matched. In 1939 he collaborated with R.E. Stetson on an article for the *Journal of the American Medical Association*, in which he described such a case when a woman had had a stillbirth. He suggested that the failure of the transfusion must have been caused by the disintegrating products of the foetus, the first time anyone had made this suggestion. In 1941, in another article in the same journal, he suggested the factor involved appeared to parallel "the anti-Rhesus agglutinin of Landsteiner and Wiener".

The Rhesus factor consists of antigens, sources of antibodies, first identified in the Rhesus monkey. About 85 per cent of humans have this factor in their blood, so they are Rh-positive; the remaining 15 per cent are Rh-negative. Landsteiner and Wiener found that continual transfusions of Rh-positive blood into a Rh-negative recipient would build up antibodies which meant there would be destruction of red blood cells. But this also happened in some pregnant women even at the first transfusion. As a result of Levine's work, it was realized that when a Rh-negative women bore a Rh-positive foetus because of a Rh-positive father, the exchange of blood through the placenta could mean the mother built up antibodies to Rh-positive blood. In her future pregnancies, the baby could suffer from anaemia or jaundice while still in the womb, leading to brain damage, and this was often fatal. Perhaps as many as one in 150 babies fitted this category, and as a result of Levine's work, many thousands of babies were saved by administering drugs to suppress the mother's formation of antibodies or by giving the baby, often still *in utero*, a complete change of blood.

Although this was Levine's most productive discovery, his further work on the classification of blood and the blood problems in the newborn led him to discover many new blood groups. These discoveries made the subject progressively more complicated, but eventually he clarified these too.

In 1944 he moved to the Ortho Research Division in Raritan, New Jersey, where he worked as director of the immunohaematology division until his retirement in 1965. His advice was sought by scientists worldwide, and his laboratory was well known for its research and training. Cancer was a target for Levine's later research, and one of his most important discoveries was that blood serum of some cancer patients could become toxic to their cancer cells. This valuable finding offers prospects of long-standing remission with some kinds of the disease.

Dr Levine continued with his work even after retirement, until he was forced by ill-health to give it up a year before he died. The fascination of the search for the unknown never left him, and he was universally admired for his capacity to solve research problems of extraordinary complexity.

Born Philip Levine. **Parents** Morris and Fay (Zirulick) Levine. **Marriage** Hilda Lillian Perlmutter, attorney, 1938. **Children** Phyllis Ann, Mark Armin, Paul Karl and Victor Raphael. **Education** Brooklyn Boys' High School; College of the City of New York, BS, 1919; Cornell University Medical School, MD, 1923, MA, 1926. **Emigration** Left Russia for USA, 1908. **Military service** Private, Students' Army Training Corps, World War I. **Career** Assistant, Rockefeller Institute, 1925–28, associate, 1928–32; instructor in pathology and bacteriology, University of Wisconsin, 1932–35; bacteriologist and immunologist, Beth Israel Hospital, New Jersey, 1935–44; director, immunohaematology division, Ortho Research Foundation, New Jersey, 1944–66, emeritus director from 1966. **Related activities** Member, advisory board, *Journal of Hematology*; seminar associate, Columbia University, from 1953; visiting investor, Sloan-Kettering Institute of Cancer Research, 1976; member, Board of Medical Control of the Blood Transfusion Association of New York; consultant: Jewish Memorial Hospital, New York, Nassau Hospital, Mineola, Muhlenburg Hospital, Plainfield, St Michael's Hospital, Newark. **Offices and memberships** Royal College of Physicians; National Academy of Science; American Society of Clinical Pathologists; American College of Physicians; American Society of Human Genetics (president, 1969); New York Academy of Science; New York Academy of Medicine; American Association for the Advancement of Science; American Association of Immunologists; Society for Experimental Biology and Medicine; Medical Association of the State of New Jersey; Harvey Society. **Awards and honours** Mead Johnson Award, 1943; Ward Burdick Award, American Society of Clinical Pathologists, 1946; Laker Ward, American Public Health Association, 1946; Phi Lambda Kappa Gold Medal, 1947; Norwegian Society of Immunohaematologists' Gold Medal, 1975; Allan Award, American

Society of Human Genetics, 1975; Passano Foundation Award; Landsteiner Award; Townsend Harris Award; Kennedy Award. **Publications** Numerous articles in academic journals. **Cause of death** Undisclosed, at age 87.

CLARE BOOTHE LUCE

American Playwright, Journalist and Diplomat

Born **New York City, New York, 10 April 1903**

Died **Washington, DC, 9 October 1987**

Looking at a photograph of Clare Boothe Luce at a certain age you see an unmistakably American face, lacking the "delicate, fragile beauty" attributed to her in her youth, but with a strength and cunning you can see has been earned over the years. Perhaps the type is best described as a combination of Nancy Reagan's slim and moneyed brand of elegance with the air of toughness given off by a smart, successful, self-made businesswoman. This, indeed, is not that far off the mark. She was certainly a self-made success story—and proud of it—but it is too limited. For Clare Boothe Luce combined in her one slight person the roles of war reporter, satirical columnist, playwright, politician, diplomat and (twice) millionaire's wife. In all of these guises she was renowned for her sharp tongue, which it must be said often came in useful. But there were also greater depths to her: a personal tragedy which tore her life in half, the fact that she was a devout Roman Catholic in later life, and her overall persona as a thoroughly emancipated woman, even if her relationship to feminism was often a problematic one.

She was born Ann Clare Boothe, the daughter of an ex-dancer and an amateur violinist-turned-businessman, in 1903. She spent most of her childhood in Memphis and Chicago, but her early years were etched with the acid of her parents' bad relationship; they separated before she had even reached adolescence. The experience left a lasting emotional scar, but the young Clare spent an enjoyable year in France with her mother before starting at secondary school. She was educated privately in New York, with her father coughing up in school fees what he could not muster in terms of personal attention; she graduated in 1919. In the meantime her mother had remarried. Dr Albert E. Austin, Clare's new stepfather, became important to her as a political example: she was to "inherit" much later—albeit under her own steam—the seat in Congress representing the fourth Connecticut District which he vacated in 1943.

After her mother's remarriage, Clare left home to go and work in New York. Temperamentally unsuited to office work, she quickly got bored in her job and enrolled at Clare Tree Major's School of Theater, planning to pursue a career on the stage and succeed where both her parents had failed. As a child she had been an understudy to Mary Pickford in *A Good Little Devil*, so a precedent had been set. But her grand design for the future took rather a different turn when, on a trip to Europe with her parents in 1919, she met Mrs O.H.P. Belmont. Through Mrs B. she became interested, and for a time actively involved, in the women's suffrage movement which was then beginning its final and most militant assault on male privilege in both the United States and Europe, especially Britain. Like many independently minded young women of her generation, Clare Boothe was absolutely devoted to the cause of justice, both as a disenfranchised female and as a Daughter of the American Revolution. During the early 1920s at least, her feminism was clear and uncompromising.

But Mrs Belmont had still another string to her bow for Clare: George Tuttle Brokaw, New York clothing manufacturer and the first of her millionaire husbands. They married in 1923, and although the marriage lasted only six years, it put paid to the young Mrs Brokaw's plans to be an actress. Adopting her own name again, Clare Boothe turned her hand to writing instead, joining the staff of *Vogue* in 1930 in the humble job of editorial assistant. Her rise in women's journalism was sensational: a year later she was promoted to associate editor on *Vanity Fair* and by 1933 she was managing editor. But having reached the top of the tree, she lost interest. What she really wanted to do was write; a first book—a collection of satirical columns—had been published in 1933 under the title *Stuffed Shirts*. Now she felt ready to write for the theatre.

After four false starts she finally got a play produced on Broadway in 1935. *Abide With Me*, a too-sombre psychological drama, according to the critics, was a phenomenal flop and closed almost as soon as it had opened. But never mind; Clare Boothe was ready to strike again, this time with *The Women*, which started in New York in December 1936, ran for 657 performances, toured the US, was made into a film and is still being performed quite regularly on a stage somewhere near you. *The Women*, a biting satire on the preoccupations of rich women and the minor wars being fought between them, had been written in three days and revised during rehearsals. It was a funny (in both senses) play for a feminist to write, with a wit and wealth of critical observation cutting relentlessly into the women who were its protagonists, but without the saving grace of social critique to put their situation into perspective. The play, therefore, has earned the dubious accolade of "controversial", a code word for misogynist; however, it is deemed to be acceptably so because it was written by a woman.

By this time Clare Boothe had become Clare Boothe Luce, the wife of Henry Robinson Luce who was then the owner and editor-in-chief of a press-empire involving *Time*, *Life* and *Fortune* magazines. Although this connection obviously could have yielded her interesting advantages in the shape of journalistic commissions, Luce preferred for the time being to continue with playwriting. In 1938 *Kiss the Boys Goodbye* was produced, a comedy which the author had meant to be taken as a "political allegory about Fascism" but which failed to have its pretensions of seriousness recognized. This was followed by *Margin for Error* in 1940, where the political reference was brought out much more clearly in a comedy-melodrama about the murder of a Nazi agent in the US. Despite the one huge and several limited successes in drama, it was evident that Clare Boothe Luce's writing would always be put in the comedy slot if she did not prove her mettle in another genre. For this, as it turned out, the outbreak of war gave ample opportunity.

In 1940 Clare Boothe Luce embarked on a trip to Europe to witness the Nazi machine roll westward and to report on the front-line situation for *Life*. The resulting *reportage*, *Europe in the Spring*, gives a detailed if hardly objective account of travels in Italy, the Netherlands, France and England during the German spring offensive of 1940. Reviews were mixed, but there was no doubt that Clare Boothe Luce had found her new medium in writing about political events abroad. Nor did she confine her political interests to outside. The year 1940 also marked the date when she got involved in election campaigns for the first time. The Republican candidate, Wendell Wilkie, was her man, but for Luce's own political career the publicity engendered by a journalistic feud between herself and fellow columnist Dorothy Thompson, who backed Roosevelt, was probably more important. For weeks the two women kept the general public entertained with their war of words over who was the most capable man to lead the country into war. In the end, Luce pronounced that "Roosevelt lied this country into war" and that Republican intervention was sorely needed to correct the "dictatorial bumbledom" of Democratic government.

All this proved a mere dress-rehearsal for Luce's own entry into politics as representative for the Fourth District of Connecticut in 1942. She had got there with the slogan "Let's fight a hard war instead of a soft war" and immediately became a member of the powerful House Military

Affairs Committee. During her term in Congress she was also concerned with the fate of war refugees, the question of which of the superpowers would control Poland after the German surrender, with UN controls on nuclear arms, and with equal pay for equal work (the feminist impulse asserting itself once more). Luce was elected for a second term in 1944, when she spent Christmas with American soldiers in Italy, thus proving that her words about the "hard war" were not just idle chat from the sidelines: she was prepared to face the danger too.

This second trip to Italy was perhaps a fateful one, for after the war, once General Eisenhower had been elected to the presidency, Clare Boothe Luce was asked to become his ambassador to Rome by way of thanks for the support she had given him in his campaign. Thanks to her notorious way with words—barbed or funny, usually both—little in Clare Boothe's political life had gone unnoticed or uncontested. But the opposition this time came from a different quarter: not so much from inside the US political establishment as from Italy, where the more conservative factions objected to a woman taking such high office and the communists on the other hand were worried about her religious leanings. In the end the problems were smoothed over and her appointment went ahead, but as the first woman to take on such an important foreign post she had a difficult time. For one thing, her sharp tongue hardly made her ideally suited to the niceties of diplomatic life; in addition, she managed to make herself unpopular by implying during the 1953 Italian elections that if the communists won, American aid would undoubtedly dry up. She left Italy in 1957 under something of a cloud.

In 1959 Eisenhower duly nominated her as ambassador to Brazil, a competitive post much fought over by career diplomats. This was a time when political appointments were wont to come under close scrutiny in Congress, and Democratic senator Wayne Morse managed to cast so much doubt on Luce's qualification for the job that she withdrew her application on the advice of her husband. From then on, apart from an edited collection of American and British fiction, *Saints for Now* (1952), and a book of her own, *Slam the Door Softly* (1969), Clare Boothe Luce was not much in the public eye, concentrating instead on journalism, script-writing and—not least importantly—matters of religion. In 1944 Clare Boothe Luce's only child, her daughter Ann Clare Brokaw, was killed in a car accident in Palo Alto, California. For this, the worst tragedy in any parent's life, there was no remedy, but it did make Luce turn more inward, away from the dazzling society of press and politicians in which she had been moving thus far. In 1946 she was received into the Roman Catholic Church, the faith which was to sustain her for the rest of her busy and often controversial life.

Born Ann Clare Boothe. **Parents** William F., a businessman, and Ann Clare, a dancer, (Snyder) Boothe. **Marriages** 1) George Tuttle Brokaw, 1923 (divorced, 1929); 2) Henry R. Luce, 1935 (deceased). **Children** Ann Clare, from first marriage (died, 1944). **Education** St Mary's, Garden City, New York, 1914–17; The Castle, Tarrytown, New York, 1917–19; Clare Tree Major's School of the Theater. **Career** Associate editor, *Vogue* magazine, 1930–31; associate editor, *Vanity Fair* magazine, 1931–32, managing editor, 1932–34; newspaper columnist, 1934; playwright, from 1935; journalist, under contract to *Life* magazine, Europe, 1940; entered active politics, campaigning for Republican presidential candidate Wendell Wilkie, 1940; reported for *Life* magazine from China, 1941, and Africa, India and Burma, 1942; member of US Congress, 1943–47; returned to writing, 1947; campaigned for successful Republican presidential candidate Dwight Eisenhower, 1952; US ambassador to Italy, 1953–57; retired from politics and resumed writing. **Other activities** Active in women's suffrage movement, early 1920s; received into Roman Catholic Church, 1946. **Offices and memberships** Former member, New Nationalist Party, early 1930s; first vice-chair, National Review Board, East-West Center; member: Academy of Political Science, American Institute of Foreign Trade, Daughters of the American Revolution; editorial board, *Encyclopaedia Britannica*. **Awards and honours** Cardinal Newman

Award, 1951; honorary degrees: Colby College, Fordham University, Mundelein College, Temple University, Creighton University, Georgetown University, Seton Hall College, St John's University. **Books** *Stuffed Shirts*, 1933; *Europe in the Spring*, published in UK as *European Spring*, 1940; (editor) *Saints For Now*, 1952. **Plays** *Abide with Me*, 1935; *The Women*, 1936 (filmed, 1939); *Kiss the Boys Goodbye*, 1938; *Margin for Error*, 1939; *Child of the Morning*, 1952; *Slam the Door Softly*, 1969. **Cause of death** Undisclosed, at age 84.

ANDRÉ MASSON

French Artist

Born **Balagny-sur-Thérain, France, 4 January 1896**

Died **Paris, France, 28 October 1987**

André Masson has never enjoyed the popularity of his fellow surrealists Dali, Ernst and Miró. Nevertheless, he made an important contribution to the surrealist movement, particularly in his "automatic" drawings and sand paintings, and though his name is unfamiliar to the average museum-goer, his importance has long been recognized by historians.

Like that of many modernists, Masson's artistic career began with a conventional academic training, first at the École des Beaux Arts in Brussels and then at the Beaux Arts in Paris, where he studied under Paul Badouin. He started art school early, in his middle teens, but his passionate love of reading meant that he missed little he would have picked up at school. His favourite reading was philosophy and at the age of 16 the young Masson worshipped Nietzsche. Philosophical speculation remained a basic habit throughout his life and gained expression in several books, the first of which, *Mythology of Nature, Mythology of Being*, came out in 1936. The title introduces Masson's other major teenage obsession—his interest in nature. Both nature and philosophy were to have a profound impact on his painting.

At the outbreak of World War I Masson enrolled immediately in the French Army. He was thrilled by the idea of war and eagerly anticipated "Wagnerian aspects of battle". Along with millions of others, he was swiftly disillusioned. Severely wounded—at one point actually believing himself to be dead—he had to spend several years in hospitals and psychiatric wards. His traumatic experiences transformed his thinking. He became acutely intolerant of rational philosophical systems and anarchic in all his ideas. The irrational mind acquired an entirely new importance for him and in the mid-1920s, having resumed painting in 1919, he gravitated naturally towards the surrealist camp, exhibiting in the first surrealist exhibition at the Galerie Pierre in Paris in 1925.

Taking their cue from Freud, the surrealists believed that Western society had been completely undermined by its stress on rational thinking. As Masson put it in 1960, "For us, the surrealists of 1924, the great prostitute was reason. It was cool reason after all which had led mankind into the war to end all wars." The necessary antidote, the surrealists argued, was to give free rein to the unconscious, irrational mind. Surrealist painters set about this in two ways. Some, like Dali and Magritte, concentrated on producing fantastic dream images, since Freud taught that in dreams the unconscious mind was expressing itself. The other approach was to make art "automatically", using pictorial techniques in which conscious decision-making by the artist had no part. Masson tried both. Works like the 1925 *Bird Pierced by the Arrow* offered dream imagery. In other pictures he worked "automatically".

In the 1920s he made a number of "automatic" drawings—doodles in which he let his hand go where it wanted. These products of Masson's "wandering line", as Gertrude Stein called it, could often be seen in *La Révolution Surréaliste*, the surrealist house magazine. Masson's other "automatic" technique was an original one. He would spatter glue randomly over a canvas and then sprinkle it with sand which stuck to the sticky areas. With the addition of some paint marks he would, in theory, achieve a completely accidental painting. The fact that these pictures usually contain recognizable figures invites some scepticism about just how automatic they actually were, but they were nevertheless held by the surrealists to be the purist expressions of the unconscious mind.

Internal politics in the surrealist group were always tempestuous and in 1929 Masson split with the ringleader, André Breton. Despite this, his links with surrealism remained strong. In 1930 he was co-founder of the surrealist review *Minotaure*. In his art he also continued to work with ideas that were entirely surrealist. Pictures from the early 1930s deal mainly with the themes of eroticism and violence, since these two impulses were for Masson basic to the unconscious.

From 1934 until the civil war broke out in 1936, Masson lived in Spain. This sojourn led to a series of works peopled by half-men, half-bulls, which, once again, derived from his obsession with the animal nature of the unconscious. In the later 1930s Masson worked on several series of pictures using the ideas of metamorphosis, anthropomorphic furniture and the mythology of nature, and in these years he was finally reconciled with Breton.

Like most of the surrealists, Masson moved to the United States in 1941 to escape the German invasion of France, staying there till the end of the war. He had always been fascinated in myth, seen in surrealist circles as yet another manifestation of the unconscious mind. In the US he became interested in the myths of the North American Indians and produced a number of abstracted evocations of them, such as *The Maize Myth* (1942). Largely due to the impact of a number of exhibitions of surrealism held in the US in the early 1940s, surrealist ideas had a strong effect on the new generation of American painters. Masson was heavily involved in the organization of these exhibitions and his interest in myth seems to have been particularly influential with the future abstract impressionists Jackson Pollock and Mark Rothko, both of whom began producing myth paintings at this time.

Masson was constantly exploring new ideas, and though a committed avant-gardist, he did not hesitate to experiment with more conventional painting ideas if they interested him. In the early 1950s, for example, he suddenly produced a series of landscapes using impressionistic colour and expressive brushwork which were far less progressive than his earlier work. Shifting again, the later 1950s saw the development of a sort of abstract calligraphy which probably derived from abstract expressionism, a borrowing that earned him some harsh criticism in the art press. This style, in several variations, was to be the dominant feature of his late work.

Masson was not solely an easel painter. At several points in his career he did designs for the stage, the first being those he made for Massine's *Les Présages* danced by the Ballet Russe in 1933. In 1963 he won a prize for his theatre designs at the Sao Paulo Biennale. He also had one major decorative commission—the ceiling for the Théâtre de Paris—which he executed in 1965. As well as these, he produced sculpture, graphic work and book illustrations, also finding time to write several philosophical books. Towards the end of his life he received several honours, being made an officer of the Legion of Merit and a Commander of Arts and Letters.

Born André Aimé René Masson. **Parents** Aimé and Marthe (Bénard) Masson. **Marriages** 2) Rose Makles, 1934. **Children** Gladys from first marriage; Diego and Luis from second marriage. **Education** Académie Royale des Beaux-Arts, Brussels; École Nationale Supérieure des Beaux-Arts, Paris, 1912. **Military service** French Army, 1914–19. **Career** Odd jobs as ceramic decorator, deliveryman, proofreader, Paris, 1920s; associate of surrealists, 1924–29; first book illustrations, 1925; first sculptures, 1928; moved to Grasse, southern France, 1932; produced theatre designs, for Ballet Russe de Monte Carlo, 1933; illustrator for *Acephale*, edited by Georges Bataille, 1933; lived and painted in Tossa de Mar, Catalonia, Spain, 1934–36, Lyons-la-Fôret, France, 1937; produced theatre designs for Jean-Louis Barrault, Léonide Massine and Jean-Paul Sartre, from 1937; co-founder, *Minotaure* review, Paris, 1939; lived in Freluc, Auvergne, France, 1940–41; lived in Connecticut, 1941–45; organized conference, *Origins of Surrealism*, Baltimore Museum of Art, 1941, Mount Holyoke College, Massachusetts, 1943; associated with exiled surrealists, organized conferences, lectures and exhibitions, New York, 1941–45; lived in Poitiers and Aix-en-Provence, France, 1946–47; produced first lithographs, 1948; travelled extensively in Europe, particularly Italy, from 1950; designed ceiling of Odéon, Théatre de France, Paris, 1965; first tapestry designs, 1967. **Other activities** Organized concerts with Karlheinz Stockhausen, 1970; participated in film, *Arts et l'emphémère* by Pierre Schneider, 1971, and television film on Matisse, with Hans Hartung and Georges Mathieu, 1973. **Offices and memberships** Member, Council of National Museums, 1962. **Awards and honours** Grand Prix National des Arts, 1954; Officer, Legion of Honour; Commander des Arts et des Lettres: Sao Paulo Biennale Prize, 1963. **Publications** *Mythology of Being*, New York, 1942; *Anatomy of My Universe*, New York, 1943; *Nocturnal Notebook*, New York, 1944; *Bestiaire*, New York, 1946; *Mythologies*, Paris, 1946; *Caret de Croquis*, Paris, 1950; *Le Plaisir de peindre*, Nice, 1950; *Voyage à Venise*, Paris, 1952; *Métamorphose de l'artiste*, Geneva, 1956; *La Mémoire du monde*, Geneva, 1974. **Books illustrated** *Soleils bas* by Georges Limbour, Paris, 1924; *L'Anus solitaire* by Georges Bataille, Paris, 1931; *Terre sur terre* by Tristan Tzara, Paris, 1946; *Le Dit du vieux marin Christobel et Koubla Khan* by Samuel Taylor Coleridge, Paris, 1948; *Un Saison en enfer* by Rimbaud, 1960; *Oeuvres complètes: essais philosophiques* by Albert Camus, Paris, 1962; *L'Idiot* by Dostoevsky, Paris, 1966. **Individual exhibitions** Galerie Simon, Paris, 1923, 1929, 1936; Pierre Matisse Gallery, New York, 1935; Wildenstein and Company, London, 1936; Baltimore Museum of Art, 1941; Buchholz Gallery, New York, 1942, 1943, 1944, 1945, 1947, 1949; Willard Gallery, New York, 1942; Arts Club of Chicago, 1942; Paul Rosenberg Gallery, New York, 1944; Galerie Louise Leiris, Paris, 1945, 1947, 1948, 1950, 1952, 1954, 1957, 1960, 1962, 1968, 1970, 1973, 1983, 1986; Palais des Beaux-Arts, Brussels, 1946; Arts Council Gallery, London, 1947; Landesamt für Museen, Fribourg, Switzerland, 1949; Kunsthalle, Basle (with Alberto Giacometti), 1950; Paul Rosenberg Gallery, New York, 1953; Curt Valentin Gallery, New York, 1953; Kunstverein, Düsseldorf (toured West Germny), 1954; Kestner-Gesellschaft, Hanover, 1955; Leicester Galleries, London, 1955; Galerie Lucien Blanc, Paris, 1956; Galerie der Spiegel, Cologne, 1957; Galerie R. Hoffman, Hamburg, 1957; Albertina Akademie, Vienna, 1958; Saidenberg Gallery, New York, 1958, 1961, 1966; *Biennale*, Venice, 1958; Marlborough Fine Art, London, 1962; Edgardo Acosta Gallery, Beverly Hills, California (travelled to the Pasadena Art Museum, California and Santa Barbara Museum of Art, California), 1958; Kunstkabinett Klihm, Munich, 1958; Galerie Furstenberg, Paris, 1958; Meijishobo, Tokyo, 1958; Galleria Bussola, Turin, 1959, 1970; Galleria Il Segno, Rome, 1960; Galerie Renée Ziegler, Zurich, 1960, 1966; Svensk-Franska Konstgalleriet, Stockholm, 1960; Richard Feigen Gallery, Chicago, 1961; Galerie Gerald Cramer, Geneva, 1963, 1965, (with Max Ernst) 1971; Galerie du Perron, Geneva, 1963; Stedelijk Museum, Amsterdam, 1964; Akademie der Künste, Berlin, 1964; Musée National d'Art Moderne, Paris, 1965; Galerie Michael Hertz, Bremen, West Germany, 1965, 1972; Tel Aviv Museum, 1965; Galerie Françoise Ledoux, Paris, 1965; Galerie les Contards, Lactose, Vaucluse, France, 1966; Galerie Wünsche, Bonn, 1966; Musée des Beaux-Arts, Lyons, 1967; La Nuova Loggia, Bologna, 1967, 1970; Galerie Vincent Kramer, Prague, 1967; Musée Cantini, Marseilles, 1968; Galerie Lucie Weil, Paris, 1968; Musée, St Étienne du

Roubray, France, 1968; Galleria Il Fauno, Turin, 1969; Galerie Sagot-le-Garée, Paris, 1969; Casino Comunal, Knokke-le-Zoute, Belgium, 1969; Palazzo dei Diamanti, Ferrara, Italy, 1969; Museum am Ostwall, Dortmund (travelled to the Klingenmuseum, Solingen, West Germany and the Pfalzgalerie, Kaiserlauten, West Germany), 1969; Galleria Schwarz, Milan, 1970, 1973; Centre d'Art, Beirut, 1971; Basil Jacobs Fine Art, London, 1971; Salle des Fêtes, Bobigny, France, 1971; Galerie Andelt, Wiesbaden, 1971; Galerie de l'Éditeur, Paris, 1971; Maison de la Culture, Amiens, France, 1971; Maison des Arts et Loisirs, Montbeliard, France, 1972; Galerie de Seine, Paris, 1972, 1975; Waddington Galleries, London, 1972; Lerner-Heller Gallery, New York, 1972, 1973, 1975, 1976; Blue Moon Gallery, New York, 1972, 1973, 1975, 1976; *Salon de la Quinzaine d'Art en Quency*, Montauban, France, 1972; Galerie Verrière, Paris, 1972; Galerie Ariane, Gothenburg, Sweden, 1972; Galleria Zanini, Rome, 1973; Galleria San Sebastianello, Rome, 1973; Centre d'Art 2, Beirut, 1973; Mayor Gallery, London, 1973; Galerie Jacques Davidson, Tours, France, 1973; Galerie du Lion, Paris, 1973; Musée de l'Art et d'Histoire, Fribourg, Switzerland (travelled to the Galerie Gerald Cramer, Geneva), 1973; Galerie Benador, Geneva, 1974; *Opere 1925–73*, Il Collezionista d'Arte Contemporanea, Rome, 1974; Galerie Claude Tchou, Paris, 1974; Musée Grand-Palais de Malte, Aix-en-Provence, 1975; Musée d'Art Moderne de la Ville, Paris, 1976; Museum of Modern Art, New York, 1976; Grand Palais, Paris, 1977; Galerie Patrick Cramer, Geneva, 1978; Orsanmichele, Florence, 1981; Marisa del Re Gallery, New York, 1981, 1987; Foundation Royaumont, Belgium, 1985; Artcurial, Paris, 1986; Galerie Jade, Colmar, France, 1987; Edward Totah Gallery, London 1988. **Selected group exhibitions** *Peintures Surréalistes*, Galerie Pierre, Paris, 1925; *International Surrealist Exhibition*, Burlington Galleries, London, 1936; *Fantastic Art, Dada, Surrealism*, Museum of Modern Art, New York, 1937; *First Papers of Surrealism*, Reed Mansion, New York, 1942; *Surrealistische Malerei in Europa*, Saarbrucken Museum, West Germany, 1952; *Art Français Contemporain*, Palais des Beaux-Arts, Brussels, 1966; *Dada, Surrealism and Their Heritage*, Museum of Modern Art, New York (travelled to the Los Angeles county Museum of Art and the Art Institute of Chicago), 1968; *Futurism: A Modern Focus*, Guggenheim Museum, New York, 1973; *Surrealism*, National Museum of Modern Art, Tokyo, 1975; *Neue Wirklichkeit: Surrealismus und Neue Sachlichkeit*, Orangerie, Schloss Charlottenburg, Berlin, 1977. **Collections** Centre Georges Pompidou, Paris; Musée d'Art Moderne de la Ville, Paris; Wallraf-Richartz Museum, Cologne; Folkwang Museum, Wessen; Nationalgalerie, Berlin; Tate Gallery, London; Museum of Modern Art, New York; Hirshhorn Museum, Washington, DC; National Gallery of Victoria, Melbourne. **Selected theatrical designs** *Les Présages* (ballet), 1933; *Numances* (play), 1937; *Medea* (opera), 1940; *Hamlet* (play), 1946; *Wozzeck* (opera), 1963. **Cause of death** Undisclosed, at age 91. **Further reading** Jean-Louis Barrault, Georges Bataille, André Breton and others, *André Masson*, Rouen, 1940; Michel Leiris and Georges Limbour, *André Masson and His Universe*, Geneva, 1947; Hubert Juin, *André Masson*, Paris, 1963; Otto Hahn, *Masson*, Paris, New York and London, 1965; Jean-Paul Clébert, *Mythologie d'André Masson*, Geneva, 1971; L.M. Sapphire, *André Masson*, New York, 1973; Michel Leiris, Paul Elouard, André Breton and others, *André Masson: Opere 1925–73* (exhibition catalogue), Rome, 1974; René Passeron, *André Masson et les puissances du signe*, Paris, 1975; William Rubin and Carolyn Lanchner, *André Masson* (exhibition catalogue), New York, 1975; William Rubin, Carolyn Lanchner and Michel Leiris, *André Masson* (exhibition catalogue), Paris, 1977; Bernard Noel, *André Masson* (exhibition catalogue with text), Royaumont, 1985; Claude Duthuit, *André Masson* (exhibition catalogue with text), Paris 1986. **Further viewing** *André Masson et les quatre eléments* by Jean Gremillon, 1959; *A la source de la femme aimée* by Nelly Kaplan, 1966; *Perspectives surréalistes: les metamorphoses*, ORTF-TV film, 1971; *Le Monde imaginaire d'André Masson*, with the sculptor Hansjorg Gesigner, TV film 1973.

SIR PETER MEDAWAR

British Medical Researcher

***Born* Rio de Janeiro, Brazil, 28 February 1915**

***Died* London, England, 2 October 1987**

Transplants of hearts, lungs and other organs, unthinkable not so long ago, are everyday occurrences now. It was for his fundamental work on tissue grafting, which provided the foundations on which organ transplants are based, that Sir Peter Medawar was made a co-recipient of a Nobel Prize in 1960.

He was born in South America, his mother being English, his father a Lebanese businessman. For his education he was sent back to Britain, where he went from Marlborough College to Magdalen College, Oxford. Here, under the influence of Sir Howard Florey who gained a Nobel Prize for his work on penicillin, he distinguished himself academically and obtained a first class honours degree in zoology. A fellow student of his was Jean Taylor whom he married in 1937. In 1938 he was appointed a fellow of the college.

Although his training had been in zoology and he was by inclination a physiologist, his determined development as an expert in clinical immunology was partly the result of chance. Early in World War II a bomber crashed close to his home, and one of the surviving airmen had third-degree burns on 60 per cent of his body. This unfortunate occurrence sparked Medawar to investigate tissue transplants. He began by studying human grafts on military casualities at the burns unit of Glasgow Royal Infirmary and was among the first to recognize the "rejection reaction". At the same time he developed a concentrated solution of fibrinogen, a biological "glue" which helps in skin grafts to unite the ends of nerves.

It had been known for a very long time that skin could be transplanted on to another part of a patient, or to an identical twin, but otherwise it was thought there would be no chance of success. However, blood transfusion had been found practical once the antigens, the substances which produce antibodies, had been classified; it had then been possible to find donors' blood for which the patient had no antigens. Would similar classification make skin grafts acceptable?

To investigate, Medawar used rabbits on which he grafted skin. He found that a graft from a genetically different rabbit was accepted at first but, after a long delay, it would be shed. A second skin graft from the same animal would be shed much more quickly and vigorously. If skin from another rabbit altogether was then grafted, it would be rejected in a similar way to the first transplant. These results indicated natural and acquired immunity. How long and how vigorously the rejection took was later shown to depend on how different the donor and recipient were in their antigens.

Medawar and his colleagues, particularly Rupert Billingham and Leslie Brent, studied cells, especially lymphocytes, as the agents of graft rejection and other immunological phenomena. As has often been the case in scientific advances, it was an experiment that went wrong which proved to be the greatest step forward. They were hoping to distinguish between fraternal and identical twin cattle while still unborn, and thought that acceptance or rejection of skin grafts would show this. However, they found that the grafts were permanently accepted, even between brother and sister cattle when the skin was transferred in the womb.

Medawar read how Dr R.D. Owen in the US had demonstrated that fraternal twin cattle, which share the same placenta and have a common blood circulation in the womb, possess each other's red blood cells even when adult, so they have acquired tolerance of each other's blood. Medawar realized he had accidentally discovered the same could occur with tissues.

Sir Macfarlane Burnet of the University of Melbourne, an expert in influenza, leukaemia and virus diseases, had been consulting with Medawar about their experiments, and came to the conclusion that immunological defences were not inherited or transmitted at the time of conception, but developed in the embryo. Full immunological protection was only acquired gradually *after* birth. By introducing a foreign element or pattern from selected donors during this period of immunological development, the body might be taught to tolerate grafts.

Dr Medawar, who had been professor at Birmingham, now moved to London University where he seized the opportunity presented by Burnet's theories to attack with experimental evidence the hallowed concept that the body has immunological defences, and "anything foreign must be harmful". This idea, he felt, was "ground out in a totally indiscriminate fashion with results that are sometimes irritating, sometimes harmful, and sometimes mortally harmful. It is far better to have immunological defences than not to have them, but this does not mean that we are to marvel at them as evidences of a high and wise design."

With his team of researchers in London, he injected mice embryos with tissue from an adult mouse and found it did not affect the embryo's development. When the mouse was fully developed, tissue from the original donor's strain was grafted on—and accepted. The mouse had "acquired immunological tolerance".

Not only had this conclusively demonstrated that the barriers to foreign tissue transplants and organ grafts could be overcome by subtle means in certain circumstancs, instead of requiring whole-body X-radiation or drastic drugs, but it also explained why the body does not normally reject its own cellular substances, and what happens when it does, in auto-immune disease for instance. Developing from this work, it is now possible to match donor and recipient so that hearts, kidneys and other organs can be accepted.

Dr Peter Medawar and Sir Macfarlane Burnet, the collaborating leaders in this research, shared the Nobel Prize in 1960. There were many other degrees, honours and awards, and Medawar, who had been elected a fellow of the Royal Society at the early age of 34, became Sir Peter Medawar in 1965. By then he had moved from London University to become director of the National Institute for Medical Research at Mill Hill, a post he held until 1971. Here he was in charge of many intelligent young scientists, and a flood of important scientific papers was generated. It was during this time that disaster struck him personally.

In 1969 the British Association, of which Sir Peter was president, was meeting in Exeter. While reading the lesson during Sunday service in the cathedral, he suffered a brain haemorrhage and was severely handicapped for the rest of his life. This was a tragedy for a relatively young man of 54 who enjoyed all sorts of sport. However, the way he coped with his afflictions was both astonishing and inspiring, every new set-back being met with a keen determination to go on with life, and he never lost his zest for conversation or his sense of humour.

His work continued. He gave up the directorship of the National Institute for Medical Research, moving to the Clinical Research Centre at Northwick Park, where he worked with a small research group on the problems of cancer. His wide-ranging interests are reflected in his numerous publications. These include *The Uniqueness of the Individual*, *The Art of the Soluble*, *Advice to a Young Scientist*, *Pluto's Republic* and the largely autobiographical *Memoirs of a Thinking Radish*. In this final book he described, without self-pity and with great humour, what it is like to be physically handicapped.

Born Peter Brian Medawar. **Parents** Nicholas, a businessman, and Edith Muriel (Dowling) Medawar. **Marriage** Jean Shinglewood Taylor, 1937. **Children** Two daughters and two sons. **Education** Marlborough College; Magdalen College, Oxford; Christopher Welch Scholar and Senior Demy of Magdalen College, 1935. **Career** Fellow of Magdalen College, 1938–44, 1946–47; senior research fellow and university demonstrator in zoology and comparitive anatomy, St

John's College, Oxford, 1944; Mason Professor of zoology, University of Birmingham, 1947–51; Jodrell Professor of zoology and comparative anatomy, University College, London, 1951–62; director, National Institute for Medical Research, Mill Hill, 1962–71, director emeritus, from 1975; professor of experimental medicine, Royal Institution, London, 1977–83. **Related activities** Lectures included: Harvey, New York, 1957, Croonian, Royal Society, 1958, Reith, British Broadcasting Corporation, 1959, Dunham, Harvard Medical School, 1959, Romanes, 1968, Danz, Washington University, St Louis, 1984; University of Otago, New Zealand; Cultural Exchange Programme, Soviet Union; professor-at-large, Cornell University, New York, 1965; president, British Association for the Advancement of Science, 1968–69; president, Royal Postgraduate Medical School, London, from 1981. **Offices and memberships** Fellow, Royal Society, 1949; member: Agricultural Research Council, 1952–62, Medical Research Council Committee investigating nuclear radiation hazards, 1955–56, University Grants Committee, 1955–59, Medical Research Council, 1962–84, Royal Commission on Medical Education, 1965–68, board of consultants, Sloan-Kettering Cancer Research Institute, New York, Institute of Cellular Pathology, Brussels, New York Academy of Sciences, 1959, American Academy of Arts and Sciences, 1959, American Philosophical Society, 1961, National Academy of Sciences, USA, 1965, Indian Academy of Sciences, 1967. **Awards and honours** Commander, Order of the British Empire, 1958; Royal Medal of the Royal Society, 1959; (with Sir Macfarlane Burnet) Nobel Prize for Medicine, 1960; knighted, 1965; Copley Medal, 1969; Companion of Honour, 1972; Order of Merit, 1981; honorary fellowships: St Catherine's College, Oxford, 1960, American College of Physicians, 1964, Royal Society of Edinburgh, 1965, Royal College of Physicians of Edinburgh, 1966, Royal College of Physicians and Surgeons of Canada, 1966, Royal College of Surgeons, 1967, Royal College of Pathology, 1971, University College, London, 1971; honorary doctorates: Aston, Birmingham, Cambridge, Dundee, Exeter, Glasgow, Hull, London, Queen's (Glasgow), Southampton, Brussels, Liège, Alberta, Dalhousie (Halifax, Nova Scotia), Harvard, Chicago, Florida, Gustavus Adolphus College (Minnesota), Brazil. **Publications** (all published in London, unless stated) (editor, with W.E. LeGros) *Essays on Growth and Form Presented to D'Arcy Wentworth Thompson*, Oxford, 1945; *An Unsolved Problem of Biology*, 1952; *The Uniqueness of the Individual*, London and New York, 1957; (editor) *Biological Problems of Grafting: A Symposium*, Liège and Springfield, 1959; *The Future of Man*, London and New York, 1960; (editor, with D.V. Glass) *A Discussion on Demography*, 1963; *The Art of the Soluble: Creativity and Originality in Science*, 1967; *Recent Advances in the Immunology of Transplantation Genetics and the Future of Man*, St Louis, 1968; *Induction and Intuition in Scientific Thought*, London and Philadelphia, 1969; *The Hope of Progress*, 1972; (with J.S. Medawar) *Life Science*, 1977; (editor, with J.H. Shelley) *Structure in Science and Art: Symposium Proceedings*, New York, 1980; *Advice to a Young Scientist*, London and New York, 1980; *Pluto's Republic*, 1982; (with J.S. Medawar) *Aristotle to Zoos: Philosophical Dictionary of Biology*, 1984; *The Limits of Science*, 1985; *Memoirs of a Thinking Radish*, 1986. **Cause of death** Series of strokes, at age 72.

W.N. MEDLICOTT

British Historian

Born **Wandsworth, London, 11 May 1900**

Died **Chiswick, London, 7 October 1987**

Professor W.N. Medlicott was one of the most influential and authoritative voices this century on the history of international relations and British foreign policy. He made an important contribution to the further professionalization of historical research through the attention he paid social and economic factors, and the meticulousness of his own research.

William Norton Medlicott was born at the turn of the century, the son of the editor of the *Church Family Newspaper*. Too young to see active service in World War I, he nevertheless spent a couple of years in the Bedfordshire & Hertfordshire Regiment from 1918 to 1920. He completed his first degree at University College, London, in 1923, and an MA at the Institute of Historical Research in 1926.

Medlicott's early academic career was outwardly unremarkable; it was not until his late thirties that the sort of painstaking research he specialized in began to bear fruit. He joined University College, Swansea, as a lecturer in 1926 and, apart from a visiting lectureship at the University of Texas from 1931 to 1932, he remained in Wales until the end of World War II.

The Congress of Berlin and After (1938) was Medlicott's first major work—a highly detailed account of the diplomatic manoeuvrings around the famous Congress of 1878. This, and the later *Bismarck, Gladstone and the Concert of Europe* (1956), are still perhaps the works for which Medlicott will be most remembered and consulted. The intervening *British Foreign Policy After Versailles* (1940) consolidated a reputation already established.

During the war Medlicott spent a year as a principal in the Board of Trade. Then, in 1942, he was recruited to the team of scholars retained by the Cabinet Office's historical section for eventual compilation of the official history of the war. This later led to the publication, in 1952 and 1959, of Medlicott's two-volume *The Economic Blockade*, a skilful history of the whole range of economic warfare deployed by Britain against Germany.

From 1945 to 1953 Medlicott was professor of history at University College of the Southwest in Exeter. It was the next stage in his career which caused surprise, when he was appointed Stevenson Professor of international history at the London School of Economics. This appointment turned out to be a sound choice. Medlicott methodically built up a small department into one of the most prestigious collection of experts in the field of international history in the world.

The way in which international history was regarded also changed because of Medlicott's influence and example. From being an often anecdotal recital of exchanges between diplomats, emphasis gradually switched to the economic and social forces which lie at the root of many of those exchanges.

Another Medlicott speciality was the detailed analysis and editing of documents. Here his lasting monument is the dozen volumes he edited for the second series of *Documents on British Foreign Policy 1919–39*, which appeared between 1969 and 1984.

If Medlicott had a weakness as an historian it was his dryness of style, of which *The Congress of Berlin and After*, again, is the outstanding example. An indispensable mine of information and insights, it is hardly the sort of book which would entice a newcomer, or most undergraduates, to its subject. To his credit, however, Medlicott saw the need to make history more accessible to the general reader and student, and from the mid-1960s onward he produced a number of books with a much broader audience in mind, and which have stood the test of time very well. Of these, *Bismarck and Modern Germany* (1965) was the earliest. With his wife, Medlicott also edited a highly useful companion volume of documents, *Bismarck and Europe*, and a collection of foreign commentary on Britain, *The Lion's Tale*, both published in 1971.

Medlicott contributed to the spread of historical study at school level as an honorary secretary of the Historical Association, and later as its president. Workmanlike rather than inspirational, he will be best remembered for his unsurpassed skills as an editor.

Born William Norton Medlicott. **Parents** William Norton, editor, *Church Family Newspaper*, and Margaret Louisa (McMillan) Medlicott. **Marriage** Dr Dorothy Kathleen Coveney, university lecturer and palaeographer, 1936 (died, 1979). **Education** Aske's School, Hatcham; University College, London, BA, 1923; Institute of Historical Research, London, MA, 1926, DLitt, 1952. **Military service** Bedfordshire & Hertfordshire Regiment, 1918–20. **Career** Lecturer, University College, Swansea, 1926–45; professor of modern history, University of Exeter, 1945–53, vice-principal, 1953; Stevenson Professor of International History, London School of Economics, 1953–67, emeritus from 1967. **Related activities** Visiting professor, University of Texas, 1931–32; member: editorial board, *Annual Register*, 1947–71, Institute for Advanced Study, Princeton University, 1952, 1957; chairman, editorial board, *International Affairs*, 1954–62; chairman, British Coordinating Committee for International Studies; council member, Chatham House, 1955–71; senior editor, *Documents on British Foreign Policy, 1919–39*, from 1965; Creighton Lecturer, University of London, 1968. **Other activities** Principal officer, Board of Trade, 1941; official historian, Ministry of Economic Warfare, 1942–58. **Offices and memberships** Member: British Historical Association, honorary secretary, 1943–46, president, 1952–55. **Awards and honours** Gladstone Prize University College, London; Hester Rothschild Prize; Lindley Student, University of London; honorary DLitt: University College, Swansea, 1970, Leeds, 1977, Buckingham, 1984; Commander of the Order of the British Empire, 1983; fellow: Royal Historical Society, University College, London; honorary fellow, London School of Economics. **Publications** *The Congress of Berlin and After: A Diplomatic History of the Near Eastern Settlement, 1878–80*, 1938, new edition, 1963; *The Origins of the Second Great War* (pamphlet), 1940; *British Foreign Policy Since Versailles: 1919–39*, 1940, new edition, 1968; *The Economic Blockade*, 2 vols, 1952, 1959; *Bismarck, Gladstone and the Concert of Europe*, 1956; *Modern European History, 1789–1945: A Select Bibliography*, 1960; *The Coming of War in 1939*, 1963; *From Metternich to Hitler: Aspects of British and Foreign History, 1814–1939*, 1963; *Bismarck and Modern Germany*, 1965; *Contemporary England, 1914–64*, 1967, revised edition, 1976; *Britain and Germany: The Search for Agreement, 1930–37*, 1969; (with D. K. Coveney) *Bismarck and Europe*, 1971; (with D. K. Coveney) *The Lion's Tale: An Anthology of Criticism and Abuse*, 1971; (editor) *Documents on British Foreign Policy, 1919–39*: second series, vols 20–21, 1969–84; numerous articles and reviews. **Cause of death** Undisclosed, at age 87.

RAYMOND MOORE

British Photographer

***Born* Wallasey, Cheshire, 26 August 1920**

***Died* Dumfriesshire, Scotland, 6 October 1987**

Raymond Moore may be remembered as the photographer who immortalized the British B and B (bed and breakfast) sign, as well as small boys, sunlit dogs and that Sunday-morning, out-of-season desolation of seaside resorts when the trippers have gone and only litter and driftwood remain. The images of Moore's photographs are everyday. They are of caravans by the sea, a game of hopscotch drawn in the sand, washing blowing in the wind, a children's playground, streets signs and graffiti. It all looks very simple, as though, in the words of the critic Clive Lancaster, "Moore did nothing more startling than point his camera at the world." He was a "magician with nothing up his sleeve".

Like that other deceptively simple photographer, Henri Cartier-Bresson, Moore had, however, trained as an artist. Influenced by the Euston Road school, the one painting which now survives is a "Coldstream-like" landscape bisected by a straggling fence, the forerunner of many later photographed fences. Moore brought an artist's sense of form and perspective to his photographs, together with an economy that left his pictures startlingly uncluttered, free from irrelevant detail.

Where Cartier-Bresson sought the "photographic moment", Moore seems rather to have sought the "photographic place", the "photographic feeling". Place was always important to him, but the places of his pictures such as Skomer Isle or the Cumbrian coast, are not always easily recognizable. The place that mattered for Moore was "the no man's land between the real and fantasy—the mystery in the commonplace—the uncommonplace". If he can best be classified as a landscape photographer, it must be added that his landscapes were as much about his inner vision as they were about the outer world.

Moore was always reticent about his work. The few statements that he was prepared to make about photography tended to be printed over and over again whenever his work was exhibited. In preparing his introduction for the 1985 collection *Every So Often*, Clive Lancaster recalled how Moore, when asked what points he would like made, responded by sending him a copy of the medieval Japanese monk Basho's *Narrow Road to the Deep North*.

In an interview published in *Creative Camera* in 1981, just before his major retrospective exhibition at the Hayward Gallery in London, Moore was, however, a little more forthcoming. He described himself as "a loner" and a "reflective pessimist" and confessed that he was always looking for "signs of finality and the end of time, impending departure and desperation". These he found in the images of graffiti "which come up in some of my pictures and which are the marks of people anxious to express themselves, to get things off their chests". He stressed that he had no "social point" to make. He was interested in the places where cultures met and in "the *Alice in Wonderland* quality which reflections present ready made". The picture of a sunlit dog reflected in a traffic mirror in a dull street in Alderney beneath a "Public Convenience" sign is an example of what he meant.

Although Moore was only the second photographer to be accorded a retrospective exhibition at the Hayward (the first was Bill Brandt in 1970) and the first ever to have an Arts Council exhibition (arranged by the Welsh Arts Council in 1968), recognition of his work was slow. For almost two decades, while teaching at Watford and at the Trent Polytechnic, Moore worked in almost total isolation. This, his Californian friend Russ Anderson said, was "frighteningly painful for him". In 1973, when the Photographer's Gallery in London at last arranged an exhibition of Moore's work, the magazine *Creative Camera* lamented the fact that Moore was so much better known and honoured in America, where he had already had three one-man exhibitions, than in his native land.

Despite his later success and his inclusion in every major photographic exhibition in the last decade, Raymond Moore is probably still more appreciated in Europe and the US than he is in Britain. Perhaps this is inevitable given the commonplace nature of the subjects he celebrates. Perhaps it is hardest of all for us, who are closest to them, to throw off our own blinkers as Moore would have us do and "become more sensitive to the import of what is around us".

Born Raymond Moore. **Marriage** Mary. **Children** One son. **Education** Wallasey School of Art, 1937–40; Royal College of Art, London, 1947–50; associate, Royal College of Art, 1950; studied with Minor White, Massachusetts Institute of Technology, 1970. **Military service** Royal Air Force, 1940–46. **Career** Instructor of painting and lithography, Watford College of Art, Hertfordshire, 1950–54, lecturer in creative photography, 1956–74; freelance photographer, 1955–87; senior lecturer, creative photography, Trent Polytechnic, Nottingham, 1975–78. **Awards and honours** Arts Council bursary, 1978. **Publications** *Murmurs at Every Turn: The Photographs of Raymond Moore*, London, 1981; *Every So Often: Photographs by Raymond Moore* edited by Neil Hanson, Newcastle-upon-Tyne, 1983. **Individual exhibitions** Regent Street Polytechnic, London, 1959; Artists International Association Gallery, London, 1962; *Modfot 1: Raymond Moore*, R.W.S. Gallery, London (toured Britain and Europe), 1967; Welsh Arts Council Gallery, Cardiff (toured Britain), 1968; International Museum of Photography, George Eastman House, Rochester, New York, 1970; Carl Siembab Gallery, Boston, 1971; Art Institute of Chicago (retrospective), 1971; The Photographers' Gallery, London, 1973; Thackrey and Robertson, San Francisco, 1976; The Photographic Gallery, Cardiff, 1978; Salzburg College, Austria, 1980; Hayward Gallery, London (retrospective), 1981; Royal Photographic Society, Bath, Avon (toured Britain), 1982; Birksted Gallery, London, 1985; *Every So Often*, Northern Centre for Contemporary Art, Newcastle-upon-Tyne (toured Sweden, Finland and Britain, 1985–86), 1985; *49 Prints*, British Council, Barcelona (toured Spain, France, Canada, Netherlands and West Germany), 1986. **Selected group exhibitions** *The Land: 20th-Century Landscape Photographs Selected by Bill Brandt*, Victoria and Albert Museum, London (travelled to the National Gallery, Edinburgh, Ulster Museum, Belfast, and National Museum of Wales, Cardiff, 1976), 1975; *Photographs: Sheldon Memorial Art Gallery Collection*, University of Nebraska, Lincoln, 1977; *Concerning Photography*, The Photographers' Gallery, London (travelled to Spectro Workshop, Newcastle-upon-Tyne), 1977; *Three Photographers: Cooper, Hill, Moore*, Focus Gallery, San Francisco (with Thomas Joshua Cooper and Paul Hill), 1977; *Three Perspectives on Photography*, Hayward Gallery, London, 1979; *Metaphysical Presence*, in *Grupa Junif '80*, Ljubljana, Yugoslavia, 1980; *Première Triennale Internationale de Photographie*, Charleroi, Belgium, 1980; *Presences of Nature*, Carlisle Museum and Art Gallery, Cumbria (toured Britain), 1982; *British Photography 1955–65*, The Photographers' Gallery, London, 1983; *Creation*, Scottish National Gallery of Modern Art, Edinburgh (toured Scotland), 1984; *The Photographic Art*, Stills Gallery, Edinburgh, 1986. **Collections** Victoria and Albert Museum, London; Welsh Arts Council, Cardiff; Contemporary Art Society for Wales, Cardiff; University College of Wales, Aberystwyth; Bibliothèque Nationale, Paris; Art Institute of Chicago; Gernsheim Collection, University of Texas at Austin; University of New Mexico, Albuquerque; British Council, London; The National Museum of Photography; Arts Council. **Cause of death** Undisclosed, at age 67. **Further reading** *Photographs by Raymond Moore* (exhibition catalogue), Cardiff, 1968.

JACQUELINE DU PRÉ

British Cellist

Born **Oxford, England, 26 January 1945**

Died **London, England, 19 October 1987**

Parents and friends called her Jackie and told how, at age 37 and already crippled by disease, her radiant smile could still make her look like a little girl. No wonder—nothing could make her smile so much, or cry so easily, as the sound of the cello.

Jacqueline du Pré's passion for the instrument had been established at the age of four. The family album has it that one winter evening, when she heard some cello music on the radio, it made such a big impression on her that she asked her parents for "the thing that makes that noise". They obliged, and from that moment on the little girl was wedded to "that thing", that great bulky beast ostensibly so little suited to the build and temperament of a young child. But then, of course, Jacqueline du Pré was no ordinary child. The myths which habitually form around great musicians would in her case undoubtedly say that she was born to play the cello and destined to relinquish it after only ten years of a brilliant career, having spent all her artistic energies in the spiritual and emotional intensity of her concerts. Fortunately, reality is always more complex than myth—if also rather more prosaic.

Gifted, Jackie du Pré certainly was, but she was also a child prodigy, one of the lucky few whose talent was recognized at an early age and carefully nurtured to full fruition. In the first instance it was her mother who, as Jacqueline later said, "guided my first steps, wrote tunes for me to play, and drew pictorial descriptions of the melodies". Later, she had distinguished teachers and mentors of world repute, such as Pablo Casals and Mstislav Rostropovich, to help her develop. Great musicians, she knew, are made not born. It was, therefore, all the more tragic that when she reached maturity as a performer, barely in her mid-twenties and poised for a long and distinguished musical career, she was struck by multiple sclerosis which put an abrupt end to it all.

Not much is known about Jacqueline du Pré's childhood, except her early love of music. She was enrolled at the London School of Violoncello at the age of six, and four years later William Pleeth, whom du Pré described as her "cello daddy", took her under his wing, despite the fact that he had never before taught children. Evidently, this was different: "She played with calm confidence and a degree of concentration that would be extraordinary in an adult," he said, "There was nothing precocious about her; she came uncorrupted...I could see the potential quite strongly on the first day. The speed with which she tackled every assignment was like letting a horse off the reins". Years later, Pablo Casals' first impression upon hearing her play was similar. He asked her where she came from, and when she replied, "England," he would not believe her. "Where," Casals wondered, "did such temperament come from?" Then, when he found out that she had a French name, he exclaimed, "Aha!", satisfied that he had found his answer. Casals, like Pleeth, was only too pleased to act as Jacqueline's mentor. And so, in later years, were others: before she reached the age of 20 she had been coached by the famous Paul Tortelier in Paris and by Rostropovich, who brought her to Moscow, as well.

Du Pré took to the concert stage with eagerness and conviction. In 1961 she made her début as a soloist at London's Wigmore Hall. On that occasion she played a 1672 Stradivari given her by an anonymous benefactor. Just 16 years old, she proved her mettle as a performer when, during the first piece, Handel's Sonata in G Minor, the A string came loose. She calmly stood up, went backstage to replace it and returned to start anew. The audience from then on was hers. William

Pleeth recalled: "Her playing was the perfect marriage between real passion and innocent reverence. It was a spiritual, not just a physical thing. She let each piece *live* so completely. People were practically crying."

A concert career began which took Jacqueline du Pré all over the world. Everywhere people wanted to hear—and see—this wunderkind who, as if enchanted, played the cello with her whole body and soul and yet gave each piece its due, whether classical or modern. For some, du Pré's intensity was too much, and she was occasionally criticized for being too emotional, too violent in her play. Others, by contrast, enjoyed the almost sexual energy she brought to the music, with her face displaying every shift of emotion from exuberant joy to anguish to mourning.

Du Pré herself experienced the wider world in which she now came to move as exciting but also threatening. For one thing, she felt herself to be "under-educated" because of her almost exclusive concentration on music hitherto, and for another, she felt lacking in social graces, never having moved much in the company of strangers before. The cello, she realized, had been her best friend until the age of 17 when she started performing. "No one who has not experienced it can know just what it means to have a private world of your own to go into, to be quite by yourself whenever you need it," she said later. "It was my gorgeous secret—an inanimate object, but I could tell it all my sadness and my problems. But I realized later that it didn't necessarily equip one to deal with one's fellow humans."

The one who did show her how to deal with one's fellow humans was Daniel Barenboim, then an up-and-coming concert pianist and conductor. They met through mutual friends in 1966. With characteristic bluntness, Barenboim's opening gambit was a comment on du Pré's size, which was rather larger than usual due to a recent stay in the Soviet Union where she had lived on a diet of pure stodge. "You don't look like a musician!" Barenboim exclaimed when they were introduced. Du Pré, feeling shy and a little insecure at the time, decided there was only one adequate response: she took her cello and played. Soon Barenboim joined in and that was, by all accounts, *it*.

"It was as if we had been playing all our lives," du Pré said. "And the shock to me was enormous, that I could have this degree of communication with another person." A year later they were married. Through the energetic and gregarious Barenboim, Jacqueline du Pré met far more people than she had time and inclination for, but she also became part of what was then known as "the Barenboim gang", an extended family of Jewish (often Israeli) musicians who performed and socialized together. This was far more important to her than the parties and the adulation—to belong to a group of friends with whom she could communicate and perform. During this time, she, Barenboim and Pinchas Zukerman recorded several of Beethoven's piano trios and other pieces in the classic chamber music repertoire.

Between 1967 and 1971 she frequently toured with her husband and recorded both live concerts and studio performances. Undoubtedly the most memorable of these was the Elgar Cello Concerto, performed and recorded in 1970 with Barenboim, for this was the piece which established her fame and name as one of the greatest cellists of this century. Although she recorded the work of many other composers—Schumann, Beethoven, Brahms, Chopin, de Falla—she made the Elgar concerto really her own. Du Pré's own assessment of the 1970 recording was that it had been her "swansong", her last and greatest achievement before succumbing to multiple sclerosis. The slow passage of the piece, she said, "tears me to bits every time I hear it. It is like the distillation of a tear."

After five brilliant years in love and work with Barenboim, having made many new friends and with her reputation established all over the world, Jacqueline du Pré was advised to give music a rest for a year when, during the Brahms Double Concerto in New York in 1971, she suddenly had difficulty in fingering and bowing the cello. Two years later multiple sclerosis was diagnosed and by that time it was clear that she would never perform in public again. Devastated, but not defeated, she turned to teaching, choosing carefully a few promising pupils to whom she would devote her now severely limited energies. Nevertheless, even when confined to a wheelchair, she would still dominate the classroom with her passion and intensity. In 1976 she was awarded the OBE; a year later she and Barenboim launched the Jacqueline du Pré Multiple Sclerosis Society Research Fund.

The rest of the story is a sad one, less that of a great musician than a victim of a wasting disease. By the time the end came, at 42, Jacqueline du Pré was completely paralysed, unable even to talk or read. Her marriage, once the perfect match between two young, gifted and successful people passionately in love with each other, had deteriorated into little more than a financial arrangement. The world, however, had not forgotten her. Julian Lloyd Webber vividly described how he remembers her: an inspiration to all, musicians and non-musicians alike. In a repeat of du Pré's own experience when she was very young, Lloyd Webber recalled hearing her play on the radio and the impact it had on him:

> From that evening I determined to find out as much as possible about the cello and its music. I immediately set about taping a library of obscure cello music off the radio. Most of those tapes I have today, yet few can match the intensity of what I heard that evening. Looking back at photos of Jackie playing the cello it is striking how often a broad grin can be seen stretching from ear to ear. What a marvellous change from the stereotype of a "serious" musician! How wonderful to see and hear someone actually enjoying the music they play!

Lloyd Webber, of course, went on to become a cellist himself. Listening to her on the radio, he also had become enthralled by "the thing that makes that noise", the thing that had been her solace, her best friend, the instrument of her success and, finally, the greatest sacrifice she had to make in a too short, too painful life.

Born Jacqueline du Pré. **Parents** Derek and Iris du Pré. **Marriage** Daniel Barenboim, conductor/pianist, 1967. **Education** London Violoncello School with Herbert Walenn, from 1951; Guildhall School of Music and Drama; studied with William Pleeth, Paul Tortelier and Mstislav Rostropovich. **Career** Professional début, Wigmore Hall, London, 1961; made many concert tours around the world, and many recordings; forced to retire from performing due to multiple sclerosis, 1973; turned to teaching cello, 1974. **Other activities** Established Jacqueline du Pré Multiple Sclerosis Society of Great Britain, 1977. **Awards and honours** Officer, Order of the British Empire, 1976. **Recordings** (include) J.S. Bach, Sonata No.2 in D major and Toccata, Adagio and Fugue in C major; Beethoven sonatas, nos 1, 2, 3, 4, 5, piano trios, nos 1, 2, 3, 4, 5, 6, 7, 8, 14, Trio in B flat major for clarinet, cello and piano, op.11, Variations, op.44 and 121a; Brahms, Sonatas 1 and 2; Bruch, *Kol Nidrei* for cello and piano, op.47; Chopin, Cello Sonata in G minor, op.65; Delius, Cello Concerto; Dvorák, Cello Concerto in B minor, op.104; Elgar, Cello Concerto in E minor, op.85; de Falla, Seven Popular Spanish Songs, no.4; Franck, Sonata in A major; Haydn, Cello Concerto in C major and in D major; Prokofiev, *Peter and the Wolf*; Saint-Saëns, Cello concerto no.1, *Le Carnaval des Animaux—Le Cygne*; and Schumann, Cello concerto in A minor. **Cause of death** Multiple sclerosis, at age 42. **Further reading** Carol Easton, *Jacqueline du Pré*, London, 1989.

CONSTANTINE TSATSOS

Greek Politician, Poet and Scholar

Born **Athens, Greece, 1 July 1899**

Died **Athens, Greece, 8 October 1987**

A distinguished and highly respected intellectual, Constantine Tsatsos had a long and dignified career as a politician and scholar during a troubled period in the history of modern Greece.

Born in Athens into a rich family (his father was a lawyer and politician), Tsatsos was educated at home by private tutors, and he showed an early and keen interest in literature which he pursued throughout his life. He studied at Athens Law School, a faculty of the university, and qualified as a doctor of law. Although he practised for a short period, he did not take over his father's practice, as expected, but went to Heidelberg University in Germany to study the philosophy of law.

After this experience he returned to his native Athens to take up the post of associate professor of the philosophy of law at the university from 1931 to 1932, becoming a fully-fledged professor there in 1932, and remaining in that position until the German occupation of Greece in 1941.

Tsatsos was an outspoken patriot, and soon had to flee the country for his own safety, along with many other intellectual Greeks. He went to the Middle East, where he became an adviser to the beleaguered government in exile. After the country was liberated in October 1944, he returned, and in 1945 joined the non-political government as social services and interior minister, then press and information minister and, temporarily, minister for the air force.

In 1946 he was elected as an MP for the small Unionist Party, and in 1949 became education minister. The following year he took on the position of deputy minister of coordination, which he held until 1951.

On the death of General Papagos in 1955, Konstantine Karamanlis formed a government and was appointed prime minister, and Tsatsos became one of his most trusted advisers. His political career flourished: he was minister to the prime minister from 1956 to 1961, on several occasions acting foreign affairs minister, and minister of social services from 1962 to 1963.

On 21 April 1967 he was appointed justice minister, but he was not to fulfil the role: on the same day the non-parliamentary government of the colonels was formed, which terrorized the country for seven years.

As everyone who knew him expected, Tsatsos never tired of plotting to overthrow the undemocratic regime stifling Greece. When the colonels eventually fell, in 1974, Tsatsos took up his place again in the new Karamanlis government, and was given the ministerial portfolio of cultural affairs, as well as the crucial role as chairman of the committee to draft the new constitution—a clear indication of his status as the respected elder statesman of Greek politics. In 1975 a referendum abolished the monarchy, and in June Parliament elected Tsatsos the first president of the new Republic of Greece.

As a corollary to this glittering career, Tsatsos was a prolific author and outstanding scholar, like his contemporary Kanellopoulos, who was twice prime minister. They were both recognized as philosophers of the Heidelberg School, and Tsatsos's published works in this field include *Kant's Theory of Knowledge* and *Social Philosophy in Ancient Greece*. Between 1964 and 1973 he wrote four volumes of aphorisms and reflections.

His legal books were numerous. He wrote, in German, *Der Begriff des Positiven Rechts*, and in Greek *The Problem of Interpreting the Law, The Problem of the Sources of Law, Introduction to Jurisprudence* and *Studies in the Philosophy of Law*.

Tsatsos was of the group known in Greece as the "Generation of 1930", which, besides a lively output of fiction, developed the study of literature and created a new school of criticism. He was both a critic and a poet, and published his complete poetical works in 1973. He wrote a monograph of the Greek lyric poet Kostis Palamas, who died in 1943, books on aesthetics and the theory of art, as well as many annotated translations of Demosthenes and Cicero and other literary works.

His talents extended to sociology and history, and he wrote a book on the roots of the American Republic and on Greece and Europe. He also contributed to the *History of the Hellenic Nation*.

Tsatsos married Jeanne Seferis, a writer and poet, whose brother George had won the Nobel Prize for literature. George Seferis published an essay on the problems of poetry and language based on conversations he had with his brother-in-law Tsatsos; entitled "Dialogue on Poetry", it can be found in Seferis's book *Dokimes*. In 1961 Tsatsos was elected a member of the prestigious Athens Academy.

He stepped down from the presidency in 1980 to make way for Karamanlis, whom he much admired. Tsatsos is often remembered for his recognition of the less attractive side of the Greek character—not something his countrymen are wont to point out. In his iconoclastic presidential address to the people on New Year's Day in 1978 he said, "We abhor discipline and teamwork. We are attracted to extremism and intransigence. We are always impatient. We Greeks plant poplars, not oak trees."

Born Constantine Tsatsos. **Marriage** Jeanne Seferis, writer and poet. **Children** Two daughters. **Education** University of Athens, doctor of law, 1930; University of Heidelberg. **Career** Practised law, Athens, 1930–31; associate professor of philosophy of law, University of Athens, 1931–32, professor, 1932–46; adviser, Greek government in exile, 1940–45; member of parliament, 1946–50, 1956–63, 1964–67; 1974–75; minister of social services and interior, 1945; minister of press and information, 1945; minister of air force, 1945; minister of education, 1949–50; deputy minister of coordination, 1950–51; minister to the prime minister, acting minister of foreign affairs, 1956–61; minister of social services, 1962–63; minister of justice, 1967; minister of cultural affairs, 1974; president of the Hellenic Republic, 1975–80. **Related activities** Chairman, committee to draft the new constitution, 1974–75. **Offices and memberships** Member, Academy of Athens, 1961. **Publications** (in German) *Der Begriff des Positiven Rechts*; (in Greek) *The Problem of Interpreting the Law*; *The Problem of the Sources of Law*; *Introduction to Jurisprudence*; *Studies in the Philosophy of Law*; *Kant's Theory of Knowledge*; *Social Philosophy in Ancient Greece*; *The Roots of the American Republic*; *Costis Palamas*; *The Vocation of Hellenism*; *Politics*; *Essays on Aesthetics and Education*; *Complete Poetical Works*, 1973; *Aphorisms and Reflections*, 4 vols, 1964–73; *Dialogues in a Monastery*; *Greece and Europe*, 1977; *Studies in Aesthetics*, 1977; *Theory of Art*, 1978; *The History of the Hellenic Nation*; numerous annotated translations of Demosthenes and Cicero; numerous minor publications on politics, sociology, philosophy and literature. **Cause of death** Undisclosed, at age 88.

LINO VENTURA

French Actor

***Born* Parma, Italy, 14 July 1919**

***Died* Paris, France, 22 October 1987**

A popular actor since 1953 whose career spanned three decades, Lino Ventura's specialties were psychological dramas and thrillers. His poker-faced tough guy, as in *The Valachi Papers*, or raspy-voiced and mournful plain-clothed detective, as in *Illustrious Corpses*, was consistently resolute and steadfast. His character always got his man—or, on occasion, his woman. His Maigret was unsurpassed, and was often a model for other actors playing the role. He was just as successful in his more lighthearted roles, but it was as the police investigator in *Garde à Vue* (1981) that he is best remembered.

Ironically enough, considering he created a specifically French character type, Ventura was born Angelino Borrini in Italy. However, he moved with his family when he was six years old, and France remained his home until his death. He had always spoken little of his youth, except to maintain that his education was gained on the street, as his neighbourhoods were rough ones. He began working at 14 and was, in turn, a mechanic, a groom and a travelling salesman. When referring to the war years, he only maintained that he knew "hunger, cold and fear...I don't regret having a tough childhood—it was an excellent grounding for life."

Ventura's stocky frame seemed to guarantee him a career in wrestling; he earned a gold medal in the 1950 European Championship. When a severely broken leg, at the age of 31, cut his career short, he organized matches and became a well-known sports personality. Ventura was noticed, in the time-honoured way, by a director, Jacques Becker, who was looking for a villain. A subsequent, successful screen test led to the first of many parts. Ventura made over 50 films and his first, *Touchez pas au grisbi*, introduced him to leading actor Jean Gabin. The two became lifelong friends.

Other films included *Ascenseur pour l'échafaud* (1957), *Un taxi pour Tobruk* (1961), *Maigret tend un piège* (1957), *Les Aventuriers* (1967), *The Valachi Papers* (1972) and *The Medusa Touch* (1977). His last major role was as Jean Valjean in the 1982 film version of *Les Misérables*, a rare opportunity for him to prove versatility. With no formal acting lessons, Ventura acknowledged his years as a wrestler to be his drama training. "It is a sport which, when you lose, you cannot make any excuses...I found it an extraordinary school of humility."

Ventura was one of the most commonly recognized and liked faces in the French cinema; however, most people were not aware of his fund-raising projects in aid of mentally handicapped children. (His own daughter was afflicted.) Personally, a private man, Ventura's humanitarianism was often anonymous. In addition, he always retained that humility he learned in the ring. "I never thought of myself as an actor. I cannot tell you what I represent in terms of the public. In the eyes of the producers I am someone who draws people into the cinema and am therefore an actor on whom they speculate without fear of losing out. One thing I can say with certainty is that I was not born to be a star."

Born Angelino Borrini. **Parents** Jean Ventura, exporter, and Luisa Borrini. **Marriage** Odette Lecomte, 1942. **Children** Three daughters, Mylène, Linda and Clélia, one son, Laurent. **Education** Primary school, Parma, Italy. **Emigration** Left Italy for France with his parents, 1927. **Career** Mechanic, groom, travelling salesman, 1930s–40s; wrestler, to 1950; boxing match organizer and sports personality, 1950–53; actor, mainly in films, 1953–87. **Related activities** Founder, Perce-Neige Foundation for mentally handicapped children. **Awards and honours**

Gold medal, European wrestling championship, 1940; Prix Grand Siècle, 1979. **Films** *Touchez pas au grisbi*, 1953; *Razzia sur la chnouf*, 1954; *Crime et châtiment*, 1956; *Ascenseur pour l'échafaud*, 1957; *Maigret tend un piège*, 1957; *Montparnasse 19 et le gorille vous salue bien*, 1957; *Marie-Octobre*, 1958; *125 rue Montmartre*, 1959; *Un taxi pour Tobruk*, 1960; *Les Lions sont lâches*, 1961; *Le Bâteau d'Émile*, 1961; *Crooks in Clover*, 1963; *100,000 dollars au soleil*, 1964; *Les Grandes gueules*, 1965; *La Métamorphose des cloportes*, 1965; *Ne nous fâchons pas*, 1966; *Avec la peau des autres*, 1966; *Le Deuxième souffle*, 1966; *Les Aventuriers*, 1967; *Le Repace*, 1968; *L'Écume des jours*, 1968; *Le Clan des siciliens*, 1969; *L'Armée des ombres*, 1969; *Dernier domicile connu*, 1970; *Fantasia chez les ploucs*, 1971; *Boulevard du rhum*, 1971; *L'Aventure*, 1971; *Cosa Nostra/The Valachi Papers*, 1972; *Wild Horses*, 1972; *Le Silencieux*, 1973; *La Raison du plus fou*, 1973; *Les Anges*, 1973; *La Bonne année*, 1973; *L'Emmerdeur*, 1973; *Les Durs*, 1974; *La Gifle*, 1974; *La Cage*, 1975; *The Pink Telephone*, 1975; *Cadavres exquis/Illustrious Corpses*, 1976; *La Grande menace*, 1978; *Les Séducteurs*, 1980; *Sunday Lovers*, 1980; *Garde à Vue*, 1981; *Espion Lève-Toi*, 1982; *Les Misérables*, 1982; *Le Ruffian*, 1983; *Le Grand échiquier* (for TV), 1979. **Cause of death** Undisclosed, at age 68.

BASIL WRIGHT

British Documentary Film-maker

Born **London, England, 12 June 1907**

Died **Oxfordshire, England, 14 October 1987**

The British documentary film movement of the 1930s boasted a wealth of talent, and one of its leaders was Basil Wright. He came from a wealthy and liberal background, receiving a traditional upper-class education at Sherborne public school before going up to Corpus Christi College, Cambridge, to read classics and economics—a useful mixture for a potential film-maker.

Shortly after graduating from university, Wright went to work at the newly-formed Empire Marketing Board's film unit. This outfit had the task of making documentary films explaining and promoting the work of the board, and Wright was employed as an assistant to the legendary John Grierson who ran the unit. Grierson, who has been called the founding father of the British documentary film, was the first person to realize the enormous potential of the cinema to promote and advertise. The films made under his auspices in the 1930s and 1940s were artistically significant in themselves and also had a profound effect on the development of British cinema, influencing it away from German romantic expressionism towards realism.

Wright displayed considerable aptitude and a year after joining the film unit he was given the opportunity of directing. A series of documentaries followed, including *Windmill in Barbados*, *Cargo from Jamaica* and *Liner Cruising South*. These all faithfully described the work of the Marketing Board, but they went further than that; each film had Wright's unique hallmark which, as Jack Ellis has put it, was "a special talent for poetic observation".

The acknowledged masterpiece of this first series was *Song of Ceylon*, made in 1934. This broke new ground in that it was a musical and poetic evocation of the Ceylonese culture and traditional way of life starkly contrasted with the effects of modern industry on the country. The film had a big impact both in Britain and abroad and won many prizes, including the Gold Medal and Prix du Gouvernement at the Brussels Film Festival in 1935.

The following year Wright made another documentary which became famous—*Night Mail*, sharing the direction of this piece with Harry Watt (q.v.). This film had a number of famous collaborators: W.H. Auden wrote the verse commentary, Benjamin Britten composed the music, and the sound track was directed by Cavalcanti, who had worked on several of Wright's earlier films.

In 1937 Wright founded the Realist Film Unit, which enabled him to produce films, as well as directing them. In fact, he directed only two more films—*Children at School* and *The Face of Scotland*—before turning most of his energies to production, where he supervised and encouraged the work of other young directors.

With the outbreak of World War II, Wright joined the Film Centre as executive producer, retaining this post until 1944, when he became director-general of the Ministry of Information. This meant that throughout the war and immediate post-war years he was responsible for the production of films for various government departments which left him with no time for directing his own work.

It was not until 1950 that Wright was able to produce his next project, *Waters of Time*, a study of the River Thames, which was commissioned for the 1951 Festival of Britain. This film, with a verse commentary by Paul Dehn, was well received.

In 1953 Wright, together with Paul Rotha who had also been one of the Grierson group of film-makers, was commissioned by UNESCO to make a joint film showing that organization's work in deprived communities. This was his largest commission and his most ambitious project to date. He and Rotha decided jointly on the theme, then Wright went to Thailand to shoot his material while Rotha went to Mexico. On their return they put the results together and, astonishingly, they worked. With a commentary by Rex Warner and music by Elisabeth Lutyens, the film was generally acclaimed as a triumph.

By contrast, Wright's next film was a very small-scale project. *The Stained Glass of Fairford* took as its subject some fine medieval glass in an English village church. Wright's affection for the subject was apparent in the film and it was also the first time he used colour.

Having had a lifelong love of Greece, its people and way of life, Wright was delighted when, in 1958, he was able to realize a long-cherished ambition to make a film about the country. The *Immortal Land*, which was to be his last project, was his longest film and it won him a Council of Europe Award.

Wright spent the later years of his life teaching and lecturing, especially in the United States. He also published two books about his film-making—*The Use of Film* (1948) and *The Long View* (1974). His contribution to the British documentary film was immense and was eloquently summed up in *The Times* obituary: "Wright was, first and foremost, a poet of the film...his films, apart from their own very considerable merits, formed a welcome oasis in the mass of the more didactic documentaries of the 1930s."

Born Basil Charles Wright. **Parents** Lawrence and Gladys (Marsden) Wright. **Education** Sherborne School, Dorset; Corpus Christi College, Cambridge (Mawson Scholar). **Career** Joined Empire Marketing Board film unit as assistant under John Grierson, 1930; directorial début, *The Country Comes to Town*, 1931; transferred with Grierson to General Post Office film unit, 1933; founded Realist Film Unit, 1937; executive producer, Film Centre, 1939–44; produced films for ministries and armed forces, travelling to Canada to advise on information film-making, World War II; producer-in-charge, Crown Film Unit, 1945; adviser to director-general, Ministry of Information, 1946; formed own documentary production company, *International Realist*, 1946–49; director of documentaries for various companies and organizations, including UNESCO, 1951–60; concentrated on lecturing and teaching, 1960 onwards. **Related activities** Visiting lecturer on film art, University of California, 1962, 1968; senior lecturer in film history, National Film School, 1971–73; visiting professor of radio, television and film, Temple University, Philadelphia, 1977–78. **Offices and memberships** Governor: Bryanston School, from 1949, British Film Institute, 1953; council member, Royal College of Art, 1954–57; fellow, British Film Academy, 1955. **Awards and honours** (include) Gold Medal and Prix du Gouvernement, Brussels, for *Song of Ceylon*, 1935; Council of Europe Award for *The Immortal Land*, 1959; Gold Cross, Royal Order of King George I, Greece, 1963. **Publications** *The Use of Film*, London, 1948; *The Long View*, London, 1974. **Films** *The Country Comes to Town*, 1931; *O'er Hill and Dale*, 1932; *Gibraltar*, 1932; *Windmill in Barbados*, 1933; *Liner Cruising South*, 1933; *Cargo from Jamaica*, 1933; *Song of Ceylon*, 1934; *Pett and Pott*, 1934; (with Harry Watt) *Night Mail*, 1936; (with Harry Watt) *6.30 Collection*, 1936; *Children at School*, 1937; *The Smoke Menace*, 1937; *The Face of Scotland*, 1938; *The Londoners*, 1939; *Evacuation*, 1939; *Harvest Help*, 1940; *This Was Japan*, 1945; *The Story of Omolo*, 1946; *Bernard Miles on Gun Dogs*, 1948; *Waters of Time*, 1950; (with Paul Rotha) *World Without End*, 1953; *Stained Glass at Fairford*, 1955; *The Immortal Land*, 1958; (with Michael Ayrton) *Greek Sculpture*, 1959; *A Place for Gold*, 1960. **Cause of death** Undisclosed, at age 80. **Further reading** Rachael Law, *Documentary and Educational Films of the 1930s*, London, 1979; Rachael Law, *Films of Comment and Persuasion of the 1930s*, London, 1979.

NOVEMBER

ÉAMONN ANDREWS

Irish Television Personality

***Born* Dublin, Éire, 19 December 1922**

***Died* London, England, 5 November 1987**

Éamonn Andrews became a British television celebrity by the deceptively simple method of always being himself—a rather naïve and charming soft-brogued Irishman.

Born the son of a carpenter, Andrews received an education with a strong religious bias at a Christian Brothers' school in Dublin. As a child he was a talented choirboy, winning several prizes for his singing, and he also became the All-Ireland Junior Boxing Champion while still at school. These early pugilistic skills later helped him to land his first job in broadcasting, when he was taken on as a part-time boxing commentator with Radio Éireann at the age of 16. The next few years were to prove an invaluable training ground. In addition to covering boxing matches, he was allowed to try his hand at rugby and soccer commentaries, and was also given the odd small role in radio plays. While doing all this, he studied acting at the Abbey Theatre, Dublin, and even managed to hold down his full-time job as an insurance clerk.

When Andrews landed his first series of radio talks and interviews, entitled *Microphone Parade*, he finally gave up the insurance job. This was obviously the right move, as the series ran for three years and his career with Irish radio continued without a break until 1949. Feeling the need for a change, he moved to England, touring the country with the Joe Loss Band Show as chairman of the *Double or Nothing* quiz. In 1950 he returned to radio, taking over the job of presenting the BBC quiz programme *Ignorance Is Bliss*, which was a huge success.

Andrews' television career began in 1951 when he was the inaugural chairman of the panel game *What's My Line*, which was to become a British institution. Four years later, when television was expanding in Britain, he began to present a programme which he had devised himself, entitled *This Is Your Life*, and it was this hugely successful series which established him as a household name and for which he will be best remembered.

Every week (often in outlandish disguises) Andrews would "ambush" a well-known personality and after uttering the immortal words "This is your life", he would whisk off his hapless victim to a television studio to endure a half-hour potted biography complete with friends and relatives who had been sworn to secrecy and brought along to surprise the guest and add their own anecdotes. The finale almost invariably involved a reunion with a long lost member of the family who had been flown halfway around the world for the occasion.

The programme ran for almost ten years, and during that time only two of Andrews' victims revolted. The international footballer Danny Blanchflower took flight, utilizing, as one commentator has put it, "the superb turn of speed over a short distance that was one of his particular assets as a wing half for Spurs and Northern Ireland", and was seen no more. Years later Richard Gordon, author of *Doctor in the House*, swore at Andrews and left the studio but was persuaded to return later and the programme continued.

Part of the phenomenal attraction of *This Is Your Life* was the initial pick-up when the audience shared in the mounting excitement as Andrews lay in wait ready to jump out at the unsuspecting subject. Indeed, this part sometimes involved some unintentionally comic or dangerous moments, such as the time when, in pursuit of the television magician David Nixon, Andrews was inserted into one of his tricks. This involved the rather large Andrews having to climb into a rather small sack. On the night Nixon unexpectedly added a whole lot of extra stage business to the performance with the result that Andrews was left cooking gently under the heat of the studio lights for a frighteningly long time. Apart from the unpredictability of the pick-up, Andrews brought to the programme a relaxed style which put guests at ease and drew reminiscences out of them, whether they were celebrities who were well used to the media or obscure and nervous relatives.

In addition to preparing and presenting this programme, Andrews also compèred the BBC children's shows *Crackerjack* and *Playbox*. These programmes built up large audiences and were much loved by children of all ages.

In 1964 the BBC decided to end the *This Is Your Life* series, so Andrews moved to the independent television channels. He worked as a link man for the Saturday afternoon programme *The World of Sport*, before developing *The Eamonn Andrews Show* in which he acted as host to a number of guest celebrities. This was the British forerunner of television chat shows and Andrews developed it from lightweight beginnings to a well-balanced show made up of a mixture of serious conversation and show business frivolity. This format proved to be extremely successful and the series ran throughout the 1970s. In addition, Andrews presented a regular current affairs programme called *Today*. In recent years, his biggest successes, the panel game *What's My Line* and *This Is Your Life*, were revived and both series again drew large audiences.

One of the secrets of Andrews' constant success in a widely disparate range of programmes was the "common touch", which he applied to all his television guests, from excitable children to nervous great-aunts and contestants, to well-known personalities. He always put his guests first, making their stories sound interesting and taking none of the limelight for himself. Andrews had a clear philosophy about the role of television, which he summed up in one interview: "Television will always fail the day it forgets that entertainment—sad and tinselly though it is—is the prime purpose". Clearly, he had found the right formula, and throughout his long career he won the prestigious award of Television Personality of the Year four times.

Apart from being a successful television presenter, Éamonn Andrews was a shrewd businessman. He became chairman of Radio Éireann in 1960 and had a sizeable stake in Irish television from its inception. He remained a committed Catholic all his life and in 1964 he received a papal knighthood for his charitable work.

Born Éamonn Andrews. **Parents** William, a carpenter, and Margaret Andrews. **Marriage** Gráinne Bourke, 1951. **Children** One son and two daughters (all adopted). **Education** Irish Christian Brothers' School, Dublin. **Career** Broadcaster, Radio Éireann, 1941–50; continued working as clerk for Dublin insurance company during early radio career; studied acting under Ria Mooney at Abbey Theatre, Dublin; acted in minor roles, Radio Éireann plays; became radio critic for the *Irish Independent*; hosted radio talk show, *Microphone Parade*, for three years; toured England with Joe Loss Band as chairman of *Double or Nothing* quiz, 1949; first BBC radio broadcast, presenting quiz programme, *Ignorance Is Bliss*, 1950; subsequently worked on various BBC radio programmes; first BBC television appearance as chairman of *What's My Line?* panel game, 1951; devised and presented *This Is Your Life*, BBC TV, 1955–64; also appeared on number of other BBC television shows, including *Crackerjack!* and *Playbox* (both for children); joined ABC Television as presenter and host of various programmes, including *The Éamonn Andrews Show*, 1964–68; joined Thames Television as presenter of current affairs programme *Today* and later *This Is Your Life*, from 1968; *What's My Line?* resuscitated with Andrews as host, 1984. **Related activities** Wrote play, *The Moon Is Black*, produced at the Peacock, Dublin, 1941; chairman, Radio Éireann Statutory Authority; helped set up Irish television, 1960–66. **Other activities** Much involvement with charitable works connected with the Catholic Church. **Awards and honours** All-Ireland Amateur Junior Boxing Champion (middleweight); Television Personality of the Year (four times); Knight of St Gregory (papal knight), 1964; Commander of the Order of the British Empire, 1970. **Publications** *This Is My Life* (autobiography), 1963; *Surprises of Your Life* (autobiography), 1978; articles for magazines and newspapers. **Radio** (all BBC, unless stated, includes) *Microphone Parade*, Radio Éireann; *Ignorance Is Bliss*; *Sports Report*; *A Book At Bedtime*; *Housewives' Choice*. **Television** *What's My Line?*; *This Is Your Life*; *Sports Report*; *Crackerjack!*; *Playbox*; *The World of Sport*; *The Éamonn Andrews Show*; *Today*; *Top of the World*. **Cause of death** Undisclosed, at age 64. **Further reading** Gus Smith, *Éamonn Andrews: A Life*, London, 1988; Gráinne Andrews, *For Ever and Ever Éamonn: The Public and Private Lives of Éamonn Andrews*, London, 1989.

JACQUES ANQUETIL

French Cycling Champion

***Born* Mont-Saint-Aignan, France, 8 January 1934**

***Died* Boos, France, 17 November 1987**

Because cycling has never made it into the top ten league of popular sports, the praises of its heroes have too often remained unsung. And while today's valiant knights of the racing bicycle can at least earn good money with their efforts and be famous for the few weeks they ride the Tour de France in summer, none but the sport's practitioners and true devotees can fully appreciate the enormity of their achievement in even completing the race—let alone winning it.

Jacques Anquetil, who deserves to be remembered as one of the greatest giants in the sport, won the Tour de France no less than five times. At a time when competition was keen but essentially still amateurish (in all senses of the word), Anquetil dominated the cycling scene with a physical force and cunning which has since only been rivalled by Eddy Merckx—and even this is open to debate. Today, the iron grip exercised by Anquetil in the 1950s and 1960s seems a remote phenomenon. Riders who make it to the top currently don't last there much longer than a few years, and there is now a clear division between sprinters and climbers, i.e. those who win on speed and good tactics, and those whose victory comes long and slow through sheer hard endurance. Only the best, and then only the very best of them, possess both qualities—the long and the short of cycling. Jacques Anquetil was one.

It is often said that the mountainous regions of France and Italy (and more recently Peru) have traditionally produced the best cyclists because of the strength required of those who live there to get about when motorized transport is not available. As folklore would have it, meat delivery boys were supposed to be best suited to championship cycling because of the weight they had to carry around in their baskets which reputedly enhanced their magnificent muscle-power. Jacques Anquetil was not born a butcher's boy, but the son of a strawberry-grower in Normandy. Growing up in rural France, he trained like his father to be a horticulturalist, but before he was ready to earn a living as such, a local acquaintance discovered Anquetil's talent for rushing about the village at breakneck speed. The man, who also happened to own a cycle shop, encouraged his young protégé to take part in local races, which were easily won. Before Anquetil had celebrated his eighteenth birthday he had chalked up his first major victory as French amateur road racing champion. In 1952 this success was followed by a bronze medal at the Helsinki Olympics, and a year later Anquetil astounded the cycling world by beating all the professionals to the Prix des Nations, a most prestigious time-trial. Five victories in the Paris–Nice, another classic in the cycling world, confirmed the fact that Jacques Anquetil, young as he was, had most definitely arrived.

A decade of great victories began in 1956 with Anquetil breaking the one-hour record set by the legendary Italian (meat delivery boy!) Fausto Coppi no less than 14 years before. The following year he won his first Tour de France, followed three years later by victory in the Giro—the Tour of Italy—which until that time had never been won by a Frenchman. He repeated this feat in 1964, having won the Tour of Spain for the first time the previous year. In between were four successive victories in the Tour de France, of which the last was the most dramatic because it was won more or less on the finishing line.

Anquetil's opponent in this latter duel (and many more) was Raymond Poulidor, the other great French cycling name of the 1960s. But while Anquetil usually emerged the stronger of the two, it was Poulidor—lovingly nicknamed Poupou by the French public—who was the most popular. It was no surprise, then, to Anquetil that even on the occasion of this, his fifth Tour de France win, he was criticized for having been too "calculating" by pipping Poulidor at the post. In fact, Anquetil had been chasing him all the time after a headlong charge down the mountain the day before in order to make up for time lost during the climb in the Pyrenees. But Anquetil realized only too well that he was being criticized for nothing more, or less, than defeating Poupou—and against such a charge there was no possible defence.

Anquetil retired from active racing in 1969 in order to spend more time with his wife and daughter, and to capitalize on the small fortune he had earned with racing. He developed his interests (of mind as well as matter) in cattle-ranching, gravel pits and real estate by way of investment, and became involved in race organization, television commentary, equipment manufacture and newspaper journalism as well. These last interests, of course, allowed him to remain involved in sport and to give new audiences the benefit of his experience, even though big changes in terms of equipment, team management and financial rewards had come about.

Despite the absence of rampant commercialism in Anquetil's day, he still had to endure many of the pressures that cyclists face today. This is illustrated by the fact that in 1967 he was denied the world one-hour record by the International Cycling Union because he had refused to undergo a drug test afterwards. Although there were rumblings of discontent at the time that Anquetil had been treated too harshly, many keen observers of the sport would no doubt applaud such action if only standards were being enforced as strictly today. Yet, despite this incident, which briefly cast a shadow over Anquetil's integrity, there can be no doubt that he was a great athlete.

Born Jacques Anquetil. **Parents** Ernst, strawberry-grower, and Victorine (Legrand) Anquetil. **Marriage** Janine Lepetit, 1958. **Children** Sophie. **Education** Collège Technique de Sotteville-les-Rouen. **Career** Professional cyclist, 1953–69; bronze medal, Helsinki Olympics, 1952; Grand Prix des Nations, Tour de la Manche, 1953; nine times winner, Grand Prix des Nations,

1953–1966; seven times winner, Grand Prix de Lugano, 1954–65; Champion de France de Poursuite, 1955–56; one-hour world record, 1956; winner, Tour de France, 1957, 1961, 1962, 1963, 1964; Les Six Jours de Paris, 1957, 1958; winner, Grand Prix de Bretagne, 1959; winner, Giro (tour of Italy), 1960, 1964; Paris–Nice, 1957, 1961, 1963, 1965, 1966; Tour of Spain, 1963; Le Critérium du Dauphiné Libéré, 1963; Le Critérium National, 1963; Le Critérium du Dauphiné Libéré et Bordeaux–Paris (both within 24 hours), 1965; Le Critérium des As, 1959, 1960, 1963, 1965; second place, world championship, 1966; winner, Critérium National de la Route, 1961, 1963, 1965, 1967; Liège—Bastogne–Liège, 1966; Tour of Sardinia, 1966; Tour of Catalonia, 1967; world record, one-hour speed test, 1967; retired, 1969. **Related activities** After retirement became involved in race organization, television commentary, equipment manufacture and newspaper journalism. **Other activities** Investments in cattle-ranching, gravel pits and property. **Offices and memberships** President, National Union of Professional Cyclists, 1967–70. **Awards and honours** Prix Deutsch-de-la-Meurthe, 1963; grand prize, Sports Academy, 1964; chevalier, Legion of Honour, 1966; chevalier, National Order of Merit; gold medal for physical education. **Publications** (with Pierre Joly) *En brûlant les étapes*, 1966; (with Pierre Joly) *Je suis comme ça*, 1967; (with Pierre Chany and Michel Scob) *Cyclisme*, 1975. **Cause of death** Cancer, at age 53.

JAMES BALDWIN

American Novelist, Playwright and Essayist

***Born* Harlem, New York City, 2 August 1924**

***Died* St Paul de Vence, France, 30 November 1987**

James Baldwin was not the only writer of the 1950s and 1960s to explore the condition of race relations in American society. Blacks had finally lost patience with the pace of civil reform and sought to express themselves politically, culturally and—some—seditiously. From Malcolm X to Martin Luther King Jr, from the Black Muslims to the Congress of Racial Equality, from Langston Hughes to Richard Wright, and from Montgomery to Memphis there was a profound movement to redress the rampant oppression. Few were able to galvanize opinion to his own, or make people feel the justice of Black people's anger like James Baldwin. "More than any other writer," says critic Martin Fagg, "Baldwin can make one begin to feel what it is really like to have a black skin in a White man's world: and he is especially expert at evoking, not merely the brutally overt physical confrontations between Black and White, but the subtle unease that lurks beneath."

Baldwin was perhaps the best of his generation at "examining his own emotions and reactions...as if he is examining those of the nation", and so holds a distinctive position in American literature. He fell out of favour in the 1970s, and was especially attacked by Black Muslim Eldridge Cleaver. Part of this was due to his homosexuality, which also contributed to his emigration to France in 1948, and partly to his notoriety in the civil rights movement. However, Baldwin always insisted that labels say more about the name-giver, and that "prophet", "visionary", "propagandist" and "militant" were signs of other people's needs. In summing up Baldwin's importance, critic Robert Sayre says "whatever deeper comprehension of the race issue Americans now possess has been in some way shaped by him....In his excursions into his psyche he has offered himself as a metaphor for our self-inflicted national injury."

New York's Harlem, one of America's most shameful examples of urban squalor and centre of several important cultural movements, was Baldwin's birthplace and home for 17 years. He was raised in accordance with the moral standards of the Southern rural background of his parents, especially of the Southern church. His father was a clergyman from New Orleans who preached fervid sermons on the Harlem circuit. Baldwin remembered him as a proud, bitter man who "was being eaten up by paranoia". The children, Baldwin the eldest of nine, were never glad to see him, nor could they forgive him for "his cruelty to our bodies and our minds".

At the age of 14 Baldwin became a preacher himself at Harlem's Fireside Pentecostal Church. As a holy roller, he became a "holy freak" for three years, "revelling", as Fern Eckman put it, "in a most unholy fashion over his ability to draw greater crowds than his father. Looking back on those years, Baldwin said, "I...was too tormented, and I didn't understand the gospel". Later he would condemn the church for its role in enslaving Blacks, but then "I believed, but I didn't know. Now—maybe I know, but I don't believe." "This religion," according to one commentator, "has been enormously influential on Baldwin's writing, but it is the music of the religion, the drama of the religion, the fire and excitement that have lingered, not the essence." In fact, only one of his novels, *Giovanni's Room*, is not set in Harlem or the revivalist movement. "In the streets of Harlem," says author Mario Puzo, "in the dark bedrooms, the dangerous hallways, the chanting churches, Baldwin is at his best."

In high school Baldwin edited a literary magazine and found "the fire of literature". The two books he read and reread were Harriet Beecher Stowe's *Uncle Tom's Cabin* and Dickens' *A Tale of Two Cities*. His teachers remembered him as a "bright, sad-looking boy" and Kenneth Clark once described him as "a little man, physically, with tremendous emotional and intellectual power....In his conversations he is the essence of spontaneity and...is incapable of communicating anything other than the total truth which he feels and thinks at that particular time." It was here, in high school, that he decided to be a writer, instead of a preacher.

Following his graduation in 1942, Baldwin lived in Greenwich Village—a popular Manhattan community for writers and artists. For the next five years he eked out a living washing dishes and working in offices, factories and restaurants while writing in the evenings. During this time he wrote polemical essays on the plight of the American Black which appeared in *Nation*, *New Leader* and *Commentary*. Although he would become more widely known as a novelist, his essays have received the more favourable critical reception. Baldwin the essayist is "one of the two or three greatest...this country has ever produced" according to critic John Howe. While R.E. Long further explains that "Baldwin's intelligence functions brilliantly, coolly, preserving always a sense of proportion....Then there is the question of America itself and its search for identity, past and present." His two greatest collections of essays are *Notes of a Native Son*, a collection of ten autobiographical essays which analyse his feelings about race relations in the United States and abroad, and *Nobody Knows My Name*, dealing with more literary topics and his growing involvement in the civil rights movement. In these pieces Baldwin rendered a uniquely "complex conception of the Negro as a man who is simultaneously like...all other men and yet profoundly, perhaps irrevocably, different. Baldwin himself saw his function as that of a "conduit" to speak for those who could not.

While living in Greenwich Village he was befriended by the novelist Richard Wright, who wrote *Native Son*. Baldwin showed Wright a manuscript which would become *Go Tell It on the Mountain*, for which Wright helped Baldwin secure a Eugene F. Saxton Memorial Award in 1945. Even so, Baldwin found life in the United States to be artistically stifling. For him America was "a suffocating society that not only seemed to lock every Black writer into the crude simplicities of propaganda and protest, but also was particularly inimical to a homosexual like himself". A second award enabled him to move to France three years later, where he spent eight years and published three of his most important works: *Go Tell It on the Mountain*, *Giovanni's Room* and *Notes of a Native Son*. The solitude was the final ingredient he needed to complete his first manuscript. He read and studied Henry James, whom he felt had the sense of form he lacked.

As a novelist, Baldwin had beautiful lyrical qualities in his work, though they were sometimes overshadowed by his Jeremaic activities later on. In *Go Tell It on the Mountain* everything is perfectly blended. It centres on the religious conversion of John Grimes on the night of his fourteenth birthday. Divided into three sections—"The Seventh Day", "The Prayers of the Saints" and "The Threshing Floor"—the novel is at once documentary, dreamlike and musical. We are introduced to Grimes's father Gabriel, the repressive, brimstone preacher who hates all White people; Aunt Florence, bitter and fearful of death by cancer; and the mother Elizabeth, whose search for an idyllic love ends in hatred, tragedy and redemption. Part II contains the rhythmic and poetic prayers and memories of each of John's relations. Gabriel relives his life from the age of 21 to 40, his affairs and sexless marriage, the death of his illegitimate son, and his contradictory feelings of piety and lust. In Florence's prayer she bitterly asks God why he "preferred her mother and her brother, the old, Black woman and the low, Black man, while she, who had only sought to walk upright, was come to die alone and in poverty, in a dirty furnished room". The book is full of grand impressionistic passages and lessons about the artistic power of hatred: "He did not *want* to love his father," says the young Grimes. "He wanted to hate him, to cherish that hatred and to give his hatred words one day."

The major conflict in this essentially autobiographical work is the boy's anguished choice between church and jail, which for Baldwin represents the historical role Christianity has played in the constriction and spiritualization of Black people. The "saints" in the book are all martyrs to their humanity: Gabriel by duties too spiritual for his desires, Florence by ambition and Elizabeth by love. The characters vacillate between surrender to body, family, church and country, but can experience no ecstasy outside praising the mysteries of God. "The Biblical enchantment of Baldwin's prose," wrote one commentator, "elevates even his scenes of animal love, and the speech of his characters is vividly true to their heritage."

In his earlier work Baldwin is passionate and angry, but confident in the power of finding words for that anger. Permeating his outrage at racial and sexual injustice is "the quest for love", both on a personal level and as "an agent of racial and national survival". His central theme, especially in his early work, is the "need to accept reality as a necessary foundation for individual identity and this is a logical prerequisite for the kind of saving love in which he places his whole faith". *Giovanni's Room* explores this kind of love and responsibility. The protagonist David recalls his homosexual lover on the eve of the lover's execution for murder. David deserts him to return to his fiancée, but is condemned by the lover for his falseness: "You are not leaving me for a *woman*. If you were really in love with this little girl, you would not have had to be so cruel to me....You want to kill [me] in the name of all your lying little moralities."

Most people consider these his best works. His next novel, *Another Country*, did not ring true for many, and some thought it was "a nightmarish round of miscegenation and sexual deviation". Baldwin replied that Americans simply refused to look into the mirror he had held up to them, nor could they see how disastrously they were living. None the less, his mood and writing had changed. As he became more actively involved in the civil rights protest, he began to doubt that mankind had the ability to save itself through love. He began to condemn outright that acceptance and love could be based on social or cultural factors, but instead must occur solely between individuals. This is the premise for the interracial and intersexual relationships in *Another Country*, which has been described as "a rejection of the moral significance [of] the categories White and Negro, heterosexual and homosexual".

This modification of Baldwin's social view ran parallel to his political activities and preceded a weakening of his powers as a novelist. He had returned to the United States in 1957 and made his first visit to the South. He was deeply moved by the crusade for reform and later said in an interview that "the depth of my involvement began then". More confrontational essays began to appear in magazines, dealing with the racial problems and the Black Muslim movement. Increasingly, his function as an artist was absorbed by his role as a spokesman for American Negroes. His two plays, *The Amen Corner* and *Blues for Mister Charlie*, were "as much civil rights pageant as drama" leaving much of his intellectual complexity oversimplified. In *If Beale Street Could Talk* Baldwin shows no love or mercy in the Black church and no truth or justice in American law. The only answer seems to lie in familiar and personal love.

In 1963 he began lecturing on the West Coast and in Harlem on behalf of the Congress of Racial Equality, and over the next several years became a familiar voice on radio and television. Later in 1963 he was part of the celebrated audience with Attorney-General Robert F. Kennedy, which tried to impress upon the Kennedy administration Black impatience with the slow rate of change.

However, his growing prominence as a campaigner signalled a decline in the quality of his literary output. In an essay from *Notes of a Native Son* Baldwin argued that writers with a cause to fight cannot write great fiction because "they reduce their characters to pawns on a chessboard". Their moral sincerity may be unimpeachable, and what they write may be socially valuable, but it is not great fiction. But Baldwin seems to have fallen into that trap, especially with *Tell Me How Long the Train's Been Gone*. Mario Puzo claimed that he was now creating "cardboard characters", and another critic suggested that "however sensitive Baldwin may be to the unique quality of the individual...he has generally been unsuccessful in creating characters who exist independently of their categorizations".

His celebrity status caused this lapse for two reasons. First, after his initial successes, he—like all writers— had to work within the context of these earlier achievements and of the new writers who had been influenced by him. Second, and perhaps more importantly, the combination of his eloquence, honesty and superb intelligence with his role as a spokesman resulted in the "vacuities of speechifying". Another commentator also gives an accurate assessment of the problem: "His fame now secure, we have accorded him the highest honour we can bestow upon a public intellectual: we have disarmed him with celebrity, fallen in love with his eccentricities and institutionalized his outrage into prime time entertainment." It was further claimed that Baldwin "now suffers from...a separation of his feelings and his voice...systematically deceiving himself through rhetorical inflation and hysteria".

He found his feelings and voice again in *Just Above My Head*, his last and longest novel. It tells the story of Arthur Montana, a gospel singer whose life is recalled by his brother Hall, and in many ways it is a return to Baldwin's original works. There is a personal frankness here that had disappeared from his writing. This return to humaneness also marks the end of a very dark and cynical period in his life.

Baldwin spent the last few years of his life quietly in the South of France. He earned huge sums of money from his writing, but generally rejected material possessions. His work still commands a vast audience, for his criticisms are still valid, his compassion still relevant and his writing still inspiring.

Born James Arthur Baldwin. **Parents** David, a lay preacher, and Berdis Emma (Jones) Baldwin. **Education** Public School 139, Harlem, New York; Frederick Douglass Junior High School, New York; DeWitt Clinton High School, Bronx, New York. **Emigration** Left USA for Europe, living mainly in Paris, 1948–56; returned to USA, 1956, but spent last years of life in France. **Career** Various jobs, including handyman, dishwasher, waiter, office boy and some defence-related work, while training himself to be a writer, 1940s; moved to France, where he wrote *Go Tell It on the Mountain*, *Giovanni's Room* and *Notes of a Native Son*, 1948–56; returned to US as full-time writer and political activist, principally for civil rights movement, 1957–1970s; spent last years in France. **Related activities** Lecturer on behalf of Congress for Racial Equality, 1963; many appearances on radio and television in connection with civil rights, 1964 onwards. **Other activities** Lay preacher, Fireside Pentecostal Church, Harlem, New York, *circa* 1938–41. **Memberships** Authors' League; Actors' Studio, New York; Dramatists' Guild; National Advisory Board of Congress on Racial Equality; International PEN; National Committee for a Sane Nuclear Policy. **Awards and honours** Saxton Fellowship, 1945; Rosenwald Fellowship, 1948; Guggenheim Fellowship, 1954; American Academy Award, 1956; *Partisan Review* Fellowship, 1956; National Institute of Arts and Letters Award, 1956; Ford Fellowship, 1958; National Conference of Christians and Jews Brotherhood Award, 1962; George Polk Award, 1963; honorary DLitt, University of British Columbia, Vancouver, 1963; Foreign Drama Critics' Award, 1964; Martin Luther King Jr Award, City University of New York, 1978. **Novels** *Go Tell It on the Mountain*, New York, 1953, London, 1954; *Giovanni's Room*, New York, 1956, London, 1957; *Another Country*, New York, 1962, London, 1963; *Tell Me How Long the Train's Been Gone*, New York and London, 1968; *If Beale Street Could Talk*, New York and London, 1974; *Just Above My Head*, New York and London, 1979. **Short stories** "Any Day Now", *Partisan Review*, Spring 1960; (collection) *Going to Meet the Man*, New York and London, 1965; "Exodus", in *American Negro Short Stories*, ed. John Henrik Clarke, New York, 1966; "Equal in Parts", *Travelers*, New York, 1972. **Plays** *The Amen Corner*, New York, 1968, produced Washington DC, 1955, New York, London and Edinburgh, 1965 and London, 1987; *Blues for Mr Charlie*, New York, 1964, London, 1965, produced New York, 1964; *One Day, When I Was Lost: A Scenario Based on "The Autobiography of Malcolm X"*, London, 1972, New York, 1973; *A Deed from the King of Spain*, produced New York, 1974. **Other** *Notes of a Native Son*, Boston, 1955, London, 1964; *Nobody Knows My Name: More Notes of a Native Son*, New York, 1961, London, 1964; *The Fire Next Time*, New York and London, 1963; *Nothing Personal*, New York and London, 1964; *A Rap on Race*, Philadelphia and London, 1971; *No Name in the Street*, New York and London, 1972; *A Dialogue: James Baldwin and Nikki Giovanni*, Philadelphia, 1973, London, 1975; *Little Man, Little Man* (for children), London, 1976, New York, 1977; *The Devil Finds Work: An Essay*, New York and London, 1976; *Jimmy's Blues: Selected Poems*, London, 1983; *The Price of a Ticket: Collected Non-fiction 1948–85*, New York and London, 1985; *Evidence of Things Not Seen*, New York, 1985, London, 1986; also contributed essays and articles to magazines including *Nation*, *New Leader* and *Commentary*. **Film** (direction and screenplay) *The Inheritance*, 1973. **Cause of death** Cancer, at age 63. **Other reading** Fern Eckman, *The Furious Passage of James Baldwin*, New York, 1966, London, 1968; Stanley Macebuh, *James Baldwin: A Critical Study*, New York, 1973, London, 1975; Keneth Kinnamon (editor), *James Baldwin: A Collection of Critical Essays*, New Jersey, 1974; Therman B. O'Daniel (editor), *James Baldwin: A Critical Evaluation*, Washington, 1977; Louis H. Pratt, *James Baldwin*, Boston, 1978; Fred L. and Nancy Standley, *James Baldwin: A Reference Guide* (bibliography), Boston, 1979; Carolyn W. Sylvander, *James Baldwin*, New York, 1980; Kenneth B. Clark and Malcolm King, *Baldwin: Three Interviews*, Connecticut, 1985; Trudier Harris, *Black Women in the Fiction of James Baldwin*, Tennessee, 1987; Horace Porter, *Stealing the Fire: The Art and Protest of James Baldwin*, Connecticut, 1988.

ROSS R. BARNETT

American Lawyer, Politician and Segregationist
Born **Standing Pine, Mississippi, 22 January 1898**
Died **Jackson, Mississippi, 6 November 1987**

In a decade rocked by political and racial strife, during which the American South moved slowly and inexorably towards racial integration, a small but prominent circle of Southern politicians battled ruthlessly to bar legislative reforms and uphold White supremacist traditions. One of its loudest spokesmen was staunch segregationist Ross R. Barnett, governor of Mississippi from 1960 to 1964. Though his economic policies did much to encourage the state's industrial growth, Barnett is best remembered for his ardent efforts to prevent Black Air Force veteran James H. Meredith from enrolling at the University of Mississippi in 1962, and for being the only Southern governor to oppose the 1960 Democratic Party platform and the Kennedy–Johnson ticket. Believing that racial segregation was divinely ordained, he dedicated his life to the effort of preserving it.

The youngest of ten children born to a Baptist farming family near Carthage, Mississippi, Barnett learned early the value of hard work. In addition to helping with farming chores, he operated a barber shop and worked as a janitor while attending Leake County public schools. Following army service in World War I, he enrolled at Mississippi College, sawing logs and selling aluminium ware to pay his expenses. He also participated in a string of extra-scholastic activities, among them music, basketball and the Baptist Young People's Union. Before entering law school at the University of Mississippi, he spent two years teaching high school and coaching athletics in northern Mississippi, then, while studying, worked as a part-time law librarian and Sunday school teacher. Two summer terms at Vanderbilt University enabled him to finish his degree in 1926, well ahead of schedule. Soon afterwards he opened a law practice in the state capital of Jackson.

Over the years Barnett built a strong client base and enjoyed a lucrative practice. He also served in numerous professional organizations, and in the 1940s rose to the presidency of the Mississippi Bar Association. In 1956 he was among a group of Southern lawyers who offered their help to racist agitator John Kasper, imprisoned for inciting violence over school integration.

In 1951 Barnett made his first bid for the governorship of Mississippi. Though he was unable to clinch the Democratic nomination, the experience gained him a strong following and allowed him to stage a mightier—though still unsuccessful—effort four years later. His opportunity finally came in 1959, when J.P. Coleman, barred from succeeding himself as Mississippi's governor, endorsed Carroll Gartin for the Democratic gubernatorial nomination. By denouncing Coleman as a moderate and making White supremacy his central campaign issue, Barnett appealed to the prejudices of legions of rural fundamentalists. He was also among the many Mississippians critical of Coleman's decision to summon the FBI to help in the investigation of the Mack Parker lynching in 1959. A strong advocate of states' rights, he believed then, as in 1961, when the Freedom Riders entered the state, that Mississippi was fully capable of handling its own problems.

Although both Gartin and Barnett campaigned as segregationists, Barnett's speeches were far more emotive and rang with extraordinary assertions. "The Negro is different because God made him different to punish him," he declared. For Barnett, the segregation issue was a burning question—a personal crusade—and one which, at the end of the 1950s, brought him a rush of supporters. He defeated Gartin by a margin of 35,000 votes in the Democratic primary of 1959, capturing 62 of Mississippi's 82 counties. As the Republicans offered no opposition, he went on to win the general election in November. He was inaugurated as Mississippi's fifty-second governor on 19 January 1960.

One of Barnett's campaign pledges had been to work hand in hand with other Southern governors in order to preserve racial segregation. This promise was put to the test after the Democratic National Convention in July 1960, when the party adopted a civil rights plank advocating "equal access for all Americans to all areas of community life, including voting booths, school-rooms, jobs, housing and public facilities". Calling the platform "horrible" and "repulsive", Barnett helped form a slate of eight unpledged Democratic electors to provide an alternative to those pledged to the national platform and the Democratic presidential nominee, John F. Kennedy. In the end, the Mississippians decided in favour of the uncommitted voters, but this had no effect on the outcome of the general election.

As governor, Barnett also served as chairman of the State Sovereignty Commission, an organization established by the Mississippi Legislature in 1956 to prevent desegregation. Within seven months of his election, he had allocated $20,000 to the Mississippi Association of Citizens Councils to help in its pro-school segregation media campaign. But throughout his term, the tide of change flowed against him.

In May 1961, when the Freedom Riders arrived in Montgomery, Alabama, to protest segregation on city buses, Barnett offered his support to Alabama governor John Patterson. But the activists persisted, and when they arrived in Jackson, Mississippi, he could do no more than order their peaceful arrest. One year later, when James Meredith attempted to register at the Oxford campus of the University of Mississippi, Barnett appealed to the state college board for the authority to prevent it. As the threat of public violence loomed, the nation looked on in anxious anticipation. Barnett conferred by telephone with President Kennedy, who advised him to capitulate. Two people were killed and hundreds injured in the riots that followed. Though Barnett finally yielded to Meredith's demand, the US Court of Appeals later charged the governor with contempt for his part in the affair. Fines were levied and he was sentenced to prison. However, the charges were eventually dropped, and Barnett completed his term as governor.

Though loath to discuss the Meredith confrontation in later years, Barnett maintained his controversial views, and once admitted, "Generally speaking, I'd do the same things again." When his term as governor expired, he could not succeed himself, so he returned to private law practice. In 1967 he staged a comeback attempt, but showed a weak performance, finishing fourth place in the Democratic primary.

In addition to his extreme political and social views, Barnett, a tall, distinguished man described by *Newsweek* magazine as "courtly and urbane", with a gift for flamboyant oratory, was noted for his extravagant personal tastes. A report disclosed that he had spent more than $300,000 refurbishing the governor's mansion; luxurious touches added during his tenancy included gold-plated taps in the bathroom. He was also reprimanded for his efforts to place his campaign supporters in government positions.

But Barnett also filled his life with charitable works. Over the years he served as chairman of the Mississippi Heart Association, president of two university alumni organizations, and deacon of the First Baptist Church in Jackson. He was also a Shriner, and an active member of the American Legion. Until the end of his life, he failed to see a contradiction between his civic and religious works and his racist beliefs. "God was the original segregationist," he contended. "He made the White man white and the Black man black, and He did not intend for them to mix.... There is no case in history where the Caucasian race has survived social integration. We will not drink from the cup of genocide."

Born Ross Robert Barnett. **Parents** John William, a farmer, and Virginia Ann (Chedwick) Barnett. **Marriage** Mary Pearl Crawford, teacher, 1929. **Children** Ross Jr, Quida and Virginia. **Education** Agricultural High School, Lena, Mississippi; Mississippi College, Clinton; University of Mississippi Law School, graduated 1926. **Military service** US Army, World War I. **Career** Teacher and athletics coach, Pontotoc High School, Mississippi, 1922–24; began practising law in Jackson, Mississippi, 1926; served as commissioner, vice-president and president, Mississippi State Bar Association, 1943–44; ran unsuccessfully for governorship of Mississippi, 1951, 1955; elected governor of Mississippi, 1959; achieved national notoriety for resistance to civil rights movement and desegregation, early 1960s; chair, State Sovereignty Commission, established in 1956 to prevent desegregation; returned to law practice at end of gubernatorial term, 1964; continued as leading spokesman for White supremacist ideology, 1965–87. **Offices and memberships** Deacon, First Baptist Church, Jackson, Mississippi. **Cause of death** Heart failure, at age 89.

BRAND BLANSHARD

American Philosopher

Born **Fredericksburg, Ohio, 27 August 1892**

Died **New Haven, Connecticut, 19 November 1987**

A reasonable idealist would perhaps be the best way to describe the liberal philosopher Brand Blanshard, one of the few twentieth-century advocates of the type of philosophy popular in the late 1800s. Although his philosophical principles were fraught with idealistic overtones, they were not, on the other hand, used to support religion or ethics. Philosophy, Blanshard felt, should be employed not as a sharpener of the mind, but in the traditional function of philosophy itself: the search for truth and values, and the extension of substantive knowledge. Because of these beliefs, Blanshard was known throughout his lifetime as a reactionary, defending reason against the scepticism and empiricism which have been advocated by Anglo–American philosophers since Bertrand Russell.

How did an American come under what were, until quite recently, considered to be outmoded methods of thought? Part of the answer lies in Blanshard's education. After graduating from the University of Michigan, he went to Oxford University to study on a Rhodes Scholarship. There Blanshard fell under the influence of F.H. Bradley and H.H. Joachim—the latter being the last of the Oxford idealists—and accordingly turned to study Bosanquet and Royce, among others. Through their metaphysical systems, the young philosopher hoped to find the rational foundations for human knowledge. Reason thus became his focus at an early age, and it was one he never abandoned. "The finest of all achievements, and the most difficult, I have come to think, is merely being reasonable," he stated. "It is difficult because it runs counter to our love of the dramatic, the temperamental, the aggressive and the spectacular, all of which we prize too highly. If men were reasonable, if they even tried to be reasonable, the world would be transformed overnight."

In *The Nature of Thought* (1939), his first major work, Blanshard redefined the coherence definition of truth usually accepted by rationalists; in essence, he added idealism to what already existed. "Truth," he asserted, "is the approximation of thought to reality...at a given time the degree of truth in our experience as a whole is the degree of system it has achieved." Reason, he went on to state, gives man knowledge of necessary connections—not only of those which exist in the actual world, but also of those which compose its fundamental structure. For decades, such views were considered out of touch with modern thought, yet recently, many philosophers have returned to Blanshard's theories, holding them to be more plausible than the beliefs of the logical positivists. Although Blanshard himself slightly modified his views in his Carus Lectures of 1959, he continued to defend rationalistic idealism against its chief opponents: logical empiricism, existentialism and, particularly, linguistic analysis. "There is no reason," he said, "why we should not think and speak meaningfully of the self, of other minds and, whether it exists or not, of a divine mind. We can freely think of non-sensible relations—of implication, of likeness and difference, of time, of causality...We can still debate the meaning of goodness and justice without fear that they will be ruled out as senseless because non-sensible."

After retiring from Yale in 1961, where he had been teaching for 16 years, Blanshard wrote a three-volume sequel to *The Nature of Thought*. The first volume, *Reason and Goodness*, defended morals against linguistic analysis; the second, *Reason and Analysis*, tried to destroy the process of linguistic analysis altogether; *Reason and Belief*, the third volume, advocated a return to religious thinking—that is, if it were devoid of emotionalism and modified by reason, for Blanshard never found historical Christianity, or any particular religion, wholly acceptable.

The philosopher was also an active supporter of the humanities in education. In *The Uses of a Liberal Education*, Blanshard stated that the aim of a liberal education was "richness of spirit". The book caused Peter Caws of the *New York Times Book Review* to say that, despite his great age, Blanshard's views remained in tune with the modern world. "He understands better than a good many younger writers, the character of our world and its problems," he said.

A liberal who denounced Senator McCarthy for being more un-American than any of those he criticized, Brand Blanshard gained numerous honorary degrees and academic awards throughout his career. He died at the age of 95, the logical end to a long and rational life.

Born Brand Blanshard. **Parents** Francis George, a minister, and Emily (Coulter) Blanshard. **Marriages** 1) Frances Margaret Bradshaw, 1918 (died, 1966); 2) Roberta Yerkes, 1969. **Education** University of Michigan, BA, 1914; Columbia University, MA, 1918; Oxford University, BSc, 1920; Harvard University, PhD, 1921. **Military service** US Army, 1918–19. **Career** Assistant professor, University of Michigan, 1921–25; Swarthmore College, Pennsylvania: associate professor, 1925–28, professor, 1928–45; professor of philosophy, Yale University, 1945–61, chairman of department, 1945–50, 1959–61. **Related activities** Dudleian Lecturer, Harvard University, 1945, Noble Lecturer, 1948, Whitehead Lecturer, 1961; Gifford Lecturer, University of St Andrews, Scotland, 1952–53; Hertz Lecturer, British Academy, 1952; Adamson Lecturer, Manchester University, 1953; Howison Lecturer, University of California, Berkeley, 1954; Matchette Lecturer, Wesleyan University, 1957; Carus Lecturer, American Philosophical Association, 1959; fellow, Wesleyan University Center for Advanced Studies, Middletown, Connecticut, 1961–62; visiting professor, University of Minnesota, 1962. **Offices and memberships** Corresponding fellow, British Academy; honorary member, Aristotelian Society, London; honorary fellow, Merton College, Oxford; member: American Academy of Arts and Sciences, American Philosophical Association (president, Eastern Division, 1942–44), American Theological Society (president, 1955–56), Phi Beta Kappa. **Awards and honours** Rhodes Scholar, 1913–15, 1919–20; Guggenheim Fellowship, 1929–30; Senior Award, American Council of Learned Societies, 1958; Medal of Honor, Rice Institute, Houston, 1962; honorary doctorates: Swarthmore College, 1947, Bucknell University, Pennsylvania, 1954, Oberlin College, Ohio, 1956, Colby College, Maine, 1956, Trinity College, Connecticut, 1957, Roosevelt University, Chicago, 1959, University of St Andrews, 1959, Kenyon College, Ohio, 1961,

Simpson College, Indiana, 1961, Concord College, West Virginia, 1962, Albion College, Michigan, 1966, University of New Mexico, 1968. **Publications** *The Nature of Thought*, 2 vols, London, 1939, New York, 1940; (with others) *Philosophy in American Education, Its Task and Opportunities*, New York and London, 1945; (with others) *Preface to Philosophy*, London, 1945; *The Uses of a Liberal Education*, New Haven, 1951; *On Philosophical Style*, Bloomington and Manchester, 1954; *The Impasse in Ethics, and a Way Out*, Berkeley, 1955; *Education in the Age of Science*, New York, 1959; *Reason and Goodness*, New York and London, 1961; *On Sanity in Thought and Art*, Tucson, 1962; *Reason and Analysis*, La Salle and London, 1962; *The Life of the Spirit in a Machine Age*, Northampton, 1967; (edited by Eugene Freeman) *The Uses of a Liberal Education, and Other Talks to Students*, La Salle, 1973, London, 1974; *Reason and Belief*, London, 1974, New Haven, 1975; (with others, edited by Paul Arthur Schilpp) *The Philosophy of Brand Blanshard*, La Salle, 1980; *Four Reasonable Men: Marcus Aurelius, John Stuart Mill, Ernest Renan, Henry Sidgwick*, Middletown, 1984; plus articles in academic and popular journals and magazines. **Cause of death** Undisclosed, at age 95.

C.E. BLUNT

British Numismatist

***Born* 16 July 1904**

***Died* Marlborough, Wiltshire, 20 November 1987**

Although one of the century's leading numismatists of British coins, Christopher Blunt's career did not attract the public attention received by his brother Anthony, the art historian, but within a rarified circle of medieval scholars he was acknowledged as the foremost authority on British, and particularly tenth-century, coins.

Together with his brothers, Anthony and Wilfrid (q.v.), he attended Marlborough College in Wiltshire as a foundation scholar. After leaving to work in the City, he joined the firm of merchant bankers Higginson and Co., becoming partner and director of its successor companies (the Hill Samuel Group). His wartime career was honourable, and on retiring from the army in 1945 with the rank of colonel, he was created an officer of the US Legion of Merit and awarded the OBE.

Rather in the manner of an eighteenth-century dilettante, Blunt pursued his scholarly researches in tandem with his professional career in the City. At school he had been fascinated by history and archaeology, and from 1931 he produced a series of standard works on the coinages of the English kings Henry VI, Edward IV and Edward V. Under the guidance of a number of authorities on numismatics, together with Michael Dolley, he began research into Anglo-Saxon coins, concentrating particularly on the eighth and ninth centuries. He is known, however, for his research which focuses on the coins of the next century: his publications in this area are *The Coinage of Athelstan* (1974), followed by a catalogue published jointly with M.M. Archibald on the British Museum's collection of Anglo-Saxon coins, AD 924 to *circa* 973. A short time before his death he had completed the correction of proofs for a forthcoming book, written jointly, on the *Coinage of Tenth-Century England*.

Although his publications were few, he was fully occupied by his activities as editor of the *British Numismatic Journal* (from 1935 to 1971), senior editor of the *Sylloge of Coins of the*

British Isles from 1953, published under the auspices of the British Academy, president of the British Numismatic Society (1946–50) and the Royal Numismatic Society (1956–61), and of the Society of Medieval Archaeology. He also contributed several articles to numismatic journals.

Through his fellowship of the Society of Antiquaries, he was closely involved in the rehabilitation of Kelmscott, the house of the English Arts and Crafts artist, William Morris. In his home village of Ramsbury, and in his county, Wiltshire, he devoted himself to service on regional archaeology and natural history societies and chaired the Wiltshire Museums Council.

For over 50 years, he gathered archaeologists, numismatists and historians at his home, where, no doubt, numismatics was the main topic of conversation. Unaware of his brother Anthony's activities as a Soviet agent, he was deeply affected by these revelations. However, he had always been proud of both his brothers' achievements as author and art historian, although their achievements in no way diminish his own, for his researches changed the course of early British numismatics.

Born Christopher Evelyn Blunt. **Parents** Reverend A.S.V. and Hilda Violet Blunt. **Marriage** Elisabeth Rachel Bazley, 1930 (died, 1980). **Children** One son and two daughters. **Education** Foundation scholar, Marlborough School, Wiltshire. **Military service** 52 anti-aircraft regiment, Territorial Army, 1939–45; general staff, General Headquarters; dispatches, British Expeditionary Force; Home Forces, 21 Army Group; Supreme Headquarters, Allied Expeditionary Force; retired as colonel, 1946. **Career** Entered Higginson and Company, merchant bankers, 1924, partner, 1947, executive director of successor companies, 1950–64. **Other activities** Numismatist; principal editor, *British Numismatic Journal*, 1935–71; senior editor, *Sylloge of Coins of the British Isles*, 38 volumes. **Offices and memberships** President: British Numismatic Society, 1946–50, Royal Numismatic Society, 1956–61, Wiltshire Archaeological and Natural History Society, 1970–74, Society of Medieval Archaeology, 1978–80; chairman, Wiltshire Museum Council. **Awards and honours** Medal: Royal Numismatic Society, British Numismatic Society, American Numismatic Society; officer, American Legion of Merit, 1945; officer, Order of the British Empire, 1945; fellow: British Academy, 1965, Society of Antiquaries. **Publications** *The Coinage of Athelstan*, 1974; (with M.M. Archibald) *Catalogue of Anglo-Saxon Coins in the British Museum, 924–c.973*, 1986; *The Coinage of Tenth-Century England*; contributor to *Numismatic Chronicle*, *British Numismatic Journal*, *Archaeologia*. **Cause of death** Undisclosed, at age 83.

LORD COBBOLD

British Banker

***Born* London, England, 14 September 1904**

***Died* Hertfordshire, England, 1 November 1987**

Lord Cobbold, KG, PC, GCVO, was deputy governor of the Bank of England from 1945 to 1949 and governor from 1949 to 1961—an important period in the bank's history which left it in a very different relationship to government from earlier times. Cobbold's efficiency and organizational skills enabled the bank to weather nationalization, devaluation, restoration of sterling convertibility and the rigours of the Radcliffe Committee enquiry and the Bank Rate tribunal and emerge a leaner and fitter, if perhaps a somewhat chastened, institution.

Cameron Fromanteel Cobbold was descended from a well-known Suffolk brewing family, his great-grandfather having been MP for Ipswich from 1847 to 1868. Cobbold's own father was a not-too-successful barrister, but he launched his son with the typical upper-class education of Eton and King's College, Cambridge, where he was a scholar and prizeman. But Cobbold's gifts lay in the practical rather than the academic realm, and he left Cambridge in his second year before taking his degree. At the age of 21 he entered the City, first with a firm of accountants in London and Paris and then with one of their clients, C.E. Heath and Excess Insurance. He quickly made his mark there and was sent out to Italy to manage the firm's Italian subsidiary. Here Cobbold met his first major professional problem in the rescue operation mounted by the Bank of England to save the British–Italian Banking Corporation. His skill in sorting out the tangle of interests brought him to the notice of the then governor, Montagu Norman, and in 1933 he was invited to join the bank as an adviser in its overseas department. Again he arrived at a critical time with the final collapse of the gold standard, and his already good relations with the staff of the Bank of France enabled him to play a big part in the Anglo–French–American Monetary Agreement of 1936 which engineered an agreed depreciation of various European currencies.

In 1938 he was elected a director of the bank and from then on was in charge of its overseas financial dealings, principally in negotiating the Anglo–French agreement of December 1939 designed to integrate the British and French economic and monetary systems with the outbreak of World War II. Cobbold's was a key influence in monetary affairs during the war and in the preparations for the post-war international system, in particular the setting up of the Bretton Woods institutions. By this time he was deputy governor and he played an important part in the Labour Government's nationalization of the bank—a difficult period in which he crossed swords with the then chancellor of the exchequer, Hugh Dalton, a clash of wills which almost lost him the governorship. Fortunately for him, Dalton was succeeded by Sir Stafford Cripps and Cobbold was ultimately appointed governor in 1949.

This was no easy appointment. A number of Tory and Labour politicians were suspicious of the new regime, primarily because of Cobbold's dislike of Keynesian economics. But for the very same reason, his appointment was welcomed in the City. In the event, Cobbold largely succeeded in keeping the bank out of politics, at least until the later part of his time as governor. And this was not easy. Almost immediately after his appointment he was faced with a sterling crisis—inevitable from the end of Lend-Lease with the cessation of hostilities in 1945. He was forced to advise the government to undertake a major devaluation of the pound when no further US loans were forthcoming, and was instrumental in organizing a general realignment of European currencies against the dollar.

The return of a Conservative government in 1951 enabled him to back a more competitive and market-dominated economy in contrast to Labour's controls, but he distrusted the stop-go policies of Harold Macmillan both as chancellor and prime minister and regretted that as governor he did not have more power to control the "dangerously unorthodox" government spending. In 1957 came a major bank crisis when leakage of prior information about a substantial increase in bank rate was rumoured. A judicial tribunal cleared all members of the court of complicity in taking advantage of their knowledge of the impending move, but thereafter all responsibility for changes in the rate was moved from the bank to the chancellor. Cobbold certainly tended to treat all monetary policy, and especially the bank rate, as wholly within the powers of the bank—an attitude which came in for criticism from the Radcliffe Committee on the Working of the Monetary System, whose report was published in 1959. Cobbold's successor as governor was more open in his approach.

Cobbold had been reappointed for a second term in 1954 and agreed to continue into a third term on the grounds that the Radcliffe enquiry was still proceeding in 1959. He was therefore responsible for successfully negotiating sterling's return to convertibility in that year. But the pressures, especially of the various enquiries and the ups and downs of relations with the Macmillan Government were beginning to tell, and he resigned on 30 June 1961. He had been elevated to the peerage in 1960 and in 1963 was appointed by the queen as lord chamberlain, a position he held until 1971, thereafter becoming a permanent lord-in-waiting. This was in many ways a happier time. Cobbold was the first lord chamberlain to be appointed from the professional world and his management skills brought many much needed reforms to the royal household. He also introduced a more modern approach to relations between monarchy and people. The guest lists for Buckingham Palace garden parties were broadened to include a much wider spectrum of the population and the system of informal lunches at the palace, with people from all walks of life, was introduced. His service to the Royal Family was rewarded with the Order of the Garter—the highest order of English chivalry—in 1970.

Cobbold also served in 1962 as chairman of a commission of enquiry investigating the attitude of the people of Sarawak and North Borneo to incorporation into the State of Malaysia. He was also a director of a number of medical charities, being chairman of the Middlesex Hospital from 1963 to 1974 and president of the British Heart Foundation until 1976. Though regarded by some of his bank associates as somewhat cold and ruthless, he gained the respect of his central bank colleagues in the Bank for International Settlements and in the Commonwealth. He was also the first governor to appear on television and initiated the making of a film to popularize knowledge about the working of the bank.

Born Cameron Fromanteel Cobbold. **Parents** Lieutenant Colonel Clement John Fromanteel, barrister, and Stella Willoughby Saville (Cameron) Cobbold. **Marriage** Lady Margaret Hermione Millicent Bulwer-Lytton, 1930. **Children** Two sons and one daughter. **Education** Eton College, Berkshire, 1917–23; King's College, Cambridge, 1923–25. **Military service** Lieutenant, London Rifle Brigade, 1925–29. **Career** Began City career with firm of accountants, 1925; joined C.E. Heath & Excess Insurance; general manager, Italian Excess Insurance Co, Milan; adviser, Bank of England, 1933–38, executive director, 1938, deputy governor, 1945, governor, 1945–61. **Related activities** Director: Bank for International Settlement, 1949–61, British Petroleum, 1963–74, Hudson Bay Company, 1964–74, Guardian Royal Exchange, 1963–74; chairman: Chemical Bank New York Advisory Commission, 1969–74, Italian International Bank, 1971–74. **Other activities** High sheriff of county of London, 1946–47; chairman, Malaysia Commission of Enquiry, 1962; lord chamberlain of Her Majesty's Household, 1963–71; chancellor, Royal Victorian Order, 1963–71; chairman, Middlesex Hospital Board of Governors and Medical School Council, 1963–74; permanent lord-in-waiting to the queen, 1971–87; vice-president, British Heart Foundation, president to 1976. **Awards and honours** Fellow of Eton, 1951–67, steward of the courts, 1973–87; privy counsellor, 1959; created first Baron of Knebworth, 1960; honorary fellow, Institute of Bankers, 1961; honorary LLD, McGill University, 1961; honorary DSc (economics), London University, 1963; Knight Grand Cross of the Royal Victorian Order, 1963; Knight of the Order of the Garter, 1970; deputy lieutenant, Hertfordshire, 1972; one of Her Majesty's lieutenants for the City of London. **Cause of death** Undisclosed, at age 83.

SIR JOHN COLVILLE

British Diplomat and Civil Servant
***Born* England, 28 January 1915**
***Died* Hampshire, England, 19 November 1987**

Sir John Colville was at the centre of power as private secretary to three British prime ministers, including Winston Churchill. He played a similar role for the future Queen Elizabeth II, and late in life made his own modest contribution to the memoir literature of the war years.

Colville's aristocratic background made his entry into the inner circle of politics easier, if not inevitable. His father was a younger son of Viscount Colville of Culross, holder of a Scottish peerage going back to the reign of James I. His mother was a lady-in-waiting to Queen Mary, George V's consort, and in line with this tradition, Colville, as a boy, acted as page of honour to the king.

His education and choice of career were equally privileged. After Harrow (as it happened, Churchill's own alma mater), Colville took a first-class honours degree in history at Trinity College, Cambridge, and entered the diplomatic service in 1937. Once embarked upon a profession that, to this day, favours the well-connected as well as the intelligent, Colville rose rapidly. At the age of 24 he was appointed assistant private secretary to Prime Minister Neville Chamberlain, and when, in the dark days of 1940, Winston Churchill took over at 10 Downing Street, Colville remained at his post, despite an initial regret at Chamberlain's forced departure.

In the event Colville became one of Churchill's most valued and trusted personal staff, and repaid this trust with a fierce loyalty. Service with Churchill, the war-time leader, was notoriously demanding; his staff had to be prepared to work all hours, and were subject to extraordinary pressures from the unorthodox working habits of their chief.

Much against Churchill's will, Colville received permission in 1941 to train as a pilot with the Royal Air Force Volunteer Reserve. In 1943, however, he returned to his place at Downing Street, where he was to remain until the end of the war, with the exception of a stint of active service with a fighter squadron during the Normandy invasion.

In May 1945 Churchill held a general election which, much to his surprise, resulted in a Conservative defeat. Colville, of whose partisanship there could now be no doubts, stood unsuccessfully as a Conservative candidate. After this setback, he continued as private secretary to the new Labour prime minister, Clement Attlee, but soon returned to the diplomatic service.

From 1945 to 1947 Colville worked in the Foreign Office, with special responsibility for the Balkans. Then, upon the marriage of Princess Elizabeth, the heir to the throne, he was appointed her private secretary. He expressed his reservations about the job to Churchill, but was bluntly told, "There is no argument where the throne is concerned". For two years Colville filled what proved to be a job almost as demanding as his war-time duties.

After marrying in 1948, Colville resumed his diplomatic career in 1949, as counsellor to the British embassy in Lisbon. Upon Churchill's return to power in 1951, however, Colville was summoned to the heart of Whitehall for the last time. As Churchill's joint principal private secretary from 1951 to 1955, he played an important role in making the wheels of government go round. He ran the prime minister's private office, gave him some assistance with his speeches, and served as a not-always-popular liaison between Churchill and the lesser lights of the Cabinet. Most questionable was Colville's share in covering up the extent to which Churchill's 1953 stroke incapacitated him, a matter which was deliberately played down, not only to the public but even to members of the government.

More clearly beneficial to posterity was Colville's success in persuading the prime minister of the need for greater emphasis on technology in British education, a development which resulted in the foundation of Churchill College, Cambridge. Colville's work in establishing the college was one of the reasons for his knighthood in 1974.

With Churchill's belated retirement in 1955, Colville also decided to leave public service. The remainder of his working career was taken up by directorships with a number of merchant banks and other private companies. He also began to make his mark as a writer. (An early effort, *Fools' Pleasure* in 1935, had not attracted much notice.) He contributed to *Action This Day: Working with Churchill* (1968), wrote a biography of Lord Gort, *Man of Valour* (1972), used his war-time diary for *Footprints in Time* (1976), and drew on his experience with the Royal Family for *The New Elizabethans* (1977). His last book, *The Fringes of Power* (1985), described the second Churchill government from his own, admittedly biased, standpoint.

Colville was once characterized, rather unkindly, as "the greatest snob in England". Perhaps a more accurate assessment would be to recognize him as a genuine diplomat, skilled in ironing out difficulties, who nevertheless identified totally with the Conservative fount of power.

Born John Rupert Colville. **Parents** Honourable George and Lady Cynthia Colville, lady-in-waiting to Queen Mary. **Marriage** Lady Margaret Egerton, 1948. **Children** Two sons and one daughter. **Education** Harrow School, Middlesex; Trinity College, Cambridge, first-class honours, history tripos, senior scholar. **Military service** Served, 1939–45, Royal Air Force Voluntary Reserve, 1941–44. **Career** Third secretary, diplomatic service, 1937; assistant private secretary to Neville Chamberlain, 1939–40, Winston Churchill, 1940–41, 1943–45, Clement Attlee, 1945; private secretary to Princess Elizabeth, 1947–49; first secretary, British Embassy, Lisbon, 1949–51; counsellor, Foreign Service, 1951; joint principal private secretary to Prime Minister Winston Churchill, 1951–55. **Related activities** Director: Grindlays Bank, Provident Life Association; chairman: London Committee, Ottoman Bank, Eucalyptus Pulp Mills Limited; president, Banque Grindlay SA, New Victoria Hospital, from 1978, Prayer Book Society, 1981–84; vice-president, National Association of Boys' Clubs. **Awards and honours** Page of honour to King George V, 1927–31; Commander of the Royal Victorian Order, 1949; Companion of the Order of the Bath, 1955; honorary fellow, Churchill College, Cambridge, 1971; knighted, 1974; officer, Legion of Honour. **Publications** *Fools' Pleasure*, 1935; (contributor) *Action This Day—Working with Churchill*, 1968; *Man of Valour*, 1972; *Footprints in Time*, 1976; *The New Elizabethans*, 1977; *The Portrait of a General*, 1980; *The Churchillians*, 1981; *Strange Inheritance*, 1983; *The Fringes of Power*, 1985. **Cause of death** Undisclosed, at age 72.

LORD DUNCAN-SANDYS

British Politician and Statesman

***Born* London, England, 24 January 1908**

***Died* London, England, 26 November 1987**

Duncan Sandys was at the centre of the substantial overhaul that British defence and foreign policies went through in the 1950s and 1960s as the nation somewhat belatedly adjusted to a changed international climate following World War II. As minister of defence in the late 1950s he implemented the strategy that for many years to come committed Britain to dependence on nuclear deterrence rather than the deployment of large conventional forces. Then, as Commonwealth and colonial secretary in the early 1960s, he negotiated independence for some of its most important overseas dependencies, as the country divested itself of the last vestiges of its imperial past.

Resilient, hard-working and loyal, he became something of a troubleshooter for successive Conservative Party leaders, making a success of a series of difficult and often unattractive assignments during a long political career. But he never quite attained any of the highest offices in the land, and his later years were overshadowed by controversy.

As the son of a Conservative member of parliament, the young Sandys naturally gravitated toward politics. Educated at the prestigious private school Eton College and Oxford University's Magdalen College, he qualified as a lawyer but opted to join the foreign service, being posted to the Berlin embassy and then representing Britain in European and world trade negotiations. At the age of 27 he was elected member of parliament for the southeast London constituency of Norwood and married the daughter of Sir Winston Churchill the same year.

Sandys took a keen interest in defence matters and, although a member of his party's executive committee, backed Churchill's campaign against the premiership of Conservative leader Neville Chamberlain. Chamberlain's policy of conciliation towards Hitler's Germany in the hope of avoiding war seemed to be leaving the country dangerously exposed if war should come. When it did, Sandys immediately enlisted in the army, serving with the expeditionary force which was sent in 1940 to aid neutral Norway's resistance to the Nazi invasion and whose ignominious withdrawal in the face of overwhelming odds toppled the Chamberlain government and brought Churchill to 10 Downing Street.

Invalided out of the service the following year, Sandys was soon recruited to the new administration as financial secretary to the War Office and then given responsibility for armament production with the Ministry of Supply. But it was in the chair of the War Cabinet's committee for defence against the German flying bombs then wreaking havoc on the south of England that Sandys really distinguished himself. The policy of sustained bombardment of the German research and rocket bases greatly influenced the conflict's course. His recompense was a place in the Cabinet as minister of works in the last months of the war, whose end saw him lose his parliamentary seat in the dramatic Labour landslide of 1945.

Sandys now devoted himself to promoting his central political ideal of European unity, founding the European Movement and becoming chairman of its international executive, and when he regained his place in parliament in 1950 as member for Streatham, near his former constituency, he continued to work enthusiastically for the European cause.

It was as minister of supply, however, that he returned to government after Churchill and the Conservatives swept back to power in the election of 1951. The new administration saw a central part of its mission as being to roll back some of the achievements of its socialist predecessor, and it fell to Sandys to push through parliament the bill to denationalize the iron and steel industry in the teeth of fierce hostility from the Opposition. Demonstrating the dogged determination that had become his political trademark, he saw the measure passed.

He was rewarded with the housing and local government portfolio and, in particular, the familiarly thankless task of abolishing rent restrictions, thus boosting the property market but creating hardship among poorer tenants. It was another parliamentary minefield which he negotiated with considerable skill to a successful conclusion.

When Sandys took over the Ministry of Defence, the priorities were rather different. Defence policy since the war had to a large extent been bipartisan, and still reflected an illusion of worldwide British military domination that the war itself had rendered obsolete. The so-called Cold War rivalry between the twin superpowers of the United States and the USSR, with their respective spheres of influence, now dominated the international agenda. This had become clearer than ever the previous year after the débâcle of the colonial-style joint attack launched by Britain and France on Egypt in an attempt to overturn that country's nationalization of the Suez Canal—an attack that had to be aborted when the US refused to support it.

The task before Sandys, therefore, was to effect radical reforms designed to sweep the cobwebs from the entire area of defence policy. This involved drastic reduction in the size of the armed forces by the abolition of the draft in favour of a well-paid, all-volunteer force within the essentially European framework of NATO, based on the central role of the nuclear deterrent.

This upheaval in the services and the scaling down of the imperial role that it implied met resistance from the Right, while the switch to a nuclear emphasis inflamed the Left. Nevertheless, by the time Sandys moved on, a pattern had been set for defence policy that would endure to the end of his lifetime.

His next important political role would prove to be his last—secretary of state for Commonwealth relations and colonial secretary. The juxtaposition of the two posts was significant, as colonies one by one became independent members of the Commonwealth.

Among those gaining their independence in Sandys' time were Jamaica, Kenya and Nigeria. But perhaps more momentous was the failure of his somewhat impromptu initiative to bring a measure of multi-racialism to the governance of Southern Rhodesia. The refusal of representatives of the White minority in the colony to concede meaningful change in the franchise that would lead to majority rule meant that Sandys' deal could offer only piecemeal reform (15 seats in parliament) to the Black majority, whose leaders had no choice but to reject it. The direct result was White Rhodesia's unilateral declaration of independence in 1965, to which Sandys, by then just a plain member of parliament following the 1964 change of government, openly and controversially gave his support.

In some quarters Sandys was now being labelled a racist, for he had also added his voice to the growing clamour on the Right for limits on Black immigration to Britain, a post-war social phenomenon reflected in his own Streatham constituency. But more than anything else, these were signs that Sandys' brand of politics had had its day, with the Conservatives now marching to the tune of the much less patrician Edward Heath.

Sandys never again held office, and he saw out his political career as a member of the House of Lords. During this period he became embroiled in further controversy, as chairman of the multinational concern Lonrho Ltd, when he was indirectly implicated in criticisms made in a government report of irregularities in the company's accounts. It was a sad swan-song.

Sandys had a penchant for performing conjuring tricks (he was a member of the Magic Circle), and at the height of his powers he could usually be relied upon to pull a rabbit out of the hat at a vital moment. If the ability failed him towards the end of his career, it had nevertheless stood him and his party in good stead over the many years in which the latter found his services indispensable to its endeavours.

Born Duncan Edwin Sandys; became Lord Duncan-Sandys on elevation to House of Lords, 1974. **Parents** Captain George, MP, and Mildred (Cameron) Sandys. **Marriages** 1) Diana Churchill, 1935 (divorved, 1960); 2) Marie-Claire Schnitt, formerly Viscountess Hudson, 1962. **Children** One daughter and two sons from first marriage; one daughter from second marriage. **Education** Eton College, Berkshire; Magdalen College, Oxford, MA. **Military service** Commissioned, Territorial Army (Royal Artillery), 1937; Expeditionary Force in Norway, 1940; promoted to lieutenant colonel, 1941; disabled on active service, 1941. **Career** Entered diplomatic service, 1931, posted to Berlin, 1931–33; Foreign Office, 1933–35; Conservative MP, Norwood, 1935–45; financial secretary, War Office, 1941–43; parliamentary secretary in charge of armament production, Ministry of Supply, 1943–44; chairman, War Cabinet Committee for defence against

German flying bombs and rockets, 1943–45; minister of works, 1944–45; founder, European Movement, 1947, chairman, international executive to 1950; Conservative MP, Streatham, 1950–74; minister of supply, 1951–54; minister of housing and local government, 1954–57; minister of defence, 1957–59; minister of aviation, 1959–60; secretary of state for Commonwealth relations, 1960–64; secretary of state for the colonies, 1962–64. **Related activities** Political columnist, *Sunday Chronicle*, 1938–39; member, national executive, Conservative Party, 1938–39; co-founder, Air Raid Protection Institute (later Institute of Civil Defence), 1938; chairman, parliamentary assembly of Council of Europe and of Western European Uneion, 1950–51, 1965–87, leader, British delegation, 1970–72; president, Europa Nostra, 1969–84, honorary life president, 1984; chairman, British section, Franco-British Council, 1972–78. **Other activities** Member, generaly Advisory Council, BBC, 1947–51; director, Ashanti Goldfields Corporation, 1947–51, 1966–72; founder, Civic Trust, president from 1956; chairman, Lonrho Limited, 1972–84, president, 1984; chairman, International Organizing Committee, European Architectural Heritage Year, 1975; vice-president, Association of District Councils, from 1979; honorary vice-president, National Chamber of Trade, from 1951. **Offices and memberships** Member, Magic Circle. **Awards and honours** Privy Counsellor, 1944; honorary member, Royal Town Planning Institute, 1956; Grand Cross, Order of Merit, Italy, 1960; freeman of Bridgetown, Barbados, 1962; honorary fellow, Royal Institute of British Architects, 1968; Companion of Honour, 1973; Order of the Sultanate of Brunei, 1973; created life peer, Baron Duncan-Sandys, 1974; medal of honour, city of Paris, 1974; Gold Cup of European Movement, 1975; Goethe Gold Medal, Hamburg Foundation, 1975; Grand Cross of Order of Crown, Belgium, 1975; Commander, Legion of Honour, France, 1979; Grand Cross, Order of Merit, Federal Republic of Germany, 1981. **Publications** *The European Movement and the Council of Europe*, 1949; *The Modern Commonwealth*, 1961. **Cause of death** Undisclosed, at age 79.

GEORGES FRANJU

French Film Director

Born **Fougères, France, 12 April 1912**

Died **Paris, France, 5 November 1987**

Georges Franju, a director noted for his treatment of fantasy, as well as the bizarre, had what can be considered a patchy career, so that, generally, his name has not become a true classic in cinema history. However, a small handful of his works remain little jewels in any survey of international film.

Trained as a stage designer between 1932 and 1933, Franju created the sets for theatres and music halls, including the Folies Bergère, before turning to the cinema. His first film, *Le Métro*, was co-directed with Henri Langlois. It did not attract great notice; however, two years later he and Langlois had founded the Cinémathèque Français, the country's national film archive which has become one of the world's finest. His interest in and love for the silent film was nourished by the association, and this had some effect upon several of his films, including his tribute to the film serialist Louis Feuillade in *Judex* (1963), regarded by some as his finest film.

Between 1938 and 1945 he was secretary of the International Federation of Film Archives, and in 1946 founded the Académie du Cinéma. After World War II, he began to make his name as a director, with a series of shorts to which he gave an intense personal expression. *Le Sang des bêtes* (1949) is one of his best known, with its shocking scenes of slaughter-houses and animal victims. *Hôtel des invalides*, two years later, was a commission to celebrate the Musée des l'Armes, the home of Napoleon's tomb. In it Franju pointed out that it also houses the victims of war, being the veteran's hospital, and transforms the emblems of military glory into sinister inconography. His 1953 tribute to Georges Méliès (the French film pioneer of illusion), *Le Grand Méliès*, was a delicate and affectionate work, also highlighting what many critics feel to be Franju's best period. While some consider him, during this time, to have been a social documentarist, others have interpreted these shorts as poetic, by a director who makes no comment but forces the viewer merely to see hypocrisy. Certainly his documentaries are idiosyncratic; he uses imagery and juxtaposition, but does not make overt statements or utilize symbolism. They carry single images that are some of the most harrowing and memorable in cinema history.

Franju turned to features in 1958 with *La Tête contre les murs*, establishing an international reputation for surrealism and a taste for the morbid world view which, along with his use of photographer Eugen Schufftan, made evident his debt to the German classic cinema. *Les Yeux sans visage* (1959), about a wicked banker and an avenger who protects his daughter's interests, was a good horror film, but possibly shallow when considered to be anything more complicated than that. Nevertheless, Franju demonstrated his control of visual narrative, and his superb grey and white photography, evident in most of his work, was excellent here.

His practical style of surrealism continued with *Thomas l'imposteur* (1964), adapted by Jean Cocteau from his World War II novel, as well as in *La Faute de l'Abbé Mouret* (1970), about a priest's descent into earthly interests. Franju also directed a series of films for television, "Chroniques de France", from 1965 to 1976. He returned to the genre of fantasy-thriller in 1974 with *L'Homme sans visage*, paying homage to comic-strip fiction, but his continuing weakness with features—including a fuzzy dedication to plot—seemed to indicate a lack of spirit. He is best remembered for the sensitive poetry of his early documentaries, which he once said seem to illustrate his ease and preference for imagination "for the most ordinary action to become imbued with disquieting meaning, for the décor of everyday life to engender a fantastic world".

Born Georges Franju. **Education** Religious school, Fougères. **Military service** French Army, Algeria, 1928–32. **Career** Worked for insurance company, 1927; trained as designer, building sets for Folies Bergère and Casino de Paris, 1932–33; with Henri Langlois began Cercle du Cinéma programmes, directed first film, 1934; with Langlois, founded the French national film archive, Cinémathèque Française, and *CINEMAtographe* magazine, 1937; executive secretary, Fédération Internationale des Archives du Film (FIAF), 1938–45; began to make name as film-maker after the war with series of documentary shorts; secretary-general, Institut de Cinématographie Scientifique, 1945–54; founder, L'Académie du Cinéma, 1946; first feature-length film, *La Tête contre les murs*, 1958; continued to make films, while also moving into television direction. **Awards and honours** Chevalier, Legion of Honour; officer, Ordre National du Mérite et des Arts et des Lettres. **Publications** *De Marey à Renoir: trésors de la cinémathèque française 1882–1939*, Paris, 1981; plus numerous articles and interviews in film journals. **Films** (co-director) *Le Métro*, 1934; *Le Sang des bêtes*, 1949; *En passant par la Lorraine*, 1950; *Hôtel des invalides*, 1951; *Le Grand Méliès*, 1952; *Monsieur et Madame Curie*, 1953; *Les Poussières*, 1954; *Navigation marchande/Marine marchande*, 1954; *A propos d'une rivière/Le Saumon Atlantique*, 1955; *Mon chien*, 1955; *Le Théâtre National Populaire/Le TNP*, 1956; *Sur le pont d'Avignon*, 1956; *Décembre, mois des enfants*, 1956; *Notre Dame, cathédrale de Paris*, 1957; *La Première nuit*, 1958; *La Tête contre les murs*, 1958; (and co-adaptor) *Les Yeux sans visage*, 1959; *Pleins feux* *sur l'assassin*, 1960; *Thérèse Desqueyroux*, 1962; *Judex*, 1963; *Thomas l'imposteur/Thomas the Imposter*, 1964; *Marcel Allain*, 1966; *La Faute de l'Abbé Mouret/The Demise of Father Mouret*, 1970; (and co-music) *Nuits rouges/L'Homme sans visage/Shadowman*, 1974. **Television** (includes) "Chroniques de France" series, 1965–76; *Les Rideaux blancs*, episode from *L'Instant de la paix*, 1965; *Pour le plaisir*, 1966–68; *La Service des affaires classées*, 1970; *La Ligne d'ombre*, 1971; (adaptor) *L'Homme sans visage*, from 1974. **Cause of death** Undisclosed, at age 75.

ERNÖ GOLDFINGER

Hungarian/British Architect

Born **Budapest, Hungary, 11 September 1902**

Died **London, England, 15 November 1987**

Perhaps the most rigorous of "modern movement" architects who practised in England, Ernö Goldfinger would never compromise the tenets of his design philosophy. A most cosmopolitan European, he was, nevertheless, an Anglophile and made his home in London from 1934 until his death. Often prickly, always crushing in argument, he nevertheless inspired genuine friendship and affection in those who knew him well.

Before the arrival in England of the wave of European architects who were forced to flee from an increasingly inhospitable Continent, a few émigrés came for reasons other than to escape from persecution. Ernö Goldfinger was one of these. He had already migrated across Europe; before his eighteenth birthday, he left Budapest for Vienna, then Vienna for Gstaad in Switzerland, travelling with his parents. From Switzerland he proceeded alone to Paris, to commence his architectural study.

Goldfinger first enrolled at the École Nationale et Supérieure des Beaux-Arts, which he entered in 1923, at the age of 21. A year later he became one of a dozen founder members of an "Atelier Moderne", a splinter group from the Beaux-Arts school. The young founders of this group initially asked the leading modernist architect in Paris, Le Corbusier, to become their master. Corbusier refused, but suggested an architect for whom he himself had worked at one time; this was Auguste Perret, who accepted their offer.

Perret's method of teaching by example was clearly very important to Goldfinger. The combination of classically-based order and proportion, with the adventurous, almost Gothic, structural possibilities of the "new" material—reinforced concrete—and the didactic, systematic planning of the Beaux-Arts school were deeply imbued in Goldfinger. He remained at the Atelier Perret until 1927 and always retained a great respect for his master—"the last classicist", as he often referred to him.

To have lived in Paris in the 1920s is the stuff of legend now; Goldfinger used to frequent the Café du Dôme and the Deux Magots, where he mixed with painters, sculptors and photographers, including Pablo Picasso, Max Ernst, Amedée Ozenfant, André Kertész and Fernand Léger. These early friendships enabled him to assemble a fine collection of modern paintings, which were to become the envy of visitors.

Another contact from Parisian café society was the radical Austrian architect and writer Adolf Loos, who had published the celebrated essay "Ornament and Crime" in 1908. Goldfinger may have learned much about the handling of fine surfaces from Loos, who was busy during the late

1920s designing houses in Paris for the Dada poet Tristan Tzara and for the exotic dancer Josephine Baker.

Auguste Perret would not meet Loos, as he was an Austrian and—Perret suspected—a "modernist". Goldfinger, however, was fascinated. He visited the 1925 Exposition des Arts et Métiers Industriels et Décoratives in the company of Loos. This was the crucial exhibition where the stylish opulence of what we now call Art Deco contrasted sharply with the stark modernism of the Pavilion de l'Ésprit Nouveau by Ozenfant and le Corbusier. Loos and Goldfinger concurred in their dislike of Corbusier's 1920s work: "I hate his 'Kasbah' architecture—all the white stuff". However, Loos certainly communicated to Goldfinger his own great appreciation of England, and of the English culture of restraint in all things: architecture, tailoring and furnishing.

Soon after the exhibition in Paris, Goldfinger made his first visit to England to design a beauty salon for Helena Rubinstein in Mayfair. He brought with him a tough-minded approach to modern architecture, combined with a dash of Parisian chic—both rather rare qualities in 1926 England. Little wonder, then, that the British firm of shopfitters thought the design drawings were unfinished. Unaccustomed to "modern" design, they interpreted the lack of applied decoration as a result of the architect's inability to draw, rather than a deliberate design intention!

In addition to these difficulties, relations between architect and client were not easy. In fact, Goldfinger had to resort to legal action to recover his full fee from Rubinstein.

Goldfinger continued to study and to practise in Paris from 1924 until 1933. After his marriage to Ursula Ruth Blackwell, an English student of painting, the couple settled in England in 1934.

When the Goldfingers arrived, London was still largely a Georgian city, although already in the process of destruction. In common with many other Continental architects, Goldfinger was impressed by the restrained simplicity and seemingly effortless elegance of Georgian squares, streets and individual buildings. He greatly admired Portland Place, and had a special fondness for Chandos House, designed by Robert Adam: "The most beautiful house in London…the most arrogant understatement that ever happened". London's modern buildings, however, did not impress him similarly: he grudgingly admitted to liking Wells Coates's flats (at Lawn Road, Hampstead) and the gorilla house (at the Regent's Park Zoo) by Tecton.

Goldfinger's commissions before the war included a number of shops for progressive retailers, several exhibition designs and a stage set for the left-wing play *Stay Down Miner*. He also made a number of designs for furniture, ignoring advice given by his old friend Loos: "Architects sit in chairs, they do not design them." In 1951 he published a book called *British Furniture Today* in which he made stern comments on the lax use of the words "modern" and "contemporary", recommending a scientific approach to furniture design.

An important statement of Goldfinger's architectural views was embodied in the three brick and concrete houses he built in Willow Road, near Hampstead Heath, just before the outbreak of World War II. At first the scheme met with fierce opposition from local residents who were outraged at the thought of a "white concrete box" facing the heath. Goldfinger nevertheless carried through his plans with a determination characteristic of his personal style.

In 1945 he co-authored a scheme for the rebuilding of London, pointing out that the wartime bombing had provided the opportunity for large-scale redevelopment. Illustrated with charming sketches by Gordon Cullen, who was working in Goldfinger's office at the time, the book was only one of many such schemes published in the cautiously optimistic aftermath of the war. However, all the problems identified in the book still seem, alas, to be in evidence today.

In 1946 came the first really large commission Goldfinger had yet been offered: the refurbishment of the offices and printing works of the *Daily Worker*, the communist newspaper. The result of the reworking produced a sort of watered-down Russian constructivism tempered with detail of a type that owes much to Auguste Perret. In collaboration with Colin Penn,

Goldfinger also revamped the Covent Garden headquarters of the British Communist Party, this time in contemporary style with a symmetrical frontage of glass bricks.

Goldfinger's *chef d'oeuvre*—Alexander Fleming House at the Elephant and Castle in South London—was built in two phases (1959 and 1963) to house the Ministry of Health. This large complex of buildings in reinforced concrete had a rectangular grid system of advancing and receding planes of windows. Liveliness in composition was introduced by variation in the size of the different blocks, though an astonishing degree of overall symmetry was preserved. Although much admired by the architectural fraternity, the building did not find favour with the general public. In 1989 it was disfigured, partly by demolition, and partly by the addition of very unsympathetic cladding.

The hard edge of Goldfinger's modernism may perhaps be best exemplified by his two tower blocks for the Greater London Council. In Balfron Tower (1964) and Trellick Tower (1967) the sheer scale is quite overwhelming, "architecture" is a matter of proportional system and faceless inhumanity may seem to prevail. To counter such charges, at least in part, Goldfinger and his wife moved into a flat on the twenty-seventh floor of the Balfron House tower in 1967—for two months. This was in order to prove the effectiveness of the design, which it did to the satisfaction of Goldfinger. He also moved his office from Piccadilly to the base of the other tower in 1972.

A close friend of Goldfinger's, H.T. Cadbury-Brown, said at his death: "What was wonderful about Ernö was that he had no *doubts*." His professional life was one of certainty. It was not crowned by the award of the Gold Medal of the RIBA, but Goldfinger must have relished to the full his election to the Royal Academy in 1975.

Born Ernö Goldfinger. **Parents** Oscar, a doctor, and Regine (Haiman) Goldfinger. **Marriage** Ursula Ruth Blackwell, 1933. **Children** Peter, Elizabeth and Michael. **Education** Budapest Gymnasium, 1912–19; Le Rosay School, Gstaad, Switzerland, 1919–20; studied architecture, Atelier Jaussely, Paris, 1922–23; École Nationale et Supérieure des Beaux-Arts, Paris, 1923 (government diploma, 1931); co-founder, breakaway Atelier Auguste Perret, 1924, Paris, 1924; École d'Urbanisme, Sorbonne, Paris, 1927–28. **Emigration** Left France for UK, 1934; naturalized, 1945. **Career** In private architectural and design practice, Paris, 1924–34, and London, 1934–79. **Related activities** London correspondent, *L'Architecture d'aujourd'hui*, Paris, 1934–74; lecture Britain, USA, France, Spain and Hungary. **Offices and memberships** Founder member, Congrès Internationaux d'Architecture Moderne (CIAM), 1928–59; honorary secretary, French Section of Athens Congress, 1933; founder member, Modern Architecture Research Society (MARS, British section on CIAM), 1935–60, and editor, *MARS News*, London, 1944–45; member: Association of Building Technicians, 1937, Royal Institute of British Architects' Foreign Relations Committee, 1937–45; council member, Architects' Registration Council of the United Kingdom, 1941–50; co-founder, with Sir Patrick Abercrombie and Auguste Perret, International Union of Architects (honorary organizing secretary, British section, 1946); council member, Architectural Association, London, 1960–63, 1965–68; member, Council of Industrial Design, 1961–65; honorary member, Association of Hungarian Architects, 1963; fellow: Royal Institute of British Architects, 1966, Royal Society of Arts, 1968; associate, Royal Academy, 1971; Royal Academician, 1975. **Publications** (with E.J. Carter) *County of London Plan Explained*, London, 1945; *British Furniture Today*, London, 1951; also contributed many articles to architectural journals. **Exhibitions** CIAM Exhibition, Athens, 1934; Housing Exhibition, Grand Palais, Paris, 1934, and Olympia, London, 1935; MARS Group Exhibition, Burlington Gallery, London, 1938; CIAM Exhibition, Aix-en-Provence, France, 1952; *This Is Tomorrow*, Whitechapel Art Gallery, London, 1955; UIA Sports Buildings Commission Exhibition, Moscow, 1968; *Thirties*, Hayward Gallery, London, 1979; *Works 1: Ernö Goldfinger*, Architectural Association, London, 1983. **Collection** Royal Institute of British Architects Drawings

Collection, London. **Works** Library in Aghion House (designed by Perret), Alexandria, Egypt, 1926; Helena Rubinstein beauty salon, 24 Grafton Street, London, 1926; Central European Express, rue Godot de Mauroy, Paris, 1927; La Portique picture gallery, Boulevard Raspail, Paris, 1928; Cheftel apartment, furniture and interiors, 6 rue d'Astorg, Paris, 1928; Grossman apartment, furniture and interiors, 6 rue d'Astorg, Paris, 1928; Alpina exhibtiton stand, *Foire de Paris*, 1928; Alpina exhibition stand, *British Industries Fair*, Olympia, London, 1928; Luteaux monument, Jardin d'Acclimatation, Algiers, 1929; hotel project, Philippeville, Algeria, 1929; housing project, Philippeville, Algeria, 1929; (with Pierre Forestier) nursery school, Vitry-Seine, near Paris, 1929; Hollender apartment interiors, Paris, 1930; Susanne Blum offices and apartment, 53 rue de Varenne, Paris, 1930; Dick Wyndham studio interiors, rue Froidevaux, Paris, 1930; Ernö Goldfinger studio and apartments interiors, 3 rue de la Cité Universitaire, Paris, 1931; Entas steel stacking chairs, Paris, 1931; Aero Club project, 1931; heliometer, 1932; 15-storey apartment building exhibition project, 1933; P. and M. Abbatt toy showroom, Endsleigh Street, London, 1933; Lahousse house and studio, near Le Touquet, France, 1933; Abbatt apartment, Tavistock Square, London, 1934; S. Weiss shop, Golders Green, London, 1935; "Easiwork" toys and furniture for P. and M. Abbatt Company, London, 1935; P. and M. Abbatt toy shop, Wimpole Street, London, 1936; (with Gerald Flower) house, Broxted, Essex, 1937; children's section, British pavilion, *World's Fair*, Paris, 1937; three terrace houses, including Goldfinger House, 1–3 Willow Road, London, 1937; ICI exhibition stand, *British Industries Fair*, Olympia, London, 1938; children's section, *MARS Group Exhibition*, Burlington Gallery, London, 1938; Benroy apartment, Hendon, London, 1938; Wordsworth House, 13 Westhill, London, 1938; education exhibitions for British Army, Royal Navy and Royal Air Force, 1939–45; air raid shelter, Bedales School, Petersfield, Hampshire, 1940; blastproof housing competition project, 1940; planetarium project, Hyde Park, London, 1945; newspaper office and printing press, 75 Farringdon Road, London, 1947; Fletcher Hardware Company warehouse and offices, Pershore Street, Birmingham, 1949; Fletcher House, Henley-in-Arden, Warwickshire, 1949; Brandlehow Road Primary School, Wandsworth, London, 1950; Westville Road Primary School, Hammersmith, London, 1950; dairy farm, Ibstone, Buckinghamshire, 1950; house with two apartments, 74 Avenue des Chênes, Uccle, Brussels, 1950; (with Lilian Ladlow) S. Weiss shop, Shaftesbury Avenue, London, 1951; kiosks, *Festival of Britain*, South Bank, London, 1951; four houses, Broadstairs, Kent, 1952; block of flats, 10 Regent's Park Road, London, 1954; Carr and Company offices, Shirley, West Midlands, 1955; office building, 45–46 Albemarle Street, London, 1956; Taylor Woods showroom, 45–46 Albemarle Street, London, 1956; (with Victor Passmore and Helen Phillips) *This Is Tomorrow* exhibition, Whitechapel Art Gallery, London, 1956; Wallis House, Amersham, Buckinghamshire, 1957; Hille factory, 134 St Albans Road, Watford, Hertfordshire, 1957–60; Abbotts Langley housing, Hertfordshire, 1958; (with Charlotte Perriand) French (now Belgian) Government Tourist Office, 66 Haymarket, London, 1958; Elephant and Castle development competition project, London, 1959; Hille house offices and showroom, 134 St Albans Road, Watford, Hertfordshire, 1960; Player House, Coombe Hill Road, Coombe Hill, Surrey, 1962; Westminister Bank, Elephant and Castle, London, 1962; Alexander Fleming House, Ministry of Health, Elephant and Castle, London, 1962–66; (with Charlotte Perriand) French Government Tourist Office, 177 Picadilly, London, 1963; Motz House, 16 Bedford Street, Oxford, England, 1965. **Cause of death** Undisclosed, at age 85. **Further reading** Mate Major, *Ernö Goldfinger*, Budapest, 1973; James Dunnett and Gavin Stamp, *Ernö Goldfinger: Works I*, London, 1983.

IRENE HANDL

British Actress and Novelist

***Born* London, England, 27 December 1901**

***Died* London, England, 29 November 1987**

The actress Irene Handl was something of an institution in British film, theatre and television. For around 40 years she held a very secure corner of the market in working-class comic characters, usually chambermaids, char ladies or similar types. At the age of 64 she produced a highly acclaimed novel which suggested a less comfortable side to her personality.

She was born in the prosperous north London neighbourhood of Maida Vale, in 1901. Her mother was French and her father a Viennese banker: "We had a cook, a housemaid and a char and we lived in a house with a big garden...I remember Caruso singing at a wedding in a neighbour's garden." Educated at a variety of schools, and widely travelled in youth, she stayed at home to look after her father following her mother's death. Writing and painting were hobbies until she was nearly 40, whereupon father declared, "Irene you must have something to do that will suit you and occupy your mind—I suggest the theatre." Consequently she attended the Embassy School and studied with Eileen (sister of Dame Sybil) Thorndike.

By starting so late in the profession, she missed the conventional romantic roles—"I sublimated all that into char women with romantic streaks," she said. It was an immediately successful formula. In 1937 she was stopping the show nightly, playing the maid throughout a long run of the comedy *George and Margaret* on London's West End stage. The next year she made her first film, and after working through a host of small parts, was a stalwart of British ciné-comedy in the 1950s and 1960s, and a national figure. She featured with the great Tony Hancock's would-be Bohemian in *The Rebel*, was excellent as Peter Sellers' disapproving wife in *I'm All Right Jack* and splendidly unbudgeable, uncomprehending in *Morgan, a Suitable Case for Treatment*. Her talent ably encompassed classical roles—Mrs Malaprop, Lady Bracknell, and her own eccentric favourite, the medium Madame Arcati in Noël Coward's *Blithe Spirit*. However, her biggest stage success was in the familiar groove as a "lovable Cockney char" in *Goodnight Mrs Puffin*.

During this time she discovered herself growing bored with the "marshmallowy" character and turned again to writing. An adventure befell Irene Handl in Paris in the 1920s. She would not say what it was, but at least some of it became *The Sioux*, a novel about an obsessive, incestuous, rich French family, the Benoirs. Written in a "totally peculiar" way, in a redolent, sensuous style, it was greeted with surprise and admiration in 1965. Equally well received was a sequel, *The Gold Tip Pfitzer*, in 1973. The title is the name of a gloomy evergreen tree she discovered in a New Zealand cemetery.

Of her own books she wrote: "I never research. The process goes on all the time subconsciously and suddenly bursts out...they may be good, bad or indifferent as literary works, but they are unique."

Irene Handl had also a busy career in television, playing within her accustomed range. The climax was the series *For the Love of Ada* about romance late in life. It ran for three years from 1970 and spawned a film, which did not transfer successfully to the big screen. She was popular on children's shows like *Metal Mickey* and *Supergran*, and continued with television, film and even the institutional Christmas pantomime until well into her eighties.

Short, tubby and plain in real life, she didn't look very different to the hundreds of cheery proletarians she acted, and had commonplace though oddly mixed interests: conversation, cooking, chihuahuas, fishing and Elvis Presley. But in conversation she spoke the extraordinary language of her books, full of unexpected images and insights. The exotic, elegant, over-charged Benoirs seemed in some sense to represent her spiritual autobiography, and their air hung thick about her. She never married, lived alone and did not care overmuch for the contemporary world: "My lovable old girls make a lot of people happy and I appreciate it. In these filthy times people must have *something*."

Born Irene Handl. **Parents** Frederick, a banker, and Marie (Schuepp) Handl. **Education** High school in London; Embassy School of Acting, 1936–37. **Career** Stage, radio, television and film actress from age of 36. **Related activities** Some writing for radio. **Other activities** Writer of novels. **Offices and memberships** British Actors' Equity Association; president, National Chihuahua Club; follow, National Geographical Society; member, Elvis Presley Fan Club. **Awards and honours** Pye Female Comedy Award for *Maggie and Her*, 1980. **Publications** *The Sioux* (novel), 1965, reissued 1984, published as *The Green and Purple Dream*, 1973; *The Gold Tip Pfitzer* (novel), 1973. **Films** *Missing, Believed Married*, 1937; *Strange Boarders*, 1938; *Mrs Pym of Scotland Yard*, 1939; *The Fugitive/On the Night of the Fire*, 1940; *Night Train/Gestapo* and *Night Train to Munich*, 1940; *Dr O'Dowd*, 1940; *Gasbags*, 1940; *George and Margaret*, 1940; *The Girl in the News*, 1941; *Get Cracking*, 1943; *The Flemish Farm*, 1943; *I'll Walk Beside You*, 1943; *It's in the Bag*, 1943; *Millions Like Us*, 1943; *Rhythm Serenade*, 1943; *Welcome, Mr Washington*, 1944; *Give Us the Moon*, 1944; *Kiss the Bridge Goodbye*, 1944; *Uncensored*, 1944; *Brief Encounter*, 1945; *For You Alone*, 1945; *Great Day*, 1945; *Mr Emmanuel*, 1945; *The Randolph Family/Dear Octopus*, 1945; *The Spell of Amy Nugent/Spellbound/Passing Clouds*, 1945; *The Gay Intruders/Medal for the General*, 1946; *I'll Turn to You*, 1946; *The Hills of Donegal*, 1947; *Code of Scotland Yard*, 1948; *The Fool and the Princess*, 1948; *The Cardboard Cavalier*, 1949; *Her Man Gilby/English Without Tears*, 1949; *Dark Secret*, 1949; *For Them That Trespass*, 1949; *The History of Mr Polly*, 1949; *Silent Dust*, 1949; *Temptation Harbour*, 1949; *Stage Fright*, 1950; *Adam and Evelyne*, 1950; *The Perfect Woman*, 1950; *One Wild Oat*, 1951; *Treasure Hunt*, 1952; *Meet Mr Lucifer*, 1953; *Mr Potts Goes to Moscow/Top Secret*, 1953; *The Wedding of Lilli Marlene*, 1953; *Burnt Evidence*, 1954; *Mad About Men*, 1954; *The Weak and the Wicked*, 1954; *Duel in the Jungle*, 1954; *Young Wives' Tale*, 1954; *Who Done It*, 1956; *A Kid for Two Farthings*, 1956; *Brothers in Law*, 1957; *The Silken Affair*, 1957; *Small Hotel*, 1957; *Happy Is the Bride*, 1958; *The Key*, 1958; *It's Never Too Late*, 1958; *Law and Disorder*, 1958; *The Crowning Touch*, 1959; *I'm All Right Jack*, 1959; *Left, Right and Centre*, 1959; *Carry on Constable*, 1960; *Doctor in Love*, 1960; *French Mistress*, 1960; *Inn for Trouble*, 1960; *Make Mine Mink*, 1960; *Next to No Time*, 1960; *Desert Mice*, 1960; *Man in a Cocked Hat/Carlton-Browne of the FO*, 1960; *School for Scoundrels*, 1960; *The Night We Got the Bird*, 1961; *Beware of Children/No Kidding*, 1961; *Call Me Genius/The Rebel*, 1961; *Double Bunk*, 1961; *Nothing Barred*, 1981; *The Pure Hell of St Trinian's*, 1961; *Two-Way Stretch*, 1961; *Upstairs and Downstairs*, 1961; *Watch It, Sailor!*, 1961; *A Weekend with Lulu*, 1961; *Make Mine a Double*, 1962; *Heavens Above!*, 1963; *Just for Fun*, 1963; *Morgan!/Morgan, a Suitable Case for Treatment*, 1966; *The Wrong Box*, 1966; *Smashing Time*, 1967; *Lionheart*, 1968; *The Mini-Affair*, 1968; *The Italian Job*, 1969; *Wonderwall*, 1969; *Doctor in Trouble*, 1970; *On a Clear Day You Can See Forever*, 1970; *The Private Life of Sherlock Holmes*, 1970; *The Last Remake of Beau Geste*, 1977; *Adventures of a Private Eye*, 1977; *Stand Up, Virgin Soldiers*, 1977; *The Great Rock and Roll Swindle*, 1979; *Riding High*, 1980; *The Hound of the Baskervilles*, 1983; *Absolute Beginners*, 1986. **Stage** (all in London, unless stated) *Night Alone*, 1937; *George and Margaret*, 1937; *Full Flavour*, 1938; *Rovina*, 1938; *Never Goodbye*, 1938; *A Star Come Home*, 1938; various productions at the Garrison Theatre, Salisbury, 1940–45; *Great Day*, 1945; *Under the Counter*, 1945; *Mr Bowling Buys a Newspaper*, 1946; *Day After Tomorrow*, 1946; *Divorce on Tuesday*, 1946; *We Proudly*

Present, 1947; *Summer in December*, 1949; *Marriage Playground*, 1949; *Cry Liberty*, 1950; *Will I Do?*, Glasgow, 1951; *Magnolia Street Story*, 1951; *Bold Lover*, Brighton, 1951; *First Person Singular*, 1952; *The Wedding Ring*, Manchester, 1952; *Goodnight, Sweet Prince*, 1953; *Strange Request*, 1955; *Home and Away*, 1955; *Jubilee Girl*, 1956; *Goodnight, Mrs Puffin*, 1961 (Australian tour, 1963); *Busybody*, 1964; *Everything Happens on Friday* (UK tour), 1964; *Dear Miss Hope*, 1966; *Busybody* (Australian and New Zealand tour), 1966; *Dear Miss Hope* (UK tour), 1967; *The Farmer's Wife*, 1967; *My Giddy Aunt* (London and UK tour), 1968; *His, Hers and Theirs* (UK tour), 1970; *Chorus of Murder*, Guildford, 1972; *Goodnight, Mrs Puffin*, Eastbourne, 1972; *Blithe Spirit* (UK tour), 1973; *Dead Easy*, 1974; *The Freeway*, 1974; *The Importance of Being Earnest*, 1975; *Night Must Fall* (UK tour), 1975; *Habeas Corpus* (UK tour), 1975; *Emu in Pantoland*, 1976; *A Family*, 1978; *Ten Times Table* (UK tour), 1979; *Mrs Perry and Her*, 1980. **Television** (includes) *A Legacy*; *For the Love of Ada*; *Hancock's Half Hour*; *You Must Be Joking*; *The Rag Trade*; *In Sickness and in Health*; *Never Say Die*; *Angels*; *Metal Mickey*; *Supergran*. **Cause of death** Undisclosed, at age 85.

CHARLES HOLLAND

American Singer

Born **Norfolk, Virginia, 27 December 1909**

Died **Amsterdam, Netherlands, 7 November 1987**

Charles Holland was one of the many Black Americans whose careers were affected by the racism so endemic in modern American society. For while, during much of this century, Black women were welcomed on American concert stages, men were not. In Holland's case, exile proved to be the only answer, and his career developed in Europe without constant reference to the colour of his skin. Yet prejudice followed him abroad too, and in 1961, another American tenor, Eddie Ruhl, was sacked by the Norwegian Opera because he refused to share a dressing-room with Holland.

Charles Holland's route to the concert stage was not an obvious or even direct one. He began singing at the age of 14 and later took lessons. His first engagements were not on the concert stage, however, but with a jazz band, and in the 1930s he worked with both Benny Carter's and Fletcher Henderson's big bands. Appearances in musical theatre, films and a 13-week series on NBC radio consolidated his reputation as a fine singer; he was described by Ross Parmenter of the *New York Times*, in a review of his concert début in New York in 1940, as "a refined and delicate artist with a light voice which was sweet and true".

By this time, Holland had switched to a classical career, helped by studying with Georges le Pyre in Hollywood and Clyde Burrows in New York. His first appearances were with the avant-garde, singing in Virgil Thomson's *Four Saints in Three Acts* and the première of Marc Blitzstein's *Airborne*, but after settling in Paris in 1949, his repertoire widened to include the full range of concert music. Holland made his European operatic début at the Paris Opéra in 1954, singing in Mozart's *Die Zauberflöte* (*The Magic Flute*) and in the following year became the first Black to sing at the Opéra-Comique. By this time, his once-light voice had darkened, and he was able to sing Verdi's *Otello* in London. Throughout the 1950s and 1960s he performed regularly throughout Europe, enjoying a successful operatic career in France, Germany and Holland, with visits as far afield as Canada and New Zealand.

In 1969 Holland returned to the United States for the first time in 20 years. Donal Henahan reported in the *New York Times* that he "sang with considerable power and elegance" and that he "lifted the programme into the realm of exciting music". Some of that exciting music could be heard when he made his belated Carnegie Hall début in 1982, at the age of 72, but by then, Holland's reputation in the US was confirmed.

The conductor and pianist Dennis Russell Davies had met Holland in 1975. "I heard this extraordinary voice and this extraordinary story...[he was] the most remarkable artist it has been my good fortune to meet." Davies arranged several American tours for Holland, during which they made a few recordings together (Holland was also to record an album of spirituals). On one such tour in California in 1977, the performance artist Laurie Anderson was in the audience. She heard Holland sing the aria "O Souverain" from Massenet's *Le Cid*, and used the piece as an inspiration for her best-selling record "O Superman", part of the *United States* performance work. Such variety of experience and exposure was typical of Holland, and he continued singing well into his seventies. Will Crutchfield reviewed a performance he gave in New York in 1984: "He sang from a full heart and with a conviction that need not give place to anyone. His voice failed him at times; his spirit never." It serves as a fitting epitaph to a great singer.

Born Charles Holland. **Marriage** Catherine. **Children** Charles and Mark. **Education** Studied with May Hamaker Henley, Georges le Pyre and Clyde Burrows. **Emigration** Left United States for France, 1949, later settling in Netherlands. **Career** Sang with Benny Carter and Fletcher Henderson jazz bands; switched to classical singing, making New York recital début, 1940; after moving to Europe, sang on French radio and television; début, Paris Opéra, 1954; first Black singer at Opéra-Comique, 1955; toured Europe in opera and recitals, 1956–69; returned to US to perform, 1969, toured, 1977–84. **Stage** *Green Pastures*, New York, 1941; *Four Saints in Three Acts*, New York; *The Airborne*, New York; *Run Little Chillun'*, New York. **Film** *Hullaballoo*, 1941. **Radio** Thirteen-week concert programme, NBC, 1941. **Opera** *Die Zauberflöte*, Paris, 1954; *Otello*, London, 1955; also sang in *Carmen*, *Boris Godunov*, Gounod's *Faust*, *The Pearl Fishers* and many others. **Recordings** *My Lord What a Mornin'* (spirituals), 1750 Arch 1796, 1983; *Songs of Innocence and Experience*, 1984. **Cause of death** Undisclosed, at age 77.

GENERAL SEYNI KOUNTCHÉ

Niger Soldier and Politician

***Born* Fandou, Niger, 1 July 1931**

***Died* Paris, France, 10 November 1987**

An austere and ascetic man and a rigorous politician, Seyni Kountché seized control of Niger, the landlocked West African republic, in a violent coup in 1974, and held on to the presidency, sometimes grimly, until his early death. He was a man of enormous energy and was known to be extraordinarily hardworking; during his regime the country flourished as never before, but he was ruthless in the extreme, and unpopular. Some would say that ruthlessness is a necessary characteristic for an African politician if he is to succeed.

Born in Fandou in 1931, into the Djerma tribe, Kountché went to primary school in Filingué and in 1944 started at the French Army School in Kati, Mali. Three years later he moved to a school in St Louis, Senegal. His military career began when he joined the French Colonial Army in 1949. He was promoted to sergeant in 1957 and in the same year was admitted to Fréjus Officers' School in France, from which he graduated two years later as second lieutenant; in 1960 he was promoted to warrant officer. During his time in the French Colonial Army he served in Indochina and Algeria.

When his country won its independence in 1960 (the same year as many other African states, including Cameroun, the Ivory Coast and Togo), he returned, and in 1961 joined the newly created Niger Army and served in Zinder, Niger's second town, and in Agadez. He went to France again in 1965, to attend the Officers' Training School in Paris for a year, and in 1967 he was promoted to deputy chief of staff of the army, a position he retained until 1973, and in addition was elevated to the rank of major in 1968.

Although reports had circulated of his "political unreliability", in July 1973 he became chief of staff of the Niger Armed Forces, at the rank of lieutenant-colonel, and this was the beginning of the end for President Diori Hamani, who had run the country since independence: Kountché ousted him in a *coup d'état* in April the following year.

Kountché claimed that he was motivated to such drastic action by the poverty of his country, starving in the drought-stricken years of the early 1970s, and the exploitation of it by corrupt officials who sold foreign aid food on the black market for personal gain. Niger is a barren country—only 3 per cent of the land is cultivated—and yet it is 90 per cent dependent on agriculture. Rainfall diminishes towards the north, which eventually becomes the Sahara Desert.

On taking power, Kountché formed a military government in the capital, Niamey, and expelled the French Army from Niger, but he somehow managed to avoid alienating the government in Paris, and good relations between the two countries were maintained.

Uranium had been discovered in Niger in 1967, and Kountché exploited this to the full by launching ambitious development programmes which, to a certain extent, covered up for the lack of legal political activity. By 1980 uranium accounted for 75 per cent of the country's export earnings, but the following year it began to dwindle seriously. Despite the continuation of a punishing drought, Kountché managed, through sound economic planning and foreign aid, to achieve self-sufficiency in Niger in staple food grains. He also improved the infrastructure of the country considerably, particularly in the fields of education and health in previously undeveloped areas.

His achievements as a reformist were, then, spectacular. But his people weighed this against his harsh style, and his economic success failed to overcome his unpopularity. He was an abrasive disciplinarian, often making unannounced visits to ministries and severely punishing officials whom he discovered taking bribes. He realized the precarious nature of his position—and it was not surprising that he did, since there were two coup attempts and many other indications of unrest—so changed his staff frequently. Those who opposed him in any way and stirred up trouble within the army were dealt with most harshly. Kountché did not allow the hapless Diori out of house arrest until 1984.

Besides being head of state and president of the Supreme Military Council from 1974 until his death, Kounché held many other government posts, including minister of development, minister of the interior, chairman of the Entente Council and minister of national defence.

He travelled a great deal during his presidency, particularly within Africa. In 1975, for example, he was instrumental in the establishment of the Economic Community of West African States (ECOWAS) in Lagos, and in the following year he was a signatory to the creation of a permanent tripartite commission of cooperation between Algeria, Libya and Niger. His activities ranged from opposition to the racist regime of South Africia to assistance for Chad in its war against Libya. In 1984 he met President Reagan in Washington to negotiate for food aid.

Kountché was a devout Muslim and very keen on morality. He rose at dawn and often worked more than 18 hours a day; unsurprisingly, under those circumstances, he rarely socialized. He was generally considered abrupt in every aspect of his personality, and rather humourless.

He promoted himself to the rank of general in 1984, ten years after taking power. He died of a brain tumour and was succeeded by a cousin, Colonel Ali Seibou, the army chief of staff.

Born Seyni Kountché. **Education** Primary school in Filingué; French Army School, Kati, Mali, 1944–47; Army School, St Louis, Senegal, 1947–49. **Career** Joined French Colonial Army, 1949; promoted to sergeant, 1957; Fréjus Training School, France, 1957–59; promoted to warrant officer, 1960; served with Niger Army, 1961–87; general, 1984; Officers' Training School, Paris, 1965–66; promoted to deputy chief of staff, Niger Armed Forces, 1966–73, chief of staff, 1973–74, lieutenant-colonel, 1974; ousted President Diori Hamani in *coup d'état*, 1974; head of state, 1974–87. **Related activities** Minister of development, of the interior, of national defence, 1974–87; chairman, Entente Council, 1974. **Cause of death** Brain tumour, at age 56.

THOMAS G. LANPHIER

American Fighter Pilot

***Born* Canal Zone, Panama, 27 November 1915**

***Died* La Jolla, California, 26 November 1987**

Thomas G. Lanphier Jr achieved fame for shooting down the plane carrying the commander-in-chief of the Imperial Japanese Navy, Admiral Isokoru Yamamoto, during World War II. He was also the first son of a man who was himself a pioneer in the development of American air power and commercial air travel. Thomas G. Lanphier Sr was an army officer who, during World War I, transferred to the American Flying Corps. Until 1928 the elder Lanphier was a commander of fighter squadrons. He also broke records on transcontinental flights, took part in an important Arctic aviation survey and, on leaving the service, was a business associate of the aviator Charles Lindbergh.

The Panama Canal Zone, where Lanphier Jr was born, was one of many army bases at which his father was stationed. Given the peripatetic military life, his early education took place in a number of schools. However, he reached Stanford University, joined the Army Air Corps and was a qualified pilot by late 1941.

The war in the Pacific showed that Lanphier Jr was a chip off the old block. He flew 112 combat missions, during which he was responsible for shooting down 17 enemy planes and, perhaps most spectacularly, sinking a Japanese destroyer. His most famous feat, however, came when American intelligence intercepted a Japanese signal giving details of an inspection tour of the Solomon Islands by Admiral Yamamoto, who was not only chief of the Japanese Navy, but had also masterminded the attack on Pearl Harbor in 1941. President Roosevelt personally gave orders for Yamamoto's plane to be intercepted and destroyed.

On 18 April 1943 the squadron of P-38 Lightnings in which Lanphier was a pilot flew 435 miles from Guadalcanal to meet Yamamoto and his escort over Bougainville. There was a brief, vicious dogfight between the Americans and the Japanese Zero escort fighters, with Lanphier accounting for one of the enemy. At the same moment, he spotted the bomber carrying Yamamoto fleeing low over the jungle:

> I fired a long steady burst across the bomber's course from approximately right angles. The bomber's right engine, then its right wing burst into flame. The men aboard the bomber were too close to the ground to jump. Just as I moved into range of Yamamoto's bomber and its cannon, the bomber's wing tore off. The bomber plunged into the jungle. It exploded. That was the end of Admiral Isokoru Yamamoto.

After the war, Lanphier worked as a newspaper editor in Boise, Idaho, then in Washington as assistant to President Truman's air secretary, Senator W. Stuart Symington. In the 1950s he supported Symington's candidacy in the Democratic presidential primaries.

At the time of his death he was working on *Fighter Pilot*, an account of his wartime experiences, but the book was never finished.

Born Thomas George Lanphier Jr. **Parents** Thomas George, soldier, businessman and pioneer airman, and Janet Irma (Cobb) Lanphier. **Marriage** Phyllis Fraser. **Children** Five daughters: Judith, Patricia, Janet, Kathleen and Phyllis. **Education** Stanford University. **Military service** US Army Air Corps, rising to lieutenant-colonel, World War II; flew more than 100 missions in the Pacific. **Career** (all post-war) Editor, the *Idaho Daily Statesman*, Boise, Idaho; special assistant to secretary of the air force, Washington; chair, National Security Resource Board; vice-president, Convair Division of General Dynamics Corporation. **Awards and honours** Distinguished Flying Cross, 1943; plus many other military decorations. **Cause of death** Cancer, at age 71.

RENÉ LÉVESQUE

French–Canadian Politician

***Born* New Carlisle, Quebec, 24 August 1922**

***Died* Montreal, Quebec, 1 November 1987**

Ever since their conquest by the British in 1759, French–Canadians have preserved an embittered national self-consciousness. Although a minority within the Canadian confederation, they have remained the overwhelming majority in their own province of Quebec, and yet until very recently, most of the commercial and industrial power in Quebec has been English–Canadian or American-owned. In the twentieth century the Québécois have seen even their language eroded, as industrialization and new technology relied increasingly on English.

René Lévesque, who was premier of Quebec from 1976 to 1985, embodied many of these resentments and anxieties. As the leader of the Quebec separatist movement, the Parti Québécois, he threatened to split Canada by taking Quebec out of confederation. In the end, however, the goal of complete independence appears to have been rejected by the voters of Quebec.

Lévesque was born at New Carlisle in the Gaspé Peninsula, the extreme southeastern tip of Quebec, opposite the province of New Brunswick. His father, Dominique Lévesque, had been an active Liberal politician but retired to the Gaspé for health reasons, buying a local radio station. Lévesque's mother, Diane Dionne, was equally gifted, and later travelled widely and became an expert in French cookery.

Lévesque was educated locally at a time when the English-speaking community still enjoyed marked advantages in school facilities. As a teenager, he stood in as an announcer on his father's radio station.

After Dominique Lévesque's death in 1938, the family moved to Quebec city, where Lévesque attended the Collège Saint-Charles-Garnier, and put in two years as a law student at Laval University.

By this time, however, Canada was at war, and the threat of conscription was proving an unpopular issue in Quebec, as it had been during World War I. Willing to do "anything to get overseas, but not in His Majesty's uniform", Lévesque fled to the United States and enlisted in the US Office of War Information in 1943. He saw overseas service as a war reporter from 1944 to 1945, and helped with broadcasts from London into occupied France.

Between 1946 and 1959 Lévesque made his name in radio, then in television journalism. By the early 1950s he was the chief reporter for the French-language Radio Canada, and did freelance work for the Canadian Broadcasting Corporation, covering the Korean War and both the American and Canadian political scene. It was in this period, too, that he married Louise l'Heureux, with whom he had two sons and a daughter.

By the mid-1950s the CBC was showing an interest in French-language programmes, and Lévesque helped prepare the first of these. He then hosted two controversial but highly popular shows, *Carrefour* (Crossroads) from 1954 to 1956, and *Point de Mire* (Bull's Eye) from 1956 to 1959. Both programmes demonstrated his frankness and skill in explaining complex subjects simply. As a political journalist he was especially effective, mining a rich seam of public scandal under the corrupt Quebec provincial government of Maurice Duplessis and his Union Nationale.

Lévesque's political career began in 1959, when a strike by Radio Canada staff ended *Point de Mire*. His active involvement in the strike revealed a considerable oratorical talent. With his heavily lined face, gravelly voice and staccato hand gestures he made a compelling speaker.

His politicization coincided with a revival of the Quebec Liberal Party, which attacked the complacency of the Union Nationale and its reliance on conservative Catholic opinion in the province, while presiding over the sale of Quebec resources to outside interests. At the urging of the Liberal leader Jean Lesage, Lévesque ran in the provincial election of 1960, and was returned for Montreal Laurier.

Lévesque was immediately offered a post in the new Liberal government, and was successively minister for public works, for Natural Resources and Family and Social Welfare. His greatest achievement in the Lesage government was undoubtedly the nationalization, or rather the takeover by the provincial authorities, of the hydroelectric power industry in Quebec.

This was part of his overall strategy of economic home rule for Quebec, with the people as "shareholders and not just as employees". Lévesque was also the driving force behind Quebec Liberalism's "quiet revolution", involving reforms in health, education, labour legislation, electoral law and women's rights.

The 1960s also saw a sea-change in the way Québécois saw themselves. An increasing number of young French–Canadians, as well as many of the liberal educated élite, were concerned about the pace at which, they believed, French–Canadian language and culture were being swamped in a sea of Americanization. Despite a Liberal government in Ottawa after 1963 which, especially once Pierre Trudeau became Canadian prime minister in 1968, was committed to a policy of "bilingualism and biculturalism", the idea of Quebec independence was finding a political voice.

René Lévesque was one of those voices. When the Quebec Liberals again lost power to the Union Nationale in 1966, Lévesque responded to the new mood with a proposal for a free Quebec which would, however, retain an economic "association" with Canada. He broke with the Liberals and founded his own Mouvement Souverainté-Association in 1967. In November 1968 the Lévesque party merged with two other separatist groups to form the Parti Québécois (PQ).

The PQ's first electoral test in 1970 showed the extent of support already for some form of separatism. Although the Liberals under Robert Bourassa turned out the Union Nationale as the provincial government, the PQ won 24.4 per cent of the votes and seven seats in the Quebec National Assembly.

In the years 1970 to 1971 separatist sentiment was behind Canada's first experience of urban terrorism, when the Quebec Liberation Front (FLQ) took the British trade commissioner in Montreal hostage, and later kidnapped and murdered the Quebec labour minister, Laporte, in an attempt to gain independence by force. The incident, which could have damaged the PQ because of the danger of becoming identified with the FLQ, was eventually defused by the release of the British hostage and the arrest of Laporte's killers. The whole episode may, in fact, have convinced Quebec voters that a political solution to the separatist issue, as offered by the PQ, was preferable to possible further violence. If this was so, it was still not enough to save the PQ from defeat in the 1973 provincial election. Nevertheless, the PQ's share of the vote rose to 30.1 per cent, relegating the Union Nationale to a firm third place.

Lévesque was convinced by now of the need to play down separatism as an election issue. In the next election in 1976 the PQ hardly mentioned the idea, apart from vague talk of a referendum. Instead, they concentrated on the economy and the abundant scandals of Bourassa's Liberal government.

The result, on 15 November 1976, was a crushing PQ victory, with 70 seats out of 110. Lévesque, now premier of a separatist government, continued to avoid the separatist issue, aware that a referendum, if held, might boomerang badly for his party.

The Lévesque administration thus sought, with some success, to show its competence in other fields. Its most controversial piece of legislation was the so-called Language Bill 101, which restricted the use and teaching of English in Quebec. Vehemently opposed by the English-speaking minority, many of the bill's provisions have since been declared unconstitutional by Quebec and Canadian courts.

Equally contentious was the Quebec government's role in the creation of a new federal constitution by Prime Minister Trudeau. Lévesque opposed the Trudeau constitution on the ground that it did not adequately safeguard Québécois rights; but in the end the agreement of the other nine provinces left the Quebec government isolated. The constitution was approved by the federal parliament with the proviso that Quebec could accept it at some later date.

In 1980 a referendum on "sovereignty-association" was finally held. Even in its watered-down version, offering independence within an economic union with the rest of Canada, Quebec voters turned down the PQ proposal by a majority of three to two. Separatism seemed to be a non-starter.

The Lévesque government, despite this setback, continued to be popular at the polls for some time after. In 1984, however, Lévesque, convinced that the retention of independence as a policy was going to lose the next election, moved to drop it from the PQ manifesto. This produced a ruinous split between hard-line separatists and pragmatists, and a dispirited Lévesque resigned the leadership and retired from politics in January 1985. The discomfiture of the PQ was completed shortly after by its defeat at the hands of the renascent Robert Bourassa's Liberals.

Lévesque was regarded by virtually everyone who had contact with him, political opponents not excepted, as a man of tremendous personal charm and honesty of purpose. His habits, which included chain-smoking and all-night poker, were somehow engagingly bohemian. In the words of one commentator, "...he was not a phony".

Born René Lévesque. **Parents** Dominique, a lawyer, and Diane Dionne (Pineault) Lévesque. **Marriages** 1) Louise l'Heureux, 1947 (divorced); 2) Corrine Cote, 1979. **Children** Pierre, Claude and Suzanne by first marriage. **Education** New Carlisle and Gaspé schools; Quebec University, BA; Laval University Law School. **Career** Announcer, station CHNC, New Carlisle, late 1930s; overseas reporter with US Army, Office of War Information, Europe, 1944–45; reporter and commentator, Canadian Broadcasting Corporation, 1946–59; member, Quebec National Assembly, 1960–70; minister, Public Works, Natural Resources and Social Welfare, 1960–66; member of opposition, 1966–70; president, Parti Québécois, 1966–85; returned to work as journalist and radio commentator, 1985–87. **Awards and honours** Grand Médaille de Vermeil, 1977; Grand Officer, Legion of Honour, 1977. **Publications** *Option–Quebec*, 1988; *La Passion de Québec*, 1978; *My Quebec*, 1979; *Oui*, 1980. **Cause of death** Heart attack, at age 65.

GWENDOLYN MacEWEN

Canadian Poet, Novelist and Playwright
***Born* Toronto, Ontario, 1 September 1941**
***Died* Toronto, Ontario, 30 November 1987**

During her 26-year career, Gwendolyn MacEwen was an important part of contemporary Canadian poetry by virtue of her bardic and mythical influences. She was most often concerned with the ambiguities of time, history and fact, and also explored the nature of myth-making. In addition to poetry, she wrote plays and radio drama, two novels and short stories, a travel book about Greece and fiction for children. She excelled in the kind of exuberant, personal, and graceful style which discovered the supernatural in everyday experience. However, she was less successful at tackling weightier material, such as the search for a cultural hero and the construction of mythological history in the manner of Jung. While she did not completely satisfy her audience, she managed to secure her place in Canadian literature as a competent poet. Her best works, the novel *King of Egypt, King of Dreams*, the poetic novel *Noman*, and the verse collection *Magic Animals* reveal that her failings by no means detracted from her performance.

MacEwen began publishing her work at a time when most poets were interested in the immediate social and political environment. According to one commentator, Canadian verse was in a "post-Williams age" in which the emphasis was on "the rhythmic arrangement of a prose line". Roughly speaking, she was a Romantic poet because of her use of specifically poetic diction and her heavy reliance on imagination to shape her poems. To her, poetry was "a means of invoking the mysterious forces which move the world and shape our destinies". The influences of Dylan Thomas and Hart Crane can be seen here, and in her love of sound and imagery. Despite her command of tone, she exhibits an unwillingness to be direct, using heavy metaphors, and altering syntax. In all her short poems, in volumes such as *A Breakfast for Barbarians*, *The*

Shadowmaker and *The Armies of the Moon*, there is a desire for escape to other times and worlds. She insists on discovery as an act of creation:

When you see the land naked, look again
(burn your maps, that is not what I mean).
I mean the moment when it seems most plain
is the moment when you must begin again.

MacEwen's longer works were applauded for their rich symbolism and the witty, urbane dialogue and description. *Julian the Magician* attempts to show in the protagonist the life of Christ as a natural manifestation of archetypal patterns. It is a work in some ways reminiscent of Fraser's *Golden Bough* and Jung's theories of collective unconscious. The novel draws extensively on a wide range of Biblical and heretical work, such as the Zohar, the Kabalah, and the *Pistis Sophia*. It is strangely ahistorical, set in a vaguely post-Renaissance period and full of modern and antiquated references. Historical credulity is also undermined in *King of Egypt, King of Dreams*, which is a work of "highly wrought myth-making". She was greatly influenced by Greek and Christian symbolism and the fairy-tale genre, which encouraged her to question and manipulate conventional history.

MacEwen's main weaknesses were lack of control over technique and subject matter, and sometimes a failure to "see the irony in the God she engages". Tom Marshall qualified his support by complaining that her "urgent and exuberant utterance [occasionally] approached incoherency". *Julian* was criticized for artificially forcing the Christ-figure identity on the reader and for its inability to allow "the image-patterns to work as naturally as they do in a fairy-tale". It would appear that her grand designs sometimes proved too much for her when long mythological references were left undigested by the story itself, or when the fable sounds slightly infantile against the framework of historical fiction. George Jonas described her novels, for instance, as "Fertile, in the way of a tropical pond, it is full of beautiful flowers and also things that creep and crawl on an altogether puzzling number of legs. One is fascinated by such a pond, without being quite sure if one ought to drink from it."

Some of her work showed an "imbalance in the direction of inner experience..." and evasion of the overwhelming external challenge of Canadian space and society. Like most incumbent, but ethnically foreign populations, Canadians are faced with the dilemma of a derivative culture, where the icons and ethos have a negative relationship to the land. MacEwen senses this when she writes, "O baby, what hell to be Greek in this country—without wings, but burning anyway..." None the less, the problem is not solved by wrapping personal and local experience in great European tapestries. This is evident both in her attempt to "construct a myth" out of the *individual* voice and in the uncritical adoption of cultural paradigms that are basically alien to her own land.

MacEwen did manage to make a strong impression on many of her colleagues and readers. Not only has she been anthologized, but there is a substantial amount of critical work devoted to her. Unfortunately, the attention did not bring financial success. Just before her death she was fighting off pressing debts. But perhaps it is better to let the poet herself have the last word: "For me, language has enormous, almost magical power....I write to communicate joy, mystery, passion; not the joy that naïvely exists without knowledge of pain, but that joy which arises out of and conquers pain."

Born Gwendolyn Margaret MacEwen. **Marriages** 1) Milton Acorn, poet; 2) Nikos Tsingos, singer, 1971 (divorced, 1977). **Career** Full-time writer, 1960–87. **Related activities** Writer-in-residence, University of Western Ontario, London, 1984–85; writer-in-residence, Toronto University, 1986. **Offices and memberships** Writers' Union of Canada. **Awards and honours**

CBC Prize, 1965; Governor-General's Award, 1970; Canada Council Grant, 1973, 1977, 1981; A.J.M. Smith Award, 1973; Du Maurier Gold and Silver Awards, 1983. **Verse** (all published in Toronto, unless stated) *Selah: The Drunken Clock*, 1961; *The Rising Fire*, 1963; *A Breakfast for Barbarians*, 1966; *The Shadow-Maker*, 1969; *The Armies of the Moon*, 1972; *Magic Animals: Selected Poems, Old and New*, 1975; *The Fire-Eaters*, 1976; *Trojan Women* (includes plays and translations from Yannis Ritsos), 1981; *The T.E. Lawrence Poems*, Ontario, 1982; *Earthlight 1968–82: Selected Poetry*, 1982; *Afterworlds*, n.d. **Plays** *Terror and Erebus* (radio, broadcast 1965), Toronto, 1974; *Tesla* (radio), 1966; *The World of Neshia* (radio), 1967; *The Last Night of James Pike* (radio), 1976; *The Trojan Women* (adapted from Euripedes, produced Toronto, 1978), Toronto, 1979. **Novels** *Julian the Magician*, Toronto and New York, 1963; *King of Egypt, King of Dreams*, Toronto, 1972. **Others** *Open Secrets* (recording), CBC, 1972; *Noman* (short stories), Ottawa, 1972; *Mermaids and Ikons: A Greek Summer*, Toronto, 1978; *The Chocolate Moose* (for children), Toronto, 1981; *The Honey Drum* (for children), Ontario, 1983; *Dragon Sandwiches* (for children), 1985. **Cause of death** Undisclosed, at age 46.

ROGER MANVELL

British Film Historian, Biographer and Novelist

***Born* Leicester, England, 10 October 1909**

***Died* Boston, Massachusetts, 30 November 1987**

Roger Manvell's principal achievement was to promote and popularize the art and history of international film at a time when there was too little knowledge or intelligent guidance available to the public. He began a dynasty of film writers and scholars, beginning with his Penguin edition of *Film* in 1944 which became a war-time best seller, plus other film "primers" which influenced generations in appreciating the medium on a variety of levels. Unlike much of the theoretical writing in the 1970s, Manvell's style was consistently enlivening, accessible and affectionate, never reducing the examination of film into bloodless sterility. His tone never strayed into the pomposity of semiotics.

Manvell was also one of the first writers to establish the upstart television as a serious medium, full of creative possibilities. He was also one of the first to explore it critically for its possible misuse of its influence.

The son of a clergyman, Manvell earned a doctorate at London University before lecturing for ten years in adult education at Leicester University. In 1937 he moved to Bristol University to teach literature, drama and film—subjects in which he was equally erudite. But his passion for film found both expression and appreciation in the 1920s and 1930s when the film society movement was catching fire in universities everywhere. He was one of the first people to promote the movement outside London.

During the war, Manvell worked in the film department of the Ministry of Information, writing scripts on the side. In 1945 he became director of the British Film Institute, then two years later the director of the British Film Academy. He held the post for 12 years, then stayed on as consultant when it re-formed into the British Academy for Film and Television Arts.

Manvell was also associate editor of the *New Humanist* magazine (1957–75), was active in the movement, and was director of the Rationalist Press Association. His anti-Fascism was rooted in his humanist convictions. In his novel *The Passion* (1960) he described how the theatrical vocation of a lapsed clergyman was just as God-given as the religious life he had left.

As a writer, Manvell was enthusiastic but discerning. He was against the trade censorship of films, especially with regard to political issues. He not only lectured and broadcast in 30 countries on film and wrote volumes on the subject, ranging from filming Shakespeare to animation design to Ingmar Bergman, but collaborated on other works as well. One of these was Rachael Low's definitive work on the history of British film. In addition, he wrote two books on British stage actresses, also finding time to write prolifically on Nazi Germany and its leaders. He was awarded the Order of Merit from both Germany and Italy, contributed to the *Encyclopaedia Britannica* and served on many international film festival juries.

Although Manvell's style of examining film was criticized by some of his students in the late 1960s and early 1970s (it had through repetition and possibly lack of expansion become too routine and self-contained), there is no doubt that his work is as crucial to an understanding of film as it was decades ago. No one could consider a film scholar's education—even into the 1990s—complete without studying Manvell's approach.

Born Arnold Roger Manvell. **Parents** Canon Arnold E.W., clergyman, and Gertrude (Baines) Manvell. **Marriage** Françoise Nautré, 1981. **Education** Wyggeston School, Leicester; King's School, Peterborough; University College, Leicester, BA with first class honours in English language and literature, 1930; University of London, PhD, 1936. **Career** Schoolmaster and lecturer in adult education, 1931–37; lecturer, literature and drama, department of extramural studies, University of Bristol, 1937–40; specialist in film, Ministry of Information, 1940–45; research officer, British Film Institute, 1945–47; director, British Film Academy, 1947–59; consultant and editor of its journal, British Academy of Film and Television Arts, 1959–76; visiting professor of film, Boston University, 1975–82, professor, 1982–87. **Related activities** Lecturer on film for British Film Institute, British Council and other groups around the world; regular broadcaster from 1946, especially on *The Critics*, BBC; editor, *Penguin Film Review*, 1946–49; editor, "National Cinema" series, Grey Walls Press, 1948–53; governor, London Film School, 1966–74; vice-chairman, National Panel for Film Festivals, 1974–76. **Other activities** Associate editor, *New Humanist*, 1967–75; Bingham Professor of Humanities, Louisville University, 1973; director: Rationalist Press Association Limited, Pemberton Publishing Company Limited. **Offices and memberships** Member, committee of management, Society of Authors, 1954–57, 1965–68; chairman: Society of Lecturers, 1959–61, Radiowriters' Association, 1962–64, Authors' Club, 1972–75. **Awards and honours** Visiting fellow, Sussex University; Commander of the Order of Merit of the Italian Republic, 1970; Order of Merit (First Class) of German Federal Republic, 1971; honorary DLitt: Sussex, 1971, Leicester, 1974, Louisville, 1979; honorary DFA, New England College, 1972; Scholar/Teacher of the Year Award, Boston University, 1984–85. **Publications** *Film*, 1944; (contributor) *Twenty Years of British Film*, 1947; (editor) *Experiment in the Film*, 1948, reprinted 1970; (with Rachael Low) *The History of the British Film: Volume I: 1896–1906*, 1948; (with Paul Rotha) *Movie Parade, 1888–1949*, 1950; (editor) *Three British Screenplays*, 1950; *A Seat at the Cinema*, 1951; (editor with R.K.N. Baxter) *Cinema*, 1952, reprinted, 1978; *On the Air*, 1953; *The Animated Film*, 1954; *The Film and the Public*, 1955; (with John Huntley) *The Technique of Film Music*, 1957, second edition, 1976; *The Dreamers* (novel), 1957; (with John Halas) *The Technique of Film Animation*, 1959, fourth edition, 1976; *The Passion* (novel), 1960; (with Heinrich Fraenkel) *Doctor Goebbels: His Life and Death*, 1960, revised edition, 1968; *The Living Screen*, 1961; (with John Halas) *Design in Motion*, 1962; (with Heinrich Fraenkel) *Goering*, 1962; (with Heinrich Fraenkel) *The Man Who Tried to Kill Hitler*, 1964; (with Heinrich Fraenkel) *Himmler*, 1965; *The July Plot* (television play), 1966; *What Is a Film?*, 1965; *New Cinema in Europe*, 1966; *This Age of Communication*,

1966; (editor with A. William Bluem) *Television: The Creative Experience*, 1967; (with Heinrich Fraenkel) *The Incomparable Crime: Mass Extermination in the Twentieth Century: The Legacy of Guilt*, 1967; *New Cinema in the USA*, 1968; *Ellen Terry*, 1968; *New Cinema in Britain*, 1969; (with Heinrich Fraenkel) *The Canaris Conspiracy: The Secret Resistance to Hitler in the German Army*, 1969; *SS and Gestapo: Rule by Terror*, 1970; *Sarah Siddons*, 1970; (with John Halas) *Art in Movement*, 1970; (with Heinrich Fraenkel) *The German Cinema*, 1971; *The Conspirators: 20 July 1944*, 1971; *Shakespeare and the Film*, 1971, revised edition, 1979; (with Heinrich Fraenkel) *Hess: A Biography*, 1971; (editor) *International Encyclopedia of Film*, 1972; *Goering*, 1972; (author of introduction) *Masterworks of the German Cinema*, 1974; *Charles Chaplin*, 1974; (with Heinrich Fraenkel) *The Hundred Days to Hitler*, 1974; *Films and the Second World War*, 1975; *The Trial of Annie Besant and Charles Bradlaugh*, 1976; *Love Goddesses of the Movies*, 1975; (with Heinrich Fraenkel) *Inside Adolph Hitler*, 1975, revised edition, 1977; *Theater and Film: A Comparative Study of the Two Forms of Dramatic Art, and of the Problems of Adaptation of Stage Plays into Films*, 1979; *Ingmar Bergman*, 1980; *Art and Animation: The Story of Halas and Batchelor Animation Studio, 1940–80*, 1980; (with Michael Fleming) *Images of Madness: The Portrayal of Madness in the Feature Film*, 1985; also contributed to many journals. **Cause of death** Undisclosed, at age 78.

PIETER MENTEN

Dutch War Criminal

***Born* Netherlands, 1899**

***Died* Loosdrecht, Netherlands, 14 November 1987**

Justice's blindness is rightly regarded as a good thing. It must be acknowledged, however, that sometimes justice cannot see what is right under her nose: crimes which, though they have been witnessed, go unrecorded and unpunished for years on end. This is the story of Pieter Menten, who was eventually convicted of taking part in a Nazi massacre and sentenced to prison—but only after having lived for 25 years in peace and prosperity in the Dutch countryside, as if nothing had ever happened.

The Pieter Menten saga has its origins in the late 1930s, when he was a businessman with oil and mining interests in Poland. When the Germans invaded in 1939, Menten instantly made it clear that he was on their side. Whether it was at first merely opportunism to safeguard his business interests in the region, or whether he was from the beginning and by deep-rooted conviction a believer in Hitler's plans for the Third Reich, has never been established. What is clear is that Pieter Nicolaas Menten was a willing participant in the execution of Jews.

By 1941 he was working for the German SS as a translator in Poland, where he served them as an officer for at least two years. Apparently, for reasons unknown, Menten returned to Holland in 1943. Without ostensibly engaging in further work for the Germans, he gradually began to establish himself as an art collector of some repute, for he had done well out of the war. Still, keeping a low profile was not wholly successful. In 1949 Menten was sentenced to eight months in prison for collaboration with the Nazis, a sentence which he dutifully served. Then, in the early 1950s, Poland and the Israeli authorities asked for his extradition on the grounds that he was wanted in both countries for alleged war crimes. Astonishingly enough, these requests for extradition were refused by the Dutch government without further explanation. Much later, in a pre-trial investigation in 1977, it was revealed that in 1952 the justice minister had granted Menten immunity from prosecution—an indefensible decision never exposed to public scrutiny which, it was rumoured, may have been motivated by personal interests.

From 1952 until the mid-1970s Pieter Menten and his wife Meta led a quiet life in a 40-room villa in Blaricum, about 20 miles from Amsterdam. After serving his prison sentence, Menten successfully sued both the Dutch and the German states for wartime "losses and damages to his art collection", and had received sums of £175,000 and £200,000 from the respective countries in compensation. The Mentens were well off and, leading a sheltered life in the polished world of art and art dealing, well respected. It is all the more ironic that it was Pieter Menten's art-dealing which in the end brought him to heel.

In 1976 the Dutch daily *De Telegraaf* published an interview with Menten about a forthcoming sale of part of his art collection. The story was published in Israeli newspapers, where it aroused the suspicion of Chaviv Kanaan, a journalist, who decided to pursue it further. In a matter of months, through the combined efforts of Kanaan, the Dutch weekly *Accent* and the TV news programme *Aktua*, enough evidence was assembled, including eyewitness reports, to warrant a full-scale investigation into Menten's wartime activities. Before the government got to that stage, however, Menten himself requested an official investigation "to clear his name". Such perversely reverse logic was typical of the man: having succeeded in getting "compensation" for what was most likely stolen (Jewish) property, he clearly felt that anything was possible and that calling the authorities' bluff was the best defence. It did not turn out quite that way. As evidence was being amassed in the course of the investigation, the net tightened around Menten. By the end of 1976 he was running scared. He and his wife fled to Switzerland, an unexpected escape facilitated by the then justice minister van Agt who had failed to read an urgent message concerning Menten. The Swiss, however, were prepared to extradite Menten on condition that he would not be allowed to go anywhere but his native country, and in 1977 the case came to court in the Netherlands.

During a total of 25 dramatic hearings, witnesses brought from Podhoroce (now in the Ukraine, but part of Poland during World War II) testified to Menten's presence in Nazi uniform at the massacre of at least 195 of their fellow residents, most of them Jews. Unfortunately, the witnesses' accounts differed greatly and the court found it impossible to establish exactly what had taken place 36 years previously. Menten was cleared of war crimes allegedly committed in a neighbouring village, but found guilty of taking part in the killing of between 20 and 30 Polish Jews in Podhoroce on 7 July 1941. This sentence was subsequently quashed on technical grounds by the Dutch Supreme Court, where Menten had lodged an appeal. Throughout the trial itself he had maintained the rather fanciful defence that he had fallen victim to a KGB conspiracy.

Fuelled by the public outrage which greeted Menten's release in 1978, the Dutch government in turn appealed the release ruling, which resulted in a retrial in 1980. This time Pieter Menten got his defence counsel to plead immunity on the grounds of insanity, but the plea was unsuccessful. The public prosecutor asked for a life sentence; instead, Menten got ten years in prison, with the argument that at his age (78) ten years would amount to life anyway.

The saga reared its head again five years later, when Menten was released, having won remission for "good behaviour". As he came out of prison, old and decrepit, he cut a pathetic figure. In 1977 his house had been fire-bombed by a man who claimed to have done it as an act of repentance for having also been a member of the SS during the war; Menten therefore returned to live, not in the mansion, but in the coach-house next to it. Under house-arrest, as before, and degenerating quickly, he entered a nursing home in the summer of 1987. There he died, apparently unrepentant, taking his secrets with him.

Born Pieter Nicolaas Menten. **Marriage** Meta. **Career** Businessman, with mining and oil interests in Poland before 1939; joined Nazis, serving as a translator for an SS unit in Poland, 1941; returned to Netherlands, 1943; began to amass art collection, much of it believed to have been stolen from Jews; continued to work in world of art as collector and dealer; served eight-month sentence for collaboration with Nazis, 1949; weathered two unsuccessful attempts by Poland to extradite him for war crimes, 1950s; case reopened, 1976; fled to Switzerland, 1976, deported as undesirable alien; stood trial in Amsterdam on charges of taking part in massacre of Jews in two Polish villages, 1977; acquitted on one count, but found guilty and sentenced to 15 years in prison on second count; verdict initially quashed; retried, found guilty and sentenced to ten years, 1980; released, 1985. **Cause of death** Undisclosed, at age 88.

GEORGE RYGA

Canadian Playwright, Scriptwriter and Novelist
***Born* Deep Creek, Alberta, 27 July 1932**
***Died* Summerland, British Columbia, 18 November 1987**

Before George Ryga became a full-time writer in 1962 he worked for a radio station in Edmonton, the capital of Alberta, and before that he was by turns in construction, the hotel industry and farming. The community he grew up in was devoted to farming and the inhabitants were mostly Ukrainian immigrants or their descendants. Ryga wrote a total of eleven stage plays, plus a number of radio and television dramas. His major concern was with the degradation of human beings who are displaced and isolated, who lack a spiritual origin. The degradation was specifically connected to the dilemmas of Canadian life and society: the effects of a foreign culture on the indigenous people and the sense of despair created by imported values that make no sense in a new landscape.

Many of Ryga's characters are initially presented as miscreants and reprobates—drunken, indolent, outcast and ignorant—then the action of the plays slowly undermines this stereotype. By the end we see that the protagonist actually bears the guilt and shame of a malicious and vindictive society, and they must choose death to preserve their humanity. There is strident social criticism, of course, because the references to racism and contemporary events are so identifiable, but Ryga's larger concern is moral rather than psychological, and philosophical rather than political. It is the way one can be true in a false society, the necessity of evil, and the horrors of loneliness which propel all Ryga's plays.

One way of characterizing his work is to look at it as an attempt to mythologize the Canadian cultural experience. Canadian contemporaries of Ryga, such as Gwendolyn MacEwen (q.v.), try to construct a metaphoric identity for the nation. But where MacEwen centred on the more religious and romantic aspects of this process, Ryga looked at the physical and social consequences of the lack of a common heritage. The dislocation and dispossession on which he builds his work is a product of, on the one hand, the confused and formless European sense of self, and on the other, the Indians' humiliated and degraded sense of self. White culture is portrayed as empty and sanctimonious because the Whites' real relationship to the environment does not support their beliefs. The Indians had this synthesis, but Ryga suggests that it has been allowed to decay as a result of White dominance. Both groups have lost a spiritual tie to the land, both need to accept the other to regain this vital connection. The tragedy of Ryga's plays is that this is the one thing which will never happen.

The main character in his first play, *Indian*, is nameless, referred to only as "Indian", and seems to embody all the misconceptions White society has of his people. At the play's climax we discover that he has also committed fratricide, though it is because of the White man's cowardice and refusal to admit Indian's humanity that he does this. Ryga's third and most popular play, *The Ecstasy of Rita Joe*, more fully develops the themes of prejudice, judgement and death. Presented variously in realistic and non-realistic scenes, Rita is brought before the magistrate's court and accused of being a VD carrier. The memories she has of her family and the events leading up to her condemnation show again how ignorance and self-hatred poison human relations. The play ends with Rita's final rejection by her White accusers, her rape and murder. The paradox in the murder, as with *Indian*, is that it is an act of freedom which oppressors can neither sanction nor admit. Indian shows compassion on his brother by releasing him from the pitiful state which he now suffers. Rita's death becomes a martyrdom which she accepts as the price of maintaining her dignity. In Ryga's plays the main characters choose evil willingly because the good is jealously guarded by those with completely selfish ends.

The lack of integration between land and people and between the individual and the group is the essential duality in Ryga's work, and is manifest in technique and staging. Many of his plays employ memory, flashback and fantasy to tell the story. The associative, rather than the logical sequence is the guiding principle in *Indian*, *Ecstasy*, *Nothing But a Man*, *Grass and Wild Strawberries* and *Captives of a Faceless Drummer*. The settings are often timeless, ahistorical and ill-defined. *Indian* is set in a "stark, non-country", and the stage of *Ecstasy* contains a large circular ramp lit with either general highlighting or localized spots. The use of dance and ballad-singing is an integral part of several works, providing the central mechanism in *Nothing* and an ironic counterpoint in *Ecstasy*. Ryga also experimented with newsreels and recorded sound effects to evoke setting and advance the story. All these devices generate a great fluidity and openness to the plays, in some sense a mimesis of the openness of the Canadian landscape and the unanchored character of the Canadian heritage. By dismantling Canadian history and the constriction of discursive narrative, Ryga tries to build his own mosaic, to reconnect the Canadian people with their surroundings.

The only play which is least like the others is *Captives of a Faceless Drummer*. Its source is the political kidnappings by the separatist Front de la Libération Québécois (FLQ) in Montreal. As before, the main characters are introduced in a bad light. The FLQ are stupid, irresponsible and abusive. Harry, the captive, initially receives the sympathy of the audience because he is civilized and refined. However, as he is interrogated by the FLQ commander, the falseness and hypocrisy of Harry's society are unearthed. The commander is the most complete character in the play because he recognizes the depravity of both his enemies and his allies. He knows the consequences of his choice, but this enables him to become the master of his own fate, whereby his death is a vision of truth. Although the usual Ryga devices are operative here, the result is not openness and fluidity; rather, it is one of confinement. Rita Joe's recollections make possible new insight and highlight hidden connections. Harry's, on the contrary, expose his narrow-mindedness and limited perceptions. Still, the thematic focus of the play is firmly in the Ryga mould. The gulf between people and the place they live, literally and figuratively, raises similar questions about myth and reality, artist and worker, youth and age, and freedom and oppression.

Ryga's purpose in all this is not dissimilar to that of American and Australian writers, who have also tried to find such relationships in their own context. The vastness of all three nations and, in fact, the very existence of their nationhood creates a problem of definition and self-certainty. All three nations have heterogenous populations who were forced to leave their ancestral homes, displacing the people they found. The identity of each nation is somehow "elsewhere", and each produces writers who try to bridge the gap. Ryga explores these issues in his essays and his plays, and claims that the cultural vacuum which exists in Canada is, in a way, the negative "myth" of Canadians. His own work attempts to create a genuine mythology in this situation, and also to discover the irony and tragedy inherent in its absence.

Born George Ryga. **Parents** George, a farmer, and Maria (Kolodka) Ryga. **Marriage** Norma Lois Campbell. **Children** Five. **Career** Worked in farming, construction and hotel industry; joined radio station, Alberta, Canada, 1950–54; full-time writer, 1962–87. **Related activities** Guest professor: University of British Columbia, Banff School of Fine Arts, Simon Fraser University. **Offices and memberships** Association of Canadian Television and Radio Artists; Writers' Guild of America, West; honorary member, British Columbia Civil Liberties Association. **Awards and honours** Imperial Order Daughters of the Empire Award, 1950, 1951; Canada Council senior arts grant, 1972; Fringe Frist Award, Edinburgh Festival, 1973. **Novels** *Hungry Hills*, Toronto, 1963; *Ballad of a Stone-Picker*, Toronto, 1966, revised edition, 1976; *Night Desk*, 1976. **Plays** (all produced in Vancouver, unless stated) *Nothing But a Man*, 1966; *The Ecstasy of Rita Joe*, 1967, and Washington, DC, 1973 (published, 1970); *Grass and Wild Strawberries*, 1969; (author of music and lyrics) *Captives of the Faceless Drummer*, 1971 (published, 1971); *The Ecstasy of Rita Joe and Other Plays* (anthology), 1971; (author of music) *Sunrise on Sarah*, Banff, 1973; *A Feast of Thunder*, 1973; *Paracelsus*, not produced (published, *Canadian Theatre Review*, fall 1974); *Indian*, Winnipeg, 1974 (published, 1967); *Twelve Ravens for the Sun*, 1975; *Country and Western* (anthology), 1976; *Ploughmen of the Glacier*, 1976 (published, 1977); *Seven Hours to Sundown*, Edmonton, 1976 (published, 1977). **Radio plays** *A Touch of Cruelty*, 1961; *Half-Caste*, 1962; *Masks and Shadows*, 1963; *Bread Route*, 1963; *Departures*, 1963; *Ballad for Bill*, 1963; *The Stone Angel*, 1965; *Seasons of a Summer Day*, 1975. **Television plays** *Indian*, 1962; *The Storm*, 1962; *Bitter Grass*, 1963; *For Want of Something Better to Do*, 1963; *The Tulip Garden*, 1963; *Two Soldiers*, 1963; *The Pear Tree*, 1963; *Man Alive*, 1965; *The Kamloops Incident*, 1965; *A Carpenter by Trade* (documentary), 1967; *Ninth Summer*, 1972; *The Mountains* (documentary), 1973; *The Ballad of Iwan Lepa* (documentary), 1976. **Other** *The Manipulators* (TV series scripts), 1968; *The Name of the Game* (TV series scripts), 1969; *Miners, Gentlemen and Other Hard Cases* (radio series scripts), 1974–75; *Advocates of Danger* (radio series scripts), 1976; *Beyond the Crimson Morning* (travel), 1979. **Cause of death** Undisclosed, at age 55.

RAPHAEL SOYER

American Artist

Born **Borisoglebsk, Russia, 25 December 1899**

Died **Manhattan, New York, 4 November 1987**

To introduce Raphael Soyer there can be nothing better than descriptions by friends. Here is Harry Salpeter in 1938, telling how Soyer, as he was approaching middle age, still bore a remarkable resemblance to his youthful self: "A fairly stiff wind might knock Raphael down, he looks that frail....His body is as thin and small as it ever was, his eyes no less tired and his voice still the husky whisper." And here, writing about Soyer's work, is another friend, the Nobel Prize-winning author Isaac Bashevis Singer: "We are both interested—he as a painter and I as a writer—in the millions and billions of variations of love between the sexes. I would say I try to write about the things I know best. He tries to paint the people he knows best."

The people Soyer knew best and chose as subjects for his paintings were primarily the people of New York: the down-and-outs, the workers, the women Singer wrote about, but also the artists and students of his own circle. In representing them, Soyer clung steadfastly to realism as the best vehicle for his art, despite the increasing dominance of abstraction art as the century wore on. In the New York art world, an environment which often seems to be ruled by the changing winds of fads and fancies, Raphael Soyer survived a respected, because principled, figure. The chairman of the Metropolitan Museum of Art, which houses some of Soyer's work, described him shortly after his death as "the grand old man of twentieth-century realist art"—something which Soyer would undoubtedly have taken as a tribute.

He was born into a family of Lithuanian Jews in Russia, on the verge of the twentieth century—Christmas Day 1899. His father, Abraham, was a journalist, writer and teacher of Hebrew; his mother, Bella, a busy housewife with five children to look after. The Soyers' (then Schoars) life in Russia was not easy. Although talented and well educated, Abraham was constantly thwarted in his efforts to raise his family and find proper employment by racial harassment and outright anti-Semitic persecution. Moses Soyer, Raphael's twin brother, later recalled how from early childhood the US had appeared to them as the promised land:

> Our favourite books were *Tom Sawyer, Uncle Tom's Cabin* and *Hiawatha*, and among the heroes of our childhood George Washington and Abraham Lincoln led all the rest. On weekends and holidays our mother would cover the large, round dining-room table with a shining oilcloth, on which, in barbaric red and green, was pictured Brooklyn Bridge spanning the East River and joining the "glass" skyscrapers of Manhattan with the slums of Brooklyn.

The dream of living in the US came true all too soon when, in 1912, Abraham Soyer was forcibly exiled from Russia. The family sailed to New York and settled in the East Bronx, where a new phase of their difficult existence began.

In Russia all the Soyer children had been educated partly by their father at home (learning French, German and Hebrew, as well as Russian) and at the local school, where Raphael in particular displayed his talents for drawing and writing. In the US, however, this learning did not work to their advantage. Having no English, it took the boys three years to get into high school, by which time they were nearly grown and expected to supplement the family income. Moses and Raphael went to school for only a year before taking up employment in factories and various other forms of arduous, low-paid work. Still, they managed to put aside just enough to attend drawing classes in the evenings at Cooper Union. Both their father, who had an interest in drawing, and their mother, who was an accomplished embroidery artist, had encouraged the children's artistic pursuits. Lacking the financial means to send them to college, Abraham and Bella Soyer supported Moses, Raphael and later Isaac in their efforts to earn a living as artists, in which all three eventually succeeded.

Raphael Soyer went from Cooper Union to the National Academy in 1918, as well as attending sketch classes at Beaux-Arts. Here he learned not only the practice but also the history of art, and he felt inspired by the work of Rembrandt, Breugel, Goya, Eakins and Homer. In the early 1920s he left the academy to go to the Art Students League, where he was offered a teaching job in 1932. This finally put an end to the tiring routine of daytime factory labour and evening art classes.

A few years earlier the exhibition of his painting *Bronx Street Scene* in the Salons of America show had brought Soyer into contact with Alexander Brook, who had introduced him to the Whitney Studio Club and the Daniel Gallery, where his work had begun to sell well almost immediately. On the proceeds, he decided he could afford to marry Rebecca Letz in 1931, and start a family of his own. The couple went on a honeymoon-cum-art-tour to Europe the following year. They also visited the USSR, where Soyer addressed the International Society of Artists.

During the 1930s the three Soyer brothers gained a collective reputation as painters of the realist school. Inevitably, given that they had been subjected to the same artistic influences and social environments, there was a family resemblance in their work, which they were ready to acknowledge but did not choose to develop. Years before they had made a decision never to share a studio and, as far as possible, to follow different schools. This unspoken agreement was only broken once when, in 1939, Moses and Raphael were commissioned to each paint a mural on opposite walls of the Kingsessing Postal Station in Philadelphia. To their own surprise the twin brothers found that collaboration on this occasion proved a serious creative effort which enhanced the work of each in their similarity as well as their individual distinctiveness.

Overall, however, Raphael emerged as the most prolific and the best known of the three Soyer painters. His works of the Depression and those painted in the 1940s all tend to focus on the plight of isolated, lonely, often dispossessed individuals set apart in the crowd. This earned him the criticism of being too "proletarian" in his tastes, but it also brought him fame and appreciation of his effort to depict New York life as it was for most people—not just the privileged few. Tramps on the Bowery, bored travellers in Penn Station, unemployed men queueing to be hired at the factory gate—all attracted Soyer's eye. Famous paintings like *Waiting Room* and *Avenue of the Americas*, which included a rather melancholy self-portrait among the crowd, were the result.

Very occasionally, Soyer's subjects benefited directly from their "picturesque" existence, as in the case of Walter Broe. This homeless wanderer discovered by Soyer became a favourite model of many artists on the Lower East Side and managed to earn his keep in moderate comfort at the Mills Hotel until his death in 1940. Few of the untold millions crowding the streets of New York in desolation today will be immortalized as often as he, or as lovingly.

Bad as the Depression was for the majority of Americans, it was a fruitful period for art and for artists who, for once in their lives, could obtain government grants to support their work. All three Soyer brothers benefited in this way from the Government Art Projects, funded by Roosevelt's New Deal, which made it possible for them to establish their reputations.

In 1939 the Soyer brothers jointly founded the New Art School, of which Moses was made director in 1941. Raphael, meanwhile, had become quite famous. In 1932 he won the Kohnstamm Prize of the Chicago Institute and two years later the PAFA Beck Gold Medal for his portrait of *Gitel*. In the same year the Metropolitan Museum purchased its first example of his work.

Throughout his artistic life Raphael Soyer espoused the realist aesthetic, which was best summed up in a 1953 letter to the arts magazine *Realism*, to which he and 45 other artists put their signatures. "We believe," they wrote, "that texture and accident, colour, design and all the other elements of painting are only a means to a larger end, which is the depiction of man and his world." With this statement, as in the rest of his writing and, indeed, always in his painting, Soyer engaged in a polemic with the adherents of abstract art. Abstraction was something he deplored, and in condemnation he did not mince his words: "This arbitrary exploitation of a single phase of painting encourages a contempt for the taste and the intelligence of the American public," Soyer wrote in the same letter to *Realism*. The controversy over abstract art continued, as is well known, for years. Soyer's stance in it, however, did not mean that he kept a safe distance from the cultural changes that were taking place in the 1950s and 1960s. He knew many of the vanguardists on the New York art scene, and his friends included Arshile Gorky, Red Grooms and Allen Ginsberg—the latter of whom he painted in 1966.

But Soyer was criticized by some of his contemporaries and especially by a younger generation of painters. In an autobiographical essay he described a confrontation with Jackson Pollock which must go down in art history as a classic statement of irreconcilable positions: "Without greeting me, he rudely said, 'Soyer, why do you paint like you do?' He pointed to an airplane. 'There are planes flying, and you still paint realistically. You don't belong to our time.' I could have said to Jackson, 'If I don't like the art of our time, must I belong to our time?' But I did not say that. I merely said that I paint the way I like to."

And what could be a better epitaph than this—"I paint the way I like to"—for the life of an artist who, when asked shortly before his death what he was doing, replied: "Painting dishevelled girls, as usual".

Born Raphael Schoar. **Parents** Abraham, a teacher of Hebrew, and Bella (Schneyer) Schoar. **Marriage** Rebecca Letz, 1931. **Children** Mary. **Education** Trained in art at Cooper Union, National Academy of Design and Art Students League, New York. **Emigration** Left Russia for USA, 1912. **Career** Factory worker while studying art at evening classes; began to show work in New York in late 1920s; came to prominence as advocate of realism in 1930s; co-founder and teacher (with brothers) of New Art School, New York, 1939; exhibited nationally and internationally into the 1980s; author of occasional articles on art. **Memberships** Artists' Equity Association; American Art Group; Society of Painters, Sculptors and Gravers; National Institute of Arts and Letters (council member); National Academy of Design; American Academy of Arts and Letters. **Awards and honours** Kohnstamm Prize of Chicago Institute, 1932; PAFA Beck Gold Medal, 1934; $1000 Prize for Art, USA, 1959; Gold Medal, American Academy of Arts and Letters, 1981. **Publications** *A Painter's Pilgrimage: Homage to Thomas Eakins*; *Self Revealment*; *Diary of an Artist* (memoirs), 1977. **Exhibitions** (include) Salons of America show; Corcoran Museum, Washington; Carnegie International; Chicago; Philadelphia. **One-man shows** (include) Daniel Rehn Gallery, Valentine Gallery, Macbeth ACA; Wehye Gallery; Association of American Artists; Forum Gallery; Whitney Museum of American Art (retrospective), 1967. **Collections** Whitney Museum of Modern Art; Phillips Memorial Gallery, Washington; Metropolitan Museum of Art, New York; New York Public Library; Baltimore Museum of Modern Art, Maryland; Addison Museum, Addison, Massachusetts; Columbus Gallery of Fine Arts, Ohio. **Cause of death** Cancer, at age 87.

HAROLD WASHINGTON

American Lawyer and Public Official

***Born* Chicago, Illinois, 15 April 1922**

***Died* Chicago, Illinois, 25 November 1987**

"I'm going to run them all the way into Lake Michigan with this reform," Harold Washington, then mayor of Chicago, is reported to have said to interviewers in 1983. By "them" he meant his alderman, members of the infamous Democratic "machine" which had ruled the city of Chicago for decades. By means of entrenched personal power combined with an "I'll scratch your back if you'll scratch mine" system of interest-based favouritism, the "machine" had worked to keep insiders in and outsiders out of Chicago politics. But no more! With "this reform" Washington was referring to a series of measures he had instigated to eliminate the influence of the "machine" and to restore democratic (as distinct from Democratic) government in the city. This was no easy task.

Firstly, Washington was seeking to dismantle the almost feudal legacy of city management as engineered by the notorious Richard J. Daley, "the Boss" who had dominated Chicago for decades. Daley, needless to say, had been a machine-man. Secondly, Washington had been elected the first Black mayor of Chicago, the city which Martin Luther King had called "the most segregated in the whole of the United States", amid high hopes of sweeping changes in living conditions of the Black people who had almost unanimously supported him. Thus, on taking office, Harold Washington was caught in the conflicting demands of past and future, between the devil of vested interests and corruption on the one hand, and the deep blue sea of radical reform to alleviate intolerable urban degeneration on the other.

When Washington came to power in 1983 it was as part of a major effort in the Black constituency at large to get more Black people elected to high office. He was not a well-known politician at the time—it was the election which really shot him to prominence. But Washington's victory, when it came, was an event of historic importance—not only because of the memory of Daley and because it was less usual for Black mayors to win election in major Northern cities, but also because it was expected that his election would increase Black voter registration across the entire United States. To illustrate the weight a Black mayor of Chicago would carry in national politics, a Democratic Party official told the *Chicago Tribune*: "I think he is going to take a very active role nationally. I cannot see the '84 presidential election going by without the national party seeking his advice and counsel."

Harold Washington was a native of the city he was later to govern. He was one of eleven children; his father was a minister, a lawyer and a Democratic precinct captain on Chicago's Black South Side, so young Harold came into contact with politics at an early age. As a boy he used to run errands for his father and other members of the Democratic organization, thus getting to know most of the important figures in the local party. He was a promising student, something of an athlete too, and fairly successful as an amateur middleweight boxer. All this was cut short by World War II. Washington joined the air force and served in the Pacific; for his services he was decorated with the Marianas Campaign Ribbon. Upon his return to the United States, he enrolled at Roosevelt University in Chicago to study political science and economics. After graduating, he went to Northwestern University Law School, ostensibly to follow in his father's footsteps. He obtained his degree in 1952 and started a private law practice. Two years later he was appointed assistant city prosecutor and from 1960 until 1964 he worked as arbitrator for the Illinois Industrial Commission. Meanwhile, his involvement in politics had begun when, in 1954, he had taken over as precinct captain from his father who died in that year.

A political career proper was embarked upon in 1965, when Washington was elected to the Illinois House of Representatives where he served for eleven years. His legislative talents manifested themselves when he entered the State Senate in 1977. A forceful yet persuasive and witty orator, he initiated legislation concerning the protection of witnesses to crimes, fair employment practices, help for poor and elderly consumers, and the establishment of a Department of Human Rights. He also drafted a bill which would make Martin Luther King's birthday a state holiday, and he founded the Illinois legislature's Black caucus.

As a lifelong Democrat, Washington loyally supported "machine" politics during his first few years in public office. But when during the 1960s and 1970s he saw the forces of law and order increasingly employed against Blacks, he began to distance himself from the Democratic establishment. Police brutality and the fact that the Democratic Party refused to share power with Blacks running on an independent ticket in local elections decided the issue for him. In 1977, when Richard J. Daley died, Washington broke altogether with the Democratic machine.

It was all the more surprising, therefore, that he managed to secure the party's backing for his mayoral campaign in 1982, albeit not without difficulty and delay. He entered the race late, but the fact that he was the only Black candidate worked in his favour. Furthermore, with his personal charisma and solid legislative track record he made a big impression on the fast-growing and increasingly assertive Black electorate which made up 40 per cent of Chicago's registered voters. Some of his opponents fought an overtly racist campaign. Washington's electoral slogan, "It's our turn", was partly a response to this, but it was also designed to appeal to all voters who had never benefited from "machine" rule, including White liberals, as well as Blacks and Hispanics. With massive Democratic Party backing and a vote which was unanimous among Blacks but split among the White electorate, Harold Washington sailed into Chicago's top job.

From the beginning—and much as expected—Washington experienced concerted opposition from many of his sitting aldermen, who were in the majority. Determined to break their pervasive influence, he repeatedly used his right of veto as well as his power to make spending proposals, to appoint officials and to withhold funding from certain council committees if he felt they were not acting responsibly. Among his measures to democratize city government were executive orders for greater access to city records, public hearings on the budget and decentralization of funding control from City Hall to neighbourhood projects. Affirmative action was also high on Washington's list of priorities. He appointed the first Black commissioner of police, and many more women, Black people and Hispanics were employed in top posts during his term of office than ever before. Probably the most important of his achievements in Chicago, however, was a significant reduction in the city's massive deficit of $80 million, something which neither liberal critics nor the most rabid of his many right-wing foes could argue with.

Undoubtedly, Washington's success in this department was attributable to the efforts of a large army of accountants and other financial wizards, but it also owed something to his own habit of lateral thinking, plus the fact that he suffered from an acute form of workaholism. He needed so little sleep that after a 16-hour working day he would feel just ready to go for a jog, have a good read and then meet up with friends to eat and talk. He had been married once for ten years, but lacking a family life he had thrown almost all his energies into work after his divorce.

At the time of his sudden death, Washington was still struggling with the massive problems which plagued Chicago. Although he had managed to introduce some measures of reform, Lake Michigan had proved further away than when in 1983 the new mayor had gleefully boasted he would dump all his recalcitrant aldermen there.

Born Harold Washington. **Parents** Roy L., lawyer and Methodist minister, and Bertha (Jones) Washington. **Education** Du Sable High School, Chicago; Roosevelt University, Chicago, BA, 1949; Northwestern University Law School, JD, 1952. **Military service** US Army Air Force, World War II. **Career** Admitted to Illinois Bar, 1953; subsequently practised in Chicago; precinct captain, Democratic Party, Chicago, from 1954; assistant city prosecutor, 1954–58; arbitrator, Illinois Industrial Commission, 1960–64; member, Illinois House of Representatives, 1965–76; member, Illinois State Senate, 1977–80; Democratic mayor of Chicago, 1983–87. **Other activities** Columnist for *Citizens' News, Metro News* and *Black Xpress* publications. **Offices and memberships** Illinois and Cook County Bar Associations; West Woodlawn Businessmen's Association (director); Nu Beta Epsilon. **Awards and honours** Illinois Independent Voters' Outstanding Legislator Award, 1970; American Federation of Labor/Congress of Industrial Organizations State Federation Outstanding Legislator Award, 1974; Breadbasket Commercial Association Affirmative Action Merit Award, 1973; Negro Relations League William L. Dawson Award, 1974; Mrs Martin Luther King Jr Citation, 1974. **Cause of death** Undisclosed, at age 65.

DECEMBER

LESLIE ARLISS

British Film Director
***Born* London, England, 1901**
***Died* England, 30 December 1987**

Leslie Arliss was responsible for two of the most popular films to come out of British studios during World War II. The first was *The Man in Grey* (1943), starring the rising cinema figures of James Mason, Margaret Lockwood, Phyllis Calvert and Stewart Granger, all of whom found their popularity at the box office greatly increased. This was followed in 1945 by *The Wicked Lady*, also with Mason and Lockwood. Both were productions of Gainsborough Films.

The formula of swashbuckling escapism in these films was absolutely right for war-ravaged Londoners. *The Man in Grey* was a Regency costume drama of jealousy and murder, while *The Wicked Lady* recounted the adventures of a highwayman and the woman who befriended him. Popular and successful though they were at the time, the latter is now mainly remembered for the depth of the star's cleavage which necessitated the re-shooting of some scenes for the American market.

Arliss was the son of George Arliss, a notable British stage actor of his time, who portrayed such flamboyant historical characters as Voltaire, Disraeli, Richelieu and the Duke of Wellington, and was one of the first to take on the challenge of cinema. He went to Hollywood in the early 1930s to recreate his stage performances on screen. It was perhaps this which inspired the young Leslie, who had spent his early adult life working in South Africa, to take on the challenge of the film industry himself.

He returned to England and joined Elstree Studios as a scriptwriter. His early productions included an adaptation of the stage farce *Orders Is Orders* (1933), *Jack Ahoy* (1934), a vehicle for the comedian Jack Hulbert, and an odd wartime comedy drama, *The Foreman Went to France* (1942), starring the comedian Tommy Trinder.

In 1941 Arliss was given his first opportunity to direct his own adaptation of the stage success by Eden Philpotts, *The Farmer's Wife*. This led him to be offered the chance to direct the two Gainsborough costume dramas that made his name. Critic Gilbert Adair commented, "These commercially profitable but heretofore critically disreputable films had always been regarded as the cinematic equivalent of Mills and Boon [publishers of romantic pulp fiction]—all doomy Regency rakes ogling their virginal brides, and amnesiac gentlewomen masquerading as Florentine spitfires..." These films, however, were revived at the National Film Theatre in 1983 and were claimed to possess "a vigour and frankness in their concern with love, marriage, desire, ambition and adventure, not usually associated with British cinema".

Adair continues, "Such iconoclastic revising of received wisdom has often enlivened film criticism. But these particular reassessments can be endorsed only if one is prepared to ignore the fact that the films in question, with narratives ostensibly fuelled by erotic passion, were actually shot with a debilitating lifelessness and performed with risible dependence on what were already dated histrionic conventions."

However, one has to remember that another popular form of escapism at the time was Georgette Heyer's historical romances which also filled the need to forget the drab reality of everyday life and the awful losses so many people were contending with because of the war.

Arliss continued directing both for the cinema and, later, for television but without achieving any great success. His reputation rests on the Gainsborough productions and these will ensure him a permanent place in the history of the British film industry, even though the critics panned them.

Born Leslie Andrews. **Father** George Arliss, actor. **Marriage** Dorothy Cumming (died, 1986). **Children** One daughter. **Education** Tonbridge School, Kent. **Career** Journalist, South Africa, 1930; script department, Elstree Studios, England; moved to Ealing Studios; film director, Gainsborough Pictures; worked mainly in television from mid-1950s to retirement. **Films** (as writer) *Orders Is Orders*, 1932; *Jack Ahoy*, 1934; *Rhodes of Africa*, 1936; *Pastor Hall*, 1939; *The Foreman Went to France*, 1942; (as director) *The Farmer's Wife*, 1941; *The Night Has Eyes*, 1942; *The Man in Grey*, 1943; *Love Story*, 1944; *The Wicked Lady*, 1945; *A Man About the House*, 1947; *Idol of Paris*, 1948; *The Woman's Angle*, 1952; *Miss Tulip Stays the Night*, 1955; *See How They Run*, 1955. **Television** (includes) *Douglas Fairbanks Presents*; *The Buccaneers*. **Cause of death** Undisclosed, at age 86.

MARGARET SCOLARI BARR

American Art Historian

***Born* Rome, Italy, 1901**

***Died* New York City, New York, 30 December 1987**

For more than half a century, Margaret Scolari Barr was one of the New York art world's most dynamic and influential figures. In addition to acting as interpreter for her husband, Alfred H. Barr, founding director of the city's Museum of Modern Art, in his conversations with Picasso, Matisse, Miró, and a host of other non-English-speaking artists, she served as a prominent member of the Emergency Rescue Committee, organized to secure the escape of talented artists from Europe during World War II. As a teacher of art history at Manhattan's prestigious Spence School for 37 years, she inspired generations of future scholars, and at the same time, earned recognition as the author of several important historical studies, including a monograph on the Italian modernist sculptor Medardo Rosso. The book was hailed as the best English work on the artist ever published.

Born in Rome, the daughter of an Irish mother and an Italian father, Margaret Scolari began her academic studies in Italy, completing a first degree in humanities and linguistics at the

University of Rome in 1922. Three years later she emigrated to the United States, where she accepted a post as professor of Italian at Vassar College. By 1929 she had also earned a master's degree in art history, and that autumn moved to New York City to continue her graduate work at New York University. Later that same year, at the inaugural exhibition of the Museum of Modern Art, she was introduced to Alfred Barr. This casual meeting marked the beginning of a fruitful and enduring personal and professional alliance. They were married in Paris the following year.

Margaret Scolari quickly revealed herself as Barr's invaluable assistant, aiding and abetting him in all his scholarly and curatorial endeavours. They shared a tremendous passion for fine modern art, coupled with a tireless and single-minded devotion to duty. In a 1953 profile of Alfred Barr, writer Dwight Macdonald of the *New Yorker* characterized the partnership as a highly organized and efficient one, leaving little time for idleness or indecision. "The day after the wedding, Barr started out to borrow pictures for a forthcoming Corot–Daumier show, with Mrs Barr acting as his translator and secretary. They continued the arrangement through the 1930s, going abroad almost every summer to beg and borrow pictures for the next year's exhibitions."

A gifted linguist, fluent in French, Italian, Spanish and German, Margaret Scolari Barr was instrumental in her husband's success. According to Hilton Kramer, editor of the journal *New Criterion*, "All of his dealings with Picasso, Matisse, Miró and virtually all non-English-speaking European artists were done with her as the interpreter. Neither of his two most important books, on Picasso and Matisse, could have been possible without her." As an expression of his gratitude, Barr dedicated his 1946 Picasso monograph to her.

Richard Oldenburg, a later director of the Museum of Modern Art, described Margaret Scolari Barr as a "remarkable person", both for her penetrating intellect and her unfailing integrity. "She was an essential partner in the achievements and legacy of Alfred Barr...a gifted art historian with a fine sense of quality...very intelligent, strong-willed and intensely honest about everything and everyone, including herself," he remembered. During the war years, her integrity led her to become actively involved in the work of the Emergency Rescue Committee, now the International Rescue Committee, which helped artists such as Jacques Lipchitz, Piet Mondrian, Max Ernst, Yves Tanguy and André Masson (q.v.) escape Nazi-occupied Europe.

In 1943 she joined the faculty at New York's Spence School. She remained there as a teacher of art history, inspiring class after class of fresh-faced secondary students, for the next 37 years. Among her young *protégées* was Joan R. Mertens, curator of Greek and Roman art at the Metropolitan Museum.

As a teacher, Margaret Scolari Barr was an enthusiastic and bewitching, if somewhat intimidating, figure. Anne d'Harnoncourt, director of the Philadelphia Museum, remembered her forceful, riveting style. "I think the remarkable thing about [her] was her emphasis. She made everyone else, including me, feel fuzzy and vague. She had a real gift for drawing your attention and not letting it go."

In her introductory remarks to her young art history students—a lecture she delivered every year—she emphasized the fundamental link between the intellectual understanding and the aesthetic appreciation of art. "The more you know about a work of art—what preceded it, what followed it, the reasons why it is the way it is—the more it will come to life for you. The tourist who goes through museums exclaiming 'Beautiful, beautiful' is something to be deplored. You jolly well must know why." But, lest the task seem too onerous, she always added, "Plan to enjoy yourselves. As Poussin, the great French painter of the seventeenth century, remarked, 'Le fin de l'art est la délectation' (the goal of art is to delight)".

In addition to teaching, and assisting her husband in his academic endeavours, Margaret Scolari Barr devoted herself to her own critical writings and translations. Over the years her projects included an Italian translation of Charles Rufus Morey's catalogue of the Vatican

Library's Museo Christiano and the first complete English translation of Matisse's *Notes of a Painter*. But her crowning academic achievement came in 1963, with the publication of *Medardo Rosso (1858–1928)*. At the time of her death she was engaged in a lengthy chronology of her life with her husband, who died in 1981. The first part, covering the years 1930 to 1944, the formative period of the Museum of Modern Art, appeared in the summer 1987 issue of the *New Criterion*. The couple's only daughter, Victoria, raised in New York's artistic mileu, is, appropriately enough, a painter.

Born Margaret Scolari. **Parents** Virgilio, antiques dealer, and Mary (Fitzmaurice) Scolari. **Marriage** Alfred H. Barr, director, Museum of Modern Art, 1930 (died, 1981). **Children** Victoria, a painter. **Education** University of Rome, 1919–22; studied art history, New York University, 1929. **Emigration** Left Italy for the United States, 1925. **Career** Teacher of art history, Spence School, New York City, 1943–80. **Related activities** Assisted husband in interviewing important artists, acting as interpreter; also helped him in efforts to borrow paintings for exhibitions. **Other activities** Helped European artists flee Nazi persecution through work with Emergency Rescue Committee. **Publications** *Medardo Rosso*, New York, 1963; (translator into Italian) *Catalogue of the Vatican Library's Museo Christiano* by Charles Rufus Morey; (translator into English) *Notes of a Painter* by Matisse. **Cause of death** Cancer of the colon, at age 86.

PATRICK BISSELL

American Ballet Dancer

***Born* Corpus Christi, Texas, 1 December 1957**

***Died* Hoboken, New Jersey, 29 December 1987**

Patrick Bissell's tragically early death robbed the ballet world of one of its most promising stars. He was encouraged to take dance lessons as an early age by his mother and sister who promised the child that the training would help him fulfil his ambition to become big and strong. He made rapid progress and at the age of 15 left home to study at various ballet academies, including those at Champaign, Illinois, San Francisco and North Carolina. Following this, Bissell gained a scholarship to the School of American Ballet, New York, where he was noticed and encouraged by Stanley Williams, one of his teachers, and Lincoln Kirstein, the director of New York City Ballet.

In spite of this attention, Bissell failed to get a place with New York City Ballet on graduating, so he opted for American Ballet Theater, where he was accepted into the *corps de ballet* in 1977. He had been with the company only three months when the director, Lucia Chase, told him he had been chosen to dance the leading role of Solor in *La Bayadère*. Bissell panicked, thinking he did not have the stamina to sustain the complicated and demanding role, but after strenuous coaching and great encouragement from the rest of the company, his début was an overwhelming success.

After this auspicious start Bissell's rise was meteoric. He danced the leading role of the Prince in Mikhail Baryshnikov's production of *The Nutcracker* and he was soon promoted to soloist at

Ballet Theater. The following year, 1979, he was appointed principal dancer and began to tackle a variety of leading roles.

Bissell's range extended through the classics from Albrecht in *Giselle* and Siegfried in *Swan Lake* to more modern parts such as Don José in Roland Petit's production of *Carmen* and leading roles in many of George Balanchine's ballets. Tall and ruggedly handsome, Bissell was ideally suited to these parts and early on in his career the chief dance critic of the *New York Times* wrote, "...he carries his tall frame with beautiful sweep and classical style". As well as these seemingly natural attributes, he soon became famous for his passionate acting and a gifted technique which made the most difficult choreography look easy to the uninitiated.

By the time he was 21 Bissell was established as one of the leading dancers in America and fêted as a star. As he recognized, this gave him a much more spectacular lifestyle than most other young people. In one interview he is quoted as saying, "I do have much more freedom than most people my age. When I got my own apartment with my own possessions around me I wanted to work hard. To work is the greatest joy."

However, so much early success also brought problems. Gelsey Kirkland, one of Bissell's partners at Ballet Theater, considered that his talents were exploited too soon. In her book, *Dancing on My Grave*, she wrote that "he had been pushed into some major roles before his time due to the shortage of male partners in the company". He worked desperately hard to measure up to these unrealistic expectations and, not surprisingly, he began to sustain a series of injuries. After this Bissell's private life became unstable. It was soon apparent that he had problems with alcohol and Kirkland, herself a victim of the "baby ballerina" syndrome, has also described their drug-taking. Bissell's dancing became uneven and unpredictable and he was twice dismissed from Ballet Theater for lateness and missing rehearsals. In 1982 he married Jolinda Menendez, a principal dancer with Ballet Theater, but this relationship soon broke down and the couple were divorced.

Bissell fought hard to overcome his problems and he continued to bounce back from the depths. Shortly before his death he discussed his roles for Ballet Theater's next season with artistic director Baryshnikov, who commented later, "I saw Patrick just before Christmas. He looked forward to performing with the company during the upcoming tour." Sadly, it was not to be.

Although Bissell never managed to fulfil his potential, he will undoubtedly occupy a place in the annals of dance history. This was summed up by Baryshnikov who, on hearing of his death, said, "Patrick Bissell was without doubt one of the brightest lights in American Ballet Theater's history, or for that matter, in the entire world".

Born Patrick Bissell. **Parents** Donald and Pat Bissell. **Marriage** Jolinda Menendez, principal dancer, Ballet Theater, 1982 (divorced). **Education** Trained in ballet and jazz dance, Toledo, Ohio, 1967–72; studied at various academies, including National Academy of Dance, Champaign, Illinois, and North Carolina School of the Arts; scholarship to School of American Ballet. **Career** Began as professional dancer with brief stint at Boston Ballet, 1976; joined *corps de ballet*, Ballet Theater, 1977, soloist, 1978, principal dancer, 1979; dismissed for chronic lateness and missed rehearsals, 1980–81; reinstated as principal dancer, 1982–87. **Related activities** Guest dancer: Stars of World Ballet, 1979, National Ballet of Canada, 1980, Edinburgh Festival, 1980, and many other companies. **Principal roles** Prince in *The Nutcracker*; Don José in *Carmen*; Franz in *Coppélia*; Basil and Espada in *Don Quixote*; Albrecht in *Giselle*; Romeo in *Romeo and Juliet*; Prince Siegfried in *Swan Lake*; James in *La Sylphide*; Prince Desire in *Sleeping Beauty*; Prince in *Cinderella*; lead roles in *Stravinsky Violin Concerto*, *Symphonie Concertante*, *Theme and Variations*. **Cause of death** Apparent suicide, at age 30. **Further reading** Gelsey Kirkland with Fred Lawrence, *Dancing on My Grave*, New York, 1986, London, 1987.

CLIFTON CHENIER

American Singer and Musician
***Born* Opelousas, Louisiana, 25 June 1925**
***Died* Lafayette, Louisiana, 12 December 1987**

One of the joys of American music is its sheer diversity. Regional, ethnic, cultural, social and religious differences have thrown up a wealth of indigenous music that, while all loosely collected together under the label of American folk music, is nevertheless infinite in its variety. None is more unique than Zydeco, the Black version of Cajun music played by French-speaking Blacks on the Louisiana and Texas Gulf coasts.

Cajun music itself mixes waltzes and two-steps, rhythm and blues, country and soul music into a sweaty dance music that is played for physical involvement, not passive appreciation. The word Cajun is a corruption of Acadian, the name of the French-speaking inhabitants of Nova Scotia who migrated to Louisiana after the British invasion of Nova Scotia in 1755. Cajun music thus has European roots, with a basic instrumentation of fiddle and accordion. But while Cajun music has developed along fairly traditional, European-based lines, Zydeco has embraced the whole wealth of Black music. The man responsible for that development, and for popularizing Zydeco around the world, was Clifton Chenier.

Chenier was the son of one accordion-player and the nephew of another. His brother Cleveland played the run board—basically an old-fashioned corrugated washboard strapped to the chest and played with metal fingerpicks—and the two of them performed together at private house parties in Louisiana in the mid-1940s. At this time Chenier's music was strongly influenced by the traditional French–Cajun two-step, but in the mid-1950s, he moved inland to Houston in Texas. There he heard other Black musics—the blues and rhythm and blues—as well as country music and the emerging rock and roll, and his style soon began to merge this aural diversity into a unique combination.

When Chenier returned to Louisiana, his eclectic approach was to change Zydeco for ever. He concentrated on playing the piano accordion, the largest of the accordion family and the most suitable for playing the blues, and recorded his new music prolifically, making more than 100 albums in all. After the success of "Clifton Blues" in 1954, Chenier became the star of Zydeco music. With his Red Hot Louisiana Band, he toured extensively throughout the Southern states and then further afield, playing a zestful dance music that denied anyone the chance to sit back and relax.

Chenier himself never sat still, and he continued to absorb new sounds and ideas within his music. Mixing traditional Cajun instrumentation with electric guitars, saxophones and a strong backbeat on drums, he was open in later years to both jazz and rock influences, notably in the elaborate guitar playing of band-member Paul Senegal. Throughout his career, Chenier sang in a funky French/English patois, impenetrable to all but a few, and accompanied himself with a fine blues harmonica.

Not that such a vocal delivery restricted his appeal in any way. In 1955 Chenier recorded for Specialty Records, a basically rock and roll label that introduced his music to a new audience, first at home in the US and then abroad, notably in Jamaica. In 1966 he performed at the Berkeley Folk Festival, and was soon in demand at folk, blues and jazz festivals throughout the world. By this time, he was acknowledged as the King of Zydeco, an inspiration to a new generation of Zydeco musicians who followed in his footsteps.

Unfortunately, Chenier himself was not to live to see the full flowering of his success, for in 1979 ill health curtailed his career. He lost one of his feet to diabetes and was eventually on thrice-weekly dialysis. Despite that, he continued to perform as regularly as possible right up to his death, playing to the full his role as world ambassador of Zydeco music.

Born Clifton Chenier. **Father** Joseph Chenier, a musician. **Marriage** Margaret, *circa* 1945. **Career** Part-time musician, 1942–54; formed Hot Sizzling Band and played in Texas and Louisiana to mid-1950s; recorded on many labels, including, Elko, Specialty, Argo, Checker, Zynn, Arhoolie, Arhoolie/Crazy Cajun, RCA Victor, from 1954; performed at many folk and blues festivals; toured US, UK and Europe, playing many club dates, 1955–87. **Awards and honours** Best Cajun Artist, *Blues Unlimited* readers' poll, 1973; National Heritage Fellowship, National Educational Association, 1984. **Films** *Dry Wood* and *Hot Pepper*, 1973; *Within Southern Louisiana*, 1974. **Recordings** "Clifton Blues", Imper 5532, 1954; "Louisiana Blues", Bayou 509, 1965; "Monifique", Arhoolie 1038, 1967; "Tu le ton son ton", Arhoolie 1052, 1970; "Jambalaya", Arhoolie 1086, 1975; *Bayou Boogie; King of Bayou*, 1964; *Bogalusa Boogie*, 1964. **Songs** (include) "Ain't Gonna Worry Any More"; "All Day Long"; "All Night Long"; "Bad Luck and Trouble"; "Bayou Drive"; "Bogalusa Boogie"; "Blues All the Time"; "Brown Skin Woman"; "Calinda"; "Come Go Along With Me"; "I Can't Stand"; "I Woke Up This Morning"; "I'm a Hog for You"; "Just a Lonely Boy"; "Louisiana Blues"; "My Mama Told Me"; "One Step at a Time"; "They Call Me Crazy"; "Something on My Mind"; "Worried Life Blues". **Cause of death** Diabetes, at age 62. **Further reading** J. Broven, *South to Louisiana: The Music of the Cajun Bayous*, Louisiana, 1983.

SEPTIMA CLARK

American Civil Rights Activist and Teacher

***Born* Charleston, South Carolina, 3 May 1898**

***Died* John's Island, South Carolina, 15 December 1987**

As the daughter of a former slave, Septima Clark must have inherited a special awareness of the injustices faced by Black people living in a White-dominated society. To say that these insights, combined with her own experiences of growing up in the American South at the turn of the century where her people were systematically denied their basic rights, must have led her naturally to a career as a teacher and civil rights activist would be glib. It must be considered an exceptional and amazing achievement that Clark found the courage and energy to take on the system and fight tirelessly for education and equality for Black people for over 70 years.

Clark attended Avery Normal Institute, graduating in 1916 at the age of 18. After this she began her teaching career when she was appointed to a post in a Black public school on John's Island. Two years later she was appointed to Avery Institute and it was at this time that she became formally involved in civil rights issues by organizing a petition to have Black teachers hired by the Charleston County School District. The petition attracted 20,000 signatures. In 1927 Clark took up a teaching post in Columbia and she also became active in a campaign for Black teachers to receive the same salary scales as their White counterparts.

Clark continued to teach while working ceaselessly for better conditions for Black Americans. Inevitably, this often put her safety at risk, as well as getting her into trouble with the authorities, and at one point she was dismissed from a teaching post in Charleston on the excuse that she was a member of the National Association for the Advancement of Colored People.

While concerned with all these issues, Clark did not neglect her own education. She enrolled at Benedict College, Columbia, and received a bachelor's degree in 1942. Subsequently, she went on to study successfully for a master's degree at Hampton Institute, Virginia.

As the civil rights movement gained momentum in the 1950s, Clark's work in this sphere continued to develop. She was particularly active in the campaign to enfranchise Black voters and while working at the Highlander Folk School in Tennessee, she implemented a programme aimed at giving Black people the skills to pass the voter literacy tests. She began to gain national recognition for her work and toured the country giving lectures. In 1957 she became director of education at the Highlander Folk School, and four years later she was appointed director of a literacy training programme. In 1962 she became director of teacher training for the Southern Christian Leadership Conference and in that year her autobiography, *Echo in My Soul*, was also published. Two years later her achievements in the civil rights movement were acknowledged when she was invited to accompany Martin Luther King to Norway when he received the Nobel Peace Prize.

Over the years Clark received many honours, including Woman of the Year in Charleston in 1956, a citation from the National Council of Negro Women in 1963 and a Living Legacy Award from President Carter in 1979. In 1982 she was presented with the Order of Palmetto, South Carolina's highest civilian award.

On her death the governor of South Carolina, Carroll A. Campbell Jr, said, "The state has lost not only a civil rights activist but a legendary educator and humanitarian". Much had changed in the 60 years since the authorities of that same state had dismissed her from her teaching post for membership of a civil rights organization. However, had Septima Clark been around to hear those words, she might well have smiled ironically when she considered how much still remains to be done.

Born Septima Poinsette. **Parents** Peter Porcher, a caterer, and Victoria (Anderson) Poinsette. **Marriage** Nerie David Clark (died). **Children** Nerie David Jr. **Education** Avery Normal Institute, 1916; Columbia University, 1930; Atlanta University, 1937; Benedict College, AB, 1942; Hampton Institute, MA, 1946. **Career** Teacher and teaching principal in public schools, John's Island, South Carolina, 1922–56; director of education, Highlander Folk School, Monteagle, Tennessee, 1957–61, director of literacy training programme, 1961; teacher and training director, Southern Christian Leadership Conference, from 1962; elected Charleston County School Board, 1974. **Offices and memberships** South Carolina Council on Human Relations; National Association for Advancement of Colored People; National Adult Education Association, chairman, rural section, 1961; Council of Southern Mountains; South Carolina Democratic Women; Citizens' Committee of Charleston County; Alpha Kappa Alpha. **Awards and honours** Woman of the Year for Civic Activities, Charleston, South Carolina, 1956; plaque for civic activities from Utility Club, New York City, 1960; citation from the National Council of Negro Women, 1963; plaque from Chatham County Crusade for Voters, 1964; Living Legacy Award, US government, 1979; Order of the Palmetto, South Carolina, 1982. **Publications** (with Legette Blythe) *Echo in My Soul* (autobiography), New York, 1962; contributor to *Freedomways* and other periodicals. **Cause of death** Undisclosed, at age 89.

HENRY COTTON

British Golfer

***Born* Holmes Chapel, Cheshire, 26 January 1907**

***Died* Portimão, Portugal, 22 December 1987**

Possibly the only professional golfer to have appeared in a music hall act, Thomas Henry Cotton was a unique, as well as an outstanding, figure within his sport. He turned professional at the age of 17, and was still winning tournaments almost 30 years later. In 1956 he finished equal sixth in the British Open, ahead of every other home-grown player, except John Panton. And, as one particular story about him helps to illustrate, even when he reached his mid-seventies, he was still keen to play well. He presented his 1948 Open-winning set of clubs to the Professional Golf Association, but when he was reminded by his wife during a later visit how well he used to play with the putter, he took it back.

Cotton's background differed from most professionals of his time in that he did not enter the profession through the caddies' ranks. For this reason, and because he was educated at a public school—Alleyn's in Dulwich—he has been described as "probably the first gentleman professional". But he mixed easily with golfers of all kinds: from caddies and assistants, to fellow professionals, and even the Duke of Windsor.

Not necessarily the most gifted of players, Cotton had an acute analytical brain and was willing to practise until his hands bled. He made his first trip to the United States in 1928 to gain experience, and learned from Tommy Armour how to draw the ball for added length. Putting was the one department of his game which occasionally appeared slightly stilted. Otherwise, Cotton's style was full of power and grace, and, despite being a "made" rather than a "born" golfer, displayed no signs of artificiality.

Cotton was recognized as *the* up-and-coming player of the 1930s. He won the Kent Open from 1926 to 1930, played in the 1929 Ryder Cup, and was in contention for the British Open several times. In 1933 he was tied for the lead after scores of 73, 72 and 71, but fell back to seventh following a disastrous final round of 79. Cotton himself later admitted that the reason he used to fall away like this was because he paid too much attention to what others were doing on the course.

But everything changed at Sandwich in 1934. His opening rounds of 67 and 65 were nothing short of brilliant—the latter round even giving a name to a golf ball: "The Dunlop 65". His third round of 72, played in a stiff breeze, left him 12 strokes ahead of his nearest challenger. And despite an attack of nervous indigestion on the final round, during which he dropped several strokes, he held on to win by five.

Cotton's win broke an eleven-year spell of American domination of the British Open. Three years later, in Ryder Cup year, he faced the entire US team at Carnoustie, where a round of 71 in driving rain and on a practically water-logged course not only gave him his second title, but also elevated him to the very pinnacle of world golf.

He was unable to travel as freely to the United States as he might have liked, but his exploits on the greens and fairways of the United Kingdom and the rest of Europe emphasized the fact that he was the finest golfer Britain had produced since World War I. By the outbreak of World War II, he had taken a total of nine European Opens, including the German Open three times in a row.

Several of his best years were nevertheless lost to the war. Commissioned in the RAF, he was invalided out in 1943 with ulcers and a burst appendix, and turned to playing exhibition matches to raise funds for the Red Cross. After the war, he picked up his career where he left off, winning the 1946 French Open, and renewing his dominance of the British game. In that same year he was awarded the MBE for his services to the sport.

His third British Open title was won at Muirfield in 1948; but after that, Cotton began to feel that enough was enough. He became an infrequent tournament player, and did not enter another British Open at all until 1952, when he finished fourth. But Henry Cotton was more than just a great player. He was a shrewd and observant businessman who never missed an opportunity to exploit a little good publicity. Even as a player, he took the time to teach, to design clubs, to write and even—as a one-off—to perform in the music hall. That famous occasion occurred in 1938 at the London Coliseum, where his 15-minute "act" consisted mainly of demonstrating shots on a darkened stage with balls, shoes and gloves treated in a luminous paint. As an encore, he hit soft balls into the auditorium with the lights full on.

In the 1950s he began to concentrate on designing courses, and was soon in great demand, especially on the Continent. At Penina in Portugal he accepted the challenge of making a course on land that was once a paddy field. He made his home there, travelling with his Argentinian wife to Britain and France each summer. During the 1975 revolution, he was forced to leave the country, having been branded as "a capitalist who works too hard". He and his wife, "Toots", who played a profound role in his golfing career and from whom he was inseparable, were nevertheless able to return to their home in Penina after the troubles were over.

Despite his success in other areas, it is as a player that Cotton will be best remembered. His three British Open titles set him apart from other British golfers, and his regular encounters in tournaments and in three Ryder Cups with the best American players illustrated his greatness on a global scale at a time when transatlantic travel was less easy than it is today.

Much of his success on the course can be traced to the constant practising which, even as a young man, left him with a pronounced tilt of the shoulders, as a result of so many hours in a golfing stance with his right shoulder set well below the left. It proved to be an early illustration of a lifetime dedicated to the sport.

Born Thomas Henry Cotton. **Marriage** Maria Isabel Estanguet Moss, 1939 (died, 1982). **Education** Alleyn's School, Dulwich. **Military service** Flight lieutenant, Royal Air Force Volunteer Reserve, invalided out, 1943. **Career** Golfer; played in first Boys' Golf Championship, 1921; turned professional, 1924; assistant, Fulwell, 1924, Rye, 1925, Cannes, 1925; professional, Langley Park, 1927, Waterloo, Brussels, 1933, Ashridge, Kent, 1936; won Kent Professional Championship, 1926–30; Belgian Open, 1930, 1934, 1938; Mar del Plata, 1930; Dunlop Tournament, 1931, 1932, 1953, runner-up, 1959; *News of the World* Tournament, 1932, 1939; British Open, 1934, 1937, 1948; Italian Open, 1936; German Open, 1937, 1938, 1939; Silver King Tournament, 1937; Czechoslovak Open, 1937, 1938; Harry Vardon Trophy, 1938; *Daily Mail* 000 Tournament, 1939; Penfold Tournament, 1939, 1954; *News Chronicle* Tournament, 1945; Star Tournament, 1946; Professional Golfers' Association Match Play Champion, 1946; represented Great Britain *v.* America, 1929, 1937, 1947, 1953; Ryder Cup Team Captain, 1939, 1947, 1953; Spaulding Tournament, 1947; led US Open Qualifying, 1956. **Related activities** Visited USA in 1929, 1931, 1947, 1948, 1956–57; visited Argentine, 1929, 1948–50; professional golf correspondent, *Golf Monthly*; designed many golf courses, including Abridge, Felixstowe, Canons Brook, Castle Eden Golf Club, Eaglescliffe, Stirling, Gourock, Windmill Hill, Bletchley, Sene Valley, Folkestone and Ely (UK), Megève and Deauville (France), Penina, Val do Lobo, Golf de Monte Gorda and Monte Velho (Portugal); director and founder, Golf Foundation for development of youthful golfers. **Offices and memberships** Vice-president: National Golf Clubs Advisory Bureau, Golf Writers' Association. **Awards and honours** Member, Order of the British Empire, 1946; honorary member, Professional Golf Association. **Publications** *Golf*,

1932; *This Game of Golf*, 1948; *My Swing*, 1952; *My Golfing Album*, 1959; *Henry Cotton Says*, 1962; *Study the Game of Golf with Henry Cotton*, 1964; *The Picture World of Golf*, 1965; *Golf in the British Isles*, 1969; *A History of Golf*, 1973; *Thanks for the Game*, 1980. **Cause of death** Undisclosed, at age 80.

PETER DARRELL

British Ballet Dancer, Choreographer and Director

Born **Richmond, Surrey, 19 September 1929**

Died **Glasgow, Scotland, 2 December 1987**

Peter Darrell's major achievement was his pioneering work in extending the scope of classical dance so that it appealed to a wider audience. He was trained at the school of the Sadler's Wells Ballet in London and on graduating in the mid-1940s he was immediately invited to join the company. At this time ballet in England was still a relatively new art form and Darrell's early years as a dancer coincided with an exciting time of innovation and expansion. In 1946 the Sadler's Wells company graduated from its small base to the larger and grander Royal Opera House, Covent Garden, which offered far more scope for its burgeoning talents. Visits to London by the American Ballet Theater and the New York City Ballet companies were having a big impact on British audiences, and in 1949 Sadler's Wells Ballet's first visit to the Metropolitan Opera House, New York, which was an outstanding success, established it as a company of international status. Darrell was to retain the liveliness, excitement and creativity which characterized the Sadler's Wells Company during these years for the rest of his life.

At first Darrell concentrated solely on dancing. He had an early success when he created a featured role in Frederick Ashton's *Valses Nobles et Sentimentales* (1947), and he went on to make notable appearances in Ashton's *Façade*, Mikhail Fokine's *Carnaval* and Ninette de Valois's *The Gods Go a-Begging*. Darrell soon extended his range. While continuing to dance in classical works, he also began to appear in musicals and to try his hand at choreography. After experimenting with various new dance forms at the Ballet Workshop held in the Mercury Theatre, London, he received his first professional commission in 1952 when he was invited to mount a new version of *Harlequinade* for Anton Dolin's Festival Ballet.

Darrell worked within the framework of classical ballet; his aims were always to extend the tradition by making use of contemporary themes and utilizing other theatrical skills. In 1956 he joined forces with Elizabeth West, who was a teacher at the renowned Old Vic Theatre School in Bristol, and together they set up the Western Theatre Ballet. This was a bold venture, in that it attemped to bring the world of dance to southwest England where there was no ready-made audience. Indeed, financial constraints obliged the company to spend part of each year touring, but Darrell, the company's resident choreographer and artistic director, remained true to the policy of using the classical technique in a more dramatic and contemporary way.

He demonstrated these ideas in his ballet *The Prisoners*, the company's first production. This was a great success and the ballet has remained in the repertoire, being constantly revived since its première in 1957. The company soon built an impressive reputation for the drama and individuality of its performances and Darrell's output was prolific, producing several new ballets a year. In 1962 Elizabeth West died tragically in a mountaineering accident and Darrell took sole charge of the company.

Although he was faced with the full responsibility of running the company, he continued to produce new works. Notable among his large output at this time were *A Wedding Present* (1962), which achieved tragic depth, and a modern version of Debussy's *Jeux* in the following year. *Mods and Rockers* (1963), which was based on the music of the Beatles, proved extremely popular, and by the mid-1960s the company had become well known nationally.

In 1966 the Sadler's Wells Opera in London offered the company better facilities and this enabled Darrell to produce his most ambitious work, *Sun into Darkness*. This was the first British three-act ballet with a contemporary setting. Darrell enlisted the help of the playwright David Rudkin to work with him on the story and a score was commissioned from Malcolm Williamson. The production was an acclaimed success.

In his drive to reach new audiences Darrell experimented with television, creating two ballets specially for that medium—*Houseparty* (1963) and *Orpheus* (1965)—and again he used a playwright, this time John Hopkins, to devise the plot. Among Darrell's other work for television was *Cool for Cats*, a pop music series for which he choreographed dance sequences during 1964, but his main work remained with his company whose talents he continued to nurture and develop.

In 1969 the company was invited to make its base in Glasgow where it became Scottish Theatre Ballet. Darrell continued to produce a stream of new works and he also mounted innovative versions of the classics, including *Giselle* (1971), *The Nutcracker* (1973), *Swan Lake* (1977) and *Cinderella* (1979). He also invited other choreographers to create works for the company but it was his own ballets that became the company's hallmark. Darrell was greatly loved and respected by his dancers, who at one point threatened to resign *en masse* when the managing board proposed to change the company's direction. Needless to say, the changes were not implemented.

In his last years Darrell struggled against a long illness and in 1986 he decided to give up his director's role to concentrate solely on choreography. However, at the time of his death no successor had been found.

Born Peter Skinner. **Education** Sadler's Wells Ballet School. **Career** Ballet dancer, Sadler's Wells Opera Ballet, performing in such works as *Valses Nobles at Sentimentales*, *Façade*, *Carnaval* and *The Gods Go a-Begging*, mid-1940s; worked in musicals and at Malmö Opera House, Sweden; turned to choreography via the Ballet Workshop, 1951; first professional commission, *Harlequinade*, for Festival Ballet, 1952; co-founder with Elizabeth West of Western Theatre Ballet, 1957, becoming sole director after her death, 1962–87; company moved to Glasgow, becoming Scottish Theatre Ballet and then Scottish Ballet, 1969. **Related activities** Occasional television choreography. **Awards and honours** Commander of the Order of the British Empire. **Works choreographed** (include) *Midsummer Watch*, 1951; *Les Chimères*, 1953; *Trio*, 1953; *Fountain*, 1954; *Celeste and Celesthina*, 1954; *Magic* 1954; *Balleto da camera*, 1955; *The Gift*, 1955; *The Prisoners*, 1957; *The Enchanted Garden*, 1958; *Chiaroscuro*, 1959; *Quatre quartières*, 1959; *Sound Barrier, 1965; Bal de la victoire*, 1960; *Salade*, 1961; *Ode*, 1961; *Non-Stop*, 1962; *A Wedding Present*, 1962; *The Unicorn, the Gorgon and the Manticore*, 1962; *Jeux*, 1963; *Mods and Rockers*, 1963; *Mayerling*, 1963; *Elegy*, 1963–64; *Lysistrata*, 1964; *Home*, 1965; *Sun into Darkness*, 1966; *Lessons in Love*, 1966; *Francesca*, 1967; *Ephemeron*, 1968; *Beauty and the Beast*, 1969; *Herodias*, 1970; *Giselle*, 1971; (act II only) *The Nutcracker*, 1972; *Variations for a Door and a Sigh*, 1972; *Othello*, 1972; *The Nutcracker*, 1973; *Tales of Hoffman*, 1973; *La Péri*, 1973; (with Joyce Graeme) *Giselle*, 1973; *Asparas*, 1974; *The Scarlet Pastorale*, 1974; *Mary, Queen of Scots*, 1976; *Swan Lake*, 1977; *Five Rocket Songs*, 1978; *Cinderella*, 1979; *Tristan and*

Iseult, 1979. **Television** (all BBC unless stated) *Houseparty*, 1963; *Cool for Cats*, 1964; *A Man Like Orpheus*, 1965; *An Engagement Party*, Granada TV, 1974. **Cause of death** Undisclosed, at age 58.

ARTHUR H. DEAN

American Lawyer and Diplomat

Born **Ithaca, New York, 16 October 1898**

Died **Glen Cove, New York, December 1987**

Arthur H. Dean was a successful international and corporate lawyer who made his name as a diplomatic negotiator for the US government and as the trusted adviser to four US presidents. On graduating from Cornell Law School in 1923, Dean joined the firm of Sullivan and Cromwell, becoming senior partner of that firm on the resignation of his mentor, John Foster Dulles, in 1949.

As a lawyer, Dean worked with Dulles on negotiations in Paris, Berlin, Rome, Milan and London on the security issues and business transactions arising out of the Dawes Plan loans to Germany after World War I. In 1972 he worked for two years in Japan on a £9 billion bond issue by the Nippon Power Company, the first ever to be offered to the American public. In 1933 President Eisenhower recruited him to the Department of Commerce Committee responsible for the 1934 Securities Exchange Act.

It was in 1953, however, as President Eisenhower's special envoy to the post-armistice talks at the end of the Korean War, that Arthur H. Dean became a world-famous figure. His assignment to negotiate on behalf of the UN Command was described by the *New York Herald Tribune* as "possibly one of the most important diplomatic roles ever assigned to an American". Nor was the romance of the situation lost as the two sides faced each other in a tent pitched across the thirty-eighth parallel high among the frozen mountains of central Korea. Dean, according to a colleague, was "like pom poms firing off verbal rockets [and] using every courtroom technique he knew". But he did not manage to break down the stony intransigence of the Communist side and eventually, after seven weeks of talks, returned to the US convinced that "the Chinese Communists are determined to keep North Korea politically and economically integrated into their own economy".

Dean's second spell of diplomatic duties, this time as President Kennedy's representative to the Geneva test ban talks in 1961, was scarcely more productive. Test ban negotiations, called off by the Soviets in December 1960 after the U-2 spy plan affair, were re-opened in 1961. In April Dean presented his draft of the first complete American test ban treaty proposal and in September helped Kennedy draft his "Proposal for General and Complete Disarmament in a Peaceful World". Both foundered on mutual mistrust and on Soviet rejection of the number of on-site inspections the Americans were proposing. By the time the first partial nuclear test ban was eventually signed in August 1963, Dean had returned to private law practice.

In view of all this, and perhaps as further illustration of the difficulties and misunderstandings of the Cold War years, it seems hard that at home Dean should also have had to face accusations of "appeasement" levelled by a senator for Idaho, Herman Welker. Publicly refuting any such charge, Dean told a press conference in 1954 that "Communism is repugnant to every idea for which I stand. In my judgment it should be fought tooth and nail. I am against the appeasement of the USSR, Red China, North Korea or any other Communist government. I am not in favour of the recognition of Red China or its admission to the United Nations."

Where Arthur Dean seems to have been most immediately successful was as adviser to President Johnson on the Vietnam War. He was a member of the Senior Advisory Committee that turned down the military request for a further 100,000 troops for the war and is widely credited with having persuaded President Johnson to stop the bombing in Vietnam and to stand down at the next presidential election.

Dean always faced his assignments, no matter how difficult, with characteristic optimism. He would no doubt be gratified at recent advances in *détente*.

Born Arthur Hobson Dean. **Parents** William Cameron, law professor, and Maud Campbell (Egan) Dean. **Marriage** Mary Talbott Clark Marden, 1932. **Children** Nicholas B. Marden and Patricia Campbell. **Education** Ithaca High School; Cornell University, 1915–18, 1919–21, AB, 1921; Cornell Law School, LLB, 1923, editor *Law Review*. **Military service** United States Navy, 1918–19; Coast Guard Reserve, 1941–45. **Career** Admitted to New York Bar, 1923; joined Sullivan and Cromwell, 1923, full partner, 1929, senior partner, 1949, specialist in international law; presidential adviser and diplomat over three decades. **Related activities** Member, Dickinson Committee, Department of Commerce, 1934; drafted Trust Indenture Act, 1939; drafted Investment Company Act, 1940; Special Deputy Secretary of State, UN/Korea peace talks, 1953; chief of delegation, nuclear test ban treaty talks, 1963; member, Senior Advisory Group on Vietnam, 1968. **Other activities** Dickinson Lecturer, Harvard Graduate School of Business Administration, 1949; member, joint administrative board, New York Hospital-Cornell Medical Center; director: Solvay American Corporation, Crowley-Republic Steel Corporation, Henry L. Crowley and Company, American Agricultural Chemical Company, Cornell Aeronautical Laboratory, Mexical Light and Power Company; general counsel, American Metal Company; director, Visiting Nurse Association, Association for the Aid of Crippled Children. **Offices and memberships** Trustee: Cornell University 1945–48, chairman, executive committee, 1948, New York Bank, North Country Hospital, Long Island, Hochschild Foundation; chairman of the board, Breen Vale School, Long Island; member, finance committee, Carnegie Foundation for the Advancement of Teaching; member: Foreign Policy Association, Japan Society, Academy of Political Science, American Academy of Political and Social Science; chairman, Institute of Pacific Relations, 1950–52. **Publications** *Business Income Under Present Price Levels*, 1949; *Test Ban and Disarmament: The Path of Negotiation*, 1966; contributed to *Fortune*, *New York Herald Tribune* and several law journals. **Cause of death** Pneumonia, at age 89.

GUSTAV FRÖHLICH

German Actor and Film Director

***Born* Hanover, Germany, 21 March 1902**

***Died* Lugano, Switzerland, 22 December 1987**

Despite a successful film career spanning five decades and more than 120 movies, Gustav Fröhlich remained largely unknown outside his native Germany. But his place in cinema history was secured forever by his first major role, in Fritz Lang's silent classic *Metropolis*.

Fröhlich rejected a career in journalism in favour of the stage at the age of 17, when he joined a company of travelling players. With the help of an influential industrialist, he was soon making his Berlin début, in Eugene O'Neill's *The Moon of the Caribbees* at the Volksbühne. He was still not 20.

Within three years he was bringing his blond, blue-eyed good looks to the screen alongside Lionel Barrymore in Danish director Benjamin Christensen's *Die Frau mit dem schlechten Ruf* (Woman of Ill-repute). The following year, after three films under Fred Sauer, *Metropolis* catapulted him to stardom.

Fröhlich played the upper-class young man whose love for a beautiful woman inspires him to join her in leading a workers' revolt against industrial serfdom in the futuristic, mechanized city of the title. The film struck a chord in the brittle Germany of the Weimar Republic, still recovering from World War I and increasingly riven by class conflicts, and Fröhlich's name was made.

He followed this *succès d'estime* with a succession of fine performances, including *Hurrah! Ich lebe!* (Hurrah, I'm Alive) for William Thiele, and *Asphalt* for Joe May, while an English version of his early talkie, Gustav Ucicky's *Der unsterbliche Lump* (The Immortal Vagabond), was an international success. In 1933 he starred in and co-directed *Rakoczy-Marsch* (The Rakoczy March), the first of eight films to come under his direction over the next 20 years.

Fröhlich was not among those German artists for whom Adolf Hitler's rise to power meant exile, a terminated career or worse. Indeed, his brand of escapist entertainment perfectly suited the Nazis' purpose, and his career flourished—except for a brief ban that apparently followed a curious episode linking Nazi propaganda minister Josef Goebbels with Fröhlich's then lover, Lieda Baarova, his co-star in *Barcarole*. Legend has it that Fröhlich slapped Goebbels's face for showing undue interest in the charms of the Czechoslovakian actress. Although he himself always denied the story, the fact remains that Baarova made an abrupt departure for Prague and between 1941 and 1943 Fröhlich was unable to appear in films, which could only be made with Goebbels's seal of approval. One casualty of the ban was Veit Harlan's lavish costume drama *Der grosse König* (The Great King), which was shelved and later reissued with drastic alterations.

Fröhlich continued to make films after World War II, both as director and as actor. His best role was in Willi Forst's *Die Sünderin* (The Sinner), a remake of *Blonde Venus* in which Hildegard Neff made her name with a brief but controversial nude scene. He also returned to the stage, notably in George Bernard Shaw's *Candida* in Düsseldorf.

From 1960 on Fröhlich limited his appearances to occasional television dramas, making something of a triumphant comeback at the age of 80 in a serial called *The Laurents*. The following year he published his autobiography, *Das waren Zeiten* (Those Were the Days), and the year after that the film that made him famous gained a whole new audience worldwide when it was re-released with colour tints and a rock score. Despite this, Fröhlich lived out his final years far from the metropolis, amid the lakeside tranquillity of Switzerland.

Born Gustav Friedrich Fröhlich. **Marriages** 1) Gitta Alpar, actress and singer (divorced); 2) Lieda Baarova, actress; 3) Maria Hajek (died). **Education** Berlin Gymnasium. **Career** Journalist, briefly; stage actor at Heilbronn Theatre, then Berlin stage début at the Volksbühne in *The Moon of the Caribbees*, 1921; worked with Piscator's left-wing People's Theatre, from 1921; film début, 1925; came to national attention in Fritz Lang's *Metropolis*, 1926; début as film director, 1933; continued acting in and directing films until 1960; switched to television roles after 1960. **Publications** *Das waren Zeiten: Ein deutsches Filmheldenleben* (Those Were the Days—My Life as a Film Hero), Munich, 1983. **Films** *Die Frau mit dem schlechten Ruf*, 1925; *Schiff in Not*, 1925; *Friesenblut*, 1925; *Die Frau, die nicht "nein" sagan kann*, 1926; *Metropolis*, 1926; *Die elf Teufel*, 1927; *Gehetzte Frauen*, 1927; *Ich hierate meine Frau*, 1927; *Jahrmarkt des Lebens*, 1927; *Jugendrausch/Eva and the Grasshopper*, 1927; *Die Meister von Nürnberg/The Meistersinger of Nuremberg*, 1927; *Die leichte Isabell*, 1927; *Die Pflicht zu schweigen*, 1927; *Schwere Jungens-Leichte Mädchen*, 1927; *Angst*, 1928; *Die Rothausgasse*, 1928; *Wenn die Schwalben heimwärts ziehn/Fremdenlegionär*, 1928; *Heimkehr/Homecoming*, 1928; *Hurrah! Ich lebe!/Hurrah, I'm Alive!*, 1928; *Asphalt*, 1929; *Das Brennende Herz/The Burning Heart*, 1929; *Hochverrat/High Treason*, 1929; *Der unsterbliche Lump/The Immortal Vagabond*, 1930; *Brand in der Oper/Fire in the Opera House*, 1930; *Zwei Menschen*, 1930; *Voruntersuchung/Inquest*, 1931; *Die heilige Flamme*, 1931; *Kismet*, 1931; *Gloria*, 1931; *Liebeslied*, 1931; *Mein Leopold*, 1931; *So lang noch ein Waltzer von Strauss erklingt*, 1931; *Liebeskommando/Love's Command*, 1931; *Unter falscher Flagge*, 1932; *Kaiserwaltzer/Johann Straus, K und I. Hofballmusikdirektor*, 1932; *Gitta entdeckt ihr Herz*, 1932; *Eine Mann mit Herz*, 1932; *Ein Lied, ein Kuss, ein Mädel*, 1932; *Die verliebte Firma*, 1932; *Sonnenstrahl*, 1933; *Die Nacht der grossen Liebe/The Night of the Great Love*, 1933; *Rund um eine Million*, 1933; *Was Frauen träumen/What Women Dream*, 1933; *Der Flüchtling aus Chikago*, 1934; *Stradivari*, 1935; *Barcarole*, 1935; *Liebesleute/Hermann und Dorothea von heute*, 1935; *Oberwachtmeister Schwenek*, 1935; *Ein Teufelskerl/A Devil of a Fellow*, 1935; *Es flüstert die liebe*, 1935; *Nacht der Verwandlung/Demaskierung*, 1935; *Die Stunde der Versuchung*, 1936; *Die Entführing*, 1936; *Stadt Anatol*, 1936; *Gleisdreieck/Alarm auf Gleis B*, 1936; *Inkognito*, 1936; *Die unmögliche Frau*, 1936; *Gabriele ein, zwei, drei*, 1937 *Alarm in Peking*, 1937 *Frau Sixta*, 1938; *Die kleine und die grosse Liebe/Minor Love and the Real Thing*, 1938; *In geheiner Mission*, 1938; *Renate im Quartett*, 1939; *Alarm aus Station III*, 1939; *Herz modern möbliert*, 1940; *Ihr Privatsekretär*, 1940; *Herz geht vor Anker*, 1940; *Alles Schwindel*, 1940; *Sechs Tage Heimaturlaub*, 1941; *Clarissa*, 1941; *Der grosse König*, 1942; *Mit den Augen einer Frau*, 1942; *Tolle Nacht*, 1943; *Das Konzert*, 1944; *Familie Buchholz/Neigungsehe*, 1944; *Der grosse Fall/Ihr grosse Fall*, 1944; *Eine alltägliche Geschichte*, 1944; *Sag'die Warheit*, 1946; *Des verlorene Gesicht/Secrets of a Soul*, 1948; *Diese Nacht vergess' ich nie*, 1949; *Diese Mann gehört mir*, 1950; *Die Sünderin/The Sinner*, 1950; *Stips*, 1951; *Haus des Lebens*, 1952; *Gefährliches Abenteuer/Abenteuer in Wien*, 1953; *Ehe für eine Nacht*, 1953; *Von der Liebe reden wir später*, 1953; *Die lkeine Stadt will schlafen gehen*, 1954; *Rosen aus dem Süden*, 1954; *Ball der Nationen*, 1954; *Der erste Frühlingstag*, 1956; *Vergiss, wenn Du kannst*, 1956; *...und keiner schämte sich/ ...and Nobody Was Ashamed*, 1960. **Films directed** (co-director) *Rakoczy-Marsch*, 1933; *Abenteuer eines jungen Herrn in Polen/Liebe und Trompetenklang*, 1934; *Leb' wohl Christina*, 1945; *Weg im Zwielicht*, 1948; *Der Bagnosträfling*, 1949; *Die Lüge*, 1950; *Torreani*, 1951; *Seine Tochter ist der Peter*, 1955. **Stage** *Celle*, 1919; *The Moon of the Caribbees*, 1921; *The Prince of Homburg*, early 1920s; *Candida*, n.d. (post-war). **Television** (includes) *The Laurents* (serial), early 1980s. **Cause of death** Undisclosed, at age 85. **Further reading** W. Holl, *Gustav Fröhlich, Kunstler und Mensch*, Berlin, 1936.

JASCHA HEIFETZ

Russian/American Violinist

Born **Vilna, Russia, 2 February 1901**

Died **Los Angeles, California, 10 December 1987**

On a warm Indian Summer evening in New York, in October 1917, a large and hypercritical audience, liberally sprinkled with veteran violin virtuosi, gathered in Carnegie Hall to hear a 16-year-old called Jascha Heifetz. The concert was a triumph—nobody had ever heard flawless intonation or virtuosic pyrotechnics to compare with this. Sitting beside his friend, the pianist Leopold Godowski, Mischa Elman was mopping his brow. "It's hot in here," he whispered. "Not for pianists," came the cheerful reply.

By the end of his life, Jascha Heifetz was universally acknowledged as the most brilliant violinist of the century. He unquestionably ranks with Paganini and Kreisler among the great violin virtuosi of history. Stony-faced and stern in his attitude, he cut an impressive figure on stage. Boris Schwarz, who knew him as a young man, described "the immobile presence, the unsmiling face, showing his profile to the public, the violin held high, hand pushed far back, the bow arm with the elbow angled up. A minimum of fuss which disguised a maximum of self-discipline."

Heifetz began to learn the violin when he was three from his father Ruben, a fine professional violinist. He seemed to be born knowing how to play. He first played in public at the age of five and at the age of six performed the Mendelssohn Violin Concerto at Kovno. He graduated from the Vilna Conservatoire when he was eight and promptly entered the St Petersburg Conservatoire. Here, Leopold Auer, the virtuoso who established what we now know as the Russian school of violin playing, heard him play and took him into his class—the youngest ever member at ten years old. Apart from conservatoire students, Jews (even the parents of students) were not allowed in the City of the Tsar. The young prodigy's family overcame this problem by enrolling the 40-year old Ruben Heifetz as a student.

Young Heifetz's first foreign tour came in 1912, with a tour of Scandinavia and Austria. He also made a sensational début at the Hochschule für Musik in Berlin, resulting in an invitation from Nikisch to return to play the Tchaikovsky concerto with the Berlin Philharmonic.

World War I and the 1917 Russian Revolution proved to be unsurmountable obstacles and Heifetz decided that his future lay outside Russia. In 1917 his triumphant conquest of the New York audience at Carnegie Hall was the first chapter of a story leading to his acquisition of American citizenship in 1925.

By then Heifetz had already played to British audiences several times, making his London début in 1920. He visited Australia and the Orient in 1925, and in 1926 toured Palestine, where, among other engagements, he gave free concerts for the Jewish population. He made a return concert in the USSR in 1934. Devoted admirers came from remote Siberian outposts to hear him play, some selling clothing or other possessions in order to be able to afford the trip, and he was followed through the streets afterwards, praise ringing in his ears. The famously "stony-faced" virtuoso declared afterwards: "That was the greatest emotional experience of my life!"

In 1944 he travelled in the southern Mediterranean "theatres of war", playing 45 concerts in eight weeks, some of them at the front lines. Mostly he concentrated on the popular classics, but on one occasion he elected to play a Bach prelude. "This number is like spinach," he said, "you may not like it but it is good for you." Afterwards, to his amazement and delight, there were loud cries of "More spinach!"

The tools of Heifetz's "trade" were two famous violins—one a 1731 Stradivarius, the other a Guarnerius, known as the "David" because it was owned at one time by Ferdinand David, a famous nineteenth-century violinist.

His career combined the triumphs of the international virtuoso—"triumph" seems to be a word that has become synonymous with Heifetz's performances—with excursions into chamber music, which he found profoundly satisfying. For a time he played and recorded with Artur Rubinstein and the cellist Piatigorsky, an ensemble which was dubbed the "Million Dollar Trio" by American audiences. He gave concerts in almost every country in the world, often in the midst of national turmoil: in Russia during the Revolution, in Ireland during the Sinn Fein uprisings, in Japan during an earthquake and in India during anti-British riots. He was involved in a political controversy during a tour of Israel where he broke an unofficial ban by performing works by Strauss, alleged to be a Nazi sympathizer. After a recital in Jerusalem, Heifetz was attacked with an iron bar, injuring his hand though not seriously or permanently. Unperturbed, he went on to perform another concert the following evening. According to an estimate made by the artist in 1940, he had spent two-fifths of his waking career at the violin and had made the equivalent of two return trips to the moon.

Heifetz was a master who relished difficulties and apparent impossibilities. His tone was always pure and sweet, but had muscularity and infallible intonation. But, as he said, "Don't imagine everything came to me out of a clear sky." He was industrious and practised assiduously. He was also an insatiable searcher after new repertoire. William Walton's violin concerto, written in 1939, was commissioned by Heifetz who relished its spectacular difficulties. Once thought impossible, the concerto is now in the repertoire of any self-respecting violin virtuoso and as such is a testament to Heifetz's influence and the concerto's stature. He also commissioned works by Castelnuovo Tedesco, Korngold and Gruenberg.

Another of Heifetz's commissions was Schoenberg's concerto but he never graced it with a public performance because he felt that the work, after a strong beginning, went off at too many intellectual tangents, which made for an unnecessary sacrifice of expressiveness. The problems were not with the player, to whom they represent an exciting challenge, but to the audience whom Heifetz felt would be alienated by the piece.

After the war Heifetz reduced his appearances. A prisoner of his own superhuman accomplishments, he could not get rid of the idea that in an audience of 2000 people, 1999 had come hoping to hear a wrong note. His public retirement finally came in 1972.

Heifetz was quiet, courteous and reserved, never displaying anything that could be described as artistic temperament. The Garbo of the violin, he hated prying questions and once took legal action against an unofficial biographer. As a result it became a critical commonplace to concentrate on his technical achievement rather than his musicality. This may be responsible for his known distate for the world of music criticism. Technique was not for its own sake, Heifetz insisted, but to serve the notes and their expression—an axiom he always lived by.

After 1962 he taught at the University of Southern California, where the Heifetz Chair of Music was established in 1975, with Heifetz as its first occupant.

Despite his eminence, Heifetz was too private and intense to be a beloved figure. He was also a prisoner of his own exceptionally high standards, causing one commentator to remark: "He has only one rival, one violinist he is trying to beat—Jascha Heifetz."

Born Jascha Heifetz. **Father** Ruben Heifetz, violinist. **Marriages** 1) Florence Vidor, film actress, 1928 (divorced, 1946); 2) Frances Spiegelberg, 1947 (divorced, 1963). **Children** Son and daughter from first marriage; one son from second marriage. **Education** Royal School of Music, Vilna, Russia; Imperial Conservatoire, St Petersburg. **Emigration** Left Russia for USA, 1917; naturalized, 1925. **Military service** Air warden, US Civilian Defense Corps, World War

II. **Career** Public début as violinist aged around five, Vilna, Russia; one year later played Mendelssohn's concerto in Kovno; St Petersburg début aged ten years, 1911; Berlin début at the Hochschule für Musik, 1912; later played in Austria and Scandinavia; left Russia for USA, via Siberia and Far East, making American début at Carnegie Hall, New York, 1920; toured England, 1920, Australia, 1921, Far East, 1923, Palestine, 1926, and South America; returned to play in Soviet Union, 1934; made fewer appearances after the war, though played at Carnegie Hall, 1964, and toured Israel, 1967; retired, 1972. **Related activities** Appeared in film, *They Shall Have Music*, 1939; toured Italian and North African theatres of war, giving troop concerts, 1944; taught at University of Southern California, from 1962; occupied Heifetz Chair of Music, University of Southern California, from 1975; made numerous recordings throughout career. **Offices and memberships** First vice-president, American Guild of Musical Artists; honorary member: Society of Concerts of Paris Conservatoire, Association des Anciens Élèves du Conservatoire, Cercle International de la Jeunesse Artistique; honorary vice-president, Mark Twain Society, USA; honorary president, Musicians' Fund of America. **Awards and honours** Commander, Legion of Honour (France), 1957. **Cause of death** Undisclosed, at age 86. **Further reading** H.R. Axelrod (editor), *Heifetz*, 1976.

ARNOLD LOBEL

Illustrator and Author of Children's Books
***Born* Los Angeles, California, 22 May 1933**
***Died* Manhattan, New York, 4 December 1987**

Arnold Lobel's contribution to children's fiction was both distinguished and distinctive. His talents as an illustrator were soon matched by an ability to produce simple but satisfying stories which sprang from an unusual empathy with children and animals. With an impressive economy of words, and a robustness of line in his drawings, Lobel produced a succession of books which explored human foibles with affection and an extremely individual humour. His most attractive and telling characters are anthropormorphic animals, and his stories move convincingly from fable and folk-tale to contemporary nursery-cosiness.

He was born in Los Angeles and grew up in New York. After graduating from the Pratt Institute in Brooklyn with a degree in fine arts in 1955, he married Anita Kempler who had been a fellow-student at Pratt. The couple collaborated successfully on one or two books. Meanwhile, Arnold Lobel provided illustrations for Sol Scharfstein's *Bibletime*, *Hebrew Dictionary* and *Holiday Dictionary* in 1958, and then, in 1961, for Fred Phleger's *Red Tag Comes Back*. The experience of illustrating this story (about the life pattern of salmon) appears to have sparked off Lobel's flair for writing and drawing for children. *A Zoo for Mister Muster* (1962), about the Prospect Park Zoo in Brooklyn, was the first of over 20 books he both illustrated and wrote.

Once asked which came first, the pictures or the words, Lobel admitted that writing was often "very painful". Apparently, it generally emerged from "a situation, or a sequence of situations" that he thought "would be fun to draw". Sometimes he found that the story popped into place "in just the right way", but more often than not it was a struggle for him.

There is little evidence of this difficulty in his zestful books. Oral storytelling was never a problem. As a small and rather delicate child he was sometimes bullied at school, but he could compensate for his lack of athletic prowess by entertaining his classmates with his original stories. He once told an interviewer that his later tales were based on his own preoccupations and childhood experiences: "I write the books for myself, I don't think 'children' as I formulate a story. If I did there would be a tendency to be condescending." He claimed to relate to his child audience through humour: "I couldn't be comfortable doing a book without some element of humour. It cuts down on the sentimentality that sometimes bogs down children's books.

Lobel's books are deceptive in appearance. Apparently simple picture-books provide amalgams of word and image that persuasively convey truths about collective and individual behaviour, and the fact that wisdom comes so often out of the mouths of animals works well for young readers. Seriousness is always counterbalanced by humour; in *Fables*, for example, we find both the earnestness of the mouse who achieves his ends through perseverance, and the bizarre situation of a camel that hopes to become a ballet-dancer.

A major theme of Lobel's books is friendship, which often takes unlikely forms. From his first book, *A Zoo for Mr Muster*, this is evident, and it is particularly well developed in his series of stories about his most memorable characters, Frog and Toad. These have achieved several literary awards, including the 1971 Caldecott Honor Book award and the 1973 Newbery Award, and seem destined to become classics of children's literature.

As well as creating his own books, Lobel continued to illustrate other authors' works, and had a hand in almost 100 books. His death is a sad loss to children everywhere.

Born Arnold Stark Lobel. **Parents** Joseph and Lucille (Stark) Lobel. **Marriage** Anita Kempler, writer and children's book illustrator, 1955. **Children** Adrianne and Adam. **Education** Pratt Institute, Brooklyn, New York, BFA, 1955. **Career** Writer and illustrator of children's books, 1955–87. **Awards and honours** American Library Association Notable Book Awards for *Frog and Toad Are Friends*, 1970, *On the Day Peter Stuyvesant Sailed Into Town*, 1971, and *Frog and Toad Together*, 1972; Caldecott Honor Book Awards for *Frog and Toad Are Friends*, 1971, and *Hildilid's Night*, 1972; National Book Award finalist for *Frog and Toad Are Friends*, 1971; *Book World* Spring Book Festival Award for *Frog and Toad Together*, 1972; Children's Showcase Book Awards for *On the Day Peter Stuyvesant Sailed Into Town, Frog and Toad Together* and *Seahorse*, 1973, *The Clay Pot Boy*, 1974; Christopher Award for *On the Day Peter Stuyvesant Sailed Into Town*, 1973, 1977; Newbery Honor Book Award for *Frog and Toad Together*, 1973; George C. Stone Center for Children's Books Award, 1978; American Book Award nominee for *Frog and Toad Are Friends*, 1980; American Library Association Caldecott Medal for *Fables*, 1981; University of Southern Missouri Medallion, 1985; Goldenkite Award for Illustration, Society of Children's Book Writers, 1988. **Fiction** *A Zoo for Mister Muster*, New York, 1962; *A Holiday for Mister Muster*, New York, 1963; *Prince Bertram the Bad*, New York, 1963, Surrey, 1970; *Giant John*, New York and Surrey, 1965; *Lucille*, New York and Surrey, 1964; *The Bears of the Air*, New York, 1965, Surrey, 1966; *The Great Blueness and Other Predicaments*, New York, 1968, Surrey, 1970; *Small Pig*, New York, 1969, Surrey, 1970; *Frog and Toad Are Friends*, New York, 1970, Surrey, 1971; *Mouse Tales*, New York, 1972, Surrey, 1973; *Frog and Toad Together*, New York, 1972, Surrey, 1973; *Owl at Home*, New York, 1975, Surrey, 1976; *Frog and Toad All Year*, New York, 1976, Surrey, 1977; (illustrated by Anita Lobel) *How the Rooster Saved the Day*, New York, 1977; *Mouse Soup*, New York, 1977, Surrey, 1978; *Grasshopper on the Road*, New York, 1978, Surrey, 1979; (illustrated by Anita Lobel) *A Treeful of Pigs*, New York, 1979, London, 1980; *Days with Frog and Toad*, New York, 1979, Surrey, 1980; *Frog and Toad Tales* (Collection), Surrey, 1981; *Uncle Elephant*, New York, 1981, Surrey, 1982; *Ming Lo Moves the Mountain*, New York and London, 1982. **Verse** *Martha, the Movie Mouse*, New York, 1966, Surrey, 1967; *The Ice-Cream Cone Coot and Other Rare Birds*,

New York, 1971; *On the Day Peter Stuyvesant Sailed into Town*, New York, 1971; *The Man Who Took the Indoors Out*, New York, 1974, Surrey, 1976; *The Book of Pigericks: Pig Limericks*, New York, 1983, London, 1984; (illustrated by Anita Lobel) *The Rose in My Garden*, New York and London, 1984. **Other** (editor) *Gregory Griggs and Other Nursery Rhyme People*, New York and London, 1978; *Fables*, New York and London, 1980; (illustrated by Anita Lobel) *On Market Street*, New York and London, 1981; *Frog and Toad Coloring Book*, New York, 1986; *The Frog and Toad Pop-up Book*, New York, 1986. **Illustrator** Sol Scharfstein: *Bibletime*, 1958, *Hebrew Dictionary*, 1958, *Holiday Dictionary*, 1958; Fred Pfleger, *Red Tag Comes Back*, 1961; Susan Oneacre, *Something Old, Something New*, 1961; Betty Baker, *Little Runner of the Longhouse*, 1962; Millicent E. Selsam: *Terry and the Caterpillars*, 1962, *Greg's Microscope*, 1963, *Let's Get Turtles*, 1965, *Benny's Animals*, 1966; Peggy Parish: *Let's Be Indians*, 1962, *Let's Be Early Settlers with Daniel Boone*, 1967, *Dinosaur Time*, 1974; *Mildred Myrick: The Secret Three*, 1963, *Ants Are Fun*, 1968; Charlotte Zolotow: *The Quarreling Book*, 1963, *Someday*, 1965; Nathaniel Benchley: *Red Fox and His Canoe* 1964, *Oscar Otter*, 1966, *The Strange Disapearance of Arthur Cluck*, 1967, *Sam the Minuteman*, 1969; Phil Ressner, *Dudley Pippin*, 1965; Felice Holman, *The Witch on the Corner*, 1966; Andrea Di Noto, *The Star Thief*, 1967; Edward Lear: *The Four Little Children Who Went Round the World*, 1968, *The New Vestments*, 1970; Sarah Catherine Martin, *The Comic Adventures of Old Mother Hubbard*, 1968; Lilian Moore, *Junk Day on Juniper Street*, 1969; Jack Prelutsky: *The Terrible Tiger*, 1969, *Circus*, 1974, *Nightmares*, 1976, *The Mean Old Hyena*, 1978, *The Headless Horseman Rides Tonight*, 1980, *The Random House Book of Poetry for Children*, 1983, *Tyrannosaurus Was a Beast*, 1988; Judith Horst, *I'll Fix Anthony*, 1969; Laura E. Cathon, *Tot Botot and His Little Flute*, 1970; Grimm Brothers, *Hansel and Gretel*, 1971; Sulamith Ish-Kishor, *The Master of Miracles*, 1971; Cheli Ryan, *Hildilid's Night*, 1971; Robert A. Morris, *Seahorse*, 1972; Miriam Young: *Miss Suzy's Easter Surprise*, 1972, *Miss Suzy's Christmas*, 1973, *Miss Suzy's Birthday*, 1974; Paula Fox, *Good Ethan*, 1973; Cynthia Jameson, *The Clay Pot Boy*, 1973; Norma Farber, *As I Was Crossing Boston Common*, 1975; Anne K. Rose, *As Right As Right Can Be*, 1976; Doris Orgel, *Merry, Merry Fibruary*, 1977; Jean Van Leeuwen: *Tales of Oliver Pig*, 1979, *More Tales of Oliver Pig*, 1981; Carol Chapman, *The Tale of Meshka the Kvetch*, 1980; Maxine Kumins, *The Microsope*, 1984; Laura Gerlinger, *A Three Hat Day*, 1985; *The Random House Book of Mother Goose*, 1986; Harriet Ziefert: *Bear All Year*, 1986, *Bear Gets Dressed*, 1986, *Bear's Busy Morning*, 1986, *Bear Goes Shopping*, 1986, *Where's the Guinea Pig*, 1987, *Where's the Turtle,* 1987, *Where's the Dog*, 1987, *Where's the Cat*, 1987; Valerie Scho Carey, *The Devil and Mother Crump*, 1987. **Cause of death** Cardiac arrest resulting from Aids, at age 54.

ROUBEN MAMOULIAN

American Film and Stage Director

***Born* Tbilisi, Russia, 8 October 1897**

***Died* Los Angeles, California, 4 December 1987**

Rouben Mamoulian was a man of boundless creative energy whose persistence of vision was largely responsible for forging the American stage musical into a sophisticated popular art form through such Broadway productions as *Porgy and Bess* and *Oklahoma*. If his talents were not always as intelligently exploited by Hollywood—he made just 16 films in almost 30 years—he nevertheless introduced in movies like *Dr Jekyll and Mr Hyde* (1931) many technical innovations which enriched the language of cinema.

Mamoulian studied stagecraft at the Moscow Art Theatre under Stanislavsky, disciple and proponent of "fantastic realism", and Yevgeny Vakhtangov, then established a successful drama studio in his home town of Tbilisi, where his mother was director of the Armenian Theatre.

After a 1920 tour of Britain with his company, he stayed on to teach drama at London University, gaining a toehold in West End theatre with a production of *The Beating on the Door* (1922). This was followed by a succession of hit plays and operettas which carried his reputation across the Atlantic, and in 1923 he travelled to the United States to take up an appointment as production director of the newly formed National American Opera Company at Rochester, New York.

After three years, during which he expanded his range of grand opera as well as straight plays and operettas, Mamoulian felt ready to try his luck on Broadway. New York's Theatre Guild, initially hesitant, eventually assigned him *Porgy* (1927), DuBose and Dorothy K. Heyward's American folk play with an all-Black cast. The play incorporated Negro spirituals, and Mamoulian was able to implement the ideas he had been refining for integrating dance, song, dialogue and dramatic action into a unified pattern that was above all rhythmic. It was a stress that was to recur throughout his work. *Porgy* was both a critical and a popular success, enjoying a run of nearly 400 performances.

The pace of Mamoulian's career began to accelerate. Eight more Broadway productions followed in under two years, and Paramount summoned him to join the exodus of stage talent to Hollywood. Talking pictures needed directiors who knew what to do with talking actors, and Mamoulian fitted the bill.

His first film was *Applause* (1929), featuring popular singer Helen Morgan. Mamoulian turned this sentimental tale into a landmark in cinema history by the simple expedient of fitting wheels to the camera, which, since the coming of the talkies, had had to be enclosed in a soundproof booth to blot out its fearsomely intrusive din. He made full use of this restored mobility with sophisticated tracking shots and imaginative use of light and shade, supplemented with a double-channel audio track to enhance sound quality. The medium had taken a sizeable step forward, and Hollywood began to sit up and take notice.

For his second film, *City Streets* (1931), basically a star vehicle for Gary Cooper, Mamoulian's inventive presentation breathed life into Dashiell Hammett's routine gangster yarn. The film is particularly noteworthy for his novel use of sound to express a character's thoughts and memories during a silent close-up.

With *Dr Jekyll and Mr Hyde*, Paramount sought to emulate the success Universal had been having with its horror pictures *Dracula* and *Frankenstein*. What it got was a cinematic *tour de force*, with an Oscar-winning performance by Fredric March at its centre. The film's depth of emotion and profound insight into humanity's potential for evil totally transcended the horror tag (although it was still horrific enough for the censors later to cut 16 of its original 98 minutes).

Once again Mamoulian showed his genius for harnessing technical virtuosity to creative imagination. He shot the stunning Jekyll-to-Hyde transformation scene in one continuous take, removing colour filters one by one to reveal March at last in full gruesome Hyde make-up. And through his use of a subjective 360-degree revolving camera, the audience was enabled to view the world through the eyes of his character.

According to Mamoulian, the production schedule for *Love Me Tonight* (1932) was too tight, and the result was a movie shot in haste. For most critics, however, it is one of the best musicals ever made, ingeniously fusing Rodgers and Hart's delightful score with witty dialogue partly in rhythmical, rhyming verse. Time constraints notwithstanding, Mamoulian had the entire music soundtrack recorded in advance, freeing him to concentrate on the non-musical aspects during the shooting itself. It was another of his innovations that became standard practice.

Despite this proven talent for musicals, which he demonstrated again in *The Gay Desperado* (1936) and *High, Wide and Handsome* (1937), it seemed that producers at this time preferred to entrust Mamoulian with the task of maintaining the lustre of their leading female stars. This he did for Marlene Dietrich in *Song of Songs* (1932), Anna Sten in *We Live Again* (1934), and Greta Garbo in *Queen Christina* (1933), probably Garbo's finest screen performance. Mamoulian, ever inventive, timed part of the action to a metronome to obtain the "sustained rhythmic quality of the dance". *Becky Sharp* (1935), starring Miriam Hopkins, was the first full-length movie to be shot in the new three-colour Technicolor process.

Towards the end of the 1930s Mamoulian's screen work, although commercially more successful than ever, began, from an artistic point of view, to mark time. His creativity and independence seemed to be subject more and more to the dead hand of Hollywood's innate conservatism. *Golden Boy* (William Holden's 1939 screen début), *The Mark of Zorro* (1940) and *Blood and Sand* (1941) were, of course, well made, and entertaining too, but in many ways they could have been the work of any competent director. It was back on Broadway, where he had freer rein, that he was wielding his talent to full effect.

Between shooting *Becky Sharp* and *The Gay Desperado*, Mamoulian brought to the stage an American musical milestone. *Porgy and Bess*, George Gershwin's operatic adaptation of *Porgy*, had a disappointingly short first run. It was nevertheless a triumph for Mamoulian, who made the most of the potent syncopations of Gershwin's evocative music.

Mamoulian had now become an American citizen, and displayed a particular fondness for tackling American subjects. With Rodgers and Hammerstein's ambitious musical *Oklahoma* (1955) he was able to distil the essence of the frontier spirit into an exhilarating union of song, dance and dynamic action. It came, he said, closer to his ideal of the theatre than anything he had ever done, and the production ran for more than five years on Broadway. The same team had met similar success with *Carousel* (1953). Under Mamoulian's direction the American musical had come of age.

Summer Holiday (1946), a lavish musical film starring Mickey Rooney, was made during this period, but in spite of its success Mamoulian was not to make another film for almost a decade. His independence was too much for the producers; he had been taken off *Laura* in 1944 when he had already commenced shooting, and a number of films originally assigned to him were given to other directors.

Happily his next picture, *Silk Stockings* (1957), which proved to be his last, was a vindication of all that he stood for. The combination of Cole Porter's tunes and Fred Astaire and Cyd Charisse's dancing, particularly in the set-piece speciality numbers that were Mamoulian's forte, assured the film's enduring popularity. It was the perfect summation of his movie career, but at the same time it showed how much he still had to give.

It was not his final experience of Hollywood, however. In 1962 he was fired from the Elizabeth Taylor–Richard Burton blockbuster, *Cleopatra*, after shooting ten minutes of film. Taken over by Joseph L. Mankiewicz, the movie became one of the greatest artistic and commercial disasters in Hollywood history, a fact which was no doubt of little consolation to Mamoulian. His talent abused just once too often, he opted for retirement. From his vantage point in Beverly Hills, he could look back on a lifetime of bold and prolific achievement.

Born Rouben Mamoulian. **Parents** Zachary David, a bank president, and Virginia, an actress, (Kalantarian) Mamoulian. **Marriage** Azadia Newman, artist, 1945. **Education** Lycée Montaigne, Paris; Tbilisi Gymnasium; Moscow University; Vakhtangov Studio Theatre, Moscow **Emigration** Left USSR for England, 1920; settled in USA, 1923; naturalized, 1930. **Career**

Acted in and directed plays, Moscow and Tbilisi, 1918–20; travelled to England with touring company, 1920; directed plays for Russian Repertory Company, England, early 1920s; London stage directorial début, 1922; moved to New Jersey and directed productions for National American Opera Company, 1923–25; founder and first director, Eastman Theater School, 1924; teacher and director, Theater Guild, New York, from 1926; directed first film, *Applause*, 1929; subsequently worked in both stage and film before concentrating on the latter from the 1950s. **Related activities** Lecturer on film in USA and elsewhere, including at King's College, London, 1920–23; founder, Rouben Mamoulian Award for Best Australian Short Film, 1974; author of various articles on film and theatre direction. **Offices and memberships** Founding member, Directors' Guild of America, board member, 1936–39, 1944–46, 1953–58, first vice-president, 1953–58; vice-president of jury, Cannes Film Festival, 1963; Dramatists' Guild of America; American Library Association; honorary member, Delta Kappa Alpha. **Awards and honours** First prize for *Dr Jekyll and Mr Hyde*, International Film Festival, 1931; honorary citation for *Queen Christina*, 1934; first prize for first colour film, *Becky Sharp*, 1936; New York Film Critics' Award for best direction, *The Gay Desperado*, 1936; Foreign Press Society Award for best direction, *The Gay Desperado*, 1936; State of California Golden Seal, 1938; prize for best colour film, *Blood and Sand*, 1941; Pulitzer Prize Committee special citation for *Oklahoma*, 1943; Donaldson Award for best direction *Carousel*, 1945; honorary citation for *Becky Sharp*, 1955; Medal of the City of Paris for *Oklahoma*, 1955; Plaque of Versailles for *Oklahoma*, 1955; guest of honour, Venice International Film Festival, 1955; Technical Progress Festival Award for introduction of colour to the screen in *Becky Sharp*, 1955; University of Southern California Silver Bowl, 1963; University of Transylvania Silver Cup, 1966; San Francisco Film Festival Polished Agate Trophy, 1971; Count Dracula Society Gold Horace Walpole Medal, 1971; Armenian–American Bicentennial Celebration Award of Excellence, 1976. **Publications** (contributor) *George Gershwin*, 1938; (contributor) *Great Composers Through the Eyes of Their Contemporaries*, 1951; *Abigail: Story of the Cat at the Manger*, New York, 1964; *Hamlet Revised and Interpreted*, New York, 1965; (contributor) *Scoundrels and Scalawags*, 1968; plus articles in various periodicals. **Films** *Applause*, 1929; *City Streets*, 1931; *Dr Jekyll and Mr Hyde*, 1931; *Love Me Tonight*, 1932; *Song of Songs*, 1932; *Queen Christina*, 1933; *We Live Again*, 1934; *Becky Sharp*, 1935; *The Gay Desperado*, 1936; *High, Wide and Handsome*, 1937; *Golden Boy*, 1939; *Mark of Zorro*, 1940; *Blood and Sand*, 1941; *Rings on Her Fingers*, 1942; *Summer Holiday*, 1946; *Carousel*, 1953; *Oklahoma*, 1955; *Silk Stockings*, 1957; (screenplay only, adapted from *The Devil's Hornpipe* with Maxwell Anderson) *Never Steal Anything Small*, 1959. **Stage** (all in New York, unless stated) *The Beating on the Door*, London, 1922; *Porgy*, 1927; *Marco Millions*, 1928; *These Modern Women*, 1928; *Cáfe Tomaza*, 1928; *Women*, 1928; *Wings Over Europe*, 1928; *R.U.R.*, 1929; *Game of Love and Death*, 1929; *A Month in the Country*, 1930; *Die Gluchliche Hant*, 1930; *Solid South*, 1930; *Farewell to Arms*, 1930; *Porgy and Bess*, 1935; *Oklahoma*, 1943; *Sadie Thompson*, 1944; *Carousel*, 1945; *St Louis Woman*, 1946; *Leaf and Bough*, 1948; *Lost in the Stars*, 1949; *Arms and the Girl*, 1950; *Shakespeare's Hamlet, A New Version*, University of Kentucky, 1966. **Plays** (translator) I. Turgenev, *A Month in the Country*, 1930; (with Howard Dietz) *Sadie Thompson*, 1944; (translator with Maxwell Anderson) Bizet's *Carmen*, Rossini's *Barber of Seville*, 1951–52; (with Maxwell Anderson) *The Devil's Hornpipe* (musical), 1951–52; *Shakespeare's Hamlet, A New Version*, 1966. **Cause of death** Undisclosed, at age 90. **Further reading** Tom Milne, *Rouben Mamoulian*, London, 1969; James Silke (ed), *Rouben Mamoulian: Style Is the Man*, Washington, DC, 1971.

RALPH NELSON

American Film Director

Born **Long Island City, New York, 12 August 1916**

Died **Santa Monica, California, 21 December 1987**

When Ralph Nelson's most graphic and controversial film, *Soldier Blue*, was released in 1970, many critics greeted it with anger and indignation. In the story, based on a real incident in the pioneering days of the American West, a group of cavalrymen invade an Indian village and massacre hundreds of inhabitants. Coming, as it did, at the height of the Vietnam War, the film had clear and distressing parallels with My Lai. Many felt Nelson was using violence purely for sensational value and commercial gain. Yet, despite the sensitive and incendiary nature of *Soldier Blue*, and many of his other dramatic works, Nelson was regarded as one of early television's most imaginative and innovative directors, and one of cinema's most provocative ones. In addition to a host of award-winning feature films, such as *Requiem for a Heavyweight*, *Charly* and *Lilies of the Field*, during his 30-year career, Nelson directed more than 1000 television plays and serials. Many, broadcast live in the 1950s and 1960s, were among TV's most memorable dramas.

Raised in Long Island City, New York, the son of a chauffeur, Nelson revealed his contrariness at an early age. Though he had a knack for dramatics, and won an oratory contest at the age of 15, his adolescence was a stormy one, marked by gang fights, criminal offences and a string of prison sentences. Years later, reflecting on his early life, he claimed that he had been jailed in 18 states before he was 16. He also travelled the United States by freight car, living rough as a hobo and observing life from all sides—unconsciously gathering material for what he later referred to as the "social comment" in many of his films.

Returning to New York in the early 1930s, Nelson made his way to Broadway and soon found work as a stage manager with the famous Lunts acting team. He also found his feet as an actor, making his first stage appearance in 1933 in *Ticket of Leave Man* at the Wharf Theater in Provincetown. A year later he made his New York stage début as a cabin boy in *False Dreams, Farewell*, and thereafter appeared in a handful of Shakespeare productions, including *Romeo and Juliet*, *Hamlet* and *The Taming of the Shrew*, once serving as understudy to Leslie Howard. During this period he also penned several plays of his own, two of which, *Mail Call* and *The Wind Is Ninety*, were later produced on Broadway.

In 1941 Nelson interrupted his stage career to serve as an air force fighter pilot in World War II. After the war, instead of returning to theatre work, he followed the wave of new technology into television. He remained there for more than 22 years, turning out hundreds of dramatic and musical programmes, and making a name for himself as a powerful and demanding director.

One of Nelson's hallmarks throughout his career was his propensity to create stirring dramas from odd or unlikely subjects—topics some critics hailed as fresh and original, and others condemned as pretentious or sentimental. One example was *Requiem for a Heavyweight*, an emotional rendition of Rod Serling's study of the world of professional boxing. Despite strong criticism, the drama, broadcast live on CBS-TV's *Playhouse 90* in 1956, won Emmy Awards for its writer, its starring actor and its director. A film version of the same story, starring Anthony Quinn, marked Nelson's big screen début in 1962. Another controversial drama, *Lilies of the Field*, portrayed the relationship between a Negro workman and a group of German nuns. In the movie version, Nelson insisted the leading role be given to Sidney Poitier—then an obscure actor—rather than one of his better-known contemporaries. Poitier won an Oscar for his performance and Nelson was nominated for best director. Five years later his skilled direction of another controversial film, *Charly*, the story of a mentally handicapped man, helped win an Oscar for Cliff Robertson.

From 1959 onwards, Nelson served as president of Rainbow Productions in Hollywood, writing, producing and directing screenplays for a host of television serials. These included *General Electric Theater*, *Desilu Playhouse*, *Climax*, *Omnibus*, *DuPont Show of the Month* and the popular comedy series *Mama*. Among his directorial innovations was his use of videotape in rehearsals—introduced to help actors recognize their strengths and weaknesses and improve their performances. At the same time, this method provided them with a clearer understanding of the production as a whole.

After the big-screen successes of such films as *Requiem for a Heavyweight* and *Lilies of the Field*, Nelson found himself increasingly drawn to cinematic work. He demonstrated his power and versatility at every turn. Controversial triumphs of the mid-1960s included *Soldier in the Rain*, *Father Goose*, *Duel at Diablo* and *The Wrath of God*, the last starring Robert Mitchum as a gun-running priest. Then, in 1970, came *Soldier Blue*. Because of the film's sensitive nature, Nelson took the unusual precaution of travelling to each country in which it opened in order to answer questions and discuss the issue of censorship. "We had just finished filming in Mexico when the Pinkville Massacre was revealed and the row broke out," he told reporters then. "The film shows the horror of a man at war, when the blood lust takes over. We show decapitation and mutilation because that is what happened. There is the same horror in Vietnam and the same thing is happening there." Nelson's next film, *Flight of the Doves*, an idyllic story of two Irish children, was a surprising contrast in its gentleness and innocence.

Towards the end of the 1970s, Nelson left the cinema and returned to television, ending his career in 1979 with a special TV production, *Christmas, Lilies of the Field*. A member of numerous professional societies, in his later years he also received an honorary doctorate from Columbia University, and served as a guest lecturer in cinema arts at a number of other institutions, including UCLA, USC and NYU. Reflecting on the many adventures in his life—particularly the contrast between his delinquent childhood and his later wealth and success—was a frequent source of amusement for him. Amid all the excitement and flamboyance, however, he valued his family life most of all. Three marriages brought him three sons and a daughter. "My most important legacy is my children," he was quoted as saying. "All the rest is make-believe."

Born Ralph Nelson. **Parents** Carl Leo, a chauffeur, and Elsa (Lagergreen) Nelson. **Marriages** 1) Celeste Holm, actress, 1936 (divorced, 1938) 2) Name unknown; 3) Barbara Powers, 1954 (deceased). **Children** Three sons, Theodor, Ralph and Peter, one daughter, Meredith. **Education** State schools, Long Island City, New York. **Military service** Fighter pilot, later captain, US Army Air Corps, 1941–45. **Career** Worked in Broadway theatre as actor and, for five years, as stage manager to the Lunts acting team, 1933–41; wrote two plays given Broadway productions, *Mail Call*, 1944, and *The Wind Is Ninety*, 1945; moved into television as director for NBC TV, 1948–49, and CBS TV, 1949–52, directing over 1000 drama productions, 1948–60; president, Rainbow Productions, Los Angeles, from 1959; film directing début, 1962; returned to television work, late 1970. **Related activities** Guest lecturer: University of California, Los Angeles, University of Southern California, San Francisco State College, New York University, Columbia University, University of Michigan. **Offices and memberships** Directors' Guild of America; Producers' Guild; Writers' Guild West; Dramatists' Guild; life member, Authors' League of America; Screen Actors' Guild; American Federation of Radio and Television Actors; Actors' Equity Association. **Awards and honours** John Golden Prize for *Mail Call*, 1943; National Theater Awards for *Mail Call*, 1943, *Angels Weep*, 1943, and *The Wind Is Ninety*, 1944; National Theater Fellowship, 1947; National Academy of Television Arts and Sciences Emmy Award for *Requiem for a Heavyweight*, 1956; Academy Award for Best Picture of the Year, plus five nominations for producing and directing, *Lilies of the Field*, 1963; Golden Globe Humanitarian Award for *Lilies of the Field*, 1963; Berlin Film Festival Golden Bear Award; Bell Ringer Award; honorary DHL, University Columbia. **Publications** *Mail Call* (play), 1943, also anthologized in John Golden (ed), *Army Play by Play*, 1943; *Angels Weep* (play), 1944; *The Wind Is Ninety* (play), 1946; plus contributions to magazines, including *Yale Review*, *American Magazine*, *Theater Arts*, *Argosy* and *Action*. **Films** (as producer/director, unless stated) (director only) *Requiem for a Heavyweight*, 1962; (director only) *Soldier in the Rain*, 1963; (director only) *Lilies of the Field*, 1963; *Fate Is the Hunter*, 1964; *Father Goose*, 1965; *Once a Thief*, 1965; *Duel at Diablo*, 1966; *Counterpoint*, 1967; *Charly*, 1968; *Tick, Tick, Tick*, 1969; *Soldier Blue*, 1970; *Flight of the Doves*, 1971; *The Wilby Conspiracy*, 1975; *Embryo*, 1976; *A Hero Ain't Nothin' But a Sandwich*, 1977; *You Can't Go Home Again*, 1978. **Screenplays** *The Man in the Funny Suit*; *The Flight of the Doves*; *The Wrath of God*. **Stage roles** *Ticket of Leave Man*, Provincetown, Massachusetts, 1933; *False Dreams, Farewell*, New York, 1934; *Romeo and Juliet*, New York, 1955; *The Taming of the Shrew*, New York, 1936; *There Shall Be No Night*, New York; (tour) *Hamlet*; (tour) *Idiot's Delight*. **Television** Directed and/or produced over 1000 plays and series, including *Requiem for a Heavyweight*, 1956; *Cinderella* (musical), 1957; *Hamlet*, 1959; *Christmas, Lilies of the Field*, 1979; *I Remember Mama*; and plays for *General Electric Theater*, *Climax*; *Du Pont Show of the Month*, *Dick Powell Theater and Desilu Playhouse*. **Cause of death** Cancer, at age 71.

ARKADY RAIKIN

Soviet Actor and Producer

***Born* Riga, Latvia, 24 October 1911**

***Died* Moscow, USSR, *circa* 21 December 1987**

Mention the name of Arkady Raikin to any inhabitant of Moscow or Leningrad, and a smile of mirth, affection and respect will signal instant recognition. He dominated the stage of Soviet satire for over five decades, witnessing the most turbulent years of Soviet post-revolutionary history. Yet there he remained, an attestation to the fact that a society which can still laugh at itself is a society not doomed.

Raikin, a Jew from Latvia, was educated at the Ostrovsky Dramatic Insitute in Leningrad. On graduation he served his dramatic apprenticeship first at the Komsomol (Youth) Theatre, and then at the Novy Theatre. He ultimately aspired to the position of producer/director when, in the 1930s, he opened his own company, the Leningrad Miniature Theatre. This step undoubtedly paved the way for a career which concentrated on monologues and small skits. His varied theatrical career and innate feeling for storytelling led him naturally from strength to strength. It was perhaps no surprise that in a society suffering from the effects of a protracted war, his humorous acts won great acclaim. Gradually, as Soviet society became less intense, Raikin obviously found his niche and began gently to tickle the sensitive spots of the system. such tactics worked, being, as they were, a kind of catharsis for the everyday frustrations of life.

In his work, Raikin frequently focused on the inefficiencies of the Soviet economic system, and in particular on "the plan", to be fulfilled at any cost, even when it meant "producing 70 bows for one violin". He was not only famed for his parodies of the system, but also for those who were part of it. In one particularly famous sketch, a bureaucrat, who merely serves to complicate people's lives, is actually paid to stay at home in bed. The pettiness of bureaucrats, the megalomania of minor officials and, above all, the endless red tape—nothing escaped his pregnant observations. He pilloried a system unable to "cope" without the plan, where everything worked (or didn't!) because of the covert manipulation of officials, begging the question: "How on earth does such an economy function?" Commenting on those targets of his satire, Raikin once said that he was always interested in the person who was negative and harmful to mankind. Such a person, he noted, ceased to be a person and deserved to be ridiculed.

With a gesture or a mime, or even merely standing mute on stage, Raikin could convey to his audience with subtlety and sophistication the idiosyncracies of Soviet life. That is not to say, however, that he had forgotten his original talents as a comedian, for there were times when his histrionics themselves were sufficient to have his audience in uproar.

As if to stress the unpredictable nature of Soviet life, Raikin's ability to ridicule the society's defects and shortcomings was greatly admired by the country's political leaders. High ranking officials, even Khrushchev and Brezhnev, as well as the man in the street, were known to be keen admirers. As if to seal his official State approval, he was awarded the title of People's Artist of the USSR in 1968, followed in 1980 and 1981 with a Lenin Prize and the title Hero of Socialist Labour, an honour indeed for a man who all his life walked the political tightrope. In an interview, Raikin once said of his position as official state "raconteur": "If the government allow Raikin to talk about it, then that must mean this is something you can talk about...after all, this is a government theatre, like all theatres. What I say has been passed by the censor. Nobody forbade it, no one told me I shouldn't talk about it."

Raikin, whom many saw as the mouthpiece of the citizens' frustrations and discontent, remained the everyman of Soviet society, in some ways the all-hearing, all-seeing "fool" who tried to communicate the hope of a slightly better world to come, and who gave his audience the strength to see through another day.

Born Arkady Isaakovich Raikin. **Education** Leningrad Ostrovsky Dramatic Institute. **Career** Actor, Leningrad Komsomol Theatre, 1935–37; Leningrad Novy Theatre, 1937–39; founded Leningrad Miniature Theatre, 1939; began to perform humorous sketches, mocking certain aspects of Soviet life, 1940s; thereafter worked largely as a comedian on stage and television. **Awards and honours** Order of the Patriotic War; People's Artist of the USSR, 1968; Lenin Prize, 1980; Hero of Socialist Labour, 1981. **Cause of death** Undisclosed, at age 76.

ERNST STEINHOFF

Soviet/American Aero-engineer

Born **Treysa, Germany, 11 February 1908**

Died **Alamogordo, New Mexico, 2 December 1987**

On 8 September 1944, in Chiswick, West London, a 15-ton rocket which had been launched in Holland landed without any warning. The one-ton warhead caused a blast which could be felt for miles. It was the first V–2 rocket attack. As a technical achievement it was astonishing, foreshadowing the success of post-war space rockets, and its success depended on the stabilizing and guidance system which had been designed by Dr Ernst Steinhoff.

Ernst August Steinhoff was born in Treysa, about 70 miles north of Frankfurt, West Germany. He graduated at Darmstadt Technical University, where he stayed on to take his master's degree, and then moved to the Polytechnic College at Bad Frankenhausen as lecturer in aeronautical engineering. It was three years later, in 1936, that he joined the German Aeronautical Research Institute, and after another three years he was appointed director of the Institute of Electronic Ballistics and Control at the German Rocket Research Centre. He had become one of the remarkable team under Wernher von Braun who developed rockets at Peenemünde before and during the war, and after the war played a crucial role in the US space programme.

Meanwhile, von Braun was developing the A–4 rocket, a project he had shown to be feasible in 1938 when a small experimental rocket went a distance of eleven miles. But a great deal more money and research was required to perfect it, and Steinhoff's contribution, designing the stabilizing and guidance system, was a crucial part of the development. On 3 October 1942, after two failures, a 45-foot long rocket weighing 12 tons took off from Peenemünde and flew perfectly, reaching an altitude of 54 miles.

At this stage Germany was searching for *Vergeltungswaffe* (vengeance weapons), and the first of these, the V–1, was a pilotless flying-bomb run on petrol and compressed air. Called "buzz-bombs" or "doodle-bugs" by the British who suffered from them, the first V–1s crossed the Channel shortly after D-Day. They flew until the fuel ran out, and when people heard their characteristic engine-noise stop, they knew highly damaging explosions would follow within 15 seconds. Within a month of the first V–1, London organized a massive evacuation of children to try to minimize loss of life from these lethal weapons.

The A–4 rocket on which Steinhoff was working, which became the V–2, was not used until three months after the V–1. Its development had been halted at one stage because Hitler had dreamt that it would never reach England; on another occasion it was halted again by a very damaging RAF raid on Peenemünde which almost killed Steinhoff.

Some 3600 V–2s landed on England, raining down long after the V–1s had been stopped by the Allies who had overrun the launch sites just across the Channel. They were terrifying because they fell entirely without warning, for they fell at greater than the speed of sound from a height of 50 miles. As they could take off from a simple concrete pad almost anywhere, it was virtually impossible for Allied forces to destroy their sites in bombing raids. German V–2s killed nearly 3000 Britons, and the millions living within range felt perpetually threatened, but the weapon came too late to save Germany. Early in 1945 Holland was captured by the Allies, and the rockets ceased as they had insufficient range from further afield.

To the scientists working at Peenemünde, the surrender of Germany was now merely a matter of time, so the team discussed whether they would prefer to be captured by the Russians or the West. They chose the West unanimously, so they left Peenemünde, which lay in the path of the

Russian advance, and made their way to Oberjoch, a resort in Bavaria. When the advancing Americans found them they were peacefully sunning themselves.

Von Braun, Steinhoff and the others went to the United States, where their previous activities, far from being held against them, were considered highly valuable. Indeed, the V–2 rocket became a central component of the US rocket programme on which they worked. Steinhoff played a crucial part in the research, occupying a progressive series of posts until he finally became chief scientist at the US Air Force Missile Development Center near Alamogordo in New Mexico. He retired in 1972, an honoured man who belonged to the International Space Hall of Fame.

Born Ernst August Steinhoff. **Marriage** 1936. **Children** Seven. **Education** Darmstadt Technical University, BS, 1931, MS, 1933, PhD in applied physics, 1940. **Emigration** Left Germany for US, 1945; subsequently naturalized. **Career** Lecturer, aeronautical engineering, Polytechnic College, Bad Frankenhausen, 1933–36; research associate, German Aeronautical Research Institute, 1936–39; director, Institute of Electronic Ballistics and Control, German Rocket Research Centre, 1939–45; chief, steering section, Rocket Research and Development Division, Fort Bliss, US Army, 1948–50; scientific adviser, Holloman Air Force Base, US Department of the Air Force, 1957; deputy technical director, Curtiss-Wright Corporation, 1957–58; director, missile engineering, Crosley Division, Avco Corporation, 1959–60, staff scientist adviser, E & O Division, 1960–61; senior staff, Rand Corporation, 1961–63; chief scientist, Air Force Missile Development Center, Holloman Air Force Base, New Mexico, 1963–70; adviser to commander, Air Force Flight Dynamics Laboratory, 1970–72; researcher and consultant, 1972–76; scientific adviser, New Mexico Research Center, Alamogordo, from 1976. **Related activities** Chairman, Panel on Control and Guidance of Guided Missiles, Germany, 1943–44; member: Joint Test Range Standardization Board, White Sands Proving Ground and Test Range Requirements Board, US Air Force Missile Test Center, Florida, and Air Research Development Command, 1949–57; member, technical management council, US Air Force Research and Development Command, 1955–57; member, Air Force Systems Command Technology Management Council, 1963–69; visiting professor, Massachusetts Institute of Technology, 1968–69; chairman of the board, New Mexico Research Institute, president from 1972; chairman of the board, Intercontinental Optics Company. **Memberships** American Geophysical Union; National Aeronautical Association. **Awards and honours** Associate fellow, American Institute of Aeronautics and Astronautics; fellow: Institute of Electrical and Electronic Engineers, American Astronomical Society; elected to International Space Hall of Fame. **Cause of death** Undisclosed, at age 79.

SIR MELFORD STEVENSON

British Lawyer and Judge

Born **England, 17 October 1902**

Died **Sussex, England, 26 December 1987**

It is one of the hallmarks of the British constitutional machinery that the judiciary, powerfully independent, yet sagaciously administering justice, is peopled by individuals who remain largely unknown to the population at large. Sir Melford Stevenson's career was such, however, that he was often in the public eye, firmly impressing his style, personality and formidable intellect on British law. He was in turn a highly successful junior barrister, and eminent King's Counsel and Queen's Counsel, and a controversial judge.

He was called to the Bar by the Inner Temple in 1925, and built up a solid practice over 15 years. During World War II, he served as a deputy judge advocate in the armed forces, holding the rank of major. In 1945 he stood as Conservative candidate for a ward in Essex, but was heavily defeated through what today would probably be called "lack of the common touch". His speeches were described by one writer as "scornful and sophisticated", not perhaps the most successful formula by which to wage a popular campaign.

Having taken silk in 1943, he continued to ascend in the profession by becoming a recorder, firstly of Rye, then of Cambridge. The Inner Temple elected him a bencher in 1950, one of the traditional honours of the four Inns of Court. In view of his excellent practice and high reputation, it is a wonder that Stevenson was not made a judge until 1957, aged 55. The received opinion of the day was that this was due to his uninhibited comments, expressed privately but given great currency throughout the profession, on colleagues, judges and politicians.

During his time as a silk, Stevenson appeared in many celebrated cases, mainly in the fields of divorce, libel and crime. He defended Ruth Ellis, the last woman to be hanged in England, and also represented the Crown in Kenya in Jomo Kenyatta's appeal against his conviction for his involvement with Mau Mau activities. He also appeared in many "society" divorce cases, where he often flamboyantly sparred with the noted advocate, Gilbert Beyfus. This was when Stevenson brought his highly developed forensic skills to the fore: a highly distinctive voice, an easy and fluent manner and an uncanny skill in finding the striking and apposite phrase or sentence.

Stevenson's first four years on the bench were spent in the Probate, Divorce and Admiralty Division, where his stay was fairly unremarkable. In 1961 he was transferred to the Queen's Bench Division, where he became one of the best known judges in the country.

To gangsters, he was very harsh. His dicta and sentences gave rise to great controversy. He made no secret of his special distaste for men who engaged in violent crimes, as the notorious Kray brothers discovered to their chagrin. In the "Garden House riots" trial in 1970, he sentenced some of the Cambridge undergraduates who had inflicted great damage to property during the course of a protest against the Greek regime, to long terms of imprisonment. There was universal uproar and protest from dons, MPs, journalists, members of the clergy and students. Stevenson was characteristically unrepentant and said that the sentences would have been harsher had the students not been "exposed to the evil influences of some senior members of the university".

He was occasionally indiscreet in his outspokenness, most notably when he referred to the act liberalizing the law on homosexuality as a "buggers charter" and had to be officially reprimanded by the lord chancellor. He once commented to a party to divorce proceedings: "He chose to live in Manchester, a wholly incomprehensible choice for any free human being to make", and described a particular rape as "a rather anaemic affair as rape goes", both of which attracted widespread protest.

To barristers he could be caustic and intolerant, in an age when judges had the general reputation of being patient, courteous and perhaps a little boring. To Quintin Hogg, Lord Hailsham, on the threshold of becoming lord chancellor, he said, "I am tired of all this legal claptrap", not perhaps particularly sensitive remarks to make to one of the foremost members of the Bar.

However, he was always helpful and courteous to witnesses and jurors, which enhanced his reputation, albeit sporadic, as a true representative of the ordinary man, upholding the sort of standards that they thought ought to be upheld in the criminal courts.

After his retirement in 1979, Stevenson remained in the public eye, mainly through frequent participation in television shows. In these appearances he brought to bear those qualities which caused close friends to describe him as a lively, witty and delightful companion. It was perhaps unfair that his controversial conduct so overshadowed his judicial competence, as evidenced by the trust placed in him to handle some of the most sensitive and difficult cases of the time.

Born Aubrey Melford Steed Stevenson. **Father** Reverend J. G. Stevenson. **Marriages** 1) Name unknown; 2) Rosalind Monica Wagner. **Children** One daughter from first marriage; one son and one daughter from second marriage. **Education** Dulwich College, London; University of London, LLB. **Career** Called to Bar, Inner Temple, 1925, bencher, 1950, treasurer, 1972; major and deputy judge advocate, 1940–45; King's Counsel, 1943; recorder of Rye, 1944–51, City of Cambridge, 1942–57; deputy chairman, West Kent Quarter Sessions, 1949–55; justice of the High Court, 1957–59, Probate, Divorce and Admiralty Division, 1957–61, Queen's Bench Division, 1961–79; presiding judge, South-Eastern Circuit, 1970–75. **Related activities** Member, Interdepartmental Committee on Human Artificial Insemination, 1958–60. **Awards and honours** Knighted, 1957; privy counsellor, 1973. **Cause of death** Undisclosed, at age 85.

"SLAM" STEWART

American Jazz Musician

***Born* Englewood, New Jersey, 21 September 1914**

***Died* Binghamton, New York, 10 December 1987**

"Sing" would have been a better nickname than "Slam" for Leroy Stewart, for he made his reputation by developing a unique way of humming in octave unison above his bass. This technique he picked up in the 1930s when he was studying at the Boston Conservatory. There he heard violinist Ray Perry singing in unison with his bowed lines. Stewart adapted the practice to his bass playing and was soon a master at accompanying his bowed improvisations with a wordless hum, of necessity, of course, an octave higher. So equipped, Stewart was assured of his name in jazz history.

Initially, the idea appealed to the singer and pianist Slim Gaillard. The two had first met at a Harlem club and in 1937 formed the duo Slim and Slam. Theirs was a novelty duo, for Slim Gaillard was incapable of treating any musical idea seriously, and they rapidly became a big success on radio. One record, "Flat Fleet Floogie" (known universally but erroneously as "Flat Foot Floogie") was a massive hit in 1938, and others followed soon after. The two worked together until 1942, when Gaillard entered the army, but this essentially comic duo disguised the fact that Stewart was now a consummate musician in his own right.

Stewart had started playing the violin as a child but soon switched to bass. His first public performances were in Newark in the early 1930s and he soon acquired his nickname Slam for his habit of slapping the bass as he played it. After the rise and demise of Slim and Slam, Stewart continued to work in New York, forming his own trio, touring as a member of the Art Tatum trio from 1943 to 1944, then with Benny Goodman until 1945. By this time he was a celebrity, appearing in Fats Waller's band in the 1943 film *Stormy Weather* and winning numerous jazz polls for his bass playing. As the 1940s drew to a close, Stewart was one of the most recorded of jazz artists, guesting on many renowned albums.

Stewart's trio attracted many favourable reviews, partly because for three and a half years pianist Erroll Garner was a member. Stewart was always at his best when playing with pianists, and he kept up his association with Art Tatum until the early 1950s. Yet sessions with Roy Eldridge, Lionel Hampton, Red Norvo and Dizzy Gillespie only served to emphasize his all-round strengths, for Stewart was a powerfully rhythmic player whose presence enhanced any rhythm section, whatever the style. Mainstream, swing or bop, Stewart was equally in control, as can be seen in the remarkable duo performances he recorded in 1945 with saxophonist Don Byas.

Stewart's bass playing skills were recognized beyond the confines of jazz, and in 1969 he worked with the Lincoln String Quartet, following that up with regular appearances in the 1970s as a featured soloist with the Indianapolis Symphony Orchestra. From 1971 he taught music at the State University of New York, Binghamton, which awarded him an honorary doctorate in 1984, and wrote instruction tutors for bass players. He also gave master classes at Yale and elsewhere, proving that he was as fine a teacher as he was performer.

In later life, he was continually in demand, touring with Goodman again between 1973 and 1975, and forming a partnership in 1978 with guitarist Bucky Pizzarelli. Busy until the end, Stewart was an original whose unique contribution to jazz is still being assessed.

Born Leroy Elliott Stewart. **Education** Studied music in Newark with Sonny Marshall; Boston Conservatory. **Military service** US Army, World War II. **Career** Jazz bass player and scat singer; worked with Peanuts Holland, Buffalo, 1936; met future partner, guitarist Slim Gaillard at Jock's Place, Harlem, 1937; formed duo as "Slim and Slam", gaining national hit with "Flat Fleet Floogie", 1938; other popular songs included "Tutti Frutti", "Spooghm" and "Groove Juice Special"; duo split, 1942; subsequently formed own trio with Johnny Collins and Billy Taylor; also worked freelance with a number of important jazz bands, including Fats Waller, Dizzy Gillespie, Don Byas, Art Tatum Trio, 1943–44, 1950s; played with Benny Goodman Band, 1944–45, 1973–75; Roy Eldridge Quartet, 1953; Beryl Booker, 1955–57; Rose Murphy, late 1950s, early 1960s; formed partnership with Bucky Pizzarelli, 1978. **Related activities** Featured in Paris Jazz Festival, 1948; taught music at State University of New York, Binghamton, from 1971. **Awards and honours** *Esquire* Silver Award, 1945–46; *Met* poll winner, 1946; honorary doctorate, SUNY, Binghamton, New York, 1984. **Film** (as member of Fats Waller's band) *Stormy Weather*, 1943. **Recordings** (include) duos with Don Byas: "Indiana", Jazz Star 47101, 1945; "I Got Rhythm", Jazz Star 47102, 1945; (as sideman) S.Gaillard, "The Flat Fleet Floogie", Voc 4021, 1938; J.Guarnieri, "Bow Singing Slam", Savoy 530, 1944; A.Tatum, "Topsy", Asch 4522, 1944; D.Gillespie, "Groovin' High", Guild 1001, 1945; A.Tatum, *Art Tatum Trio*, Cap H408, 1952. **Cause of death** Undisclosed, at age 73.

LESLIE THOMPSON

Jamaican Jazz Musician

Born **Kingston, Jamaica, 17 October 1901**

Died **London, England, 26 December 1987**

The history of jazz in Britain has been enormously enriched by the many people who, as immigrants, have chosen or been forced to make Britain their home. One such person was the Jamaican-born trumpeter Leslie Thompson, one of the finest British jazz musicians ever. In him, the many strands that weave together to make British jazz what is today are clearly personified.

Thompson was a graduate of Alpha Boys' Catholic School, renowned in Jamaican educational circles as the place where many of Jamaica's foremost musicians, notably the saxophonist Joe Harriot, received their first musical education. The school was founded as an industrial institute in 1880 and was run by a London–based religious order. Under the guiding eye of the nuns, music had been on the curriculum from the 1890s and bandmasters coached generations of children to love and to learn music. Thompson remembered that when he went there in 1912, he was just one of many "barefoot boys enjoying life".

> Life to us was a song! We didn't have to worry about what we wore or what we ate, we just lived for amusing ourselves. But Alpha was the music factory for jazz musicians, a place where they were willing to turn the natural ability of the children into something practical. The nuns looked after us, and of course those who had this gift in them, it just sort of worked itself out.

For Thompson, this education was to prove invaluable when, in 1919, he decided to study in Britain at the Military Music Academy at Kneller Hall. There he won a silver medal, the highest possible award for a trooper. But further advancement to becoming a bandmaster or conductor was denied him because of his colour—British military regulations did not allow officers of non-European descent at that time—so he returned to Jamaica. He joined the West India Regiment, making two brief visits to Canada and Britain, but for most of the time he was a "man about town, artistically", playing accompaniment for silent films and in dance groups.

In 1929 Thompson was forced to return to Britain, for in that year, Al Jolson's film *The Jazz Singer* was on release. It was a talkie, and it put paid to Thompson's career in cinemas. Musicians in Britain had been similarly affected by the innovation, but Thompson fell on his feet in a matter of days when he met a Jewish bandleader from Dalston in London who hired him to play at Jewish weddings. Further engagements followed, and Thompson was soon much in demand, for he could play both orchestral and dance-band music. "I was hall-marked insofar as I was Black. The chaps I played with, I don't think they'd ever had the pleasure—or we could use the word 'displeasure'—to play with a coloured person. But the chaps, they were marvellous. We were just musicians together."

It was during his early years in Britain that Thompson first heard jazz. He soon mastered the new music and joined several bands whose skills easily matched their American counterparts and inspirations, even if, unlike the Americans, the British preferred their music toned down. "In America people really like it 'hot'. In England we'd just talk about the heat but it really wasn't so hot. The type of music that we played over here was what you would call 'milk-and-water' jazz, compared to the other stuff!" But it was interesting work, and Thompson gained because of his colour, for several dance-band leaders hired him because they felt he would give their music the "authenticity" it so obviously lacked.

In 1930 Thompson joined Spike Hughes's group, Britain's foremost jazz band, playing trumpet, trombone and occasionally double bass for two years. Hughes had a policy of bringing over guest American musicians to play with his band, which gave Thompson some much needed exposure to the source of jazz itself. His big break came in 1934 when, after a stint playing in Noël Coward's *Words and Music* at the Adelphi Theatre in London, he was asked to join Louis Armstrong's band for its first European tour. Thompson was well prepared, for he had had several years experience in impresario C.B.Cochrane's theatre orchestra pits where he had played everything from new works by Stravinsky and William Walton to the latest jazz. Where that had made demands on his sight-reading ability, Armstrong stretched his ability to improvise and play from memory. It was "a rare treat. I was able to enjoy Armstrong at his best. It was absolutely marvellous." As Thompson remarked, in a typically self-effacing way, "I'm a bit of a musician myself, but I really was thrilled night after night to hear that man play. He was such a perfectionist..."

Thompson recorded with Armstrong in Paris in 1934 and, when he returned to Britain, formed his own big band in 1936. It was not a success and was soon taken over by the dancer Ken "Snakehips" Johnson, but its claim to fame is that it was the first all-Black outfit of any size to work in Britain. Back on his own again, he played in several London shows, recorded and worked with American bandleader Benny Carter when he visited London from 1936 to 1937, and played classical music in a number of concerts at the Albert Hall. Until the outbreak of war, Thompson found a place with Edmundo Ros, pioneering the Latin-American music that was about to sweep the dance-floors. During the war, Thompson started as a gunner with the Royal Artillery but soon joined the "Stars in Battledress" unit and played for the troops. Demobbed in 1945, he returned to the West End nightclub circuit, performing by night and studying composition and cello at the Guildhall School of Music during the day.

Although Thompson had made his career as a musician, there was another side to the man. Throughout his life he was devoutly religious, reading his Bible every day. So it was no surprise when, in 1954, he gave up professional music and became the warden of the Alliance Club, a Christian-based London student's hostel. In 1963, at the age of 62, he qualified as a probation officer and worked at London's Pentonville Prison. Predictably, he started up a prison jazz band, of which he was a leading member. On his retirement at the age of 70, he continued to give jazz lessons part-time to the inmates.

That selflessness was typical of the man, for Thompson was considerate to everyone and much in demand in churches of all denominations for his abilities as a preacher, counsellor and a trumpet player. In his life came together the different strands of Black music, military bands, church and dance hall that have done so much to shape the face of modern British jazz.

Born Leslie Anthony Joseph Thompson. **Education** Alpha Boys' Catholic School, Jamaica; trained as military bandsman, Kneller Hall Army School, England, and the West India Regiment; graduated in trumpet and cello, Guildhall School of Music, post World War II. **Emigration** Left Jamaica for England, 1919; settled permanently, 1929. **Military service** Royal Artillery, briefly; "Stars in Battledress" unit, World War II. **Career** Played cinemas and recitals, including concerts of classical music at the Albert Hall, London; played trumpet, double bass and trombone in Spike Hughes's band, 1930–32; worked with C.B.Cochrane and "Snakehips" Johnson; with Louis Armstrong, recorded in Paris, 1934, toured Italy, Switzerland and France, 1934–35; formed own band, 1935 (later led by Ken Johnson); with band led by Edmundo Ros, 1937–39; performed in nightclubs and dance halls in London, 1946–54; quit professional music, becoming warden of Christian students' hostel, Alliance Club, 1954; qualified as probation officer, 1963; subsequently worked in Pentonville Prison, London, founding and playing in prison jazz band and continuing to give jazz lessons after retirement in 1971.

Other activities Active Christian, preaching, counselling and playing trumpet at church services of various denominations. **Publications** (with J.P. Green) *An Autobiography*, Crawley, 1985. **Recordings** (include) Spike Hughes's group, "Sirocco", Decca F2844, 1932; Billy Merrin's Commanders, "Organ Grinder's Swing", Crown 275, 1936. **Cause of death** Undisclosed, at age 86.

TERENCE TILLER

British Poet, Broadcaster and Producer
Born **Truro, Cornwall, 19 September 1916**
Died **London, England, 24 December 1987**

Terence Tiller was a minor, scholarly poet who readily admitted of himself that, "I don't and can't and would never have been able to, earn my living as a poet". Critics, however, praised particularly two collections of his poems—*The Inward Animal*, published in 1943, and *Unarm Eros*, published in 1947. Both reflected Tiller's wartime experience as a civilian lecturer in English history and literature at Fuad I University in Cairo.

Tiller himself said that these experiences of war, exile and single strangeness "must have shaken and perhaps destroyed, many a customary self. There will have been a shocked and defensive rebellion; reconciliation must follow; the birth of some mutual thing in which the old and the new, the self and the alien, are combined after war....The birth of something at once myself, the new self and 'Egypt' is the 'inward animal'." Certainly, according to the critic Ian Fletcher, the poems "are strongest when they rise from some observed scene or persons, least sensuous when 'Egypt' is missing from the record".

While in Cairo, Tiller became associated with the "Personal Landscape" group of poets, which included Lawrence Durrell and Bernard Spencer. "I have been called," Tiller wrote, "and am willing to call myself, a modern metaphysical," admitting that he had been more influenced by the "metaphysicals" than by any other poets, except Dante and Rilke. For the spirit of his times he was, perhaps, too much of a "traditionalist" to achieve great popularity. Later volumes did not suit the fashion of the day and Tiller remained always something of a "poet's poet".

Before going to Egypt, Terence Tiller had been a lecturer in medieval history at Cambridge University. Jesus College, where he had been a history student, awarded him the Chancellor's Medal in 1936 and made him a research fellow and director of studies in 1937. When he returned from Egypt in 1946, he went, however, not to Cambridge but to London and the BBC, where he was to work for the next 30 years in the features and drama departments.

Tiller, it seems, eventually found his true haven in that traditional delight of the English intellectual—BBC Radio's Third Programme (now known as Radio 3). The numerous plays he wrote, re-wrote or produced are evidence of his continuing concern for poetry, myth and medieval literature. His own plays included *Lilith*, *The Play of Noah* and *The Tower of Hunger*. But he also adapted for radio Chaucer's *Parlement of Foules*, Greene's *Carde of Fancie*, Langland's *Vision of Piers Plowman*, *The Cornish Cycle of Mystery Plays* and Nabokov's *The Defence*.

The writer of Tiller's obituary in the London *Times* noted that "any feature or production by Terence was as good as a guarantee that thousands of intelligent listeners would switch on for it. He may be said to have been a member of that select band who advanced the art of radio."

Tiller's wide-ranging knowledge that embraced not only the world of English literature, but also that of music and of chess, would certainly seem to have earned him, in an age of specialists, his own claim to have been something of an old-fashioned polymath.

Born Terence Rogers Tiller. **Marriage** Doreen Hugh Watson, 1945. **Children** Two daughters. **Education** Latymer Upper School, Hammersmith; Jesus College, Cambridge University, BA, honours, 1937, MA, 1940. **Career** Research scholar and director of studies, Cambridge University, 1937–39, lecturer in medieval history, 1939; lecturer in English history and literature, Fuad I University, Cairo, Egypt, 1939–46; radio writer and producer, features department, BBC Radio 3, 1946–65, drama department, 1965–76. **Awards and honours** Chancellor's Medal, Jesus College, 1936; Cholmondeley Award, 1980. **Verse** *Poems*, 1941; *The Inward Animal*, 1943; *Unarm Eros*, 1947; *Reading a Medal and Other Poems*, 1957; *Notes for a Myth and Other Poems*, 1968; *The Singing Mesh and Other Poems*, 1979. **Plays** *The Death of Adam*, 1950; *The Vision of Piers Plowman* (adaptation), 1980. **Radio** *The Wakefield Shepherds' Play*, 1947–48; *Play of Noah*, 1947–48; *The Death of a Friend*, 1949; *The Cornish Cycle of Mystery Plays*, 1949–62; *Lilith*, 1950; *The Tower of Hunger*, 1952; *The Parlement of Foules* (adapted from Chaucer), 1958; *Final Meeting*, 1966; *The Carde of Fancie* (adapted from Robert Greene), 1966; *The Diversions of Hawthornden*, 1967; *The Assembly of Ladies*, 1968; *Zeus the Barnstormer*, 1969; *After Ten Years* (adapted from C.S. Lewis), 1969; *The Flower and the Leaf*, 1970; *The Batchelar's Banquet* (adapted from Thomas Dekker), 1971; *Four of a Kind* (adapted from Verlaine), 1976; *The Defence* (adapted from Nabokov), 1979; *The Romance of the Rose* (adapted from Chaucer), 1982; *Ladies Lost and Found* (adapted from Chaucer), 1984. **Other** *Egypt*, 1936; (editor) *Personal Landscape: An Anthology of Exile*, 1945; (editor) *New Poems 1960: A PEN Anthology*, 1960; (editor and translator) *Confessio Amantis*, 1963; (editor) *Chess Treasury of the Air*, 1966; (editor and co-translator) *The Inferno* by Dante, 1967. **Cause of death** Undisclosed, at age 71.

JOOP den UYL

Dutch Politician

***Born* Hilversum, Netherlands, 9 August 1919**

***Died* Amsterdam, Netherlands, 24 December 1987**

Joop den Uyl, prime minister of the Netherlands during much of the turbulent 1970s, joined the Dutch Labour Party on the day of its foundation in 1946. During the 40 years of active political life that followed, he ran the gamut of political offices from local councillor to director of the party's research institute, to leader of the opposition, to prime minister, and back again to become an ordinary member of parliament towards the end of his life.

A pragmatic leader, Joop den Uyl saw the Labour Party through some of its most painful changes of direction in the post-war period, first under the influence of the new left and later in response to the "new realism" occasioned by the oil shortages of the early 1970s. He also steered the country through a minefield of national crises during his term as prime minister, and became known internationally for his tireless opposition to the siting of cruise missiles on Dutch soil. In this, as in his protests against the expansion of nuclear energy, history proved him right, as witnessed by Chernobyl and the rise of glasnost. When den Uyl died at 68 years of age, it was acknowledged by friend and foe alike that he, one of Holland's foremost elder statesmen, had gone before his time.

Johannes Marten den Uyl, Joop for short, was born in Hilversum in the heart of the Netherlands in 1919, the son of a basket-weaver. After leaving school, he went to Amsterdam University, where he read economics. During World War II when the country was under Nazi occupation, he fought in the Resistance and worked as a journalist on daily and weekly papers such as *Het Parool* and *Vrij Nederland*, both of which were part of the underground press. In the immediate post-war years den Uyl continued writing for these (now legalized) papers, until in 1947 he accepted the directorship of the Labour Party's research institute—the Dr Wiardi-Beckman Foundation. In his capacity as chief of the party's think-tank, den Uyl published a number of important reports and books which showed the way forward for Dutch socialism. Among them was *De Weg Naar de Vrijheid* (The Road to Liberty), published in 1951, which was, in effect, a comprehensive party programme and policy blueprint for the decade to come.

In 1953 den Uyl won a seat on Amsterdam's city council, where, in 1962, he was promoted to *wethouder* (the equivalent of a government minister or secretary with budgetary responsibilities). At the same time he was also a member of parliament from 1956 until 1965, when he became minister of economic affairs in a coalition cabinet with the Catholic centre-right party. From the parliamentary elections in February 1967 onwards, den Uyl became the most important opposition spokesperson as leader of its biggest party—Labour. This was the role in which the country got to know him well: dogged, persistent, vociferous and indefatigable in his questioning of government orthodoxy and received Christian–Democrat opinion.

In May 1973 Joop den Uyl was elected prime minister for the first time, heading up a coalition cabinet of the broad left with a few representatives of the denominational centre-right parties thrown in. Amid hopes of radical reform, he set to work on a programme of social welfare expansion, increased foreign aid and cuts in defence, but his sincere efforts at implementing this broadly socialist agenda were soon thwarted by the energy crisis of the early to mid-1970s. Best remembered from that time in the Netherlands are the "carless Sundays" when children could be seen roller-skating on the motorways since virtually all other means of transport had been declared illegal for the day. But while it gained him some fans among youngsters, carless Sundays did not do much for den Uyl's popularity with the electorate at large, even though it became clear to Dutch voters soon enough that the oil crisis had set the whole of Western Europe on course for an inflationary spiral leading to economic recession, and that it was not the fault of den Uyl *or* his brand of socialism. Still, as prime minister he had to live with the consequences.

However, the economic crisis of the 1970s, serious though it was, was not the most difficult matter den Uyl had to deal with during his term in office. Far more tricky was the threat of constitutional crisis in 1976 caused by allegations that Prince Bernhard, husband to the then Queen Juliana, had accepted bribes from the Lockheed aircraft company in return for his royal influence in securing lucrative defence contracts with the Dutch Army. An official investigation ordered by den Uyl revealed no firm evidence of bribe-taking, but it did criticize the prince for poor judgement and dishonourable contacts with Lockheed. In the end, a constitutional crisis was avoided when den Uyl decided not to prosecute the prince, but to issue a code of conduct instead. Thus, Queen Juliana was saved from early abdication (she handed over the reins to her daughter Beatrix in 1980), and the prince, who up till then had been extremely popular with the Dutch people, henceforth kept a very low profile.

Still, den Uyl's problems during his time as prime minister were not over. In 1977 the Netherlands' colonial past came back to haunt it, when 55 people travelling on a commuter train were taken hostage by South Moluccan militants (their country of origin, the South Moluccan Islands, is now part of Indonesia). After days of national panic, frantic negotiations and fearful uncertainty, den Uyl approved an assault on the train by the marines. Two hostages and six hijackers were killed, and the country was rudely alerted to the fact that all was not as quiet as it seemed in this small North Sea delta, haven of social democracy. The spectre of internal armed resistance disrupted a political scene which, up till then, had been governed by consensus, more or less. It was no wonder, then, that soon after the hostage crisis the coalition between broad left and Christian-Democrats fell apart. Den Uyl was relegated to his familiar role as leader of the opposition once more. But this did not mean he merely returned to the old routine. He was also vice-president of the Socialist International for a time and helped lead a very effective opposition to NATO against the siting of 48 cruise missiles in the late 1970s, when Holland became a focus for the international peace movement.

In Parliament during the 1980s den Uyl remained as combative a debater as ever, although after handing over the leadership of the party to younger lights he was rather less in the public eye than previously. In partnership with his wife, Liesbeth—an equally articulate and forceful personality in her own right—Joop den Uyl promoted in his political work and embodied in his personal history a specifically Western European post-war ideal of welfare socialism and equal opportunity. During much of his political career, his forceful personality and brand of democratic socialism dominated the Labour Party and heavily influenced Dutch politics as a whole, an influence which continues to be apparent today.

Born Johannes Marten den Uyl. **Father** Basket-weaver. **Education** University of Amsterdam, economics degree. **Career** Newspaper journalist, *Het Parool* and *Vrij Nederland*, 1940–47; joined Dutch Labour Party, 1946; director, Dr Wiardi-Beckman Foundation (Labour Party research institute), 1947–53; won seat on Amsterdam city council, 1953, promoted to *wethouder*, 1962; concurrently member of parliament, 1956–65; minister of economic affairs, 1965–66; leader of the opposition, 1967–73; prime minister, 1973–77; leader of the opposition, 1977–86. **Related activities** Led opposition to NATO deployment of cruise missiles in The Netherlands, 1977; vice-president, Socialist International. **Publications** (include) *De Weg Naar de Vrijheid* (The Road to Liberty), 1951. **Cause of death** Cancer, at age 68.

ANTHONY WEST

British Novelist, Biographer, Essayist and Critic

***Born* Norfolk, England, 4 August 1914**

***Died* Fisher's Island, New York, 27 December 1987**

An understanding of Anthony Panther West can only be achieved by looking closely into the facts surrounding his birth, the lives of his particularly illustrious parents, and their own relationship.

In 1912 a 19-year-old reviewer for a long dead feminist weekly called *The Free Woman* slated a novel written by the eminent writer and political commentator H.G. Wells. This aroused the curiosity of Wells's wife, Jane, and the reviewer was invited to spend a weekend with the couple. From their very first meeting the young woman, who later became Dame Rebecca West, made it clear that she wanted an affair with Wells. At first Wells backed off. Not that he was averse to having affairs; throughout his life he had many, but for him they were light-hearted interludes, not to be taken seriously. Anthony West later wrote of them meeting at a time when Rebecca was "deeply involved in a post-adolescent crisis of unusual severity...and [had] come on in the role of the wholly liberated woman, and had overplayed the part". Wells had found her "affected, silly and pretentious", and said goodbye. However, the following year, in a review of another of Wells's novels, Rebecca West wrote that occasions could arise in which casual sex could be appropriate, and Wells's interest in her was revived. He described her as a "young woman of quite extraordinary quality" and wrote that he had never met anything quite like her before.

A passionate affair developed, resulting in the birth of Anthony West the following year. Wells delighted in their private life, later recalling his lover as witty, lively and warm. They invented fantasy worlds together: in one she kept a pub and he drove a gig; in another they were two sad and furry animals called the Pussteads; a third produced Wells's nickname for her, which later was passed to their son—she was a "Legendary Panther" who pursued bishops at dinner parties.

The downfall in their relationship sprang from the time it became clear to West that Wells would never marry her. Although she accepted that he would never leave his wife, it is probable that she had hopes of marriage after Jane's death in 1927, by which time Anthony was 13. Of this period Anthony West himself has written: "From the time I reached the age of puberty, and she came to the point of a final rupture with my father, she was minded to do me what hurt she could, and she remained set in that determination as long as there was breath in her body to sustain her malice." Her first action in this direction was to adopt Anthony. The process was explained as one of expediency. Rather than go through life with a birth certificate which declared his mother a spinster and thus disclosing his illegitimacy, he was to have two documents: one recording the fact of birth, the other his adoption 14 years later. West has said, "It was not pointed out to me...that this highly symbolic performance also removed my father from my pedigree..." It is significant that he did not, in later years at least, realize that it effectively removed his mother from his pedigree—something he might have welcomed.

West was educated at Stowe, a then recently founded private school with rather more liberal attitudes than those prevailing at the more august Eton or Rugby, which date back several centuries. He was not a good student and achieved no academic success. However, this could not have been the result of any intellectual failing on his part. His subsequent writing demonstrates a keen mind, and his economy of style shows similarities with his father's. In particular, his biography of Wells is remarkably perceptive in its grasp of international affairs throughout the first half of the twentieth century.

West suffered a comparatively brief spell of ill health. He had TB and it was this that later exempted him from serving in World War II. It did not, however, hinder him in taking a four-year vagabond trip round the world after leaving school nor, in his subsequent years, becoming a farmer and cattle breeder.

But writing was in his blood and within a very short time he was reviewing new fiction for the left-wing weekly, *New Statesman*. During the war itself he worked in radio for the BBC, but resigned in 1946 to begin his career as a writer. His first novel, *The Vintage* (entitled *On a Dark Night* in the UK), was generally praised for the quality of its writing. It also demonstrated a strong sense of disillusion with the twentieth century. But this disillusion seems to have related more to Europe than to the Western world as a whole. When he moved to the US in 1950, West cited the narrowing of the intellectual climate in England as his reason for leaving. He found it repulsive. The US he found "still fundamentally liberal and the spirit...alive".

However, this was by no means the sole reason for his move. Later he wrote that he had "transplanted myself to the United States to make a fresh start in life, 3000 miles out of [my mother's] way, but...found myself pursued by her animosity even at that distance". She promptly set about "queering" West's pitch by trying to discourage people she knew from helping him. Fortunately for West, she was not entirely successful. He landed a staff job with the *New Yorker* and became a reviewer for *Time* magazine. It was also the time he wrote his autobiographical novel, *Heritage*, published in 1955. Just how autobiographical it was did not become clear until after his mother's death. It was thus only in 1984 that it was able to be published in England with a preface written in 1983. Also published in that year was the biography of Wells. The preface and the biography show that it is entirely the story of his parents and himself, even in such minute points as the father's "squeaky" voice that emerged in public speaking, something which George Bernard Shaw had once berated Wells about.

Rebecca West's bitterness towards her son seems never to have abated. Nothing he wrote concerning his background could be published in England during her lifetime because she threatened legal action. Very much earlier she had determined he should never be allowed to publish anything in the UK. While West was at school his mother had eventually married a rich man who made him his heir. Rebecca took pains to inform Wells of this. Having checked it out, Wells subsequently made his will leaving West any personal souvenirs he might choose but nothing from his estate as he understood he had "substantial expectations from another quarter".

Three years after Wells's death (in 1946) the reason for this became apparent. A couple of newspapers had carried a publisher's advertisement for current books, one of which was by West. This was accompanied by a snippet of information to the effect that he showed promise and was working on a biography of his father. His stepfather immediately visited to remonstrate with him about the raking up of old scandals and the distress it was causing his mother. If West was not prepared to rethink the matter he would have to reconsider his will. A week's thinking time elapsed, the will was changed and the following year West left England for good.

In the US he found something of what he was looking for: a second marriage and family and a very successful career. He loved the land with a visual passion for its "dynamic landscape, primary colours [and] clear air". He called it "my America, my new found land", a place where the individual was free and unconstrained. Sadly, however, he was not able to leave his pain behind him. Throughout his life and work he carried with him the anguish of his mother's vengeance: he could not exorcize her. Had he survived her by a few more years he might have been able to do so.

Born Anthony Panther West. **Parents** H.G. Wells, writer, and Rebecca West, writer. **Marriages** 1) Katherine Church, 1936 (divorced); 2) Lily Dulany Emmet, 1952. **Children** One son, one daughter from first marriage; one son, one daughter from second marriage. **Education** Stowe School, Buckinghamshire; Central School of Art, London. **Emigration** Left England for USA, 1950. **Career** Travelled around world for four years before resettling in England; dairy farmer and Guernsey cattle breeder, 1937–43; journalist, Far Eastern Desk, BBC radio, 1943–45, Japanese Service, 1945–47; worked on first novel, 1947–50; staff writer, *New Yorker* magazine, 1950–79. **Related activities** Critic and book reviewer, *New Statesman* and *Nation*, 1930s; book reviewer, *Time* magazine, from 1950s. **Awards and honours** Houghton Mifflin Literary Fellowship for *The Vintage*, 1950. **Novels** *On a Dark Night*, London, 1949, published as *The Vintage*, Boston, 1950; *Another Kind*, London, 1951, Boston, 1952; *Heritage*, New York, 1955, revised edition, London and New York, 1984; *The Trend Is Up*, New York, 1960, London, 1961; *David Rees, Among Others*, New York and London, 1970. **Other** *Gloucestershire* (guide book), London, 1939; *D. H. Lawrence*, London, 1951, revised edition, 1966; *The Crusades* (juvenile), New York, 1954, published as *All About the Crusades*, London, 1967; *Principles and Persuasions: Literary Essays*, New York, 1957, London, 1958; *Elizabethan England*, New York and London, 1965; (editor) *The Galsworthy Reader*, New York, 1968; *Mortal Wounds: The Lives of Three Tormented Women*, New York, 1973, London, 1975; *John Piper*, London, 1979; *H. G. Wells: Aspects of a Life*, New York and London, 1984; plus numerous articles for newspapers and magazines. **Cause of death** Undisclosed, at age 73. **Further reading** ed. G. P. Wells, *H. G. Wells in Love: Postscript to an Experiment in Autobiography*, London, 1984.

FREDERICK WILLEY

British Politician

***Born* Durham, England, 13 November 1910**

***Died* Wiltshire, England, 13 December 1987**

Frederick Willey's political career in the British Labour Party spanned 40 years. As a moderate he always occupied the centre ground which, on occasion, got him into trouble with the left-wingers of his party. However, he was respected for staying true to his traditionalist principles and was generally acknowledged as being an honest and decent man.

Willey was educated at Johnston School, Durham, before winning a place to Cambridge University where he read law at St John's College. In addition to obtaining a first-class degree, Willey demonstrated considerable prowess at sports and he had the distinction of gaining a soccer blue. Further study followed and he was called to the Bar as a barrister in 1936.

He soon built up a successful practice on the northeast judicial circuit, and he also found himself much in demand as a lecturer. This promising career was to be interrupted by the outbreak of World War II in 1939. Undaunted, Willey became an auxiliary fireman in London's East End, an area which was to be particularly affected throughout the war years by heavy bombing. He flourished in his new role and also found time to become London regional officer of the Fire Brigades' Union.

When the war ended, Willey, who was already a staunch member of the Labour Party, decided to enter politics. He was successful in the 1945 general election in which the Labour Party won a landslide victory and he became the member for Sunderland, a deprived industrial city in northeast England.

This was an exhilarating and challenging time to be active in British politics. The country had to come to terms with the loss of so many of its younger generation in the fighting abroad and deal with the large-scale destruction of homes and industries from enemy bombing at home. Other things had changed too. The historian A. J. P. Taylor, writing of post-war Britain, noted that "Traditional values lost much of their force. Other values took their place. Imperial greatness was on the way out; the welfare state was on the way in. The British Empire declined; the condition of the people improved." The Labour Party, which had pledged itself not just to repair the damage but to make radical improvements in social conditions, now set about the huge task of introducing the Welfare State which was to incorporate the socialist ideals of free education and health provision, and improved standards of living for all.

Although Willey was a newcomer to politics, his talents were quickly noticed and he was appointed parliamentary private secretary to the home secretary, J. Chuter Ede, in 1946. He was also made chairman of the Select Committee on Estimates which involved scrutinizing the spending plans of the various government departments. In 1950 Willey was promoted to the post of parliamentary secretary at the Ministry of Food—not an easy job, as he inherited policies which made the ministry a constant target for criticism. The following year the Labour government fell and for the next few years Willey became an opposition member of parliament. In 1960 Hugh Gaitskell, the leader of the Labour opposition, appointed Willey spokesman on education and a busy period followed in which he drew up the Labour Party's plans for radical reforms in the school system.

When Labour came to power again in 1964, Willey was appointed minister of land and natural resources. Under his auspices the ministry set up the controversial Land Commission which allowed for compulsory purchase of land so that development could be regulated. This measure attracted a great deal of criticism. The ministry was later subsumed into the Ministry of Housing and Local Government and Willey remained there as minister of state, where his next task was to tackle the vexed question of leasehold reform. He found himself increasingly at odds with government policy and in 1967 resigned his post so that, as he said in his letter of resignation, "he could speak with a more independent voice".

Although he was now a backbench member of parliament, Willey continued to be extremely active. He chaired a Select Committee on Education and Science which examined the relationship between students and their universities, and following this he was chair of the Select Committee on Members' Interests. This committee recommended that members of parliament should have to disclose any outside financial interests, such as company directorships, which might have an influence on the way they voted.

In common with other members of parliament, Willey suffered the tedium of late-night sittings, when debates would go on until the early hours of the morning and he would have to stay to the bitter end in order to cast his vote in the division. He put this time to good use by writing a book, *The Honourable Member* (1974), which was a lively and incisive account of life as a member of parliament.

In the latter half of the 1970s Willey continued to sit on several key committees which reported on such crucial subjects as abortion and race relations. In 1979 he was elected chairman of the Parliamentary Labour Party, a taxing role. By this time Labour had again become the party of opposition and the Conservative government, led by Margaret Thatcher, which was to dominate British politics for the next decade, was firmly in power. In 1981 Willey decided the time had come to retire and he announced his decision not to contest the next election. It was a graceful departure from the hurly-burly world of politics.

Born Frederick Thomas Wiley. **Parents** Frederick and Mary Willey. **Marriage** Eleanor Snowdon, 1939 (died, 1987). **Children** Two sons (one deceased) and one daughter. **Education** Johnston School, Durham; St John's College, Cambridge University, first class honours in law. **Career** Called to Bar, Middle Temple, 1936; practised law on northeast judicial circuit, 1936–45; Labour member of parliament, Sunderland, 1945–50, Sunderland North, 1950–83; parliamentary private secretary to Home Secretary J. Chuter Ede, 1946–50; parliamentary secretary, Ministry of Food, 1950–51; opposition member, 1951–64; minister of land and natural resources, 1965–67; minister of housing and local government, 1967–68; returned to back benches, 1968–79; opposition member, 1979–83. **Related activities** Chairman, Select Committee on Estimates; member, Select Committees on Statutory Instruments and Public Accounts, to 1950; member, Select Committee on Privileges; former chairman: Select Committees on Members' Interests, 1974–75, Race Relations and Immigration, Selection, Abortion (Amendment) Bill; chairman, Parliamentary and Scientific Committee, Parliamentary Labour Party, 1979–81, member, Consultative Assembly of the Council of Europe and Assembly of Western European Union. **Other activities** Director, North-Eastern Trading Estates, Limited, to 1950; River Wear Commissioner, to 1950; director, Introductions Limited, 1960–64; vice-president: Youth Hostels' Trust of England and Wales, Save the Children Fund. **Awards and honours** Blackstone Prizeman, Cambridge University; Harmsworth Studentship; McMahon Studentship; honorary fellow, Sunderland Polytechnic; privy counsellor, 1964. **Publications** *Plan for Shipbuilding*, 1956; *Education, Today and Tomorrow*, 1964; *An Enquiry into Teacher Training*, 1971; *The Honourable Member*, 1974; articles in various periodicals, legal and political. **Cause of death** Undisclosed, at age 77.

MARGUERITE YOURCENAR

French Novelist, Poet, Playwright and Translator
Born **Brussels, Belgium, 8 June 1903**
Died **Mount Desert Island, Maine, 18 December 1987**

Before 1981 the Académie Française, France's most elevated body of scholars and thinkers, had been an all-male, all-French affair. But in that fateful year, more than a decade after the arrival of second-wave feminism, the revolution finally occurred when Marguerite Yourcenar was elected to membership. Dressed in a cape designed by Yves Saint Laurent and wearing a pendant with the image of Hadrian instead of the traditional sword, Yourcenar gave a gracious speech of acceptance in which she did not let on too much that she had known about the vigorous (anti-female) opposition to her candidacy in certain quarters. According to the official version, the academy had unanimously chosen her to join its illustrious company of "immortals" because of her numerous and erudite contributions to French culture. Yourcenar became the first woman in French intellectual history to be bestowed this honour—and also the first foreigner. For, having lived in the US since the outbreak of World War II, she had taken American citizenship and the French Academy therefore had to give her a special dispensation to join the club. This was duly granted, and thus Marguerite Yourcenar became not only an honorary man for the occasion, but an honorary Frenchman to boot.

It is only a slight exaggeration to say that Yourcenar's first steps were guided towards the path of intellectual distinction. She was born in Belgium of a Belgian mother, who died when Marguerite was still very young. Her father, the Frenchman Michel de Crayencour (of which Yourcenar is an anagram) in effect raised her, and she grew up with an absolute devotion to him. And no wonder: he was a man of letters, but also something of a bon viveur, and he reared her on a diet of privilege involving personal tuition plus frequent travel and holidays in the South of France. Under her father's guidance, the young Marguerite learnt to read in four languages. By the age of eight she was studying Racine's *Phèdre* in anticipation of the classics which she would read in Latin and Greek a few years later.

In 1916 father and daughter sailed to England in the Crayencours' private yacht. They spent a year there before returning to live in Paris; their house in French Flanders had been bombed and was no longer habitable. From the age of 14 Marguerite had been writing verse; by the time she was 18 her father arranged for private publication of *Le Jardin des chimères* (The Garden of Chimeras, 1921), followed in 1922 by another volume of poetry *Les Dieux ne sont pas morts* (The Gods Are Not Dead). Yourcenar later dismissed these works as youthful folly "feebly imitative of poets in vogue at the time whose techniques I was seriously studying".

She was 24 when her father died and was devastated by his loss. In her grief, she turned to the only sources of comfort she knew: travel and the study of classical culture. What came out of this was a first novel, *Alexis ou la Traité du vain combat* (Alexis or the Treatise on Useless Combat, 1929) which earned praise for the handling of the difficult and, in those days, controversial theme of homosexuality—something she was to return to in her masterpiece *Memoirs of Hadrian*. The second novel, *La Nouvelle Eurydice* (1931), was less enthusiastically received, but with *Denier du rêve* (*A Coin in Nine Hands*, 1934), Yourcenar established herself as a serious novelist. The book dealt with a highly apposite political theme in a story centring around assassination attempts on Mussolini. Yourcenar disclosed in this novel "the hollow reality hidden beneath the bloated façade of Fascism". Its successor, *Coup de grâce* (1939), a story of love, betrayal and masochistic revenge, also set in the international arena of war and resistance, is counted by many critics as one of Yourcenar's major works. It rounded off her period of apprenticeship during the 1930s, which had also included *Nouvelles orientales (Oriental Tales*, 1938) and a prose poem, *Feux* (*Fires*, 1936.) About the latter Yourcenar commented later—rather harshly—that it had been "the product of a love crisis" and that her prose poetry suffered from "excessive expressionism".

This was easy to say from the vantage point of maturity and happiness which she found towards the end of the decade with the American scholar Grace Frick, who had invited her to come over to the US at the outbreak of war. Yourcenar, who, until that time, had never held a job for a living, took up the offer to teach literature and art at Sarah Lawrence College, New York. Maybe at that time neither she nor her friend were aware of the permanent nature of her stay, but that was how it turned out. They settled down together, first in Connecticut, and a few years later in Mount Desert Island, Maine, a place they both fell in love with. Both women died there at their beloved home "Petite Plaisance"—Grace Frick in 1979, after nearly 40 years in devoted partnership with Marguerite, much of whose work she translated into English.

Yourcenar did not do much original work during the 1940s, preoccupied as she was with her new existence in the US and with her teaching. But she was nothing if not a cultural omnivore, and some of her efforts in coming to terms with American culture resulted in a translation of Henry James's *What Maisie Knew* (1947) and—rather more adventurously—of Negro spirituals in the collection *Fleuve profond, sombre rivière* (Deep, Dark River, not published until 1964), which she wanted to introduce to the French public.

Yourcenar's approach to translation was hardly orthodox, even if it was effective. "I try to give an idea, an emotion," she said, "as close as I can to what the author wanted to be felt by the reader. Even if we have to use another form, to reach the French reader by another channel, I'll still try to give his emotions, his feelings."

In an important way, this identification with the emotions of another people in another time was also what fuelled Yourcenar's imagination when she wrote her undisputed masterpiece, *Memoires d'Hadrien* (*Memoirs of Hadrian*, 1951). The central theme, Hadrian's love for the beautiful young Antinous, was one that had interested Yourcenar for a long time. She finally succeeded in writing the story of that love when she hit upon the structure of having Hadrian, on his deathbed, write out his life in letters to his grandson Marcus Aurelius—a time-honoured but, here, extremely well-used device.

It is tempting to speculate that the fascination with male homosexuality, so brilliantly rendered in this book within the safe setting of history, was also a way for Yourcenar to displace her own transgressions of sex and gender. Unfortunately, this is a subject on which she herself always maintained a resounding silence. What is clear, however, is that she managed to identify with Hadrian to such a degree that she really managed to recreate the man and his times and make him present to a twentieth-century audience. She described this process of identification herself as one of "absorption in that *sympathetic magic* which operates when one transports oneself, in thought, into another's body and soul".

Throughout her writing life, Yourcenar was engaged in demonstrating that "one can contract the distance between the centuries at will". She had a strong preference for classical themes in all her work (apart from Hadrian also Icarus, Alceste, Pindar, Electra and the earlier mentioned Eurydice), but she also turned her hand to other periods. *L'Oeuvre en noir* (*The Abyss*, 1968) is about "a Renaissance man lurking in the lingering shadows of the Dark Ages", a kind of alchemist/philosopher/engineer whose quest for science is nevertheless still dominated by the magical world-view of an earlier age. This novel has been criticized, not so much for the grim quality of the Hieronymous Bosch-like pictures it evokes, but for its badly-drawn protagonist Zeno who gives off an impression of lifelessness which Hadrian, even on his deathbed, never managed to put across. Another criticism which has been levelled at some of Yourcenar's work is the rather lofty tone she adopted, something which the foreign reader is tempted to identify as "typically French": large themes, great passions and a tendency towards pomposity. Yet all this does not detract from the fact that Yourcenar's novels have—as they must—invariably been read as works of art, scholarship and philosophical meditation rolled into one. They are not light reading, nor do they pretend to be, but they are an education in themselves.

Apart from novels and poetry Yourcenar published several plays, collections of essays and literary criticism, more translations (including the modern Greek poetry of Cavafy), and two volumes of autobiography. The latter were rather grandly entitled *Le Labyrinth du monde* (The Labyrinth of the World), volume one being a family history of her father's side, and volume two being a maternal history set in her native Belgium.

Yet despite the fact that she covered so many genres, used such a wide range of historical material and was so conversant with a number of different cultures, there are two glaring absences in Yourcenar's erudite and prolific repertoire: feminism and psychoanalysis. This is all the more remarkable for a Frenchwoman and for someone who was in the same league with, for example, Simone de Beauvoir. The absence in Yourcenar's work of any engagement with either feminism or psychoanalysis, two major areas of twentieth-century scholarship, cannot be explained by a mere generational difference and must lead us to conclude that Yourcenar simply had no interest in them.

This is not to say, though, that she lived in a world of her own (roughly "the past"), and was not at all concerned with the state of contemporary affairs. As she grew older, she became increasingly involved in environmental issues. In *Le Temps, ce grand sculpteur* (Time, the Great Sculptor, 1983) she wrote at length about ecology and conservation, especially the welfare of animals and the preservation of endangered species. Although it is not so evident in the rest of her work, Yourcenar's love of nature was very much at the root of her intellectual energy and the pleasure she took in exploration and discovery of all kinds. In *Les Yeux ouverts* (*With Open Eyes*, 1984), a collection of interviews, Jacqueline Piatier wrote: "She feels she is linked to everything, to the past as well as the present, to human beings but also to animals, landscapes, buildings". An intensely private person, Yourcenar donated her papers, journals and letters (including the correspondence with Grace Frick) to Harvard University with the characteristic stipulation that the collection must remain sealed for 50 years. It is going to be a long wait for Yourcenar scholars—but there can be little doubt that it will be worth it.

Born Marguerite Antoinette Jeanne Marie Ghislaine de Crayencour. **Parents** Michel and Fernande (de Cartier de Marchienne) de Crayencour. **Education** Private tutors. **Emigration** Left Europe for USA, 1939; took dual French–US nationality, 1947. **Career** Writer. **Related activities** Part-time lecturer in comparative literature, Sarah Lawrence College, Bronxville, New York, 1939–49; various lecture tours. **Offices and memberships** Foreign member, Royal Belgian Academy, 1971; French Academy, 1980; American Academy and Institute of Arts and Letters, 1982. **Awards and honours** Prix Fémina-Vacaresco, 1952; Newspaper Guild of New York Award, 1955; Prix Combat, 1963; Prix Fémina, 1968; Monaco Grand Prize, 1972; Grand Prix National des Lettres, 1974; French Academy Grand Prize, 1977; Erasmus Prize (Amsterdam), 1983; National Arts Club Medal (USA), 1986; officer, Order Leopold (Belgium); officer, Legion of Honour; honorary degrees: Smith College, Massachusetts, 1961, Bowdoin College, Maine, 1968, Colby College, Maine, 1972, Harvard University, Massachusetts, 1981. **Fiction** (all published in Paris, unless stated) *Alexis, ou la traité de vain combat*, 1929, revised edition, 1952, and Henley, 1984; *La Nouvelle Eurydice*, 1931; *Denier du rêve*, 1934, revised edition, 1959, published as *A Coin in Nine Hands*, New York, 1982, Henley, 1983; *Le Mort conduit l'attelage*, 1935; *Nouvelles orientales*, 1938, revised edition, 1963, as *Oriental Tales*, Henley, 1985, New York, 1986; *Le Coup de grâce*, 1939, revised edition, 1953, published as *Coup de Grace*, New York and London, 1957; *Mémoires d'Hadrien*, 1951, published as *Memoirs of Hadrian*, New

York, 1954, London, 1955; *L'Oeuvre en noir*, 1968, published as *The Abyss*, New York and London, 1976; *Anna, soror*, 1981; *Comme l'eau qui coule*, 1982; *Oeuvres romanesque*, 1982; *Two Lives and a Dream*, New York and Henley, 1987. **Plays** (all published in Paris, unless stated) *Electre, ou la chute des masques*, 1954; *Le Mystère d'Alceste, suivi de qui n'a pas son minotaure?*, 1963, 1971; *Théâtre*, including *Rendre à César, La Petite sirène, Le Dialogue dans le marécage*, 1971. **Verse** (all published in Paris, unless stated) *Le Jardin des chimères*, 1921; *Les Dieux ne sont pas morts*, 1922; *Feux* (prose poems), 1936, published as *Fires*, New York, 1981, Henley, 1982; *Les Charités d'Alcippe et autres poèmes*, Liège, 1956, published as *The Alms of Alcippe*, New York, 1982; *La Couronne et la lyre: poèmes traduits du grec*, 1979. **Other** (all published in Paris, unless stated) *Pindare*, 1932; (translator) *Les Vagues* by Virginia Woolf, 1937; *Les Songes et les sorts*, 1938; (translator) *Ce qui savait* (What Maisie Knew) by Henry James, 1947; *Préface à la Gita-Govinda*, 1958; (translator with Constantin Dimaras) *Présentation critique de Constantin Cavafy 1863–1933*, 1958; *Sous bénéfice d'inventaire*, 1962; (editor and translator) *Fleuve profond, sombre rivière: les "Nègro spirituals"* 1964; (translator) *Présentation critique d'Hortense Flexner*, 1969; *Le Labrynthe du monde* (memoirs): vol 1 *Souvenirs pieux*, 1974; vol 2 *Archives du nord*, 1977; *Comment Wang-Fô fut sauvé* (for children), 1979; *Les Yeux ouverts* (interview), 1980, published as *With Open Eyes*, Boston, 1984; *Mishima, ou La Vision du vide*, 1981, published as *Mishima: A Vision of the Void*, New York and Henley, 1986; *Nôtre Dame des Hirondelles* (for children), 1982; *Le Temps, ce grand sculpteur: Essais*, 1983; *The Dark Brain of Piranesi: Essays*, New York and Henley, 1984. **Cause of death** Undisclosed, at age 84. **Further reading** Jean Blot, *Yourcenar*, Paris, 1971.

YAKOV ZELDOVICH

Soviet Physicist

***Born* Minsk, Russia, 8 March 1914**

***Died* Moscow, USSR, 2 December 1987**

Yakov Zeldovich made important advances in the physics of explosions, elementary particles and astronomy. In addition, he played an important part in the discovery of "black holes" and the debate on the origin of the universe.

He was born in Minsk, not far from the Polish border, the year World War I began. After graduating from Leningrad University he joined the staff of the Institute of Chemical Physics. In the years leading up to World War II he was involved in a number of defence projects, and it was then that he studied the physics of explosions in depth.

An explosion is a very sudden increase in pressure, accompanied by heat, light, sound and mechanical shock, caused by a release of energy. Explosions can have mechanical causes, as when a large quantity of water comes into contact with a massive, hot solid and is very rapidly evaporated. The explosion of Krakatoa in 1883 demonstrated how powerful a mechanical explosion can be.

Zeldovich, however, was more involved with chemical explosions, where an unrestrained chemical reaction provides the energy, and he managed to work out the mechanism of nitrogen oxidation is such explosions. Later, in World War II, a new form of explosion was being developed, and Zeldovich conceived a method of calculating the chain reaction in nuclear fission.

In 1966 he was made a professor at Moscow University. His country rewarded him for his distinguished work in the study of explosives and other branches of physics with a cluster of decorations, including three Orders of Lenin, four State Prizes of the USSR, and a Lenin Prize, and he was also made a Hero of the Soviet Union on three occasions. In addition, he received numerous honours abroad, including an honorary doctorate from Cambridge University, which he was twice prevented from leaving the Soviet Union to receive in person.

The nature of the cosmos was a prime interest of Zeldovich, and his work in developing the concept of the black hole was especially important. When a star collapses, it goes through various stages. When the atoms are crushed and packed so tightly together that there is little waste, it is a white dwarf. Then the protons and electrons are forced together to produce neutrons, so that neutron star material is far denser than that of a white dwarf. If it still continues to contract, it enters a stage of gravitational collapse where no known physical process can halt the contraction, and when it gets down to a certain size—the Schwarzschild radius—not even light can escape. Hence the title black hole. All the normal laws of physics fail, and it has been suggested it may be crushed out of existence altogether.

As well as his interest in these aspects of astronomy, Zeldovich was intrigued by the origin of the universe, and was a strong advocate of the Big Bang theory. On these topics he was co-author of *The Theory of Gravity and the Evolution of Stars* and *The Structure and Evolution of the Universe*. Other publications of his included a mathematics textbook, and on a lighter note, his book on the possibility of communicating with extraterrestrial civilizations. We have not yet had the chance of putting his ideas into practice.

Born Yakov Borisovich Zeldovich. **Education** Leningrad University. **Career** Physicist, Institute of Chemical Physics, 1931–64; Institute of Applied Mathematics of USSR Academy of Sciences, from 1964; professor, Moscow University, 1966–87. **Offices and memberships** Member, USSR Academy of Sciences, 1958. **Awards and honours** Hero of Socialist Labour (three times); Lenin Prize; State prizes of the USSR (four times); Order of Lenin (three times); honorary doctorate, Cambridge University. **Publications** *Higher Mathematics for Beginners*, 1968; *The Theory of Gravity and the Evolution of Stars*, 1971; *The Structure and Evolution of the Universe*; *The Problem of the Century: Is Communication Possible with Extraterrestrial Civilizations?* **Cause of death** Undisclosed, at age 73.

Cumulative Alphabetical Index

Cumulative Index of Entrants by Profession

The index is divided into the following categories:

Actors, Actresses and Entertainers

Advertising and Public Relations Executives

Anthropologists and Archaeologists

Architects and Planners

Arms Control Experts

Art Historians, Collectors, Critics and Dealers

Artists and Craftsmen

Arts Administrators

Astronomers and Astrophysicists

Aviators, Aviation Experts, Aerodynamicists and Astronauts

Biographers and Memoirists

Biologists, Botanists, Naturalists and Zoologists

Business Executives and Industrialists

Chefs and Food Writers

Chemists and Biochemists

Children's Writers

Clergy and Religious Scholars and Theorists

Composers, Arrangers, Songwriters and Librettists

Criminals

Dancers, Choreographers and Dance Critics

Designers

Diplomats

Directors

Earth Scientists (including Geographers, Geologists, Meteorologists,Seismologists, Oceanographers and Demographers)

Economists, Financial Specialists and Bankers

Educators, Educationists and Educational and Foundation/Association Administrators

Engineers and Technologists

Essayists

Explorers

Farmers, Horticulturists and Agriculturists

Heads of State, Presidents, Premiers and Governors General

Historians, Classicists, Genealogists and Folklorists

Illustrators, Cartoonists and Animators

Intelligence Officers and Agents

International Affairs Officials

Inventors

Journalists and Editors (including Travel Writers)

Judges, Lawyers and Criminologists

Labour Leaders

Librarians, Museum Curators, Archivists and Antiquarians

Linguistics Experts

Literary Scholars and Critics

Management and Industrial Relations Specialists

Mathematicians, Statisticians and Cryptographers

Medical Practitioners and Researchers

Military Officers and Strategists

Musical Performers and Conductors

Novelists and Short Story Writers (including Humorists)

Performing Arts Critics and Scholars

Philanthropists

Philosophers

Photographers and Cinematographers

Physicists

Playwrights and Scriptwriters

Poets

Political Scientists

Politicians

Pollsters

Producers and Administrators (Film, Stage, Radio, TV and Music)

Psychiatrists and Psychologists

Public and Government Officials

Publishers, Newspaper Proprietors and Literary Agents

Radio and Television Personalities

Royalty and Socialites (including notable spouses of famous people)

Social, Political and Human Rights Activists

Social Workers

Sociologists

Sovietologists

Sports and Games Figures

Theatrical/Music Impresarios, Managers and Agents

Translators